FORENSIC MENTAL HEALTH

A SOURCE GUIDE FOR PROFESSIONALS

EDITORS

Jerrod Brown & Erv Weinkauf

Forensic Press International

P.O. Box 14183

St. Paul, Minnesota 55114-1802

Printed in the United States of America

Publisher's Cataloging-in-Publication data

Names:	Brown, Jerrod, editor	Weinkauf, Erv, editor.
Title:	Forensic Mental Health: A Source Guide for Professionals / Jerrod Brown and Erv Weinkauf.
Description:	First trade paperback original edition.	St. Paul [Minnesota] : Forensic Press International, 2018.	Includes index.
Identifiers:	ISBN 978-1-547132-3-79
Subjects:	Psychology–Mental Health–Forensics	Mental Health–United States.	Forensics–Mental Health.	BISAC: PSYCHOLOGY / Forensic Psychology
Classification:	DDC 362.1—362.4

First Edition

18 19 20 21 22 23 24 25 | 12 11 10 9 8 7 6 5 4 3 2 1

FORENSIC
MENTAL
HEALTH

A SOURCE GUIDE
FOR PROFESSIONALS

EDITORS

Jerrod Brown & Erv Weinkauf

FORENSIC PRESS
INTERNATIONAL
—— A Publication Company ——

St. Paul, Minnesota

ABOUT THE BOOK

Forensic Mental Health: A Source Guide for Professionals is an innovative, yet practical new textbook that addresses the nexus of mental health and legal systems. Specifically, forensic mental health can be defined as the utilization of psychological strategies and techniques (e.g., diagnosis and treatment) to assist criminal justice-involved clients with mental health issues. These clients benefit from mental health care at all points in the criminal justice system, including prior to prosecution, during trial, and after adjudication. In these settings, mental health care can encompass everything from assessment and treatment services to casework management and collaboration with stakeholders. Such services are provided by a diverse group of professionals from different vocational and academic backgrounds (e.g., psychiatrists, psychologists, nurses, social workers, counselors, and others). The importance of forensic mental health services is highlighted by the fact that criminal justice-involved clients with mental health issues are disproportionately likely, relative to the general population, to be re-arrested, re-incarcerated, and victimized by others.

Necessitated by the rapid development of the field, this practitioner-oriented textbook adopts a multidisciplinary perspective on several timely, prominent, and often overlooked issues in the field of forensic mental health. This textbook features 20 standalone chapters written by a diverse collection of authors drawn from a wide variety of disciplines. Topics covered include but are not limited to the role of mental illness in criminal behavior, special populations and neurobehavioral disorders, memory-related disturbances, competency to stand trial, and re-entry into the community. Although extensively referenced, each chapter is written in an engaging and easy-to-follow manner that is appropriate for undergraduate students, graduate students, and established professionals alike. As such, *Forensic Mental Health: A Source Guide for Professionals* serves as an incomparable tool for those learning about how to assist current or future clients.

The value of *Forensic Mental Health: A Source Guide for Professionals* is based in its ability to serve a wide variety of roles for different people. First, the textbook can serve as a great introduction to forensic mental health for students considering a career in this field. This could include students from criminal justice, psychology, and human service programs. Second, the textbook has the potential to provide additional professional seasoning or training for professionals already working in the field, but who may be unfamiliar with some topics such as legal concepts (e.g., competency to stand trial). Third, the textbook can simply be an essential resource for experienced legal professionals, clinicians, or others who might need a refresher on a given topic. Fourth, this textbook could be valuable to professionals and organizations that are collaborating with forensic mental health professionals in an effort to serve criminal justice-involved clients. In light of this versatility, *Forensic Mental Health: A Source Guide for Professionals* is a valuable addition to any library.

EDITORS

JERROD BROWN

Jerrod Brown, Ph.D., is an Assistant Professor and Program Director for the Master of Arts degree in Human Services with an emphasis in Forensic Behavioral Health for Concordia University, St. Paul, Minnesota. Jerrod has also been employed with Pathways Counseling Center in St. Paul, Minnesota for the past fifteen years. Pathways provides programs and services benefiting individuals impacted by mental illness and addictions. Jerrod is also the founder and CEO of the American Institute for the Advancement of Forensic Studies (AIAFS), and the Editor-in-Chief of Forensic Scholars Today (FST) and the Journal of Special Populations (JSP). Jerrod has completed four separate master's degree programs and holds graduate certificates in Autism Spectrum Disorder (ASD), Other Health Disabilities (OHD), and Traumatic-Brain Injuries (TBI).

ERV WEINKAUF

Erv Weinkauf, MA, is a retired Criminal Justice Department Chair (online) at Concordia University, Saint Paul, Minnesota. He directed and taught in the university's BA Criminal Justice program, MA Criminal Justice Leadership program, and MA program in Forensic Mental Health. The Forensic Mental Health program was developed by Jerrod Brown and Janina Cich from the American Institute for the Advancement of Forensic Studies (AIAFS) and Erv. He has co-authored and edited articles covering a variety of mental health topics such as autism, confabulation, family violence, fetal alcohol syndrome, malingering, offender reentry, sex offenders, and youth fire setting. Prior to working at Concordia University, Erv served as a police officer and deputy sheriff for thirty-seven years in Brown County, Minnesota, and retired as the New Ulm Police Department's Chief of Police in 2009. He is a graduate of the FBI National Academy. Erv was an adjunct instructor at several colleges and universities for twenty years and guest instructor for the Minnesota Chiefs of Police Chief Law Enforcement Officer (CLEO) and Leadership Academies. He was a member of the Minnesota Chiefs of Police Advisory Board and South Central Technical College Advisory Board. Erv held a variety of positions: Pro Kinship for Kids Mentor, Guardian ad Litem, Children's Justice Initiative Panel, and was instrumental in the development of Teen and Adult Drug Courts in Brown County, Minnesota. He was an Advisory Board member and president of the Association of Training Officers of Minnesota (ATOM), Charter Board member and president of New Ulm Area Youth Wrestling Association, church president, and junior high school football and wrestling coach. Erv was selected as Police Officer of the Year by both the American Legion, State of Minnesota, and Veterans of Foreign Wars, State of Minnesota, was recipient of the City of New Ulm Service to Mankind Award, Minnesota Public Safety Award of Honor, and Association of Training Officers of Minnesota (ATOM) Hall of Fame Award.

FORENSIC MENTAL HEALTH: A BRIEF OVERVIEW

OVERVIEW

Forensic mental health is an area of study concerned with the intersection of mental health and the criminal justice system. In particular, professionals working within the field of forensic mental health may utilize screening and assessment and treatment and intervention techniques to improve the outcomes of individuals with mental health-related problems who are involved in the criminal justice system. The importance of this task is emphasized by the fact that individuals with mental illness are at a higher risk for arrest, imprisonment, and victimization than the general population. Working on behalf of these individuals, the field of forensic mental health is composed of a diverse group of professionals who may have lower level or advanced degrees. These professionals can be tasked to provide an incredibly diverse set of services, including screening and assessment evaluations, treatment services, casework management, and forging relationships with other stakeholders in the community. Given this important service, this review provides a brief overview of forensic mental health as a field.

FORENSIC MENTAL HEALTH

Forensic mental health is the intersection of the mental health and legal systems. In fact, the term "forensic" simply refers to the use of science in legal contexts. In this case, mental health screening and assessment and treatment and intervention techniques are employed to better understand and potentially improve the psychological functioning of clients entangled in the criminal justice system. Clients could be at any of several time points in the criminal justice system, ranging from pretrial or during trial to incarceration or community supervision. Across these time points, psychologists, psychiatrists, nurses, case managers, counselors, and other professionals are tasked with providing mental health services to a range of clients. To increase awareness of forensic mental health, this brief introduction overviews the prominence of mental illness in the criminal justice system, the backgrounds of forensic mental health professionals, the roles served by these professionals, and a summary of recommended training for these professionals.

Forensic mental health exists because those involved in the criminal justice system are more likely to have mental illness than the general population. In fact, individuals with mental illness are at a higher risk for arrest, imprisonment, and crime victimization than the general population. As such, many inmates in jails and prisons have a severe need for mental health treatment. Referrals for mental health care commonly come from law enforcement officers, corrections officials, community supervision specialists, and the courts. Although effective mental health interventions prior to involvement in the legal system are ideal, criminal behavior is often the precipitating factor that results in individuals finally receiving mental health treatment.

The field of forensic mental health is composed of a diverse group of professionals united by a single purpose: improving the mental health and long-term outcomes of criminal justice-involved clients. Forensic mental health professionals may have lower level or advanced degrees. For example, forensic mental health professionals include those with a master's degree in social work, marriage and family counseling, addiction counseling, and other areas. Alternatively, technicians who are supervised by licensed professionals can also play an important role in the field of forensic mental health. In some cases, this group of professionals can be broadened to include professionals from law enforcement, corrections, legal, medical, and education settings.

Together, this consortium of professionals works on behalf of clients with mental health issues who are involved in the criminal justice system.

Forensic mental health professionals can be tasked to provide an incredibly diverse set of services for criminal justice-involved clients. At the outset, these professionals are often called upon to provide screening and assessment evaluations. Evaluations can serve to inform the ideal placement and course of treatment or determine the individual's competency to stand trial or make legal decisions such as waiving *Miranda* rights. Further, forensic mental health professionals are commonly tasked with providing treatment services in the community, hospitals, and jail or prison. Treatment services often have to deal with difficult issues, including severe psychopathology like psychosis and mania, sex offending, intellectual disabilities, substance use, and competency restoration. In many cases, these treatment services are mandated by the courts. Beyond assessment and treatment, forensic mental health professionals often perform casework management, coordinate and oversee services, and supervise other mental health professionals who work with criminal justice-involved clients. Throughout these roles, forensic mental health professionals often need to forge and maintain relationships with others in the community, such as the client's family, educators, health care providers, social workers, lawyers, judges, and other stakeholders. The quality of these mental health services and the strength of these multidisciplinary relationships are important in improving the client's mental health and reducing their likelihood of recidivism.

To be effective in these varied and essential roles, forensic mental health professionals would greatly benefit from advanced training and education. In particular, education and training programs need to emphasize evidence-based practices. This should include assessment and treatment strategies and techniques with empirical support in criminal justice populations. Similarly, a greater understanding of the research on etiologies of different mental illnesses and criminal behaviors would be helpful. Further, a greater familiarity with the different arenas of the criminal justice system (i.e., law enforcement, the courts, jails and prisons, and community supervision) and how to function in each arena (e.g., providing expert testimony) is imperative. That said, such education and training programs are sometimes limited in their scope, which means obtaining such training will likely take increased effort on the part of the forensic mental health professional.

As this brief introduction highlights, there is a strong need for mental health treatment in forensic settings. The task of ensuring that criminal justice-involved individuals receive the appropriate mental health services falls to a diverse group of professionals. These forensic mental health professionals provide a wide variety of services, from case management to assessment and treatment. Advanced training and education can help improve the effectiveness of forensic mental health professionals. In turn, accurate assessment and appropriate treatment have the potential to improve long-term outcomes and reduce the likelihood of recidivism.

About the Contributors

Aaron Trnka, MA, LMFT, *is the Clinical Director and CEO of Lighthouse Psychological Services, Inc., a sexual offender program for special needs adult males. Aaron has practiced in the field since 2004. He has specialized in trauma-informed care, is certified in EMDR, and currently directs an adult day treatment program for maladaptive sexual behaviors. Aaron has experience working with children, adults, families, and couples.*

Adam L Piccolino, PsyD, ABN, *is the lead neuropsychologist for the Minnesota Department of Corrections,where he provides neuropsychological assessment to individuals with a variety of brain-related diseases or syndromes. He has taught a variety of psychology courses at the graduate level and is currently an Associate Professor at the Chicago School of Professional Psychology.*

The Hon. Allison L. Krehbiel *has a bachelor's degree from the University of Minnesota and a J.D. from the William Mitchell College of Law. She has served as a prosecutor for the City of Minneapolis and as a public defender for the Fifth Judicial District of Minnesota. She is presently a District Court Judge chambered in St. Peter, Minnesota.*

Amanda Fenrich, MA, *is a Sex Offender Treatment Specialist with the Washington State Department of Corrections, treating and providing both group and individual therapy to adult male sex offenders. She is currently completing her PhD in the Advanced Studies of Human Behavior at Capella University. Amanda obtained her Master of Arts degree in Human Services with an Emphasis in Forensic Mental Health and her Bachelor of Criminal Justice from Concordia University, St. Paul, Minnesota. Previous experience includes working as a probation officer, where Amanda supervised offenders in the Special Needs Unit with various neurocognitive and neurodevelopmental disorders including Fetal Alcohol Spectrum Disorder (FASD).*

Andrea Patrick, MA, *recently graduated from John Jay College with her degree in Forensic Psychology. She completed her thesis on the reliability of a stalking risk assessment tool. She is interested in continuing her concentration with risk assessment tools and forensic populations.*

Ann Marie Winskowski PsyD, LP, *is a licensed psychologist working in St. Paul, Minnesota. Dr. Winskowski received her Masters and Doctorate degrees from the University of St. Thomas. Dr. Winskowski currently works in private practice, providing forensic psychological evaluations for the courts throughout the Twin Cities metro area.*

Ann Yurcek *has been mentoring and supporting parents and caregivers in the FASD, Foster, Adoption and mental health systems since 1999. She has been an advocate, trainer and writer in FASD, Trauma, and Special needs children, teens and adults. She and her husband are parents to 12 children, 6 adopted through the foster care system with FASD and other mental health and medical challenges.*

Anne Russell *is the mother of two adult children with Fetal Alcohol Spectrum Disorder (FASD). Anne established the Russell Family Fetal Alcohol Disorders Association (rffada) in 2007 and has attended and presented at national and international conferences and workshops in New Zealand, Canada, the United States, and around Australia.*

Anthony P. Wartnik *was a trial judge for 34 years, serving as presiding Judge of Juvenile Court, Family Law Court Chief Judge, Dean Emeritus of the Washington Judicial College, Judicial College Board of Trustees chair and the Washington Supreme Court's Judicial Conference Education Committee chair. Judge Wartnik is a nationally and internationally recognized speaker, author and trainer on issues involving FASD and the law and teaches post-graduate courses on forensic mental health and special needs populations at Concordia University, St. Paul, MN.*

Barbara Luskin, PhD, LP, *is a licensed psychologist with a focus on ASD. She received her PhD from the University of Chicago. She has worked at the Autism Society of Minnesota for the past 16 years, primarily seeing adults with autism spectrum disorder.*

Beth Jordan, MA, LPCC, LADC, *is a retired police officer with 21 years of service. She also worked as an EMT and is trained in Crisis Negotiations, CISM, and Chaplaincy work. Her duties as an officer also included working as the Training Officer, Gun Instructor, and as a member of the S.W.A.T. unit. Since retiring after an injury, she has completed Master's level training and licensing for both counseling and addictions, and works in private practice providing counseling, training, and crisis response to Law Enforcement agencies in Minnesota. In addition, Beth serves on the board for the Law Enforcement Family Support Network and specializes in PTSD, trauma, communication, and addictions.*

Bethany Hastings, MA, *is the Program Supervisor at People Incorporated-Riverwind, an adult crisis residence. She has her Master's degree in Adlerian Psychology, clinical counseling, marriage and family therapy and art therapy. Bethany is currently working towards LPCC licensure and obtaining a board certification in art therapy.*

Blake R. Harris, PhD, *is a Licensed Clinical Forensic Psychologist practicing in Austin, Texas. He currently works as a psychological services manager with the Travis County Juvenile Probation Department and oversees the clinical services in secured residential placement and outpatient settings. Dr. Harris has also been involved in the treatment and evaluation of violent offenders, individuals adjudicated Incompetent to Stand Trial, and those found Not Guilty by Reason of Insanity.*

Cameron R. Wiley *is a graduate student pursuing a PhD in Neuropsychology at Howard University. He received a Bachelor of Science in Psychology with a minor in Neuroscience from The Ohio State University in May of 2017. His current research focuses on the relationship between autonomic stability and emotion regulation.*

Carlie J. Bolin, MA, *is a graduate of the University of Minnesota-Twin Cities with a double degree in psychology and sociology of law, criminology, and a deviance minor. She is a graduate of Condordia University – St. Paul Master's degree in Human Services with an emphaisis in Forensic Mental Health.*

Carlo A. Giacomoni, PsyD, ABPP, *is a psychologist at North Star Mental Health, LLC, in Minnesota. He is board certified in clinical psychology and has considerable experience in a variety of forensic evaluations.*

Casie M. Nauman, PhD, MEd, *is a school counselor and an adjunct professor at Concordia University, St. Paul. Casie has her Doctorate in Educational Administration and Policy from The University of Georgia. She specializes in issues of multicultural education, law and mental health as it pertains to K-12 students.*

Charlotte Gerth Haanen, PhD, LP, *has worked in the field of psychology with at-risk and adjudicated adolescents, children with emotional and behavioral disorders, adults with serious and persistent mental illness, adults who sustained traumatic brain injury, and both adults and children with developmental disabilities. Services provided have included individual and group therapy, diagnostic assessments, neuropsychological evaluations, and psychosexual assessments.*

Cheryl Arndt, PhD, *is a research psychologist with experience in quantitative and qualitative research and mental health program administration and evaluation. She is the Director of Performance Improvement for KidsPeace. Dr. Arndt is a peer reviewer for the Journal of Special Populations and is on the Board of the American Psychological Association's Society for Child and Family Policy.*

Cody Charette, PhD, *from the Psychology, Policy, and Law program of the California School of Forensic Studies at Alliant International University located in Fresno, CA. He specializes in threat assessment, deception detection, intelligence analysis, data analysis, and the use of technology for indirect assessment of offenders. He is currently a data analyst for the Fresno Fire Department in Fresno, California.*

Danielle Price, LPC, ADC, LPCC, LADC, *is currently the Clinical Coordinator at a Juvenile Residential Facility in West Virginia. The facility houses 40 youth, who all have a dual diagnosis of substance abuse and mental illness coupled with trauma. Danielle graduated with her Bachelor degree from West Virginia University in 2010 and her Master's in Clinical Psychology from The University of St. Thomas in 2013.*

Deborah A. Eckberg, PhD, *is a Professor of Criminal Justice at Metropolitan State University (MN). Dr. Eckberg has published research spanning a wide variety of topics in journals such as Race and Justice, American Sociologist, the Journal of Special Populations, and the Journal of Marriage and the Family. Dr. Eckberg earned her Bachelor of Arts degree from Dartmouth College and her Master of Arts and Doctorate from the University of Minnesota, all in sociology with an emphasis in criminology.*

Debra Huntley, PhD, *teaches in the Social and Behavioral Sciences department at Concordia University, St. Paul. She is a licensed psychologist and earned her doctorate in clinical psychology from the University of Houston. Her research and areas of professional interest include child and family issues, psychopathology, and forensic mental health. She is currently a member of the editorial review board for The Family Journal, Forensic Scholars Today, and the Journal of Special Populations.*

Diane Harr, PhD, *is the Coordinator of Graduate Special Education Programs at Concordia University, St. Paul. Previously, Diane taught and coordinated special education programs at the K-12 grade levels in a suburban school district. Her public-school experience has included assessing, identifying and implementing instructional strategies geared to meet the needs of all students, including those with Autism Spectrum Disorder, Emotional Behavioral Disorders, Specific Learning Disabilities, and other neurological and/or functional impairments.*

Diane Neal, MS, LPCC, *is the Executive Director of Project Pathfinder, Inc. PPI provides programs and services for problematic and offending sexual behaviors. Diane has over 25 years working with mental health issues and specializes in sexualized behaviors, targeting highest risk and special needs clients. Diane provides consults and training to multi-faceted organizations and universities, addressing primary prevention and responding to sexual assault. Diane holds multiple certifications in Trauma Treatment, Trauma Informed Care, Autism Spectrum and Developmental Disorders, Sexual Offending and Healthy Sexuality.*

Elizabeth Cardwell, BA, *is a volunteer researcher. She graduated from the University of Minnesota in 2014 with Bachelor of Arts degrees in Psychology and Sociology of Law, Criminology, and Deviance. Her experience includes assisting with research at the Center for Homicide Research and in the University of Minnesota's Cognitive Psychology Department.*

Elizabeth Quinby, MA, *received her Masters of Arts in Counseling and Psychological Services from Saint Mary's University of Minnesota in 2015. Elizabeth works as Lead Event Coordinator for the American Institute for the Advancement of Forensic Studies (AIAFS). She is also currently working at Integrity Living Options in Minneapolis as a Community Supports Director, overseeing the creation and implementation of behavior plans and behavior services for individuals with serious and persistent mental illness. Elizabeth is also volunteering with the Innocence Project of Minnesota, as a consultant.*

Eric Skog, MA, *is a Sergeant with the St. Paul Police Department and currently serves in the Homicide/Robbery unit as an investigator. He has eighteen years' experience with the St. Paul Police Department.*

Erik Asp, PhD, *is an Assistant Professor in the Department of Psychology at Hamline University in St. Paul, MN. He is the director of the Wesley and Lorene Artz Cognitive Neuroscience Research Center. His central research interests concern the neural substrates of belief and doubt, egocentric biases, prejudice, ERN, N400, and prefrontal cortex function. Dr. Asp received his PhD in Neuroscience from the University of Iowa in 2012. His dissertation garnered the University of Iowa's Graduated Dean's Distinguished Dissertation Award in 2014. Dr. Asp has also done postdoctoral work at the University of Chicago's Center for Cognitive and Social Neuroscience Lab, investigating the neural bases of* social and physical pain, and at the University of Iowa's Psychiatry Iowa Neuroimaging Consortium Group, researching functional connectivity abnormalities in schizophrenia.

Erin Watts, MSW, LICSW, *has worked as a mental health professional providing clinical services to people with complex mental health diagnosis and is working towards building capacity of services providers through training and technical assistance. She is currently with the University of Minnesota's Institute on Community Integration, overseeing statewide initiatives to integrate person-centered practices and positive behavior supports into agencies and systems supporting people with disabilities.*

Erin Rafferty-Bugher, ATR-BC, LPCC, *received her Master's degree (1998) in art therapy from the school of the Art Institute of Chicago. Erin started in the field in 1998; she has a wide variety of experience working with children and adolescents with various challenges including Autism Spectrum Disorder, Attachment Trauma as well as PTSD. Erin is currently working as an instructor in the art therapy program at the Adler Graduate School in Richfield, Minnesota. She also supervises and is the field experience coordinator.*

Erwin E. Concepcion, PhD, LP, *Clinical Neuropsychologist, is a manager with the Minnesota Department of Human Services Direct Care and Treatment Division, with over 25 years of clinical and administrative experience in psychology and neuropsychology. Dr. Concepcion provides clinical consultation and evaluation focusing on adults with developmental and mental health conditions. In addition, he specializes in working with individuals who present with co-occurring conditions related to brain injury and substance use disorders.*

Gennae Falconer, MA, *has worked in the non-profit sector for over 20 years, creating and facilitating trainings designed to help people understand the complexities of poverty, mental health issues, the criminal justice system, and our interactions within varying cultures. She is an adjunct professor with Concordia University, St. Paul, and is currently the Learning and Development Manager for Mental Health Resources. She has her Master's degree in Forensic Psychology.*

Hal Pickett PsyD, LP, ABPP, *has been a Clinical Psychologist for over twenty years, working in clinical, academic and administrative roles. His clinical passion is youth forensic work and neurobehavioral assessment through a trauma-informed lens. He champions a mutually respectful model of intertwining the clinical and juvenile justice worlds.*

Hannah Fordice, MA, *is a graduate of Concordia University, St. Paul. She is interested specifically in the areas of trauma, family homicide, domestic abuse, and sexual offending. Hannah plans to pursue a career in program development for non-profit-based crisis centers, shelters, and legal services set up for victims of abuse.*

Janina Cich, MA, *is a retired Law Enforcement Officer with two decades of Criminal Justice experience. She recently took on the role of CJ Program Director at Concordia University, St. Paul. Janina is also Professor of Criminal Justice & Forensic Mental Health Programs at local colleges and Universities and a frequent lecturer. She conducts Crisis Intervention Training for Law Enforcement and Mental Health Practitioners focusing on awareness, assessment, intervention, de-escalation techniques, and prevention approaches for mental health populations in the criminal justice systems. She currently serves as the Chief Operating Officer of the American Institute for the Advancement of Forensic Studies (AIAFS).*

Jason Weaver, PhD, *earned his doctorate degree in Psychology from the University of Minnesota in Minneapolis, MN. He currently teaches social psychology and research design at Colorado College. His research primarily examines identity and responses to psychological threat.*

Jeffrey Riley, BA, *graduated from the St. Olaf Psychology program in 2016 with concentrations in Neuroscience and Linguistics. Current research interests include addiction and trauma rehabilitation, as well as the role of positive psychology in effective rehabilitation efforts. He is presently employed by Pathways Counseling Center.*

Jessica Marsolek, MSW, LGSW, *is the social worker for the Minnesota Chapter of The Huntington's Disease Society of America (HDSA). HDSA is the largest volunteer organization dedicated to improving the lives of those affected by HD. Jessica is also an elementary school social worker for the Independent School District #15, MN.*

Jodee Kulp *has spent 40 years working in the field of foster care, kinship care, and adoptive care. Since 1997, she has dedicated her research and advocacy to the field of FASD and today specializes in working with the adult population. She is the author, co-author and contributing author of twelve books in supporting professionals, families and other caregivers working with persons prenatally exposed to alcohol. She publishes and reviews articles and presents for national and international audiences.*

Jody Allen Crowe, MSc, *Public School Administration, professor, Concordia St. Paul University. Crowe authored "The Fatal Link: The Connection Between School Shooters and the Brain Damage from Prenatal Exposure to Alcohol." He is the founder and president of Healthy Brains for Children.*

John Von Eschen, MA, LMFT, *is a licensed marriage and family counselor and has been practicing at Pathways Counseling center as a gambling therapist for the last 12 years. He also works with Northstar Problem Gambling Alliance as a trainer and educator about the dangers of problem gambling dual addictions and prevention.*

Jolene Rebertus, MA, LPCC, LICSW, *holds a Master's degree in Forensic Psychology. Ms. Rebertus is currently working for the MN Department of Corrections as a State Program Administrative Manager, managing Health Services Release Planning services statewide. Ms. Rebertus' practice is focused on offender reentry and access to treatment post release, serving on numerous committees throughout the state of Minnesota, and providing various trainings on helping individuals with health needs exiting a correctional facility.*

Joseph H. Metzen, BA, JD, *has a BA in History and German from the University of Minnesota at Morris, and a J.D. from the University of Minnesota Law School. He presently works for the Nicollet County Court in St. Peter, Minnesota.*

Julia Besser, MA, *is a former humanitarian aid worker who is currently earning her PhD in Counseling Psychology, with a focus on corrections and policy making. She teaches undergraduate coursework in Psychopathology and Professional Development and serves as the President of the Graduate Student Council at Texas Woman's University. Her current research focuses on how the punitive criminal dilemma is affected by issues of competency and the complexity of detecting malingering. Her doctoral research is guided by her years of experience within the Texas state prison system, a forensic psychiatric hospital and a substance use treatment center.*

Julie Anderson, MA, LMFT, *is a Master's level Licensed Marriage and Family Therapist with over 11 years' experience in the mental health field, working with children, adolescents, adults, and couples. Julie has worked in a variety of settings, which include residential treatment, group therapy treatment, clinical agencies, and in the community. Julie's clinical specialties include adults with severe persistent mental illness (SPMI), pre- and post-marriage education, and relationship dynamics.*

Kate Bailey, MPP, *is the Development Director and former coordinator of the Trauma-Informed Care Technical Assistance Center at Minnesota Communities Caring for Children (MCCC), a nonprofit organization dedicated to the prevention of child abuse and neglect. Kate has a Master's degree in Public Policy from the Hubert H. Humphrey School of Public Affairs in Minneapolis, Minnesota.*

Kathy J. Harowski, PhD, LP, *is a clinical psychologist with expertise in forensic and health psychology. She has worked in a wide range of public-sector settings and is currently working for the Minnesota Department of Human Services as a behavioral medicine practitioner at St. Peter Security Hospital. Dr. Harowski is an experienced teacher and trainer who has worked in higher education, teaching and developing curriculum for undergraduate and graduate students in psychology, criminal justice and forensic psychology.*

Kayla Vorlicky, BA, *is a graduate of Hamline University whose studies focused on the intersections of criminal justice and psychology. Her specific interests in the realm of criminal justice and psychology focus on the criminal behavior or involvement of individuals with developmental deficits, such as those associated with Autism Spectrum Disorder (ASD) and FASD, as well as delusional issues, such as those associated with schizophrenia.*

Kimberly D. Dodson, PhD, *is an Associate Professor and Criminology Program Director in the Department of Social and Cultural Sciences at the University of Houston – Clear Lake. Her research interests include evidence-based assessment of correctional policies and programs and the rehabilitation and treatment needs of women, minorities, and special needs offenders.*

Kristin Turner, MA, LPCC, DBTC, *received her Master's in Counseling Psychology from the University of St. Thomas in Minneapolis, Minnesota. She is independently licensed in the state of Minnesota as a Licensed Professional Clinical Counselor, providing therapy to individuals with serious and persistent mental illness. Kristin is trained in Dialectical Behavior Therapy and has experience facilitating DBT groups in intensive outpatient programs.*

Laura Cooney-Koss, PsyD, MCJ, *is a licensed Clinical Psychologist in Delaware and New Jersey and is the owner and Clinical Director of Forensic Associates of Delaware, LLC. Dr. Cooney-Koss and the clinicians in this practice specialize in conducting psychological evaluations for a variety of legal referral questions and providing training for the community and professionals on forensic clinical issues.*

Leslie Barfknecht, LCSW, *is Co-Founder of Change Partnership, LLC, an organization dedicated to the implementation of evidence-based practices, and The Healthy Mind Institute, a private practice offering psychotherapy and wellness classes. Ms. Barfknecht is currently a Treatment Supervisor at Sand Ridge Secure Treatment Center in Mauston, WI, and has expertise in working with offender and high-risk populations in both an administrative and direct practice role, specializing in sexual offender treatment program development and delivery in a forensic setting. She is a Member of the Motivational Interviewing Network of Trainers (MINT) and a Certified Trainer for the International Center for Clinical Excellence (ICCE).*

Margaret R. Wimberley, MA, *was a Field Operations Manager for News, Sports and Entertainment for ABC-TV, New York. Shows included: World News Tonight, Monday Night Football, Nightline, World Series Baseball, The Academy Awards, Good Morning America, The Tour de France. Subsequent to a career change, she turned her focus to forensic study, and has a strong research interest in topics related to the criminal justice and forensic mental health aspects of Fetal Alcohol Spectrum Disorder (FASD).*

Mario L. Hesse, PhD, *is a Professor of Criminal Justice at St. Cloud State University (MN). Dr. Hesse's research and teaching interests focus on corrections, gangs and media and crime. Mario has extensive practitioner-based experience working in the corrections field (adult community-based programs, juvenile detention centers and juvenile probation).*

Marissa Zappala, MA, *has a Bachelor's in Psychology and Criminal Justice from Penn State University, as well as a Master's in Forensic Psychology from John Jay College of Criminal Justice. Her clinical interests include cognitive biases and clinical deacon-making in forensic psychology.*

Martha Nance, MD, *is a board-certified neurologist and clinical geneticist, who has been the Director of the HD Center of Excellence at Hennepin County Medical Center since 1991. She is an Adjunct Professor in the Department of Neurology at the University of Minnesota, and also the Medical Director of the Struthers Parkinson's Center.*

Matthew D. Krasowski, MD, PhD, *is a pathologist, Clinical Professor, and Vice Chair of Clinical Pathology and Laboratory Services in the Department of Pathology at the University of Iowa Hospitals and Clinics. He has interest in the pharmacology and analytical toxicology of drugs of abuse. He has published multiple articles and book chapters on pharmacology and drugs of abuse.*

Megan Moeller, MSW, LICSW, *holds a Master's degree in Social Work. Ms. Moeller is currently working for the MN Department of Corrections as a Corrections Program Director, supervising Health Services Release Planning services statewide. Over the last ten years she has provided mental health care to adults within community and correctional, focusing on offender reentry and access to treatment post release.*

Nina Ross, LICSW-MPH, *has worked as a senior social worker at the Huntington's Disease Center of Excellence at Hennepin County Medical Center since 2007. She has been the social worker for the ALS Center of Excellence there since 2003. She has been part of mental health teams in several adult and pediatric emergency departments and was a child protection social worker for a number of years. She also worked at the Centers for Disuse Control and Prevention in the then Violence Epidemiology branch.*

Olivia Johnson, DM, *holds a doctorate in Organizational Leadership Management from the University of Phoenix, School of Advanced Studies. She is the Illinois State Representative and active Board Member for the National Police Suicide Foundation, she holds a three-year term with the Illinois Suicide Prevention Alliance (ISPA) as a suicidology researcher, and is an active ISPA member. Her life's work is focused on suicide awareness and prevention efforts through research, publication, and community efforts.*

Pamela Oberoi, MA, *is a psychotherapist and the director of refugee and immigrant services at Pathways Counseling Center. She is a researcher in the field of trauma, war trauma, and other topics connected to psychopathology. Pamela has authored and co-authored articles related to these topics, including the topic of confabulation.*

Phyllis Burger, EdS, *is a Doctoral Candidate and full-time faculty in the Department of Graduate Teacher Education at Concordia University, St. Paul, MN. Her research, work, and teaching focus is childhood trauma, incarcerated women, and mental illness. Phyl works in partnership with the American Institute for the Advancement of Forensic Studies (AIAFS).*

Rachel Tiede, MA, LMFT, *is a therapist with Pathways Counseling Center in St. Paul and has a private practice in Burnsville, Minnesota. She is also adjunct faculty for Concordia University, St. Paul, and provides trainings for different organizations Her specialties include working with domestic violence and individuals with intellectual and developmental delays.*

Randy Stinchfield, PhD, *Clinical Psychologist and Associate Director, Center for Adolescent Substance Abuse Research, Department of Psychiatry, University of Minnesota Medical School. Dr. Stinchfield has conducted clinical studies and survey research in the area of problem gambling with both adult and youth samples. He has published this research in journal articles and book chapters. His current work in problem gambling focuses on the prevalence of gambling among youth and adults, assessment of gambling treatment outcome, and the development of instruments to measure problem gambling. His research on classification accuracy of DSM-IV diagnostic criteria for Pathological Gambling is credited as the rationale for lowering the diagnostic threshold in DSM-5.*

Resmiye Oral, MD, *is a Professor of Pediatrics and Director of Child Protection Program at the University of Iowa Children's Hospital. She is the co-chair of UIHC Trauma Informed Care Initiative and a member of the UI Trauma Informed Practices Initiative and Central Iowa ACEs Steering Committee. She engages in multiple community-based activities related to Adverse Childhood Experiences, (ACEs) and child abuse prevention and publishes regularly on child abuse-related topics.*

Robin L. Brown, PhD, LP, ABPP/CN, *received her doctorate from the University of Michigan. She is a licensed psychologist with ABPP Board Certification in Clinical Neuropsychology. She has over twenty-five years of clinical experience and has worked in a variety of settings, including outpatient clinics, inpatient psychiatry, correctional facilities, and private practice, as well as having held adjunct faculty positions.*

Ryan Chukuske, MA, *is the Director of Staff Learning and Development at a forensic facility in Minnesota. Prior to this appointment, he was a Clinical Program Therapist for 10 years, working specifically with sex offenders diagnosed with various developmental disorders. Ryan is also an adjunct professor with Concordia University, St. Paul.*

Samantha Carter, MBA, EJD, *has worked for county governments for seven years, spending the majority of her time in Human Service and the Criminal Justice areas. Samantha is interested in promoting criminal justice systems that are inclusive to the needs of offenders with mental health issues.*

Sara Hartigan *is a second-year Forensic Psychology Master's student at John Jay and will be joining Richard Rogers' lab at the University of North Texas for her PhD studies. Her main areas of interest include clinical evaluations and developing treatment interventions within the forensic population.*

Sarah Herrick, MA, LP, LPCC, CCFC, *has worked with sexual abusers ranging in age from ten to elderly since 1991, in residential, community mental health, and secured settings. Currently, she is working with civilly committed sexual abusers and is an adjunct professor with Concordia University's (St. Paul, MN) Forensic Mental Health on-line graduate program.*

Stefanie Varga, PhD, LP, *is a licensed clinical neuropsychologist in MN with expertise in traumatic brain injury, prenatal exposure, and neurological injury and illness. She owns and operates an outpatient clinic, Treehouse Psychology, PLLC, in Hugo, MN. Dr. Varga also works privately as a court-appointed neutral evaluator completing juvenile and adult forensic psychological and neuropsychological evaluations.*

Stephanie A. Kolakowsky-Hayner, PhD, CBIST, FACRM, *is an Associate Professor of Research in the Department of Rehabilitation Medicine at the Icahn School of Medicine at Mt. Sinai in New York, NY. She serves as the Immediate Past Chairman of the Board of the Brain Injury Association of California. She is a member of the Academy of Certified Brain Injury Specialists' Board of Governors and the American Congress of Rehabilitation Medicine Board of Governors.*

Tina Jay, MA, *has been an advocate for children as a Guardian ad Litem since 1998, with a background in Early Childhood Education, a Bachelor's degree in Social Work, and a Master's degree in Forensic Mental Health. Tina has extensive training and experience in the area of Fetal Alcohol Spectrum Disorder (FASD).*

Trisha M. Kivisalu, Ph.D., *is a Staff Psychologist at the University of Texas Health Science Center, San Antonio. She completed her doctorate in Clinical Psychology at the California School of Professional Psychology at Alliant International University in Fresno, California, an APA accredited Ph.D. program. She has experience working with children, youth, adults, and older adults in academic, clinical, research and assessment settings. She has over 15 years of experience working in the mental health field. She has worked in the community, university and hospital settings, clinics, private practice, and non-profit organizations. She enjoys the combination of clinical work with research, supervision, outreach, and teaching in university hospital settings as well as engaging in information sharing through publications and presentations at local and national conferences.*

Valerie Gonsalves, PhD, MLS, *is the Psychologist Manager for the Wisconsin Division of Community Corrections. Previously, she worked at Sand Ridge Secure Treatment center where she implemented a DBT program and assisted in the development of programs focused on treatment engagement. She specialized in working with individuals with disordered personalities.*

SPECIAL RECOGNITION

We sincerely appreciate the numerous edits and countless hours Sharon Weinkauf devoted to the completion of this textbook. Her dedication was influenced, in part, by the amount of information she gained while editing each chapter. Sharon expressed how the knowledge gained from this experience enhanced her understanding of mental health issues experienced by family members, friends and acquaintances she holds near and dear to her heart.

We also appreciate the numerous amount of hours Jodee Kulp devoted to design, production, edits, and indexing of this source guide. Her dedication to this project has proven invaluable and we are grateful for the many years in book design and publication work she has. Now that this project is under her belt, she can add APA styling to her many skills.

TABLE OF CONTENTS

About the Book 5

About the Editors: Jerrod Brown and Erv Weinkauf 6

Overview of Forensic Mental Health 7

About the Contributors 9

Special Recognition 17

Chapter Titles:

1. **Autism Spectrum Disorder (ASD) in the Criminal Justice System** 21
   Jerrod Brown, Hannah Fordice, Barbara Luskin, Diane Harr, Bethany R. Hastings,
   Amanda Beltrani, Phyllis Burger, Erin Rafferty-Bugher, Erv Weinkauf, Gennae Falconer,
   Casie Nauman & Ryan Chukuske

2. **Borderline Personality Disorder in the Criminal Justice System** 49
   Kristin Turner & Beth Jordan

3. **Competency to Stand Trial (CST): A Beginner's Guide** 82
   Amanda Beltrani, Marissa Zappala, Laura Cooney-Koss, Ann Marie Winskowski & Jerrod Brown

4. **Confabulation: A Beginner's Guide for Criminal Justice
   and Forensic Mental Health Professionals** 93
   Jerrod Brown, Cody Charette, Jason Weaver, Cameron R. Wiley, Erik W. Asp, Erin Watts,
   Pamela Oberoi, Janina Cich, Erv Weinkauf, Kayla Vorlicky, Deb Huntley, Erwin Concepcion,
   Carlo Giacomoni, & Mario L. Hesse

5. **Dementia in the Criminal Justice System** 114
   Robin L. Brown & Carlie J. Bolin

6. **Evidence-Based Practice: Applying General Principles of
   Effective Psychotherapy in Forensic Mental Health Settings** 142
   Leslie Barfknecht, Valerie M. Gonsalves, Samantha L. Carter, Marissa Zappala & Sara Hartigan

7. **Fetal Alcohol Spectrum Disorder (FASD): A Beginner's Guide for
   Clinical and Forensic Professionals** 160
   Jerrod Brown, Cody Charette, Stefanie Varga, Sarah E. Herrick, Anthony Wartnik, Tina Jay,
   Amanda Fenrich, Phyllis Burger, Rachel Tiede, Anne Russell, Stephanie A. Kolakowsky-Hayner,
   Julie R. Anderson, Erv Weinkauf, Jodee Kulp, Jody Allen Crowe, Ann Yurcek, Diane Neil,
   & Margaret Wimberley

8. **Forensic Risk Assessment: A Beginner's Guide**..................184
    Jerrod Brown & Jay P. Singh

9. **Huntington's Disease and the Criminal Justice System**..................193
    Martha Nance, Nina Ross, Jessica Marsolek, & Adam Piccolino

10. **Illegal Street Drugs and Prescription Medications in the Criminal Justice System**..................216
    Matthew D. Krasowski

11. **Malingering and Deception: A Practitioner's Guide**..................242
    Erv Weinkauf, Sara Hartigan, Marissa Zappala, Julia Besser, Cody Charette,
    Laura Cooney-Koss, Kathy Harowski, Blake Harris, & Kayla Vorlicky

12. **Obsessive Compulsive Disorder (OCD) and Compulsive Hoarding in the Criminal Justice System**..................268
    Deb Huntley, Janina Cich, Hal Pickett, Deborah Eckberg, Olivia Johnson,
    & Kimberly D. Dodson

13. **Offender Reentry: A Summary of History, Existing Barriers, and Best Practices**..................284
    Megan Moeller & Jolene Rebertus

14. **Pediatric Abusive Head Trauma: A Practitioner's Guide**..................299
    Jerrod Brown & Resmiye Oral

15. **Problem Gambling: A Beginner's Guide for Clinical and Forensic Professionals**..................317
    Jerrod Brown, Randy Stinchfield, Mario L. Hesse, Matthew D. Krasowski, Blake Harris,
    John Von Eschen, Elizabeth Cardwell, & Phyllis Burger

16. **Problem-Solving Courts: An Overview**..................353
    Allison Krehbiel & Joseph H. Metzen

17. **Schizophrenia: A Beginner's Guide for Clinical and Forensic Considerations**..................371
    Jerrod Brown, Beth Jordan, Erin J. Watts, Cheryl Arndt, Matthew D. Krasowski,
    Amanda Beltrani, Andrea Patrick, Erik Asp, Aaron Trnka, Phyllis Burger, Debra Huntley,
    Trisha M. Kivisalu, Deborah A. Eckberg, Erwin Concepcion, & Samantha L. Carter

18. **Suggestibility: A Beginner's Guide for Criminal Justice and Forensic Mental Health Professionals**..................404
    Jerrod Brown, Elizabeth Quinby, Erv Weinkauf, Charlotte Gerth Haanen,
    Hal Pickett, Danielle Price, & Eric Skog

19.   **Trauma-Informed Care (TIC): An Overview with Applications
      for the Criminal Justice System** 422
      Kate Bailey & Jerrod Brown

20.   **Traumatic Brain Injury (TBI) in the Criminal Justice System:
      A Practitioner's Guide** 439
      Erwin Concepcion, Jerrod Brown, Deborah Eckberg, Margaret Wimberley,
      Cameron Wiley, & Jeffrey Riley

      Subject Index 476

CHAPTER 1

AUTISM SPECTRUM DISORDER (ASD) IN THE CRIMINAL JUSTICE SYSTEM

JERROD BROWN, HANNAH FORDICE, BARBARA LUSKIN, DIANE HARR,
BETHANY R. HASTINGS, AMANDA BELTRANI, PHYLLIS BURGER, ERIN RAFFERTY-BUGHER,
ERV WEINKAUF, GENNAE FALCONER, CASIE NAUMAN, & RYAN CHUKUSKE

CHAPTER OVERVIEW

Autism spectrum disorder (ASD) is a pervasive developmental disability that is characterized by deficits in social and communications skills, cognitive rigidity, as well as a wide range of behavioral symptoms. The presence of impaired social and communication skills can be particularly debilitating and isolating to these individuals. Autism spectrum disorder is highly individualized; an individual's level of impairment ultimately falls within a continuum ranging from mild to severe. This chapter discusses scenarios in which people with ASD may find themselves in contact with the justice system and reviews the specific challenges that they may face within those contexts. In light of the unique difficulties inherent to this population, a discourse regarding the diagnostic criteria and manifestation of ASD is imperative to increasing education and awareness among those who are involved in the intersection of ASD and the criminal justice system.

WHAT IS AUTISM SPECTRUM DISORDER?

The *Diagnostic and Statistical Manual of Mental Disorders (DSM)* is the most widely used classification or diagnostic tool for practitioners and researchers within the field of psychology (American Psychiatric Association [APA], 2013). The fourth edition of the DSM (DSM-IV) characterized autistic disorder, Asperger's syndrome, childhood disintegrative disorder, and pervasive developmental disorder as separate and distinct diagnoses under the general heading of pervasive developmental disorders. However, in the fifth edition (DSM-5), these disorders were combined into one diagnosis (APA, 2013). Although peer-reviewed journal articles prior to 2013 refer to these disorders as separate conditions, the DSM-5 was modified to reflect the evolving conceptualization of autism as a singular diagnosis, as supported by current research examining the disorder

(APA, 2013). It is important to note that this chapter will discuss autism as presented in the DSM-5 diagnostic criteria. Current practice suggests that a previous diagnosis of autism, Asperger syndrome or PDD-NOS will automatically convert to autism spectrum diagnosis.

The key diagnostic features of autism spectrum disorder are persistent impairment of social communication and interaction, and restrictive or repetitive behaviors (APA, 2013). Although individuals affected by ASD share these common characteristics to varying degrees, no two cases generate identical symptom profiles (Lord & Cook, 2013). Autism spectrum disorder symptoms develop in early childhood, prior to the age of three, although they may not be recognized at that time based on the severity of the disorder. Recent research has demonstrated a marked increase in adult diagnoses, due to lack of recognition of symptoms earlier (Fountain, King, & Bearman, 2011). Individual manifestations, severity, developmental level, presence of a support system, and early intervention may mask difficulties associated with ASD in some contexts, perhaps lending to the prevalence of later diagnosis (APA, 2013).

According to the DSM-5, ASD is four times more common in males than females, and is even more prevalent in males when milder forms are taken into consideration (APA, 2013). Furthermore, the number of individuals being diagnosed with ASD has increased substantially over the last decade (Centers for Disease Control and Prevention [CDC], 2014; Richler, Huerta, Bishop, & Lord, 2010). Autism spectrum disorder is now considered the fastest growing developmental disability in the United States (CDC, 2015). The Center for Disease Control estimates that one in 68 individuals has been diagnosed with ASD (CDC, 2015), and that autism diagnoses are increasing at a rate of 10% to 17% each year (National Human Genome Research Institute [NHGRI], 2012). This sharp growth in diagnoses may be attributed to several factors, including broader diagnostic criteria, increased awareness, and improved identification (Salsedaa, Dixona, Fass, Miora, & Leark, 2011).

Although there is not yet a specific known cause for ASD, there are multiple different beliefs regarding the development of the disorder (Grzadzinski, Luyster, Spencer, & Lord, 2012; Higgs & Carter, 2015). Estimates for heritability of ASD range from 37% to more than 90%, and about 15% of ASD cases are associated with several known genetic mutations (APA, 2013). Brain scans of individuals with ASD have shown differences in the shape and structure of the brain. The amygdala, prefrontal cortex, and fusiform gyrus, all of which are associated with social functioning, have been found to be atypical among those diagnosed with ASD (Baron-Cohen, O'Riordan, Stone, Jones, & Plaisted, 1999; Critchley et al., 2000; Dalton et al., 2005; Schultz et al., 2000). Murphy (2010) proposes that the etiology of ASD is likely to be multifactorial, with a neuro-genetic basis closely associated with abnormal brain development, specifically a disconnection between brain regions. Environmental factors that may increase the risk of developing ASD have been identified, including older parental age, low birth weight and fetal exposure to hazardous substances, such as the anticonvulsant medication *Valproate* (APA, 2013). Higgs and Carter (2015) note evidence of a bio-psychosocial model that suggests the etiology and developmental trajectories of the disorder are most likely a result of the complex interplay of several different biological and environmental factors.

DIAGNOSTIC CO-MORBIDITY

Between 70% and 74% of children with autism spectrum disorder (ASD) are diagnosed with a co-morbid mental disorder, and about 40% have two or more co-morbid mental disorders (APA, 2013; Mattila et al., 2010). Psychopathology and intellectual disabilities are more likely to occur in individuals with ASD than in those with intellectual disabilities alone, signaling that autism itself may be a risk factor for psychopathology (Helverschou, Bakken, & Martinsen, 2011). Some of the most commonly found disorders in combination with ASD are anxiety disorder, Attention-Deficit hyperactivity disorder (ADHD), and oppositional defiant disorder (ODD) (Simonoff et al., 2008). Depression is also related to ASD and appears to correlate with higher developmental age and IQ, as well as greater ASD symptom severity (Mayes, Calhoun, Murray, & Zahid, 2011). Individuals with ASD may also have an increased risk of developing a substance use disorder (SUD); a twin study from Washington University School of Medicine found that the presence of autistic traits is associated with a greater likelihood of abuse and addiction to alcohol and drugs, possibly due to the tendency for repetitive behavior which increases the risk of addiction (De Alwis et al., 2014).

Co-morbid health conditions, such as epilepsy, diabetes, and asthma, are also common in individuals with autism (Freeman, Roberts, & Daneman, 2005; Kotey, Ertel, & Whitcomb, 2014; Tuchman, Moshe, & Rapin, 2009). Epilepsy, in particular, has an extremely high co-occurrence with ASD; a recent study found that around 22% of those with ASD develop epilepsy by adulthood (Bolton et al., 2011). Children who have co-morbid ASD and seizure disorder may also retain greater cognitive impairments, lower adaptive skills, emotional problems, and higher rates of psychiatric drug use (Hara, 2007). A study in 2010 found that children with ASD who experienced seizures also tended to exhibit greater impairments across all domains of functioning (Matson, Neal, Hess, Mahan, & Fodstad, 2010). The presence of health conditions in someone with autism increases the risk of injury, medical emergencies, and early death (Forsgren et al., 2005).

Adults, especially those who reached adulthood before 1980, may have multiple but inaccurate diagnoses (including personality disorders), as the symptoms of autism were not recognized. The difficulty diagnosing ASD is exacerbated by ambiguity on how autism presents during adulthood and how it should be differentiated from other conditions, such as cluster A personality disorders (Allen et al., 2008; Haskins & Silva, 2006). The presence of secondary conditions in someone with ASD may complicate not only the diagnosis and treatment of all disorders, but could also lead to an increased propensity for involvement in the criminal justice system (Alexander, Chester, Green, Gunaratna, & Hoare, 2015; Gómez de la Cuesta, 2010; Newman & Ghaziuddin, 2008; Palermo, 2004). Co-morbid mental health conditions that are often associated with ASD may be a compounding factor when someone on the autism spectrum comes into contact with the legal system, due to perceived antisocial behavior, inability to interpret social cues, and communication challenges (Cohen, Dickerson & Forbes, 2014; Långström, Grann, Ruchkin, Sjöstedt, & Fazel, 2009; Newman & Ghaziuddin, 2008).

OVERVIEW OF ASD IN THE CRIMINAL JUSTICE SYSTEM

Individuals with autism spectrum disorder may come in contact with the criminal justice system for a variety of reasons. However, the exact prevalence rate of criminal justice contact within this population is unknown due to the small sample size utilized in the studies on this intersection (Baron-Cohen, 1988; Ghaziuddin, Tsai, & Ghaziuddin, 1991; Haskins & Silva, 2006; Kristiansson & Sorman, 2008; Mawson, Grounds, & Tantam, 1985; Mouridsen, Rich, Isager, & Nedergaard, 2008; Schwartz-Watts, 2005). Additionally, these studies may not account for the number of individuals who did not have a diagnosis when they entered the criminal justice system. Despite the lack of major research, the general consensus of existing studies is that individuals with ASD may be at an increased risk of committing illegal acts and are more likely to experience abuse, neglect, and violent victimization than the general population (Ghaziuddin et al., 1991; Mouridsen, 2012; Petersilia, Foote, Crowell, & National Research Council [U.S.], 2001). The possibility exists that contact with the justice system among individuals with ASD may not be driven by nefarious or malicious acts (Howlin, 2004); however, the underlying factors that contribute to criminal behavior among those with ASD are still uncertain, and it is likely that they are multifactorial and heterogeneous in nature (Freckelton, 2013). Some suggested risk factors for offending include, but are not limited to, low levels of intelligence, poor school performance and attendance, co-occurring mental disorders, restricted empathy, cognitive rigidity, a history of aggression, and limited ability to appreciate the social context of situations (Farrington, 2002; Haskins & Silva, 2006; Kawakami et al., 2012; Murrie, Warren, Kristiansson, & Dietz, 2002).

ASD Symptoms and Features

Misinterpretation of Social Cues

For an individual with autism spectrum disorder, difficulty understanding social etiquette and misinterpretation of social cues are deficits of the disorder. These deficits manifest in difficulty reading nonverbal cues and problems understanding others' thoughts and feelings, which may lead to inappropriate and possibly criminal behavior (Haskins & Silva, 2006; Murrie et al., 2002; Palermo, 2004). Criminal behavior resulting from social deficits may include: unwitting participation in illegal acts, unwanted sexual advances, inappropriate touching or physical contact, harassment, stalking, and a lack of understanding of social etiquette of private and public acts such as masturbation and exhibitionism (Freckelton, 2013).

Obsessive Interests

Obsessive interests are a commonly reported behavior amid individuals with ASD (Howlin, 2004; Mouridsen et al., 2008; Woodbury-Smith et al., 2005). Fixation or obsession with a particular idea, interest, or person may eventually lead to unintentional law breaking (Barry-Walsh & Mullen, 2004; Chen et al., 2003; Silva, Ferrari, & Leong, 2002). Some studies have highlighted that individuals with autism who have a fascination with fire are at an increased risk of committing arson (Barry-Walsh & Mullen, 2004; Everall & LeCouteur, 1990; Woodbury-Smith et al., 2010). Siponmaa, Kristiansson, Jonson, Nyden, and Gillberg (2001) found in their study of 16 arsonists, that almost two-thirds were diagnosed with ASD. Other unhealthy fixations and obsessions in someone with autism may lead to stalking, obsessive sexual interests, harassment, self-harm, and violent fascinations (Hagland & Webb, 2009; Freckelton, 2013). Obsessive interests that are not overtly dangerous may lead to illegal behavior, such as trespassing to access an object of intense interest. The Internet provides a convenient platform for persons with ASD to act out their obsessions in relative anonymity and from the safety of their own homes, potentially leading them to commit a cybercrime (Freckelton, 2013). The concrete and rigid thinking of someone with ASD who is hyper-focused on their obsession, may lead him or her to be negligent of environmental surroundings and the effect his or her actions could have on others. Early identification and treatment of rigid and fixated special interests (e.g., fire, violence, sexually inappropriate behaviors, single person obsession, etc.) that could potentially lead to criminal acts is highly recommended (Ray, Marks, & Bray-Garretson, 2004; Woodbury-Smith et al., 2010).

Language Deficits

Individuals with ASD also commonly display language deficits, with about 25% of children with this disorder failing to develop any verbal language skills (National Institute on Deafness and Other Communication Disorders [NIDCD], 2010). Even the highest-functioning individuals with ASD may have difficulty communicating when subjected to anxiety-provoking situations, such as the stress of an emergency event. According to a law enforcement guide by Petersilia et al. (2001), persons with ASD usually display a more concrete or "literal" type of communication and may struggle with abstract language, concepts, and ideas, and have difficulty understanding sarcasm or irony. In addition, those affected by ASD universally struggle with pragmatics, or the appropriate use of language for the situation at hand (Landa, 2000; Tager-Flusberg, Paul, & Lord, 2005). These language deficits can cause an individual with autism to have no response or a delayed response during questioning. Further, the individual may repeat what an officer or interviewer has just said, or may make blunt and inappropriate comments. A response from an individual with autism may be misinterpreted as disrespectful or challenging the authority figure. This breakdown in communication may result in anger, frustration, and fear of law enforcement and other professionals present during an emergency situation (Browning & Caulfield,

2011). To avoid misinterpretation, first responders should be aware of the common manifestations of language and communication deficits.

Due in part to language deficits, traditional investigative interviewing strategies are likely to be less effective on those with ASD compared to non-impacted persons (Maras & Bowler, 2010). Individuals with autism may be more likely to demonstrate acquiescence during interviews, interrogations, or testimony (Maras & Bowler, 2010). Acquiescence refers to the act of agreeing to a statement or question out of a desire to please someone else or do what is expected (Woodbury-Smith & Dein, 2014). It may occur more often in individuals with autism because of their desire to make friends and be socially accepted or from motivation to quickly end an interview that is uncomfortable and over-stimulating (North, Russell, & Gudjonsson, 2008; Woodbury-Smith & Dein, 2014).

DIFFICULTY WITH NOVELTY AND CHANGE

During adulthood, individuals with ASD often have trouble establishing independence, due to continued pattern rigidity, decision-making issues, and difficulty with novelty and change (APA, 2013; Luke, Clare, Ring, Redley, & Watson, 2012). Violent behaviors may be exhibited as a reaction to deviation from their established daily routine (Baron-Cohen, 1988; Mawson et al., 1985). Changes can cause severe tantrums that result in unintentional harm to the individual or those around them (Adler et al., 2015; Bronsard, Botbol, & Tordjman, 2010).

HYPER- OR HYPOSENSITIVITY TO STIMULI

Hyper- or hyposensitivity to sensory stimuli is a common issue associated with ASD. An inability to tolerate or process multiple stimuli simultaneously, such as sirens, loud noises, strong smells, bright lights, lots of questions, and other sensory integration difficulties, may lead someone with autism to shut down or act out. Emergency and law enforcement personnel who may potentially engage with individuals with ASD should be aware that anxiety, fear, and confusion may be caused by inappropriately handled encounters during high-stress situations. Increases in external stimuli may cause the individual to quickly escalate from simple, comforting or self-stimulating movements (e.g., rocking) into more violent movement (i.e., hitting, screaming, pushing, and kicking) (Browning & Caulfield, 2011).

Delayed ASD diagnosis is associated with a greater likelihood of criminal behavior, which reinforces the importance of early identification and intervention (Kawakami et al., 2012; Lord, 1995). For individuals who have ASD, a supervised environment may act as a protective factor against running away, victimization, perpetration, and medical emergencies (Mouridsen, 2012; National Autistic Society, 2008). Within the criminal justice system, it is crucial for professionals to identify those with ASD, including those who may not have been properly diagnosed prior to coming into contact with the criminal justice system, and accurately evaluate the person's strengths, limitations, and abilities (Katz & Zemishlanv, 2006; Wing, 1997). Without proper identification and evaluation, individuals with ASD may not receive adequate services and treatment, may not understand their constitutional rights, and may be unable to engage in legal counsel for their own defense (Mayes, 2003; Mouridsen, 2012).

SEXUALLY INAPPROPRIATE BEHAVIORS

Currently, research is very limited in the areas of sexuality, sexual offending, and sexual abuse among those with ASD (Sevlever, Roth, & Gillis, 2013; Walters et al., 2013). The lack of information about this topic likely reflects the general focus on ASD as a childhood disorder, as well as society's discomfort with discussing sexual issues (Ousley & Mesiov, 1991). However, many caregivers of children with ASD express concern that their child may involve themselves in inappropriate sexual behaviors as they reach adolescence and adulthood (Nichols & Blakeley-Smith, 2010). Limited research, mostly in the form of case studies, has revealed several sexual offenders diagnosed with ASD (Sevlever et al., 2013). Misunderstood behavior, social skill limitations, occasional obsessive behavior, and lack of education all play a role in the increased possibility that those with ASD will either engage in inappropriate sexual behavior or become the victim of it (Sevlever et al., 2013).

One of the reasons that sexuality is a problem for some individuals with ASD is due to the lack of acquired age-appropriate sexual and social knowledge (Griffiths, Quinsey, & Hingsburger, 1989; Price, 2003; Sutton et al., 2013). Individuals with ASD might miss opportunities to learn about normative sexual development from important resources like peers and mainstream educational health classes. Missing these opportunities may create an increased dependence on media sources to learn about sex, such as online pornography (Higgs & Carter, 2015). Teaching children with ASD about normal sexual development and interests may reduce the risk of them acting out inappropriately later in life (Mandall, Walrath, Manteuffel, Sgro, & Pinto-Martin, 2005); however, even when taught appropriate sexual behavior, individuals with ASD are likely to struggle when it comes to putting theory into practice. Hellemans, Colson, Verbraeken, Vermeiren and Deboutte (2007) highlighted that high-functioning adolescent males with ASD who have learned appropriate socio-sexual skills still tended to engage in problematic behaviors (i.e., masturbating in public, touching of the genitals in public, and having excessively frank conversations about sex). The gap between cognitive awareness of normative sexual behavior and the practice of this behavior is due in part to social skill limitations (Realmuto & Ruble, 1999; Sutton et al., 2013). Most people with ASD desire normal consenting sexual relationships, but may be unable to achieve them due to social, emotional, and contextual deficits (Higgs & Carter, 2015; Attwood, 2007). Therefore, it has been suggested that sex offender treatment programs providing services to those with ASD consider incorporating practical social skills training into their curriculum (Murrie et al., 2002; Sutton et al., 2013). Additionally, sexual offenders with autism may be completely unaware that they have caused harm to their victims, due to social and emotional deficits (Payne & Hollin, 2014); thus, treatment for sexual offenses committed by those with ASD should include empathy training as a key component (Ray et al., 2004).

A lack of socio-sexual knowledge, coupled with deficits in emotional regulation may increase sexually lewd behaviors among individuals with ASD (Konstantareas & Lunsky, 1997; Price, 2003; Realmuto & Ruble, 1999; Stokes & Kaur, 2005; Walters et al., 2013). Emotional labeling and coping strategies, such as cognitive reappraisal or ability to reframe a situation, have been identified as deficits to this population (Samson, Huber, & Gross, 2012). Autism Spectrum Disorder may also inhibit the ability to accurately detect, identify, and analyze others' emotions, in turn increasing the prospect that someone with ASD could misread the rejection or fear of a sexual partner (Adolphs, Sears, & Piven, 2001; Hill & Berthoz, 2004). Moreover, a 2007 study specifically reported that those with ASD lacked the ability to differentiate between desired and undesired physical contact. This could cause someone with ASD to be unaware of personal and physical boundary violations (Hellemans et al., 2007).

In some ASD cases, the presence of repetitive behaviors, hyper-focused interests, and sensory fascination may lead to an unusual fixation of sexual behaviors. Compulsive masturbation, fetishism, paraphilia, pornography, and sex-associated fears are some of the possible expressions of unusual sexual tendencies (Haskins & Silva, 2006; Hellemans et al., 2007; Ray et al., 2004). Individuals with autism may also have trouble distinguishing between public and private acts, creating an increase of inappropriate displays of compulsive sexual behaviors in public (Kalyva, 2010; Ruble & Dalrymple, 1993; Sevlever et al., 2013; Van Bourgondien & Reichle, 1997).

VIOLENCE AND AGGRESSION

Heightened media attention on ASD-associated crimes has raised public alarm over the possible link between an autism diagnosis and violent behavior (Mouridsen, 2012). Despite this speculation, there is very little research on the prevalence of aggression among individuals with ASD, and the existing research presents mixed findings (Lerner, Haque, Northrop, Lawer, & Bursztajn, 2012; Strickland, 2013). A 2009 meta-analysis found a significant relationship between high-functioning individuals with ASD and violence in only 11 of 147 reviewed studies, therefore deeming this relationship inconclusive (Bjørkly, 2009). However, several other case studies have suggested that the presence of certain traits, such as lack of social skills, restricted empathy, and intellectual deficits, may cause individuals with ASD to act out in certain situations (Barry-Walsh & Mullen, 2004; Holland, Clare & Mukhopadhyay, 2002; Lerner et al., 2012; Murrie et al., 2002). For example, Kohn, Fahum, Ratzoni and Apter (1998) presented a case study of a violent individual with autism whose behavior was significantly associated with deficits in Theory of Mind, (TOM), which is the lack of his or her ability to recognize that the behavior of others is driven by their mental states (i.e., beliefs and desires) and that one's behavior can affect the mental states of others (Baron-Cohen, 1995). Although not specified as diagnostic criteria, deficits in theory of mind are considered common in persons with autism (Attwood, 2007; Baron-Cohen, Jolliffe, Mortimore, & Robertson, 1997). Additionally, several other studies have supported the possibility of violent outbreaks and social misunderstandings among people with ASD, due to a lack of theory of mind (Haskins & Silva, 2006; Strickland, 2013).

Deficits in emotional regulation, which may manifest as lack of impulse control, aggression, and poor peer interaction, are also extremely common among people with ASD (Eisenberg et al., 1995; Loveland, 2005). Physiological arousal in individuals with autism with poor emotional regulation can cause violent and angry outbursts (Clements, 2005; Laurent & Rubin, 2004). Lerner et al. (2012) suggest that poor emotional regulation in combination with a lack of theory of mind may potentiate violent behavior in people with autism; for example, theory of mind difficulties could cause social confusion, which in turn could lead to an inability to contain frustration and, finally, physically acting out.

One example of a violent and aggressive "tantrum" describes the story of 11-year-old boy (Ferriss, 2015). In 2014, the boy, who was diagnosed with ASD, kicked a trashcan while being scolded for misbehaving at school. A school resource officer witnessed the outburst and promptly filed a disorderly conduct charge within the juvenile court system. Just a few weeks later, he tried to leave at the end of class with his peers, even though his teacher had instructed him to stay behind. The principal sent the same resource officer from the earlier incident to retrieve him, who resisted going with the officer. He ended up in handcuffs and was charged with a misdemeanor and felony assault of a police officer. Five months later, he was found guilty on all charges, a ruling that will likely affect the rest of his life (Ferriss, 2015). Cases like his are an example of how a child diagnosed with ASD may quickly end up in the criminal justice system due to acting out as a result of a lack of understanding regarding how to appropriately respond to authority figures.

When an individual with ASD displays violent behaviors, clinicians should assess for the presence of co-morbid psychiatric and substance use disorders (Ghaziuddin, 2005; Långström et al., 2009). A comprehensive evaluation may identify secondary conditions or stressors that might be contributing to problematic and dangerous behaviors (Palermo, 2004). For example, conduct disorder and oppositional defiant disorder are common co-morbidities among children diagnosed with ASD (Brereton, Tonge, & Einfeld, 2006; Kamp-Becker et al., 2011; Simonoff et al., 2008). Both of these disorders, by definition, are strongly associated with defiance, anger, and violent behavior (APA, 2013). Substance use disorder (SUD) is also associated with autistic symptoms, and up to 75% of individuals with ASD who begin addiction treatment report engaging in violent behaviors such as mugging, physical attacks, and assault with a weapon (Burnette et al., 2008; Chermack et al., 2008; De Alwis et al., 2014). Identification and treatment of co-morbid psychiatric disorders is essential in reducing the risk of violence among individuals with ASD (Långström et al., 2009).

SUICIDE AND SELF-INJURIOUS BEHAVIOR

Physical injuries, accidental or intentional, are another common reason individuals with ASD may come into contact with emergency and criminal justice personnel. Problems with motor skills and movement, such as clumsiness, poor coordination, and strange posture, may be present among those with ASD (Allen et al., 2008;

Bjørkly, 2009). These abnormalities may bolster higher frequency of accidents and injuries than their general population counterparts. In addition, repetitive movements, co-occurring disorders, and higher rates of suicidal ideation may all increase the risk that someone with ASD engages in self-harm behaviors.

Although restricted and repetitive behaviors constitute one of the diagnostic criteria for ASD, these characteristics are both historically less studied compared to the social/communication deficits portion of the disorder (Bodfish, Symons, Parker, & Lewis, 2000). Repetitive behaviors are usually harmless (i.e., rocking, arm flapping, snapping fingers, vocal sounds, repetitive blinking, etc.) but can become an emergency situation if they begin to cause harm to the individual or others. Self-injurious behavior (SIB) is a common problem for those with autism, with prevalence estimates as high as 50% (Adler et al., 2015; Baghdadli, Pascal, Grisi, & Aussilloux, 2003). Two of the most frequently seen SIBs in children with ASD are head-hitting and hand/skin-biting (Canitano, 2006). Self-injurious behavior may become aggravated while someone is incarcerated due to the unfamiliar environment, change in routine, and increased stress levels (The National Autistic Society, 2008). It is important to note that SIB is not limited to individuals with an ASD diagnosis: associated perinatal conditions, severe intellectual disability, and young age are all considered risk factors for SIB (Bodfish et al., 2000; Murphy, Hall, Oliver, & Kissi-Debra, 1999; Baghdadli et al., 2003).

Epilepsy and ASD are common co-occurring disorders that may result in unintentional self-injury and create an increased risk of suicide (Pompili, Girardi, Roberto, & Tatarelli, 2005). The most common type of seizure for individuals with autism who have epilepsy is a generalized tonic-clonic seizure, a classic manifestation of which is characterized by three phases: a) the body will flex/contract, extend, and tremor, followed by b) a "clonic" phase that includes contraction and relaxation of muscles, and finally c) a postictal phase characterized by an altered state of consciousness (Bolton et al., 2011; John Hopkins Medicine, 2014). Generalized tonic-clonic seizures may result in physical injuries from falling and/or depressive episodes during the postictal phase (Verrotti et al., 2008). Postictal-phase depressive episodes are coupled with an increased risk of suicide for the extent of the depressive episode (Fukuchi et al., 2002).

Suicidal ideation and a history of suicide attempts are 28 times more common in those with autism than those without (Mayes, Gorman, Hillwig-Garcia, & Syed, 2013). Depression, behavioral problems, or being bullied are all indications of suicide risk. A 2013 study suggested that nearly 50% of children with autism faced with the aforementioned difficulties have attempted suicide in the past or have indicated a high suicidal ideation (Mayes et al., 2013). Adjustment disorders and post-traumatic stress disorder have also been identified as significantly more common in individuals who have co-occurring ASD and display suicidal thoughts or behaviors (Kato et al., 2013; Storch et al., 2013). Time spent in an intensive care unit and the length of hospital stays after suicide attempts have both been found to be significantly longer for those with ASD compared to those without (Kato et al., 2013).

VICTIMIZATION

Those with disabilities such as ASD may be especially vulnerable to maltreatment, as they often are unable to recognize danger, defend themselves, or obtain assistance (Petersilia, 2001). In addition, the communication deficits commonly found in individuals with ASD may impede their ability to report being the victim of a crime or a crime they witnessed against someone else (Phipps & Ells, 1995; Sevlever et al., 2013). Moreover, some people with ASD experience difficulty differentiating between "safe" and "unsafe" individuals and the ability to recognize situations that typically evoke a fear response (Sevlever et al., 2013; Woodbury-Smith et al., 2005; Woodbury-Smith et al., 2010). In the absence of fear, persons with ASD may inadvertently place themselves in dangerous situations. Peer pressure, bullying, and caretaker or parental abuses are some of the possible ways that an individual with ASD may become a victim or unwilling participant in criminal behavior.

Those with ASD often desire social contact and relationships, but may lack the necessary skills to maintain positive relations with others (Bauminger, Shulman, & Agam, 2003; White & Schry, 2011). As a result, common consequences associated with ASD are isolation, rejection, and increased anxiety in social situations (Bellini, 2004; Wood & Gadow, 2010). The desire for acceptance among peers and misinterpretation of social situations may cause someone with ASD to behave in a manner they do not like or would not normally engage in, including unwitting participation in a crime (Petersilia, 2001). Individuals with ASD may also be more likely to confess to a crime they did not commit when being interrogated by law enforcement, in order to placate a peer or make a new "friend" happy (Debbaudt, 2002). Children with ASD are also much more likely to endure bullying at school and occasionally become bullies themselves, as a result of social anxiety (Humphrey & Symes, 2010; Zablotsky, Bradshaw, Anderson & Law, 2013).

A relevant example of social naivety and peer pressure is a 2014 news story of a 16-year-old boy with autism in southern Maryland who was tortured by two female classmates over the course of three months (Shapira & Hedgpeth, 2014; Wagner, 2014). The 17- and 15-year-old girls recorded themselves holding a knife to the boy's throat, forcing him to perform various sexual acts, physically assaulting him, and forcing him repeatedly into a frozen pond. The victim's mother stated that he believed the two girls were his friends and were just "playing around" (Shapira & Hedgpeth, 2014; Wagner, 2014). Sevlever et al. (2013) indicated that individuals with ASD may be unaware of what constitutes abuse and thus are less likely to report it and defend themselves. Unfortunately, submission to unwanted acts is not limited to peer and social interactions, but may also occur at the hands of a caretaker or family member.

Raising a child with disabilities has been identified as escalating parental stress levels, in turn putting these children at an increased risk of abuse (Hayes & Watson, 2013; Petersilia, 2001). The demands faced when raising a child with ASD may contribute to depression among caregivers, with the severity of the child's ASD-related symptoms negatively correlated to the caregiver's overall well-being and life satisfaction (Benson & Karlof, 2009; Bristol, Gallaghar, & Holt, 1993). Marital problems as a result of increased parental stress, financial difficulties related to cost of care, and family disruptions are common among those who have a child with autism (Benson, 2006; Benson & Karlof, 2009; Hastings, 2002). Higher levels of stress, depression, anxiety, social isolation, and marital dissatisfaction in parents are significantly correlated with an increase in abusive behavior toward a child (Rodriguez & Murphy, 1997; Whipple & Webster-Stratton, 1991). Furthermore, symptoms commonly present in children suffering from ASD, such as provoking behaviors, externalizing symptoms, and demanding or needy attitudes, have been associated with caregiver maltreatment (Chance & Scannapieco, 2002; Sprang, Clark, & Bass, 2005; Turner, Vanderminden, Finkelhor, Hamby, & Shattuck, 2011).

Changes in behavior and an increase in acting out may be signs of victimization in someone with ASD. Unfortunately, the normal fluctuation in behavioral issues across the lifespan of someone with ASD makes it difficult to use such traits as indicators of abuse (Sevlever et al., 2013). Furthermore, if there is limited or no communication with the victim regarding the problem, it is nearly impossible to identify occurrences of abuse by behavioral changes alone (Sevlever et al., 2013). Caretakers and other people that regularly come into contact with individuals with ASD should look for bruising, cuts, lacerations, decreased weight, unkempt appearance, and aggravated symptoms, in addition to behavioral problems, as possible warning signs of victimization.

MINORS WITH ASD AND JUVENILE COURT

Poor parental control, a chaotic environment, psychiatric co-morbidity, and a family history of mental health disorders or criminality are risk factors for violent behavior in children with ASD (Ghaziuddin, 2005; Vermeiren, Jespers, & Moffit, 2006). Furthermore, the cognitive, social, and behavioral impairments of ASD may make it difficult for youth with ASD to recognize the consequences of criminal behavior, further decreasing already low levels of self-control (Mayes, 2003; Woodbury-Smith et al., 2005).

ASD develops in early childhood, leaving many of those affected by it with disrupted and insecure attachment patterns with caregivers, especially for individuals with co-occurring intellectual or developmental disabilities (Grzadzinski et al., 2012; Rutgers, Bakermans-Kranenburg, van Ijzendoorn, & van Berckelaer-Onnes, 2004). A recent meta-analysis indicated that poor attachment is significantly associated with delinquent behavior, and that the association is strongest when attachment to parents or caretakers is insecure at a very young age, as it tends to be in those with ASD (Hoeve et al., 2012). Increased risk of poor attachment or attachment disorders in this population, paired with stressful, chaotic, or abusive home-lives, may place children with autism on the pathway to repeat offending during adolescence and adulthood.

Although attachment problems and familial stress can cause acting out at home, delinquent behavior in youths with ASD is likely to come out in the context of school; childhood offenses are more likely to occur when there is peer rejection, low popularity, and social isolation, all of which are common experiences for students with ASD (Cheely et al., 2012; Farrington, 2005). Students with disabilities are more likely to be suspended from school, referred to police, arrested, and charged in juvenile court for school-related incidents than students who do not have disabilities (Losen & Martinez, 2013; Larson & Turner, 2002; Quinn, Rutherford, & Leone, 2001). Attempts to fit in may also cause youths with ASD to be highly susceptible to negative peer influences, increasing their risk of participating in illegal behaviors in the future (Sutton et al., 2013). Sexually acting out at school or elsewhere may also be a problem for individuals with ASD as they reach physical maturity but often lack age-appropriate knowledge of normative sexual behavior (Griffiths et al., 1989; Price, 2003; Sutton et al., 2013). This reality is reflected in a 2009 study which found that juvenile sex offenders had a significantly higher rate of ASD symptoms than healthy controls had (Hart-Kerkhoffs et al., 2009). In general, crimes committed by juveniles with ASD are committed against a person instead of property (likely as a reactionary event) and tend to be milder offenses than those committed by juveniles without ASD (Cheely et al., 2012).

Approximately two-thirds of all arrested youths go to juvenile court; therefore, it is reasonable to assume that children with ASD who act out may end up in a courtroom (Office of Juvenile Justice and Delinquency Prevention, 2015). Due in part to milder criminal behavior, juvenile offenders diagnosed with ASD are less likely to be prosecuted than their counterparts, but rather, tend to be diverted into pre-trial interventions (Cheely et al., 2012). In addition, those who are given court-ordered interventions instead of being charged are more likely to have a co-occurring intellectual disability (Cheely et al., 2012). The Royal College of Psychiatrists (2006) strongly recommends that youths with autism who come in contact with the juvenile justice system be given routine screenings as well as access to psychiatric care. This care should include differentiation of ASD from other disorders, recognition of the impact that ASD may have on responsibility and mental capacity, and adequate provision of resources and treatment during the court process and subsequent sentence.

However, before firm policy recommendations regarding prevention services, intervention, and differential sentencing can be made for the juvenile justice system, there must be research done on the prevalence of disorders like ASD in offending adolescents (Vermeiren et al., 2006). A series of methodologically sound evaluations focusing on prevalence and co-morbidity of ASD in the juvenile justice system would be helpful in providing information on intervention and prevention recommendations and leading to recidivism reduction in juvenile offenders with the disorder (Teplin, Abram, McClelland, Dulcan, & Mericle, 2002).

ASD IN THE COURTS

Depending on symptomatology and individual circumstance, criminal responsibility and culpability may be mitigated in legal proceedings due to a diagnosis of autism spectrum disorder (ASD) (Freckelton, 2013). In addition to a diagnosis of ASD being a mitigating factor, it has been considered integral in decisions involving criminal intent, responsibility, and sanity (Freckelton, 2013). Autism may provide an alternative explanation for the *actus reus* (criminal act) or for the *mens rea* (the mental state of the individual at the time of the criminal act) in cases involving a defendant with autism (Cea, 2014).

Deficits commonly associated with ASD may impair an individual's ability to fully comprehend their legal rights and their ability to assist legal counsel in a criminal trial (Mayes, 2003). Furthermore, cognitive, communication, and social-emotional deficits may also make participating in personal defense during a criminal hearing difficult. According to Paterson (2008), an additional component of ASD is diminished emotional regulation, which can manifest as a lack of emotional expression when speaking. This absence of visible emotion may be misunderstood as apathy and/or lack of remorse for a criminal behavior. Paterson (2008) also found that individuals with autism lacked emotion when describing attacks or aggressive behaviors they had experienced. In addition to inhibited facial expressions, persons with ASD almost universally struggle with pragmatics, or the use of language that is appropriate for the setting (Landa, 2000; Tager-Flusberg et al., 2005). Testimony given with pragmatic errors may sound like the defendant is rude, inappropriate, careless, or crass. In cases where the individual is testifying for the prosecution, they may come across as though they are lying or unaffected by the crime they are alleging was committed against them. Expert testimony from a medical or mental health professional is one way to accurately relay to the court the effects of ASD on an individual's behavior and communicative ability in front of others (Cea, 2014).

Those with ASD experience and often interact with the world in a way that is unique to their symptom profile (Freckelton & List, 2009). Offenders and victims with ASD have risks and needs that are different than the general population, which can complicate the legal process (Murphy, 2003). Despite the evidence that deficits of ASD significantly alter a defendant's ability to function optimally during the legal process, some courts do not afford special treatment to defendants with autism (Freckelton, 2012; Freckelton, 2013; Mayes, 2003). Defendants with ASD would benefit from the help of trained advocates who understand their disability and can assist them with navigating the criminal justice system (Autism Speaks, 2015). Consideration by the court of the role autism and its associated symptoms play in the commission of crime increases the likelihood that an appropriate sentence, considerate of the defendant's disabilities, will be granted for the crime (Cea, 2014).

COMPETENCY TO STAND TRIAL

Intent, criminal responsibility, and culpability can be challenged in some cases involving a criminal defendant with autism (Cashin & Newman, 2009; Freckelton, 2012). An attorney for a client with ASD may request a competency evaluation as established in Dusky v. U.S. (1960). This landmark case held that for a defendant to be considered competent to stand trial, he must have "sufficient ability to consult with his lawyer with a reasonable degree of rational understanding" and a "rational as well as factual understanding of the proceedings against him" (Dusky v. U.S., 1960, p.362). Currently, all states use some modification of the Dusky Standard. If the client does not meet this two-prong legal standard for adjudicated competency at the time of the trial proceedings, the state must suspend prosecution of the client. A prosecutor may request a hearing at a later date to determine if the client is still legally incompetent. If at this point a judge determines that a client has been restored to capacity, the state may then resume prosecuting the client.

The Center for Disease Control and Prevention reported that, in 2011, roughly 38% of children with ASD also had a co-occurring intellectual disability that was severe enough to support incompetence to stand trial. Cases in which a defendant with ASD is found to be incompetent are likely to be dropped within several years, as autism and intellectual disability are incurable, and it is unlikely that competency will be restored (Strickland, 2013).

The principle of competency to stand trial has been established in the law for a long time, but the exact definition remains ambiguous (Roesch, Zapf, Golding, & Skeem, 2014). The Dusky standard, although clear in intent, does not elaborate what exactly constitutes "sufficient ability" or "reasonable degree of rational understanding" (Dusky v. U.S., 1960, p.362). Due to these conceptual ambiguities, interpretation of the Dusky standard and trial competency tends to fall heavily on mental health professionals, resulting in expert witnesses being called upon frequently in criminal cases involving persons with ASD (Freckelton, 2013). In an effort to give practical guidance to mental health professionals, the American Academy of Psychiatry and the Law (AAPL) has created a guideline for forensic psychiatric evaluation of competence to stand trial (Mossman et al., 2015); this guide may be useful in the assessment of ASD criminal defendants.

INSANITY DEFENSE

Pleading "not guilty by reason of insanity" means a person may concede to committing a crime but claim that they are not responsible due to their mental illness or disability (Legal Information Institute (b), 2015). The insanity defense was originally based off of M'Naghten's Case in 1843, which resulted in the M'Naghten rule being established by the English House of Lords in the 19th century and adopted in both the United States and Great Britain (Legal Information Institute (b), 2015). The M'Naghten rule presumes sanity unless the defense proves that "at the time of the committing of the act, the party accused was laboring under such a defect of reason, from disease of mind, as not to know the nature and quality of the act he was doing; or if he did know it, that he did not know he was doing what was wrong" (FindLaw (b), 2014; Legal Information Institute (b), 2015; Strickland, 2013).

Outside of the M'Naghten rule there are three other common tests used by the courts, depending on the jurisdiction, to determine legal insanity: the irresistible impulse test, the Durham rule, and the Model Penal Code test (FindLaw (a), 2014). The irresistible impulse test holds that the defendant was unable to control his or her impulses due to mental illness, the Durham rule holds that the criminal act was a direct result of mental illness, and the Model Penal Code test holds that the defendant failed to understand that his or her act was criminal or was unable to act within the confines of the law due to his or her mental illness (FindLaw (a), 2014). Most states use the M'Naghten rule, sometimes in combination with the irresistible impulse test or the Model Penal Code test; only New Hampshire uses the Durham rule; whereas Idaho, Kansas, Montana, and Utah do not uphold the insanity defense at all (FindLaw (a), 2014).

As explained above, the crux of the insanity defense depends upon the presence of a mental illness that causes criminal acts, impulses that may lead to criminal acts, or the inability to differentiate between what acts are criminal and what are not. According to the National Alliance on Mental Illness (2015), ASD falls under the category of mental illness, as do many of its commonly co-occurring disorders. However, since the Insanity Defense Reform Act of 1984, the burden of providing clear and convincing evidence of insanity at the time of the crime lies with the defendant, not the government (Offices of the United States Attorneys, 2015). This means that although ASD and many of its accompanying disorders are indeed mental illnesses, for the insanity defense to be used, the defendant must still prove that the symptoms and/or deficits of ASD were intense enough to inhibit understanding of the crime committed, that it caused the crime by impulse, or that the crime was a direct result of ASD symptoms.

In some cases ASD may excuse criminal responsibility, given its link to socio-emotional and intellectual impairments that affect rationality and understanding (Woodbury-Smith & Dein, 2014).

INCARCERATION

Currently, prevalence rates of inmates with autism spectrum disorder serving sentences within correctional settings are unknown (Robinson et al., 2012). In some ways, the strict routines and predictability of life in prison may provide the stability that someone on the spectrum needs to maximally function; on the other hand, many of the traits and deficits associated with ASD (i.e., communication deficits, sensory problems, difficulty with change, etc.) could make adjusting to the physical and social environment of prison difficult (McAdam, 2012; Robertson & McGillivray, 2015; Underwood, Forrester, Chaplin, & McCarthy, 2013;). Myers (2004) reported that individuals with ASD or learning disabilities are more likely to be taken advantage of, bullied, and ostracized while in prison than their peers without disabilities are. Furthermore, inmates with ASD tend to have higher levels of suicidality and are more likely to experience episodes of depression and generalized anxiety than inmates without ASD (McCarthy et al., 2015).

The lack of social skills common in individuals with ASD, collated with a desire for peer acceptance and friendship, likely play a role in the increased risk of prisoners with autism being targets for bullying and victimization (Allen et al., 2008; Bauminger et al., 2003; White & Schry, 2011). Some researchers have proposed that as an attempt to cope with victimization, individuals with autism may displace anger and hurt by acting out against other inmates or staff (Freckelton & List, 2009; Murrie et al., 2002; Robertson & McGillivray, 2015). Misinterpretation of maladaptive behavior stemming from victimization or difficulty adjusting can lead to an increased risk of forced isolation of the individual with ASD to protect those around (Paterson, 2008; Robertson & McGillivray, 2015). Although seclusion can effectively protect a vulnerable prisoner with ASD, it also limits his or her ability to engage in rehabilitation services and to further adapt to a correctional setting (Myers, 2004; Robertson, & McGillivray, 2015). Due to the nature of conditional release from prison often requiring improvements in adaptive living skills and completion of a treatment/rehabilitation program, inmates with autism that are frequently isolated may be incarcerated for longer periods of time (Robertson, & McGillivray, 2015). If conditional release is achieved, or upon completion of their sentence, offenders with ASD may have greater difficulty reintegrating into the community due to difficulties with independent living, lack of access to necessary services, change in routine, lack of structure, and poor social and economic support (Myers & Plauché-Johnson, 2007).

The ability of the criminal justice system to effectively deal with individuals with ASD is limited by the fact that many individuals are not accurately diagnosed before or upon admission (Talbot, 2009). Early identification of inmates with ASD allows better care and appropriate management, which can lead to overall outcome improvement (Robinson et al., 2012). Unfortunately, the support necessary for individuals with autism is often lacking in correctional facilities; for example, prison staff surveyed in a 2004 study reported a substantial shortage of resources, training, and ability to care for offenders with disabilities such as ASD (Myers, 2004).

PROBATION

During the criminal sentencing of an individual with ASD, the defense may state that a convict with autism may find the experience of incarceration more burdensome than the typical offender does, due to his or her disorder (*Shtukaturov v. Russia*, 2008). An alternative to prison in these cases is probation. Probation is a court-ordered substitute for prison wherein an individual is released to the community under supervision of a U.S. probation officer, with the stipulation of certain conditions (United States Courts, 2015). Although probation initially sounds like an ideal solution to the challenges of incarceration for someone with ASD, one major concern is whether these individuals are capable of adhering to the conditions of probation (Allen et al., 2008; Schellack, 2014).

Conditions of probation may or often include remaining in a certain geographical area, refraining from going to certain locations, performing community service, reporting regularly to a probation officer and court hearings, participating in treatment, and finding employment or engaging in vocational training (Legal Information Institute (a), 2015). These stipulations may be difficult for many to uphold, especially for someone with a developmental disability such as ASD. Violation of any of the aforementioned probationary terms may result in an issued warning, extension of probation, brief jail time, revocation of probation and a prison sentence, additional community service hours, or monetary fines/restitution (FindLaw, 2015). Social service programs that provide appropriate training and support for those with disabilities have long waiting lists and may not coordinate well with the criminal justice system. Common deficits in ASD, such as learning disabilities, lack of language development, social deficits, difficulty understanding abstract concepts, and other communication problems, may make meaningful engagement in court-ordered rehabilitation programs difficult (Ray et al., 2004; Robertson & McGillivray, 2015). In addition, adults with ASD often have trouble finding employment, adjusting to new jobs, and maintaining a job long-term (Hendricks, 2009); with or without intellectual disability, the majority of individuals with ASD are unemployed or underemployed (Gerhardt & Lainer, 2011).

Although probation is not a perfect solution for offenders with a diagnosis of ASD, it may be a viable alternative to incarceration. Probation allows for the individual to maintain his or her current support system and remain in any ongoing treatment or rehabilitation. In addition, probation allows the individual to access community mental health resources that the prison system often does not offer.

TREATMENT AND PREVENTION STRATEGIES

When an individual with autism spectrum disorder commits a crime, his or her behavior may be caused by deficits associated with the disorder rather than with risk factors identified by traditional offender risk assessment tools (Barry-Walsh & Mullen, 2004; Browning & Caulfield, 2011; Murphy, 2013). This reality brings into question the ability of common forensic risk assessment tools to effectively predict the degree of risk that an offender with autism presents. Use of evidence-based models for offender rehabilitation may be complicated by deficits associated with the disorder. As of 2015, no known large-scale studies had been conducted researching the dynamic risk factors that are associated with ASD and criminal offending. Additionally, no proposed programs adapted specifically to this client base had been developed (Higgs & Carter, 2015).

The most common approach for ASD treatment is educational and behavioral intervention, supported by pharmacological therapy for co-morbid mental health disorders. (Leskovec, Rowles, & Findling, 2008; Matson, Sipes, Fodstad, & Fitzgerald, 2011; Myers & Plauché-Johnson, 2007). A treatment approach that focuses on relapse prevention through skill building in the areas of social interaction and environmental context has shown particular promise in effectively reducing recidivism (Allen et al., 2008). In addition, treatment programs which integrate the variability in ASD symptoms, common co-occurring disorders, and individual capacities for arousal and change are likely to be more effective than a one-size-fits-all approach (Higgs, & Carter, 2015; Woodbury-Smith, Clare, Holland, & Kearns, 2006). For many people with ASD, visual communication is easier to understand than spoken communication; therefore, the use of visual aids in treatment may dramatically increase program participation and outcomes (The National Autistic Society, 2008). Alternative forms of therapy, such as detoxification, immunoregulatory intervention, supplements, music therapy, dolphin-assisted therapy, craniosacral manipulation, audio integral training, etc., have very little empirical evidence to either support or refute their effectiveness in reducing symptoms of ASD (Leskovec et al., 2008; Myers & Plauché-Johnson, 2007).

An additional barrier that is faced when developing an effective treatment for offenders with ASD is that those with ASD have difficulty responding to criticism, due to deficits in their ability to comprehend the motivation and goals others maintain (Ray et al., 2004). Furthermore, emotional deficits and heightened alexithymia may cause those with ASD to struggle with identifying, verbalizing, and analyzing their emotions (Berthoz & Hill, 2005). They may also internalize problems such as blame and self-criticism or, conversely, externalize problems by becoming angry and blaming others (Attwood, 2007). Providing education to offenders about their ASD diagnosis, especially if diagnosed later in life, may be valuable in a treatment setting (Katz & Zemishlany, 2006; Murphy, 2010).

Treatment of any co-occurring mental or behavioral disorder(s) lowers an individual's risk of becoming involved in the justice system (Allen et al., 2008). Unfortunately, traditional treatment programs for secondary disorders often require integration of those with ASD into settings that may not meet the unique needs of this population, such as requiring an ASD client with social deficits to interact with other offenders as a key component of treatment (Higgs & Carter, 2015).

PROFESSIONAL AWARENESS

The high prevalence of Autism Spectrum Disorder in high security, psychiatric settings suggests that ASD may be underdiagnosed in the criminal justice system, due to the absence of proper assessment and identification (Hare, Gould, Mills, & Wing, 1999; Scragg & Shah, 1994). Because of this, criminal justice professionals may regularly encounter individuals with ASD as victims, witnesses, or suspects of a crime and be completely unaware of the individual's diagnosis (Browning & Caulfield, 2011; Maras & Bowler, 2014). This is especially true with undiagnosed adolescent and adult offenders who may present with symptoms that are different from those typically seen in children at autism clinics and individuals with no intellectual disabilities, communication deficits, or history of specialist contact (Anckarsäter, Nilsson, Saury, Råstam, & Gillberg, 2008; Woodbury-Smith & Dein, 2014). Without proper recognition of ASD, the possibility of a fair defense during legal proceedings is limited (Robinson et al., 2012).

Because ASD is a "hidden" disorder (i.e., it does not affect the individual's appearance and can be present without intellectual deficits), professionals who retain vast levels of awareness regarding ASD and its related consequences may be better equipped to serve this population and aid in the reduction of future legal involvement (Allen et al., 2008; Salsedaa, Dixona, Fass, Miora, & Leark, 2011). In addition, the broader diagnosis of ASD embraced in the DSM-IV has likely played a role in the increase of mental health professionals (i.e., psychiatrists and psychologists) who have been called upon to provide expert testimony and forensic reports to the court on the mental state and ability of persons with ASD (Freckelton, 2013). The education provided by these clinicians during legal proceedings and sentencing is integral to illuminating the cause of criminal behavior, culpability, and future prevention of recidivism in defendants with ASD (Bishop, 2008; Browning & Caulfield, 2011; Freckelton & List, 2009).

Unfortunately, many mental health and other criminal justice professionals lack the proper training to effectively testify about, recognize, intervene, and communicate with individuals on the spectrum. Freckelton (2013) stressed a number of challenges faced by mental health professionals who are evaluating ASD or testifying about ASD in legal settings: (1) an accurate diagnosis, (2) effectively communicating how ASD impacts an individual's global functioning, (3) providing context for the behavior of individuals with ASD, particularly during interviews and legal proceedings, (4) evaluating the potential co-morbidity of ASD with internalizing and externalizing disorders, (5) conveying how ASD contributes to criminal behavior and understanding of consequences, and (6) avoiding stigmatizing ASD or the defendant.

In 2005, The National Autistic Society of Great Britain identified that over 90% of law enforcement officials and solicitors in Great Britain received no training on the symptoms and behaviors of individuals with ASD. Even criminal justice professionals that are familiar with ASD often lack an adequate understanding of autism in the context of emergency situations and the justice system (Browning & Caulfield, 2011). The need for regular and ongoing training pertaining to the complexities and challenges of ASD within criminal justice arenas is strongly recommended. In addition, Robinson and colleagues (2012) suggest that institutions such as jails and prisons, which may not have the resources to conduct their own assessments, should have referral plans in place for specialized ASD services in the area.

CONCLUSION

The majority of people with autism spectrum disorder (ASD) are law-abiding citizens and, according to limited empirical evidence, may not be more likely to engage in criminal behavior than their general population counterparts (Bjørkly, 2009; Browning & Caulfield, 2011; Ghaziuddin et al., 1991; Gómez de la Cuesta, 2010; Mouridsen, 2012). However, due to the deficits inherent in ASD, some of those affected by the disorder are at risk of being either victimized or acting out in illegal ways (Bishop, 2008).

Unlike the wealth of research on intellectual disabilities (ID) and crime, the decades-long delay of incorporating autism into the third version of The Diagnostic and Statistical Manual of Mental Disorders in 1980 likely limited research on offenders with ASD. Nonetheless, the co-occurring nature of ASD and ID may mean that some of the findings on ID and crime can be generalized to ASD and crime (King & Murphy, 2014). Additional research is needed in many areas to better understand the complex relationship between individuals with ASD and the criminal justice system (Howlin, 2004; Woodbury-Smith et al., 2006). Careful consideration of all the potential categories of crime that someone with ASD may engage in and the links between specific deficits and types of crime is a viable starting point for future studies in this area (Freckelton, 2013; Sevlever et al., 2013). Research on ASD and the criminal justice system would enable the development of treatment and education service standards for offenders with autism (Woodbury-Smith & Dein, 2014).

The development of an offender risk-factor assessment tool specifically for individuals with ASD and careful consideration of how to improve and tailor therapeutic programs for this population could effectively lower the risk of recidivism for ASD offenders (Higgs & Carter, 2015). Furthermore, the formation of professional associations that provide integrated services such as legal counsel, disorder screening, advocacy, risk assessment services, education and awareness training, and rehabilitation services for offenders and victims with autism would help close the gap in the criminal justice system into which this misunderstood population tends to fall.

REFERENCES

Adler, B. A., Wink, L. K., Early, M., Shaffer, R., Minshawi, N., McDougle, C. J., & Erickson, C. A. (2015). Drug-refractory aggression, self-injurious behavior, and severe tantrums in autism spectrum disorders: A chart review study. *Autism, 19*(1) 102-106. doi:10.1177/1362361314524641

Adolphs, R., Sears, L., & Piven, J. (2001). Abnormal processing of social information from faces in autism. *Journal of Cognitive Neuroscience, 13*(2), 232-240. doi:10.1162/089892901564289

Alexander, R. T., Chester, V., Green, F. N., Gunaratna, I., & Hoare, S. (2015). Arson or fire setting in offenders with intellectual disability: Clinical characteristics, forensic histories, and treatment outcomes. *Journal of Intellectual and Developmental Disability, 40*(2), 189-197. doi:10.3109/13668250.2014.998182

Allen, D., Evans, C., Hider, A., Hawkins, S., Peckett, H., & Morgan, H. (2008). Offending behavior in adults with Asperger syndrome. *Journal of Autism and Developmental Disorders, 38*(4), 748-758. doi:10.1007/s10803-007-0442-9

American Psychiatric Association. (2013). *Diagnostic and Statistical Manual of mental disorders.* (5th ed., pp. 99-105). Washington D.C: American Psychiatric Publishing.

Anckarsäter, H., Nilsson, T., Saury, J. M., Råstam, M., & Gillberg, C. (2008). Autism spectrum disorders in institutionalized subjects. *Nordic Journal of Psychiatry, 62*(2), 160-167. doi:10.1080/08039480801957269

Andrews, D. A., & Bonta, J. (2010). *The psychology of criminal conduct* (5th ed.). New Providence, NJ: Lexis Nexis.

Attwood, T. (2007). *The complete guide to Asperger's syndrome.* London, UK: Jessica Kingsley.

Autism Speaks. (2015, January 1). Legal Matters to Consider. Retrieved from http://www.autismspeaks.org/family-services/tool-kits/transition-tool-kit/legal-matters

Baghdadli, A., Pascal, C., Grisi, S., & Aussilloux, C. (2003). Risk factors for self-injurious behaviors among 222 young children with autistic disorders. *Journal of Intellectual Disability Research, 47*(8), 622-627. doi:10.1046/j.1365-2788.2003.00507.x

Baron-Cohen, S. (1988). An assessment of violence in a young man with Asperger's syndrome. *Journal of Child Psychology and Psychiatry, 29*(3), 351-360. http://dx.doi.org/10.1111/j.1469-7610.1988.tb00723.x

Baron-Cohen, S. (1995). *Mindblindness: An essay on autism and theory of mind.* Boston, MA: MIT Press/Bradford Books.

Baron-Cohen, S., Jolliffe, T., Mortimore, C. & Robertson, M. (1997). Another advanced test of theory of mind: Evidence from very high functioning adults with autism or Asperger's syndrome. *Journal of Child Psychology and Psychiatry, 38*(7), 813-822. doi:10.1111/j.1469-7610.1997.tb01599.x

Baron-Cohen, S., O'Riordan, M., Stone, V., Jones, R., & Plaisted, K. (1999). Recognition of faux pas by normally developing children and children with Asperger syndrome or high-functioning autism. *Journal of Autism and Developmental Disorders, 29*(5), 407-418.

Barry-Walsh, J. B., & Mullen, P. E. (2004). Forensic aspects of Asperger's syndrome. *Journal of Forensic Psychiatry & Psychology, 15*(1), 96-107. doi:10.1080/14789940310001638628

Bauminger, N., Shulman, C., & Agam, G. (2003). Peer interaction and loneliness in high-functioning children with autism. *Journal of Autism and Developmental Disorders, 33*(5), 489-507.

Bellini, S. (2004). Social skill deficits and anxiety in high-functioning adolescents with autism spectrum disorders. *Focus on Autism and Other Developmental Disabilities, 19*(2), 78-86. doi: 10.1177/10883576040190020201

Benson, P. R. (2006). The impact of child symptom severity on depressed mood among parents of children with ASD: The mediating role of stress proliferation. *Journal of Autism and Developmental Disorders, 36*(5), 685-695. doi:10.1007/s10803-006-0112-3

Benson, P. R., & Karlof, K. L. (2009). Anger, stress proliferation, and depressed mood among parents of children with autism spectrum disorders: A longitudinal replication. *Journal of Autism and Developmental Disorders, 39*(2), 350-362. doi:10.1007/s10803-008-0632-0

Berthoz, S., & Hill, E. (2005). The validity of using self-reports to assess emotion regulation abilities in adults with autism spectrum disorder. *European Psychiatry, 20*(3), 291-298. doi: 10.1016/j.eurpsy.2004.06.013

Bishop, D. (2008). An examination of the links between autistic spectrum disorders and offending behavior in young people. *Internet Journal of Criminology*, 1-32.

Bjørkly, S. (2009). Risk and dynamics of violence in Asperger's syndrome: A systematic review of the literature. *Aggression and Violent Behavior, 14*(5), 306-312. doi:10.1016/j.avb.2009.04.003

Bodfish, J. W., Symons, F. J., Parker, D. E., & Lewis, M. H. (2000). Varieties of repetitive behavior in autism: Comparisons to mental retardation. *Journal of Autism and Developmental Disorders, 30*(3), 237-243. doi:10.1023/A:1005596502855

Bolton, P. F., Carcani-Rathwell, I., Hutton, J., Goode, S., Howlin, P., & Rutter, M. (2011). Epilepsy in autism: Features and correlates. *The British Journal of Psychiatry, 198*(4), 289-294. doi:10.1192/bjp.bp.109.076877

Brereton, A. V., Tonge, B. J., & Einfeld, S. L. (2006). Psychopathology in children and adolescents with autism compared to young people with intellectual disability. *Journal of Autism and Developmental Disorders, 36*(7), 863-870. doi:10.1007/s10803-006-0125-y

Bristol, M. M., Gallagher, J. J., & Holt, K. D. (1993). Maternal depressive symptoms in autism: Response to psychoeducational intervention. *Rehabilitation Psychology, 38*(1), 3-9. http://dx.doi.org/10.1037/h0080290

Bronsard, G., Botbol, M., & Tordjman, S. (2010). Aggression in low functioning children and adolescents with autistic disorder. *Plus ONE, 5*(12), e14358. doi:10.1371/journal.pone.0014358

Browning, A., & Caulfield, L. (2011). The prevalence and treatment of people with Asperger's syndrome in the criminal justice system. *Criminology & Criminal Justice, 11*(2), 165-180. doi:10.1177/174889 581 1398455

Burnette, M. L., Ilgen, M., Frayne, S. M., Lucas, E., Mayo, J., & Weitlauf, J. C. (2008). Violence perpetration and childhood abuse among men and women in substance abuse treatment. *Journal of Substance Abuse Treatment, 35*(2), 217-222. doi:10.1016/j.jsat.2007.10.002

Canitano, R. (2006). Self-injurious behavior in autism: Clinical aspects and treatment with risperidone. *Journal of Neural Transmission, 113*(3), 425-431. doi:10.1007/s00702-005-0337-x

Cashin, A., & Newman, C. (2009). Autism in the criminal justice detention system: A review of the literature. *Journal Forensic Nurses, 5*(2), 70-75. doi:10.1111/j.1939-3938.2009.01037.x

Cea, C. N. (2014). Autism and the Criminal Defendant. *St. John's Law Review, 88*(2), 495-529.

Center for Disease Control and Prevention. (2011). Autism spectrum disorders: Data and statistics. Retrieved from http://www.cdc.gov/ncbddd/autism/data.html

Center for Disease Control and Prevention. (2015). Facts About ASD. Retrieved from http://www.cdc.gov/ ncbddd/autism/facts.html

Chance, T., & Scannapieco, M. (2002). Ecological correlates of child maltreatment: Similarities and differences between child fatality and nonfatality cases. *Child & Adolescent Social Work Journal, 19*(2), 139-161.

Cheely, C. A., Carpenter, L. A., Letourneau, E. J., Nicholas, J. S., Charles, J., & King, L. B. (2012). The prevalence of youth with autism spectrum disorders in the criminal justice system. *Journal of Autism and Developmental Disorders, 42*(9), 1856-1862. doi:10.1007/s10803-011-1427-2

Chen, P. S., Chen, S. J., Yang, Y. K., Yeh, T. L., Chen, C. C., & Lo, H. Y. (2003). Asperger's disorder: A case report of repeated stealing and the collecting behaviours of an adolescent patient. *Acta Psychiatrica Scandinavica, 107*(1), 73-76. doi:10.1034/j.1600-0447.2003.01354.x

Chermack, S. T., Murray, R. L., Walton, M. A., Booth, B. A., Wryobeck, J., & Blow, F. C. (2008). Partner aggression among men and women in substance use disorder treatment: Correlates of psychological and physical aggression and injury. *Drug Alcohol Dependence, 98*(1-2), 35-44. doi:10.1016/j.drugalcdep.2008.04.010

Clements, J. (2005). *People with Autism behaving badly: Helping people with ASD move on from behavioral and emotional challenges.* London, UK: Jessica Kingsley.

Critchley, H. D., Daly, E. M., Bullmore, E. T., Williams, S. C., Van Amelsvoort, T., Robertson, D. M., ... Murphy, D. G. (2000). The functional neuroanatomy of social behavior: Changes in cerebral blood flow when people with autistic disorder process facial expressions. *Brain, 123*(11), 2203-2212. http:// dx.doi.org/10.1093/brain/123.11.2203

Dalton, K. M., Nacewicz, B. M., Johnstone, T., Schaefer, H. S., Gernsbacher, M. A., Goldsmith, H. H., ... Davidson, R. J. (2005). Gaze fixation and the neural circuitry of face processing in autism. *Nature Neuroscience, 8*(4), 519-526. doi:10.1038/nn1421

De Alwis, D., Agrawal, A., Reieren, A. M., Constantino, J. N., Henders, A., Martin, N. G., & Lynskey, M. T. (2014). ADHD symptoms, autistic traits, and substance use and misuse in adult Australian twins. *Journal of Studies on Alcohol and Drugs, 75*(2), 211-221.

Debbaudt, D. (2002) *Autism, advocates, and law enforcement professionals.* London, UK: Jessica Kingsley Publishers. *Dusky v. U.S.*, 362 U.S. (1960), U.S. 402, p.362.

Eisenberg, N., Fabes, R. A., Murphy, B., Maszk, P., Smith, M., & Karbon, M. (1995). The role of emotionality and regulation in children's social functioning: A longitudinal study. *Child Development, 66*(5), 1360-1384.

Everall, I. P., & Lecouteur, A. (1990). Firesetting in an adolescent boy with Asperger's syndrome. *British Journal of Psychiatry, 157*, 284-287. doi:10.1192/bjp.157.2.284

Farrington, D. P. (2002). Families and crime. In J.Q. Wilson & J. Petersilia (Eds.), *Crime: Public policies for crime control* (2nd ed., pp.129-148). Oakland, CA: Institute for Contemporary Studies Press.

Farrington, D. P. (2005). *Introduction to integrated developmental and life-course theories of offending.* (pp. 1-14). New Brunswick, NJ: Transaction Publishers.

Ferriss, S. (2015). How kicking a trash can became criminal for a 6th grader. Public Radio International: The Center for Public Integrity. Retrieved from http://www.pri.org/stories/2015-04-10/how-kicking-trash-can-became-criminal-6th-grader

FindLaw (a). (2014). Insanity Defense. Retrieved from http://criminal.findlaw.com/criminal-procedure/insanity-defense.html

FindLaw (b). (2014). The M'Naghten Rule. Retrieved from http://criminal.findlaw.com/criminal-procedure/the-m-naghten-rule.html

FindLaw. (2015). Probation violation. Retrieved from http://criminal.findlaw.com/criminalcharges/probation-violation.html

Fisman, S., Wolf, L. C., & Noh, S. (1989). Marital intimacy in parents of exceptional children. *Canadian Journal of Psychiatry, 34*, 519-525.

Forsgren, L., Hauser, W. A., Olafsson, E., Sander, J. W., Sillanpaa, M., & Tomson, T. (2005). Mortality of epilepsy in developed countries: A review. *Epilepsia, 46*(11), 18-27.

Fountain, C., King, M. D., & Bearman, P. S. (2011). Age of diagnosis for autism: Individual and community factors across 10 birth cohorts. *Journal of Epidemiology and Community Health, 65*(6), 503-510. doi:10.1136/jech.2009.104588

Freckelton, I. (2012). Expert evidence by mental health professionals: The communication challenge posed by evidence about autism spectrum disorder, brain injuries, and Huntington's disease. *International Journal of Law and Psychiatry, 35*(5-6), 372-379. doi:10.1016/j.ijlp.2012.09.008

Freckelton, I. (2013). Autism spectrum disorder: Forensic issues and challenges for mental health professionals and courts. *Journal of Applied Research in Intellectual Disabilities, 26*(5), 420-434. doi:10.1111/jar.12036

Freckelton, I., & List, D. (2009). Asperger's disorder, criminal responsibility and criminal culpability. *Psychiatry, Psychology and Law, 16*(1), 16-40. doi:10.1080/13218710902887483

Freeman, S. J., Roberts, W., & Daneman, D. (2005). Type 1 diabetes and autism: Is there a link? *Diabetes Care, 28*(4), 925-926. doi: 10.2337/diacare.28.4.925

Fukuchi, T., Kanemoto, K., Kato, M., Ishida, S., Yuasa, S., Kawasaki, J., Suzuki, S., & Onuma, T. (2002). Death in epilepsy with special attention to suicide cases. *Epilepsy Research, 51*(3), 233-236. doi:10.1016/S0920-1211(02)00151-1

Gerhardt, P. F., & Lainer, I. (2011). Addressing the needs of adolescents and adults with autism: A crisis on the horizon. *Journal of Contemporary Psychotherapy, 41*(1), 37-45. doi:10.1007/s10879-010-9160-2

Ghaziuddin, M. (2005). *Mental health aspects of autism and Asperger's syndrome.* London, UK: Jessica Kingsley Publishers.

Ghaziuddin, M., Tsai, L., & Ghaziuddin, N. (1991). Brief report: Violence in Asperger syndrome, a critique. *Journal of Autism and Developmental Disorders, 21*(3), 349-354. http://dx.doi.org/10.1007/BF02207331

Gómez de la Cuesta, G. (2010). A selective review of offending behavior in individuals with autism spectrum disorders. *Journal of Learning Disabilities and Offending Behavior, 1*(2), 47-58.

Griffiths, D., Quinsey, V. I., & Hingsburger, D. (1989). *Changing inappropriate sexual behavior*. Baltimore, MD: Paul H. Brooks.

Grzadzinski, R., Luyster, R., Spencer, A., & Lord, C. (2012). Attachment in young children with autism spectrum disorders: An examination of separation and reunion behaviors with both mothers and fathers. *Autism, 18*(2) 85-96. doi:10.1177/1362361312467235

Hagland, C., & Webb, Z. (2009). *Working with adults with Asperger Syndrome: A practical toolkit*. Philadelphia, PA: Jessica Kingsley.

Hara, H. (2007). Autism and epilepsy: A retrospective follow-up study. *Brain and Development, 29*(8), 486-490. doi:10.1016/j.braindev.2006.12.012

Hare, D. J., Gould, J., Mills, R., & Wing, L. (1999). A preliminary study of individuals with autistic spectrum disorders in three special hospitals in England. *London: National Autistic Society*.

Hart-Kerkhoffs, L. A., Jansen, L. M., Doreleijers, T. A., Vermeiren, R., Minderaa, R. B., & Hartman, C. A. (2009). Autism spectrum disorder symptoms in juvenile suspects of sex offenses. *Journal of Clinical Psychiatry, 70*(2), 266-272. Retrieved from http://www.ncbi.nlm.nih.gov/pubmed/19210944

Haskins, B. G., & Silva, J. A. (2006). Asperger's disorder and criminal behavior: Forensic-Psychiatric considerations. *Journal of the American Academy of Psychiatry and the Law, 34*(3), 374-384.

Hastings, R. P. (2002). Parental stress and behavior problems of children with developmental disability. *Journal of Intellectual and Developmental Disability, 27*(3), 149-160. doi:10.1080/1366825021000008657

Hayes, S., & Watson, S. (2013). The impact of parenting stress: A meta-analysis of studies comparing the experience of parenting stress in parents of children with and without autism spectrum disorder. *Journal of Autism and Developmental Disorders, 43*(3), 629-642. doi:10.1007/s10803-012-1604-y

Hellemans, H., Colson, K., Verbraeken, C., Vermeiren, R., & Deboutte, D. (2007). Sexual behavior in high-functioning male adolescents and young adults with autism spectrum disorder. *Journal of Autism and Developmental Disorders, 37*(2), 260-269. doi:10.1007/s10803-006-0159-1

Helverschou, S.B., Bakken, T., & Martinsen, H. (2011). Psychiatric disorders in people with autism spectrum disorders: Phenomenology and recognition. In J. L. Matson & P. Sturmey (Eds.), *International handbook of autism and pervasive developmental disorders* (pp. 53-74). New York, NY: Springer.

Hendricks, D. (2009). Employment and adults with autism spectrum disorders: Challenges and strategies for success. *Journal for Vocational Rehabilitation, 32*(2), 125-134. doi:10.3233/JVR-2010-0502

Higgs, T., & Carter, A. J. (2015). Autism spectrum disorder and sexual offending: Responsivity in forensic interventions. *Aggression and Violent Behavior, 22*, 112-119. doi:10.1016/j.avb.2015.04.003 http://dx.doi.org/10.1016/j.avb.2015.04.003

Hill, E. & Berthoz, S. (2004). Brief report: Cognitive processing of own emotions in individuals with autistic spectrum disorder and in their relatives. *Journal of Autism Developmental Disorders, 34*(2), 229-235. doi:10.1023/B:JADD.0000022613.41399.14

Hoeve, M., Stams, G. J. J. M., van der Put, C. E., Semon Dubas, J., van der Laan, P. H., & Gerris, J. R. M. (2012). A meta-analysis of attachment to parents and delinquency. *Journal of Abnormal Child Psychology, 40*(5), 771-785. http://dx.doi.org/10.1007/s10802-011-9608-1

Holland, T., Clare, I. C. H., & Mukhopadhyay, T. (2002). Prevalence of 'criminal offending' by men and women with intellectual disability and the characteristics of 'offenders': Implications for research and service development. *Journal of Intellectual Disability Research, 46*, 6-20. doi:10.1046/j.1365-2788.2002.00001.x

Howlin, P. (2004). *Autism and Asperger syndrome: Preparing for adulthood* (2nd. Ed.). London, UK/New York, NY: Routledge.

Humphrey, N., & Symes, W. (2010). Perceptions of social support and experience of bullying among pupils with autistic spectrum disorders in mainstream secondary school. *European Journal of Special Needs Education, 25*(1), 77-91.

John Hopkins Medicine. (2014). Epilepsy and Seizures. *Health Library.* Retrieved from http://www.hopkinsmedicine.org/healthlibrary/conditions/nervous_system_disorders/epilepsy_and_seizures_85,P00779/\

Kalyva, E. (2010). Teachers' perspectives of the sexuality of children with autism spectrum disorders. *Research Autism Spectrum Disorders, 4*(3), 433-437. doi:10.1016/j.rasd.2009.10.014 http://dx.doi.org /10.1016/j.rasd.2009.10.014

Kamp-Becker, I., Schröder, J., Muehlan, H., Remschmidt, H., Becker, K., & Bachmann, C. J. (2011). Health-related quality of life in children and adolescents with autism spectrum disorder. *Zeitschrift für Kinder-und Jugendpsychiatrie und Psychotherapie, 39*(2), 123-131. doi:10.1024/1422-4917/ a000098

Kato, K., Mikami, K., Akama, F., Yamada, K., Maehara, M., Kimoto, K., ... Matsumoto, H. (2013). Clinical features of suicide attempts in adults with autism spectrum disorders. *General Hospital Psychiatry, 35*(1), 50-53. doi:10.1016/j.genhosppsych.2012.09.006

Katz, N., & Zemishlany, Z. (2006). Criminal responsibility in Asperger's syndrome. *Israel Journal of Psychiatry and Related Science, 43*(3), 166-173.

Kawakami, C., Ohnishi, M., Sugiyamac, T., Someki, F., Nakamurae, K., & Tsujiif, M. (2012). The risk factors for criminal behavior in high-functioning autism spectrum disorders (HFASDs): A comparison of childhood adversities between individuals with HFASDs who exhibit criminal behavior and those with HFASD and no criminal histories. *Research in Autism Spectrum Disorders, 6*(2), 949-957.

King, C., & Murphy, G. H. (2014). A systematic review of people with autism spectrum disorder and the criminal justice system. *Journal of autism and developmental disorders, 44*(11), 2717-2733.

Kohn, Y., Fahum, T., Ratzoni, G., & Apter, A. (1998). Aggression and sexual offense in Asperger's syndrome. *The Israel Journal of Psychiatry and Related Sciences, 35*(4), 293-299.

Konstantareas, M. M., & Lunsky, Y. J. (1997). Sociosexual knowledge, experience, attitudes, and interests of individuals with autistic disorder and developmental delay. *Journal of Autism and Developmental Disorders, 27*(4), 397-413. doi:10.1023/A:1025805405188

Kotey, S., Ertel, K., & Whitcomb, B. (2014). Co-occurrence of autism and asthma in a nationally-representative sample of children in the United States. *Journal of Autism and Developmental Disorder, 44*(12), 3083-3088. doi:10.1007/s10803-014-2174-y

Kristiansson, M., & Sorman, K. (2008). Autism spectrum disorders: Legal and forensic psychiatric aspects and reflections. *Clinical Neuropsychiatry: Journal of Treatment Evaluation, 5*(1), 55-61. Referenced from http://www.clinicalneuropsychiatry.org /pdf/07_kristians.pdf

Landa, R. (2000). Social language use in Asperger syndrome and high-functioning autism. In A. Kiln, F.V. Volkmar, & S.S. Sparrow (Eds.) *Asperger Syndrome* (pp. 125-155). New York, NY: Guilford Press.

Långström, N., Grann, M., Ruchkin, V., Sjöstedt, G., & Fazel, S. (2009). Risk factors for violent offending in autism spectrum disorder: A national study of hospitalized individuals. *Journal of Interpersonal Violence, 24*(8), 1358-1370. doi:10.1177/0886260508322195

Larson, K. A., & Turner, K.D. (2002). *Best practices for serving court involved youth with learning, attention, and behavioral disabilities.* Washington, DC: U.S. Department of Education and U.S. Department of Justice.

Laurent, A. C., & Rubin, E. (2004). Challenges in emotional regulation in Asperger's syndrome and high functioning autism. *Topics in Language Disorders, 24*(4), 286-297. Retrieved from http://journals.lww.com/topicsinlanguagedisorders/Abstract/2004/10000/Challenges_in_Emotional_Regulation_in_Asperger.6.aspx

Legal Information Institute (a). (2015). 18 U.S. code chapter 227, subchapter B: Probation. Cornell University Law School. Retrieved from https://www.law.cornell.edu/uscode/text/18/part-II/chapter-227/subchapter-B

Legal Information Institute (b). (2015). Insanity Defense. Cornell University Law School. Retrieved from https://www.law.cornell.edu/wex/insanity_defense

Lerner, M. D., Haque, O. S., Northrop, E. C., Lawer, L., & Bursztajn, H. J. (2012). Emerging perspectives on adolescents and young adults with high-functioning autism spectrum disorders, violence, and criminal law. *Journal of the American Academy of Psychiatric Law, 40*(2), 177-190. Referenced from http://www.jaapl.org/content/40/2/177.short

Leskovec, T. L., Rowles, B. M., & Findling, R. L. (2008). Pharmacological treatment options for autism spectrum disorders in children and adolescents. *Harvard Review of Psychiatry, 16*(2), 97-112. doi:10.1080/10673220802075852

Lord, C. (1995). Follow-up of two-year-olds referred for possible autism. *Journal of Child Psychology and Psychiatry, 36*(8), 1365-1382. doi: 10.1111/j.1469-7610.1995.tb01669.x

Lord, C., & Cook, E. H. (2013). Autism spectrum disorders. *Autism: The Science of Mental Health, 28*(2), 217-221. Retrieved from http://www.ncbi.nlm.nih.gov/pubmed/11144346

Losen, D., & Martinez, T. A. (2013). *Out of school and off track: The overuse of suspensions in American middle and high schools.* Los Angeles, CA: The civil rights project at USLA.

Loveland, K. A. (2005). Social-emotional impairment and self-regulation in autism spectrum disorder. In J. Nadel, & D. Muir. (Eds.), *Emotional developmental: Recent research advance* (pp. 365-382). New York, NY: Oxford University Press.

Luke, L., Clare, I., Ring, H., Redley, M., & Watson, P. (2012). Decision making difficulties experienced by adults with autism spectrum conditions. *Autism, 16*(6), 612-621. doi:10.1177/1362361311415876

Mandall, D. S., Walrath, C. M., Manteuffel, B., Sgro, G., & Pinto-Martin, J. A. (2005). The prevalence and correlates of abuse among children with autism served in comprehensive community-based mental health settings. *Child Abuse & Neglect, 29*(12), 1359-1372. doi:10.1016/j.chiabu.2005.06.006

Maras, K. L., & Bowler, D. M. (2010). The cognitive interview for eyewitnesses with autism spectrum disorder. *Journal of Autism and Developmental Disorders, 40*(11), 1350-1360. doi:10.1007/s10803-010-0997-8

Maras, K. L., & Bowler, D. M. (2011). Brief report: Schema consistent misinformation effects in eyewitnesses with autism spectrum disorder. *Journal of Autism and Developmental Disorders, 41*(3), 815-820. doi:10.1111/j.2044-8295.2011.02077.x

Maras, K. L., & Bowler, D. M. (2014). Eyewitness testimony in autism spectrum disorder: A review. *Journal of Autism and Developmental Disorders, 44*(11), 2682-2697. doi:10.1007/s10803-012-1502-3

Matson, J. L., Neal, D., Hess, J. A., Mahan, S., & Fodstad, J. C. (2010). The effect of seizure disorder on symptom presentation in atypically developing children and children with autism spectrum disorders based on the BDI-2. *Developmental Neurorehabilitation, 13*(5), 310-314. doi: 10.3109/17518421003782192

Matson, J. L., Sipes, M., Fodstad, J. C., & Fitzgerald, M. E. (2011). Issues in the management of challenging behaviors of adults with autism spectrum disorder. *CNS Drugs, 25*(7), 597-606. Retrieved from http://link.springer.com/article/10.2165/11591700-000000000-00000#/page-1

Mattila, M. L., Hurtig, T., Haapsamo, H., Jussila, K., Kuusikko-Gauffin, S., Kielinen, M., Moilanen, L. (2010). Co-morbid psychiatric disorders associated with Asperger syndrome/high-functioning autism: A community-and clinic-based study. *Journal of Autism and Developmental Disorders, 40*(9), 1080-1093. doi: 10.1007/s10803-010-0958-2

Mawson, D., Grounds, A., & Tantam, D. (1985). Violence and Asperger's syndrome: A case study. *British Journal of Psychiatry, 147*(5), 566-569. doi: 10.1192/bjp.147.5.566

Mayes, S., Calhoun, S., Murray, M., & Zahid, J. (2011). Variables associated with anxiety and depression in children with autism. *Journal of Developmental & Physical Disabilities, 23*(4), 325-337. doi: 10.1007/s10882-011-9231-7

Mayes, S. D., Gorman, A. A., Hillwig-Garcia, J., & Syed, E. (2013). Suicide ideation and attempts in children with autism. *Research in Autism Spectrum Disorders, 7*(1), 109-119. doi:10.1016/j.rasd.2012.07.009

Mayes, T. A. (2003). Persons with autism and criminal justice. *Journal of Positive Behavior Intervention, 5*(2), 92-100. doi: 10.1177/10983007030050020401

McAdam, P. (2012). Knowledge and understanding of the autism spectrum amongst prison staff. *Good Autism Practice, 10*(1), 19-25.

McCarthy, J., Underwood, L., Hayward, H., Chaplin, E., Forrester, A., Mills, R., & Murphy, D. (2015). Autism spectrum disorder and mental health problems among prisoners. *European Psychiatry, 30*(1), 28-31. doi:10.1016/S0924-9338(15)30674-X

Mossman, D., Noffsinger, S. G., Ash, P., Frierson, R. L., Gerbasi, J., Hackett, M., ... Zonana, H. V. (2015). AAPL practice guideline for the forensic psychiatric evaluation of competence to stand trial. *Journal of the American Academy of Psychiatry and the Law, 35*(4), S3-S72.

Mouridsen, S. (2012). Current status of research on autism spectrum disorders and offending. *Research in Autism Spectrum Disorders, 6*(1), 79-86. doi:10.1016/j.rasd.2011.09.003

Mouridsen, S. E., Rich, B., Isager, T., & Nedergaard, N. J. (2008). Pervasive developmental disorders and criminal behavior: A case control study. *International Journal of Offender Therapy and Comparative Criminology, 52*(2), 196-205.

Murphy, D. (2003). Admission and cognitive details of male patients diagnosed with Asperger's syndrome detained in a special hospital: Comparison with a schizophrenia and personality disorder sample. *Journal of Forensic Psychiatry & Psychology, 14*(3), 506-524. doi:10.1080/1478994031000152736

Murphy, D. (2010). Extreme violence in a man with an autistic spectrum disorder: Assessment and treatment within high security psychiatric care. *Journal of Forensic Psychiatry and Psychology, 21*(3), 462-477. doi:10.1080/14789940903426885

Murphy, D. (2013). Risk assessment of offenders with an autism spectrum disorder. *Journal of Intellectual Disabilities and Offending, 4*(1-2), 33-41.

Murphy, G., Hall, S., Oliver, C., Kissi-Debra, R. (1999). Identification of early self-injurious behavior in children with intellectual disability. *Journal of Intellectual Disability Research, 43*(3), 149-163. doi: 10.1046/j.1365-2788.1999.00183.x

Murrie, D. C., Warren, J. I., Kristiansson, M., & Dietz, P. E. (2002). Asperger's syndrome in forensic settings. *International Journal of Forensic Mental Health, 1*(1), 59-70. doi:10.1080/14999013.2002.10471161

Myers, F. (2004). *On the borderline? People with learning disabilities and/or autistic spectrum disorders in secure, forensic and other specialist settings*. Edinburgh, UK: Scottish Development Centre for Mental Health.

Myers, S. M., & Plauché-Johnson, C. (2007). Management of children with autism spectrum disorders. *Pediatrics, 120*(5), 1162-1182. doi: 10.1542/peds.2007-2362

National Alliance on Mental Illness. (2015). Mental Health Conditions. Retrieved from http://www.nami.org/Learn-More/Mental-Health-Conditions

National Autistic Society. (2005). *Autism: A guide for criminal justice professionals [online]*. Retrieved from www.nas.org.uk/content/1/c4/80/67/cjp_guide.pdf

National Autistic Society. (2008). *Autism: A guide for criminal justice professionals*. London, UK. Retrieved from http://www.autism.org.uk/working-with/criminal-justice/a-guide.aspx

National Human Genome Research Institute. Learning About Autism. (2012, October 22). Retrieved from http://www.genome.gov/25522099

National Institute on Deafness and Other Communication Disorders. NIH Workshop on Nonverbal School-Aged Children with Autism. (2010, June 23). Retrieved from http://www.nidcd.nih.gov/funding/programs/10aut

Newman, S., & Ghaziuddin, M. (2008). Violent crime in Asperger syndrome: The role of psychiatric co-morbidity. *Journal of Autism and Developmental Disorders, 38*(10), 1848-1852. doi: 10.1007/s10803-008-0580-8

Nichols, S., & Blakeley-Smith, A. (2010). "I'm not sure we're ready for this …": working with families toward facilitating healthy sexuality for individuals with autism spectrum disorders. *Social Work and Mental Health, 8*(1), 72-91. doi: 10.1080/15332980902932383

North, A. S., Russell, A. J., & Gudjonsson, G. H. (2008). High functioning autism spectrum disorders: An investigation of psychological vulnerabilities during interrogative interview. *The Journal of Forensic Psychiatry & Psychology, 19*(3), 323-334. doi:10.1080/14789940701871621

Office of Juvenile Justice and Delinquency Prevention. (2015). Statistical briefing book: Juveniles in court. Office of Justice Programs, U.S. Department of Justice. Retrieved from http://www.ojjdp.gov/ojstatbb/court/overview.html

Offices of the United States Attorneys. (2015). 634. Insanity Defense Reform Act of 1984. United States Department of Justice. Retrieved from http://www.justice.gov/usam/criminal-resource-manual-634-insanity-defense-reform-act-1984

Ousley, O. Y., & Mesibov, G. B. (1991). Sexual attitudes and knowledge of high-functioning adolescents and adults with autism. *Journal of Autism and Developmental Disorders, 21*(4), 471-481. doi: 10.1007/BF02206871

Palermo, M. T. (2004). Pervasive developmental disorders, psychiatric co-morbidities, and the law. *International Journal of Offender Therapy and Comparative Criminology, 48*(1), 40-48. doi: 10.1177/0306624X03257713

Paterson, P. (2008). How well do young offenders with Asperger syndrome cope in custody? *British Journal of Learning Disabilities, 36*(1), 54-58.

Payne, K. L., & Hollin, C. (2014). Alexithymia, Asperger's syndrome and criminal behavior: A review. *Journal of Criminal Psychology, 4*(2), 155-162.

Petersilia, J., Foote, J., Crowell, N. A., & National Research Council (U.S.) (2001). *Crime victims with developmental disabilities: Report of a workshop*. Washington, DC: National Academy Press.

Petersilia, J. R. (2001). Crime victims with developmental disabilities: A review essay. *Criminal Justice and Behavior, 28*(6), 655-694. doi: 10.1177/009385480102800601

Phipps, C. A., & Ells, M. L. (1995). Facilitated communication: Novel scientific evidence or novel communication? *Nebraska Law Review, 74*(4), 601-657.

Pompili, M., Girardi, P., Ruberto, A., & Tatarelli, R. (2005). Suicide in the epilepsies: A meta-analytic investigation of 29 cohorts. *Epilepsy Behavior, 7*(2), 305-310.

Price, D. (2003). A developmental perspective of treatment for sexually vulnerable youth. *Sexual Addiction & Compulsivity, 10*(4), 225-245. doi: 10.1080/713775412

Quinn, M. M., Rutherford, R. B., & Leone, P. E. (2001). *Students with disabilities in correctional facilities.* Arlington, VA: ERIC Clearing House on Disabilities and Gifted Education.

Ray, F., Marks, C., & Bray-Garretson, H. (2004). Challenges to treating adolescents with Asperger's syndrome who are sexually abusive. *Sexual Addiction & Compulsivity, 11*(4), 265-285. doi: 10.1080/10720160490900614

Realmuto, G. M., & Ruble, L. A. (1999). Sexual behaviors in Autism: Problems of definition and management. *Journal of Autism and Developmental Disorders, 29*(2), 121-127. Retrieved from http://newdirections. mb.ca/services/sbp_resources/For%20Parents/Autism%20%26%20Management%20of%20SBP.pdf

Richler, J., Huerta, M., Bishop, S. L., & Lord, C. (2010). Developmental trajectories of restricted and repetitive behaviors and interests in children with autism spectrum disorders. *Development and psychopathology, 22*(01), 55-69. doi: http://dx.doi.org/10.1017/S0954579409990265

Robertson, C. E., & McGillivray, J. A. (2015). Autism behind bars: A review of the research literature and discussion of key issues. *Journal of Forensic Psychiatry and Psychology,* 1-18. doi: 10.1080/14789949.2015.1062994

Robinson, L., Spencer, M. D., Thomson, L. D., Stanfield, A. C., Owens, D. G., Hall, J., & Johnstone, E. C. (2012). Evaluation of a screening instrument for autism spectrum disorders in prisoners. *PluS one, 7*(5), 1-8. doi: 10.1371/journal.pone.0036078

Rodriguez, C. M., & Murphy, L. E. (1997). Parenting stress and abuse potential in mothers of children with developmental disabilities. *Child Maltreatment, 2*(3), 245-251. Retrieved from http://libres.uncg.edu/ ir/uncg/f/C_Rodriguez_Parenting_1997.pdf

Roesch, R., Zapf, P. A., Golding, S. L., & Skeem, J. L. (2014). *Defining and assessing competency to stand trial.* United States Department of Justice. Retrieved from http://www.justice.gov/sites/default/files/ eoir/legacy/2014/08/15/Defining_and_Assessing_Competency_to_Stand_Trial.pdf

Royal College of Psychiatrists. (2006). *Psychiatric services of adolescents and adults with Asperger syndrome and other autistic spectrum disorders.* London, UK: Council Report CR136.

Ruble, L., & Dalrymple, J. (1993). Social/sexual awareness of persons with autism: A parental perspective. *Archives of Sexual Behavior, 22*(3), 229-240. doi: 10.1007/BF01541768

Rutgers, A. H., Bakermans-Kranenburg, M. J., van Ijzendoorn, M. H., & van Berckelaer-Onnes, A. (2004). Autism and attachment: A meta-analytic review. *Journal of Child Psychology and Psychiatry, 45*(6), 1123-1134 doi:10.1111/j.1469-7610.2004.t01-1-00305.x

Salsedaa, L., Dixona, D., Fass, T., Miora, D., Leark, R. (2011). An evaluation of Miranda rights and interrogation in autism spectrum disorders. *Research in Autism Spectrum Disorders, 5*(1), 79-85. doi:10.1016/j. rasd.2010.06.014

Samson, A. C., Huber, O., & Gross, J. J. (2012). Emotion regulation in Asperger's syndrome and high-functioning autism. *Emotion, 12*(4), 659-665. doi: 10.1037/a0027975

Schellack, J. (2014). *Autism in the criminal justice system.* Autism Advocacy and Law Center. Retrieved from http://autismlawcenter.com/2014/01/autism-in-the-criminal-justice-system/

Schultz, R. T., Gauthier, I., Klin, A., Fulbright, R. K., Anderson, A. W., ... Gore, J. C. (2000). Abnormal ventral temporal cortical activity during face discrimination among individuals with autism and Asperger syndrome. *Archives of General Psychiatry, 57*(4), 331-340. doi:10.1001/archpsyc.57.4.331

Schwartz-Watts, D. M. (2005). Asperger's Disorder and Murder. *Journal of the American Academy of Psychiatry and Law, 33*(3), 390-393. Retrieved from http://www.jaapl.org/content/33/3/390.full.pdf

Scragg, P., & Shah, A. (1994). Prevalence of Asperger's syndrome in a secure hospital. *British Journal of Psychiatry, 165*(5), 679-682. doi: 10.1192/bjp.165.5.679

Selkirk, C. G., McCarthy Veach, P., Lian, F., Schimmenti, L., & LeRoy, B. S. (2009). Parents' perceptions of autism spectrum disorder etiology and recurrence risk and effects of their perceptions on family planning: Recommendations for genetic counselors. *Journal of Genetic Counseling, 18*(5), 501-519. doi: 10.1007/s10897-009-9233-0

Sevlever, M., Roth, M. E., & Gillis, J. M. (2013). Sexual abuse and offending in autism spectrum disorders. *Sexuality and Disability, 31*(2), 189-200. doi: 10.1007/s11195-013-9286-8

Shapira, I., & Hedgpeth, D. (2014). Autistic boy allegedly abused by two girls in St. Mary's considered them friends, mom says. The Washington Post, March 12, 2014. Retrieved from http://www.washingtonpost.com/local/crime/in-st-marys-two-female-teens-charged-with-sexually-abusing-disabled-16-year-old-boy/2014/03/12/2d4dd568-a9f9-11e3-9e82-8064fcd31b5b_story.html

Shtukaturov v. Russia. (2008). ECHR 223

Silva, J. A., Ferrari, J. A., & Leong, G. B. (2002). The case of Jeffrey Dahmer: Sexual serial homicide from a neuropsychiatric developmental perspective. *Journal of Forensic Science, 47*(6), 1347-1359. Retrieved from http://www.murderpedia.org/male.D/images/dahmer-jeffrey/docs/jeffrey-dahmer-silva-et-al.pdf

Simonoff, E., Pickles, A., Charman, T., Chandler, S., Loucas, T., & Baird, G. (2008). Psychiatric disorders in children with autism spectrum disorders: Prevalence, co-morbidity, and associated factors in a population-derived sample. *Journal of the American Academy of Child and Adolescent Psychiatry, 47*(8), 921-929. doi:10.1097/CHI.0b013e318179964f

Siponmaa, L., Kristiansson, M., Jonson, C., Nyden, A., & Gillberg, C. (2001). Juvenile and young mentally disordered offenders: The role of child neuropsychiatric disorders. *Journal of the American Academy of Psychiatry and Law, 29*(4), 420-426. Retrieved from http://www.jaapl.org/content/29/4/420.short

Sprang, G., Clark, J. J., & Bass, S. (2005). Factors that contribute to child maltreatment severity: A multi-method and multidimensional investigation. *Child Abuse & Neglect, 29*(4), 335-350. doi:10.1016/j.chiabu.2004.08.008

Stokes, M. A., & Kaur, A. (2005). High functioning Autism and sexuality: A parental perspective. *Autism, 9*(3), 266-289. doi: 10.1177/1362361305053258

Storch, E. A., Sulkowski, M. L., Nadeau, J., Lewin, A. B., Arnold, E. B., Mutch, P. J., ... Murphy, T. K. (2013). The phenomenology and clinical correlates of suicidal thoughts and behaviors in youth with autism spectrum disorders. *Journal of Autism and Developmental Disorders, 43*, 2450-2459. doi: 10.1007/s10803-013-1795-x

Strickland, H. A. (2013). Autism and crime: Should autistic individuals be afforded the use of an "autism" defense? Retrieved from http://www.udclawreview.com/wpcontent/uploads/2013/02/Autism-and-Crime_final-2-2.pdf

Sutton, L., Hughes, T., Huang, A., Lehman, C., Paserba, D., Talkington, V., ... Marshall, S. (2013). Identifying individuals with autism in a state facility for adolescents adjudicated as sexual offenders: A pilot study. *Focus on Autism and Other Developmental Disabilities, 28*(3) 175-183. doi:10.1177/1088357612462060

Tager-Flusberg, H., Paul, R., & Lord, C. E. (2005). Language and communication in autism. In F. Volkmar, R. Paul, A. Klin, & D. J. Cohen (Eds.), *Handbook of autism and pervasive developmental disorders: Vol. 1. Diagnosis, development, neurobiology, and behavior* (3rd ed.) (pp. 335-364). New York, NY: Wiley.

Talbot, J. (2009). No one knows: Offenders with learning disabilities and learning difficulties. *International Journal of Prisoner Health, 5*(3), 141-152. http://dx.doi.org/10.1108/13595474200900004

Teplin, L. A., Abram, K. M., McClelland, G. M., Dulcan, M. K., & Mericle, A. A. (2002). Psychiatric disorders in youth in juvenile detention. *Archives of General Psychiatry, 59*(2), 1133-1143. Retrieved from http://www.ncbi.nlm.nih.gov/pmc/articles/PMC2861992/

Tuchman, R., Moshe, S. L., & Rapin, I. (2009). Convulsing toward the pathophysiology of autism. *Brain Development, 31*(2), 95-103. doi: 10.1016/j.braindev.2008.09.009

Turner, H. A., Vanderminden, J., Finkelhor, D., Hamby, H., & Shattuck, A. (2011). Disability and victimization in a national sample of children and youth. *Child Maltreatment, 16*(4), 275-286. doi: 10.1177/1077559511427178

Underwood, L., Forrester, A., Chaplin, E., & McCarthy, J. (2013). Prisoners with neurodevelopmental disorders. *Journal of Intellectual Disabilities and Offending Behavior, 4*(½), 17-23. doi:10.1108/JIDOB-05-2013-0011

United States Courts. (2015). Glossary of Legal Terms. Administrative Office of the U.S. Courts. Retrieved from http://www.uscourts.gov/glossary

Van Bourgondien, E., & Reichle, C. (1997). Sexual behavior in adults with autism. *Journal of Autism and Development Disorders, 27*, 113-125.

Vermeiren, R., Jespers, I., & Moffit, T. (2006). Mental health problems in juvenile justice populations. *Child and Adolescent Psychiatry Clinics of North America, 15*, 333-351.

Verrotti, A., Cicconetti, A., Scorrano, B., De Berardis, D., Cotellessa, C., Chiarelli, F., & Ferro, F. M. (2008). Epilepsy and suicide: Pathogenesis, risk factors, and prevention. *Journal of Neuropsychiatric Disease and Treatment, 4*(2), 365-370. Retrieved from http://www.ncbi.nlm.nih.gov/pmc/articles/PMC2518384/

Wagner, M. (2014). Maryland teen sentenced to time in juvenile jail for torturing autistic boy. New York Daily News, June 6, 2014. Retrieved from http://www.nydailynews.com/news/crime/md-teen-4-years-torturing-autistic-boy-article-1.1819510

Walters, J., Hughes, T., Sutton, L., Marshall, S., Crothers, L., Lehman, C., ... Huang, A. (2013). Maltreatment and depression in adolescent sexual offenders with an autism spectrum disorder. *Journal of Child Sexual Abuse, 22*(1), 72-89. doi:10.1080/10538712.2013.735357

Whipple, E. E., & Webster-Stratton, C. (1991). The role of parental stress in physically abusive families. *Child Abuse and Neglect, 15*(3), 279-291. doi:10.1016/0145-2134(91)90072-L

White, S. W., & Schry, A. R. (2011). Social anxiety in adolescents on the autism spectrum. C.A. Alfano & D. C. Beidel (Eds.), *Social anxiety in adolescents and adults: Translating developmental science into practice* (pp. 183-201). American Psychological Association (APA).

Wing, L. (1997). Asperger's syndrome: Management requires diagnosis. *Journal of Forensic Psychiatry & Psychology, 8*(2), 253-257. doi:10.1080/09585189708412008

Wood, J. J., & Gadow, K. D. (2010). Exploring the nature and function of anxiety in youth with autism spectrum disorders. *Clinical Psychology: Science and Practice, 17*(4), 281-292. doi: 10.1111/j.1468-2850.2010.01220.x

Woodbury-Smith, M. R., Clare, I. C. H., Holland, A. J., & Kearns, A. (2006). High functioning autistic spectrum disorder, offending and other law-breaking: Findings from a community sample. *Journal of Forensic Psychiatry and Psychology, 17*(1), 108-120. doi:10.1080/14789940600589464

Woodbury-Smith, M. R., Clare, I. C. H., Holland, A. J., Kearns, A., Staufenberg, E., & Watson, P. (2005). A case-control study of offenders with high functioning autistic spectrum disorders. *Journal of Forensic Psychiatry and Psychology, 16*(4), 747-763. doi: 10.1080/14789940500302554

Woodbury-Smith, M. R., Clare, I. C. H., Holland, A. J., Watson, P. C., Bambrick, M., Kearns, A., & Staugenberg, E. (2010). Circumscribed interests and 'offenders' with autism spectrum disorders: A case-control study. *Journal of Forensic Psychiatry and Psychology, 21*(3), 366-377. doi: 10.1080/14789940903426877

Woodbury-Smith, M., & Dein, K. (2014). Autism spectrum disorder (ASD) and unlawful behaviour: Where do we go from here? *Journal of Autism and Developmental Disorders, 44*(11), 2734-2741. doi: 10.1007/s10803-014-2216-5

Zablotsky, B., Bradshaw, C. P., Anderson, C. & Law, P. A. (2013). The association between bullying and the psychological functioning of children with autism spectrum disorders. *Journal of Developmental Behavioral Pediatrics, 34*(1), 1-8. doi: 10.1097/DBP.0b013e31827a7c3a

CHAPTER 2

BORDERLINE PERSONALITY DISORDER IN THE CRIMINAL JUSTICE SYSTEM

KRISTIN TURNER & BETH JORDAN

CHAPTER OVERVIEW

Borderline Personality Disorder is a serious mental illness affecting 1%-2% of the general population. Individuals with Borderline Personality Disorder may suffer from unstable relationships, difficulty regulating mood, intense anger, self-injury, impulsivity and chronic suicidal ideation and behaviors. It is common for individuals with Borderline Personality Disorder to experience frequent psychiatric hospitalizations and high utilization of crisis resources. Law enforcement is most likely to encounter an individual with Borderline Personality Disorder in crisis situations such as suicide attempts or threats, or in situations related to substance use, as a significant percentage of individuals with Borderline Personality Disorder have Co-morbid substance use disorders. Rather than symptoms of Borderline Personality directly contributing to their offense, individuals with Borderline Personality Disorder who become incarcerated generally committed crimes related to Co-morbid substance use (e.g., possession offenses) or while under the influence of substances. This chapter focuses on educating readers about causes, symptoms, treatment and effective ways to interact with individuals suffering from this illness.

INTRODUCTION

Unfamiliarity surrounding mental health often leads individuals suffering from mental illness to be stigmatized and feared. This chapter focuses on providing an unbiased view of criminal offenders diagnosed with Borderline Personality Disorder (BPD). Approximately 1.6% of the general population meets criteria for BPD (American Psychiatric Association, 2013; Gardner, Dodsworth, & Selby, 2015). Of the number of people diagnosed with BPD, a small number of individuals become involved with the criminal justice system. Most of these offenders have a Co-morbid diagnosis that influences their behavior (Gardner et al., 2015; Sansone, Lam, & Wiederman, 2012). According to the Diagnostic and Statistical Manual of Mental Disorders (DSM-5), the manifestation of BPD symptoms can vary greatly from person to person (Sisti & Caplan, 2012). Therefore, diagnosing BPD and other personality disorders is a complex process that often relies on clinical judgment and, as a consequence, may result in diagnosis errors. This chapter attempts to highlight difficult behaviors commonly displayed by individuals with BPD, as well as increase awareness of how these behaviors develop. We aim to shed light on the inner world of an individual with BPD, to help increase empathy and understanding, in hopes that this will help those in the criminal justice system effectively and compassionately work with these individuals.

CLINICAL PRESENTATION

According to the Diagnostic and Statistical Manual of Mental Disorders, 5th Edition, (DSM-5) personality disorders are a pervasive pattern of behavior and traits that begin during adolescence or young adulthood and may persist throughout an individual's life. These traits deviate significantly from cultural expectations such as norms, values, and religious or other culture-specific beliefs. Symptoms cause distress and impair individuals' daily functioning, such as an individual's ability to care for themselves, hygiene, ability to hold a steady job, and their ability to maintain meaningful relationships. There are three clusters of personality disorders—Cluster A, Cluster B, and Cluster C—each distinguished by a set of common behaviors and traits. BPD falls under Cluster B, which also includes Antisocial Personality Disorder, Histrionic Personality Disorder, and Narcissistic Personality Disorder (American Psychiatric Association, 2013).

Approximately 6% of individuals in primary care settings, 10% in outpatient mental health settings, and 20% in inpatient mental health settings are diagnosed with BPD (American Psychiatric Association, 2013; Gianoli, Jane, O'Brien, & Ralevski, 2012). However, the actual prevalence of BPD in the prison system is unknown. Some studies report estimates of 25%-50% of prisoners meeting criteria for BPD, and others report estimates comparable with the general population (Nee & Farman, 2005; Sansone et al., 2012).

BPD is a pervasive pattern of instability related to domains of interpersonal relationships, self-image, affect, impulsivity, and lack of a sense of self (Leppanen, Karki, Saariaho, Lindeman, & Hakko, 2015; Sijtsema, Baan, & Bogaerts, 2014; Sisti & Caplan, 2012). Individuals with BPD often experience intense anger that is difficult to control and disproportionate to the situation (Sijtsema et al., 2014). In addition, these individuals may interpret normal life events as abandonment. For example, an individual with BPD may react with disproportionate anger if his/her partner is a few minutes late due to traffic, or if a health care provider needs to cancel an appointment due to a family emergency. These feelings of abandonment may lead individuals to harbor negative feelings about themselves and increase the need to be constantly around others (American Psychiatric Association, 2013).

Relationships involving an individual with BPD tend to be intense and unstable. These individuals attach quickly in relationships, resulting in idealizing the other person in the relationship and engaging in intimate self-disclosure within the first or second encounter. This intense idealization frequently changes to devaluation as the other person is unable to meet the individual's unrealistic demands (i.e., amount of time spent together) and the individual with BPD views their partner as not caring enough, invested enough, or present enough. In addition to rapid changes in relationships, individuals with BPD also have sudden changes in identity, including career goals, sexual identity, personal values, and social groups. Their self-image tends to generally consist of a core belief that they are deficient or defective. They may also experience chronic feelings of emptiness, or feeling as if they do not exist at all (American Psychiatric Association, 2013). The symptoms of BPD can make it difficult for individuals diagnosed with this condition to form productive working relationships (SAMHSA, 2011).

Due to the complexity of the diagnosis, it may be most effective to adopt a team approach for treatment, which would include a case manager or social worker, mental health provider, substance abuse counselor, psychiatrist, and other supportive services. These professionals will need to have strong (but flexible) boundaries and be aware of how the diagnosis affects the individual's overall functioning and ability to engage in treatment. Effective communication between providers is essential to avoid splitting behaviors and provide consistency.

ETIOLOGY

The exact etiology of BPD remains unknown. Research indicates that BPD seems to be, in part, hereditary, since a first-degree biological relative of an individual with BPD is approximately five times more likely to develop the disorder than an individual with no first-degree relatives suffering from the disorder (American Psychiatric Association, 2013). At this time, the general consensus is that BPD is a combination of heritable vulnerability coupled with environmental factors that interact to bring about the full presentation of the disorder (Goodman, New, Triebwasser, Collins, & Siever, 2010).

SUICIDE AND SELF-HARM

Suicidal tendencies and self-mutilation are also extremely common and indicative symptoms of BPD (Gardner et al., 2015). In fact, this is the only personality disorder diagnosis that includes self-harm as a diagnostic criteria (SAMHSA, 2011). Paris (2005) indicates that about half of individuals diagnosed with BPD utilize self-injurious behavior, which generally involves superficial cuts to wrists and arms. This behavior is frequently perceived as attention-seeking by others, but self-harm in individuals with BPD serves various functions. It may help individuals alleviate distress, release or express emotions, use physical pain to distract themselves from emotional pain, deal with unaccepted realities of the present moment, communicate the intensity of their distress to others, or cope with dissociation by grounding themselves (Gardner et al., 2015; Linehan, 1993a; Linehan, 1993b; Linehan, 2015; Paris, 2005; Wupperman, Fickling, Klemanski, Berking & Whitman, 2013). Researchers recently developed a novel theory suggesting that self-injurious behavior may provide relief at a biological level by activating the body's *relief-from-stress* response with endogenous opioids (Kirtley, O'Carroll, & O'Connor, 2015). Thus, self-injurious behavior may be a survival tool for people with BPD that helps them tolerate short-term distress. However, this coping mechanism tends to be ineffective in the long-term. People with BPD can benefit from learning alternative strategies to replace these self-harm habits with more effective coping strategies (Linehan, 1993a; Linehan, 1993b; Linehan, 2015).

In addition to non-suicidal self-harm, a high percentage of individuals with BPD experience chronic suicidal ideation, and eventually, 8%-10% commit suicide (American Psychiatric Association, 2013). There are two types of suicidal ideation: passive and active. Passive suicidal ideation includes thoughts of death, wanting to die, or wishing to not be in this world. For example, if an individual wishes she/he would be hit by a bus, this would be passive suicidal ideation. Active ideation consists of an actual plan with intent to commit suicide; for example, if an individual has a plan to end their life by jumping in front of a bus. When active ideation is present, the individual's intent and access to means (i.e., firearm or medications) should be assessed, along with protective factors that may prevent them from acting on their thoughts. If an individual appears to be experiencing any suicidal ideation, a thorough suicide assessment should be used, because passive ideation can very quickly become active. Both should be treated with equal weight in an assessment of the person's risk (Simon, 2014).

CO-MORBIDITY

Most adults presenting with BPD commonly experience an array of Co-morbid conditions. It is estimated that 84.5% of individuals with BPD also have at least one other non-personality disorder diagnosis, and 73.9% have a Co-morbid personality disorder (Kaess, von Ceumern-Lindenstjerna, Parzer, Chanen, Mundt, Resch, & Brunner, 2013). The most common Co-morbid disorders in adults with BPD tend to be substance use disorders (Grant et al., 2008; Kienast, Stoffers, Bermpohl, & Lieb, 2014; Sansone et al., 2012), mood disorders, anxiety, post-traumatic stress disorder (PTSD), and eating disorders (Grant et al., 2008; Kaess et al., 2013).

Other Co-morbid diagnoses include attention-deficit/hyperactivity disorder, and other personality disorders (American Psychiatric Association, 2013).

BPD often co-occurs with Bipolar Disorder and depressive disorders (American Psychiatric Association, 2013). It was questioned at one point if BPD and Bipolar Disorder were actually the same construct or if they were, in fact, separate disorders (Galione & Zimmerman, 2010). Research has concluded that they are, indeed, separate diagnoses; therefore, when co-occurring, each diagnosis should be treated independently. Researchers Galione & Zimmerman (2010) also found that when comparing individuals diagnosed with depression to individuals with BPD and Co-morbid depression, the latter had a younger age of onset, more depressive episodes, an increased likelihood of presenting with uncommon symptoms, and a higher prevalence of added anxiety and substance use disorders as well as previous suicide attempts. Clinicians can differentiate BPD from other Cluster B personality disorders by identifying the individual's focus on self-destructive behavior, dysregulated and angry interpersonal relationships, and chronic identification of emptiness and loneliness (American Psychiatric Association, 2013). Individuals with BPD frequently suffer from past trauma, unemployment, recurrent job losses, interrupted education, and marital discord. (American Psychiatric Association, 2013).

DEVELOPMENT AND COURSE OF BORDERLINE PERSONALITY DISORDER

The overall trajectory of this disorder has common themes, regardless of the causative factors which will be described in this section. There are common risk factors for BPD, and the development of BPD varies widely (American Psychiatric Association, 2013). Data shows that BPD symptoms may begin in childhood, but attention to these symptoms often occurs in late adolescence or early adulthood (American Psychiatric Association, 2013; Lieb, Zanarini, Schmahl, Linehan, & Bohus, 2004). People with BPD often show progress in their 30s or 40s in vocational goals and relationship stability, even though there may be a tendency toward experiencing emotions with an intensity that affects daily functioning (Kreisman & Straus, 2010; Zanarini, Frankenburg, Hennen, & Silk, 2004). Community mental health clinics show that many people no longer meet criteria for BPD after a 10-year follow-up (American Psychiatric Association, 2013).

There is evidence for the remission of BPD over time, in terms of no longer meeting full criteria for the disorder. While some 5-year studies show little change, some 15- and 27-year follow-up studies show remission for participants with BPD by ages 40-50 (American Psychiatric Association, 2013; Paris, 2002). Symptoms and functioning have been shown to fluctuate: while relapses or a return to a lower level of functioning may sometimes occur across the lifespan, symptoms often decline over time (Quigley, 2003; Zanarini et al., 2003). Data shows that people with BPD appear to be more highly functioning and stable in their elderly years (American Psychiatric Association, 2010). However, despite possible remission over time, suicide rates of 10% across the lifespan remain a concern (American Psychiatric Association, 2013; Paris, 2002), and it is common for people with BPD to show high rates of utilization of the medical health system (American Psychiatric Association, 2013). Therefore, assisting people with this disorder in navigating effective treatment options is a vital part of an effective community response and a necessity in the corrections milieu.

ATTACHMENT FACTORS
People with BPD often experience insecure attachments to caregivers, supporting the relationship between attachment factors and development of BPD (Bartholomew, Kwong, & Hart, 2001; Keinänen, Johnson, Richards, & Courtney, 2012; Sharp & Romero, 2007; Skodol et al., 2002). Similarly, parental loss or separation is also a risk factor for development of BPD (Paris, Zweig-Frank, & Guzder, 1994).

Healthy attachment to caregivers in childhood creates the ability to psychologically connect with others (Bowlby, 1969). When it occurs, the caregiver is sensitive and responsive to the child's needs, and the child is able to rely upon the caregiver as a stable source of care. The child is then able to develop in other healthy ways, such as feeling secure enough to engage in activities without clinging to or avoiding the caregiver and developing healthy coping skills to manage difficult emotions. In this way, healthy attachment is an important factor in emotion regulation and identity development (Ainsworth, 1973; Bowlby, 1969; Ludolph, 2010).

Insecure attachment styles involve a relationship in which children often show clingy, rejecting, avoidant, and/or disorganized behaviors towards their caregiver. This type of attachment often leads children to have difficulties with emotion regulation (Ainsworth, 1979; Bowlby, 1969; Fonagy, Target, & Gergely, 2000; Ludolph, 2010). For example, children who demonstrate a disorganized response toward their caregiver both seek and retreat from the caregiver (Hesse & Main, 2000). When upset, children with insecure attachments may not be as readily soothed by the caregiver. This can lead to other problems, such as difficulty managing emotions, distorted views of the world, harmful or ineffective coping strategies, and ineffective ways of obtaining responses for their needs in interpersonal relationships. This may contribute to emotional lability and intense, unstable relationship patterns that later develop in people with BPD.

Studies demonstrate that offenders have higher rates of insecure attachment styles or disorganized attachment styles, compared to the general population (Timmerman & Emmelkamp, 2006). While the majority of people with insecure attachment do not necessarily develop criminal behaviors, it is common for people with criminal behavior histories to have insecure attachments (Hoeve et al., 2012; Timmerman & Emmelkamp, 2006).

It is noteworthy to remember two points on attachment as a factor in development of BPD. First, the relationship between attachment styles and BPD is not a causal one. That is, insecure attachment styles do not cause individuals to develop BPD. Second, data has suggested that caregivers in insecure attachment relationships with their children may be dealing with their own wounds from their insecure attachment relationships as children, thus passing on insecure attachment styles generationally (Hesse & Main, 2000; Perepletchikova, Ansell, & Axelrod, 2012; Schroeder, Higgins, & Mowen, 2012). Instead of blaming parents, it is important to raise awareness of attachment patterns, intervene early when attachments are not secure, and provide interventions so that parents learn how to respond to their children in ways that promote healthy attachment. It is likely that addressing such issues can be a protective factor for anyone suffering from BPD, especially for those individuals who have come in contact with the criminal justice system.

INVALIDATING ENVIRONMENTS

Certain environmental factors are commonly associated with people diagnosed with BPD. Invalidating environments and experiences during childhood are thought to play a key role in the development of BPD later in life, especially in regard to emotional dysregulation (Feigenbaum, 2007; Feigenbaum, 2008; Linehan, 1993a; Linehan, 1993b; Linehan, 2015; Robertson, Kimbrel, & Nelson-Gray, 2013; Rochefort, 2014; Sturrock & Mellor, 2014). Invalidation from caregivers involves either inconsistent or ineffective responses to the emotional experiences of children. Children need to be able to understand emotions, communicate them, understand that their communication was received by caregivers, and respond effectively in order to manage emotions appropriately for their developmental stage (Feigenbaum, 2007; Feigenbaum, 2008; Linehan, 1993a; Linehan, 1993b; Linehan, 2015). Imagine a child who is upset and crying about a negative experience. A validating response might involve the caregiver identifying and validating the emotion (e.g., "That's sad, isn't it?" or "I can see you're upset. How about if we play a game to feel better?"). However, a caregiver may sometimes respond with invalidation (e.g., "You're fine, get up, stop crying. There's nothing wrong—quit crying"). In this example, the child is left confused—with the message that her or his internal emotion is not valid and with the discrepancy between internal experiences of an emotion and public responses to that emotion. Invalidating responses may also include providing inconsistent responses that are confusing to the child; for example, if one time the caregiver responds with empathy, but another time the caregiver does not respond at all. Sometimes this behavior may be the result of substance use or mental health disorders, which prevents the caregiver from consistently responding to the child's needs. If invalidation occurs on an emotional level, a child may learn not to trust his or her emotional experience. If BPD develops, the emotional experience would also be an intense experience for which the child may have no skills to understand or manage (Linehan, 1993a; Linehan, 1993b; Linehan, 2015). As the child grows older, he or she feels even more alone in their intense emotional experiences, with no skills to manage them (Feigenbaum, 2007; Feigenbaum, 2008).

ABUSE, NEGLECT, AND TRAUMA

There is a widely supported correlation between the development of BPD and experiences of abuse, neglect, or trauma (American Psychiatric Association, 2013; van Dijke, Ford, van Son, & van der Hart, 2013; Feigenbaum, 2007; Feigenbaum, 2008; Hopwood & Zanarini, 2012; Linehan, 1993a; Linehan, 1993b; Linehan, 2015). Childhood abuse is reported in 66%-75% of people with BPD (Feigenbaum, 2007; Johnson, Cohen, Brown, Smalles, & Bernstein, 1999; Zanarini, 2000). These traumatic or abusive experiences may often be received from a primary caregiver (van Dijke, Ford, van Son, Frank, & van der Hart, 2013). While these experiences do not necessarily cause BPD, they may play a critical role in its development by disrupting healthy mood regulation and developing mood dysregulation (van Dijke & Ford, 2013; Linehan, 1993a; Linehan, 1993b; Linehan, 2015). Abuse can be understood as the ultimate form of invalidation, as the child's safety and needs are directly violated. Types of abuse include emotional, verbal, physical, or sexual. Sexual abuse is a particularly high-risk factor, although the experience of sexual abuse alone does not mean that BPD will develop (Feigenbaum, 2007; Feigenbaum, 2008; Hopwood & Zanarini, 2012; Sharp & Romero, 2007).

BIOLOGICAL VULNERABILITY AND TEMPERAMENT

The biopsychosocial model for understanding BPD highlights the cumulative effects of multiple factors in its development. Factors include biological vulnerability and temperament, social experiences that cue this vulnerability, and psychological processes that disrupt emotion regulation, thought processes, and identity development (Feigenbaum, 2007; Feigenbaum, 2008; Linehan, 1993a; Linehan, 1993b; Linehan, 2015). In addition to the genetic factors already discussed in this chapter, people with BPD experience emotions in a heightened and sensitized fashion (Linehan, 1993a; Linehan, 1993b; Linehan, 2015). This can be understood at a biological level in terms of sensitized arousal of the central nervous system, resulting in more intense physiological arousal in response to emotional experiences (Deckers, Lobbestael, van Wingen, Kessels, Arntz, & Egger, 2015; Lieb et al., 2004). For example, increased heart rate may be triggered more easily and experienced more intensely in daily situations, or parts of the body that control stress response may experience hyper-responsiveness (Sharp & Romero, 2007).

Recent data also shows a sensitized stress response in the brain among people with BPD. Areas of the brain that involve emotional experiences and fight-or-flight stress responses (such as the amygdala and the hypothalamic-pituitary-adrenal axis [HPA]) appear to be overactive, while areas of the brain involving impulse control and thought processing (i.e., the prefrontal cortex) are under-activated (Donegan et al., 2003; Kreisman & Straus, 2010; Lieb et al., 2004; Rinne et al., 2002). This amounts to a hyper-sensitized physiological response to emotions at a biological and neurological level, as well as a reduced ability to counteract emotional experiences with impulse control. In addition, there is some evidence that people with BPD interpret neutral facial expressions as threatening rather than neutral (Donegan et al., 2003). Thus, current data shows that when people with BPD experience an emotional trigger, the other person's response is often perceived as a threat by the person with BPD; this threat is experienced intensely and the physiological response escalates quickly (Ebner-Priemer et al., 2015). Instead of slowly experiencing an increase in emotions at a manageable pace, a person with BPD may experience an intense increase in emotions at an overwhelmingly fast pace. Thus, people with BPD need access to specific skills to manage emotions more effectively. For this reason, some therapies, such as Dialectical-Behavior Therapy (DBT), teach specific skills to manage this intense, physiological, emotional reactivity (Linehan, 1993a; Linehan, 1993b; Linehan, 2015).

INTERACTION BETWEEN ENVIRONMENTAL AND BIOLOGICAL FACTORS

While all of these factors have been associated with the development of BPD, this does not mean that they cause BPD or that all need to be present for an individual to develop BPD. However, theories have suggested that BPD develops as a result of the interaction between a sensitized nervous system (i.e., temperament factors) and environmental factors such as attachment style, invalidation, or exposure to trauma (Fosse, Monestes, & Bakhache, 2008; Linehan, 1993a; Linehan, 1993b; Linehan, 2015). While there is some evidence for this interaction theory, how this interaction develops is still being studied (Carlson, Egeland, & Sroufe, 2009; Paris, 2005; Sauer & Baer, 2010). For example, invalidation becomes a two-way street for a child with a sensitized emotional process or a difficult temperament. While a difficult temperament may not always occur in people with BPD, this diagnosis is at risk of developing when a child has a biological predisposition toward sensitized emotional responses, and it often occurs in the context of an invalidating environment (Linehan, 1993a; Linehan, 1993b; Linehan, 2015). In this case, a trait that leads to more negative inner states interacts with the invalidation of the caregiver. The child's tendency toward perceiving insults is met with a negative reaction from the caregiver, which validates the perception (Hopwood & Zanarini, 2012) and may increase symptomology. Or, another way to understand this interaction: a child with a difficult temperament tries to communicate distress to a caregiver and is met with invalidation, and his or her attempt at communicating distress is not acknowledged; therefore, the child increases communication about distress in increasingly unhealthy ways in order to be heard by the caregiver (Linehan, 2015). At times the caregiver's lack of validation to the child may also be understandably related to low resources within the family, such as low social support, high demands on time, or financial stress that inhibits the family's ability to be attuned to the child's needs (Linehan, 2015).

Caregivers may try to make a child stop crying or exhibiting negative behaviors, but without effective parenting tools. The child's problem behaviors and emotional sensitivity may continue to escalate. A caregiver may be left feeling the child is insatiable or impossible to soothe, and the child may be left feeling he or she is unheard by the caregiver (Linehan, 2015). When the child responds negatively to invalidation, the caregiver may in turn feel invalidated by the child regarding her or his ability to fulfill the role of caregiver. The child's behavior may continue to escalate, as they are not receiving what they need from caregivers. This may lead to increasing frustration on the part of the caregiver and further reduce the effectiveness of the caregiver responses to the child (Linehan, 2015).

CHILDHOOD DIAGNOSES AND OTHER CONTRIBUTING FACTORS

There are several childhood diagnoses that are commonly predictive of later developing BPD as adults, although these diagnoses do not necessarily mean that BPD will develop. For example, children who are diagnosed with Attention-Deficit Hyperactivity Disorder (ADHD) are more likely to be diagnosed with BPD as an adult. This relationship may occur, in part, due to the difficulty children with ADHD have in controlling their impulses (Burke & Stepp, 2012; Eppright et al., 1993; Speranza et al., 2011). Oppositional-Defiant Disorder is another common childhood diagnosis among people with BPD (Burke & Steppe, 2012), and Antisocial Personality Disorder has also been associated with the development of BPD. Goodman, Hull, Clarkin, and Yeomans (1999) found that Antisocial Personality Disorder diagnosed before age 15 is a predictor of BPD. Eppright et al. (1993) found a high Co-morbidity rate between female adolescents with conduct disorder and BPD, and between male adolescents with Antisocial Personality Disorder and BPD.

As previously mentioned, individuals with symptoms of BPD may develop self-injurious behaviors as a way to manage distressing symptoms or to communicate distress to others (Substance Abuse and Mental Health Services Administration, 2014; Linehan, 1993a; Linehan, 1993b; Linehan, 2015). While BPD is often associated with self-harm, individuals diagnosed with BPD can sometimes act aggressively toward others, due to their inability to effectively manage stress, paired with low impulse control (Newhill, Eack, & Mulvey, 2012; Sansone & Sansone, 2012).

RISK AND PROTECTIVE FACTORS IN THE DEVELOPMENT OF BPD

Risk and protective factors include those that either decrease or increase the likelihood of a positive prognosis and help inform professionals about levels of risk for people with BPD. They also guide professionals implementing interventions on how to minimize risk. Therefore, it is beneficial to be aware of risk and protecting factors when dealing with individuals who suffer from BPD.

SUPPORT SYSTEMS

High social support has been shown as a protective factor, while low social support has been shown as a risk factor (Kleinman & Liu, 2013; Quigley, 2003; Soloff & Chiappetta, 2012). It can be helpful to ask a person with BPD about their support system, in terms of whom he or she can speak to for support (Soloff & Chiappetta, 2012). People in a support system may include friends or family members; connections at school or work; connections at local churches, clubs or organizations; or sponsors or participants in local support groups. People with low support systems can often connect with professional supports such as therapists, counselors, social workers, psychologists, case managers, psychiatrists, doctors, nurses, or personal care attendants (PCAs). In addition, there are community resources which can help increase social support, such as National Alliance for Mental Illness (NAMI). National and local crisis phone lines are important numbers to have access to in case of thoughts of harm to self or others. Local or national "warm lines" offer a listening ear for individuals who are not in a state of crisis, but who need to speak with someone to avoid their thoughts and feelings from escalating further.

FAMILY IMPLICATIONS

As summarized earlier in this chapter, trauma, abuse, or neglect are often experienced by people who develop BPD. Parents who are involved with child protective services and experience symptoms of BPD have likely experienced maltreatment themselves as children; abuse cycles may be passed down through generations if interventions are not offered (Hesse & Main, 2000; Perepletchikova et al., 2012). Without intervention, interpersonal problems have been shown to persist among people with BPD (Wright, Hallquist, Beeney, & Pilkonis, 2013), with clear implications for family structure. Current data suggests that individual or family-focused interventions for parents with BPD may be beneficial in strengthening families and interrupting cycles of abuse or neglect (Perepletchikova et al., 2012; Stobie & Tromski-Klingshirn 2009; Zeichner, 2013). If abuse is present in a home, it is important to provide treatment interventions to interrupt the abuse and provide a safe environment for children at risk of developing BPD, as severity of childhood abuse increases the likelihood of suicide attempts for individuals with BDP (Links, Kolla, Guimond, & McMain, 2013).

WORK AND SCHOOL CONNECTIONS

While there is need for further research, there is some evidence that connections at work or school can act as protective factors for both healthy community members and for people with BPD (Buehringer, 1995; Quigley, 2003). For example, positive work environments can provide a positive structure separate from chaotic social relationships. However, a critical boss or co-worker can also trigger an increase in symptoms (Kreisman & Strauss, 2010). Therefore, assisting a person in continued engagement in positive work or school functions may be a helpful intervention. This may include prompting about when to go to class or work, breaking this task down into manageable steps, encouraging him or her to engage in these activities, and addressing barriers to engaging.

BULLYING

In a large-scale study with over 6,000 participants, experiences with peer bullying were associated with increases in the risk of developing symptoms of BPD (Wolke, Schreier, Zanarini, & Winsper, 2012). This suggests the possible utility of legislative anti-bullying programs, although more data is needed to support the efficacy of interventions for bullying in reducing risk of developing symptoms of BPD.

CULTURAL FACTORS AND DEVELOPMENT OF BPD

Due to the evaluative nature of diagnosing a person with BPD, there is a risk of assessing a person as having maladaptive traits when those traits are culturally adaptive or normative (American Psychiatric Association, 2010). For example, personality assessments have been shown to over-assess people of color as "mistrustful," "paranoid," or "suspicious." Yet these traits can also be understood as adaptive in the historical context of people of color responding protectively after years of slavery and discrimination. In this light, mistrust of white people, especially those in authority, is not pathological but adaptive (Sue & Sue, 2013). Therefore, it is essential to distinguish between normative development and pathology in terms of personality disorder. This difference is important in both the mental health and medical health systems, in the school system, and in the criminal justice system, so that responses to people are appropriate. For example, a person of color who appears guarded may not be pathological, but may instead be exhibiting strengths in learning how to survive discrimination. Effective responses involve awareness of how cultural identity impacts people in the community, awareness of personal beliefs or stereotypes, and avoiding personalizing responses from members of cultural communities as a personal attack (American Psychiatric Association, 2010; Sue & Sue, 2013).

ADOLESCENTS AND YOUNG ADULTS

It is important to note that young adults often have difficulty with identity development (Newman & Newman, 2015) and may even be predisposed to act similarly to people with BPD in terms of emotional dysregulation and impulsivity (Walsh, 2012). Although not all adolescents display such behaviors, they have a predisposition to them as a part of how the brain develops at a biological level. Impulsivity and emotional reactivity, which are quite common among adolescents, are understandable because the parts of the brain that control emotions are sensitized during adolescence, while those that control higher thinking and impulse control are not yet fully developed (Walsh, 2012). It is therefore important to avoid diagnosing a teenager or young adult with a personality disorder too early, as they may experience difficulties with identity problems and emotion management that are normal developmental processes rather than mental health concerns. For this reason, the American Psychiatric Association (2010) cautions clinicians about diagnosing BPD before a person is well into adulthood.

SOCIOECONOMIC STATUS

While people from all socio-economic statuses experience symptoms of BPD, it is more common for people with BPD to have lower income and education. A study examining the effects of sociodemographic factors on the prevalence of BPD showed that having a high school education has a low correlation with higher rates of BPD, especially among men. In addition, lower financial status (incomes under $69,999) and being single after a serious relationship (widowed, divorced, separated) also correlated with higher rates of BPD for both men and women (Grant et al., 2008).

More specifically, people who live in poverty are more likely to experience trauma and discrimination that may affect development (Sue & Sue, 2013), since these individuals experience higher levels of stress, are more likely to be malnourished, are less likely to be educated, and are less likely to have access to child care and psychiatric care (Kreisman, 2010). Food insecurity is also linked to developmental and emotional difficulties as well as acting-out behaviors and suspensions from school (Children's Defense Fund, 2012). Awareness of these factors and the daily realities of people of low socio-economic status help increase intervention effectiveness (Sue & Sue, 2013).

MULTICULTURAL ASSESSMENT AND PLACEMENT IN THE MENTAL HEALTH SYSTEM

Early treatment and connection with the mental health system can help reduce later developmental problems such as mental illness. However, recent data shows that different ethnic groups have varying personality disorder diagnostic rates and varying referrals to treatment (Ryder, Sunohara, & Kirmayer, 2015). There is data to show that people of color are disproportionately more likely to be placed in the juvenile justice system than referred to mental health services. On the contrary, non-Hispanic whites are three times more likely to receive substance use treatment than people of color. Latino children are also less likely to be assessed by a primary care physician as having a mental health condition. In the foster care system, African Americans are less likely to receive mental health treatment, less likely to have stable placement, and more likely to show lower test scores, higher dropout rates, and higher rates of being absent or tardy from school. When African American children age out of the system, they are more likely to be homeless or incarcerated and less likely to graduate from high school (Children's Defense Fund, 2012). While studies show that Caucasians, Hispanics, and African Americans use and sell drugs at similar rates, Hispanics and African Americans are disproportionally incarcerated for drug crimes (Alexander, 2012).

It appears that African Americans and Hispanics are more likely to fall through the cracks and do not receive needed treatment for mental health and substance-use issues (Ryder, Sunohara, & Kirmayer, 2015). People across systems of education, mental health, and criminal justice need to work together by being aware of how cultural factors intersect with placement in healthcare or the justice system, and assessing carefully for adequate follow-up care and referrals. Appropriate referrals by people across fields can aide in effective community response and treatment for mental health.

ANTISOCIAL PERSONALITY AND BPD

There is limited research related to offenders in the criminal justice system with BPD as their only diagnosis; offenders usually have a secondary substance-related diagnosis or a Co-morbid diagnosis of Antisocial Personality Disorder (ASPD) (Gardner et al., 2015; Howard, Khalifa, & Duggan, 2014). Several authors have noted that a substantial portion of offending behaviors committed by individuals with BPD may be associated with substance use or a Co-morbid diagnosis of ASPD (Sansone et al., 2012). Individuals with BPD and combined ASPD tend to have worse treatment and correctional outcomes and higher recidivism, likely due to ASPD behaviors, such as violence without remorse and a disregard for the rights of others, rather than BPD behaviors. Individuals with BPD as their primary diagnosis tend to show symptom improvement in response to clinical treatment (Oldham, 2006; Zanarini, 2009).

Although symptoms of BPD have been associated with higher rates of reported partner violence (Weinstein, Gleason, & Oltmanns, 2012), individuals with ASPD and BPD may show differences in factors that predict aggression. In one large study of over 700 undergraduate participants, predicting factors for BPD included motor impulsiveness, irritability, resentment, and guilt, while predictors for ASPD included motor impulsiveness, physical aggression, indirect aggression, and negativism (Fossati et al., 2004). This shows that while ASPD and BPD have commonality in impulsive behaviors, behaviors associated with aggression are more closely linked to ASPD than BPD (Fossati et al., 2004). This again reinforces the importance of focusing on behaviors, accurately assessing for the diagnosis of BPD versus ASPD, and avoiding an assumption that a diagnosis of BPD will automatically denote aggressive behaviors.

Myths and Controversies about BPD

Ability to Make Progress over Time

A common misconception involves the idea that people diagnosed with BPD are "beyond help" or have a lifetime diagnosis. This myth may have evolved by comparing BPD to other disorders such as Bipolar and Schizophrenia that have been shown to be less responsive to treatments (Lieb et al., 2004). While people with personality disorders tend to experience more long-standing difficulties with functioning, there is good evidence to show that people with BPD can and do get better with treatment and support (Oldham, 2006; Zanarini et al., 2009; Substance Abuse and Mental Health Services Administration, 2014). Those with BPD progress over time when treatment is effectively matched to the presenting issues (American Psychiatric Association, 2013; Paris, 2002; SAMHSA, 2011). In fact, people with BPD who are able to obtain evidence-based treatments typically begin to show progress within one year (American Psychiatric Association, 2013; Paris, 2002).

Stereotypes about People with BPD

Others may perceive people with BPD negatively. Staff members at mental health facilities may have stigmas about individuals suffering from BPD as being manipulative or attention-seeking (Kreisman & Straus, 2010; Millar, Gillanders, & Saleem, 2012; Stroud & Parsons, 2013), possibly in response to emotionally intense dynamics that play out as a part of the symptoms of BPD (American Psychiatric Association, 2010). These negative views may be related to a lack of understanding about the function of behaviors of people with BPD (Kreisman & Straus, 2010). As reviewed earlier, it is clear that presentations such as self-injurious behavior, which may initially be difficult to understand, serve a function in managing symptoms of BPD (Gardner et al., 2015; Linehan, 1993a; Linehan, 1993b; Linehan, 2015; Paris, 2005; Wupperman et al., 2013). It is also clear that intense and unstable relationships are a difficult symptom of BPD, rather than an intentionally malicious behavior (American Psychiatric Association, 2010). For this reason, it is recommended to carefully reflect on one's personal reactions to people with BPD, to increase awareness, and to ensure that staff members understand the causes of the behavior displayed by individuals with BPD (American Psychiatric Association, 2010).

Some preliminary studies suggest that making a conscious effort to understand the behavior of people with BPD can help mitigate negative attitudes, highlighting a framework of understanding that these behaviors have developed to manage emotional experiences rather than seek attention or "manipulate" (Millar, Gillanders, & Saleem, 2012; Stroud & Parsons, 2013). It may also be helpful to identify alternative coping strategies without dismissing the individual as helpless (Linehan, 1993a; Linehan, 1993b; Linehan, 2015; Kreisman & Straus, 2010). More research is needed in terms of what is helpful in shifting mental health staff perceptions about individuals with BPD.

Gender Differences

While the rates of BPD in the general population tend to be similar for men and women, the types of Co-morbidities are different (Zanarini et al., 1998). Males have been shown to be more likely to have substance abuse disorders, while females have a noticeably higher rate of eating disorders. There is some evidence of a higher level of disability shown in women with BPD than in men. Some behavioral differences are also evident, such as more anger and ASPD in men with BPD and more anxiety disorders, eating disorders, and PTSD in women with this diagnosis (SAMHSA, 2011). In the UK, it is estimated that 20% of the female prison population meets criteria for BPD compared to 2% of the general population (Nee & Farman, 2005). A more recent study of newly committed offenders found 29.5% of all offenders from the Iowa Department of Corrections met criteria for BPD, and 93.2% had at least one BPD trait. The study also found that the number of women who met criteria for BPD was more than twice the male rate. The study concluded that symptoms of BPD in both genders likely contribute to criminogenic behavior. The authors suggest early detection and treatment for BPD and that BPD should not be overlooked in the male population (Black et al., 2007). Although ASPD and BPD both have components of impulsivity, ASPD is more common in males than females, and individuals with ASPD are generally more emotionally stable than individuals with BPD (Fossati et al., 2004). It is common for men to be stereotypically diagnosed with ASPD without considering BPD and for women to be diagnosed with BPD without considering ASPD, due to BPD being thought of as a "female" disorder and ASPD as being a "male" disorder. ASPD and BPD need to be considered for both genders displaying symptoms of impulsivity and intense emotional responses, as both are possible options despite an individual's gender.

While there is limited research on the prevalence of personality disorders within the Lesbian, Gay, Bisexual, Transgender, Queer (LGBTQ) population, one study found significant differences between individuals diagnosed with Gender Identity Disorder (GID) and the general population (Duisin et al., 2014). GID occurs when an individual's biological sex is not congruent with their experienced gender, which causes significant discomfort and impairment in functioning. Individuals with GID were shown to be significantly more likely to be diagnosed with a personality disorder (Duisin et al., 2014). Future research needs to focus on gaining a better understanding of personality disorders and other psychopathology in the LGBTQ population.

TREATING BORDERLINE PERSONALITY DISORDER

Treating BPD is complex due to the nature of the disorder. The primary treatment modalities that will be discussed in this chapter fall into two basic categories. The first is comprised of Cognitive Behavioral Therapies, including Dialectical Behavior Therapy (DBT), Schema-Focused Therapy (SFT), and Systems Training for Emotional Predictability and Problem Solving (STEPPS). The second general category is Psychodynamic Therapies, including Transference Focused Psychotherapy (TFP), Dynamic Deconstructive Psychotherapy (DDP) and Mentalization-Based Therapy (MBT). All of these treatments are evidence-based, primarily differentiated by the theoretical orientation behind the two categories. An overview of each therapy is described in more detail below.

COGNITIVE BEHAVIORAL THERAPY

Cognitive Behavioral Therapy (CBT) was originally developed in the early 1960s as a short-term, highly structured psychotherapy for depression. It focused on problem-solving, educating clients, and identifying and restructuring dysfunctional thinking and behavior. This model works on the premise that distorted and dysfunctional thinking are common to all psychological disturbances and influence individuals' moods and behaviors (Beck, 1995). Since its development, CBT has been successfully adapted to diverse populations and diagnoses, and ultimately modified by other major theorists such as Albert Ellis (Beck, 1995). Clients with BPD commonly have beliefs that consist of seeing themselves as "bad," "unlovable," and "deserving of punishment." They view others as "neglectful," "untrustworthy," "rejecting," or "harmful." CBT highly emphasizes psycho-education, or directly teaching patients about how to recognize, manage and/or modify painful emotions (Yeomans, Levy, & Meehan, 2012). The following treatments were developed based on the basic principles of CBT.

DIALECTICAL BEHAVIOR THERAPY (DBT)

DBT is a skills-based treatment originally developed by Marsha Linehan. This model takes the perspective that emotional dysregulation is at the heart of BPD (Linehan, 1993a; Linehan, 1993b; Linehan, 2015). Validating the client's experience and accepting the client while continuing to encourage behavioral changes is a key component therapists practice in DBT (Linehan, 2015; Yeomans et al., 2012). It combines group skills training along with weekly individual psychotherapy and consists of four modules: core mindfulness, emotion regulation, interpersonal effectiveness and distress tolerance.

The overall goals of DBT are to decrease self-injurious behavior (SIB), decrease suicidal ideation (SI) and suicide attempts, teach clients how to effectively manage intense emotions and unhealthy urges in ways that do not make situations worse, increase problem-solving skills, and increase interpersonal communication skills (Linehan, 1993a; Linehan, 1993b; Linehan, 2015). Besides being cost-effective, DBT programs have been found to be successful compared to standard group therapy (Soler et al., 2009). Multiple DBT pilot studies have been implemented within the male and female prison populations, with promising results in decreasing criminogenic risk, decreasing self-harm and aggressive behaviors, and improving quality of life (Nee & Farman, 2005, 2007; van den Bosch, Hysaj, & Jacobs, 2012; Shelton, Sampl, Kesten, Zhang, & Trestman, 2009). Sampl, Wakai, & Trestman (2010) discuss the need to modify original DBT materials in order to accommodate typical needs of offenders within the prison system. They suggest incorporating more visual learning, changing language and terminology to that of a 5th-grade reading level, and adapting life examples to fit typical prison-related scenarios. Despite these positive findings, authors acknowledge that significantly more research is needed regarding effective implementation and outcomes of DBT in prisons.

Schema-Focused Therapy (SFT)

SFT was developed by psychologist Jeffrey Young and his colleagues. A schema is the lens through which we see and make sense of the world. It consists of stereotypes, prejudices, biases, thoughts, feelings, values, beliefs, etc., and is shaped through our experiences. Schemas influence the way individuals view themselves, their relationship with others, and the world at large. Maladaptive schemas influence our behavior and communication patterns and may prevent individuals from forming healthy attachments and interactions within interpersonal relationships. The general premise of SFT and BPD is that individuals with BPD develop specific maladaptive schemas in childhood that carry into adulthood and cause maladaptive coping, impairment, and relational difficulties (Leppanen, Karki, Saariaho, Lindeman, & Hakko, 2015). An example of a maladaptive schema within a BPD individual could be the belief that "I am a bad person."

SFT was developed as a long-term treatment option for patients who do not respond well to other treatment options (Leppanen et al., 2015). SFT is delivered on an individual basis twice a week and combines techniques from several theoretical orientations, including CBT and attachment, psychodynamic, and emotion-focused therapies. The four main techniques used in SFT are limited re-parenting, experiential imagery and dialogue work, cognitive restructuring and education, as well as behavioral pattern breaking. The goal of this therapy is for the client to experience their therapist as a healthy parental figure, internalizing this through the therapist's warmth, nurturance, limit-setting and firmness. Other specific techniques used are relaxation exercises, imagery, role-playing, assertiveness training, and letter-writing. Cognitive techniques challenge the client's negative schemas, thoughts, and beliefs. The therapeutic relationship is also used to increase healthy attachment to others (Yeomans et al., 2012). Research has shown positive outcomes when implementing SFT with BPD clients in the community (Leppanen et al., 2015).

Systems Training for Emotional Predictability and Problem Solving (STEPPS)

STEPPS is a manualized adjunctive treatment that couples CBT and group systems interventions. This treatment modality conceptualizes BPD as an "emotional intensity disorder," treated by skills training to monitor and manage intense emotions and moods (Yeomans et al., 2012). It incorporates family members and significant others into treatment as an added support (Harvey, Black, & Blum, 2010). It is delivered in a group format two hours a week for twenty weeks and does not require additional weekly individual therapy, although clients are welcome to seek out individual therapy in addition to STEPPS, if desired (Brown, Blum, & Black, 2014).

The program was designed to supplement and enhance treatments such as individual therapy, case management, medications, etc. (Harvey et al., 2010). STEPPS is generally led by two facilitators, and the curriculum is highly structured, with detailed lesson plans, homework assignments, and packets with materials for the program.

There are three main components in STEPPS: awareness of illness, emotion management, and behavior management. Awareness of illness is psycho-educational in nature. It redefines BPD as an "emotional intensity disorder" (EID) and assists in increasing awareness of the symptoms of the disorder, so clients can learn to manage them. It also provides education on schemas, which are referred to as "cognitive filters," and how to challenge and correct these distortions. Emotion management aims to teach skills that assist clients in predicting the course of emotional states and stressful situations, as well as increasing healthy and adaptive coping mechanisms for distressful states. Behavior management includes skills such as goal setting, healthy eating habits, sleep hygiene, exercise, physical health, and interpersonal relationship management. It emphasizes the importance of daily routine to assist in managing the disorder (Brown et al., 2014).

The STEPPS program has specific advantages for correctional settings compared to other BPD treatment programs. STEPPS is only a twenty-week program in both the community corrections and correctional settings. This is advantageous for the correctional setting due to differences in length of sentencing among offenders, as well as transfers and releases occurring with minimal notice. STEPPS is easily implemented by therapists, requires minimal training, and can be implemented with limited budgets in a correctional setting. An additional advantage to this program is that it offers a two-hour evening session that is open to offenders' families, visitors, and correctional officers, in order to educate them on the "language" of STEPPS and provide the knowledge needed to help reinforce the skills offenders learn throughout the program (Brown et al., 2014). In 2005, the Iowa Department of Corrections (IDOC) implemented the STEPPS program as part of routine mental health care. IDOC collected data to track the effectiveness of this program and concluded that STEPPS resulted in significant improvement in mood, as well as a decrease in self-harming behaviors, suicidal behaviors, and disciplinary infractions (Brown et al., 2014). In 2013, Black, Blum, McCormick, & Allen conducted a study of 77 offenders within the Iowa DOC. This study concluded that STEPPS was also successful in decreasing BPD symptoms, suicidal behaviors, and disciplinary infractions. The authors determined that STEPPS can be successfully implemented within prison and community corrections to treat BPD. STEPPS has been successfully implemented and accepted in the United Kingdom and The Netherlands, showing it is adaptable across some cultures (Harvey, Black, & Blum, 2010). This is positive in that if the program is able to be applied across cultures, it would be reasonable to assume that the program will be beneficial for diverse cultural backgrounds within U.S. correctional systems.

PSYCHODYNAMIC THERAPIES

TRANSFERENCE-FOCUSED PSYCHOTHERAPY (TFP)

TFP is based on Kernberg's object relations model of BPD and was originally created as treatment for severe personality pathology (Bliss & McCardle, 2014; Yeomans, Levy, & Caligor, 2013). TFP views BPD as stemming from a lack of understanding of self and others and an inability to successfully integrate a stable and consistent personal identity. Individuals with BPD do not know how to integrate strengths and weaknesses, good and bad, into one cohesive personality or identity. This leads an individual to rely heavily on defense mechanisms and leaves them vulnerable to adopting cognitive distortions about themselves and the world around them. This theory is based on the premise that interactions and relationships in early childhood are internalized and carried throughout the course of development (Yeomans et al., 2013).

Individuals with BPD view the world in black and white extremes (i.e., all good or all bad). Therefore, the goal of TFP is to help the client think more flexibly, realistically, and compassionately (Bliss & McCardle,

2014). It attempts to assist individuals in understanding how their view of the world contributes to perception and misperception of daily interactions and produces intense emotions (Hopwood, Swenson, Bateman, Yeomans, & Gunderson, 2014). This approach uses clarification, confrontation, and transference interpretations as the primary interventions. FTP focuses on the "here and now" and different themes and affects that play out in the relationship between the therapist and client (Bliss & McCardle, 2014). Transference is the tendency for a client to unintentionally and unknowingly transfer their feelings, wishes, desires, fears and perceptions onto their therapist. Transference can be positive (such as affectionate feelings toward their therapist) or negative (such as hostile feelings or feelings of rejection or abandonment by their therapist) (Faiver, Eisengart, & Colonna, 2004). The therapist is able to use this process to address the maladaptive difficulties of individuals with BPD and create healthier, more adaptive patterns. One strength of TFP is the evidence that it is the only treatment to be associated with improvement in secure attachment (Bliss & McCardle, 2014). TFP has also been shown to be effective in reducing symptoms of anger and impulsivity (Madeddu, Aquaro, & Preti, 2012).

MENTALIZATION-BASED TREATMENT (MBT)

MBT is a modified form of psychodynamic therapy for BPD developed by Bateman and Fonagy (Bliss, & McCardle, 2014). This model conceptualizes BPD as a difficulty with attachment, separation tolerance, and mentalization, and focuses on mentalization rather than cognitions, behaviors, or insight (Bliss & McCardle, 2014; Laurenssen et al., 2014). Mentalization, sometimes referred to as "reflective capacity" or "reflective function," is defined as "the client's ability to think about oneself in relation to others, and to understand another's state of mind" (Bliss & McCardle, 2014, p. 64). Difficulty with mentalization happens when a client assumes that whatever is on his or her mind is an accurate reflection of reality. An example of this would be "I feel he does not love me, therefore he does not" (Hopwood, Swenson, Bateman, Yeomans, & Gunderson, 2014). The client struggles to consider and identify other possible explanations for others' behaviors. Interventions for MBT include support and validation, as well as ways of facilitating perspective-taking and understanding states of mind. The initial intervention in MBT is to assist clients in regulating emotions, which is necessary for additional therapeutic work (Bliss & McCardle, 2014). Studies show MBT is effective in reducing distress, self-harm, and suicidal behavior. MBT has also shown effectiveness in increasing psychosocial, occupational and interpersonal functioning (Morken, Karterud, & Arefjord, 2014; Kvarstein, Pedersen, Urnes, Hummelen, Wilberg, & Karterud, 2015). There have been positive results when adapting this model to adolescents (Laurenssen et al., 2014). While these findings are promising, authors acknowledged limitations to the studies and call for the need for continued research.

DYNAMIC DECONSTRUCTIVE PSYCHOTHERAPY (DDP)

DDP is a manualized, individual therapy for BPD clients who are resistant to treatment or difficult to engage, as well as individuals with co-occurring substance use disorders (Goldman & Gregory, 2010; Gregory & Remen, 2008). Recent studies predict that approximately 78% of individuals with BPD currently have or will develop a substance use disorder. Individuals with Co-morbid substance use disorders tend to be more impulsive and less stable than BPD individuals without substance use disorders (Kienast, Stoffers, Bermpohl, & Lieb, 2014). While DDP can be used on its own, it can also be used along with other treatments such as group therapy, medications, and self-help groups (Goldman & Gregory, 2009). It is a 12- to18-month program where clients meet once a week for one-hour sessions that address BPD along with other complex behaviors such as self-harm, eating disorders, and recurrent suicide attempts (Gregory, 2014). DDP is based on the belief that BPD clients lack three neurocognitive capacities that are needed for processing emotional experiences (Goldman & Gregory, 2010; Gregory & Remen, 2008).

The first deficit is *Association*, which is "the capacity to identify, acknowledge, and sequence emotional experiences" (Goldman & Gregory, 2010, p. 360). Individuals with BPD tend to struggle to verbalize their experiences and create narratives (Gregory & Remen, 2008). The second deficit is *Attribution*, which is "the ability to view oneself and others as having ambiguous, multifaceted, and/or complex motivations and emotions" (Goldman & Gregory, 2010, p. 361). Individuals with BPD tend to have polarized attributions that rapidly alternate between each other, which results in an inconsistent and unstable sense of self, as well as emotional dysregulation (Gregory & Remen, 2008). Clients are intolerant of ambiguity and tend to see things in black and white categories (Goldman & Gregory, 2010). The last deficit is *Alterity*, which is "the ability to reflect on oneself and others from an outside or 'objective perspective'" (Goldman & Gregory, 2010, p. 361). This deficit leads clients to make inaccurate assumptions about the motivations and intentions of others, due to their inability to realistically assess their experiences and others' intentions (Goldman & Gregory, 2010; Gregory & Remen, 2008).

The effectiveness of DDP in treating BPD and substance use is unclear. The manualized approach of DDP has been shown to rectify deficits and moderately improve the BPD symptoms of dissociation and depression, as well as decrease behavioral problems of self-harm, substance misuse, and suicide attempts (Gregory, 2014). Research has also shown promising results for treating BPD and Dissociative Identity Disorder (DID), which is commonly Co-morbid with BPD (Chlebowski & Gregory, 2012). DDP yields moderate positive results (Kienast et al., 2014), which could be a reflection of the difficult population it is designed to treat. Some studies show DDP to be effective in treating BPD behaviors and symptoms, but it has been shown to be less successful in treating substance use. While DDP has been shown to be moderately effective for treating particularly difficult clients, future research should focus on pilot programs within correctional settings, as there is little known of its effectiveness in that setting.

SUMMARY OF TREATMENT APPROACHES

The literature on treatment for BPD supports multiple treatment approaches for reducing symptoms—one treatment has not been shown to be better than another (Bliss & McCardle, 2014). Common components of each of these treatments are structure, increase in awareness, ability to think dialectically, and validation. It may be the combination of these common elements that are behind the improvement in symptoms, regardless of the specific model used (Bliss & McCardle, 2014). Some research suggests that different models are helpful in addressing specific symptoms of BPD, such as TFP helping with core BPD symptoms of depression and DDP being most beneficial for improving social support and alcohol misuse (Goldman & Gregory, 2010). Adapted DBT and STEPPS programs seem to be the most heavily applied and researched within corrections populations; however, even this research is highly limited. Madeddu, Aquaro, & Preti, (2012) conducted a literature review of MBT, TFP, DBT and SFT. All four of these approaches were shown to be effective in reducing self-harm, suicidal behavior, and parasuicidal behavior. TFP was found to be the most effective in reducing anger and impulsivity, and DBT was most effective in reducing emotional dysregulation behaviors. TFP was found to be helpful in increasing an individual's capacity for reflective function. They concluded that all four models were effective in treating BPD. According to the study, DBT, SFT, and TFP all met criteria for "well-established treatments for BPD." Interestingly, while MBT was shown to be effective, it did not meet criteria for "well-established" (Madeddu, Aquaro, & Preti, 2012). All research behind treatment for BPD acknowledges limitations and calls for future research on the topic.

It seems reasonable that the most effective treatment for the correctional population would be a model that is easily adaptable to different environments, intellectual abilities, and short-term rather than long-term therapy, as well as being deliverable in a group setting in order to reach as many offenders as possible in a cost-effective manner. This is likely why STEPPS and DBT seem to be the most widely studied approaches within corrections.

MEDICATIONS

Unlike many mental disorders, medication is not the primary treatment for BPD, since the disorder is one of personality rather than a chemical imbalance in the brain like depression or psychosis (Australian Government National Health and Medical Research Council, 2012). However, recent research indicates that antipsychotics may be helpful. One study found that low doses of the antipsychotic Seroquel significantly reduced the severity of BPD symptoms (Black et al., 2014). Other research on antipsychotic and mood-stabilizing medications indicates a possibility of decreasing rates of violent crime—a consideration when working with any individual with a history of psychiatric conditions and violent crimes (Fazel, Zetterqvist, Larsson, Långström, & Lichtenstein, 2014). These results imply that individuals within the criminal justice system who meet criteria for BPD should have access to psychotropic medications to use as prescribed by a medical professional. Although encouraging, research is still developing, and psychotherapy is needed in conjunction with medications for optimal results.

CO-OCCURRING SUBSTANCE-USE DISORDERS

As noted earlier in this chapter, there is a high Co-morbidity rate between BPD and substance use disorders (Grant et al., 2006; Oldham, 2006). As a risk factor in BPD, substance use has been shown to predict a higher risk of recidivism (Erickson, 2014; Scott, Grella, Dennis, & Funk, 2014), as well as a continuation of BPD symptoms (Zanarini, Frankenburg, Hennen, Reich, & Silk, 2004). Interventions related to addressing substance use may include assisting individuals in scheduling chemical dependency assessments or accessing treatment, reducing exposure to substances and triggers to using, removing access to substances in the home, distancing from friends or contacts who use, and connecting with sober supports, among others. Due to a reluctance to engage in sobriety, effective interventions to address substance use include motivational interviewing, a well-established, evidence-based approach for chemical dependency. This approach assists the individual in exploring and talking about his or her personal goals and how sobriety may aide in reaching those goals, rather than having an outside person tell the individual how it will help, which more often results in power struggles (SAMHSA, 2011).

INPATIENT HOSPITALIZATION AND CIVIL COMMITMENT

It is common for individuals with BPD to be hospitalized due to suicidal ideation, suicide attempts, and self-harming behaviors; however, inpatient hospitalization should not be considered as treatment for BPD, but rather, a short-term, goal-oriented option for crisis management (Australian Government National Health and Medical Research Council, 2012). If individuals are experiencing many hospital stays for chronic suicidal ideation and/or attempts and refusing treatment or not following through on treatment recommendations, civil commitment may be necessary for BPD individuals to get the care and treatment they need while minimizing safety risks.

According to the National Alliance on Mental Illness (NAMI) in Minnesota, the court will allow an involuntary civil commitment if the individual has a mental health diagnosis and (1) is unable to care for themselves, (2) is a danger to themselves or others, (3) is engaging in voluntary damage to property, (4) if lack of medical care will result in a significant medical or psychological deterioration, or (5) if there is no less-restrictive course of action to assist the person.

Civil commitment is for individuals 18 years and older. An individual may commit a crime, be charged, and be civilly committed rather than execute their sentence in prison, or they may execute their sentence in prison and then be placed on civil commitment (National Alliance on Mental Health Minnesota, 2006). There are no black-and-white rules on which setting in which an individual would be placed—it depends on the mental health treatment options available, as well as the severity of mental illness (Slovenko, 2012; Stredny,

Parker, & Dibble, 2012). If an individual is found "not guilty by reason of insanity," this is an acquittal, and they will likely be placed on civil commitment and sent to a state-operated, inpatient hospital to be stabilized. There is also the option of "diminished" or "partial" responsibility for a crime, which would lessen the degree of criminal responsibility placed on the defendant, without fully acquitting them of charges (Kinscherff, 2010).

There is some controversy regarding whether or not individuals with BPD have the insight and capacity to recognize an action as right or wrong, which results in questions about whether or not they are fully responsible for their actions. Some scholars argue that because an individual with BPD has capacity for some insight and empathy, an insanity defense would not be appropriate. Others argue that individuals with BPD should be considered in the same category as minors and those with intellectual disabilities and low IQ (Bonnie, 2010; Kinscherff, 2010; Sisti & Caplan, 2012).

BORDERLINE PERSONALITY DISORDER AND THE CRIMINAL JUSTICE SYSTEM

The focus of corrections has changed over time; however, the main goals can be summed up as deterrence, incapacitation, retribution and rehabilitation (Kifer, Hemmens, & Stohr, 2003). Until the mid-1970s, rehabilitation was a significant part of prison policy (Benson, 2003). Since then, the "tough on crime" viewpoint has turned the focus to punishment. Tough on crime policies significantly increased the number of individuals incarcerated but did not decrease crime rates (Benson, 2003; Harty, 2012). In 2003, Kifer et al. found that individuals working in the correctional field ranked incapacitation as the main goal, followed by deterrence, rehabilitation and retribution. Recent research on meta-analyses of differing prison focuses concluded that punitive approaches such as supervision and sanctions showed only modest reductions in recidivism and, at times, increased re-offense rates, while rehabilitation treatment approaches revealed consistently positive, large results. The difficulty of implementing research findings into practice continues to be a challenge (Lipsey & Cullen, 2007). This research supports implementing programs such as STEPPS and DBT into prison structure to reduce recidivism and alleviate mental health symptoms, rather than focusing on punishment, which does not address the root cause of offending behaviors. One study approached the problem from a racial disparity perspective, taking into account socio-demographics, cultural, and historical trauma with African Americans recently released from prison, by addressing structural barriers to improving mental and physical health and economic gains as a way to reduce recidivism (Windsor, Jemal, & Benoit, 2014). Participants reportedly were more engaged in treatment and felt it was beneficial, regardless of their personal difficulties or circumstances (Windsor et al., 2014).

INCARCERATION

A disproportionate number of individuals with mental illness end up in criminal justice environments (Gee & Ogloff, 2015). The Australian court case of R v. Verdins, Buckley and Vo [2007] resulted in recommendations to address this fact, acknowledging that forensic mental health and its interface with criminal justice requires expertise and knowledge regarding mental health. It further discussed the line between 'insanity' and moral culpability with regard to mental health diagnoses. How much does the diagnosis matter, with respect to the placement, treatment, or deterrence offered through the current criminal justice system of punishment, and can the punishment actually negatively impact individuals with certain illnesses, further deteriorating their mental health? Based on this discussion, a broader spectrum of options would be necessary to address the grey area between legal insanity and full culpability (Gee & Ogloff, 2015). What impairment does a diagnosis like Borderline Personality Disorder cause, and how does it impact both the intention formation for criminal behavior and the ability to accept treatment or deterrence? Further, there needs to be assessment related to the cause of any pathology or diagnosis, including brain injury or cognitive impairment from BPD or other disorders (as opposed to psychopathology or pure criminal intent), and these factors necessarily must be weighed against community safety.

As discussed earlier in this chapter, individuals with BPD are more likely to use and abuse substances, have poor interpersonal skills, and have great difficulty regulating their emotions and controlling impulses. These deficits create circumstances that make it likely that an individual with BPD will encounter the criminal justice system—frequently as victims of crimes (e.g., interpersonal violence or childhood abuse). Research also indicates a strong correlation between Borderline Personality Organization (a framework defining the structural organization and severity of BPD) and Antisocial Features in prison inmates convicted of violent offenses (Leichsenring, Kunst, & Hoyer, 2003). This finding supports the notion that individuals with BPD *and* ASPD are more likely to commit violent offenses. A recent study of a sampling of men convicted of violent crimes in Sweden examined whether antipsychotics or mood stabilizers could reduce incidence of violent crime. Results showed a significant reduction in criminal behavior. (Fazel et al., 2014).

It is relatively common for both male and female offenders to have a BPD diagnosis, which has been found to be overrepresented in the prison population. Some have found that prevalence to be between 25% and 50%, with the number of incarcerated women meeting criteria for BPD ten times that of men (Gardner et al., 2015). This high percentage of women diagnosed with BPD may be related to gender biases in clinical diagnosis. (Gardner et al., 2015). More research on specific expressions of BPD symptoms for males and females in the prison systems is needed.

Research indicates that young men with BPD are more likely to engage in certain types of criminal behaviors: aggravated and simple assault, disorderly conduct, driving under the influence, drug abuse violations, and public intoxication (Sansone et al., 2012), reflecting the high Co-morbidity of BPD and substance use. Other contact with authorities may be in the form of crisis calls to emergency services as a result of self-harm or suicidal behavior. A concerned party or the individual with BPD may call 911 in hopes that the emergency responder can assist in de-escalating the situation or transporting the individual to a hospital where they can be assessed by a mental health professional.

The stigma and behaviors associated with BPD can directly affect how practitioners and criminal justice professionals interact with individuals with BPD (Aviram, Brodsky, & Stanley, 2006). Distancing oneself can be misinterpreted as abandonment or dislike, which can trigger negative responses to the perceived abandonment. Another study (Deckers et al., 2015) shows that stress can increase the subjective negative emotions and negative cognitions in BPD without increasing physiological arousal. Individuals with BPD are not necessarily more sensitive to social cues, leading to emotional dysregulation, but are more likely to have stronger reactions and more emotional dysregulation under stress (Deckers et al., 2015). Gardner et al. (2015) discussed characteristic behaviors, including affect-regulation problems, impulse control, self-harm, and anger-control problems.

Some of the most effective treatment modalities, such as DBT, can be considered too demanding on time, money, and resources in corrections. This study also posed that rumination can precede emotional cascades and dysregulated emotional states. The stress and isolation in corrections and difficulty connecting with others (including staff), along with the limited number of activities and distractions available, can be considered potential precursors to dysregulated emotional states (Gardner et al., 2015). Ineffective coping skills can further lead to self-injurous behavior (SIB) and other negative behaviors.

A study of the effects of stress on impulsivity showed that stress increases impulsivity in people with BPD more than in healthy controls (Cackowski et al., 2014). There are two prevalent models for viewing the effects of stress from incarceration: the deprivation model and the importation model (Goncalves, Goncalves, Martins, & Dirkzwager, 2014). The deprivation model assumes characteristics and limitations of prison lead to the stress. The importation model assumes that problems among inmates are caused by characteristics of the inmates themselves. This study suggests both as mitigating factors, and that impulsivity and aggression (each of which can be increased by stress) are both strong predictors of misconduct (Goncalves et al., 2014; Houser & Welsh, 2014).

Misconduct includes not just rule-breaking or criminal acts while incarcerated, but also includes self-harm behaviors. Wakai, Sampl, Hilton, & Ligon (2014) examined incarcerated women and their need for specific interventions to treat the underlying causes of self-harm and to help them develop coping skills. Motivational interviewing and CBT offer two approaches which are easier to integrate into all levels of corrections. Left unaddressed, SIB will become increasingly serious, which may subsequently lead to suicide attempts. Left untreated, the behavior also has a negative impact on staff morale, requiring significant resources and interventions (Wakai et al., 2014). A perceived lack of social support is a factor of SIB, even in a prison setting. Social support from outside the prison system (e.g., family visits) are a protective factor against SIB (Goncalve et al., 2014). Stress and isolation can increase such behavior, so punitive measures which isolate prisoners with SIB might be contraindicated. Substance use can increase SIB (Suicide Prevention Resource Center, 2001). Individual who have BPD and substance use disorders are most likely to engage in suicidal behaviors. Factors which need to be assessed and monitored include the individual's motive for self-harm, past suicide attempts, and impulsivity levels. A team approach by medical, correctional staff, and mental health professionals should be used.

CRISIS DE-ESCALATION

Since individuals with BPD have the potential to be chronically unstable and have difficulty controlling their impulses (APA, 2013), it is important for professionals working within the criminal justice system to recognize the onset of a crisis and have the necessary training to successfully de-escalate the situation. Common punishment for acting-out behaviors for incarcerated individuals includes restraints and seclusion. However, a review of the use of these techniques in psychiatric facilities showed them to be more harmful to the clients (Gaskin, Elsom, Happell, 2007). This review included a study in which a psychiatric unit utilized a behavioral consultation team to assess clients' plans and behaviors in order to reduce the use of seclusion. This approach could be applied to prison or jail settings to address specific behaviors and needs. For example, individuals with BPD tend to feel constantly invalidated by others and are frequently looking to be heard. Validation is a tool which can be used to begin to calm a dysregulated individual (Loewenstein & McManus, 2014). By validating the individual during a crisis, the staff communicate to the person that he or she is being heard and understood. Inserting validation remarks before a request (e.g., "I can see you are having an especially tough night; could you please sit down and talk with me about it?") can be helpful. It is crucial to note that a dysregulated individual is likely reacting to prolonged stress in the form of glucocorticoids related to the "fight or flight" reaction, which over time can lead to dopamine depletion, depression, and dysphoria or restlessness (Sapolsky, 2004), potentially increasing BPD symptoms.

De-escalation techniques help the client regain a feeling of self-control. Nonverbal communication is extremely important in crisis de-escalation. While it is important to protect oneself from potential physical harm, it is also important to note how tone of voice, facial expressions, and body language can de-escalate or escalate someone (Loewenstein & McManus, 2014). Rather than raising one's voice, it may be more beneficial to become quieter and calmer. Escalated individuals will often unconsciously mimic the calmer, quieter tone. Giving an escalated individual two options is also frequently helpful. When presented with two options, they are less likely to be overwhelmed and more likely to feel they have control because they are able to make a choice (e.g., "Would you like to sit down here or in the living room and talk with me?"). Either option implies that the person will sit down and talk, but giving them a choice is likely to help them feel in control, which in turn helps them to regulate their emotions. Richmond and colleagues (2012) describe ten domains of de-escalation. These advise on body language and personal space, concrete language and respectful communication, and slowing down interactions enough to allow the person to contain emotions and make choices. It involves coaching the person through the crisis event and helping them regain self-control in order to problem solve. This process can look different depending on the person's diagnosis and the context of the situation (Richmond et al., 2012). These techniques can be used in community and correctional settings.

SAFETY PLANNING

Given the risk of suicide attempts and self-injurious behavior, safety planning plays an important role in responding to people with BPD. Effective safety planning typically involves several elements: (1) identification of warning signs, (2) list of useful coping skills, (3) list of social and professional support contacts, (4) emergency resources to utilize during a crisis, and (5) elimination of access to any means of suicide and self-injury (Stanley & Brown, 2012; Pederson, 2015). Effective coping skills should be straightforward, simple, and concrete, so as to be manageable when one feels overwhelmed (Linehan, 1993a; Linehan, 1993b; Linehan, 2015). For example, the individual can be asked to stop and breathe, listen to music, or take a warm or cold shower (Linehan, 1993b; Chapman & Gratz, 2007). However, it is typically more effective to provide individuals with multiple coping options, so the person can freely choose which one to use (Stanley & Brown, 2012).

Writing down a detailed plan can help the person remember what to do if he or she feels emotionally overwhelmed (Pederson, 2015). This plan should be kept in a place that is easily accessible and, if possible, should be shared with the individual's support system (Stanley & Brown, 2012). By knowing the plan, friends and family can help remind the person suffering from BDP to engage in coping skills and make any necessary calls. It may be advantageous to include a list of medications and professionals in the safety plan in case hospitalization is necessary.

If safety concerns arise, it is important to follow up with a mental health provider and consult with other professionals involved with the client (Pederson, 2015). For example, notifying a provider that a client has been hospitalized will bridge the gap of care so that the mental health provider can follow up as needed. In other situations, notifying a mental health provider that police were called to the home can help the provider more accurately assess the functioning level and safety of the client. This collateral information can be key to the mental health provider's ability to properly intervene. Notably, the provider may not be able to return the call, due to confidentiality laws, unless a release of information form has been completed and signed by the client or if the situation constitutes an emergency. Regardless, a person in the legal or criminal justice system can always leave information for the mental health provider to respond to, as appropriate.

REMOVING ACCESS TO MEANS OF SELF-HARM OR HARM TO OTHERS

One important step in safety planning is to remove the access to means of acting on urges to harm self or others (Suicide Prevention Resource Center, 2001; Stanley & Brown, 2012). For example, remove a gun from the premises if a person has thoughts of shooting himself or herself, or ask a family member to hold or administer a person's medications if they have thoughts of overdosing. Though a person may still find a way to act on thoughts of harm, removing the means creates an added barrier to engaging in such acts. This extra time can mean the difference between acting and pausing long enough for a clinician or caregiver to redirect the suicidal urge.

Law enforcement officers need to be familiar with their state's procedures for emergency holds. These are usually included in state statutes, giving licensed peace officers the ability to transport someone in crisis to an appropriate emergency room or crisis facility, even against the person's wishes. They may be commonly referred to as transport holds, emergency holds, or 72-hour holds (a designated maximum-hold period). It is frequently the responding officer's responsibility to decide where to take an escalated individual for further evaluation. Indicators that a hospital may be more appropriate for the individual than jail would include a current or previous mental health diagnosis, suicidal gestures, threats, visible indications of self-injurious behaviors (e.g., cuts or burns to forearms), and indications that the individual may be experiencing a break from reality (e.g., paranoia, delusions, auditory or visual hallucinations, or speaking in a nonsensical manner). An emergency responder collaborating with a county (mobile) crisis team will likely have access to a social worker, registered nurse, or other mental health professional who can assess the individual and make appropriate recommendations. For example, in the state of Minnesota, a Licensed Peace Officer, RN, or a licensed independent clinical social worker (LICSW) can place a transportation hold on an individual to ensure he or she is transported to a hospital for evaluation. The transportation hold ensures the individual gets to the hospital and is held temporarily until an assessment can be completed. If the hospital staff decide the individual needs to be admitted to the hospital for psychiatric reasons, they can then place a health-and-welfare hold on the individual, or an individual can admit themself.

RISK ASSESSMENT FOR RECIDIVISM

Recidivism, mental health, substance use, motivation, readiness for change, history of previous treatments, and length or conditions of sentencing need to be considered before assigning any placement or treatment within the corrections setting (Center for Substance Abuse Treatment, 2005). Appropriate substance abuse and mental health services can improve an individual's behavior both in the corrections setting and after release, to reduce recidivism (Fisher et al., 2014).

Criminal thinking, hostility, or anger problems may need to be challenged with pro-social values. Treatment in pretrial settings is necessarily brief and might be impacted by the client's beliefs about how it affects their due process rights or about coercion or stigma that might influence their case. They might have overriding concerns about loss of jobs or children, which keep them from engaging in treatment (Center for Substance Abuse Treatment, 2005).

Substance abuse treatment followed by community treatment upon release can be an effective way to reduce recidivism, as can relapse prevention incorporated into parole or probation. Dynamic risk factors such as continued substance abuse, homelessness, or other negative environmental factors can directly affect recidivism. A history of trauma or abuse might cause an offender under the forced sobriety of incarceration to experience negative emotional states, dysregulation, suicidal ideation or behavior for lack of their primary coping mechanism of substance abuse. The availability of services within the corrections setting can address this. Other factors to consider in predicting recidivism are treatment non-adherence, environmental stress, impulsivity, antisocial attitudes, and active mental health symptoms (Center for Substance Abuse Treatment, 2005).

In some jurisdictions, diversion into a mental health court program is an option. A recent study showed that these diversion programs were appropriate options so long as the offender had a stable residential location and had been diagnosed with a single disorder. Those with concurrent disorders or who lacked stable housing were less likely to complete the program (Verhaaff & Scott, 2015).

Assessment for the purpose of corrections placement for substance abuse treatment needs to consider how the substance abuse has impacted all facets of the individual's life. Professional screenings are more expensive but show improved placement decisions for treatment (Center for Substance Abuse Treatment, 2005). It is important to remember that motivation and willingness for treatment changes over time. Therefore, a systematic assessment for offenders should screen for mental health or other co-occurring disorders such as substance use with BPD, trauma, or self-harm. Screenings of this sort also help identify offenders who may be more vulnerable after release or on probation. Cardarelli et al. (2015), in studying the probationary population, found that 13% in a study of over 2000 individuals were at risk for suicide, and those with a mental health diagnosis had a 2-8 times higher likelihood of suicide. Recommendations from that study included offering more mental health services for offenders while incarcerated and more coordination between probationary agencies and the community mental health and substance abuse services, as well as specialty probation agents (Cardarelli et al., 2015; Angell, Matthews, Barrenger, Watson, & Draine, 2014; Wolff et al., 2013). Further consideration needs to be given to the issue of substance abuse as a contributing factor to the co-occurring disorder. Sobriety due to incarceration allows this distinction, and re-assessment is recommended after 4-6 weeks (Center for Substance Abuse Treatment, 2005). Assessments need to be normed for the particular group. No one treatment modality is effective for everyone, so the best approach will require a variety of options and levels of services appropriate for a wide variety of clients. While this might initially appear to be a more expensive choice, it increases treatment adherence and lowers overall costs by improving the quality of services and overall outcomes (Center for Substance Abuse Treatment, 2005; Wolff et al., 2013). This might also be one way to address scheduling and the ability to include treatment options as well as job duties or schooling in the prison setting. Combining options such as DBT into substance abuse treatment can also increase its effectiveness, especially with co-occurring disorders such as BPD and substance abuse, which further lowers recidivism risks (Center for Substance Abuse Treatment, 2005).

Some of the most reliable predictors of recidivism are age, not having custody of one's children, substance misuse or abuse, and frequent substance use (Scott, Grella, Dennis, & Funk, 2014). Scott and colleagues' study looked at a sample of women over a three-year period, post-release. The study highlighted the fact that women overall have more complex re-entry needs after incarceration than men typically do, related to these risk factors. Interestingly, the recidivism triggers seem to change over the initial months after release. Substance use issues may be the largest mitigating factor during the first year, while not having custody of one's children becomes the overriding factor after a year (Scott et al., 2014). Child custody status has also been shown to be a significant risk factor for recidivism. While having custody of a child or children appears to predict a lower risk of recidivism, having no custody appears to predict a higher risk of recidivism among women offenders (Scott et al., 2014). This data supports the importance of creating re-entry programs that allow mothers to return from correctional settings and regain custody privileges to reduce overall risk of recidivism.

Another research study found that 73% of individuals with a BPD diagnosis from an outpatient psychiatry clinic engaged in violence within a one-year time period during the study (Newhill et al., 2009). However, the shared variance with psychopathy and ASPD led to the conclusion that BPD alone does not predict future violence. As noted, people with BPD experience interpersonal problems, which have been shown to be a mediating factor that leads to victimization and/or aggressive behavior (Stepp, Smith, Morse, Hallquist, & Pilkonis, 2012).

Some data shows that lower financial status increases risk of recidivism; in fact, the lower the financial ability, the higher the risk of recidivism (Erickson, 2014). This is also a risk factor for suicide (Page et al., 2014; Soloff & Chiappetta, 2012). This data supports financial and vocational planning with offenders, even while in the correctional setting, both to reduce recidivism and to increase safety upon discharge. This is especially necessary with co-occurring disorders such as BPD with substance abuse.

CONCLUSION

Much of the treatment research discussed in this chapter emphasizes the need for early detection and early intervention for BPD. The research also emphasizes the need for BPD treatment separate from treatment for specific Co-morbid disorders such as substance disorders; an individual with BPD should have BPD-specific treatment as well as an adjunct service to address substance use or other Co-morbid diagnoses. Early detection of a mental illness would provide individuals with opportunities to understand their illness and make changes before they commit a crime.

There is minimal research related to treatment programs in correctional settings, because treatment and rehabilitation may not be the top priority in a prison. Future research should address the impact of prison treatment programs and their relationship with recidivism. Since BPD is no longer perceived as an "untreatable" mental illness, it would be reasonable to assume that treatment while incarcerated could decrease recidivism in individuals without an Antisocial Personality Disorder diagnosis.

REFERENCES

Ainsworth, M. S. (1973). The development of infant-mother attachment. In B. Cardwell & H. Ricciuti (Eds.), *Review of child development research* (Vol. 3, pp. 1-94) Chicago: University of Chicago Press.

Ainsworth, M. S. (1979). Infant-mother attachment. *American Psychologist, 34*, 932-937.

Alexander, M. (2012). *The New Jim Crow: Mass incarceration in the age of colorblindness.* New York: The New Press.

American Psychiatric Association. (2010). *Diagnostic and statistical manual of mental disorders* (4th Ed.). Washington, DC.

American Psychiatric Association. (2013). *Diagnostic and statistical manual of mental disorders* (5th Ed.). Washington, DC.

Angell, B., Matthews, E., Barrenger, S., Watson, A. C., Draine, J. (2014). Engagement processes in model programs for community reentry from prison for people with serious mental illness. *International Journal of Law and Psychiatry, 37*, 490-500. doi:10.1016/j.ijlp.2014.02.022

Australian Government, National Health and Medical Research Council. (2012). *Clinical practical guidelines for the management of Borderline Personality Disorder.* Retrieved from www.nhmrc.gov.au/guidelines- publications/mh25_borderline_personality_guideline.pdf

Aviram, R. B., Brodsky, B. S., & Stanley, B. (2006). Borderline personality disorder, stigma, and treatment implications. *Harvard Review of Psychiatry, 14*, 249-256. doi:10.1080/10673220600975121

Bartholomew, K., Kwong, M. J., & Hart, S. D. (2001). Attachment. In Livesley, & John W. (Eds.), *Handbook of personality disorders: Theory, research, and treatment* (pp. 196-230). New York, NY: Guilford Press.

Beck, J. S. (1995). *Cognitive Therapy: Basics and Beyond.* New York, NY: Guilford Press.

Benson, E. (2003). Rehabilitate or punish? *Monitor on Psychology, 34*(7), 46.

Black, D. W., Blum, N., McCormick, B., Allen, J. (2013). Systems Training for Emotional Predictability and Problem Solving (STEPPS) group treatment for offenders with borderline personality disorder. *Journal of Nervous and Mental Disease, 201*(2) 124-129.

Black, D. W., Gunter, T., Allen, J., Blum, N., Arndt, S., Wenman, G., & Sieleni, B. (2007). Borderline personality disorder in male and female offenders newly committed to prison. *Comprehensive Psychiatry, 48,* 400-405. doi:10.1016/j.comppsych.2007.04.006

Black, D. W., Zanarini, M. L., Romine, A., Shaw, M., Allen, J., & Schulz, S. C. (2014). Comparison of low and moderate dosages of extended-release Quetiapine in borderline personality disorder: A randomized, double-blind, placebo-controlled trial. *American Journal of Psychiatry, 171*,1174-1182.

Bliss, S., & McCardle, M. (2014). An exploration of common elements in dialectical behavior therapy, mentalization-based treatment and transference focused psychotherapy in the treatment of borderline personality disorder. *Clinical Social Work Journal, 42*, 61-69. doi:10.1007/s10615-013-0456-z

Bonnie, R. J. (2010). Should a personality disorder qualify as a mental disease in insanity adjudication? *Journal of Law, Medicine, & Ethics,* winter, 2010.

Bowlby, J. (1969), *Attachment and loss, Vol. 1: Attachment.* New York: Basic Books.

Brown, J., Blum, N., & Black, D. W. (2014). Systems training for emotional predictability and problem solving: An advanced understanding. *The Journal of Law Enforcement, 3*(4), 1-8.

Buehringer, G. (1995). Relapse and prevention in substance abuse. In C.N. Stefanis, H. Hippius, et al. (Eds.), *Research in addiction: An update. Psychiatry in progress series, Vol 2* (pp. 83-93). Goettingen, Germany: Hogrefe and Huber Publishers.

Burke, J. D., & Stepp, S. D. (2012). Adolescent disruptive behavior and Borderline Personality Disorder symptoms in young adult men. *Journal of Abnormal Childhood Psychology, 40*, 35-44. doi:10.1007/s10802-011-9558-7

Cackowski, S., Reitz, A. C., Ende, G., Kleindienst, N., Bohus, M., Schmahl, C., & Krause-Utz, A. (2014). Impact of stress on different components of impulsivity in borderline personality disorder. *Psychological Medicine, 44*, 3329-3340. doi:10.1017/S0033291714000427

Cardarelli, R., Balyakina, E., Malone, K., Fulda, K. G., Ellison, M, Sivernell, R., & Shabu, T. (2015). Suicide risk and mental health co-morbidities in a probationer population. *Community Mental Health Journal, 51*,145-152. doi:10.1007/s10597-014-9771-2

Carlson, E. A., Egeland, B., & Sroufe, L. A. (2009). A prospective investigation of the development of borderline personality symptoms. *Development and Psychopathology, 21*, 1311-1334. doi:10.1017/S0954579409990174

Center for Substance Abuse Treatment. (2005). Substance Abuse Treatment for Adults in the Criminal Justice System. Treatment Improvement Protocol (TIP) Series 44. HHS Publication No. (SMA) 13-4056. Rockville, MD: Substance Abuse and Mental Health Services Administration.

Chapman, A. L., & Gratz, K. L. (2007). *The Borderline Personality Disorder Survival Guide.* Oakland, CA: New Harbinger.

Children's Defense Fund. (2012). Children's health. Retrieved from http://www.childrensdefense.org/policy-priorities/childrens-health/

Children's Defense Fund. (2012). The state of American's children 2012 handbook. Retrieved from http://www.childrensdefense.org/child-research-data-publications/data/soac-2012-handbook.html

Chlebowski, S. M., & Gregory, R. J. (2012). Three cases of dissociative identity disorder and co-occurring borderline personality disorder treated with dynamic deconstructive psychotherapy. *American Journal of Psychotherapy, 66*, 165-180.

Deckers, J. W. M., Lobbestael, J., van Wingen, G. A., Kessels, R. P. C., Arntz, A., & Egger, J. I. M. (2015). The influence of stress on social cognition in patients with Borderline Personality Disorder. *Psychoneuroendocrinology, 52*, 119-129.

Donegan, N. H., Sanislow, C. A., Blumberg, H. P., Fulbright, R. K., Lacadie, C., Skudlarski, P., Gore, J. C., ... & Wexler, B. E. (2003). Amygdala hyperreactivity in borderline personality disorder: Implications for emotional dysregulation. *Biological Psychiatry, 54*, 1284-1293. doi: 10.1016/S0006-3223(03)00636-X

Duisin, D., Batinic, B., Barisic, J., Djordjevic, M. L., Vujovic, S., & Bizic, M. (2014). Personality disorders in persons with gender identity disorder. *The Scientific World Journal*, vol. 2014, Article ID 809058, 7 pages, 2014. doi: 10.1155/2014/809058

Ebner-Priemer, U. W., Houben, M., Santangelo, P., Kleindienst, N., Tuerlinckx, F., Oravecz, Z., Verleysen, G., ... & Kuppens, P. (2015). Unraveling affective dysregulation in borderline personality disorder: A theoretical model and empirical evidence. *Journal of Abnormal Psychology, 124*, 186-198. doi:10.1037/abn0000021

Eppright, T.D., Kashani, J. H., Robison, B.D., & Reid, J.C. (1993). Co-morbidity of conduct disorder and personality disorders in an incarcerated juvenile population. *American Journal of Psychiatry, 150*, 1233-1236.

Erickson, J. R. (2014). *Risk factors for criminal recidivism in female offenders.* (Unpublished master's thesis). Drexel University, Philadelphia, PA.

Faiver, C., Eisengart, S., & Colonna, R. (2004). The Counselor Intern's Handbook. Belmont, CA: Brooks/ Cole.

Fazel, S., Zetterqvist, J., Larsson, H., Langstrom, N., & Lichtenstein, P. (2014). Antipsychotics, mood stabilizers, and risk of violent crime. *Lancet, 384*, 1206-1214.

Feigenbaum, J. (2007). Dialectical behavior therapy: An increasing evidence base. *Journal of Mental Health, 16*, 51-68.

Feigenbaum, J. (2008). Dialectical behavior therapy. *Psychiatry, 7*(3), 112-116.

Fisher, W. H., Hartwell, S. W., Deng, X., Pinals, D. A., Fulwiler, C., & Roy-Bujnowski, K. (2014). Recidivism among released state prison inmates who received mental health treatment while incarcerated. *Crime & Delinquency, 60*, 811-832. doi:10.1177/0011128714541204

Fonagy, P., Target, M., & Gergely, G. (2000). Attachment and borderline personality disorder: A theory and some evidence. *The Psychiatric Clinics of North America, 23*, 103-122.

Fossati, A., Barratt, E. S., Carretta, I., Leonardi, B., Grazioli, F., & Maffei, C. (2004). Predicting borderline and antisocial personality disorder features in nonclinical subjects using measures of impulsivity and aggressiveness. *Psychiatry Research, 125*, 161-170. doi:10.1016/j.psychres.2003.12.001

Fosse, X., Monestes, J. L., & Bakhache, B. (2008). Disorganized attachment and genetics in the development of borderline personality disorder. *European Psychiatry, 3*, S94.

Galione, J., & Zimmerman, M. (2010). A comparison of depressed patients with and without borderline personality disorder: Implications for interpreting studies of the validity of the bipolar spectrum. *Journal of Personality Disorders, 24*, 763-772.

Gardner, K. J., Dodsworth, J., & Selby, E. A. (2015). Borderline personality traits, rumination, and self-injurious behavior: An empirical test of the emotional cascades model in adult male offenders. *Journal of Forensic Psychiatry Practice, 14*, 398-417.

Gaskin, C. J., Elsom, S. J., & Happell, B. (2007). Interventions for reducing the use of seclusion in psychiatric facilities: Review of the literature. *British Journal of Psychiatry, 191*, 298- 303. doi:10.1192/bjp. bp.106.034538

Gee, D. G., & Ogloff, J. R. P. (2015). Sentencing offenders with impaired mental functioning: R v Verdins, Buckley and Vo [2007] at the Clinical Coalface. *Psychiatry, Psychology, and Law, 21*(1), 46-66. doi :10.1080/13218719.2013.774682

Gianolo, M. O., Jane, J. S., O'Brien, E., & Ralevski, E. (2012). Treatment for Co-morbid borderline personality disorder and alcohol use disorders: A review of the evidence and future recommendations. *Experimental and Clinical Psychopharmacology, 20*(4), 333-344. doi:10.1037/a0027999

Goldman, G. A., & Gregory, R. J. (2009). Preliminary relationships between adherence and outcome in dynamic deconstructive psychotherapy. *Psychotherapy Theory, Research, Practice, Training, 46*(4), 480-485. doi:10.1037/a0017947

Goldman, G. A., & Gregory, R. J. (2010). Relationships between techniques and outcomes for Borderline Personality Disorder. *American Journal of Psychotherapy, 64*(4), 359-371.

Goncalves, L. C., Goncalves, R. A., Martins, C., & Dirkzwager, A. J. E. (2014). Predicting infractions and health care utilization in prison. *Criminal Justice and Behavior, 41*(8), 921-942. doi:10.1177/0093854814524402

Goodman, G., Hull, J. W., Clarkin, J. F., & Yeomans, F. E. (1999). Childhood antisocial behaviors as predictors of psychotic symptoms and DSM-III-R borderline criteria among inpatients with borderline personality disorder. *Journal of Personality Disorders, 3*, 35-46.

Goodman, M., New, A. S., Triebwasser, J., Collins, K. A., & Siever, L. (2010). Phenotype, endophenotype, and genotype comparisons between borderline personality disorder and major depressive disorder. *Journal of Personality Disorders, 24*, 38-59.

Grant, B. F., Chou, S. P., Goldstein, R. B., Huang, B., Stinson, F. S., Saha, T. D., Smith, S. M., Dawson, D. A., Pulay, A. J., Pickering, R. P., & Ruan, W. J. (2008). Prevalence, correlates, disability, and Co-morbidity of DSM-IV borderline personality disorder: Results from the Wave 2 National Epidemiological Survey on alcohol and related conditions. *Journal of Clinical Psychiatry, 69*(4), 533-545.

Grattagliano, I., Cassibba, R., Costantini, A., Laquale, G. M., Latrofa, A., Papagna, S., Sette, G., Taurino, A., & Terlizzi, M. (2015). Attachment models in incarcerated sex offenders: A preliminary Italian study using the adult attachment interview. *Journal of Forensic Sciences, 60*(Suppl 1), 2015, S138-S142.

Gregory, R. J. (2012). Managing suicide risk in borderline personality disorder: Distinguishing real risk from attention seeking. *Psychiatric Times, 29*(5), 25. Retrieved from go.galegroup.com.ezproxy.stthomas.edu/ps/i.do?id=GALE|A288628656&v=2.1&u=clic_stthomas&it=r&p=HRCA&sw=w&authCount=1#

Gregory, R. J. (2014). *Clinical, Training, and Research Manual of Dynamic Deconstructive Psychotherapy*, Department of Psychiatry and Behavioral Sciences, SUNY Upstate Medical University, Syracuse, New York. Retrieved from http://www.upstate.edu/psych/pdf/education/psychotherapy/ddp_manual.pdf

Gregory, R. J., & Remen, A. L. (2008). A manual-based psychodynamic therapy for treatment-resistant borderline personality disorder. *Psychotherapy Theory, Research, Practice, Training, 45*(1), 15-27. doi:10.1037/0033-3204.45.1.15

Harlow, H., & Zimmermann, R. R. (1959). Affectional responses in the infant monkey. *Science, 130*, 421-432. doi:10.1126/science.130.3373.421

Harty, C. M. (2012). The causes and effects of get tough: A look at how tough-on-crime policies rose to the agenda and an examination of their effects on prison populations and crime. *Graduate Thesis and Dissertations*. Retrieved from http://scholarcommons.usf.edu/etd/1066

Harvey, R., Black, D. W., & Blum, Nancee. (2010). Systems Training for emotional Predictability and Problem Solving (STEPPS) in the United Kingdom: A preliminary report. *Journal of Contemporary Psychotherapy, 40*, 225-232. doi:10.1007/s10879-010-9150-4

Hernandez, A., Arntz, A., Gaviria, A. M., Labad, A., & Gutierrez-Zotes, J. A. (2012). Relationships between childhood maltreatment, parenting style, and borderline personality disorder criteria. *Journal of Personality Disorders, 26*(5), 727-736.

Hesse, E., & Main, M. (2000). Disorganized infant, child, and adult attachment: Collapse in behavioral and attentional strategies. *Journal of the American Psychoanalytic Association, 48*, 1097-1127. doi:10.1177/00030651000480041101

Hoeve, M., Stams, G. J. J. M., van der Put, C. E., Dubas, J. S., van der Laan, P. H., & Gerris, J. R. M. (2012). A meta-analysis of attachment to parents and delinquency. *Journal of Abnormal Child Psychology, 40*, 771-785. doi:10.1007/s10802-011-9608-1

Hopwood, C. J., Swenson, C., Bateman, A., Yeomans, F. E., & Gunderson, J. G. (2014). Approaches to psychotherapy for borderline personality: Demonstrations by four master clinicians. *Personality Disorders: Theory, Research, and Treatment, 5*(1), 108-116. doi:10.1037/per0000055

Hopwood, C. J., & Zanarini, M. C. (2012). The contributions of neuroticism and childhood maltreatment to hyperbolic temperament. *Journal of Personality Disorders, 26*, 815-820.

Houser, K. A., & Welsh, W. (2014). Examining the association between co-occurring disorders and seriousness of misconduct by female prison inmates. *Criminal Justice and Behavior, 41*(5), 650-666. doi:10.1177/0093854814521195

Howard, R. C., Khalifa, N., & Duggan, C. (2014). Antisocial personality disorder Co-morbid with borderline pathology and psychopathy is associated with severe violence in a forensic sample. *The Journal of Forensic Psychiatry & Psychology, 25*(6), 658-672. doi:10.1080/14789949.2014.943797

Johnson, J. G., Cohen, P., Brown, J., Smalles, E. M., & Bernstein, D. P. (1999). Childhood maltreatment increases risk for personality disorders during early adulthood. *Archives of General Psychiatry, 56*, 600-606. doi:10.1001/archpsyc.56.7.600

Kaess, M., von Ceumern-Lindenstjerna, I., Parzer, P., Chanen, A., Mundt, C., Resch, F., & Brunner, R. (2013). Axis I and II Co-morbidity and psychosocial functioning in female adolescents with Borderline Personality Disorder. *Psychopathology, 46*, 55-62. doi:10.1159/000338715

Keinanen, M. T., Johnson, J. G., Richards, E. S., & Courtney, E. A. (2012). A systematic review of the evidence-based psychosocial risk factors for understanding of borderline personality disorder. *Psychoanalytic Psychotherapy, 26*, 65-91. doi:10.1080/02668734.2011.652659

Kienast, T., Stoffers, J., Bermpohl, F., & Lieb, K. (2014). Borderline personality disorder and Co-morbid addiction: Epidemiology and treatment. *Deutsches Arzteblatt International, 111*(16), 280-286.

Kifer, M., Hemmens, C., & Stohr, M. K. (2003). The goals of corrections: Perspectives from the line. *Criminal Justice Review, 28*(1), 47-69.

Kinscherff, R. (2010). Proposition: A personality disorder may nullify responsibility for a criminal act. *Conundrums and Controversies in Mental Health and Illness,* winter 2010, 745-759.

Kirtley, O. J., O'Carroll, R. E., O'Connor, R. C. (2015). The role of endogenous opioids in non-suicidal self-injurious behavior: Methodological challenges. *Neuroscience and Behavioral Reviews, 48*,186-189.

Kleinman, E. M., & Liu, R. T. (2013). Social support as a protective factor in suicide: Findings from two nationally representative samples. *Journal of Affective Disorders, 150*, 540-545.

Kreisman, J., & Strauss, H. (2010). *I hate you don't leave me.* New York: Penguin Group.

Kvarstein, E. H., Pedersen, G., Urnes, O., Hummelen, B., Wilberg, T., & Karterud, S. (2015). Changing from a traditional psychodynamic treatment programme to mentalization-based treatment for patients with borderline personality disorder—Does it make a difference? *Psychology and Psychotherapy: Theory, Research and Practice, 88*, 71-86. doi:10.1111/papt.12036

Laurenssen, E. M. P., Hutsebaut, J., Feenstra, D. J., Bales, D. L., Noom, M. J., Busschbach, J. J. V., Verheul, R., & Luyten, P. (2014). Feasibility of mentalization-based treatment for adolescents with borderline symptoms: A pilot study. *Psychotherapy, 51*(1), 150-166. doi:10.1037/a0033513

Leichsenring, F., Kunst, H., & Hoyer, J. (2003). Borderline personality organization in violent offenders: Correlations of identity diffusion and primitive defense mechanisms with antisocial features, neuroticism, and interpersonal problems. *Bulletin of the Menninger Clinic, 67*(4), 314-327.

Leppanen, V., Karki, A., Saariaho, T., Lindeman, S., & Hakko, H. (2015). Changes in schemas of patients with severe borderline personality disorder: The Oulu BPD study. *Scandinavian Journal of Psychology, 56*, 78-85. doi:10.1111/sjop.12172

Lieb, K., Zanarini, M. C., Schmahl, C., Linehan, M. M., & Bohus, M. (2004). Borderline personality disorder. *Lancet, 364*, 453-461.

Liebman, R. E., & Burnette, M. (2013). It's not you, it's me: An examination of clinician- and client-level influences on countertransference toward borderline personality disorder. *American Journal of Orthopsychiatry, 83*(1), 115-125.

Lindberg, M. A., Fugett, A., & Lounder, L. (2014). The Attachment and Clinical Issues Questionnaire: A new methodology for science and practice in criminology and forensics. International Journal of Offender Therapy and Comparative Criminology, *58*(10), 1166-1185. doi: 10.1177/0306624X13492397

Linehan, M. M. (1993a). *Cognitive-Behavioral Treatment of Borderline Personality Disorder*. New York: Guilford.

Linehan, M. M. (1993b). *Skills Training Manual for Treating Borderline Personality Disorder*. New York: Guilford.

Linehan, M. M. (2015). *DBT Skills Training Manual* (2nd Edition). New York: Guilford.

Links, P. S., Kolla, N. J., Guimond, T., & McMain, S. (2013). Prospective risk factors for suicide attempts in a treated sample of patients with borderline personality disorder. *Canadian Journal of Psychiatry, 58*, 99-106.

Lipsey, M. W., & Cullen, F. T. (2007). The effectiveness of correctional rehabilitation: A review of systematic reviews. *The Annual Review of Law and Social Science 3*, 297-320. doi:10.1146/annurev.lawsosci.3.081806.112833

Loewenstein, K., & McManus, M. (2014). "Don't tell me to calm down!" De-escalation of the agitated patient in a hospital setting. In K. Gallo & L. G. Smith (Eds.) *Building a Culture of Patient Safety Through Simulation: An Interprofessional Learning Model* (pp. 171-186). New York, NY: Springer Publishing.

Ludolph, P. S. (2010). Answered and unanswered questions in attachment theory with implications for children of divorce. *Journal of Child Custody, 6,* 8-24. doi:10.1080/15379410902894817

Madeddu, F., Aquaro, P., Preti, E. (2012). Psychotherapy for borderline personality disorder: A review of literature on the efficacy of four manualized treatments. *Journal of Psychopathology, 18*(3).

McCormick, B., Blum, N., Hansel, R., Franklin, J. A., St. John, D., Pfohl, B., Allen, J., & Black, D. W. (2007). Relationship of sex to symptom severity, psychiatric Co-morbidity, and health care utilization in 163 subjects with borderline personality disorder. *Comprehensive Psychiatry, 48*, 406-412. doi:10.1016/j.comppsych.2007.05.005

Millar, H., Gillanders, D., & Saleem, J. (2012). Trying to make sense of the chaos: Clinical psychologists' experiences and perceptions of clients with 'borderline personality disorder'. *Personality and Mental Health, 6,* 111-125. doi:10.1002/pmh.1178

Morken, K., Karterud, S., & Arefjord, N. (2014). Transforming disorganized attachment through mentalization-based treatment. *Journal of Contemporary Psychotherapy, 44,* 117-126. doi:10.1007/s10879-013-9246-8

National Alliance on Mental Illness Minnesota. (2006). Understanding the Minnesota civil commitment process. Author. Retrieved from www.namihelps.org/assets/PDFs/civilcommitmentSinglePg102108.pdf

Nee, C., & Farman, S. (2005). Female prisoners with borderline personality disorder: Some promising treatment developments. *Criminal Behaviour and Mental Health, 15,* 2-16.

Nee, C., & Farman, S. (2007). Dialectical behavior therapy as a treatment for borderline personality disorder in prisons: Three illustrative case studies. *The Journal of Forensic Psychiatry & Psychology, 18,* 160-180. doi: 10.1080/14789940601104792

Newhill, C. E., Eack, S. M., & Mulvey, E. P. (2009). Violent behavior in borderline personality. *Journal of Personality Disorders, 23,* 541-554.

Newman, B.M., & Newman, P.R. (2015). Development Through Life: A Psychosocial Approach (12th Ed.). Stamford, CT: Cengage Learning.

Oldham, J. M. (2006). Borderline personality disorder: An overview. *Psychiatric Times, 11*(8). Retrieved from www.psychiatrictimes.com/articles/borderline-personality-disorder-overview-0

Oldham, J. M., Gabbard, G. O., Goin, M. K., Gunderson, J., Soloff, P., Spiegel, D. Stone, M., & Phillips, K. A. (2010). Practice guideline for the treatment of patients with Borderline Personality Disorder. American Psychiatric Association.

Page, A., Morrell, S., Hobbs, C., Carter, G., Dudley, M., Duflou, J., & Taylor, R. (2014). Suicide in young adults: Psychiatric and socio-economic factors from a case-control study. *BMC Psychiatry, 14*, 68.

Paris, J. P. (2002). Implications of long-term outcome research for the management of patients with borderline personality disorder. *President and Fellows of Harvard College*, 315-323.

Paris, J. P. (2005). Understanding self-mutilation in borderline personality disorder. *Harvard Review of Psychiatry, 13*, 179-185. doi:10.1080/10673220591003614

Paris, J., Zweig-Frank, H., & Guzder, J. (1994). Psychological risk factors for borderline personality disorder in female patients. *Comprehensive Psychiatry, 35*, 301-305.

Pederson, L. (2015). Dialectical Behavior Therapy: A Contemporary Guide for Practitioners. West Sussex, UK: John Wiley & Sons, Ltd.

Perepletchikova, F., Ansell, E., & Axelrod, S. (2012). Borderline Personality Disorder features and history of childhood maltreatment in mothers involved with child protective services. *Child Maltreatment, 17*, 182-190. doi:10.1177/1077559512448471

Quigley, B. D. (2003). *Diagnostic relapse in borderline personality disorder: Risk and protective factors* (Doctoral dissertation, Texas A&M University). Retrieved from http://repository.tamu.edu/bitstream/handle/1969.1/1237/etd-tamu-2003B-2003061217-Quig-1.pdf?sequence=1&isAllowed=y

Rawal, P., Romansky, J., Jenuwine, M., & Lyons, J. S. (2004). Racial differences in the mental health needs of youth in the juvenile justice system. *The Journal of Behavioral Health Services and Research, 31*(3), 242-254.

Richmond, J. S., Berlin, J. S., Fishkind, A. B., Holloman, G. H. Jr., Zeller, S. L., Wilson, M. P., Rifai, M. A., & Ng, A. T. (2012). Verbal de-escalation of the agitated patient: Consensus statement of the American Association for Emergency Psychiatry Project Beta de-escalation workgroup. *Western Journal of Emergency Medicine, 13*(1), 17-25. doi:10.5811/westjem.2011.9.6864

Rinne, T., de Kloet, E. R., Wouters, L., Goekoop, J. G., DeRijk, R. H., & van den Brink, W. (2002). Hyperresponsiveness of hypothalamic-pituitary-adrenal axis to combined dexamethasone/corticotrophin-releasing hormone challenge in female borderline personality disorder subjects with a history of sustained childhood abuse. *Society of Biological Psychiatry, 52*, 1102-1112.

Robertson, C. D., Kimbrel, N. A., & Nelson-Gray, R. O. (2013). The invalidating childhood environment scale (ICES): Psychometric properties and relationship to borderline personality symptomatology. *Journal of Personality Disorders, 27*, 402-410.

Rochefort, S. M. (2014). *The role of attachment security and invalidation in borderline symptomology (Unpublished master's thesis)*. Simon Frazer University, Burnaby, British Columbia, Canada.

Ryder, A.G., Sunohara, M., & Kirmayer, L.J. (2015). Culture and personality disorder: From a fragmented literature to a contextually grounded alternative. *Current Opinion in Psychiatry, 28*(1), 40-45.

Salter Ainsworth, M. D., & Bell, S. M. (1970). Attachment, exploration, and separation: Illustrated by the behavior of one-year-olds in a strange situation. *Child Development, 41*(1), 49-67.

SAMHSA National GAINS Center. (2011, January). *Motivational interviewing*.

Sampl, S., Wakai, S., & Trestman, R. L. (2010). Translating evidence-based practices from community to corrections: An example of implementing DBT-CM. *JOBA-OVTP, 2*(2), 114-123.

Sansone, R. A., Lam, C., & Wiederman, M. W. (2012). The relationship between illegal behaviors and borderline personality symptoms among internal medicine outpatients. *Comprehensive Psychiatry, 53*, 176-180. doi:10.1016/j.comppsych.2011.03.006

Sansone, R. A., & Sansone, L. A. (2012). Borderline personality disorder and externalized aggression. *Innovations in Clinical Neuroscience, 9*, 23-26.

Sapolsky, R. M. (2004). *Why zebras don't get ulcers.* New York: Holt Paperbacks.

Sauer, S. E., & Baer, R. A. (2010). Validation of measures of biosocial precursors to borderline personality disorder: Childhood emotional vulnerability and environmental invalidation. *Assessment, 17*, 454-466. doi:10.1177/1073191110373226

Schroeder, R. D., Higgins, G. E., & Mowen, T. J. (2012). Maternal attachment trajectories and criminal offending by race. *American Journal of Criminal Justice, 39,*155-171. doi:10.1007/s12103-012-9192-0

Scott, C. K., Grella, C. E., Dennis, M. L., & Funk, R. R. (2014). Predictors of recidivism over 3 years among substance-using women released from jail. *Criminal Justice and Behavior, 41*(11), 1257-1289. doi:10.1177/0093854814546894

Sharp, C., & Romero, C. (2007). Borderline personality disorder: A comparison between children and adults. *Bulletin of the Menninger Clinic, 71*, 85-114.

Shelton, D., Sampl, S., Kesten, K. L., Zhang, W., & Trestman, R. L. (2009). Treatment of impulsive aggression in correctional settings. *Behavioral Sciences and the Law, 27*, 787-800. doi:10.1002/bsl.889

Sijtsema, J. J., Baan, L., & Bogaerts, S. (2014). Association between dysfunctional personality traits and intimate partner violence in perpetrators and victims. *Journal of Interpersonal Violence, 29*, 2418-2438. doi:10.1177/0886260513520228

Simon, R. I. (2014). Passive suicidal ideation: Still a high risk clinical scenario. *Current Psychiatry, 13*, 13-15. Retrieved from www.currentpsychiatry.com/the-publication/issue-single-view/passive-suicidal-ideation-still-a-high-risk-clinical-scenario/651a76321f5ec282d271b194343a9bfd.html

Sisti, D. A., & Caplan, A. L. (2012) Accommodation without exculpation? The ethical and legal paradoxes of borderline personality disorder. *Journal of Psychiatry and Law, 40*, 75-92.

Skodol, A. E., Siever, L. J., Livesley, W. J., Gunderson, J. G., Pfohl, B., & Widiger, T. A. (2002). The borderline diagnosis II: Biology, genetics, and clinical course. *Society of Biological Psychiatry, 51*, 951-963.

Slovenko, R. (2012). Criminal law standards in civil commitment. *Journal of Psychiatry & Law,* summer, 135-166.

Soler, J., Pascual, J. C., Tiana, T., Cebria, A., Barrachina, J., Campins, M. J., Gich, I., Alvarez, E., & Perez, V. (2009). Dialectical behavior therapy skills training compared to standard group therapy in borderline personality disorder: A 3-month randomized controlled clinical trial. *Behaviour Research and Therapy, 47*, 353-358. doi: 10.1016/j.brat.2009.01.013

Soloff, P. H., & Chiappetta, L. (2012). Prospective predictors of suicidal behavior in borderline personality disorder at 6-year follow-up. *American Journal of Psychiatry, 169*, 484-490.

Speranza, M., Revah-Levy, A., Cortese, S., Falissard, B., Pham-Scottez, A., & Corcos, M. (2011). ADHD in adolescents with borderline personality disorder. *BMC Psychiatry, 11*, 158.

Stanley, B., & Brown, G. K. (2012). Safety Planning Intervention: A brief intervention to mitigate suicide risk. *Cognitive and Behavioral Practice, 19,* 256-264.

Stepp, S. D., Smith, T. D., Morse, J. Q., Hallquist, M. N., & Pilkonis, P. A. (2012). Prospective associations among borderline personality disorder symptoms, interpersonal problems, and aggressive behaviors. *Journal of Interpersonal Violence, 27*(1),103-24. doi: 10.1177/0886260511416468

Stobie, M. R., & Tromski-Klingshirn, D. M. (2009). Borderline Personality Disorder, divorce and family therapy: The need for family crisis intervention strategies. *The American Journal of Family Therapy, 37,* 414-432. doi:10.1080/01926180902754760

Stredny, R. V., Parker, A. L., & Dibble, A. E. (2012). Evaluator agreement in placement recommendations for insanity acquittees. *Behavioral Sciences and the Law, 30*, 297-307. doi:10.1002/bsl.1995

Stroud, J., & Parsons, R. (2013). Working with borderline personality disorder: A small-scale qualitative investigation into community psychiatric nurses' constructs of borderline personality disorder. *Personality and Mental Health, 7*, 242-253. doi:10.1002/pmh.1214

Sturrock, B., & Mellor, D. (2014). Perceived emotional invalidation and borderline personality disorder features: A test of theory. *Personality and Mental Health, 8,* 128-142. doi:10.1002/pmh.1249

Substance Abuse and Mental Health Services Administration. (2014, Fall). An introduction to co-occurring borderline personality disorder and substance use disorders. *In Brief, 8*(3).

Sue, D. W., & Sue, D. (2013). *Counseling the culturally diverse: Theory and practice* (5th Ed.). New York: John Wiley & Sons.

Suicide Prevention Resource Center. (2001). Risk and protective factors for suicide. *National Strategy for Suicide Prevention: Goals and Objectives for Action.* Retrieved from http://www.sprc.org/sites/sprc.org/files/library/srisk.pdf

Timmerman, I. G. H., & Emmelkamp, P. M. G. (2006). The relationship between attachment styles and cluster B personality disorders in prisoners and forensic inpatients. *International Journal of Law and Psychiatry, 29,* 48-56. doi:10.1016/j.ijlp.2005.04.005

van den Bosch, L.M.C., Hysaj, M., & Jacobs, P. (2012). DBT in an outpatient forensic setting. *International Journal of Law and Psychiatry, 35,* 311-316. doi:10.1016/j.ijlp.2012.04.009

van Dijke, A., Ford, J. D., van Son, M., Frank, L., & van der Hart, O. (2013). Association of childhood-trauma-by-primary caregiver and affect dysregulation with Borderline Personality Disorder symptoms in adulthood. *Psychological Trauma: Theory, Research, Practice, and Policy, 5*(3), 217-234. doi:10.1037/a0027256

Verhaaff, A., & Scott, H. (2015). Individual factors predicting mental health court diversion outcome. *Research on Social Work Practice, 25,* 213-228. doi:10.1177/1049731514523507

Wakai, S., Sampl, S., Hilton, L., & Ligon, B. (2014). Women in prison: Self-injurious behavior, risk factors, psychological function, and gender-specific interventions. *The Prison Journal, 94,* 347-364. doi:10.1177/0032885514537602

Walsh, D. (2012). Why do they act that way: A survival guide to the adolescent brain for you and your teenager. New York: Free Press.

Weinstein, Y., Gleason, M. E. J., & Oltmanns, T. F. (2012). Borderline but not antisocial personality disorder symptoms are related to self-reported partner aggression in late middle-age. *Journal of Abnormal Psychology, 121,* 692-698. doi: 10.1037/a0028994

Windsor, L. C., Jemal, A., & Benoit, E. (2014). Community Wise: Paving the way for empowerment in community reentry. *International Journal of Law and Psychiatry, 37,* 501-511. doi: 10.1016/j.ijlp.2014.02.023

Wolff, N., Frueh, B. C., Huening, J., Shi, J., Epperson, M. W., Morgan, R., & Fisher, W. (2013). Practice informs the next generation of behavioral health and criminal justice interventions. *International Journal of Law and Psychiatry, 36,* 1-10. doi: 10.1016/j.ijlp.2012.11.001

Wolke, D., Schreier, A., Zanarini, M. C., & Winsper, C. (2012). Bullied by peers in childhood and borderline personality symptoms at 11 years of age: A prospective study. *Journal of Child Psychiatry and Psychology, 53,* 846-855. doi:10.1111/j.1469-7610.2012.02542.x

Wright, A. G. C., Hallquist, M. N., Beeney, J. E., & Pilkonis, P. A. (2013). Borderline personality pathology and the stability of interpersonal problems. *Journal of Abnormal Psychology, 122,* 1094-1100. doi:10.1037/a0034658

Wupperman, P., Fickling, M., Klemanski, D. H., Berking, M., & Whitman, J. B. (2013). Borderline personality features and harmful dysregulated behavior: The meditational effect of mindfulness. *Journal of Clinical Psychology, 69,* 903-911. doi:10.1002/jclp.21969

Yeomans, F. E., Levy, K. N., & Caligor, E. (2013). Transference-focused psychotherapy. *Psychotherapy, 50,* 449-453. doi:10.1037/a0033417

Yeomans, F. E., Levy, K. N., & Meehan, K. B. (2012, April). Treatment approaches for borderline personality disorder. *Psychiatric Times,* 42-44.

Zanarini, M. C. (2009). Psychotherapy of borderline personality disorder. Acta Psychiatrica Scandinavica, *120*, 373-377. doi:10.1111/j.1600-0447.2009.01448.x

Zanarini, M. C., Frankenberg, F. R., Dubo, E. D., Sickel, A. E., Trikha, A., Levin, A., & Reynolds, V. (1998). Axis I Co-morbidity of borderline personality disorder. *American Journal of Psychiatry, 155,* 1733-1739.

Zanarini, M. C., Frankenburg, F. R., Hennen, J., Reich, D. B., & Silk, K. R. (2003). The longitudinal course of borderline personality psychopathology: 6-year prospective follow-up of the phenomenology of borderline personality disorder. *American Journal of Psychiatry, 160*, 274-283.

Zanarini, M. C., Frankenburg, F. R., Hennen, J., Reich, D. B., & Silk, K. R. (2004). Axis I Co-morbidity in patients with borderline personality disorder: 6-year follow-up and prediction of time to remission. *American Journal of Psychiatry, 161*(11), 2108-2114.

Zeichner, S. (2013). Borderline personality disorder: Implications in family and pediatric practice. *Journal of Psychology and Psychotherapy, 3*, 122. doi:10.4172/2161=0487.1000122

CHAPTER 3

COMPETENCY TO STAND TRIAL (CST): A BEGINNER'S GUIDE

AMANDA BELTRANI, MARISSA ZAPPALA, LAURA COONEY-KOSS,
ANN MARIE WINSKOWSKI & JERROD BROWN

CHAPTER OVERVIEW

A core principal of modern-day law is that all defendants maintain the right to a fair trial (Davidson, Kovacevic, Cave, Hart, & Dark, 2015; Murrie & Zelle, 2015). Competency to stand trial (CST) is a doctrine of jurisprudence which allows criminal proceedings to be postponed should a defendant be unable to efficiently participate in his or her defense on account of mental disease or defect (Roesch, Zapf, Golding, & Skeem, 2004; United States v. Duhon, 2000; Zapf & Roesch, 2009). CST concerns a defendant's present mental capacity to comprehend the trial proceedings, as well as the ability to participate and assist counsel in formulating a defense (Chauhan, Warren, Kois, & Wellbeloved-Stone, 2015; Denney & Tyner, 2010; Everington, DeBerge, & Mauer, 2000; Grisso & Appelbaum, 1998; Mossman, 2007; Stafford & Sellbom, 2013). An individual's competency impacts everything from pre-arrest interactions with investigating officers to formal legal proceedings through sentencing (Murrie & Zelle, 2015). It is important for forensic mental health evaluators to clearly understand the reason for referral, concerns about competency, and demands of the case (Davidson, Kovacevic, Cave, Hart, & Dark, 2015). The formal decision regarding a defendant's competency is a legal issue rather than a clinical decision: the judge, in light of the mental health expert's evaluation, renders the ultimate decision (Otto, 2006). Nonetheless, a judge's competency ruling closely follows the recommendations made by mental health professionals a majority of the time (Cooper & Zapf, 2003; Hubbard, Zapf, & Ronan, 2003; Melton et al., 2007; Mossman, 2007; Zapf, Hubbard, Cooper, Wheeles, & Ronan, 2004).

BELOW WE PRESENT VARIOUS FACTS ABOUT THE COMPLEX TOPIC OF CST THAT ALL PROFESSIONALS SHOULD KNOW:

ORIGINS OF CST

The origins of competency to stand trial (CST) can be traced to Babylonian Talmud and early Judeo-Christian texts (Nussbaum, Hancock, Turner, Arrowood & Melodick, 2007), along with English common law that emerged prior to the 14th century (Otto, 2006). Impeding on trial proceedings, defendants frequently remained mute in lieu of making a plea, thus requiring English courts to determine whether this muteness was a function of "malice" or "visitation of God" (e.g., deaf, mute or suffering psychiatric illnes) (Melton et al., 2007). This began the judicial system's distinction between crimes committed by those suffering from mental illness and crimes committed with malicious intent. In light of this distinction it was determined that those defendants who suffer from mental illness are neither able to stand trial, nor are they deserving of the same punishment as those who committed a crime with malicious intent.

Dusky v. United States (1960)

The United States Supreme Court's ruling in Dusky v. United States (1960) serves as the standard for determining competency. The court in Dusky held that a defendant must have "sufficient present ability to consult with his lawyer with a reasonable degree of rational understanding" and a "rational as well as factual understanding of the proceedings against him" (p. 402). However, the ruling in Dusky left several ambiguities within the definition of competency, such as what is "sufficient present ability"? And how is it determined if a defendant "has a rational as well as factual understanding of the proceedings against him"?

Godinez v. Moran (1993)

The U.S. Supreme Court case of Godinez v. Moran (1993) called into question whether, after being found competent to stand trial, a defendant could still have other legal incompetencies. The Court ruled that the standard for trial competence would be the same standard as competence to waive counsel, act as one's own lawyer, plead guilty, etc. Essentially, this determination says that if an individual is competent in one area, he/she is automatically said to be competent in all other realms related to the legal proceedings. However, states still maintain the right to set higher standards for a defendant to engage in self-representation.

Fairness of the Legal System

For legal proceedings to remain fair, defendants need to demonstrate sufficient competence to actively participate in their own defense and comprehend ongoing legal proceedings (Murrie & Zelle, 2015). A basic level of competence is needed for a defendant to have a fair trial. Because competence is so valued, attorneys from either side or the court itself may raise the issue of CST at any point before a verdict is rendered during trial. Only a bona fide doubt concerning a defendant's current mental status is required to raise the issue of competency (Drope v. Missouri, 1975; Pate v. Robinson, 1966). By keeping this low legal threshold, the court is better able to maintain a commitment to due process.

Frequency

The bona fide doubt standard, which was established in Drope v. Missouri (1975), makes a CST evaluation fairly easy to request. This helps to explain the high frequency in which these evaluations are conducted (approximately 60,000 per year) (Bonnie & Grisso, 2000; Morris & DeYoung, 2012; Pirelli, Gottdiener, & Zapf, 2011; Poythress, Bonnie, Monahan, Otto, & Hoge, 2002). In fact, evaluating fitness to stand trial is the most common assessment completed by forensic mental health professionals (Bonnie & Grisso, 2000; Poythress, Bonnie, Monahan, Otto, & Hoge, 2002). About 5% of defendants charged with a felony receive competency evaluations each year in the Unites States (Bonnie & Grisso, 2000; Morris & DeYoung, 2012; Pirelli, Gottdiener, & Zapf, 2011; Poythress, Bonnie, Monahan, Otto, & Hoge, 2002). Even though either side or the court may raise the issue of competency, defense attorneys request the vast majority of competency evaluations (Chauhan et al., 2015).

COSTS

Over the years, competency evaluations have shifted from institution-based evaluation to community-based evaluations, thus significantly lowering the financial burden the evaluation of competency has on the United States (Zapf, Roesch, & Pirelli, 2014). Only 20%-30% of the approximately 60,000 competency evaluations that occur each year find that the defendant is incompetent (Pirelli et al., 2011; Otto & Weiner, 2013). The majority of financial resources that jurisdictions devote to forensic mental health services are consumed by evaluating, adjudicating, and restoring competence (Murrie & Zelle, 2015).

CST AND CULPABILITY

CST evaluations do not determine culpability, but instead identify whether a defendant can sufficiently participate in legal proceedings (Chauhan et al., 2015). A competency evaluation relies heavily on a defendant's present ability, and should be considered separate from the defendant's mental functioning at the time the crime was committed (an issue referred to as criminal responsibility) (Chauhan et al., 2015; Dusky v. United States, 1960). While CST falls under a larger umbrella of adjudicative competencies (i.e., competency to waive Miranda, competency to plead guilty, competency to be sentenced), it is important to understand that CST is distinct in that it requires specific evaluation of the defendant's current psycholegal capabilities as they pertain to his/her charges and legal proceedings (Piel, Finkle, Giske, & Leong, 2015).

DEFINING COMPETENCY

The assessment of competency is unique, because it requires consideration of both mental status as well as psycholegal abilities (Murrie & Zelle, 2015). A psychiatric diagnosis does not automatically equate to incompetence (Murrie & Zelle, 2015). To render an individual incompetent, the presence of a mental disease or defect must significantly impair a defendant's rational and factual understanding of the trial proceedings (Murrie & Zelle, 2015; Dusky v. United States, 1960). Defendants who possess a mental disease or defect may be found competent if their impairment does not hinder their ability to rationally or factually understand the legal proceedings against them or to consult with and assist defense counsel. CST evaluations assess basic cognitive processes in relation to the defendant's present psycholegal abilities such as understanding relevant legal information, appreciating the workings of the adjudicative system and the potential consequences they face, the ability to use logical thinking and reasoning, being motivated to assist counsel, and the ability to effectively formulate and communicate decisions (Murrie & Zelle, 2015). Competence may vary across different legal contexts, and it maintains various operational definitions; therefore, it can never be adequately captured by one fixed set of facts (Grisso, 2003). Assessments of CST concentrate on several clinical and legal issues, including mental and physical health, comprehension of legal proceedings, and capacity to communicate with legal counsel (Chauhan et al., 2015).

INCOMPETENT DEFENDANTS

Those individuals found to be incompetent to stand trial as adults are more likely to be older, non-white, male, unemployed, unmarried and have had previous contact with the criminal justice system, compared to their competent counterparts (Pirelli et al., 2011). Those who are deemed incompetent often have a history of previous psychiatric hospitalizations and current diagnoses on the psychotic spectrum (Pirelli et al., 2011). Other research has reported that a high number of defendants found incompetent to stand trial also have a co-occurring substance or alcohol use disorder (Weinborn, Orr, Woods, Conover, & Feix, 2003).

MENTAL ILLNESS

The legal issue of competency has no single, easily identifiable psychological correlate (Golding, 2008; Grisso, 2003; Ho & Henderson, 1998; Meehl, 1970; Nicholson & Johnson, 1991; Nicholson & Kugler, 1991). It has been argued that a defendant's fitness should be considered contextually, meaning that the abilities required by the defendant in his or her specific case should be taken into account when assessing competence (Zapf et al., 2014). Although most individuals suffering from a mental illness are deemed competent to stand trial, given the overwhelming prevalence of serious mental illness in the criminal justice system (approximately 74% of inmates), it is inevitable that there will be defendants who are unable to comprehend and participate in different stages of their trial, jeopardizing a number of the defendant's fundamental rights (Murrie & Zelle, 2015). This emphasizes the substantial need for mental health professionals to provide competency evaluations and restorative treatment.

PSYCHOTIC DISORDERS

Historically, incompetency was equated with psychosis; however, research has since provided evidence that the presence of psychosis itself is not sufficient for a defendant to be adjudicated incompetent (Zapf et al., 2014). To be found incompetent, the psychotic symptoms must directly impact the defendant's ability to understand their legal situation and participate in their own defense. A defendant with a psychotic disorder may present with hallucinations, delusions, grossly disorganized behavior and/or the inability to differentiate between reality and what is not real (Murrie & Zelle, 2015). Most defendants who are found incompetent have a diagnosed psychotic disorder (e.g., schizophrenia). While defendants with psychotic disorders are eight times more likely to be found incompetent to stand trial, compared to defendants without psychotic disorders, the majority of defendants who carried a psychotic disorder diagnosis were still found competent (Pirelli et al., 2011). Pirelli et al. (2011) identified that, of those referred for a CST evaluation and found to be competent to stand trial, 22.2% were diagnosed with a psychotic disorder. It was also found that the majority of defendant's who carried a psychotic disorder diagnosis were still found competent (Pirelli et al., 2011).

COGNITIVE FUNCTIONING

A competency evaluation may not require a cognitive assessment, depending on the individual's history. However, an examination of their history may reveal cognitive issues that have a profound impact on CST and restoration (Kirkish & Sreenivasan, 1999; Marcopulos, Morgan, & Denney, 2008; Martell, 1992; Simpler & Parmenter, 2011). Along with psychosis, cognitive impairments have been identified as a common symptom present in incompetent defendants (Mossman, 2007). "Cognitive impairment" is a term that encompasses several cognitive deficits. In a study of competency evaluation reports by mental health professionals, White and colleagues (2012) reported an association between a defendant's ability to participate in legal proceedings and several cognitive functions (e.g., memory, attention, and processing speed abilities). Additionally, several researchers have found that low intelligence test scores increase the likelihood of a defendant being rendered Incompetent to Stand Trial (IST) (Everington & Dunn, 1995; Hoge, Bonnie, Poythress, Monahan, & Eisenberg, 1997; Nicholson & Kugler, 1991; Otto et al., 1998; Rogers, Ustad, Sewell, & Reinhardt, 1996). This may be due to the fact that intellectual or developmental disabilities and neurological disorders can cause cognitive impairments, which in turn may negatively impact an individual's ability to understand and participate meaningfully in trial proceedings, make rational decisions or understand basic legal distinctions (White, Meares, & Batchelor, 2014). Examples of these diagnoses include: Attention-Deficit/Hyperactivity Disorder (ADHD), Fetal Alcohol Spectrum Disorder (FASD), Autism Spectrum Disorder (ASD), and frontal lobe impairments that are congenital or acquired through head injury or substance use. Evaluators and legal decision-makers must carefully assess an individual's cognitive functioning to identify if the defendant maintains deficits that may contribute to the inability to meet the standards for adjudicative competency (Piel et al., 2015). Although not designed to assess CST, several instruments that have been developed to measure specific cognitive constructs (e.g., Minnesota Multiphasic Personality Inventory-2, Personality Assessment Inventory, Brown ADD scales, or neuropsychological tests) are commonly used in competency evaluations (Hathaway & McKinley, 1989; Brown, 1996; Pirelli et al., 2011).

INTELLECTUAL DISABILITY

Defendants with intellectual disabilities may lack the necessary components to meet the Dusky standard for competency, since intellectual deficits may inhibit the ability of the defendant to communicate effectively with counsel or to understand the legal proceedings that are surrounding them. Relatively few researchers and scholars have addressed the problems faced by intellectually disabled individuals in the criminal justice system (Zapf & Roesch, 2009). A recent study found that 12.6% of defendants in its sample who were found IST maintained a primary diagnosis of mental retardation (Bath & Gerring, 2014). Intellectual disability does not in and of itself render a defendant incompetent. It is the impact of the intellectual disability on the individual's assessed psycholegal functioning, which provides the basis for the competency opinion.

It is important that when individuals with intellectual disabilities are identified within the criminal justice system, they are evaluated by a mental health professional who is familiar with specific issues that are relevant to intellectual disability. The Competence Assessment for Standing Trial for Defendants with Mental Retardation (CAST-MR) (Everington & Dunn, 1995) is the only competency assessment tool designed for adult individuals with intellectual disabilities. The use of the CAST-MR, allows for a structured assessment relevant to competency standards that can be used in conjunction with other data points, such as results of intellectual functioning assessment and achievement testing, to provide an informed decision about a defendant's competence (Anderson & Hewitt, 2002; Nestor, Daggett, Haycock, & Price, 1999).

ADULT VS. JUVENILE COMPETENCY STANDARDS

Juvenile-specific statutes have been crafted to allow for developmental concerns in informing opinions about competency in juvenile defendants. Twenty-one states retain adolescent-specific statutes; however the majority of states in the U.S. extend adult competency standards to juveniles without incorporating important developmental considerations (Bath & Gerring, 2014). Although considerations such as age and maturity have been included to a certain extent in competency doctrines, developmental psychologists often consider the concept of CST in juveniles to be paradoxical, since youths often lack the developmental maturity that is necessary to competently participate in their own legal proceedings (Grisso, 2003). Developmental and cognitive differences between juveniles and adults make it difficult, and perhaps even ethically questionable, to directly apply adult competence standards to juveniles (Otto, 2006). When the evaluation of cognitive deficits, intellectual or functional abilities, and psychiatric impairment is relevant to a competency evaluation in this population, it is suggested that developmentally appropriate instruments should be used as foundational sources of information (Mart, 2006). Viable instruments that have been identified for competency assessments of juveniles include the Wechsler Intelligence Scales for Children –V, Millon Adolescent Clinical Inventory (MACI), Minnesota Multiphasic Personality Inventory – Adolescent, and the Jesness Inventory (JI) (Butcher et al., 1992; Jesness, 1966; Mart, 2006; Millon, 1994; Weschler, 2014). The Juvenile Adjudicative Competence Interview (JACI) (Grisso, 2005) is a semi-structured interview that is designed specifically as a guided clinical assessment to use with youth who may be of questionable adjudicative competence. In addition, with juveniles, it is especially important to obtain collateral information about their functioning, since they may not be the most reliable and accurate historians. A supplemental parent interview guide for the JACI is available for use. Also, records about the youth's functioning in an academic and/or therapeutic setting are often informative.

GENDER AND RACE

Some research suggests that women are more likely to be found incompetent by an evaluator or court (Crocker, Favreau, & Caulet, 2002; Rogers, Seman, & Stampley, 1984; Warren et al., 2006), while other studies find no such evidence (Cox & Zapf, 2004; Warren et al., 2006). Therefore, it is clear that research surrounding the impact a defendant's gender may have on the evaluation of their trial competency is varied (Pirelli et al., 2011).

Research focused on the impact of race in competency evaluations has suggested that ethnic minorities may be more likely to be found incompetent (Pirelli et al., 2011; Kois, Pearson, Chauhan, Goni, & Saraydarian, 2013).

PROCEDURES

PROFESSIONAL QUALIFICATIONS

Psycho-legal judgments may be impacted by evaluation length, use of psychological instruments, and collection of collateral information (Chauhan et al., 2015). Mental health professionals who perform CST evaluations need to be licensed and are typically required to have PhD/PsyD in psychology or MD in psychiatry, with advanced specialized training in forensic assessments of competence (Murrie & Zelle, 2015). Not all states require specific training and continuing education for evaluators prior to eligibility for conducting criminal competency evaluations; however, these psychologists have an ethical duty, set forth by the Specialty Guidelines for Forensic Psychology, to demonstrate their own competence, specific to the evaluation and the case at hand (Murrie & Zelle, 2015).

CST ASSESSMENTS

A number of instruments from informal checklists to structured assessments have been designed to assess competency over the past 50 years (Pirelli et al., 2011). Some of the more commonly used assessment tools are Fitness Interview Test-Revised (FIT-R), the MacArthur Competence Assessment Tool-Criminal Adjudication (MacCAT-CA), and the Evaluation of Competency to Stand Trial–Revised (ECST-R) (Hoge, Bonnie, Poythress, & Monahan, 1999; Roesch, Zapf, & Eaves, 2006; Rogers, Tillbrook, & Sewell, 2004). Using information collected from the interview, collateral information, and data gathered from forensic assessment instruments, evaluators must form an opinion in regard to the degree of impairment a defendant maintains, while referencing the context of his or her legal proceedings.

MALINGERING AND CST

Rogers (1997) called for the systematic screening of defendants for malingering and other deviant response styles. Research estimates that malingering impacts somewhere between 4,800-10,200 defendants referred for competency evaluations each year (Jackson, Rogers, & Sewell, 2005). Instruments designed to detect malingering of psychiatric symptoms may be used in conjunction with competency-specific instruments, in order for evaluators to gauge the genuineness of symptom presentation. Examples of these tools include: the Minnesota Multiphasic Personality Inventory-2, the Structured Interview of Reported Symptoms-2 (SIRS-2), and the Inventory of Legal Knowledge (ILK) (Hathaway & McKinley, 1989; Musick & Otto, 2010; Rogers, Sewell, & Gillard, 2010).

JACKSON V. INDIANA

The majority of adult defendants found to be incompetent are restored to competence after a short stay in an inpatient psychiatric facility (Colwell & Gianesini, 2011; Morris & DeYoung, 2012; Samuel & Michals, 2011). However, prior to 1972, defendants who were found incompetent in some jurisdictions were automatically and indefinitely committed. The U.S. Supreme Court case Jackson v. Indiana (1972) held that defendants committed solely on the basis of incompetency "cannot be held more than the reasonable period of time necessary to determine whether there is a substantial probability that he will attain that capacity in the foreseeable future" (p. 738). The court in Jackson further stated that a defendant should either be released or civilly committed if restoration to competency is not likely in a practical amount of time. The Jackson decision was seminal in the modifications that states made to their statutes, providing alternatives to commitment and limiting the length of time. The procedure to determine a reasonable amount of time for an incompetent defendant's commitment varies state to state, as Jackson did not specifically define what a "reasonable period of time" might be. For some states the duration of commitment may have a set limit (e.g., 18 months) and others use a proportion of the length of sentence the defendant would have been given if convicted (Zapf et al., 2014).

INCOMPETENT TO STAND TRIAL (IST)

Once a person is adjudicated incompetent, a judge must weigh factors such as dangerousness and availability of resources when determining the appropriateness of inpatient or outpatient restoration treatment (Johnson & Candilis, 2015). Defendants who are rendered IST as adults are usually treated in a hospital setting until competence is restored (Miller, 2003; Pinals, 2005). Restoration to fitness for trial is most often completed through the use of medication (Mueller & Wylie, 2007). The U.S. Supreme Court has ruled on specific factors that must be considered prior to forcibly medicating a defendant. The Court found that an individual can be forcibly medicated if it is justifiable and medically appropriate (Riggins v. Nevada, 1992), necessary for the safety of the defendant or others (Washignton v. Harper, 1990), or if it is likely to restore competency with minimal side effects and less-intrusive methods are not possible (Sell v. U.S., 2003). The goal of restorative treatment is to return a defendant to legal competence as delineated in Dusky v. United States (1960), rather than address broader mental health issues and improve global functioning (Jackson, Warren, & Coburn, 2014). For juveniles who are determined to be incompetent for adjudication, the outcome is dependent on the state-specific legal code (Bonnie & Grisso, 2000; Gorter-Hines et al., 2014; Johnson, 2006; Viljoen & Grisso, 2007). The juvenile Court will typically find that if the youth can receive treatment and/or education which will assist them in acquiring or restoring their competency in a reasonable amount of time, then legal proceedings will be delayed until competence has been achieved (Viljoen & Grisso, 2007). However, if the Court finds that the child is not competent and is unable to have competency acquired or restored in a timely fashion, the Court may choose to dismiss the charges or dismiss the charges once treatment services have been completed.

CONCLUSION

It is evident that the issue of CST is one that appears quite frequently in trial proceedings. The facts and issues surrounding this topic are relevant to mental health and legal professionals, as these individuals are responsible for evaluating and adjudicating defendants whose competency is in question. The information provided here aims to serve as a basic outline of topics necessary for a general understanding of CST. Though research is still emerging, CST remains the most widely studied and perhaps the most understood of psycholegal issues in criminal court proceedings.

REFERENCES

Anderson, S. D., & Hewitt, J. (2002). The effect of competency restoration training on defendants with mental retardation found not competent to proceed. *Behavioral Sciences and the Law, 26*, 343-351.

Bath, E., & Gerring, J. (2014). National trends in juvenile competency to stand trial. *Journal of The American Academy of Child & Adolescent Psychiatry, 53*, 265-268. doi:10.1016/j.jaac.2013.11.015

Bonnie, R. J., & Grisso, T. (2000). Adjudicative competence and youthful offenders. In T. Grisso, R. G. Schwartz, T. Grisso, R. G. Schwartz (Eds.), *Youth on trial: A developmental perspective on juvenile justice* (pp. 73-103). Chicago, IL, US: University of Chicago Press.

Brown, T. E. (1996). *Brown ADD scales*. San Antonio, TX: Psychological Corporation.

Butcher, J.N., Williams, C.L., Graham, J.R., Tellegen, A., Ben-Porath, Y.S., & Kaemmer, B. (1992). Minnesota Multiphasic Personality Inventory-Adolescent (MMPI-A).

Chauhan, P., Warren, J., Kois, L., & Wellbeloved-Stone, J. (2015). The significance of combining evaluations of competency to stand trial and sanity at the time of the offense. *Psychology, Public Policy, and Law, 21*, 50-59. doi:10.1037/law0000026

Colwell, L. H., & Gianesini, J. (2011). Demographic, criminogenic, and psychiatric factors that predict competency restoration. *Journal of the American Academy of Psychiatry and the Law, 39*, 297-306.

Cooper, V. G., & Zapf, P. A. (2003). Predictor variables in competency to stand trial decisions. *Law and Human Behavior, 27*, 423-436. doi:10.1023/A:1024089117535

Cox, M. L., & Zapf, P. A. (2004). An investigation of discrepancies between mental health professionals and the courts in decisions about competency. *Law & Psychology Review, 28,*109-132.

Crocker, A. G., Favreau, O. E., & Caulet, M. (2002). Gender and fitness to stand trial: A 5-year review of remands in Quebec. *International Journal of Law and Psychiatry, 25,* 67-84.

Davidson, F., Kovacevic, V., Cave, M., Hart, K., & Dark, F. (2015). Assessing fitness for trial of deaf defendants. *Psychiatry, Psychology and Law, 22*, 145-156. doi:10.1080/13218719.2014.919690

Denney, R. L., & Tyner, E. A. (2010). Criminal law, competency, insanity, and dangerousness: Competency to proceed. In A. M. Horton Jr. & L. C. Hartlage (Eds.), *The Handbook of Forensic Neuropsychology* second edition (pp. 211-233). New York, NY: Springer Publishing Company.

Drope v. Missouri, 420 U.S. 162 (1975).

Dusky v. United States, 362 U.S. 402 (1960).

Everington, C.T., DeBerge, K., & Mauer, D. (2000). The relationship between language skills and competence to stand trial abilities in persons with mental retardation. *Journal of Psychiatry and Law, 28*, 475-492.

Everington, C., & Dunn, C. (1995). A second validation study of the Competence Assessment for Standing Trial for Defendants with Mental Retardation (CAST-MR). *Criminal Justice and Behavior, 22*, 44-59. doi:10.1177/0093854895022001004

Godinez v. Moran, 509 U.S. 389 (1993).

Golding, S. L. (2008). *Evaluations of adult adjudicative competency*. In R. Jackson (Ed.), Learning forensic assessment (pp. 75-108). New York, NY: Routledge/Taylor & Francis Group.

Gorter-Hines, E., Lexcen, F., Ward, B., & Kuniyoshi, J. (2014). Challenges to Restoring Juvenile Competence with Involuntary Medications. *Journal of Forensic Psychology Practice, 14*, 247-262.

Grisso, T. (2003). *Evaluating competencies: Forensic assessments and instruments* (2nd ed.). New York, NY, US: Kluwer Academic/Plenum Publishers.

Grisso, T. (2005). *Evaluating juveniles' adjudicative competence: A guide for clinical practice*. Sarasota, FL: Professional Resource Press/Professional Resource Exchange.

Grisso, T., & Appelbaum, P. S. (1998). *Assessing competence to consent to treatment: A guide for physicians and other health professionals*. New York, NY: Oxford University Press.

Hathaway, S.R. & McKinley, J.C. (1989). *Manual for the Minnesota Multiphasic Personality Inventory-2* (MMPI-2). Minneapolis, MN: University of Minnesota Press.

Ho, T., & Henderson, B.B. (1998). Relationship of psychological, demographic, and legal variables to court decisions of competency to stand trial among mentally retarded criminal defendants. *Journal of Criminal Justice, 26*, 307-329.

Hoge, S. K., Bonnie, R. J., Poythress, N. G., & Monahan, J. (1999) *The MacArthur Competence Assessment Tool—Criminal Adjudication*. Odessa, FL: Psychological Assessment Resources.

Hoge, S. K., Bonnie, R. J., Poythress, N. G., Monahan, J., & Eisenberg, M. (1997). The MacArthur Adjudicative Competence Study: Development and validation of a research instrument. *Law and Human Behavior, 21*, 141-179.

Hubbard, K. L., Zapf, P. A., & Ronan, K. A. (2003). Competency restoration: An examination of the differences between defendants predicted restorable and not restorable to competency. *Law And Human Behavior, 27*, 127-139. doi:10.1023/A:1022566328781

Jackson v. Indiana, 406 U.S. 715 (1972).

Jackson, R. L., Rogers, R., & Sewell, K. W. (2005). Forensic Applications of the Miller Forensic Assessment of Symptoms Test (MFAST): Screening for Feigned Disorders in Competency to Stand Trial Evaluations. *Law And Human Behavior, 29*, 199-210. doi:10.1007/s10979-005-2193-5

Jackson, S. L., Warren, J. I., & Coburn, J. J. (2014). A Community-Based Model for Remediating Juveniles Adjudicated Incompetent to Stand Trial: Feedback from Youth, Attorneys, and Judges. *Juvenile and Family Court Journal, 65*, 23-38.

Jesness, C. F. (1966). *Manual: the Jesness inventory*. Palo Alto, California.

Johnson, K. M. (2006). Juvenile competency statutes: A model for state legislation. *Indiana Law Journal, 81*, 1067-1095.

Johnson, N. R., & Candilis, P. J. (2015). Outpatient competence restoration: A model and outcomes. *World Journal of Psychiatry, 5*, 228.

Kirkish, P., & Sreenivasan, S. (1999). Neuropsychological assessment of competency to stand trial evaluations: A practical conceptual model. *Journal of the American Academy of Psychiatry and the Law, 27*, 101-113.

Kois, L., Pearson, J., Chauhan, P., Goni, M., & Saraydarian, L. (2013). Competency to stand trial among female inpatients. *Law and Human Behavior, 37*, 231-240. doi:10.1037/lhb0000014

Marcopulos, B. A., Morgan, J. E., & Denney, R. L. (2008). Neuropsychological evaluation of competency to proceed. In R. L. Denney, J. P. Sullivan, R. L. Denney, J. P. Sullivan (Eds.), *Clinical neuropsychology in the criminal forensic setting* (pp. 176-203). New York, NY, US: Guilford Press.

Mart, E. G. (2006). *Getting started in forensic psychology practice: How to create a forensic specialty in your mental health practice*. Hoboken, NJ, US: Wiley Publishing.

Martell, D. A. (1992). Forensic neuropsychology and the criminal law. *Law and Human Behavior, 16*, 313-336. Doi:10.1007/BF01044772

Meehl, P. (1970). Some methodological reflections on the difficulties of psychoanalytic research. In M. Radner & S. Winokur (Eds.), *Minnesota studies in the philosophy of science* (Vol. 4, pp. 403-416). Minneapolis: University of Minnesota Press.

Melton, G. B., Petrila, J., Poythress, N. G., Slobogin, C., Lyons, P. J., & Otto, R. K. (2007). *Psychological evaluations for the courts: A handbook for mental health professionals and lawyers* (3rd Ed.). New York, NY, US: Guilford Press.

Miller, R. D. (2003). Hospitalization of criminal defendants for evaluation of competence to stand trial or for restoration of competence: Clinical and legal issues. *Behavioral Sciences and the Law, 21*, 369-391.

Millon, T. (1994). Millon Adolescent Clinical Inventory (MACI). Minneapolis: Nacional Computers Systems.

Morris, D. R., & DeYoung, N. J. (2012). Psycholegal abilities and restoration of competence to stand trial. *Behavioral Sciences and the Law, 30*, 710-728. doi:10.1002/bsl.2040

Mossman, D. (2007). Predicting restorability of incompetent criminal defendants. *Journal of the American Academy of Psychiatry and the Law, 35*, 34-43.

Mueller, C. & Wylie, M. (2007). Examining the effectiveness of an intervention designed for the restoration of competency to stand trial. *Behavioral Sciences and the Law, 25*, 891-900.

Murrie, D. C., & Zelle, H. (2015). Criminal competencies. In B. L. Cutler, P. A. Zapf, B. L. Cutler, P. A. Zapf (Eds.), *APA handbook of forensic psychology, Vol. 1: Individual and situational influences in criminal and civil contexts* (pp. 115-157). Washington, DC, US: American Psychological Association. doi:10.1037/14461-005

Musick, J., & Otto, R. (2010). *The inventory of legal knowledge*. Lutz, FL: Psychological Assessment Resources.

Nestor, P. G., Daggett, D., Haycock, J., & Price, M. (1999). Competence to stand trial: A neuropsychological inquiry. *Law and Human Behavior, 23*, 397-412.

Nicholson, R.A., & Johnson, W.G. (1991). Prediction of competency to stand trial: Contribution of demographics, type of offense, clinical characteristics, and psycholegal ability. *International Journal of Law and Psychiatry, 14*, 287-297.

Nicholson, R. A., & Kugler, K. E. (1991). Competent and incompetent criminal defendants: A quantitative review of comparative research. *Psychological Bulletin, 109*, 355-370.

Nussbaum, D., Hancock, M., Turner, I., Arrowood, J., & Melodick, S. (2007). Fitness/competency to stand trial: A conceptual overview, review of existing instruments, and cross-validation of the Nussbaum Fitness Questionnaire. *Brief Treatment and Crisis Intervention, 8*, 43-72. doi:10.1093/brief-treatment/mhm026

Otto, R. K. (2006). Competency to stand trial. *Applied Psychology in Criminal Justice, 2*(3,SpecIss), 82-113.

Otto, R. K., Poythress, N. G., Nicholson, R. A., Edens, J. F., Monahan, J., Bonnie, R. J., & ... Eisenberg, M. (1998). Psychometric properties of the MacArthur Competence Assessment Tool–Criminal Adjudication. *Psychological Assessment, 10*, 435-443. doi:10.1037/1040-3590.10.4.435

Otto, R. K., & Weiner, I. B. (2013). *Handbook of psychology: Forensic psychology* (Vol. 11) (2nd ed.). Hoboken, NJ, US: John Wiley & Sons Inc.

Pate v. Robinson, 383 U.S. 375 (1966).

Piel, J., Finkle, M. J., Giske, M., & Leong, G. B. (2015). Determining a criminal defendant's competency to proceed with an extradition hearing. *Journal of the American Academy of Psychiatry and the Law Online, 43*, 201-209.

Pinals, D. A. (2005). Where two roads meet: Restoration of competence to stand trial from a clinical perspective. *New England Journal of Criminal Civil Confinement, 31*, 81-108.

Pirelli, G., Gottdiener, W. H., & Zapf, P. A. (2011). A meta-analytic review of competency to stand trial research. *Psychology, Public Policy, and Law, 17*,1-53. doi:10.1037/a0021713

Poythress, N., Bonnie, R., Monahan, J., Otto, R. K., & Hoge, S. (2002). *Adjudicative competence: The MacArthur studies*. New York: Kluwer/Plenum.

Riggins v. Nevada 504 U.S. 127 (1992).

Roesch, R., Zapf, P.A., & Eaves, D. (2006). *Fitness Interview Test-Revised: A structured interview for assessing competency to stand trial*. Sarasota, FL: Professional Resource Press.

Roesch, R., Zapf, P.A., Golding, S.L., & Skeem, J.L. (2004). Defining and assessing competency to stand trial. *The Handbook of Forensic Psychology*. Hoboken, NJ, US: John Wiley & Sons Inc.

Rogers, R. (1997). *Clinical assessment of malingering and deception* (2nd ed.). New York: The Guilford Press.

Rogers, R., Seman, W., & Stampley, J. (1984). A study of socio-demographic characteristics of individuals evaluated for insanity. *International Journal of Offender Therapy and Comparative Criminology, 28*, 3-10.

Rogers, R., Sewell, K. W., & Gillard, N. D. (2010). *SIRS-2: Structured Interview of Reported Symptoms: Professional manual*. Psychological Assessment Resources, Incorporated.

Rogers, R., Tillbrook, C.E., & Sewell, K.W. (2004). *Evaluation of Competency to Stand Trial – Revised professional manual*. Lutz, FL: Psychological Assessment Resources.

Rogers, R., Ustad, K. L., Sewell, K. W., & Reinhardt, V. (1996). Dimensions of incompetency: A factor analytic study of the Georgia court competency test. *Behavioral Sciences and the Law, 14*, 323-330. doi:10.1002/(SICI)1099-0798(199622)14:3<323::AID-BSL243>3.0.CO;2-Z

Samuel, S. E., & Michals, T. J. (2011). Competency restoration. In E. Y. Drogin, F. M. Dattilio, R. L. Sadoff, T. G. Gutheil, E. Y. Drogin, F. M. Dattilio, ... T. G. Gutheil (Eds.), *Handbook of forensic assessment: Psychological and psychiatric perspectives* (pp. 79-96). Hoboken, NJ, US: John Wiley & Sons Inc. doi:10.1002/9781118093399.ch4

Sell v. United States 539 U.S. 166 (2003).

Simpler, A. H., & Parmenter, B. A. (2011). Can neuropsychological assessment inform forensic evaluators' psycholegal opinions? Evidence through a case report. *Journal of Forensic Psychology Practice, 11*, 351-360.

Stafford, K., & Sellbom, M. (2013). Assessment of competence to stand trial. In R. K. Otto & I. Weiner (Eds.), *Handbook of Psychology: Forensic Psychology* (2nd ed., Vol. 11), (pp. 412-439). New Jersey: John Wiley & Sons, Inc.

U.S. v. Duhon, 104 F.Supp. 2d. 663 (W.D.La. 2000).

Viljoen, J. L., & Grisso, T. (2007). Prospects for remediating juveniles' adjudicative incompetence. Psychology, *Public Policy, and Law, 13*, 87-114.

Warren, J. I., Murrie, D. C., Stejskal, W., Colwell, L. H., Morris, J., Chauhan, P., & Dietz, P. (2006). Opinion Formation in Evaluating the Adjudicative Competence and Restorability of Criminal Defendants: A Review of 8,000 Evaluations. *Behavioral Sciences & the Law, 24*, 113-132. doi:10.1002/bsl.699

Washington v. Harper, 494 U.S. 210 (1990).

Wechsler, D. (2014). Wechsler Intelligence Scale for Children–Fifth Edition. San Antonio, TX: Pearson.

Weinborn, M., Orr, T., Woods, S. P., Conover, E., & Feix J. (2003). A Validation of the Test of Memory Malingering in a Forensic Psychiatric Setting. *Journal of Clinical and Experimental Neuropsychology, 25*, 979-990. doi:10.1076/jcen.25.7.979.16481

White, A. J., Batchelor, J., Pulman, S., & Howard, D. (2012). The role of cognitive assessment in determining fitness to stand trial. *International Journal of Forensic Mental Health, 11*, 102-109.

White, A. J., Meares, S., & Batchelor, J. (2014). The role of cognition in fitness to stand trial: A systematic review. *The Journal of Forensic Psychiatry and Psychology, 25*, 77-99.

Zapf, P. A., Hubbard, K. L., Cooper, V. G., Wheeles, M. C., & Ronan, K. A. (2004). Have the Courts Abdicated Their Responsibility for Determination of Competency to Stand Trial to Clinicians?. *Journal of Forensic Psychology Practice, 4*, 27-44. doi:10.1300/J158v04n01_02

Zapf, P. A., & Roesch, R. (2009). *Evaluation of competence to stand trial*. New York, NY, US: Oxford University Press.

Zapf, P. A., Roesch, R., & Pirelli, G. (2014). Assessing competency to stand trial. In I. B. Weiner, R. K. Otto, I. B. Weiner, R. K. Otto (Eds.), *The handbook of forensic psychology* (4th ed.) (pp. 281-314). Hoboken, NJ, US: John Wiley & Sons Inc.

CHAPTER 4

CONFABULATION: A BEGINNER'S GUIDE FOR CRIMINAL JUSTICE AND FORENSIC MENTAL HEALTH PROFESSIONALS

JERROD BROWN, CODY CHARETTE, JASON WEAVER, CAMERON R. WILEY, ERIK W. ASP, ERIN WATTS, PAMELA OBEROI, JANINA CICH, ERV WEINKAUF, KAYLA VORLICKY, DEB HUNTLEY, ERWIN CONCEPCION, CARLO GIACOMONI, & MARIO L. HESSE

CHAPTER OVERVIEW

The integrity of the judicial process is often contingent upon accurate and reliable eyewitness testimony from suspects, defendants, victims, and witnesses. However, there are instances when individuals may unknowingly and unintentionally produce statements, confessions, and other accounts that are partially or even entirely false. This phenomenon is known as confabulation, the act of providing inaccurate information based on distorted or fabricated memories without the intention to deceive. Confabulation can arise from a number of factors and conditions that the criminal justice and forensic mental health systems may not regularly consider. Broader awareness of confabulation is essential because this phenomenon may negatively impact the outcome of a particular case. As such, this chapter examines the complex and multifaceted nature of confabulation by defining different types of confabulation, identifying potential causes of confabulation, considering different clinical conditions that may increase the likelihood of confabulation, and discussing how real and confabulated memories may be distinguished from each other.

INTRODUCTION

Confabulation is the act of providing information based on unintentionally inaccurate memories that are provoked by questions or arise spontaneously (Moscovitch, 1989, p.133). This could simply be the act of filling in blank memory spaces or creating a semblance of coherency and continuity while attempting to improve the quality of narrative (Gallagher, 2003). This may be driven by a subconscious attempt to create and hold false memories or as an act of self-deception (Burgess & Shallice, 1996; Schnider, von Daniken, & Gutbrod, 1996). Recently, the description of confabulation has been broadened to include a range of memory errors (e.g., distortions and descriptions of false realities) as well as less dramatic errors (e.g., memory intrusions, embellishments, elaborations, and the paraphrasing of existing memories) (Guerri, Bazinet, & Riley, 2009). This phenomenon differs greatly from lying in the traditional sense. Although lying occurs when the individual in question is aware of the falsehood of their statements, confabulation is not motivated by malicious or willful deception for either the gain of external benefit or avoidance of punishment (LoPiccolo et al., 1999; Moscovitch, 1995). As such, confabulation has been described as "honest lying." Depending on the pathology, individuals with neurological impairments can be prone to confabulation. In addition, confabulation, when defined as unintentional and unaware communication of falsehoods, can also occur in healthy individuals in particular situations. When this seemingly innocent act occurs within the criminal justice system in the form of testimony or confession, the results can have an adverse, corrupting impact on the judicial process (Brown et al., 2014).

A testimonial confession is the strongest, most convincing evidence provided to juries (Kassin & Neumann, 1997). According to Supreme Court Justice William Brennan, "The introduction of a confession makes other aspects of a trial in court superfluous" (Colorado v. Connelly, 1986). In courtroom settings, there is the tenuous assumption in the minds of many jurors and judges that only a guilty person would confess to a crime. However, this opinion fails to account for the tendency of all people (but in particular, individuals with poor cognitive function) to believe the narrative of which they have been accused. Moreover, under interrogation, conditions of mental resource depletion, and deliberate deception (e.g., asserting a suspect is guilty), as used in the Reid technique, false confessions are more common. Although it remains difficult to determine the exact number of individuals who have falsely confessed, a European study found that 27 out of 229 prisoners (12%) claimed to have falsely confessed (Gudjonsson, 2003). In a separate study of Icelandic students with Attention-Deficit and Hyperactivity Disorder (ADHD), 12.4% of the participants were identified as falsely confessing to law enforcement (Gudjonsson et al., 2012). In addition to these studies, there are also certain individuals and organizations that specifically keep track of the prevalence of false confessions in criminal justice settings. United States researcher Robert Perske maintains "Perske's List," which documents cases of false confessions by individuals with an intellectual disability. As of October 2011, 75 separate cases have been documented (Perske, 2011). Similarly, the Innocence Project is an organization that was established to exonerate individuals who have been falsely convicted due to a lack of proper DNA testing in conjunction with false confessions or unreliable eyewitness reports. As of April 2014, 79 of 316 exonerated individuals (25%) were convicted based on false confessions (Scheck & Neufeld, 2015). Furthermore, Kassin and colleagues (2012) reported that false confessions appear to have a corrupting effect on the entire criminal investigation process. For example, false confessions increased the likelihood of other subsequent errors associated with forensic science, eyewitness accounts, and informant evidence. A potential driving factor may be the inferred guilt and biases by those who would otherwise be considered impartial, such as a jury or witnesses. A collective confirmation bias may spread during the justice process, where the objective data are made to fit the prevailing confession theory of the crime rather than the objective data leading to the optimal theory.

Limitations to testimony do not end with the possible occurrence of false confessions. Despite the wealth of knowledge regarding its potential lack of reliability, testimony from defendants, accusers, eyewitnesses, and informants remain integral to the criminal justice system (Wells & Loftus, 1984). In fact, testimony is often given more weight than may be appropriate by juries who are unaware of published findings or salient deficiencies in a person's ability to testify (Imwinkelried, 1989). Lending credence to this perspective, false testimony (including false confessions, false eyewitnesses, and false informants/cooperating witnesses) was found to be integral to the conviction of 195 of the 200 individuals who later had their convictions overturned as a result of the work of the Innocence Project (Garrett, 2008). Although it is possible that some false testimony occurred due to deliberate lying, research suggests many false convictions are caused by confabulation or unintentional false memory (Loftus & Pickrell, 1995; Loftus & Zanni, 1975). The context and situations which produce confabulation largely remain unanswered and are worthy of future exploration.

In light of the consequences of wrongful convictions, such as unintentional loss of liberty and a host of other negative consequences, the veracity and reliability of testimony are crucial in legal proceedings focused on understanding criminal actions (Brown et al., 2014; Gudjonsson, 1992; Sharrock, 1988). Distinguishing confabulated recall from deliberate lying is an important part of the process in uncovering truth and separating fact from fiction. As highlighted above, this concern is particularly salient in legal settings when individuals with neurological impairments serve as defendants, convicts, witnesses, bystanders, or victims (Clare & Gudjonsson, 2010; Gudjonsson & Clare, 1995). The aim of this chapter is to improve understanding of confabulation through a systematic review of the nature and existence of conditions and situations conducive to this disturbance.

CONFABULATION: AN OVERVIEW

Confabulation is a term that is surrounded by persistent confusion, controversies, and misconceptions. These problems are driven, at least in part, by difficulties in simply defining confabulation. Although there is a lack of consensus, confabulation can be broadly defined as the communication of falsely constructed answers and information by an individual recounting an event that he or she genuinely believes to be the truth (Anastasi, 2006; Macleod, Gross, & Hayne, 2016; Shingaki, Park, Ueda, Murai, & Tsukiura, 2016). This typically includes additions, deletions, and distortions in both the content and temporal context of memories (DeLuca, 2009). Individuals often claim that they can relive these memories and, in fact, sometimes act on or respond to their confabulations (Ciaramelli & Ghetti, 2007). For example, this behavior may be seen as bereavement over the death of an imaginary friend. Other emotional responses may include constructed memories and situations, such as the search for a phone number of an imagined person (Schnider, 2003). These types of behaviors suggest that confabulators subjectively experience memories as being real and may potentially base actions and decisions on false or distorted beliefs (Goel & Dolan, 2003). Nonetheless, confabulation has multiple definitions, an unclear etiology, and high levels of Co-morbidity with psychiatric disorders and other neuroclinical conditions. As a result, there has been a struggle in simply defining confabulation and raising awareness of how confabulation can impact different long-term outcomes in places such as criminal justice settings.

Highlighting this complexity, several attempts have been made to classify this phenomenon. For example, confabulation was initially placed along a continuum ranging from minor distortions to completely bizarre or delusional false memories. This placement was based on the level of cognitive or executive dysfunction associated with the incident of confabulation (Schnider, von Däniken, & Gutbrod, 1996). Consistent with this idea of confabulation falling on a continuum is the concept that there are subtypes of confabulation. In an effort to clarify several subtypes of confabulation, Schnider (2008, p. 53) proposed four forms of confabulation. First, *intrusions or simple provoked confabulations* are distortions of a single element or aspect of memory. Second, *momentary confabulations* are false statements upon incitement. Possibly plausible, these provoked or spontaneous confabulations can range from simple statements to elaborate stories. Third, *fantastic confabulations* have no "basis in reality" and are not associated with acting upon the false belief. Fourth, *behaviorally spontaneous confabulations* are primarily identified by people acting out their false beliefs and occur concurrently with severe amnesia and disorientation. Zannino and colleagues (2008) characterized spontaneous confabulations as "untrue, sometimes bizarre statements that are readily evident in the patient's everyday conversations, which express false beliefs that they sometimes act on" (p. 832). This classification model highlights the complexities of simply defining confabulation.

Despite these diverse definitions and subtypes of confabulation, some commonalities exist in how confabulation has been described. Specifically, most definitions of confabulation have included three components: (1) Falsehood (Falsity), (2) reporting method (Reports) and (3) memory basis (Memories) (Gilboa & Verfaellie, 2010; Huntley, Brown, & Wiley, 2016; Turner, Cipolotti, Yousry, & Shallice, 2008; Xie et al., 2010). First, *falsity* alone has the potential for arbitrary results. For example, when an individual is asked for the time, he or she may initially state the correct time. However, if he or she persists in stating the same time, then the subsequent statements of the time would be inaccurate. Second, *reporting method* refers to how (i.e., verbal versus non-verbal) confabulation is conveyed. In fact, several researchers have identified the occurrence of confabulation in drawing, physically pointing to items, and other non-linguistic responses (Hirstein, 2009). Therefore, it is important for those who encounter confabulation to be cognizant of the varieties of ways in which this phenomenon can manifest itself. Third, although some argue confabulation is confined to actual memories, our definition of confabulation is broader in regards to unintentional communication of a falsehood. Thus, some incidents of confabulation are not traceable to any previous recollections and are spontaneously conjectured (Hirstein, 2009). As shown above, closer examination of these criteria reveals a number of issues that challenge the definition and application of confabulation.

The lack of consensus and ensuing confusion on the topic of confabulation has contributed to the lack of awareness about this phenomenon and its consequences. Although amnesia is a well-known and widely researched condition of memory loss that leads to errors of omission and execution, less is known about confabulation (Fotopoulou, Conway, Solms, Tyrer, & Kopelman, 2008). For example, there is relatively little awareness in mental health and criminal justice professionals about confabulation's contribution to the fallibility of human memory in regard to omission (i.e., forgetting of details and experiences) and execution (i.e., inaccurately recalling or distorting memories). This is problematic because of the profound consequences that confabulation can produce on criminal justice outcomes. This can range from false confessions and inaccurate eyewitness testimony to wrongful convictions and imprisonment. As such, greater familiarity with the concept of confabulation and its causes is needed in mental health and criminal justice settings.

CAUSES OF CONFABULATION

Many existing theories attempt to explain the etiology and driving factors behind confabulation. The most widely-accepted explanation suggests that a combination of memory impairment and compromised executive function increases the likelihood of its occurrence (Johnson, O'Connor, & Cantor, 1997). Since these disturbances can be exhibited by those affected by various phenomena involving executive dysfunction (e.g., amnesia, Wernicke-Korsakoff Syndrome, ruptured anterior communicating artery aneurysms), it is often theorized that issues with cognition contribute to confabulation (Johnson, Hayes, D'Esposito, & Raye, 2000; Turner et al., 2008). This difficulty in identifying the neurological sources of confabulation may be the result of heterogeneous patient samples that were used in these previous studies (Fischer, Alexander, D'esposito, & Otto, 1995). Further, both spontaneous and provoked confabulation may have different potential sources that include varying degrees of memory and executive functioning deficits (Dalla Barba, 1993; Kessels, Kortrijk, Wester, & Nys, 2008; Kopelman, 1987; Schnider et al., 1996). This section identifies possible contributing factors in different types of confabulation.

SPONTANEOUS CONFABULATION

Spontaneous confabulation may arise from a confusion of events due to a disturbed sense of chronology or an impaired ability to process and filter information (Kopelman, 1987; Schnider et al., 1996). Specifically, spontaneous confabulation has been associated with an inability to recognize the temporal order of stored information, which results in the erroneous recollection of different elements of memories that do not correspond with one another (Schnider et al., 1996). Such confusion does not result from an external cue, but may arise when there are difficulties in differentiation between new information and previously stored information. This old information, regardless of its relevance to the current situation, often fails to be suppressed or filtered, adding to the creation of false accounts of memory (Schnider, 2008). In these cases, a persistent outpouring of irrelevant memories occurs (Kopelman, 2010). Thus, spontaneous confabulation can occur when memories from an older period are determined to be currently relevant (Turner & Coltheart, 2010).

Habits and recurring events may also play a role in the presentation of spontaneous confabulation (Nahum et al., 2009). Individuals who are at a greater risk of confabulating may rely on past habits and memories when attempting to fill in gaps in their recall, overestimating the likelihood that their past behavior is relevant to the present. This failure to disregard previously accurate information is indicative of a failure of extinction, which is how "one learns that certain expectations no longer apply" (Ouyang & Thomas, 2005, p. 9347). Of course, another likely possibility is that extinction failure and confabulation are both derived from the same core cognitive dysfunction (Asp & Tranel, 2013). Moreover, individuals have a tendency to rely on the availability heuristic, a mental shortcut based on past habits and experiences that is used to make decisions in the present (Tversky & Kahneman, 1973). Those who confabulate may be more susceptible to relying on this method of processing, unknowingly incorporating familiar pieces of memory into their accounts (Asp et al., 2013).

PROVOKED CONFABULATION

Provoked confabulation refers to errors or distortions that are incorporated into memories in response to an external cue or challenge (Kopelman, 1987). Provoked confabulation occurs when the person is prompted for an answer or has received external cues, placing the expectation for a memory that does not exist while simultaneously communicating that it should exist (Kessels, Kortrijk, Wester, & Nys, 2008). Because provoked confabulation results from the inadequate or incomplete search for information in memory, fleeting intrusion errors or distortions often occur in response to a direct query (Kopelman, 2010; Schnider et al., 1996). Below, we summarize a few of the established external cues of provoked confabulation.

Perhaps the most extensively researched situational predictor of confabulation is the misinformation effect (Loftus, 2003; Loftus & Hoffman, 1989). In this line of research, a participant witnesses an event and then is subsequently presented with inaccurate information about the event. Later on, the participant is asked to recount the event. Across several circumstances and research studies, participants consistently incorporate some or all of the inaccurate information into their memories of the event (Henkel, 2011; Kassin, 2005; Loftus, 2003). This effect is particularly acute when the misinformation is quite subtle. For example, participants are significantly more likely to report having seen a broken headlight when asked "Did you see *the* broken headlight?" than when asked "Did you see *a* broken headlight?" (Loftus & Zanni, 1975, p. 86). In this case, the mere substitution of the word "the" for the word "a" was enough to cause people to alter the details of their memory. Similarly, Loftus and Palmer (1974, p. 587) observed the use of prompting in confabulation when evaluating the importance of word choice during the questioning of a witness. In this study of 150 participants, the word "smashed" was substituted for the word "hit" when questioning witnesses about car accident videos. Participants falsely recalled seeing broken glass at a greater rate when the word "smashed" (32%) was used instead of the word "hit" (14%). Further, the participants judged the speed of the car to be an average of 7 mph faster when the word "smashed" was used rather than the word "hit." Across several studies, multiple factors have been identified that moderate the degree to which misinformation causes confabulation. When given an alcohol placebo (tonic water), for example, participants are more likely to accept misinformation and confabulate (Assefi & Garry, 2003). In contrast, being in a bad mood reduces the influence of misinformation and generally improves the accuracy of memory, as research shows that negative mood states lead to increased effort in processing details and gathering additional information (Forgas, Goldenberg, & Unkelbach, 2009; Forgas, Laham, & Vargas, 2005).

In addition to the misinformation effect, false memories can be conjured by one's imagination (Hyman & Pentland, 1996). For example, people who have been asked to imagine completing a set of mundane tasks will often report that they actually completed those tasks when questioned later (Goff & Roediger, 1998). This tendency to mistake imagination for an actual memory is even stronger when people are shown photographs of the completed work or are provided with manipulated photographic or video evidence of their experiences (Henkel, 2011; Nash & Wade, 2009; Wade, Garry, Read, & Lindsay, 2002). Other examples include studies in which people were told that they were lost in a shopping mall as a child (Loftus & Pickrell, 1995) or became ill after eating a particular food (Bernstein & Loftus, 2009b). In each study, participants would often recall these events as real memories at a later date. Even seeing a manipulated advertisement for Disney World that features Bugs Bunny is enough to conjure detailed but inaccurate childhood memories of meeting Bugs Bunny at Disney World. These memories are clearly false, as Bugs Bunny is a Warner Brothers' character and would never appear at Disney World (Braun, Ellis, & Loftus, 2002; Loftus, 2003). In these cases, it seems that the imaginations of participants use the researchers' suggestion of an event to create a false memory. These false memories are even more prevalent when multiple sensory experiences are involved, such as both hearing about and imagining an event (Henkel, Franklin, & Johnson, 2000).

Indeed, even events that seem seared into our memory are as susceptible to error as other memories. Flashbulb memories are a class of memory characterized by their vividness and sensory detail, which increases an individual's confidence in the accuracy of the memory (Brown & Kulik, 1977; Talarico, 2009; Talarico & Rubin, 2003). For example, most Americans can recall in great detail where they were and what they were doing when they learned of a significant historical event such as the assassination of President Kennedy (Brown & Kulik, 1977) or the September 11 attacks on the World Trade Center Twin Towers in New York City (Curci & Luminet, 2006). Flashbulb memories generally include an emotional component that makes them particularly salient and more likely to be remembered and revisited than other less meaningful memories. Nonetheless, flashbulb memories are no more accurate than ordinary memories (Talarico & Rubin, 2003), which makes them particularly vulnerable to confabulation.

One explanation for the inaccuracies in flashbulb memory is the tendency for individuals to share experiences following a significant historical event (Finkenauer et al., 1998; Pennebaker & Harber, 1993; Skowronski & Walker, 2004). As an individual repeatedly accesses their memory of the experience while hearing the vivid descriptions of others, the individual may begin to incorporate elements of others' accounts into their own memories. Because of the vivid descriptions in each person's story, it is easy for an individual to imagine themselves in someone else's experience. The mechanism at work during this process might be quite similar to the imagination manipulations that memory researchers use to create confabulation in the laboratory. The vulnerability of flashbulb memories to confabulation is of particular concern to justice professionals dealing with victims of violent crime.

Although these experimental laboratory studies established that relatively minor external cues can elicit confabulation in a non-clinical population, these studies do not necessarily generalize to more realistic circumstances (Yuille & Cutshall, 1986). Indeed, there are concerns that people may have better memories for the details of stressful and personal real-life events. However, people who witness a crime have been shown to have worse memories of the details of the incident than those shown videotapes of a crime (Ihlebaek, Love, Eilertsen, & Magnussen, 2003). Additionally, people who witness a violent crime are less accurate in identifying the perpetrators than those people who witness a non-violent crime (Clifford & Hollin, 1981). As such, memory may actually be limited in stressful and personal real-life situations, rather than improved.

CLINICAL RELEVANCE

Confabulation is often the result of a combination of both situational and dispositional factors. As outlined above, situational context can increase confabulation in healthy individuals. In addition, a variety of psychological and neurological attributes affect the likelihood for confabulation. Provoked and spontaneous confabulation occurs following damage to specific brain structures (i.e., basal forebrain, hypothalamus, and dorsomedial thalamic nucleus) (Schnider, 2008). The ventromedial prefrontal cortex (vmPFC) has been heavily implicated in the editing and inhibiting of inaccurate memories (Moscovitch & Melo, 1997; DeLuca & Diamond, 1995); thus, lesions to the vmPFC have been strongly associated with confabulation (both spontaneous and provoked). Damage to the prefrontal cortex can also lead to impaired recognition of perceptual context features (i.e., the format in which an item was presented) (Ciaramelli & Spaniol, 2009) and result in difficulties distinguishing memories from other thoughts, ideas, or experiences, as might be evidenced in provoked confabulation (Fotopoulou et al., 2008). In confabulation, this often occurs with autobiographical content, such as: (a) the man who questioned his wife one evening about why she kept telling other people that they were married when they were not; (b) the hospital employee who recounted regular visits from her parents, despite their being dead many years; and (c) the 61-year-old man who talked about having recently taken his girlfriend home to meet his parents, both of whom had died many years earlier (Kopelman, 2010). Such instances can have a devastating impact in court proceedings, where provoked and spontaneous confabulation can result in inaccurate testimony. As a result, mental health and legal professionals should be aware of these potential contributing factors to confabulation.

From a neurological perspective, there are a number of clinical disorders that compromise the functional integrity of neural structures putatively important for accurate memory recall. This section explores some relevant clinical disorders that are commonly implicated in confabulation.

FETAL ALCOHOL SPECTRUM DISORDER

From an early-life developmental perspective, believing fictional stories typically occurs in younger, healthy children (Schacter, Kagan, & Leichtman, 1995). Older individuals with Fetal Alcohol Spectrum Disorder (FASD) or with other neurological damage may exhibit similar symptoms due to an arrested cognitive development. The presence of such disorders may result in the demonstration of behaviors that would be appropriate for much younger individuals (Nedjam, Devouche, & Dalla Barba, 2004). As such, developmental impairment constitutes one of the many complex causes of this disturbance (Gibbard, Wass, & Clarke, 2003).

Prenatal alcohol exposure (PAE) has been associated with widespread neuropsychological deficits across several domains, leading to significant impairments and disadvantages for affected individuals (Petrenko et al., 2014; Rangmar et al., 2015; Wheeler, Stevens, Sheard, & Rovet, 2012). These damages and deficits related to PAE can impact general intelligence, memory, language, attention, verbal and nonverbal learning, visuospatial abilities, executive functioning, fine and gross motor skills, and social and adaptive functioning (Edwards & Greenspan, 2010; Rasmussen, 2005; Rasmussen & Bisanz, 2009; Schnider, 2008). Further, these individuals are disproportionately likely to be neglected, abused, and mistreated relative to the general population (LaDue, Streissguth, & Randels, 1992; Thiel et al., 2011). In combination with these other life circumstances, the executive functioning and higher order cognitive processing impairments of FASD likely increase the risk of memory issues, including confabulation.

Executive functioning is crucial for the capacity to comprehend, plan, organize, strategize, notice, and contextualize details (Welsh & Pennington, 1988; Jirikowic, Kartin, & Olson, 2008; Schonfeld, Paley, Frankel, & O'Connor, 2006). The ability to tell stories (verbal or written) or recount situations and experiences in a detailed, organized, and sequential manner can be impaired. Such deficiencies in language and memory contribute to the presentation of confabulation. Specifically, some have theorized that individuals affected by prenatal alcohol exposure suffer from a disturbed sense of chronology, and this confusion of events may cause confabulation if earlier memories are judged as currently relevant (Clare & Gudjonsson, 2010; Fast & Conry, 2006; Pezdek et al., 2009; Turner & Coltheart, 2010). These difficulties can be exacerbated in stressful situations, where the individual may become overwhelmed and faced with confusing evidence of guilt in regard to the crime, when attempting to solve a problem or recall a memory (Horselenberg et al., 2003; Kassin & Kiechel, 1996; Nash & Wade, 2009).

Complicating matters, the impulsivity and inhibitory control issues of FASD increase the risk of criminal justice involvement (Rasmussen, 2005). Although the actual prevalence of FASD in offenders is unknown (Burd, Selfridge, Klug, & Bakko, 2004), one study estimated the frequency of individuals with FASD in one federal correctional facility to be as high as 10% (MacPherson & Chudley, 2007). In another study of criminal justice-involved adolescents undergoing mandated psychiatric or psychological assessments, the rate of FASD was 23.3% (Fast, Conry, & Loock, 1999). The accuracy of these estimates is hindered by the fact that individuals with FASD often do not have low IQ or physical symptoms, highlighting why many refer to FASD as an "invisible disability" (Olson, Oti, Gelo, & Beck, 2009). To prevent FASD from remaining unidentified and leading to severe legal consequences, mental health and criminal justice professionals must receive advanced training in identifying and working with offenders with FASD (Sanders & Buck, 2010).

The presence of FASD correlates with poor executive function, which is a key factor in higher rates of confabulation. However, a direct examination of the link between FASD and confabulation has yet to be confirmed though empirical studies More research is needed to establish this connection.

KORSAKOFF'S SYNDROME

Korsakoff's syndrome is a neuropsychiatric condition characterized by severe amnesia in the absence of dementia (Krabbendam et al., 2000). In most cases, chronic alcohol abuse compounded with malnutrition results in lesions of the diencephalon, leading to problems with executive functioning and memory (Van Oort & Kessels, 2009). Perhaps as a function of these memory impairments, patients suffering from Korsakoff's syndrome often exhibit severe confabulatory behavior (Kessels et al., 2008). Research indicates that a high percentage of patients exhibit spontaneous confabulation due to source-memory impairments caused by temporal confusion (Kessels et al., 2008; Van Oort & Kessels, 2009). Patients with Korsakoff's syndrome often create new, false memories to fill in amnesic gaps. As such, care providers and professionals should be aware of the high incidence of confabulation when working with patients with Korsakoff's syndrome.

ALZHEIMER'S DISEASE

Alzheimer's disease impairs memory and increases the likelihood of confabulation (Barba, Nedjam, & Dubois, 1999). In fact, affected individuals with advanced forms of the disorder are often unaware that they even have the disorder (Weinstein, Friedland, & Wagner, 1994). In one study conducted by Attali and colleagues (2009), Alzheimer's patients were presented with different fairy tales and then asked to recall their content. These stories were similar versions of classic fairy tales. The typical plot was modified for some patients and not modified for other patients. Alzheimer's patients produced significantly more confabulations in the recall of modified fairy tales compared to non-modified stories. This recall points to a greater preservation of over-learned and well-known information (Attali, De Anna, Dubois, & Dalla Barba, 2009), and could mean that gaps in memory are filled with experiences or knowledge from remote memory storage. In a review of the literature, Kopelman (2010) notes that when these confabulating patients were asked what activities they had planned for the day, their response often included well-established memories from their distant past (Kopelman, 2010), which also suggests a tendency to refer to over-learned information from the past, indicating temporal malfunctioning. In contrast, other research in Alzheimer's patients suggests that confabulation may result from the disruption of the brain's encoding processes rather than the retrieval of memories (Attali et al., 2009). In particular, research participants (healthy controls and individuals with Alzheimer's) were more likely to confabulate on a fairy tale when their attention was divided, indicating a more shallow level of encoding. In light of these findings, the severity of cognitive decline in individuals with Alzheimer's is positively correlated with the frequency of confabulatory behavior (Tallberg & Almkvist, 2001).

TRAUMATIC BRAIN INJURY (TBI)

Although confabulation is a common symptom of many neurocognitive and neuropsychiatric disorders and phenomena, it can also stem from external factors such as traumatic brain injury (TBI). This is an alteration of brain function and pathology caused by an external, physical force coming into contact with the skull and brain in the form of a strike, blow, or percussive blast (Brain Injury Association of America, 2015; Centers for Disease Control, 2015; Troncoso & Pletnikova, 2010). TBI is very common among criminal offenders, with prevalence estimates ranging from 25% to 87% of incarcerated individuals (Wood & Agharkar, 2015). Similarly, a recent study of 384 juveniles that were newly admitted into the New York City jail system found that approximately 50% of these youth had at least one incident of TBI (Kaba, Diamond, Haque, MacDonald, & Venters, 2014). Not only is TBI positively associated with behavioral problems in custodial settings like prison (Kaba et al., 2014), but damage to certain regions of the brain can also lead to the presentation of confabulation. Specifically, research has found that any blunt trauma causing damage to the prefrontal cortex may trigger confabulatory behaviors (Brown et al., 2014). However, for suspects with strong motives to obscure the truth, disentangling confabulation from purposeful deception (i.e., lying or malingering) is not easy or straightforward. Because of the elusiveness in diagnosing confabulation, it may be helpful to systematically screen and test for TBI. When TBI is present, careful screening for confabulation is warranted. Such an approach has the potential to combat a general lack of knowledge or awareness in justice-related professionals regarding confabulation. The importance of these efforts are emphasized by the fact that not correctly identifying the presence of confabulation negatively impacts all subsequent steps of the criminal justice and legal processes, and may ultimately lead to false confessions and inappropriate court rulings (Brown et al., 2014)

SCHIZOPHRENIA

Confabulation has also been witnessed in patients with schizophrenia, regardless of their level of intelligence (Nathaniel-James & Frith, 1996). Relative to those without schizophrenia, individuals suffering from schizophrenia show significant increases in intrusion errors, which are typical for confabulation (Kopelman, 2010; Lorente-Rovira et al., 2010). Further, preoccupations related to an individual's delusional beliefs and content, which are often bizarre or implausible in reality, have also been linked to confabulation (Kopelman, 2010). Additionally, some authors have found that patients with schizophrenia are unable to differentiate plausible mistakes from implausible ones. As a result, these patients have difficulty identifying and correcting their errors (Kopelman, 2010). Interestingly, Morias and colleagues (2004) have hypothesized that confabulation in those with schizophrenia may be more of a function of verbal comprehension difficulties than memory impairment.

One core sign of schizophrenia is delusion, which some researchers argue, stems from a shared deficit with confabulation (Asp & Tranel, 2013; Turner & Coltheart). The DSM-5 (American Psychiatric Association, 2013) outlines delusions as a false belief that is strongly held and exceptionally resistant to contrary evidence. Such a delusion is likely to persist, regardless of the strength of contrary evidence. In contrast, delusional memories consist of a true memory that becomes subject to a deluded interpretation or arises as a false memory due to psychosis (Kopelman, 1997). Two types of delusional memories have been identified. The first occurs when new and special significance is attributed to an otherwise common event that took place in the past. For example, a patient might believe that he or she is of royal descent because he or she recalled using a fork with a crown on it as a child. The second type of delusional memory involves describing memories of events and experiences that are impossible (McKenna, Lorente-Rovira, & Berrios, 2009). Examples include giving birth to thousands of children or recalling the presence of alien life forms at one's own birth. Delusional memories can be differentiated from confabulation because confabulations can occur independently from any existing dysfunction (Kopelman, 1999).

ABUSE, TRAUMA, AND THE RECOVERY OF MEMORIES

Psychological trauma has been shown to affect memory and cause a broad range of memory impairments, including amnesia, dissociation, and confabulation (Davies et al., 1998). For example, Kopelman (2010) identified difficulties in the accurate retrieval of childhood sexual abuse memories, particularly for events that occurred during early childhood. Such fragments of memories are likely to be inaccurate or distorted due to difficulties with locating these memories in a temporal or other spatial context (Kopelman, 2010). Further, children are particularly prone to suggestion and confabulation (Brainerd, Reyna, & Ceci, 2008; Ceci, Papierno, & Kulkofsky, 2007; Lindsay & Read, 1994). As such, the integrity of childhood trauma memories faces several other serious challenges (Morgan et al., 2004).

The methods by which memories of childhood trauma are "recovered" may encourage confabulation. Research indicates that therapists sometimes suggest to patients that they experienced some type of trauma as a child. In some cases, the therapist may ask the patient to review old childhood photographs to stimulate forgotten memories or even ask the patient to imagine if there are any traumas that they may have experienced during childhood (Lindsay & Read, 1994; Loftus, 1993). An even more extreme technique previously used for "recovering" memories was hypnotizing patients before providing the suggestion or imagination instruction of childhood trauma (Lindsay & Read, 1994). Because hypnosis puts patients in an extremely suggestible state, it can amplify the conditions that encourage confabulation during the memory recovery process (Kirsch & Braffman, 2001). Although these techniques are performed with good intentions, these conditions can promote confabulation in laboratory studies (Hyman & Pentland, 1996; Lindsay, Hagen, Read, Wade, & Garry, 2004; Loftus, 1993; Mazzoni & Memon, 2003). In fact, recent research has even noted that the experience of being in a therapy session was the most significant discrepancy between corroborated and uncorroborated reports of child sexual abuse remembered later in life (Geraerts et al., 2007).

Not all people are equally likely to confabulate when prompted to recover memories. Independent factors such as high suggestibility, a predisposition for dissociative experiences, and attachment style have been linked to an increased likelihood of confabulation (Heaps & Nash, 1999; Hyman & Billings, 1998). According to research on attachment theory, individuals with an avoidant attachment style tend to ignore or avoid painful emotional information (Bowlby, 1980; Edelstein, 2006; Edelstein & Shaver, 2004; Fraley, Garner, & Shaver, 2000). An avoidant attachment style is typically characterized by the lack of an intimate or supportive connection with one's partner or caregiver, which detracts from one's emotional and social development (Ainsworth, 1978). Further, people with an avoidant attachment style have less accurate memories about stressful or traumatic events, which may be due to their limited processing of distressing information as a way to avoid any need for attachment (Edelstein et al., 2005). Further, children who have avoidant parents also tend to have worse memories for painful experiences. This could be due to the fact that avoidant parents are not as responsive to the child's experiences (Alexander et al., 2002; Edelstein et al., 2004; Goodman, Quas, Batterman-Faunce, Riddlesberger, & Kuhn, 1997). These poorer levels of memory could potentially increase the likelihood of confabulation, since information is provided to fill in the gaps.

It should be noted that not all recovered memories are the result of confabulation (Hyman & Billings, 1998). Many people do experience extreme trauma as children and may not remember or fully understand it until they are adults (e.g., Williams, 1994). However, the conditions which bring about the recovery of such memories are critical to their accuracy. Confabulated childhood experiences can severely impact the lives of the patient and their families, depending on how the information contained in the memories is managed. Further, confabulated "memories" of childhood abuse can cast doubt on the real experiences of others who actually experienced childhood traumas (Lindsay & Read, 1994; Loftus, 1993). As such, mental health professionals must be careful when exploring the possibility of abuse during childhood with their patients.

TESTIMONY: CONFABULATION AND RELIABILITY

Awareness about confabulation must be increased in society as a whole. This includes educating the public, particularly those who work in mental health and criminal justice settings, about the terminology and etiology of confabulation. Once that foundation has been established, clear, easily understood examples of confabulation can be employed to make this phenomenon appear meaningful and vivid. These are critical steps to increasing the ability to recognize confabulation and how it relates to effective and reliable communication in a variety of settings.

Improved recognition and understanding of confabulation by mental health and legal professionals is necessary to limit the potential impact of false confessions or inaccurate testimony on criminal justice outcomes. Suspects suffering from neuropsychological impairments are at a profound cognitive disadvantage in the judicial process. These individuals with neuropsychological impairments are especially vulnerable to suggestion when interviewed or questioned by police. Further, an individual's impaired understanding of his/her legal rights and their increased susceptibility to acquiescence, suggestibility, and compliance with authority can lead to confabulation (Clare & Gudjonsson, 2010). As such, legal professionals must be familiar with the possibility that suspects with neuropsychological deficits could create new memories and confess to acts that they did not commit. Effort should be put forth to identify individuals with obvious deficits before they are allowed to disclose pertinent data to the investigation. The occurrence of confabulation can be greatly reduced if comprehensive medical and psychiatric assessments evaluate the individual's ability to accurately and honestly testify (Fast & Conry, 2006). Thus, one strategy for minimizing the impact of confabulation in the legal system is to identify *who* is likely to confabulate, so that a cautious approach is used when interpreting testimony from populations who are known or suspected to confabulate.

In addition to identifying those who might be at a greater risk of confabulating, it is imperative to consider the situations and factors that lead non-clinical populations to exhibit such behavior. Social motivational factors and interview dynamics have proven to be relevant to the development of false memories as well (Zaragosa, Payment, Ackil, Drivdahl, & Beck, 2001). For example, suggestive questioning is highly unreliable and can result in false testimony (Pezdek et al., 2009), especially since temporal confusion tends to provoke unchecked responses to external cues (Kopelman, 2010). Other studies have documented circumstances in which participants confabulated false confessions due to high suggestibility, long interview duration, amnesia-related circumstances, lack of confidence in their own memories, or a general absence of genuine memories (Kopelman, 2010). In particular, Henkel and Coffman (2004) identified interrogation techniques that lead to false memories and confabulation. These include having suspects imagine what might have happened, hearing details of reports that are similar to the crime, repeatedly being accused while also having their statements discounted, being told that the evidence connects them to the crime scene, and using techniques to increase stress and discomfort. Henkel and Coffman (2004) add that the likelihood of false memories in therapy situations are increased by long delays between the occurrence of the event and the recall of the memory, the presence of authority figures who make suggestions that certain events occurred, repetition of suggestions that are viewed as plausible, and encouragement of guessing or imagining what happened. To help limit the possibility of such circumstances, extensive attempts by researchers have been made to create relevant interviewing technique recommendations that reduce false testimony, false recovered memories, and false confessions for clinicians and law enforcement officials (Henkel & Coffman, 2004; Lindsay & Read, 1994; Wakefield & Underwager, 1998; Wells, Small, Penrod, Malpass, Fulero, & Brimacombe, 1998; Wells et al., 2000).

Approaches that systematically test which characteristics and situations are most likely to produce confabulation are useful in a scientific context, (Bernstein & Loftus, 2009a). However, statistical approaches are less helpful in a legal context, because the practitioner can only draw probabilistic generalities from research findings, which people are notoriously poor at understanding (Tversky & Kahneman, 1974). For example, if a 39-year-old man with schizophrenia who was abused as a child is suggestively questioned about a crime that he witnessed, it is safe to conclude that his testimony is much more prone to confabulation than a non-disordered witness of the same event. Nonetheless, this man may possess many accurate memories despite his increased risk to confabulate, and it is possible that his testimony is entirely accurate. In this court case, the most important concern is whether a specific memory is confabulated. Therefore, the most beneficial approach in considering the possibility of confabulation is to identify differences between real and confabulated memories rather than factors that lead to confabulation (Bernstein & Loftus, 2009a). Ideally, this approach would allow practitioners to assess the veracity of a memory without having to evaluate the individual or the circumstances.

Perhaps the most intuitive difference between a real memory and a confabulated memory is a person's confidence in the accuracy of the memory. Indeed, laypeople believe confidence is a critical marker of memory accuracy (Lieppe & Eisenstadt, 2007; Simons & Chabris, 2011), and jurors place great importance on the level of confidence communicated by the witness when deciding whether or not to believe his or her testimony (Whitley & Greenberg, 1986). Although confidence is positively correlated with precision, and people who are more confident in their memories are less likely to confabulate (Brewer & Weber, 2008; Sporer, Penrod, Read, & Cutler, 1995), this relationship is not nearly strong enough to be indicative of memory accuracy. In fact, the association between confidence and accuracy is not as high as most might believe (Simons & Chabris, 2011). This correlation ranges from .12 to .41. This means that, at best, confidence explains less than 17% of the variation in accuracy (Sporer et al., 1995).

Another difference between real and confabulated memories can be found in their level of detail. Real memories tend to be more vivid and have greater sensory detail than false memories (Bernstein & Loftus, 2009a; Schooler, Gerhard, & Loftus, 1986; Suengas & Johnson, 1988). However, just as in the case of confidence, this relationship is not strong enough to be used as an indicator of memory accuracy. In particular, flashbulb memories are distinctive for their sensory detail and vividness, but are no more accurate than other memories (Talarico & Rubin, 2003). Both real and false memories have comparable levels of detail when rehearsed (Suengas & Johnson, 1988). Further, testimony is often rehearsed many times throughout the investigation and trial preparation process. As such, the level of detail in a memory may be a rather poor indicator of memory accuracy in a court setting.

Research has begun to investigate differences in patterns of brain activation between genuine and false memories (Chua, Rand-Giovannetti, Schacter, Albert, & Sperling, 2004). This study found that real memories tend to activate medial temporal lobe structures more strongly than false memories. However, this tendency is purely correlational and no more indicative of memory accuracy than confidence or vividness are. Interestingly, confidence activates the left dorsolateral prefrontal cortex, independent of accuracy. It is hoped that future research in this promising area will increase the ability of clinicians to differentiate between genuine and false memories by allowing for the identification of false memories held with high confidence.

CONCLUSION

Confabulation is of great concern in the criminal justice system where eyewitness testimony and confessions are often the most compelling evidence presented in a criminal court case. As discussed above, this is problematic because the human memory is fallible, particularly in the set of stressful circumstances that often characterize the legal process. As such, broader awareness of confabulation and its precipitating factors is imperative among mental health and criminal justice professionals. This includes the clinical conditions that increase the likelihood of spontaneous confabulation and the interview and interrogation techniques that lead to provoked confabulation. Advanced training and education are central in limiting the impact of confabulation on criminal court case outcomes. The importance of such efforts is emphasized by the potential consequences of false confessions and wrongful convictions.

REFERENCES

Ainsworth, M. D. S. (1978). The Bowlby-Ainsworth attachment theory. *Behavioral and brain sciences*, *1*(03), 436-438.

Alexander, K. W., Goodman, G. S., Schaaf, J. M., Edelstein, R. S., Quas, J. A., & Shaver, P. R. (2002). The role of attachment and cognitive inhibition in children's memory and suggestibility for a stressful event. *Journal of Experimental Child Psychology*, *83*, 262-290.

American Psychiatric Association. (2013). *DSM 5*. American Psychiatric Association.

Anastasi, J.S. (2006). Understanding confabulation: A multidisciplinary approach. *Applied Cognitive Psychology*, *20*, 275-278.

Asp, E.W., Manzel, K., Koestner, B., Denburg, N.L., Tranel, D. (2013). Benefit of the doubt: A new view of the role of the prefrontal cortex in executive functioning and decision making. *Froniters in Neuroscience*, *7*, 1-13.

Asp, E.W., & Tranel, D. (2013). False Tagging Theory: Toward a unitary account of prefrontal cortex function. In D.T. Stuss & R.T. Knight (Eds.), *Principles of Frontal Lobe Function* (2nd ed.), pp. 383-416. New York: Oxford University Press.

Assefi, S. L., & Garry, M. (2003). Absolut memory distortions: Alcohol placebos influence the misinformation effect. *Psychological Science*, *14*, 77-80.

Attali, E., De Anna, F., Dubois, B., & Dalla Barba, G. (2009). Confabulation in Alzheimer's disease: poor encoding and retrieval of over-learned information. *Brain, A Journal of Neurology*, *132*, 204-212.

Barba, G., Boissé, M., Bartolomeo, P., & Bachoud-Lévi, A. (1997). Confabulation following rupture of posterior communicating artery. *Cortex; A Journal Devoted To The Study Of The Nervous System and Behavior*, *33*, 563-570.

Barba, G. D., Nedjam, Z., & Dubois, B. (1999). Confabulation, executive functions, and source memory in Alzheimer's disease. *Cognitive Neuropsychology, 16,* 385-398.

Bernstein, D. M., & Loftus, E. F. (2009a). How to tell if a particular memory is true or false. *Perspectives on Psychological Science*, *4*, 370-374.

Bernstein, D. M., & Loftus, E. F. (2009b). The consequences of false memories for food preferences and choices. *Perspectives on Psychological Science*, *4*, 135-139.

Bowlby, J. (1980). *Attachment and loss: Vol. I. Attachment*. New York: Basic Books.

Brain Injury Association of America, National Brain Injury Information Center. (2015). Brain Injury Statistics: Traumatic Brain Injury. Retrieved from www.biausa.org

Brainerd, C. J., Reyna, V. F., & Ceci, S. J. (2008). Developmental reversals in false memory: A review of data and theory. *Psychological Bulletin*, *134*, 343-382.

Braun, K. A., Ellis, R., & Loftus, E. F. (2002). Make my memory: How advertising can change our memories of the past. *Psychology and Marketing*, *19*, 1-23.

Brewer, N., & Weber, N. (2008). Eyewitness confidence and latency: Indices of memory processes not just markers of accuracy. *Applied Cognitive Psychology*, *22*, 827-840.

Brown, J., Long-McGie, J., Oberoi, P., Wartnik, A., Wresh, J., Weinkauf, E., & Falconer, G. (2014). Confabulation: Connections between brain damage, memory, and testimony. *The Journal of Law Enforcement, 3*(5), 1-11.

Brown, R., & Kulik, J. (1977) Flashbulb memories. *Cognition, 5,* 73-99.

Burd, L., Selfridge, R., Klug, M., & Bakko, S. (2004). Fetal alcohol syndrome in the United States corrections system. *Addiction Biology, 9*(2), 169-176.

Burgess, P. W., & Shallice, T. (1996). Confabulation and the control of recollection. *Memory, 4,* 359-412.

Ceci, S. J., Papierno, P. B., & Kulkofsky, S. (2007). Representational constraints on children's suggestibility. *Psychological Science, 18,* 503-509.

Centers for Disease Control and Prevention (2015). Traumatic brain injury in the United States: Fact sheet. Online. Retrieved from www.cdc.gov/traumaticbraininjury/get_the_facts.html

Chua, E. F., Rand-Giovannetti, E., Schacter, D. L., Albert, M. S., & Sperling, R. A. (2004). Dissociating confidence and accuracy: Magnetic resonance imaging shows origins of the subjective memory experience. *Journal of Cognitive Neuroscience, 16,* 1131-1142.

Ciaramelli, E., & Ghetti, S. (2007). What are confabulators' memories made of? A study of subjective and objective measures of recollection in confabulation. *Neuropsychologia, 45,* 1489-1500.

Ciaramelli, E., & Spaniol, J. (2009). Ventromedial Prefrontal Damage and Memory for Context: Perceptual Versus Semantic Features. *Neuropsychology, 23,* 649-657.

Clare, I.C.H., & Gudjonsson, G.H. (2010). The Vulnerability of Suspects with Intellectual Disabilities During Police Interviews: A Review and Experimental Study of Decision-Making. *Mental Handicap, 8,* 110-128.

Clifford, B. R., & Hollin, C. R. (1981). Effects of the type of incident and the number of perpetrators on eyewitness memory. *Journal of Applied Psychology, 66,* 364-370.

Colorado v. Connelly, 479 U.S. 157 (1986).

Coltheart, M., & Turner, M. (2009). *Confabulation and Delusion.* In Hirstein, W (Ed.), Confabulation: Views from neuroscience, psychiatry, psychology, and philosophy (pp. 173-187). New York: Oxford University Press.

Curci, A., & Luminet, O. (2006). Follow-up of a cross-national comparison on flashbulb and event memory for the September 11th attacks. *Memory, 14,* 329-344.

Dalla Barba, G. (1993). Confabulation: Knowledge and recollective experience. *Cognitive Neuropsychology, 10,* 1-20.

Davies, G., Morton, J., Mollon, P., & Robertson, N. (1998). Recovered memory in theory and practice. *Psychology, Public Policy, and Law, 4,* 1079-1090.

DeLuca, J. (2009). *Confabulation in anterior communicating artery syndrome.* In Hirstein, W. (Ed)., Confabulation: Views from neuroscience, psychiatry, psychology, and philosophy (pp. 13-32). New York: Oxford Publishing Company.

DeLuca, J. & Diamond, B.J. (1995). Aneurysm of the anterior communicating artery: A review of neuroanatomical and neuropsychological sequelae. *Journal of Clinical and Experimental Neuropsychology, 17,* 100-121.

Edelstein, R. S. (2006). Attachment and emotional memory: Investigating the source and extent of avoidant memory impairments. *Emotion, 6,* 340-345.

Edelstein, R. S., Alexander, K. W., Shaver, P. R., Schaaf, J. M., Quas, J. A., Lovas, G. S., & Goodman, G. S. (2004). Adult attachment style and parental responsiveness during a stressful event. *Attachment and Human Development, 6,* 31-52.

Edelstein, R. S., Ghetti, S., Quas, J. A., Goodman, G. S. Alexander, K. W., Redlich, A. D., & Cordon, I. M. (2005). Individual differences in emotional memory: Adult attachment and long-term memory for child sexual abuse. *Personality and Social Psychology Bulletin, 31*, 1537-1548.

Edelstein, R. S., & Shaver, P. R. (2004). Avoidant attachment: Exploration of an oxymoron. In D. Mashek & A. Aron (Eds.), *Handbook of closeness and intimacy* (pp. 397-412). Mahwah, NJ: Lawrence Erlbaum.

Edwards, W. J., & Greenspan, S. (2010). Adaptive Behavior Alcohol Spectrum and Fetal Disorders. *The Journal of Psychiatry & Law, 38*(4), 419-447.

Fast, D., & Conry, J. (2006). The Challenge of Fetal Alcohol Syndrome in the Criminal Legal System. *Addiction Biology, 9*, 161-166.

Fast, D. K., Conry, J., & Loock, C. A. (1999). Identifying fetal alcohol syndrome among youth in the criminal justice system. *Journal of Developmental & Behavioral Pediatrics, 20*(5), 370-372.

Finkenauer, C., Luminet, O., Gisle, L., El-Ahmadi, A., van der Linden, M., & Philippot, P. (1998). Flashbulb memories and the underlying mechanisms of their formation: Toward an emotional-integrative model. *Memory and Cognition, 26*, 516-531.

Fischer, R. S., Alexander, M. P., D'esposito, M., & Otto, R. (1995). Neuropsychological and neuroanatomical correlates of confabulation. *Journal of Clinical and Experimental Neuropsychology, 17*(1), 20-28.

Forgas, J. P., Goldenberg, L., Unkelbach, C. (2009). Can bad weather improve your memory? An unobtrusive field study of natural mood effects on real-life memory. *Journal of Experimental Social Psychology, 45*, 254-257.

Forgas, J. P., Laham, S. M., & Vargas, P. T. (2005). Mood effects on eyewitness memory: Affective influences on susceptibility to misinformation. *Journal of Experimental Social Psychology, 41*, 574-588.

Fotopoulou, A. (2010). The affective neuropsychology of confabulation and delusion. *Cognitive Neuropsychiatry, 15*, 38-63.

Fotopoulou, A., Conway. M. A., Solms, M., Tyrer, S., & Kopelman, M. (2008). Self-serving confabulation in prose recall. *Neuropsychologia, 46*, 1429-1441.

Fraley, R. C., Garner, J. P., & Shaver, P. R. (2000). Adult attachment and the defensive regulation of attention and memory: Examining the role of preemptive and postemptive defensive processes. *Journal of Personality and Social Psychology, 79*, 816-826.

French, L, Garry, M., & Loftus, E. (2009). False memories: A kind of confabulation in non-clinical subjects. In Hirstein, W (Ed.), *Confabulation: Views from neuroscience, psychiatry, psychology, and philosophy* (pp. 33-66). New York: Oxford University Press.

Fryer, S.L., Tapert, S.F., Mattson, S.N., Paulus, M.P., Spadoni, A.D., & Riley, E.P. (2007). Prenatal Alcohol Exposure Affects Frontal-Striatal BOLD Response During Inhibitory Control. *Alcoholism: Clinical and Experimental Research, 31*, 1415-1424.

Gallagher, S. (2003). Self-narrative in schizophrenia. *The self in neuroscience and psychiatry*, 336-357.

Garrett, B. (2008). Judging Innocence. *Columbia Law Review, 1*, 55-142.

Geraerts, E., Schooler, J. Merckelbach, H., Jelicic, M., Hauer, B., & Ambadar, Z. (2007). The reality of recovered memories: Corroborating continuous and discontinuous memories of childhood sexual abuse. *Psychological Science, 18(7)*, 564-568.

Gibbard, W. B., Wass, P., & Clarke, M. E. (2003). The neuropsychological implications of prenatal alcohol exposure. *The Canadian child and adolescent psychiatry review, 12*, 72.

Gilboa, A., & Verfaellie, M. (2010). Telling it like it isn't: The cognitive neuroscience of confabulation. *Journal of the International Neuropsychological Society, 16*(2), 961-966.

Goel, V., & Dolan, R. J. (2003). Explaining modulation of reasoning by belief. *Cognition*, *87*, 11-22.

Goff, L. M., & Roediger, H. L. (1998). Imagination inflation for action events: Repeated imaginings lead to illusory recollections. *Memory and Cognition*, *26*, 20-33.

Goodman, G. S., Quas, J. A., Batterman-Faunce, J. M., Riddlesberger, M. M., & Kuhn, J. (1997). Children's reactions to and memory for a stressful event: Influences of age, anatomical dolls, knowledge, and parental attachment. *Applied Developmental Science*, *1*, 54-75.

Gorman, W. F. (1982). Defining malingering. *Journal of Forensic Sciences*, *27*(2), 401-407.

Gudjonsson, G. H. (1992). *The psychology of interrogations, confessions, and testimony*. Chichester: John Wiley.

Gudjonsson, G. H. (2003). *The science of interrogations and confessions: A handbook*. Chichester, UK: Wiley.

Gudjonsson, G. H., & Clare, I. C. (1995). The relationship between confabulation and intellectual ability, memory, interrogative suggestibility and acquiescence. *Personality and Individual Differences*, *19*(3), 333-338.

Gudjonsson, G. H., Sigurdsson, J. F., Sigfusdottir, I. D., & Young, S. (2012). False confessions to police and their relationship with conduct disorder, ADHD, and life adversity. *Personality and Individual Differences*, *52*, 696-701.

Guerri, C., Bazinet, A., & Riley, E.P. (2009). Fetal Alcohol Spectrum Disorders and Alterations in Brain and Behavior. *Alcohol & Alcoholism*, *44*, 108-114.

Heaps, C., & Nash, M. (1999). Individual differences in imagination inflation. *Psychonomic Bulletin and Review*, *6*, 313-318.

Henkel, L. A. (2011). Photograph-induced memory errors: When photographs make people claim they have done things they have not. *Applied Cognitive Psychology*, *25*, 78-86.

Henkel, L. A., & Coffman, K. J. (2004). Memory distortions in coerced false confessions: A source monitoring framework analysis. *Applied Cognitive Psychology*, *18*, 567-588.

Henkel, L. A., Franklin, N., & Johnson, M. K. (2000). Cross-modal source monitoring confusions between perceived and imagined events. *Journal of Experimental Psychology: Learning, Memory, and Cognition*, *26*, 321-335.

Hirstein, W. (2009). Introduction: What is confabulation? In Hirstein, W (Ed.), *Confabulation: Views from neuroscience, psychiatry, psychology, and philosophy* (pp. 1-14). New York: Oxford University Press.

Horselenberg, R., Merckelbach, H., & Josephs, S. (2003). Individual differences and false confessions: A conceptual replication of Kassin and Kiechel (1996). *Psychology, Crime and law*, *9*, 1-8.

Huntley, D., Brown, J., & Wiley, C. R. (2016). Confabulation and Mental Health: A Beginner's Guide. *Behavioral Health*, *4*(2), 1-9.

Hyman, I. E., & Billings, F. J. (1998). Individual differences and the creation of false childhood memories. *Memory*, *6*, 1-20.

Hyman, I. E., & Pentland, J. (1996). The role of mental imagery in the creation of false childhood memories. *Journal of memory and language*, *35*, 101-117.

Ihlebaek, C., Love, T., Eilertsen, D. E., & Magnussen, S. (2003). Memory for a staged criminal event witnessed live and on video. *Memory*, *11*, 319-327.

Imwinkelried, E. J. (1989). Importance of the Memory Factor in Analyzing the Reliability of Hearsay Testimony: A Lesson Slowly Learnt—And Quickly Forgotten, The. *Fla. L. Rev.*, *41*, 215.

Jirikowic, T., Kartin, D., & Olson, H. C. (2008). Children with fetal alcohol spectrum disorders: a descriptive profile of adaptive function. *Canadian Journal of Occupational Therapy*, *75*, 238-248.

Johnson, M. K., Hayes, S. M., D'Esposito, M., & Raye, C. (2000). Confabulation. In F. Boller & J. Grafman (Eds.), *Handbook of neuropsychology: Memory and its disorders* (2nd ed., Vol. 2, pp. 383-407). Amsterdam, The Netherlands: Elsevier Science.

Johnson, M. K., O'Connor, M., & Cantor, J. (1997). Confabulation, memory deficits, and frontal dysfunction. *Brain and cognition, 34*(2), 189-206.

Kaba, F., Diamond, P., Haque, A., MacDonald, R., & Venters, H. (2014). Traumatic Brain Injury Among Newly Admitted Adolescents in the New York City Jail System. *Journal of Adolescent Health, 54*(5), 615-617.

Kassin, S. M. (2005). On the psychology of confessions: Does innocence put innocents at risk? *American Psychologist, 60*, 215-228.

Kassin, S. M., Bogart, D., & Kerner, J. (2012). Confessions That Corrupt Evidence From the DNA Exoneration Case Files. *Psychological science, 23*, 41-45.

Kassin, S. M., & Kiechel, K. L. (1996). The social psychology of false confessions: Compliance, Internalization, and Confabulation. *American Psychological Society, 7*, 125-128.

Kassin, S. M., & Neumann, K. (1997). On the power of confession evidence: An experimental test of the fundamental difference hypothesis. *Law and Human Behavior, 21*(5), 469.

Kern, R. S., Van Gorp, W. G., Cummings, J. L., Brown, W. S., & Osato, S. S. (1992). Confabulation in Alzheimer's disease. *Brain and cognition, 19*, 172-182.

Kessels R., Kortrijk, H., Wester, A., & Nys, G. (2008). Confabulation behavior and false memories in Korsakoff's syndrome: Role of source memory and executive functioning. *Psychiatry and Clinical Neurosciences, 62*, 220-225.

Kirsch, I., & Braffman, W. (2001). Imaginative suggestibility and hypnotizability. *Current Directions in Psychological Science, 10*, 57-61.

Kopelman, M. D. (1987). Two types of confabulation. *Journal of Neurology, Neurosurgery & Psychiatry, 50*, 1482-1487.

Kopelman, M. D. (1997). Anomalies of autobiographical memory: Retrograde amnesia, confabulation, delusional memory, psychogenic amnesia, and false memories. In J. D. Read & D. S. Lindsay (Eds.), *Recollections of trauma: Scientific research and clinical Practice.* New York and London: Plenum Press. 273-303.

Kopelman, M. D. (1999). Varieties of false memory. *Cognitive neuropsychology, 16*, 197-214.

Kopelman, M. D. (2010). Varieties of confabulation and delusion. *Cognitive Neuropsychiatry, 15*, 14-37.

Krabbendam, L., Visser, P. J., Derix, M. M., Verhey, F., Hofman, P., Verhoeven, W., & Jolles, J. (2000). Normal cognitive performance in patients with chronic alcoholism in contrast to patients with Korsakoff's syndrome. *The Journal of Neuropsychiatry and Clinical Neurosciences, 12*, 44-50.

LaDue, R. A., Streissguth, A. P., & Randels, S. P. (1992). *Clinical considerations pertaining to adolescents and adults with fetal alcohol syndrome. Perinatal Substance Abuse: Research Findings and Clinical Implications.* (pp. 104-131). Baltimore: John Hopkins University Press.

Lieppe, M. R., & Eisenstadt, D. (2007). Eyewitness confidence and the confidence-accuracy relationship in memory for people. In R. C. L. Lindsay, D. F. Ross, J. D. Read, & M. P. Toglia (Eds.), *The Handbook of Eyewitness Psychology: Vol 2, Memory for People.* New Jersey: Lawrence Erlbaum Associates, Inc. 377-425.

Lindsay, D. S., Hagen, L., Read, J. D., Wade, K. A., & Garry, M. (2004). True photographs and false memories. *Psychological Science, 15*, 149-154.

Lindsay, D. S., & Read, J. D. (1994). Psychotherapy and memories of childhood sexual abuse: A cognitive perspective. *Applied Cognitive Psychology, 8,* 281-338.

Loftus, E. F. (1993). The reality of repressed memories. *American Psychologist, 48,* 518-537.

Loftus, E. F. (2003). Make-believe memories. *American Psychologist, 58,* 867-873.

Loftus, E. F., & Hoffman, H. G. (1989). Misinformation and memory: The creation of memory. *Journal of Experimental Psychology: General, 118,* 100-104.

Loftus, E. F., & Palmer, J. C. (1974). Reconstruction of automobile destruction: An example of the interaction between language and memory. *Journal of Verbal Learning and Verbal Behavior, 13,* 585-589.

Loftus, E. F., & Pickrell, J. Q. (1995). The formation of false memories. *Psychiatric Annals, 25,* 720-725.

Loftus, E. F., & Zanni, G. (1975). Eyewitness testimony: The influence of the wording of a question. *Bulletin of the Psychonomic Society, 5,* 86-88.

LoPiccolo, C. J., Goodkin, K., & Baldewicz, T. T. (1999). Current issues in the diagnosis and management of malingering. *Annals of Medicine, 31,* 166-174.

Lorente-Rovira, E., Santos-Gomez, J.L., Moro, M., Villagran, J. M., & McKenna, P. J. (2010). Confabulation in schizophrenia: a neuropsychological study. *Journal of the International Neuropsychological Society, 16*(6), 1018-1026.

Macleod, E., Gross, J., & Hayne, H. (2016). Drawing conclusions: The effect of instructions on children's confabulation and fantasy errors. *Memory, 24*(1), 21-31.

MacPherson, P., & A.E. Chudley. (2007, March). Fetal Alcohol Spectrum Disorder (FASD): Screening and estimating incidence in an adult correctional population. In *2nd International Conference on Fetal Alcohol Spectrum Disorder: Research, Policy, and Practice Around the World.* Victoria, BC.

Mattson, S.N., Crocker, N., Nguyen, T.T. (2011). Fetal Alcohol Spectrum Disorders: Neuropsychological and Behavioral Features. *Neuropsychology Review, 21,* 81-101.

Mattson, S.N., Gramling, L., & Delis, D. (1996). Global–Local Processing in Children Prenatally Exposed to Alcohol. *Child Neuropsychology, 2,* 165-175.

Mazzoni, G. & Memon, A. (2003). Imagination can create false autobiographical memories. *Psychological Science, 14,* 186-188.

McKenna, P.J., Lorente-Rovira, E., & Berrios, G.E. (2009). Confabulation as a psychiatric symptoms. In Hirstein, W (Ed.), *Confabulation: Views from neuroscience, psychiatry, psychology, and philosophy* (pp. 159-172). New York: Oxford University Press.

Morais, J., Frith, C., & Dab, S. (2004). Comprehension, encoding, and monitoring in the production of confabulation in memory: A study with schizophrenic patients. *Cognitive neuropsychiatry, 9*(3), 153-182.

Morgan III, C. A., Hazlett, G., Doran, A., Garrett, S., Hoyt, G., Thomas, P., Baranoski, M., & Southwick, S. M. (2004). Accuracy of eyewitness memory for persons encountered during exposure to highly intense stress. *International Journal of Law and Psychiatry, 27,* 265-279.

Moscovitch, M. (1989). *Confabulation and the frontal system: Strategic versus associative retrieval in neuropsychological theories of memory.* In H. R. Roediger & F. I. Craik (Eds.), Varieties of memory and consciousness: Essays in the honour of Endel Tulving.Hillsdale: Lawrence Erlbaum Associates.

Moscovitch, M. (1995). Confabulation. In D. L. Schacter (Ed.), *Memory distortions.* Cambridge: Harvard University Press.

Moscovitch, M., & Melo, B. (1997). Strategic retrieval and the frontal lobes: Evidence from confabulation and amnesia. *Neuropsychologia, 35,* 1017-1034.

Nahum, L., Ptak, R., Leemann, B., & Schnider, A. (2009). Disorientation, Confabulation, and Extinction Capacity: Clues On How the Brain Creates Reality. *Biological Psychiatry, 65,* 966-972.

Nash, R. A., & Wade, K. A. (2009). Innocent but proven guilty: Eliciting internalized false confessions using doctored video evidence. *Applied Cognitive Psychology, 23*, 624-637.

Nathaniel-James, D. A., & Frith, C. D. (1996). Confabulation in schizophrenia: Evidence of a new form. *Psychological Medicine, 26*, 391-400.

Nedjam, Z., Devouche, E., & DallaBarba, G. (2004). Confabulation, But Not Executive Dysfunction Discriminate AD From Frontotemporal Dementia. *European Journal of Neurology, 11*, 728-733.

Olson, H.C., Oti, R., Gelo, J., & Beck, S. (2009). Family matters: Fetal Alcohol Spectrum Disorders and the family. *Developmental Disabilities Research Reviews, 15*(3), 235-249.

Ouyang, M., & Thomas, S. A. (2005). A requirement for memory retrieval during and after long-term extinction learning. *Proceedings of the National Academy of Sciences of the United States of America, 102*(26), 9347-9352.

Parwatikar, S. D., Holcomb, W. R., & Menninger, K. A. (1985). The detection of malingered amnesia in accused murderers. *Journal of the American Academy of Psychiatry and the Law Online, 13*(1), 97-103.

Pei, J. R., Rinaldi, C. M., Rasmussen, C., Massey, V., & Massey, D. (2008). Memory patterns of acquisition and retention of verbal and nonverbal information in children with fetal alcohol spectrum disorders. *Canadian Journal of Clinical Pharmacology, 15*(1), e44-e56.

Pennebaker, J. W., & Harber, K. D. (1993). A social stage model of collective coping: The Loma Prieta earthquake and the Persian Gulf War. *Journal of Social Issues, 49*, 125-145.

Perske, R. (2011). Perske's List: False Confessions From 75 Persons With Intellectual Disability. *Intellectual and developmental disabilities, 49*(5), 365-373.

Petrenko, C. L., Tahir, N., Mahoney, E. C., & Chin, N. P. (2014). Prevention of secondary conditions in fetal alcohol spectrum disorders: identification of systems-level barriers. *Maternal and Child Health Journal, 18*(6), 1496-1505.

Pezdek, K., Lam, S.T., & Sperry, K. (2009). Forced Confabulation More Strongly Influences Event Memory If Suggestions Are Other-Generated Than Self-Generated. *Legal and Criminological Psychology, 14*, 241-252.

Rangmar, J., Hjern, A., Vinnerljung, B., Strömland, K., Aronson, M., & Fahlke, C. (2015). Psychosocial outcomes of Fetal Alcohol Syndrome in adulthood. *Pediatrics, 135*(1), 52-58.

Rasmussen, C. (2005). Executive functioning and working memory in fetal alcohol spectrum disorder. *Alcoholism: Clinical and Experimental Research, 29*(8), 1359-1367.

Rasmussen, C., & Bisanz, J. (2009). Executive functioning in children with Fetal Alcohol Spectrum Disorder: Profiles and age-related differences. *Child Neuropsychology, 15*(3), 201-215.

Sanders, J. L., & Buck, G. (2010). A long journey: Biological and non-biological parents' experiences raising children with FASD. *Journal of Population Therapeutics and Clinical Pharmacology, 17*, 308-322.

Schacter, D.L., Kagan, J. & Leichtman, M.D. (1995). True and false memories in children and adults: A cognitive neuroscience perspective. *Psychology, Public Policy, and the Law, 1*, 411-428.

Scheck, B., & Neufeld, P. (2015, April 17). *The Innocence Project.* Retrieved from http://www.innocenceproject.org

Schnider, A. (2003). Spontaneous confabulation and the adaptation of thought to ongoing reality. *Nature Reviews Neuroscience, 4*, 662-671.

Schnider, A. (2008). The Confabulating Mind: How the Brain Creates Reality. Oxford: Oxford University.

Schnider A., von Däniken C., & Gutbrod K. (1996). The mechanisms of spontaneous and provoked confabulations. *Brain, Journal of Neuropsychology, 19*, 1365-1375.

Schonfeld, A. M., Paley, B., Frankel, F., & O'Connor, M. J. (2006). Executive functioning predicts social skills following prenatal alcohol exposure. *Child Neuropsychology, 12*, 439-452.

Schooler, J. W., Gerhard, D., & Loftus, E. F. (1986). Qualities of the unreal. *Journal of Experimental Psychology: Learning, Memory, and Cognition, 12*, 171-181.

Sharrock, R. (1988). Eyewitness testimony: Some implications for clinical interviewing and forensic psychology. In F. N. Watts (Ed.). *New developments in clinical psychology* (Vol. 2, pp. 208-225). Chichester: John Wiley.

Shingaki, H., Park, P., Ueda, K., Murai, T., & Tsukiura, T. (2016). Disturbance of time orientation, attention, and verbal memory in amnesic patients with confabulation. *Journal of clinical and experimental neuropsychology, 38*(2), 171-182.

Simons, D. J., & Chabris, C. F. (2011). What people believe about how memory works: A representative survey of the U.S. population. *PLos ONE, 6*, e22757.

Skowronski, J. J., & Walker, W. R. (2004). How describing autobiographical events can affect autobiographical memories. *Social Cognition, 22*, 555-590.

Sporer, S. L., Penrod, S., Read, D., & Cutler, B. (1995). Choosing, confidence, and accuracy: A meta-analysis of the confidence-accuracy relation in eyewitness identification studies. *Psychological Bulletin, 118*, 315-327.

Suengas, A. G., & Johnson, M. K. (1988). Qualitative effects of rehearsal on memories for perceived and imagined complex events. *Journal of Experimental Psychology, 117*, 377-389.

Talarico, J. M. (2009). Freshman flashbulbs: Memories of unique and first-time events in starting college. *Memory, 17*, 256-265.

Talarico, J. M., & Rubin, D. C. (2003). Confidence, not consistency, characterizes flashbulb memories. *Psychological Science, 14*, 455-461.

Tallberg, I., & Almkvist, O. (2001). Confabulation and memory in patients with Alzheimer's Disease. *Journal of Clinical and Experimental Neuropsychology, 23*, 172-184.

Thiel, K. S., Baladerian, N. J., Boyce, K. R., Cantos, O. D., Davis, L. A., Kelly, K., ... & Stream, J. (2011). Fetal alcohol spectrum disorders and victimization: implications for families, educators, social services, law enforcement, and the judicial system. *The Journal of Psychiatry & Law, 39*(1), 121-157.

Troncoso, J.C. & Pletnikova, O. (2010). Traumatic brain injuries and dural hemorrhages. In J. C. Troncoso, A. Rubio, & D. R. Fowler (Authors), *Essential forensic neuropathology* (pp. 71-81). Baltimore, MD: Wolters Kluwer Health/Lippincott Williams & Wilkins.

Turner, M. S., Cipolotti, L., Yousry, T. A., & Shallice, T. (2008). Confabulation: Damage to a specific inferior medial prefrontal system. *Cortex, 44*, 637-648.

Turner, M., & Coltheart, M. (2010). Confabulation and Delusion: A Common Monitoring Framework. *Cognitive Neuropsychiatry, 15*, 346-376.

Tversky, A., & Kahneman, D. (1973). Availability: A heuristic for judging frequency and probability. *Cognitive psychology, 5*(2), 207-232.

Tversky, A., & Kahneman, D. (1974). Judgment under uncertainty: Heuristics and biases. *Science, 185*, 1124-1131.

Van Oort, R., & Kessels, R. (2009). Executive dysfunction in Korsakoff's 's syndrome: Time to revise the DSM criteria for alcohol-induced persisting amnestic disorder. *International Journal of Psychiatry in Clinical Practice, 13*, 78-81.

Wade, K. A., Garry, M., Read, J. D., & Lindsay, S. (2002). A picture is worth a thousand lies: Using false photographs to create false childhood memories. *Psychonomic Bulletin & Review, 9*, 597-603.

Wakefield, H., & Underwager, R. (1998). Coerced or nonvoluntary confessions. *Behavioral Sciences and the Law, 16*, 423-440.

Weinstein, E. A., Friedland, R. P., & Wagner, E. E. (1994). Denial/unawareness of impairment and symbolic behavior in Alzheimer's disease. *Cognitive and Behavioral Neurology, 7*, 176-184.

Wells, G. L., & Loftus, E. F. (Eds.). (1984). *Eyewitness testimony: Psychological Perspectives.* Cambridge University Press.

Wells, G. L., Malpass, R. S., Lindsay, R. C. L., Fisher, R. P., Turtle, J. W., & Fulero, S. M. (2000). From the lab to the police station: A successful application of eyewitness research. *American Psychologist, 55*, 581-598.

Wells, G., L., Small, M., Penrod, S., Malpass, R. S., Fulero, S. M., & Brimacombe, C. A. E. (1998). Eyewitness identification procedures: Recommendations for lineups and photospreads. *Law and Human Behavior, 22*, 603-647.

Welsh, M.C., & Pennington, B.F. (1988). Assessing Frontal Lobe Functioning in Children: Views from Developmental Psychology. *Developmental Neuropsychology, 4*, 199-230.

Wheeler, S. M., Stevens, S. A., Sheard, E. D., & Rovet, J. F. (2012). Facial memory deficits in children with fetal alcohol spectrum disorders. *Child Neuropsychology, 18*(4), 339-346.

Whitley, B. E., & Greenberg, M. S. (1986). The role of eyewitness confidence in juror perceptions of credibility. *Journal of Applied Social Psychology, 16*, 387-409.

Williams, L. M. (1994). Recall of childhood trauma: A prospective study of women's memories of child sexual abuse. *Journal of Consulting and Clinical Psychology, 62*, 1167-1176.

Wood, S. & Agharkar, B. (2015). Traumatic Brain Injury in Criminal Litigation. *UMKC Law Review, 84*(2), 411-422.

Xie, S., Libon, D., Wang, X., Massimo, L., Moore, P., Vesely, L. Khan, A., Chatterjee, A., Coslett, H.B., Hurtig, H.I., & Liang, T.W. (2010). Longitudinal patterns of semantic and episodic memory in frontotemporal lobar degeneration and Alzheimer's disease. *Journal of the International Neuropsychological Society, 16*(2), 278-286.

Yuille, J. C. & Cutshall, J. L. (1986). A case study of eyewitness memory of a crime. *Journal of Applied Psychology, 71*, 291-301.

Zannino, G.D., Barban, F., Caltagirone, C., & Carlesimo, G.A. (2008). Do Confabulators Really Try To Remember When They Confabulate? *Cognitive Neuropsychology, 25*, 831-852.

Zaragosa, M.S., Payment, K.E., Ackil, J.K., Drivdahl, S.B., & Beck, M. (2001). Interviewing witnesses: Forced confabulation and confirmatory feedback increase false memories. *American Psychological Society, 12*, 473-477.

CHAPTER 5

DEMENTIA IN THE CRIMINAL JUSTICE SYSTEM

ROBIN L. BROWN & CARLIE J. BOLIN

CHAPTER OVERVIEW

Dementia is commonly thought of as a single disease. In fact, dementia is an umbrella term that refers to a group of disorders characterized by a loss of cognitive functioning that interferes with an individual's ability to perform daily activities such as personal care, household chores, managing finances, and socializing. The severity of dementia ranges from a mild stage, when it just begins to affect a person's functioning, to a severe stage, when the person becomes completely dependent on others for basic activities of daily living. This chapter explains the basics of dementia, provides an overview of the common causes and types of dementia, describes how dementia is diagnosed, and explores the ways dementia can impact various areas of an individual's life, particularly those areas likely to result in involvement with the criminal justice and legal systems.

INTRODUCTION

In the United States, there are over 5 million people living with dementia (CDC, 2017). The most significant risk factor for developing dementia is age. According to the World Health Organization (WHO, 2015), about one in six people between ages 80 and 85 years, one in three people between ages 85 and 90, and almost half of those over age 90 develop dementia. Given the aging of the population, it is anticipated that the number of Americans age 65 and older living with dementia could more than double by 2050.

Although the risk of dementia increases with aging, dementia is not a normal part of the aging process. Contrary to what was once believed, recent studies indicate that as we age, the number of nerve cells (neurons) in the brain remains relatively stable, with little if any neuronal death in areas supporting cognition. Although structural, microscopic and biochemical changes do occur to the brain during normal aging, the extensive neuronal death that occurs in dementia is not seen (Freeman et al., 2008; Uylings & de Brabandera, 2002). While the changes that are part of normal aging result in decline in some aspects of cognition, many areas of cognition (e.g., general intellectual level and verbal skills including vocabulary, word, usage, reading, and writing) remain stable. In normal aging, there is a slowing in speed of cognitive processing, with a decrease in the amount of information that can be processed in a given amount of time. Thus, as we age we are likely to need more time to process information, complete mental tasks and problem-solve. While normal cognitive aging may result in a person needing more time to process new information, it does not reduce the amount of new information a person can learn. This slower, less efficient cognitive functioning often seen in normal aging is in sharp contrast to the loss of brain function and cognitive abilities seen in dementia. Occasional memory lapses, such as difficulty recalling a person's name or purpose of entering a room, become more common as we age.

Basics of Dementia

Common to all forms of dementia is a significant loss of cognitive function due to changes in the brain caused by an underlying disease or condition. All forms of dementia result from the death of neurons (nerve cells) in the brain and/or the loss of communication among these cells. Neurons are specialized information-processing cells of the brain that receive and send information. Information is communicated through chemicals, called neurotransmitters, which produce electrical impulses. All cognitive and bodily functions are controlled by these transmissions. This neuronal network functions much like the electrical circuits that control lights, appliances and other machinery. When there is a "short" or disconnection in the circuit, the lights, appliances, etc., do not function properly. Similarly, damage to any part of a neuron interferes with the transmission of messages within the brain and between the brain and the body. Symptoms of dementia emerge as the underlying neurodegenerative disease causes previously healthy neurons in the brain to stop functioning, lose connections with other neurons, and eventually die. Each type of dementia is characterized by different pathological or structural changes in the brain. The symptoms and progression of dementia vary depending on the underlying cause and the location and number of damaged brain cells. Each type of dementia has a characteristic course; however, variations occur from individual to individual (Cummings, 2003; National Institute of Neurological Disorders and Stroke [NINDS], 2013).

Guidelines for diagnosing different types of dementia have been developed by a variety of expert groups. In clinical practice, the Diagnostic and Statistical Manual of Mental Disorders (DSM) is generally used to guide the diagnosis of dementia. In the latest edition, DSM-5 (American Psychiatric Association - APA, 2013), dementia is subsumed under a newly named category, Neurocognitive Disorders, and is replaced by the term "major neurocognitive disorder." The DSM-5 states that the term "dementia" may continue to be used for those neurocognitive disorders caused by neurodegenerative diseases. According to the DSM-5, a diagnosis of major neurocognitive disorder requires evidence of significant cognitive decline from a previous level of functioning in one or more cognitive domains (e.g., complex attention, language, executive function, learning and memory, perceptual-motor and social judgment), and the cognitive deficits must interfere with independence in everyday activities. A notable change in the DSM-5 is the elimination of the requirement for memory impairment as a criterion for all types of dementia, which was present in the prior edition of the DSM (DSM-IV). The DSM-IV criteria were developed based on the typical progression of Alzheimer's disease, and a diagnosis of dementia required the presence of memory impairment regardless of the underlying cause of the dementia syndrome. However, it is now recognized that memory impairment is not present in all types of dementia. In addition, consistent with research support for conditions such as mild cognitive impairment (MCI), which can at times precede dementia (Albert et al., 2011), the DSM-5 also provides criteria for diagnosing minor neurocognitive disorders. The criteria are similar to those for major neurocognitive disorders; however, the cognitive impairments are milder and do not interfere with independent functioning. Although mild neurocognitive disorders may progress to dementia, they may remain a static condition (APA, 2013).

TYPES OF DEMENTIA

There are many diseases and medical conditions that may cause neurocognitive disorders, including progressive neurodegenerative diseases such as Alzheimer's disease, Lewy Body disease and frontotemporal disorders. Neurocognitive disorders may also result from neurotoxic effects of alcohol or other substances, cerebrovascular disease; traumatic brain injury; exposure to toxins; or from metabolic, autoimmune, or infectious processes. While the neurodegenerative diseases result in a progressive and irreversible loss of neurons and brain functions, there are other causes of major neurocognitive disorders that are potentially reversible. Vitamin deficiencies (e.g., vitamin B-12 deficiency), infectious diseases, brain tumors, metabolic conditions, endocrine disorders (e.g., hypothyroidism), normal pressure hydrocephalus, and alcohol abuse can cause neurological deficits and cognitive impairments such as those seen in dementia (National Institute of Neurological Disorders and Stroke - NINDS, 2013; Tripathi & Vibha, 2009). The majority of these conditions are treatable, with treatment halting and, at times, reversing cognitive impairment. A review of all possible etiologies and types of dementia is beyond the scope of this chapter. The causes and characteristics of the most common types of dementia will be reviewed.

ALZHEIMER'S DISEASE

Alzheimer's disease (AD) is the most common cause of dementia in individuals age 65 and older, making up 60%-80% of cases. The risk for AD increases after age 65 and doubles every 5 years thereafter (Alzheimer's Association, 2015a). Alzheimer's disease is an irreversible, progressive neurodegenerative disorder. Hallmark abnormalities of Alzheimer's disease are the presence of beta-amyloid plaques and tau tangles in the brain. These abnormal protein deposits may begin to form 20 or more years before symptoms appear (Jack, 2012; Villemagne et al., 2013). Beta-amyloid plaques, consisting of clumps of beta-amyloid protein and degenerated bits of other cells, form outside the neurons, and tangles of tau protein form inside neurons. The beta-amyloid plaques and tau tangles interfere with the ability of neurons to communicate and prevent cells from receiving essential nutrients, eventually leading to cell death. These plaques and tangles tend to start forming in the hippocampal region of the brain, a part of the brain essential to learning and memory (Braak & Braak, 1991; Cummings, 2003). As the plaques and tangles spread and more neurons die, additional areas of the brain are affected, and the brain begins to atrophy (shrink). By the final stage of Alzheimer's, there is widespread damage in the brain, and the volume of the brain is significantly reduced. The cause of Alzheimer's is not fully understood. A small percentage of Alzheimer's cases (1 percent or less) are caused by mutations to any of three genes: the gene for amyloid precursor protein and the genes for presenilin 1 and presenilin 2 proteins (Bateman et al., 2011; Bekris, Yu, Bird, & Tsuang, 2010). These genetic mutations are present in individuals with early-onset Alzheimer's, which develops between ages 30 and 60. The majority of individuals with Down's syndrome also develop early Alzheimer's dementia. This is believed to be because the extra copy of chromosome 21 that is present in Down's syndrome contains the amyloid precursor protein gene. Late-onset Alzheimer's, occurring at age 65 or later, is most common. Late-onset Alzheimer's is thought to result from a combination of factors, including genetic, environmental, and lifestyle.

Alzheimer's dementia has an insidious onset, with a gradually progressive increase in the number and severity of symptoms. The average survival time is 8 to 10 years from the time of diagnosis, but survival times vary and may extend to 20 years (Alzheimer's Association, 2015a; Helzner et al., 2008; Larson et al., 2004). Because the pathological changes in the brain begin in the hippocampus, the early symptoms of Alzheimer's dementia are often problems with short-term memory, learning and recall of new information, and word-finding difficulty (Cummings, 2003). Early signs of Alzheimer's include repetitive questioning and misplacing belongings (McKhann et al., 1984). Individuals may remember childhood stories, yet forget conversations that happened five minutes earlier (Cohen, 2015). Visuospatial difficulties, which can result in getting lost in familiar places, are also often seen in the early stage (Alzheimer's Association, 2015a; Cohen, 2015). As the disease progresses, memory problems increase and executive function deficits (e.g., organization, planning, and judgment) are evident. Individuals experience confusion with time or place and have impaired judgment, difficulty problem-solving, trouble recognizing family and friends, and increased difficulty communicating. While some individuals lack insight into their symptoms, others are painfully aware of their cognitive difficulties, resulting in acute anxiety and embarrassment (Cumming, 2003; NINDS, 2013). Changes in mood or personality occur, and many individuals with Alzheimer's develop behavioral and psychiatric symptoms, including agitation, sleeplessness, wandering, anxiety, aggression, delusions, paranoia, and at times—hallucinations. In the later stages of Alzheimer's, individuals are disoriented (do not know time and place), have severe memory impairment, no longer recognize family members, and are unable to bathe, dress, toilet, and feed themselves. In the final stage, individuals lose the ability to control motor functions and are often no longer able to speak or walk and have difficulty swallowing.

Alzheimer's disease cannot be stopped or reversed; there is no cure. Cognitive symptoms of Alzheimer's dementia are often treated with cholinesterase inhibitors (e.g., Aricept, Rivastigmine, Memantine). The medications currently available temporarily improve symptoms, but do not slow or stop damage to neurons caused by the disease. The effects of the medications last from only 6 to 12 months and are effective in only about half of the individuals who take them (Cohen, 2015). Currently, treatment of Alzheimer's focuses on maintenance of cognitive skills, management of behavioral symptoms, slowing /delaying symptoms, and improving quality of life for the individual.

Vascular Dementia

Vascular dementia (previously called multi-infarct or post-stroke dementia), a loss of cognitive function due predominantly, if not exclusively, to cerebrovascular disease, is the second-most-common cause of dementia (APA, 2013). Vascular dementia as the sole cause is estimated to account for 10% to 20% of dementia cases (Roman, 2003). However, almost half of all older individuals with other types of dementia also have pathologic evidence of vascular dementia (Fernando & Ince, 2004). Vascular dementia often co-occurs with Alzheimer's disease (Alzheimer's Society, 2015; Roman, 2003). In the United States, prevalence estimates for vascular dementia are 0.2% in those ages 65 to 70, 13% in those 70 to 79, 16% in those 80 to 89, and as much as 45% in those 90 years or older. Risk factors for vascular dementia include hypertension, diabetes, high cholesterol, obesity, smoking, and cardiovascular pathology such as arteriosclerosis and atrial fibrillation. Vascular dementia is also associated with two genetic disorders: cerebral amyloid angiopathy (a condition in which amyloid plaques build up in the walls of blood vessels, causing them to break down and rupture) and CADASIL (cerebral autosomal dominant arteriopathy with subcortical infarcts and leukoencephalopathy) (NINDS, 2013; Roman, Erkinjuntti, Wallin, Pantoni & Chui, 2002).

A variety of cerebrovascular diseases, ranging from large-vessel stroke to microvascular disease, can lead to vascular dementia. All of these conditions cause damage to or blockage in blood vessels in the brain, resulting in infarcts (strokes) or bleeding in the brain (hemorrhage). In fact, the diagnosis of vascular dementia requires the demonstration of ischemic abnormalities or lesions on neural imaging. Vascular dementia is divided into types, depending on the cause of the damage and the regions of the brain affected. The clinical presentation varies depending on the location, number and size of blood vessels involved. Whereas Alzheimer's dementia is a chronic progressive condition, vascular dementia can be progressive or static (stop progressing) depending on the underlying pathology (Roman, 2003).

Vascular dementia resulting from a major stroke or caused by one or more small strokes is often called post-stroke dementia or stroke-related dementia. Large-vessel subtype of post-stroke dementia is the most common form of acute-onset vascular dementia (Roman, 2003). A major stroke occurs when a large blood vessel becomes abruptly and permanently blocked, causing a sudden interruption in the blood supply, which deprives neurons of oxygen and leads to death of a large volume of brain tissue. Symptoms following a major stroke can include confusion, disorientation, acute sensory motor symptoms including loss of motor function on one side of the body (hemiparesis) and/or aphasia (impaired ability to speak or understand language). About 20% of people who have a major stroke develop dementia within three months following the stroke (APA, 2013).

More often, individuals can also have a series of small strokes over a period of weeks or months. Symptoms of such small strokes are often temporary, because the blockage clears itself. These interruptions of the blood supply, though brief, result in an infarct: death of a small area of tissue in the brain. Vascular dementia, in this case, results from the total damage of all of the infarcts together. In cases of multiple infarcts, there is often acute onset of cognitive and focal neurological symptoms, followed by a stepwise-fluctuating decline in cognition with intervening periods of stability or, at times, some improvement.

Small-vessel vascular dementia, which is caused by diseases of the very small blood vessels deep within the brain, is thought to be the most common type of vascular dementia (Alzheimer's Society, 2015). Reduced blood flow from these small vessels causes damage (lesions) in the white matter (nerve fibers that carry signals), basal ganglia and/or thalamus. Small-vessel vascular dementia typically has a gradual onset and slow progression. The cognitive deficits that occur are due to disruption of cortical–subcortical circuits, which cause impairments in complex attention and executive functioning. Typical symptoms include problems in complex attention, psychomotor slowness, problems with organization and planning, difficulty initiating or starting behaviors, as well as depression and apathy. Although individuals with subcortical vascular dementia are able to learn and retain information, forgetfulness is common. The forgetfulness is due to problems with spontaneous recall and, unlike those with Alzheimer's, when provided with cues/prompts, recall improves. Typically, language, math skills, and other higher cortical functions are preserved.

There is no cure for vascular dementia—the brain damage caused cannot be reversed. Although there are currently no drugs approved by the FDA to treat vascular dementias, there is some evidence that drugs used for Alzheimer's may benefit people with mild to moderate vascular dementia (Kavirajan & Schneider, 2007). The main goal of treatment is to prevent further damage to the brain by reducing risk factors for additional cerebral vascular damage.

LEWY BODY DEMENTIAS

Lewy body dementia is not a single disorder; it is a spectrum of disorders involving disturbances of cognition, behavior, sleep, movement, and autonomic function (Galvin et al., 2008; NINDS, 2013). Lewy body dementia is the third most common cause of dementia (NINDS, 2013) and is thought to account for 4.2% of all diagnosed dementias in the community and 7.5% of diagnosed dementias in clinical settings (Vann Jones & O'Brien, 2014). Lewy body dementia is more common in males than females with a ratio of 1.5:1 (APA, 2013). It is estimated that about 1 million people in the United States are affected by Lewy body dementia (NIA / NINDS, 2015).

Lewy body dementia includes Dementia with Lewy bodies (DLB) and Parkinson's disease Dementia (PDD). The two types are caused by the same underlying neurodegenerative disease. The hallmark of both DLB and PDD are abnormal deposits called Lewy bodies, named for Dr. Friedreich Lewy, who first identified the deposits (Donaghy & McKeith, 2014). Lewy bodies are abnormal accumulations of alpha-synuclein protein, a protein involved in communication between neurons. As these abnormal clumps of alpha-synuclein protein accumulate in neurons, the neurons function less effectively, lose their ability to communicate with other neurons, and eventually die. The cause of Lewy body dementia is not known. Although Parkinson's disease and rapid eye movement (REM) sleep behavior disorder are linked to a higher risk of Lewy body dementia, no specific lifestyle factor has been shown to increase one's risk for the disorder, nor is Lewy body dementia considered a genetic disease (Vann Jones & O'Brien, 2014; NIA/NINDS, 2015).

The primary difference between Dementia with Lewy bodies (DLB) and Parkinson's disease dementia (PDD) is the order in which the cognitive and motor symptoms emerge. In DLB, Lewy bodies initially accumulate in neurons in the cortical areas of the brain (areas responsible for attention, thinking, memory), giving rise to cognitive symptoms. As the disease spreads to other areas of the brain, individuals with DLB begin to have Parkinsonian symptoms (masked face, resting tremor, rigidity, slow movements, and postural instability). In PDD, the Lewy bodies are primarily located in the basal ganglia and brain stem, causing the motor stiffness, rigid muscles, difficulty walking and other motor symptoms, (the hallmarks of Parkinson's disease) to emerge first. As the disease spreads into higher cortical areas of the brain, individuals with PDD begin to exhibit cognitive decline. Although the early symptoms of the types differ, over time, individuals with DLB and PDD may look very similar.

DEMENTIA WITH LEWY BODIES

Dementia with Lewy bodies (DLB) has an insidious onset, followed by a gradually progressive decline. Although the progression is characterized by occasional plateaus, there is a continuous downhill decline, leading to severe dementia and then death. Onset of symptoms is typically between the ages of 60 and 90, with most common onset in mid-70s. Average duration of survival is 5 to 7 years, although the time-span can range from 2 to 20 years. Dementia with Lewy bodies includes progressive cognitive impairment, with early changes in complex attention and executive functions—rather than learning and memory. Memory impairment is less pronounced, and visual spatial, attentional, and executive function impairments are more severe in DLB than in Alzheimer's dementia. In addition to cognitive decline, the diagnosis of DLB requires two of at least three core diagnostic features or one core feature and one suggestive diagnostic feature (APA, 2013). The DSM-5 defines the three core features as fluctuations in attention, alertness and cognition; recurrent visual hallucinations that are well formed and detailed; and spontaneous parkinsonism that begins subsequent to development of cognitive decline. Suggestive features are defined as having a diagnosis of REM sleep disorder and sensitivity to neuroleptics (antipsychotic medication). By consensus agreement, in DLB the onset of cognitive decline is at least one year before the onset of motor symptoms (APA, 2013; Galvin et al., 2008). At times, visual hallucinations, depression and REM disorder may be present before the cognitive symptoms. Falls, syncope and transient episodes of unexplained loss of consciousness are frequent in individuals with DLB. Autonomic dysfunction such as orthostatic hypotension (dizziness upon standing from a lying/seated position) and urinary incontinence may be observed. Depression, while not uncommon, is not as frequent as anxiety and psychotic symptoms, which are prominent features of DLB. In addition to the visual hallucinations (usually of people and/or animals) (Hanson & Lippa, 2009), delusions that a loved one is an imposter (Capgras phenomenon) or that an unfamiliar location (e.g., hospital) is their home (reduplicative paramnesia) (Nagahama, Okina, Suzuki, & Matsuda, 2010) often occur.

Individuals with DLB are more functionally impaired than would be expected for their cognitive deficits, when compared to individuals with other neurodegenerative diseases such as Alzheimer's. This is primarily because of the motor and autonomic impairments, which cause problems with toileting, transferring, and eating. Sleep disorders and psychiatric symptoms further contribute to functional difficulties.

PARKINSON'S DISEASE DEMENTIA

A diagnosis of Parkinson's disease dementia (PDD) requires the individual to have an established diagnosis of Parkinson's disease before the onset of cognitive decline. By consensus, the motor symptoms of Parkinson's disease (i.e., bradykinesia, tremor, rigidity, and a shuffling walk) must be present at least one year before cognitive decline has reached the level of neurocognitive disorder (APA, 2013; Galvin et al. , 2008). The cognitive deficits in PDD must develop gradually (APA, 2013). Prevalence of Parkinson's disease in the United States increases with age from approximately 0.5% between ages 65 and 69 to 3% at age 85 and older (APA, 2013). Although in the majority of those with Parkinson's disease, symptoms first appear after age 60, a small percentage of individuals have early-onset Parkinson's disease in which symptoms occur around age 40 and, at times, earlier. Not everyone with Parkinson's disease develops dementia. Among those with Parkinson's disease, as many as 75% will develop dementia sometime in the course of their disease (APA, 2013). Dementia is relatively rare in people with onset of Parkinson's disease before age 50 years, even when the disease is of long duration (Ferman & Boeve, 2007).

Although the cognitive symptoms in PDD are similar to those of DLB, individuals with PDD do not exhibit the fluctuations in alertness and cognition that are common in DLB. In addition, individuals with PDD typically have more problems learning new material and deficits in memory and language. Cognitive symptoms include difficulty concentrating; problems with planning, sequencing, decision-making, and visuospatial awareness (way-finding difficulty in familiar surroundings); and inflexibility in adapting to changes. Frequent symptoms of PDD include apathy, depression, anxious mood, personality changes, and REM sleep behavior disorder. Hallucinations and delusions also occur in PDD.

Some medications used to treat Alzheimer's disease are also used to treat the cognitive symptoms of LBD (NIA/NINDS, 2015). Motor symptoms of LBD are treated with dopamine-increasing medications (e.g., carbidopa-levodopa). However, these medications can worsen confusion and hallucinations. While these drugs can improve functioning, they cannot stop or reverse the progress of the disease. Currently there is no way to prevent or cure Lewy body dementia—either DLB or PDD. As with other types of neurodegenerative dementias, the primary focus of treatment is on improving the individual's quality of life by involving the person in activities and events they enjoy, supporting existing abilities, relieving symptoms, and providing emotional support.

FRONTOTEMPORAL DEMENTIAS

Frontotemporal dementias (FTD) are a group of neurodegenerative disorders characterized by prominent, progressive changes in behavior, personality and/or language, accompanied by degeneration of the frontal and/or temporal lobes. The term FTD refers to three clinical syndromes: behavioral-variant frontotemporal dementia and two language variants: semantic primary progressive aphasia and non-fluent (also called agrammatic) primary progressive aphasia (NIA/NIND, 2014). In some cases, FTD is associated with progressive neuromuscular weakness otherwise known as amyotrophic lateral sclerosis (ALS, or Lou Gehrig's disease) (Association for Frontal Temporal Degeneration - AFTD, 2013). Previously thought to be rare, FTD is now believed to rival Alzheimer's as the cause of early-onset dementia (Prince et al., 2013). Prevalence estimates are in the range of 2 to 10 per 100,000 (APA, 2013), with FTD making up 5% to 10 % of all cases of dementia (NIA/NIND, 2014). Although age of onset varies, approximately 60% of individuals with FTD are between 45 and 64 years of age (NIA/NIND, 2014; Ratnavalli, Brayne, Dawson, & Hodges, 2002). Prevalence estimates of behavioral variant and semantic language variant are higher among males, while prevalence estimates of non-fluent language variant are higher among females (APA, 2013).

The pathology of FTD is heterogeneous; there are a number of underlying neuropathological processes connected to FTD. Four varieties of abnormal protein aggregates are associated with FTD: tau, TDP-43, ubiquitin, and FUS (Johnson et al., 2005; Piguet, Hornberger, Mioshi, & Hodges, 2011). In the healthy brain, tau is involved in stabilizing microtubules, which support the structure and shape of neurons; ubiquitin is involved in clearing waste products from neurons; TDP-43 and FUS are involved in production of other proteins. In FTD, one or more of these proteins begin to change shape or quantity (either too little or too much), resulting in the buildup of abnormal clumps of protein (inclusions) in neurons. One type of inclusion, called a "Pick body" (named after the neurologist who discovered them), was first identified almost one hundred years ago as present in Pick's disease. While it was once believed that all individuals with FTD had Pick's disease, it has now been established that Pick bodies are present in only about 20% of those with FTD (Cognitive Neurology and Alzheimer's Disease Center – CNADC, n.d.). The various inclusions interfere with the functioning of cells, which in turn leads to neuronal death. As neurons die, scar tissue (gliosis) develops in the damaged region, causing tissue loss (atrophy). The abnormal inclusions tend to start forming in the frontal and anterior temporal lobes and gradually spread to other regions of the brain. The hallmarks of FTD are loss of neurons and atrophy (shrinking of tissue) in the frontal lobes, parts of the temporal lobes, and in deeper brain structures that link to them. The loss of neurons and damage in these areas lead to changes in behavior, language and/or motor skills. The posterior regions (back) of the brain are spared in FTD; therefore, many day-to-day functions are normal.

The cause of the brain changes that lead to FTD is not fully understood. Although several genetic mutations have been linked to FTD, in the majority of cases, the cause of FTD is unknown. A genetic (hereditary) cause can be identified in 15% to 40% of individuals with FTD (NIA/NINDS, 2014). Familial forms of FTD are most often caused by inherited mutations in either the MAPT gene (causes abnormalities in tau protein), the PGRN gene (causes TDP-43 protein to go awry), or the C9ORF72 gene. Mutations in the VCP, CHMP2B, TARDBP and FUS genes result in very rare Familial types of FTD (NIA/ NINDS, 2014).

Frontotemporal dementia is a progressive, degenerative brain disease with an insidious onset. In all types of FTD, there is a continual decline in cognition and functioning, leading to complete dependence and then death. Survival is shorter, and decline is more rapid than in typical Alzheimer's disease. The average life expectancy of an individual is 6 to 11 years after symptom onset and 3 to 4 years after diagnosis (Johnson et al., 2005). Although the three types of FTD are distinguished by the earliest symptoms and progression of symptoms, there is considerable variability in course of FTD within types. Due to the relatively early age of onset, FTD has a greater impact on the workplace and family life than other types of dementia. Although cognitive deficits tend to be minimal, the behavioral and language impairments of FTD lead to severely impaired functioning early in the disease.

Behavioral Variant FTD

Behavioral variant FTD (bvFTD) is the most common type, comprising about half of all cases of FTD (Piguet et al., 2011). The areas of the frontal and temporal lobes affected in bvFTD cause disruption in the frontal lobe and frontal circuits, contributing to aspects of personality and executive functions. As a result, changes in personality and inappropriate social behaviors are the primary characteristics of bvFT (Johnson et al., 2005). According to the DSM-5, the diagnosis of bvFTD requires a prominent decline in social cognition and/or executive abilities and at least three of the following behavioral symptoms: behavioral disinhibition, apathy or lack of initiation, loss of empathy, perseverative or compulsive/ritualistic behavior, and hyperorality and dietary changes (APA, 2013). The most common initial symptoms of bvFTD are disinhibition and impulsivity or apathy, lack of initiative, and inactivity. Behavioral disinhibition may be manifested by socially inappropriate behaviors such as being overly familiar with strangers, public urination, using obscene language or making inappropriate sexual remarks, or invading others' personal space (CNADC, n.d.) (Piguet et al., 2011). Apathy is associated with loss of interest and/or motivation for activities and social relationships, social withdrawal, lack of initiative, and emotional blunting. Apathy is often mistaken for depression, although the individual with bvFTD does not experience sad feelings.

Changes in the person's usual emotional responsiveness, such as loss of empathy or compassion in someone who was responsive to others' distress or heightened emotionality in someone who was typically less emotionally responsive, is common (CNADC, n.d.). Decline in self-care and personal responsibilities frequently occur. Individuals with bvFTD also often develop repetitive movements (pacing, rubbing, or picking) and/or complex ritualistic behaviors such as hoarding, checking, and cleaning.

Cognitive decline is less prominent in bvFTD. Early cognitive symptoms reflect diminished executive functioning and include decreased self-awareness and decreased judgment. Almost universally, individuals with bvFTD lack insight into their behavioral and cognitive changes and the distress experienced by family members/significant others (Williamson et al., 2010). Difficulty recognizing consequences of behavior and lack of self-awareness leads to poor judgment and decision-making, which in turn often result in financial and legal problems and threats to safety (Association for Frontal Temporal Degeneration [AFTD], 2013). Additional cognitive deficits, including impairments in planning and organization, decreased mental flexibility, distractibility, impaired response inhibition, and diminished abstract reasoning appear as bvFTD progresses. Visuospatial abilities, learning and memory are relatively spared, although executive function deficits may give the appearance of memory problems (Hornberger, Piguet, Graham, Nestor & Hodges, 2010; Rascovsky et al., 2007).

PRIMARY PROGRESSIVE APHASIA

Primary progressive aphasia (PPA), the language variant FTD, is characterized by a progressive loss of language function. According to the DSM-5, the diagnosis of language variant FTD requires prominent decline in language ability, in the form of speech production, word finding, object naming, grammar, or word comprehension (APA, 2013). PPA results when the underlying disease process damages regions of the temporal and frontal lobes in the language-dominant hemisphere. Two types of PPA are classified as frontotemporal dementia: agrammatic (nonfluent) PPA and semantic PPA. The type of PPA depends on which areas of the neural networks underlying speech and language are damaged. Neuroimaging typically reveals atrophy in the left posterior fronto-insular cortex in nonfluent PPA and anterior temporal atrophy in semantic PPA (Gorno-Tempini et al., 2004).

Nonfluent/aggrammatic PPA is characterized by aggrammatical speech output with effortful production of sounds (Gorno-Tempini et al., 2011). Individuals with nonfluent PPA have slow, labored speech production and shortened sentences. As the disease progresses, speech becomes increasingly hesitant and sentences become gradually shorter—leading to eventual mutism. Speech of those with nonfluent PPA typically contains distortions, deletions, substitutions, insertions, or transpositions of speech sounds, of which the person is often not aware. Omissions of pronouns, conjunctions and articles occur frequently, and distortions, deletions, substitutions, insertions, or transpositions of speech sounds are common, leading to speech sometimes described as telegraphic (Gorno-Tempini et al., 2011). The person is often not aware of the errors. Word order may be incorrect, especially in writing or e-mails. Early on, comprehension is relatively intact; however, as the disease progresses, individuals have difficulty understanding lengthy, complex sentences (Gorno-Tempini et al., 2011). Comprehension of single words and object knowledge are typically spared until the later stages of the disease. Activities of daily living, except for those depending on language, are maintained. In contrast to bvFTD, social decorum remains intact. Cognitive deficits are often restricted to expressive language function for a few to several years before global dementia develops (Mesulam, 2013).

Semantic PPA is characterized by anomia (i.e., difficulty recalling the names of objects) and impaired single-word comprehension, with preserved fluency, repetition, and grammar. The earliest symptom is word-finding difficulty. In the early stage of semantic PPA, individuals often understand complete sentences, but are unable to understand single words (Mesulam, 2013). As the disease progresses, individuals lose not only the ability to name things, but also the meaning of the words and knowledge of the object they are trying to name. In the early stage of semantic PPA, words for low-frequency items are lost, and later on, more common words are lost. For instance, when shown a picture of a cat, a person with semantic PPA will neither be able to generate the correct word nor be able to pick the word "cat" from a list of words, and even if told that it is a cat, they may still have difficulty understanding the concept of "cat." As the disease progresses, individuals have increasing trouble understanding conversation. Some individuals also develop impaired ability to recognize familiar faces, a condition referred to as prosopagnosia. Memory for events, executive functions and visuospatial abilities are usually spared until the later stages of semantic PPA. In the late stages of semantic PPA, behavioral changes (disinhibited, inappropriate behaviors) similar to those seen in bvFTD may emerge. Semantic variant PPA accounts for 20% of FTD cases (Davies et al., 2005).

There is no cure for and no treatment that will slow down or prevent FTD. Current treatment of FTD focuses on symptom management and supports for the individual, family members/significant others, and caregivers. While there are no medications approved for the treatment of FTD, antidepressants (particularly SSRIs), antipsychotics, and other drugs used to treat Parkinson's and Alzheimer's symptoms may help manage the symptoms and behavioral problems associated with FTD (NIA/NINDS, 2014).

MIXED DEMENTIA

Mixed dementia is characterized by hallmark abnormalities of more than one cause of dementia. Alzheimer's combined with vascular dementia is the most common. Alzheimer's combined with Dementia with Lewy bodies is the second-most common, followed by Alzheimer's with vascular dementia and Dementia with Lewy bodies (Schneider, Arvanitakis, Bang, & Bennett, 2007). Autopsy studies suggest that mixed dementia is quite common, with about half of those with dementia having pathologic evidence of more than one cause of dementia (Schneider et al., 2007). While symptoms from the different types of dementia will be present in mixed dementia, the proportion of symptoms attributable to any one type is unknown. The manner in which the underlying disease processes in mixed dementia impact each other is not understood. Questions as to whether having pathology of two or more causes of dementia leads to symptoms being worse, the course of progression to be faster, or greater variation in clinical presentation among individuals are still to be answered.

EVALUATION AND DIAGNOSIS OF DEMENTIA

The American Academy of Neurology (AAN) along with numerous other expert groups have published guidelines for the evaluation of dementia (AAN, 2010). Any person suspected of having dementia should undergo a formal evaluation, which typically consists of a thorough medical history obtained from the patient and care partner, a physical/neurological examination, cognitive screening, laboratory studies, and neuropsychological testing. There is generally agreement among the various guidelines that structural neuroimaging, either CT or MRI, can be used to rule out reversible causes and should be performed at least once (Ngo & Holroyd-Leduc, 2015).

HISTORY

In the clinical setting, cognitive impairment may be unrecognized by primary care physicians 40% of the time (Chodosh et al., 2004). Individuals with dementia often show poor insight into their condition, and thus, a family member or friend should be present to describe any cognitive or behavioral decline. Frequently, friends and distant family may be unaware of cognitive decline due to relatively intact social functioning. The common misconception that "normal aging" allows for a certain degree of forgetfulness also contributes to cognitive impairment going unrecognized. From the physician's standpoint, there are inherent challenges in making a diagnosis of dementia due to the lack of definitive lab tests for this condition. In addition, increasing time constraints for providers may limit ability to perform the comprehensive evaluation necessary for a diagnosis.

LABORATORY STUDIES

Although treatable causes of neurocognitive disorders occur in only about 9% of cases (Clarfield, 2003), assessment for potentially reversible conditions contributing to cognitive dysfunction should be part of the evaluation process. According to AAN (2010) guidelines, all individuals presenting with memory and/or cognitive complaints should undergo routine lab tests (complete blood count, electrolytes, BUN (blood urea nitrogen), creatinine, calcium, liver function tests, and fasting glucose) as well as lab tests for thyroid function (TSH), vitamin B12 and folate. Additional tests for HIV, syphilis, or heavy metals (such as lead) should be done when the individual has a suggestive history.

NEUROPSYCHOLOGICAL TESTING

As stated in the DSM-5, neuropsychological testing is part of the standard evaluation of dementia (APA, 2013). However, formal neuropsychological testing is not always available and may not be feasible in some instances. In such cases, brief standardized cognitive screening instruments, such as the Mini-Mental Status Exam (MMSE) or the Montreal Cognitive Assessment (MoCA), may be used. Except in instances in which cognitive screening indicates moderate to severe impairment, screening should be followed by formal neuro-psychological testing. Formal neuropsychological testing is also recommended when screening results in a normal score, yet there are persistent, unexplained changes in cognition or daily functioning.

Neuropsychologists assess brain function and impairment by drawing inferences from an individual's performance on standardized tests. The neuropsychologist is able to differentiate the cognitive profiles of the various types of neurodegenerative disorders. A comprehensive neuropsychological evaluation generally consists of a battery of standardized tests designed to assess a range of cognitive domains, including intelligence, attention, processing speed, learning/memory, executive function, language, visuospatial, perceptual-motor, and social cognition, as well as mood /personality. The battery of tests is typically tailored for the individual being assessed. Administration time can range from 1.5 to 6 hours, depending on the number of tests administered. Based on an individual's test performance, the neuropsychologist is able to determine whether there has been a cognitive decline, identify the nature and extent (severity) of the cognitive impairment, and identify the underlying etiology for cognitive dysfunction. Neuropsychological evaluation is particularly helpful in diagnosing for diagnostic clarification when a neurocognitive disorder is suspected, but there are no clearly identifiable biomarkers, as is the case with most neurodegenerative dementias. For example, neuropsychological evaluation can distinguish mild Alzheimer disease from normal aging with close to 90 percent accuracy (Salmon & Bondi, 2009). In addition to assisting in differential diagnosis of dementia, neuropsychological evaluation is often essential for making determinations about an individual's capacity to work, manage finances, or make complex medical decisions.

IMPACT OF DEMENTIA

The functioning and independence of the individual with dementia are significantly impacted, as are the lives of family and friends. Regardless of the type of dementia, as it progresses, the individual's ability to manage his or her own daily activities and self-care declines. As the loss of cognitive functioning increases, the individual's ability to comprehend and communicate diminishes, and his or her judgment declines, leading to inability to respond appropriately in social situations, deal with emergencies, manage finances, or make medical decisions. This diminished ability to care for self and impaired judgment lead to situations and/or behaviors that bring individuals with dementia into contact with law enforcement officials, attorneys, and the criminal justice system. Common to the majority of these situations are issues of autonomy and capacity (civil competence), safety and vulnerability, and criminal competence.

AUTONOMY AND CAPACITY

Autonomy is generally understood to be the ability to understand and act on choices rationally and without coercion or controlling interference by others. Over the past two decades, the importance of respecting the autonomy of individuals with dementia has received increasing attention and support in medical, legal and social arenas (Long, Lines, Wiener & Gould, 2014). The United Nations Convention on the Rights of Persons with Disabilities states that persons with disabilities (defined loosely as persons with impairments and barriers to participation in society) have inherent dignity, individual autonomy (including the freedom to make their own choices), and independence, and they have a right to full and effective participation and inclusion in society (Pineda & UNICEF, 2008). The convention mandates participants (United States and 157 other countries) develop person-centered approaches to decision-making for people with dementia (Smith & Sullivan, 2012). This approach requires that the individual's abilities and preferences be taken into account when decisions are made about care and other aspects of living.

The Alzheimer's Association (2015c) and Alzheimer's Disease Education and Referral Center (ADEAR- NIA, 2008) highlight the importance of advance planning to ensure an individual's preferences are respected and wishes carried out. Advance planning should take place as soon as possible after the diagnosis and/or in early-stage dementia, when people are typically able to understand and participate in the majority of personal, legal and medical decisions (Moye, Karel, Azar, & Gurrera, 2004). Advanced directives for health-care such as a living will and a durable power of attorney for health care allow a person to communicate their desired medical treatment and assign authority for health care decisions to a particular person once the individual with dementia can no longer do so. Advanced directives for financial and estate management, durable power of attorney for finances, living trusts, and estate wills provide instructions and authority for making decisions about finances and property when the individual is no longer able to manage his or her affairs.

A diagnosis of dementia does not immediately rob a person of the ability to make rational decisions or to manage his or her life. However, as dementia progresses and the severity of cognitive impairment increases, there inevitably comes a time when the person's ability to make their own decisions—that is, his or her capacity—is questioned. When questions of capacity arise, family members, partners, friends, and caregivers often turn to medical and legal professionals to help determine a course of action. Making such determinations requires balancing the safety and the autonomy of the individual with dementia. According to the Alzheimer's Association Ethics Advisory Panel, "people with dementia should be allowed to exercise their remaining capacities for choice," and professionals have an obligation to protect a person with dementia from seriously harmful consequences, and an equal obligation to respect his or her competent decisions (Alzheimer's Association, 2015c). Accomplishing this balance requires assessment of an individual's capacity or competence to make and carry out decisions. The law states that capacity is not "all or nothing" (Geriatrics and Ethics Project, n.d.); a person may be competent to make decisions in some areas and not in others (Mossman & Farrell, 2015).

CAPACITY AND COMPETENCE

The terms capacity and competence are often used interchangeably. Competence is the legal term for one's decision-making capacity, while the terms capacity and decision-making capacity are more widely used by professionals in clinical settings. Technically, whether or not an individual is competent can only be adjudicated by the court. However, there are many circumstances in which clinicians and other professionals are called upon to determine whether an individual with dementia has the ability to make decisions about a specific issue or situation. Determination of an individual's capacity, whether made by professionals or by courts, is based on the same key elements: the ability to understand the options, the ability to understand the consequences of choosing each of the options, and the ability to understand the personal cost and benefit of each of the consequences and relate them to their own set of values and priorities (Mossman & Farrell, 2015). The cognitive impairments that occur as dementia progresses can impact the individual's ability to understand information that is relevant to the options, retain the information, weigh the available information, appreciate the consequences of a particular task or decision, and communicate his or her decision. Questions about an individual's competence can arise in the context of a number of areas. The most common areas of concern for individuals with dementia are competence to consent to or refuse medical treatment, competence to manage personal affairs, (including independent living and finances), sexual consent, and driving ability (Mossman & Farrell, 2015).

MEDICAL CONSENT

Among the various areas of competence, the criteria for determining the capacity of an individual with dementia to consent to or refuse medical treatment are the most well-established. Criteria for determining decisional capacity for medical treatment are rooted in the concept of informed consent, which requires that one's consent to treatment be competent, voluntary, and informed (Meisel, 2005; Furrow, Greaney, Johnson, Jost, & Schwartz, 2000). The standards for what constitutes informed consent are spelled out in federal regulations and by The Joint Commission. The competent aspect of informed consent is defined by law. All 50 states have laws that address capacity to make medical decisions; in most states medical decisions-making capacity is defined by statute under their advance directives laws.

Although statutes vary from state to state, most are based on the framework laid out by Applebaum and Grisso (1998), which identifies four key abilities needed for medical decision-making capacity: (1) ability to comprehend diagnostic and treatment-related information; (2) appreciation or acknowledgement that a carefully considered medical diagnosis is valid and that treatment may be beneficial; (3) ability to weigh risks and benefits of options and relate them to personal preferences; and (4) ability to express or communicate one's preferences and choice. Diminished capacity for medical consent is associated with impairments in memory, executive functions, and comprehension that occur in dementia. Difficulties understanding diagnostic and treatment information has been shown to be related to impairments in memory, conceptualization, and comprehension (Gurrera et al., 2006; Marson, Chatterjee, Ingram, & Harrell, 1996; Marson, Ingram, Cody, & Harrell, 1995). Reduced ability to appreciate the impact of the diagnosis and treatment is associated with impaired executive functions and conceptualization. Impairments in attention, executive functions (particularly, cognitive flexibility), and inability to recall information after a delay impact ability to contrast risks and benefits and relate them to personal preferences.

Although there is a high rate of lack of capacity for medical decisions in individuals with dementia (Kim, Karalwish, & Caine, 2002), the diagnosis of dementia does not in and of itself mean an individual does not have medical decision-making capacity. An individual's capacity to make medical decisions can vary from situation to situation, depending on the complexity of the particular health problem and the number of treatment options. Thus, a patient's capacity for medical treatment, especially in the early stages of dementia, may need to be assessed on multiple occasions. A number of standardized instruments have been developed for assessing capacity for medical consent. These instruments have been shown to have respectable levels of reliability and validity (ABA Commission on Law and Aging & APA [ABA/APA], 2008; Mossman & Farrell, 2015). The most commonly used of these instruments include the McArthur Competence Assessment Tool for Treatment (MacCAT-T) (Grisso & Appelbaum, 1998), Capacity to Consent to Treatment Instrument (CCTI) (Marson et al., 1995), Hopkins Competency Assessment Test (HCAT) (Janofsky, McCarthy, & Folstein, 1992), the Hopemont Capacity Assessment Interview (HCAI) (Edelstein, 1999), and Assessment of Capacity to Consent to Treatment (ACCT) (Moye et al., 2008).

FINANCIAL CAPACITY

Financial capacity is a medical-legal construct that represents the ability to independently manage one's financial affairs in a manner consistent with personal self-interest and values (Marson, 2013). Legal determination of financial capacity is based on whether an individual has the financial skills sufficient for handling one's estate and financial affairs, and is the basis for determinations of conservatorship or guardianship of the estate (ABA/APA, 2008). Financial capacity is often understood to include more specific legal capacities, such as contractual capacity, capacity to make gifts/donations, and testamentary capacity (ABA/APA, 2008).

A clinical model of financial capacity developed by Marson and colleagues (Griffith et al., 2003; Marson & Hebert, 2005) is often used as a framework for evaluating an individual's financial capacity. This model identifies the functional abilities required for financial capacity. The model conceptualizes financial capacity as having two components: performance and judgment. The performance component encompasses the various tasks and skills a person must be able to perform to meet his or her financial needs (e.g., counting coins/currency accurately; understanding the monetary values of money; completing cash transactions; managing a check book; understanding and using bank statements; paying bills; and understanding basic financial terms and concepts such as loans, investments, rates of return and wills). In addition to such knowledge and skills, the individual must be able to exercise judgment and make decisions that are in his or her financial self-interest. Judgment involves the ability to make reasonably sound financial decisions in novel or ambiguous social situations, such as being sensitive to fraud, invulnerable to coercion, and prudent in making investments. To have financial capacity, an individual must be able to carry out financial activities in ways that promote and protect self-interest (Marson, 2013).

A wide variety of cognitive abilities are involved in financial capacity, including verbal conceptual knowledge, visual attention, memory (verbal and visual), mental and written arithmetic abilities, procedural learning, abstract reasoning and executive functions underlying varieties of judgment. Because it is highly cognitively mediated, financial capacity is more vulnerable to medical conditions that affect cognition, such as neurodegenerative diseases, than other consent capacities (Marson, 2013).

Concerns about declining financial skills, including problems managing household finances, making poor financial decisions, or being exploited, are often raised by family members of individuals being evaluated for dementia (Widera et al., 2011). Studies focused on changes in financial capacity occurring in individuals with neurodegenerative diseases indicate that financial capacity shows emerging impairment in individuals in the prodrome or transitional stage of Alzheimer's, widespread impairment in individuals with mild Alzheimer's disease, and advanced global impairment in all financial areas in individuals with moderate Alzheimer's (Griffith et al., 2003; Marson et al., 2000). Studies also show that the performance and judgment components of financial capacity are separate; one may be impaired, while the other is intact. Thus, while the financial skills of individuals with Parkinson's dementia or early Frontotemporal dementias may be intact, due to impaired judgment, they may be unable to use these skills in ways that meet their basic needs or protect their interests (Marson, 2013).

Unlike medical consent capacity, which involves making a specific decision at a particular point in time, financial capacity involves a wide range of activities and time frames and a variety of settings. Thus, assessment of financial capacity requires a more formal and comprehensive evaluation than does assessment of capacity for medical consent. Unlike the area of medical consent, few instruments have been developed for assessment of financial capacity. The Financial Capacity Instrument (FCI-9) (Marson, 2001; Marson et al., 2000) is one of few measures specifically designed to assess financial capacity. One of the instruments used in assessing medical consent capacity, the Hopemont Capacity Assessment Interview, has three vignettes that assess social judgment in financial situations. Measures of limited financial skills are also contained in a number of independent living skills instruments.

INDEPENDENT LIVING

According to available national and regional data, a significant percentage of people with dementia live alone. Studies indicate 13%-25% percent of individuals age 65 and older diagnosed with Alzheimer's disease or other types of dementia are living alone in a private residence (Alzheimer's Association, 2015a; Kasper, Freedman, & Spillman, 2014). Since many people with dementia have not been diagnosed, and the data does not include nonelderly people with dementia who live alone, these figures are likely an underestimate. Thus, for many persons with dementia, the issue of whether the individual is safe to live independently is likely to arise.

Although there is no specific set of criteria for "the capacity to live independently," the legal standards defined in guardianship laws are often used in determining an individual's capacity to do so. Statutes for determining and establishing guardianship vary from state to state. However, in many states guardianship laws are based on the model set out in the Uniform Guardianship and Protective Proceedings Act (UGPPA) (National Conference of Commissioners on Uniform State Laws, 1997). The UGPPA defines an incapacitated person as someone who is unable to "receive and evaluate information or make or communicate decisions to the extent that the individual lacks the ability to meet essential requirements for physical health, safety, or self-care even with appropriate technological assistance" (National Conference of Commissioners on Uniform State Laws, 1997, p.1). Adult protective services (APS) statutes also provide legal guidance regarding an individual's capacity for independent living. According to APS, indications that a person with dementia living alone is not able to adequately manage his or her personal care needs and daily activities include frequent emergency medical visits, little or no food in the home, unkempt appearance, dirty clothes, and inappropriate clothing for the weather. Appointment of a guardian, however, should be a last resort, and when necessary, should be limited to only those areas in which the individual lacks competence.

Because a considerable range of skills and abilities are potentially relevant to the capacity for independent living, assessment of a wide range of areas is necessary. Determining capacity for independent living is a complex process that ideally involves professionals from multiple disciplines (Skelton, Kunik, Regev, & Naik, 2010). The ABA Commission on Law and Aging & APA (ABA/APA, 2008) has proposed a framework for determining capacity for independent living that reflects legal standards found in guardianship laws that emphasize cognitive and functional components, as well as cognitive, functional, and judgmental components of independent living cited in APS laws. This framework identifies three components needed for independent living: (1) Understanding—does the person understand the basic responsibilities and tasks needed to live alone, and can he or she foresee possible problems related to performing or not performing tasks; (2) Application—is the person able to perform activities of daily living (ADLs) such as dressing themselves, toileting, bathing, meal preparation, cleaning, laundry, and communication; (3) Judgment—does the person have the ability to problem solve, handle emergencies, compensate for areas of incapacitation, appreciate consequences of potential choices, and minimize risk to self and others. There are a number of tests for assessing basic ADLs and instrumental activities of daily living (IDLs) and general decision-making ability. The more commonly used instruments include the Independent Living Scales (ILS) (Loeb, 1996); the Direct Assessment of Functional Status-Revised (DAFS-R) (McDougall et al., 2010); the Capacity Assessment Tool (CAT) (Carney et al., 2001); the Everyday Problems Test (EPT) (Willis & Marsiske, 1993); and the Revised Observed Tasks of Daily Living (OTDL-R) (Diehl et al., 2005).

DRIVING ABILITY

Driving is a complex activity that requires a variety of cognitive skills, including processing speed; visual perception, visual processing, and visuospatial skills; selective and divided attention; multitasking; and decision-making and judgment (National Highway Traffic and Safety Administration [NHSTA], 2014). Driving safety is frequently a concern in individuals with a dementia diagnosis, as cognitive impairment is a significant risk factor for motor vehicle accidents (Spenceley, Sedgwick, & Keegan, 2015). The declining cognitive ability of a person with dementia will eventually necessitate the need for the individual to stop driving. The need to restrict or give up driving raises a number of issues for individuals with dementia and their families. Loss of driving can impact the non-driving spouse and brings added responsibilities (e.g., transporting the person to appointments and activities, shopping) for others in the individual's life. Alternative methods of transportation may be limited or nonexistent, and the loss of the ability to drive can result in social isolation and limit access to a variety of services.

Determining at what point driving restrictions are needed is difficult because there is little evidence that links the stages of dementia to driving behavior (Alzheimer's Association, 2015b). A number of studies have revealed an increased crash rate for drivers with dementia compared to age-matched individuals without dementia (Carr & Ott, 2010; Rizzo et al., 2001). While there is consensus that the cognitive deficits of individuals with moderate to severe dementia prevent them from being able to safely or practically operate a motor vehicle, there is less agreement about the driving ability of individuals in the early stages of dementia (Ott et al., 2008). Although some individuals with mild dementia voluntarily restrict their driving, more often, individuals with dementia lack insight and judgment into their impairments and do not willingly limit or give up driving. Thus, the responsibility for driving restrictions falls on others—in many instances, family members or caregivers.

Laws addressing impaired drivers vary from state to state. A number of states have established driver licensing regulations and restrictions for older drivers in order to reduce accidents (Greene et al., 2007; Grabowski, Campbell, & Morrisey, 2004). Though the states vary in the ways they handle these laws, most include vision tests, in-person renewals, and/or a shortened time period between license renewals (NHSTA, 2014). The shortened time periods between renewals are in place to recognize rapid declines in physical and mental health of aging adults (Greene et al., 2007). Although most states have policies or laws for the identification of drivers with physical or mental impairments, the majority rely on voluntary reporting by physicians or other healthcare professionals, and only a few have mandatory reporting (Berger, Rosner, Kark, & Bennett, 2000; Greene et al., 2007).

Complicating matters is the fact that there is no one historical feature and no test result that accurately quantifies driving risk (Iversen et al., 2010). Recent evidence-based reviews provide guidelines and recommendations for assessing driving ability in individuals with dementia (Carr & Ott, 2010; Iversen et al., 2010). There is general agreement that brief mental status screens such as the Mini Mental State Exam (MMSE), the St. Louis University Mental Status Examination (SLUMS), and the Montréal Cognitive Assessment (MoCA) should not be used as the sole determinant of driving recommendations (Iversen et al., 2010). Although neuropsychological testing offers a means to assess cognitive abilities such as attention, executive functioning, visual spatial ability and information processing, which are essential to driving, there is insufficient evidence that results of neuropsychological testing give an accurate estimate of driving risk (Iversen et al., 2010; Wheatley, Carr & Marottoli, 2014). These reviews indicate that interactive driving simulators and performance-based road tests provide the most objective measure of driving ability and are the best predictors of driving risk (Berger et al., 2000; Iversen et al., 2010; Wheatley, Carr & Marottoli, 2014).

VICTIMIZATION

Older adults with dementia are thought to be at greater risk of abuse and neglect than those of the general elderly population (National Center on Elder Abuse [NCEA], 2015). The National Center on Elder Abuse (NCEA, 2015) divides elder abuse into domestic and institutional abuse. Domestic abuse refers to mistreatment committed by someone with whom the elder has a special relationship, such as a spouse, sibling, child, friend, or caregiver. Institutional abuse refers to mistreatment that occurs in residential facilities (such as a nursing home, assisted living facility, group home, board and care facility, foster home, etc.) and is usually perpetrated by someone with a legal or contractual obligation to provide some element of care or protection. Abuse includes any of the following types of maltreatment: physical, emotional, and sexual abuse; caregiver neglect or abandonment; and exploitation (illegal taking, misuse, or concealment of funds, property, or assets).

ABUSE AND NEGLECT

People with dementia are particularly vulnerable to abuse because of impairments in memory, communication abilities, and judgment. In addition, individuals with dementia are likely to be in relationships of dependency, which renders them vulnerable to abuse. A number of studies have shown that as dementia progresses, so does the risk of all types of abuse (Dong et al., 2014).

Each state has adult protective service laws that define abuse and neglect and mandate programs that provide protection and assistance for vulnerable adults. Laws and definitions vary from state to state. In a number of states, "elder abuse" is now a criminal violation (Jackson, 2016). In most states, social service and health care providers are mandated to report suspected abuse and neglect. Despite these laws and programs, abuse of older adults with dementia is underreported (Dong et al., 2014; NCEA, 2015). Many people with dementia are unable, frightened, or embarrassed to report abuse (Cooper & Livingston, 2014). Estimates of prevalence rates for abuse and neglect in people with dementia are reported to range from 5.4% to 62.3% (Dong et al., 2014) and from 27.5% to 55% (Tronetti, 2014).

In a U.S. study, caregiver abuse and neglect of people with dementia was detected in 47.3% of the surveyed caregivers (Wiglesworth, 2010). Other studies looking at rates of abuse among older adults with dementia have found that 27.9% to 62.3% had experienced psychological abuse, 3.5% to 23.1% experienced physical abuse, 13.6% to 29.5% experienced neglect, and 31% of those abused experienced multiple forms of abuse (Dong et al., 2014; Tronetti, 2014; Wiglesworth et al., 2010). According to the nationally representative survey of adults age 60 and older, 76% of perpetrators of physical abuse were family members. Of those perpetrators, 57% were partners or spouses, 10% were children or grandchildren, and 9% were other relatives; acquaintances accounted for 19% of physical abuse, and strangers made up 3% (Acierno, Hernandez-Tejada, Muzzy, & Steve, 2009).

FINANCIAL EXPLOITATION AND FRAUD

Financial exploitation is one of the most commonly reported types of elder abuse in people with dementia living alone (NCEA, 2015), with perpetrators often being friends or family members who have a relationship of trust with the victim. Risk for financial exploitation or money mismanagement increases when individuals with dementia are unable to get to the bank without assistance; have multiple care providers; or leave money, bills, and other financial information around the house. An individual with dementia is also at risk if they are socially isolated or feel pressured by family or friends for money.

Each year, millions of elderly Americans become the target of telemarketing and internet fraud, as well as other forms of financial scams (Pak & Shadel, 2011), which results in an annual loss of $2.9 billion from elder victims alone (MetLife Mature Market Institute, 2011). There are numerous fraud schemes that target vulnerable populations, including money transfer fraud, home repair fraud, and sweepstake scams. The same factors that make individuals with dementia vulnerable to financial exploitation leave them at increased risk of consumer fraud, particularly financial fraud. The vulnerability, social isolation, cognitive impairments, and loss of independence of elderly people with dementia make them easy targets for fraud (Friedman, 1992; Jackson & Hafemeister, 2011).

Because of their cognitive impairments, individuals with dementia may be unable to connect their actions (e.g., providing personal banking information to gain earnings) with the loss of funds and the devastating financial outcome. As a result, individuals with dementia may fall victim of fraud multiple times before family, friends or professionals become aware of the situation. The signs of financial abuse, financial exploitation and fraud include increased worry about finances, peculiar banking or credit card activity, deficient food and necessities, and an unusual type or number of purchases (Cohen, 2008). Recently, there has been an increased focus on developing programs and resources to prevent financial exploitation of individuals with dementia. A number of these resources are available through the Consumer Financial Protection Bureau, the National Center for Elder Abuse, and the American Bar Association Commission on Law and Aging.

ABUSE, EXPLOITATION AND THE CRIMINAL JUSTICE SYSTEM

The conceptualization of elder abuse has shifted radically over the past 25 years (Jackson, 2016). Prior to the 1990s, elder abuse was viewed as a problem of caregiving similar to that of child abuse. However, during the 1990s elder abuse began to be viewed as more similar to family violence. The inclusion of elder abuse as a form of family violence transformed it from a social services issue to a criminal justice issue (Wolf, Hodge, & Roberts, 1998). The introduction of the Elder Justice Act in 2002 firmly established elder abuse as a crime. Older adult victims of abuse became seen as not merely "in need of assistance," but rather, as entitled to justice (Jackson, 2016).

As a result of the intensified recognition and focus on prosecution of cases of elder abuse and financial exploitation, law enforcement and legal professionals are increasingly likely to find themselves working with individuals with dementia. As victims/witnesses, individuals with dementia pose challenges for law enforcement. Cognitive deficits may prevent individuals with dementia from accurately reporting information and events. Individuals with dementia who are the victims of abuse and exploitation may not be able to understand or explain what happened to them. They also may be fearful of their abuser, on whom they may be dependent, and/or wary of others. Because individuals with dementia sometimes make allegations of theft or intrusion that are due to cognitive deficits, their reports of actual victimization may not be believed. Individuals with dementia also tend to be suggestible and are susceptible to misinformation (Brank & Wylie, 2015). It is therefore important that allegations made by individuals with dementia be carefully assessed.

Along with the increased recognition focus on prosecution of cases of elder abuse, neglect and financial exploitation, there has been an increased emphasis on training prosecutors, lawyers and law enforcement officers on unique aspects of the elderly as potential or actual victims of crime (Aprile, 2012). A number of organizations offer training and other resources for responding effectively to the needs of individuals with dementia. For example, the following offer a variety of materials as well as websites which provide tips for effective interactions: The Community Oriented Policing Service (COPS) Office's Physical and Emotional Abuse of the Elderly Problem Specific Guide; USDOJ: Elder Justice Initiative; The International Association of Chiefs of Police (IACP) Alzheimer's Initiative Program; The Alzheimer's Association Safe Return Guide for Law Enforcement; and The Alzheimer's Association First Responders Training Program.

CRIMINAL VIOLATIONS, AGGRESSION, AND VIOLENCE

According to United States arrest data, in general, the elderly are less likely to commit crimes, and most of the crimes committed by elders consist of relatively minor offenses (Dunlop, Rothman, & Hirt, 2001). Studies indicate that while there is a high incidence of "low level" aggression (does not cause injuries) in individuals with dementia, violent acts do occur (Cohen, 2004; Dunlop et al., 2001). There have, however, been few studies of the prevalence, risk factors, and clinical patterns of criminal behaviors, aggression, and violence perpetrated by individuals with dementia (Cohen, 2004; Cipriani, Lucetti, Danti, Carlesi & Nuti, 2016). Available data shows that crimes committed by people with dementia range from theft, traffic violations, trespassing, inappropriate sexual advances, and minor aggressive acts to more severe violence and homicide (Liljegren et al., 2015; Cipriani et al., 2016).

Evidence from recent studies indicates that new onset criminal behavior can be one of the earliest signs of dementia (Liljegren et al., 2015; Cipriani, Lucetti, et al., 2016). Neurodegenerative diseases can cause dysfunction in regions of the brain involved in judgment, executive function, emotional processing, sexual behavior, violence, and self-awareness, and these deficits can result in antisocial and criminal behavior in individuals with no history of antisocial activities (Liljegren et al., 2015). Although criminal and antisocial behaviors have been documented in a variety of neurodegenerative disorders, new criminal behaviors are more likely to emerge in association with some neurodegenerative diseases than others (Liljegren et al., 2015; Cipriani et al., 2016). In their study of 2,397 patients diagnosed with dementia, Liljegren et al. (2015) found new criminal behaviors were most prevalent in individuals with behavioral variant frontotemporal dementia (bvFTD—37.4%), followed by individuals with semantic variant primary progressive aphasia (svPPA—27%). Criminal behaviors were far less frequent in Alzheimer's dementia (7.7%). Previous studies, albeit with smaller samples, have reported similar differences in prevalence of criminal behaviors between individuals with bvFTSD and Alzheimer's dementia (Miller et al., 1997; Mendez, Chen, Shapira, & Miller, 2005). In addition to higher frequency of criminal behaviors, these investigators found that the nature of criminal behavior also differs in different types of dementia.

Criminal behaviors in those with Alzheimer's disease, which primarily affects brain areas that are responsible for memory (hippocampal and posterior brain regions), tend to be less violent and involve more instances of poor judgment, resulting in traffic violations, trespassing, shoplifting, public urination and sexually inappropriate behavior (Miller et al., 1997; Liljegren et al., 2015; Cipriani et al., 2016). These behaviors often result from confusion, disorientation, or misinterpreting the environment. While aggressive behaviors are not uncommon in individuals with Alzheimer's dementia, they tend to be "low level" and to be associated with agitation and paranoia (e.g., perceiving intimate care as a threat, failure to recognize non-family/friend and believing them an intruder) and are often directed at caregivers (Patel & Hope, 1993; Liljegren et al., 2015; Cipriani et al., 2016).

In contrast, individuals with bvFTD and svPPA, disorders which affect frontal brain circuits responsible for regulating socially appropriate behavior, have a higher frequency of antisocial behaviors and violence, with theft, unethical job conduct, inappropriate sexual behavior, indecent exposure, public urination, illegal driving acts, and physical assaults or violence being the most common criminal behaviors (Miller et al., 1997; Mendez et al., 2005; Liljegren et al., 2015; Cipriani et al., 2016). As noted by Mendez (2010), the behavior of individuals with FTD, particularly bvFTD, is reminiscent of the famous case of Phineas Gage, who developed "acquired sociopathy" after sustaining a frontal lobe injury from an explosion that drove a railroad spike through his brain.

HOMICIDE

Little is known about the prevalence and patterns of violence escalating to homicide in persons with dementia. While homicides committed by individuals with dementia are relatively rare, they are of concern to family members, caretakers and law enforcement. Cohen (2004) conducted a two-year retrospective newspaper surveillance study using the BurrelleLuce's Information Service (the media monitoring service) to identify news stories in which a person with dementia killed another person. The BurrelleLuce service surveyed 1734 United States daily newspapers from 2002-2003. A total of nine cases in which an individual with dementia committed homicide were identified. The individuals with dementia ranged in age from 68 to 74 years, 90% were men, 90% killed a spouse or intimate, 20% were homicide–suicides, 80% used a firearm, and 90% of the incidents occurred at home. This computes to an estimated prevalence for dementia-perpetrated homicide of 0.22 per 100,000 persons with dementia. Cohen noted that a previous newspaper surveillance study on homicide and dementia conducted by her program showed that more than half of all incidents reported occurred in long-term-care facilities. Review of the incidents suggested vascular dementia, paranoia, and psychotic symptoms in combination with environmental stressors and the availability of firearms and other lethal means were likely risk factors for serious aggression and violence (Cohen, 2004).

LEGAL PROCEEDINGS

The legal process presents challenges for individuals with dementia and the professionals involved. Cognitive impairments associated with dementia impact the individual's ability to comprehend and participate in every stage of the legal process. Difficulties are likely to arise in the initial contacts with law enforcement personnel, as many individuals with dementia do not fully comprehend events around them, do not consistently recall events and details of those events, and often lack awareness or insight into the ramifications of their own behavior or the behaviors of others. Memory impairment can lead to individuals with dementia providing inaccurate or contradictory information (noted previously), and the cognitive impairments of dementia also contribute to vulnerability to suggestibility. Dementia can undermine an accused's confession, consent to search, or similar decisions (Aprile, 2012; Brank & Wylie, 2015). Dementia, depending on the severity of cognitive impairments, could render a person mentally incompetent to stand trial. Even in cases where dementia does justify the exclusion of evidence and the individual is competent to proceed, the accused's dementia may be relevant to the jury's view of credibility of information obtained from or other decisions made by him or her (Aprile, 2012). As many individuals with dementia are not diagnosed until late in the disease, it is incumbent on clinical, legal and law enforcement professionals who are dealing with the elderly to be alert to the possibility that an individual may be experiencing cognitive impairment that is not obvious.

COMPETENCE TO STAND TRIAL

As previously stated, dementia may render an individual incompetent to stand trial. Cognitive limitations have long been recognized as a significant problem warranting competence evaluations (Aprile, 2012; Mossman & Farrell, 2015). Few studies have focused on competence to stand trial in elderly and demented defendants; however, of those done, findings consistently show that defendants with dementia are at high risk of being found incompetent to stand trial (Morris & Parker, 2009). Adjudicating such individuals raises a number of questions for courts and mental health authorities involved in competency restoration. One question has to do with the fairness of institutionalizing individuals with dementia, for whom there is little chance of attaining competence to stand trial and who have not been convicted of a crime (Morris & Parker, 2009). In the case of Jackson v. Indiana (1972), the U.S. Supreme Court held that indefinite commitment of an individual solely on account of his incompetence to stand trial is unconstitutional, and that the nature and duration of commitment must bear some reasonable relation to the purpose for which an individual was committed. In addition, the court ruled that continued commitment for restoration to competency "must be justified by progress toward that goal," and that those individuals deemed permanently incompetent, without a substantial probability of attaining competence in the foreseeable future, must either be released or undergo civil commitment proceedings (Jackson v. Indiana, 1972, p. 739). As individuals diagnosed with dementia have been found to be less likely to be restored to competence within one year of hospitalization (Morris & Parker, 2009), this ruling has significance for legal proceedings and decisions regarding defendants with dementia. Questions of responsibility for a crime and competence to stand trial are also challenging due to the progressive nature of neurodegenerative disorders. The neurocognitive and behavioral impairments associated with these disorders progress and change over the course of legal proceedings.

Individuals with frontotemporal dementia (FTD) present additional challenges in the areas of criminal responsibility and competence to stand trial. Core features of bvFTD are disturbances to social and moral decision-making, profound difficulty following legal and moral rules and norms, and commission of social and often legal transgressions (Mendez, 2010). Typically, individuals in early stages of FTD exhibit a loss of social tact and propriety, improper verbal or nonverbal communication and unacceptable physical contact. In greater than 50% of individuals with FTD, socially inappropriate behavior develops into failure to conform to lawful behavior (Mendez et al., 2005). Despite the changes in their brain causing these changes in personality and behavior, individuals with FTD, particularly in the early stages, often have relatively normal performance on traditional cognitive tests of memory and even of executive control and are able to recognize and verbalize that what they did was wrong (Brower & Price, 2001; Kramer et al., 2003). Although individuals with FTD are able to understand their actions, they lack the inhibitory circuitry in the frontal lobe to prevent inappropriate behavior. This ability makes individuals with FTD particularly vulnerable in legal proceedings, as the traditional insanity defense requires that defendants do not understand that their actions are wrong (Mendez, 2010; Berryessa, 2016). Nevertheless, individuals with FTD have a specific brain-based impairment in moral reasoning and may not possess the faculties sufficient to bring reason to bear on their impulses and abstain from criminal violations (Mendez, 2010). Further, if the individual is deemed competent to stand trial and is found to be responsible for his or her actions, questions then arise regarding the appropriate nature and objective of the sentence for an offender with bvFTD (Berryessea, 2016). It is likely that traditional sentences, aimed at retribution and deterrence, are ineffective and obsolete punishments for offenders with FTD (Aprile, 2012; Berryessa, 2016).

CONCLUSION

Neurodegenerative diseases have significant impact on an individual's cognitive and behavioral functioning. The diagnosis of dementia poses several risks and raises a variety of concerns/questions regarding aspects of the individual's welfare as well as ethical and legal issues. As the population continues to age, clinical and legal professionals within the criminal justice system will increasingly be faced with challenges and grappling with issues associated with this population. To ensure individuals with dementia are identified and treated justly and that their safety and that of the public is maintained, clinical professionals, legal professionals, and law enforcement personnel need to have increased knowledge and understanding of neurodegenerative disorders and their impact and be given resources to work with these individuals.

REFERENCES

Acierno, R., Hernandez-Tejada, M., Muzzy, W. & Steve, K. (2009). *National Elder Mistreatment Study*. U.S. Department of Justice grant report, NCJ 226456. Retrieved from https://www.ncjrs.gov/pdffiles1/nij/grants/226456.pdf

Albert, M.S., DeKosky, S.T., Dickson, D., Dubois, B., Feldman, H.H., Fox, N.C., Gamst, A., Holtzman, D.M., Jagust, W.J., Petersen, R.C., & Snyder, P.J. (2011). The diagnosis of mild cognitive impairment due to Alzheimer's disease: Reccomendations from the National Institute on Aging-Alzheimer's Association workgroups on diagnostic guidelines for Alzheimer's disease. *Alzheimer's and Dementia, 7*, 270-279.

Alzheimer's Association. (2015a). *2015 Alzheimer's disease Facts and Figures*. Retrieved from http://www.alz.org/facts/downloads/facts_figures_2015.pdf

Alzheimer's Association. (2015b). *Driving and Dementia*. Retrieved from http://www.alz.org/documents_custom/statements/Driving_and_Dementia.pdf

Alzheimer's Association. (2015c). *Respect for Autonomy*. Retrieved from http://www.alz.org/documents_custom/statements/Respect_for_Autonomy.pdf

Alzheimer's Disease Education and Referral Center (ADEAR). (2008). *Legal and Financial Planning for People with Alzheimer's Disease Fact Sheet*. Bethesda: NIH. Retrieved from https://d2cauhfh6h4x0p.cloudfront.net/s3fs-public/legal_and_financial_planning-final_10-14-13.pdf

Alzheimer's Society. (2015). *What is Vascular Dementia?* Retrieved from https://www.alzheimers.org.uk/site/scripts/download_info.php?downloadID=1094

American Academy of Neurology (AAN). (2010). *Detection, diagnosis and management of dementia.* Retrieved from http://tools.aan.com/professionals/practice/pdfs/dementia_guideline.pdf

American Bar Association Commission on Law and Aging & American Psychological Association – ABA/APA. (2008). *Assessment of older adults with diminished capacity: A handbook for psychologists.* Washington, D.C: American Bar Association Commission on Law and Aging.

American Psychiatric Association (APA). (2013). *Diagnostic and Statistical Manual of Mental Disorders: DSM-5, 5th edition.* Washington, DC: American Psychiatric Association.

Appelbaum, P. S., & Grisso, T. (1988). Assessing patients' capacities to consent to treatment. *New England Journal of Medicine, 319*, 1635-1638.

Aprile, J. V. (2012). Defending the elderly. *Criminal Justice, 27*, 55-56, 63.

Association for Frontal Temporal Degeneration (AFTD). (2013). *The Doctor Thinks It's FTD. Now What?* Radnor, PA: AFTD.

Bateman, R.J., Aisen, P.S., De Strooper, B., Fox, N.C., Lemere, C.A., Ringman, J.M., Salloway, S., Sperling, R.A., Windisch, M., & Xiong, C. (2011). Autosomal-dominant Alzheimer's disease: a review and proposal for the prevention of Alzheimer's disease. *Alzheimer's Research & Therapy, 3*, 1. Retrieved from http://alzres.biomedcentral.com/articles/10.1186/alzrt59

Bekris, L.M., Yu C.E., Bird, T.D., & Tsuang, DW. (2010). Genetics of Alzheimer disease. *Journal of Geriatric Psychiatry and Neurology, 23*, 213-27.

Berger, J. T., Rosner, F., Kark, P., & Bennett, A. J. (2000). Reporting by physicians of impaired drivers and potentially impaired drivers. *Journal of General Internal Medicine, 15*, 667-672.

Berryessa, C. (2016). Behavioral and neural impairments of frontotemporal dementia: Potential implications for criminal responsibility and sentencing. *International Journal of Law and Psychiatry, 46*, 1-6.

Braak, H., & Braak, E. (1991). Neuropathological staging of Alzheimer-related changes. *Acta Neuropathology, 82*, 239-259.

Brank, E. M., & Wylie, L. E. (2015). Elders and the justice system. In B. L. Cutler & P. A. Zapf (Eds.), *APA Handbook of Forensic Psychology Vol. 2: Criminal Investigation, Adjudication, and Sentencing Outcomes* (pp. 59-77). Washington, DC: APA.

Brower, M., & Price, B. (2001). Neuropsychiatry of frontal lobe dysfunction in violent criminal behavior: A critical review. *Journal of Neurology, Neurosurgery, and Psychiatry, 71*, 720-726.

Carney, M. T., Neugroschl, J., Morrison, R. S., Marin, D., & Siu, A. L. (2001). The development and piloting of a capacity assessment tool. *The Journal of Clinical Ethics, 12*, 17-23.

Carr, D. B., & Ott, B. R. (2010). The older adult driver with cognitive impairment: "It's a very frustrating life". *Journal of the American Medical Association, 303(*16), 1632-1641.

Centers for Disease Control and Prevention. (2015) Retrieved from https://www.cdc.gov/aging/aginginfo/alzheimers.htm

Chodosh, J., Petitti, D.B., Elliott, M., Hays, R.D., Crooks, V.C., Reuben, D.B., Galen Buckwalter, J., & Wenger, N. (2004). Physician recognition of cognitive impairment: Evaluating the need for improvement. *Journal of the American Geriatrics Society, 52*, 1051-1059.

Cipriani, G., Lucetti, C., Danti, S., Carlesi, C. & Nuti, A. (2016). Violent and criminal manifestations in dementia patients. *Geriatrics and Gerontology International, 16*, 541-549.

Clarfield, A. M. (2003). The decreasing prevalence of reversible dementias: An updated meta-analysis. *Archives of International Medicine, 163*, 2219-2229.

Cognitive Neurology and Alzheimer's Disease Center (CNADC) (n.d.). *What is frontotemporal degeneration (bvFTD)? Northwestern University Feinberg School of Medicine.* Retrieved from http://www.brain. northwestern.edu/pdfs/Disease%20Summaries/bvFTD.pdf

Cohen, C. (2008). Consumer fraud and dementia: Lessons learned from conmen. *Dementia, 7*, 283-285.

Cohen, D. (2004). *Violent crimes and dementia: A Hearing on crimes without criminals? Seniors, dementia, and the aftermath.* Retrieved from http://www.aging.senate.gov/imo/media/doc/hr119dc.pdf

Cohen, M. (2015). Dementia 101. *Neurology Now, 11*, 44-50.

Cooper, C., & Livingston, G. (2014). Mental health/psychiatric issues in elder abuse and neglect. *Clinic in Geriatric Medicine, 30*(4), 839-850. doi: 10.1016/j.cger.2014.08.011

Cummings, J. L. (2003). *The Neuropsychiatry of Alzheimer's Disease and Related Dementias.* New York: Taylor & Francis.

Davies, R. R., Hodges, J. R., Kril, J. J., Patterson, K., Halliday, G. M., & Xuereb, J. H. (2005). The pathological basis of semantic dementia. *Brain, 128*, 1984-1995.

Diehl, M., Marsiske, M., Horgas, A. L., Rosenberg, A., Saczynski, J. S., & Willis, S. L. (2005). The Revised Observed Tasks of Daily Living: A performance-based assessment of everyday problem solving in older adults. *Journal of Applied Gerontology, 24*, 211-230. doi:10.1177/0733464804273772

Donaghy, P. C., & McKeith, I. G. (2014). The clinical characteristics of dementia with Lewy bodies and consideration of prodromal diagnosis. *Alzheimer's Research & Therapy, 6*(4), 46. Retrieved from https:// alzres.biomedcentral.com/articles/10.1186/alzrt274

Dong, X., Chen, R., & Simon, M. A. (2014). Elder abuse and dementia: A review of the research and health policy. *Health Affairs, 33*, 642-649.

Dunlop, B., Rothman, M. B., & Hirt, G. M. (2001). Elders and criminal justice: International issues for the 21st century. *International Journal of Law and Psychiatry, 24*, 285-303.

Edelstein, B. (1999). *Hopemont Capacity Assessment Interview manual and scoring guide.* Morgantown: West Virginia University.

Ferman, T. J., & Boeve, B. F. (2007). Dementia with Lewy bodies. *Neurologic Clinics, 25*, 741-760.

Fernando M.S., & Ince P.G. (2004). MRC Cognitive Function and Ageing Neuropathology Study Group: Vascular pathologies and cognition in a population-based cohort of elderly people. *Journal of the Neurological Sciences, 226*, 13-27.

Freeman, S. H., Kandel, R., Cruz, L., Rozkalne, A., Newell, K., Frosch, M. P., Hedley-Whyte, E. T., Locascio, J. J., Lipsitz, L.A., & Hyman, B. T. (2008). Preservation of neuronal number despite age-related cortical brain atrophy in elderly subjects without Alzheimer disease. *Journal of Neuropathology & Experimental Neurology, 67*, 1205-1212.

Friedman, M. (1992). Confidence swindles of older consumers. *Journal of Consumer Affairs, 26*, 20-46.

Furrow, B. R., Greaney, T. L., Johnson, S. H., Jost, T. S., & Schwartz, R. L. (2000). *The doctrine of informed consent* (2nd ed.). St. Paul, MN: Thomson-West.

Galvin, J. E., Boeve, B. F., Duda, J. E., Galasko, D. R., Kaufer, D., Leverenz, J. B., Lippa, C. F., & Lopez, O. L. (2008). *Current Issues in Lewy Body Dementia: Diagnosis, Treatment and Research.* Lilburn, GA: Lewy Body Association.

Geriatrics Ethics Project. (n.d.) *Geriatrics: Decision-Making, Autonomy, Valid Consent and Guardianship.* Retrieved from http://www.miami.edu/index.php/ethics/projects/geriatrics_and_ethics/decision- making_autonomy_valid_consent_and_guardianship/

Gorno-Tempini, M. L., Dronkers, N. F., Rankin, K. P., Ogar, J. M., Phengrasamy, L., Rosen, H. J., Johnson, J. K., Weiner, M. W., & Miller, B. L. (2004). Cognition and anatomy in three variants of primary progressive aphasia. *Annals of Neurology, 55*, 335-346.

Gorno-Tempini, M.L., Hillis, A.E., Weintraub, S., Kertesz, A., Mendez, M., Cappa, S.E.E.A., Ogar, J.M., Rohrer, J.D., Black, S., Boeve, B.F., & Manes, F. (2011). Classification of primary progressive aphasia and its variants. *Neurology, 76*, 1006-1014.

Grabowski, D. C., Campbell, C. M., & Morrisey, M. A. (2004). Elderly licensure laws and motor vehicle fatalities. *JAMA. 291*(23), 2840-2846.

Greene, E., Bornstein, B., & Dietrich, H. (2007). Granny, (don't) get your gun: competency issues in gun ownership by older adults. *Behavioral Sciences and the Law, 25*, 405-423.

Griffith, H. R., Belue, K., Sicola, A., Krzywanski, S., Zamrini, E., Harrell, L., & Marson, D. C. (2003). Impaired financial abilities in mild cognitive impairment: A direct assessment approach. *Neurology, 60*, 449-457.

Grisso, T., & Appelbaum, P. S. (1995). Comparison of standards for assessing patients' capacities to make treatment decisions. *The American Journal of Psychiatry, 152*(7), 1033.

Grisso, T., & Applebaum, P. S. (1998). *Assessing Competence to Consent to Treatment.* New York: Oxford University Press.

Grisso, T., & Appelbaum, P. S. (1998). *MacArthur Competence Assessment Tool for Treatment (MacCAT-T).* Professional Resource Press/Professional Resource Exchange.

Gurrera, R. J., Moye, J., Karel, M. J., Azar, A. R., & Armesto, J. C. (2006). Cognitive performance predicts treatment decisional abilities in mild to moderate dementia. *Neurology, 66*, 1367-1372.

Hanson, J. C., & Lippa, C. F. (2009). Lewy body dementia. *International Review of Neurobiology, 84,* 215-228.

Helzner, E. P., Scarmeas, N., Cosentino, S., Tang, M. X., Schupf, N., & Stern, Y. (2008). Survival in Alzheimer disease: A multiethnic, population-based study of incident cases. *Neurology, 71*, 1489-1495.

Hirst, M. (2005). Carer distress: A prospective, population-based study. *Social Science & Medicine, 61*, 697-708.

Hornberger, M., Piguet, O., Graham, A.J., Nestor, P.J., & Hodges, J.R. (2010). How preserved is episodic memory in behavioral variant frontotemporal dementia? *Neurology, 74*, 472-479.

Iverson, D. J., Gronseth, G. S., Reger, M. A., Classen, S., Dubinsky, R. M., & Rizzo, M. (2010). Practice parameter update: Evaluation and management of driving risk in dementia: Report of the quality standards subcommittee of the American academy of neurology. *Neurology, 74*, 1316-1324.

Jack, C. R. Jr. (2012). Alzheimer disease: New concepts on its neurobiology and the clinical role imaging will play. *Radiology, 263*, 344-361.

Jackson, S. L. (2016). The shifting conceptualization of elder abuse in the United States: from social services, to criminal justice, and beyond. *International Psychogeriatrics, 28*, 1-8.

Jackson, S. L., & Hafemeister, T. L. (2011). Financial abuse of elderly people vs. other forms of elder abuse: Assessing their dynamics, risk factors, and society's response. *Final Report Presented to the National Institute of Justice. Jackson v. Indiana,* 406 U.S. 715, 92 S. Ct 1845 (1972).

Jackson v. Indiana, (1972). 406 U.S. 715, 92S. Ct1845

Janofsky, J. S., McCarthy, R. J., & Folstein, M. (1992). The Hopkins Competency Assessment Test: A brief method for evaluating patients' capacity to give informed consent. *Hospital and Community Psychiatry, 43*, 132-136.

Johnson, J. K., Diehl, J., Mendez, M. F., Neuhaus, J., Shapira, J. S., Forman, M., Chute, D. J., Roberson, E. D., Pace-Savitsky, C., Neumann, M., & Chow, T. W. (2005). Frontotemporal lobar degeneration: Demographic characteristics of 353 patients. *Archives of Neurology, 62*, 925-930.

Kasper, J. D., Freedman, V. A., & Spillman, B. C. (2014). *Disability and care needs of older Americans by dementia status: An analysis of the 2011 National Health and Aging Trends Study.* Prepared for the Office of Disability, Aging and Long Term Care Policy, Office of the Assistant Secretary for Planning and Evaluation, U.S. Department of Health and Human Services, Contract # HHSP23337003T. Retrieved from http://aspe.hhs.gov/daltcp/reports/2014/NHATSDS.cfm

Kavirajan, H., & Schneider, L. S. (2007). The efficacy and adverse effects of cholinesterase inhibitors and memantine in vascular dementia: a systematic review and meta-analysis of controlled trials. *Lancet Neurology, 6*, 782-792.

Kim, S. Y., Karlawish, J. H. T., & Caine, E. D. (2002). Current state of research on decision-making competence of cognitively impaired elderly persons. *American Journal of Geriatric Psychiatry, 10*, 151-165.

Kramer, J. H., Jurik, J., Sha, S. J., Rankin, K. P., Rosen, H. J., Johnson, J. K., & Miller, B. L. (2003). Distinctive neuropsychological patterns in frontotemporal dementia, semantic dementia, and Alzheimer disease. *Cognitive and Behavioral Neurology: Official Journal of the Society for Behavioral and Cognitive Neurology, 16*, 211-218.

Larson, E. B., Shadlen, M., Wang, L., McCormick, W. C., Bowen, J. D., Teri, L., & Kukull, W. A. (2004). Survival after initial diagnosis of Alzheimer disease. *Annals of Internal Medicine, 140*, 501.

Liljegren, M., Naasan, G., Temlett, J., Perry, D.C., Rankin, K.P., Merrilees, J., Grinberg, L.T., Seeley, W.W., Englund, E., & Miller, B.L. (2015). Criminal behavior in frontotemporal dementia and Alzheimer disease. *JAMA neurology, 72*(3), 295-300.

Loeb, P.A. (1996). *Independent Living Scales*. San Antonio: Psychological Corporation.

Long, E., Lines, L. M., Wiener, J. M., & Gould, E. (2014). *The Alzheimer's Voice: Person-Centered and Person-Directed Dementia Care Report*. Retrieved from www.aoa.acl.gov/AoA_Programs/HPW/Alz.../AD_voice_2014-12-18-14.docx

Marsiske, M., & Willis, S. L. (1995). Dimensionality of everyday problem solving in older adults. *Psychology and Aging, 10*, 269-283.

Marson, D. C. (2001). Loss of competency in Alzheimer's disease: Conceptual and psychometric approaches. *International Journal of Law and Psychiatry, 8*, 109-119.

Marson, D. C. (2013). Clinical and ethical aspects of financial capacity in dementia: A commentary. *The American Journal of Geriatric Psychiatry: Official Journal of the American Association for Geriatric Psychiatry, 21*(4), 392-390.

Marson, D. C., Chatterjee, A., Ingram, K. K., & Harrell, L. E. (1996). Toward a neurologic model of competency: Cognitive predictors of capacity to consent in Alzheimer's disease using three different legal standards. *Neurology, 46*, 666-672.

Marson, D. C., & Hebert, T. (2005). Assessing civil competencies in older adults with dementia: Medical decision making capacity, financial capacity, and testamentary capacity. In G. J. Larrabee, (Ed.), *Forensic neuropsychology: A scientific approach* (pp. 334-377). New York: Oxford University Press.

Marson, D. C., Ingram, K. K., Cody, H. A., & Harrell, L. E. (1995). Assessing the competency of patients with Alzheimer's disease under different legal standards: A prototype instrument. *Archives of Neurology, 52*, 949-954.

Marson, D. C., Sawrie, S., McInturff, B., Snyder, S., Chatterjee, A., Stalvey, T., Boothe, A., & Harrell, L. (2000). Assessing financial capacity in patients with Alzheimer's disease: A conceptual model and prototype instrument. *Archives of Neurology, 57,* 877-884.

McDougall, G. J., Becker, H., Vaughan, P. W., Acee, T. W., & Delville, C. L. (2010). The revised direct assessment of functional status for independent older adults. *Gerontologist, 50,* 363-370.

McKhann, G., Drachman, D., Folstein, M., Katzman, R., Price, D., & Stadlan, E. M. (1984). Clinical diagnosis of Alzheimer's disease: Report of the NINCDS-ADRDA Work Group under the auspices of department of health and human services task force on Alzheimer's disease. *Neurology, 34,* 939-944.

Meisel, A. (2005). Ethics and law: Physician-assisted dying. *Journal of Palliative Medicine, 8,* 609-623.

Mendez, M. F. (2010). The unique predisposition to criminal violations in frontotemporal dementia. *Journal of American Academy of Psychiatry and Law, 38,* 318-323.

Mendez, M. F., Chen, A. K., Shapira, J. S., & Miller, B. L. (2005). Acquired sociopathy and frontotemporal dementia. *Dementia Geriatrics Cognitive Disorder, 20,* 99-104.

Mesulam, M. M. (2013). Primary progressive aphasia and the language network: The 2013 Houston Merritt Lecture. *Neurology, 81,* 456-462.

MetLife Mature Market Institute. (2011). *The MetLife study of. elder financial abuse: Crimes of occasion, desperation, and predation against America's elders.* New York: Author. Retrieved from https://www.metlife.com/assets/cao/mmi/publications/studies/2011/mmielder-financial-abuse.pdf

Miller, B. L., Darby, A., Benson, D. F., Cummings, J. L., & Miller, M. H. (1997). Aggressive, socially disruptive and antisocial behaviour associated with fronto-temporal dementia. *British Journal of Psychiatry, 170,* 150-154.

Morris, D. R., & Parker, G. F. (2009). Effects of advanced age and dementia on restoration of competence to stand trial. *International Journal of Law and Psychiatry, 32,* 156-160.

Morse, S. J. (2011). Mental disorder and criminal law. *Journal and Criminal Law and Criminology, 101,* 885-968.

Mossman, D., & Farrell, H. M. (2015). Civil Competencies. In B. L. Cutler & P. A. Zapf (Eds.), *APA Handbook of Forensic Psychology Vol. 1: Individual and Situational Influences in Criminal and Civil Contexts* (pp. 533-558). Washington, DC: APA.

Moye, J., Karel, M. J., Azar, A. R., & Gurrera, R. J. (2004). Capacity to consent to treatment: Empirical comparison of three instruments in older adults with and without dementia. *Gerontologist, 44*(2), 166-175.

Moye, J., Karel, M. J., Edelstein, B., Hicken, B., Armesto, J. C., & Gurrera, R. J. (2008). Assessment of capacity to consent to treatment: Current research, the "ACCT" approach, future directions. *Clinical Gerontologist, 31,* 37-66.

Nagahama, Y., Okina, T., Suzuki, N., & Matsuda, M. (2010). Neural correlates of psychotic symptoms in dementia with Lewy bodies. *Brain, 133,* 557-567.

National Center on Elder Abuse (NCEA), Administration on Aging (AOA). (2015). *FAQs.* Retrieved from http://www.ncea.aoa.gov/faq/index.aspx

National Conference of Commissioners on Uniform State Laws. (1997). *Uniform Guardianship and Protective Proceedings Act (1997).* Chicago, IL: Author. Retrieved from http://www.azcourts.gov/Portals/83/pdf/UniformProbateCode1997.pdf

National Highway Traffic and Safety Administration (NHTSA). (2014). *Physician's guide to assessing and counseling older drivers: Chapter 3: Formally assess function.* Retrieved from http://www.nhtsa.gov/people/injury/olddrive/olderdriversbook/pages/Chapter3.html

National Institute of Aging / National Institute of Neurological Disorders and Stroke (NIA/NINDS). (2014). *Frontotemporal Disorders: Information for Patients, Families and Professionals*. Bethesda: NIH. Retrieved from https://www.nia.nih.gov/alzheimers/publication/frontotemporal-disorders/introduction

National Institute of Aging / National Institute of Neurological Disorders and Stroke (NIA/NINDS). (2015). *Lewy Body Dementia: Information for Patients, Families and Professionals*. Bethesda: NIH. Retrieved from https://catalog.ninds.nih.gov/pubstatic/15-7907/15-7907.pdf

National Institute of Neurological Disorders and Stroke (NINDS). (2013). *The Dementias-Hope Through Research*. Bethesda: NIH. Retrieved from http://www.ninds.nih.gov/disorders/dementias/the-dementias.pdf

Ngo, J., & Holroyd-Leduc, J. M. (2015). Systematic review of recent dementia practice guidelines. *Age and Ageing, 44*, 25-33.

Ott, B. R., Heindel, W. C., Papandonatos, G. D., Festa, E. K., Davis, J. D., Daiello, L. A., & Morris, J. C. (2008). A longitudinal study of drivers with Alzheimer disease. *Neurology, 70*(14), 1171-1178.

Pak, K., & Shadel, D. (2011). *AARP Foundation national fraud victim study*. Washington D.C.: AARP.

Patel, V., & Hope, T. (1993). Aggressive behavior in elderly people with dementia: A review. *International Journal of Geriatric Psychiatry, 8*, 457-472.

Piguet, O., Hornberger, M., Mioshi, E., & Hodges, J. R. (2011). Behavioural-variant frontotemporal dementia: Diagnosis, clinical staging, and management. *Lancet Neurology, 10*, 162-172.

Pineda, V., & UNICEF. (2008). *It's about ability: An explanation of the Convention on the Rights of Persons with Disabilities*. Available at http://www.unicef.org/publications/index_43893.html

Prince, M., Bryce, R., Albanese, E., Wilmo, A., Ribeiro, W., & Ferri, C. P. (2013). The global prevalence of dementia: A systematic review and meta-analysis. *Alzheimer's Dementia, 9*, 63-75.

Rascovsky, K., Hodges, J. R., Kipps, C. M., Johnson, J. K., Seeley, W. W., Mendez, M. F., Knopman, D., Kertesz, A., Mesulam, M., Salmon, D. P., & Galasko, D. (2007). Diagnostic criteria for the behavioral variant of frontotemporal dementia (bvFTD): Current limitations and future directions. *Alzheimer Disease and Associated Disorders, 21*, S14-S18.

Ratnavalli, E., Brayne, C., Dawson, K., & Hodges, J. R. (2002). The prevalence of frontotemporal dementia. *Neurology, 58*, 1615-1621.

Rizzo, M., McGehee, D. V., Dawson, J. D., & Anderson, S. N. (2001). Simulated car crashes in drivers with Alzheimer disease. *Alzheimer Disease and Associated Disorders, 15*(1), 10-20.

Roman, G. C. (2003). Vascular dementia: Distinguishing characteristics, treatment, and prevention. *Journal of the American Geriatric Society, 51*, S296-S304.

Roman, G. C., Erkinjuntti, T., Wallin, A., Pantoni, L., & Chui, H. C. (2002). Subcortical ischaemic vascular dementia. *The Lancet Neurology, 1*, 426-436.

Salmon, D. P., & Bondi, M. W. (2009). Neuropsychological assessment of dementia. *Annual Review of Psychology, 60*, 257-282.

Schneider, J. A., Arvanitakis, Z., Bang, W., & Bennett, D. A. (2007). Mixed brain pathologies account for most dementia cases in community dwelling older persons. *Neurology, 69*, 2197-2204.

Skelton, F., Kunik, M. E., Regev, T., & Naik, A. D. (2010). Determining if an older adult can make and execute decisions to live safely at home: A capacity assessment and intervention model. *Archives of Gerontology and Geriatrics, 50*, 300-305. doi:10.1016/j.archger.2009.04.016

Smith, A., & Sullivan, D. (2012). A new ball game: The United Nations Convention on the Rights of Persons with Disabilities and assumptions in care for people with dementia. *Journal of Law and Medicine, 20*(1), 28-34.

Sörensen, S., Duberstein, P., Gill, D., & Pinquart, M. (2006). Dementia care: Mental health effects, intervention strategies, and clinical implications. *The Lancet Neurology, 5*, 961-973.

Spenceley, S. M., Sedgwick, N., & Keenan, J. (2015). Dementia care in the context of primary care reform: An integrative review. *Aging & Mental Health, 19*, 107-120.

Tripathi, M., & Vibha, D. (2009). Reversible dementias. *Indian Journal of Psychiatry, 51*(Suppl1), S52-S55.

Tronetti, P. (2014). Evaluating abuse in the patient with dementia. *Clinics in Geriatric Medicine, 30*(4), 825-838. doi: 10.1016/j.cger.2014.08.010

Uylings, H.B.M. & de Brabandera, J.M. (2002). Neuronal changes in normal human aging and Alzheimer's disease. *Brain and Cognition, 49,* 268-276.

Vann Jones, S. A., & O'Brien, J. T. (2014). The prevalence and incidence of dementia with Lewy bodies: a systematic review of population and clinical studies. *Psychological Medicine, 44*, 673-683.

Villemagne, V.L., Burnham, S., Bourgeat, P., Brown, B., Ellis, K.A., Salvado, O., Szoeke, C., Macaulay, S.L., Martins, R., Maruff, P., & Ames, D. (2013). Amyloid β deposition, neurodegeneration, and cognitive decline in sporadic Alzheimer's disease: A prospective cohort study. *Lancet Neurology, 12*, 357-367.

Wheatley, C., Carr, D., & Marottoli, R. (2014). Consensus statements on driving for persons with dementia. *Occupational Therapy in Health Care, 28*, 132-139.

Widera, E., Steenpass, V., Marson, D., & Sudore, R. (2011). Finances in the older patient with cognitive impairment. *Journal of the American Medical Association, 305*, 698-706.

Wiglesworth, A., Mosqueda, L., Mulnard, R., Liao, S., Gibbs, L., & Fitzgerald, W. (2010). Screening for abuse and neglect of people with dementia. *Journal of the American Geriatrics Society, 58*(3), 493-500.

Williamson, C., Alcantar, O., Rothlind, J., Cahn-Weiner, D., Miller, B. L., & Rosen, H. J. (2010). Standardised measurement of self-awareness deficits in FTD and AD. *Journal of Neurology, Neurosurgery and Psychiatry, 81*, 140-145.

Willis, S. L., & Marsiske, M. (1993). *Manual for the Everyday Problems Test*. University Park: Pennsylvania State University.

Wolf, R. S., Hodge, P., & Roberts, P. (1998). Elder abuse and neglect: prosecution and prevention. *Critical Issues In Aging: An Annual Magazine Of The American Society On Aging, 2*, 35-38.

World Health Organization (WHO). (2015). *Dementia Fact Sheet No. 362*. Retrieved from http://www.who.int/mediacentre/factsheets/fs362/en/

CHAPTER 6

EVIDENCE-BASED PRACTICE: APPLYING GENERAL PRINCIPLES OF EFFECTIVE PSYCHOTHERAPY IN FORENSIC MENTAL HEALTH SETTINGS

LESLIE BARFKNECHT, VALERIE M. GONSALVES, SAMANTHA L. CARTER, MARISSA ZAPPALA, & SARA HARTIGAN

CHAPTER OVERVIEW

Individuals entangled in the legal system are disproportionately likely to suffer from mental illness and substance abuse issues (James & Glaze, 2006; National Institute of Health, 2010). In fact, according to Swartz & Lurigo (2007), the criminal justice system has become one of the largest mental health care providers in the United States. Considering the disproportions of substance abusers and mentally ill in the criminal justice system, it is clear reactive measures must be implemented to mitigate this overpopulation. Recent professional movements encourage implementing a variety of Evidence-Based Practices (EBP) in mental health or criminal settings; in other words, protocols and practices have begun to rely on the use of empirical evidence as the backing for their development. These implementations have led to positive outcomes primarily because EBP is the implementation of "interventions intended to improve, or ameliorate, the social or clinical problems of affected individuals, including offenders with drug abuse" (Pendergast, 2011). Evidence-based practices are used for a much wider range of topics in forensic psychology itself (such as police psychology, criminal profiling) and also in other professional areas. The leading theoretic EBP model for dealing with the abundance of incarcerated mental ill persons is the Risk Needs Responsivity (RNR) model (Andrews, Bonta, & Hoge, 1990). RNR has three guiding principles. First, individuals with the highest level of criminogenic needs require the highest level of services. Second, a client should be offered services that target their personal criminogenic needs. Third, the intervention should be tailored to a client's abilities and learning styles in an effort to maximize effectiveness (Bonta & Andrews, 2007). According to Bonta & Andrews (2007), the implied impact of introducing RNR and improving mental health services to the mentally ill can significantly reduce recidivism, thus reducing the number of individuals re-encountering the legal system because of unaddressed mental health needs. Possible solutions to these growth opportunities may be integrating current psychotherapy practices in community settings with interventions currently used in forensic settings.

INTRODUCTION

Evidence-based practice in psychology (EBPP) is defined by the American Psychological Association (APA) as "the integration of the best available research with clinical expertise in the context of patient characteristics, culture, and preferences" (APA, 2006, p. 284). Over the last few decades, there has been an increase on the emphasis of evidence-based interventions (EBI) and evidence-based practice (EBP) in the forensic mental health setting, resulting in increased funding for research. Subsequently, emerging research has led to an increase in successful evidence-based practices that cater to the needs of mentally ill offenders. This chapter offers a brief overview of the prevalence of mental health needs within criminal justice systems, pendulum shifts in approaches for addressing forensic mental health needs, and identification of a few evidence-based interventions used within criminal justice and forensic mental health institutions.

INTERVENTIONS IN FORENSIC MENTAL HEALTH SETTINGS

The Bureau of Justice Statistics (BJS) has reported that over 1.2 million inmates (not including those on community supervision) have a diagnosed mental illness (James & Glaze, 2006). Approximately 75% of those inmates with a mental illness also met the criteria for a substance use disorder (National Institute of Health, 2010). Likewise, a dependency or abuse of alcohol or drugs was observed for approximately 74% of state prisoners with a mental illness and 56% of those without a mental illness (Bureau of Justice Statistics, 2004). According to the National Institute of Health (NIH), substance abuse and dependence rates are four times greater in criminal offenders than the general population (2010). Taken together, these statistics demonstrate a relationship between criminal activity, substance abuse or dependency, and mental health, which has increased awareness to the mental health needs of offenders and forensic patients.

The combination of these mental health needs with the appeal of reducing the risk of re-offense resulted in significant paradigm shifts in forensic mental health treatment. Initially, treatment interventions were implemented based on widely understood psychotherapeutic principles. However, after the conclusion that offender rehabilitation was ineffective because treatment deviated from traditional psychotherapeutic principles (Martinson, 1974), those initial treatment interventions were questioned. The premise for such a conclusion stemmed from the analysis of programs with the "get tough" model, where the emphasis was on accountability and confrontational techniques, rather than contemporary client-centered interventions (Cullen & Gendreau, 2001). "Get tough" models made logical sense and certainly appealed to a sense of justice and retribution inherent in the public perception of offenders at the time. Unfortunately, the programs were largely ineffective at achieving the desired goal of reducing recidivism. For example, boot camps are an intervention in which individuals, typically juveniles, undergo rigorous daily routines, including military-type activities in the context of a rather harsh, less client-centered interaction styles. Despite wide adoption, boot camps have been found to be largely ineffective at producing substantial reductions to recidivism rates (Cullen, Blevins, Trager, & Gendreau, 2005; Wilson, MacKenzie, & Mitchell, 2003). In fact, some studies examining such punitive-based models indicate that recidivism rates rose in response to such interventions (Gendreau, Goggin, Cullen & Andrews, 2001; Pratt & Cullen, 2005; Smith, Goggin, & Gendreau, 2002).

Although the "get tough" model was not an effective EBP or EBI, the information from studying this model provided important insight to forensic mental health interventions. Meta-analytic studies demonstrated three important conclusions concerning forensic mental health interventions (Hanson et al., 2002):

- In general, treatment with offenders produces measureable positive changes in recidivism.
- The effect size of treatment interventions selected was not homogeneous. That is, some treatment programs were more effective than others.
- Programs aimed at punitive styles of intervention demonstrated no effectiveness.

These findings underscore the importance of developing and evaluating approaches to determine effective interventions. According to Andrews and Bonta (2007) as well as Miller, Zweben, and Johnson (2005), EBP in forensic mental health refers to programs that have been derived from empirical research and have been shown to reduce recidivism. EBP that can successfully reduce recidivism among mentally ill offenders will not only reduce the financial burden of re-incarcerating repeat offenders, but will also address concerns of public safety once those offenders are released.

OVERARCHING PRINCIPLES OF EFFECTIVE INTERVENTIONS: RISK, NEED, RESPONSIVITY

As practitioners and researchers began empirical evaluations on treatment interventions, the RNR model emerged as the predominant theoretical model of rehabilitation (Andrews, Bonta, & Hoge, 1990). Treatment programs that adhere to this model of intervention demonstrate positive outcomes with respect to reductions in recidivism among a wide variety of offender types (Andrews & Bonta, 2007; Marlowe et. al., 2006).

RISK
The risk principle of the RNR model states that individuals with the highest level of criminogenic needs require the highest level of services. In contrast, individuals with low needs require few, if any, services (Andrews & Bonta, 2007). Although this conclusion may seem obvious, there is pressure to apply a high level of service to low-risk offenders in practice. This may be due to the fact that low-risk offenders are a more compliant and motivated population (Andrews & Bonta, 2007). Treatment for low-risk individuals results in minimal recidivism reduction, as these individuals already have a low base rate of re-offense (Andrews & Dowden, 2006). According to Andrews and Bonta (2007), inappropriate matching of resources in conjunction with offender risk level can make matters worse and create a waste of resources. This seemingly paradoxical finding could be the result of exposing low-risk offenders to contact with high-risk offenders (Bonta, Wallace-Capretta, & Rooney, 2000).

The risk principle can be applied to other fields besides forensic mental health settings. For example, an individual who presents with no risk markers for a heart attack may receive information regarding maintenance of their health, but rarely will they require specialized services. When an individual with high blood pressure or obesity visits a doctor, the physician often identifies this person as high risk. As a result, the doctor discusses the myriad of treatment interventions available to reduce that patient's risk of adverse medical consequences. In this example, more interventions are offered to a client as their level of risk increases. The principle of risk in the RNR model works in much the same way, where the amount and types of services are tailored to the offender's level of need.

To determine an offender's level of risk, a variety of options are available, including risk assessments based on algorithms, structured clinical judgment, and non-structured clinical judgment. The method of assessment used to determine risk varies by site and clinician preference. For more information on specific assessments, readers are encouraged to view the Risk Assessment chapter of this book. From a treatment perspective, the most important aspect of this principle of service delivery is to ensure that treatment intensity accurately reflects risk severity.

NEED

The need principle of RNR asserts that a client should be offered services that target their criminogenic needs (Andrews et al., 1990). Criminogenic needs are dynamic risk factors that are directly related to criminal behavior (Andrews & Bonta, 2006). The major areas of criminogenic need include antisocial personality pattern, pro-criminal attitudes, social supports for crime, substance abuse, family/marital relationships, school/work, and (lack of) prosocial recreational activities (Andrews & Bonta, 2006). Although certain variables such as criminal history may be related to recidivism, these variables are static, or unchangeable, and cannot be addressed through treatment. Therefore, static variables are not primary targets for interventions.

It is critical to mention that "needs" also encompass other treatment needs not related to recidivism, which are important to address but are not a priority in a forensic mental health setting, and thus will not be explored in this section.

RESPONSIVITY

Responsivity refers to tailoring the intervention to a client's abilities and learning styles in an effort to maximize effectiveness. There are two elements of responsivity: general and specific (Andrews & Bonta, 2006). The general responsivity factor dictates that most interventions should be based on cognitive social learning techniques, which may be the most effective way to teach people new behaviors (Andrews & Bonta, 2006; Walters, Clark, Gingerich, & Meltzer, 2007). Furthermore, to increase responsivity, services should be delivered under conditions that include warmth and structure (Walters et al., 2007). Creating conditions that are supportive and structured are critical to elevated function in psychotherapy and further support the notion that deviation from traditional psychotherapy techniques is unnecessary in a forensic setting.

The second element of the responsivity principle is specific responsivity. This tenet refers to matching selected interventions to the individual learning approaches and needs of a client. The therapist must account for personal strengths, personality factors, cognitive impairments, and learning style. During this process, practitioners are encouraged to consider client reactance levels. This is the extent to which a client rejects or opposes participation in therapy or the adaptation of a particular opinion (Brehm, 1966). Another often-overlooked element related to responsivity is the client's motivation to participate in treatment. Clinicians must address motivational factors, particularly in mandated treatment, to maximize the likelihood that the offender will benefit from the intervention. Attention to these dynamics will maximize the likelihood of positive outcomes for an offender (Osher, 2012).

A proper parallelism is the notion that medicine does not work if it is not taken. Thus, an intervention will not be effective if the offender does not find value in making the change or is unable to apply the skills necessary to bring about the change. William Miller (2012) suggests four components for encouraging behavioral change: express empathy, develop discrepancy, roll with resistance, support self-efficacy. He contends that these will assist in facilitating the appropriate environment to increase responsivity. Additional discussion concerning motivational interviewing will be discussed in the treatment modalities section below.

APPLICATION OF COMMUNITY INTERVENTIONS

It is necessary to emphasize the importance of minimizing the distinction between forensic and community patients. Historically, forensic patients were considered qualitatively different from individuals in the community. Practitioners have frequently been reluctant to utilize community-based interventions in forensic settings. As described, this trend was particularly common during the "get tough" era of forensic mental health. With more evaluations of program effectiveness, research has found that many of the interventions used in the community are also applicable to forensic mental health.

Triage systems are one example of overlapping treatment concepts between community mental health and forensic mental health. This system includes assessing the need for mental health services, assessing the level of risk to self or others, and identifying the situation's urgency and the type of response required. The Victorian Government Department of Health Statewide mental health triage scale - Guidelines (2010) asserts that the triage aspects are clearly interrelated and require adequate assessment, and the presence or absence of any one aspect should not be used to preclude further assessment. Table 1 illustrates the similarities between the triage system and RNR principles.

TABLE 1

Comparison of community mental health triage and RNR.

	Mental Health Triage	Risk Need Responsivity
Level of Risk	Assess level of risk to the person and/or others to the type and intensity of specialized mental health services. Higher risk of harm would lead to more intense and urgent assignment of services; less risk of harm would lead to less-intrusive and less-urgent interventions.	Match the intensity of treatment and services to risk of future offending behavior. Those that present a higher risk of future offending behavior (recidivism) would receive increased services and those that present a lower risk of recidivism would receive fewer services.
Treatment Target	Consider all factors contributing to continued perseverance of mental illness symptoms and target those areas that are most likely to assist in reducing symptoms and sustaining management of symptoms (presence, severity and complexity of mental illness symptoms, AODA, co-morbidities [e.g., medical], social/environmental vulnerabilities and supports, and functional status).	Provide evidenced-based treatment and services which directly target the needs that are most associated with recidivism and can be changed (dynamic) (e.g, criminal thinking and anti-social peer group).
Intervention	Determine the urgency and type of response required from mental health or other services based both on what works for their current symptomatology.	Applying EBP that target criminogenic needs in a manner in which it is effective for the individual, taking into account preferences, abilities and willingness.

Applying this systematic approach to emergency settings and mental health caseloads has increased the effectiveness of services provided to individuals in crisis and long-term caseloads. Engagement in behavioral health systems and psychotropic medications following psychiatric hospitalization predicts a reduced likelihood of arrest (Van Dorn, Desmarais, Petrila, Haynes, & Singh, 2013). This example demonstrates the overlap between community interventions and forensic mental health practices. Consideration of how to adapt, rather than reinvent, interventions used with non-forensic patients to forensic patients is paramount to efficient remediation.

TREATMENT MODALITIES

As indicated above, RNR includes cognitive-based interventions as a general principle of effective treatment. In this section, we outline examples of cognitive-behavior therapy (CBT) interventions. In addition to CBT as a general principle, we will describe motivational interviewing (MI), which can serve as an effective interaction style. Finally, the discussion of these two general techniques will be supplemented with an overview of additional interventions.

COGNITIVE BEHAVIORAL THERAPY (CBT)

Cognitive Behavioral Therapy (CBT) is a form of treatment examining the relationship between thoughts, feelings, and behaviors. CBT operates under the assumption that distressing feelings can be ameliorated by identifying and disputing the automatic thoughts that generate those feelings (Rotter & Carr, 2013). Research has demonstrated that offenders who will benefit from CBT have distinctive thinking styles with limited problem-solving skills (Ross & Fabiano, 1985). Cognitive skills training (designed to help offenders learn how to problem solve and make decisions) is one of the best evidence-based approaches for reducing recidivism, particularly in sexual and violent offenders (i.e., murder, assault, offense with weapon, arson, criminal and malicious damage) versus acquisitive offenses (Traverse, Mann, & Hollin, 2014). These cognitive skills training programs are structured and skills-based; they target the most predictive elements of crime (antisocial attitudes and values) by teaching impulse control skills, emotion regulation, flexible and rational thinking, and problem-solving. Cognitive skill training programs are consistent with the responsivity principle of RNR because they follow cognitive-behavioral and social-learning theories and principles (Traverse, Mann, & Hollin, 2014). Such CBT-based interventions can lead to 8.2% reductions in felony re-convictions of general offenders (Aos, Miller, & Drake, 2006). Table 2 highlights a selection of CBT interventions, each of which is discussed below.

TABLE 2

Sample of CBT forensic mental health interventions.

Treatment Target	Evidence-based Interventions
Criminal Thinking	Thinking for a Change (T4C)
Anger Management	Aggression Replacement Training® (ART®)
Mental Illness	Illness Management & Recovery
Values & Moral Reasoning	Moral Recognition Therapy® (MRT®)
Emotion Regulation	Systems Training for Emotional Predictability and Problem Solving (STEPPS™) Dialectical Behavior Therapy (DBT)
Substance Abuse & Mental Illness	Integrated Dual Disorders Treatment (IDDT)
Trauma	Seeking Safety TARGET TREM

AGGRESSION REPLACEMENT TRAINING (ART)

ART (Goldstein, Glick, & Gibbs, 1998) is a CBT intervention that teaches strategies to offenders for managing aggressive and antisocial behaviors. Originally developed as an intervention for juveniles, ART has been adapted and applied for use with adults in a forensic setting. The ten-week program is a total of 30 intervention hours. ART is composed of three techniques: structured learning (behavioral component), anger control (affective/emotional component), and moral reasoning (thought and values component). Structured learning training teaches social interaction skills through direct instruction, role-play, and feedback. In particular, clients are asked to focus on distressing or high-risk situations and problem-solve these scenarios during group therapy sessions. Training in anger control aims to assist offenders in the identification of internal and external triggers associated with aggression. Participants must bring at least one example of their anger in a recent situation to their session. This example is used to help train them to manage their anger responses in a more efficient way. Morality is taught via higher learning, ethical dilemmas, discussion, and exercises focused on perspective. Moral analysis focuses on the reasoning aspects of aggressive behavior and enhances morality in participants. Studies have found that lower recidivism rates are associated with program completion (Gibbs, Potter, & Goldstein, 1995).

THINKING FOR A CHANGE (T4C)

T4C was developed by Bush, Glick, and Taymans (1997) with the support of the National Institute of Corrections. T4C is designed to teach offenders prosocial skills and attitudes by using problem-solving strategies. The curriculum is divided into 25 lessons, each lasting between one and two hours. No more than one lesson should be addressed per day. Optimally, the group would meet twice per week. Several studies have identified that T4C is effective at reducing recidivism (Golden, Gatchel, & Cahill, 2006; Landenberger & Lipsey, 2005; Lowenkamp, Hubbard, Makarios, & Latessa, 2009).

MORAL RECOGNITION THERAPY (MRT)

MRT (Little & Robinson, 2006) is a cognitive-behavior therapy approach that systematically addresses the moral reasoning of offenders. The underlying goal of MRT is to change conscious decision-making by increasing levels of moral reasoning (Little & Robinson, 2006). MRT combines a variety of psychological traditions that address growth in the areas of ego, social and moral behavior.

The core workbook *How to Escape Your Prison*, which was first published in 1986, is structured around 16 steps focusing on seven basic treatment issues:

1. Confrontation of beliefs, attitudes and behaviors
2. Assessment of current relationships
3. Reinforcement of positive behavior and habits
4. Positive identity formation
5. Enhancement of self-concept
6. Decrease in hedonism and frustration tolerance
7. Development of higher stages of moral reasoning

The curriculum covers the first 12 steps to bring an offender to "normal" levels in moral reasoning. Groups can meet up to twice a week, and all 12 steps can be completed in a minimum of 3-6 months. MRT is recognized as an evidence-based practice on the National Registry of Evidence-based Programs and Practices (NREPP).

INTEGRATED DUAL DISORDERS TREATMENT (IDDT)

IDDT (Mueser et al., 2003) is an intensive program designed for individuals experiencing elements of both mental illness and addiction. Developed at Dartmouth Medical School, IDDT embraces a collaborative approach to coordinate service delivery, addressing all areas of the client's recovery (Surface, 2008). IDDT is an evidence-based program featuring 26 domains and endorsed by the Substance Abuse and Mental Health Services Administration (SAMSHA). Both treatment and organizational elements are viewed as essential for providing treatment services (e.g., multidisciplinary team approach, time-unlimited services, substance abuse treatment, pharmacological treatment, etc.). Integrated within this approach are case management (housing, employment), family inclusion, Illness Management & Recovery (IMR) (Gingerich & Mueser, 2010), Assertive Community Treatment (ACT) (Goldstein et al., 1998), and Intensive Case Management (ICM) (Hangan, 2006). In addition, IDDT asserts Stage-Wise Interventions, which means that all interventions must be consistent with the client's stage of recovery.

The four Stage-Wise Interventions are:
1. **Engagement** – forming a solid therapeutic alliance with the client.
2. **Persuasion** – guiding the engaged client toward participation in a recovery-oriented process.
3. **Active Treatment** – helping the motivated client to acquire skills and supports for management of their illnesses and achieving goals.
4. **Maintenance/Relapse Prevention** – assisting clients to apply management strategies for recovery maintenance.

ILLNESS MANAGEMENT AND RECOVERY (IMR)

IMR teaches strategies for symptom management to people with chronic and serious mental illness (Drake et al., 2001; Mueser, Torrey, Lynde, Singer, & Drake, 2003; Mueser et al., 2002). IMR is a standardized program based on a recovery-oriented approach to help people with a severe mental illness gain control and set individual and meaningful life goals (Mueser et al., 2002).The core values of IMR include hope, the importance of personal choice, collaboration and respect (Mueser et al., 2002).

IMR consists of 10 modules, which are designed for the practitioner and client to complete together during a series of one-hour sessions that occur once or twice a week over a ten-month period (Roe et al., 2007). The first module assists the client in discovering their personal recovery goal. The second module covers three basic mental health diagnoses: depression, bipolar disorder, and schizophrenia (Roe et al., 2007). The purpose of providing a diagnosis is to assist the client in understanding his or her diagnosis and its effect on global functioning. A large portion of this module discusses stigma reduction and assists the client in reducing the shame related to their mental health disorder. The third module outlines treatment options and targets individual vulnerabilities, including both environmental and biological stressors. The fourth module emphasizes the importance of social support as it relates to symptom management. The fifth module targets effective use of medication. The sixth module focuses on drug and alcohol use and their interactions with mental illness. The seventh module normalizes the nonlinear progression of illness management, with specific attention paid to the possibility of symptom re-emergence and relapse prevention. Finally, the last module examines coping with stress (Mueser et al., 2006).

The goal of IMR is to teach the client skills that are needed to independently manage their mental illness. Notably, this program is designed to be used in conjunction with other EBPs (evidence-based practices) that reduce risk. Mueser (2013) reported that IMR had positive effects on illness management outcomes and disciplinary problems, particularly in comparison to standard treatment in a correctional population.

Motivational Interviewing (MI)

MI is a therapeutic technique that was first introduced to target substance use (Miller, 1983). MI is a foundational, evidence-based, service-delivery component in local, state, and federal criminal justice systems (Bonta & Andrews, 2007). The widespread application of MI in corrections has typically yielded positive results (Walters et al., 2007). For example, a meta-analysis by McMurran (2009) found that applying MI in criminal justice systems within the RNR model can lead to improved retention in treatment, enhanced motivation to change, and a reduction in recidivism.

At its most basic level, "motivational interviewing is a collaborative conversational style for strengthening a person's own motivation and commitment to change" (Miller & Rollnick, 2013, p. 12). In other words, MI is a way to assist clients in weighing the "pros" and "cons" of changing or maintaining a behavior, by identifying and questioning their own internal personal motivations through specific techniques. When utilizing this technique, the therapist focuses on different aspects of the client to address ambivalence about change in a non-confrontational way. MI is comprised of both the "spirit" and specific techniques. The "spirit" of MI is described by the acronym PACE (Partnership, Autonomy, Compassion and Evocation) (Miller & Rollnick, 2013). Each of these characteristics must be present when practicing MI.

MI can be challenging for professionals in forensic settings. More specifically, the beliefs or values of the professionals may increase the judgment of clients, because clients in forensics systems have often demonstrated behavior that lends itself to judgment. Thus, there may be additional barriers to employing non-judgmental compassion as prescribed in delivering MI. In addition, MI presents a shift from a more authoritative and confrontational style of supervision.

The basic techniques of MI contain open-ended questions, affirmations, reflections and summaries (OARS) (Miller & Rollnick, 2013). The OARS acronym guides how a professional should verbally interact with a client. Studies on the effectiveness of MI have found that OARS, and in particular–affirmations, are essential to the change process (Farber & Doolin, 2011).

Motivational Interviewing provides a basis for carrying out the principle of responsivity from the RNR model. Specifically, MI suggests a style of communication that makes it more likely for offenders to engage in treatment and make behavioral changes (Walters et al., 2007). MI respects client self-efficacy and autonomy, and promotes collaboration (Miller & Rolnick, 2013). As a basic form of communication and a strategy of engagement, MI can help improve clinical outcomes for forensic mental health patients and is most effective when applied with other treatment interventions.

The ability to measure and ensure fidelity is one benefit of implementing and utilizing MI in forensic systems. For example, the Motivational Interviewing Treatment Integrity (MITI) (Moyers et al., 2005) is behavioral coding system that focuses on the professional's behavior within interactions. Utilization of the MITI allows supervisors to ensure that MI is applied as intended and maintains integrity as an evidence-based practice.

Dialectical Behavior Therapy (DBT)

Originally developed to treat persons with Borderline Personality Disorder (BPD), DBT is a cognitive-behavioral form of psychotherapy used for the treatment of various mental health disorders and complex trauma reactions in clients who exhibit patterns of problematic behavior. These behaviors include emotional dysregulation, alterations in attention and consciousness, distortions about self and others, disruption in the ability to form meaningful relationships, and somatizations (for a review of symptoms of reactions to complex trauma, see Courtois, 2004; for a review of BPD, see Lieb, Zanarini, Schmahl, Linehan, & Bohus, 2004). DBT has been modified and adapted for individuals with developmental disabilities (Lew, Matta, Tripp-Tebo, & Watts, 2006), substance abuse disorders (Linehan et al., 2002), eating disorders (Hill, Craighead, & Safer, 2011; Safer

& Jo, 2010; Safer, Telch, & Agras, 2001), and depression (Harley, Sprich, Sagren, & Jacobo, 2008). In forensic settings, DBT has been associated with reductions in anger, hostility, depression, and staff burnout (Evershed et al., 2003; Shelton et al., 2009). Treatment involves weekly skills training groups, individual therapy, and phone consultation with the therapist outside of scheduled meeting times. Additionally, DBT therapists are required to participate in a consultation team, which allows for the therapist to receive support in working with this challenging population.

It is important to note that the goal of DBT varies radically by setting. In the community, DBT strives to help patients achieve a life worth living, as determined by the client. A fundamental assumption in DBT is that the patient's life is currently distressful (Linehan, 1993), with the primary goal of enhacing motivation in the patient so as to improve quality of life and reduce dysfunctional behaviors (Chapman, 2006).

However, in a forensic setting, the primary goal of treatment is to reduce re-offense rates. One method to achieve this objective is targeting the factors that increase the risk for re-offending. For these forms of intervention to be successful, the patient must be meaningfully engaged in treatment. Emotion dysregulation, interpersonal disruption, or a distorted sense of self can all serve as barriers to meaningful treatment engagement. Therefore, targeting factors that may interfere with treatment engagement is one method of working toward reducing recidivism. In addition, there is increasing emphasis on enhancing the protective factors as a means of preventing recidivism. Because DBT is designed to enhance the quality of one's life, helping offenders improve internal motivation for pro-social behavior may decrease offending.

SYSTEMS TRAINING FOR EMOTIONAL PREDICTABILITY AND PROBLEM SOLVING (STEPPS)

STEPPS is a 20-week (one two-hour session per week), manualized cognitive-behavioral, skills-based group treatment program for persons with Borderline Personality Disorder (BPD) (Blum et al., 2008; Blum, Bartels, St. John, & Pfohl, 2012). Each lesson focuses on specific increased emotional management or behavioral skills. Considerable research, including several uncontrolled studies and two randomized controlled trials, has found that the STEPPS program was associated with improvements in mood, BPD symptoms, impulsivity, and negative affectivity when compared with treatment as usual (Blum, Pfohl, Monahan, & Black, 2002; Blum et al., 2008; Boccalon et al., 2012; Bos, van Wel, Appelo, & Verbrakk, 2010; Harvey, Black, & Blum, 2010).

TRAUMA

According to a report by Reavis and colleagues (2013), the prevalence of Adverse Childhood Effects (ACE) was four times higher in offenders than a normative sample. This staggering statistic emphasizes the importance of understanding and responding to trauma reactions when providing interventions that are designed to reduce recidivism.

TRAUMA INFORMED CARE (TIC)

TIC is a strengths-based framework designed for trauma victims that aims to understand the impact of trauma and empowers the survivors to regain control and emotional stability. TIC is an approach that implements and adheres to six key principles: (a) safety; (b) trustworthiness and transparency; (c) peer support; (d) collaboration and mutuality; (e) empowerment, voice, and choice; and (d) cultural, historical, and gender issues. The primary goals of TIC are identifying trauma and related symptoms, training staff to be aware of the impact of trauma, reducing triggers and situations that may lead to a trigger, and a fundamental "do no harm" approach (Harris & Fallot, 2001; Hodes, 2006). A trauma-informed approach can be employed in any setting, but there are many challenges in implementing TIC in a forensic context (e.g., limited privacy, focus on maintaining order, pat-downs and strip searches, restricted movement) (Owens et al., 2008). If implemented successfully,

TIC can result in reductions of trauma reactions, which in turn improve stabilization, reduce critical incidents, and require fewer uses of restraint and seclusion (Miller & Najavits, 2012). Further, TIC can provide a stable platform for change. If an offender feels safe, there is a higher likelihood of meaningful engagement in treatments that reduce recidivism.

TRAUMA AFFECT REGULATION: GUIDE FOR EDUCATION AND THERAPY (TARGET)

TARGET is a psycho-educational structured approach for teaching skills to individuals (adolescents and adults) who exhibit trauma-related symptoms that are triggered by stress and traumatic experiences (Ford, 2006). TARGET's aim is to help those who experience trauma to understand it, by explaining the biological correlates of trauma exposure, and to then reinforce their sense and ability of control. Delivered in 10-12 individual or group sessions, TARGET focuses on the skills encapsulated by the acronym FREEDOM:

- Focus
- Recognize triggers
- Emotion self-check
- Evaluate thoughts
- Define goals
- Options
- Make a contribution

TRAUMA RECOVERY AND EMPOWERMENT MODEL (TREM AND M-TREM)

TREM and the men's version (M-TREM) were originally developed by Harris and colleagues at a Community Connections treatment center in the 1990s. Both the TREM and M-TREM are psycho-educational and structured group interventions that focus on the development of trauma recovery skills and current functioning in the individual (TREM, 2008). Typically, the program is administered in weekly 75-minute, recovery-topic group sessions over the course of 29 sessions (TREM) or 24 sessions (M-TREM).

The TREM is a female gender-specific curriculum organized into three major parts (TREM, 2008):

1. **Empowerment** – learn strategies for self-comfort and accurate self-monitoring, such as skills to establish healthy physical and emotional boundaries

2. **Trauma education** – education on the direct effects of abuse while exploring and learning to reframe the connections between past abuse and current experiences and stressors

3. **Skill-building** – focus on skills to address problem-solving, communication, interpersonal relationships, and emotion regulation.

M-TREM is organized in a similar manner, but the content differs:

1. **Emotions and relationships** – learn an emotional vocabulary, increase abilities to develop healthy relationships, and improve understanding of relationship dynamics

2. **Trauma education** – similar to TREM

3. **Skill-building** – similar to TREM, but with an alternative ordering and different content issues.

TREM and M-TREM aim to intervene and address trauma in people with severe mental illnesses and/or substance abuse problems.

FUTURE OF EBP IN FORENSIC MENTAL HEALTH SETTINGS

Complications have been identified by the significant number of forensic clients who are unmotivated to participate in treatment, particularly in light of the mandatory nature of treatment in these settings. As such, measurement of treatment motivation must be incorporated when developing instruments that index change in needs during treatment. This is a key area to explore with clients to adhere to RNR principles, specifically responsivity.

Primarily, measuring the correct level of need is of paramount importance, particularly in forensic mental health settings. First, attention to level of need is essential because forensic facilities have limited resources. As previously discussed, mixing low-risk clients with high needs is a potential waste of resources. Second, relative to risk, there is mixed research on how much treatment is enough and whether too much treatment may result in diminishing effectiveness (Loughran et al., 2009; Sperber, Latessa, & Makarios, 2013). There is a dearth of empirical evidence available to assist practitioners in determining the threshold at which treatment begins to lose its effectiveness (Sperber et al., 2013). As such, continued attention to the measurement of progress is essential.

Finally, additional interventions should be aimed at individuals who do not admit to criminal activity, who are also commonly labeled as "deniers." Many programs include the expectation that offenders will admit responsibility (McGrath, Cumming, Burchard, Zeoli, & Ellerby, 2009); however, a growing body of literature suggests that denial is not generally a factor that increases recidivism risk. Some studies have even found that treated "deniers" recidivated at similar rates as treated admitters (Hanson & Morton-Bourgon, 2004; Seager, Jellicoe, & Dhaliwal, 2005). This is troubling because individuals who do not admit to their crimes are often excluded from participating in treatment programs (Lund, 2000). Moving forward, researchers and clinicians need to develop treatments that target "deniers" who may still benefit from interventions.

CONCLUSION

The primary objective of EBP in forensic mental health systems is to reduce recidivism in the most economical and effective way possible. Historically, there has been resistance to the adaptation of community-based interventions for use in forensic settings. This is problematic because attending to variables that are relevant to therapy in the community can also be important in forensic settings. Further, applying some of these community interventions to forensic patients can help reduce the likelihood of recidivism in a more effective and economical manner.

The Risk Need Responsivity (RNR) model (Andrews & Bonta et al., 1990) provides a framework for practitioners and administrators to not only provide policy and systems management in a responsible manner, but to guide daily work and interventions in an effective and evidenced-based approach. This model stresses the need to individualize interventions to an individual's risk level, criminogenic needs, and learning style. As such, clinicians in forensic mental health settings must have a variety of options available to allow the individualization of services. There are many structured cognitively-based interventions available to provide effective interventions reviewed in this chapter.

An ongoing challenge for clinicians in these environments is measuring intervention effectiveness. Although clinicians can measure symptom reduction, tracking the long-term impact of the interventions on recidivism is a much more challenging endeavor. Additionally, the interaction between motivation issues and treatment outcomes presents a unique challenge to researchers. Despite significant advances in forensic mental health since its inception, this field remains greatly in need of improving outcomes for individuals. Integrating our current knowledge in psychotherapy from community settings with the goals of a forensic setting can improve the likelihood that clinicians will achieve more favorable outcomes.

References

American Psychological Association Presidential Task Force on Evidence-Based Practice. (2006). Evidence-based practice in psychology. *American Psychologist, 61,* 271-285.

Andrews, D. A., & Bonta, J. (2006). The psychology of criminal conduct (4th ed.). Newark, NJ: LexisNexis.

Andrews, D. A., & Dowden, C. (2006). Risk Principle of Case Classification in Correctional Treatment. A Meta-Analytic Investigation. *International Journal of Offender Therapy and Comparative Criminolgy, 50*(1), 88-100.

Andrews, D. A., Zinger, I., Hoge, R. D., Bonta, J., Gendreau, P., & Cullen, F. T. (1990). Does correctional treatment work? A clinically relevant and psychologically informed meta-analysis. *Criminology, 28,* 369-404.

Aos, S., Miller, M., & Drake, E. (2006). Evidence-based adult corrections programs: What works and what does not? Olympia: Washington State Institute for Public Policy.

Blum, N., Bartels, N., St. John, D., & Pfohl, B. (2012). *STEPPS: Systems Training for Emotional Predictability and Problem Solving (Second Edition).* Coralville, IA, Level One Publishing.

Blum, N., Pfohl, B., Monahan, P., & Black, D.W. (2002). STEPPS: A cognitive behavioral systems based group treatment for outpatients with borderline personality disorder—a preliminary report. *Comprehensive Psychiatry, 43,* 301-310.

Blum, N., St. John, D., Pfohl, B., Stuart, S., McCormick, B., Allen, J., Arndt, S., & Arndt, S. (2008). Systems training for emotional predictability and problem solving (STEPPS) for outpatients with borderline personality disorder: A randomized controlled trial and 1-year follow-up. *American Journal of Psychiatry, 165,* 468-478.

Boccalon, S., Alesiana, R., Giarolli, L., Franchini, L., Colombo, C., Blum, N., & Fossati, A. (2012). Systems Training for Emotional Predictability and Problem Solving (STEPPS): Theoretical model, clinical application, and preliminary efficacy data in a sample of inpatients with personality disorders in Co-morbidity with mood disorders. *Journal of Psychopathology, 18,* 335-343.

Bonta, J., & Andrews, D. (2007). Risk-Need-Responsivity Model for Offender Assessment and Rehabilitation. Ottawa: Public Safety Canada.

Bonta, J., Wallace-Capretta, S., & Rooney, J. (2000). A quasi-experimental evaluation of an intensive rehabilitation supervision program. *Criminal Justice and Behavior 27,* 312-329.

Bos, E.H., van Wel, E B., Appelo, M.T., Verbraak, M.J. (2010). A randomized controlled trial of a Dutch version of Systems Training for Emotional Predictability and Problem Solving for borderline personality disorder. *Journal of Nervous and Mental Diseases, 198,* 299-304.

Brehm, J. (1966). *A Theory of Psychological Reactance.* New York: Academic Press.

Bureau of Justice Statistics, (2014). *Drugs and Crime Facts: Drug Use and Crime.* Retrieved from http://www.bjs.gov/content/dcf/duc.cfm

Bush, J., Glick, B., & Taymans, J. (1997). *Thinking for a change: Integrated cognitive behavior change program.* National Institute of Corrections. Washington, DC: U.S. Department of Justice.

Chapman, A. L. (2006). Dialectical behavior therapy: Current indications and unique elements. *Psychiatry, 3*(9), 62-68.

Courtois, C.A. (2004). Complex trauma, complex reactions: Assessment and treatment. P*sychotherapy: Theory, Research, Practice and Training, 41,* 412-425.

Cullen, F. (2012). Taking rehabilitation seriously: Creativity, science, and the challenge of offender change. *Punishment & Society, 14,* 94. doi: 10.1177/1462474510385973

Cullen, F, Blevins, K., Trager, J. and Gendreau, P. (2005). The rise and fall of boot camps: Acase study in Common-Sense Corrections. *Journal of Offender Rehabilitation, 40,* 53-70.

Cullen, F. & Gendreau, P. (2001). From nothing works to what works: Changing professional ideaology in the 21st century. *The Prison Journal, 81,* 313-338. doi: 10.1177/0032885501081003002

De Vogel, V., de Ruiter, C., Bouman, Y., & de Vries Robbé, M. (2012). *SAPROF. Guidelines for the assessment of protective factors for violence risk, English version.* (2nd ed.). Uterecht: De Forensische Zorgspe-cialisten.

De Vogel, V., de Ruiter, C., Y., & de Vries Robbé, M. (2009). *SAPROF. Guidelines for the assessment of* bou-man *protective factors for violence risk, English version.* Uterecht: Forum Educatief.

Drake, R. E., Goldman, H. H., Leff, H. S., Lehman, A. F., Dixon, L., Mueser, K. T. (2001). Implementing evidence-based practices in routine mental health service settings. *Psychiatric Services, 52,* 179-182.

Epperson, M. W., Wolff, N., Morgan, R., Fisher, W. H., Frueh, B. C., & Huening, J. (2011). *The next genera-tion of behavioral health and criminal justice interventions: Improving outcomes by improving inter-ventions.* New Brunswich, NJ: Center for Behavioral Health Services & Criminal Justice Research: Rutgers University.

Evershed, S., Tennant, A., Boomer, D., Rees, A., Barkham, M., & Watson, A. (2003). Practice-based outcomes of dialectical behaviour therapy (DBT) targeting anger and violence, with male forensic patients: A pragmatic and non-contemporaneous comparison. *Criminal Behaviour and Mental Health, 13,* 198-213. doi:10.1002/cbm.542

Farber, B. A. & Doolin, E. M. (2011). Positive regard. *Psychotherapy, 48,* 58-64.

Ford, Julian D., & Eileen Russo. (2006). "Trauma-Focused, Present-Centered, Emotional Self-Regulation Approach to Integrated Treatment for Post-traumatic Stress and Addiction: Trauma Adaptive Recov-ery Group Education and Therapy (TARGET)." *American Journal of Psychotherapy 60*(4), 335-355.

Gendreua, P., Goggin, C., Cullen, F. & Andrews, D. (2001). The effects of community sanctions and incar-ceration on recidivism. *Compendium of Effective Correctional Programs.* Vol 1 Chapter 4. Ottawa, Ontario: Public Works & Government Services Canada.

Gibbs, J. C., Potter, G. B., & Goldstein, A. P. (1995). *The equip program: Teaching youth to think and act responsibly through a peer-helping approach.* Champaign, IL: Research Press.

Gingerich, S., & Mueser, K. T. (2010). *Illness management and recovery implementation resource kit* (re-vised ed.). Rockville, MD: Center for Mental Health Services, Substance Abuse and Mental Health Services Administration.

Golden, L. S., Gatchel, R. J., & Cahill, M. A. (2006). Evaluation the effectiveness of the National Institute of Corrections' "Thinking for a Change" program among probationers. *Journal of Offender Rehabilita-tion, 42,* 52-73.

Goldstein, A. P., Glick, B., & Gibbs, J. C. (1998). *Aggression Replacement Training: A Comprehensive Inter-vention for Aggressive Youth (revised ed.).* Champaign, IL: Research Press.

Hangan, C. (2006). Introduction of an intensive case management style of delivery for a new mental health service. *International journal of mental health nursing, 15*(3), 157-162.

Hanson, K., Gordon, A., Harris, A., Marques, J., Murphy, W., Quinsey, V., & Seto, M. (2002). First report of the Collaborative Outcome Data Project on the effectiveness of psychological treatment for sex offenders. *Sexual Abuse: A Journal of Research and Treatment, 14,* 169-194.

Hanson, R. K., & Morton-Bourgon, K. E. (2004). *Predictors of sexual recidivism: An updated meta-analysis* (Corrections Research User Report No. 2004–02). Ontario, Canada: Public Safety and Emergency Preparedness Canada.

Harley, R., Sprich, S., Safren, S., Jacobo, M., & Fava, M. (2008). Adaptation of dialectical behavior therapy skills training group for treatment resistant depression. *Journal of Nervous and Mental Disease, 196,*136-143. doi:10.1097/NMD.0b013e318162aa3f

Harris, M., & Fallot, R. D. (2001). *Using trauma theory to design service systems.* San Francisco, CA: Jossey-Bass.

Harvey, R., Black, D. W., & Blum, N. (2010). STEPPS (Systems Training for Emotional Predictability and Problem Solving) in the United Kingdom: A preliminary report. *Journal of Contemporary Psychotherapy, 40*, 225-232.

Hill, D. M., Craighead, L. W., & Safer, D. L. (2011). Appetite-focused dialectical behavior therapy for the treatment of binge eating with purging: A preliminary trial. *International Journal of Eating Disorders, 44,* 249-261. doi:10.1002/eat.20812

Hodes, G. R. (2006). *Responding to childhood trauma: The promise and practice of trauma informed care.* Pennsylvania Office of Mental Health and Substance Abuse Services.

James, D.J, & Glaze, L.E. (2006). *Mental health problems of prison and jail inmates.* (Report No. NCJ 213600). Retrieved from Bureau of Justice Statistics, http://www.bjs.gov/content/pub/pdf/mhppji.pdf

Landenberger, N. A. & Lipsey, M. W. (2005). The positive effects of cognitive–behavioral programs for offenders: A meta-analysis of factors associated with effective treatment. *Journal of Experimental Criminology, 1*(4), 451-476.

Lew, M., Matta, C., Tripp-Tebo, C., & Watts, D. (2006). *Dialectical behavior therapy for individuals with intellectual disabilities: a program description.* Mental Health Aspects of Developmental Disabilities. Vol. 9, No. 1.

Lieb, K., Zanarini, M. C., Schmahl, C., Linehan, M. M., & Bohus, M. (2004). Borderline personality disorder. *The Lancet, 364,* 453-461.

Linehan, M. (1993). *Cognitive Behavioral Treatment of Borderline Personality Disorder.* Guilford Press: New York.

Linehan, M. M., Dimeff, L. A., Reynolds, S. K., Comtois, K. A., Shaw Welch, S., Heagerty, P., & Kivlahan, D. R. (2002). Dialectical behavior therapy versus comprehensive validation therapy plus 12-step for the treatment of opioid dependent women meeting criteria for borderline personality disorder. *Drug and Alcohol Dependence, 67,* 13-26. doi: 10.1016/S0376-8716(02)00011-X

Lipsey, M., Landenberger, N. A., & Wilson, S. J. (2007). Effects of Cognitive-Behavioral Programs for Criminal Offenders: A Systematic Review. *Campbell systematic reviews, 3*(6), 1-30.

Lipsey, M. W. (1992). Juvenile delinquency treatment: A meta-analytic inquiry into the variability of effects. In: Cook, T.D., Cooper, H., Cordray, D.S., et al. (eds) *Meta-analysis for explanation: A casebook.* New York: Russell Sage, 83-127.

Lipsey, M. W. & Wilson, D. B. (1998). Effective interventional for serious juvenile offenders: A synthesis of research. In: Loeber, R. and Farrington, D.P. (eds). *Serious and violent juvenile offenders: Risk factors and successful interventions.* Los Angeles, CA: SAGE, 313-366.

Little, G. L. & Robinson, K. D. (2006). How to escape your prison: A moral recognition therapy workbook. Memphis, TN: Eagle Wing Books, Inc.

Loughran, T. A., Mulvey, E. P., Schubert, C. A., Fagan, J., Piquero, A. R., & Losoya, S. H., (2009). Estimating a dose-response relationship between length of stay and future recidivism in serious juvenile offenders. *Criminology, 47*(3), 699-740.

Lowenkamp C. T., Hubbard D., Makarios, M. D., & Latessa, E. J. (2009.). A quasi-experimental evaluation of thinking for a change: A "real-world" application. *Criminal Justice and Behavior, 36,* 137-146.

Lund, C. A. (2000). Predictors of sexual recidivism: Did meta-analysis clarify the role and relevance of denial? *Sexual Abuse: A Journal of Research and Treatment, 12, 275-287.*

Maletzky, B. M. & Steinhauser, C. (1998). The Portland Sexual Abuse Clinic. InW. L. Marshall, Y. M. Fernandez, S. M. Hudson, & T. Ward (Eds.), *Sourcebook of treatment programs for sexual offenders* (pp. 105-116). New York: Plenum.

Mann, R. E., Hanson, R. K., & Thornton, D. (2010). Assessing risk for sexual recidivism; Some proposals on the nature of psychologically meaningful risk factors. *Sexual Abuse: A Journal of Research and Treatment, 22*(2), 191-217. doi:10.1177/1079063210366039

Marlowe, D. B., Festinger, D. S., Arabia, P. L., Dugosh, K. L., Benasutti, K. M., Croft, J. R., McKay, J. R., (2006). Adaptive intervention in drug court: A pilot experiment. *Criminal Justice Review, 33,* 343-360.

McGrath, R., Cumming, G., Burchard, B., Zeoli, S., & Ellerby, L. (2009). Current Practices and Emerging Trends in Sexual Abuser Management. The Safer Society 2009 North American Survey. Retrieved February 16, 2015 from http://www.safersociety.org/uploads/WP141-Current_Practices_Emerging_Trends.pdf

McGuire, J. (Ed). (1995). What works: Reducing reoffending: Guidelines from research and practice. Wiley series in offender rehabilitation. Oxford, England: John Wiley & Sons. xiii 242 pp.

McMurran, M., (2009). Motivational Interviewing with offenders: a systematic review. *Legal and Criminological Psychology, 14,* 83-100.

Miller, N. A. & Najavits, L. M. (2012). Creating trauma-informed correctional care: A balance of goals and environment. *European Journal of Psychotraumatology, 3,* 17246. doi:10.3402/ejpt.v3i0.17246

Miller, W. R. (1983). Motivational interviewing with problem drinkers. *Behavioral Psychotherapy, 11,* 147-172.

Miller, W. R. (2012). William Miller on Motivational Interviewing. Retrieved from http://www.psychotherapy.net/data/uploads/51194e1c160b2.pdf

Miller, W. R. & Rollnick, S. (2012) Motivational Interviewing: Helping People Change (3rd ed.). Guilford Press.

Miller, W. R., Zweben, J., & Johnson, W. R. (2005). Evidence-based treatment: Why, what, where, when, and how? *Journal of Substance Abuse Treatment, 29*(4), 267-276.

Moyers, T. B., Martin, T., Manuel, J. K., Hendrickson, S. M. L., & Miller, W. R. (2005). Assessing competence in the use of motivational interviewing. *Journal of Substance Abuse Treatment, 28*(1), 19-26. doi:10.1016/j.jsat.2004.11.001

Mueser, K. T. (2013). Illness Management and Recovery. *SAMHSA's Gains Center for Behavioral Health and Justice Transformation.* Retrieved from http://gainscenter.samhsa.gov/cms-assets/documents/141803-531013.imr-fact-sheet—-kim-mueser.pdf

Mueser, K. T., Corrigan, P. W., Hilton, D., Tanzman, B., Schaub, A., & Gingerich, S., (2002). Illness management and recovery for severe mental illness: A review of the research. *Psychiatric Services, 53,* 1272-1284.

Mueser, K. T., Meyer P.S., Penn D.L., Clancy R., Clancy D.M., Salyers M.P., (2006). The Illness Management and Recovery program: Rationale, development, and preliminary findings. *Schizophrenia Bulletin, 32,* 32-43.

Mueser, K. T., Noordsy, D., Drake, R., & Fox, L. (2003). Integrated Treatment for Dual Disorders. Guilford Press.

Mueser, K. T., Torrey, W. C., Lynde, D., Singer, P., & Drake, R. E. (2003). Implementing evidence-based practices for people with severe mental illness. *Behavior Modification, 27,* 387-411.

Olver, M. E., Wong, S. C. P., Nicholaichuk, T., & Gordon, A. (2007). The validity and reliability of the Violence Risk Scale-Sexual Offender version: Assessing sex offender risk and evaluating therapeutic change. *Psychological Assessment, 19*, 318-329.

Osher, F., D'Amora, D. A., Plotkin, J. D., Jarrett, N., & Eggleston, A. (2012). *Adults with behavioral health needs under correctional supervision: A shared framework for reducing recidivism and promoting recovery.* Council of State Governments Justice Center. http://csgjusticecenter.org/wp-content/uploads /2013/05/9-24-12_Behavioral-Health-Framwork-final.pdf

Owens, B., Wells, J., Pollock., Muscat, B., & Torres, S. (2008). *Gendered violence and safety: A contextual approach to improving security in women's' facilities.* Washington, DC: US Department of Justice, Office of Justice Programs, National Institute of Justice.

Pratt, T. & Cullen, F. (2005). Assessing macro-level predictors and theories of crime: A meta-analysis. *Crime and Justice, 32,* 373-450.

Prendergast, M. L. (2011). Issues in defining and applying evidence-based practices criteria for treatment of criminal-justice involved clients [Abstract]. *Journal of Psychoactive Drugs,* 7, 10-18.

Reavis, J. A., Looman, J., Franco, K., & Rojas, B. (2013). Adverse childhood experiences and adult criminality: How long must we live before we possess our own lives? *The Permanente Journal, 17*(2), 44-48.

Roe, D., Penn, D., Bortz, L., Hasson-Ohayon, I., Hartwell, K., & Roe, S. (2007). Illness management and recovery: Generic issues of group format implementation. *American Journal of Psychiatric Rehabilitation, 10,* 131-147.

Ross, R. R., & Fabiano, E. A. (1985). *Time to Think: A Cognitive Model of Delinquency Prevention and Offender Rehabilitation.* Tennessee: Institute of Social Sciences and Arts.

Rotter, M. and Carr, W. A., (2013). Reducing Criminal Recidivism for Justice-Involved Persons with Mental Illness: Risk/Needs/Responsivity and Cognitive-Behavioral Interventions. *SAMHSA's GAINS Center for Behavioral Health and Justice Transformation.* October 2013.

Safer, D. L., & Jo, B. (2010). Outcome from a randomized controlled trial of group therapy for binge eating disorder: Comparing dialectical behavior therapy adapted for binge eating to an active comparison group therapy. *Behavior Therapy, 41,* 106-120. doi:10.1016/j.beth.2009.01.006

Safer, D. L., Telch, C. F., & Agras, W. S. (2001). Dialectical behavior therapy for bulimia nervosa, *The American Journal of Psychiatry, 158,* 632-634. doi:10.1176/appi.ajp.158.4.632

Seager, J. A., Jellicoe, D., & Dhaliwal, G. K. (2005). Refusers, dropouts, and completers: Measuring sex offender treatment efficacy. *International journal of offender therapy and comparative criminology, 48*(5), 600-612.

Shelton, D. Sample, S, Kesten, K. L., Zang, W., & Trestman, R .L. (2009) Treatment of impulsive aggression in correctional settings. *Behavioral sciences and the Law, 27,* 787-800.

Skeem, J. (2009, March). *Offenders with mental illness: What (really) works? Part I* [PDF https://webfiles.uci.edu/skeem/Downloads_files/FMHAC_Seaside2009.pdf

Skeem, J., Nicholson, E., & Kregg, C. (2008, March). Understanding barriers to re-entry for parolees with mental disorder. In D. Kroner (Chair), *Mentally disordered offenders: A special population requiring special attention.* Symposium conducted at the meeting of the American Psychology-Law Society (Jacksonville, FL).

Smith, P., Goggin, M., & Gendreau, P. (2002). The Effects of Prison Sentences and Intermediate Sanctions on Recidivism: General Effects and Individual Difference. *Public Works and Government Services Canada.*

Sperber, K. G., Latessa, E. J., and Makarios, M. D., (2013). Examining the interaction between level of risk and dosage of treatment. *Criminal Justice and Behavior, 40,* 338. doi:10.1177/0093854812467942

Surface, D. (2008). Integrated Dual Disorders Treatment: A new wave in recovery. *Social Work Today, 8*(6), 14.

TARGET©, (n.d.). Advanced Trauma Solutions, Inc. Retrieved from http://www.advancedtrauma.com/Services.html

Travers, R., Mann, R. E., & Hollin, C. R. (2014). Who benefits from cognitive skills programs? Differential impact by risk and offense type. *Criminal Justice and Behavior, 41*(9), 1103-1129.

TREM©, (2008). *Community Connections*. Retrieved from http://www.communityconnectionsdc.org/web/page/657/interior.html

United States Department of Justice, (2013). *Smart on Crime: Reforming the Criminal Justice System for the 21st Century*. Retrieved from http://www.justice.gov/sites/default/files/ag/legacy/2013/08/12/smart-on-crime.pdf

Van Dorn R. A., Desmarais S. L., Petrila J., Haynes D., & Singh J. P. (2013). Effects of outpatient treatment on risk of arrest of adults with serious mental illness and associated costs. *Psychiatric Services, 64*(9), 856-862. doi: 10.1176/appi.ps.201200406

Victorian Government Department of Health, (2010). *Statewide mental health triage scale – Guidelines* Retrieved from http://www.health.vic.gov.au/mentalhealth/triage/triage-guidelines-0510.pdf

Walters, S. T., Clark, M. D., Gingerich, R., & Meltzer, M. L. (2007). *A guide for probation and parole: Motivating offenders to change*. Washington, DC: U.S. Department of Justice, Office of Justice Programs, National Institute of Corrections.

Wilson, D., MacKenzie, D., & Mitchell, F. N. (2005). Effects of Correctional Boot Camps on Offending: A Systematic Review. *Campbell Systematic Reviews, 1*(6), 1-45.

CHAPTER 7

Fetal Alcohol Spectrum Disorder (FASD): A Beginner's Guide for Criminal Justice and Forensic Mental Health Professionals

Jerrod Brown, Cody Charette, Stefanie Varga, Sarah E. Herrick,
Anthony Wartnik, Tina Jay, Amanda Fenrich, Phyllis Burger,
Rachel Tiede, Anne Russell, Stephanie A. Kolakowsky-Hayner,
Julie R. Anderson, Erv Weinkauf, Jodee Kulp, Jody Allen Crowe,
Ann Yurcek, Diane Neal & Margaret Wimberley

Chapter Overview

Fetal Alcohol Spectrum Disorder (FASD) is the term used to describe a group of neuro-cognitive, neuro behavioral, and physical malformations caused by prenatal alcohol exposure (PAE). This condition is caused by the effects of ethanol, the principal teratogenic toxin in alcohol, when exposed to the fetal brain (Centers for Disease Control and Prevention, 2014; McMurtrie, 2011; Wheeler, Stevens, Sheard, & Rovet, 2012). This chapter reviews the definition, recognition, Co-morbid conditions, secondary challenges, intervention, and the role of FASD in criminal justice matters. Early detection and effective treatment of individuals with FASD should be a public health and safety priority—certainly after arrest, but preferably long before.

Introduction

Fetal Alcohol Spectrum Disorder (FASD) is an umbrella term used to describe life-long neurocognitive and neurobehavioral disorders, brain damage, and specific physical malformations associated with the effects of prenatal alcohol exposure (PAE) on a developing embryo (Jacobson et al., 1993; Mattson, Schoenfield, & Riley, 2001). Specifically, alcohol consumed during pregnancy passes directly through the placenta, causing damage across a wide spectrum of severity. Damage can range from facial deformities, organ malformation, stunted growth stature, and microcephaly. Additionally, diminished IQ can result from brain damage associated with executive functioning deficits (Lebel, Roussotte, & Sowell, 2011). Research has shown that brain cells exposed to alcohol *in utero* can become damaged, resulting in structural abnormalities of the brain. This damage can be irreversible in some cases due to cell death, reduction or cessation of cell growth, or simply an overgrowth of brain cortex matter (Wozniak & Muetzel, 2011). The consequences of severe brain damage such as this are associated with long-term neuropsychological, physical, developmental, and behavioral consequences. Treatment often requires extensive and long-standing clinical and social service interventions (Popova, Lange, Burd, & Rehm, 2015; Ware et al., 2015). The range and severity of deficits an individual with FASD may experience directly correlates with the timing and dosage of alcohol exposure to the developing fetus and do not often improve as the individual ages (Brown & Connor, 2013).

Although diagnoses under the FASD umbrella include some generally agreed-upon diagnostic terms, the specific criteria for each remain varied. The most commonly employed diagnostic terms, despite subtle differences in protocol or technique, are Fetal Alcohol Syndrome (FAS), partial Fetal Alcohol Syndrome (pFAS), Alcohol-Related Birth Defects (ARBD), and Alcohol-Related Neurodevelopmental Disorder (ARND). It was not until the publication of the most recent fifth edition of the Diagnostic and Statistical Manual for Mental Disorders (DSM-5) that a mental health diagnosis was available to address FASD-related conditions (American Psychiatric Association, 2013). This includes the specifier of "Associated with Prenatal Exposure to Alcohol" in the classification of Neurodevelopment Disorders–a diagnosis of Other Specified Neurodevelopmental Disorder. Further, the DSM-5 goes on to identify Neurobehavioral Disorder Associated with Prenatal Alcohol Exposure (ND-PAE) as an area in need of further study (American Psychiatric Association, 2013).

Prenatal alcohol exposure has been recognized as the leading preventable cause of Developmental Disability (DD) and Intellectual Disability (ID) in the United States (American Psychiatric Association, 2013; Brems, Boschma-Wynn, Dewane, Edwards & Robinson, 2011).

As a direct result of PAE, 2%-5% of the population of the United States suffers from some level of dysfunction (May et al., 2009). Further, recent studies indicate that this may be considerably higher in communities where rates of binge drinking among women of childbearing age are high (May et al., 2014). Higher rates of alcohol-exposed individuals are also found in at-risk communities such as child services, criminal justice systems, and foster care settings (Muralidharan, Sarmah, Zhou & Marrs, 2013). It is estimated that a juvenile with FASD is 19 times more likely than the rest of the population to be arrested (Popova, Lange, Bekmuradov, Mihic, & Rehm, 2011). Sample studies indicate 60% of individuals with FASD will, at some point during their lifetime, become involved in the criminal justice system (Streissguth, Barr, Kogan, & Bookstein, 1996).

Despite the fact that the prevalence rate of FASD in the United States is believed to be as high as 5% (May et al., 2009), this estimate is likely low because of poor access to assessments involving at-risk populations and the absence of readily available, affordable, and accessible means of diagnosis. Other problems associated with difficulty of diagnosis include definitional misconceptions of FASD, stigmas related to the conditions, lack of funding, limited array of forensically focused screening tools, and a paucity of adequately trained personnel. Further challenges include symptoms overlapping with other disorders and the lack of FASD-specific training for providers within medical and mental health fields (Gahagan et al., 2006). Consequently, there are a scant number of opportunities for juveniles having, or suspected of having, FASD receiving a proper diagnosis prior to becoming involved in the criminal justice system (Boland, Chudley, & Grant, 2002; Brown, Connor, & Adler, 2012; Brown et al., 2015). Far fewer opportunities exist for adults with FASD, diagnosed or not, to receive support and services (Olson, 2015).

PRENATAL ALCOHOL CONSUMPTION

Half of all pregnancies in the United States are estimated to be unplanned (Centers for Disease Control and Prevention, 2014). Time is most of the essence during the early days and weeks of a pregnancy, since those are the most critical for fetal development. Unfortunately, the consumption of alcohol before recognition and confirmation of the pregnancy may contribute to underreporting of alcohol exposure during gestation (Floyd & Sidhu, 2004). Given the high alcohol use during childbearing age by women in the United States, the rate of alcohol consumption at the onset of pregnancy could be much higher than reported in most research. For example, women may be unaware they are pregnant for several weeks or more after conception, thereby leaving their unborn child unintentionally exposed to alcohol during the important early stages of fetal development (Cannon et al., 2015). Supporting this, one study found that half of the participants reported alcohol consumption during the three months prior to learning about their pregnancies (Floyd, Decoufle, & Hungerford, 1999). In one community, 30% of those tested were found to have elevated levels of fatty acid ethyl esters (FAEEs), a marker used to check for metabolized alcohol present *in utero* (Ethen et al., 2009)—five times higher than was determined through maternal self-reporting (Gareri, Lynn, Handley, Rao, & Koren, 2008). As these studies indicate, assembling a realistic baseline established on acknowledged fetal alcohol exposure is difficult due to challenges associated with gaining accurate information.

Despite attempts to educate the public, alcohol consumption during pregnancy within the United States has remained constant in recent years (Rasmussen et al., 2012). Approximately 12% of women consume alcohol during pregnancy, with the highest reported demographic consisting of women ranging in age from 35 to 44 (Centers for Disease Control, 2014). It has been estimated that 1.9% of women report binge drinking. Binge drinking is defined as four or more drinks in a two-hour period (Centers for Disease Control, 2014). In summary, the findings of past FASD research appear to vastly underestimate this phenomenon. Further study, heightened awareness, and improved education regarding alcohol, pregnancy, and FASD, are crucial to the reduction of the prevalence rate of this life-long disorder.

RECOGNIZING FASD

Evidence-based diagnostic guidelines for FASD have been developed by a variety of organizations, including the Institute of Medicine (IOM), The Centers for Disease Control and Prevention (CDC) and The Washington State Fetal Alcohol Syndrome Diagnostic & Prevention Network's 4-Digit Diagnostic Code (Astley & Clarren, 2000; CDC, 2014; Hoyme et al., 2005). Even though criteria for diagnosis may vary slightly depending on a given set of guidelines, presentation of abnormalities in three specific areas of physical development and a documented history of PAE are standard (Astley, 2013; Riley, Varga, & Warren, 2011). The three abnormalities most commonly associated with FASD are: (1) specific pathognomonic facial features, including small palpebral fissures, thin upper lip, and a smooth philtrum (the vertical groove above the upper lip) (2) a significant growth deficiency; and (3) significant central nervous system damage (Astley, 2013; Chapman, 2008; Chudley et al., 2005; Meintjes et al., 2002). In cases where these abnormalities are consistent with FAS and other possible conditions have been eliminated, documentation of PAE is not considered necessary for a positive diagnosis (Bertrand et al., 2011).

In the absence of documented PAE, differential diagnosis presents a significant challenge. The teratogenic effects of alcohol resemble numerous genetic and environmentally activated conditions (Riley et al., 2011; O'Leary-Moore, Parnell, Lipinski & Sulik, 2011). Diagnosis without evidence of PAE can be further complicated by apparent Co-morbidity with other disorders such as Attention-Deficit/ Hyperactivity Disorder (ADHD). Recent neuropsychological studies comparing children diagnosed with ADHD versus FASD show that the child with FASD typically has a lower IQ score, greater overall deficits in letter fluency, and more difficulty encoding verbal information (Crocker, Vaurio, Riley & Mattson, 2011; Vaurio, Riley, & Mattson, 2008).

Symptom clusters define an array of FASD-related disorders. For example, pFAS requires confirmed PAE, central nervous system (CNS) damage, and at least two of three facial anomalies considered diagnostically significant to FAS (Astley, 2013). According to a CDC (2014) guideline, a diagnosis of Alcohol-Related Neurodevelopmental Disorder (ARND) typically requires deficits associated with brain impairment that cannot be explained by genetics or family associations, in spite of the absence of facial abnormalities or outwardly distinctive visual signs of a disability (Doyle & Mattson, 2015; Stratton, Howe, & Battaglia, 1996). Alcohol-Related Birth Defects (ARBD) focuses on physical symptoms and medical conditions related to PAE. These may include scoliosis, malformations of the kidneys, malformations of the heart, ureteral duplications, hearing loss, optic nerve hypoplasia, sunken chest, and "railroad" malformations of the ears (Hoyme et al., 2005).

It is important to note that a diagnosis of FAS, characterized by a distinctive facial dysmorphia, does not mean this individual has the most severe form of FASD. Dependent on the timing and level of alcohol exposure during gestation, individuals with pFAS, ARBD, ARND, or ND-PAE may appear outwardly typical. However, these individuals could experience more severe clinical, social, and cognitive deficits requiring intensive interventions and medication to prevent or reduce adverse life outcomes (American Psychiatric Association, 2013; Rasmussen, 2005; Streissguth et al., 2004). Consistent with these observations, animal studies show that outward manifestations of FASD (such as facial dysmorphia) occur with alcohol exposure during a very short window in gestation, but do not indicate the severity of exposure or damage (O'Leary-Moore, Parnell & Lipinski, 2011). The same level of alcohol consumption occurring at a later time in gestation may not be outwardly perceptible, but can be equally as, if not more, damaging to the developing brain (Murawski, Moore, Thomas, & Riley, 2015). In summary, although nearly all diagnostic criteria specify physical markers such as dysmorphia of facial features or overall growth stuntedness, significant brain impairment may occur without observable physical markers (Nuñez, Roussotte, & Sowell, 2011).

Because FASD is a brain-based disability with behavioral and often hidden maladies, gathering historic secondary source data may provide a more complete picture of the complications by which an individual is beset. No two individuals will be alike due to the myriad of primary, secondary, and tertiary disabilities. The individual may also have been screened, assessed and treated by many different professionals.

The following types of professionals may be involved in an individual with FASD's life:

- Audiologist
- Cardiologist
- Dysmorphologist
- Endocrinologist
- Endodontists
- Gastroenterologist
- Geneticist
- Immunologist
- Internalist
- Nephrologist
- Neurologist
- Nutritionist
- Occupational therapist
- Ophthalmologist
- Optometrist
- Physical therapist
- Plastic surgeon
- General practitioner or pediatrician
- Speech-language pathologist

The following types of mental health professionals may be involved in an individual with FASD's life:

- Psychiatrist
- Psychologist
- Behavior management specialist
- Eating disorder specialist
- Chemical treatment specialist

Insightful additional information may be provided by obtaining an extensive dental history, cumulative educational record, and all pertinent child welfare records.

FASD Symptoms

Symptoms associated with damage caused by prenatal alcohol exposure are many and varied and can range from mild to severe. The symptoms are a result of a coalescing of a number of different facets, including the type and severity. The type and severity of damage is dependent not only on duration and amount of alcohol consumed, but also several other factors, including genetics, epigenetics, maternal health, and exposure to toxins. Alcohol exposure during the first trimester of pregnancy inhibits organ development, alters craniofacial development, and results in abnormalities to the structure of the brain, cardiac system, and other organs (Day et al., 1989; Day et al., 2002). During first and second trimesters, alcohol exposure also leads to increased rates of miscarriage (Andersen, Andersen, Olsen, Grønbæk, & Strandberg-Larsen, 2012). In the third trimester, birth weight and length have also been shown to be impacted by exposure to alcohol (Day et al., 1990).

Growth rates in children with FAS are often inhibited due to exposure to alcohol during the first trimester; however, not all children with FASD will exhibit stunted growth (Patra et al., 2011). Stunted growth is defined by birth weight at or below the 10th percentile, slowness to gain weight as the child ages (in comparison to other children), and a disproportionally low weight to height ratio (Centers for Disease Control, 2014; Riley et al., 2011).

Despite its presence in most diagnostic criteria, facial dysmorphia occurs in only about 10% of those exposed to alcohol prenatally (Jones et al., 2010; Leibson, Neuman, Chudley, & Koren, 2014). When the individual's face does not exhibit dysmorphic features, diagnosis can be significantly more challenging. Further complicating the diagnostic process is that even if dysmorphic facial features are present during childhood, these abnormalities can become indistinct or fade after the onset of puberty (Spohr, Willms, & Steinhausen, 1993; Spohr, Willms, & Steinhausen, 1994; Steinhausen, Willms, & Spohr, 1993).

Children with FAS are likely to be diagnosed as being within the FASD umbrella because of their facial dysmorphology. However, individuals with pFAS, ARND and ARBD are often overlooked as candidates for FASD because of the physical invisibility of their disability (Chudley, Kilgour, Cranston, & Edwards, 2007; Malbin, 2004). For this reason, FASD has been referred to by many as an invisible disability. Despite the lack of facial dysmorphology, these individuals may have undiagnosed brain damage that impacts their day-to-day functioning. Further, this brain damage may result in behavioral disorders that can hinder their response to interventions and treatment (Clarke & Gibbard, 2003). The structural damage can impact intellectual and adaptive functioning, language, learning, numerous academic skills, attention, working memory, processing speed, ability to reason, and comprehension of even basic mathematical concepts (Mattson & Riley, 1998; Norman et al., 2013; Nuñez, Roussotte, & Sowell, 2011; Riley, McGee & Sowell, 2004). Table 1 highlights the various invisible deficits associated with FASD. These deficits are more likely to become more pronounced when the individual is stressed or under pressure.

Table 1

Invisible Disabilities often associated with FASD

• Attention-deficits	• Immature behavior
• Maladaptive social skills	• Memory deficits
• Difficulty learning from consequences	• Poor impulse control
• Difficulty with abstract concepts such as mathematics, time, and money	• Poor judgment
	• Poor problem-solving skills
• Hyperactivity	• Poor decision-making skills

Note. Used with permission from the National Organization on Fetal Alcohol Syndrome-UK

Many organs and body systems can be affected in fetal development from prenatal alcohol exposure. Each time exposure to alcohol occurs, the resultant brain and body damage is unique to that stage of development. The CNS and the fetal brain develop continuously and can be affected at every stage of gestation (Burd, Cohen, Shah, & Norris, 2011). These structural abnormalities in the fetal brain emerge as causal factors for continued deficit manifestation in the growing postnatal brain (Brown & Connor, 2013). Normal neurological growth pathways associated with childhood and adolescence that typically create effortless access to efficient and effective responses to situations, reasoned decisions, and other executive functions are impaired when the structure of the newborn's brain has been damaged. This damage results in inhibited development (Brown & Connor, 2013), which can result in subsequent behavioral manifestations. For example, most individuals with FASD have deficits in response inhibition, whereby individuals with FASD will typically act or react without being able to identify the consequences of their actions (Jirikowic, Kartin, & Olson, 2008).

As result of the aforementioned executive functioning impairments, this population tends to have difficulty regulating emotion (Schonfeld, Paley, Frankel, & O'Connor, 2006; Thiel et al., 2011) and recognizing how their behavior impacts others. In turn, this may affect the ability of these individuals to accept responsibility for problematic behavior. This can also play a role in preventing them from learning from their mistakes, misdeeds, or crimes (Dewhurst, 2009). Further, individuals with FASD are also at risk for victimization by others, including their caregivers (Fast & Conry, 2004; Thiel et al., 2011). Exacerbating issues, those with FASD are likely to lack awareness of personal boundaries as well as normal means of self-protection (Thiel et al., 2011). Factors such as impaired reasoning, lack of judgment, poor self-regulation and other deficits often lead to involvement with the legal system (Chartrand & Forbes-Chilibeck, 2003).

CO-OCCURRING DISORDERS AND SECONDARY CONSEQUENCES

CO-OCCURRING CONDITIONS

Recognizing Co-morbidity in people with FASD is necessary to fully understand the etiology of the behaviors and the needs of the individuals (Mattson et al., 2011). More than 90% of individuals with FASD have at least one Co-morbid mental health diagnosis (Streissguth et al., 1996). Co-morbid diagnoses often associated with FASD include (Amos-Kroohs et al., 2016; Clarke & Gibbard, 2003; Famy, Streissguth & Unis, 1998; Green et al., 2009; Lutke, 2004; May et al., 2009; O'Malley & Rich, 2013; Streissguth et al., 1996):

- Attention-Deficit/Hyperactivity Disorder (ADHD)
- Conduct Disorder (CD)
- Eating disorders
- Reactive Attachment Disorder (RAD)
- Post-traumatic Stress Disorder (PTSD)
- Learning Disorders
- Sleep Disorders
- Seizure Disorders
- Substance Use Disorders

Recent research highlights autism as a prevailing Co-morbid condition, yet the exact nature of the connection remains unclear (Westrup, 2013). Although conclusions should be tempered by the study's sample size, 16 out of 21 youth (72%) diagnosed with FASD also met the diagnostic criteria for Autism Spectrum Disorder (ASD) (Mukherjee, Layton, Yacoub, & Turk, 2011). Further research with larger samples is necessary to better understand the potential links between FASD, ASD, and other conditions.

It is possible that widespread Co-morbidity is merely due to the high prevalence rates of FASD. Alternatively, many individuals with FASD may be misdiagnosed with other conditions whose symptoms overlap because both the diagnostic capacities for FASD and the general awareness of the condition are so low. Consistent with this possibility, individuals with FASD often receive multiple diagnoses of other conditions before finally finding a clinician with the expertise to diagnose FASD.

Co-morbid mental health conditions can be treated and managed through appropriate intervention techniques (Streissguth et al., 2004). Failure to diagnose the primary brain injury of FASD may hinder treating both FASD and the other presenting Co-morbid disorders. The established treatment protocols for the Co-morbid conditions alone may not be as effective in individuals with FASD (Elias, 2013; Peadon & Elliott, 2010). Furthermore, in conjunction with other mental health conditions, FASD may place an individual at a higher risk of adverse life outcomes, especially when the individual lacks appropriate services, supports, and guidance.

LEARNING DISABILITIES AND MEMORY-RELATED DEFICITS

Prenatal alcohol exposure directly impacts learning and memory (Streissguth, Barr, Bookstein, & Sampson, 1993; Streissguth, Barr, Carmichael, & Sampson, 1994). Children with FASD may exhibit both auditory and visual learning and memory deficits (Kodituwakku, 2007). Additionally, deficits associated with verbal learning and the processing of odor identification are common (Bower, Szajer, Mattson, Riley, & Murphy, 2013).

In a sample of children who were exposed to prenatal binge drinking during the first trimester, suffered deficits in verbal learning, including problems encoding, storing, and retrieving information (Willford, Richardson, Leech, & Day, 2004). Noted deficits occurred in their recollection of word-pairs presented verbally after both short and long delays, but no effect was found for visual measures (Willford et al., 2004). Nonetheless, visual memory and learning were as impaired as verbal domains in other studies (Coles, Lynch, Kable, Johnson, & Goldstein, 2010; Pei, Rinaldi, Rasmussen, Massey, & Massey, 2008). Further, many individuals impacted by FASD with relatively high IQ scores do not appear to have significant learning difficulties (Streissguth, Randels, & Smith, 1991), but present with deficits that persist throughout development, including social-emotional development, hyperactivity, and deficiencies in planning, sensory processing, and problem solving (Blackburn, Carpenter, & Egerton, 2010; Streissguth et al., 2004).

Kodituwakku and colleagues (1995) found that individuals with FASD have an inability to maintain and utilize encoded information. They also have deficits in the prioritization of goals corresponding to working memory (Kodituwakku, Handmaker, Cutler, Weathersby, & Handmaker, 1995). Confounding caregivers and law enforcement personnel as well as others who interact with this population, short-term verbal recall abilities can present a false impression of a functional, non-impaired individual (Blackburn et al., 2010; Mattson, & Riley, 1999). Mathematics, specifically mathematical processing and cognitive estimation, also appears to be an area of weakness (Mattson, Crocker, & Nguyen, 2011).

Fundamental deficits in learning and memory may impede successful educational outcomes for those with FASD (Kalberg & Buckley, 2007). These students consistently demonstrate lower achievement rates compared to peers without FASD (Streissguth, Barr, Kogan, & Bookstein, 1996). Students with FASD are also characterized by truancy, behavioral problems, and eventually–elevated dropout rates (Gunn, 2013; Kalberg & Buckley, 2007; Streissguth et al., 1996).

SUBSTANCE ABUSE

Substance use disorders (SUD) are prevalent among individuals with FASD. In a large study of adults with Fetal Alcohol Effects (FAE) (an outdated term), researchers found that 53% of males and 70% of females had substance abuse issues (Streissguth et al., 1996). Another study estimated that one-half of the participants with FASD had experienced substance use disorders (May et al., 2009). This increased risk of developing substance use disorders is due in part to the lack of support for primary disabilities, in conjunction with family substance abuse histories (Totten, 2009). Further, substance abuse may be associated with abuse of all forms, which in turn creates additional environmental adversity, complicating familial relationships and contributing to guardianship instability (Streissguth et al., 1996). This is believed to be partially the result of disruptions in their dopamine receptors during the gestation process. This disruption creates increased deficits in their executive and inhibitory control (Schneider, Moore, & Adkins, 2011). The continuation of this cycle results in an increasing number of young people with FASD who experience adverse environments and are therefore at an increased risk of encountering the criminal justice system in some form.

The Co-morbidity of FASD and SUD is more difficult to treat than either alone, given the already implicit impairments in behavioral regulation and decision-making of an individual with FASD. The implementation of a successful treatment regimen is also hindered by the individual's cognitive issues. When combined with impairments in executive functioning, such as organizing, cognitive fluidity, and coping ability, the chances for a successful outcome diminish greatly. In particular, Grant et al. (2014) surmised that women with FASD had difficulty attending to completion of both inpatient and outpatient treatment programs; they were more successful with inpatient therapy because it was structured and required fewer independent decisions.

GUARDIANSHIP INSTABILITY

Children with FASD are often not raised by their birth parents. For that reason, a high proportion of children with FASD, diagnosed or suspected, are placed into foster care each year. Some estimates of this population run as high as 70% (Burd et al., 2011; LaFrance et al., 2014; Lange, Shield, Rehm, & Popova, 2013). Because many foster caregivers are unaware of the child's history and possible PAE, appropriate parenting techniques found effective for this population are often not employed—resulting in possible secondary disabilities.

Secondary disabilities are conditions that arise from the chronic stress and frustration of not having FASD-related disabilities diagnosed and treated. They include depression, conduct disorder, lying, confabulation, substance addiction, dropping out of school, inability to parent and undertake employment, sex-offending, and trouble with the law (Popova et al., 2015). Once these secondary disabilities have developed, medical professionals often misdiagnose these as an individual's primary disability (Popova et al., 2015). The lack of historical context regarding a child results in other problems as well.

Placement in foster care without knowledge that the child has PAE can create untenable situations for both the caregiver and the child. Even if caregivers could use the best commonly accepted parenting techniques available, for individuals with FASD the consequences are likely to result in secondary disabilities with increasingly severe presentation. These include deterioration of mental health and other Co-morbid disorders, unless techniques specifically developed and tailored for children with FASD are brought to bear (Burd, Lange, Popova, & Rehm, 2014; LaFrance et al., 2014). Children with PAE are subjected to high rates of foster parent turnover (Lange et al., 2013), intensifying the challenge for young people with FASD to establish meaningful, lasting relationships with peers and adults. This limits their social supports and increases both real and perceived isolation (Lange et al., 2013). Further, children in the foster system are at an increased risk for a range of negative physical and psychological outcomes beyond prenatal alcohol exposure. These outcomes can include substance-abusing parents, physical abuse, or neglect (Burd, Fast, Conry, & Williams, 2010).

Similar issues affect children with FASD who are adopted. Landgren, Svensson, Stromland, and Gronlund (2010) found in their research that approximately half of their samples of internationally adopted children were affected by FASD. The adoption process often complicates recognition of PAE. As previously noted, because of the current lack of available biomarkers denoting FASD, definitive confirmation of FASD is difficult to obtain. These children typically lack personal medical histories, in particular prenatal data, and scant secondary information is available. This lack of documentation hinders diagnosis of any of the disorders within the FASD spectrum, because documented PAE is required at a minimum. It is also difficult for these individuals to access appropriate clinical and social services (Centers for Disease Control, 2014).

DOMESTIC VIOLENCE

Due to traits associated with impaired judgment and indiscriminate trust, females with FASD can be at an elevated risk for domestic violence and abuse and are at a significantly higher risk of sexual exploitation and trafficking (May et al., 2005; May et al., 2008). Difficulties with reading, understanding facial expressions, and body language are also prevalent (May et al., 2005; May et al., 2008). Domestic violence is known to contribute to mental and physical illness, substance abuse, suicidal thinking, and numerous other issues (Edward, Sterling, Joanne, & Egon, 2010). Another aspect of domestic violence involves non-existent or fragile communication with an individual's family of origin. The individual may also lack an accessible support system or be constrained from asking for help. All of these challenges taken together may bring about unhealthy coping behaviors such as substance abuse (May et al., 2008). Unfortunately, abuse of drugs and alcohol will often perpetuate in a vicious cycle, latently increasing the probability of FASD-affected children in subsequent generations.

SUICIDE

Individuals with FASD have an elevated risk of suicidal behavior (Baldwin, 2007; Huggins, Grant, O'Malley, & Streissguth, 2008). Rates of attempted suicide are approximately 10 times higher for individuals with FASD than in the general population (Merrick & Kandel, 2007). In a study of 473 individuals with FASD, the mean age was 25.6 years and most participants suffered from clinical depression (Streissguth et al., 1996). Within this group, 23% had attempted suicide and 43% had made suicidal threats. Suicidal risk in individuals with FASD was highlighted again in a pilot study where 6 of the 11 participants between the ages of 18 and 30 had attempted suicide—a rate of 54% (Huggins, Connor, O'Malley, Barr, & Streissguth, 2001; O'Malley & Huggins, 2005). In another life history study, roughly 46% had attempted suicide (Grant et al., 2013).

High rates of suicidality may not only be linked to the cognitive deficits found in FASD, but also to Co-morbid disorders and other biological, psychological, and sociological factors (Huggins et al., 2008). The U.S. Surgeon General's Report on Mental Health (1999) listed sixteen risk factors that were identified as contributing to suicide (Shalala, 1999). Eight of these risk factors are commonly found in individuals with FASD (Shalala, 1999). These risk factors include mental health disorders, substance abuse disorders, impulsivity and/or aggressive tendencies, barriers to accessing medical or psychiatric care, history of trauma/abuse, job or financial loss, relational or social loss, and lack of social supports (Shalala, 1999). Suicide attempts and thoughts about suicide may take place throughout an individual's lifetime and are difficult to treat when left untreated for too long.

Suicidal ideation and actions also affect mothers who give birth to children with FASD. In a study of 70 women with a mean age of 26 who had delivered children on the FASD spectrum, 60% had attempted suicide and 72% had "significant" suicidal thoughts (Rasmussen et al., 2012). These high rates are likely a combination of the grief and guilt associated with giving birth to a child with FASD, combined with their own substance use disorders that may be being used as coping mechanisms in the absence of more efficacious treatment.

FASD AND THE CRIMINAL JUSTICE SYSTEM

Involvement in the criminal justice system is common among individuals with FASD (Brown et al., 2011; Riley, Clarren, Weinberg, & Jonsson, 2011; Wartnik & Carlson, 2011). Although few epidemiological studies investigating FASD have been conducted in U.S. correctional settings, individuals with FASD may comprise a sizable percentage of the corrections population (Fast, Conry, & Loock, 1999). A large study at the University of Washington found that about 60% of individuals with FASD had contact with the criminal justice system and 50% had a history of confinement in a jail, prison, residential drug treatment facility, or psychiatric hospital (Streissguth et al., 1996). In fact, youth with FASD are 19 times more likely to be arrested than peers without FASD (Popova et al., 2011). This elevated risk is likely caused by aggressive acting-out behaviors; impulsivity; executive and adaptive functioning impairments; and untreated trauma, mental health-related issues and substance use concerns (Edwards & Greenspan, 2010; Greenspan, Switzky, & Woods, 2011; Kully-Martens, Treit, Pei, & Rasmussen, 2013). It may also be due in part to the cognitive deficits associated with FASD, such as the impaired ability to cope with environmental adversity (Brown, Connor, & Adler, 2012). Stressful situations involving the courts, police, and persons of authority tend to cause youth with FASD to experience sensory overload and may result in additional acts of aggression (Popova et al., 2011). When left unaddressed, behavioral symptoms associated with FASD may lead to or exacerbate co-occurring conditions and secondary disabilities such as substance abuse, mental disorders, or impulsive behavior. These additional conditions and disabilities place the individual at an even higher risk for illegal activity (Idrus, McGough, Riley, & Thomas, 2011).

Youth with FASD who become involved in the criminal justice system are at a profound disadvantage in all stages of the legal process, from arrest to sentencing and even beyond in post-release community settings (Brown et al., 2012; Brown, Wartnik, Connor, & Adler, 2010; Edwards & Greenspan, 2010). As a result of the brain damage associated with PAE, this population tends to be naïve, lack foresight about their decisions, and may even make a false confession based on a mistaken appraisal of a situation (Popova et al., 2011). This population tends to be easily and excessively influenced by social peer pressure, which can result in the individual being unwittingly led into compromising positions, particularly given their inability to foresee consequences (Brown et al., 2012; Clark, Lutke, Minnes, & Ouellette-Kuntz, 2004; Pollard et al., 2004). Therefore, adolescents with FASD are easy targets for victimization and manipulation (Fast & Conry, 2009).

Forensic professionals working in mental health and criminal justice settings need to cultivate an increased awareness of how to effectively approach and interact with individuals that have, or are suspected to have, FASD. Having such knowledge has been shown to improve treatment outcomes (Paley & O'Connor, 2011). After working with the Alaska FASD Partnership to pass a state law that would allow FASD to be a mitigating factor during judicial sentencing, State Senator Kevin Meyer stated, "Studies have repeatedly shown that recidivists with FASD and other brain impairments are more likely to stop committing crimes when they are given the same support as people with mental illness" (Kelly, 2012). Thus, understanding the implications of FASD will prove beneficial for criminal justice professionals, especially when developing client-based approaches and treatment strategies to reduce recidivism.

Juvenile justice programs have traditionally been particularly ill-equipped to identify and address the various issues posed by youth with FASD (Brown et al., 2012). Recognizing this, the Office of Juvenile Justice and Delinquency Prevention was involved with launching the American Bar Association's advocacy for FASD education in the criminal justice system in 2013. It has raised importance for authorities in the criminal justice system to be aware of the impact of FASD on the juvenile offender population. Professionals are also encouraged to educate staff so that the guidelines regarding FASD are well understood (Kable, Reynolds, Valenzuela, & Medina, 2014).

INAPPROPRIATE SEXUAL BEHAVIORS AND SEXUAL VICTIMIZATION

The likelihood of sexual misconduct may be increased for those with FASD. Characteristics such as the inability to learn from mistakes, difficulty with abstract reasoning, lack of understanding personal boundaries, poor impulse control, and being unable to grasp the concept of consequences may result in the individual with FASD engaging in sexually inappropriate behaviors (Baumbach, 2002; Fast & Conry, 2004; Novick, 1997; Popova et al., 2011; Streissguth et al., 1996; Streissguth, LaDue, & Randels, 1988). For example, one of the most frequently noted issues associated with the FASD-impacted individual's tendency to engage in sexual misconduct concerns their lack of developmental maturity. This may contribute to sexual interest in someone who is not of the FASD individual's chronological age, but of his or her developmental age (Boulding, 2007). Individuals with FASD may associate and possibly engage in sexual behavior with younger individuals who are closer to them in developmental age than chronological age (McMurtrie, 2011). In some states, if the FASD-impacted individual is 18 or older, they may be charged with statutory rape, leading to the arrest and incarceration of a person whose developmental age may be as young as a 6- or 7-year-old (Boulding, 2007). It has been estimated that as many as 49% of all persons with FASD were found to have participated in sexual misconduct by the time they became adults (Streissguth et al., 1996). It is important to stress that these statistics apply most frequently to conditions where the FASD-impacted individual has not been provided with early interventions and, in many cases, may have developed patterns of coping strategies that include sexualized behavior (Baumbach, 2002; Fast & Conry, 2004; Novick, 1997; Popova et al., 2011; Streissguth et al., 1996; Streissguth et al., 1988). As such, professionals serving individuals suspected of having FASD with histories of sexually inappropriate behaviors should consider the disorder when establishing services and supports for these highly vulnerable and at-risk persons (Baumbach, 2002; Fast & Conry, 2004; Novick, 1997; Popova et al., 2011; Streissguth et al., 1996; Streissguth et al., 1988).

In addition to increasing the risk of sexual misconduct, the symptoms of FASD also increase the likelihood of becoming victims of sexual misconduct (Baumbach, 2002; Fast & Conry, 2004; Novick, 1997; Popova et al., 2011; Streissguth et al., 1996; Streissguth, LaDue, & Randels, 1988). Some individuals with FASD may be incapable of comprehending the dangerous consequences of violating social norms related to sexual behavior, such as seeking affection from strangers and unwittingly presenting themselves as someone open to sexual contact. This is especially true of adolescents and children (Thiel et al., 2011). Some estimate that as many as 55%-60% of the FASD population are victims of sexual abuse or assault (Streissguth et al., 1996). Further, in what seems like a double-bind situation, if an individual with FASD engages in consensual sexual activity with someone their own age, this individual with FASD may automatically be considered a rape victim in some states, due to their mental incapacities (McMurtrie, 2011).

VICTIMIZATION

Individuals with FASD are at an elevated risk of not only committing crimes, but also becoming victims of crime. Although likely to be grossly underestimated due to the under-reporting of crimes (Thiel et al., 2011), research suggests that individuals with FASD may have victimization rates as high as 25%-50% (Baladerian, 1999). As with all cases of victimization, reports must be carefully evaluated to ensure they are not mishandled or incorrectly dismissed (Thiel et al., 2011). Thiel and colleagues (2011) posit victimization by caregivers often goes under-reported. Furthermore, when reporting or giving a witness statement regarding criminal activity, the cognitive deficits of an individual with FASD may prevent them from providing an accurate statement of events (Fast & Conry, 2004). Thus, increasing awareness about the extent of victimization in this population is important to reduce criminal behavior towards those with FASD (Petersilia, 2009). Specialized programs have been designed to train individuals with cognitive deficits on how to properly report victimization when confronted with unavoidable situations (Petersilia, 2009). However, such training programs must overcome many challenges such as lower levels of positive social interactions and poor social supports for individuals with FASD. To decrease the under-reporting of victimization, family members of individuals with FASD should be trained to recognize the emotional and behavioral changes associated with victimization (Thiel et al., 2011).

LEGAL PROCEEDINGS

The legal process is challenging for individuals. This is especially true for individuals with FASD. These individuals have greater difficulty when it comes to understanding the intricacies of the legal system and recognizing the significance of personal rights (McLachlan et al., 2014). Reduced reasoning capacity may impair their ability to comprehend the specifics of the criminal justice processes, including *Miranda* rights, interrogative procedures, and legal proceedings. In addition, they may not understand the importance of plea bargains, testimony, and giving of consent to search (Douds, Stevens, & Sumner, 2012; McLachlan, Roesch, Viljoen, & Douglas, 2014).

In a study of 50 young offenders with FASD and an equal number of neuro-typical offenders, comparisons were made to determine their understanding of basic legal rights (McLachlan et al., 2014). The results showed that 76% of the offenders in the FASD group were incapable of understanding court proceedings, in comparison to just 28% in the neuro-typical group (McLachlan et al., 2014). Complicating matters, it is not uncommon for individuals with FASD to state that they understand what qualifies as personal rights, even though they actually do lack such comprehension when tested (Katner, 2006; National Organization on Fetal Alcohol Syndrome, 2012).

Considerations need to be made when obtaining statements from individuals with FASD. There is a tendency for this population to try to please others, which can significantly diminish their ability to provide accurate testimony (Thiel et al., 2011). Those with FASD may even falsely confess to crimes they did not commit, which may stem, in part, from a high degree of emotional discomfort with being questioned (National Organization on Fetal Alcohol Syndrome, 2012; Peadon & Elliott, 2010; Thiel et al., 2011). They may lack the capacity to understand the consequences of confessing to a crime they did not commit and may view their confession as simply a means to escape an uncomfortable situation, such as that experienced during an interrogation (Douds et al., 2012). In fact, they may even portray events in a way that deviates from reality to align their experience with prompts given during questioning (Conry & Fast, 2000). Conry and Fast (2000) described a defendant with FASD confessing to a double murder. The defendant, who could not have committed the crime because he was incarcerated at the time, later explained that he confessed to end the interrogation and please the officer who questioned him. Deliberate reporting of inaccurate information may trigger further negative legal consequences, such as a wrongful conviction and incarceration (Brown, Gudjonsson & Connor, 2011; Fast & Conry, 2004).

CONFABULATION

Confabulation is the provision of false information by someone who cannot differentiate between a genuine event and an event that only *seems* genuine (Nedjam, Devouche, & Barba, 2004). Individuals with FASD are known to confabulate frequently. Damage to the frontal lobe related to PAE, specifically to the ventromedial frontal cortex, may be linked to confabulation. Most often the damage is found in the context of memory impairment and communication issues (Brown, Long-McGie, Oberoi et al., 2014; Fotopoulou, 2008, Moscovitch & Melo, 1997). Memory gaps associated with FASD-related brain damage may backfill, creating congruent memories of events that are not real or are only partially accurate (Brown, Oberoi, Wartnik, Weinkauf, & Wresh, 2013; Pei, Job, Kully-Martens, & Rasmussen, 2011). Executive functioning impairment and the inability to organize complex or voluminous information may also play a role in confabulation (Pei et al., 2011). Despite confusing real and fictional events, false self-reports may hold some element of truth, which can create an impression of accurate reporting. Those who confabulate may truly believe their false memories are true, despite evidence to the contrary (Brown et al., 2013).

Although not investigated directly, people with FASD are particularly vulnerable to false confessions, as observed in individuals with mental disabilities common to FASD (Perske, 2011). Even though the court may consider a diagnosis of FASD as relevant in an arrest, confession, or testimony, it is unusual for courts to distinguish between IQ, which has little correlation with social judgment and behavior, and executive functioning, which determines a defendant's ability to control his or her behavior (Douds et al., 2012). Examples of this occur in court cases when the defense is compelled to request a competency evaluation to prove the defendant was incompetent during confession or even back to when the crime originally took place. Because of inadequate understanding of FASD-related issues the competency evaluation may be declined because the court decides alcohol exposure in an FASD diagnosis does not warrant a court-ordered evaluation (*Dunn v. Johnson*, 1998).

Selected courts examined by Douds et al. (2012) were found to allow witnesses to dispute claims of FASD inhibiting the portrayal of accurate information. In an extreme example of this, a 9-year-old child diagnosed with FAS, who was called upon as a witness in a trial (*U.S. v. Allen J.*, 1997), was deemed competent because he understood the difference between a lie and the truth, and therefore would be able to stand up to questioning. The article relating this case cites that although the child with FAS may have been competent to differentiate between truth and lies, he would not understand the difference between truth and fantasy (Thiel et al., 2011).

LAW ENFORCEMENT AND INTERROGATION

Individuals with FASD may encounter the criminal justice system from the position of a witness, defendant, or complainant. Law enforcement officers should be aware as to how people with FASD are vulnerable to suggestive techniques and may unknowingly provide inaccurate information and contradictory statements as victims, witnesses, or suspects (Baumbach, 2002; Conry & Fast, 2000; Brown et al., 2011; Moore & Green, 2004). For example, individuals with mild learning disabilities and other cognitive complications are more susceptible to suggestive questioning (Clare & Gudjonsson, 1993). Fast and Conry (2004) cited an instance where an individual with FASD who conveyed false information suggested to him during questioning by police was subjected to a substantial incarceration. Thus, suggestive interrogation techniques employed by law enforcement have the potential of significantly influencing an individual with FASD's capacity to recall, and consequently may diminish the accuracy of testimony given by these individuals (*R. v. Sterling*, 1995). This mistaken recollection of events through suggestive questioning can hold serious implications for defendants with FASD.

To protect against this possibility, suspects, witnesses, and victims with suspected cases of FASD should be tested for suggestibility. One option may be the Gudjonsson Suggestibility Scale (GSS), which consists of the interviewer reading a short narrative and then asking specific questions based on the narrative (Gudjonsson, 1997). This has been proposed as a technique that could be used to ensure objectivity and provide documentation regarding the extent to which the individual being tested demonstrates his or her level of yielding to suggestive questions (Gudjonsson, 1997). The incorporation of such an approach could reduce the number of wrongful convictions.

SENTENCING CONCERNS

FASD complicates the implementation of differential culpability. This is the concept of determining punishment by applying a relative value to the intention of harm caused in a crime and the related amount of guilt. Individuals with FASD may not always have the cognitive capacity to foresee the consequences of their actions, much less control their emotions or urges (Brown et al., 2011; McLachlan et al., 2014). This creates a scenario where weighing differential culpability in relation to criminal behavior is particularly relevant (McMurtrie, 2011). This enables a defense attorney to argue that a defendant lacked all impulse control and that he or she did not have time to form criminal intent as a direct result of the impairments associated with FASD.

In *Weeks v. State* (1998), the Supreme Court of Indiana stated that a judicial ruling must consider an individual's capacity to control his or her behavior along with any limitation on the actions. The Court went on to state that it must consider whether this limitation is at all connected to the crime committed (*Weeks v. State*, 1998). If the defense can establish that a defendant's impulsive behavior was directly connected to the crime committed, sentencing may be reduced or mitigated. However, some courts have narrowly construed the U.S. Supreme Court's ruling by only considering FASD as a mitigating factor in capital or death penalty cases. As of the summer of 2015, the United States Supreme Court had not addressed the issue in non-death-penalty cases.

A 2002 case involving a male defendant is an example that highlights the frustrations associated with FASD and the courts. The male defendant in this case was accused of killing a nine-year-old girl, a fact that was not in dispute (Chartrand & Forbes-Chillibeck, 2003). He had been in and out of the courts his entire life. The day prior to the girl's murder, he had been in jail awaiting psychological assessment. When the person scheduled to do the assessment did not arrive, the judge released him. This defendant's lawyer acknowledged the defendant had "the attention span of a gnat" (Chartrand & Forbes-Chillibeck, 2003, p. 36). Aware of the defendant's FAS diagnosis, the defense submitted a defense of not guilty by reason of insanity (NGRI). The defendant refused to support this defense based solely on the belief that he could smoke if he went to the state penitentiary. The defendantt's lawyer, frustrated by what he claimed was a complete injustice, renounced practicing law over this case (Chartrand & Forbes-Chillibeck, 2003).

CORRECTIONAL SETTINGS & OFFENDER REENTRY

The correctional system can be a difficult environment for individuals with FASD. Often perceived as vulnerable by their fellow inmates, individuals with FASD are profoundly at risk for victimization while incarcerated (Fast & Conry, 2004; Malbin, 2004). These individuals may demonstrate considerable rule-breaking behavior because they have difficulty managing their impulses, remembering rules, generalizing rules, and comprehending the consequences of their behavior (Kully-Martens, Pei, Job & Rasmussen, 2012). Social skill deficits (Malbin, 2004) may contribute to these individuals being used as scapegoats, often succumbing to peer pressure (Brintnell, Bailey, Sawhney, & Kreftin, 2011). Further, as frequent recidivism may cause individuals with FASD to become known to corrections professionals, the resultant familiarity has been cited as a factor that contributes to their deficits being ignored (Mela & Luther, 2013).

Leaving the correctional facility and reintegrating into society can be an especially challenging task for offenders with FASD (Brown, Herrick, & Long-McGie, 2014). They will often fail to successfully navigate the conditions of their release (Brintnell et al., 2011). Homelessness, lack of family support, substance abuse, unemployment, financial instability, and inherent deficiencies associated with adaptive behavior and executive function can result in the individual failing to reintegrate successfully into society (Brown et al., 2014). Recidivism rates are high for this population (Fast & Conry, 2009; Malbin, 2004), as the obligations required of some ex-offenders with FASD, including appearing at scheduled parole meetings or testing centers, can be all but impossible to achieve without additional support and monitoring. Accurate reporting, remembering bail requirements, and cautiously navigating life with a suspended sentence can be almost impossible for a person with FASD. Failing at any one of these critical activities may mean a return to prison.

INTERVENTION STRATEGIES

Screening and the subsequent identification of individuals with FASD of all ages and within all social strata are required to ensure that the specific needs of these individuals are met. In a study of 415 individuals with FASD, 60% had dropped out of school, 60% had been in trouble with the law, and 35% had substance abuse problems (Streissguth et al., 1996). Of those who were 21 years or older, 79% had trouble with employment (Streissguth et al., 1996). Although early identification and access to resources were key predictors of success, only 11% of the participants in their study had been diagnosed with FASD prior to age six (Streissguth et al., 1996). Because the intellectual abilities of children with FASD generally fell within the normal range of standard IQ tests, they did not obtain the necessary resources. As recently as 2014, routine screening remained lacking despite the high prevalence estimates of FASD in criminal justice settings (Yan, Bell, & Racine, 2014). Unfortunately, this ongoing need for screening is made even more relevant by the magnitude of the financial, social, emotional, and community burdens that this under-served population places on the criminal justice system (Brown et al., 2014; Burd, Selfridge, Klug, & Bakko, 2004).

Criminal justice professionals would be well served by employing appropriate strategies for working with individuals who may have FASD. One such strategy is utilization of the D.E.A.R. model, developed by the first author to assist professionals with individuals involved with the criminal justice system, which is outlined as follows:

Direct Language – When communicating with an individual with FASD, always use simple and direct language, as this population has problems thinking abstractly. Explain things slowly to allow the individual plenty of time to process what is being said. To ensure comprehension, periodically ask the individual to explain—in his or her own words—what you have just said.

Engage Support System – When interviewing an individual with FASD, be sure to ask if they carry the card of a mentor, advocate, or caseworker who can offer support or act as an interpreter. This population frequently does not understand the consequences of providing police with self-incriminating statements. This is particularly problematic in the case of confabulation, which results from a poor working memory. People with FASD will incriminate themselves for what seems to be no logical reason. To prevent delays in the judicial process or the individual from harming themselves, it is important to avoid the use of leading questions until a member of their support system is present.

Accommodate Needs – When communicating with an individual with FASD, the session should be conducted in a quiet place without distractions whenever possible. Give the individual time, space, and avoid verbal confrontation. This population usually functions at a lower developmental level than their chronological age. Adapt your choice of words and your style of communication accordingly.

Remain Calm – When communicating with an individual with FASD, do not rush them. This will cause stress and may result in the individual becoming overwhelmed. This population is characterized by an inability to manage their emotions, causing situations to escalate quickly. It is preferable that people around the individual maintain a calm and measured demeanor.

CONCLUSION

Despite being 100% preventable, PAE is one of the leading causes of birth defects and cognitive impairments in the United States (Centers for Disease Control, 2014). Although facial abnormalities and other physical malformations are sometimes observed in individuals who suffer from two of the diagnoses within the FASD spectrum (FAS and pFAS), the most significant damage to individuals with FASD is invisible (Riley et al., 2011). Alcohol exposure to the developing brain often results in deficits in reasoning and difficulty managing and maintaining social attachments. Complicating matters, it is common for people with FASD to experience childhood trauma, substance abuse, mental illness, and social isolation. These difficulties work in conjunction with each other to create extreme challenges the FASD population experiences in obtaining and maintaining employment or living independently. As such, the need for early detection of individuals with FASD should be prominently highlighted as a public health and safety priority.

The combination of FASD and secondary disabilities can increase the likelihood of entanglement in the criminal justice system. The inability of these individuals to comprehend and exhibit lawful behavior without the aid of professional support will continue to place them on the path of the criminal justice system. Once involved, individuals with FASD are at a significant disadvantage—a fact seldom recognized by criminal justice professionals. Without a thorough understanding of the dynamics of this growing population, the relationship of FASD-impacted individuals to the courts will remain problematic at best. To avoid miscarriages of justice, inhibit recidivism, and promote community safety, it is essential that members of law enforcement, defense attorneys, prosecutors, judicial officials, and forensic mental health professionals be given the tools and training needed to work with this often severely misunderstood population. Promotion of FASD educational programs and resources for those professionals working within the criminal justice system is strongly recommended with all deliberate speed.

References

American Psychiatric Association. (2013). *Diagnostic and statistical manual of mental disorders* (5th ed.). Washington, DC: Author.

Amos-Kroohs, RM, Fink, B. A., Smith, C. J., Chin, L, Van Calcar, S.C., Wozniak, J.R., Smith, S.M. (2016). Abnormal Eating Behaviors Are Common in Children with Fetal Alcohol Spectrum Disorder, *The Journal of Pediatrics, 169,* 194-200.

Andersen, A. M. N., Andersen, P. K., Olsen, J., Grønbæk, M., & Strandberg-Larsen, K. (2012). Moderate alcohol intake during pregnancy and risk of fetal death. *International journal of epidemiology, 41*(2), 405-413.

Astley, S.J. (2013). Validation of the fetal alcohol spectrum disorder 4-digit diagnostic code. *Canadian Journal of Clinical Pharmacology, 20*(3), 416-467.

Astley, S. J., Bailey, D., Talbot, C., & Clarren, S. K. (2000). Fetal alcohol syndrome (FAS) primary prevention through FAS diagnosis: II. A comprehensive profile of 80 birth mothers of children with FAS. *Alcohol and Alcoholism, 35*(5), 509-519.

Astley, S. J., & Clarren, S. K. (2000). Diagnosing the full spectrum of fetal alcohol-exposed individuals: Introducing the 4-digit diagnostic code. *Alcohol and Alcoholism, 35*(4), 400-410.

Baladerian, N.J. (1999). *Abuse of children and adults with developmental disabilities: A risk reduction guidebook.* Los Angeles, CA: Mental Health Consultants.

Baldwin, M. (2007). Fetal alcohol spectrum disorders and suicidality in a healthcare setting. *International Journal of Circumpolar Health, 66,* 54-60.

Baumbach, J. (2002). Some implications of prenatal alcohol exposure for the treatment of adolescents with sexual offending behaviors. *Sexual Abuse: A Journal of Research and Treatment, 14,* 313-327.

Bertrand, J., Floyd, R. L., Weber, M. K., O'Connor, M., Riley, E. P., Johnson, K. A., & Cohen, D. E. (2011). National Task Force on FAS/FAE (2004). Fetal alcohol syndrome: Guidelines for referral and diagnosis. *Centers for Disease Control and Prevention,* Atlanta, GA.

Bishop, S., Gahagan, S. & Lord, C. (2007). Re-examining the core features of autism: A comparison of autism spectrum disorder and fetal alcohol spectrum disorder. *Journal of Child Psychology and Psychiatry, 48*(11), 1111-1121.

Blackburn, C., Carpenter, B., & Egerton, J. (2010). Shaping the future for children with fetal alcohol spectrum disorders. *Support for Learning, 25*(3), 139-145.

Boland, F.J., Chudley, A.E. & Grant, B.A. (2002). The challenge of fetal alcohol syndrome in adult offender population. *Forum on Corrections Research, 14,* 61-64.

Boulding, D. (2007). What judges and lawyers need to know about fetal alcohol spectrum disorder and witnesses. Retrieved from http://www.davidboulding.com/pdfs/14-1.pdf

Bower, E., Szajer, J., Mattson, S.N., Riley, E.P., & Murphy, C. (2013). Impaired odor identification in children with histories of heavy prenatal alcohol exposure. *Alcohol Journal, 47,* 275-278.

Brems, C., Boschma-Wynn, R., Dewane, S.L., Edwards, A., & Robinson, R.V. (2011). Prevention of fetal alcohol spectrum disorders: Educational needs in academia. *Journal of Alcohol and Drug Education, 55.1,* 15-37.

Brintnell, S.E., Bailey, P.G., Sawhney, A., & Kreftin, L. (2011). Understanding FASD: Disability and social supports for adult offenders. In E.P. Riley, S. Clarren, J. Weinberg & E. Jonsson (Eds.). *Fetal Alcohol Spectrum Disorder: Management and Policy Perspectives of FASD* (pp. 233-257). Germany: Wiley-Blackwell.

Brown, N. N., Burd, L., Grant, T., Edwards, W., Adler, R., & Streissguth, A. (2015). Prenatal alcohol exposure: An assessment strategy for the legal context. *International journal of law and psychiatry, 42*, 144-148.

Brown, N. N., & Connor, P. (2013). Executive dysfunction and learning in children with fetal alcohol spectrum disorders (FASD). *Cognitive Sciences, 8*(1), 47-105.

Brown, N., Connor, P., & Adler, R. (2012). Conduct-disordered adolescents with fetal alcohol spectrum disorder intervention in secure treatment settings. *Criminal Justice and Behavior, 39*, 770-793.

Brown, N. N., Gudjonsson, G., & Connor, P. (2011). Suggestibility and fetal alcohol spectrum disorders: I'll tell you anything you want to hear. *The Journal of Psychiatry & Law, 39*(1), 39-71.

Brown, J., Herrick, S., & Long-McGie, J. (2014). Fetal alcohol spectrum disorders and offender reentry: A review for criminal justice and mental health professionals. *Behavioral Health, 1*(1), 1-19.

Brown, J., Long-McGie, J., Oberoi, P., Wartnik, A., Wresh, J., & Falconer, G. (2014). Confabulation: Connections between brain damage, memory, and testimony. *Journal of Law Enforcement, 3*(5), 1-11.

Brown, J., Oberoi, P., Wartnik, A., Weinkauf, E., & Wresh, J. (2013). Fetal alcohol spectrum disorder (FASD) and confabulation: A basic understanding. Retrieved from www.mosfas.org

Brown, N. N., Wartnik, A. P., Connor, P. D., & Adler, R. S. (2010). A proposed model standard for forensic assessment of fetal alcohol spectrum disorders. *Journal of Psychiatry & Law, 38*(4), 383-418.

Burd, L., Cohen, C., Shah, R., & Norris, J. (2011). A court team model for young children in foster care: The role of prenatal alcohol exposure and fetal alcohol spectrum disorders. *The Journal of Psychiatry & Law, 39*(1), 179-191.

Burd, L., Fast, D., Conry, J. & Williams, A. (2010). Fetal alcohol spectrum disorder as a marker for increased risk of involvement with correction systems. *Journal of Psychiatry and Law, 38*(4), 559-583.

Burd, L., Lange, S., Popova, S. & Rehm, J. (2014). Canadian children and youth in care: The cost of fetal alcohol spectrum disorder. *Child Youth Care Forum, 1*(43), 83-96.

Burd, L., Selfridge, R., Klug, M., & Bakko, S. (2004). Fetal alcohol syndrome in the United States corrections system. *Addiction Biology, 9*(2), 169-176.

Cannon, M. J., Guo, J., Denny, C. H., Green, P. P., Miracle, H., Sniezek, J. E., & Floyd, R. L. (2015). Prevalence and characteristics of women at risk for an alcohol-exposed pregnancy (AEP) in the United States: Estimates from the National Survey of Family Growth. *Maternal and child health journal, 19*(4), 776-782.

Centers for Disease Control and Prevention, National Center on Birth Defects and Developmental Disabilities, Division of Birth Defects and Developmental Disabilities. (2014). Fetal Alcohol Spectrum Disorders (FASDs). Retrieved from http://www.cdc.gov/ncbddd/fasd/

Chapman, J. L. (2008). Fetal alcohol spectrum disorder (FASD) and the criminal justice system: An exploratory look at current treatment practices (Doctoral dissertation, School of Criminology-Simon Fraser University).

Chartrand, L.N, & Forbes-Chilibeck, E.M. (2003). The Sentencing of offenders with fetal alcohol syndrome. *Health Law Journal, 11*, 35-70.

Chudley, A. E., Conry, J., Cook, J. L., Loock, C., Rosales, T., & LeBlanc, N. (2005). Fetal alcohol spectrum disorder: Canadian guidelines for diagnosis. *Canadian Medical Association Journal, 172*(5 suppl), S1-S21.

Chudley, A. E., Kilgour, A. R., Cranston, M., & Edwards, M. (2007). Challenges of diagnosis in fetal alcohol syndrome and fetal alcohol spectrum disorder in the adult. *American Journal of Medical Genetics Part C: Seminars in Medical Genetics, 145*(3), 261-272.

Clare, I. & Gudjonsson, G. (1993). Interrogative suggestibility, confabulation, and acquiescence in people with mild learning disabilities (mental handicap): Implications for reliability during police interrogations. *British Journal of Clinical Psychology, 32*, 295-301.

Clark, E., Lutke, J., Minnes, P., & Ouellette-Kuntz, H. (2004). Secondary disabilities among adults with fetal alcohol spectrum disorder in British Columbia. *Journal of Fetal Alcohol Syndrome International, 2*(13), 1-12.

Clarke, M. & Gibbard, W. (2003). Overview of fetal alcohol spectrum disorders for mental health professionals. *The Canadian Child and Adolescent Psychiatry Review, 12*(3), 57-63.

Coles, C. D., Lynch, M. E., Kable, J. A., Johnson, K. C., & Goldstein, F. C. (2010). Verbal and nonverbal memory in adults prenatally exposed to alcohol. *Alcoholism: Clinical and Experimental Research, 34*(5), 897-906.

Conry, J. & Fast, D. (2000). *Fetal alcohol syndrome and the criminal justice system.* Vancouver, British Columbia: Fetal Alcohol Syndrome Resource Society.

Crocker, N., Vaurio, L., Riley, E. P., & Mattson, S. N. (2011). Comparison of verbal learning and memory in children with heavy prenatal alcohol exposure or attention-deficit/hyperactivity disorder. *Alcoholism: Clinical and Experimental Research, 35*(6), 1114-1121.

Day, N. L., Jasperse, D., Richardson, G., Robles, N., Sambamoorthi, U., Taylor, P., & Cornelius, M. (1989). Prenatal exposure to alcohol: Effect on infant growth and morphologic characteristics. *Pediatrics, 84*(3), 536-541.

Day, N. L., Leech, S. L., Richardson, G. A., Cornelius, M. D., Robles, N., & Larkby, C. (2002). Prenatal alcohol exposure predicts continued deficits in offspring size at 14 years of age. *Alcoholism: Clinical and Experimental Research, 26*(10), 1584-1591.

Day, N. L., Richardson, G., Robles, N., Sambamoorthi, U., Taylor, P., Scher, M., & Cornelius, M. (1990). Effect of prenatal alcohol exposure on growth and morphology of offspring at 8 months of age. *Pediatrics, 85*(5), 748-752.

Dewhurst, A. M. (2009). *Forensic assessments of youth affected by FASD.* Edmonton, Canada: Government of Alberta.

Douds, A., Stevens, H., & Sumner, W. (2012). Sword or shield? A systematic review of the roles FASD evidence plays in judicial proceedings. *Criminal Justice Policy Review, 24*(4), 492-509.

Doyle, L.R. & Mattson, S. N. (2015). Neurobehavioral disorder associated with prenatal alcohol exposure (ND-PAE): Review of evidence and guidelines for assessment. *Current Developmental Disorders Reports, 2,* 175-186.

Dunn v. Johnson, 162 F.3d 302 (1998).

Edward, P. R., Sterling, C., Joanne, W., & Egon, J. (2010). *Fetal alcohol spectrum disorder: Management and policy perspectives of FASD.* Weinheim, Germany: Wiley-Blackwell.

Edwards, W. J., & Greenspan, S. (2010). Adaptive behavior and fetal alcohol spectrum disorders. *Journal of Psychiatry & Law, 38*(4), 419-447.

Elias, E. (Ed.). (Jan. 2013). Improving awareness and treatment of children with fetal alcohol spectrum disorders and co-occurring psychiatric disorders. Retrieved from http://www.jbsinternational.com/sites/default/files/FASDpaperfinal_INT.pdf

Ethen, M. K., Ramadhani, T. A., Scheuerle, A. E., Canfield, M. A., Wyszynski, D. F., Druschel, C. M., & Romitti, P. A. (2009). Alcohol consumption by women before and during pregnancy. *Maternal and Child Health Journal, 13*(2), 274-285.

Famy, C., Streissguth, A., & Unis, A. (1998). Mental illness in adults with fetal alcohol syndrome or fetal alcohol effects. *American Journal Psychiatry, 155,* 553-554.

Fast, D., & Conry, J. (2004). The challenge of fetal alcohol syndrome in the criminal legal system. *Addiction Biology, 9,* 161-166.

Fast, D. & Conry, J. (2009). Fetal alcohol spectrum disorders and the criminal justice system. *Developmental Disabilities Research Review, 15*(3), 250-257.

Fast, D., Conry, J., & Loock, C. (1999). Identifying fetal alcohol syndrome (FAS) among youth in the criminal justice system. *Journal of Developmental & Behavioral Pediatrics, 20,* 370-372.

Feldman, H., Jones, K., Lindsay, S., Slymen, D., Klonoff-Cohen, H., Kao, K., & Chambers, C. (2012). Prenatal alcohol exposure patterns and alcohol-related birth defects and growth deficiencies: A prospective study. *Alcoholism: Clinical and Experimental Research, 36*(4), 670-676.

Floyd, R., Decoufle, P., & Hungerford, D. (1999). Alcohol use prior to pregnancy recognition. *American Journal of Preventive Medicine, 17,* 101-107.

Floyd, R. & Sidhu, J. (2004). Monitoring prenatal alcohol exposure. *American Journal of Medical Genetics Part C Seminars in Medical Genetics, 127,* 3-9.

Fotopoulou, A. (2008). False selves in neuropsychological rehabilitation: The challenge of confabulation. *Neuropsychological Rehabilitation, 18,* 541-565.

Gahagan, S., Sharpe, T. T., Brimacombe, M., Fry-Johnson, Y., Levine, R., Mengel, M., & Brenneman, G. (2006). Pediatricians' knowledge, training, and experience in the care of children with fetal alcohol syndrome. *Pediatrics, 118*(3), e657-e668.

Gareri, J., Lynn, H., Handley, M., Rao, C. & Koren, G. (2008). Prevalence of fetal ethanol exposure in a regional population-based sample by meconium analysis of fatty acid ethyl esters. *Therapeutic Drug Monitoring, 30*(2), 239-245.

Goodlett, C. R., & Horn, K. H. (2001). Mechanisms of alcohol-induced damage to the developing nervous system. *Alcohol Research and Health, 25*(3), 175-184.

Grant, T. M., Brown, N. N., Graham, J. C., & Ernst, C. C. (2014). Substance abuse treatment outcomes in women with Fetal Alcohol Spectrum Disorder. *The International Journal of Alcohol and Drug Research, 3*(1), 43-49.

Grant, T. M., Brown, N. N., Graham, J. C., Whitney, N., Dubovsky, D., & Nelson, L. A. (2013). Screening in treatment programs for fetal alcohol spectrum disorders that could affect therapeutic progress. *The International Journal of Alcohol and Drug Research, 2*(3), 37-49.

Green, C. R., Mihic, A. M., Nikkel, S. M., Stade, B. C., Rasmussen, C., Munoz, D. P., & Reynolds, J. N. (2009). Executive function deficits in children with fetal alcohol spectrum disorders (FASD) measured using the Cambridge Neuropsychological Tests Automated Battery (CANTAB). *Journal of Child Psychology and Psychiatry, 50*(6), 688-697.

Greenspan, S., Switzky, H. N., & Woods, G. W. (2011). Intelligence involves risk-awareness and intellectual disability involves risk-unawareness: Implications of a theory of common sense. *Journal of Intellectual and Developmental Disability, 36*(4), 246-257.

Gudjonsson, G. (1997). *The Gudjonsson suggestibility scales manual.* London: Psychology Press.

Gunn, J. (2013). Meeting the needs of children with fetal alcohol spectrum disorder through research based interventions. *New Zealand Journal of Teachers' Work, 10,* 148-168.

Hoyme, H. E., May, P. A., Kalberg, W. O., Kodituwakku, P., Gossage, J. P., Trujillo, P. M., & Robinson, L. K. (2005). A practical clinical approach to diagnosis of fetal alcohol spectrum disorders: clarification of the 1996 institute of medicine criteria. *Pediatrics, 115*(1), 39-47.

Huggins, J. E., Connor, P. D., O'Malley, K., Barr, H. M., & Streissguth, A. P. (2001). Suicide/parasuicide behavior in adults with fetal alcohol spectrum disorders (FASD). Poster presentation at Research Society on Alcoholism 24th Annual Meeting; 2001 June 23-28; Montreal (QC).

Huggins, J. E., Grant, T., O'Malley, K., & Streissguth, A. P. (2008). Suicide attempts among adults with fetal alcohol spectrum disorders: Clinical considerations. *Mental Health Aspects of Developmental Disabilities, 11*, 33-41.

Idrus, N. M., McGough, N. N., Riley, E. P., & Thomas, J. D. (2011). Administration of memantine during ethanol withdrawal in neonatal rats: Effects on long-term etanol-induced motor incoordination and cerebellar purkinje cell loss. *Alcoholism: Clinical and Experimental Research, 35*(e), 355-364.

Jacobson, J. L., Jacobson, S. W., Sokol, R. J., Martier, S. S., Ager, J. W., & Kaplan-Estrin, M. G. (1993). Teratogenic effects of alcohol on infant development. *Alcoholism: Clinical and Experimental Research, 17*(1), 174-183.

Jirikowic, T., Kartin, D., & Olson, H. (2008). Children with fetal alcohol spectrum disorders: A descriptive profile of adaptive functioning. *Canadian Journal of Occupational Therapy, 75*(4), 238-248.

Jones, K. L., Hoyme, H. E., Robinson, L. K., del Campo, M., Manning, M. A., Prewitt, L. M., & Chambers, C. D. (2010). Fetal alcohol spectrum disorders: Extending the range of structural defects. *American Journal of Medical Genetics Part A, 152*(11), 2731-2735.

Kable, J. A., Reynolds, J. N., Valenzuela, C. F., & Medina, A. E. (2014). Proceedings of the 2013 annual meeting of the fetal alcohol spectrum disorders study group. *Alcohol, 48*(7), 623-630.

Kalberg, W. & Buckley, D. (2007). FASD: What types of intervention and rehabilitation are useful? *Neuroscience and Biobehavioral Reviews, 31*(2), 278-285.

Katner, D. R. (2006). The mental health paradigm and the MacArthur study: Emerging issues challenging the competence of juveniles in delinquency systems. *American Journal of Law and Medicine, 32*(4), 503-583.

Kelly, C. (2012). Bill would add FASD as mitigating factor in criminal sentencing. *KTOO Public Media*, 4.2.12.

Kodituwakku, P. W. (2007). Defining the behavioral phenotype in children with fetal alcohol spectrum disorders: A review. *Neuroscience & Biobehavioral Reviews, 31*(2), 192-201.

Kodituwakku, P. W., Handmaker, N. S., Cutler, S. K., Weathersby, E. K., & Handmaker, S. D. (1995). Specific impairments in self-regulation in children exposed to alcohol prenatally. *Alcoholism: Clinical and Experimental Research, 19*(6), 1558-1564.

Kully-Martens, K., Pei, J., Job, J., & Rasmussen, C. (2012). Source monitoring in children with and without fetal alcohol spectrum disorders. *Journal of Pediatric Psychology, 37*(7), 725-735.

Kully-Martens, K., Treit, S., Pei, J., & Rasmussen, C. (2013). Affective decision-making on the Iowa Gambling Task in children and adolescents with fetal alcohol spectrum disorders. *Journal of the International Neuropsychological Society, 19*(02), 137-144.

LaFrance, M. A., McLachlan, K., Nash, K., Andrew, G., Loock, C., Oberlander, T. F., & Rasmussen, C. (2014). Evaluation of the neurobehavioral screening tool in children with fetal alcohol spectrum disorders (FASD). *Journal of Population Therapeutics and Clinical Pharmacology, 21*(2), e197-210.

Landgren, M., Svensson, L., Stromland, K., & Gronlund, M. (2010). Prenatal alcohol exposure and neurodevelopmental disorders in children adopted from Eastern Europe. *Pediatrics, 125*(5), 1178-1185.

Lange, S., Shield, K., Rehm, J., & Popova, S. (2013). Prevalence of fetal alcohol spectrum disorders in child care settings: a meta-analysis. *Pediatrics, 132*(4), e980-e995.

Lebel, C., Roussotte, F., & Sowell, E. R. (2011). Imaging the impact of prenatal alcohol exposure on the structure of the developing human brain. *Neuropsychology Review, 21*(2), 102-118.

Leibson, T., Neuman, G., Chudley, A. E., & Koren, G. (2014). The differential diagnosis of fetal alcohol spectrum disorder. *Journal of Population Therapeutics and Clinical Pharmacology, 21*(1), e1-e30.

Lutke, J. (2004). Fetal alcohol spectrum disorder (FASD) and corrections. Provided by New Beginnings Group.

Malbin, D. V. (2004). Fetal alcohol spectrum disorder (FASD) and the role of family court judges in improving outcomes for children and families. *Juvenile and Family Court Journal, 55*(2), 53-63.

Mattson, S. N., Crocker, N., & Nguyen, T. T. (2011). Fetal alcohol spectrum disorders: neuropsychological and behavioral features. *Neuropsychology Review, 21*(2), 81-101.

Mattson S. N. & Riley E. P. (1998). A review of the neurobehavioral deficits in children with Fetal Alcohol Syndrome or prenatal exposure to alcohol. *Alcoholism: Clinical and Experimental Research, 22,* 279-294.

Mattson S. N. & Riley E. P. (1999). Implicit and explicit memory functioning in children with heavy prenatal alcohol exposure. *Journal of the International Neuropsychological Society, 5*(5), 462-471.

Mattson, S. N., Schoenfeld, A. M., & Riley, E. P. (2001). Teratogenic effects of alcohol on brain and behavior. *Alcohol Research and Health, 25*(3), 185-191.

May, P. A., Baete, A., Russo, J., Elliott, A. J., Blankenship, J., Kalberg, W. O., ... & Hoyme, H. E. (2014). Prevalence and characteristics of fetal alcohol spectrum disorders. *Pediatrics, 134*(5), 855-866.

May, P., Gossage, J., Brooke, L., Croxford, J., Adnams, C., Jones, K., & Viljoen, D. (2005). Maternal risk factors for fetal alcohol syndrome in the Western Cape Province of South Africa: A population- based study. *American Journal of Public Health, 95,* 1190-1199.

May, P., Gossage, J, Kalberg, W., Robinson, L., Buckley, D., Manning, M., & Hoyme H. (2009). Prevalence and epidemiologic characteristics of FASD from various research methods with an emphasis on recent in-school studies. *Developmental Disabilities Research Review, 15*(3), 176-192.

May, P., Gossage, J., Marais, A., Hendricks, L., Snell, C., Tabachnick, B., & Viljoen, D. (2008). Maternal risk factors for fetal alcohol syndrome and partial fetal alcohol syndrome in South Africa: A third study. *Alcoholism: Clinical and Experimental Research, 32,* 738-753.

McLachlan, K., Roesch, R., Viljoen, J., & Douglas, K. (2014). Evaluating the psycholegal abilities of young offenders with fetal alcohol spectrum disorder. *Law and Human Behavior, 38,* 10-22.

McMurtrie, J. (2011). The criminal justice system's disparate treatment of individuals with fetal alcohol spectrum disorders in cases involving sexual activity. *Journal of Psychiatry and Law, 39,* 159-177.

Meintjes, E. M., Douglas, T. S., Martinez, F., Vaughan, C. L., Adams, L. P., Stekhoven, A., & Viljoen, D. (2002). A stereo-photogrammetric method to measure the facial dysmorphology of children in the diagnosis of fetal alcohol syndrome. *Medical Engineering & physics, 24*(10), 683-689.

Mela, M., & Luther, G. (2013). Fetal alcohol spectrum disorder: Can diminished responsibility diminish criminal behavior? *International Journal of Law and Psychiatry, 36,* 46-54.

Merrick, J., & Kandel, I. (2007). Fetal alcohol syndrome and suicide: A review. *International Journal on Disability and Human Development, 6*(3), 237-240.

Moore, T. E., & Green, M. (2004). Fetal alcohol spectrum disorder (FASD): A need for closer examination by the criminal justice system. *Criminal Reports, 19,* 99-108.

Mooring v. Lewis, 2003 U.S. Dist. LEXIS 4827 (2003).

Moscovitch, M., & Melo, B. (1997). Strategic retrieval and the frontal lobes: Evidence from confabulation and amnesia. *Neuropsychologia, 35*(7), 1017-1034.

Mukherjee, R., Layton, M., Yacoub, E., & Turk, J. (2011). Autism and autistic traits in people exposed to heavy prenatal alcohol: data from a clinical series of 21 individuals and nested case control study. *Advances in Mental Health and Intellectual Disabilities, 5,* 42-49.

Muralidharan, P., Sarmah, S., Zhou, F. C., & Marrs, J. A. (2013). Fetal alcohol spectrum disorder (FASD) associated neural defects: complex mechanisms and potential therapeutic targets. *Brain sciences*, *3*(2), 964-991.

Murawski, N. J., Moore, E. M., Thomas, J. D., & Riley, E. P. (2015). Advances in diagnosis and treatment of fetal alcohol spectrum disorders: From animal models to human studies. Retrieved from http://pubs. niaaa.nih.gov/arcr/arcr371/article07.htm

National Organization on Fetal Alcohol Syndrome. (2012). *FASD: What the justice system should know.* Washington, DC: Author.

Nedjam Z, Devouche, Z., & Barba, G. (2004). Confabulation but not executive dysfunction discriminates AD from frontotemporal dementia. *European Journal of Neurology, 11,* 728-733.

Norman, A. L., O'Brien, J. W., Spadoni, A. D., Tapert, S. F., Jones, K. L., Riley, E. P., & Mattson, S. N. (2013). A functional magnetic resonance imaging study of spatial working memory in children with prenatal alcohol exposure: Contribution of familial history of alcohol use disorders. *Alcoholism: Clinical and Experimental Research, 37*(1), 132-140.

Novick, N. (1997). FAS: Preventing and treating sexual deviancy. In A.P. Streissguth & J. Kanter, (eds.). *The challenge of fetal alcohol syndrome: Overcoming secondary disabilities* (pp. 162-170). Seattle, WA: University of Washington Press.

Nuñez, , S. C., Roussotte, F., & Sowell, E. R. (2011). Focus on: Structural and functional brain abnormalities in fetal alcohol spectrum disorders. *Alcohol Research & Health, 34*(1), 1.

O'Leary-Moore, S.K., Parnell, S. E., Lipinski, R. J., & Sulik, K. K. (2011). Magnetic resonance-based imaging in animal models of fetal alcohol spectrum disorder. *Neuropsychology Review, 21,* 167-185.

Olson, H. C. (2015). Advancing recognition of fatal alcohol spectrum disorders: The proposed DSM-5 diagnosis of "Neurobehavioral Disorder Associated with Prenatal Alcohol. *Current Developmental Disorders Report, 2,* 187-198.O'Malley, K., & Huggins, J. (2005). Suicidality in adolescents and adults with fetal alcohol spectrum disorders. *Canadian Journal of Psychiatry, 50*(2), 125.

O'Malley, K. & Rich, S. (2013). *Clinical implications of a link between fetal alcohol spectrum disorders (FASD) and autism or Asperger's disorder - A neurodevelopmental frame for helping understanding and management.* Recent advances in autism spectrum disorders - Volume I, Prof. M. Fitzgerald (Ed.), ISBN: 978-953-51-1021-7, InTech, DOI: 10.5772/54924.

Paley, B. & O'Connor, M. (2011). Behavioral interventions for children and adolescents with fetal alcohol spectrum disorders. *Alcohol Research and Health, 34,* 64-75.

Patra, J., Bakker, R., Irving, H., Jaddoe, V. W., Malini, S., & Rehm, J. (2011). Dose-response relationship between alcohol consumption before and during pregnancy and the risks of low birthweight, preterm birth and small for gestational age (SGA): A systematic review and meta-analyses. BJOG: *An International Journal of Obstetrics & Gynaecology, 118*(12), 1411-1421.

Peadon, E. & Elliott, E. J. (2010). Distinguishing between attention-deficit hyperactivity and fetal alcohol spectrum disorders in children: clinical guidelines. *Journal of Neuropsychiatric Disease and Treatment, 6,* 509-515.

Pei, J., Job, J., Kully-Martens, K., & Rasmussen, C. (2011). Executive function and memory in children with fetal alcohol spectrum disorder. *Child Neuropsychology, 17*(3), 290-309.

Pei, J. R., Rinaldi, C. M., Rasmussen, C., Massey, V., & Massey, D. (2008). Memory patterns of acquisition and retention of verbal and nonverbal information in children with fetal alcohol spectrum disorders. *The Canadian Journal of Clinical Pharmacology. 15*(1), e44-e56.

Perske, R. (2011). Perske's list: False confessions from 75 persons with intellectual disability. *Intellectual and developmental disabilities, 49*(5), 365-373.

Petersilia, J. (2009). Invisible victims: Violence against persons with developmental disabilities. *Human Rights, 27*(1), 9-12. Petrenko, C. L., Tahir, N., Mahoney, E. C., & Chin, N. P. (2014). Prevention of secondary conditions in fetal alcohol spectrum disorders: Identification of systems-level barriers. *Maternal and Child Health Journal, 18*(6), 1496-1505.

Pollard, R., Trowbridge, B., Slade, P. D., Streissguth, A. P., Laktonen, A., & Townes, B. D. (2004). Interrogative suggestibility in a U.S. context: Some preliminary data on normal and FAS/FAE subjects. *Personality and Individual Differences, 37*, 1101-1108.

Popova, S., Lange, S., Bekmuradov, D., Mihic, A., & Rehm, J. (2011). Fetal alcohol spectrum disorder prevalence estimates in correctional systems: A systematic literature review.*Canadian Journal of Public Health, 102*(5), 336-340.

Popova, S., Lange, S., Burd, L., & Rehm, J. (2015). The burden and economic impact of fetal alcohol spectrum disorder in Canada. Centre for addiction and mental health. Retrieved from http://www.camh. ca/en/research/news_and_publications/reports_and_books/DocumentsBurden%20and%20Eco%20 Costs%20FASD%20Feb%202015.pdf

R. v. Sterling, 4037 SK CA (1995).

Rasmussen, C. (2005). Executive functioning and working memory in fetal alcohol spectrum disorder. *Alcoholism: Clinical and Experimental Research, 29*(8), 1359-1367.

Rasmussen, C., Kully-Martens, K., Denys, K., Badry, D., Heneveld, D., Wyper, K., & Grant, T. (2012). The effectiveness of a community-based intervention program for women at-risk for giving birth to a child with fetal alcohol spectrum disorder (FASD). *Community Mental Health Journal, 48*, 12-21.

Riley, E. P., Clarren, S., Weinberg, J., & Jonsson, E. (Eds.). (2011). *Fetal alcohol spectrum disorder: Management and policy perspectives of FASD*. John Wiley & Sons.

Riley, E.P., Infante, M.A. & Warren, K.R. (2011). Fetal alcohol spectrum disorders: An overview. *Neuropsychological Review, 21*, 73-80.

Riley, E. P., McGee, C. L., & Sowell, E. R. (2004). Teratogenic effects of alcohol: A decade of brain imaging. *American Journal of Medical Genetics Part C: Seminars in Medical Genetics, 127*(1), 35-41.

Schneider, M.L., Moore, C.F. & Adkins, M.M. (2011). The effects of prenatal alcohol exposure on behavior: Rodents and primate studies. *Neuropsychology Review, 2*, 186-203.

Schonfeld, A. M., Paley, B., Frankel, F., & O'Connor, M. J. (2006). Executive functioning predicts social skills following prenatal alcohol exposure. *Child Neuropsychology, 12*(6), 439-452. Senate passes bill allowing judges to consider FASD as factor during sentencing. (2012, Apr 04). *Targeted News Service*. Retrieved from http://search.proquest.com/docview/964279493?accountid=35803

Shalala, D.E. (1999). Mental Health: A Report of the Surgeon General. Department of Health and Human Services. U.S. Public Health Service. Retrieved from http://profiles.nlm.nih.gov/ps/access/NNBBHS.pdf

Spohr, H.L., Willms, J., & Steinhausen H.C. (1993). Prenatal alcohol exposure and long-term developmental consequences. *Lancet, 341*, 907-910.

Spohr, H.L., Willms, J., & Steinhausen, H.C. (1994). The fetal alcohol syndrome in adolescence. *Acta Paediatr, 404*, 19-26.

Steinhausen, H,C,, Willms, J., & Spohr, H.L. (1993). Long-term psychopathological and cognitive outcome of children with fetal alcohol syndrome. *Journal of the American Academy of Child and Adolescent Psychiatry, 32*(5), 990-994.

Stevens, S., Nash, K., Koren, G., & Rovet, J. (2013). Autism characteristics in children with fetal alcohol spectrum disorders. *Child Neuropsychology, 19*(6), 579-587.

Stratton, K.R., Howe, C.J., & Battaglia, F.C. (1996). *Fetal alcohol syndrome: Diagnosis, epidemiology, prevention, and treatment*. Washington, DC: National Academy Press.

Streissguth, A., Barr, H., Bookstein, F., & Sampson, P. (1993). *The enduring effects of prenatal alcohol exposure on child development: Birth through 7 years: A partial least squares solution.* Ann Arbor, MI: University of Michigan.

Streissguth, A., Barr, H., Carmichael, O., & Sampson, P. (1994). Drinking during pregnancy decreases word attack and arithmetic scores on standardized tests: Adolescent data from a population-based prospective study. *Alcoholism: Clinical and Experimental Research, 18,* 248-254.

Streissguth, A., Barr, H., Kogan, J., & Bookstein, F. (1996). *Understanding the occurrence of secondary disabilities in clients with fetal alcohol syndrome (FAS) and fetal alcohol effects (FAE). Final report to the Centers for Disease Control and prevention (CDC).* Seattle, WA: University of Washington, Fetal Alcohol & Drug Unit, Tech. Rep. No. 96-06.

Streissguth, A., Bookstein, F., Barr, H., Sampson, P., O'Malley, K., & Young, J. (2004). Risk factors for adverse life outcomes in fetal alcohol syndrome and fetal alcohol effects. *Journal of Developmental and Behavioral Pediatrics, 25*(4), 228-238.

Streissguth, A., LaDue, R., & Randels, S. (1988). A manual on adolescents and adults with fetal alcohol syndrome with special reference to American Indians. (2nd ed.). Albuquerque, NM: University of Washington.

Streissguth, A. P., Randels, S. P., & Smith, D. F. (1991). A test-retest study of intelligence in patients with fetal alcohol syndrome: implications for care. *Journal of the American Academy of Child & Adolescent Psychiatry, 30*(4), 584-587.

Thiel, K., Baladerian, N., Boyce, K., Cantos VII, O., Davis L., Kelly, K., & Stream, J. (2011). Fetal alcohol spectrum disorders and victimization: Implications for families, educators, social services, law enforcement, and the judicial system. *Journal of Psychiatry & Law, 39,* 121-157.

Totten, M. (2009). Investigating the linkages between FASD, gangs, sexual exploitation and women abuse in the Canadian Aboriginal population: a preliminary study. *Native Women's Association of Canada, 5*(2), 1-25.

U.S. Department of Health and Human Services. (n.d.).: SAMHSA: Fetal alcohol spectrum disorders center for excellence. Retrieved from http://fasdcenter.samhsa.gov/documents/WYNK_Numbers.pdf

Vaurio, L., Riley, E. P., & Mattson, S. N. (2008). Differences in executive functioning in children with heavy prenatal alcohol exposure or attention-deficit/hyperactivity disorder. *Journal of the International Neuropsychological Society, 14,* 119-129.

Ware, A., Infante, M., O'Brien, J., Tapert, S., Jones, K., Riley, E., & Mattson, S. (2015). An fMRI study of behavioral response inhibition in adolescents with and without histories of heavy prenatal alcohol exposure. *Behavioral Brain Research, 278,* 137-146.

Weeks v. State, 697 N.E.2d 28, 30 (Ind. 1998)

Westrup, S. (2013). Foetal alcohol spectrum disorders: As prevalent as autism?. *Educational Psychology in Practice, 29*(3), 309-325.

Wheeler, S.M., Stevens, S.A., Sheard, E.D. & Rovet, J.F. (2012). Facial memory deficits in children with fetal alcohol spectrum disorders. *Child Neuropsychology, 18*(4), 339-346.

Willford, J., Richardson, G., Leech, S., & Day, N. (2004). Verbal and visuospatial learning and memory function in children with moderate prenatal alcohol exposure. *Alcoholism: Clinical and Experimental Research, 28,* 497-507.

Wozniak, J.R. & Muetzel, R.L. (2011). What does diffusion tensor imaging reveal about the brain and cognition in fetal alcohol spectrum disorders? *Neuropsychology Review, 21,* 133-147.

Yan, A., Bell, E., & Racine, E. (2014). Ethical and social challenges in newborn screening for prenatal alcohol exposure. *Canadian Journal of Neurological Sciences, 41,* 115-118.

CHAPTER 8

FORENSIC RISK ASSESSMENT: A BEGINNER'S GUIDE

JERROD BROWN & JAY P. SINGH

CHAPTER OVERVIEW

Forensic risk assessment refers to the attempt to predict the likelihood of future offending in order to identify individuals in need of intervention. Risk assessment protocols have been implemented in mental health and criminal justice settings around the globe to prioritize risk reduction strategies for those most at need. Helping to allocate scarce resources more effectively and efficiently while protecting our communities, forensic risk assessment has come to be a cornerstone of forensic practice in many jurisdictions. The present chapter is intended to provide practitioners and policymakers with a general introduction to this fast-growing field of research. The process of identifying those static and dynamic risk and protective factors that are incorporated into the risk assessment process is examined. Thereafter, strengths and weaknesses of the three most common approaches to risk assessment are described, and requirements under *Tarasoff* liability are discussed.

FORENSIC RISK ASSESSMENT: A BEGINNER'S GUIDE

In 1972, Alberta Lessard, a mentally ill woman involuntarily committed to a psychiatric hospital in Wisconsin, filed a class action suit on behalf of all individuals aged 18 and older who had been committed under the Wisconsin State Mental Health Act. This legislation allowed mentally ill individuals who were "gravely disabled" (Wis. Stat. § 51.001 et seq.) to be involuntarily hospitalized for treatment. Overruling this law, the U.S. Supreme Court held that in order to be involuntarily hospitalized: "The risk of violence to self or others must be established, with such dangerousness being demonstrated by a recent overt act plus the substantial probability of recurrence" (*Lessard v. Schmidt*, 1972, p. 1093).

Dangerousness was defined as "having a high probability of inflicting imminent substantial physical harm" (Drake, Clemente, & Perrin, 2006, p. 2). This emphasis on the likelihood of inflicting harm reflected a growing preference in 20th century America for probabilistic estimates of the risk of antisocial behavior such as violence as opposed to clinicians' dichotomous judgments of dangerousness that had been used throughout the first half of the century. It was this need to accurately establish the risk of future offending that gave birth to one of the largest fields in forensic mental health: forensic risk assessment.

Originally published in *Archives of Forensic Psychology, 1*(1), 2014.
The editor of this journal has granted permission to reprint.

Historically, the construct of *risk* referred to the probability of gain or loss weighted by the value of what stood to be gained or lost. Beginning largely in the 20th century, this construct was applied to the area of forensic mental health. *Forensic risk assessment* refers to the process by which the likelihood of future antisocial behavior is evaluated (Singh, 2012). The antisocial behavior being predicted may constitute a first-time offense or a repeat offense, the latter of which is referred to as *recidivism*. Risk assessments routinely involve the structured examination of a number of *risk factors* (biological, psychological, or sociological characteristics that increase the likelihood of antisocial behavior) and *protective factors* (biological, psychological, or sociological characteristics that decrease the likelihood of antisocial behavior). These may be either *static* (historical or unchanging), *acutely dynamic* (modifiable and likely to change), or *stably dynamic* (modifiable but unlikely to change) in nature (Andrews & Bonta, 2010). An example of a static risk factor for antisocial behavior is a history of violence (Quinsey, Harris, Rice, & Cormier, 2006), whereas an acute dynamic risk factor would be stress (Borum, 1996), and a stable dynamic risk factor would be marital status (Andrews & Bonta, 1995). An example of a static protective factor against antisocial behavior is intelligence (de Vogel, de Ruiter, Bouman, & de Vries Robbe, 2007), whereas an acute dynamic protective factor would be medication adherence (Webster, Martin, Brink, Nicholls, & Desmarais, 2009), and a stable dynamic protective factor would be healthy peer relationships (Webster et al., 2009).

IDENTIFYING RISK AND PROTECTIVE FACTORS

According to the guidelines set forth by Grann and Långström (2007), risk and protective factors – be they static or dynamic in nature – can be identified using one of three techniques: (a) the empirical method, (b) the theoretical method, or (c) the clinical method. Each of these three techniques has its own merit, albeit they vary in terms of their focus on psychometrics versus practical application. In the empirical method, risk and protective factors are identified through research in which a sample is followed for such a duration as to allow for the possibility of offending. The biopsychosocial characteristics of those who offend are analyzed to see if they systematically differ from those who do not. If the presence of a given characteristic increases the likelihood of offending to a statistically significant extent, it is considered a risk factor. If the presence of that characteristic decreases this likelihood, the characteristic is considered a protective factor.

In the theoretical method, a particular theory (e.g., psychoanalytic, behavioral, cognitive) is used to guide decisions as to which characteristics place an individual at a higher or lower risk of antisocial behavior (Grann & Långström, 2007). Different theoretical orientations offer different conceptualizations of what constitutes an "at risk" person and propose different mechanisms concerning how that individual came to be at risk. For example, risk assessments formulated from a psychoanalytic perspective may take into consideration information concerning disorganized attachment styles as well as an individual's sexual history. (For an overview of forensic risk assessment and psychodynamic theory, see Doctor & Nettleton, 2003). Behavioral measures, on the other hand, would be more likely to include consideration of the individual's previous offending history, social competence, and his or her parents' style of discipline. (For an overview of forensic risk assessment and behavioral theory, see Eifert & Feldner, 2004). Risk tools adopting a cognitive approach would likely include consideration of an individual's capacity for emotion regulation, tendency to ruminate, and level of impulsivity. (For an overview of cognitive approaches to forensic risk management, see Lipsey, Hapman, & Landenberger, 2001).

In contrast to the previous two approaches, the clinical method of identifying risk and protective factors involves identifying individual characteristics which, regardless of whether they are empirically or theoretically associated with offending, are changeable and thus can be addressed through clinical intervention (Grann & Långström, 2007). For example, although traits such as an individual's history of antisocial behavior or severe mental illness cannot be altered, other characteristics such as employment status or level of education can. Hence, the clinical method places an emphasis on dynamic factors.

CONTEMPORARY APPROACHES TO FORENSIC RISK ASSESSMENT

Although there are numerous adverse outcomes that can be evaluated through forensic risk assessment (e.g., substance use, absconsion, self-harm), this chapter will focus on evidence-based approaches to violence, sex offender, and general recidivism risk assessment. Specifically, we will explore the three leading approaches to risk assessment currently used in practice and examples of key tools that follow each. In addition, we will examine the importance of understanding *Tarasoff* liability in the context of forensic risk assessment.

Systematic reviews and meta-analyses of the research base on forensic risk assessment have established three leading approaches to this form of evaluation: (a) unstructured clinical judgment, (b) actuarial assessment, and (c) structured professional judgment (Singh & Fazel, 2010). In the following section, we will examine the relative strengths and weaknesses of each.

UNSTRUCTURED CLINICAL JUDGMENT

Unstructured clinical judgment (UCJ) refers to the subjective process of evaluating the likelihood of an adverse outcome without the use of a structured method (e.g., a risk assessment tool). Instead, clinical skills and experience with the given individual whose risk is being assessed are relied upon (Murray & Thomson, 2010). The key benefits of the UCJ approach include its flexibility, its utility in tailoring risk assessments to a given individual, its incorporation of a variety of case-specific risk and protective static and dynamic factors, and its inexpensiveness (i.e., no materials need to be purchased). The key drawback of the UCJ approach is its inherent subjectivity, resulting in poor rates of reliability and predictive validity. Of particular concern is this approach's vulnerability to human judgment biases in the decision-making process. For example, hindsight bias due to recent tragic events involving high-profile homicides by individuals diagnosed with a mental illness may result in the overestimation of violence-risk in persons with quite low base rates of interpersonal aggression (Arkes, 1991; Large, Ryan, Singh, Paton, & Nielssen, 2011). If evaluating a college-aged adolescent in Newtown, Connecticut, in the United States, who was diagnosed with Asperger's Syndrome and raised by a single mother who had taught him to fire guns, this adolescent would likely be perceived as a higher risk immediately after an armed gunman reportedly diagnosed with Asperger's Syndrome entered Sandy Hook Elementary School in Newtown in 2012 and fatally shot 20 children and six adult staff members. This, despite epidemiological research findings suggesting that individuals diagnosed with Asperger's Syndrome are not at increased risk of violence compared to the general population (Ghaziuddin, 2013), and that the large majority of individuals with this diagnosis who do go on to be violent do not commit crimes involving weapons (Harmon, 2012).

Perhaps the best-known criticism of unstructured clinical judgment in forensic risk assessment is the seminal monograph by Monahan (1981), entitled *The Clinical Prediction of Violent Behavior*. A spiritual successor to Meehl's (1954) *Clinical vs. Statistical Prediction: A Theoretical Analysis and a Review of the Evidence*, in which it was argued that professionals cannot predict outcomes as successfully as statistical formulae, Monahan reviewed the research literature on unstructured clinical judgment and found that clinicians are unable to predict violence at rates above chance, concluding:

> [P]sychiatrists and psychologists are accurate in no more than one out of three predictions of violent behavior over a several-year period among institutionalized populations that had both committed violence in the past (and thus had high base rates for it) and those who were diagnosed as 'mentally ill' (Monahan, 1981, pp. 48-49).

ACTUARIAL ASSESSMENT

Actuarial risk assessment tools are structured instruments composed of risk and/or protective, static and/or dynamic factors that are found to be associated with the adverse event of interest using a statistical methodology (e.g., logistic regression, Cox regression, Chi-Squared Automatic Interaction Detection [CHAID]). Each item is weighted in accordance with the amount of variance it accounts for in the prediction of the adverse event of interest. Total scores are cross-referenced with a manual in which estimates of recidivism rates are provided for either each score or for ranges of scores (referred to as "risk bins" or "risk categories"). These estimates are derived from the actual rates of recidivism seen in groups with the same score or ranges of scores in the sample on which the tool was calibrated (i.e., the group whose data was used to develop the tool).

The key benefits of actuarial risk assessment tools include their objectivity and transparency in the risk assessment process, their speed of administration, their requiring mostly historical information (i.e., incorporating mostly static risk factors) that are routinely available in criminal/court/medical records, their removal of human judgment biases inherent in the clinical decision-making process, and the generation of an estimated recidivism rate. The latter is perceived as the most significant strength of actuarial risk assessment tools, making them of higher perceived usefulness in legal settings (Singh, 2013).

The key drawbacks of actuarial risk assessment tools are the inability to apply group-based recidivism rates to individual patients (Hart, Michie, & Cook, 2007), the instability of estimated recidivism rates when applied to groups in different jurisdictions (Singh, Fazel, Gueorguieva, & Buchanan, 2014), and the inability to incorporate case-specific information to modify estimated recidivism rates. Concerning the latter, the preponderance of the research literature on modifying the findings of actuarial risk assessment tools suggests that such modification weakens rather than strengthens their reliability and predictive validity (Quinsey et al., 2006). In addition, adding or removing additional items on actuarial risk assessment tools or using them with unintended populations or to predict unintended outcomes has been found to weaken their predictive validity (Quinsey et al., 2006).

Examples of commonly-used actuarial risk assessment schemes include the Violence Risk Appraisal Guide (VRAG) (Quinsey et al., 2006), the Static-99 (Hanson & Thornton, 1999), and the Level of Service Inventory (Andrews & Bonta, 1995). All three of these schemes have been revised over the past decade to take into consideration new research findings concerning violence, sex offenders, and general recidivism risk assessment (respectively). New statistical analyses have recently been conducted to construct the Violence Risk Appraisal Guide-Revised (VRAG-R) (Rice, Harris, & Lang, 2013), the Static-99-Revised (Static-99R; Helmus, Thornton, Hanson, & Babchishin, 2012), and the Level of Service/Case Management Inventory (LS/CMI) (Andrews, Bonta, & Wormith, 2004).

The VRAG-R is a 12-item instrument including static risk factors that capture seven domains: living situation, school performance, substance use, marital status, criminal history, index offense characteristics, and antisocial personality. Items are weighted using Nuffield's (1982) base rate weighting strategy and total scores are used to place individuals into one of nine risk bins, each of which has associated recidivism rate estimates. As the instrument is intended for use in predicting violence in mentally disordered offenders, the VRAG-R may be particularly useful in psychiatric hospitals and clinics for determining the allocation of therapeutic resources as well as in aiding discharge decisions. Albeit a new scheme, the VRAG-R is based on an instrument that is amongst the most validated actuarial instruments available (Waypoint Centre for Mental Health Care, 2014).

The Static-99R is a 10-item instrument including static risk factors that capture four domains: age, living situation, index offense characteristics, and prior offense characteristics. Items are weighted according to logistic regression weights and total scores are used to place individuals into one of four risk bins, each of which has associated recidivism rate estimates. As the instrument is intended for use in predicting sexual recidivism in adult sexual offenders, the Static-99R may be particularly useful in court settings for assisting in decisions such as bail determination and the need for community supervision in sexual offenders. Although the revision to the Static-99 is a relatively new instrument, the original scheme has been extensively validated across populations and settings (Helmus, 2008; Singh, Fazel, Gueorguieva, & Buchanan, 2013).

The LS/CMI is a 43-item instrument including static and dynamic risk factors that capture eight domains: criminal history, leisure/recreation, alcohol/drug problems, education/employment, companions, procriminal attitudes, family/marital, and antisocial patterns. Items are weighted in a present vs. absent fashion and total scores are used to place individuals into one of five risk bins, each of which has associated recidivism rate estimates. As the instrument is intended for use in predicting general recidivism in late adolescent and adult offender populations, the LS/CMI may be particularly useful in jail, prison, and re-entry settings for identifying criminogenic needs and promoting responsive approaches to treatment for high-risk offenders. The LS/CMI is based on the highly-regarded Risk-Needs-Responsivity principles which emphasize prioritizing interventions for individuals at highest risk, focusing on criminogenic needs to reduce risk, and tailoring treatments to the characteristics of the individual case (Andrews & Bonta, 2010).

STRUCTURED PROFESSIONAL JUDGMENT

Structured professional judgment (SPJ) risk assessment tools were developed to address the inflexibility of actuarial schemes. SPJ instruments are composed of risk and/or protective, static and/or dynamic factors that research or theory suggests are associated with the adverse event of interest. Total scores are used as an aide-memoire, guiding administrators in making a categorical risk judgment (e.g., Low, Moderate, or High) when combined with case-specific information gained through clinical experience with the client being evaluated. Hence, total scores are not to be used as statistical predictors of risk but rather as an important piece of a larger formulation process.

SPJ schemes seek to address the weaknesses of actuarial schemes. Thus, the key benefits of SPJ risk assessment tools include being more focused on individual clients than groups and the ability to take into consideration information not included in the item content of specific tools. The predictive validity of SPJ tools has been found to be non-significantly different than that of actuarial tools (Fazel, Singh, Doll, & Grann, 2012). In addition, practitioners generally perceive SPJ instruments to be more accurate and reliable than actuarial instruments and also of greater interest to mental health boards (Singh, 2013). The key drawbacks of SPJ risk assessment tools include a less objective evaluation process as well as the re-introduction of human decision-making biases into risk assessments. In addition, SPJ instruments are generally perceived as taking longer to administer than actuarial instruments (Singh, 2013). Examples of commonly-used SPJ risk assessment schemes include the Historical, Clinical, Risk Management-20 (HCR-20) (Douglas, Hart, Webster, & Belfrage, 2013), the Sexual Violence Risk-20 (SVR-20) (Boer, Hart, Kropp, & Webster, 1997), and the Short-Term Assessment of Risk and Treatability (START) (Webster, Martin, Brink, Nicholls, & Desmarais, 2009).

The HCR-20 is a 20-item instrument including both static and dynamic risk factors that capture three domains: historical risk factors, clinical risk factors, and risk management factors. As the instrument is intended for use in predicting violence in mentally disordered civil and forensic patients, the HCR-20 may be particularly useful in mental health settings. Though the third version of this instrument was recently released, the HCR-20 scheme is amongst the most validated available (Douglas, Shaffer, Blanchard, Guy, Reeves, & Weir, 2014).

The SVR-20 is a 20-item instrument including both static and dynamic risk factors that capture three domains: psychosocial adjustment risk factors, sexual offense risk factors, and future plans risk factors. As the instrument is intended for use in predicting violence in sexual offenders, the SVR-20 may be particularly useful in Sexually Violent Predator hearings for determining whether indeterminate detention might be necessary for convicted sexual offenders. The second version of this instrument is scheduled to be released within the next year, but the reliability and validity of the original scheme has been evidenced internationally (Rettenberger, Hucker, Boer, & Eher, 2009).

The START is a 20-item instrument including dynamic risk and protective factors. As the instrument is intended for use in predicting violence in psychiatric populations, the START may be particularly useful in civil and forensic psychiatric hospitals and clinics for identifying treatment targets. Albeit comparatively newer than alternative schemes such as the HCR-20 and SVR-20, the START has become one of the most widely used risk assessment tools for the purposes of risk monitoring (Singh, 2013) and has been found to be a reliable and valid predictor of future violence (O'Shea & Dickens, 2014).

TARASOFF LIABILITY AND FORENSIC RISK ASSESSMENT

In the case of *Tarasoff v. Regents of the University of California* (1976), a 25-year-old Masters student at the University of California, Berkeley, who had been diagnosed with paranoid schizophrenia, murdered a 19-year-old girl named Tatiana Tarasoff (Slovenko, 1988). Tarasoff's murderer had been receiving counselling and had disclosed his obsession with the girl and his fantasies about harming her to his therapist, who claimed that he did not inform the proper authorities due to doctor-patient confidentiality. Tarasoff's parents sued their daughter's murderer's therapist as well as other members of the University for negligence. The Supreme Court of California held that:

> When a therapist determines, or pursuant to the standards of his profession should determine, that his patient presents a serious danger of violence to another, he incurs an obligation to use reasonable care to protect the intended victim against such danger. The discharge of this duty may require the therapist to take one or more of various steps, depending upon the nature of the case. Thus it may call for him to warn the intended victim or others likely to apprise the victim of the danger, to notify the police, or to take whatever other steps are reasonably necessary under the circumstances (*Tarasoff v. Regents of the University of California*, 1976, p. 431).

The ruling that mental health professionals have a duty to protect those individuals whom their patients threaten with bodily harm established a legal precedent that clinicians could be held partially responsible for their patients' crimes, unless they could prove that they thoroughly assessed their patients' risk of harming others (Cooper, Griesel, & Yuille, 2008). Thus, the introduction of "*Tarasoff* liability" (Mason, 1998, p. 109) also increased the importance of forensic risk assessment tools, which could be cited as evidence against clinical negligence (Monahan, 2006). Although the *Tarasoff* ruling has not been upheld in all 50 U.S. states (Kaser-Boyd, 2015), the American Psychological Association continues to expect mental health professionals to be competent in the use of violence risk assessment tools when evaluating the risk of harm to others as part of civil commitment hearings (Gilfoyle et al., 2011).

CONCLUSION

Over the past 30 years, more than 400 forensic risk assessment tools have been developed for the purposes of predicting the likelihood of future violence, sex offending, and general recidivism (Singh, 2013). In accordance with a recent *amicus curiae* brief from the American Psychological Association (Gilfoyle et al., 2011), we recommend that such structured instruments be routinely used by mental health and criminal justice professionals and that judges and lawyers seek out evaluators who use such instruments rather than unstructured clinical judgments. This said, risk assessment tools should not be the sole determinants of decisions concerning civil liberties, especially when the base rate of the outcome of interest is particularly low (McSherry & Keyzer, 2009).

Though currently used in over 40 countries for prediction, management, and monitoring purposes (Singh, 2013), no single risk assessment tool has emerged as being more accurate than others (Yang, Wong, & Coid, 2010). To decide which tool to use, meta-analytic research suggests focusing on the intended population and outcome for which a tool was designed, and then trying to find a "best fit" with the population and outcome of interest (Singh, Grann, & Fazel, 2011). The more deviations from a tool manual (e.g., item omissions, changes in scoring procedures), the weaker the tool's performance – this extends to using a "clinical override" on estimates established by actuarial risk assessment tools (Quinsey et al., 2006).

As new risk assessment tools have recently been developed for more specific populations (for example, intellectually disabled offenders [Lofthouse, Lindsay, Totsika, Hasting, & Roberts, 2014]), to assess the likelihood of more specific outcomes (for example, spousal assault [Kropp, Hart, & Belfrage, 2010] and suicide [Steeg et al., 2012]), there has been a renewed focus on moving beyond static risk factors and moving toward incorporating more dynamic and protective factors in the item content of these increasingly important instruments. With the knowledge gained in this chapter on the broad approaches used in forensic risk assessment, it is recommended that interested readers continue their education on available tools using resources such as the Risk Management Authority's (2007) *Risk Assessment Tool Evaluation Directory* or the Global Institute of Forensic Research's monthly Executive Bulletin on risk assessment tools (www.gifrinc.com).

REFERENCES

Andrews, D. A., & Bonta, J. (1995). *LSI-R: The Level of Service Inventory-Revised.* Toronto, ON: Multi-Health Systems.

Andrews, D. A., & Bonta, J. (2010). *The psychology of criminal conduct* (5th ed.). New Providence, NJ: Matthew Bender & Company, Inc.

Andrews, D. A., Bonta, J., & Wormith, J. S. (2004). *LS/CMI: Level of Service/Case Management Inventory.* Toronto, ON: Multi-Health Systems.

Arkes, H. R. (1991). Costs and benefits of judgment errors: Implications for debiasing. *Psychological Bulletin, 110,* 486-498. doi: 10.1037/0033-2909.110.3.486

Boer, D. P., Hart, S. D., Kropp, P. R., & Webster, C. D. (1997). *Manual for the Sexual Violence Risk-20. Professional guidelines for assessing risk of sexual violence.* Burnaby, BC: Mental Health, Law, and Policy Institute, Simon Fraser University.

Borum, R. (1996). Improving the clinical practice of violence risk assessment: Technology, guidelines, and training. *American Psychologist, 9,* 945-956. doi: 10.1037/0003-066X.51.9.945

Cooper, B. S., Griesel, D., & Yuille, J. C. (2008). Clinical-forensic risk assessment: The past and current state of affairs. *Journal of Forensic Psychology Practice, 7,* 1-63. doi: 10.1300/J158v07n04_01

de Vogel, V., de Ruiter, C., Bouman, Y., & de Vries Robbe, M. (2007). *Handleiding bij de SAPROF. Structured Assessment of Protective Factors for violence risk. Versie 1.* [Guide to the SAPROF. Structured Assessment of Protective Factors for violence risk. Version 1]. Utrecht: Forum Educatief.

Doctor, R., & Nettleton, S. (2003). *Dangerous patients: A psychodynamic approach to risk assessment and management.* London: Karnac.

Douglas, K. S., Shaffer, C., Blanchard, A. J. E., Guy, L. S., Reeves, K., & Weir, J. (2014). *HCR-20 violence risk assessment scheme: Overview and annotated bibliography.* Burnaby, BC: Mental Health, Law, and Policy Institute, Simon Fraser University.

Drake, C., Clemente, L., & Perrin, G. (2006). *Violence risk assessment in clinical practice.* Phoenix, AZ: Arizona Psychologist. Retrieved from http://azpsychologist.com/sourcebook_Violence_Risk-Lia%5B1%5D.doc

Eifert, G. H., & Feldner, M. T. (2004). Conceptual foundations of behavioral assessment strategies: From theory to assessment. In M. Hersen (Ed.), *Comprehensive handbook of psychological assessment: Behavioral assessment* (pp. 95-107).

Fazel, S., Singh, J. P., Doll, H., & Grann, M. (2012). The prediction of violence and antisocial behaviour: A systematic review and meta-analysis of the utility of risk assessment instruments in 73 samples involving 24,827 individuals. *British Medical Journal, 345*, e4692.

Gilfoyle, N. F. P., Ogden, D. W., Tran, D. H., Friedman, S. S., Owens, A. L., & Pickering, W. C. (2011). Brief for amici curiae American Psychological Association and Texas Psychological Association in support of petition for a writ of certiorari. Washington, DC: American Psychological Association.

Grann, M., & Långström, N. (2007). Actuarial assessment of violence risk: To weigh or not to weigh? *Criminal Justice & Behavior, 34*, 22-36.

Hanson, R. K., & Thornton, D. (1999). *Static-99: Improving actuarial risk assessments for sex offenders* (User Report 99-02). Ottawa, ON: Department of the Solicitor General of Canada.

Hart, S. D., Michie, C., & Cooke, D. J. (2007). Precision of actuarial risk assessment instruments: Evaluating the 'margins of error' of group v. individual predictions of violence. *British Journal of Psychiatry, 49*, S60-S65. doi: 10.1192/bjp.190.5.s60

Helmus, L. (2008). *Annotated bibliography of Static-99 replications*. Retrieved from http://www.static99.org/pdfdocs/static-99annotatedbibliography.pdf

Helmus, L., Thornton, D., Hanson, R. K., & Babchishin, K. M. (2012). Improving the predictive accuracy of Static-99 and Static-2002 with older sex offenders: Revised age weights. *Sexual Abuse: A Journal of Research and Treatment, 24*, 64-101. doi: 10.1177/1079063211409951

Kaser-Boyd, N. (2015). Threat assessment in homicide/suicide: The duty to warn. In: C. de Ruiter & N. Kaser-Boyd (2015). *Forensic psychological assessment in practice: Case studies*. New York, NY: Routledge.

Kropp, P. R., Hart, S. D., & Belfrage, H. (2010). *The Brief Spousal Assault Form for the Evaluation of Risk (B-SAFER), Version 2: User manual*. Vancouver, BC: ProActive ReSolutions.

Large, M. M., Ryan, C. J., Singh, S. P., Paton, M. B., & Nielssen, O. B. (2011). The predictive value of risk categorization in schizophrenia. *Harvard Law Review, 19*, 25-33. doi: 10.3109/10673229.2011.549770

Lessard v. Schmidt, 349 F. Supp. 1078 (E.D. Wis. 1972).

Lipsey, M. W., Chapman, G. L., & Landenberger, N. A. (2001). Cognitive-behavioral programs for offenders. *Annals of the American Academy of Political & Social Science, 578*, 144-157.

Lofthouse, R. E., Lindsay, W. R., Totsika, V., Hastings, R. P., & Roberts, D. (2014). Dynamic risk and violence in individuals with an intellectual disability: Tool development and initial validation. *Journal of Forensic Psychiatry & Psychology, 25,* 288-306.

Mason, T. (1998). Tarasoff liability: Its impact for working with patients who threaten others. *International Journal of Nursing Studies, 35*, 109-114.

McSherry, B., & Keyzer, P. (2009). *Sex offenders and preventive detention: Politics, policy and practice*. Annandale, VA: The Federation Press.

Meehl, P. E. (1954). *Clinical versus statistical prediction: A theoretical analysis and review of the evidence*. Minneapolis: University of Minnesota Press.

Monahan, J. (1981). *The clinical prediction of violent behavior*. Rockville, MD: U.S. Department of Health and Human Services.

Monahan, J. (2006). *Tarasoff* at thirty: How developments in science and policy shape the common law. *University of Cincinnati Law Review, 75*, 497-521.

Murray, J., & Thomson, M. (2010). Clinical judgement in violence risk assessment. *Europe's Journal of Psychology, 1*, 128-149.

Novaco, R. (1994). Anger as a risk factor for violence among the mentally disordered. In J. Monahan & H. J. Steadman (Eds.), *Violence and mental disorder* (pp. 21-59). Chicago, IL: University of Chicago Press.

Nuffield, J. (1982). *Parole decision making in Canada: Research towards decision guidelines.* Ottawa, ON: Ministry of Supply and Services Canada.

O'Shea, L. E., & Dickens, G. L. (2014). Short-term Assessment of Risk and Treatability (START): Systematic review and meta-analysis. *Psychological Assessment, 26*, 990-1002. doi: 10.1037/a0036794

Quinsey, V. L., Harris, G. T., Rice, M. E., & Cormier, C. A. (2006). *Violent offenders: Appraising and managing risk* (2nd ed.). Washington, DC: American Psychological Association.

Rettenberger, M., Hucker, S. J., Boer, D. P., & Eher, R. (2009). The reliability and validity of the *Sexual Violence Risk-20* (SVR-20): An international review. *Sexual Offender Treatment, 4*, 1-14.

Rice, M. E., Harris, G. T., & Lang, C. (2013). Validation of and revision to the VRAG and SORAG: The Violence Risk Appraisal Guide-Revised (VRAG-R). *Psychological Assessment, 25*, 951-965. doi: 10.1037/a0032878

Risk Management Authority. (2007). *Risk assessment tools evaluation directory (RATED).* Paisley: Risk Management Authority.

Singh, J. P. (2013). *The International Risk Survey (IRiS) project: Perspectives on the practical application of violence risk assessment tools.* Paper presented at the Annual Conference of the American Psychology-Law Society, Portland, OR.

Singh, J. P. (2012). The history, development, and testing of forensic risk assessment tools. In E. Grigorenko (Ed.), *Handbook of juvenile forensic psychology and psychiatry.* New York: Springer.

Singh, J. P., & Fazel, S. (2010). Forensic risk assessment: A metareview. *Criminal Justice & Behavior, 37*, 965-988. doi: 10.1177/0093854810374274

Singh, J. P., Fazel, S., Gueorguieva, R., & Buchanan, A. (2013). Rates of sexual recidivism in high risk sex offenders: A meta-analysis of 10,422 participants. *Sexual Offender Treatment, 7*, 44-57.

Singh, J. P., Fazel, S., Gueorguieva, R., & Buchanan, A. (2014). Rates of violence in patients classified as high risk by structured risk assessment instruments. *British Journal of Psychiatry, 204*, 180-187. doi: 10.1192/bjp.bp.113.131938

Singh, J. P., Grann, M., & Fazel, S. (2011). A comparative study of violence risk assessment tools: A systematic review and metaregression analysis of 68 studies involving 25,980 participants. *Clinical Psychology Review, 31*, 499-513. doi: 10.1016/j.cpr.2010.11.009

Slovenko, R. (1975). Psychotherapy and confidentiality. *Cleveland State Law Review, 24*, 375-391.

Steeg, S., Kapur, N., Webb, R., Applegate, E., Stewart, S. L. K., Hawton, K., ... Cooper, J. (2012). *Psychological Medicine, 42*, 2383-2394. doi: 10.1017/S0033291712000347

Waypoint Centre for Mental Health Care. (2014). *Research department bibliography on assessment and communication of violence risk.* Retrieved from http://static.squarespace.com/static/520a76a0e4b03ad-27abae1e3/t/53f52df0e4b07b3557c47122/1408577008298/Risk.pdf

Webster, C. D., & Belfrage, H. (2013). *HCR-20 (Version 3): Assessing Risk for Violence.* Burnaby, BC, Canada: Mental Health, Law, and Policy Institute, Simon Fraser University.

Webster, C. D., Martin, M. L., Brink, J., Nicholls, T. L., & Desmarais, S. (2009). *Manual for the Short-Term Assessment of Risk and Treatability (START). Version 1.1.* Hamilton, ON: Forensic Psychiatric Services Commission.

Yang, M., Wong, S. C., & Coid. J. (2010). The efficacy of violence prediction: A meta-analytic comparison of nine risk assessment tools. *Psychological Bulletin, 136*, 740-767. doi:10.1037/a0020473

CHAPTER 9

HUNTINGTON'S DISEASE AND THE CRIMINAL JUSTICE SYSTEM

MARTHA NANCE, NINA ROSS, JESSICA MARSOLEK,
& ADAM PICCOLINO

CHAPTER OVERVIEW

Huntington's Disease (HD) is an adult-onset neurodegenerative disease that leads to dementia, lack of coordination, involuntary movements called chorea, and various manifestations of psychological and behavioral disturbances. This disorder may be characterized by the combination of psychological symptoms (e.g., depression, anxiety, irritability, apathy, perseveration/obsessiveness, and impulsivity), cognitive symptoms (e.g., dementia, anosognosia) and motor symptoms (e.g., the presence of involuntary movements along with disturbance of volitional movements, and disorganized speech). All symptoms differ in severity per patient affected and progress over 10-20 years, until the affected person can no longer care for themselves independently until death, which is often caused by swallowing disturbance. Each offspring of a person affected by HD has a 50% chance of inheriting the gene that causes HD. Due to psychological, cognitive symptoms, and anosognosia, individuals with HD are more likely than the general public to have a criminal record or to have encounters with law enforcement. Stage of disease and associated symptoms may contribute to the risk that a person with HD will commit a crime. In the early stages of the disease, cognitive changes affecting executive functioning and decision-making may provoke criminal behavior. However, as symptoms progress further, it becomes more difficult to multi-task and problem solve, and subsequently, it becomes more difficult for the person to have the organizational skills to commit more complex crimes. Eventually the person with HD will be physically unable to create any crime. This chapter will review: (1) what is known and has been studied about the correlation between those affected with HD and their involvement in the criminal justice system; (2) disposition planning for those with HD and how to plan for appropriate settings when in the correctional system; (3) child maltreatment, neglect and domestic violence as it pertains to a family affected by HD; (4) considerations for police and first responders when contact is made with an individual affected by HD; (5) driving and pedestrian considerations; and (6) treatment options available. The goals of this chapter are to raise awareness about HD within the clinical, forensic and criminal justice settings. We hope that police, fire and first responder professionals will have a better understanding of the unique circumstances that are common for patients and families who have HD, but may not be common for those who do not.

HUNTINGTON'S DISEASE

Huntington's disease (HD) is a genetic disorder of the central nervous system that occurs in 1 out of 10,000 people in the United States (Crozier, Robertson, & Dale, 2015; Doria et al., 2015), with onset being more frequent in adulthood. The variant that begins earlier is called juvenile Huntington's disease (JHD), and people often live to young adulthood. It has been referred to as "perhaps the most unpleasant disease of all" (Kakoschke v. Draper, 2006, at [30]). Historically, patients who have suffered from what is now known as Huntington's were often ostracized, even treated as if they were witches due to their awkward, involuntary movements (or "chorea"), once called St. Vitus Dance, named after a young martyr in the 4th century who prayed for salvation of those afflicted with the "dancing plague" just prior to being boiled alive in molten lead and pitch (Hayden, 1981; Wexler, 2008). Persons with JHD tend to develop stiffness and don't develop chorea. Aspects of the disease that make it particularly likely for affected individuals to come into contact with the criminal justice system include disinhibition, paranoia, strong sexual urges, and psychosis, which often appear as the first symptoms and cause misdirection in diagnosis (Walker, 2007). We will review below the important medical, genetic, and psychosocial aspects of the disease, as well as discuss some of the special challenges that HD presents to affected individuals, their families, law enforcement, courts, correctional facilities, and the community. Resources for families, law enforcement and the forensic community are listed at the end of this chapter.

HISTORY OF HUNTINGTON'S DISEASE: THE STIGMA

Early documentation of the debilitating, progressive, and fatal genetic disease now known as Huntington's disease was published in 1872 by Dr. George Huntington, a physician in East Hampton, New York, who came from a family of doctors who had treated and observed for several generations a ravaging disease that struck only adults in certain families in their community (Hayden, 1981). A later work by the eugenicist Charles Davenport in 1916, entitled *Huntington's chorea in relation to heredity and eugenics,* served to establish the severely negative perception of HD both within and outside the HD community—a stigma that persists today (Davenport & Muncey, 1916). Laws were passed in many states in the early 20th century which led to the involuntary sterilization of adults and minors with a variety of genetic and non-genetic disabilities. HD was specifically targeted by the Nazi racial hygiene laws of the 1930s as a condition necessitating identification and involuntary sterilization. In the United States, sterilization of individuals with disabilities was legal well into the 1960s, and it is not known how many individuals in the U.S. with HD were sterilized as a result of these laws. These and other aspects of the history of HD are well detailed by Alice Wexler, a historian whose family carries the Huntington's genetic strain (Wexler, 2008).

Up until late in the 20th century, prior to the development of effective pharmacotherapy for the psychiatric and behavioral aspects of HD, people with HD were often hidden away at home or placed in state-funded psychiatric long-term treatment facilities. Historically, members of HD families were often stigmatized, as they still are today, due to difficulties with insurance and employment (Wexler, 2008; Røthing, Malterud, & Frich, 2014). This background may impact the attitude of a person with HD who finds themselves in a confrontational situation with an authority figure such as a police officer, judge, physician, or even a family member.

CLINICAL OVERVIEW OF HUNTINGTON'S DISEASE

HD is a neurodegenerative disease that leads to dementia, lack of coordination, involuntary movements called chorea, and various manifestations of psychological and behavioral disturbances. The cognitive and motor features of the disease gradually worsen from initial onset, which typically occurs between ages 30 and 50, over a 10- to 20-year course until death (An et al., 2012; Arran, Craufurd, & Simpson, 2014; Jacobs, Boyd, Hogarth, & Horak, 2015). The prevalence is about 4-8/100,000 in Caucasian populations and is ten-fold lower in Asian populations (Harper, 1992; Pringsheim et al., 2012). Approximately 30,000 people in the United States have HD, although this estimate is based on outdated epidemiological studies and should be viewed as only a rough idea of the order of magnitude. There are perhaps one thousand people with HD in each state (Cina, Smith, Collins, & Conradi, 1996; Oster, Shoulson, Quaid & Dorsey, 2010; Varshney & Ehrlich, 2003). Although there is no treatment known to slow, reverse, or cure HD, medications can relieve some of the involuntary movements and mood disturbances (Kowalski, Belcher, Keltner, & Dowben, 2015). In addition, assistive devices and environmental adaptations are used to optimize an affected individual's ability to function and to support the family as they cope with the effects of the disease.

MEDICAL AND BIOLOGICAL ASPECTS OF HD

ROLE OF GENETICS

HD is an autosomal dominant genetic disorder, affecting males and females with equal likelihood. Each biological child of an affected individual has a 50% chance of inheriting the disease-causing gene (An et al., 2012; MacLeod et al., 2013). The gene is present throughout life, and its presence does not determine whether or not a person has symptoms of the disease. The clinical diagnosis of HD is made by a neurological examination and can take into consideration positive gene test results. (Crozier, Robertson, & Dale, 2015). Affected individuals have often completed their families before their symptoms develop, and spouses marrying into the family face the difficult task of witnessing the impact of the disease first on the spouse and then on one or more of their children (and even grandchildren). Children are placed in the situation where they must watch the affected parent's course, knowing that they have a 50% chance of developing symptoms later in life. "At-risk" individuals of decision-making capacity (i.e., adults) may choose to have a blood test to determine whether they carry the Huntington's gene (de Die-Smulders, De Wert, Liebaers, Tibben, & Evers Kiebooms, 2013; van der Meer & Vervoort, 2012). This is known as a "predictive" or "pre-symptomatic" genetic test, which carries with it a number of psychosocial considerations and should be performed according to published guidelines that emphasize the importance of pre-test genetic counseling (Clément, Gargiulo, Feingold, & Durr, 2015; MacLeod et al., 2013). Only a small percentage of the at-risk population in the United States (about 5%-10%) undergo predictive testing for HD. It is not performed in the U.S. as a routine procedure prior to adoption, and employers and insurers are prohibited by the (federal) Genetic Information Non-discrimination Act (GINA) from requiring or utilizing genetic information prior to decisions about employment or individual health insurance coverage (http://www.ginahelp.org/). Predictive testing does not determine whether a person's current symptoms or problems are caused by HD, and therefore does not resolve issues that concern legal competence, child custody, ability to work, or any other situation where the question has to do with the individual's current level of function. Prenatal genetic testing and in-vitro fertilization with pre-implantation genetic diagnosis is also available and is chosen by a small minority of individuals. Adoption and surrogate parenthood are other reproductive options for affected and at-risk individuals (Keenan, Miedzybrodzka, & Eden, 2012)

AGE OF ONSET

Like Alzheimer's and Parkinson's disease, HD is categorized as a neurodegenerative disorder. However, the onset age of HD symptoms varies widely and is generally much younger than those more common conditions. About 5%-10% of affected individuals have onset of symptoms before age 20 ("juvenile onset HD"), and an equal percentage may have onset in the 8th-9th decade. Most commonly, however, a person genetically disposed to HD will present symptoms between the ages of 30 and 50, during or after the reproductive years, and certainly during the time of life when he or she is most likely working and raising a family (Aylward et al., 2012; Hoss et al., 2015; Lee et al., 2012; Simonin et al., 2013; Valcárcel-Ocete et al., 2015; Vittori et al., 2014; Weydt, Soyal, Landwehrmeyer, Patsch, 2014; Tabrizi et al., 2012).

PSYCHOLOGICAL FACTORS

The psychological and behavioral features of HD vary widely, not only from one person to another, but also across the span of the disease. In some cases, the psychological impact is minimal; however, for others, this may present as the most disabling aspect of the disease. Depression, anxiety, irritability, perseveration/obsessiveness, and impulsivity are most common to HD (Almqvist, Brinkman, Wiggins, & Hayden, 2003; Arran, Craufurd, & Simpson, 2014; Licklederer, Wolff, & Barth, 2008). Reclusiveness, paranoia, and suspiciousness occur somewhat less frequently, and incidence of overt hallucinations appears only rarely (Tsuang et al., 2014). Individuals with HD sometimes engage in substance abuse, inappropriate behavior, and criminal activity (Byars, Beglinger, Moser, Gonzalez-Alegre, & Nopoulos, 2012; Chu, Knight, O'Neill, & Purkayastha, 2014; Kalkhoven, Sennef, Peeters, & Van Den Bos, 2014). Disorganized behaviors, exacerbated by unawareness or denial of the need for help and leading to vulnerability is common. Suicidal thinking, gestures, and attempts are much more common among the HD population than in general, particularly in the early stages of the disease. In our experience, premeditated acts of violence are uncommon in the person diagnosed with HD, particularly as his or her progressing cognitive impairment interferes with the ability to plan for and complete an organized activity. Impulsive, explosive, and threatening behaviors, however, are quite common throughout the course of the disease and impact others in the individual's living environment (Fisher, Sewell, Brown, & Churchyard, 2014).

In some communities, the categorization of HD as a neurological disorder can negatively impact a person's access to appropriate psychiatric care, because the treating neurologists may be uncomfortable with the management of severe psychiatric or behavioral symptoms. Psychiatrists, psychiatric care extenders, nurse practitioners and PAs may be relatively unfamiliar with the disease. It should be noted that, unlike the cognitive and motor impairments which progress over time, psychiatric and behavioral symptoms wax and wane over the course of the disease and do not necessarily progress.

THE COURSE OF HD

HD progresses inexorably to death over 10-20 years, with morbidity and death often being related to a swallowing disturbance (dysphagia), which in turn leads to aspiration pneumonia or simply to weight loss and a gradual weakening. The Shoulson-Fahn scale is a validated measure used to assess the functional aspects of disease progression (Shoulson & Fahn, 1979). The scale measures a person's ability to work, manage money, and perform household chores; to do self-care activities such as bathing, dressing, and toileting; and to live independently. Scores run from 0-13 and are divided into five "stages." Affected individuals lose an average of 0.7 points/year on the scale. A person without medical background can complete the scale based on responses from the affected person, family member, or caregiver. Certain issues predictably arise at certain stages of the disease. In Stage 1, an affected person is just beginning to be aware of changes, which ultimately lead to work-related disability. Stage 2 is a relatively quiescent time, when the person is largely safe at home but not working and, at some point, not driving. Stage 3 is a time of transition, as others need to take over the overall decision-making and household organization and begin to assist with daily cares. By Stages 4 and 5, people with HD need 24-hour care. A Danish study found that pneumonia and cardiovascular disease accounted for the greatest number of deaths from HD (Sorensen, 1992). The table below lists the typical level of capacity to do certain activities by disease stage.

TABLE 1

Ability to perform life activities through the stages of Huntington's disease

Life Activity	Stage 1	Stage 2	Stage 3	Stage 4	Stage 5
Competitive Work	Capable to Impaired	Unable	Unable	Unable	Unable
Drive	Capable	Capable to Unable	Unable	Unable	Unable
Household Management	Capable	Capable to Impaired	Impaired to Unable	Unable	Unable
Routine Self-Care	Capable	Capable	Capable to Impaired	Impaired to Unable	Unable

The abnormal gene that causes HD is present in all body cells from time of conception, but the clinical diagnosis is generally not made until the adult years, when motor symptoms and declining function become evident. Recent research has proven that subtle cognitive, behavioral, and functional changes begin long before a diagnosis can confidently be made (Chisholm et al., 2013). Combined with the affected person's tendency to deny or be unaware of his or her symptoms, there is the potential for functional, criminal, or legal issues to arise during this time—when the person has no diagnosis, either because he/she is truly in the prodromal period, has not sought medical care, or because the physician was not able to make a formal diagnosis of HD. In our experience, physicians are often reluctant to diagnose HD when there are only behavioral and/or mental health symptoms, without the presence of clear motor symptoms. However, this is the best time for the family to emphasize exercise, proper nutrition, having a routine, and social contact as ways to optimize function as the person moves towards the diagnosis of HD.

SYMPTOM CATEGORIES

DEMENTIA

Like Alzheimer's disease, HD causes dementia—but the nature of the dementia is quite different from that of Alzheimer's. Although people with HD may have speech problems, they do not have the grammatical errors or other language problems that are common in Alzheimer's disease. And unlike Alzheimer's, people with HD are likely to retain personality and social interaction throughout the course of their disease. "Executive functions" such as planning, sequencing, multitasking, decision-making, and judgment are typically affected first. There is difficulty learning new material, and some affected individuals can become perseverative—repeatedly concerning themselves with the same issue, over and over again. A challenging aspect of cognitive impairment in HD is a tendency to lack awareness, or denial of symptoms (anosognosia). Anosognosia is actually subtly different from denial of symptoms, which represents a psychological defense response to stress. Anosognosia is the impairment of the cognitive ability to recognize the nature of one's own illness. In this situation, the person may observe and recognize the illness state in others, but literally be unable to see it in himself or herself. This deficit in self-awareness ranges in severity and may be selective, involving only certain aspects of the disease (e.g., only for motor disturbances) (Sitek, Thompson, Craufurd, & Snowden, 2014). This can make the provision of care or support, or even an understanding of the facts of a situation, extremely difficult, as the affected person denies having problems and makes excuses or blames others for troubles or situations that have arisen.

In combination with other features of the disease, dementia gradually leads to disability from work, inability to care for others (e.g., children), inability to drive or manage financial and household affairs, and eventually to perform self-care. People in the late stages of HD require assistance with all aspects of daily living (meal preparation, feeding, bathing, dressing, management of incontinence, etc.) (Booij, Engberts, Rödig, Tibben, & Roos, 2012; Fonteijn et al., 2012). Although medications to treat the dementia of Alzheimer's disease are available, there is no evidence that these drugs help the dementia of HD.

MOVEMENT DISORDER

The movement disorder of HD has two parts: the presence of involuntary movements and the disturbance of volitional movements (Guo et al., 2012). These combine to create impairments of gait, handwriting, other fine and gross arm movements, and slurring of speech. People with HD may walk erratically, stagger, or fall, as well as waver or wobble, even as they stand still. The involuntary movements are generally not rhythmic (like a tremor), but rather more dance-like (as in "chorea") or tic-like (Jankovic & Roos, 2014). Movements can be low in amplitude, somewhat fidgety, or more writhing, twisting, or ballistic (high in amplitude, shooting or lurching in nature)—or all of these combined. Later in the course, stiffness or rigidity (dystonia) can be intermixed with the chorea, or replace it entirely. Incoordination and involuntary movements can lead to substantial social distress, as strangers misinterpret the gait or speech changes as "walking (or talking) like a drunk" or an involuntary ballistic movement as an intentional hitting movement. To make matters worse, the movement symptoms are exacerbated by stress, and thus are likely to be more prominent if a person is in a stressful or confrontational situation. Wrist or ankle restraints should never be used on a person with HD, as they will not prevent involuntary movements and will likely cause injury when those movements occur. Medications can be used to reduce chorea if it is severe and bothersome to the affected person.

DISORGANIZED SPEECH

Slurred speech (dysarthria) is common in HD, ranging from very mild in the early stages of the disease to very severe later on. In the late stages, individuals with HD are often mute, but may communicate basic feelings through grunts, screams, or body language. Difficulty with communication can be frustrating for people with HD and may lead to increased irritability or aggressiveness (Rusz, Klempíř, Tykalová, Baborová, Čmejla, Růžička, & Roth, 2014). A speech pathologist can help the affected person to maintain useful speech for as long as possible and to develop other simple communication strategies in the late stages.

HALLUCINATIONS, DELUSIONS, AND PARANOIA

Actual hallucinations—seeing or hearing things that are not there—are relatively uncommon in HD, but paranoid or suspicious thinking is common. Some people with HD become reclusive and resistant to interactions with others, or only accept assistance from specific, well-known individuals (Corey-Bloom, Herndon, & Howell, 2015). Antipsychotic medications can help to reduce hallucinations and paranoia.

CONFABULATION

"Confabulation" is an interesting term and might be considered a lie without the intention of lying. It occurs when normal memory function is inadequate (Brown et al., 2015) and imaginary information fills the missing patches of memory, existing in the mind of the confabulator as real information and a genuine part of his or her memory (Gudjonsson, 1992).

The term "confabulate" seems appropriate in describing the phenomenon that occurs in certain people with HD. Confabulation is related to unawareness/denial, as the person comes up with alternative explanations for events or behaviors that are subtly or dramatically different from those of other viewers. Confabulation can reach absurd extremes, as in the example of a woman who had lived in the nursing home for two years because of her HD and who, when asked, would say, "I don't have HD. I am just visiting." There are no medications known to prevent confabulation; caregivers and family members have to decide how to address the situation. As in the case with the patient just described, the family was able to get her moved to a care facility even in the face of her (apparent) unawareness of her diagnosis.

EXPLOSIVENESS, IMPULSIVENESS, IRRITABILITY, AND CONDUCT DISORDER

Perhaps the most challenging behavioral symptoms associated with HD involve the tendency toward irritability and explosive or impulsive behaviors (Fisher, Sewell, Brown, & Churchyard, 2014). These probably occur in relation to the impact of HD on the frontal lobes of the brain, which work to suppress inappropriate urges, behaviors, and thoughts. The frontal lobes mature late in development, not until the end of the second or early third decade. Injury to this part of the brain in a person with HD, particularly when combined with depression, suspiciousness, and testosterone, predisposes the person to negativistic, irritable, or aggressive behaviors. When they occur, these behaviors are generally not premeditated, although they may repeatedly occur in a similar situation or in relation to a particular family member or caregiver. A minority of people with HD have an ongoing or pre-existing proclivity to antisocial or aggressive behavior. Medications, cognitive-behavioral therapy, family counseling, and environmental adaptations can help to reduce a person's tendency to irritability and explosiveness.

APATHY

Apathy represents one of the most common behavioral symptoms of HD and is broadly characterized by a lack of motivation that manifests in affective, behavioral and cognitive domains (Van Duijn, Reedeker, Giltay, Eindhoven, Roos, & Van Der Mast, 2014). Apathetic individuals may show reduced interest in their surroundings, lack initiation, and are inclined to have others structure their activities. The presentation of apathy may look similar to depression and, while both conditions may co-exist, apathy is considered a distinct syndrome from depression, especially in neurologically compromised patients such as those with HD. A key distinction between the two conditions is the HD individual's lack of sadness and discontent common to depression. Stimulant medications or stimulating antidepressants are sometimes used to relieve apathy, and most individuals benefit from structured daily activities.

CAUSE OF HUNTINGTON'S DISEASE

The sole cause of HD is a mutation in the gene that encodes a protein called "huntingtin." The mutation causes the cell to make a protein that is larger but more fragile than the normal protein. Over years, the abnormal protein is easily broken into smaller pieces with "sticky ends" which tend to accumulate inside brain cells (Moss et al., 2014; Schapira, Olanow, Greenamyre, & Bezard, 2014). Although the protein is present in many cells in the body, the damaging effects of its accumulation seem to be exclusively in the brain; people with HD do not have trouble with the heart, lungs, kidneys, any other organs, or bones. The effects of HD appear first in a part of the brain called the caudate nucleus but eventually lead to an overall shrinkage of the white matter of the brain and widespread loss of nerve cells, particularly affecting the frontal lobes.

The size of the gene mutation varies from one person to the next, and there is a correlation between the mutation size and the age when symptoms begin, so that larger mutations tend to result in earlier onset ages. The size of the mutation tends to increase as it passes from parent to child, but it can get smaller. There is a greater tendency for the gene mutation to increase in size when it is passed on by a father, which explains the tendency for children with "juvenile onset" HD (onset before age 18) to have affected fathers (Roos et al., 1991; Stine, 1993).

CO-MORBID CONDITIONS

A challenging issue for patients and caregivers associated with HD is the potential for co-morbidity (Arran, Craufurd, & Simpson, 2014). Depression, attention-deficit disorder, anxiety, substance abuse, and antisocial behaviors commonly occur in people who do not have HD, and the presence of HD does not protect people from having these problems. Similarly, the presence of these symptoms, particularly at a young age, in a person who is at risk for HD (the child of an affected individual) does not necessarily mean that HD has begun. People with HD have often grown up in psychosocially and financially stressed families because of the presence and erratic behavior of a parent with HD and, as a result, may be more likely to have mood and substance abuse issues. Errors can be made in both directions, over-attributing symptoms and problems to HD, or failing to recognize the constellation of features that comprise HD. Patients who have HD are frequently diagnosed with a psychiatric disorder first—before the HD diagnosis is made (Cusin, Franco, Fernandex-Roloer, DeBois, Welch, 2013; Sprengelmeyer et al., 2014; Thompson et al., 2012; Van Duijn et al., 2014).

People with HD are generally otherwise medically healthy, probably because of the relatively young age of onset. As previously noted, the disease itself does not directly impact other body organs such as the heart, liver, or kidneys, nor do people with HD have a higher risk of other chronic medical conditions such as diabetes, heart disease, or arthritis.

DEPRESSION AND ANXIETY

Depression is seen in 40% of people with HD and contributes significantly to irritability, suicidality, and reduced quality of life (Nance et al., 2011). Both depression and anxiety are treatable with medications and/or non-pharmacologic treatments. Therefore, people with HD who have these symptoms should be referred to a physician for treatment. Counseling and pharmacotherapy are both possible modes of treatment, but due to the cognitive impairment associated with HD, pharmacotherapy may be the best option (Nance, Paulsen, Rosenblatt, & Wheelock, 2011). There are no specific medications used to treat depression or anxiety in HD; the physician would prescribe the same medication as would be used by a similar person without HD. A primary care doctor, psychiatrist, or neurologist can prescribe medications for HD.

SUBSTANCE ABUSE

Substance abuse is estimated to occur in patients who have HD at a higher rate than the general public (Byars, Beglinger, Moser, Gonzalez-Alegre, & Nopoulos, 2012). The most common substance of choice is alcohol. HD choreic symptoms already mimic displays of intoxication from alcohol, so the abuse of alcohol further complicates symptoms, creating a more unsteady gait and more heavily slurred speech than usual. Intoxication will also increase the risk of injury associated with unsteady gait and poor judgment. Individuals who have HD are advised to refrain from substance abuse, as it complicates treatment and may counteract important medications. Those who have HD and also abuse alcohol or other drugs have a higher risk of county human service and law enforcement involvement, hospitalizations, divorce, and loss of parental rights.

People with HD should be asked about drug and alcohol use and abuse, as appropriate, and referred for treatment. Urine or blood testing for drugs or alcohol use might be appropriate in certain acute situations, as it might for a person without HD. Both HD and chemical dependency can negatively affect relationships, families, and parenting and increase the probability of interaction with the criminal justice system. Often there is synergism between the two. As the disease progresses, drug or alcohol use might have to be facilitated by another member of the household, as the affected individual loses the ability to leave the home or make purchases; thus, assessment or counseling of family members may be necessary.

SUICIDE

There is an increased risk for suicidality and completed suicide among individuals with HD (Black & Andreasen, 2011; Wahlin, Bäckman, Lundin, Haegermark, Winblad, & Anvret, 2000). Suicide is more likely to occur in the earlier stages, when the affected person has greater cognitive and motor capacity to complete the act. For this reason, it contributes greatly to "lost years of life," a public health measure of the impact of mortality. Suicide also has serious impact on surviving family members and caregivers.

While not lethal, suicidal ideation and suicide attempts can be devastating to the individual, family, and the community around them and requires the dedication of appropriate resources. Life and disease milestones such as predictive genetic diagnosis; loss of parent with HD; and loss of ability to work, to drive, or to live independently are key factors in an escalation of the risk of suicidality. Factors that compound suicide risk in the general population include being male, social isolation, and access to firearms. Awareness of the danger, consistent screening, and other prevention strategies may help to reduce risk in this area (Whalin, Baeckman, Lundin, Haegermark, Winblad, Anyret, 2000).

The increased risk of suicidality around the time of predictive genetic testing for HD has been the focus of several studies. Findings indicate that genetic testing for HD should be done in the context of a prescribed protocol that includes careful screening for depression and suicidality, along with support for the individual who is undergoing predictive testing (Wahlin, 2006). Individuals with symptoms of depression who initiate the pre-testing process need additional support (Lawson et al., 1996), and severe depression at this juncture needs to be evaluated before testing, with the possibility of rescheduling at a later time being an option. Another study, focused on suicides in the testing phase and the subsequent two years, found a high level of suicidal ideation prior to testing. Depression scores and frequency of suicidal ideation increased for individuals who tested positive for HD, as compared to those who were found not to have HD (Larsson, Luszcz, Bui, & Wahlin, 2006).

Suicidality in the prodromal phase, the period of time prior to when a gene-positive person has noticeable symptoms, is another focus of research. Based on a study of 735 prodromal, HD-positive individuals and 194 non-gene-expanded individuals identified by "Predict HD," the Pre-Enroll-HD North American data collection system found several risk factors for suicidality in the prodromal group. This included a history of suicide attempts and the presence of depression (Fiedorowicz, Mills, Ruggle, Langbehn, & Paulsen 2011).

Depression is a major indicator of suicide risk in individuals with HD (Wetzel et al., 2011). Anxiety, aggression, and irritability have also been identified as risk factors (Wetzel et al., 2011). The phase of the disease is also found to be a risk factor, with the majority of HD suicides occurring in the early and late phases (Baliko, 2004).

A review of 506 deceased former residents of the New England states who had HD found age-stratified differences in risk of death by suicide when compared to Massachusetts' suicide rates for the general population. For persons age 50- to 69-years old, the rate of suicide among HD patients was 8.2 times higher compared to the general population. In the 10- to 49-year-old cohort, there was no difference in the rate of suicide between persons with HD and the general population in MA. It was also found that the rate of suicide was higher among persons in the earlier stages of the disease (Schoenfeld et al., 1984).

People with HD, particularly in acutely confrontational or psychosocially difficult situations, should be screened for suicidality and re-screened as necessary. The Columbia Suicide Severity Rating Scale (C-SSRS) is a useful screening tool for both medical professionals and for police and other first responders (cssrs.columbia.edu).

FAMILY IMPACT

Due to the hereditary nature of HD, the disease impacts not just the individual but also the individual's family (Aubeeluck, Buchanan, & Stupple, 2012; Røthing, Malterud, & Frich, 2014). HD creates complex relationships and experiences for those living in a family where HD exists. When a child is growing up in a family that is affected by HD, he or she may have the experience of seeing a grandparent, aunt, uncle or parent affected with the disease. As a biological child being raised in a family with HD, at some point the individual will become aware of their own at-risk status for inheriting HD. For some children in families affected by HD, being around someone with the disease may be very difficult, as they consider the possibility that HD may be included in their own future (Williams et al., 2013).

Huntington's disease patients and families are most likely confronted by many aspects of grief and loss throughout their lifetime (Hubers et al., 2014). *Ambiguous loss* is pertinent to HD. It means that a person may be physically but not psychologically present (Boss, 2006) and incapable of expressing themselves for a major portion of the time when they are symptomatic with the disease.

Grief within families with HD can be complicated, affecting various family members in many ways: physically, psychologically, socially and spiritually. Along with HD, families may also be struggling with other illnesses and disabilities (i.e., developmental disability, Alzheimer's disease) (Klodniski, 2004). Patients, significant others, children and other friends and family all grieve in their own way along the HD journey. Klodniski (2004) points out that some of the signs of grief may become confused with signs of HD. Forgetfulness, depression and irritability are particularly relevant. Secrecy often exists within the family. Some members deny the presence of HD in their family or their own symptoms. This can reduce access to support and healthcare.

"HD YO" is an international web site translated into multiple languages for the younger person at risk of developing HD, who has tested positive, or who has Juvenile-HD (JHD). It has four sections that meet specific developmental needs: children, teens, young adults, and JHDs. It also has a section for parents and professionals. In addition to providing educational information, it allows for interaction between persons affected by HD and has become an important source of support to children, adolescents, and young adults whose lives are affected by HD.

Support to the non-affected parent will also benefit the child. This can include therapy for that parent and participation in HD caregiver in-person support groups and, when not available, support groups online, or a general caregiver group when neither are available. The non-affected parent may need encouragement to accept help for themselves and their children. As symptoms progress, some individuals with HD and their families choose placement in either a group home or nursing home. Placement may allow for more normal family relationships and allow for more typical child development.

LIMITED DATA REGARDING HUNTINGTON'S DISEASE

HD is an uncommon disease without systematically collected registry information in most countries or regions—even in HD Centers of Excellence. Where clinical data is collected, it is generally done by health professionals regarding medical and psychological symptoms. A world-wide observational study called Enroll-HD is collecting more psychosocial information about affected and at-risk individuals and their families and may ultimately provide better information about the frequency and types of interactions that HD families have with the criminal justice system.

Huntington's disease meets the criteria as a rare or orphan disease, defined as a prevalence of less than 1/1,500 in the United States and less than 1/ 2,500 in Japan. The European Commission on Public Health defines these diseases as "life threatening or chronically debilitating with a prevalence of less than 1/2000"

(U.S. Food and Drug Administration, 2015). Despite this designation, HD is one of the most common neuro-degenerative diseases, after Alzheimer's and Parkinson's (Bertram & Tanzi, 2005).

Unlike other diseases such as Cancer and Amyotrophic Lateral Sclerosis (ALS), there is no registry for HD in most countries that uses active surveillance strategies to chronicle individuals with HD, with the exception of Denmark—where the "Registry for Huntington's Disease" is maintained at the University of Medicine, Biochemistry, and Genetics at the University of Copenhagen, and where all cases of the disease in Denmark are assumed to be enrolled. The benefit of a registry not only allows for the accurate calculation of rates, but also identifies traits associated with the disease in question (Fenger & Sorensen, 1986).

Prevalence rates of HD reflect individuals who have been diagnosed with the disease. Prevalence implies that the person is counted from the time they are diagnosed through the course of their disease. These rates do not include individuals who have received genetic testing and are not yet symptomatic for the disease. Nor does "prevalence" of HD encompass individuals at risk of developing the disease because they had a parent or grandparent who had the disease, followed by an untested parent. This group, however, does have special needs as a result of their status, and may seek therapy and/or participate in support groups. The impact of prodromal symptoms influencing judgment and behavior associated with this important subgroup is being researched.

The Huntington's Disease Society of America has developed a program for HD Centers of Excellence, where patients and families can obtain multidisciplinary care and participate in clinical research (www.hdsa.org). However, current data suggests that fewer than 25% of affected individuals receive care at a Center of Excellence for a variety of reasons: distance, perceived benefits, insurance coverage, lack of awareness of their need, denial of need, etc.. Because of the perception that "there is nothing that doctors can do" and the past stigma associated with the diagnosis of HD, some affected persons who know or suspect their diagnosis do not seek medical care. And the rarity of the disease means that the general practitioner or even the neurology or mental health specialist may have little experience in the management of a patient or family with HD. This is different from other diseases, as with ALS or cancer, where the patient would have more immediate health needs which would bring them to care and there are fewer barriers.

Unfortunately, data obtained from a sample of individuals attending a Huntington's Disease Center of Excellence, where an interdisciplinary team follows them, may not be representative of the HD population as a whole. Families attending such clinics may represent more proactive and supportive families who actively seek out such programs, and they may in turn benefit from the case management, medical, and other services available at these Centers. They may, therefore, be somewhat less likely than the HD population as a whole to have violent or disruptive behaviors.

"Enroll-HD" is an international, longitudinal, observational study collecting demographic information, symptom surveys, neurological assessments and bio-samples on an annual basis from individuals symptomatic or at-risk for HD and other family members. While it uses a passive surveillance strategy, it has a strong number (>20,000, drawn internationally) and has the potential to provide excellent data for hypothesis generating and for identification of service needs. (Seay, Giuliano, & Handley, 2012).

HUNTINGTON'S DISEASE AND CRIMINAL JUSTICE

Individuals with HD are more likely than the general public to have a criminal record or to have encounters with law enforcement. Jensen, Fenger, Bolwig and Sorensen (1998) found that males who carried the HD gene had a higher rate of criminal activity than the normal male population. It has also been noted that the majority of the crimes committed by individuals with HD are minor in severity, related to the progression and personality changes associated with the disease (Jensen et al., 1998).

Stage of disease and associated symptoms may contribute to the risk that a person with HD will commit a crime. In the early stages of the disease, cognitive changes affecting executive functioning and decision-making may provoke criminal behavior. However, as symptoms progress, it becomes more difficult to multi-task and problem solve, and it subsequently becomes more difficult for the person to have the organizational skills to commit more complex crimes. People with end-stage HD are also more likely to be in residential placements that prevent involvement in crimes, and where access to drugs and alcohol is limited. As the physical symptoms of the disease progress, there becomes a point at which committing a crime becomes impossible.

CRIMINAL ACTIVITY

We are aware of only one published study to date on the incidence and types of crimes committed by people with HD. Jensen et al. (1998) conducted a case control study linking data from three registries maintained in Denmark. Their subjects—individuals who were symptomatic for HD and their first-degree relative controls—were drawn from the Registry for Huntington's disease maintained at the Institute of Medical, Biochemistry and Genetics at the University of Copenhagen. The second group of non-related controls, matched on age and gender, were drawn from the Danish Central Registry of Citizens. All were reviewed in the Danish Central Registry Criminal Registry.

They found that among the 99 males who were symptomatic for HD, crime rates overall were significantly increased as compared to first-degree relatives (RR=2.8) and non-related controls (RR=2.3). However, the crimes committed appeared to be of "minor severity" and reflected disease-related personality changes. These crimes included stealing other than robbery, animal maltreatment, and illegal hunting. They also identified "offenses against drug laws," "minor sex crimes," and "absence from the military." The rates of "drunk driving" were significantly increased as compared to rates for relatives (RR=3.8) and non-relatives (RR=7.1). Of interest, they found no cases of rape and murder. This work did not make mention of domestic violence (Jensen et al., 1998).

It is likely that a study of this nature could not be replicated in other countries: the registries where data was obtained appear to be unique to Denmark; classification of crimes varies between political entities; similar to other variables studied in social science research; and there are differences in crime rates between reference populations. It is noted that the murder rate is five times higher in the United States compared to Denmark.

Premeditated crimes such as murder, burglary, and other felonies seem to be much less likely. The majority of crimes committed by individuals who have HD seem to be nuisance crimes rather than violent crimes; although, due to the psychiatric symptoms, irritability, impulsivity and the compromised ability to communicate effectively, violence is typically toward those in the person's immediate environment, such as partners, children and caregivers. Sexual disinhibition can occur, and some patients were convicted of criminal sexual acts. Poor judgment and lack of awareness may contribute to the individual committing minor or nuisance crimes such as traffic crimes, both as a driver and pedestrian, and disturbing the peace (Mendez, 1994).

DISPOSITION PLANNING

Meeting the special needs of a person with HD in the correctional system may create a challenge, even in the jail where they are initially held. After conviction, disposition planning may be difficult because correctional programs may not meet the needs of a person with HD. Residential programs for late-stage HD patients will not accept persons with active violent behaviors. A person with HD may not benefit from a chemical dependency treatment program that is cognitively based, due to their cognitive deficits.

Many states have laws about placement of registered sex offenders in nursing homes, which has sometimes made it impossible to place a person with HD in an HD-specific nursing home unit. Additionally, community notification may make group home placement difficult or impossible for higher level sexual offenders. Thus, a person who is both a registered sex offender and has HD may have significant barriers to suitable placement. These barriers will continue throughout the lives of HD offenders, regardless of the limitations that develop as a result of their disease progression.

CHILD MALTREATMENT, NEGLECT AND DOMESTIC VIOLENCE

Child abuse includes neglect and emotional, verbal, physical, and sexual abuse (Klevens, Barnett, Florence, & Moore, 2015). There is very limited information about child abuse involving parents with HD, and it only appears to have been collected in the late 1800s to early 1900s. Clinic staff needs to be aware of the risks to children of HD patients. This includes putting children at risk for motor vehicle-related injuries and fires. The caring parent with HD whose balance is impaired as a result of HD may unintentionally injure an infant or small child they are holding if they fall or drop their offspring. HD also affects judgment, frustration, tolerance, and memory, all implicated in child caring. However, many symptomatic parents clearly understand their child's needs and request or agree to services that will benefit their child. Parents with HD continue to demonstrate strong empathy for their child throughout the course of their disease, even if it means that they play less of a parental role.

Psychological symptoms associated with HD (including psychosis, paranoia, depression and obsessive tendencies) can contribute to the emotional abuse of a child. It is likely the parent is not doing this intentionally; but, common to persons with HD, they may not be aware of the impact of their behavior and actions. Children may be upset by having a parent who has affected speech and/or gait, trouble swallowing, or is cognitively impaired. This may be heightened during adolescence, when embarrassment about difference is developmentally normal. Furthermore, the child with a parent who has HD may live in a constant state of vigilance for unpredictable behaviors, and they may also have caregiver and household responsibilities beyond normal expectations.

There are varieties of interventions, depending on the situation, which could support child safety as well as any developmental needs that may be neglected. Childcare support while the non-affected parent is working could prevent unintentional injuries to young children. Schools can play an important role in providing extra support services. In some cases, particularly when an infant or young child is involved, supportive home visiting by a public health nurse or social worker may be helpful, either for the parent in earlier stages of HD or for the non-affected spouse who may have added stress as a result of balancing parenting, caregiving, and work/wage responsibilities.

A report of abuse or neglect should be made to child protection (also called Child and Family Services or other names, depending on location) in the jurisdiction where the child lives, but this does not guarantee intervention. Standards for opening a case are driven by state statute and the policies of the local agency, with the age of the child taken into consideration. Typically, these services are not in place to prevent injury, and service is not provided until abuse or neglect has occurred. Simply having a parent with HD alone will not open a case unless there are allegations of abuse or neglect, or there is substantial history of this behavior.

Individual therapy for the child might be helpful, and there may be benefits from family therapy as well. Depending on the situation, this could involve both parents or only the non-affected parent. Allowing the child to form attachments to adults outside the family of origin could provide needed support. This could be within the extended family, at school, within the family's social network, or with a person from the greater community who has been screened. Participation in extracurricular activities, part of normal child development, would allow the school-aged child to spend less time exposed to their parent's negative behaviors. Physical activity for the child should also be promoted because research has shown that it may delay symptoms and onset of HD.

While there has not been formal research on HD and domestic violence, it is an issue that families bring up in HD Clinics. Features of the disease (including irritability, poor judgment, and lack of awareness) put the person with HD at greater risk of perpetrating domestic violence. Frustration as a result of lack of control over one's life and conflicts over the necessity of setting limits on activities such as driving may also contribute to Intimate Partner Violence (IPV). Additionally, features of HD may provoke conditions making the individual with HD the victim of domestic violence. For instance, difficult behaviors and a stressed caregiver can lead to domestic violence or neglect by the caregiver. Support groups, psychotherapy, and education can help the caregiver to cope and manage better. Individuals with HD should be screened for evidence of victimization and asked if they feel safe in their living situations and with their care providers.

While changing patterns in relationships can be difficult in general, HD makes it difficult to learn new concepts and change behaviors. Substitute care that allows the person with HD and their non-affected partner to spend time together may help, and caregiver support may also be beneficial. As the disease progresses, the person with HD may become more passive and less physically capable of inflicting physical abuse, decreasing the risk of domestic violence.

HOMICIDE

Murder is rare among individuals with HD, although there have been a few cases highlighted by popular media. It appears that the common factors in these cases were not wanting family members to suffer and feelings of inadequacy in the caretaker's ability to meet the care needs of the family member with HD. One of the most publicized cases was that of Carol Carr, who shot two of her three sons who were suffering from HD and who were living in a nursing home (Scott, 2002). Carr had watched her husband suffer from the disease and did not want her sons to have the same experience (Scott, 2002). Another media case was that of Sanford "Sandy" Garfinkel, who killed his wife Mary because of his inability to cope with her HD (Smith, 2012).

INTERACTION WITH POLICE AND FIRST RESPONDERS

Individuals who are symptomatic for HD are at greater risk of having interactions with the police for several reasons. Chorea, unstable gait, and slurred speech may incorrectly give the impression that the individual is intoxicated. Concerned community members may report that the person is either driving or has small children in their care, or an officer may observe them directly. Patients have reported this type of event as humiliating and a barrier to being part of the community. In the clinical setting, information about interaction with law enforcement varies. While there have been instances when the person has been able to explain their situation as being a result of having HD, it may be difficult or impossible for the person with the disease to explain that HD causes them to be mistaken as intoxicated. This is particularly true when the person is under increased stress associated with being stopped by the police.

Some individuals with HD carry an identification card produced by the Huntington's Disease Society of America and made available through Huntington's Disease Centers of Excellence that explain they have the disease and may appear intoxicated as a result of their symptoms. However, the individual must be able to remember to carry the card and be able to show it to law enforcement when needed. This requires that they reach into their pocket to get the card—likely at a time of increased stress. Another option is for them to wear a medical alert bracelet that has "HUNTINGTON'S DISEASE" imprinted on the reverse side. The individual has to be able to overcome the stigma of having a disability associated with the bracelet and be willing to wear it has to remember to have it on. The police officer or other first responder has to find it and understand the meaning.

Some disabled individuals now wear photo identification badges like those worn in the workplace, and this could be of benefit if adapted for persons with HD. These badges are used by the general population and don't carry a stigma, can contain some information about HD, and are easy to wear and easy for a first responder to see. Increased awareness about HD among police officers, EMTs, and other first responders would be beneficial. Making sure the individual with HD is well identified, along with improved awareness by first responders about HD and its symptoms, including an understanding of chorea, may reduce negative incidents. We encourage HD families to identify themselves to local law enforcement at a time when there is not a crisis, in the hope of creating a mutually supportive and understanding relationship. The Huntington's Disease Society of America has also created an educational pamphlet about HD for law enforcement and first responders.

As symptoms progress, it is typical for an individual with HD to have "long response latency," which is characterized by a delay in answering questions and participating in discussion. This can feel unnatural or frustrating for the non-affected person, and the natural response is to repeat the question or begin to provide answers. This can be confusing and frustrating and may feel disrespectful to the affected person, resulting in them answering in the affirmative in order to be seen as giving an answer. They may potentially not totally understand the implication of the response they are giving. In clinical settings, providers should be conscious of a 'knee jerk' type of response. This is also true when interacting in the community with a person who has HD.

When a complex discussion is involved, the affected person may comprehend only a portion of what is said to them before attempting to respond. Someone with HD may also not appear to respond at all, even if they are being complimented or thanked. Even if the speaker is not receiving the response that he expects from the affected person, it is best to proceed as though the person is understanding some or most of what is being said. It is permissible to repeat a question or statement a couple of times or to phrase it in slightly different ways in order to try getting an appropriate response.

Research has found that individuals with HD may have an impaired ability to interpret emotions, including anger and disgust (Calder et al., 2010). This has implications when interacting with law enforcement and other first responders. It is important to be aware of these communication limitations and to take them into consideration during intervention by law enforcement, crisis mental health teams and other first responders.

When the service is the result of a domestic or family crisis, the non-affected household member may find comfort and support if the first responder is able to tell them they are familiar with or know something about HD. The non-affected household member may benefit from hearing that they need to receive help in caring for the person with HD. If they bring up that they have considered placement outside the home, this can be supported.

DRIVING AND PEDESTRIAN ISSUES

There are compelling reasons that, after a particular point in the progression of the disease, a person with HD should not be driving and should give up their license. Reasons may include impaired judgment, chorea, and lack of awareness. Law enforcement may play a role either directly or when family turns to them for assistance with the matter. No longer being able to drive is a major milestone for a person with HD and may cause a great deal of conflict within the family. However, addressing it in a timely manner can prevent serious injury or death to the person with HD, a relative, or a community member. Using an independent center to assess driving ability may help to lessen the risk, as a professional experienced in handling this difficult discussion can help the person with HD process the decision to end driving. Using this strategy takes the focus off the family and the physician. Some people with HD reach this decision on their own, or their family is able to distract them from driving. Lack of access to the car or the car keys is helpful.

In some cases, persons with HD have been known to walk inappropriately into traffic, including freeways. Intoxication may also be a factor when this happens. These situations have the potential to put the person with HD, motorists, and law enforcement at risk for injury or death.

From the clinical setting, it appears there are several milestones during the middle phases of HD when the risk of suicidality needs to be carefully screened. This includes the period around ending driving and the loss and adjustment to this major change in lifestyle. Having an alternative to driving may help lessen the risk of resultant depression. This is likely to be less of an issue in communities where individuals are less dependent on personal cars.

VICTIMIZATION

Law enforcement, EMTs and other first responders may be called to provide service to a person who has HD as a victim of crime. Poor judgment, lack of awareness, and an inability to interpret behavioral cues contribute to increased risk of crimes against the person with HD, including sexual assault. Co-morbidities such as chemical dependency and Bipolar Disorder would further increase this risk. Possibly because of the previously stated data collection limitations, there is no formal documentation of crimes committed against persons with HD.

ABILITY TO FORM CRIMINAL INTENT

The progressive loss of higher cortical functions such as planning, sequencing, multitasking, and decision-making impacts the ability to make sound judgment, form criminal intent and, at times, for a person with HD to even understand the consequences of his or her actions (Freckelton, 2012). At some point, the individual will no longer be capable of criminal intent due to cognitive decline. Timeliness is a factor for an individual's ability to stand trial.

The use of expert witnesses and input of neurologists who work with individuals with HD is highly recommended during criminal proceedings, to assist in determining the stage of disease of the patient, to provide needed education, as well as to present an insightful and informed contribution toward understanding the individual's current state (Freckelton, 2012). Formal cognitive testing and/or formal psychiatric/competency evaluation may be necessary in some situations.

TREATMENT

There is currently no cure or treatment to slow the progression of HD. However, it is a treatable disease. Medications can relieve many of the symptoms, and many types of interventions can improve the quality of life for the affected individual as well as his or her family. At HD Centers of Excellence, interdisciplinary teams of health professionals work with the core group of neurologists, psychiatrists, and physicians. These health professionals include physical therapists, occupational therapists, speech pathologists, dietitians, psychologists, neuropsychologists, social workers, nurses, and genetic counselors.

MEDICAL INTERVENTIONS
There is an FDA-approved medication to treat the chorea, and physicians often use other medications such as neuroleptic (antipsychotic) drugs or benzodiazepines (sedative or anti-anxiety drugs) on an off-label basis to reduce the involuntary movements. There is no medication for the cognitive decline (dementia) associated with HD. Many medications are used (including antidepressants, anti-anxiety agents, antipsychotics, mood stabilizing anticonvulsants, and others); however, none specifically have been proven to work in HD for the myriad of psychiatric and behavioral symptoms of the disease. Electroconvulsive therapy is rarely used, but not contraindicated. There are other treatments that are experimental at this time.

Family therapy

Individual and family therapy can be very beneficial for the family affected by HD. Due to the complexities associated with genetic risk, symptoms of those affected and their changing roles are added stressors for families. Therapy for unaffected family members separate from the affected person may be more beneficial when the affected person lacks awareness. And it may be necessary and have great benefit for other family members when the affected person refuses to participate.

Support group meetings are highly beneficial for individuals and families. HD-specific support groups offer families the chance to be with other families experiencing similar struggles. There is great benefit in speaking with a family who has been in similar situations; to be able to share what worked best and to provide differing perspectives can be beneficial. The Huntington's Disease Society of America provides support groups throughout the United States.

Independent Living Transitions

Individuals with HD require a variety of levels of support and care for activities of daily living due to the debilitating, progressive nature of the disease. Individuals gradually lose the ability to take care of household and self-care routines, possibly due to the decline of cognitive abilities needed to plan, organize, initiate, and maintain attention (Nance et al., 2011). As noted in Table 1, people with Stage 2 and 3 HD begin with deficits in household management and routine self-care. To try and have the individual remain in their home or community setting longer, cohabitating members may assist in areas the individual is no longer able to complete. If living independently, deficits can be more pronounced than if living with others and may require a move into a setting offering supervision and care earlier.

Lack of awareness (i.e., anosognosia) may play a role in the individual's inability to live independently. Self-care, hygiene and bathing may not be considered a priority by a person with HD. If the individual has chorea, bathing, changing clothes, and washing clothes or dishes may be stressful and simply avoided. If not a priority to the individual, if it creates stress, or if it simply takes too long, tasks necessary to remain independent often are neglected.

County services or law enforcement involvement may be required if living alone is no longer safe. Individuals with HD may receive 24-hour supervision and necessary care supports through in-home services or assisted living, group or adult foster home or nursing home settings. Options often depend on financial resources, benefits available, and location (Nance et al., 2011).

Placement away from home in a group home or nursing home is another time of elevated risk of suicide. This is particularly true when the need for this transition is sudden or is poorly explained. It is advisable to discuss the possibility for future placement soon after diagnosis, so the person with HD can process this information while they can still display good judgment. This discussion should include information about what would be necessary if the non-affected spouse cannot be available to provide care, particularly if they are away for their own medical treatment. When placement is well understood and the person with HD is involved in the process, transition is more likely to happen smoothly.

Finding a long-term care facility in the United States to care for someone who has HD can be complicated. The majority of states in the United States currently lack HD-specific care options for individuals. There are group homes in the authors' home state of Minnesota and a few nursing homes around the country (one in Minnesota) that specialize in HD. Although it is a minority of individuals who present significant behavioral problems (Zarowitz, O'Shea, and Nance, 2014), it appears that a care center that has had a negative experience with an individual with HD often refuses to consider another patient with the disease. This is unfortunate and reflects a lack of sensitivity to the variable nature and severity of disease symptoms from one patient to the next.

CONCLUSION

Huntington's disease is a complex disease that has a progressive impact on an individual and his or her family over many years, and ultimately over generations. Because it is a genetic disease, the experiences of a single individual with HD—good or bad—are recounted over generations and have an impact on the attitude and behavior of family members for years to come. Positive interactions with knowledgeable first responders in a time of crisis and with authority figures in the clinic, courtroom, and community are therefore particularly critical. Increased awareness of the pharmacologic and nonpharmacologic strategies available to improve function and reduce symptoms in people with this disease can help to reduce the stigma that has afflicted affected families over many generations.

RESOURCES

* The Huntington's Disease Society of America provides support groups, social work professionals and "Centers of Excellence" around the country. All provide specialized education, support and care for people who are affected and their family members who may be at risk of the disease or who may themselves be caring for someone who has the disease (www.hdsa.org).
* The Huntington's Disease Youth Organization (HDYO) provides accurate and age-appropriate information and support for young people impacted by Huntington 's disease (www.hdyo.org).
* The Huntington Study Group (www.huntington-study-group.org) is a consortium of clinical research centers in the United States and around the world whose goal is to develop new treatments for HD.

REFERENCES

Almqvist, E.W., Brinkman, R. R., Wiggins, S., & Hayden, M. R. (2003). Psychological consequences and predictors of adverse events in the first 5 years after predictive testing for Huntington's disease. *Clinical Genetics, 64,* 300-309.

An, M. C., Zhang, N., Scott, G., Montoro, D., Wittkop, T., Mooney, S., ... & Ellerby, L. M. (2012). Genetic correction of Huntington's disease phenotypes in induced pluripotent stem cells. *Cell Stem Cell, 11*(2), 253-263.

Arran, N., Craufurd, D., & Simpson, J. (2014). Illness perceptions, coping styles and psychological distress in adults with Huntington's disease. *Psychology, Health & Medicine, 19,* 169-179.

Aubeeluck, A. V., Buchanan, H., & Stupple, E. J. (2012). 'All the burden on all the carers': exploring quality of life with family caregivers of Huntington's disease patients. *Quality of Life Research, 21*(8), 1425-1435.

Avila-Giron, R. (1973). Medical and social aspects of Huntington's chorea in the state of Zulia, Venezuela. *Adv Neurol, 1,* 261-266.

Aylward, E. H., Liu, D., Nopoulos, P. C., Ross, C. A., Pierson, R. K., Mills, J. A., ... & Coordinators of the Huntington Study Group. (2012). Striatal volume contributes to the prediction of onset of Huntington disease in incident cases. *Biological Psychiatry, 71*(9), 822-828.

Baliko, L., Csala, B., & Czopf, J. (2004). Suicide in Hungarian Huntington's disease patients. *Neuroepidemiology, 23*(5), 258-260.

Berridge, K.C., & Robinson, T.E., (1998). What is the role of dopamine in reward: Hedonic impact, reward learning, and or insensitive salience? *Research Reviews, 28,* 309-369.

Bertram, L., & Tanzi, R. E. (2005). The genetic epidemiology of neurodegenerative disease. *Journal of Clinical Investigation, 115*(6), 1449-1457.

Black, D.W., & Andreasen, N.C. (2011). *Introductory textbook of psychiatry (3rd. ed.).* Arlington, VA: American Psychiatric Publishing, Inc.

Booij, S. J., Engberts, D. P., Rödig, V., Tibben, A., & Roos, R. A. (2012). A plea for end-of-life discussions with patients suffering from Huntington's disease: the role of the physician. *Journal of Medical Ethics*, medethics-2011.

Boss, P. (2006). *Loss, trauma, and resilience: Therapeutic work with ambiguous loss.* New York: WW Norton & Co.

Brown, J., Hesse, M., Rosenbloom, M., Harris, B., Weaver, J., Wartnik, A., Concepcion, E., Mertz, C., Weinkauf, E., Oberoi, P., & Kolakowsky-Hayner, S. (2015). Confabulation in Correctional Settings: An Exploratory Review. *The Journal of Law Enforcement*, 4(3), 1-8.

Byars, J. A., Beglinger, L. J., Moser, D. J., Gonzalez-Alegre, P., & Nopoulos, P. (2012). Substance abuse may be a risk factor for earlier onset of Huntington disease. *Journal of Neurology*, 259(9), 1824-1831.

Calder, A. J., Keane, J., Young, A. W., Lawrence, A. D., Mason, S., & Barker, R. A. (2010). The relation between anger and different forms of disgust: implications for emotion recognition impairments in Huntington's disease. *Neuropsychologia*, 48(9), 2719-2729.

Chisholm, L.Z., Flavin, K.T., Paulsen, J.S. & Ready, R. (2013). Psychological well-being in persons affected by Huntington's disease: A comparison of at-risk, prodromal, and symptomatic groups.

Chu, E., Knight, C., O'Neill, M., & Purkayastha, D. D. (2014). H17 Huntington's Disease And Forensic Risk Factors In Females. *Journal of Neurology, Neurosurgery & Psychiatry*, 85(Suppl 1), A57-A57.

Cina, S. J., Smith, M. T., Collins, K. A., & Conradi, S. E. (1996). Dyadic deaths involving Huntington's disease: a case report. *The American Journal of Forensic Medicine and Pathology*, 17(1), 49-52.

Clément, S., Gargiulo, M., Feingold, J., & Durr, A. (2015). Guidelines for presymptomatic testing for Huntington's disease: Past, present and future in France. *Revue Neurologique*, 171, 572-580.

Corey-Bloom, J., Herndon, A., & Howell, S. (2015). Assessing psychiatric symptoms in individuals with, and at risk for, Huntington's disease (P5. 290). *Neurology*, 84(14 Supplement), P5-290.

Crozier, S., Robertson, N., & Dale, M. (2015). The Psychological Impact of Predictive Genetic Testing for Huntington' s Disease: A Systematic Review of the Literature. *Journal of Genetic Counseling*, 24(1), 29-39.

Cusin, C., Franco, F. B., Fernandez-Robles, C., DuBois, C. M., & Welch, C. A. (2013). Rapid improvement of depression and psychotic symptoms in Huntington's disease: A retrospective chart review of seven patients treated with electroconvulsive therapy. *General Hospital Psychiatry*, 35(6), 678-683.

Davenport, C.B., & Muncey, E.B. (1916). Huntington's chorea in relation to heredity and eugenics. *American Journal of Psychiatry*, 73, 195-222.

de Die-Smulders, C. E. M., De Wert, G. M. W. R., Liebaers, I., Tibben, A., & Evers Kiebooms, G. (2013). Reproductive options for prospective parents in families with Huntington's disease: clinical, psychological and ethical reflections. *Human Reproduction Update*, 19(3), 304-315.

Doria, J. G., de Souza, J. M., Andrade, J. N., Rodrigues, H. A., Guimaraes, I. M., Carvalho, T. G., ... & Ribeiro, F. M. (2015). The mGluR5 positive allosteric modulator, CDPPB, ameliorates pathology and phenotypic signs of a mouse model of Huntington's disease. *Neurobiology of Disease, 73*, 163-173.

Fedorowicz, J.G., Mills, J.A., Ruggle, A., langbehn, D., Paulsen, J.S. (2011). Suicidal behavior in prodromal Huntington's disease. *Neurodegenerative Diseases, 8*(6), 483-490.

Fenger, K. and Sørensen, S. A. (1986). A computerised register for Huntington's chorea in Denmark. *Clinical Genetics, 29*, 460-461.

Fisher, C. A., Sewell, K., Brown, A., & Churchyard, A. (2014). Aggression in Huntington's Disease: A Systematic Review of Rates of Aggression and Treatment Methods. *Journal of Huntington's Disease, 3,* 319-332.

Fonteijn, H. M., Modat, M., Clarkson, M. J., Barnes, J., Lehmann, M., Hobbs, N. Z., ... & Alexander, D. C. (2012). An event-based model for disease progression and its application in familial Alzheimer's disease and Huntington's disease. *NeuroImage, 60*(3), 1880-1889.

Freckelton, S. (2012). Expert evidence by mental health professionals: The communication challenge posed by evidence about autism spectrum disorder, brain injuries, and huntington's disease. *Internal Journal of Law and Psychiatry, 35,* 372-379.

Gudjonsson, G. H. (1992). *The psychology interrogations, confessions, and testimony.* Chichester: John Wiley.

Guo, Z., Rudow, G., Pletnikova, O., Codispoti, K. E., Orr, B. A., Crain, B. J., ... & Troncoso, J. C. (2012). Striatal neuronal loss correlates with clinical motor impairment in Huntington's disease. *Movement Disorders, 27*(11), 1379-1386.

Harper, P. S. (1992). The epidemiology of Huntington's disease. *Human Genetics, 89*(4), 365-376.

Hayden, M. (1981) *Huntington's chorea.* Springer-Verlag. Berlin.

Holmes, D. (2013). Serial groper is given a suspended prison term. *The Chronicle.* Retrieved from http://ezproxy.stthomas.edu/login?url=http://search.proquest.com/docview/1323333248?accountid=14756

Hoss, A. G., Labadorf, A., Latourelle, J. C., Kartha, V. K., Hadzi, T. C., Gusella, J. F., ...& Myers, R. H. (2015). miR-10b-5p expression in Huntington's disease brain relates to age of onset and the extent of striatal involvement. *BMC Medical Genomics, 8*(1), 10.

Hubers, A. A. M., Hamming, A., Giltay, E. J., von Faber, M., Roos, R. A. C., van der Mast, R. C., & van Duijn, E. (2014). J41 Suicidality in huntington's disease: A qualitative study on coping strategies and treatment options. *Journal of Neurology, Neurosurgery & Psychiatry, 85*(Suppl 1), A78-A79.

Hubers, A.A.M., Reedeker, N, Giltay, E.J., Roos, R.A.C., van Dujin, E., & Van der Mast, R.C. (2012). Suicidality in Huntington's disease. *Journal of Affective Disorders, 136*(3), 550-557.

Huntington's Disease Society of America (HDSA) (2013). *Talking With Kids About HD.* New York: HDSA Huntington's disease; new huntington's disease study findings reported from University of Iowa. (2012). *Biotech Week,* 731. Retrieved from http://ezproxy.stthomas.edu/login?url=http//search.proquest.com/docview/1081920745?accountid=14756

Jacobs, J. V., Boyd, J. T., Hogarth, P., & Horak, F. B. (2015). Domains and correlates of clinical balance impairment associated with Huntington's disease. *Gait & Posture, 41*(3), 867-870.

Jankovic, J., & Roos, R. A. (2014). Chorea associated with Huntington's disease: To treat or not to treat? *Movement Disorders, 29*(11), 1414-1418.

Jensen, P., Fenger, K., Bolwig, T. & Sorensoen, S. (1998). Crime in Huntington's disease: a study of registered offences among patients, relatives and controls. *Journal of Neurology, Neurosurgery, and Psychiatry, 65,* 467-471.

Kakoschke v Draper (2006). Queensland Supreme Court 386.

Kalkhoven, C., Sennef, C., Peeters, A., & Van Den Bos, R. (2014). Risk-taking and pathological gambling behavior in Huntington's disease. *Frontiers in Behavioral Neuroscience, 8,* 103.

Keenan, K. F., Miedzybrodzka, Z., & Eden, J. (2012). N05 Fostering, adoption and Huntington's disease: Improving clients' experience. *Journal of Neurology, Neurosurgery & Psychiatry, 83*(Suppl 1), A50-A50.

Klevens, J., Barnett, S. B. L., Florence, C., & Moore, D. (2015). Exploring policies for the reduction of child physical abuse and neglect. *Child abuse & neglect, 40,* 1-11.

Klodniski, P. (2004). *Loss and grief: Coping with the death of a loved one and with other losses related to Huntington Disease.* Canada: New Directions Publishing.

Kowalski, P. C., Belcher, D. C., Keltner, N. L., & Dowben, J. S. (2015). Huntington's Disease. *Perspectives in psychiatric care*, *51*, 157-161.

Larsson, M.U., Luszcz, M.A. Bui, T.H., & Wahlin, T.B. (2006). Depression and suicidal ideation after predictive testing for Huntington's disease: a two year follow-up study. *Journal of Genetic counseling*, *15*(5), 361-374.

Lawson, K, Wiggins, S., Green, T. Adam, S. Bloch, M., & Hayden, M.R. (1996). Adverse psychological events occurring in the first year after predictive testing for Huntington's disease. The Canadian Collaborative Study predictive testing. *Journal of Genetics and Medicine, 33*(10), 856-862.

Lee, J. M., Ramos, E. M., Lee, J. H., Gillis, T., Mysore, J. S., Hayden, M. R., ... & Ames, D. (2012). CAG repeat expansion in Huntington disease determines age at onset in a fully dominant fashion. *Neurology*, *78*(10), 690-695.

Licklederer, C., Wolff, G., & Barth, J. (2008). Mental health and quality of life after genetic testing for Huntington disease: A long term effect study in Germany. *American Journal of Medical Genetics. Part A, 146*, 2078-2085.

Lindholm, C. (2015). Parallel realities: The interactional management of confabulation in dementia care encounters. *Research on Language and Social Interaction, 48*(2), 176-199.

MacLeod, R., Tibben, A., Frontali, M., Evers-Kiebooms, G., Jones, A., Martinez Descales, A., & Roos, R. A. (2013). Recommendations for the predictive genetic test in Huntington's disease. *Clinical genetics, 83*(3), 221-231.

Mendez, M.F. (1994). Huntington's disease: update and review of neuropsychiatric aspects. *The International Journal of Psychiatry in Medicine, 24*(3), 189-208.

Moss, D. J. H., Poulter, M., Beck, J., Hehir, J., Polke, J. M., Campbell, T., ... & Tabrizi, S. J. (2014). C9orf72 expansions are the most common genetic cause of Huntington disease phenocopies. *Neurology, 82*(4), 292-299.

Nance, M., Paulsen, J.S., Rosenblatt, A., & Wheelock, V. (2011). *A physician's guide to the management of Huntington's Disease* (3rd ed.). United States: Huntington's Disease Society of America.

Oster, E., Shoulson, I., Quaid, K., & Dorsey, E. R. (2010). Genetic adverse selection: Evidence from long-term care insurance and Huntington disease. *Journal of Public Economics*, *94*(11), 1041-1050.

Physical activity could delay onset of Huntington's disease. (2008, Apr 01). *The Hindustan Times*. Retrieved from:http://ezproxy.stthomas.edu/login?url=http://search.proquest.com/docview/470318537?accountid=14756

Pringsheim T, K Wiltshire, L Day, J Dykeman, T Steeves, & N Jette, (2012). The incidence and prevalence of Huntington's disease: A systematic review and meta analysis. *Movement Disorders, 27,* 1083-1091.

Roos, R.A.,Vegter-van der Vlis, M., Hermans, J., Elshove, H. M., Moll, A.C., van de Kamp, J.J., & Bruyn, G.W. (1991). Age at onset in Huntington's disease: Effect of line of inheritance and patient's sex. *Journal of Medical Genetics. 28,* 515-519.

Røthing, M., Malterud, K., & Frich, J. C. (2014). Caregiver roles in families affected by Huntington's disease: a qualitative interview study. *Scandinavian Journal of Caring Sciences*, *28*(4), 700-705.

Rusz, J., Klempíř, J., Tykalová, T., Baborová, E., Čmejla, R., Růžička, E., & Roth, J. (2014). Characteristics and occurrence of speech impairment in Huntington's disease: possible influence of antipsychotic medication. *Journal of Neural Transmission, 121*(12), 1529-1539.

Schapira, A. H., Olanow, C. W., Greenamyre, J. T., & Bezard, E. (2014). Slowing of neurodegeneration in Parkinson's disease and Huntington's disease: future therapeutic perspectives. *The Lancet, 384*(9942), 545-555.

Schoenfeld, M., Myers, R.H., Cupples, L.A., Berkman, B., Sax, D.S., & Clark, E. (1984). Increased rates of suicide among patients with Huntington's Disease. *Journal of Neurology, Neurosurgery, and Psychiatry, 47*, 1283-1287.

Scott, J. (2002, Aug 24). Mom faces murder trial car shot disabled sons, ignited furor. *The Atlanta Journal - Constitution*. Retrieved from http://ezproxy.stthomas.edu/login?url=http://search.proquest.com/docview/336913604?accountid=14756

Seay, M., Giuliano, J., & Handley, O. (2012). M02 Enroll-HD: a prospective observational study in a global huntington's disease cohort. *Journal of Neurology, Neurosurgery & Psychiatry, 83*(Suppl 1), A46-A47.

Shanks, M. F., McGeown, W. J., Guerrini, C., & Venneri, A. (2014). Awareness and confabulation. *Neuropsychology, 28*(3), 406.

Shoulson I., Fahn, S. (1979). Huntington's disease: clinical care and evaluation. *Neurology, 29*, 1-3.

Simonin, C., Duru, C., Salleron, J., Hincker, P., Charles, P., Delval, A., ... & REGISTRY Study of the European Huntington's Disease Network. (2013). Association between caffeine intake and age at onset in Huntington's disease. *Neurobiology of Disease, 58*, 179-182.

Sitek, E. J., Thompson, J. C., Craufurd, D., & Snowden, J. S. (2014). Unawareness of deficits in huntington's disease. *Journal of Huntington's Disease, 3*(2), 125-135.

Smith, K. (2012, Jan 18). 16 years for man who killed his ill wife. *McClatchy - Tribune Business News* Retrieved from:http://ezproxy.stthomas.edu/login?url=http://search.proquest.com/docview/916491420?accountid=14756

Sorensen, S.A., & Fenger, K., (1992). Causes of death in patients with Huntington's disease and unaffected first degree relatives. *Journal of Medical Genetics, 29*(12), 911-914.

Sprengelmeyer, R., Orth, M., Müller, H. P., Wolf, R. C., Grön, G., Depping, M. S., ... & Landwehrmeyer, G. B. (2014). The neuroanatomy of subthreshold depressive symptoms in Huntington's disease: A combined diffusion tensor imaging (DTI) and voxel-based morphometry (VBM) study. *Psychological Medicine, 44*(09), 1867-1878.

Stine, O.C., Pleasant, N., Franz, M.L., Folstein, S.E. & Ross, C.A. (1993). Correlation between the onset age of Huntington's disease and length of the trinucleotide repeat in IT-15.*Human Molecular Genetics*. 2 (10): 1547-1549 doi:10.1093/hmg/2.10.1547

Tabrizi, S. J., Reilmann, R., Roos, R. A., Durr, A., Leavitt, B., Owen, G., ... & Langbehn, D. R. (2012). Potential endpoints for clinical trials in premanifest and early Huntington's disease in the TRACK-HD study: analysis of 24 month observational data. *The Lancet Neurology, 11*(1), 42-53.

The Genetic Information Nondiscrimination Act. Retrieved from http://www.ginahelp.org

Thompson, J. C., Harris, J., Sollom, A. C., Stopford, C. L., Howard, E., Snowden, J. S., & Craufurd, D. (2012). Longitudinal evaluation of neuropsychiatric symptoms in Huntington's disease. *The Journal of Neuropsychiatry and Clinical Neurosciences, 24*(1), 53-60.

Tsuang, D., Almqvist, E. W., Lipe, H., Strgar, F., DiGiacomo, L., Hoff, D., ... & Bird, T. D. (2014). Familial aggregation of psychotic symptoms in Huntington's disease. *American Journal of Psychiatry, 157*, 1955-1959. The Genetic Information Nondiscrimination Act. Retrieved from http://www.ginahelp.org

U.S. Food and Drug Administration (2015). Retrieved from http://www.fda.gov/RegulatoryInformation/Legislation/FederalFoodDrugandCosmeticActFDCAct/SignificantAmendmentstotheFDCAct/OrphanDrugA ct/default.htm

Valcárcel-Ocete, L., Alkorta-Aranburu, G., Iriondo, M., Fullaondo, A., García-Barcina, M., Fernández-García, J. M., ... & REGISTRY investigators of the European Huntington's Disease Network. (2015). Exploring Genetic Factors Involved in Huntington Disease Age of Onset: E2F2 as a New Potential Modifier Gene. *PloS one, 10*(7), e0131573.

van der Meer, L., & Vervoort, I. (2012). O04 Parents and children in families with Huntington's disease: Dutch professional's experiences. *Journal of Neurology, Neurosurgery & Psychiatry, 83*(Suppl 1), A51-A51.

Van Duijn, E., Reedeker, N., Giltay, E. J., Eindhoven, D., Roos, R. A., & Van Der Mast, R. C. (2014). Course of irritability, depression and apathy in Huntington's disease in relation to motor symptoms during a two-year follow-up period. *Neurodegenerative Diseases, 13*(1), 9-16.

Varshney, A., & Ehrlich, B. E. (2003). Intracellular Ca 2+ signaling and human disease: the hunt begins with Huntington's. *Neuron, 39*(2), 195-197.

Vittori, A., Breda, C., Repici, M., Orth, M., Roos, R. A., Outeiro, T. F., ... & REGISTRY investigators of the European Huntington's Disease Network. (2014). Copy-number variation of the neuronal glucose transporter gene SLC2A3 and age of onset in Huntington's disease. *Human Molecular Genetics, 23*(12), 3129-3137.

Wahlin, R., (2006). To know or not to know: A review of behavior and suicidal ideation in preclinical Huntington's disease. *Patient Education and Counseling, 65*(3), 279-286.

Wahlin, T. B. R., Bäckman, L., Lundin, A., Haegermark, A., Winblad, B., & Anvret, M. (2000). High suicidal ideation in persons testing for Huntington's disease. *Acta Neurologica Scandinavica, 102,* 150-161.

Walker, F.O. (2007) Huntington's disease, *Lancet 369,* 218-228.

Wetzel, H.H., Gehl, C.R., Delafave-Castillio, L., Schiffman, J.F., Shannon, K.M., & Paulsen, J.S. (2011). Suicidal ideation in huntington's disease: The role of co-morbidity. *Psychiatry Research, 188*(3), 372-376.

Wexler A. (2008). *The woman who walked into the sea. Huntington's and the making of a genetic disease.* Yale University Press.

Weydt, P., Soyal, S. M., Landwehrmeyer, G. B., & Patsch, W. (2014). A single nucleotide polymorphism in the coding region of PGC-1α is a male-specific modifier of Huntington disease age-at-onset in a large European cohort. *BMC Neurology, 14*(1), 1.

Williams, J. K., Driessnack, M., Barnette, J. J., Sparbel, K. J., Leserman, A., Thompson, S., & Paulsen, J. S. (2013). Strategies used by teens growing up in families with Huntington Disease. *Journal of Pediatric Nursing, 28*(5), 464-446.

Zarowitz B.J., O'Shea, T., Nance, M. (2014). Clinical, demographic, and pharmacologic features of nursing home residents with Huntington's disease. *J Am Med Dir Assoc., 6,* 423-428.

CHAPTER 10

ILLEGAL STREET DRUGS AND PRESCRIPTION MEDICATIONS IN THE CRIMINAL JUSTICE SYSTEM

MATTHEW D. KRASOWSKI

CHAPTER OVERVIEW

Drug abuse is a major public health and criminal justice issue. Drug-related offenses are very common reasons for incarceration, and drug abuse continues to be a serious challenge within correctional facilities. The last decade has seen two major drug abuse trends. The first trend is a dramatic rise in abuse of prescription medications, especially opioids such as hydrocodone, oxycodone, and fentanyl. Addiction to prescription opioids has led to a large increase in overdoses. The second trend is a proliferation of synthetic "designer" drugs related to either amphetamines or cannabis. This chapter will review (1) scheduling and regulation of drugs; (2) drug-of-abuse testing; (3) opiates and opioids; (4) stimulants, including cocaine, amphetamine, methamphetamine, and designer amphetamine-like drugs; (5) phencyclidine and ketamine; (6) sedative-hypnotics, including barbiturates, GHB, benzodiazepines; (7) muscle relaxants; (8) marijuana and synthetic cannabinoids; and (9) prescription drug abuse in the criminal justice system. The goals of this chapter are to provide a detailed overview of drugs of abuse and to highlight the impact within the criminal justice system.

INTRODUCTION

Drug abuse continues to be a major public health and criminal justice issue (Cartwright, 2008; Whiteford et al., 2013). Possession and distribution of drugs, along with activities associated with illicit drug synthesis, are very common reasons for incarceration. Drug abuse often co-occurs with mental illness, and some drugs may worsen mental health symptoms (Zweben, 2000). Within correctional facilities, drug abuse can be a major challenge.

The patterns of drug use vary regionally and temporally. "Designer drugs" such as the synthetic cannabinoids and cathinones may have rapidly fluctuating popularity (Albertson, Chenoweth, Colby, & Sutter,

2016; Baumann & Volkow, 2016; Nelson, Bryant, & Aks, 2014; Rech, Donahey, Cappiello Dziedzic, Oh, & Greenhalgh, 2014; Thornton & Baum, 2014), with some drugs only circulating on the streets for a short period of time before other drugs replace them. In addition, the last two decades have seen a steady increase in the diversion and misuse of prescription medications, particularly opioids and benzodiazepines, resulting in a dramatic rise in overdoses of these drugs (Dodrill, Helmer, & Kosten, 2011; Gilson & Kreis, 2009; Hernandez & Nelson, 2010; Ling, Mooney, & Hillhouse, 2011; Strassels, 2009). Methods of diversion include fraudulent prescriptions, thefts, and prescription drug trafficking networks. The decline in world markets for cocaine, heroin, and cannabis in the last 20 years is almost entirely offset by a rise in prescription opioid abuse. In correctional facilities, prescription medications uncommonly misused in the general public (e.g., bupropion and quetiapine) may be commonly abused medications (Hilliard, Barloon, Farley, Penn, & Koranek, 2013; Pilkinton & Pilkinton, 2014).

This chapter describes the common illegal street drugs and prescription medications that impact the criminal justice system. The generic, street, and trade names for drugs are listed in Tables 1-3, along with their common metabolites and urine test detection windows. This data is summarized from multiple sources ("Drug Enforcement Administration Drug Fact Sheets," 2014; Hammett-Stabler, Pesce, & Cannon, 2002; Melanson, 2012; Moeller, Lee, & Kissack, 2008; Tenore, 2010; Verstraete, 2004).

SCHEDULING OF DRUGS

The Controlled Substances Act enacted in 1970 placed drugs into five schedules, based on their potential for abuse and harm (Rocha, 2013; "Schedule of Controlled Substances," 2014). Within the United States, the Drug Enforcement Administration (DEA) and the Food and Drug Administration (FDA) regulate drugs. The scheduling of drugs influences ability for health providers such as physicians to prescribe medications. Drugs in Schedules I and II have tighter restrictions than those of Schedules III, IV, and V.

Schedule I drugs are those considered to have the highest abuse potential and no accepted medical use. Prescriptions for these drugs are not allowed, and legal use in humans is confined to highly restricted research studies. Drugs in Schedule I include heroin, methylenedioxymethamphetamine (MDMA, "ecstasy"), gamma-hydroxybutyrate (GHB), marijuana/tetrahydrocannabinol (THC), methaqualone, cathinone, and some hallucinogens (e.g., lysergic acid diethylamide, LSD). Recent additions to Schedule I include the synthetic cannabinoids (e.g., "K2/Spice") and designer amphetamine-like drugs (e.g., mephedrone, methylone, "bath salts"). The placement of marijuana in Schedule I is a controversial and evolving issue (Ammerman, 2014; Durkin, 2014). Current United States federal law has this drug in Schedule I, but some states have passed laws allowing for medical and/or recreational use.

Schedule II drugs have high abuse potential but can be legally prescribed in the United States. Prescriptions for Schedule II drugs typically require extra security measures such as triplicate forms, no automatic refills, and/or limitation on third parties picking up prescriptions. Drugs in Schedule II include amphetamine, methamphetamine, cocaine, methylphenidate, and many of the prescription opioids (e.g., fentanyl, hydromorphone, methadone, morphine, oxycodone, and oxymorphone). Hydrocodone combination products (e.g., hydrocodone mixed with acetaminophen) were originally in Schedule III but were moved into Schedule II in October 2014.

The remaining schedules are for drugs with lower abuse liability. Schedule III is an intermediate category that contains anabolic steroids (e.g., methyltestosterone, stanozolol), buprenorphine, ketamine, and dronabinol (synthetic drug containing a component found in marijuana). Schedule IV contains a number of sedative/hypnotics ("sleeping pills," tranquilizers, anxiolytics). These include benzodiazepines (e.g, alprazolam, clonazepam, diazepam, lorazepam), eszopiclone, phenobarbital, and zolpidem. In August 2014, the widely prescribed opiate tramadol was added to Schedule IV. Schedule V drugs are in the lowest category of abuse potential. Examples include cough suppressants with low doses of codeine and the chronic pain medication pregabalin.

"Designer" drugs of abuse present a difficult legal challenge, as these compounds initially are not listed as scheduled drugs (German, Fleckenstein, & Hanson, 2013; Gunderson, 2013; Gunderson, Kirkpatrick, Willing, & Holstege, 2013; Zawilska & Wojcieszak, 2013). Inventive drug chemists can make minor modifications to a wide range of chemical structures to create novel psychoactive compounds. This opens up almost unlimited possibilities. The amphetamine-like and synthetic cannabinoid drugs each have hundreds of compounds already synthesized but not abused, with thousands more theoretically possible. The Federal Analogue Act of 1986 was passed in an attempt to regulate compounds very close in chemical structure to existing drugs in Schedule I or II. This law is legally tricky to apply (Rocha, 2013). The DEA has the authority to temporarily schedule drugs pending a final decision to permanently schedule, a power which has been exercised for the designer amphetamine-like and synthetic cannabinoid drugs ("Schedule of Controlled Substances," 2014).

DRUG-OF-ABUSE TESTING

Laboratory testing for drugs of abuse plays an important role in the medical and criminal justice system (Melanson, 2012; Wyman, 2012). Rapid screening for drugs can be valuable in the acute management of patients who may be intoxicated. Testing may also be helpful in determining whether someone has been abstaining from drugs (e.g., as part of a condition for parole or in the context of a substance abuse treatment program). Health providers prescribing controlled substances may use drug-of-abuse testing as part of a medication contract with the patient. In that context, testing can verify that the patient is taking the prescribed medication (seeing that the expected drug tests are positive) and not using other drugs that are not prescribed (Ling et al., 2011). Drug testing is also used in competitive athletics and may include detailed testing for "performance-enhancing drugs" (e.g., anabolic steroids) along with commonly abused drugs such as cocaine, heroin, or marijuana (Thevis, Kuuranne, Geyer, & Schanzer, 2013).

The interpretation of drug-of-abuse testing can be complicated (Melanson, 2012; Tenore, 2010). Much of the challenge is with the limitations of screening tests, which can show false positives and false negatives, although confirmatory testing can also present interpretive difficulties (Johnson-Davis, Sadler, & Genzen, 2016). There are a number of technical issues that arise with drug-of-abuse testing. First, some classes of drugs (especially the benzodiazepines and opiates) contain many compounds with medical or criminal justice importance. Screening tests for these classes of drugs may not be able to detect all drugs within that class, leading to what may be perceived as false negatives. Second, some drugs have complicated metabolism which can make interpretation difficult. For instance, morphine is a common prescription drug, a component of poppy seeds, and also a metabolite (breakdown product) of codeine and heroin. Consequently, the detection of morphine may have multiple explanations. Third, some drugs require specialized detection methods and may not be tested for routinely. For example, fentanyl is a potent opioid drug that is given at low dose compared to most other opioids. The levels of fentanyl found in urine or blood are generally very low and beyond the ability of routine screening methods to detect.

There are a number of specimens that can be used for drug-of-abuse testing. Common specimens include urine, blood, saliva (oral fluid), and hair. Urine has traditionally been the most common specimen for drug-of-abuse analysis (Hammett-Stabler et al., 2002; Melanson, 2012; Moeller et al., 2008; Tenore, 2010). Drugs and their metabolites accumulate in urine, leading to a wider window of detection compared to blood. However, one downside to the use of urine is the challenge of collection. In trauma settings, especially those that involve injury to the pelvic region, collection of urine may be difficult. In addition, individuals may attempt to evade testing by a variety of methods such as substituting clean urine (or artificial urine) for their own specimen, adulterating their own urine using chemicals or water (sometimes adding yellow color with substances such as lemon juice or goldenseal tea), or drinking lots of fluids prior to collection to dilute out any drugs present. Some laboratories perform tests such as urine creatinine or urine specific gravity ("density") to detect adulteration of the specimen. Diluting specimens with water will lead to very low urine creatinine and specific gravity levels that are unlikely to be found in normal urine. More sophisticated analysis for adulteration will test for common adulterants such as bleach, glutaraldehyde, chromates, and nitrites (e.g., Klear®, Whizzies®). In forensic or workplace drug testing, specimens that are too dilute or that show other evidence of adulteration will be rejected.

To limit specimen tampering, collection of urine specimen may be directly observed. This reduces risk of adulteration or specimen substitution but is time-consuming for personnel, requiring availability of both male and female employees. Other measures that may be taken for urine collection include using a collection bathroom without a sink and with a colored dye in toilet water. Both of these measures reduce risk of diluting urine with water.

Blood is a possible specimen for drug-of-abuse testing (Verstraete, 2004). Use of blood avoids the specimen tampering issues that may be seen with urine. Blood is also the main alternative specimen for patients that cannot produce urine (e.g., due to kidney failure). The main downside of using blood is a more-limited time window of detection compared to urine. Drugs and their metabolites do not circulate in blood nearly as long as they may be present in urine. Therefore, drug exposure that may be detected in urine may be missed if testing only blood. Saliva (oral fluid) has emerged as a viable specimen type for drug-of-abuse testing (Allen, 2011; Bosker & Huestis, 2009; Verstraete, 2004). This specimen has appeal as an alternative to observed urine collections. The collection is not as simple as spitting in a collection cup, but is not very time-consuming. A special device is placed in the mouth for several minutes. This device absorbs the oral fluid and is then sent to the laboratory for analysis. Oral fluid testing methods have improved over the last decade and, for some drugs, are close to the detection in urine.

Hair is a specimen that can assess longer-term drug use (Kintz, Villain, & Cirimele, 2006). For many drugs, it is possible to detect prior exposure going back 60-90 days. Hair testing may be used in cases involving children to assess drug exposure that may be indicative of child abuse or neglect. In these types of cases, urine testing may not reveal the exposure to the child if there is a significant delay from the exposure to when the child comes to medical or law enforcement attention. There are different methods of hair analysis that can distinguish between environmental/passive exposure (e.g., child living in a house with a methamphetamine laboratory or with caregivers smoking cannabis) and systemic exposure such as ingestion or injection of drugs. These methods detect whether a drug has simply coated the hair (from environmental exposure) or incorporated in the hair shafts (from systemic exposure). The use of hair drug analysis has been expanding in the adult population, especially as a means to assess abstinence from drugs of abuse. It is important to keep in mind that hair analysis may not detect very recent use of drugs (drugs and drug metabolites often take at least several days or longer to be incorporated into the growing hair shaft). Also, the long-time window of hair drug analysis means that it can take several months for hair to become negative even after an individual has stopped using a drug.

Given the limitations of drug screening tests, confirmatory testing may be needed in some circumstances (Levine, 2003; Wyman, 2012). Confirmatory methods provide definitive identification of drugs and their metabolites. Currently, nearly all confirmatory methods use chromatography with mass spectrometry (MS). Common methods include gas chromatography/mass spectrometry (GC/MS) and liquid chromatography/tandem mass spectrometry (LC/MS/MS). GC/MS has traditionally been the "gold standard" for forensic drug analysis. When performed by a certified laboratory, GC/MS can provide drug identification with extremely high degree of certainty. However, LC/MS//MS is increasing in usage and also provides very accurate drug identification. Specialty toxicology reference laboratories can identify a very wide range of drugs, even including the designer drugs.

OPIATES AND OPIOIDS

The term *opiates* technically refers to compounds derived from the opium poppy plant (Karch, 2009). This includes compounds such as codeine and morphine that can be directly found in poppy seeds, but also other compounds such as heroin (diacetylmorphine), hydrocodone, and oxycodone that are synthetically derived from the natural opiates ("semi-synthetic" opiates). *Opioid* is a broader designation that includes opiates but also synthetic molecules structurally dissimilar to opiates (e.g., fentanyl, methadone, and meperidine).

The opioids interact with opioid receptors in the brain (Waldhoer, Bartlett, & Whistler, 2004). There are three main types of opioid receptors: mu (μ), kappa (κ), and delta (δ). Common effects of opioids include analgesia (pain relief), cough suppression, constipation, urinary retention, nausea, and respiratory depression. All three opioid receptors are involved in analgesia, although the mu receptor mediates many of the classic effects of opioids including respiratory depression. Many opiates, including morphine, activate all three opioid receptors. Some opiates, termed mixed agonist-antagonists, activate some opioid receptors but block (antagonize) others. An example is nalbuphine.

Chronic use of opioids can lead to dependence and tolerance (Gilson & Kreis, 2009; Hill, Rice, Connery, & Weiss, 2012; Ling et al., 2011). The withdrawal symptoms from stopping opioid use can be severe and may include anxiety, lacrimation (tears), rhinorrhea (runny nose), sweating, yawning, hot flashes, muscle cramps, and diarrhea. Opioid overdose is a medical emergency and often presents with a triad of pinpoint pupils (miosis), unconsciousness, and respiratory depression. The medication *naloxone* (Narcan®) is an antagonist ('blocker') of opioid effects and can be used in emergency situations to manage opioid overdose. When naloxone is used, there is a risk of precipitating withdrawal symptoms.

Morphine is the prototype opiate and is found in the opium poppy (Karch, 2009). Morphine is very effective for the relief of severe pain. Morphine is marketed under a range of generic and trade names (e.g., MS-Contin®, oramorph SR®, Kadian®, Roxanol®) and is a schedule II controlled substance. Morphine is not very well absorbed orally; consequently, morphine has been traditionally used almost exclusively by injection. However, within the last two decades, a variety of other morphine formulations have been approved and now include oral solutions, immediate- and sustained-release capsules and tablets, and rectal suppositories (Walsh, 2005). Those who abuse morphine tend to prefer injection because of the much more rapid and euphoric effects.

Because morphine is a natural constituent of poppy seeds (codeine is also, to a lesser degree), recent ingestion of food containing poppy seeds can cause positive urine opiate drug screens, especially at the lower 300 ng/mL opiate cutoff commonly used in medical settings. Workplace (employee) drug testing uses a higher opiate cutoff of 2,000 ng/mL; at this higher cut off, positive test results due to dietary poppy seeds are less likely (Lachenmeier, Sproll, & Musshoff, 2010).

Codeine is an opiate found in many products, including some over-the-counter medications. Most commonly, codeine is prescribed in combination products such as codeine/acetaminophen. Abusers of codeine tend to rapidly ingest the drug at high doses.

Heroin (diacetylmorphine) is the most rapidly acting of the opiates and is highly addictive (Karch, 2009). Heroin is produced by acetylation of morphine (derived from the opium poppy). Heroin is usually sold on the streets as a white or brown powder, or as a black sticky substance known as "black tar heroin." Heroin is typically injected or smoked. A trend seen over the last decade is the increasing prevalence of high purity heroin that may be snorted or smoked. Heroin produces very rapid euphoric effects, followed by a "twilight" state of sleep and wakefulness. Use of heroin carries high risk of addiction. Users rapidly develop tolerance to the drug and escalate to higher doses to achieve the same intensity. With the variable content of heroin sold on the streets, abusers may be unaware of the dose they are taking, resulting in risk of respiratory depression, convulsions, coma, and death. With the increasing abuse of prescription opiates (e.g., hydrocodone, oxycodone), heroin has seen a resurgence. In some locations, the street value of prescription opiates exceeds that of heroin, leading some abusers to choose the cheaper heroin. In addition to the risk of acute overdose, long-term heroin use has risk of infections (especially from repeated injections and sharing needles) and heart damage.

Hydrocodone is the most frequently prescribed opioid in the United States (Ling et al., 2011; Wightman, Perrone, Portelli, & Nelson, 2012). Until 2013, hydrocodone was only marketed in formulations mixed with other drugs such as acetaminophen (Lortab®, Vicodin®) or ibuprofen (Vicoprofen®). These combined formulations reduce the ability of users to crush pills and snort or inject them. However, a formulation of pure hydrocodone (Zohydro®) was approved in 2013 in the United States. Due to rising concerns about non-medical use of hydrocodone, the DEA moved hydrocodone combination products from Schedule III to II in October 2014 ("Schedule of Controlled Substances," 2014).

Hydromorphone (Dilaudid®) is an opiate that is several times more potent than morphine, but with a shorter duration of action (Ling et al., 2011; Wightman et al., 2012). In hospital settings, hydromorphone is commonly used to manage acute pain. Tablets of hydromorphone tend to be the most common form used. These may be crushed, dissolved, and injected, with similar effects to heroin.

Oxycodone is a semi-synthetic opiate that has greatly increased in popularity over the last 15 years (Ordonez, Gonzalez, & Espinosa, 2007). Originally marketed for severe cancer pain, oxycodone has shifted to much wider medical usage. Abuse of oxycodone has also become a significant public health problem (Gilson & Kreis, 2009; Ling et al., 2011; Strassels, 2009). Oxycodone tablets may be crushed and sniffed, dissolved in water and injected, or heated on foil and inhaled. Like hydrocodone, many prescriptions for oxycodone are for formulations combined with acetaminophen (e.g., Endocet®, Percocet®). Pure oxycodone products (e.g., OxyContin®, Roxicodone®) are preferred for abuse. When abused, the effects of oxycodone resemble those of heroin.

Oxymorphone is a potent Schedule II synthetic opiate with a pharmacology profile very similar to oxycodone (Chamberlin, Cottle, Neville, & Tan, 2007; Karch, 2009). In fact, oxymorphone is one of the metabolites produced by humans from oxycodone. Oxymorphone was first marketed the United States in 1959 as injectable and rectal suppository forms. Prescriptions for oxymorphone increased starting in 2006, with the approval of immediate- and extended-release oxymorphone tablets (Opana® and Opana ER®). By 2012, prescriptions for oxymorphone had increased over fourfold. Emergency department visits associated with adverse effects of oxymorphone more than doubled from 2010 to 2011, as estimated by the Drug-of-Abuse Warning Network (DAWN) (Ling et al., 2011; Young, Glover, & Havens, 2012). Like oxycodone, oxymorphone is used for the treatment of moderate to severe pain. Oxymorphone is slightly more potent than oxycodone, with oxymorphone doses generally being one-half that of oxycodone. Health professionals or abusers of oxymorphone that are unaware of the dosing differences can inadvertently run the risk of severe adverse effects by assuming that both drugs use the same dosing.

Methadone (Dolophile®, Methadose®) is a synthetic opioid traditionally used to manage opioid addiction as part of treatment programs (Bonhomme, Shim, Gooden, Tyus, & Rust, 2012). Methadone has a long duration of action and produces less of a "high," relative to the more commonly abused opioids. Methadone treatment programs are designed to provide methadone in a manner that limits cravings and reduces abuse of other opiates. There has been a major shift in methadone usage over the last 10 years, with increasing use of methadone in treating chronic pain, as opposed to managing opioid addiction. This has resulted in a nearly tenfold increase in methadone prescriptions in the last decade. Health and correctional facility employees sometimes underestimate the safety risk of methadone, believing it to be much safer than other opioids. While methadone is generally safe at prescribed dosages, methadone overdose is very dangerous (Corkery, Schifano, Ghodse, & Oyefeso, 2004). One-third of all opioid deaths involve methadone, even though methadone only represents approximately 5% of total opioid prescriptions. The main causes of death in methadone overdoses are cardiac arrhythmias and respiratory arrest.

Fentanyl (Dolophile®, Methadose®) is an extremely potent synthetic opioid (Karch, 2009). Prior to 2000, fentanyl was mainly used in the hospital setting for management of pain during surgery and other invasive procedures. The last 15 years has seen a shift from hospital use of fentanyl to outpatient use for chronic pain (Bonhomme et al., 2012; Gilson & Kreis, 2009; Ling et al., 2011; Rich & Webster, 2011; Wightman et al., 2012). Fentanyl has a short duration of action, and chronic use requires a means of continuous administration, such as that obtained by use of fentanyl transdermal (skin) patches. Fentanyl abuse takes two main forms. One is the misuse of fentanyl by those with access to the injectable forms. This may include health professionals such as anesthesiologists and nurses. The other common form of fentanyl abuse involves the transdermal patches which may be retrieved from the trash after the intended users discard them (Nelson & Schwaner, 2009). Even after several days of use, a significant amount of drug still remains in the gel inside the patch. Abusers of fentanyl may remove the gel contents and inject or ingest it, or use other means such as heating pads to promote faster release of drug from patches. Abuse of fentanyl carries a high risk of overdose, and addicts may die suddenly due to respiratory arrest. In the last 10 years, the United States has seen several outbreaks of street heroin laced with fentanyl. This caused hundreds of deaths in 2005–2007, with many deaths resulting from rapid overdose and respiratory arrest from the combination of the two opioid drugs (Centers for Disease Control and Prevention, 2008).

Buprenorphine is a synthetic opiate used for the treatment of pain and for managing opioid addiction (Bonhomme et al., 2012). Buprenorphine is a long acting (24-72 hours) opiate that produces much less respiratory depression at high doses, compared to other opioids such as morphine or fentanyl. This is because buprenorphine is an opioid "partial agonist" which does not produce the same maximal opioid effects as seen with "full agonists" like morphine. The relative safety of buprenorphine in overdose contrasts with the danger of overdose seen with methadone, another drug frequently used in the outpatient management of opioid addiction.

Buprenorphine was first marketed in the United States in 1985 as an injectable formulation for the management of pain (Buprenex®). Diversion and abuse of this injectable product occurred in the United States, Europe, and other parts of the world (Ling et al., 2011). In 2002, two sublingual buprenorphine products (Suboxone® and Subutex®) were approved in United States for the treatment of opioid addiction. Suboxone® is a combination product of buprenorphine and the opioid antagonist naloxone. When used as intended, the buprenorphine in Suboxone® is absorbed in the mouth while the naloxone is not (naloxone is only active if injected). However, if someone tries to inject Suboxone®, the naloxone will block the effect. Subutex® and a more recently approved transdermal buprenorphine product (Butrans®) contain buprenorphine without naloxone and are more highly targeted by addicts.

To more tightly manage prescriptions of buprenorphine, the Narcotic Addict Treatment Act was amended in 2001 and again in 2006 to allow qualified physicians with special certification to prescribe certain scheduled drugs for the treatment of narcotic addiction (Bonhomme et al., 2012). Currently, certified physicians can treat up to 100 patients outside of the context of a clinic-based narcotic treatment program. Buprenorphine was originally Schedule V when approved in 1985, but has since been moved to Schedule III. Despite the restrictions on buprenorphine prescribing, non-medical use of buprenorphine has increased in the last decade (Bonhomme et al., 2012; Ling et al., 2011; Rich & Webster, 2011). Emergency department visits related to nonmedical use of buprenorphine increased nearly fivefold from 2006 to 2011. For abuse, the most desired formulations are those without naloxone. Some addicts use buprenorphine intranasally as a heroin substitute. The rising use of buprenorphine for chronic pain has greatly increased the number of prescriptions and thus the potential for diversion.

Tramadol is an opiate-like analgesic drug that was approved in the United States in 1995 (Ultram®) (Nossaman, Ramadhyani, Kadowitz, & Nossaman, 2010). Soon after approval, there were reports related to diversion and abuse of tramadol (Gilson & Kreis, 2009; Hill et al., 2012; Ling et al., 2011; Rich & Webster, 2011). Tramadol was originally not scheduled but was placed into Schedule IV in August 2014 ("Schedule of Controlled Substances," 2014). DAWN estimated 20,000 emergency department visits related to nonmedical use of tramadol in the United States in 2011. Abusers of tramadol often take the drug at much higher dose than intended. At these high doses, the effects of tramadol resemble those of other opioid analgesics such as morphine or oxycodone. However, high doses of tramadol, especially in combination with certain antidepressants, have been associated with a "serotonin syndrome" consisting of hyperthermia (very high body temperature), convulsions, pain, and muscle rigidity (Nelson & Philbrick, 2012). This syndrome can result because tramadol blocks an enzyme (monoamine oxidase, MAO) that the body uses to break down the neurotransmitter serotonin. When tramadol is combined with other drugs (especially antidepressants such as the selective serotonin reuptake inhibitors [e.g., fluoxetine, paroxetine]), the total interference with serotonin breakdown can lead to dangerously high levels of serotonin.

Meperidine (Demerol®) is an opioid analgesic first introduced in the 1930s (Karch, 2009). Meperidine has effects that are similar to morphine but with a shorter duration of action and less antitussive (cough suppressant) effect. Prescriptions of meperidine declined in the United States, as other short-acting opioids (e.g., fentanyl, hydrocodone, and hydromorphone) increased in usage. In the hospital setting, meperidine used to be a very common drug sought out by opioid addicts. The adverse effects of meperidine resemble that of other opioids. In addition, similar to tramadol, meperidine has been associated with a serotonin syndrome, especially when used at high dose and in combination with antidepressants that affect serotonin (Gillman, 2005).

Nalbuphine (Nubain®) is a synthetic opiate that has considerably less abuse potential than other opiates (Anderson, 2011). Nalbuphine is in a class of opiates referred to as mixed agonist-antagonists. Nalbuphine blocks the mu opioid receptor but activates the kappa receptor. Nalbuphine was originally placed in Schedule II but, following petitioning by the manufacturer, was removed from the list of controlled substances. Nalbuphine is approved for use in the United States as an injectable formulation. Nalbuphine is generally not attractive as a drug-of-abuse. The antagonist effects of nalbuphine at the mu opioid receptor will block the effects of other opiates such as heroin and oxycodone, and may even precipitate withdrawal symptoms in a chronic user of other opiates. Nalbuphine is rarely encountered by law enforcement personnel.

Dextromethorphan (DXM) is a cough suppressant found in over 100 over-the-counter medications, either alone or in combination with other drugs such as analgesics (e.g., acetaminophen), antihistamines (e.g., chlorpheniramine), or expectorants (e.g., guaifenesin) (Burns & Boyer, 2013). The typical adult dose is in the range of 45-120 mg per day. When used as directed, DXM has low risk of side effects. Abusers of DXM take the drug at very high dose in a single ingestion, consuming up to 1500 mg or more (Burns & Boyer, 2013; Romanelli & Smith, 2009; Schwartz, 2005). This type of illicit use of DXM is known as "Robotripping" (after Robitussin®), "dexing," or "skittling." DXM abuse traditionally entailed consuming large volumes of the over-the-counter liquid cough suppressant preparations. However, abuse of gel capsule and tablet preparations has increased over the last 5 years. DXM powder is also sold illegally over the Internet and poses risks due to variable dose and composition. DXM may also be mixed with other drugs such as MDMA or methamphetamine. DXM abuse is most common in teenagers and young adults.

At high dose, DXM can produce psychoactive effects that include agitation, confusion, inappropriate laughter, paranoia, and hallucinations. Depending on the dose, DXM intoxication can resemble that of MDMA, ketamine, or PCP. Deaths have been reported when DXM was abused in combination with ethanol or other central nervous system depressants. The other risk of abusing high-dose DXM is toxicity from other drugs contained in combination DXM products (Monte, Chuang, & Bodmer, 2010; Romanelli & Smith, 2009;

Schwartz, 2005). Acetaminophen overdose can cause liver damage. High doses of chlorpheniramine and guaifenesin can themselves affect the heart and brain. A variety of Internet sources publish methods to extract DXM from the other drugs and cough syrups. DXM is currently not scheduled.

Detection of opioids by drug testing is complicated by the large number of drugs and variable detection by assays (Krasowski et al., 2009; Moeller et al., 2008). Standard opiate urine screens readily detect codeine, morphine, hydrocodone, hydromorphone, and 6-acetylmorphine (diagnostic of heroin). However, opiate screens often miss oxycodone, oxymorphone, buprenorphine, and tramadol, even though these are technically opiates. Synthetic opioids such as fentanyl, meperidine, and methadone are also not detected. Consequently, there are now separate screening tests available for oxycodone/oxymorphone, buprenorphine, tramadol, meperidine, and methadone. When interpreting drug-of-abuse screening results, it is important to look carefully to see which drugs were tested for and which were not. Confirmatory testing by mass spectrometry can detect all of the opioids.

STIMULANTS

COCAINE

Cocaine is a stimulant drug that targets the norepinephrine (noradrenaline) and dopamine systems (Karch, 2009). Increasing norepinephrine levels in the body increases blood pressure and heart rate. Cocaine is a Schedule II drug that has limited clinical use as a local anesthetic in specialized ear-nose-throat surgeries. "Crack" cocaine is cocaine hydrochloride mixed with bicarbonate and water and boiled. The cocaine base precipitates out and forms pellets and rocks when cooled.

The most common routes of cocaine abuse are snorting (insufflation), smoking, and intravenous administration (Karila, Petit, Lowenstein, & Reynaud, 2012). Intravenous use of cocaine generally achieves the highest blood levels and also carries the highest risk of death. Long-term complications result from needle use, including risk of infections and heart damage. In 2003, cocaine was the most frequent cause of death due to drug abuse; however, cocaine has since been surpassed by the prescription opioids in this regard (Hernandez & Nelson, 2010; Ling et al., 2011; Strassels, 2009).

In the transport of cocaine, individuals may conceal it in body cavities (e.g., rectum or vagina) or swallow packets of cocaine to be retrieved after defecation (Mandava et al., 2011). This practice is called body packing or stuffing. There is very high risk of death if packets of cocaine rupture prior to retrieval. Law enforcement should be aware of this risk when identifying individuals suspected of transporting illicit drugs, especially when the individual is showing signs of gastrointestinal discomfort. There are reports of medical therapy (e.g., administration of laxatives) inadvertently causing rupture of packets in body packers (Karch, 2009).

Cocaine blood concentrations do not correlate well with intoxication. Chronic addicts can build up significant tolerance to cocaine, but then may die from a variety of causes. Many cocaine-related deaths are likely misclassified due to lack of recognition of the chronic health effects of cocaine. Autopsy of individuals who die from cocaine use often show hearts that are enlarged and fibrotic. A history of cocaine use in conjunction with typical heart pathology is strong evidence of a cocaine-related death.

A variety of physical signs may be clues to cocaine use (Karch, 2009). Chronic inhalation of cocaine through the nose can cause perforation of the nasal septum (tissue that divides the two nostrils). Users of crack cocaine may show evidence of burn trauma to their fingers and nails (e.g., "parrot-beak" nails, "crack thumb") or lips. Stigma of needle injection sites may also be visible on the skin.

A controversial topic with cocaine is a phenomenon known as "excited delirium"—a combination of hyperthermia (high body temperature) and delirium with agitation (Karch, 2009). Users may present with paranoid and psychotic symptoms, and what may be described as "superhuman" strength. In some cities, medical examiners estimate that excited delirium accounts for up to 10% of cocaine-related deaths. The cause of death can be a source of litigation when individuals die in police custody or a hospital setting (Vilke, Bozeman, Dawes, Demers, & Wilson, 2012).

Detection of cocaine is relatively straightforward. All urine screening methods on the market target one of the main metabolites of cocaine: benzoylecgonine (Hammett-Stabler et al., 2002; Verstraete, 2004). Cocaine itself is metabolized very quickly. Cocaine is not structurally similar to other drugs that are commonly encountered; thus, false positives with drug testing are uncommon. Other drugs with the "-caine" ending (e.g., lidocaine, procaine, bupivacaine, etc.) do not cross-react with cocaine screens, despite a similar name. The main challenge of cocaine detection is that the drug and its metabolites may not stay in the system for more than 1-2 days, unless there is very heavy use. One research study looked at whether passive exposure to crack cocaine vapor can cause positive cocaine testing. This study did not find evidence that this can occur; in fact, most of the research subjects exposed passively to cocaine vapor had undetectable amounts of cocaine metabolites in their urine (Cone, Yousefnejad, Hillsgrove, Holicky, & Darwin, 1995).

AMPHETAMINE AND METHAMPHETAMINE

Amphetamines are a class of compounds that share a common chemical structure (Karch, 2009). Similar to cocaine, amphetamines affect the norepinephrine and dopamine systems. Ephedrine and pseudoephedrine are chemically close to the amphetamines and share some similar effects.

Methamphetamine (technically d-methamphetamine) is a Schedule II drug (Vearrier, Greenberg, Miller, Okaneku, & Haggerty, 2012). It has narrow medical use limited to treatment of obesity and Attention-Deficit hyperactivity disorder (ADHD). Methamphetamine was originally used in nasal ingestions (e.g., Desoxyn®) and bronchial inhalers; the less-active levo or l-isomer of methamphetamine is still used in some over-the-counter products (e.g., Vicks® Nasal Inhaler).

Methamphetamine is a highly addictive drug with strong central nervous system stimulant properties (Karch, 2009; Vearrier et al., 2012). Methamphetamine was widely abused in the 1960s, with a reduction in abuse in the 1970s. It was placed as a controlled substance in 1971, and the injectable formulation (which had been highly abused) was removed from the market. Methamphetamine has seen a resurgence of abuse from the 1980s to the present. In some areas, methamphetamine abuse has outpaced that of heroin and cocaine, with ready availability of the drug fueled by large and small clandestine laboratories. Methamphetamine is abused for stimulants and euphoric effects. The drug may be taken orally, snorted, smoked, or injected. Smoking or injecting methamphetamine results in intense euphoria and is often associated with binge use.

Methamphetamine synthesis can be done even in small scale settings such as homes, farm buildings, or mobile vans (Vearrier et al., 2012). Multiple nonprescription products, including pseudoephedrine, ephedrine, and phenylpropanolamine, can be used as a precursor material for the manufacture of methamphetamine. This has led to a proliferation of "meth labs" in rural settings that can escape the attention of law enforcement. Methamphetamine production is a highly explosive process that can release toxic chemicals such as hydrochloric acid, phosphine, and vaporized methamphetamine. Various flammable chemicals may be used in methamphetamine synthesis, including acetone, ammonia, Coleman® fuel, diethyl ether, mineral spirits, and toluene. Fires and explosions in methamphetamine labs are common and can result in severe burn injuries. In a survey of Midwest regional burn centers, 10% of burn patients tested positive for methamphetamine (Burke et al., 2008). Methamphetamine users tended to have more severe burns, greater inhalation trauma, and more associated non-thermal injuries.

In an attempt to limit production of methamphetamine, the Combat Methamphetamine Epidemic Act was passed in 2005 (Karch, 2009; Vearrier et al., 2012). This law required retailers of nonprescription products containing pseudoephedrine, ephedrine, and phenylpropanolamine to place these products behind the counter or in a locked cabinet. Consumers must show identification, and a registry is kept of purchasers of these products. Law enforcement has also restricted other precursors of methamphetamine such as phenyl-2-propanone.

Amphetamine (d-amphetamine) has similar pharmacologic properties to methamphetamine but has much wider therapeutic use (Karch, 2009). Amphetamine is commonly used in the treatment of ADHD (e.g., Adderall® and Vyvanse®) and also for some other disorders such as narcolepsy. Consequently, there is a wide availability of prescription amphetamine that can be diverted for illicit usage. The common use of amphetamine to treat ADHD in elementary, junior high, and high school students requires schools to be vigilant to the possibility that medication may be stolen for non-medical use.

In terms of drug testing, amphetamine and methamphetamine are usually detected well by standard amphetamine drug-of-abuse screens (Melanson, 2012; Moeller et al., 2008). As discussed below, these screens may also detect other amphetamines such as MDMA. Confirmatory testing is needed to distinguish between the presence of amphetamine and methamphetamine. Because amphetamine is a metabolite of methamphetamine, both compounds are often detected in urine of methamphetamine users.

THE "DESIGNER" AMPHETAMINE AND AMPHETAMINE-LIKE DRUGS

In addition to amphetamine and methamphetamine, there is a wide array of other amphetamine-like drugs (Christophersen, 2000; Cottencin, Rolland, & Karila, 2013; German et al., 2013; Gunderson et al., 2013; Zawilska & Wojcieszak, 2013). MDMA (ecstasy) is a drug closely related to methamphetamine, but with strong hallucinogenic properties (Meyer, 2013). MDMA has a reputation as a "party drug"—popular at clubs and rave parties. MDMA use is associated with euphoria, energizing effects, distortions in time and perception, and enhanced enjoyment of tactile and sexual experiences. MDMA may be abused with other drugs. An example is "candy flipping," which is abuse of LSD and MDMA together. Medical management of suspected MDMA use may be complicated by the misleading sale of reported MDMA tablets that actually contain other drugs such as DXM, methamphetamine, ketamine, and ephedrine. One unusual adverse effect that may be seen with MDMA use is severe hyperthermia (with body temperature exceeding 104°F, 40°C) and dehydration. This presents as a medical emergency and requires rapid cooling and supportive hydration of the user.

There are a variety of other "designer" amphetamine-like drugs that have circulated as street drugs from time to time (Christophersen, 2000; Cottencin et al., 2013; German et al., 2013; Gunderson et al., 2013; Zawilska & Wojcieszak, 2013). Many of these are sold with misleading names like "bath salts," which gained a lot of popular and media attention starting around 2010. This broad class of amphetamine-like drugs is actually not new, with some having been first synthesized as early as the 1930s. Alexander Shulgin popularized amphetamine-like drugs in two books: PiHKAL (Phenethylamines I Have Known and Loved) (Shulgin & Shulgin, 1991) and TiHKAL (Tryptamines I Have Known and Loved) (Shulgin & Shulgin, 1997), in which he and his wife describe both the chemical synthesis and pharmacologic effects (assumed to be from testing the compounds on themselves) for hundreds of amphetamine-like drugs. A comprehensive description of the amphetamine-like drugs is beyond the scope of this chapter, but some of the more common examples will be described below.

The amphetamine-like compounds that became popularized by the misleading name "bath salts" are mostly a group of drugs related to cathinone (Capriola, 2013; Coppola & Mondola, 2012; Cottencin et al., 2013; German et al., 2013; Gunderson et al., 2013; Rech et al., 2014; Thornton & Baum, 2014; Zawilska & Wojcieszak, 2013). Cathinone is a compound found in khat (qat), a green leafy plant cultivated throughout Eastern Africa (especially Ethiopia and Somalia) and Yemen. Khat is typically chewed in social sessions that may last up to 12 hours. Khat use began to be seen in the United States following increased immigration from Eastern Africa and Yemen. Cathinone and khat became Schedule I controlled substances in United States in 1993. Methcathinone, a derivative of cathinone, has even more powerful psychoactive effects and is also Schedule I.

Three of the most common "bath salts" are mephedrone, methylenedioxypyrovalerone (MDPV), and methylone (German et al., 2013; Gunderson et al., 2013). These three drugs were placed under an emergency DEA order in Schedule I in 2011 ("Schedule of Controlled Substances," 2014). Understanding the clinical effects and toxicity of these amphetamine-like drugs is complicated by lack of systematic study. The illicit drugs distributed as "bath salts" have varied composition and may not get analyzed by laboratories possessing the analytical techniques to resolve all the compounds present. Snorting and swallowing are the most common routes of administration for the "bath salts." Hallucinations and panic attacks have been reported in users of these drugs. MDPV and mephedrone can produce psychosis, confusion, and rapid heart rate. Similar to MDMA, overdoses have been associated with very high body temperature, resulting in some deaths.

Detection of amphetamine-like drugs can be difficult, but MDMA is detected by some amphetamine drug screens. The cathinones and other designer amphetamines are missed by most amphetamines screens (Petrie et al., 2013). Specialized forensic toxicology laboratories have developed tests using mass spectrometry that can detect designer amphetamines.

PHENCYCLIDINE AND KETAMINE

Phencyclidine (PCP, "Angel dust") is a Schedule I stimulant drug whose use has shown substantial variation across the last several decades (Karch, 2009). The 1980s had the highest overall use of PCP, but the drug faded significantly in the 1990s. However, the drug has more recently shown resurgence in the club-drug scene. PCP is relatively easy to manufacture and may be mixed in with other drugs. PCP is pharmacologically related to the general anesthetic ketamine (discussed below) and can produce powerful hallucinations, euphoria, paranoia, and depersonalization. Classically, PCP is often associated with aggressive behavior, with reports of users having "superhuman strength" and sometimes causing severe injury to themselves or others without being aware of what they are doing. Such reports have been popularized by the media and may overestimate how frequently PCP induces such behavior. Nevertheless, medical and law enforcement personnel can be at personal risk when users are in an agitated and aggressive state. It is important to note that aggressiveness may be caused by other drugs of abuse, especially cocaine, amphetamines and amphetamine-like drugs. There are urine drug-of-abuse screening assays for PCP, although not all drug-of-abuse panels include testing for PCP, especially if PCP use is uncommon in the local region.

Ketamine (Ketolar®, "Special K") is a Schedule III drug used medically as a general anesthetic (Corazza, Assi, & Schifano, 2013; Morgan & Curran, 2012). Ketamine produces "dissociative anesthesia," an unusual state in which the patient may have open eyes yet be unconscious to the surroundings. Ketamine has limited effects on respiration and the cardiac system, making it a useful anesthetic in settings where depressing respiration function is not desirable (e.g., treating a broken bone or a separated joint in a remote setting such as a rock-climbing fall). Ketamine can produce hallucinations and powerful distortions of perception. Prior to 2000, ketamine was rarely encountered outside of the medical setting, but the drug began to be popular for its hallucinatory effects in the club-drug scene. Ketamine is also used in veterinary medicine, and users may divert the drug from veterinary sources for abuse. Ketamine is not detected by standard drug abuse screens. Specialized testing, typically by mass spectrometry, is needed for detection.

SEDATIVE-HYPNOTICS

BARBITURATES

The barbiturates were the dominant sedative-hypnotic medications for several decades starting in the 1950s and were heavily prescribed and misused as "sleeping pills" (Karch, 2009). Barbiturates have found other clinical uses, such as treatment of seizures (phenobarbital), anesthesia (pentobarbital, thiopental), and headaches (butalbital, now found mainly in headache preparations such as Fiorinol®). While clinically effective, a major downside to barbiturates is their danger in overdose, which is magnified when used together with other central nervous system depressants such as ethanol. Historically, many high-profile celebrity deaths (e.g., Marilyn Monroe, Elvis Presley, Abbie Hoffman) have been attributed at least in part to barbiturate overdose. Unlike opioids and benzodiazepines, there is no specific antidote to the barbiturates. Management of overdose is thus supportive and consists of supporting the respiratory and cardiac systems until the effects of the drug wear off.

Abusers of barbiturates tend to prefer short-acting and intermediate acting barbiturates, namely *amobarbital* (Amytal®), *pentobarbital* (Nembutal®), and *secobarbital* (Seconal®). Depending on abuse liability, the barbiturates are found in Schedule II (amobarbital, pentobarbital), III (butalbital), or IV (*phenobarbital*, Luminal®) in the United States ("Schedule of Controlled Substances," 2014). Occasionally, found in combination products such as Fiorinol®, barbiturates are used to offset the withdrawal effects of stimulants such as cocaine and the amphetamines.

There are urine drug-of-abuse screening assays for barbiturates, although not all drug-of-abuse panels still include testing for barbiturates. Many laboratories have discontinued routine testing barbiturates, as this class of drugs becomes less common in terms of non-medical use.

GHB

Gamma-hydroxybutyrate (GHB) is a drug that has gained notoriety as a "date rape" drug (Schep, Knudsen, Slaughter, Vale, & Megarbane, 2012). GHB was originally investigated as an anesthetic but was never marketed in the United States for that purpose. GHB is sold illicitly for a variety of deceptive claims, including as a supplement for bodybuilding, weight loss, insomnia, and reversal of baldness. Two analogs of GHB, gamma-butyrolactone (GBL) and 1,4-butanediol (BD), are available legally as industrial solvents that are sometimes sold to potential abusers with misleading names such as "ink stain remover" or "nail enamel remover." GBL and BD are rapidly converted to GHB in the body after ingestion.

GHB, GBL, and BD are abused for their euphoric or calming effects. All three substances can be slipped into beverages with minimal change in taste. This can make users vulnerable to sexual assault or other criminal acts. The combination of GHB and ethanol or other central nervous system depressants can lead to life-threatening adverse effects. GHB can also unpredictably cause visual hallucinations and, occasionally, aggressive behavior. Overdose of GHB rapidly causes unconsciousness, respiratory depression, and slowed heart rate. There is currently no antidote for GHB intoxication. GHB itself is regulated as a Schedule I controlled substance; however, a specialized GHB pharmaceutical product (Xyrem®) is Schedule III and used primarily for the treatment of narcolepsy.

GHB is often considered in the criminal investigation of alleged sexual assault facilitated by drug intoxication (Hall & Moore, 2008). Other drugs commonly implicated in drug-facilitated sexual assault are ethanol and the benzodiazepine flunitrazepam (Rohypnol®). GHB is difficult to detect by laboratory analysis and is missed by routine drug screens. In addition, GHB is rapidly cleared from the body and is often undetectable by 24 hours after use.

BENZODIAZEPINES AND RELATED DRUGS

The benzodiazepines, in essence, replaced the barbiturates as the dominant sedative, sleeping pill, and anxiety-reducing medications (O'Brien, 2005). In the United States, *diazepam* (Valium®) was the overall most-prescribed drug for much of the 1970s and 80s. Since then, use of diazepam has declined, while other benzodiazepines such as *alprazolam* (Xanax®), *clonazepam* (Klonopin®), and *lorazepam* (Ativan®) have increased. Other commonly prescribed benzodiazepines include *chlordiazepoxide* (Librium®), *oxazepam* (Serax®), and *temazepam* (Restoril®). The benzodiazepines have a wide range of clinical applications, including sedation, management of seizures, muscle relaxation, treatment of withdrawal symptoms from other drugs, and management of anxiety. Benzodiazepines may be abused for their euphoric effects or to relieve the withdrawal symptoms associated with the use of other drugs such as cocaine (Jones, Mogali, & Comer, 2012; O'Brien, 2005). Unlike the barbiturates, there is a specific antagonist for benzodiazepines—flumazenil, Romazicon®—that may be used in managing overdoses.

Drug-of-abuse screening panels commonly include tests for benzodiazepines, but a limitation of the screens is that they may not detect all of the clinically important benzodiazepines (Krasowski et al., 2009), including designer benzodiazepines such as flubromazolam that have recently appeared on the illicit drug scene (Lukasik-Glebocka et al., 2016). Detection of diazepam, chlordiazepoxide, temazepam, and oxazepam tends to be very good. On the other hand, currently marketed assays may not have good sensitivity for alprazolam, clonazepam, and/or lorazepam. Confirmatory testing may be needed for detection of the benzodiazepines.

There are also other drugs that are similar to benzodiazepines in pharmacologic action, but which are technically not *benzodiazepines* (Zammit, 2009). The two most common current examples are *zolpidem* (Ambien®) and *eszopiclone* (Lunesta®), both of which are mainly used as sleeping pills. These drugs tend to be safer than benzodiazepines. Zolpidem and eszopiclone will not be detected by standard benzodiazepines screens.

Flunitrazepam (Rohypnol®) is a benzodiazepine that has gained specific notoriety for its use in drug-facilitated sexual assault (Hall & Moore, 2008; Parkin & Brailsford, 2009). Flunitrazepam is a Schedule IV controlled substance, but has never been approved for medical use in the United States. However, in many other countries, flunitrazepam is widely used as a sedative-hypnotic. Prior to 1997, Rohypnol® was manufactured as a small white tablet which, when mixed into drinks, dissolved easily without changing the color or taste and could render the victim physically and psychologically incapacitated. After 1997, the manufacturer responded to concerns about the use of the drug in sexual assault and changed Rohypnol® into an oblong green tablet with a blue core. When dissolved into drinks, these tablets would dye the drink blue. However, generic or illicit forms of the drug may not have the blue dye.

Flunitrazepam can be detected by urine benzodiazepine drug screens and confirmatory testing. Flunitrazepam has a half-life in the body of 18-24 hours and may be detectable in urine for up to several days after ingestion. Testing for flunitrazepam may be performed in the workup of suspected drug-facilitated sexual assault, often together with testing for other drugs such as ethanol and GHB. Even though flunitrazepam is categorized as a Schedule IV substance, penalties for possession, trafficking, and distribution involving one gram or more of flunitrazepam are the same as those of a Schedule I drug ("Schedule of Controlled Substances," 2014).

MUSCLE RELAXANTS AND ANTIEPILEPTIC DRUGS

Carisoprodol (Soma®) is a prescription drug marketed since the 1950s (Reeves & Burke, 2010; Reeves, Burke, & Kose, 2012). It is primarily used as a muscle relaxant for the relief of painful musculoskeletal conditions and is regulated as a Schedule IV drug in the United States. Carisoprodol is formulated both as single-drug tablets and also as combination tablets with other drugs such as aspirin and codeine. Carisoprodol has a rapid onset of action, and the effects last 4 to 6 hours. It is metabolized to meprobamate, which is also a prescription drug (discussed below). Overuse of carisoprodol can lead to central nervous system depressant effects, cardiac instability, and gastrointestinal effects. Severe overdose can result in coma, shock, respiratory arrest, and death. Carisoprodol abuse has increased significantly in the United States in the last decade, with an estimated 3.6 million people using this drug for nonmedical purposes in their lifetime. Chronic abuse of carisoprodol can lead to tolerance, dependence, and withdrawal symptoms. Health providers and law enforcement personnel should be aware that carisprodol is a frequently diverted and abused prescription medication.

Meprobamate (Miltown®, Equanil®) is a prescription drug marketed in the United States since the 1950s (Reeves & Burke, 2010; Reeves et al., 2012). Meprobamate was heavily used as a tranquilizer in the 1950s and '60s and accounted for one-third of all prescriptions in the United States in 1957. It is now primarily used to treat anxiety, tension, and muscle spasms. As mentioned above, meprobamate is a metabolite of carisoprodol. Excessive use of meprobamate can result in physical and psychological dependence. Meprobamate prescriptions have decreased over the years, as safer drugs such as the benzodiazepines entered clinical use. Similar to carisoprodol, meprobamate can cause serious adverse effects in overdose.

There are also other prescription medications that are less-commonly abused. *Pregabalin* (Lyrica®) is a medication used primarily for the management of chronic pain and less commonly for the management of epilepsy. While pregabalin has low potential for abuse, there are case reports of patients abusing large amounts of these drugs, often obtained from multiple health providers ("doctor shopping") (Schifano, 2014). As a result, the DEA placed pregabalin in Schedule V. Lacosamide (Vimpat®) is a drug used for the management of seizures that also has a low potential for abuse. Like pregabalin, lacosamide is also in Schedule V ("Schedule of Controlled Substances," 2014).

Standard urine drug-of-abuse screens will not detect carisoprodol, meprobamate, pregabalin, and lacosamide. Detection of these drugs typically requires specialized testing using chromatography and mass spectrometry.

MARIJUANA (CANNABIS)

Marijuana refers to products obtained from the plant Cannabis sativa (Degenhardt et al., 2013; Karch, 2009). The psychoactive compounds are concentrated in the leaves and flowering tops. There are over 500 natural compounds in the cannabis plant. Marijuana acts on cannabinoid receptors (CB1 and CB2) found in the brain (Appendino, Chianese, & Taglialatela-Scafati, 2011). These receptors are involved in the control of anxiety, blood pressure, immune function, food cravings, and pain.

The major psychoactive component is δ-9-tetrahydrocannabinol (THC) (Karch, 2009). Cannabis leaves contain 1% to 10% THC by weight, although the level of THC has been rising with improvements in breeding. This can have a dramatic effect on naïve users. Hashish resin contains approximately 15% THC. Hash oil, derived by solvent extraction of the cannabis buds, may have THC content exceeding 30%. The production of hash oil typically uses the flammable compound butane, with risks of fires and explosions during manufacture.

The use of marijuana among adults in the United States has remained relatively steady over the last two decades at approximately 4%, with approximately 6 million active users (Degenhardt et al., 2013; Karch, 2009). An estimated 20 million adults in the United States have used marijuana more than once. Despite the widespread use of marijuana, there are few reports of severe acute adverse effects. Nevertheless, use of marijuana can impair judgment and lead to secondary harm such as accidental injury or driving while intoxicated. The best documented chronic adverse effect of marijuana smoking is damage to the lungs. In this regard, the lung pathology closely resembles that produced by long-term tobacco smoking. Long-term chronic use of marijuana is also associated with "Amotivational Syndrome," which is associated with apathy, difficulty with memory and concentration, and loss of motivation and interest.

At the federal level in the United States, marijuana continues to be regulated as a Schedule I drug (no acceptable medical use); however, some states have passed laws allowing for medicinal or even recreational use of marijuana ("Schedule of Controlled Substances," 2014). The medicinal benefits of marijuana are controversial, but there are reported benefits of marijuana in treating glaucoma (increased pressure within the eye), chronic pain, lack of appetite, and nausea/vomiting (especially in patients receiving chemotherapy) (Gerra et al., 2010). A synthetic version of the active component of THC, *dronabinol* (Marinol®), is available as a Schedule III controlled medication. Dronabinol is primarily used to manage nausea and vomiting in chemotherapy patients and to stimulate appetite in HIV/AIDS patients.

THC is often included in many routine drug-of- abuse screens (Melanson, 2012; Moeller et al., 2008). Due to the frequent use of cannabis, positive screens are common in medical and criminal justice settings. Because THC is slowly cleared from the body, a positive screen may result from use as much as 3 months prior. This can present challenges in interpreting whether positive THC results impact situations such as alleged driving while intoxicated. Even with confirmatory testing, quantitative THC levels in blood or urine may not correlate with acute symptoms (Karch, 2009). As an active component of THC, dronabinol is expected to cause positive THC drug screens. A common defense for positive THC testing is that exposure was from passive inhalation. A number of research studies have looked at this issue. Passive inhalation of marijuana smoke can cause positive screening tests, although very heavy passive exposure is required (Cone et al., 1987; Hayden, 1991).

THE SYNTHETIC CANNABINOIDS

The *synthetic cannabinoids* are a diverse group of chemical compounds, many originally synthesized by J. W. Huffman (hence the abbreviation "JWH" in the codename of many of the drugs) (Castaneto et al., 2014; Cottencin et al., 2013; Gunderson, 2013; Kronstrand, Roman, Andersson, & Eklund, 2013; Logan, Reinhold, Xu, & Diamond, 2012; Tofighi & Lee, 2012). Similar to the amphetamine-like "bath salts," the synthetic cannabinoids are often sold with deceptive names such as "incense," "fertilizer," "research chemicals," and "potpourri." The common names "K2" and "Spice" were originally associated with JWH-018 and JWH-073, two of the original synthetic cannabinoids that were abused. When the synthetic cannabinoids first appeared on the market after 2000, the compounds were originally legal and not regulated as controlled substances. Some stores and Internet sources further attempted to evade regulation by labeling products "not for human consumption" (Musselman & Hampton, 2014).

Despite the common reference to these drugs as "synthetic marijuana" or "fake weed," the synthetic cannabinoids have a different adverse effect profile from THC, even though they target the same cannabinoid receptors in the brain (Durand, Delgado, Parra-Pellot, & Nichols-Vinueza, 2015; Monte et al., 2014; Takematsu et al., 2014; van Amsterdam, Brunt, & van den Brink, 2015). In response to the growing abuse of these drugs, expanding legislation in the United States and other countries has made many of these compounds illegal. Temporary placement into Schedule I by the DEA has been used for a number of the amphetamine-like drugs and synthetic cannabinoids ("Schedule of Controlled Substances," 2014).

Understanding the adverse effects of synthetic cannabinoids has been difficult (Tait, Caldicott, Mountain, Hill, & Lenton, 2016). The drugs are not picked up by routine urine drug screens, and few laboratories have the capability to do detailed analysis of these compounds. Common reported adverse effects include hallucinations, delusions, disorganized speech, and bizarre behavior (Brents & Prather, 2014; Cottencin et al., 2013; Every-Palmer, 2010; Forrester, Kleinschmidt, Schwarz, & Young, 2012; Harris & Brown, 2013; Lapoint et al., 2011; van Amsterdam et al., 2015). Less-common adverse effects include seizures and encephalopathic symptoms (Louh & Freeman, 2014). There are case reports of suicide associated with chronic use (Hermanns-Clausen, Kneisel, Hutter, Szabo, & Auwarter, 2013; Hermanns-Clausen, Kneisel, Szabo, & Auwarter, 2013; Kronstrand et al., 2013). Kidney failure has been reported with use of XLR-11, UR-144, and AM-2201 (van Amsterdam et al., 2015). Liver failure has been associated with 5F-PB-22 (Behonick et al., 2014). An important lesson is that the synthetic cannabinoids should not be assumed to be equivalent to THC. These compounds have a complicated toxicology that clearly differs from the known risks of marijuana. For example, kidney and liver failure have not been associated with cannabis use.

Detection of synthetic cannabinoids is difficult. The compounds are totally missed by standard THC (marijuana) immunoassay screens and confirmations (Krasowski & Ekins, 2014). A limited number of specialized forensic toxicology laboratories have developed tests using mass spectrometry that can detect a wide number of the synthetic cannabinoids currently circulating on the streets. However, in the emergency management of patients suspected to have used synthetic cannabinoids, there are no assays that can provide rapid results.

PRESCRIPTION DRUG ABUSE IN THE CRIMINAL JUSTICE SYSTEM

There is growing literature on the extent of prescription drug abuse in correctional facilities (Hilliard et al., 2013; Pilkinton & Pilkinton, 2014). As in the general population, there is a high rate of abuse of prescription opioids, stimulants, and benzodiazepines. Patterns of medical misuse may be influenced by prison formularies and prescribing algorithms (Hassan, Senior, Frisher, Edge, & Shaw, 2014). Additionally, correctional facilities can have patterns of drug abuse that are uncommon on the outside. This includes abuse of antidepressants and antipsychotics (Hilliard et al., 2013). Multiple factors have been identified that influence the diversion of prescription medications within correctional facilities (Pilkinton & Pilkinton, 2014). First, for some prisoners, prescription drugs may be the main or even only item of value for obtaining other desired goods. Second, limited staffing and the pressure of managing many prisoners may lead to overuse of psychiatric medications in the management of mental illness. Third, there can be a lack of knowledge of the addiction potential of medications, especially those uncommonly abused outside of correctional facilities.

The most commonly diverted medications fall into the categories of sedative-hypnotic and "euphoric" drugs. Commonly abused sedative-hypnotic medications include *benzodiazepines, zolpidem* (Ambien®)*, diphenhydramine* (Benadryl®)*, doxepin* (Sinequan®)*, quetiapine* (Seroquel®)*, chlorpromazine* (Thorazine®)*, amitriptyline* (Elavil®)*, and *paroxetine* (Paxil®). These drugs may be abused to offset withdrawal or other unpleasant symptoms resulting from misuse of other drugs.

Given that stimulants such as amphetamine or *methylphenidate* (Ritalin®) may be difficult to obtain within a correctional facility, other prescription medications may be used in unusual ways to achieve euphoric properties. This includes intranasal use of pulverized *bupropion* (Wellbutrin®)*, quetiapine*, and *ziprasidone* (Geodon®); intravenous administration of pseudoephedrine; and rapid ingestion of large amounts of cough syrup containing DXM (Hilliard et al., 2013; Oppek, Koller, Zwergal, & Pogarell, 2014; Pilkinton & Pilkinton, 2014; Tamburello, Lieberman, Baum, & Reeves, 2012).

There are a variety of tactics individuals within correctional facilities may use to obtain desired prescription medications (Pilkinton & Pilkinton, 2014). Certain behaviors should serve as a warning flag for risk of diversion. Common tactics include (1) asking for medication by name, first letter, or approximate sound (then allowing the prescriber to "identify" the drug name) (2) providing past psychiatric history, symptoms, or treatment that cannot be corroborated (3) providing vague complaints to get medications changed (4) and asking for additional dosing times.

To minimize diversion, correctional systems have implemented a variety of strategies (Pilkinton & Pilkinton, 2014; Reeves, 2011). Some of the published literature specifically addresses quetiapine, as this medication has been consistently identified as one of the most frequently abused drugs within correctional facilities. Some systems have limited or restricted their formulary drugs, in some cases even removing drugs like quetiapine from the formulary (there is published data from the state of New Jersey and from Australia on this issue) (Reeves, 2011; Tamburello et al., 2012). A second common strategy is to implement directly observed therapy, where personnel watch the inmate ingest the medication. The challenge of this strategy is that this practice is time-consuming, and inmates may try strategies such as "cheeking" or otherwise concealing medications to feign personnel. A third prevention strategy is to crush pills/tablets and mix with substances like applesauce, to limit the potential for diversion. Unfortunately, there is limited evidence that this strategy works, and the manipulation may interfere with the effectiveness of the medication.

CONCLUSION

Drug abuse represents a major challenge for the healthcare and criminal justice systems. In addition to street drugs such as cocaine and heroin, new challenges of prescription medication and designer-drug abuse have emerged in the last two decades. Mortality from prescription opioids now exceeds that of street drugs. Thus, law enforcement needs to be vigilant to the problem of fraudulent prescriptions, pharmacy thefts, and prescription-drug trafficking networks. Designer drugs such as the amphetamine-like drugs and synthetic cannabinoids present special issues of their own. Drugs in this category may have fleeting popularity or, like MDMA/ecstasy, have longer appeal. Current drug testing methods are not well-suited toward detection of rapidly changing designer drugs, making it difficult to identify the true scope of the problem. Lastly, recent literature better documents the problem of prescription drug abuse within correctional facilities and provides concrete methods for limiting abuse.

REFERENCES

Albertson, T. E., Chenoweth, J. A., Colby, D. K., & Sutter, M. E. (2016). The Changing Drug Culture: Emerging Drugs of Abuse and Legal Highs. *FP Essent, 441*, 18-24.

Allen, K. R. (2011). Screening for drugs of abuse: which matrix, oral fluid or urine? *Ann Clin Biochem, 48*, 531-541.

Ammerman, S. (2014). Marijuana. *Adolesc Med State Art Rev, 25*, 70-88.

Anderson, D. (2011). A review of systemic opioids commonly used for labor pain relief. *J Midwifery Womens Health, 56*, 222-239.

Appendino, G., Chianese, G., & Taglialatela-Scafati, O. (2011). Cannabinoids: occurrence and medicinal chemistry. *Curr Med Chem, 18*, 1085-1099.

Baumann, M. H., & Volkow, N. D. (2016). Abuse of New Psychoactive Substances: Threats and Solutions. *Neuropsychopharmacology, 41*, 663-665.

Behonick, G., Shanks, K. G., Firchau, D. J., Mathur, G., Lynch, C. F., Nashelsky, M., et al. (2014). Four postmortem case reports with quantitative detection of the synthetic cannabinoid, 5F-PB-22. *J Anal Toxicol, 38*, 559-562.

Bonhomme, J., Shim, R. S., Gooden, R., Tyus, D., & Rust, G. (2012). Opioid addiction and abuse in primary care practice: a comparison of methadone and buprenorphine as treatment options. *J Natl Med Assoc, 104*, 342-350.

Bosker, W. M., & Huestis, M. A. (2009). Oral fluid testing for drugs of abuse. *Clin Chem, 55*, 1910-1931.

Brents, L. K., & Prather, P. L. (2014). The K2/Spice Phenomenon: emergence, identification, legislation and metabolic characterization of synthetic cannabinoids in herbal incense products. *Drug Metab Rev, 46*, 72-85.

Burke, B. A., Lewis, R. W., 2nd, Latenser, B. A., Chung, J. Y., Willoughby, C., Kealey, G. P., et al. (2008). Methamphetamine-related burns in the cornbelt. *J Burn Care Res, 29*, 574-579.

Burns, J. M., & Boyer, E. W. (2013). Antitussives and substance abuse. *Subst Abuse Rehabil, 4*, 75-82.

Capriola, M. (2013). Synthetic cathinone abuse. *Clin Pharmacol, 5*, 109-115.

Cartwright, W. S. (2008). Economic costs of drug abuse: financial, cost of illness, and services. *J Subst Abuse Treat, 34*, 224-233.

Castaneto, M. S., Gorelick, D. A., Desrosiers, N. A., Hartman, R. L., Pirard, S., & Huestis, M. A. (2014). Synthetic cannabinoids: epidemiology, pharmacodynamics, and clinical implications. *Drug Alcohol Depend, 144*, 12-41.

Chamberlin, K. W., Cottle, M., Neville, R., & Tan, J. (2007). Oral oxymorphone for pain management. *Ann Pharmacother, 41*, 1144-1152.

Christophersen, A. S. (2000). Amphetamine designer drugs - an overview and epidemiology. *Toxicol Lett, 112-113*, 127-131.

Cone, E. J., Johnson, R. E., Darwin, W. D., Yousefnejad, D., Mell, L. D., Paul, B. D., et al. (1987). Passive inhalation of marijuana smoke: Urinalysis and room air levels of delta-9-tetrahydrocannabinol. *J Anal Toxicol, 11*, 89-96.

Cone, E. J., Yousefnejad, D., Hillsgrove, M. J., Holicky, B., & Darwin, W. D. (1995). Passive inhalation of cocaine. *J Anal Toxicol, 19*, 399-411.

Coppola, M., & Mondola, R. (2012). Synthetic cathinones: Chemistry, pharmacology and toxicology of a new class of designer drugs of abuse marketed as "bath salts" or "plant food". *Toxicol Lett, 211*, 144-149.

Corazza, O., Assi, S., & Schifano, F. (2013). From "Special K" to "Special M": The evolution of the recreational use of ketamine and methoxetamine. *CNS Neurosci Ther, 19*, 454-460.

Corkery, J. M., Schifano, F., Ghodse, A. H., & Oyefeso, A. (2004). The effects of methadone and its role in fatalities. *Hum Psychopharmacol, 19*, 565-576.

Cottencin, O., Rolland, B., & Karila, L. (2013). New designer drugs (synthetic cannabinoids and synthetic cathinones): review of literature. *Curr Pharm Des, In press*.

Degenhardt, L., Ferrari, A. J., Calabria, B., Hall, W. D., Norman, R. E., McGrath, J., et al. (2013). The global epidemiology and contribution of cannabis use and dependence to the global burden of disease: results from the GBD 2010 study. *PLoS One, 8*, e76635.

Dodrill, C. L., Helmer, D. A., & Kosten, T. R. (2011). Prescription pain medication dependence. *Am J Psychiatry, 168*, 466-471.

Drug Enforcement Administration Drug Fact Sheets. (2014). from http://www.justice.gov/dea/druginfo/factsheets.shtml

Durand, D., Delgado, L. L., Parra-Pellot, D. M., & Nichols-Vinueza, D. (2015). Psychosis and severe rhabdomyolysis associated with synthetic cannabinoid use. *Clin Schizophr Relat Psychoses, 8*, 205-208.

Durkin, A. (2014). Legalization of Marijuana for Non-Medical Use: Health, Policy, Socioeconomic, and Nursing Implications. *J Psychosoc Nurs Ment Health Serv*, 1-5.

Every-Palmer, S. (2010). Warning: legal synthetic cannabinoid-receptor agonists such as JWH-018 may precipitate psychosis in vulnerable individuals. *Addiction, 105*, 1859-1860.

Forrester, M. B., Kleinschmidt, K., Schwarz, E., & Young, A. (2012). Synthetic cannabinoid and marijuana exposures reported to poison centers. *Hum Exp Toxicol, 31*, 1006-1011.

German, C. L., Fleckenstein, A. E., & Hanson, G. R. (2013). Bath salts and synthetic cathinones: An emerging designer drug phenomenon. *Life Sciences, 97*(1), 2-8.

Gerra, G., Zaimovic, A., Gerra, M. L., Ciccocioppo, R., Cippitelli, A., Serpelloni, G., et al. (2010). Pharmacology and toxicology of Cannabis derivatives and endocannabinoid agonists. *Recent Pat CNS Drug Discov, 5*, 46-52.

Gillman, P. K. (2005). Monoamine oxidase inhibitors, opioid analgesics and serotonin toxicity. *Br J Anaesth, 95*, 434-441.

Gilson, A. M., & Kreis, P. G. (2009). The burden of the nonmedical use of prescription opioid analgesics. *Pain Med, 10 Suppl 2*, S89-100.

Gunderson, E. W. (2013). Synthetic Cannabinoids: A New Frontier of Designer Drugs. *Ann Intern Med, 159*, 563-564.

Gunderson, E. W., Kirkpatrick, M. G., Willing, L. M., & Holstege, C. P. (2013). Substituted cathinone products: a new trend in "bath salts" and other designer stimulant drug use. *J Addict Med, 7*, 153-162.

Hall, J. A., & Moore, C. B. (2008). Drug facilitated sexual assault—a review. *J Forensic Leg Med, 15,* 291-297.

Hammett-Stabler, C. A., Pesce, A. J., & Cannon, D. J. (2002). Urine drug screening in the medical setting. *Clin Chim Acta, 315,* 125-135.

Harris, C. R., & Brown, A. (2013). Synthetic cannabinoid intoxication: a case series and review. *J Emerg Med, 44,* 360-366.

Hassan, L., Senior, J., Frisher, M., Edge, D., & Shaw, J. (2014). A comparison of psychotropic medication prescribing patterns in East of England prisons and the general population. *J Psychopharmacol, 28,* 357-362.

Hayden, J. W. (1991). Passive inhalation of marijuana smoke: a critical review. *J Subst Abuse, 3,* 85-90.

Hermanns-Clausen, M., Kneisel, S., Hutter, M., Szabo, B., & Auwarter, V. (2013). Acute intoxication by synthetic cannabinoids - Four case reports. *Drug Test Anal., 5*(9-10), 790-794.

Hermanns-Clausen, M., Kneisel, S., Szabo, B., & Auwarter, V. (2013). Acute toxicity due to the confirmed consumption of synthetic cannabinoids: clinical and laboratory findings. *Addiction, 108,* 534-544.

Hernandez, S. H., & Nelson, L. S. (2010). Prescription drug abuse: insight into the epidemic. *Clin Pharmacol Ther, 88,* 307-317.

Hill, K. P., Rice, L. S., Connery, H. S., & Weiss, R. D. (2012). Diagnosing and treating opioid dependence. *J Fam Pract, 61,* 588-597.

Hilliard, W. T., Barloon, L., Farley, P., Penn, J. V., & Koranek, A. (2013). Bupropion diversion and misuse in the correctional facility. *J Correct Health Care, 19,* 211-217.

Johnson-Davis, K. L., Sadler, A. J., & Genzen, J. R. (2016). A Retrospective Analysis of Urine Drugs of Abuse Immunoassay True Positive Rates at a National Reference Laboratory. *J Anal Toxicol, 40,* 97-107.

Jones, J. D., Mogali, S., & Comer, S. D. (2012). Polydrug abuse: a review of opioid and benzodiazepine combination use. *Drug Alcohol Depend, 125,* 8-18.

Karch, S. B. (Ed.). (2009). *Karch's Pathology of Drug Abuse.* Boca Raton, FL: CRC Press.

Karila, L., Petit, A., Lowenstein, W., & Reynaud, M. (2012). Diagnosis and consequences of cocaine addiction. *Curr Med Chem, 19,* 5612-5618.

Kintz, P., Villain, M., & Cirimele, V. (2006). Hair analysis for drug detection. *Ther Drug Monit, 28,* 442-446.

Krasowski, M. D., & Ekins, S. (2014). Using cheminformatics to predict cross reactivity of "designer drugs" to their currently available immunoassays. *J Cheminform, 6,* 22.

Krasowski, M. D., Pizon, A. F., Siam, M. G., Giannoutsos, S., Iyer, M., & Ekins, S. (2009). Using molecular similarity to highlight the challenges of routine immunoassay-based drug of abuse/toxicology screening in emergency medicine. *BMC Emerg Med, 9,* 5.

Kronstrand, R., Roman, M., Andersson, M., & Eklund, A. (2013). Toxicological findings of synthetic cannabinoids in recreational users. *J Anal Toxicol, 37,* 534-541.

Lachenmeier, D. W., Sproll, C., & Musshoff, F. (2010). Poppy seed foods and opiate drug testing—where are we today? *Ther Drug Monit, 32,* 11-18.

Lapoint, J., James, L. P., Moran, C. L., Nelson, L. S., Hoffman, R. S., & Moran, J. H. (2011). Severe toxicity following synthetic cannabinoid ingestion. *Clin Toxicol (Phila), 49,* 760-764.

Levine, B. (Ed.). (2003). *Principles of Forensic Toxicology.* Washington, DC: AACC Press.

Ling, W., Mooney, L., & Hillhouse, M. (2011). Prescription opioid abuse, pain and addiction: Clinical issues and implications. *Drug Alcohol Rev, 30,* 300-305.

Logan, B. K., Reinhold, L. E., Xu, A., & Diamond, F. X. (2012). Identification of synthetic cannabinoids in herbal incense blends in the United States. *J Forensic Sci, 57*, 1168-1180.

Louh, I. K., & Freeman, W. D. (2014). A 'spicy' encephalopathy: Synthetic cannabinoids as cause of encephalopathy and seizure. *Crit Care, 18*, 553.

Lukasik-Glebocka, M., Sommerfeld, K., Tezyk, A., Zielinska-Psuja, B., Panienski, P., & Zaba, C. (2016). Flubromazolam—A new life-threatening designer benzodiazepine. *Clin Toxicol (Phila), 54*, 66-68.

Mandava, N., Chang, R. S., Wang, J. H., Bertocchi, M., Yrad, J., Allamaneni, S., et al. (2011). Establishment of a definitive protocol for the diagnosis and management of body packers (drug mules). *Emerg Med J, 28*, 98-101.

Melanson, S. E. (2012). The utility of immunoassays for urine drug testing. *Clin Lab Med, 32*, 429-447.

Meyer, J. S. (2013). 3,4-methylenedioxymethamphetamine (MDMA): Current perspectives. *Subst Abuse Rehabil, 4*, 83-99.

Moeller, K. E., Lee, K. C., & Kissack, J. C. (2008). Urine drug screening: Practical guide for clinicians. *Mayo Clinic Proc, 83*, 66-76.

Monte, A. A., Bronstein, A. C., Cao, D. J., Heard, K. J., Hoppe, J. A., Hoyte, C. O., et al. (2014). An outbreak of exposure to a novel synthetic cannabinoid. *N Engl J Med, 370*, 389-390.

Monte, A. A., Chuang, R., & Bodmer, M. (2010). Dextromethorphan, chlorphenamine and serotonin toxicity: Case report and systematic literature review. *Br J Clin Pharmacol, 70*, 794-798.

Morgan, C. J., & Curran, H. V. (2012). Ketamine use: A review. *Addiction, 107*, 27-38.

Musselman, M. E., & Hampton, J. P. (2014). "Not for human consumption": A review of emerging designer drugs. *Pharmacotherapy, 34*, 745-757.

Nelson, E. M., & Philbrick, A. M. (2012). Avoiding serotonin syndrome: The nature of the interaction between tramadol and selective serotonin reuptake inhibitors. *Ann Pharmacother, 46*, 1712-1716.

Nelson, L., & Schwaner, R. (2009). Transdermal fentanyl: Pharmacology and toxicology. *J Med Toxicol, 5*, 230-241.

Nelson, M. E., Bryant, S. M., & Aks, S. E. (2014). Emerging drugs of abuse. *Emerg Med Clin North Am, 32*, 1-28.

Nonpharmaceutical fentanyl-related deaths—multiple states, April 2005-March 2007. (2008). *MMWR Morb Mortal Wkly Rep, 57*, 793-796.

Nossaman, V. E., Ramadhyani, U., Kadowitz, P. J., & Nossaman, B. D. (2010). Advances in perioperative pain management: Use of medications with dual analgesic mechanisms, tramadol & tapentadol. *Anesthesiol Clin, 28*, 647-666.

O'Brien C, P. (2005). Benzodiazepine use, abuse, and dependence. *J Clin Psychiatry, 66 Suppl 2*, 28-33.

Oppek, K., Koller, G., Zwergal, A., & Pogarell, O. (2014). Intravenous administration and abuse of bupropion: A case report and a review of the literature. *J Addict Med, 8*, 290-293.

Ordonez Gallego, A., Gonzalez Baron, M., & Espinosa Arranz, E. (2007). Oxycodone: A pharmacological and clinical review. *Clin Transl Oncol, 9*, 298-307.

Parkin, M. C., & Brailsford, A. D. (2009). Retrospective drug detection in cases of drug-facilitated sexual assault: Challenges and perspectives for the forensic toxicologist. *Bioanalysis, 1*, 1001-1013.

Petrie, M., Lynch, K. L., Ekins, S., Chang, J. S., Goetz, R. J., Wu, A. H., et al. (2013). Cross-reactivity studies and predictive modeling of "Bath Salts" and other amphetamine-type stimulants with amphetamine screening immunoassays. *Clin Toxicol (Phila), 51*, 83-91.

Pilkinton, P. D., & Pilkinton, J. C. (2014). Prescribing in prison: Minimizing psychotropic drug diversion in correctional practice. *J Correct Health Care, 20*, 95-104.

Rech, M. A., Donahey, E., Cappiello Dziedzic, J. M., Oh, L., & Greenhalgh, E. (2015). New Drugs of Abuse. *Pharmacotherapy, 35*(20), 189-197.

Reeves, R. (2011). Guideline, education, and peer comparison to reduce prescriptions of benzodiazepines and low-dose quetiapine in prison. *J Correct Health Care, 18*, 45-52.

Reeves, R. R., & Burke, R. S. (2010). Carisoprodol: Abuse potential and withdrawal syndrome. *Curr Drug Abuse Rev, 3*, 33-38.

Reeves, R. R., Burke, R. S., & Kose, S. (2012). Carisoprodol: Update on abuse potential and legal status. *South Med J, 105*, 619-623.

Rich, B. A., & Webster, L. R. (2011). A review of forensic implications of opioid prescribing with examples from malpractice cases involving opioid-related overdose. *Pain Med, 12 Suppl 2*, S59-65.

Rocha, B. A. (2013). Principles of assessment of abuse liability: US legal framework and regulatory environment. *Behav Pharmacol, 24*, 403-409.

Romanelli, F., & Smith, K. M. (2009). Dextromethorphan abuse: Clinical effects and management. *J Am Pharm Assoc (2003), 49*, e20-25; quiz e26-27.

Schedule of Controlled Substances. (2014). from http://www.deadiversion.usdoj.gov/schedules

Schep, L. J., Knudsen, K., Slaughter, R. J., Vale, J. A., & Megarbane, B. (2012). The clinical toxicology of gamma-hydroxybutyrate, gamma-butyrolactone and 1,4-butanediol. *Clin Toxicol (Phila), 50*, 458-470.

Schifano, F. (2014). Misuse and abuse of pregabalin and gabapentin: Cause for concern? *CNS Drugs, 28*, 491-496.

Schwartz, R. H. (2005). Adolescent abuse of dextromethorphan. *Clin Pediatr (Phila), 44*, 565-568.

Shulgin, A., & Shulgin, A. (1991). *PIHKAL: A Chemical Love Story*. Berkeley, CA: Transform Press.

Shulgin, A., & Shulgin, A. (1997). *TIHKAL: The Continuation*. Berkeley, CA: Transform Press.

Strassels, S. A. (2009). Economic burden of prescription opioid misuse and abuse. *J Manag Care Pharm, 15*, 556-562.

Tait, R. J., Caldicott, D., Mountain, D., Hill, S. L., & Lenton, S. (2016). A systematic review of adverse events arising from the use of synthetic cannabinoids and their associated treatment. *Clin Toxicol (Phila), 54*, 1-13.

Takematsu, M., Hoffman, R. S., Nelson, L. S., Schechter, J. M., Moran, J. H., & Wiener, S. W. (2014). A case of acute cerebral ischemia following inhalation of a synthetic cannabinoid. *Clin Toxicol (Phila), 52*, 973-975.

Tamburello, A. C., Lieberman, J. A., Baum, R. M., & Reeves, R. (2012). Successful removal of quetiapine from a correctional formulary. *J Am Acad Psychiatry Law, 40*, 502-508.

Tenore, P. L. (2010). Advanced urine toxicology testing. *J Addict Dis, 29*, 436-448.

Thevis, M., Kuuranne, T., Geyer, H., & Schanzer, W. (2013). Annual banned-substance review: Analytical approaches in human sports drug testing. *Drug Test Anal, 5*, 1-19.

Thornton, M. D., & Baum, C. R. (2014). Bath salts and other emerging toxins. *Pediatr Emerg Care, 30*, 47-52; quiz 53-45.

Tofighi, B., & Lee, J. D. (2012). Internet highs—seizures after consumption of synthetic cannabinoids purchased online. *J Addict Med, 6*, 240-241.

van Amsterdam, J., Brunt, T., & van den Brink, W. (2015). The adverse health effects of synthetic cannabinoids with emphasis on psychosis-like effects. *J Psychopharmacol, in press, 29*(3) 254-263.

Vearrier, D., Greenberg, M. I., Miller, S. N., Okaneku, J. T., & Haggerty, D. A. (2012). Methamphetamine: history, pathophysiology, adverse health effects, current trends, and hazards associated with the clandestine manufacture of methamphetamine. *Dis Mon, 58,* 38-89.

Verstraete, A. G. (2004). Detection times of drugs of abuse in blood, urine, and oral fluid. *Ther Drug Monit, 26,* 200-205.

Vilke, G. M., Bozeman, W. P., Dawes, D. M., Demers, G., & Wilson, M. P. (2012). Excited delirium syndrome (ExDS): Treatment options and considerations. *J Forensic Leg Med, 19,* 117-121.

Waldhoer, M., Bartlett, S. E., & Whistler, J. L. (2004). Opioid receptors. *Annu Rev Biochem, 73,* 953-990.

Walsh, D. (2005). Advances in opioid therapy and formulations. *Support Care Cancer, 13,* 138-144.

Whiteford, H. A., Degenhardt, L., Rehm, J., Baxter, A. J., Ferrari, A. J., Erskine, H. E., et al. (2013). Global burden of disease attributable to mental and substance use disorders: findings from the Global Burden of Disease Study 2010. *Lancet, 382,* 1575-1586.

Wightman, R., Perrone, J., Portelli, I., & Nelson, L. (2012). Likeability and abuse liability of commonly prescribed opioids. *J Med Toxicol, 8,* 335-340.

Wyman, J. F. (2012). Principles and procedures in forensic toxicology. *Clin Lab Med, 32,* 493-507.

Young, A. M., Glover, N., & Havens, J. R. (2012). Nonmedical use of prescription medications among adolescents in the United States: A systematic review. *J Adolesc Health, 51,* 6-17.

Zammit, G. (2009). Comparative tolerability of newer agents for insomnia. *Drug Saf, 32,* 735-748.

Zawilska, J. B., & Wojcieszak, J. (2013). Designer cathinones—an emerging class of novel recreational drugs. *Forensic Sci Int, 231,* 42-53.

Zweben, J. E. (2000). Severely and persistently mentally ill substance abusers: Clinical and policy issues. *J Psychoactive Drugs, 32,* 383-389.

TABLE 1

Opioid Drug Names, Main Metabolites, and Urine Detection Window

Drug	Main Metabolite(s)	Common Trade and Street Names	Urine detection window
Buprenorphine	Norbuprenorphine	Buprenex®, Suboxone®, Subutex®	1-3 days
		Bupe, Stop Signs, Subbies, Subs	
Codeine	Morphine Hydrocodone	Included in many combination prescriptions (e.g., Tylenol 3®)	2-3 days
		Captain Cody, Cody, Empi, T-3s	
Fentanyl	Norfentanyl	Actiq®, Duragesic®, Fentora®, Sublimaze®	1-3 days
		Apache, China Girl, China White, Goodfella, Tango, TNT	
Heroin (diacetylmorphine)	6-Acetylmorphine (6-AM) Morphine	Big H, Black Tar, Horse, Smack, Thunder	1 day (as 6-AM)
Hydrocodone	Hydromorphone Dihydrocodeine	Hycodan®, Lortab®, Maxidone®, Vicodin®, Zohydro®	2-3 days
		Hydro, Norco, Vikes	
Hydromorphone		Dilaudid®	2-3 days
		D, Dillies, Footballs, Juice, Smack	
Morphine	Hydromorphone	Astromorph®, Avinza®, DepoDur®, Duramorph®, Kadian®, MS Contin; also found in poppy seeds	2-3 days
		Dreamer, Emsel, M.S., Morpho, Unkie	
Oxycodone	Oxymorphone Noroxycodone	Endocet®, Oxycontin®, Percocet®, Roxicet®	2-3 days
		Hillbilly heroin, Kicker, Oxy, Perc, Roxy	
Oxymorphone	Noroxymorphone	Numorphan®, Opana®	2-3 days
		Blues, Octagons, Pink Heaven	
Meperidine	Normeperidine	Demerol®	2-3 days
		D, Dillies, Dust, Juice	
Methadone	EDDP	Dolophine®, Methadose®	1-14 days
		Amidone, Fizzies, Maria, Salvia, Wafer	
Tramadol	N-Desmethyltramadol	Ultram®	2-4 days
	O-Desmethyltramadol	Chill Pills, Ultras	

Data summarized from multiple sources: "Drug Enforcement Administration Drug Fact Sheets," 2014; Hammett-Stabler et al., 2002; Melanson, 2012; Moeller et al., 2008; Tenore, 2010; Verstraete, 2004.

TABLE 2

Stimulant Drug Names, Main Metabolites, and Urine Detection Window

Drug	Main Metabolite(s)	Common Trade and Street Names	Urine detection window
Amphetamine (*d*-)		Adderall®, Benzedrine®, Dexedrine®, Vyvanse®	3-5 days
		Bennies, Speed, Uppers	
Cocaine	Benzoylecgonine Ecgonine methyl ester	Coke, Crack, Snow	1-2 days (metabolite)
Gamma-hydroxybutyrate (GHB)		Xyrem®	3-12 hours
		Easy Lay, G, Georgia Home Boy, Grievous Bodily Harm, Liquid Ecstasy, Liquid X, Scoop	
Ketamine		Ketalar®	1-2 days
		Cat Tranquilizer, Jet K, K, Kit Kat, Purple, Special K, Super K, Vitamin K	
MDMA	MDA	E, Ecstasy, XTC, Molly, STP	1-2 days
MDPV		Bath Salts, Ivory Wave, Vanilla Sky	Unknown
Mephedrone		Bath Salts, Meow Meow	Unknown
Methamphetamine (*d*-)	Amphetamine	Desoxyn®, Vicks® Nasal Inhaler (*l*-isomer)	3-5 days
		Crystal, Ice, Meth	
Methylone		Bath Salts, Explosion	Unknown
Phencyclidine		PCP, Angel dust	3-7 days

Data summarized from multiple sources: "Drug Enforcement Administration Drug Fact Sheets," 2014; Hammett-Stabler et al., 2002; Melanson, 2012; Moeller et al., 2008; Tenore, 2010; Verstraete, 2004.

TABLE 3

Sedative-Hypnotic and Cannabinoid Drug Names, Main Metabolites, and Urine Detection Window

Drug	Main Metabolite(s)	Common Trade and Street Names	Urine detection window
Alprazolam	α-Hydroyalprazolam	Xanax®	Up to 5 days
		Bars, Totem Poles	
Amobarbital		Amytal®	Up to 3 days
		Blue Devils, Blue Heaven, Blue Velvet	
Butalbital		Found in combination products (e.g., Fiorinol®)	Up to 7 days
Clonazepam	7-Aminoclonazepam	Klonopin®	Up to 5 days
		Downers, Tranqs	
Diazepam	Nordiazepam	Valium®	Up to 2 weeks
	Oxazepam	Moggies, Vallies	
	Temazepam		
Flunitrazepam		Rohypnol®	Up to 5 days
		Roche, Roofies, Ruffles	
Lorazepam		Ativan®	Up to 5 days
		Control, Silence	
Marijuana (cannabis)	11-OH-THC	Marinol®	1-4 weeks (maximum 12)
	THC-COOH	Blubbers, Boom, Ganja, Grass, Hashish, Pot, Reefer, Weed	
Oxazepam		Serax®	Up to 5 days
Pentobarbital		Nembutal®	Up to 3 days
		Nembies, Yellow Jackets	
Phenobarbital		Luminal®	Up to 15 days
		Goofballs, Purple Hearts	
Secobarbital		Seconal®	Up to 3 days
		Dolls, Red Birds, Red Devils	
Synthetic cannabinoids		JWH-018, JWH-073, HU-210, XLR-11, UR-144, AM-2201	Variable, mostly unknown
		Bliss, Black Mamba, Fake Weed, Genie, Incense, K2, Spice	
Temazepam	Oxazepam	Restoril®	Up to 5 days
		Rugby Balls	

Data summarized from multiple sources: "Drug Enforcement Administration Drug Fact Sheets," 2014; Hammett-Stabler et al., 2002; Melanson, 2012; Moeller et al., 2008; Tenore, 2010; Verstraete, 2004.

CHAPTER 11

Malingering and Deception: A Beginner's Guide

Erv Weinkauf, Sara Hartigan, Marissa Zappala, Julia Besser, Cody Charette, Laura Cooney-Koss, Kathy Harowski, Blake Harris, & Kayla Vorlicky

Chapter Overview

Malingering is the conscious, intentional fabrication or exaggeration of dysfunction for the sake of personal gain. Feigned dysfunction may include physical disability or mental/neurological impairment such as learning disorders, dementia, severe amnesia, and perceptual disorders (Batt, Shores, & Chekaluk, 2008; Browndyke et al., 2008; Dean, Victor, Boone, & Arnold, 2008). The distinguishing feature of malingering is the pursuit of externalized benefits or secondary gain, which may include financial compensation, a reduction in criminal culpability, a more lenient sentencing, avoidance of military duty, avoidance of work, obtaining of drugs, retention of child custody, or continued employment (American Psychiatric Association, 2013). The topic of malingered psychiatric symptoms is of considerable significance, since the full extent of civil and criminal justice is dependent upon a comprehensive awareness of an individual's motivational factors, mens rea, and behavioral capacity. This chapter will review: (1) malingering as a behavioral continuum, (2) motivational factors that may serve as antecedents to malingering, (3) ethical issues and considerations, (4) the differentiation of commonly co-occurring (Co-morbid) disorders, (5) patterns and detection of feigning, and (6) clinical assessment techniques for accurately identifying malingering. The goals of this chapter are to bring awareness to the phenomenon of malingering and its impact on the criminal justice system while simultaneously establishing the merit for further empirical inquiry into the nature and detection of malingering.

Introduction

The purpose of this chapter is to provide a cursory overview of the complexities involved in accurately detecting malingering. This chapter serves as a beginner's guide to the complex topic of malingering. Interested scholars and practitioners should consult additional reference material to reach a competent level of mastery. Understanding the topic of malingering is of great importance to those who are employed in the various facets of the criminal justice and mental health systems. For professionals who interview, observe, and assess individuals in contact with the criminal justice system, the complex topic of malingering is particularly salient. Similarly, note that individuals involved in other aspects of the legal system who are seeking benefits, including compensation or the avoidance of consequences, may use malingering and symptom exaggeration.

Masquerading under the guise of mental illness in order to avoid responsibility, accountability, or culpability is not a new ploy. Even the ancient hero of Homer's epic, Odysseus, attempted to feign psychosis by running about his fields with oxen, sowing salt into the ground instead of seeds (in an effort to appear insane) when he learned he was being drafted as a soldier in the Trojan War (Harris & Michael, 2012). More modern forms of malingering include feigning physical dysfunctions (e.g., neurological and perceptual disorders) and psychological or psychiatric dysfunctions (e.g., learning disability, dementia, severe amnesia, depression, anxiety, psychosis) (Batt et al., 2008; Browndyke et al., 2008; Dean et al., 2008). The benefits sought by malingerers generally involve obtaining a positive outcome (such as financial compensation, excusal from work, avoidance of criminal charges, or obtaining prescription medication) or avoiding a negative outcome (such as a legal conviction) (American Psychiatric Association, 2013). Since the 1890s, as society sought to understand the connection between mental health and the law, malingering has been a topic of considerable interest to researchers. While one of the earliest uses of the term was the aforementioned Odysseus, malingering as a clinical label has existed for approximately 150 years and is often influenced by current civil and political climates (Carroll, 2003). Over the years the term has been used in many other domains. Psychologists estimate malingering is present in 30% of disability/worker compensation claims, 29% of personal injury cases, 19% of criminal evaluations, and 8% of medical cases (Mittenberg, Patton, Canyock, & Condit, 2002). Unfortunately, the precise prevalence of malingering is unknown because there is no method currently available to accurately capture/detect examples of successful attempts.

Rogers (1990) suggested there were three models of malingering: Pathogenic, Criminological, and Adaptation Models. The "Pathogenic Model," also known as "partial malingering," refers to individuals who have a treatable, diagnosed mental dysfunction, but who continue to feign symptoms after they have ceased to experience them (Rogers, 2008a; Rogers, Sewell, & Goldstein, 1994). For example, an individual who has been diagnosed with bipolar disorder may seek additional medication by claiming his or her symptoms have not abated when, in fact, they have. In another example, an employee on leave for a medical disability continues to complain of symptoms beyond the point when they recovered, in order to remain on leave.

The "Criminological Model" refers to legal defendants who seek external gain related to criminal proceedings (Rogers, 2008d; Rogers et al., 1994). These gains may include a reduction of sentence, delays in court proceedings, or alternative accommodations while incarcerated.

The "Adaptation Model" refers to individuals who, in response to feeling overwhelmed, attempt to cope with extreme stressors by feigning symptoms. These individuals create presentations designed to shut down communication with others (McDermott & Feldman, 2007; Rogers et al., 1994). For example, an individual may present with hallucinations, because this can be an effective tool to interrupt the stress of interrogation. This behavior could be an act of desperation or a demonstration of insufficient coping skills. There are cases where these individuals may still genuinely be in need of services, despite the fact they are exaggerating their dysfunction (Martin & Schroeder, 2015; Rogers et al., 1994). Rogers and Bender (2003) stated, "the Adaptation Model views malingering as a situational response based on the appraisal of alternatives" (p. 111). Just as the incentives to malinger vary, so too do the strategies implemented by individuals to successfully complete the ruse. There are numerous approaches employed by people feigning cognitive impairment as opposed to other forms of mental disorders (Rogers & Bender, 2003). For example, individuals attempting to feign cognitive impairment must commit credible mistakes on cognitive measures; whereas, individuals feigning other types of mental disorders must establish, from the beginning, a convincing story about the progression of their disorder. Therefore, detection strategies must be tailored specifically to each case.

The ability to determine whether someone is malingering involves gathering and integrating subjective (e.g., individual accounts/testimonials) and objective (e.g., clinical observations, standardized test results, collateral data) information. Based solely on a single interview, malingering is difficult to detect. Samuel and Wittenberg (2005) suggest mental health professionals use as many secondary sources of information as possible, including collateral information from family members, care providers, public records, clinical records, coworker reports, prior psychological reports, and laboratory investigations. Any applied assessment measures should be methodically evaluated for validity and reliability in regard to malingering, in order to guard against Type I (false-positive) and Type II (false-negative) errors (Heilbronner, Sweet, Morgan, Larrabee, & Millis, 2009).

Even highly trained mental health professionals have great difficulty accurately assessing malingering when using unstructured interviews (Rosen, Mullsant, Bruce, Mittal, & Fox, 2004). Specifically, psychiatrists can only detect approximately 50% of malingering (the same rate as pure chance) through interviews or patient self-reports alone (Rosen et al., 2004). Research also suggests psychologists often use assessment instruments that fail to detect response bias and malingering, which may lead to incorrect diagnoses (Cassidy & Shaver, 2008). Many researchers have recommended that malingering should be a consideration in any forensic evaluation (Felthous, 2006; Resnick & Knoll, 2005b).

Recent advances in assessment techniques have provided insight to mental health professionals, enhancing the ability to accurately evaluate behavioral presentations and subjective reports of dysfunction (Iverson & Binder, 2000; Meyers & Diep, 2000). Still, many researchers agree that not all malingerers perform similarly on these tests. The best approach remains examining the individual's responses for consistency across psychological tests (i.e., a comparison of the individual themselves against group norms). In addition to looking for consistency across tests, it can also be beneficial to assess the individual on different days or in different settings. This allows the clinician to determine if they will present with the same symptoms over time and under diverse conditions. Individuals may also display credible, but erratic, response styles simply due to the stress of being involved in litigation—an occurrence some researchers have named Litigation Response Syndrome (LRS) (Lees-Haley, 1988; Nichols & Gass, 2015). Similar to what might be described as "stage fright" or performance anxiety, individuals may become overwhelmed by the legal process. The overwhelming feelings inhibit the individual's ability to act in their own best interest, which, in turn, may impact damage awards, competency evaluations, and findings of fitness as a parent, soldier, or other professional (Rogers & Payne, 2006).

MALINGERING AS A CONTINUUM

The detection of malingering is complex because feigned symptoms range on a continuum from mild or slight impairment to the severely impaired ability to complete tasks of daily living. Symptoms of disorders commonly feigned include depression, psychosis, and schizophrenia; memory disturbances such as amnesia and fugue states, and physical features such as pain, dizziness, and loss of sensory functioning in the form of lost vision or restricted range of motion (Egeland, Andersson, Sundseth, & Schanke, 2015). When malingering is present, it is not uncommon for individuals to endorse a full range of psychotic symptoms, such as hallucinations, delusions, and catatonia (Iverson & Binder, 2000). The malingering continuum involves distinguishing between possible, probable, and definitive cases of malingering (also referred to as pure, partial, and false cases). While these terms are commonly used interchangeably due to their considerable overlap, researchers have worked diligently to distinguish between feigning symptoms, exaggerating existing symptoms, and attributing existing symptoms to an unrelated cause (Resnick, West, & Payne, 2008). Instances of malingering are complex to determine and, as such, individual cases must meet some combination of the following criteria in order to reliably determine that malingering is occurring:

- Presence of a substantial external incentive (secondary gain)
- Evidence from psychological testing indicating potential of intentional misdirection
- Significant inconsistencies or discrepancies in self-reported symptoms, suggesting fabrication or exaggeration (Resnick et al., 2008).

For the sake of clarity, a brief definition of terms is provided in Table 1 below.

TABLE 1
Subtle Differences in Terminology

Item

- *Deception* – evidence of malingering including dishonesty and nondisclosure
- *Dissimulation* – "concealment of genuine psychiatric or other medical symptoms in an attempt to present a picture of psychiatric or organic health" (Durst, Fastovsky, Michnik, & *Raskin, 2011, p. 696)*
- *Factitious Presentation* – "intentional production or feigning of symptoms that are motivated by the desire to assume a sick role" (American Psychiatric Association, 2000, p. 517)
- *Feigning* – "the deliberate fabrication or gross exaggeration of psychological or physical symptoms without any assumptions about its goals" (Rogers & Bender, 2003, p. 6)
- *Malingering* – "the intentional production of false or grossly exaggerated physical or psychological symptoms, motivated by external incentives" (American Psychiatric Association, 2000, p. 739)
- *Poor Effort* – intentional underperformance during evaluation procedures

Note. Adapted from Rogers (2008a)

MOTIVATIONS FOR MALINGERING

As noted at the beginning of this chapter, the motivation to malinger can vary greatly, from the avoidance of possible negative outcomes (such as physical or emotional distress/discomfort) to the attainment of positive outcomes (such as personal benefit, including financial or interpersonal gain) (Hargan, 2011). The potential rewards for successful malingering are often significant enough to outweigh the negative consequences of being detected, as determined by the individual's risk-benefit analysis. In correctional or pretrial detainment settings, individuals may be motivated to malinger psychiatric symptoms to obtain modified living arrangements for special populations, receive narcotic prescriptions, buttress a claim of incompetence or, on occasion, to bolster an insanity defense (Jasinski & Ranseen, 2011; Norris & May, 1998). Defendants who successfully malinger can delay or completely evade criminal consequences if they are found incompetent to stand trial or not guilty by reason of insanity. Those found not guilty by reason of insanity may be subject to civil commitment if they are found to be an imminent danger to themselves or the community. Some defendants may find this preferable, as psychiatric hospitals are designed to be non-punitive environments that provide more liberties and accommodations than a normal punitive correctional institution. Although highly unlikely, if a defendant successfully feigns a psychiatric disorder but is not found to present a substantial risk, theoretically, that defendant could be released from custody without any criminal consequences (Kucharski, Duncan, Egan, & Falkenbach, 2006). In more likely scenarios, successful malingering can result in the imposition of a shorter period of incarceration than would have been given in the absence of the presenting symptoms (Kucharski et al., 2006). As an example, when facing serious charges, juvenile offenders may malinger in order to avoid being tried as adult offenders (Gast & Hart, 2010). Additionally, the motivation to malinger does not end with the pre-adjudication process, as there is a continuous benefit from perceived impairment by the legal system. For example, sentenced offenders in correctional institutions may feign symptoms to be transferred to more accommodating housing, avoid work details, obtain pain and psychiatric medication, gain an earlier release, or gain an earlier transition back into the community.

In Atkins v. Virginia (2002), the United States Supreme Court determined that individuals with intellectual disabilities (ID) are not eligible for the death penalty. Specifically, this ruling stipulates that cognitive and behavioral impairments, such as "the diminished ability to understand and process information, to learn from experience, to engage in logical reasoning, or to control impulses" rendered the retributive and deterrent value of the death penalty invalid and, as such, was in direct violation of the 8th Amendment of the United States Constitution. This edict provides ample motivation for defendants in capital cases to try to avoid the death penalty by feigning such a disability.

Defendants may also malinger simply to prolong the judicial process, since any delay buys more time to seek a better personal outcome or simply further delay the removal of special services or benefits related to the claimed disorder or impairment. Over the past several decades, defendants and their attorneys have become more aware of empirical research focused on mental illness and criminality. Such awareness of these findings and practices could result in more attempts at feigning disorders. Successful feigning of disorders may prompt judges and attorneys to unnecessarily request competency evaluations and time-intensive competency restoration services. Each new evaluation further lengthens the trial process. Fortunately, it is expected that the occurrences of successful feigning will decline as the criminal justice system becomes more familiar with the phenomenon and methods of accurately detecting malingering improve, commensurate with the field's increased understanding of the processes at work.

Despite the statistical rarity of successfully presenting a defense of "Not Guilty by Reason of Insanity," (NGRI) defendants continue to show a strong willingness to malinger, exaggerate, or withhold information with the goal of an NGRI verdict in mind (Callahan, Steadman, McGreevy, & Robbins, 1991; Rogers, 2008c). However, individuals who successfully malinger, thereby evading criminal prosecution, may, as an alternative, be civilly committed to an inpatient hospital setting. Ironically, these commitments are often longer than the traditional correctional sentence would have been. Contrary to the public perception that individuals who receive a NGRI sentence for murder spend little time in a psychiatric facility, the actual average is over six years (76.4 months) (Miller, 2003). To deter attempts at malingering, defendants determined to be feigning symptoms to avoid prosecution run the risk of accruing additional charges—including obstruction of justice, which can lead to harsher sentencing (e.g., U.S. COA 3rd District or U.S. v. Gigante, 1997, Fed. E.D.N.Y; U.S. v. Greer, 1998).

While this chapter is primarily focused on the occurrence of malingering in the criminal justice setting, feigning dysfunction is attempted in many other arenas. Of particular concern is the possibility of fraudulently attaining disability services and payments for malingered symptoms (Angrist, Chen, & Frandsen, 2010: Harrison & Edwards, 2010). Recently, military veterans have come under increased scrutiny, as claims related to Post-traumatic Stress Disorder (PTSD) occur more frequently (David, Duggan, & Lyle, 2011; McNally & Frueh, 2013; Veterans for Common Sense, 2012). Accommodations for those suffering from PTSD and other trauma-related disorders can include the avoidance of military deployments, avoidance of active duty for first responders, and increased disability payments.

Ethical Issues and Considerations in Malingering

The topic of malingering brings up considerable ethical issues, since an assertion that one is malingering would likely have a drastic impact on not only the individual identified as a malingerer but also on other stakeholders whose lives may be changed by the subsequent legal processes. It is important to reiterate that malingering is not considered a mental health disorder and, therefore, is not a traditional diagnostic condition. This lack of formal status greatly complicates examinations and diagnoses of legitimate disorders by introducing confounding variables into the equation (American Psychiatric Association, 2013). In response to criticism that differentiation is subjective, mental health professionals are urged to exhaust alternative explanations and diagnoses before arriving at a conclusion of malingering.

It is incumbent on the mental health professional to monitor behavior and performance during the entire evaluation (Iverson, 2006). In order to minimize false positives (finding significance where there is none), higher cutoff scores are set, which have the direct result of increasing the chance for false negatives (not finding significance when it is present) (Ju & Varney, 2000). However, mental health professionals must remain aware that individuals, on the advice of their counsel, may intentionally underperform on tests and assessments (Victor & Abeles, 2004). Still, it is important to note that there are no documented findings conclusively showing the influence of malicious coaching and deliberate interference with psychological instruments on the performance of the individuals being evaluated. While some studies indicate the effects may be minimal (Hall & Hall, 2006), other studies indicate significant declines in the effectiveness of assessment measures to detect feigning when coaching is involved (Rohling & Boone, 2007). Two approaches to coaching have been identified: (1) symptom coaching, which involves conveying the particularities of specific disorders and (2) test coaching, which provides individuals with information on how to defeat symptom validity testing (Powell, Gfeller, Hendricks, & Sharland, 2004). New threats to the validity of these tests are constantly emerging, with the Internet providing near instantaneous access to instruments, advice, and other people's experiences (Harrison & Edwards, 2010; Suhr & Gunstad, 2007; Victor & Abeles, 2004). If the integrity of the test is compromised (e.g., through online exposure), then the chances of the test validity and reliability being undermined increase exponentially (Suhr & Gunstad, 2007). Still, the negative effects of this are mitigated by competent practice, as capable examiners utilize multiple sources and a wide array of assessment tools to reach conclusions.

Professional organizations such as the APA require examiners to abide by ethical and professional obligations by only allowing those certified to administer and interpret the test protocols to access them (American Psychological Association; 2013; American Psychological Association, 2002). However, these same organizations also maintain psychologists have an ethical responsibility to make sure clients have a clear, informed understanding of the meaning and purpose of test procedures. Approximately half of attorneys and law students surveyed believe clients should be educated about psychological testing validity procedures, since this is an important component of legally and ethically required informed consent procedures (Bauer & McCaffrey, 2006). Consequently, one ramification of this is that the public has become better at emulating symptoms of specific disorders (Gutheil, 2003; Harrison & Edwards, 2010). The data on the accessibility of psychological information on the Internet highlights the importance of conducting a comprehensive malingering evaluation consisting of multiple assessment types (McDermott, 2012).

There is conflicting research regarding the effectiveness of directly informing participants that they are being tested for malingering as a part of the exam (Gunstad & Suhr, 2001; Suhr & Gunstad, 2000). While warnings advising participants as to the purpose of testing have shown to have a negligible impact on honest participants, some research has shown a difference for those individuals that malingered (Suhr & Gunstad, 2000). As it stands, there are no conclusive results. Thus, researchers are left with two schools of thought: the first argues that making participants aware of the purpose of the evaluation results in increased malingering, and the second line of thought states that warnings have no appreciable (or at best, a negligible) impact on participant performance (Suhr & Gunstad, 2000). As such, improving the field's understanding of the effectiveness of malingering warnings and how to best employ them in practical settings remains an aspirational goal (Slick, Tan, Strauss, & Hultsch, 2004).

Forensic examiners and mental health professionals may be apprehensive to offer warnings and opinions regarding malingering because of concerns about making errors, legal liabilities, and/or the stigma associated with the term (Sweet, Moberg, & Suchy, 2000). Recommendations exist to create an alternative definition for malingering by reframing the concept in terms of poor motivation (Bianchini, Mathias, & Greve, 2001; Binder & Willis, 1991). However, this idea remains controversial in the field, due to the imprecise and unstandardized nature of malingering, as well as the absence of an accepted universal definition for it (Rogers & Bender, 2003).

It is also important to note what it takes to meet and abide by the professional requirements of licensure. Mental health professionals are ethically obligated to provide services only within their own expertise and are required to take continuing education courses each year in order to develop, enhance, and maintain their competence within the field (American Psychological Association, 2002). They should maintain a thorough understanding of current research on evaluating and assessing malingering (Seward & Connor, 2008). This includes the importance of recognizing bias, maintaining awareness of misconceptions regarding malingering, and keeping current with research advancements in the field.

DIFFERENTIAL DIAGNOSES

It is important to note that malingering and mental illness are not mutually exclusive (APA, 2013). Individuals with mental illness who experience inconsistent thoughts, beliefs, or attitudes, especially as relating to behavioral decisions and attitude change, may appear deceptive even when it is not their deliberate intention (Drob & Berger, 1987; Scott, 2016). Researchers have disagreed for many years whether malingering can ever definitely be detected and differentiated from other psychological conditions. Feigned concentration difficulties, fatigue, and pain are more difficult to detect than conditions with obvious biological markers such as high-blood pressure or an obstructed airway (Turner, 2006). Differentiation of psychological symptoms largely relies on the interpretation of self-report and other subjective data.

Separate from malingering, but similar in presentation, is what is known as a factitious disorder. Individuals presenting with factitious disorder falsely report or exaggerate symptoms in the absence of secondary gain beyond adopting the role of a patient. It is posited that the motivation in a factitious disorder may be partially conscious, with a strong underlying unconscious element, rather than the fully conscious and deliberate effort that is present in instances of malingering (American Psychological Association, 2013). Symptoms of a factitious disorder can range from mild (slight exaggeration of symptoms) to severe (previously called Munchausen Syndrome) (Feldman, Hamilton, & Deemer, 2001). The person may concoct symptoms or even tamper with medical tests in order to convince others that treatment, such as a high-risk surgery, is needed (Oldham & Riba, 2001).

Care must also be taken to not diagnose somatoform disorders as malingering. Individuals with somatoform disorders present with symptoms suggestive of a general medical condition, but medical exams cannot fully account for the physical symptoms (Mayou, Kirmayer, Simon, Kroenke, & Sharpe, 2005). One such example is conversion disorder, which involves evidence of symptoms consisting of deficits affecting voluntary motor or sensory function (i.e., loss of voice or vision, difficulty swallowing, partial/full paralysis, seizures, etc.) that suggest neurological or other general medical conditions without detectible physical impairment (Boone, 2007; Bourgeois, Chang, Hilty, & Servis, 2002; Merten, 2001). Individuals with somatoform disorders often lack the vocabulary to clearly articulate their symptoms in conjunction with laboratory results that do not support their personal description of their perceived illness. Studies indicate 30% of patients with somatoform-like symptoms fail at least one symptom validity test, and 11% fail on two symptom validity tests (Kemp et al., 2008). Individuals who simulate symptoms often cannot be differentiated from patients with actual, non-simulated symptomatology (Boone, 2007; Krahn, Bostwick, & Stonnington, 2008; Merten, 2001).

However, as noted, the symptoms presented in somatoform disorders are not considered intentional in regard to the seeking of external gain.

The commonality of mental disorder symptoms feigned is not uniform. While it is less common for individuals to attempt to feign organic central nervous system damage, it is more common for individuals to feign mild brain injury or other cognitive impairment (Daniel & Resnick, 1987; Greve, Ord, Bianchini, & Curtis, 2009). Individuals with more severe traumatic brain injuries demonstrate a lack of awareness of their impairment, (also referred to as insight), which consequently leads to underreporting actual neurobehavioral symptoms (Hart et al., 2003). Individuals with traumatic brain injury can also display a limited awareness of impairment based on the magnitude of injury, pre-existing adaptive inflexibility, cycles of maladaptive behavior, and emotional instability that typically prompt the pursuit of litigation (Hart et al., 2003). While neuroimaging may provide an objective measure to determine if there is a biological reason for failure, it is far from a magic bullet for completely understanding the issue. This should not diminish the importance of neuroimaging, as both it and neuropsychological testing are often necessary to definitively determine credible impairments in cases of suspected traumatic brain injury.

Co-Occurrence with Antisocial Personality Disorder

The American Psychiatric Association's (2013) Diagnostic and Statistical Manual of Mental Disorders-Fifth Edition, (DSM-5) notes that individuals diagnosed with antisocial personality disorder (APD) are more likely to malinger than those without. Contrary to what is suggested in the DSM-5 guidelines, some research suggests forensic psychiatric defendants with APD may not demonstrate a greater likelihood of malingering than those without APD (Kucharski, Falkenbach, Egan, & Duncan, 2006; Pierson, Rosenfeld, Green, & Belfi, 2011). Researchers have argued that the view that malingering and APD are connected is "too preoccupied with one form of faking, has a weak empirical basis, and is plagued by conceptual problems" (Niesten, Nentjes, Merckelbach, & Bernstein, 2015, p. 40). One conceptual problem cited is a disregard for APD as a dimensional construct. However, APD and histrionic personality style are still considered to be associated with malingering and, thus, it is still held that examiners should use caution when considering malingering with individuals diagnosed with APD (Faust, 1995). To help differentiate malingering from other potential conditions, mental health professionals must specifically investigate the underlying motivations for behavior.

Malingering and Trauma Disorders

Distinguishing post-traumatic stress disorder (PTSD) and other trauma-based disorders from malingering presents specific challenges, due to the subjective experience of the individual experiencing trauma and the highly varied expressions of such phenomenon across all domains of function. The clinician's training, experience, knowledge, and awareness of the individual's personal history are crucial in the assessment process. This further reinforces the point of this chapter—that when considering malingering of symptoms, information from as many sources as possible is needed to make an accurate determination. The criteria for a clinical diagnosis of PTSD are largely determined by subjective experience in response to a traumatic event, usually involving a death or near-death experience, and self-reported symptoms of trauma (Elhai, Gold, Sellers, & Dorfman, 2001), which include internal experiences such as flashbacks, nightmares, and anxiety. The weight placed on these subjectively experienced criteria makes the diagnostic process particularly perilous. Further contributing to the complexity of a PTSD diagnosis is the nature of the onset of symptoms, which may occur at any age, during any stage of the lifespan, with or without other pre-existing mental disorders, and with substantial individual differences in recovery rates (Penk, Rierdan, Losardo, & Robinowitz, 2006). Diagnosis of, and compensation for, PTSD requires a direct link to an identifiable traumatic event or circumstance experienced prior to the reported symptoms (Pitman et al., 1996). In cases of malingering, the symptoms have both been feigned by non-traumatized persons and by persons who have been traumatized but who never actually developed diagnosable PTSD (Penk et al., 2006). Hence, differentiating the symptoms of an actual PTSD diagnosis and malingering is very difficult, and this difficulty is reflected in the nebulous research results presently available regarding the prevalence rates of feigned PTSD (Young, 2014).

A structured clinical interview is the foundation for both diagnosing PTSD and detecting possible malingering. The chance of successful malingering is enhanced when an individual familiar with the symptoms of the disorder is provided uniform, self-reporting checklists (Burges & McMillan, 2001; Bury & Bagby, 2002; Elhai et al., 2007; Morel & Marshman, 2008). Careful attention must be paid not only to the individual's traumatic experience but also to his or her background, financial situation, and legal situation, as these may serve as motivating factors for malingering. The examining clinician should also ask the individual open-ended questions that address the symptoms being experienced and document accurate notes of the individual's behavior, explanation of symptoms, level of cooperation, and demeanor during the interview (Elhai et al., 2007; Ingram, Dowben, Froehlich, & Keltner, 2012). The individual should be encouraged to tell his or her recollection of the related traumatic event or events in detail, with as little prompting and interruption as possible on the part of the clinician.

Recording a thorough life history is also critical to diagnosing any psychiatric illness (Penk et al., 2006). In order to get a complete picture of the patient, a review of all available medical, psychiatric, military, public, civilian, and criminal records should be conducted. With PTSD, it is tempting to focus mainly on the issue of the response to the immediate trauma. However, along with a focus on the contemporary trauma and the individual's response to it, a review of an individual's background and history is imperative. This review may provide information about previous exposure to trauma, as well as factors that support resilience and recovery (Penk et al., 2006). Additionally, throughout a comprehensive interview, the examiner can assess the internal consistency of the answers provided by the individuals in regard to their general history. It would not be uncommon for an individual who is malingering to respond to seemingly unrelated questions in an inconsistent or exaggerated fashion, as compared to what their history or collateral information indicates.

OTHER COMMONLY FEIGNED DISORDERS

Offenders who attempt to avoid arrest, conviction, and punishment often claim crime-related amnesia (Kopelman, 1995; Parwatikar, Holcomb, & Menninger, 1985). Often this is not an elaborate, cognitively taxing strategy; it may not involve anything more than a simple claim of not remembering the act in question (Jelicic & Merckelbach, 2015; Kopelman, 1995). While post-traumatic, crime-related amnesia can genuinely occur as a result of stress, it is a rare occurrence and most likely takes place when the offender is incoherent due to a state of shock. Rather than being long-term, this form of amnesia is often short in duration (Giger, Merten, Merkelbach, & Oswald, 2010).

It is not uncommon for defendants to feign psychiatric symptoms consistent, in whole or in part, with psychotic and delusional disorders (Oorsouw & Merkelbach, 2010). These symptoms may be presented objectively (i.e., quantitative, measurable, and verifiable) or subjectively (i.e., reported by the defendant, subjective and unobservable). For example, hallucinations may be feigned. Hallucinations are often associated with psychotic diagnoses such as schizophrenia. Visual hallucinations are reported at a rate of 24%-30% in individuals diagnosed with schizophrenia and are accompanied by delusions 88% of the time (Resnick & Knoll, 2005b). Visual hallucinations are also reported at a rate of 46% in malingering cases (Resnick & Knoll, 2005b). Those who malinger also report hallucinations similar to schizophrenia and other psychotic disorders (Chesterman,

Terbeck, & Vaughan, 2008). Authentic hallucinations generally become less frequent when individuals become involved in activities, socialize with others, and take their medications as directed. Additionally, these hallucinations tend to be more intermittent, rather than constant (Resnick & Knoll, 2005a). Also, true cases of schizophrenia tend to include having more auditory hallucinations than visual ones; however, malingerers tend to endorse visual hallucinations more frequently (Chesterman et al., 2008). These behaviors need to be considered when determining if an individual's symptoms are authentic or a result of malingering.

Individuals may also feign cognitive impairment and neurological disorders, including Alzheimer's disease and other forms of dementia, head injuries, autism spectrum disorder, and intellectual or learning disabilities (Oorsouw & Merkelbach, 2010). As might be expected, individuals who simulate neurological disorders and deficits often exhibit inconsistent symptoms (Resnick & Knoll, 2005b). For example, an individual who is malingering may report several symptoms from various disorders. It is important to discern this, because poor performance across cognitive ability measures attributed to an incorrect neurologic etiology can potentially lead to a misallocation of clinical and financial resources (Armistead-Jehle & Denney, 2015; Green, 2007).

A wide breadth of literature remains available on malingering related to psychiatric disorders as well; however, it is beyond the current scope of this introductory chapter (Young, 2014). The following sections will focus on patterns and detection of malingering specifically related to neurocognitive deficits.

PATTERNS OF MALINGERING: NEUROCOGNITIVE DEFICITS

Relevant to the malingering of neurocognitive deficits, four patterns have been defined for both clinical referrals and criminal justice-involved individuals (Hebben & Milberg, 2002). The first pattern is "symptom exaggeration," wherein actual impairment is presented as more intense than what is truly experienced (Hebben & Milberg, 2002). For example, on the Wechsler Memory Scale-3rd Edition (WMS-III) individuals with genuine memory impairment may still consciously choose to withhold details on the Logical Memory and Visual Reproduction Delayed Recall tests.

The second pattern identified by Hebben & Milberg (2002) involves continuing to demonstrate symptoms after they have already abated. For example, individuals may sustain a head injury and demonstrate post-concussion symptoms such as headaches, blurred vision, or loss of memory, which typically dissipate over time. Individuals attempting to malinger may utilize the opportunity to maintain an image of low cognitive functioning or impairment (Hebben & Milberg, 2002).

The third pattern of malingering involves attributing the presence of symptoms caused by a previous brain injury incident to a current incident (Hebben & Milberg, 2002). In this pattern, an occurrence of previous injury is brought up again as a way of explaining the development of newer neurocognitive symptoms. The discernment of current symptoms from preexisting ones is difficult, because neuropsychological tests can be influenced by pre-existing learning disabilities or cognitive dysfunctions.

The fourth pattern of malingering involves a blatant manifestation of symptoms or impairment (Hebben & Milberg, 2002). For example, when an individual with probable mild traumatic brain injury makes an abnormal or exaggerated number of prolonged responses when testing using the Gudjonsson Suggestibility Scales, they are likely feigning symptoms (Woolston, Bain, & Baxter, 2006). This pattern is most commonly identified in forensic populations (Woolston et al., 2006). When conducting a forensic examination, an essential initial step (regardless of the archetype) is to gather all applicable information about the individual's psychological, educational, and substance abuse history that could have an influence on current functioning and performance levels (Hebben & Milberg, 2002).

Detection of Malingering

The detection of malingering is not an easy task, regardless of the methods utilized. Prior to employing psychometric measures to assess malingering, mental health professionals (especially forensic examiners) should review the literature to determine which assessments would be most applicable to the individual, based on their initial complaints and litigation status. Multiple types of both formal and informal assessments should be utilized in all cases, including standardized measures that have been validated for the corresponding population, structured and unstructured clinical interviews, a review of medical history records, and other relevant data (Raine, 2009). It must also be understood that evidence of malingering does not rule out the co-morbid presence of an actual mental disorder (American Psychiatric Association, 2013). Additionally, evidence of malingering does not mean that the individual's legal case does not have merit. Conclusions about the meaning of the label of malingering should be differentiated from the presence of the pattern of symptoms. In other words, while two individuals may both present as malingering (based on their testing data), the reasons for their malingering, the suggested treatment, and the legal implications for each can vary considerably. As such, it is important to not only identify the presence of malingering, but also the motivation behind it.

A large part of the value of any assessment is dependent upon the reliability and validity of the uncompromised assessment tool. By using standardized assessment tools, various incongruences between performance and actual ability can be assessed. Incongruent responses can be purposeful (e.g., the tendency to offer responses that are socially acceptable) or unconscious (e.g., not taking the test seriously, poor concentration, or answering randomly) (Fugett, Thomas, & Lindberg, 2014). Typically, performance validity tests are either dichotomized as instruments designed and standardized to evaluate effort (Heilbronner et al., 2009) or indexes embedded in cognitive ability tests (e.g., Forced Choice Test) (Armistead-Jehle & Denney, 2015; Frederick & Foster, 1991).

Measures that are not designed to detect malingering should only be used to determine a performance discrepancy (Rogers & Correa, 2008). Such discrepancies are abnormal responses, which may indicate the possibility of malingering but could also result from confusion or reading difficulties (Rogers & Correa, 2008). For example, cognitive assessment measures are designed with the intent of measuring cognitive faculties; however, studies indicate standardized cognitive assessments are poor tools for detecting simulation of cognitive impairment (Boyd, McLearen, Meyer, & Denney, 2007; Rogers & Correa, 2008).

Because of the possibility of underperformance on standard assessment measures, implementing a variety of assessment tools and strategies is critical (Kessels, Aleman, Verhagen, & Van Luijtelaar, 2000). While some assessment measures are typically embedded with measures for effort, they are generally not designed to identify malingering (Berthelson, Mulchan, Odland, Miller, & Mittenberg, 2013). Differences between self-reporting, official records, and observed behavior should be considered, in addition to discrepant patterns on tests of cognition (Mittenberg et al., 2002; Sharland & Gfeller, 2007). Due to these possibilities, there have been some authors who have cautioned the use of "effort" tests in litigation and other types of cases (McCarter, Walton, Brooks, & Powell, 2009). However, on the whole, such tests are still viewed favorably by clinicians and practitioners, such as neuropsychologists. They are also still considered effective when used in conjunction with other tests and used by experienced neuropsychologists (Merten, Bossink, & Schmand, 2007). Effort tests may consist of, but are not limited to, consistency, neurocognitive, psychological, and forced-choice tests.

Other indicators of inconsistency should also be noted. These include passing difficult items but failing less-difficult items, abnormally high "I don't know" responses, near misses, and elevated recognition scores on memory items (Boone, 2007). Attending to these factors contemporaneously with all the other elements of the assessment will assist the evaluator in determining response validity and differentiating between discrepancies of responses due to true disorders (unconscious) from those that are malingering (purposeful). For this reason, there is a growing consensus that multiple tests should be conducted to determine a more accurate assessment of response validity (Larrabee, 2007; Strauss, Sherman, & Spreen, 2006), with malingering assessed in most, if not all, of the chosen evaluations (Heilbronner et al., 2009).

In some cases, it can be helpful to determine the motive for malingered symptoms. Some researchers suggest that the evaluator's responsibility might go beyond the mere identification of malingered symptoms and extend to understanding an individual's motives for deliberate feigning of symptoms (Rogers, 2008c). Often individuals who malinger symptoms have legitimate desires; however, they feel ineffective in terms of their ability to attain their goal. As such, they engage in maladaptive behaviors such as malingering to achieve their goal. Understanding what led the individual to malinger their symptoms can offer suggestions in terms of potential interventions, as well as offering mitigating factors that led to their poor choices. For example, financial incentive has been shown to directly impact the validity of an individual's performance (Bianchini, Curtis, & Greve, 2006). Malingerers who "had received compensation reported higher symptom levels than those who had not" (Kunst & Winkel, 2015, p. 318). This can be seen as suggesting potential compensation incentivizes feigning symptoms (Kunst, Winkel, & Bogaerts, 2010). However, the evaluator would gain a much better understanding of the individual if they sought to understand why financial motives were so particularly strong for the person at this time.

In order to effectively rule out malingering, the evaluator must consider the consistency of symptoms with the history and facts of the injury, the compatibility of symptoms with each other, and the conformity of symptom development with known outcomes of similar injuries (Egeland et al., 2015). To aid this process, Egeland et al. (2015) suggest testing a variety of important symptoms, including cognitive, somatic, and psychological issues reported by the individual, to ensure an accurate diagnosis. Alternatively, other research suggests malingering may also be detected by assessment measures that focus on the nature of the feigned dysfunction rather than a targeted assessment of deception (Iverson & Binder, 2000).

DEVELOPMENT OF ASSESSMENT TECHNIQUES

Early assessment techniques utilized to detect malingering in forensic settings were often limited to personality tests that tangentially produced inferential data but did not include measures designed explicitly to detect malingering (Green, Allen, & Astner, 2003). During the initial development of the Minnesota Multiphasic Personality Inventory (MMPI), the most widely used personality assessment in the world (Butcher, 1989; Butcher & Williams, 2009; Lufi & Awwad, 2013), two techniques were included to assess response patterns: over-reporting (a more elementary attempt at feigning) and under-reporting (a more sophisticated attempt at feigning) (Green et al., 2003). Scales were added to evaluate the validity of responses. The MMPI-2 revisions allowed for additional interpretation of inconsistent responses as well as random endorsement of items and answering in an all-true or all-false response style. These built-in validity scales were incorporated into the MMPI (Butcher et al., 2015). While the MMPI-2 or the MMPI-2-RF are typically used in assessments for a wide range of reasons, including assessment of inconsistent responses and symptom exaggeration, these instruments are not able to confirm the motivation for giving a misleading account, which is viewed by some researchers as important in determining malingering (Rogers & Bender, 2003).

An entirely new generation of malingering assessments have been developed specifically to address the needs of the legal system regarding litigation and criminal sentencing (Robbennolt & Studebaker, 2003). This second generation of instruments focuses on the detection of the triad of motivation, compliance, and effort (Hebben & Milberg, 2002). In particular, forced-choice examinations were created. These tests evaluate an individual's performance and effort levels, with obtained scores then compared against the performance levels of the researched and normed group (Hebben & Milberg, 2002).

One of the most commonly used forced-choice tests to determine effort levels is the Test of Memory Malingering (TOMM) (Tombaugh, 1996). This test is intended to detect the malingering of memory disorders. The TOMM has been demonstrated as having adequate classification accuracy when discriminating between individuals with cognitive impairment and malingerers (Rees, Tombaugh, Gansler, & Moczynski, 1998; Tombaugh, 1997; Vallabhajosula & van Gorp, 2001). It also compensates for other factors such as age and education (Rees et al., 1998), depression (Rees, Tombaugh, & Boulay, 2001), and other neurological conditions (Rivera et al., 2015; Tombaugh, 1997). A criticism of this measure includes insensitivity to people with dementia who have actual severe memory impairment. In those cases, there is a significant risk of false-positive results (i.e., malingering is falsely detected when there are real symptoms of dementia present). Research emphasizes the need for "further scientific investigation regarding populations at risk for failing effort and validity indicators despite best effort" (Egeland et al., 2015, p. 216). These individuals may exhibit random false memories (Schnider, 2001; Schnider, Ptak, von Daniken, & Remonda, 2000; Schnider, von Daniken, & Gutbrod, 1996). Additionally, they may produce false memories in response to cues (Cirelli, Dickinson, & Poirier, 2015; Moscovitch & Melo, 1997). Also, they may exhibit increased false recognition during word-list learning (Melo, Winocur, & Moscovitch, 1999; Olszewska, Reuter-Lorenz, Munier, & Bendler, 2015). Finally, they may also exhibit increased false-positive responses during a visual recognition task (Gilboa, Alain, He, Stuss, & Moscovitch, 2009).

Another forced-choice test is The Digit Recognition Test (DRT) (Binder, 1993), which assesses the motivation to perform on tests of recent memory. Prior to beginning the assessment, the examinee is informed they will be given a memory test and the tasks will become increasingly difficult. Malingerers should score 50%, or below chance (Tan, Slick, Strause, & Hultsch, 2010), but most malingerers are known to not perform as poorly on forced-choice techniques (Bianchini, Mathias, Greve, Houston, & Crouch, 2001; Nicholson & Martelli, 2007; Vickery, Berry, Inman, Harris, & Orey, 2001).

In addition to forced-choice tests, a number of strategies have been introduced to assess symptom validity in medical and legal cases. One such strategy is the cross-referencing of test results; for example, if an examinee performs poorly on attention and concentration tests, but does well on memory tests, it may imply underperformance on some of the tests (Iverson, 2006). In an effort to expand the pool of symptom validity tests, cognitive tests were designed to measure poor effort, and self-report tests were designed to measure exaggeration of symptoms (Iverson, 2006). Still other assessments target behavioral presentations. These tests assume individuals who attempt to exaggerate or feign have limited awareness of the diagnostic criteria for mental and behavioral disorders (Larrabee, 2007). Individuals who aim to simulate a sickness or disorder will most often exhibit more unusual behavior than truthful patients, in what might be described as "over-acting the part."

The Structured Interview of Reported Symptoms-Second Edition (SIRS-2) (Rogers, Sewell, & Gillard, 2010) and the Miller Forensic Assessment Test (M-FAST) (Miller, 2001) assess exaggeration of psychotic symptoms. The M-FAST score provides an estimate of the likelihood the individual is feigning a mental disorder. The subscales then relay information about the individual's response styles that may help explain how the individual is attempting to malinger (Miller, 2001). The SIRS-2 assesses feigned psychological distress and psychosis, with the knowledge of the types of behavioral symptoms malingerers feign in mind. Several detection strategies are embedded within the test. While this measure has been vetted on a normed sample, it is important to reiterate no single instrument should be relied upon exclusively to make conclusive decisions (Rogers et al., 2010).

The Structured Inventory of Malingered Symptomatology (SIMS) (Jelicic, Merckelbach, Giesbrecht, & de Ruiter, 2008) is a universal screening instrument developed to detect exaggeration of symptoms in five domains: (1) affective disorders, (2) psychosis, (3) low intelligence, (4) amnesia, and (5) neurological impairment (Jelicic, Hessels, & Merckelbach, 2006). The measure is considered "a good candidate for a standalone symptom validity test," in part because it covers a broad spectrum of symptoms (Egeland et al., 2015, p. 215). However, it is recommended to be part of a battery of tests in order to make a more accurate determination of malingering.

The Word Memory Test (WMT) (Green, 2003) is a computer-based test that assesses verbal memory in addition to the feigning of symptoms (Green, Lees-Haley, & Allen, 2003b). The WMT contains measures that are very sensitive to exaggeration or poor effort but insensitive to all but the most extreme forms of cognitive impairment. The WMT differs from other symptom-validity tests due to its extensive validation in clinical forensic settings, while others rely on simulation research using healthy volunteers (Green et al., 2003).

The Medical Symptom Validity Test (MSVT) (Green, 2004) and the nonverbal MSVT (NV-MSVT) (Green, 2008) were created to address the issue of low test scores produced by people with severe cognitive impairment (Singhal, Green, Ashaye, Shankar, & Gill, 2009). These tests are able to differentiate low scores between individuals attempting to simulate impairment and those with severe impairment. Research has shown that the MSVT and NV-MSVT produce minimal false positives in individuals with critical memory impairment and predict even fewer false-positive scores in people with minimal or no memory impairment (Singhal et al., 2009).

The Conners' Continuous Performance Test–II (CPT–II) (Conners, 2000) is a frequently used measure of attention and concentration. Attention-related deficits are commonly reported following traumatic brain injuries (TBI) (Rabin, Barr, & Burton, 2005). Continuous performance tasks, such as the CPT–II, may be especially sensitive to TBI-related impairments (Cicerone & Azulay, 2002; Ord, Boettcher, Greve, & Bianchini, 2010) and can, therefore, often be used as a lens to focus on identifying mild cognitive deficits. Continuous performance tasks have also proven useful for identifying malingering when feigning a TBI (Henry & Enders, 2007; Larrabee, 2008; Ord et al., 2010) or attention-deficit disorders (Quinn, 2003).

There are also multiple assessment measures that focus solely on neurological impairments. For example, the Forced Choice Test and the Portland Digit Recognition Test (PDRT) are useful in developing introductory hypotheses about behavior, but are not useful for other neuropsychological interpretations (Allen, 2011). Creating additional validity tests in existing neuropsychological instruments may be more efficient, while simultaneously enhancing overall validity, than creating entirely new instruments (Tan et al., 2010).

The Pattern of Performance Method (PPM) is one of the most effective ways to detect malingering with common neuropsychological evaluations (Meyers & Volbrecht, 2003). There are four procedures that are considered to be PPMs. One PPM inspects performance for uncommon mistakes (Slick, Sherman, & Iverson, 1999) by comparing scores of easy and difficult items. A second PPM evaluates scores for consistency with patterns of function or impairment, such as memory tests (Bernard, 1991; Russel, Spector, & Kelly, 1993), comparison of recall to recognition (Beetar & Williams, 1995; Bernard, 1991; Binder, 1992), and comparison of tests for attention and memory (Mittenberg, Arzin, Millsaps, & Heilbronner, 1993). The third PPM is an evaluation of errors normal for a reported injury. The fourth PPM is an evaluation of scores obtained from contrast groups such as non-litigating patients, malingerers, and individuals who were feigning malingering (Meyers & Volbrecht, 2003).

Since the early 1990s, there has been a surge in malingering measures (Heilbronner et al., 2009). Patterns of memory errors that might otherwise be mistaken for malingering have been examined and related to aspects of memory such as attention, encoding, storage, and retrieval (Fotopoulou, 2009; Johnson, 1991). This research has led to the creation of embedded measures of effort in a slew of cognitive tests such as Reliable Digits (Babikian, Boone, Lu, & Arnold, 2006), Sentence Repetition (Meyers, Volkert, & Diep, 2000), and the Rey Complex Figure and Recognition Test (ROCFT) (Lu, Boone, Cozolino, & Mitchell, 2003). Additional measures have been created based on the Forced Choice (Bogacz, Brown, Moehlis, Holmes, & Cohen, 2006) and Judgment of Line Orientation (Irani, 2011). Research is still emerging on these newer assessment tools; however, they are predominately used as supplemental measures to a comprehensive assessment battery (Duncan & Ausborn, 2002; Heilbronner et al., 2009). It is important to repeat that in to order adequately answer any referral question, the competent evaluator must rely on multiple tools and collateral data points, whenever possible, to build a comprehensive assessment. This is of particular importance for matters such as malingering, which can have significant and meaningful ramifications.

Internal validity indicators from commonly used measures such as the Wechsler Adult Intelligence Scale (Mittenberg et al., 2001), Wechsler Memory Scale (Ord, Greve, & Bianchini, 2008), and California Verbal Learning Test (Curtis, Greve, Bianchini, & Brennan, 2006) have also been useful for the recognition of malingering, when used as part of a comprehensive classification system targeting Malingered Neurocognitive Dysfunction (MND) (Larrabee, 2003). In this process, analysis from standard neuropsychological measures are considered questionable when they are markedly different from expected results, given the individual's history, behavior, or known patterns of brain function. However, intelligence measures should not be used independently to ascertain malingering, as IQ has not been shown to be related to outcomes on performance validity tests (Demakis, Rimland, Reeve, & Ward, 2015).

The underlying intentions behind malingering may motivate individuals to gather as much information as possible about these tests before they are administered. The integrity of the tests may in turn be compromised, as information is made increasingly available to the public via the Internet (Cunningham & Feldman, 2011). The availability to the public of certain aspects of malingering evaluations can create issues with test security, as the details about what evaluators look for during these tests may fall into the wrong hands (Bauer & McCaffrey, 2006; Ruiz, Drake, Glass, Marcotte, & van Gorp, 2002). However, current research is addressing these issues by continuing to study what responses are less likely to be affected by memory issues or forgetfulness, to avoid misidentifying malingerers and truthful responders (Buddin et al., 2014, p. 536).

CONCLUSION

The detection of malingering continues to be an important issue in both clinical and forensic settings. The assessment process is immensely complex, since the measures used to detect malingering must cover a wide range of information, including the feigning of mental disorders, cognitive impairment, common ailments, debilitating symptoms, and systemic diseases (Rogers, 2008a). The attending mental health professional must have a strong clinical background in recognizing malingering response styles, feigned symptom presentations, target symptoms, and the differentiation between malingered and real symptom presentations (Richter, 2014). When mental health professionals are not familiar with malingering, they will likely fail to recognize it (Finsterer & Stefan, 2016; Rogers, 1997). Conversely, when examiners are familiar with malingering, they are more likely to detect it (Heilbronner et al., 2009). As such, mental health professionals who administrator malingering inventories should seek out ongoing education and training to be able to better recognize the subtle signs and symptoms of those attempting to engage in this type of behavior.

After years of research on the assessment of malingering, Rogers (2008b) concluded that the ability to detect and evaluate malingering has indeed made great strides. Researchers and evaluators are far more aware of attitudinal and motivational influences that affect accuracy of test performance than ever before (Armistead-Jehle & Denney, 2015). The use of multiple mental and physical health assessment tools to assess suspected malingering is currently considered best practice (Rogers & Granacher, 2011). While no specific tests or guidelines have perfected malingering detection, mental health professionals are in a much better position today than at any previous time to decipher genuine performance from feigned performance, using a range of assessment tools, interviewing strategies, and the integration of collateral information.

REFERENCES

Allen, D. N. (2011). Portland Digit Recognition Test. In J. S. Kreutzer, J. DeLuca, & B. Caplan (Eds.), *Encyclopedia of Clinical Neuropsychology* (pp. 1966-1968). New York, NY: Springer.

American Psychiatric Association. (2000). *Diagnostic and statistical manual of mental disorders* (4th ed.). Washington, DC: American Psychiatric Association.

American Psychiatric Association (2013). *Diagnostic and statistical manual of mental disorders* (5th ed.). Arlington VA: American Psychiatric Association.

American Psychological Association. (2002). Ethical principles of psychologists and code of conduct. *American psychologist, 57*(12), 1060-1073. Retrieved from http://www.apa.org/ethics/code2002.html

American Psychological Association. (2013). Specialty guidelines for forensic psychology. *The American Psychologist, 68*(1), 7.

Angrist, J., Chen, S., & Frandsen, B. (2010). Did Vietnam veterans get sicker in the 1990s? The complicated effects of military service on self-reported health. *Journal of Public Economics, 94*, 824-837. doi:10.1016/j.jpubeco.2010.06.001

Armistead-Jehle, P., & Denney, R. L. (2015). The detection of feigned impairment using the WMT, MSVT, and NV-MSVT. *Applied Neuropsychology: Adult, 22*(2), 147-155. doi:10.1080/23279095.2014.880842

Atkins v. Virginia, 536 U.S. 304. (2002).

Australia Psychological Society. (2005). *Code of ethics*. Victoria: Australian Psychological Society.

Babikian, T., Boone, K., Lu, P., & Arnold, G. (2006). Sensitivity and specificity of various digit span scores in the detection of suspect effort. *The Clinical Neuropsychologist, 20,* 145-159. doi:10.1080/13854040590947362

Batt, K., Shores, A. E., & Chekaluk, E. (2008). The effect of distraction on the Word Memory Test and Test of Memory Malingering performance in patients with a severe brain injury. *Journal of the International Neuropsychological Society, 14*, 1074-1080. doi:10.1017/S135561770808137X

Bauer, L., & McCaffrey, R. (2006). Coverage of the test of memory malingering, Victoria symptom validity test, and word memory test on the Internet: Is test security threatened? *Archives of Clinical Neuropsychology, 21*(1), 121-126.

Beetar, J., & Williams, J. (1995). Malingering response styles on the Memory Assessment Scales and symptom validity tests. *Archives of Clinical Neuropsychology, 10*, 57-72.

Bernard, L. (1991). The detection of faked deficits on the Rey Auditory Verbal Learning Test: The effect of serial position. *Archives of Clinical Neuropsychology, 6*, 81-88.

Berry, D. T., Baer, R. A., Rinaldo, J. C., & Wetter, M. W. (2002). Assessment of malingering. In J. N. Butcher (Ed.), *Clinical personality assessment: Practical approaches*. New York, NY: Oxford University Press.

Berthelson, L., Mulchan, S. S., Odland, A. P., Miller, L. J., & Mittenberg, W. (2013). False positive diagnosis of malingering due to the use of multiple effort tests. *Brain Injury, 27*(7-8), 909-916. doi:10.3109/02699052.2013.793400

Bianchini, K., Curtis, K., & Greve, K. (2006). Compensation and malingering in traumatic brain injury: A dose–response relationship? *The Clinical Neuropsychologist, 20*, 831-847.

Bianchini, K. J., Mathias, C. W., & Greve, K. W. (2001). Symptom validity testing: A critical review. *The Clinical Neuropsychologist, 15*, 19-45.

Bianchini, K. J., Mathias, C. W., Greve, K. W, Houston, R. J., & Crouch, J. A. (2001). Classification accuracy of the Portland Digit Recognition Test in traumatic brain injury. *The Clinical Neuropsychologist, 15*, 461-470.

Binder, L. M. (1992). Malingering detected by forced choice testing of memory and tactile sensation: A case report. *Archives of Clinical Neuropsychology, 7*, 155-163.

Binder, L. M. (1993). *Portland digit recognition test manual.* Beaverton, OR: Laurence Binder.

Binder, L. M., & Willis, S. C. (1991). Assessment of motivation after financially compensable minor head trauma. *Psychological Assessment: A Journal of Consulting and Clinica Psychology, 3*(2),175. doi:10.1037/1040-3590.3.2.175

Blume, J. H., Johnson, S. L., & Seeds, C. (2009). An empirical look at Atkins v. Virginia and its application in capital cases. *Tennessee Law Review, 76*, 625-629.

Bogacz, R., Brown, E., Moehlis, J., Holmes, P., & Cohen, J. (2006). The physics of optimal decision making: A formal analysis of models of performance in two-alternative forced-choice tasks. *Psychological Review, 113*, 700-765. doi:10.1037/0033-295X.113.4.700

Boone, K. (2007). *Assessment of feigned cognitive impairment: A neuropsychological perspective.* New York, NY: The Guilford Press.

Bourgeois, J., Chang, C., Hilty, D., & Servis, M. (2002). Clinical manifestations and management of conversion disorders. *Current Treatment Options in Neurology, 4*(6), 487-497. doi:10.1007/s11940-002-0016-2

Boyd, A., McLearen, A., Meyer, R., & Denney, R. (2007). *Detection of deception.* Sarasota, FL: Professional Resource Press.

Browndyke, J., Paskavitz, J., Sweet, L., Cohen, R., Tucker, K., Welsh-Bohmer, K., Bohmer, K. A., Burke, J. R., & Schmechel, D. (2008). Neuroanatomical correlates of malingered memory impairment: Event-related fMRI of deception on a recognition memory task. *Brain Injury, 22*, 481-489. doi:10.1080/02699050802084894

Buddin, W. J., Schroeder, R. W., Hargrave, D. D., Von Dran, E. J., Campbell, E. B., Brockman, C. J., Heinrichs, R. J., & Baade, L. E. (2014). An examination of the frequency of invalid forgetting on the Test of Memory Malingering. *The Clinical Neuropsychologist, 28*(3), 525-542. doi:10.1080/13854046.2014.906658

Burges, C., & McMillan, T. (2001). The ability of naïve participants to report symptoms of post-traumatic stress disorder. *British Journal of Clinical Psychology, 40*, 209-214. doi:10.1348/014466501163544

Bury, A., & Bagby, R. (2002). The detection of feigned uncoached and coached post-traumatic stress disorder with the MMPI-2 in a sample of workplace accident victims. *Psychological Assessment, 14*, 472-484. doi:10.1037//1040-3590.14.4.472

Butcher, J. N. (1989). Minnesota multiphasic personality inventory. In I. B. Weiner & W. E. Craighead (Eds.), *Corsini Encyclopedia of Psychology.* Hoboken, NJ: John Wiley & Sons, Incorporated.

Butcher, J. N., & Williams, C. L. (2009). Personality assessment with the MMPI-2: Historical roots, international adaptations and current challenges. *Applied Psychology: Health and Wellbeing, 1*, 105-135.

Callahan, L. A., Steadman, H. J., McGreevy, M. A., & Robbins, P. C. (1991). The volume and characteristics of insanity defense pleas: An eight-state study. *Journal of the American Academy of Psychiatry and the Law Online, 19*(4), 331-338.

Carroll, M. F. (2003). Malingering in the military. *Psychiatric Annals, 33*(11), 732-736.

Cassidy, J., & Shaver, P. (2008). *Handbook of attachment: Theory, research, and clinical applications* (2nd ed.). New York, NY: The Guilford Press.

Chesterman, L. P., Terbeck, S., & Vaughan, F. (2008). Malingered psychosis. *Journal of Forensic Psychiatry & Psychology, 19*(3), 275-300. doi:10.1080/14789940701841129

Cicerone, K., & Azulay, J. (2002). Diagnostic utility of attention measures in post-concussion syndrome. *The Clinical Neuropsychologist, 16*, 280-289.

Cirelli, L. K., Dickinson, J., & Poirier, M. (2015). Using Implicit Instructional Cues to Influence False Memory Induction. *Journal of psycholinguistic research, 44*(5), 485-494.

Conners, C. (2000). *Conners' Continuous Performance Test II.* Toronto: Multi-Health Systems. Cunningham, J. M., & Feldman, M. D. (2011). Munchausen by Internet: Current Perspectives and Three New Cases. *Psychosomatics, 52*(2), 185-189.

Curtis, K., Greve, K., Bianchini, K., & Brennan, A. (2006). California verbal learning test indicators of malingered neurocognitive dysfunction: Sensitivity and specificity in traumatic brain injury. *Assessment, 13*(1), 46-61. doi:10.1177/1073191105285210

Daniel, A. E., & Resnick, P. J. (1987). Mutism, malingering, and competency to stand trial. *Journal of the American Academy of Psychiatry and the Law Online, 15*(3), 301-308.

David, H., Duggan, M. G., & Lyle, D. S. (2011). Battle scars? The puzzling decline in employment and rise in disability receipt among Vietnam era veterans. *The American Economic Review, 101*(3), 339-344.

Dean, A., Victor, T., Boone, K., & Arnold, G. (2008). The relationship of IQ to effort test performance. *The Clinical Neuropsychologist, 22*, 705-722.

Demakis, G., Rimland, C., Reeve, C., & Ward, J. (2015). Intelligence and psychopathy do not influence malingering. *Applied Neuropsychology: Adult,* (ahead-of-print), 1-9.

Denney, R. L., & Sullivan, J. P. (2008). *Clinical neuropsychology in the criminal forensic setting.* New York, NY: Guilford Press.

Drob, S. L., & Berger, R. H. (1987). Determination of Malingering: A Comprehensive Clinical-Forensic Approach. *The Journal of Psychiatry & Law, 15*, 519.

Duncan, S. A., & Ausborn, D. L. (2002). The use of reliable digits to detect malingering in a criminal forensic pretrial population. *Assessment, 9*(1), 56-61.

Durst, R., Fastovsky, N., Michnik, T., & Raskin, S. (2011). [Phenomenology of malingering, dissimulation and aspiration]. *Harefuah, 150*(9), 696-699.

Egeland, J., Andersson, S., Sundseth, Ø. Ø., & Schanke, A. K. (2015). Types or modes of malingering? A confirmatory factor analysis of performance and symptom validity tests. *Applied Neuropsychology: Adult, 22*(3), 215-226. doi:10.1080/23279095.2014.910212

Elhai, J., Butcher, J., Reeves, A., Baugher, S., Gray, M., Jacobs, G., Fricker-Elhai, A., North, T., & Arbisi, P. (2007). Varying cautionary instructions, monetary incentives, and Co-morbid diagnostic training in malingered psychopathology research. *Journal of Personality Assessment, 88*, 328-337. doi:10.1080/00223890701332136

Elhai, J., Gold, S., Sellers, A., & Dorfman, W. (2001). The detection of malingered post-traumatic stress disorder with MMPI-2 fake bad indices. *Assessment, 8*, 221-236.

Erdal, K. (2004). The effects of motivation, coaching, and knowledge of neuropsychology on the simulated malingering of head injury. *Archives of Clinical Neuropsychology, 19*, 73-88.

Faust, D. (1995). The detection of deception. *Neurologic Clinics. 13*(2), 255-265.

Feldman, M. D., Hamilton, J. C., & Deemer, H. (2001). Factitious disorder. In K. A. Philipps (Ed.), *Somatoform and Factitious Disorders. Review of Psychiatry, Vol. 20.* Washington, DC: American Psychiatric Press, pp.129-159.

Felthous, A. (2006). Introduction to this issue: Malingering. *Behavioral Sciences & the Law, 24,* 629-631.

Finsterer, J., & Stefan, L. (2016). Malingering and factitious disorder (Münchausen-syndrome) can be mitochondrial. *Indian Journal of Psychological Medicine, 38*(4), 348.

Fotopoulou, A. (2009). Disentangling the motivational theories of confabulation. W. Hirstein (Ed.), *Confabulation: Views From Neuroscience, Psychiatry, Psychology, and Philosophy.* (pp. 263-285). New York, NY; Oxford University Press.

Frederick, R. I., & Foster, H. G. (1991). Multiple measures of malingering on a forced-choice test of cognitive ability. *Psychological Assessment: A Journal of Consulting and Clinical Psychology, 3*(4), 596.

Fugett, A., Thomas, S. W., & Lindberg, M. A. (2014). The many faces of malingering and participant response strategies: New methodologies in the Attachment and Clinical Issues Questionnaire (ACIQ). *Journal of General Psychology, 141*(2), 80-97. doi:10.1080/00221309.2013.866538

Gast, J., & Hart, K. (2010). The performance of juvenile offenders on the test of memory malingering. *Journal of Forensic Psychology Practice, 10*, 53-68. doi:10.1080/15228930903173062

Giger, P., Merten, T., & Merkelbach, H., & Oswald, M. (2010). Detection of feigned crime-related amnesia: A multi-method approach. *Journal of Forensic Psychology Practice, 10*(5), 440-463, doi:10.1080/15 228932.2010.489875

Gilboa, A., Alain, C., He, Y., Stuss, D. T., & Moscovitch, M. (2009). Ventromedial prefrontal cortex lesions produce early functional alterations during remote memory retrieval. *Journal of Neuroscience 29*(15), 4871-4881.

Green, P. (2003). *Word Memory Test for Windows: User's manual and program.* Edmonton, Alberta: Green's Publishing.

Green, P. (2004). *Green's Medical Symptom Validity Test (MSVT) for Microsoft Windows: User's manual.* Edmonton, Canada: Green's Publishing.

Green, P. (2007). The pervasive influence of effort on neuropsychological tests. *Physical Medicine Rehabilitation Clinics of North America, 18*, 43-68.

Green, P. (2008). *Green's Nonverbal Medical Symptom Validity Test (NV-MSVT) for Microsoft Windows: User's manual 1.0.* Edmonton, AB, Canada: Green's Publishing.

Green, P., Allen, L. M., & Astner, K. (2003). *The word memory test.* Edmonton, Alberta: Green Publishing.

Green, P., Lees-Haley, P. R., & Allen III, L. M. (2003). The Word Memory Test and the validity of neuropsychological test scores. *Journal of Forensic Neuropsychology, 2*(3-4), 97-124.

Greve, K. W., Ord, J. S., Bianchini, K. J., & Curtis, K. L. (2009). Prevalence of malingering in patients with chronic pain referred for psychologic evaluation in a medico-legal context. *Archives of physical medicine and rehabilitation, 90*(7), 1117-1126.

Groth-Marnat, G. (2009). *Handbook of psychological assessment* (4th ed.). Hoboken, NJ: John Wiley & Sons.

Gunstad, J., & Suhr, J. (2001). Courting the clinician: Efficacy of the full and abbreviated forms of the Portland digit recognition test: Vulnerability to coaching. *The Clinical Neuropsychologist, 15*, 397-404.

Gunstad, J., & Suhr, J. (2004). Use of the abbreviated Portland digit recognition test in simulated malingering and neurological groups. *Journal of Forensic Neuropsychology, 4*, 33-47.

Gutheil, T. (2003). Reflections on coaching by attorneys. *Journal of the American Academy of Psychiatry and the Law, 31*, 6-9.

Hall, R., & Hall, R. (2006). Malingering of PTSD: Forensic and diagnostic consideration, characteristics of malingerers, and clinical presentations. *General Hospital Psychiatry, 28*, 525-535.

Hargan, V. (2011). *Are they faking it? A look at malingering incompetency to stand trial (IST).* Lexington, KY: Create Space Independent Publishing Platform.

Harris, A., Fisher, M., Veysey, B., Ragusa, L., & Lurigio, A. (2010). Sex offending and serious mental illness: Directions for policy and research. *Criminal Justice and Behavior, 37*(5), 596-612. doi: 10.1177/0093854810363773

Harris, M. D., & Michael, R. (2012). The malingering of psychotic disorders. *Jefferson journal of psychiatry, 15*(1), 7.

Harrison, A. G., & Edwards, M. J. (2010). Symptom exaggeration in post-secondary students: Preliminary base rates in a Canadian sample. *Applied Neuropsychology, 17*(2), 135-143.

Hart, T., Whyte, J., Polansky, M., Millis, S., Hammond, F., Sherer, M., Bushnik, T., Hanks, R., & Kreutzer, J. (2003). Concordance of patient and family report of neurobehavioral symptoms at 1 year after traumatic brain injury. *Archives of Physical Medicine and Rehabilitation, 84*(2), 204-213.

Hatcher, S., & Arroll, B. (2008). Assessment and management of medically unexplained symptoms. *British Medical Journal, 336*, 1124-1128.

Hebben, N., & Milberg, W. (2002). *Essentials of neuropsychological assessment.* Hoboken, NJ: Wiley.

Heilbronner, R., Sweet, J., Morgan, J., Larrabee, G., Millis, S., & Conference Participants. (2009). American Academy of Clinical Neuropsychology consensus conference statement on the neuropsychological assessment of effort, response bias, and malingering. *The Clinical Neuropsychologist, 23*(7), 1093-1129.

Henry, G., & Enders, C. (2007). Probable malingering and performance on the Continuous Visual Memory Test. *Applied Neuropsychology, 14*, 267-274. doi:10.1080/09084280701719245

Ingram, T., Dowben, J., Froehlich, K., & Keltner, N. (2012). Biological perspectives: Detecting malingering of post-traumatic stress disorder (PTSD) in adults. *Perspectives in Psychiatric Care. 48*(2), 70-75.

Inman, T., & Berry, D. (2002). Cross-validation of indicators of malingering: A comparison of nine neurological tests, four tests of malingering, and behavioral observations. *Archives of Clinical Neuropsychology, 17*, 1-23.

Irani, F. (2011). Judgment of line orientation. In J. S. Kreutzer, J. DeLuca, & B. Caplan (Eds.), *The Encyclopedia of Clinical Neuropsychology.* (pp. 1372-1374). Springer, New York. doi:10.1007/978-0-387-79948-3_1376

Iverson, G. (2006). Ethical issues associated with the assessment of exaggeration, poor effort, and malingering. *Applied Neuropsychology, 13*, 77-90.

Iverson, G., & Binder, L. (2000). Detecting exaggeration and malingering in neuropsychological assessment. *Journal of Head Trauma Rehabilitation, 15*, 829-858.

Jasinski, L. J., & Ranseen, J. D. (2011). Malingered ADHD evaluations: A further complication for accommodations reviews. *The Bar Examiner, 79*, 6-16.

Jelicic, M., Hessels, A., & Merckelbach, H. (2006). Detection of feigned psychosis with the structured inventory of malingered symptomatology (SIMS): A study of coached and uncoached simulators. *Journal of the Psychopathology and Behavioral Assessment, 28*(1), 19-22. doi:10.1007/s10862-006-4535-0

Jelicic, M., & Merckelbach, H. (2015). Amnesic Defense. In R. L. Cautin & S. O. Lilienfeld (Eds.), *The Encyclopedia of Clinical Psychology* (Vol 1). Wiley-Blackwell.

Jelicic, M., Merckelbach, H. L. G. J., Giesbrecht, T., & de Ruiter, C. (2008). Structured inventory of malingered symptomatology. In T. Gijsbrecht, C. de Ruiter, & M. Jelicic (Eds.), *Forensisch psychodiagnostisch gereedschap: malingering psychopathie en andere persoonlijkheidstrekken*, 151-160. Amsterdam: Harcourt.

Johnson, M. K. (1991). Reality monitoring: Evidence from confabulation in organic brain disease patients. In G. P. Prigatano & G. L. Schacter (Eds.), *Awareness of Deficit after Brain Injury: Clinical and Theoretical Issues*, pp. 176-197. New York, Oxford University Press.

Ju, D., & Varney, N. R. (2000). Can head injury patients simulate malingering? *Applied Neuropsychology, 7*(4), 201-207. doi:10.1207/S15324826AN0704_1

Kadlubek, R. M. (2012). *Adaptive Behavior Malingering in Legal Claims of Mental Retardation.* (Dissertation), Las Vegas, NV: University of Nevada.

Kemp, S., Coughlan, A., Rowbottom, C., Wilkinson, K., Teggart, V., & Baker, G. (2008). The base rate of effort test failure in patients with medically unexplained symptoms. *Journal of Psychosomatic Research, 65*, 319-325.

Kessels, R. P., Aleman, A., Verhagen, W. I., & Van Luijtelaar, E. L. (2000). Cognitive functioning after whiplash injury: A meta-analysis. *Journal of the International Neuropsychological Society, 6*(3), 271-278. doi:10.1017/S1355617700633027

Kopelman, M. D. (1995). The assessment of psychogenic amnesia. In A. D. Badely, B. A. Wilson, & F. N. Watts (Eds.). *Handbook of memory disorders* (pp. 427-448). West-Sussex: Wiley.

Kopelman, M. (2000). Focal retrograde amnesia and the attribution of causality: An exceptionally critical review. *Cognitive Neuropsychology, 17*, 585-621.

Krahn, L., Bostwick, J., & Stonnnington, C. (2008). Looking toward DSM-V: Should fictitious disorders become a subtype of somatoform disorder? *Psychosomatics, 49*, 277-282.

Kucharski, L. T., Duncan, S., Egan, S. S., & Falkenbach, D. M. (2006). Psychopathy and malingering of psychiatric disorder in criminal defendants. *Behavioral Sciences & the Law, 24*(5), 633-644.

Kucharski, L., Falkenbach, D., Egan, S., & Duncan, S. (2006). Antisocial personality disorder and the malingering of psychiatric disorder: A study of criminal defendants. *International Journal of Forensic Mental Health, 5*, 195-204.

Kunst, M., & Winkel, F. (2015). PTSD symptom reporting and persistent malingering in recipients of state compensation for violent crime victimization: An exploratory study. *Journal of Forensic Psychiatry & Psychology, 26*(3), 309-324.

Kunst, M., Winkel, F. W., & Bogaerts, S. (2010). Prevalence and predictors of post-traumatic stress disorder among victims of violence applying for state compensation. *Journal of Interpersonal Violence, 25*(9), 1631-1654. doi:10.1177/0886260509354591

Larrabee, G. (2003). Exaggerated pain report in litigants with malingered neurocognitive dysfunction. *The Clinical Neuropsychologist, 17*, 395-401. doi:10.1076/clin.17.3.395.18087

Larrabee, G. (2007). *Assessment of malingered neuropsychological deficits*. New York, NY: Oxford University Press.

Larrabee, G. (2008). Malingering scales for the continuous recognition memory test and the continuous visual memory test. *The Clinical Neuropsychologist, 23*, 167-180.

Lees-Haley, P. R. (1988). Litigation Response Syndrome. *American Journal of Forensic Psychology, 6*(1), 3-12.

Lees-Haley, P. R., English, L. T., & Glenn, W. J. (1991). A Fake Bad Scale on the MMPI-2 for personal injury claimants. *Psychological reports, 68*(1), 203-210.

Lu, P., Boone, K., Cozolino, L., & Mitchell, C. (2003). Effectiveness of the Rey-Osterrieth complex figure test and the Meyers recognition trial in the detection of suspect effort. *The Clinical Neuropsychologist, 17*(3), 426-440.

Lufi, D., & Awwad, A. (2013). Using the Minnesota Multiphasic Personality Inventory-2 to develop a scale to identify test anxiety among students with learning disabilities. *Learning Disability Quarterly, 36*(4), 242-249.

Martin, P. K., & Schroeder, R. W. (2015). Challenges in assessing and managing malingering, factitious disorder, and related somatic disorders. *Psychiatric Times, 32*(10), 19.

Mayou, R., Kirmayer, L. J., Simon, G., Kroenke, K., & Sharpe, M. (2005). Somatoform disorders: Time for a new approach in DSM-V. *American Journal of Psychiatry, 162*(5), 847-855.

McCarter, R., Walton, N., Brooks, D., & Powell, G. (2009). Effort testing in contemporary clinical neuropsychology practice. *The Clinical Neuropsychologists, 23*(6), 1050-1066.

McDermott, B. E. (2012). Psychological testing and the assessment of malingering. *Psychiatric Clinics of North America, 35*(4), 855-876.

McDermott, B. E., & Feldman, M. D. (2007). Malingering in the medical setting. *Psychiatric Clinics of North America, 30*(4), 645-662.

McNally, R. J., & Frueh, B. C. (2013). Why are Iraq and Afghanistan War veterans seeking PTSD disability compensation at unprecedented rates? *Journal of anxiety disorders, 27*(5), 520-526.

Melo, B., Winocur, G., & Moscovitch, M. (1999). False recall and false recognition: An examination of the effects of selective and combined lesions to the medial temporal lobe/diencephalon and frontal lobe structures. *Cognitive Neuropsychology, 16*, 343-359. doi:10.1080/026432999380825

Merten, T. (2001). Uber Simulation, artifizielle und somatoforme Storungen – eine konzeptionelle Verwirrung [On malingering, factitious and somatoform disorders: A conceptual confusion]. *Zeitschrift fur klinische Psychologie, Psychiatrie und Psychotherapie, 4*, 417-434.

Merten, T., Bossink, L., & Schmand, B. (2007). On the limits of effort testing: Symptom validity tests and severity of neurocognitive symptoms in nonlitigant patients. *Journal of Clinical and Experimental Neuropsychology, 29*(3), 308-318.

Meyers, J., & Diep, A. (2000). Assessment of malingering in chronic pain patients using neuropsychological tests. *Applied Neuropsychology, 7*, 133-139. doi:10.1207/S15324826AN0703_3

Meyers, J., & Volbrecht, M. (2003). A validation of multiple malingering detection methods in a large clinical sample. *Archives of Clinical Neuropsychology, 18*, 261-276.

Meyers, J., Volkert, K., & Diep, A. (2000). Sentence repetition test: Updated norms and clinical utility. *Applied Neuropsychology, 7*, 154-159.

Miller, D. (2003). Hospitalization of criminal defendants for evaluation of competence to stand trial for restoration of competence: Clinical and legal issues. *Behavioral Sciences and the Law, 21*, 369-391. doi:10.1002/bsl.546

Miller, H. A. (2001). *M-FAST: Miller Forensic Assessment of Symptoms Test*. Odessa, FL: Psychological Assessment Resources.

Mittenberg, W., Azrin, R., Millsap, C., & Heilbronner, R. (1993). Identification of malingered head injury on the Wechsler Memory Scale—Revised. *Psychological Assessment, 5*(1), 34-40.

Mittenberg, W., Patton, C., Canyock, E. M., & Condit, D. C. (2002). Base rates of malingering and symptom exaggeration. *Journal of Clinical and Experimental Neuropsychology, 24*(8), 1094-1102.

Mittenberg, W., Theroux, S., Aguila-Puentes, G., Bianchini, K., Greve, K., & Rayls, K. (2001). Identification of malingered head injury on the Wechsler Adult Intelligence Scale (3rd Ed.), *The Clinical Neuropsychologist, 15*, 440-445.

Morel, K., & Marshman, K. (2008). Critiquing symptom validity tests for post-traumatic stress disorder: A modification of Hartman's criteria. *Journal of Anxiety Disorders, 22*, 1542-1550.

Moscovitch, M., & Melo, B. (1997). Strategic retrieval and the frontal lobes: evidence from confabulation and amnesia. *Neuropsychologia, 35*,1017-1034.

Myers, W. C., Hall, R. C., & Tolou-Shams, M. (2012). Prevalence and assessment of malingering in homicide defendants using the Mini-Mental State Examination and the Rey 15-Item Memory Test. *Homicide studies, 17*(3), 314-328.

Nichols, D. S., & Gass, C. S. (2015). The Fake Bad Scale: Malingering or Litigation Response Syndrome—Which is It? *Archives of Assessment Psychology, 5*(1), 5-10.

Nicholson, K., & Martelli, M. F. (2007). Malingering: Traumatic brain injury. In G. Young, A. W. Kane, & K. Nicholson (Eds.), *Causality of psychological injury,* (pp. 427-475). Springer US.

Niesten, I. J., Nentjes, L., Merckelbach, H., & Bernstein, D. P. (2015). Antisocial features and "faking bad": A critical note. *International Journal of Law and Psychiatry, 41,* 34-42.

Norris, M. P., & May, M. C. (1998). Screening for malingering in a correctional setting. *Law and human behavior, 22*(3), 315-323.

Oldham, J., & Riba, M. (2001). *Somatoform & Factitious Disorders. Review of Psychiatry.* Vol 20, Washington DC: American Psychiatric Publishing, Inc.

Olszewska, J. M., Reuter-Lorenz, P. A., Munier, E., & Bendler, S. A. (2015). Misremembering what you see or hear: Dissociable effects of modality on short-and long-term false recognition. *Journal of Experimental Psychology: Learning, Memory, and Cognition, 41*(5), 1316.

Oorsouw, K., & Merkelbach, H. (2010). Detecting malingered memory problems in the civil and c r i m i n a l arena. *Legal and Criminological Psychology, 15*(1), 97-114. doi:10.1348/135532509X451304

Ord, J. S., Boettcher, A. C., Greve, K. W., & Bianchini, K. J. (2010). Detection of malingering in mild traumatic brain injury with the Conners' Continuous Performance Test–II. *Journal of Clinical and Experimental Neuropsychology, 32*(4), 380-387.

Ord, J., Greve, K., & Bianchini, K. (2008). Using the Wechsler Memory Scale–III to detect malingering in mild traumatic brain injury. *The Clinical Neuropsychologist, 22*, 689-704.

Parwatikar, S. D., Holcomb, W. R., & Menninger, K. A. (1985). The detection of malingered amnesia in accused murderers. *Bulletin of the American Academy of Psychiatry and the Law, 13*, 97-103.

Penk, W., Rierdan, J., Losardo, M., & Robinowitz, R. (2006). The MMPI-2 and assessment of post-traumatic stress disorder (PTSD). In J. N. Butcher (Ed.), *MMPI-2: A practitioner's guide* (pp. 121-141). Washington, DC: American Psychological Press.

Pierson, A. M., Rosenfeld, B., Green, D., & Belfi, B. (2011). Investigating the relationship between antisocial personality disorder and malingering. *Criminal Justice and Behavior, 38*(2), 146-156.

Pitman, R.K., Sparr, L.F., Saunders, L.S., & McFarland, A.C. (1996). Legal issues in post-traumatic stress disorder. In B.A. vanderKolg, A.C. McFarland and L. Weisaeth (eds), *Traumatic Stress: The effects of overwhelming experience on mind, body, and society* (pp. 378-397). New York: Guilford.

Powell, M., Gfeller, J., Hendricks, B., & Sharland, M. (2004). Detecting symptom- and test-coached simulators with the test of memory malingering. *Archives of Clinical Neuropsychology, 19*, 693-702.

Quinn, C. (2003). Detection of malingering in assessment of adult ADHD. *Archives of Clinical Neuropsychology, 18*, 379-395.

Rabin, L., Barr, W., & Burton, L. (2005). Assessment practices of clinical neuropsychologists in the United States and Canada: A survey of INS, NAN, and APA division 40 members. *Archives of Clinical Neuropsychology, 20*, 33-65.

Raine, M. (2009). Helping advocates to understand the psychological diagnosis and assessment of malingering. *Psychiatry, Psychology and Law [serial online], 16*(2), 322-328.

Rees, L., Tombaugh, T., & Boulay, L. (2001). Depression and the test of memory malingering (TOMM). *Archives of Clinical Neuropsychology, 16*, 501-506.

Rees, L. M., Tombaugh, T. N., Gansler, D. A., & Moczynski, N. P. (1998). Five validation experiments of the Test of Memory Malingering (TOMM). *Psychological Assessment, 10*, 10-20.

Resnick, P. J., & Knoll, J. (2005a). How to detect malingered psychosis. *Current Psychiatry, 4*, 13.

Resnick, P., & Knoll, J. (2005b). *Insanity defense evaluation: Toward a model for evidence-based practice.* Oxford, UK: Oxford University Press. www.btci.edina.clockss.org/cgi/content/full/8/1/92

Resnick, P., West, S., & Payne, J. (2008). Malingering of post-traumatic stress disorders. In R. Rogers (Ed.), *Clinical assessment of malingering and deception* (pp. 109-127). New York, NY: Guilford Press.

Richter, J. (2014). Assessment of malingered psychosis in mental health counseling. *Journal of Mental Health Counseling, 36*(3), 208-227. doi:10.17744/mehc.36.3.f78x346103782313

Rivera, D., Perrin, P. B., Weiler, G., Ocampo-Barba, N., Aliaga, A., Rodriguez, W., Rodríguez-Agudelo, Y., Aguayo, A., Longoni, M., Trapp, S., & Esenarro, L. (2015). Test of Memory Malingering (TOMM): Normative data for the Latin American Spanish speaking adult population. *NeuroRehabilitation, 37*(4), 719-735.

Robbennolt, J., & Studebaker, C. (2003). News media reporting on civil litigation and its influence on civil justice decision making. *Law and Human Behavior, 27*(1), 5-27. doi:10.1023/A:1021622827154

Rogers, R. (1990). Development of a new classificatory model of malingering. *Bulletin of the American Academy of Psychiatry and Law, 18*, 323-333.

Rogers, R. (1997). Current status of clinical methods. In R. Rogers (Ed.), *Clinical assessment of malingering and deception* (2nd ed., p. 373-397). New York: Guilford.

Rogers, R. (2008a). An introduction to response styles. In R. Rogers (Ed.), *Clinical assessment of malingering and deception* (3rd ed.) (pp. 3-13). New York, NY: Guilford Press.

Rogers, R. (2008b). Current status of clinical methods. In R. Rogers (Ed.), *Clinical assessment of malingering and deception* (3rd ed.) (pp. 391-410). New York, NY: Guilford Press.

Rogers, R. (2008c). *Clinical assessment of malingering and deception* (3rd ed.). New York, NY: Guilford Press.

Rogers, R. (2008d). Detection strategies for malingering and defensiveness. In R. Rogers (Ed.), *Clinical assessment of malingering and deception* (3rd ed., pp. 14-32). New York, NY: Guilford Press.

Rogers, R., & Bender, S. (2003). Evaluation of malingering and deception. In A. Goldstein, & I. B. Weiner (Eds.), *Handbook of psychology: Vol. 11. Forensic Psychology,* (pp. 109-129). Hoboken, NJ: John Wiley & Sons, Inc.

Rogers, R., & Correa, A. (2008). Determinations of malingering: Evolution from case-based methods to detection strategies. *Psychiatry, Psychology and Law, 15*(2), 213-223. doi:10.1080/13218710802014501

Rogers, R., & Granacher, P. (2011). Conceptualization and assessment of malingering. In E. Y. Drogin, F. M. Dattilio, R. L. Sadoff, & T. G. Gutheil (Eds.), *Handbook of forensic assessment* (p. 659-678). Hoboken, NJ: John Wiley & Sons, Incorporated.

Rogers, R., & Payne, J. (2006). Damages and rewards: Assessment of malingered disorders in compensation cases. *Behavioral Sciences and the Law, 24*, 645-658. doi: 10.1002/bsi.687

Rogers, R., Sewell, K. W., & Gillard, N. D. (2010). *SIRS-2: Structured Interview of Reported Symptoms: Professional manual*. Psychological Assessment Resources, Incorporated.

Rogers, R., Sewell, K. W., & Goldstein, A. M. (1994). Explanatory models of malingering: A prototypical analysis. *Law and Human Behavior, 18*(5), 543-552. doi:10.1007/BF01499173

Rohling, M. L., & Boone, K. B. (2007). Future directions in effort assessment. In K. B. Boone (Ed.), *Assessment of feigned cognitive impairment* (pp. 453-469). New York, NY: Guilford.

Rosen, J., Mullsant, B., Bruce, M., Mittal, V., & Fox, D. (2004). Actors' portrayals of depression to test interrater reliability in clinical trials. *American Journal of Psychiatry, 161*, 1909-1911.

Ruiz, M. A., Drake, E. B., Glass, A., Marcotte, D., & van Gorp, W. G. (2002). Trying to beat the system: Misuse of the Internet to assist in avoiding the detection of psychological symptom dissimilation. *Professional Psychology: Research and Practice, 33*, 294-299.

Russell, M. L., Spector, J., & Kelly, M. (1993, February). *Primary and recency effects in the detection of malingering using the WMS-R Logical Memory Subtests*. Poster presented at the 21st annual meeting of the International Neuropsychological Society, Galveston, TX, USA.

Samuel, R., & Wittenberg, W. (2005). Determination of malingering in disability evaluations. *Primary Psychiatry: The Leading Voice of Clinical Psychiatric Medicine, 12*, 60-68.

Schnider, A. (2001). Spontaneous confabulation, reality monitoring, and the limbic system: A review. *Brain Research Reviews, 36*, 150-160.

Schnider, A., Ptak, R., von Daniken, C., & Remonda, L. (2000). Recovery from spontaneous confabulations parallels recovery of temporal confusion in memory. *Neurology, 55,* 74-83.

Schnider, A., von Daniken, C., & Gutbrod, K. (1996). Disorientation in amnesia: A confusion of memory traces. *Brain, 119,* 1627-1632.

Scott, C. L. (2016). *The assessment of malingering: An evidence-based approach.* University of California, Davis.

Seward, D., & Connor, D. (2008). Ethical issues in assigning (or withholding) a diagnosis of malingering. In J. E. Morgan & J. J. Sweet (Eds.), *Neuropsychology of Malingering Casebook* (pp. 517-529). New York, NY: Taylor & Francis.

Sharland, M., & Gfeller, J. (2007). A survey of neuropsychologists' beliefs and practices with respect to the assessment of effort. *Archives of Clinical Neuropsychology, 22,* 213-223.

Singhal, A., Green, P., Ashaye, K., Shankar, K., & Gill, D. (2009). High specificity of the Medical Symptom Validity Test in patients with very severe memory impairment. *Archives of Clinical Neuropsychology, 24,* 721-728.

Slick, D. J., Sherman, E. M. S., & Iverson, G. L. (1999). Forum: Diagnostic criteria for malingered neurocognitive dysfunction: Proposed standards for clinical practice and research. *The Clinical Neuropsychologist, 13*(4), 545-561.

Slick, D., Tan, J., Strauss, E., & Hultsch, D. (2004). Detecting malingering: A survey of experts' practices. *Archives of Clinical Neuropsychology, 19,* 465-473.

Sreenivasan, S., Eth, S., Kirkish, P., & Garrick, T. (2003). A practical method for the evaluation of symptom exaggeration in minor head trauma among civil litigants. *Journal of American Academy of Psychiatry Law, 31,* 220-231.

Strauss, F., Sherman, F., & Spreen, O. (2006). *A compendium of neuropsychological tests: Administration, norms, and commentary.* New York, NY: Oxford University Press.

Suhr, J., & Gunstad, J. (2000). The effects of coaching on the sensitivity and specificity of malingering measures. *Archives of Clinical Neuropsychology, 15,* 415-424.

Suhr, J. A., & Gunstad, J. (2007). Coaching and malingering: A review. In G. J. Larrabee (Ed.), *Assessment of malingered neuropsychological deficits* (pp. 287-311). New York, NY: Oxford University Press.

Sweet, J., Moberg, P., & Suchy, Y. (2000). Ten-year follow-up survey of clinical neuropsychologists: Part I. Practices and beliefs. *Clinical Neuropsychologist, 14,* 18-37.

Tan, J., Slick, D., Strause, E., & Hultsch, D. (2010). How'd they do it? Malingering strategies on symptom validity tests. *The Clinical Neuropsychologist. 16,* 4. doi: 10.1016/clin.16.4.495.113909

Tombaugh, T. N. (1996). *Test of memory malingering: TOMM.* North Tonawanda, NY: Multi-Health Systems.

Tombaugh, T. N. (1997). The Test of Memory Malingering (TOMM): Normative data from cognitively intact and cognitively impaired individuals. *Psychological Assessment, 9,* 260-268.

Turner, M. (2006). Factitious disorders: Reformulating the DSM-IV criteria. *Psychosomatics, 47,* 23-32.

U.S. v. Gigante, 982 F. Supp. 140 (E.D.N.Y. 1997).

U.S. v. Greer. (US Court of Appeals, 5th Cir. 1998).

Vallabhajosula, B., & van Gorp, W. G. (2001). Post-Daubert admissibility of scientific evidence on malingering of cognitive deficits. *Journal of the American Academy of Psychiatry and the Law, 29,* 207-215.

Veterans for Common Sense. (2012). *Iraq and Afghanistan impact report, January 2012.* Retrieved from http://veteransforcommonsense.org/ wp-content/uploads/2012/01/VCS IAIR JAN 2012.pdf

Vickery, C. D., Berry, D. T. R., Inman, T. H., Harris, M. J., & Orey, S. A. (2001). Detection of inadequate effort on neuropsychological testing: A meta-analytic review of selected procedures. *Archives of Clinical Neuropsychology, 16,* 45-73.

Victor, T. L., & Abeles, N. (2004). Coaching clients to take psychological and neuropsychological tests: A clash of ethical obligations. *Professional Psychology: Research and Practice, 35*(4), 373-379. doi:10.1037/0735-7028.35.4.373

Weissman, H. N., & Debow, D. M. (2003). Ethical principles and professional competencies. *Handbook of psychology.* In A. Goldstein, & I.B. Weiner (Eds.), *Handbook of psychology: Vol. 11. Forensic Psychology*, (pp. 33-53). Hoboken, NJ: John Wiley & Sons, Inc.

Wilson v. United States, 391 F.2d 460 (D.C. Cir. 1968).

Woolston, R., Bain, S. A., & Baxter, J. S. (2006). Patterns of malingering and compliance in measures of interrogative suggestibility. *Personality and individual differences, 40*(3), 453-461.

Worthen, M. D., & Moering, R. G. (2011). A practical guide to conducting VA compensation and pension exams for PTSD and other mental disorders. *Psychological Injury and Law, 4*(3), 187-216. doi:10.1007/s12207-011-9115-2

Young, G. (2014). PTSD and Malingering: Tests, Diagnostics, Cut Scores, and Cautions. In *Malingering, Feigning, and Response Bias in Psychiatric/Psychological Injury* (pp. 855-880). Springer Netherlands.

CHAPTER 12

OBSESSIVE-COMPULSIVE DISORDERS (OCD) AND COMPULSIVE HOARDING IN THE CRIMINAL JUSTICE SYSTEM

DEB HUNTLEY, JANINA CICH, HAL PICKETT, DEBORAH ECKBERG, OLIVIA JOHNSON, & KIMBERLY D. DODSON

CHAPTER OVERVIEW

Hoarding disorder and obsessive-compulsive disorder are mental illnesses that can significantly interfere with an individual's healthy functioning and may lead to behaviors that catch the attention of forensic and criminal justice systems. This chapter will present information on the characteristics of each disorder, with a brief review of etiology, Co-morbidity and brain physiology for each. The chapter will cover specific health issues that may occur, as well as criminal behaviors that can be a result of hoarding and obsessive-compulsive disorders. Finally, screening and treatment information for those working in criminal justice and mental health settings will be discussed.

DIAGNOSTIC HISTORY OF OBSESSIVE-COMPULSIVE DISORDER AND HOARDING

Obsessive-compulsive disorder (OCD) is classified among the top ten most-disabling mental health and anxiety conditions, worldwide (Gupta, Avasthi, Grover, & Singh, 2014; Podea, Suciu, Suciu, & Mihai, 2009), exacerbated by the fact that approximately 90% of those with OCD endure Co-morbid disorders such as anxiety and mood disorders, impulse control, and substance use disorders (Gilihan, Williams, Malcoun, Yadin, & Foa, 2012; McMurran et al., 2000). OCD, which had been characterized by intrusive ideas, repetitive behaviors, compulsive accumulation of possessions, and the inability to discard worthless items, is a poorly understood disorder that creates significant dysfunction, affecting quality of life for individuals, families, and communities (Pertusa, Frost, Mataix-Cols, 2010; Pertusa et al., 2010; Podea et al., 2009; Saxena et al., 2011). Considered an incapacitating mental illness affecting approximately 2.5% of the general adult population (Bornheimer, 2015) (Podea et al., 2009), it is complicated by some of its co-occurring characteristics. While the previous edition of The Diagnostic and Statistical Manual of Mental Disorders (4th ed.; DSM-IV) (American Psychiatric Association, 1994) listed hoarding as one characteristic of OCD, hoarding disorder became a separate diagnostic category in the most recent revision (The Diagnostic and Statistical Manual of Mental Disorders, 5th ed.; DSM-5) (American Psychiatric Association, 2013).

Like OCD, hoarding is unquestionably comprised of obsessive thinking and compulsive behaviors; however, the two have distinct differences categorizing them as separate entities— differences in clinical profile, response to treatment, and brain activity (Calamari, Pontarelli, & Armstrong, 2012; Samuels et al., 2007). In a study by Pertusa et al. (2008), patients with hoarding and an OCD diagnosis were compared with patients who only had a hoarding diagnosis. Those with both disorders were more likely to hoard bizarre items (e.g., feces, nails, and rotten food); more likely to report other obsessions related to their hoarding (e.g., something catastrophic happening if the items were thrown away); tended to be concerned with more frequent symmetry, ordering, and checking behaviors related to the items; and displayed a higher prevalence of other diagnoses, such as generalized anxiety disorder and/or depression. The authors finally note that the hoarding-only group had subclinical OCD symptoms comparable to control groups, and therefore, hoarding can occur outside of the context of OCD. In addition to differences in characteristics, research also indicates differences in brain activity between hoarding and OCD behaviors of checking and washing (Mataix-Cols et al., 2004).

CHARACTERISTICS OF OBSESSIVE-COMPULSIVE DISORDER AND HOARDING

The DSM-5's classification of obsessive-compulsive disorder is diagnosed by the presence of "obsessions, compulsions, or both" (APA, 2013, p. 237). Obsessions are typically thoughts, but can also be images or more ambiguous urges. These thoughts intrude upon the individual's consciousness and create significant distress for the sufferer, because of the inability to ignore or dispel the intrusive thoughts (APA, 2013; Calamari et al., 2012; O'Connor, Koszegi, Aardema, van Niekerk, & Taillon, 2009). Research surmises that the inability to ignore or dispel intrusive thoughts generates behaviors that are carried out in compulsive rituals and behavioral patterns, ill-aligned with the obsession and conducted to dissipate the thoughts and reduce anxiety (APA, 2013; Bornheimer, 2014).

Hoarding disorder, which is now in the Obsessive-Compulsive and Related Disorders section of the DSM-5, is diagnosed as compulsively collecting and saving items, whereby the mere thought of discarding possessions is cause for significant stress and anxiety (APA, 2013). Hoarding disorder occurs twice as often as OCD in the public, and up to four times as often as schizophrenia or bipolar disorder (Pertusa et al., 2010)—consequently affecting six to fifteen million individuals in the United States (Otte & Steketee, 2011). Hoarding disorder has been linked to neuropsychiatric disorders, such as dementia, psychosis, Asperger syndrome, autism, schizophrenia, eating disorders, and developmental disabilities, as well as OCD (Mataix-Cols & Pertusa, 2012; Pertusa et al., 2010; Saxena et al., 2011; Torres et al., 2012; Wakabayashi, Baron-Cohen, & Ashwin 2012). The accumulation of possessions creates clutter predicaments, leading to unsafe living conditions that pose life-threatening health risks. Severe hoarding causes hazardous fire-safety issues, personal distress and, inevitably, disability impairment (APA, 2013; Bornheimer, 2014; Pertusa et al., 2010).

Both OCD and hoarding disorder have socio-economic consequences, including reduced education levels, heightened unemployment, and an increased use of government support systems (Saxena et al., 2011; Torres et al., 2012). Thirty-eight percent of self-identified hoarders reported annual incomes grossly below the United States poverty line (Saxena et al., 2011).

HOARDING

As noted earlier, hoarding became a separate mental health diagnosis in the latest version of The Diagnostic and Statistical Manual of Mental Disorders (5th ed.; DSM-5) (American Psychiatric Association, 2013). The criteria for diagnosis include: (1) persistent difficulty discarding or parting with possessions, regardless of their actual value; (2) perceived need to save the items, and distress associated with discarding them; (3) difficulty discarding possessions, resulting in the accumulation of possessions that congest and clutter active living areas and substantially compromise their intended use; (4) clinically significant distress or impairment in social, occupational, or other important areas of functioning, including maintaining a safe environment for self and others; (5) symptoms not attributable to another medical condition or better explained by the symptoms of another mental disorder. Hoarding behaviors seem to be particularly complex, with as many as 92% of those with a hoarding disorder (HD) having a Co-morbid mental health or personality disorder (Frost, Tolin, & Maltby, 2010). The literature indicates that 18% to 33% of those with obsessive-compulsive disorder acknowledge hoarding as a major symptom (Samuels et al., 2007). Kellet (2007) identified three categories of hoarding: instrumental hoarders collect such things as newspapers, based on an urge to keep information or records; intrinsic hoarders collect unique or distinctive objects; and sentimental hoarders keep objects that have a memory or sentimental value to them. The obvious assumption is that the first and third types may have anxiety related to forgetting some fact or memory, while the middle type may be driven by the belief that the hoarded objects have some monetary value (Kellet, 2007).

There is evidence that hoarding is linked to the experience of traumatic life events, with a positive correlation between the number of traumatic events and the severity of hoarding (Samuels et al., 2008). This may have an impact on the development of normative attachment. In addition, hoarding severity increases with age (Samuels et al., 2008). Samuels et al. (2008) noted that this does not necessarily mean that hoarding is more likely to begin as individuals reach later adulthood, but hoarding could become more problematic over time. Hoarding in later adulthood may also be related to cognitive decline or physical ailments that prevent individuals from disposing of items. Samuels et al. (2008) also noted that for this population, there is a relationship between hoarding and income, with those at the lower range more likely to engage in hoarding behaviors, perhaps to feel more financially secure. Finally, Samuels et al. (2008) found positive correlations between hoarding and alcohol dependence, as well as a relationship between hoarding and gender, with twice as many men as women engaged in hoarding behaviors.

There has been little conclusive research on the etiology of hoarding. One study completed by Wheaton, Abramowitz, Farnklin, Berman, and Fabricant (2010) explored the cognitive behavioral concepts of "experiential avoidance" (p. 512) and "saving cognitions" (p. 511). The authors described experiential avoidance as an "unwillingness to endure upsetting emotions, thoughts, memories and other private experiences, and deliberate efforts to control or escape from them" (Wheaton et al., 2010, p. 511). On the other hand, saving cognitions are those beliefs that lead the individual to "save" possessions, and include cognitive explanations such as hyper-sentimentality and the reliance on the objects to serve as memory aids ("I'll forget about my experiences unless these objects are here to remind me"). The authors found that the presence of experiential avoidance and saving cognitions were correlated with hoarding behaviors, but the evidence supported that they may drive different elements of hoarding practices. Experiential avoidance correlated more with hoarding and less with discarding behaviors. Discarding behaviors seemed to be more correlated with saving cognitions.

An etiological perspective described by Timpano and Schmidt (2013) found that self-control was negatively associated with the three identified aspects of hoarding: clutter, acquiring, and difficulty discarding. In general, hoarding has been associated with deficits in executive functioning, impulse control, and the ability to understand the value of rewards typical of daily life for non-hoarders (Tolin, 2011). In comparison, hoarding may differ from obsessive-compulsive disorder in the need, motivation, and capability for self-control. Those with obsessive-compulsive disorder tend to want to control their environment—a secondary motivation to anxiety that something catastrophic may occur if they do not (Timpano & Schmidt, 2013).

One tool for measuring hoarding behavior is the Saving Inventory-Revised (SI-R) (Frost, Steketee, & Grisham, 2004). The SI-R is a 23-item measure, with each item scored on a scale from 0 to 4. Higher scores indicate greater severity. In one study, elders who had an identified problem with hoarding scored an average of 44.6 on this measure (Frost, Steketee, & Grisham, 2004). Although this measure is useful and reliable for determining severity of the behavior, diagnosis of hoarding disorder is determined through a clinical interview by a trained professional.

OBSESSIVE-COMPULSIVE DISORDER

The Diagnostic and Statistical Manual of Mental Disorders (5th ed. DSM-5) (American Psychiatric Association, 2013) includes the following criteria for a diagnosis of obsessive-compulsive disorder: (1) The obsessions and compulsions must significantly impact daily life; (2) Individuals may or may not realize that the obsessions and compulsions are excessive or unreasonable or that they pose a true threat; (3) Obsessions are intrusive, repetitive, and persistent thoughts, urges, or images that cause distress; (4) Obsessive thoughts do not just excessively focus on real problems in the individual's life; (5) The individual has unsuccessfully tried to suppress or ignore the disturbing thoughts, images, or urges; (6) Compulsions are excessive and repetitive ritualistic behaviors that the person feels compelled to perform to keep something bad from happening; (7) Compulsions take up at least one hour or more per day; (8) Performing rituals or mental acts serves to reduce the severe anxiety caused by the obsessive thoughts. (p. 237).

While obsessive-compulsive disorder (OCD) is marked by obsessions and/or compulsions, it is the obsessions that create anxiety; however, the individual typically engages in ritualistic compulsions to reduce the anxiety. Common obsessions include contamination, perfectionism, loss of control, harm, unwanted sexual thoughts, and religious or moral thoughts. Common compulsions include washing/cleaning, order/symmetry, checking, and mental compulsions such as counting (5th ed.; DSM-5) (American Psychiatric Association, 2013). Obsessive-compulsive disorder has a lifetime rate of 2%-3% and tends to begin in adolescence or early adulthood, affecting men and women equally (Abramowitz, Taylor, & McKay, 2009).

One common perspective about the cause of OCD is the cognitive-behavioral view that while intrusive and unwanted thoughts are common for all individuals, those with increased levels of anxiety have difficulty dismissing them or distracting themselves. The anxiety increases until the individual engages in an elaborate behavioral pattern which reduces the anxiety. This behavioral pattern becomes ritualistic and stereotypical as the individual continues to repeat it to ward off anxiety-producing obsessions (Abramowitz, Taylor, & McKay, 2009).

Neurochemistry and neuroanatomy have also been implicated in the etiology of OCD. Dysfunctions in the regulation of serotonin have been linked to OCD, in addition to increased activity in the frontal orbito-striatal area (Abramowitz et al., 2009). Other biological factors connected to OCD include genetic transmission, since probability increases significantly with heritability, and in some cases, streptococcal infection, which leads to inflammation of the basal ganglia (Abramowitz et al., 2009).

One reliable tool that can assess the severity of obsessive-compulsive disorder is the Yale-Brown Obsessive Compulsive Scale (Goodman et al., 1989). While it is not meant to be a diagnostic test, the scale rates the severity of symptoms, regardless of the type of obsession or compulsion. It is a 10-item scale, with each item scored on a scale from 0 to 4, where higher scores reflect greater severity. Scores higher than 16 typically indicate a clinical sample (Frost et al., 2004).

BRAIN PHYSIOLOGY IN OCD AND HD

Several researchers have launched investigations into the brains of those with OCD and hoarding behavior (Mataix-Cols et al., 2010; Pertusa et al., 2010). There is specific evidence that the neural functioning of the brain of those with OCD is affected by the disorder, and preliminary research indicates that the brain functioning of those with either OCD or hoarding disorder have distinct differences (Mataix-Cols et al., 2010; Pertusa et al., 2010). Mataix-Cols and colleagues (2010) described brain imaging of those with OCD as showing increased activity in the "orbitofrontal-striatal-pallidal-thalamic circuits" (p. 561). Data supports that multiple areas of the brain in those diagnosed with OCD experience being engrossed with obsessions and compulsions, including areas that control executive functioning, inter-cerebral communication, and voluntary movement (Mataix-Cols et al., 2010). This might explain the diversity of symptomatology in individuals with OCD. Connections to the globus pallidus and striatum could provide insight into the urges that result in physical compulsive behaviors.

In comparison, hoarding behaviors tend to involve the cingulate gyrus, ventromedial prefrontal cortex, fronto-limbic circuits, and structures of the limbic system (An et al., 2009; Mataix-Cols et al., 2010; Saxena et al., 2004; Tolin, Frost, Steketee, & Fitch, 2008). Specifically, the collection of possessions in relation to the emotional brain drives the strong personal connection to the hoarded possessions. Sudden onset of hoarding behaviors has also been studied in those with frontotemporal dementia, schizophrenia, and brain injuries to the prefrontal and orbitofrontal cortices (Levy & Dubois, 2006; Nakaaki et al., 2007; Ohtuschi, Matsuo, Akimoto, & Watanabe, 2010; Tolin, 2011). As more sophisticated brain imaging becomes available, researchers may gain additional insight into the neurological cause and maintenance of hoarding and obsessive-compulsive disorders, and such insight may result in more efficient and effective treatments (Tolin, 2011).

COMPLEXITIES OF CO-MORBIDITY

As mentioned previously, many individuals with symptoms of obsessions, compulsions, and hoarding tend to exhibit Co-morbid mental health problems. In their research, Frost et al. (2010) found hoarding to co-occur 53% of the time with depression, 24% of the time with generalized anxiety, 24% of the time with exhibits of social phobia and 18% of the time with obsessive-compulsive disorder. Potentially related to executive functioning deficits, Grisham et al. (2007) found a 20% correlation between hoarding and attention-deficit/hyperactivity disorder. In comparison, the DSM-5 (APA, 2013) indicates those with an obsessive-compulsive disorder have about a 76% Co-morbidity rate with an anxiety disorder and 63% Co-morbidity with mood disorders, including bipolar disorder. It is also noted that lifetime tic disorders tend to be Co-morbid with obsessive-compulsive disorder at a frequency of approximately 30%. Both disorders share the strong pull or urge to act physically in a certain way.

Grisham, Brown, and Savage (2006) and Tolin et al. (2010) posit that individuals with later onset hoarding behaviors reported increased adverse life events and early childhood stress such as parental psychiatric history. According to Torres et al. (2012), the onset commonly compounds severe anxiety symptoms and leads to additional Co-morbidities such as depression, PTSD, ADHD and tic disorders. In contrast, Matthews, Kaur, and Stein (2008) found that adolescent onset of symptoms of obsessive-compulsive disorder correlated directly with trauma history, showing a significant increase when the adolescent had suffered emotional rather than physical abuse.

Also relevant is the connection between OCD and suicidal tendencies. Suicidal behavior is the leading cause of death worldwide, with 90% of suicides arising from psychiatric illness (Gupta, Avasthi, Grover, & Singh, 2014). Research indicates that individuals diagnosed with OCD were evaluated with suicidal tendencies in for 6% to 7% of subjects (Rudd, Dahm, & Rajab, 1993). Balci and Sevincock (2010) discovered between 5%-25% of those suffering from obsessive-compulsive disorder had a previous suicide attempt, but insufficient attention has been paid to suicidal behavior and tendencies in patients with OCD (Gupta et al., 2014).

FORENSIC IMPLICATIONS

In the realm of forensic mental health, hoarding disorders intersect with criminal behavior, specifically in behaviors such as kleptomania and theft (Hawyard & Coles, 2009; Pertusa et al., 2010). While animal companionship is not uncommon, dysfunctional hoarding of animals is a deviant behavior associated with harmful living conditions and self-neglect (Nathanson, 2009). Accumulating large numbers of animals and neglecting their nutrition, sanitation, and veterinary care constitutes animal endangerment, which is a criminal offense, and endangers self-health and family well-being (Pertusa et al., 2010).

Some individuals diagnosed with OCD are faced with fears of harming others (in general or specifically) with certain weapons; abusing children; attacking, molesting or raping others; or obsessions related to killing parents or siblings (Tolin, 2012). There is some evidence that obsessive relationship behaviors may result in intimate partner control or stalking. It is easier to understand the commission of petty or nuisance crimes around an urge to hoard or obsessively have something; it is more complicated to understand the commission of heinous person-related felonies such as murder, which are a consequence of obsessive thinking, compulsive behaviors or looseness of reality testing (MacMurran et al., 2000; Sheeran, 2012).

HOARDING AS A PUBLIC HEALTH ISSUE

Hoarding has recently gained more public attention from television and social media, and the most common perspective of the public is that hoarders create a cluttered or "trash house" (Tolin, 2011). Trendy television cable shows have fueled voyeuristic interest, but what is less well-understood is how this disorder can create real public health problems, with real economic costs and life-threatening consequences (Gilliam & Tolin, 2010; Mataix-Cols, 2010; Thompkins, 2011; Tolin, 2011). Tolin (2011) states that 64% of public health officials reported receiving at least one call, mostly from neighbors, to a house that was unfit because of hoarding. Neighbors can become concerned about the safety of fellow neighbors, but also about the spread of disease and attraction of unwanted animals to their properties. The general laws to maintain safe rental properties or address the public nuisance issues created by trash on certain properties can create a significant cost to the city or the owners of rental properties (San Francisco Task Force on Compulsive Hoarding, 2009). In 2009, the San Francisco Task Force on Compulsive Hoarding reported a $6.4 million annual cost to public officials and landlords related to hoarding in homes. Some specific public health and safety issues are presented below.

FIRE HAZARDS

Accumulating an excessive amount of materials by simultaneously acquiring new possessions while not discarding previously acquired items of no worth can pose a fire hazard. Firefighters or emergency personnel may enter a home with no preparation for what is behind the door. As it relates to hoarding and fire safety, a household fire becomes more dangerous if exit avenues are blocked, if flammable materials such as papers or trash are stacked next to heat sources, or if the house becomes so crowded that a fire would be difficult to control (Frost, Steketee, & Williams, 2000). In a survey of health officers who responded to 471 complaints related to hoarding, 67% of the cases were noted as posing fire hazards (Frost et al., 2000). The authors noted that the hoarder is not only secretive regarding hoarding behavior, but also in denial about the seriousness of the problem, making it highly unlikely that they will seek out help. Hoarding results in increased fire risk and in increased cost of human lives. Many public officials recognize the serious safety concerns identified by a study completed in Worchester, Massachusetts (Colpas, Zulueta, & Pappas, 2012). This study revealed that compulsive hoarding was involved in 24% of preventable fire fatalities. Research also indicates that in 6% of cases, hoarding behavior is directly related to health risks and fire fatalities involving papers and clutter stacked near a heating unit, rather than indirectly and accidently dropping a cigarette into a pile of combustibles (Frost et al., 2000). Many cities, including Minneapolis, Minnesota, have created hoarding taskforces that "offer a variety of options for addressing hoarding-related concerns, including reduced-fee therapy services, consultation, support groups, and Safety Days" (or coordinated clean-outs with a focus on harm and stress reduction) (The Hoarding Project, Treatment; para 2).

PET ABUSE

Another problem created by hoarding disorders occurs when individuals hoard many animals with inadequate "nutrition, sanitation and veterinary care" (Pertusa et al., 2010, para 1.6), creating additional public health concerns (Bronwen, 2014; Patronek & Nathanson, 2009). An example includes houses consumed by garbage, non-managed animal feces, or even more concerning—diseased and dying animals, all of which are secondary to crowding or neglect (Bronwen, 2014; Frost, Patronek, & Rosenfield, 2011). Animal hoarders accumulate animals in a multitude of ways. Some hoarders collect animals as an altruistic campaign to rescue animals in need (Frost et al., 2011), while others may accumulate animals as part of their self-identity (e.g. "I LOVE cats") or to increase a sense of control (Brown, 2011; Patronek & Nathanson, 2009). Hoarders' homes then become unorganized and overwhelmed, because they are emotionally unable to adopt out animals for better care, and are faced with inadequate money to feed or provide sufficient space for healthy housing of the animals (Frost et al., 2011).

The legal system needs training and education in dealing with animal hoarders, as well as in setting clearly defined laws. Most laws require a vague standard for providing proper and adequate care, food, and shelter to animals. The legal system is commonly at a loss regarding dealing with and promoting awareness and understanding and reducing recidivism (Renwick, 2009). Many states and cities have laws that attempt to prevent animal hoarding from happening. In Minneapolis, Minnesota, a resident can legally house three animals over four months of age, which includes dogs, cats, rabbits and ferrets (Minneapolis Animal Control and Care, 2005). Special licenses are required to have four or more pets, in which case the resident then agrees to be monitored by Animal Control. However, for most cities, vague legal and statutory language invites minimal requirement satisfaction and unconstitutional arguments (Renwick, 2009). Research has indicated that object hoarding tends to have an onset during adolescence, whereas the onset of animal hoarding typically occurs later in adulthood (Landau, Iervolino, & Pertusa, 2010). Persons with hoarding disorders involving animals seem to struggle with what appears to be delusional thinking patterns (Lockwood, 1994; Steketee et al., 2010). They often attribute human characteristics to pets and will claim an almost magical understanding of their animals' thoughts. Research also supports the notion that animal hoarders may be a group that has less insight into personal hoarding behaviors, as compared with others with obsessive-compulsive disorders (Tolin et al., 2010).

SANITATION ISSUES

While the most common items that are hoarded tend to be paper, such as newspapers and magazines or bags and wrappers, other items may accumulate that pose additional health risks (Frost et al., 2000). Rotting food can cause food poisoning if consumed, but also may attract insects and rodents. Excess accumulation of any objects likely prevents a home from being cleaned thoroughly, thus exposing the individual to dust, mildew, bacteria, and fungus, which can lead to respiratory problems as well as more-serious health consequences. In one study of those individuals identified as hoarders and visited by health officers, only half acknowledged a sanitation issue in the home, and less than a third willingly acted to solve the problem (Frost et al., 2000).

CHILD PROTECTIVE ISSUES/CUSTODY

Hoarding poses health and safety risks to children. If a homeowner is identified as a hoarder, social services can become involved. The parent could face charges of child neglect, and the child may be removed from the home. Law enforcement officers in many jurisdictions have the authority to petition the courts for an emergency removal of children from their homes if there is evidence of neglect or abuse such as hoarding. In some situations, hoarding may lead to divorce, and child custody may be determined by the court (Weiss, 2010). Courts are likely to rule in favor of the parent who can provide a safe and healthy environment for the children, rather than someone who is suspected of hoarding. Hoarding parents seeking to regain custody of their children may need to undergo a psychological evaluation, treatment, and an inspection of the home. In addition, hoarding parents often need to provide the court with evidence on their ongoing treatment, and they must be willing to allow case workers to conduct scheduled and unscheduled home visits to ensure that living conditions are acceptable and the home is a safe environment for their children.

OBSESSIVE-COMPULSIVE DISORDERS AND ANTISOCIAL/DYSFUNCTIONAL BEHAVIOR

There is little readily available forensic mental health literature examining obsessions, compulsions, and hoarding through a forensic lens. It is plausible that a person with an obsession to steal, a compulsion to take things, and a drive to hoard might become involved in petty shoplifting crimes or misdemeanor thefts. Unfortunately, with the data disconnects between mental health and the justice systems, the extent of such scenarios are not well documented. Miles, Ellis and Sheeran (2012) found that 73% of youth offenders in the United Kingdom were positively evaluated for obsessive-compulsive disorders. Research indicates that many of the youth reported that obsessions and compulsions began after incarceration. The study also revealed that the onset of anxiety after incarceration was likely due to the predisposed stress of being incarcerated and poor insight regarding previously experienced mental health problems. This anxiety may be a contributing factor for OCD symptoms (Sheeran, 2012). McMurren et al. (2000) found a significant correlation between anger, aggression and obsessive-compulsive disorder. The authors hypothesized that in situations where one feels out of control of potentially disastrous consequences for aggressive acts, the obsessive and compulsive reactions may be a way to exercise control over these situations. Specific antisocial behaviors associated with obsessive-compulsive disorders are discussed in the following sections.

PATHOLOGICAL GAMBLING

Pathological gambling has historically been categorized as an impulse disorder, but in the most recent edition of the Diagnostic and Statistical Manual of Mental Disorders (DSM-5) (American Psychiatric Association, 2013), it has been moved to the category of Substance-Related and Addictive Disorders. Addictive disorders are often connected to criminal behavior. For instance, the addict may need to steal, lie, or cheat to obtain finances that will support the habit. Additionally, under the influence of a substance or addiction, the addict makes immoral choices or engages in criminal behavior. Recent research has shown that individuals diagnosed with pathological gambling are also significantly likely to score high on measures of obsessive-compulsive behavior (Dannon, Lowengrub, Aizer, & Kotler, 2006). Hollander and Wong (1995) noted that impulsive disorders, which had included pathological gambling, are associated with strong compulsive and impulsive features. In fact, they can be thought of as an impulsive subtype of the obsessive-compulsive spectrum disorders and respond to treatments typically given for OCD.

MURDER

Kellehar and Kellehar (1998) were leaders in the development of a rubric for classifying serial murderers. An identified category included "place killer" behavior, whereby the killing behavioral pattern of the murderer is rigid, including killing in a particular environment, which suggests OCD tendencies. In his description of male serial killers, Hickey (2006) identified these murderers as "Place-Specific Killers." In both gender groups, the murderers have a preferred weapon and typically use it exclusively in a very specific murder scene (Farrell, Keppel, & Titterington, 2013). Mass murderers, in contrast, have a higher incidence of mood disorders and paranoia, with narcissistic, schizoid and antisocial traits (Meloy et al., 2011). Veale, Freeston, Krebs, Haymen & Salkovskis (2009) report that there is very little research showing that individuals with OCD act out intrusive thoughts to hurt, rape, or mutilate others. The authors further discussed that a person diagnosed with OCD is at higher risk for compulsively hurting himself or herself when they are trying to avoid the unreasonable urge to hurt another. In other words, there is also evidence that individuals with OCD may be less likely to hurt others. Other research also supports the view that while some murderers may demonstrate obsessions or compulsions, the clear majority of people diagnosed with obsessive-compulsive disorder do NOT engage in murderous behavior (Booth, Friedman, Curry, Ward, & Stewart, 2014; Friedman & Resnick, 2015). Booth et al. (2014) surmised that individuals presenting with OCD symptoms commonly develop a sense of over-responsibility for criminality, and confessing to their crimes may reduce their anxiety.

CHILD PORNOGRAPHY

Research conducted by Marshall et al. (2012) addressed criminal behavior of sexual child molesters, evaluating those who had direct contact with a child compared to those who viewed child pornography on the internet. They examined whether those who view child pornography, a form of sexual exploitation, had more obsessive thinking and compulsive behaviors than the contact offenders. They hypothesized that the need to control the fear of acting on one's child abuse urges was the driving force for this obsessive-compulsive behavior (Marshall et al., 2012), and having direct access to internet child pornography may be a protective diversion from acting on urges. Although internet offenders typically hoard hundreds to thousands of child pornography images, seemingly unable to delete them, the literature lacks sufficient support for the idea that internet child pornography users meet the criteria for hoarding disorders (Marshall et al., 2012). Another sexual child offense, pedophilia, has also been linked to obsessive-compulsive behavior, particularly compulsive-aggressive behavior which is "planned with the intention of relieving internal pressures or urges" (Hall & Hall, 2007, p. 462). Hall and Hall (2007) report research demonstrating that brain abnormalities, as evidenced by an MRI, show similar pathological abnormalities for pedophiles and individuals diagnosed with OCD. In addition, those individuals diagnosed with OCD and/or pedophilia show serotonin disturbances.

In an article by Quayle, Vaughan and Taylor (2005), the authors noted that the obsessions and compulsions that may accompany child pornography cannot be treated using the same cognitive-behavioral interventions typically used to treat OCD. Cognitive-behavioral therapy has successfully used exposure and response prevention to treat OCD; the image or thought is presented, but then the client is prevented from engaging in the compulsive behavior. However, with child pornography, the obsession does not produce anxiety, but instead produces pleasure. The authors noted that Functional Analytic Psychotherapy may be a more successful method of treating individuals who collect child pornography. This approach focuses on a willingness to experience the emotions, thoughts, memories, and bodily states without changing, escaping from, or avoiding them. The behaviors of looking at pornographic images on the internet are not permitted, but the feeling that these urges are controlling the individual are greatly reduced when it can be accepted. An important aspect of this approach is also to have the individual understand how the behavior of viewing child pornography prevents them from attaining their desired goals (Quayle et al., 2005).

OBSESSIONAL LOVE AND STALKING

Another controversial concept associated with obsessive-compulsive disorders is obsessional love. According to Doron, Derby and Szepsenwol (2014), a relationship obsessive-compulsive disorder (ROCDO) exists when a relationship suffers cognitive intrusions because one partner experiences obsessive doubts about a partner's fidelity, which ultimately interferes with relationship satisfaction. There is minimal current data which identifies the point at which these obsessive doubts develop into stalking behaviors (should the relationship end) or become overly controlling emotional abuse (should the relationship persist) (Doron, Derby, Szepsenwol, & Talmor, 2012). Pathological fixation or obsessive love can become dangerous, leading to stalking behaviors and dating violence (Kerrigan, Forfar, Farnham, & Preston, 2010; Revilla, 2013). In situations where an obsessive individual fixates on another individual, they are commonly driven by anxious obsessiveness, and the compulsion to control the other can quickly evolve into emotional captivity or delusional jealousy (Morrison, 2008). While evaluating stalking, terroristic threats, and assaults on public figures, Kerrigan et al. (2010) found that 81% of individuals involved in stalking public figures were reported to have previously received psychiatric care.

According to research, manifestations of OCD are often accompanied by extreme and distressing thoughts of violence that are intrusive and unwanted (Booth, Friedman, Curry, Ward, & Stewart, 2014). Physically violent stalkers have an extreme attachment to their targets, perceived adverse effect on their victims, and a history of physical violence or domestic abuse towards the victims. Stalking and obsessive behaviors commonly emerge in underlying anger, retaliation, emotional arousal, shame, and insecure attachment pathology, thereby increasing the rate of violence between 25%-40% (Morrison, 2008). Research indicates that the violence in domestic violence cases increases 55%-89% when obsessive disorders are involved (Morrison, 2008). The literature on stalking and intimate partner violence has profiled over-controlling, obsessive and dangerous behaviors, commonly committed by males (Morrison, 2008).

TREATMENT

Treatment efficacy for obsessive-compulsive disorder has been established for decades; however, the evolution of effective treatment relative to different OCD presentations continues to be a point of focus (Podea et al., 2009; Ponniah, Magiati, & Hollon, 2013). Treatment involves exposure, or allowing the obsessive thought to emerge, with response prevention by delaying, stopping or replacing the compulsion with an incompatible behavior. These treatments tend to involve stress inoculation or practice skills to deal with the potentially resultant anxiety created by treatment, with training in how to monitor stress levels (Gillihan, Williams, Malcoun, Yadin, & Foa, 2012). Over time, the person with OCD learns that they can tolerate the distressful obsessions for periods of time, before needing to follow through with the compulsive ritual, and no catastrophic disaster ensues. Eventually, the urge to complete the compulsive behavior subsides, and the obsessive thought, though perhaps never completely dissipated, becomes absent of stress (Gillihan et al., 2012). As noted earlier, however, this treatment approach has been less successful in treating pedophilia, as the obsession creates pleasure as opposed to anxiety.

Treatment efficacy for hoarding disorder lacks thorough research. Originally conceptualized as a symptom of OCD, hoarding disorder was treated in a similar manner. Now that hoarding is viewed as a separate disorder, research is examining how to effectively modify approaches to specifically target hoarding. One study demonstrated the effectiveness of a modified cognitive-behavioral approach. This approach added components of motivational interviewing (for those who were ambivalent about treatment) and skills training for organizing and problem-solving, as well as direct exposure and response prevention related to non-acquiring and discarding of possessions (Steketee, Frost, Tolin, Rasmussen, & Brown, 2010). Tolin (2011) postulates another promising treatment, described as harm reduction, where the goal is to not immediately eliminate hoarding but to remove the harm that it creates in the client's life.

In exploring prospective psychopharmacological treatments, research conducted by Saxena and Madment (2004) found that using the serotonin reuptake inhibitor paroxetine could provide some relief of hoarding symptoms, equal to results from its use with clients with OCD. In the same research, venlafaxine, which is a serotonin-norepinephrine reuptake inhibitor, has shown promise in decreasing hoarding symptoms. As with most mental health struggles, medication tends to be more efficient when coupled with a psychotherapeutic treatment.

CONCLUSION

Obsessive-compulsive disorder and the subdivided hoarding disorder of the DSM-5 are mental health disorders that range from personal nuisance, managed by the sufferer without outside intervention, to complex disorders that can manifest into disruptions of psychosocial functioning or even criminal behavior (APA, 2013). Obsessive-compulsive disorder, which previously existed in a list of anxiety disorders in the DSM-IV-TR (2000) 4th ed., text rev., now is included in the category of obsessive-compulsive and related disorders in the DSM-5, along with hoarding disorder. Hoarding disorder previously was only a symptom of obsessive and compulsive behaviors (APA, 2013; APA, 2000).

These diagnoses define complex neurological disorders with high incidences of Co-morbidity with other mental health problems. As in the case of hoarding disorder, they not only create dysfunctions for the sufferers, but also create disruptions for friends, families, and communities (Gillihan et al., 2012; Mataix-Cols & Pertusa, 2012; Pertusa et al., 2010; Saxena et al., 2011; Torres et al., 2012; Wakabayashi et al., 2012). As mentioned previously, this disorder, which comes with a high personal cost to the person struggling with it, also results in a high cost to the public in clean up, use of emergency and fire services, criminal behavior, or loss of life (Gilliam & Tolin, 2010; Mataix-Cols et al., 2010; Thompkins, 2011; Tolin, 2011).

When viewing hoarding or obsessive-compulsive disorders through a forensic lens, a host of exploratory hypotheses arise, indicating the need for additional research. There is limited documented or published literature on the prevalence of obsessive-compulsive disorders or hoarding disorders in individuals exhibiting criminal behaviors. However, according to Laajasalo, Ylipekka and Hakkanen-Nyholm (2013), anxious-avoidant and dependent and obsessive-compulsive characteristics are among the most prevalent personality disorders in the general population, ranging from 3%-11% (Laajasalo et al., 2013). It is imperative that we explore the efficacy of treating individuals who might be released from prison with the appropriate mental health techniques to decrease the risk for recidivism, as well as to reduce the cost to public funds or loss of life.

REFERENCES

Abramowitz, J. S., Taylor, S., & McKay, D. (2009). Obsessive-compulsive disorder. *The Lancet, 374*(9688), 491-499.

American Psychiatric Association. (2000). *Diagnostic and statistical manual of mental disorders.* (4th Edition, Text Revision). Washington, DC: American Psychiatric Publishing.

American Psychiatric Association. (2013). *Diagnostic and statistical manual of mental disorders.* (5th Edition). Arlington, VA: American Psychiatric Publishing.

An S., Mataix-Cols D., Lawrence N., Wooderson, S., Giampietro, V., Speckens, A., & Phillips, M. L. (2009). To discard or not to discard: The neural basis of hoarding symptoms in obsessive-compulsive disorder. *Molecular Psychiatry, 14*, 318-331. doi: 10.1038/sj.,p.4002129

Balci, V., & Sevincok, L. (2010). Suicidal ideation patients with obsessive-compulsive disorder. *Psychiatry Research, 175*(1-2), 104-108. doi: 10.1016/psychres.2009.03.012

Booth, B. D., Friedman, S. H.., Curry, S., Ward, H., & Stewart, S. E. (2014). Obsessions of child murder: Under recognized manifestations of obsessive-compulsive disorder. *Journal of the American Academy of Psychiatry & the Law, 42*(1), 66-74.

Bornheimer, L. A. (2015). Exposure and response prevention as an evidence-based treatment for obsessive-compulsive disorder: Considerations for social work practice. *Clinical Social Work Journal, 43*(1), 38-49. doi: 10.1007/s10615-014-0483-4

Bronwen, W. (2014). Animal hoarding: Devastating, complex, and everyone's concern. *Mental Health Practice, 17*(6), 35-39. doi: 10.7748/mhp2014.03.17.6.35.e868

Brown, S.E. (2011). Theoretical concepts from self-psychology applied to animal hoarding. *Society & Animals, 19*(2), 175-193. doi: 10.1163/156853011X563006

Calamari, J., Pontarelli, N., & Armstrong, K. (2012). Obsessive-compulsive disorder in late life. *Cognitive and Behavioral Practice, 19*(1), 136-150. doi: 10.1016/j.cbpra.2010.10.004

Colpas, E., Zulueta, J. & Pappas, D. (2012). An analysis of hoarding fire incidents and MFB organizational response. *Worchester Polytechnic Institute.* Retrieved from www.wpi.edu

Dannon, P., Lowengrub, K., Aizer, A., & Kotler, M. (2006). Pathological gambling: Co-morbid psychiatric diagnoses in patients and their families. *Israel Journal of Psychiatry and Related Sciences, 43*(2), 88-92.

Doron, G., Derby, D., Szepsenwol, O., & Talmor, D. (2012). Tainted love: Exploring relationship-centered obsessive-compulsive symptoms in two non-clinical cohorts. *Journal of Obsessive-Compulsive and Related Disorders, 1*(1), 16-24 doi: /10.1016/j.jocrd.2011.11.002

Farrell, A., Keppel, R. & Titterington, V. (2013). Testing existing classifications of serial murder considering gender: An exploratory of solo female serial murderers. *Journal of Investigative Psychology and Offender Profiling, 10,* 268-288. doi: 10.1002/jip.1392

Friedman, S. H., & Resnick, P. J. (2015). Parents who kill: Clinical and legal perspectives. *Psychiatric Times, 32*(10), 17.

Frost, R. O., Patronek, G. & Rosenfield, E. (2011). Comparison of object and animal hoarding. *Depression and Anxiety, 28*(10), 885-891. doi: 10.1002/da.20826

Frost, R. O., Steketee, G., & Grisham, J. (2004). Measurement of compulsive hoarding: Saving inventory-revised. *Behaviour Research and Therapy, 42*(10), 1163-1182. doi: 10.1016.j.brat.2003.07.006

Frost, R. O., Steketee, G., Williams, L. (2000). Hoarding: A community health problem. *Health and Social Care in the Community, 8*(4), 229-234. doi: 10.1046/j.1365-2524.2000.00245.x

Frost, R. O., Steketee, G., Williams, L. F., & Warren, R. (2000). Mood personality disorder symptoms and disability in obsessive compulsive hoarders: A comparison with clinical and nonclinical controls. *Behaviour Research and Therapy, 38*(11), 1071-1081.

Frost, R. O., Tolin, D. F., & Maltby, N. (2010). Insight-related challenges in the treatment of hoarding. *Cognitive and Behavioral Practice, 17*(4), 404-413. doi: 10.1016/j.cbpra.2009.07.004

Gilliam, C. & Tolin, D. (2010). Compulsive hoarding. *Bulletin of the Menninger Clinic, Spring,* 93-121. doi: 10.1821/bumc.2010.74.2.93

Gillihan, S. J., Williams, M. T., Malcoun, E., Yadin, E., & Foa, E. B. (2012). Common pitfalls in exposure and response prevention (EX/RP) for OCD. *Journal of Obsessive-Compulsive and Related Disorders, 1*(4), 251-257. doi: 10.1016/jocrd.2012.05.002

Goodman, W. K., Price, L. H., Rasmussen, S. A., Mazure, C., Fleischmann, R. L., Hill, C. L., Heninger, G. R., Charney, D. S. (1989). The Yale-Brown Obsessive Compulsive Scale: I. development, use, and reliability. *Archives of General Psychiatry, 46*(11), 1006-1011. doi: 10.1001/archpsyc.1989.01810110048007

Grisham J., Brown T., & Savage C. (2007). Neuropsychological impairment associated with compulsive hoarding. *Behaviour Research and Therapy, 45*(7), 1471-1483. doi: 10.1016/j.brat.2006.12.008

Grisham, J., Frost, R., Steketee, G., Kim, H., & Hood, S. (2006). Age of onset of compulsive hoarding. *Journal of Anxiety Disorders, 20,* 675-686. doi: 10.1016.j.janxdis.2005.07.004

Gupta, G., Avasthi A., Grover, S., & Singh, S.M. (2014). Factors associated with suicidal ideations and suicidal attempts in patients with obsessive compulsive disorder. *Asian Journal of Psychiatry, 12,* 140-146. doi: 10.1016/j.ajp.2014.09.004

Hall, R. & Hall, R. (2007). A profile of pedophilia: Definition, characteristics of offenders, recidivism, treatment outcomes, and forensic issues. *Mayo Clinic Proceedings, 82*(4), 457-471. doi: 10.4065/82.4.457

Hawyard, L.C., & Coles, M.E. (2009). Elucidating the relation of hoarding to obsessive-compulsive disorder and impulse control disorders. *Psychopathology and Behavioral Assessment, 31*(3), 220-227. doi: 10.1007/s10862-008-9106-0

Hickey, E. W. (2006). *Serial murderers and their victims (4th ed.)*. Belmont, CA: Thompson Wadsworth.

Hollander, E., & Wong, C. (1995). Body dysmorphic disorder, pathological gambling, and sexual compulsions. *Journal of Clinical Psychiatry, 56*(4), 7-12.

James, D. V., Kerrigan, T. R., Forfar, R., Farnham, F. R., & Preston, L. F. (2010). The Fixated Threat Assessment Centre: Preventing harm and facilitating care. *Journal of Forensic Psychiatry & Psychology, 21*(4), 521-536. doi: 10.1080/14789941003596981

Kelleher, M. D., & Kelleher, C. L. (1998). *Murder most rare: The female serial killer.* Westport: Dell Publishing.

Kellett, S. (2007). Compulsive hoarding: A site-security model and associated psychological treatment strategies. *Clinical Psychology and Psychotherapy, 14*, 412-427. doi: 10.1002/cpp.550

Laajasalo, T., Ylipekka, M., & Hakkanen-Nyholm, H. (2013). Homicidal behaviour among people with avoidant, dependent and obsessive-compulsive (Cluster c) personality disorder. *Criminal Behaviour and Mental Health, 23*, 18-29. doi: 10.1002/cbm.1844

Landau D, Iervolino, A., & Pertusa A, (2010). Stressful life events and material deprivation in hoarding disorder. *Journal of Anxiety Disorders, 25*, 192-202. doi: 10.1016/j.janxdis.210.09.002

Levy, R., & Dubois, B. (2006). Apathy and the functional anatomy of the prefrontal cortex-basal ganglia circuits. *Cerebral Cortex, 16(7)*, 916-928. doi: 10.1093/cercor/bhj043

Lockwood R. (1994). The psychology of animal collectors. *American Animal Hospital Association Trends Magazine, 9*, 18-21.

Marshall. L., O'Brien, M., Marshall, W., Booth, B., & Davis, A. (2012). Obsessive-compulsive disorder, social phobia and loneliness in incarcerated in child pornography offenders. *Sexual Addiction and Compulsivity, 19*(1-2), 41-52. doi: 10.1080/10720162.2012.665291

Mataix-Cols, D., Frost, R., Pertusa, A., Clark, L., Saxena, S., Leckman, J., Stein, D., Matsunaga, H., & Wilhelm, S. (2010). Hoarding disorder: Aa new diagnosis for DSM-V? *Depression and Anxiety, 27*, 556-572. doi: 10.1002/da.20693

Mataix-Cols, D., & Pertusa, A. (2012). Annual research review: Hoarding disorder – potential benefits and pitfalls of a new mental disorder. *Journal of Child Psychology and Psychiatry, 53*(5), 608-618. doi: 10.1111/j.1469-7610.2011.02464.x

Mataix-Cols, D., Wooderson, S., Lawrence, N., Brammer, M., Speckens, A., & Phillips, M. (2004). Distinct neural correlates of washing, checking, and hoarding symptom dimensions in obsessive-compulsive disorder. *Archives of General Psychiatry, 61*(6), 564-576. doi: 10.1001/archpsyc.61.6.564

Matthews, C., Kaur, N. & Stein, M. (2008). Childhood trauma and obsessive-compulsive symptoms. *Depression and Anxiety, 25*, 742-751. doi: 10.1002/da.20316

McMurran, M., Egan, V., Richardson, C., Street, H., Ahmadi, S. & Cooper, G. (2000). Referrals for anger and aggression in forensic psychology outpatient services. *The Journal of Forensic Psychiatry, 11*(1), 206-213. doi: 10.1080/095851800362481

Miles, H., Ellis, K., & Sheeran, E. (2012). 'Coping inside?' A prevalence of anxiety and OCD amongst incarcerated young offenders and an evaluation of a one-day CBT workshop. *The Journal of Forensic Psychiatry and Psychology, 23*(5-6), 698-705. doi:10.1080/14789949.2012.719535

Minneapolis Animal Control and Care. (2005). Chapter 64 – dogs, cats, ferrets and rabbits. *Minneapolis, Minnesota Code of Ordinances*. Retrieved from www.municode.com.

Morrison, K.A. (2008). Differentiating between physically violent and nonviolent stalkers: An examination of Canadian cases. *Journal of Forensic Science, 53*(3), 742-751. doi: 10.111/j.1556-4029.2008.00722.x

Muroff, J., Bratiotis, C. & Steketee, G. (2011). Treatment for hoarding disorders: A review of the evidence. *Clinical Social Work Journal, 39*, 406-423. doi:10.1007/s10615-010-0311-4

Nakaaki S., Murata Y., Sato J., Shinagawa Y., Tatsumi, H., Hirono, N., & Furukawa, T. (2007). Greater impairment of ability in the divided attention task is seen in Alzheimer's disease patients with depression than in those without depression. *Dementia and Geriatric Cognitive Disorders, 23*(4), 231-40. doi:10.1159/000099633

Nathanson, J.N. (2009). Animal hoarding: Slipping into the darkness of Co-morbid animal and self-neglect. *Journal of Elder Abuse & Neglect, 21*(4), 307-324. doi: 10.1080/08946560903004839

O'Connor, K., Koszegi, N., Aardema, F., van Niekerk, J., & Taillon, A. (2009). An inference-based approach to treating obsessive-compulsive disorders. *Cognitive and Behavioral Practice, 16*(4), 420-429. doi: 10.1016/j.cbpra.2009.05.001

Ohtsuchi, H., Matsuo, K., Akimoto, T. & Watanabe, Y. (2010). Fronto-limbic abnormalities in a patient with compulsive hoarding: A 99MTc-ECD SPECT study. *Psychiatry and Clinical Neurosciences, 64*, 580-583. doi:10.1111/j.14401819.2010.02120.x

Otte, S., & Steketee, G. (2011). Psychiatric issues in hoarding. *Psychiatric Times*. Retrieved from www.psychiatrictimes.

Patronek, G.J., & Nathanson, J.N., (2009). A theoretical perspective to inform assessment and treatment strategies for animal hoarders. *Clinical Psychology Review, 29*(3), 274-281. doi:10.1016/j.cpr.2009.01.006

Pertusa, A., Frost, R., Fullana, M., Samuels, J., Steketee, G., Tolin, D., & Mataix-Cols, D. (2010). Refining the diagnostic boundaries of compulsive hoarding: A critical review. *Clinical Psychology Review, 30*, 371-386. _doi:10.1016/j.cpr.2010.01.007

Pertusa A., Frost, R.O., Fullana, M.A., Samuels, J., Steketee, G., Tolin, D., Saxena, S., Leckman, J. F., & Mataix-Cols, D. (2010). Refining the diagnostic boundaries of compulsive hoarding: A critical review. *Clinical Psychology Review, 30*(4), 371-386. doi: 10.1016/j.cpr.2010.01.007

Pertusa, A., Frost, R.O., & Mataix-Cols, D. (2010). When hoarding is a symptom of OCD: A case series and implications for DSM-V. *Behaviour Research and Therapy, 48*(10), 1012-1020. doi: 10.1016/j.brat.2010.07.003

Pertusa, A., Fullana, M., Singh, S., Alonso, P., Menchon, J., & Mataix-Cols, D. (2008). Compulsive hoarding: OCD symptom, distinct clinical syndrome, or both? *The American Journal of Psychiatry, 165*(10), 1289-1298. doi: 10.1176/appi.ajp.2008.07111730

Podea, D., Suciu, R., Suciu, C., & Mihai, A. (2009). An update on the cognitive behavior therapy of obsessive compulsive disorder in adults. *Journal of Cognitive & Behavioral Psychotherapies, 9*(2), 221-233.

Ponniah, K., Magiati, I., & Hollon, S.D. (2013). An update on the efficacy of psychological treatment for obsessive-compulsive disorder in adults. *Journal of Obsessive-Compulsive Related Disorders, 2*(2), 207-218. doi: 10.1016/j.jocrd.2013.02.005

Quayle, E., Vaughan, M., & Taylor, M. (2005). Sex offenders, internet child abuse images and emotional avoidance: The importance of values. *Aggression and Violent Behavior, 11*, 1-11. doi: 10.1016/j.avb.2005.02.005

Renwick, M.L. (2009). Animal hoarding: A legislative solution. *University of Louisville Law Review, 47*(3), 585-606.

Revilla, L. (2013). Warning signs of a dangerous obsessive relationship. Retrieved from www.livestrong.com

Rudd, M. D., Dahm, P. F., Rajab, M. H. (1993). Diagnostic Co-morbidity in persons with SI and behavior. *American Journal of Psychiatry, 150,* 928-934. doi: 10.1176/ajp..150.6.928

Samuels, J. Bienvenu, O.J., Grados, M., Cullen, B., Riddle, M., Liang, K., Eaton, W., & Nestadt, G. (2008). Prevalence and correlates of hoarding behavior in a community-based sample. *Behavior Research and Therapy, 46*(7), 836-844. doi: 10.1016/j.brat.2008.04.004

Samuels, J. F., Bienvenu, O. J., Pinto, A., Fyer, A. J., McCracken, J. T., Rauch, S. L., & Nestadt, G. (2007). Hoarding in obsessive-compulsive disorder: Results from the OCD Collaborative Genetics Study. *Behaviour Research and Therapy, 45,* 673-686. doi: 10.1016/j.brat.2006.05.008

San Francisco Task Force on Compulsive Hoarding. (2009). *Beyond overwhelmed: The impact of compulsive hoarding and cluttering in San Francisco and recommendations to reduce negative impacts and improve care.* San Francisco, CA: San Francisco Task Force on Compulsive Hoarding.

Saxena, S., Ayers, C.R., Maidment, K.M., Vapnik, T., Wetherell, J.L., & Bystritsky, A. (2011). Quality of life and functional impairment in compulsive hoarding. *Journal of Psychiatric Research, 45*(5), 475-480. doi: 10.1016/j.psychires.2010.08.007

Saxena, S. & Madment, K. (2004). Treatment of compulsive hoarding. *Journal of Clinical Psychology, 60*(11), 1143-1154. doi: 10.1176/foc.5.3.foc381

Steketee, G., Frost, R. Tolin, D., Rasmussen, J., & Brown, T. (2010). Waitlist-controlled trial of cognitive behavior therapy for hoarding disorder. *Depression and Anxiety, 27,* 476-484. doi:10.1002/da.20673.

The Hoarding Project. (2016). *Hoarding.* Retrieved from www.thehoardingproject.org

Thompkins, M. (2011). Working with families of people who hoard: A harm reduction approach. *Journal of Clinical Psychology, 67,* 497-506. doi: 10.1002/jclp.20797

Timpano, K. & Schmidt, N. (2013). A relationship between self-control deficits and hoarding: A multi-method investigation across three samples. *Journal of Abnormal Psychology, 122*(1), 13-25. doi: 10.1037a0 029760

Tolin, D. (2011). Understanding and treating hoarding: A bio-psychosocial perspective. *The Journal of Clinical Psychology, 67,* 517-526. doi: 10.1002/jclp.20795

Tolin, D. (2012). *AARP face your fears: A proven plan to beat anxiety, panic, phobias, and obsessions.* New York: NY: John Wiley & Sons.

Tolin, D. F., Frost, R. O., Steketee, G., & Fitch, K. E. (2008). Family burden of compulsive hoarding: Results of an internet survey. *Behavior Research and Therapy, 46,* 334-344. doi: 10.1016/j.brat.2007.12.008

Tolin, D., Meunier, S., Frost, R. O. & Steketee, G. (2010). Course of compulsive hoarding and its relationship to life events. *Depression and Anxiety, 27,* 829-838. doi: 10.1002/da.20684

Tolin, D., & Steketee, G. (2007). General issues in psychological treatment for obsessive-compulsive disorder. *Psychological treatment of obsessive-compulsive disorder: Fundamentals and beyond* (pp. 31-59). Washington, DC: American Psychological Association.

Torres, A.R., Fontenelle, L.F., Ferrao, Y.A., Conceicao do Rosario, M., Torresan, R.C., Miguel, E.C., & Shavitt, R.G. (2012). Clinical features of obsessive-compulsive disorder with hoarding symptoms: A multi-center study. *Journal of Psychiatric Research, 26*(6), 724-732. doi: 10.1016/j.jpsychires.2012.03.005

Veale, D., Freeston, M., Krebs, G., Haymen, I. & Salkovskis., P. (2009). Risk assessment and management in obsessive-compulsive disorder. *Advances in Psychiatric Treatment, 15,* 332-343. doi: 10.1192/apt. bp.107.004705

Wakabayashi, A., Baron-Cohen, S., & Ashwin, C, (2012). Do the traits of autism spectrum overlap with those of schizophrenia or obsessive-compulsive disorder in the general population? *Research in Autism Spectrum Disorders, 6*(2), 717-725. doi: 10.1016/j.rasd.2011.09.008

Wakin, A., & Vo, D. (2008). Love-variant: The Wakin-Vo I.D.R. model of limerence. Retrieved fromhttp://www.interdisciplinary.net/ptb/persons/pil/pil2/wakinvo%20paper.pdf

Weiss, K. (2010). Hoarding, hermitage and the law: Why we love the Collyer Brothers. *Journal of the American Academy of Psychiatry Law, 38,* 251-257.

Wheaton, M., Abramowitz, J., Farnklin, J., Berman, N., & Fabricant, L. (2011). Experiential avoidance and saving cognitions in the prediction of hoarding symptoms. *Cognitive Therapy and Research, 35,* 511-516. doi: 10.1007/s10608-010-9338-7

CHAPTER 13

OFFENDER REENTRY: A SUMMARY OF HISTORY, EXISTING BARRIERS, AND BEST PRACTICES

MEGAN MOELLER & JOLENE REBERTUS

CHAPTER OVERVIEW

Offender reentry is defined as "all the activities and programming conducted to prepare ex-convicts to return safely to the community and to live as law-abiding citizens" (James, 2011, p. 1). Effective reintegration practices are critical to improving offender functioning and enhancing public safety. Initiatives should be highly structured around the use of best practices—having external evidence gained from systematic research supporting them (Listwan, Cullen, & Latessa, 2006). This chapter will introduce the history of reentry practices, individual barriers to reentry, present-day reentry practices and interventions supported by research, and reintegration work with special populations, such as those with mental health and substance use issues.

INTRODUCTION

The topic of offenders leaving correctional institutions and reentering into the community has gained significant momentum over the last decade. A December 2013 U.S. Department of Justice report stated that, for the first time in 31 years, 2009 prison releases surpassed prison admissions (Carson & Golinelli, 2014). Prisoners ages 44 and younger represented 80% of the prison population and 77% of releases (Carson & Golinelli, 2014). The National Institute of Justice reported that, in 2011, there were 1,885 releases per day from state and federal institutions, and approximately 4.8 million individuals were on community supervision (Carson & Sobel, 2012; National Institute of Justice, 2015). A Bureau of Justice Statistics report stated that during the year of 2012, 637,400 individuals were released from federal and state institutions (Carson & Golinelli, 2014). The numbers of offenders and releases into the community generates a need to assure proper reentry practices.

Strong resource allocations, current practices, and reentry efforts over the last several years have been motivated by the need to reduce high recidivism rates among those paroled into the community. Zhang,

Roberts and Farabee (2014) cited a study conducted by Langan and Levin in 2002 that followed individuals released from correctional facilities in 1994 for 3 years and found that more than two-thirds of the individuals had been rearrested. Further research published by The National Institute of Justice in 2014 supports a 67.8% recidivism rate within three years post release (Durose, Cooper, & Snyder, 2014). "The sheer volume of offenders returning to the street has stretched the limits of parole services and reentry programming, and those who are returning home are characterized by deficiencies and needs above and beyond those of past releases" (Wright & Cesar, 2013, p. 376).

History has shaped present-day corrections and reentry practices. Whether it is due to failed rehabilitation attempts, public outcry, or government initiatives toward reduction of crime, public safety is of high importance. In order to fully conceptualize modern correctional practice, including reentry, one must know the paradigms of its development throughout our history.

HISTORY OF REENTRY

The United States has experimented with a myriad of philosophical approaches to crime, incarceration, and reentry. Prior to the 1800s, minimal consideration was given to individuals' release from prison facilities. The primary focus was warehousing and punishing individuals who broke the law (Seiter & Kadela, 2003). During this period, sentence length was often tailored to the severity of the offense, believing that instituting this form of punishment alone would deter individuals from committing crime (Wodahl & Garland, 2009). Since then, distinct paradigm shifts have occurred, concerning the way sentencing and release should be implemented.

By the turn of the 20th century, the United States began to consider the possibility of early release of offenders back into the community and implemented the first Parole Board (Wodahl & Garland, 2009). Individuals who were granted parole could be released into the community while remaining under correctional jurisdiction. During this period, release conditions were limited and under-developed. Nonetheless, the creation of the first Parole Board helped provide the underpinnings for a modern-day community corrections movement (Seiter & Kadela, 2003).

Throughout the 1900s there were several initiatives based on beliefs of what worked best for society and public safety. From the 1930s to 1960s, the medical model was the primary emphasis of one's incarceration. The medical model encompassed a theoretical framework that supported the presence of environmental, biological, and psychological factors of each individual related to their offending. According to this model, treating offending behavior required an individualized treatment approach. The medical model utilized time inside a correctional facility as an opportunity to correct maladaptive behaviors (Wodahl & Garland, 2009).

Community corrections made a strong emergence in the 1960s and 1970s, because the medical model was failing. Community interventions were now deemed necessary for rehabilitation, as prison isolated the individual from realistic life scenarios and basic human needs (Wodahl & Garland, 2009). Although the idea of community supervision had existed for several years, it was during these two decades that further development and structure occurred. Correctional departments realized that prison was not sufficient to deter crime. A stronger emphasis on community corrections was developed, and individual intervention activities initiated in the community continued to gain prominence.

Scrutiny of the community corrections model and dissenting viewpoints about rehabilitation arose in the 1970s. Research published by Robert Martinson (1974) sparked the "nothing works" movement, reporting that studies on rehabilitation programs were unsuccessful at reducing reoffending (Andrews & Bonta, 2010; Gendreau, French, & Gionet, 2004). Federal funding was eliminated for community initiatives, and there was a move toward mass incarceration. In addition, the general public viewed indeterminate sentencing as too subjective and lenient. Arguments for punishment shifted from crime prevention through rehabilitation to a focus on having sentences reflect the harm caused by the offender (Andrews & Bonta, 2010). Some of this debate was sparked by the lack of changes in recidivism rates after the implementation of the rehabilitation model (Wodahl & Garland, 2009).

As a result, legislators and their constituents felt it was necessary to institute "tough on crime" sentencing. Federal mandates such as mandatory minimum sentences, increases in sentence severity for drug offenses, three-strike laws, firm-oriented sentencing guidelines, and the abolishment of parole were implemented (Currie, 1998; Gendreau, Goggin, & Cullin, 1999; Haimowitz, 2004). These mandates represented a move toward a control model and the emergence of "truth-in-sentencing" laws. Deterrence strategies were further supported by Martinson's statement: "It is possible that there is indeed something that works...that might be made to work better—something that deters rather than cures" (Martinson, 1974, p. 50). The prison population dramatically rose, leading to serious issues of overcrowding. Elliot Currie (1998) noted that there were fewer than 200,000 offenders in our prisons in 1971 and close to 1.2 million by the end of 1996.

Due to mass incarceration numbers, fiscal concerns, poor prison conditions, and evidentiary failure of the "tough on crime" policies, the United States was forced to re-examine the release of offenders and re-implement the use of community corrections (Andrews & Bonta, 2010; Church, 2013). The idea of punishment and control by incarceration was still being utilized, but movement toward enhancement of community alternatives emerged. Common practices during this period included more defined conditions of release; home confinement; and correctional, transitional housing placements. This allowed for release into the community, with the continued ability to monitor the individual (Wodahl & Garland, 2009).

REENTRY DEFINITIONS

The following are common reentry-related definitions within present-day, contemporary corrections and reentry practices. It should be noted that various states may use correctional terminology interchangeably. For example, parole in the traditional sense may be recognized in certain states as probation with conditions of release.

- **Prison** – Long-term confinement facilities operated by the 50 state governments and the Federal Bureau of Prisons. Private correctional facilities also operate under contracts for a wide variety of local, state, and federal agencies (Bureau of Justice Statistics, 2014).
- **Jail** – A facility overseen by an agency of local government—typically a law enforcement agency—intended for confinement of adults, but sometimes also containing juveniles. Individuals are detained pending adjudication or committed after adjudication, usually on sentences of a year or less (National Institute of Corrections, 2008).
- **Parole** – "The conditional release of a convicted offender from prison before the end of his sentence, based upon requirements for the offender's behavior set and supervised by a parole agency" (National Institute of Corrections, 2008, p. 140).
- **Conditional Release** – "Mandatory release of an offender from prison after completion of a portion of the term as prescribed by law to parole supervision for the remainder of the sentence" (National Institute of Corrections, 2008, p. 139). Individuals will serve the conditions of release until completion of the full term of sentence, also known as expiration.
- **Recidivism** – "...the re-arrest, reconviction, or re-incarceration of an ex-offender within a given time frame" (James, 2011, p. 6). This includes technical violations, or violations of an offender's parole or probation, also known as being in violation of their conditions of release. Examples of such violations can include substance use, violation of curfew, failure to report to supervising agent, etc., and may result in the parolee's return to prison.

BARRIERS TO REENTRY

There are numerous barriers for individuals transitioning from prison to the community. As an illustration, imagine a male offender released from prison after a 2½-year sentence. Although he completed his General Education Diploma (GED) during his incarceration, he is now homeless, unemployed, and is medically uninsured. The parolee has mild mental health symptoms, along with a substance use history. While incarcerated, he was not provided an opportunity to complete substance use treatment. His family support is limited, and his previous friends continue to engage in criminal activities. He will be supervised by a parole officer for a period of one year upon his release from the institution. He will have both general and specific terms and conditions of release to which he must adhere, such as electronic monitoring, refraining from illicit and licit substances, and supervision and restitution fees. Take a moment to review this individual's release. Think about the challenges he will face. Consider what may be imperative to enhance the possibility of a successful reentry into the community.

EDUCATION AND EMPLOYMENT

Incarcerated individuals are often faced with low education levels and minimal full-time employment histories. "Roughly half of returning offenders are functionally illiterate, and 70% are high school drop outs" (NGA Center for Best Practices, 2005, p. 5). While GED programming may be available for offenders inside, lack of education and employment preparation lead to individuals returning to the community with significant limitations regarding their ability to gain employment.

Once in the community, research demonstrates that African American males with a criminal history are less likely to be offered employment in comparison to Caucasian male offenders (Holzer, Raphael, & Stoll, 2003). Furthermore, a study showed that Caucasians with a criminal history were as likely to be offered job interviews as African Americans with similar credentials but without a criminal history (Frazier, 2014).

Employers often have criminal history restrictions and policies that limit the ability to hire individuals with a criminal record. Having been convicted of a felony significantly limits an individual's ability to be hired for full-time employment. Research suggests that agencies willing to hire offender populations are those primarily in construction trades and/or manufacturing and least likely to be in service-related fields, such as retail. If asked for an interview, offenders tend to have a difficult time explaining their gaps in employment and properly disclosing their criminal history. Interestingly, research shows that approximately 40% of employers are willing to consider individuals with significant criminal histories for a job vacancy (Holzer et al., 2003).

Pogrebin, West-Smith, Walker, & Unnithan (2014) suggest that employment alone is not enough to help individuals reintegrate back into society and find financial stability. Often, financial obligations such as parole expenses and supervision fees (urine analysis, restitution, etc.), previous debt, transportation, housing, and so forth, can prevent economic stability. Such expenses quickly add up and often exceed an individual's income.

HOUSING

Consequences of unemployment and financial instability are many, including the inability to sustain permanent housing. Some individuals are able to stay with family and/or friends following release, but this is often a temporary solution. Landlords often restrict housing opportunities to those individuals with felony histories, limiting their ability to maintain a stable residence. At least 10% of individuals returning to the community become homeless. This figure significantly increases for individuals returning to metropolitan areas, where the range of homelessness increases to 30%-50% (NGA Center for Best Practices, 2005). Being released in an urban area makes it more difficult to gain employment, as the labor market is saturated by individuals with felony backgrounds who compete for the same resources. In contrast, individuals who are able to maintain some form of stable housing generally feel more confident about their ability to remain in the community permanently (Walker, Hempel, Unnithan, & Pogrebin, 2014).

While returning to an urban area has it challenges, those returning to small rural communities also face significant barriers. Rural housing, employment, post-release programming, and health services are all limited (Wodahl, 2006). "To this point, most if not all of the focus on prisoner reentry has been from an urban perspective, with little attention on how these obstacles affect inmates returning to rural areas" (Wodahl, 2006, p. 32).

SOCIAL SUPPORTS

When a person is incarcerated, time continues on for the family members. The family structure changes: significant others may find a new companion or there may be a death in the family (Visher & Travis, 2003). A more-general finding notes that those who are incarcerated have minimal identifiable supports. Specifically, individuals are only able to identify, on average, three individuals whom they deem supportive. The majority of these individuals are family members (Shinkfield & Graffam, 2008). Research conducted in the state of Minnesota has shown that visits from fathers, siblings, in-laws, and clergy while an individual is incarcerated are associated with reduction in recidivism (Duwey & Clark, 2013).

Women and men face various unique challenges upon reentry due to gender-specific roles and family structure. A recent study found that women had greater difficulties throughout release and reported larger treatment needs for substance use and mental health issues (Spjeldnes, Jung, & Yamatani, 2014). Further vulnerabilities for women include increased need for alternative housing due to custody of children, stress related to establishing and sustaining a parenting role, low education attainment, higher rates of unemployment, and unstable and often abusive relationships (Few-Demo & Arditti, 2014; Richie, 2001; Spjeldnes et al., 2014; Visher & Bakken, 2014).

HEALTH

A qualitative study of health experiences of recently released offenders reported elevated mortality rates and inadequate or absent continuity of mental and medical healthcare, post-release. Addiction, asthma, anxiety, Bipolar Disorder, cancer, cardiovascular disease, dental issues, depression, diabetes, gastrointestinal and/or gynecologic issues, head trauma, Hepatitis C, Human Immunodeficiency Syndrome (HIV), musculoskeletal concerns, chronic pain, paranoia, PTSD, pregnancy, Schizophrenia, seizure disorder, suicide risk, shortness of breath, stroke, Tuberculosis, vision, and weight control were all concerns reported during the qualitative analysis (Binswanger et al., 2011). "Estimates of HIV and Hepatitis rates in correctional populations are 8 to 10 times higher than in the general population…" (Inciardi et al., 2007. p. 111). In 2006, the Urban Institute's Justice Policy Center reported that an Illinois study found that less than 10% of individuals being released were given referrals for follow-up health care in the community. To add further complications, even when a referral was provided, there were poor outcomes for securing medical insurance following release. The same report indicated that only 10%-20% of released prisoners were able to acquire insurance four to eight months following release.

It should be noted that some criminal offenses hold greater weight of stigmatization in the community, which ultimately has a greater negative impact on an individual's reentry process. These offenses may include sexual offenses (Burchfield & Mingus, 2008), arson, and serious violent offenses such as assault and/or murder. Reporting indicated such offenses may further limit a parolee's access to housing, treatment programs, and social supports.

INTERVENTIONS

Offender reentry is defined as "all the activities and programming conducted to prepare ex-convicts to return safely to the community and to live as law-abiding citizens" (James, 2011, p. 1). Present-day reentry can be conceptualized as a three-phase process. Phase 1 incorporates programs available throughout the incarceration period that prepare inmates for reentry. Phase 2 involves program coordination to connect individuals to community supports and resources immediately following release. Phase 3 involves providing long-term support and supervision as these individuals acclimate permanently into a community (James, 2011).

Reentry has become a focal point of the present correctional paradigm. Research shows that effective reintegration practices are critical to improving offender functioning and enhancing public safety (Listwan, Cullen, & Latessa, 2006). Current initiatives are structured by Evidenced-Based Practices (EBP). EBP is defined as "the conscientious, explicit, and judicious use of current best evidence in making decisions about the care of the individual patient." It means integrating individual clinical expertise with the best available external evidence from systematic research (Sackett, Rosenberg, Gray, Haynes, & Richardson, 1996, p. 71).

The Transition from Prison to Community (TPC) initiative was created by a compilation of national experts utilizing EBP for effective reentry initiatives. In 2002, eight states were chosen to embrace the TPC framework, and in 2009, they were joined by six additional states. The overarching structure "is a framework that can assist jurisdictions to undertake system change designed to reduce recidivism among transitioning offenders, reduce future victimization, enhance public safety; and improve the lives of communities, victims, and offenders" (National Institute of Corrections, 2008, p.11).

The National Institute of Corrections (2008) defines nine model components of TPC:
- Mobilize interdisciplinary, collaborative leadership teams to guide reentry efforts.
- Engage in a rational planning process for reentering offender populations.
- Integrate stages of offender processing, beginning at commitment to prison.
- Involve non-correctional stakeholders who can provide services in reentry efforts.
- Assure that transitioning offenders are provided basic survival resources.
- Implement valid offender assessment.
- Target effective interventions to address offender risk and need.
- Expand on the traditional roles of correctional staff by engaging an offender in change.
- Develop the capacity to measure change toward specific outcomes.

The overarching goals of TPC are informed by the Risk-Need-Responsivity Model. This model provides three principles to target effective offender intervention: risk, need, and responsivity (Andrews, Bonta ,and Worthmith, 2006). Current research demonstrates an external validity that allows for generalization and utilization of assessment across correctional settings and diverse populations.

The **risk principle** is defined as "matching the intensity of the individual's treatment to their level of risk for re-offending" (Osher, D'Amora, Plotkin, Jarrett, & Eggleston, 2012, p. 21). Research demonstrates a need to target and expand our resources on high-risk individuals (Lowenkamp & Latessa, 2004). High-intensity programming would not be appropriate for an individual determined to be at a lower risk of re-offending; providing high-intensity supervision to a low-risk offender will not impact recidivism and may foster antisocial attitudes and behaviors by having the low-risk individual in contact with high-risk individuals. "Simply stated, the risk principle indicates that offenders should be provided with supervision and treatment levels that are commensurate with their risk level" (Lowenkamp & Latessa, 2004, p. 3).

There are several validated tools and actuarial assessments available to determine the probability of the risk for reoffending. Risk assessments in a forensic setting "attempt to predict the likelihood of future offending in order to identify individuals in need of intervention" (Brown & Singh, 2014, p. 49). Often actuarial assessments utilize statistical procedures to create profiles of individuals based on characteristics proven to be associated with re-offending (Zhang, Roberts, & Farabee, 2014).

Assessments may also look at dynamic, static, and protective factors in structured examination (Brown & Singh, 2014). Static factors include items identified that are historically based and cannot be changed through intervention. Examples may include age, gender, criminal history, and race. In comparison, dynamic factors are items that an individual can change through appropriate intervention. Dynamic factors may include the quality of interpersonal relationships, anger management, and maladaptive coping skills. In comparison, some factors are acute in nature and may have immediate mitigations, such as intoxication and/or mood based on current disposition (Yesberg & Polaschek, 2015).

While dynamic factors are essential in promoting offender change, equal importance should be placed on an individual's strengths at the time of the assessment. These strengths are often defined as protective factors, and by fostering such strengths, individuals may decrease the likelihood of recidivism (Yesberg & Polaschek, 2015). For example, an individual may possess known static or dynamic risk factors; however, identifying protective factors (e.g., family, high school diploma, steady employment, etc.) may mitigate recidivism when these factors are fostered through appropriate case planning (Brown & Singh, 2014; Yesberg & Polaschek, 2015).

The **need principle** instructs interventions to target the dynamic risk factors of a particular individual (Osher et al., 2012). These dynamic factors are also referred to as criminogenic needs. Andrews et al. (2006) categorize the following as major risk-need factors that should be targeted to reduce recidivism:

- **Antisocial behavior** – early and continuing involvement in antisocial acts
- **Antisocial personality pattern** – adventurous pleasure seeking, weak self-control, restlessly aggressive
- **Antisocial cognition** – attitudes, values, beliefs, and rationalizations supportive of crime; cognitive emotional states of anger, resentment, and defiance; criminal versus reformed identity; criminal versus anti-criminal identity
- **Antisocial associates** – close associations with criminals and relative isolation from anti-criminals; immediate social support for crime
- **Family and/or marital** – two key elements are nurturance and/or caring and monitoring and/or supervision
- **School and/or work** – low levels of performance and satisfaction in school and/or work
- **Leisure and/or recreation** – low levels of involvement and satisfactions in anti-criminal leisure pursuits
- **Substance abuse** – abuse of alcohol and/or other drugs

The top four factors (antisocial behavior, antisocial personality patterns, antisocial cognition, and antisocial associates) need to be addressed in order for the remaining factors to be effective (Osher et al., 2012). For example, Bucklen and Zajac (2009) found that parole challenges and failures correlated with antisocial attitudes, poor problem solving, poor coping skills, and unrealistic expectations regarding their release. It is important to note that release planning, continuum of care, treatment, and supervision should address the identified criminogenic needs. How these criminogenic needs are addressed is defined as responsivity. An important characteristic of responsivity is to "address individual's barriers to learning in the design of treatment interventions" (Osher et al., 2012, p. 22). For example, research supports the need to provide gender-responsive programming in order to facilitate further reduction in recidivism (Spjeldnes et al., 2014).

Researchers have described several behavioral treatment approaches, such as social learning theory, cognitive behavioral therapy, and family-based therapy, as effective for those who have offended. Social learning theory postulates that "individuals acquire attitudes, behavior or knowledge from the persons around them" (Latessa, 2008). Significance is placed on appropriate modeling of these skills toward the goal of conditioning the person(s) for whom they are being modeled. These interpersonal interactions should lead to intrinsic motivation. Supervising agents and other individuals critical to the reentry process can utilize motivational interviewing and social learning principles to change routine interactions into interventions (Burke & Tonry, 2006).

Core correctional practice and the responsivity principle define the need for officers and program staff to "establish high-quality relationships with offenders (e.g., respectful, caring, enthusiastic, valuing of personal autonomy) and apply high-quality structuring skills (e.g., prosocial modeling, effective reinforcement, problem-solving strategies, service advocacy)" (Kennealy, Skeem, Manchak, & Eno Louden, 2012, p. 496). The need for rapport and alliance with offenders is especially salient for probation officers. Research supports the notion that appropriate modeling and interpersonal interactions are more influential in a community setting than within an institution (Kennealy et al., 2012).

Cognitive behavioral therapy (CBT) focuses on the thoughts of the individual and the impact of those thoughts on emotions and behaviors. CBT provides structured and active learning that addresses the antisocial attitudes and cognitive distortions proven to be ineffective. Scientific evidence has shown that thoughts can be influenced and restructured, which will lead to changes in the offenders' feelings and behavior. "Skills are not only taught but are practiced, and pro-social attitudes and behaviors are positively reinforced" (Burke & Tonry, 2006, p. 17). CBT and similar behavioral programs are the most effective interventions in reducing recidivism (Lowenkamp, Latessa, & Smith, 2006).

Social support has been further defined as "the perceived or actual instrumental and/or expressive provisions supplied by the community, social networks, and confiding partners" (Wright & Cesar, 2013, p. 376). It is important to involve prosocial networks and community in the transition from prison to community (Burke & Tonry, 2006). People important to the individual (such as family members) can reinforce positive behavior and prosocial attitudes, and provide necessary support throughout transition. **Family-based interventions** are designed to train the family on particular behavioral approaches found to be effective in reducing recidivism (Lowenkamp & Latessa, 2004).

Research shows that while social learning theory, cognitive behavioral therapy, and family-based programming impact recidivism, fidelity should be taken into account. Evidenced-based programs can be ineffective if integrity is lacking and programs are not delivered in the manner they were designed (Latessa, 2008). For example, treatment dosage, poor matching of needs, ineffective delivery, and timing are as important as the principles themselves (Visher & Travis, 2011).

Research indicates programs that focus on fear; personal shaming; psychoanalytic-talking cures; scared-straight tactics; unstructured programming; and non-directive, client-centered approaches are ineffective in reducing recidivism. These ineffective interventions have been utilized during the progression of corrections, and ultimately have been demonstrated to have little to no change in increasing public safety and reducing recidivism (Latessa, 2008).

SPECIAL POPULATIONS

Considering the prevalence of mental health symptoms and substance use in the correctional system, it is imperative that various healthcare needs are addressed when discussing offender reentry. In 2013, the Substance Abuse and Mental Health Service Administration (SAMHSA) reported that the percentage of individuals with serious mental health disorders in state prisons was 16%, compared to 5.4% in the general public (Blandford & Osher, 2013). Substance use disorders were found to be as high as 53% compared to 16% in the general public (Blandford & Osher, 2013). SAMHSA also noted the critical nature of an individuals' transition to the community, as there is a "twelvefold increase risk of death in the first two weeks of release" (Blandford & Osher, 2013, p. 1).

The United States witnessed a sharp increase in the incarceration of individuals with serious mental health issues in the 1960s. During this period, newly developed psychotropic medications were being disseminated and there was a movement toward the deinstitutionalization of patients previously placed in state hospitals. In addition, the burgeoning influence of drug-related offenses contributed to an increase in behavioral health awareness inside our institutions (Baillargeon et al., 2009). Research has shown that approximately 59% of individuals in state prisons have a co-occurring substance use and mental health disorder (Blandford & Osher, 2013). Complex mental health presentations can lead to a revolving-door phenomenon for individuals within the correctional system (Baillargeon et al., 2009).

The revolving-door phenomenon refers to the consistent finding that offenders with mental disorders are more likely to be reincarcerated while on community supervision than those without mentally disabling conditions (Haimowitz, 2004). In 2002, The Council of State Governments in the Criminal Justice/Mental Health Consensus report stated that recidivism rates for those with mental health disorders was up to 70%. The general public and those responsible for upholding conditions of release may view those with mental illness as high-risk and dangerous, ultimately affecting their rate of return to an institution (Eno Louden & Skeem, 2013). However, research suggests that those with mental illnesses are no more likely to commit new offenses than their counterparts. Technical violations and subsequent revocation of probation/parole is disproportionately more likely to occur, compared to those without a mental illness (Skeem, Winter, Kennealy, Eno Louden, & Tatar, 2014).

Individuals with mental health issues may present with functional impairments or acute symptomology that can negatively affect their ability to respond to interventions that assist in the transition from prison to the community (Osher et al., 2012). The effect of mental health symptomology ultimately affects clients' abilities to respond to treatment programs designed to address criminogenic factors. An appropriate programming response would address the individualized barriers each client faces, based on their mental health concerns, for the use of psychotropic medications and therapeutic interventions. Addressing such barriers and responsivity needs on an individualized basis will then further allow for targeting criminogenic needs.

It is important to note that while attention should be paid to mental health concerns and symptoms, mental health alone is not a major criminogenic risk factor (Osher et al., 2012). "Although individuals with serious mental illness clearly need psychiatric services, managing offenders' mental health problems may do little to reduce their risk of recidivism. Untreated mental illness is, at best, a weak predictor of recidivism among criminal offenders" (Skeem et al., 2014, p. 212). Recent research supports the framework that correctional programming should not ignore criminogenic risk factors for those with significant mental illness. In fact, it demonstrates that those with mental health concerns have higher occurrence of beliefs and values related to antisocial attitudes associated with crime, when compared to offenders without mental health concerns (Fisher et al., 2014; Ostermann & Matejkowski, 2014; Skeem et al., 2014; Wilson et al., 2014). In addition, research has found that participants with mental health concerns demonstrate cognitions associated with impulsivity, hostility and emotionality (Wilson et al., 2014).

When the findings of these studies are looked at collectively, it becomes clear that therapeutic programs for offenders with SMI [Serious Mental Illness] must develop a multipronged treatment approach that integrates interventions for individual's criminal thinking and antisocial attitudes specifically, and likely criminogenic risk (e.g., associates), with treatment for their mental illness and substance abuse issues (Wilson et. al., 2014, p. 599).

It is important to address and manage mental health symptoms with the idea that stabilization will improve an individual's ability to address criminogenic factors. For example, an individual with paranoid schizophrenia who is experiencing hallucinations (such as hearing voices) may not be able to participate in structured programming until his or her condition is stabilized. Current literature suggests the imperative need to develop programs that are tailored to meet the needs of this particular population, as well as to study correctional treatment programs for mental illness that are designed to change criminal thinking and antisocial attitudes of offenders (Fisher et al., 2014; Ostermann & Matejkowski, 2014; Skeem et al., 2014; Wilson et al., 2014).

Although research is limited on the correlation between mental health and substance use within a correctional population and the reduction of recidivism, it is apparent that not having a plan for individuals with co-occurring disorders may lead to severe consequences, such as homelessness, relapse, hospitalizations, suicide, and further criminal activities (Osher et al., 2012). Although corrections places weight on reduction of recidivism and assurance of public safety, many state and federal programs have implemented strategies to enhance mental health integration due to an ethical obligation to fulfill an individual's continuum-of-care needs.

Unlike mental health concerns, substance use can be directly correlated to crime and risk. Not only is it a criminogenic risk factor, it can also affect individuals' responsivity. The use of substances has a negative effect on proposed interventions and structured treatment programming. Use of substances sometimes leads to associations with antisocial peers, reduces daily living skills, impacts prosocial relationships, and lends itself to further criminal activity. However, if an individual has entered treatment with some autonomy, substance use can be addressed to assist in positive-outcome change regarding transitions to the community (Osher et al., 2012).

Research from the Urban Institute in 2006 reports that a majority of offenders have a history of pervasive substance use. Relatively few received substance use treatment while incarcerated, and those who engaged in use after being released were at a higher risk of reoffending. A national sample of women released from federal institutions over a ten-year period ending in 2007 found that women who did not get substance use treatment post-release were ten times more likely to be re-incarcerated within one year (Enos, 2011). "Less than 20% of inmates with drug abuse or dependence receive formal treatment" (Chandler, Fletcher, & Volkow, 2009, p. 185). Conversely, those who engage in treatment while in an institution and followed by aftercare in the community are likely to have higher rates of success—not only with reduction of substance use, but also reoffending (Urban Institute, 2006).

Applying the theoretical approach of Risk-Need-Responsivity, one must assess the severity of mental health symptoms and substance use. Again, those with higher risk for behavioral health needs should be provided with more intense treatment programming (Baillargeon et al., 2009). When developing a framework to address the transitional needs of the individual, it is essential to break down the severity of each element: mental health concerns, substance use, and criminogenic factors. (Osher et al., 2012). For example, an individual identified as low substance use risk, medium-high criminogenic factors, and high mental health needs would be best served in an integrated program that addresses mental health symptoms and has structured appointments and a higher level of correctional supervision programming.

SECOND CHANCE ACT

As long as the need exists to increase public safety and reduce recidivism, so do continued efforts with reentry strategies. The Second Chance Act was signed into law on April 9, 2008 (Pogorzelski, Wolff, Pan, & Blitz, 2005; James, 2011). This Act expanded state and local reentry demonstration projects for adult and juvenile offenders and provided eligible funding for seven broad-purpose areas:

1. Education, literacy, vocational, and job placement services
2. Substance use treatment and services, including programs that start in placement and continue through the community
3. Programs that provide comprehensive supervision and offer services in the community, including programs that provide housing assistance and mental and physical health services
4. Programs that focus on family integration during and after placement for both offenders and their families
5. Mentoring programs that start in placement and continue into the community
6. Programs that provide victim-appropriate services, including those that promote the timely payment of restitution by offenders and those that offer services to victims when offenders are released
7. Programs that protect communities from those deemed as dangerous offenders, including developing and implementing the use of risk assessment tools to determine when offenders should be released from prison

Prioritization of funding was given to agencies that could demonstrate that services were focused on disproportionate populations, inclusion of non-profit organizational input, consultation with victims, family coordination, effective case management, comprehensive review of the parole violation process, independent evaluation of program efficacy, and the targeting of high-risk individuals through the use of validated risk assessment tools (James, 2011).

It is required of grantees to develop and implement strategic reentry planning that is measurable, with performance outcomes every five years. The ultimate goal of the performance outcomes is to reduce recidivism by 50%. Community stakeholders, various law enforcement entities, nonprofit organizations, and state agencies all play a vital role in the implementation of reentry efforts under the Second Chance Act (James, 2011).

CONCLUSION

Offender reentry remains a focal point for public safety and recidivism reduction efforts. Efforts to address the multiple barriers and improve reentry programs continue to happen across the nation and are primarily focused on the use of evidenced-based practices to initiate successful transition from prison to community. Risk, needs, and responsivity principles are key to these strategies. They stress the importance of the use of actuarial assessment and resource allocation and management, in conjunction with high fidelity programming to address each individual's capacity of response.

Current practices and initiatives, such as the Transition from Prison to Community (TPC) and Second Chance Act aim to address the many barriers to reentry. With the continued implementation of core correctional programs, progress continues to develop in dismantling these hurdles. In addition, special consideration needs to be made when working with individuals with mental health symptoms and/or substance use, as these issues create further complexities in the reentry process.

Further research in the area of prisoner reentry is of great importance, as the Council of State Governments reports that we release up to 95% of individuals in our state correctional institutions (Justice Center, 2014). Continued efforts to develop and refine existing practices will further allow the implementation of best practices and, consequently, cultivate our efforts to reduce recidivism and increase public safety.

References

Andrews, D. A. & Bonta, J. (2010). Rehabilitating criminal justice policy and practice. *Psychology, Public Policy, and Law, 16*, 39-55.

Andrews, D. A., Bonta, J., & Worthmith, J. S. (2006). The recent past and near future of risk and/or need assessment. *Crime & Delinquency, 52*, 7-27.

Baillargeon, J., Binswanger, I. A., Penn, J. V., Williams, B. A., & Murray, D. O. (2009). Psychiatric disorder and repeat incarcerations: The revolving prison door. *The American Journal of Psychiatry, 166*, 103-108.

Binswanger, I. A., Nowels, C., Corsi, K. F., Long, J., Booth, R. E., Kutner, J., & Steiner, J. F. (2011). "From the prison door right to the sidewalk, everything went downhill", a qualitative study of the health experience of recently released inmate. *International Journal of Law and Psychiatry, 34*, 249-255.

Blandford, A. M., & Osher, F. C. (2013). *Guidelines for the successful transition of individual with behavioral health disorders from jail and prison*. Delmar, NY: Samhsa's Gains Center for Behavior Health and Justice Transformation.

Brown, J., & Singh, J. P. (2014). Forensic risk assessment: A beginner's guide. *Archives of Forensic Psychology, 1*, 49-59.

Bucklen, K. B., & Zajac, G. (2009). But some of them don't come back (to prison): Resource deprivation and thinking errors as determinants of parole success and failure. *The Prison Journal, 89*, 239-264.

Burchfield, K. B., & Mingus, W. (2008). Not in my neighborhood: Assessing registered sex offenders' experiences with local social capital and social control. *Criminal Justice and Behavior, 35*, 356-373.

Bureau of Justice Statistics. (2014). *Terms & definitions: State and federal prisoners and prison facilities.* Retrieved from http://www.bjs.gov/index.cfm?ty=tdtp&tid=13

Burke, P., & Tonry, M. (2006). *Successful transition and reentry for safer communities: A call to action for parole.* Silver Spring, MD: Center for Effective Public Policy.

Carson, E. A., & Golinelli, D. (2014). *Prisoners in 2012, trends in admissions and release, 1991 – 2012.* U.S. Department of Justice. Retrieved from http://www.bjs.gov/content/pub/pdf/p12tar9112.pdf

Carson, E. A., & Sobel, W., J. (2012). *Prisoners in 2011.* U.S. Department of Justice. Retrieved from http://www.bjs.gov/content/pub/pdf/p11.pdf

Chandler, R. K., Fletcher, B. W., & Volkow, N.D. (2009). Treating drug abuse and addiction in the criminal justice system: Improving public health and safety. *Journal of the American Medical Association, 301*, 183-190.

Church, W. T., II. (2013). Book review: Prisoner reentry at work: Adding business to the mix. Research on *Social Work Practice, 23*, 239.

Council of State Governments (2002). Criminal justice/Mental health consensus project. Retrieved from http://www.consensusproject.org

Currie, E. (1998). Assessing the prison experiment. Crime and Punishment in America. New York, NY: Picador.

Durose, M.R., Cooper, A.D., & Snyder, H.N. (2014). Recidivism of prison released in 30 states in 2005: Patterns from 2005 to 2010. U.S. Department of Justice.

Duwey, G., & Clark, V. (2013). Blessed be the social tie that binds: The effects of prison visitation on offender recidivism. *Criminal Justice Policy Review, 24*, 271-296.

Eno Louden, J., & Skeem, J. L. (2013). How do probation officers assess and manage recidivism and violence risk for probationers with mental disorder? An experimental investigation. *Law and Human Behavior, 37*, 22-34.

Enos, G. (2011). Post-release treatment cuts risk return to prison. *Alcoholism & Drug Abuse Weekly, 23,* (22), 6-7.

Few-Demo, A., & Arditti, J. (2014). Relational vulnerabilities of incarcerated and reentry mothers: Therapeutic implications. *International Journal of Offender Therapy and Comparative Criminology, 58,* 1297-1320.

Fisher, W. H., Hartwell, S. W, Deng, X., Pinals, D. A., Fulwiler, C., & Roy-Bujnowki, K. (2014). Recidivism among released state prison inmates who received mental health treatment while incarcerated. *Crime & Delinquency, 60,* 811-832.

Frazier, B. D. (2014). African Americans and reentry: The threat of greater challenges. *Journal of Ethnicity in Criminal Justice, 12,* 140-157.

Gendreau, P., French, S. A., & Gionet, A. (2004). What works (what doesn't work): The principles of effective correctional treatment. *Journal of Community Corrections, 13,* 4-30.

Gendreau, P., Goggin, C., & Cullen, F. T. (March 1999). *The effects of prison sentences on recidivism.* Public Works and Government Services Canada.

Haimowitz, S. (2004). Slowing the revolving door: Community reentry of offenders with mental illness. *Psychiatric Services, 55,* (4), 373-375.

Holzer, H. J., Raphael, S., & Stoll, M. A. (2003). *Employment dimensions of reentry: Understanding the nexus between prisoner reentry and work.* Washington, DC: Urban Institute.

Inciardi, J. A., Surratt, H. L., Martin, S. S., O'Connell, D. J., Salady, A. D., & Beard, R. A. (2007). Developing a multimedia HIV and hepatitis intervention for drug-involved offenders reentering the community. *The Prison Journal, 81,* 111-142.

James, N. (2011). *Offender reentry: Correctional statistics, reintegration into the community and recidivism.* Retrieved from www.nationalcia.org/.../Correctional-Statistics-Reintegration-into-the-Community.pdf

Justice Center. (2014). NRRC facts & trends. Retrieved from http://csgjusticecenter.org/nrrc/facts-and-trends/

Kennealy, P. J., Skeem, J. L., Manchak, S. M., & Eno Louden, J. (2012). Firm, fair, and caring officer-offender relationships protect against supervision failure. *Law and Human Behavior, 36,* 496-505.

Latessa, E. J. (2008). *How to prevent prisoner reentry programs from failing: Insights from evidence based corrections.* Presented at the Center for Criminal Justice Research Division of Criminal Justice.

Listwan, S. J., Cullen, F. T., & Latessa, E. J. (2006). How to prevent prisoner re-entry programs from failing: Insights from evidence-based corrections. *Federal Probation, 70,* 19-25.

Lowenkamp, C.T., & Latessa, E. J. (2004). Understanding the risk principle: How and why correctional interventions can harm low-risk offenders. *Topics in Community Corrections,* 3-8.

Lowenkamp, C. T., Latessa, E. J. & Smith, P. (2006). Does correctional program quality really matter? The impact of adhering to the principles of effective intervention. *Criminology and Public Policy, 5,* 575-594.

Martinson, R. (1974). What works? – Questions and answer about prison reform. *The Public Interest, 35,* 22-54.

National Institute of Corrections. (2008). *Transition from prison to community initiative.* Retrieved from http://nicic.gov/library/022669

National Institute of Justice. (2015). *Offender reentry.* Retrieved from http://www.nij.gov/topics/corrections/reentry/pages/welcome.aspx

NGA Center for Best Practices. (2005). *Improving prisoner reentry through strategic policy innovations.* Retrieved from http://www.nga.org/files/live/sites/NGA/files/pdf/0509PRISONERREENTRY.PDF

Osher, F., D'Amora, D. A., Plotkin, M., Jarrett, N., & Eggleston, A. (2012). *Adults with behavioral health needs under correctional supervision: A shared framework for reducing recidivism and promoting recovery.* New York, NY: Council of State Governments Justice Center and Criminal Justice/Mental Health Consensus Project.

Ostermann, M., & Matejkowski, J. (2014). Estimating the impact of mental illness on costs of crimes: A matched samples comparison. *Criminal Justice and Behavior, 41*, 20-40.

Pager, D., Western, B., & Sugie, N. (2009). Sequencing disadvantage: Barriers to employment facing young black and white men with criminal records. *Annals of the American Academy of Political and Social Sciences, 623*, 195-213.

Pogorzelski, W., Wolff, N., Pan, K., & Blitz, C. L. (2005). Behavioral health problems, ex-offender reentry policies and the "second chance act." *Public Health Consequences of Imprisonment, 95*, 1718-1724.

Pogrebin, M., West-Smith, M., Walker, A., & Unnithan, N. P. (2014). Employment isn't enough: Financial obstacles experienced by ex-prisoners during the reentry process. *Criminal Justice Review*, 39, 394-410.

Richie, B., E. (2001). Challenges Incarcerated Women Face as They Return to Their Communities: Findings From Life History Interviews. *Crime & Delinquency, 47*(3), 368-389.

Sackett, D. L., Rosenberg, W. M., Gray, J. A., Haynes, R. B., & Richardson, W. S. (1996). Evidenced based medicine: What it is and what it isn't. *British Medical Journal, 312*, 71-72.

Seiter, R. P., & Kadela, K. R. (2003). Prisoner reentry: What works, what does not, and what is promising. *Crime and Delinquency, 49*, 360-388.

Shinkfield, A.J., & Graffam, J. (2008). Community reintegration of ex-prisoners: Type and degree of change in variables influencing successful reintegration. *International Journal of Offender Therapy and Comparative Criminology, 53*, 29-42.

Skeem, J. L., Winter, E., Kennealy, P. J., Eno Louden, J., & Tatar, J. R., II. (2014). Offenders with mental illness have criminogenic needs, too: Toward recidivism reduction. *Law and Human Behavior, 8*, 212-224.

Spjeldnes, S., Jung, H., & Yamatani, H. (2014). Gender differences in jail populations: Factors to consider in reentry strategies. *Journal of Offender Rehabilitation, 53*, 75-94.

Urban Institute. (2006). Understanding the challenges of prisoner reentry: Research findings from the urban institute's prisoner reentry portfolio. Retrieved from http://www.urban.org/sites/default/files/alfresco/publication-pdfs/411289-Understanding-the-Challenges-of-Prisoner-Reentry.PDF

Visher, C. A., & Bakken, N. W. (2014). Reentry challenges facing women with mental health problems. *Women & Health, 54*, 768-780.

Visher, C. A., & Travis, J. (2003). Transitions from prison to community: Understanding individual pathways. *Annual Review Sociology, 29*, 89-113.

Visher, C. A., & Travis, J. (2011). Life on the outside: Returning home after incarceration. *The Prison Journal, 91*, 1-24.

Walker, A., Hempel, L., Unnithan, N. P., & Pogrebin, M. R. (2014). Parole, reentry and social capital: The centrality of homeless. *Journal of Poverty, 18*, 315-334.

Wilson, A. B., Farkas, K., Ishler, K. J., Gearhart, M., Morgan, R., & Ashe, M. (2014). Criminal thinking styles among people with serious mental illness in jail. *Law and Human Behavior, 38*, 592-601.

Wodahl, E. J. (2006). The challenges of prisoner reentry from a rural perspective. *Western Criminology Review, 7* (2), 32-47.

Wodahl, E. J., & Garland, B. (2009). The Evolution of Community Corrections: the Enduring Influence of the Prison. *The Prison Journal, 86*,(4), 1-24. M.

Wright, K. A., & Cesar, G. T. (2013). Toward a more complete model of offender reintegration: Linking the individual-, community-, and system-level components of recidivism. *Victims and Offenders, 8*, 373-398.

Yesberg, J. A., & Polaschek. (2015). Assessing dynamic risk and protective factors in the community: Examining the validity of the dynamic risk assessment for offender re-entry. *Psychology, Crime & Law, 21*, 80-99.

Zhang, S. X., Roberts, R. E., & Farabee, D. (2014). An analysis of prisoner reentry and paroles risk using COMPAS and traditional criminal history measures. *Crime & Delinquency, 60*, 167-192.

CHAPTER 14

PEDIATRIC ABUSIVE HEAD TRAUMA: A PRACTITIONER'S GUIDE

JERROD BROWN & RESMIYE ORAL

CHAPTER OVERVIEW

Abusive Head Trauma (AHT) is one of the most prevalent forms of fatal child abuse worldwide. Every year in the U.S., approximately 1,200-1,400 children become victims of AHT with or without shaking. Twenty-five to thirty percent of those children will die from their injuries. The severity of AHT cases covers a wide spectrum. Field studies suggest that only a portion of all AHT cases receive medical care; milder forms of AHT will most likely never reach health facilities. Those that reach health care facilities may not be recognized as AHT. As a result, cases of AHT may be underreported. Abusive Head Trauma can result in a variety of long-term, irreversible deficits involving the physiological, developmental, and cognitive domains of infant and child growth, making it imperative for professionals to recognize the risk factors, warning signs, and consequences associated with AHT. The present literature review seeks to fill the gaps in published material for practitioners, providing an accessible guide and general overview pertaining to the complex topic of AHT. This chapter will provide the reader with a general understanding of AHT, the signs and symptoms, and prevention approaches and measures. In addition, this chapter will address AHT issues and terminology for practitioners who may encounter cases of pediatric abusive head trauma, current research findings and key variables associated with AHT, and information and evaluation about various prevention initiatives.

ABUSIVE HEAD TRAUMA

In recent years, child abuse has been at the forefront of domestic and international law, in an attempt to increase public awareness and mitigate negative health and social outcomes. The World Health Organization (2014) defined child maltreatment as all forms of physical, emotional, and sexual abuse, and neglectful behavior resulting in harm to the health, development, or dignity of a child. Coined by the American Academy of Pediatrics as an update to the term Shaken Baby Syndrome (SBS), Abusive Head Trauma (AHT) is one of the most prevalent forms of fatal child physical abuse (Administration for Children & Families, 2010; Laurent-Vannier, Toure, Vieux, Brugel, & Chevignard, 2009). While "Shaken Baby Syndrome" prevails in common parlance, the terminology is inferior to AHT for several reasons. Shaken Baby Syndrome does not encompass all pathology observed in cases of "AHT" that involve injuries originating from (but not limited to) shaking, since a substantial number of cases also present with signs of impact and secondary trauma due to oxygen deprivation. Additionally, there is a scarcity of experimental and reproducible data regarding the exact process by which injuries are inflicted in SBS cases, since it is unethical to conduct such studies in human subjects. Finally, there are other forms of AHT that *do not involve shaking forces at all*, such as inflicted asphyxiation; AHT is a more generalized category of trauma that includes, among other forms, SBS (Barr, 2012; Christian & Block, 2009).

Abusive Head Trauma terminology encompasses any-and-all cranial, cervical, or cerebral injuries to an infant or child due to shaking, impact, suffocation/asphyxiation, and/or any combination of these (Christian & Block, 2009; Nakagawa & Conway, 2004; Oral, Koc, Smith, & Sato, 2011). However, a significant portion of AHT cases involve violent, rapid, and most commonly—repetitive shaking motion, with or without a final impact that can cause death or irreversible brain damage (Nakagawa & Conway, 2004; Oral, Yagmur, Nashelsky, Turkmen, & Kirby, 2008). A study conducted by Starling, Patel, Burke, Sirotnak, Stronks, and Rosquist (2004) examined 69 cases of AHT in children. Of the 69 cases, 32 perpetrators admitted to only shaking the child, 20 admitted to impact without shaking, and 17 admitted to shaking and impact. It was concluded that children whose perpetrator admitted to shaking them with no impact were 2.39 times more likely to experience retinal hemorrhages than those cases where impact was indicated; hence, shaking alone, regardless of the presence of an impact, can lead to brain damage (Starling et al., 2004).

EPIDEMIOLOGY

The prevalence and consequences of AHT are alarming. It is reported that per 100,000 births, there are between 14 and 32 subsequent cases of AHT (Barr, 2012; Fanconi & Lips, 2010; Parks, Sugerman, Xu, & Coronado, 2012). Approximately 1,200-1,400 American children are the victims of shaking and AHT every year, and estimates are that between 25% and 30% will die from their injuries (Bravo, 2014). Approximately 80% of all AHT cases occur in children under one year of age, with peak incidence between 4-6 months of age (Frasier, 2008; Leventhal, Martin, & Asnes, 2010)—much earlier than accidental head injuries, which peak around 10 months of age (Molina, Clarkson, Farley, & Farley, 2012; Parks, Kegler, Annest, & Mercey, 2012). The rate of AHT is almost twice as high as non-abusive head trauma incidents for children under one year of age. Children with AHT have mortality rates five times higher than children with non-abusive head trauma have (Niederkrotenthaler, Xu, Parks, & Sugerman, 2013). The Centers for Disease Control and Prevention (CDC) noted that the incidence of fatal AHT was 0.76/100,000 in children less than four years of age, compared to 2.16/100,000 in children less than one year of age (Parks, Kegler, Annest, & Mercey, 2012). Due to difficulties building consensus and possibly high rates of unrecognized cases of AHT, incidence rates are likely underreported (Parks et al., 2012; Runyan, 2008).

SUSCEPTIBILITY TO HEAD TRAUMA

Infants are at greater risk of head trauma compared to other age groups due to the age-related behavioral characteristics and developmental physiology of the head and neck. In an infant, the head is proportionally larger and heavier compared to the rest of body. An infant's neck muscle tone has not developed to the capacity of older children, leading to a subsequent inability to fully absorb the shock of impact and limit the range of head movement during shaking (Lopes, Eisenstein, & Williams, 2013; Oral, Rahhal, Elshershari, & Menezes,

2006). The ability to control head movement in an upright position is not attained until around 3-4 months of age, rendering an infant more susceptible to rapid and jerky neck movements over a wider arch of movement (Health Canada, 2001). The shallowness of an infant's vertebral joint facets also increases neck flexibility and range of extension compared to an older child (Oral et al., 2006).

Due to having larger subarachnoid (between the brain and the skull, containing cerebrospinal fluid) spaces, the brain of an infant is also more vulnerable to differential movements than that of an older child or adult, and immature nerves can become easily damaged (Caffey, 1974; Lewin, 2008; Lukefahr, 2008). As the infant grows and matures, myelination (the process in which a sheath of electrically insulating material, myelin, covers and protects nerve fibers and axons against shear injuries) begins and is completed around two years of age (Lewin, 2008). Before this, the brain is more vulnerable to impact and the shearing forces of shaking.

When a child is shaken, rapid acceleration and deceleration occur, causing the brain and other intracranial structures to move in kind within the skull, leading to diffuse shear injuries (or diffuse axonal injuries, or DAI) (Lopes et al., 2013). A common type of brain trauma, this kind of shear-induced injury can cause unconsciousness and even coma. Finally, an infant's brain also has higher water content and less developed glia (non-neuronal cells that, among other supportive roles, surround and insulate neurons), further increasing the risk of shear damage (Lukefahr, 2008).

RISK FACTORS ASSOCIATED WITH AHT

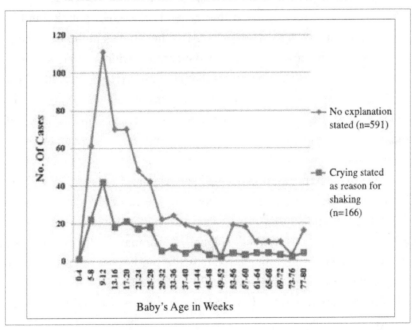

FIGURE 1

Comparing the crying curve to the rate of AHT indicates that an infant's crying relates to the rate of SBS cases. Reprinted with permission from the authors of "Age-related incidence curve of hospitalized Shaken Baby Syndrome cases: Convergent evidence for crying as a trigger to shaking" by R. G. Barr, R. B. Trent, and J. Cross, 2006, Child Abuse & Neglect, 30, pp. 7-16.

Myriad personal and environmental factors can place children at greater risk of experiencing AHT. These factors revolve around child and caregiver characteristics, as well as various situational and environmental factors, including socioeconomic status, although AHT can occur in all socioeconomic strata. Infants born prematurely, with low birth weight, are at an even greater risk of injury from AHT due to underdeveloped body structures. Such infants may also exhibit certain developmental patterns in self-regulation, such as more erratic crying patterns, which may then trigger abuse from caregivers (Hennes, Kini, & Palusci, 2001). Additionally, infants with a developmental disability, physical problems or behavioral issues are more likely to experience AHT compared to their peers, due to the increased stress levels that these conditions elicit (Flaherty, Stirling, & The Committee on Child Abuse and Neglect, 2010).

While crying is a natural and adaptive form of communication for infants, research by Russell (2010) indicated that crying increases frustration within the caregiver, especially when compounded with other psychosocial risk factors (Barr, Paterson, MacMartin, Lehtonen, & Yong, 2005; Stifter, 2005). The prevalence of inconsolable crying and duration of outbursts peak around six weeks, shortly after which infant AHT rates reach their zenith (Brazelton, 1962; Horner, 2005; Lee, Barr, Catherine, & Wicks, 2007). Given the temporal proximity of these apeces, it seems likely that crying and AHT are correlated (Lee et al., 2007). The delay following the peak of crying to the peak of AHT may represent time for increasing parental stress levels to build up and reach a breaking point (Lee et al., 2007).

While victim behavior may precipitate occurrences of AHT, caregiver characteristics and beliefs also play a significant role. Young caregivers with little experience in child rearing, and especially those with lower educational levels, are at considerably higher risk for abusing their children, particularly in single-parent households where the mother is under the age of 18 (Hennes et al., 2001; Horner, 2005; Keenan, Runyan, Marshall, Nocera, Merten, & Sinal, 2003). Johnson and Showers (1985) reported that over 50% of high school students perceived shaking as a discipline method and did not understand the associated risks. Similarly, Barr et al. (2009a) found that 2% of mothers and 3% of the general Vancouver population believed that shaking was an appropriate means of dealing with a crying infant. In other studies in the U.S., between 50% and 75% of those surveyed did not believe shaking an infant was dangerous, while 2.6% to 4.4% of those with a child under the age of 2 admitted to having shaken their infant at least once (Reynolds, 2008; Runyan, 2008; Theodore, Chang, Runyan, Hunter, Bangdiwala, & Agans, 2005). Runyan et al. (2008) reported that while 2.6% of parents of children under 2 years of age in the U.S. reported shaking their child as an act of discipline, survey data suggested that shaking as discipline occurs far more often in less-developed countries.

Gender and family dynamics may play a role in AHT. The risk of abuse differs highly between male and female caregivers (Esenio-Jennsen, Tai, & Kodsi, 2011). Altman, Canter, Patrick, Daley, Butt, and Brand (2011) found that fathers and male caregivers were five times more likely to shake an infant than mothers were. Numerous other studies found similar results in which males offended more often than their female counterparts did (Kesler, Dias, Shaffer, Rottmund, Cappos, & Thomas, 2008; Starling et al., 2004). Overall, the biological parents are most likely to commit AHT, while the boyfriend of the female caregiver is the second most-likely perpetrator (Esernio-Jennsen et al., 2011). Social isolation, substance abuse, and psychological problems (including depression) in families and caregivers are also major risk factors associated with abuse within the family (Lewin, 2008).

CLINICAL PRESENTATION OF AHT

Various signs and symptoms may raise suspicion of AHT among practitioners. It is important to be aware of potential warning signs to prevent further abuse. Victims of AHT may suffer nausea-related symptoms like vomiting in 15%-56% of cases (American Academy of Pediatrics, 2001; Guenther, Powers, Srivastava, & Bonkowsky, 2010; Ricci, Giantris, Merriam, Hodge, & Doyle, 2003; Sieswerda-Hoogendoorn, Boos, Spivack, Bilo, & van Rijn, 2012; Stoll & Anderson, 2013). Meanwhile, neurological and cognitive symptoms of seizures and altered states of consciousness occur in 43%-50% and 77% of cases, respectively (Hobbs, Childs, Wynne, Livingston, & Seal, 2005; Talvik, Metsvaht, Leito, Poder, Kool, Vali, & Talvik, 2006). Other potential symptoms in cases of AHT include loss of appetite, loss of interest in and interaction with the environment, respiratory infection, diarrhea, loss of muscle tone, cardiac arrest, and apnea (Fortin & Stipanicic, 2010; Lopes et al., 2013).

Although a majority of AHT cases may present with external bruising, unexplained fractures, and a prior history of abuse, the lack of such is not a reliable indicator to credibly rule out a diagnosis of AHT. In one series of confirmed cases of AHT, external bruising was shown to be absent in as much as 21% of the victims (Atwal, Rutty, Carter, & Green, 1998). In Shaken Baby Syndrome (SBS) in particular, external physical manifestations of abuse may often be missing (Morad, Wygnansky-Jaffe, & Levin, 2010). In a study by King, MacKay, and Sirnick (2003), prior history of abuse, which may help practitioners in identifying present cases of AHT, were absent in 40% of AHT cases. This is consistent with the fact that an overwhelming majority of AHT cases occur in the backdrop of increased parental stress levels (Oral et al., 2008).

A constellation of medical findings such as subdural hematoma (SDH), retinal hemorrhages (RH), and cerebral edema/damage (Bandak, 2005; Frasier, 2008; Gerber, & Coffman, 2007; Lopes et al., 2013) may indicate AHT in the absence of a plausible medical condition or accidental trauma. A collection of blood between tissue layers outside the brain, SDH can lead to immediate loss of consciousness, confusion and delayed unconsciousness, nausea, vomiting, and seizures, among other symptoms; MRI and CT scans can both detect a subdural hematoma. A retinal hemorrhage is the abnormal bleeding in the light sensitive retinal tissue at the back wall of the eye, and as such, only an ophthalmologic procedure can determine RH. Edema, accumulation of fluid between the skin and internal body cavities, manifests as swelling and can cause drowsiness or loss of consciousness. It is important to note that an assemblage of these signs can also occur in a severe *accidental* traumatic head injury, such as being thrown out of a motor vehicle during a collision, a crush injury, or in medical conditions such as glutaric aciduria Type 1 (Morris et al., 1999).

The most common intracranial abnormality found in cases of AHT is SDH, found in 83%-90% of children experiencing confirmed AHT (Brennan et al., 2009; Sieswerda-Hoogendoorn et al., 2012). Subdural Hematoma in AHT occurs when one or more of the bridging veins encompassing the distance between the brain and the superior sagittal sinus rupture. The superior sagittal sinus is a large vein that carries deoxygenated blood from the brain to the lungs. The bridging veins rupture at the entry into the dural space, caused by shaking and simultaneous differential movement of the intracranial structures, including the veins themselves (Sieswerda-Hoogendoorn et al., 2012). Since the musculature at this particular location is circular rather than longitudinal (thus, more vulnerable to shear injury), the blood extravasated (forced out) from the bridging veins commonly spills into the intradural (between layers of the dura mater) space, which is often mislabeled as subdural space (Hedlund, 2012). The blood then pools within the intradural space, creating SDH within the layers of the dura (Lukefahr, 2008). Although SDH is one of the major indicators of injuries associated with shaking, with or without impact, it rarely is the cause of death and disability in cases of AHT. Subdural Hematoma is most commonly a thin layer of blood over the brain convexity, sometimes limited to the interhemispheric fissures. The SDH seen in a variety of other medical conditions may have mechanisms different from traumatic-inflicted SDH (Mraz, 2009).

Shaking, itself, leads to damage within the brain tissue, since shearing forces set different layers of the brain into motion at different paces, depending on differential density of various layers. This differential movement results in a variety of neurological injuries, including injury to axons, cell death, infarction, and subsequent encephalopathy or global brain dysfunction (Lukefahr, 2008). The central nuclei and the brainstem control vital functions such as heart rate, breathing, consciousness, etc. Injuries to these structures may be primary, resulting from the initial trauma (shaking, impact, or both), but some are the result of secondary damage originating from intracranial responses to the primary trauma (Sieswerda-Hoogendoorn et al., 2012). In the latter scenario, the brain cells begin swelling in response to the primary trauma, with resultant focal or diffuse brain edema, which leads to increased intracranial pressure with subsequent herniation if brain edema is diffused and not controlled early enough. As a result of these changes and responses, damage to the brain itself, whether primary, secondary, or both, is indeed the cause of severe neurological compromise, and possibly death (Sieswerda-Hoogendoorn et al., 2012).

Retinal hemorrhages (RH) (i.e., bleeding in the back of the eye wall) are commonly found in cases of AHT (Bazelon, 2011; Kemp, 2011; Nakagawa & Conway, 2004; Salvatori & Lantz, 2014; Togioka et al., 2009). During violent shaking, acceleration and deceleration forces are exerted upon the layers of the retina as well as the intracranial structures. Due to aforementioned differential movements, the bridging veins within the optic nerve may tear, leading to intra-optic hemorrhages. Moreover, retinal layers may separate from one another as well as from the vitreus, due to the traction forces and the differential movement of various layers, forming RH that may involve intraretinal, pre-retinal, subretinal, and intra-vitreous layers (Levin, 2010). The prevalence of RH in cases of AHT ranges from 65%-100%, depending on the severity of the cases included in the case series (Bhardwaj, Chowdhury, Jacobs, Moran, Martin, & Coroneo, 2010; Forbes & Goldstein, 2008; Kobayashi, Yamada, Ohba, Nishina, Okuyama, & Azuma, 2009). On autopsy, retinal hemorrhages have been found to be more common in fatal cases of AHT—ranging from 82% to 100% (Bhardwaj et al., 2010; Oral et al., 2008). Most household or other minor accidental head trauma presents with RH in only 6%-8% of such cases, compared to 80% prevalence of RH in AHT (Forbes & Goldstein, 2008; Jenny, Hymel, Ritzen, Reinert, & Hay, 1999; Kobayashi et al., 2009). Among the cases of accidental head trauma, RH is much less severe than in cases of AHT (Frasier, 2008; Levin, 2010). Retinal hemorrhages in household head trauma usually present in the posterior pole, are few in number, and resolve very quickly, suggesting that acceleration-deceleration forces do not lead to severe RH without sufficient force (Levin, 2010). A pediatric ophthalmologist should evaluate retinal hemorrhages, since pediatricians are not equipped to assess the full spectrum of RH (Levin, 2010).

The type of RH, whether diffuse and extending to the ora serrata (the periphery of the eye globes) or focal in the posterior pole, numerous or few, multilayer or superficial, involving the macula (causing macular folds or not) is an important consideration in determining whether or not the RH is indicative of AHT. Diffuse, numerous, multilayer RH, especially if associated with macular folds near the center of the retina, are considered a significant indicator of AHT (Sieswerda-Hoogendoorn et al., 2012; Levin, 2010). This specific type of RH often correlates with rotational acceleration-deceleration forces, with or without impact. Such forces have been documented in accidental head trauma only when it involves falls from significant heights (i.e., a story high or more), motor vehicle crashes, or crush injury (Sieswerda-Hoogendoorn et al., 2012; Levin, 2010).

When sufficient force is present, skeletal injuries may occur in AHT. Although not all skeletal injuries are a sign of abuse in children, metaphyseal fractures of the long bones and rib fractures are significantly associated with AHT (Case, Graham, Handy, Jentzen, & Monteleone, 2001). Posterior rib fractures adjacent to the spine and metaphyseal fractures (along the wide portion) of the long bones are most specific for abusive trauma, while transverse long-bone-shaft fractures and simple linear skull fractures are equally commonly observed in both abusive and accidental trauma (Case et al., 2001; Maguire, Kemp, Lumb, & Farewell, 2011). Solitary skull fractures are more commonly seen in accidental head trauma and in cases of abuse. However, brain trauma can occur without the presence of skull fractures, especially in cases that experience only shaking, suffocation, or impact from a soft surface with or without shaking (Sieswerda-Hoogendoorn et al., 2012). In less-severe cases of abuse, the symptoms of AHT may be missed or confused with symptoms of other disorders, creating a diagnostic problem. In such cases, indicators of abuse may be attributed to viral infection, colic, or food intolerance (Jenny et al., 1999), and symptoms may have a delayed onset; as the amount of force exerted on the victim increases, the onset of symptoms becomes more immediate (Case et al., 2001; Health Canada, 2001).

DIAGNOSIS OF AHT

The diagnostic process begins with a thorough history from the child's caretakers, including a timeline of events before and after the child's deterioration. Every team assessing an alleged case of AHT should consider the trauma history and mechanism, the child's age and developmental level, and the type and severity of symptoms and findings in establishing or ruling out a diagnosis of AHT (see Figure 2).

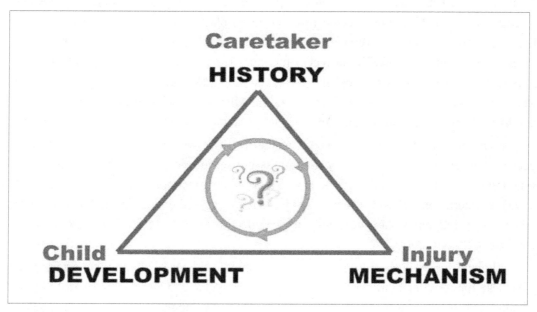

FIGURE 2

If all three components of history taking and examination are not compatible, AHT should be considered in assessing an alleged case. Reference: Used by permission from Oral, R. (February 25, 2002). Abusive Head Trauma in infants. Annual Medical Student Conference, (2002), Iowa City, IA.

Once concern for AHT is raised, the diagnostic work-up process will include the efforts of various pediatric health experts and should, at a minimum, include:

a. A skeletal survey should be completed on all infants less than two years of age—to be repeated in 10-14 days, especially in infants under one year of age. During the repeat skeletal survey, skull, pelvis, and spine X-rays do not need to be repeated. A skeletal survey assesses the injuries located within the appendicular skeleton (humeri, forearms, hands, femora, lower legs and feet) and the axial skeleton (thorax [bilateral, oblique], pelvis, lumbar spine, cervical spine, and skull) (Mandelstam, Cook, Fitzgerald, & Ditchfield, 2003). Youth ages 2 to 5 should receive a skeletal survey only in highly suspicious cases of abuse. In youth ages 5 and older, x-rays should only be performed in areas of concern. In the case of disability, all children should receive a skeletal survey when abuse is suspected, regardless of age (American Academy of Pediatrics Committee on Child Abuse and Neglect, 2001; Christian, Block, and the Committee on Child Abuse and Neglect, 2009).

b. During the acute phase, a head Computerized Tomography (CT) without contrast could capture all injuries, including intracranial hemorrhages, skull fractures, and brain damage such as brain edema, infarction, etc., that may require surgical intervention (Bradford, Choudhary, & Dias, 2013). However, it does not show the full scope of injuries in the cranium. While the head CT is the most widely used test for the early assessment of AHT, the full spectrum head Magnetic Resonance Imaging (MRI) is better for analyzing the entire range of head injuries. A head CT should be performed in the presence of any intra-cranial injury in children; in infants under one year of age if rib fractures, multiple fractures, and/or facial injuries are present; and in all infants under six months of age suspected to be physically abused (American College of Radiology, 1995).

c. A full spectrum head MRI with and without contrast should be conducted shortly after the head CT and, if possible, before surgical intervention (American Academy of Pediatrics Committee on Child Abuse and Neglect, 2001). If a head MRI is performed very early on, it should be repeated after one week to capture evolving damage/healing that takes place in the brain (Stranzinger, Kellenberger, Braunschweig, Hopper, & Huisman, 2007). Head MRI is not only good for depicting the full spectrum of intracranial injuries in AHT, but recent literature indicates that cervical spinal MRI is of utmost importance in determining cervical soft tissue, cord, and skeletal injuries (Goradia, Linnau, Cohen, Mirza, Hallam, & Blackmore, 2007). In addition, MRI is a good imaging technique in determining epiphyseal separations and fractures of the epiphyseal plate in long bones (Stranzinger et al., 2007).

d. Abdomen and chest CT scans are recommended in cases where thoraco-abdominal trauma is suspected or when the child is in a coma, exhibits impact injuries, and/or shows abnormal-end organ function tests such as of the liver, pancreas, and/or kidney functions (American College of Radiology, 1995). Furthermore, a chest CT may be useful in detecting and dating rib fractures and abnormalities when bone scintigraphy show negative initial results (Wootton-Gorges, Stein-Wexler, Walton, Rosas, Coulter, & Rogers, 2008).

e. If the skeletal survey does not show any physical manifestations of abuse, a bone scintigraphy (a nuclear scan for detecting bone abnormalities) may be considered to increase the probability of detecting rib and shaft bone fractures. However, bone scintigraphy should not be used as the sole method to detect rib fractures (Flaherty et al., 2014).

f. Electrolytes, liver function tests, amylase, lipase, blood urea, creatinine, uric acid, urinalysis, and urine myoglobin as well as cardiac markers should all be analyzed in the presence of head, chest, or abdominal injuries, as they may provide information on indicators of other forms of abuse and neglect including trauma to internal organs (Flaherty et al., 2014). As part of this process, total blood cell count (including platelets, prothrombin time, partial thromboplastin time, Von Willebrand Panel, fibrinogen, and platelet function analysis) should be performed to rule out common bleeding/coagulation diathesis and explore the presence of anemia and infection. Serum copper and ceruloplasmin levels should be obtained in select cases.

g. In select cases, genetic testing may be needed to differentiate abuse from other medical conditions, including copper deficiency, glutaric aciduria Type I, and osteogenesis imperfecta. Urine organic acids are ordered routinely to rule out glutaric aciduria Type I. However, it should be noted that low copper levels that may lead to bone fractures might develop as a result of malnutrition in children (Marquardt, Done, Sandrock, Berdon, & Feldman, 2012). Thus, identifying deficient copper levels in youth suspected of physical abuse may uncover other forms of abuse and neglect in children. Similarly, genetic testing and consultation may be necessary in children presenting with unexplained multiple fractures, to rule out osteogenesis imperfecta (Flaherty et al., 2014).

h. Depending on the specifics of the case, if there are fresh bite marks and the skin has not been washed, the skin is swabbed with moistened sterile gauze, air-dried in a paper envelope for saliva identification (Oral et al., 2008).

i. Lastly, it is recommended that a urine and/or hair sample be sent for toxicology testing for illicit drugs in all suspected cases of AHT (Oral et al., 2008).

LONG-TERM CONSEQUENCES OF AHT

The long-term consequences of AHT can be severe: death occurs in 25% to 30% of all hospitalized cases (Barr, 2012; Oral et al., 2008). Lifelong neurological impairment occurs in 80% of all surviving AHT cases, while only 15% of surviving victims of AHT survive without any sequelae (Barr, 2012). Brain damage associated with AHT may result in cerebral atrophy, a state of brain-cell degeneration in which neurons in the brain are lost (Mraz, 2009). These children show sequelae with a multitude of medical, cognitive, and developmental deficits, even if they obtain the proper treatment upon diagnosis.

Chronic seizure disorder occurs in about 20% of all surviving victims of AHT, with seizures significantly more common in children with AHT than in children with accidental head trauma—53% compared to 6%, respectively (Ashton, 2010; Barlow, Thomson, Johnson, & Minns, 2005; Chiesa & Duhaime, 2009). Additionally, while children with accidental head trauma more often present with scalp hematomas, those who experienced AHT are more likely to present with seizures (Bechtel et al., 2004). The type of seizures that surviving children develop may vary: the most common types are partial seizures (affecting only one side of the brain), myoclonic seizures (involving brief muscle contraction), and migrating clonic seizures (Bourgeois et al., 2008). One study reported that more than one type of seizure could be observed in over 50% of the patients (Bourgeois et al., 2008).

Retinal hemorrhages or damage to the occipital cortex of the brain can cause a plethora of vision problems, from visual impairment to total blindness—the latter of which may be seen in approximately half of surviving victims of severe AHT (Barlow et al., 2005). Papilledema, or swelling of the optic disc, which can also affect vision, is observed in a very small portion of victims of AHT (Levin, 2010; Mraz, 2009). Most commonly, blindness is due to the damage in the occipital cortex, where the central vision center resides (Banks & Lessell, 2002; Levin, 2010). Difficulties with vision or total blindness often contribute to other disabilities in AHT survivors, leading to worsening of limitations in learning, development, social skills, and behavioral regulation (Makaroff & Putman, 2003). Additionally, since infants with AHT are more likely to have RH, fractures, seizures and an abnormal mental status than infants with accidental brain injuries, the length of hospital stay and costs are higher than for infants with accidental head trauma (Bechtel et al., 2004; Chiesa & Duhaime, 2009).

Extensive research has examined possible influences of head trauma on language skills. Multiple research groups showed significant impairment in language skills in as high as two-thirds of recovering victims of AHT (Ashton, 2010; Barlow et al., 2005; Stipanicic, Nolin, Fortin, & Gobeil, 2008). Furthermore, complications from AHT may contribute to problems with memory, attention, and other cognitive deficits (Makaroff & Putman, 2003). Ewing-Cobbs and Bloom (1999) reported that 45% of the patients with AHT scored low on cognitive tests, and 25% of them scored low on motor tests about 1.3 months after the injury (Makaroff & Putman, 2003). They also found that 25% of patients had visual impairments, including occipital lobe atrophy and retinal fibrosis. Many child victims of AHT display developmental delays such as mental retardation (Ewing-Cobbs, Prasad, & Swank, 2006) and motor function impairment (King, MacKay, & Sirnick, 2003). Ewing-Cobbs and colleagues (2006) conducted a study in which they assessed 23 children who suffered AHT at 1 to 2 years of age and then assessed them again at 7 years of age. In comparing these children to others without AHT, researchers found that the children studied scored significantly lower on intelligence tests, and almost half of the children had IQs below the 10th percentile. Over time, the abused children continued to display mental deficits (Ewing-Cobbs et al., 2006).

A larger array of sensory, cognitive, and executive functioning may also be affected by AHT, depending on the extent and scope of damage to the brain (Ashton, 2010). The age at which head trauma occurs also has a great impact on the neurological outcome. Ashton (2010) as well as Verger et al. (2000) reported that children who experienced head trauma after the age of eight performed similarly to their peers. However, children who experienced head trauma at a younger age demonstrated slower development of, and considerable deficits in, basic motor skills and information processing. Since most AHT occurs before the age of two, at least some of this dichotomy may be due to AHT versus accidental trauma in children before and after eight years of age. Infants who experienced head trauma were shown to have disabilities in cognitive processing, including verbal and performance skills, with recovery to normal functioning taking longer than older children (Ewing-Cobbs, Barnes, & Fletcher, 2003). These findings portray the increased severity of the consequences that early AHT would lead to with regard to cognitive and motor skill development.

PREVENTION

In the last decade, Abusive Head Trauma prevention efforts have gained momentum and are largely focused on parent and caretaker education (Barr et al., 2009; Dias et al., 2005; Foley et al., 2013; Goulet, Frappier, Fortin, Deziel, & Boulanger, 2009). In addition to the efforts in the United States, Canada has developed guidelines to prevent child abuse, including AHT (Goulet et al., 2009). Experts in Quebec developed an educational program called the *Perinatal Shaken Baby Syndrome Prevention Program (PSBSPP)* to decrease the number of AHT cases (Goulet et al., 2009). This program focuses on educating parents on ways to deal with the anger and stress that may arise from taking care of a newborn. The program utilizes note cards with important information regarding AHT and teaches stress-management skills to cope with caring for an infant. During a six-month piloting of the program, the parents participating in the program reported 98% appreciation rate for this program, and the majority of nurses agreed that the program was beneficial for the prevention of AHT (Goulet et al., 2009). As a result of this pilot, staff changed their practice to following up with new parents at approximately six-weeks—during the intense crying period.

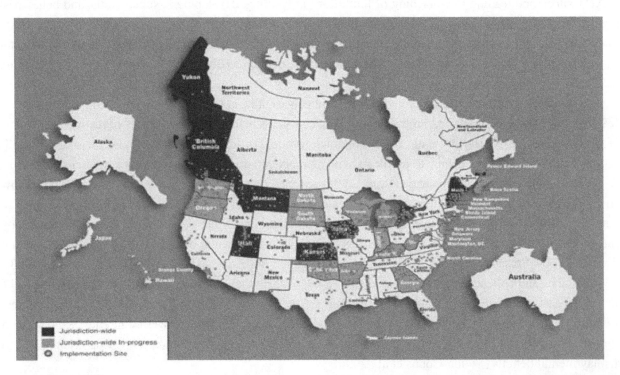

FIGURE 3

Distribution of Period of Purple Crying Programs across the globe. Retrieved from http://www.donshake.org *(With courtesy from Marilyn Barr)*

The Period of PURPLE Crying Program® has also greatly impacted the knowledge of new parents on the subject of how to manage infant crying and AHT (Barr et al., 2009; Stewart, Polgar, Gilliland, Tanner, Girrotti, Parry, & Fraser, 2011). This program mainly focuses on the period of inconsolable crying that can frustrate new parents. This program has now been implemented in six countries, including the U.S., Canada, Japan, South Korea, Australia, and Israel. In the U.S., 49 states have at least one site where the program has been implemented as the main AHT prevention program (see Figure 3) (www.dontshake.org). The effective triple-dose strategy includes educating parents in the hospital, visiting the home to follow up, and educating the public about the dangers of AHT (Stewart et al., 2011). Videos have proven to be beneficial tools in aiding the education process. Some states have also enacted campaigns for the advertisement of SBS/AHT, to publicize the consequences and symptoms in an attempt to reduce and prevent incidents (Lewin, 2008). Reaching out and aiding parents during this peak period can help significantly lower the prevalence rates (Barr et al., 2009).

The Hudson Valley Shaken Baby Prevention Initiative in the U.S., along with previous programs in the region, recognizes that to be most effective, parent education must begin in the hospital soon after delivery (Altman et al., 2011; Dias et al., 2005). The idea is to teach parents strategies to manage a crying infant appropriately, before they have experienced the stress of crying. This program was fully operational by 05/01/2005 in 20 hospitals in the seven counties of upstate New York. Nurses provide a leaflet for parents, have them watch a video, and obtain parental commitment to follow the recommendations by signing a commitment statement. In the first five years of the program, there was a 47% decrease in shaking injuries documented in the participating hospitals.

In Australia, a similar program, *The Westmead (NSW Australia) Shaken Baby Prevention Project (SBPP)*, began in 2001. A television and print media campaign, *Handle With Care* was evaluated; collaboration between government agencies and a non-governmental organization, KidsWest, funded the film and other additional resources for this project. The project uses a 4-minute animated film, pamphlets, postcards and posters, which are available online at no cost (Nutbeam, 1986). This project has been implemented in 25 countries via collaboration with the International Society for the Prevention of Child Abuse and Neglect (Foley, 2004; 2006; Kozlowska & Foley, 2006; Lopes et al., 2013; Pereira, D'Affonseca, & Williams, 2013; Runyan & Foley, 2011; Tolliday Simons, Foley, Benson, Stephens, & Rose, 2010).

Unfortunately, interventions reach mothers and female caretakers more frequently than fathers and male caretakers, despite males being responsible for almost 75% of perpetration of AHT (Personal communication with National Center on Shaken Baby Syndrome). These findings highlight the need for greater interventions at the family level. Further, organizations focused on child abuse prevention should continue to devise ways to reach the general public, especially young males and females, in order to combat AHT prior to even conception.

CONCLUSION

Abusive Head Trauma (AHT) is a pervasive global issue that affects infants of every background, often with severe consequences ranging from physical and cognitive-neurological symptoms to death. Among the survivors, 80% are afflicted with a lifelong brain injury. Victims may suffer from debilitating, altered states of consciousness, vomiting, apnea, and seizures, among other signs. Subdural hematoma, RH, and cerebral edema with rare AHT-related characteristics are common in moderate to severe cases. Approximately 30% of all hospitalized children with AHT die. The call to action, whether in treatment or prevention, is loud and clear.

A vital component of AHT diagnosis involves ascertaining the nature of the causative incident. Unfortunately, abusive caretakers may not always be honest. The most difficult part of diagnosing AHT is the lack of a reliable history. In a significant number of cases, external physical manifestations may also be non-existent. Bone fractures and even external injuries may not be pathognomonic. The constellation of RH, SDH, and diffuse brain damage presenting in the specific patterns may be very specific to SBS-type AHT, when all other potential medical explanations are ruled out. The path toward an accurate diagnosis of AHT is complicated and requires thorough understanding of the relevant syndromes.

When diagnostic opportunity during the acute phase is missed, the long-term diagnosis may pose difficulty. Sequelae of AHT such as developmental and cognitive deficits, including language, motor skills, and information processing, may not appear until later stages of development. Thus, by the time symptoms/ deficits emerge or are diagnosed, they may have very low sensitivity and specificity in diagnosis. On the other hand, long-term damage caused by AHT can be irreversible and can diminish a child's functions in social, cognitive, and academic domains when left unaddressed. Missed diagnosis of AHT can lead to multiple offenses and increased severity of abuse on the same child and/or by the same perpetrator on other children. As such, doctors and close relatives must be cognizant of any physical manifestations that do appear uncharacteristic in infants and young children, as these may be signs of early abuse.

In some ways, prevention is even more vital than treatment where AHT is concerned. While some effective preventive programs exist to educate new caregivers of the dangers of shaking an infant and the proper methods of handling a crying infant, more work is needed to define populations that most need intervention. Increased and improved professional continuing education is needed in the health and human services and in educational and criminal justice systems to identify instances of AHT more accurately and intervene on behalf of the abused infant.

Beyond the moral imperative, even financial reasoning suggests that prevention is more efficient than treatment. The lifetime cost of taking care of an AHT victim greatly outweighs the cost of the three-hour training necessary to inform medical personnel on how best to educate caregivers, especially considering an estimated $124 billion are spent each year on AHT (Barr, 2012). Education and awareness programs have proven effective in updating individuals on the risks of shaking and abuse in infants, though recognition of factors that endanger children (i.e., child and parent characteristics, or other social and economic factors) is necessary to further advance these intervention programs and significantly curb infant/child abuse rates. This starts with informed practitioners advocating for AHT victims and all infants. Their lives depend on it.

REFERENCES

Administration for Children & Families (2010). *Child Maltreatment 2010*. Washington, DC: Government Printing Office.

Altman, R. L., Canter, J., Patrick, P. A., Daley, M., Butt, N. K., & Brand, D. A. (2011). Parent education by maternity nurses and prevention of abusive head trauma. *Pediatrics, 128*(5), 1164-1172.

American Academy of Pediatrics Committee on Child Abuse and Neglect (2001). Shaken baby syndrome: Rotational cranial injuries technical report. *Pediatrics, 108*, 206-210.

Ashton, R. (2010). Practitioner Review: Beyond shaken baby syndrome: What influences the outcome for infants following traumatic brain injury? *Journal of Child Psychology and Psychiatry, 51*(9), 967-980.

Atwal, G., Rutty, G., Carter, N., & Green, M. (1998). Bruising in nonaccidental head injured children: A retrospective study of the prevalence, distribution and pathological associations in 24 cases. *Forensic Science International, 96*(2-3), 215-230.

Bandak, F. A. (2005). Shaken baby syndrome: A biomechanics analysis of injury mechanisms. *Forensic Science International, 151*, 71-79.

Banks, M. & Lessell, S. (2002). Neuroophthalmology and trauma. *International Ophthalmology Clinics, 42*(3), 1-12.

Barlow, K.M., Thomson, E., Johnson, D., & Minns, R.A. (2005). Late neurologic and cognitive sequelae of inflicted traumatic brain injury in infancy. *Pediatrics, 116*(2), 174-185.

Barr, R. (2012). Preventing abusive head trauma resulting from a failure of normal interaction between infants and their caregivers. *Proceedings of the National Academy of Sciences of the United States of America, 109*, 17294-17301. doi:10.1073/pnas.1121267109

Barr, R., Barr, M., Fugiwara, T., Conway, J., Catherine, N., & Brant, R. (2009a). Do educational materials change knowledge and behaviour about crying and shaken baby syndrome? A randomized controlled trial. *Canadian Medical Association Journal, 180*(7), 727-733. doi:10.1503/cmaj

Barr, R., Paterson, J., MacMartin, L., Lehtonen, L., & Yong, S. (2005). Pro-longed and unsoothable crying bouts in infants with and without colic. *Journal of Developmental and Behavioral Pediatrics, 26*, 14-23.

Barr, R., Rivara, F., Barr, M., Cummings, P., Taylor, J., Lengua, L., & Meredith-Benitz, E. (2009b). Effectiveness of educational materials designed to change knowledge and behaviors regarding crying and shaken-baby syndrome in mothers of newborns: Arandomized, controlled trial. *Pediatrics, 123*(3), 972-980. doi: 10.1542/peds.2008-0908

Barr, R., Trent, R. B., & Cross, J. (2006). Age-related incidence curve of hospitalized shaken baby syndrome cases: Convergent evidence for crying as a trigger to shaking. *Child Abuse & Neglect, 30,* 7-16.

Bazelon, E. (2011, February 2). Shaken-baby syndrome faces new questions in court. *The New York Times.* Retrieved from http://www.peterdale.co.uk/wpcontent/uploads/2012/02/SBSnytFeb2011.pdf

Bechtel, K., Stoessel, K., Leventhal, J.M., Ogle, E., Teague, B., Lavietes, S., … Duncan, C. (2004). Characteristics that distinguish accidental from abusive injury in hospitalized young children with head trauma. *American Academy of Pediatrics, 114*(1), 165-168.

Bhardwaj, G., Chowdhury, V., Jacobs, M., Moran, K., Martin, F., & Coroneo, M. (2010). A systematic review of the diagnostic accuracy of ocular signs in pediatric abusive head trauma. *Ophthalmology, 117*(5), 983-992. doi: 10.1016/j.ophtha.2009.09.040

Bourgeois, M., Di Rocco, F., Garnett, M., Charron, B., Boddaert, N., Soufflet, C., & Renier, D. (2008). Epilepsy associated with shaken baby syndrome. *Child's Nervous System, 24*(2), 169-172.

Bradford, R., Choudhary, A. K., & Dias, M. S. (2013). Serial neuroimaging in infants with abusive head trauma: timing abusive injuries. *Journal of Neurosurgical Pediatrics, 12*(2), 110-119.

Bravo, M.S. (2014). Shaken baby syndrome: The implementation and evaluation of an education program for parents. *Journal of Nursing Education and Practice, 4*(9), 91- 99.

Brazelton, T. (1962). Crying in infancy. *Pediatrics, 29,* 579-588.

Brennan, L. K., Rubin, D., Christian, C. W., Duhaime, A. C., Mirchandani, H. G., & Rorke-Adams, L. B. (2009). Neck injuries in young pediatric homicide victims: Clinical article. *Journal of Neurosurgery: Pediatrics, 3*(3), 232-239.

Caffey, J. (1974). The whiplash shaken infant syndrome: manual shaking by the extremities with whiplash-induced intracranial and intraocular bleedings, linked with residual permanent brain damage and mental retaewingrdation. *Pediatrics, 54*(4), 396-403.

Case, M., Graham, M., Handy, T., Jentzen, J., & Monteleone, J. (2001). Position paper on fatal abusive head injuries in infants and young children. *The American Journal of Forensic Medicine and Pathology, 22*(2), 112-122.

Chiesa, A., & Duhaime, A.C. (2009). Abusive Head Trauma. *Pediatric Clinics of North America, 56,* 317-331.

Christian, C., Block, R., & The Committee on Child Abuse and Neglect. (2009). Abusive head trauma in infants and children. *Pediatrics, 123*(5), 1409-1411. doi:10.1542/peds.2009-0408

Dias, M., Smith, K., deGuehery, K., Mazur, P., Li, V., & Shaffer, M. (2005). Preventing abusive head trauma among infants and young children: A hospital-based, parent education program. *Pediatrics, 115*, 470-477.

Esenio-Jennsen, D., Tai, J., & Kodsi, S. (2011). Abusive head trauma in children: A comparison of male and female perpetrators. *Pediatrics, 127*(4), 649-657.

Ewing-Cobbs, L., Barnes, M., & Fletcher, J. (2003). Early brain injury in children: Development and reorganization of cognitive function. *Developmental Neuropsychology, 24*(2-3), 669-704.

Ewing-Cobbs, L., & Bloom, D. R. (1999). Traumatic brain injury. In R. Brown (Ed.), *Cognitive aspects of chronic illness in children* (pp. 262-285). New York, NY: The Guilford Press.

Ewing-Cobbs, L., Kramer, L., Prasad, M., Canales, D.N., Louis, P.T., Fletcher, J.M., … Cheung, K. (2006). Neuroimaging, physical, and developmental findings after inflicted and noninflicted traumatic brain injury in young children. *Pediatrics, 102*(2), 300-307.

Ewing-Cobbs, L., Prasad, M.R., & Swank, P. (2006). Late intellectual and academic outcomes following traumatic brain injury sustained during early childhood. *Journal of Neurosurgery, 105*(4), 287-296.

Fanconi, M., & Lips, U. (2010). Shaken baby syndrome in Switzerland: Results of a prospective follow-up study, 2002-2007. *European Journal of Pediatrics, 169*(8), 1023-1028. doi: 10.1007/s00431-010-1175-x

Flaherty, E. G., Perez-Rossello, J. M., Levine, M. A., Hennrikus, W. L., Christian, C. W., Crawford-Jakubiak, J. E., … Esposito, P. W. (2014). Evaluating children with fractures for child physical abuse. *Pediatrics, 133*(2), 477-489.

Flaherty, E.G., Stirling, Jr., J., & The Committee on Child Abuse and Neglect (2010). The pediatrician's role in child maltreatment prevention. *Pediatrics, 126*, 833-841.

Foley, S. (2004). From inspiration to action. *HUSITA.* Hong Kong, China: HUSITA.

Foley, S. (2006). Undertaking a risk assessment in non-accidental injury - can we restore? Retrieved from http://www.lawsociety.com.au/cs/groups/public/documents/internetcontent/023719.pdf

Foley, S., Kovacs, Z., Rosec, J., Lamb, R., Tolliday, F., Simons-Coghill, M., & Sarten, T. (2013). International collaboration on prevention of shaken baby syndrome- an ongoing project/ intervention. *Paediatrics and International Child Health, 33*(4), 233-238. doi: 10.1179/2046905513Y.0000000093

Forbes, B., & Goldstein, S. (2008). Ocular trauma in infancy and childhood. In D.M. Albert & J.W. Miller (Eds.), *Principles and practice of ophthalmology* (pp.4263-4269). Amsterdam: Elsevier.

Fortin, G., & Stipanicic, A. (2010). How to recognize and diagnose abusive head trauma in infants. *Annals of Physical and Rehabilitation Medicine, 53*, 693-710.

Frasier L. (2008). Abusive head trauma in infants and young children: A unique contributor to developmental disabilities. *Pediatric Clinics of North America, 55*(6), 1269-1285. doi: 10.1016/j.pcl.2008.08.003

Gerber, P., & Coffman, K. (2007). Nonaccidental head trauma in infants. *Child's Nervous System, 23*(5), 499-507.

Goradia, D., Linnau, K., Cohen, W., Mirza, S., Hallam, D., & Blackmore, C. (2007). Correlations of MR imaging findings after cervical spine trauma. *American Journal of Neurologhaty, 28*, 209-215.

Goulet, C., Frappier, J., Fortin, S., Deziel, L., & Boulanger, M. (2009). Development and evaluation of a shaken baby syndrome prevention program. *The Association of Women's Health, Obstetric and Neonatal Nurses, 38*, 7-21.

Guenther, E., Powers, A., Srivastava, R., & Bonkowsky, J. (2010). Abusive head trauma in children presenting with an apparent life-threatening event. *Journal of Pediatrics, 157*(5), 821-825.

Health Canada (2001). Joint statement on shaken baby syndrome. *Minister of Public Works and Government Services, Ottawa.*

Hedlund, G.L. (2012). Subdural hemorrhage in abusive head trauma: Imaging challenges and controversies. *Journal of the American Osteopathic College of Radiology, 1*(1), 23-30.

Hennes, H., Kini, N., & Palusci, V. (2001). The epidemiology, clinical characteristics and public health implications of shaken baby syndrome. In S. Lazoritz & V. Palusci (Eds.), *The shaken baby syndrome: A multidisciplinary approach* (pp. 19-40). Binghamton: The Haworth Maltreatment & Trauma Press.

Hobbs, C., Childs, A., Wynne, J., Livingston, J., & Seal, A. (2005). Subdural haematoma and effusion in infancy: an epidemiological study. *Archives of Disease in Childhood, 90*(9), 952-955.

Horner, G. (2005). Physical abuse: Recognition and reporting. *Journal of Pediatric Health Care, 19*, 4-11.

Jenny, C., Hymel, K., Ritzen, A., Reinert, S., & Hay, T. (1999). Analysis of missed cases of abusive head trauma. *Journal of the American Medical Association, 281*(7), 621-626.

Johnson, C. F. & Showers, J. (1985). Child development, child health and child rearing knowledge among urban adolescents: Are they adequately prepared for the challenges of parenthood? *Health Education, 16*(5), 37-41.

Keenan, H., Runyan, D., Marshall, S., Nocera, M., Merten, D., & Sinal, S. (2003). A population-based study of inflicted traumatic brain injury in young children. *Journal of American Medical Association, 290*(5), 621-626.

Kemp, A. (2011). Abusive head trauma: recognition and the essential investigation. *Archives of Disease in Childhood- Education and Practice, 96*(6), 202-208. doi: 10.1136/adc.2009.170449

Kesler, H., Dias, M., Shaffer, M., Rottmund, C., Cappos, K., & Thomas, N. (2008). Demographics of abusive head trauma in the Commonwealth of Pennsylvania. *Journal of Neurosurgery: Pediatrics, 1*, 351-356.

King, W., MacKay, M., & Sirnick, A. (2003). Shaken baby syndrome in Canada: Clinical characteristics and outcomes of hospital cases. *Canadian Medical Association Journal, 168*(2), 155-159.

Kobayashi, Y., Yamada, K., Ohba, S., Nishina, S., Okuyama, M., & Azuma, N. (2009). Ocular manifestations and prognosis of shaken baby syndrome in two Japanese children's hospitals. *Japanese Journal of Ophthalmology, 53*(4), 384-388. doi: 10.1007/s10384-009-0681-8

Kozlowska, K., & S. Foley (2006). Attachment and risk of future harm: A case of non-accidental brain injury. *Australian and New Zealand Journal of Family Therapy. 27,* (2), 75-82.

Laurent–Vannier, A., Toure, H., Vieux, E., Brugel, D., & Chevignard, M. (2009). Long-term outcome of the shaken baby syndrome and medicolegal consequences: A case report. *Annals of physical and rehabilitation medicine, 52*(2), 436-447. doi: 10.1016/j.rehab.2009.03.001

Lee, C., Barr, R., Catherine, N., & Wicks, A. (2007). Age-related incidence of publicly reported shaken baby syndrome cases: is crying a trigger for shaking? *Journal of Developmental and Behavioral Pediatrics, 28*(4), 288-293.

Leventhal, J., Martin, K., & Asnes, A. (2010). Fractures and traumatic brain injuries: Abuse versus accidents in a US database of hospitalized children. *Pediatrics 126*, 104-115. doi: 10.1542/peds.2009-1076

Levin A. (2010). Retinal hemorrhage in abusive head trauma. *Pediatrics, 126*(5), 961-970. doi:10.1542/peds. 2010-1220

Lewin, L. (2008). Shaken baby syndrome: facts, education, and advocacy. *Nursing of Women's Health, 12*(3), 235-239. doi: 10.1111/j.1751-486X.2008.00328.x

Lopes, N. R., Eisenstein, E., & Williams, L. C. (2013). Abusive head trauma in children: A literature review. *Jornal de pediatria, 89*(5), 426-433.

Lukefahr, J. (2008). Abusive head trauma in infants. Retrieved from http://www.utmb.edu /pedi_ed/CORE/ Abuse/page_11.htm

Maguire, S. A., Kemp, A. M., Lumb, R. C., & Farewell, D. M. (2011). Estimating the probability of abusive head trauma: A pooled analysis. *Pediatrics, 128*(3), e550-e564.

Makaroff, K., & Putman, F. (2003). Outcomes of infants and children with inflicted traumatic brain injury. *Developmental Medicine & Child Neurology, 45*, 497-502.

Mandelstam, S. A., Cook, D., Fitzgerald, M., & Ditchfield, M. R. (2003). Complementary use of radiological skeletal survey and bone scintigraphy in detection of bony injuries in suspected child abuse. *Archives of Disease in Childhood, 88*(5), 387-390.

Marquardt, M. L., Done, S. L., Sandrock, M., Berdon, W. E., & Feldman, K. W. (2012). Copper deficiency presenting as metabolic bone disease in extremely low birth weight, short-gut infants. *Pediatrics, 130*(3), e695-e698.

Molina, D., Clarkson, A., Farley, K., & Farley, N. (2012). A review of blunt force injury homicides of children aged 0 to 5 years in Bexar County, Texas, from 1998 to 2009. *The American Journal of Forensic Medicine and Pathology, 33*(4), 344-348. doi: 10.1097/PAF.0b013e31821a88c4

Morad, Y., Wygnansky-Jaffe, T., & Levin, A. (2010). Retinal haemorrhage in abusive head trauma. *Clinical and Experimental Ophthalmology, 38*(5), 514-520. doi: 10.1111/j.1442-9071.2010.02291.x

Morris, A. A. M., Hoffmann, G. F., Naughten, E. R., Monavari, A. A., Collins, J. E., & Leonard, J. V. (1999). Glutaric aciduria and suspected child abuse. *Archives of disease in childhood, 80*(5), 404-405.

Mraz, M. (2009). The physical manifestations of shaken baby syndrome. *Journal of Forensic Nursing, 5*, 26-30. doi:10.1111/j.1939-3938.2009.01027.x

Nakagawa, T. A., & Conway, E. E. (2004). Shaken baby syndrome: Recognizing and responding to a lethal danger. *Contemporary Pediatrics, 21*, 37-48.

National Center on Shaken Baby Syndrome. Retrieved from http://www.purplecrying.info/subpages/protecting/the-relations-of-crying-to-sbs.php

Niederkrotenthaler, T., Xu, L., Parks, S.E., & Sugerman, D.E. (2013). Descriptive factors of abusive head trauma in young children—United States, 2000-2009. *Child Abuse & Neglect, 37*, 446-455.

Nutbeam, D. (1986). Health promotion glossary. *Health Promotion, 1*(1). Retrieved from http://kidshealth.schn.health.nsw.gov.au/crying-baby

Oral, R., Koc, F., Smith, J., & Sato, Y. (2011). Abusive suffocation presenting as new-onset seizure. *Pediatric Emergency Care, 27*(11), 1072-1074.

Oral, R., Rahhal, R., Elshershari, H., & Menezes, A.H. (2006). Intentional avulsion fracture of the second cervical vertebra in a hypotonic child. *Pediatric Emergency Care, 22*(5), 352-354.

Oral, R., Yagmur, F., Nashelsky, M., Turkmen, M., & Kirby, P. (2008). Fatal abusive head trauma cases: Consequence of medical staff missing milder forms of physical abuse. *Pediatric Emergency Care, 24*(12), 816-821.

Parks, S., Kegler, S., Annest, J., & Mercey, J. (2012). Characteristics of fatal abusive head trauma among children in the USA: 2003-2007: An application of the CDC operational case definition to national vital statistics data. *Injury Prevention, 18*(3), 193-199. doi: 10.1136/injuryprev-2011-040128

Parks, S., Sugerman, D., Xu, L., & Coronado, V. (2012). Characteristics of non-fatal abusive head trauma among children in the USA, 2003-2008: Application of the CDC operational case definition to national hospital inpatient data. *Injury Prevention, 18*, 392-398. doi:10.1136/injuryprev-2011-040234

Pereira, P.C., D'Affonesca, S.M., & Williams, P.C.A. (2013). A feasibility pilot intervention program to teach parenting skills to mothers of poly-victimized children. *Journal of Family Violence, 28*(1), 5-15.

Reynolds, A. (2008). Shaken baby syndrome: Diagnosis and treatment. *Radiologic Technology, 80*(2), 151-170.

Ricci, L., Giantris, A., Merriam, P., Hodge, S., & Doyle, T. (2003). Abusive head trauma in Maine infants: medical, child protective, and law enforcement analysis. *Child Abuse & Neglect, 27*, 271-283.

Runyan, D., & Foley, S. (2011). The prevention of abusive head trauma in infants and young children: Is prevention working? *9th ISPCAN ASIA PACIFIC Regional Conference on Child Abuse and Neglect.* Delhi, India: ISPCAN.

Runyan, D. K. (2008). The challenges of assessing the incidence of inflicted traumatic brain injury: A world perspective. *American Journal of Preventive Medicine, 34*(4), 112-115.

Russell, B. S. (2010). Revisiting the measurement of shaken baby syndrome awareness. *Child Abuse & Neglect, 34*(9), 671-676.

Salvatori, M., & Lantz, P. (2015). Retinal haemorrhages associated with fatal pediatric infections. *Medicine, Science, and the Law 54*(2), 121-128. doi: 10.1177/0025802414527077

Sieswerda-Hoogendoorn, T., Boos, S., Spivack, B., Bilo, R., & van Rijn, R. (2012). Abusive head trauma: Part 1. Clinical aspects. *European Journal of Pediatrics, 171*(3), 415-423. doi: 10.1007/s00431-011-1598-z

Starling, S., Patel, S., Burke, B., Sirotnak, A., Stronks, S., Rosquist, P. (2004). Analysis of perpetrator admissions to inflicted traumatic brain injury in children. *Archives of Pediatric and Adolescent Medicine, 158*(5), 454-458.

Stewart, T., Polgar, D., Gilliland, J., Tanner, D. A., Girrotti, M. J., Parry, N., & Fraser, D. (2011). Shaken baby syndrome and a triple dose syndrome for its prevention. *The Journal of Trauma, 71*(6), 1801-1807. doi: 10.1097/TA.0b013e31823c484a

Stifter, C. (2005). Crying behavior and its impact on psychosocial child development. *Encyclopedia on Early Childhood Development.* Retrieved from http://www.childencyclopedia.com/Pages/PDF/StifterANGxp.pdf

Stipanicic, A., Nolin, P., Fortin, G., & Gobeil, M.F. (2008). Comparative study of the cognitive sequelae of school aged victims of shaken baby syndrome. *Child Abuse and Neglect, 32*(3), 415-428. doi: 10.1016/j.chiabu.2007.07.008

Stoll, B., & Anderson, J. (2013). Prevention of abusive head trauma: A literature review. *Pediatric Nursing, 39*(6), 300-308.

Stranzinger, E., Kellenberger, C., Braunschweig, S., Hopper, R., & Huisman, T. (2007). Whole-body STIR MR imaging in suspected child abuse: An alternative to skeletal survey radiology? *European Journal of Radiology Extra, 63*, 43-47.

Talvik, I., Metsvaht, T., Leito, K., Poder, H., Kool, P., Vali, M., & Talvik, T. (2006). Inflicted traumatic brain injury (ITBI) or shaken baby syndrome (SBS) in Estonia. *Acta Paediatrica, 95*(7), 799-804.

Theodore, A., Chang, J., Runyan, D., Hunter, W., Bangdiwala, S., & Agans, R. (2005). Epidemiologic features of the physical and sexual maltreatment of children in the Carolinas. *Pediatrics 115*, 331-337.

Togioka, B., Arnold, M., Bathurst, M., Ziegfeld, S., Nabaweesi, R., Colombani, P., & Abdullah, F. (2009). Retinal hemorrhages and shaken baby syndrome: An evidence-based review. *The Journal of Emergency Medicine, 37*, 98-106. doi: 10.1016/j.jemermed.2008.06.022

Tolliday, F., Simons, M., Foley, S., Benson, S., Stephens, A., & Rose, D. (2010). From inspiration to action: The shaken baby prevention project in Western Sydney. *Communities, Children and Families Australia, 5*(2), 31.

Verger, K., Junque, C., Jurado, M.A., Tresserras, P., Bartumeus, F., Nogues, P., & Poch, J. (2000). Age effects on long-term neuropsychological outcome in pediatric traumatic brain injury. *Brain Injury, 14*(6), 495-503.

Wootton-Gorges, S. L., Stein-Wexler, R., Walton, J. W., Rosas, A. J., Coulter, K. P., & Rogers, K. K. (2008). Comparison of computed tomography and chest radiography in the detection of rib fractures in abused infants. *Child abuse & neglect, 32*(6), 659-663.

World Health Organization (2014). *Child Maltreatment*. Retrieved from http://www.who.int/mediacentre/factsheets/fs150/en/

CHAPTER 15

Problem Gambling:
A Beginner's Guide for Clinical and Forensic Professionals

Jerrod Brown, Randy Stinchfield, Mario L. Hesse, Matthew D. Krasowski, Blake Harris, John Von Eschen, Elizabeth Cardwell, & Phyllis Burger

Chapter Overview

Gambling is an activity where individuals wager something of value, most often money, to win something of greater value (American Psychiatric Association, 2013; Potenza, 2008). An estimated 70%-90% of people worldwide have participated in some form of gambling, such as casino gambling, sports betting, or the lottery (Abbott, Volberg, & Rönnberg, 2004; Raylu & Oei, 2002; Wardle, Moody, Griffiths, Orford, & Volberg, 2011). Gamblers wager over $90 billion per year in the United States on various forms of gambling (American Gaming Association, 2014). Many gamble as a means of social entertainment. For some, this simple act of entertainment can progress into a serious addiction, resulting in severe consequences. In addition to the potential for extreme financial loss, a gambling addiction can negatively affect interpersonal functioning, family relationships, and employment goals (American Psychiatric Association, 2013). A gambling disorder may also lead to criminal activity and involvement in the criminal justice system. The primary focus of this chapter is to highlight the impact problem gambling has on clinical and forensic populations.

Pathological Gambling (PG) or Problem Gambling

Gambling can be a relaxing recreational activity resulting in no adverse consequences. However, when gambling behaviors become impulsive and out of control, these habits can lead to a host of difficulties and problems. Recognized as a psychiatric disorder, Pathological Gambling (PG) is considered the most severe and chronic form of gambling (Ashley & Boehlke, 2012). Pathological Gambling was previously identified in the Diagnostic and Statistical Manual of Mental Disorders, Fourth Edition (DSM-IV), as an impulse-control disorder with a failure to control urges, temptations and/or impulses, and leading to negative cascading effects in other domains of the individual's life (Knezevic & Ledgerwood, 2012). The Diagnostic and Statistical Man-

Originally published in *Behavioral Health*, 2(2), 2015.
The editor of this journal has granted permission to reprint.

ual of Mental Disorders, Fifth Edition (DSM-5) categorizes this condition as Gambling Disorder (GD (Petry, Blanco, Stinchfield, & Volberg, 2013) and lists it under the section titled "Substance-Related and Addictive Disorders," specifically located in the area of "Non-Substance Related and Addictive Disorders" (O'Brien, 2011; Petry et al., 2013).

Approximately 1%-5% of Americans have or have had a pathological gambling disorder (Ladouceur & Lachance, 2007; Petry, 2005). The characterization of a pathological gambler is impulsive, lacking control over spending habits, chronic lying, and a willingness to commit illegal acts to facilitate gambling habits (Petry & Armentano, 1999). Gambling addiction creates a compulsion that is difficult to control. Pathological gamblers exhibit an inability to reduce the amount of money and time spent on gambling (Neal, Delfabbro, & O'Neil, 2005). For the problem gambler, there is a psychological need underlying the individual's inclination to gamble, despite the risk of serious financial loss (Raylu & Oei, 2002). Problem gamblers often have difficulty admitting their gambling habits cause significant harm to themselves and others (Rockloff, 2012).

Four reported subtypes exist among those with a pathological gambling disorder: gamblers who have co-morbid psychological problems (35%), gamblers without co-morbidities (27%), gamblers with co-morbid alcohol abuse (25%), and multimorbid gamblers (13%). Gamblers with co-morbid psychiatric conditions are more likely to be low-income females, have a family history of mental illness, and predominantly use electronic betting machines (Suomi, Dowling, & Jackson, 2014). Gamblers without co-morbid disorders display a lower severity of problem gambling. Problem gamblers with co-morbid alcohol abuse are usually young men who work full time. Multimorbid gamblers have more problems with their health and may exhibit increased hostility and aggressiveness (Suomi, Dowling, & Jackson, 2014).

ADOLESCENT PROBLEM GAMBLING

Severe problematic gambling habits affect as many as 4%-8% of youth (Hardoon & Derevensky 2002; Jacobs, 2000; Nower & Blaszczynski, 2004; Petry, 2005). Additional studies have shown an estimated 24%-40% of youth participate in some form of gambling on a weekly basis (Welte, Barnes, Tidwell, & Hoffman, 2008). Rates of adolescent non-problem gambling have occurred among 66%-86% of youth (Hardoon, Gupta, & Derevensky, 2004). However, multiple researchers noted significant differences in the prevalence rates of problem gambling among youth and young adults (Forrest & McHale, 2012; Petry, Blanco, Jin, & Grant, 2014; Volberg, Gupta, Griffiths, Ólasson, & Delfabbro, 2010; Welte et al., 2008). Martins, Lee, Kim, Letourneau, and Storr (2014) suggested impulsiveness might be a link between co-occurring rates of gambling and sexual behaviors in adolescents. Of the 678 students researched, 49% had gambled at least once by age 18. Another 35% had engaged in sexual intercourse by age 13 and 89% had sexual intercourse by age 18. They also found gamblers had high impulsivity levels at the age of 13, which suggests a link between gambling and impulsivity. While younger people are less likely than older adults to seek treatment for gambling problems (Petry, 2005), early identification and intervention for youth involved with gambling may reduce adverse outcomes later in life.

A family history of gambling is another risk factor in the development of compulsive gambling habits during childhood (Pietrzak, Ladd, & Petry, 2003). Children who grew up in a home where a problem gambler was present were more likely to develop similar harmful gambling habits, creating a new generation of gamblers (Abbott, Cramer, & Sherrets, 1995; Lesieur & Rothschild, 1989). This is a significant implication, as the early development of gambling habits is associated with more problem gambling habits later in life (Jacobs, 2000; Scherrer et al., 2007). In many instances, youth who engage in gambling do so with other family members or friends (American Psychiatric Association, 2013). Adolescents may also emulate the gambling behaviors of close family members and caregivers. This appears especially true for those who begin regular gambling between the ages of eight and ten (Gupta & Derevensky, 1998). Family life influences gambling behavior significantly, particularly when a parent gambles or is not active in a young person's daily life (Lussier,

Derevensky, Gupta, & Vitaro, 2014). The main risk factor for adolescent gambling is the strength and nature of relationships formed with others who gamble. Having friends who are active gamblers is also a significant risk factor (Lussier et al., 2014).

The very nature of adolescence may be a risk factor for the development of problem gambling habits (Derevensky & Gupta, 2006; Jacobs, 2004). Moreover, the presence of childhood behavioral disorders such as Attention-Deficit/Hyperactivity Disorder (ADHD), Conduct Disorder (CD), and Oppositional Defiant Disorder (ODD) may be contributing factors among some youth who engage in problem gambling practices (Slutske et al., 2014). Additionally, a childhood diagnosis of CD (Kessler et al., 2008; Slutske et al., 2014) or ADHD (Slutske et al., 2014) may be one factor that contributes to problem gambling habits later in life.

Gambling problems often develop in later adolescence (i.e., 18 to 21 years of age) (Huang, Jacobs, Derevensky, Gupta, & Paskus 2007; Winters, Stinchfield, Botzet, & Anderson, 2002). A national survey of adolescents found gambling problems were more prevalent in individuals 18-22 years old, as compared to younger adolescents ages 13-16 (Barnes, Welte, Hoffman, & Dintcheff, 2005). One study found 86% of adult pathological gamblers participated in gambling before their 19th birthday (Petry, 2005). Other studies have indicated youth who engaged in problematic gambling practices are more likely to abuse alcohol, drugs, and tobacco products (Cheung, 2014; Petry, 2005; Westphal, Rush, Stevens, & Johnson, 2000), and that poor self-control is often correlated with that abuse (Cheung, 2014). Youth gamblers also reported higher rates of sexual behaviors, which have been linked to impulsiveness (Martins et al., 2014). Adolescents are at a higher risk for truancy and financial issues if they have gambling problems (Lussier et al., 2014). Youth who show moderate to severe gambling patterns, based upon the frequency of such behaviors, indicate having some friends who also participate in moderate to severe gambling habits (Gupta & Derevensky, 1997). Brown and colleagues (2003) also found that juvenile gang members were more likely to gamble compared to non-gang members. Gang affiliation may produce greater peer pressure to begin and continue gambling.

Adolescent problem gambling may be an indicator of other underlying concerns and symptoms warranting the attention of caregivers, school professionals, mental health professionals, and other important figures in the individual's life (Welte, Barnes, Tidwell, & Hoffman, 2009). Betancourt and colleagues (2012) argued that youth gambling could develop as a means of coping with and avoiding problems among those with deficient coping strategies, such as abnormally highstress responses to negative stimuli. Adolescent gamblers showed increased rates of internalizing and externalizing behaviors as measured with the Youth Self-Report (YSR) (Achenbach & Rescorla, 2001; Betancourt et al., 2012). In the YSR, higher levels of reported internalized behaviors measure more anxiety, depression, and withdrawal, while higher levels of externalized behaviors measure increased problems with other individuals (e.g., aggression, illicit activity) (Achenbach & Rescorla, 2001). Higher levels of both internalized and externalized behaviors represent weaker coping mechanisms for everyday stressors found in the adolescent gamblers (Betancourt et al., 2012). Lussier and colleagues (2013) suggested social bonding decreases problem gambling in adolescents; therefore, it could be used as part of a treatment method for youth.

PROBLEM GAMBLING IN OLDER ADULTS

Older adults represent one of the largest potential at-risk populations for problem gambling (Subramaniam et al., 2015), as this population has demonstrated the largest increase in gambling rates: from 35% in 1975 to 80% in 1998 (Ashley & Boehlke, 2012; Hong, Sacco, & Cunningham-Williams, 2009; Lichtenberg, Martin, & Anderson, 2009). According to Hong et al. (2009), from 2008 to 2009 gambling rates in older adults jumped from 23% to 50%. On average, seniors (65 years and older) enjoy much more leisure time and a more stable income in comparison to the rest of the population, affording them more opportunity to gamble (Desai, Maciejewski, Dausey, Caldarone, & Potenza, 2004). Older adults who develop gambling problems are usually unemployed, married women (Grant, Kim, Odlaung, Buchanan, & Potenza, 2009). Late-onset gamblers are more likely to have a co-morbid anxiety disorder, which indicates that gambling could be used as an escape from stress (Grant, Kim, Odlaug, Buchanan, & Potenza, 2009). Ashley and Boehlke (2012) noted the death of a spouse and boredom as additional factors that may motivate behavioral changes towards gambling. Accessibility to gambling sites may also help to explain why pathological gambling is so prevalent in seniors, as the availability for gambling trips is elevated for those living near casinos (Desai et al., 2004). Elderly gamblers have fewer substance abuse issues and tend to have fewer financial problems than younger adults (Grant, Kim, Odlaug, Buchanan, & Potenza, 2009). For people who use wheelchairs or walkers, gambling is a seated activity that allows for hours of entertainment (Humphrey-Jones, 2009). In cases where mobility is an issue for seniors, residential living centers often host gambling activities such as bingo events as a means of promoting a sense of community and interaction (Parehk & Morano, 2009).

GENDER DIFFERENCES

Researchers have noted differences between problem gambling habits among men and women (Blanco, Hasin, Petry, Stinson, & Grant, 2006; Ibáñez, Blanco, Moreryra, & Sáiz-Ruiz, 2003; Tavares et al., 2003). Men are significantly more likely than women to have problematic gambling habits (Petry, 2005). The reasons women tend to start gambling later in life and progress more quickly to problem levels compared to men are not well understood (American Psychiatric Association, 2013). One proposed reason for the increased progression by women is the gambling format selected (Oliveira & Silva, 2001). Women often gamble via slot machines, while men tend to gamble via casino games believed to require skill (i.e., poker, blackjack) (American Psychiatric Association, 2013; Potenza et al., 2001). In addition to having different gambling format preferences than males, as a group, females seem to differ from males in terms of the reasons they choose to gamble. The development of a gambling disorder among some females may be a response to escaping an abusive relationship, loneliness, or psychological distress. Women who are classified as problem gamblers are more likely to be single or divorced (Weatherly, Montes, Peters, & Wilson, 2012). Many of them suffer from more co-morbid mental health concerns than women without gambling problems (Abbott & McKenna, 2005). These factors contrast to the proposed hypothesis for male problem gambling, which involves gambling addiction and positive stimulation (Abbott & McKenna, 2005; Humphrey-Jones, 2009; Lesieur, 1994; Lesieur & Blume, 1991; Steel & Blaszczynski, 1996; Strachan & Custer, 1993). When it comes to online gambling, women generally play casino games and bingo, and men generally make bets on sporting events and races (Gainsbury, Russell, Blaszczynski, & Hing, 2015). Past research has shown that these factors account for some of the problem gambling, according to self-reports of individual gamblers (Abbott & McKenna, 2005; Lesieur, 1994; Lesieur & Blume, 1991; Steel & Blaszczynski, 1996; Strachan & Custer, 1993).

ONLINE GAMBLING

Easily accessible gambling via the Internet, with the ability to transcend any barriers relating to location and mobility, has attracted many (Gainsbury et al., 2015; Scholes-Balog & Hemphill, 2012). Internet gambling is open 24 hours a day, providing users unlimited access to gambling opportunities. Online gambling is more economical compared to physical casino gambling, due to limited incidental expenses and lower fees and commissions (Griffiths, Parke, Wood, & Parke, 2006). While pathological gambling can be associated with a stigma of obsession and a lack of control, there is a sense of anonymity with online gambling that is not possible with in-person visits to casinos. The anonymity can reduce the negative perception gamblers experience from others, while allowing for carefree behavior (Griffiths et al., 2006). The Internet provides a separation between the gambler and his or her money. Gambling with electronic cash (e-cash) has proven easier than gambling with real cash, because individuals do not feel as attached to e-cash (Griffiths et al., 2006). This idea has been referred to as "suspension of judgment" and is the reason many casinos use chips as monetary units for betting (Griffiths, 1993). By betting online, individuals may bet in a riskier manner.

People who gamble via the Internet may also bet on sporting events or purchase lottery tickets (Gainsbury et al., 2015). Those who use both the Internet and offline means of gambling tend to have more serious gambling problems than those who only gamble online (Gainsbury et al., 2015). Online gamblers are more likely than offline gamblers to have a high-ranking job and more education, live in large cities, and consider themselves professionals at gambling (Gainsbury et al., 2015).

Online gambling can be associated with Internet crimes (McMullan & Rege, 2010). There are lone hackers who alter the odds of winning online poker matches, while others siphon money from other players' winnings. Corporations and organized crime groups can play a role in affecting who wins in online tournaments, as well. Phishing, extortion, and money laundering are involved in some online gambling websites. Internet crime can be untraceable, impersonal, automated, and not tied to any particular location (McMullan and Rege, 2010).

ACCURATE DIAGNOSIS OF PATHOLOGICAL GAMBLING AND GAMBLING DISORDER

Pathological Gambling (PG) was first included as a psychiatric disorder in 1980 in DSM-III (American Psychiatric Association, 1980), and the diagnostic criteria were revised in 1987 for DSM-III-R (American Psychiatric Association, 1987; Lesieur, 1988) and again in 1994 for DSM-IV (American Psychiatric Association, 1994). The original criteria and subsequent revisions were written by committees of experts, based primarily on a review of the literature and clinical experience. Lesieur and Rosenthal (1991) reviewed the literature for the DSM-IV committee and found little empirical data regarding the diagnostic criteria other than clinician opinions and anecdotal reports. While none of the DSM versions present an exhaustive list of PG symptoms, they are thought to include symptoms that are sufficiently relevant to provide an accurate diagnosis (Gebauer, LaBrie, & Shaffer, 2010). Following the publication of DSM-IV, there were a small number of empirical studies on the accuracy of diagnostic criteria for PG (National Research Council, 1999; Petry, Blanco, Stinchfield, & Volberg, 2013; Zimmerman, Chelminski, & Young, 2006).

The DSM-5 (American Psychiatric Association, 2013) includes the following revisions from DSM-IV: (a) renaming the disorder from Pathological Gambling to Gambling Disorder; (b) reclassifying from Impulse Control Disorders to Substance-Related and Addictive Disorders; (c) reducing the threshold for diagnosis from five criteria to four criteria; (d) eliminating the criterion, "has committed illegal acts such as forgery, fraud, theft, or embezzlement to finance gambling;" (e) making minor revisions to the wording of three criteria (such as adding the word "often" in the criterion about preoccupation with gambling), but leaving six of the nine criteria unchanged; and (f) specifying that symptoms occur within a 12- month period. The reduction of the threshold from five criteria to four was based on three studies in three different countries: USA (Stinchfield, 2003), Canada (Stinchfield et al., 2005), and Spain (Jimenez-Murcia et al., 2009). All three studies found a modest improvement in classification accuracy using a cut score of four, and most importantly, resulted in a reduction in false negatives—the error of saying the person does not have the disorder when they do.

The reason for the elimination of the illegal acts criterion was based primarily on two studies that found low prevalence rates for this criterion (Strong & Kahler 2007; Zimmerman et al., 2006). These two studies noted that the illegal acts criterion was rarely endorsed in the absence of other criteria and thus did not add to diagnostic accuracy. Illegal acts had been a criterion since PG was first introduced in DSM-III in 1980 and had been present in DSM-III-R and DSM-IV. The illegal acts criterion was not without its problems: patients could misunderstand the criterion. For example, many problem gamblers write bad checks, but they may not consider that act to be illegal, particularly if they plan to put money into the account later to cover the bad check or if they were not arrested. This criterion required clarification and probing questions during the diagnostic interview to determine whether an act, such as writing a bad check, satisfied the criterion of illegal acts. Some individuals may not report illegal behavior in a clinical assessment for fear of being reported to legal authorities. Therapists report that some individuals who deny illegal activity during the initial diagnostic assessment will later, in the course of treatment, admit to illegal acts to fund their gambling or pay gambling debts. This initial under-reporting of illegal acts may have contributed to low prevalence rates found in prior studies, which is partly why it was eliminated and may have been so without sufficient data to support its elimination.

In recognition of these issues, the DSM-5 includes the assessment of illegal acts under the criterion about lying to others and states, "these instances of deceit may also include, but are not limited to, covering up illegal behaviors such as forgery, fraud, theft or embezzlement to obtain money with which to gamble (Criterion A7)" (American Psychiatric Association, 2013, p. 586). Thus, if clinicians inquire about illegal acts and especially low-threshold illegal acts such as "taking or borrowing money from others to gamble without telling them" as examples of lying to others, then even fewer individuals with GD should be misclassified.

GAMBLING SCREENING TOOLS
Screening tools are used to identify potential gambling problems (see Table 2). The use of these tools is a crucial first step in identifying and providing the necessary interventions to alleviate the negative impact of this disorder.

Table 1
Problem Gambling Screening Tools

- Canadian Problem Gambling Index (CPGI)
- Consumption Screen for Problem Gambling (CSPG)
- Early Intervention Gambling Health Test (EIGHT)
- Gamblers Anonymous Twenty Questions (GA-20)
- Gambling Motives Questionnaire
- Georgia State Offender Gambling Screen (GSOGS)
- Lie/Bet Questionnaire
- Massachusetts Gambling Screen (MAGS)
- National Opinion Research Center DSM Screen for Gambling Problems (NODS)
- Pathological Problem Gambling Measure (PPGM)
- Problem Gambling Severity Index (PGSI, which is a component of the CPGI)
- South Oaks Gambling Screen–Revised (SOGS-R)
- South Oaks Gambling Screen–Revised for Adolescents (SOGS-RA)
- Stinchfield's Measure of DSM-IV Diagnostic Criteria for Pathological Gambling
- Victorian Gambling Screen

CANADIAN PROBLEM GAMBLING INDEX (CPGI) INCLUDING THE PROBLEM GAMBLING SEVERITY INDEX (PGSI)
One means to assess the severity of a pathological gambling disorder is by administering the Problem Gambling Severity Index (PGSI) test. The PGSI asks individuals how often they participate in gambling activities (i.e., casino gambling, sports betting, lottery), how much money one brings to the gambling venue, how much money is risked per occasion, and the harmful consequences the individual has experienced as a result of gambling (i.e., health consequences, ability to cope with stressful events). The PGSI scores range from zero to

eight or higher, with higher scores indicating an elevated risk of gambling with higher amounts of money, as well as a higher gambling frequency, generally associated with more severe negative effects on a person's life (i.e., familial alienation, high levels of debt and poor coping abilities associated with their problem gambling habits) (Ferris & Wynne, 2001). The PGSI is a highly reliable and valid instrument for measuring the severity of problem gambling (Ferris & Wynne, 2001).

Williams and Wood (2004) classified five levels of gambling: (1) non-gamblers who score a zero on the PGSI and have not gambled in the past year; (2) at-risk gamblers who score a zero on the PGSI but report some gambling in the past year, and who may be vulnerable to developing gambling habits due to family exposure, stressors, etc.; (3) low-risk gamblers who score a one or two, report little negative consequences, and exhibit few gambling habits; (4) moderate-risk gamblers who score a three to a seven and report moderate levels of negative consequences; and (5) severe-risk gamblers who are individuals who score an eight or higher and report severe negative outcomes.

South Oaks Gambling Screen—Revised (SOGS-R)

The South Oaks Gambling Screen is a commonly used tool to assess the severity of gambling problems. The SOGS was originally based on the DSM-III definition of pathological gambling and questions developed by Gamblers Anonymous (Lesieur & Blume, 1987). It consists of twenty questions and is frequently the tool of choice for researchers to determine the severity of problem gambling among those involved in the criminal justice system (Zurhold, Verthein, & Kalke, 2014) (Goodie et al., 2013; Stinchfield, 2002). The tool is easy to administer, cost-effective and requires little training (Petry, 2005). However, some of the items on the SOGS are subjective in nature and may contribute to a false positive for gambling-related concerns (Goodie et al., 2013; Stinchfield, 2002).

Rule 82 Assessment

Courts in the State of Minnesota utilize a Rule 82 Assessment that is performed by a trained, certified gambling therapist. Typically, a probation officer may request this type of assessment when a defendant is suspected of having a gambling problem, to determine its level of severity. This evaluation assists in the recommendation of services appropriate to each individual. A Rule 82 Assessment is somewhat similar to a pre-sentence investigation (PSI), and the information gathered through the assessment may be used in later court proceedings. This evaluation considers prior, if any, white-collar crimes, as well as medical records and psychological assessments. Other information such as phone logs, police records, financial records, emails, social media evidence, military records, school records, and driving records may also be requested in completing this assessment.

Causes of Pathological Gambling

The impetus for problem gambling is best explored from a biopsychosocial perspective, meaning that there are varieties of biological, psychological, and social factors that affect the development of gambling habits. The most attractive aspect enticing gamblers is the prospect for grand earnings with minimal effort. Another factor driving continued gambling is the perceived need to regain prior gambling losses (Blaszczynski & Nower, 2002). Furthermore, emotionally vulnerable individuals, such as those who are depressed or anxious, are at an increased risk to develop pathological gambling habits as an ineffective coping mechanism to deal with insecure emotions. Feelings of shame are also associated with individuals who have gambling problems, and this shame can directly affect the individual's personal propensity to gamble, as well as their reaction to gambling losses (Yi, 2012). Gambling is often used as an outlet to alleviate stress, since the prospect of winning assists in the mitigation of uncomfortable feelings of depression and anxiety. The act of gambling, like other addictions, is pleasurable in the moment. In studying adult gambling, various deficits in executive functioning—including working memory, reward processing, and control over cognitive functions—have been found (Betancourt et al., 2012; Goudriaan, Oosterlaan, de Beurs, & van den Brink, 2006).

GENETIC FACTORS

Familial heritability is regarded as a possible factor in the development of pathological gambling (Gupta & Derevensky, 1998). This hypothesis considers that when all situational variables and opportunities are equal, only certain individuals will develop pathological gambling habits (Kennedy, Muglia, Jain, & Turner, 2003). Among a sample of pathological gamblers, 86% of the individuals reported having at least one parent who also was a pathological gambler (Gupta & Derevensky, 1998). Another study found that only 45% of problem gamblers believed they had a problem, and 41% believed one of their parents had gambling issues (Abbott, McKenna, & Giles, 2000). Also, studies on twins found 35%-54% heritability rates of pathological gambling symptoms, suggesting a genetic variable that increases the risk for gambling problems (Eisen et al., 1998).

Genetic differences affecting the brain's reward system may be present in those with problem gambling. Genetic researchers found that the dopamine D2A1 allele receptor gene may contribute to impulsive gambling patterns (Derevensky & Gupta, 2004). When this gene is present, deficits in dopamine reward pathways can develop through D2A1 receptor inhibition. This deficiency leads to individuals seeking out stimulating experiences through high-risk activities like pathological gambling and/or substance abuse to make up the deficient reward perception (Ashley & Boehlke, 2012; Derevensky & Gupta, 2004). The DRD4 gene has been reported to be highly common among pathological gamblers (Kennedy et al., 2003; Kennedy, Turner, & Lobo, 2007). Specifically, the 7-repeat allele (representing the DRD4 gene connected seven times in a row among the genetic code) was highly prevalent among the sample of pathological gamblers and was not significantly present among the low-risk gambling control group (Kennedy et al., 2003; Kennedy et al., 2007). This gene has been linked to the development of attention-deficit hyperactivity disorder (ADHD), another condition characterized by an extreme lack of impulse control and issues with inattentiveness (Fernández-Aranda et al., 2013). Lastly, the DAT1 gene and the COMT gene, while not found to be directly connected to pathological gambling habits, were found at an increased rate among the individuals who showed lower levels of impulse control (Kennedy et al., 2003). This finding suggests the presence of DAT1 and COMT genes may act as risk factors for impulsive behaviors. Variations in the D2 receptor and the DA receptor gene may predispose a person towards gambling problems (Conversano et al., 2012). Antipsychotic medication blocks DA receptors and, in this way, may improve problem gambling symptoms (Conversano et al., 2012).

ADVERSE CHILDHOOD EVENTS

Trauma may act as the trigger for the development of problem gambling habits (Kausch, Rugle, & Rowland, 2006), and recent research has begun to link traumatic childhood events with an increased risk for problematic gambling in adulthood (Ashley & Boehlke, 2012; Larsen, Curtis, & Bjerregaard, 2013). Kausch et al. (2006) examined a sample of 111 problem gamblers seeking treatment in a facility in Virginia and found an estimated 64% of the individuals experienced some form of childhood abuse (e.g., physical, sexual, and emotional abuse). Approximately 42% of the sample reported experiencing more than one account of abuse, with approximately 16% reporting histories of both physical and sexual abuse.

There is high co-morbidity found between family violence and problem gambling (Dowling et al., 2014). Perhaps many of the stressors influencing gambling may also be similar to those leading one to be violent in the home. Some of these stressors include financial issues, mistrust, and communication problems. Although an explanation of the correlation between family violence and problem gambling has not been conclusively identified, Dowling et al. (2014) noted the need for routine screening, assessment, and management of problem gambling and family violence.

GEOGRAPHIC LOCATION

The proximity of individuals to gambling venues (e.g., casinos, racetracks) is directly correlated to pathological gambling. Closer radius and greater accessibility to casinos and other gambling venues may significantly increase the risk of developing pathological gambling habits (Welte, Barnes, Tidwell, & Hoffman, 2008). In fact, rates of pathological gambling in populations within a 50-mile radius of a casino are nearly double the rates for populations outside the 50-mile accessibility-zone radius (Gerstein et al., 1999). However, this finding cannot make any causal claim towards geographic location as a reason for maladaptive gambling. Instead, it may be attributed to location variables affecting gambling rates or the possibility of problem gamblers relocating to areas where gambling venues are numerous and easily accessible. Individuals living within a 50-mile radius of a casino or other major gambling venue can be categorized as an at-risk population for the development of pathological gambling. As technology advances, geographic location may no longer limit an individual's ability to gamble.

EXECUTIVE FUNCTIONING DEFICITS

Impairment of executive functioning, which consists of higher-level behavioral regulation and cognition, could enable problem gambling. Executive functioning affects numerous aspects of one's life, from the ability to adapt to new situations, to communicating effectively, to organizing a consistent schedule. Impulsiveness, combined with the anticipation of a reward, is often enough to enable the continuation of gambling behavior, despite low chances of success (Conversano et al., 2012). Deficits in executive functioning, including deficiencies in working memory, reward processing, and control over cognitive functions, have been found in adult gamblers (Betancourt et al., 2012). But Betancourt and colleagues (2012) found no significant cognitive deficits in youth gamblers, compared to their non-gambling peers. One reason given is that executive functioning and cognitive processes are still developing in this population, and deficits are not always easily detected. This may complicate attempts at early identification of at-risk youth. Impulsiveness and deficits in executive functioning are characteristic of both problem gambling and ADHD.

Problem gamblers display decision-making impairments. This deficit, in part, can be explained by the reactions and motivations tied to processing rewards and punishments. Problem gamblers are typically hypersensitive to rewards more than punishments. Simply stated, they are motivated to seek a reward and are insensitive to losing (Ochoa et al., 2013). Problem gamblers also have impairments in problem solving, controlling emotional responses, and working through future-oriented tasks. These individuals have problems resisting or delaying gratification, possibly related to impulsivity, further complicating gambling behaviors (Reid, McKittrick, Davtian, & Fong, 2012).

DIAGNOSTIC CO-MORBIDITY

Research identifies an array of co-morbidities that are highly associated with problem gambling. Petry (2005) suggested that higher rates of compulsive shopping, sexual behaviors, intermittent explosive behaviors, and kleptomania are common in this population. In addition, a high percentage of pathological gamblers experience mental health concerns, specifically mood disorders (Grant & Potenza, 2004; Petry, 2005; Raylu & Oei, 2002). Cognitive distortions occur at a higher rate when problem gamblers have co-occurring psychiatric disorders (Xian et al., 2008). These distortions may relate to perceptions and beliefs of controlling the odds of winning. Cognitive distortions are more likely to be found in problem gamblers with multiple co-morbid conditions and those with severe symptoms of gambling addiction (Xian et al., 2008). The most common co-occurring conditions associated with problem gambling are depression, anxiety, alcohol misuse, and impulsivity (Suomi et al., 2014). Depression is among the most common mental health concerns co-morbid with gambling, with as many as 76% of pathological gamblers experiencing major depression (Thomas & Jackson, 2008; Unwin, Davis, & Leeuw, 2000). Depressive symptoms are more closely associated with pathological gamblers compared to low risk gamblers and at-risk gamblers (Yip et al., 2011). It has been estimated that 37.9% of all gamblers have mood disorders and 32.4% have anxiety disorders (Lorains, Cowlishaw, & Thomas, 2011). Generalized anxiety disorder, panic disorder, and social phobias all appear more often in individuals with pathological gambling compared to non-gambling peers (Petry, Stinson, & Grant, 2005). Gambling concerns have been known to increase during times of stress and depression (American Psychiatric Association, 2013). Furthermore, Yip and colleagues (2011) found pathological gamblers were at an elevated risk of exhibiting aggression and were 2.9 times more likely to carry a weapon, compared to the general population. This is not surprising, given impulsivity is a significant component of all risky behaviors, including aggression, excessive gambling, and substance abuse. Furthermore, these correlations may be attributed to the belief among some that more money equates to increased protection. Finally, research suggests that as many as 30% of pathological gamblers may have ADHD or ADD (see Humphrey-Jones, 2009).

PERSONALITY DISORDERS

Personality disorders should be another variable to consider when exploring the topic of co-morbid pathological gambling (Humphrey-Jones, 2009). Risk-related characteristics of personality such as impulsiveness, thrill seeking, and a lack of self-control are correlated with gambling and antisocial behavior (Mishra, Lalumière, Morgan, & Williams, 2011). Borderline Personality Disorder (BPD) ties into gambling behavior as well as a propensity for criminal behavior, often because of poorly regulated emotional responses to people and situations (Steel & Blaszczynski, 1998). Narcissism can play a role in a person's belief that they can win and are more capable at winning than others (Humphrey-Jones, 2009; Petry, 2005; Steel & Blaszczynski, 1998). Two core personality traits, extraversion and neuroticism, are also associated with gambling behavior (Mishra et al., 2011).

Antisocial Personality Disorder (APD) is associated with pathological gambling and may relate to violent behaviors (Petry, 2005). When pathological gamblers with APD were compared to pathological gamblers without this personality disorder, many differences in physical traits and gambling habits were noted. The pathological gamblers with APD were typically younger, male, and divorced. They also began gambling at a younger age, gambled more frequently, and had increased medical and drug problems, compared to pathological gamblers without APD (Pietrzak & Petry, 2005). Male problem gamblers have a higher rate of conduct disorder and antisocial personality disorder (Abbott et al., 2000).

ATTENTION-DEFICIT/HYPERACTIVITY DISORDER (ADHD)

Impulsivity, which is a significant issue for problem gamblers, is a diagnostic criterion of ADHD (Breyer et al., 2009). As previously mentioned, adolescents with ADHD may be more likely to develop gambling problems compared to adolescents without ADHD (Breyer et al., 2009). A co-morbidity of ADHD increases the likelihood of substance abuse and dependence (Breyer et al., 2009). Treating ADHD is important in preventing problems with social interaction and criminal conduct (Breyer et al., 2009).

POST-TRAUMATIC STRESS DISORDER (PTSD)

Individuals who use pathological gambling as a means of coping with trauma may also be at an increased risk of developing post-traumatic stress disorder (PTSD), compared to non-problem gamblers (Kessler et al., 2008). Ledgerwood and Petry (2006) found that 12.5% to 29% of problem gamblers have PTSD. When analyzing the onset of co-morbid PTSD, it was significantly more likely to develop after the onset of pathological gambling (Kessler et al., 2008). This finding was also relevant to major depressive symptoms and substance use problems, where post-pathological gambling onset was significantly more likely, compared to pre-pathological gambling onset (Kessler et al., 2008). This may be due to risk-taking behaviors, sometimes associated with problem gambling behaviors, leading to events that may cause the onset of PTSD.

In our professional experience, some pathological gamblers who are suffering from PTSD reported gambling as a way to self-medicate and escape from their problematic symptoms. In some of these cases, the problem gambler will also misuse alcohol and/or drugs. It is important to note that alcohol can heighten problem-gambling behaviors by inhibiting control and impairing judgment (Biddle, Hawthorne, Forbes, & Coman, 2005). As such, these behaviors could lead to a destructive life style that may exacerbate PTSD-related symptoms and continue to fuel the need to engage in problem-gambling behaviors.

SUBSTANCE ABUSE

A high co-morbidity of substance use has been reported in the gambling population (Abbott et al., 2000; Cowlishaw, Merkouris, Chapman, & Radermacher, 2014; Oleski, Cox, Clara, & Hills, 2011). An estimated 75% of problem gamblers indicate alcohol abuse and 40% to 63% report drug abuse problems (Battersby, Tolchard, Scurrah, & Thomas, 2006; Petry et al., 2005; Welte, Barnes, Wieczorek, Tidwell, & Parker, 2001; Zimmerman, Chelminski & Young, 2006). Substance abuse problems have been found among individuals exhibiting lower levels of problem gambling; however, as the severity of problem gambling increases, so have substance abuse problems. It is therefore suggested that screening processes for substance use be recommended for all individuals entering treatment for gambling problems (Lorains, Cowlishaw, & Thomas, 2011). The most-commonly abused substances among pathological gamblers are tobacco products, marijuana, and alcohol (Momper et al., 2010; Odlaug, Stinchfield, Golberstein, & Grant, 2013; Yip et al., 2011). The severity of the problem may also depend on the environment in which the individual gambles. Scholes-Balog and Hemphill (2012) reported that online problem gamblers abuse substances more than venue problem gamblers.

There are common occurrences of gambling and substance use in adolescents, such that as one problem behavior increases (i.e., gambling/substance misuse), the likelihood of the other increases as well. Researchers sampled over 20,000 school students (grade school, middle school, and high school) and reported that students were 3.8 times more likely to gamble frequently (weekly or daily) if they also used drugs frequently (weekly or daily), in comparison to those who did not use drugs as much or at all (Barnes, Welte, Hoffman, & Tidwell, 2011). Also, early onset gambling is correlated with future severe substance use (Barnes et al., 2011). These findings suggested that when problem gambling and substance abuse co-occur, frequency and severity of issues increase.

TOBACCO USE

The use of cigarettes is another consideration to take into account when examining the topic of problematic gambling. Elevated tobacco use has been reported among individuals who engage in gambling (Grant, Desai, & Potenza, 2009; Grant, Kim, Odlaug, & Potenza, 2008; McGrath & Barrett, 2009; Odlaug et al., 2013). Increased tobacco use has been correlated with an increased risk in gambling severity and psychiatric problems. Odlaug and colleagues (2013) assessed 385 pathological gamblers seeking treatment in Minnesota. Of the gamblers assessed, 63.4% reported using tobacco daily. Those who used tobacco daily were more likely to have an onset of problem gambling at a young age, to have more mental health issues, and to have had previous treatment for gambling (Odlaug et al., 2013). It has been reported that tobacco use among individuals attending problem gambling treatment may negatively impact program outcomes (Grant, Kim, Odlaug, & Potenza, 2008). Screening problem gambling treatment patients regularly for tobacco use may serve as an intended benefit for overall health and wellbeing (Odlaug et al., 2013).

SUICIDE AND SUICIDAL BEHAVIOR

When a problem gambler is suicidal and has problems at home, gambling is most often a significant factor causing those problems (Smith, Wynne, & Hartnagel, 2003). Suicide among pathological gamblers is a significant concern. Raylu and Oei (2002) estimate that between 12%-24% of problem gamblers will attempt to take their life. One study found that suicidal ideation was prominent in around 1 in 5 gamblers who were looking for treatment (Wong, Kwok, Tang, Blaszczynski, & Tse, 2014). Moreover, other scholars and sources have reported that 50% of problem gamblers seeking treatment report having suicidal ideations (American Psychiatric Association, 2013; Knezevic & Ledgerwood, 2012). There are a variety of reasons why suicide rates are high among pathological gamblers. Gamblers may see suicide as a way out of financial problems or as a way to alleviate family-related stress (Wong et al., 2014).

Suicidal ideation may be influenced by untreated mental disorders. Depression and dysphoria rates are significantly higher among the pathological gambling population and may influence suicidal ideation in individuals as a way to cope with depressive states. Serotonin influences impulsive behaviors, which include violent and self-harming acts (Conversano et al., 2012). The lifetime risk of suicide among individuals with untreated major depressive disorder is 20% (Gotlib & Hammen, 2002). Bipolar disorder can also influence and elevate the risks for suicide attempts and ideation in pathological gamblers (Perlis et al., 2010). Individuals who experience the manic episodes of bipolar disorder are more likely to be involved in riskier behavior, such as pathological gambling, (Kim, Grant, Eckert, Faris, & Hartman, 2006). Of individuals diagnosed as bipolar, 41.7% reported a prior history of suicidal attempts (Perlis et al., 2010).

Chronic stress from gambling, loss of family connections, and substance use may also play a pivotal role in the contemplation of suicidal behaviors (Blaszczynski & Farrell, 1998). Guilt and shame may be significant factors, as well, when the gambling problem is discovered and the gambler has difficulty controlling their impulses (Humphrey-Jones, 2009). Gambling is a factor, but not necessarily the sole factor, in suicidal ideation and attempts. Of problem gamblers who had attempted suicide, Hodgins, Mansley, and Thygesen (2006) found that 21% of the attempts related specifically to gambling. The same study reported that almost 75% of the participants had suicidal thinking and/or attempts. Suicide attempts are often co-morbid with psychological disorders (particularly mood disorders) and substance abuse (Hodgins et al., 2006). Kausch (2003) found that in problem gamblers who have those co-morbidities, impulsiveness is likely the link between them and suicide attempts (as cited in Hodgins et al., 2006).

MEDICAL HEALTH CONSEQUENCES

Engaging in chronic gambling habits increases the risk of experiencing many of the physical phenomena associated with chronic stress, including cardiac complications, insomnia, gastrointestinal disorders, high blood pressure, and headaches (Bergh & Kühlhorn, 1994; Ladd & Petry, 2002; Lorenz & Yaffee, 1986). Pathological gamblers are significantly more likely to develop tachycardia (abnormally fast heart rates), angina (chest pain—a common symptom of coronary heart disease), and liver disease (Morasco et al., 2006). Liver disease is often exacerbated by alcohol abuse, which is common in the pathological gambling community (Walsh & Alexander, 2000). Additionally, Morasco and colleagues (2006) found that pathological gamblers were significantly more likely to utilize emergency medical services when compared to the general population. The need for constant care can worsen the workload, financial situation, and stress for family members who consistently provide care and supervision.

The environment may account for some of these medical health consequences. Problem and pathological gamblers might spend many hours sitting and inhaling smoke. A sedentary lifestyle mixed with constant second-hand smoke can negatively affect one's health (Erickson, Molina, Ladd, Pietrzak, & Petry, 2005). Problem gamblers have higher rates of obesity, nicotine, and alcohol dependence (Desai, Desai, & Potenza, 2007). They are also less realistic about their physical health; thus, they are more likely to view themselves as healthy, often ignoring health-related warning signs. It has been hypothesized that although the environment is detrimental to physical health, perhaps individuals with poor health are attracted to casinos because gambling is a sedentary activity that allows them to smoke and drink (Desai et al., 2007). Table 3 lists the numerous detrimental effects of problem gambling.

TABLE 2

Consequences Associated with Problem Gambling

- Alcohol Use
- Anger/Emotional Outbursts
- Anxiety/Worry/Nervousness
- Attempted Suicide
- Avoiding Responsibilities
- Banishment from Area Establishments
- Bankruptcy
- Blaming Others for Mistakes
- Car Accident
- Causeing Pain to Others
- Changed Identity
- Child Abuse and Neglect
- Civil Law Suits
- Closed Bank Account
- Collection Agencies Calling
- Criminal Involvement
- Depression
- Destroyed Property
- Divorce
- Domestic Violence
- Drug Use
- DUI/DWI
- Employment Concerns
- Encouraging Others to Gamble
- Falling Asleep While Driving
- Feeling Trapped
- Feelings of Emptiness
- Feelings of Guilt/Shame
- Feelings of Hopelessness/Hopelessness
- Fired from Job
- Flashbacks
- Having to move in with Parents/Relatives
- Headaches/Migraines
- Homelessness
- Homicidal Thoughts
- Impulsive Behaviors

- Incarceration
- Increased Caffeine Use
- Increased Fears
- Isolation from Others
- Lack of Self-Confidence
- Late Rent
- Loss of Automobile/Repossession
- Loss of Driver's License
- Loss of Self-Respect
- Loss of a Significant Relationship
- Loss of Time
- Lying-Type Behaviors
- Negative Attitude
- Nightmares
- Not Having Enough Money for Food
- Panic Attacks
- Poor Credit
- Probation
- Putting Someone Else at Risk
- Relationship Conflict
- Required to Obtain Payee Services
- Secretiveness/Hiding from Others
- Sleeping Difficulties
- Spent Retirement Money
- Stealing
- Suicide of Family Member/Significant Relationship Conflict
- Tarnished Reputation
- Termination of Parental Rights
- Thoughts of Suicide
- Threats by Others
- Transportation Concerns
- Urging/Fighting
- Writing Bad Checks

CRIMINAL JUSTICE SYSTEM INVOLVEMENT

Some researchers have examined the relationship between problem gambling and criminal behavior (Bell-ringer et al., 2009; Clark & Walker 2009; Folino & Abait, 2009; Lahn, 2005; Magoon, Gupta, & Derevensky, 2005). Humphrey-Jones (2009) found that according to self-reports, as many as 88% of problem gamblers had been involved in crime. The majority of crimes committed by gamblers are property or financial crimes, non-violent in nature (Lloyd, Chadwick, & Serin, 2014; Smith et al., 2003). In cases of a person murdering their immediate family, and for some, subsequently committing suicide, gambling has not been established as a significant factor (Wong et al., 2014). Problem gamblers who commit crimes are not what would be considered "career criminals," but instead, do so as a last resort to resolve problems stemming from their gambling addiction (Smith et al., 2003). White-collar crimes such as fraud are common among gamblers; however, violent crime rates are growing for this population (Humphrey-Jones, 2009). Pathological gambling is believed to prevail in approximately 4% of the general population, with severe pathological gambling impacting an estimated 1%-2% of the population (Delfabbro, 2013; Petry, 2005; Preston et al., 2012). A high percentage of these individuals may become involved in the criminal justice system in some capacity. As many as 60% of problem gamblers commit a crime associated with their gambling habits, often as a means to pay for gambling debts (Potenza et al., 2001). These criminal behaviors may include credit card fraud, theft, embezzlement, tax evasion, forgery, check fraud, or stealing from employers (American Psychiatric Association, 2013; Lesieur & Rosenthal, 1991; Schwer, Thompson, & Nakamuro, 2003). The majority of these white-collar crimes are committed by 21%-85% of pathological gamblers—the percentage depending on the type of crime in question (Nower, 2003).

Aborn and Bennett (2005) reviewed the impact of casinos in various cities in the U.S. and found that building casinos greatly increases the amount of crimes that occur in the surrounding area. This includes violent crime, bank robberies, prostitution, fraud, and essentially any incident involving alcohol and/or drugs. It was estimated that crime increased 84% in these communities (Aborn & Bennett, 2005). Crime rates also seem to increase in nearby areas, though generally not immediately after a casino is built (Aborn & Bennett, 2005). There are a number of explanations as to why problem gamblers tend to congregate around casinos. Slot machines are the most likely gambling machine to enable a person to become a problem gambler and are generally the largest source of profits for casinos (Aborn & Bennett, 2005).

Does gambling lead to criminal activity? Does criminal activity lead to gambling? Or do these habits develop alongside each other? For moderate pathological gamblers, gambling has usually been reported as a part of a criminal lifestyle, meaning that gambling habits develop in response to illicit exposure on the streets or in prison—as a means of extra income and gaining acceptance from other criminals and inmates (Turner, Preston, Saunders, McAvoy, & Jain, 2009; Williams, Royston, & Hagen, 2005). However, individuals considered severe pathological gamblers generally report criminal activity as a byproduct of poor gambling habits and a means to pay back gambling debts (Turner et al., 2009). The increased risk of criminal activity consequently leads to increased incarceration rates among problem gamblers.

SEXUALLY INAPPROPRIATE BEHAVIORS

The impulsivity and risky behaviors associated with pathological gambling have been observed with problematic sexualized behavior (Martins et al, 2014). Severe pathological gamblers are significantly more likely to be involved in risky sexual behavior, such as earlier initiation of sex and increased number of sexual partners, compared to non-gamblers (Ladd & Petry, 2002; Martins et al., 2014). However, the prevalence of sexual risks is not uniformly distributed among all pathological gamblers. Male gamblers are more likely to be involved in these behaviors compared to their female counterparts (Grant, Potenza, Weinstein, & Gorelick,

2010; Grant & Steinberg, 2005; Martins, Tavares, da Silva Lobo, Galetti, & Gentil, 2004). Younger gamblers are also more likely to be involved in these risky behaviors compared to older adults (Zuckerman & Kuhlman, 2000). Unlike non-problem gamblers, problem gamblers tend to have more sex partners, use condoms less frequently, and engage in casual and paid sexual behaviors more often (Petry, 2000). Petry's study used the South Oaks Gambling Screen (SOGS), which evaluated lifetime problem gambling. The SOGS scores revealed that the more severe the problem gambling, the riskier the sexual behaviors. According to the SOGS scores, pathological gamblers showed impulsive and addictive behaviors. This could explain why compulsive sexual behaviors are so prevalent among pathological gamblers. Grant and Steinberg (2005) assessed 225 pathological gamblers and found that 19.6% showed signs of compulsive sexual behaviors.

CORRECTIONAL SETTINGS

Problem gambling is quite common among prison inmates, with rates in correctional settings being reported as high as 38%, though ranges may fluctuate depending on the facility (Abbott & Volberg, 1999; Williams et al., 2005). In an Australian study of newly incarcerated male prisoners, it was found that 84% had participated in gambling of some form within the six months before imprisonment (Abbott et al., 2000), and 96% of the inmates had gambled at some point in their life. Among problem gamblers, 51% had gambling-related offenses, and 35% had gambling-related convictions (Abbott et al., 2000). Problem gamblers are more likely than non-problem gamblers to offend at a young age. Most early offenses were reportedly unrelated to gambling, which suggests that inmates generally were exhibiting offending behavior prior to their gambling behavior (Abbott et al., 2000). Higher proportions of problem gamblers and those at-risk of becoming problem gamblers exist within prison than in the general population (May-Chahal, Wilson, Humphreys, & Anderson, 2012; Nixon, Leigh, & Nowatzki, 2006; Sullivan, Brown, & Skinner, 2008). According to Abbott et al. (2000), the most common form of gambling behavior found in male prisoners before their incarceration consisted of activities that required skill and were repetitive. Males who were later incarcerated tended to engage in gambling behavior more often, for longer time lengths, and would spend almost six times more money at it than males in the general population (Abbott et al., 2000). Zurhold et al. (2014) examined records of 1,236 juvenile and adult prisoners in Germany. They found that 90 of the prisoners (7.3%) were problem gamblers, and of those 90 prisoners, 46.7% of them were in prison for crimes related to their gambling behaviors. The prisoners displaying problem-gambling behaviors served longer sentences than the other inmates (61 months compared to 49 months) (Zurhold et al., 2014).

One-third of criminal offenders display symptoms of problem or pathological gambling (Williams et al., 2005). Utilizing pre-trial screening with the Lie/Bet Questionnaire and in-depth analysis of prison records, Zurhold et al. (2014) found that nearly half of the prisoners identified as problem gamblers were serving sentences for crimes associated with their gambling habits and payment for subsequent losses (i.e., theft, forgery, and/or check fraud). The questionnaire asked subjects if they have lied to others regarding their gambling behavior and/or felt an urge to continue betting money within the last year. Case-study examples have indicated that inmates may engage in drug dealing and prostitution in order to continue their gambling habits or as an attempt to pay off debt associated with their addiction. Abbott and colleagues (2000) found that nearly 15% of male inmates in the study broke the law in order to settle gambling debts or to get more money in order to continue gambling. The most common crimes were burglary, theft, fraud, and robbery. Female inmates, in contrast, reported fraud and shoplifting due to gambling and were more likely to have committed a gambling-related crime (Abbott et al., 2000). Many gambling behaviors in female inmates paralleled those of male inmates. Nine percent of male inmates had been convicted of a gambling-related crime, compared to 19% of female inmates, and most had at least five convictions relating to gambling (Abbott et al., 2000). Approximately 26% of male and female inmates frequently participate in gambling activities while incarcerated. In some cases, individuals may develop a gambling problem while incarcerated (McEvoy & Spirgen, 2012), and upon release, this may contribute to a host of offender reentry challenges. Ten percent of male inmates in the study were deemed pathological gamblers, and 31% had serious gambling problems (Abbott et al., 2000).

Numerous reasons have been brought forth to account for the high gambling rates within prison populations. Williams (2008) found that prisoners viewed and used gambling as a coping strategy to deal with correctional settings during free time and as a brief escape from the mundane nature of the prison environment. When asked by Abbott (2000), the majority of prisoners answered that relieving boredom was the main reason for gambling in prison, while before prison, they gambled for the chance of winning money. Many participate in gambling games for the fun of it. Approximately 15% of the inmates reported that gambling had an impact on their life, and about half of them described the effect as negative (Abbott et al., 2000). Certain offenders may also use gambling as a means to fit in with the cultural values of prison, where high-risk betting is commonplace (McEvoy & Spirgen, 2012).

While restricted access to money is a significant factor for inmates deciding not to gamble in prison, it may lead some inmates to borrow money from others (Beauregard & Brochu, 2013). The resulting debts, if not settled, may be repaid through physical assault or theft. The risk of violence and physical injury over betting outcomes is a serious issue facing some inmates who engage in gambling activities. Gambling-related fights or arguments are products from gambling losses (May-Chahal et al., 2012; Turner & McAvoy, 2011). It is common for inmates to avoid gambling with an inmate who is in debt. Most inmates do not report dealing with direct negative consequences of gambling, though many may perceive a possible threat of physical assault (Beauregard & Brochu, 2013). Overall, the consequences of gambling are generally less severe within the prison setting.

While not universal within correctional settings, McEvoy and Spirgen (2012) found that prison administrators generally do not monitor or moderate gambling activities. This attitude toward gambling may be perceived by inmates as permission to engage in behaviors related to gambling. Prisons that do not already limit or ban gambling activities should consider doing so if there is a high prevalence of gambling with related negative consequences (Williams, 2013). Family members can also fuel gambling among incarcerated individuals, whether that is knowingly or unwittingly. McEvoy and Spirgen (2012) discussed the reality of outside family members indirectly promoting the activity by funneling money into prisoner accounts. Typically, prisoners do not experience the same degree of monetary loss while incarcerated as they do on the outside, since they are guaranteed basic amenities in the institution, which can mitigate the perceived seriousness of gambling losses (Beauregard & Brochu, 2013). Offering recreational activities that can serve as an alternative could help prevent gambling in those who engage in it out of boredom and as a stress reliever (Williams, 2013).

Due to this issue of monetary misuse, there is a need for proper education about the risks of gambling in correctional settings for inmates, family members, and prison staff. Teaching prison staff and inmates about the potential negative consequences of gambling in prison is an important consideration (Marotta, 2013). It would likely increase understanding of how a problem gambler may be better prepared for reentry if they are able to avoid gambling while incarcerated (Marotta, 2013).

Building awareness of gambling habits in prison settings may help administration identify inmates most likely to participate in gambling activities. Screening offenders for the potential of problem gambling behaviors upon entry to correctional facilities is also highly recommended. It could provide the opportunity for successful treatment implementation aimed at reducing future gambling-related offenses (Cuadrado & Lieberman, 2012) and ultimately assist the individual upon release back into the community. Introducing a gambling-related screening process could help prison staff become aware of the presence of problem gamblers (Williams, 2013). This could be especially useful if combined with training the staff in gambling prevention.

IMPACT ON FAMILY LIFE

The consequences associated with pathological gambling often place family members in a position of financial vulnerability and emotional distress (Cheung, 2015) due to financial issues, abuse, exposure to dangerous situations, and dealing with depressive symptoms (Mathews & Volberg, 2013). According to Cheung, large amounts of stress placed on the spouse of an occasional gambler can indirectly increase the likelihood that they will develop gambling problems (2015). Problem gambling can create serious debts, even leading to bankruptcy (Griffiths, 2004), which is significantly associated with severe pathological gambling habits (Shaffer & Korn, 2002). One reason for this may be the impulsive nature of pathological gamblers and the person's inability to stop gambling after severe losses. In the face of massive debts, many pathological gamblers lack the ability to settle unpaid debts, which can result in lower credit scores, potential legal sanctions, loss of property, and ultimately—bankruptcy. Filing for bankruptcy can affect not only the problem gambler, but other family members as well.

Outside family members often feel pressured to help inmates pay off prison gambling debts (Williams & Walker, 2009). Family members may feel a sense of duty toward paying back a problem gambler's debts (Mathews & Volberg, 2013). Even after a divorce, the former spouse may continue experiencing the burden of helping with repayments (Mathews & Volberg, 2013). In other cases, loan sharks may target the family of a problem gambler and pressure them to make the payment (Mathews & Volberg, 2013).

Pathological gambling is extremely detrimental to the stability of a family, since it can cause significant stress and alienate the gambler from other family members (Sullivan, 1994). Pathological gamblers often attempt to hide their actions from other family members (Borch, 2012; Williams & Walker, 2009). Family members, as well as the gamblers themselves, may be living in intense denial of the situation and its detrimental effects on the household (Borch, 2012). Once the problem is brought to light, the damage caused by this addiction can leave families with shock, disbelief, and feelings of betrayal (Sullivan, 1994). It is common for some pathological gamblers to have secret credit card accounts devoted to supporting gambling habits. In some instances, the problem gambler will lie, cheat, and steal from immediate family members to obtain additional funding for his or her addiction (Williams & Walker, 2009). Subsequently, this can lead to destroyed marriages, divorce, guilt, shame, and a loss of trust amongst all family members (Griffiths, 2004; Volberg, Nysse-Carris, & Gerstein, 2006).

DOMESTIC VIOLENCE AND CHILD MALTREATMENT

Unfortunately, problem gambling is associated with higher rates of domestic violence and child maltreatment (Afifi, Brownridge, MacMillan, & Sareen, 2010; Korman et al., 2008). The stress and financial hardship can frequently progress into family violence (Afifi et al., 2010). This finding is not surprising, given the significantly higher levels of aggression found in pathological gamblers when compared to the general population (Yip et al., 2011). Research findings suggest that a high percentage of problem gamblers seeking treatment often present with co-morbid anger and substance use problems (Korman et al., 2008). Domestic violence encompasses physical abuse (e.g., hitting/striking family members, punching walls, etc.) and emotional abuse (e.g., threats, degrading statements, harassment) (Shaw, Forbush, Schlinder, Rosenman, & Black, 2007). Often, problem gamblers become so fixated on gambling that they neglect parental and spousal duties, severely affecting the children. Child maltreatment can exist in the form of neglect (Shaw et al., 2007). Some parents who gamble excessively may lack the adequate ability to care for their children and may leave them unattended for prolonged periods to gamble, because it is common for some individuals to lose track of time while gambling (McNeilly & Burke, 2002). It has been estimated that parental gambling affects as many as 2.5 million children in the United States (Jacobs et al., 1989). Many gamblers fail to connect their gambling habits to long-term consequences that may harm other family members.

Internet gambling can also contribute to child neglect within the home, because Internet gambling is accessible 24 hours a day and it is common for gamblers to sit at their computers for the entire day (Scholes-Balog & Hemphill, 2012). This practice can interfere with the parent's ability to be present for child rearing or to tend to parental responsibilities. Children living in these situations often show poor academic performance, anxiety, depression, and a host of medical health conditions (Berman & Siegel, 1992; George & Murali, 2005). These children are at increased risk of committing suicide, compared to peers who reside in a home without a problem gambler. Children living with a parent who gambles excessively may feel rejected, alone, abandoned, and angry and experience greater attachment concerns (Lesieur, 1992). In school, these children may present themselves as unmotivated, inattentive, moody, and irritable. Children of pathological gamblers often exhibit poor interpersonal skills (George & Murali, 2005). Furthermore, children of pathological gamblers also develop inadequate coping systems, because they are more likely to have low confidence rates and greater insecurities (George & Murali, 2005). Children who grow up in a household where problem gambling is present are more likely to use tobacco products, alcohol, and drugs and to overeat, compared to youth who are not exposed to gambling concerns (Gupta & Derevensky, 1997).

Intimate partner violence (IPV) was found to be approximately ten times greater when one partner was categorized as a pathological gambler (Muelleman, DenOtter, Wadman, Tran, & Anderson, 2002). IPV is also associated with higher SOGS scores: the more severe the problem gambling, the more common the violence in the home (Liao, 2008). Korman and colleagues (2008) assessed 248 problem gamblers, noting 62.9% of the participants were either the perpetrator or the victim of IPV. Moreover, 25.4% of these problem gamblers admitted to severely perpetrating violence against their partners, and 64.5% of the participants had clinically significant anger problems. When combined with alcohol, the risk of violence was increased (Korman et al., 2008).

Overcoming the devastating effects of problem gambling in the family usually requires the assistance of outside support. When families are faced with pathological gambling, the assistance of a skilled gambling therapist is recommended. Early interventions are essential in assisting families impacted by the consequences of problem gambling. In many cases, domestic violence can ultimately lead to filing an Order of Protection (OP), child custody disputes, and even divorce (Shaw et al., 2007). To efficiently resolve conflict and minimize the risk of injury within families, Child Protective Services (CPS) and the police may become involved (Shaw et al., 2007).

TREATMENT

A variety of interventions exist for the treatment of problem gambling. These options include individual, group, and family therapy, as well as pharmacological interventions. Inpatient and outpatient treatment options are also available. Inpatient treatment programs offer 24-hour care and support and are helpful for people who have been unsuccessful in other attempts to manage their gambling. Outpatient programs can provide treatment while helping individuals maintain personal commitments at work and home, providing a new environment, which often removes stress and temptation from daily life. Given that only 2%-3% of all pathological gamblers seek services, there is a significant need for the proper identification and treatment for problem gamblers (Potenza et al., 2001). Of those who seek assistance, approximately one-half drop out after the first or second session (Ladouceur, Lachance, & Fournier, 2009).

GAMBLERS ANONYMOUS

One of the most widely used programs is Gamblers Anonymous (GA) (Petry, 2005). When transitioning out of therapy sessions, GA can be an effective resource in preventing relapse (Ladouceur & Lachance, 2007). Debt-relief counseling is offered through GA after an individual has been involved in the program for approximately one month (Humphrey-Jones, 2009). Among the individuals involved with GA, 50% showed a reduction in the frequency of gambling habits when used alongside outpatient treatment methods (Weatherly, Montes, Peters, & Wilson, 2012). The main weakness of GA is that the efficacy rate is limited: only 8% of individuals showed complete abstinence from gambling habits at the two-year mark of treatment (Weatherly et al., 2012).

COGNITIVE-BEHAVIORAL THERAPY (CBT)

Cognitive-behavioral methods are regarded as the most effective approaches when working with individuals with a gambling addiction (Grant et al., 2009b; Pallesen, Mitsem, Kvale, Johnsen, & Molde, 2005). The cognitive aspect of the therapy is especially effective during the first stages of abstaining from gambling, while the behavioral aspect aids in maintaining long-term resistance to gambling (Petry, 2005). The main goal of cognitive-behavioral therapy (CBT) is to identify thought processes and behavioral responses that lead to gambling. By understanding the causes of the addictive and excitatory response of chronic gambling, the therapy can condition individuals to avoid certain cues or thought processes that act as triggers. One gambling fallacy is the belief that the losses indicate an increased likelihood that one will win the next time (Goodie & Fortune, 2013). There is also the opposite idea: that a series of wins indicate that success is more likely to continue (Goodie & Fortune, 2013). The common element is that separate events can influence each other—that one roll of the dice has an impact on subsequent rolls. These fallacies of thinking mainly pertain to the idea that there are means of increasing one's chance of winning and controlling the outcome (Goodie & Fortune, 2013). The general success of CBT is supported by research finding significant reductions in the severity and prevalence of gambling habits in individuals (Dowling, Smith, & Thomas, 2006; Petry et al., 2006; Sylvain, Ladouceur, & Boisvert, 1997). Dowling and colleagues (2006) stated that 89% of the pathological gambling group no longer met the criteria for pathological gambling at the six-month mark of treatment. Gambling abstinence rates have also increased in individuals seeking treatment for pathological gambling (Petry et al., 2006).

In the absence of gambling, the individual will likely need something new to occupy their free time. Simultaneously, they will be less able to escape the psychological stress from which gambling had been a distraction. The temptation to gamble has a cyclical effect, often perpetuated by a constant attempt to regain losses (Ladouceur & Lachance, 2007). The individual may voluntarily ban themselves from casinos, but as with any addiction, the temptation remains. To aid in understanding the individual's specific factors contributing to gambling, it is highly beneficial for a therapist to directly observe an instance of gambling (Ladouceur & Lachance, 2007). If the gambler finds themselves in a situation where gambling is a great temptation, a therapist can work with the individual to develop a plan for similar triggering events. Self-reporting behavior and completing questionnaires are two ways in which an individual involved in CBT can develop increased awareness of their motivations for seeking treatment (Ladouceur & Lachance, 2007). With those who have a co-morbid addiction, the method of treating both addictions can vary. Treatment can be integrated, parallel, sequential, or singular (see Ladouceur & Lachance, 2007). Treating co-morbid conditions may help a patient avoid situations in which they are more likely to gamble. Overall, effective treatment is adjusted to the individual's risk factors and thought processes.

Treating problem gambling does not need to occur only on the individual level. Because financial and relationship issues that result from pathological gambling involve the family directly (Ladouceur & Lachance, 2007), family and close friends can benefit from receiving therapy. This can further prevent a relapse in gambling behavior by addressing enabling behaviors of those closest to the problem gambler (Petry, 2005). Educating the community has its benefits as well. In one Australian study (Victoria State Government, 2009), it was found that misconceptions about gambling were widespread throughout a community. Addressing those beliefs may influence the likelihood of individuals engaging in problem gambling. Reducing the stigma attached to gambling problems could increase the likelihood that families and at-risk groups would seek help (Victoria State Government, 2009). The perspective that gambling is an illness, and thus curable, is helpful to some families in working with a problem gambler's addiction. When the community perpetuates this point of view and treats gambling from a medical perspective, it restructures the problem as something curable and less shameful (Borch, 2012).

PHARMACOLOGICAL INTERVENTIONS

Pharmacological interventions are approaches taken by specialists to counteract the negative effects of cognitive and dopamine system deficits associated with pathological gambling. To date, there is no FDA-approved treatment for pathological gambling, although some medications may be effective in reducing symptoms (Bartley & Bloch, 2013; Grant, Odlaug, & Schreiber, 2014; Labuzek et al., 2014; Stea & Hodgins, 2011; Yip & Potenza, 2014). Pathological gambling may present together with other psychiatric diagnoses such as affective, anxiety, personality, and substance use disorders. The clinical diversity of pathological gambling patients has spurred investigators to study a wide-range of medications, including selective serotonin reuptake inhibitor (SSRI) antidepressants, atypical antipsychotics, mood stabilizers, opioid receptor antagonists, and psychostimulants (Grant et al., 2014; van den Brink, 2012). A common approach is to select one of these classes of medications based on the dominant presenting co-morbid psychiatric disorder. A limitation is that most published studies of such treatment have involved relatively small sample sizes, limited study duration, and non-representative clinical groups (Grant, Odlaug, & Schreiber, 2014). Antidepressants, atypical antipsychotics, mood stabilizers, and psychostimulants have demonstrated mixed results in controlled clinical trials—a number of studies failing to show any significant advantage over treatment of placebo. Other medications, however, such as opioid antagonists, did show promise in some clinical trials (Grant, Odlaug, & Schreiber, 2014). Thus, some medications used to treat co-morbid conditions may help with pathological gambling (Petry, 1999; Petry, 2005). Table 4 provides an overview of possible medications for problem gambling.

Medications used to treat problem gambling include opioid antagonists and antidepressants (Grant & Kim, 2006). The medications that currently show the most promise for the treatment of pathological gambling are the opioid antagonists (Grant et al., 2014; van den Brink, 2012; Yip & Potenza, 2014). Opioid receptor antagonists were originally designed to block the effects of opioids, as may be clinically valuable in the management of opioid overdose (Nguyen, Hahn, & Strakowski, 2013). The impulsive nature of problem gambling can be attributed to increased dopamine release (Kim, 1998). Opioid antagonists work to inhibit dopamine release in the body and reduce impulsivity (Grant & Kim, 2006). The prototype opioid antagonist is naloxone (Narcan®), a medication frequently used in emergency medicine. Naloxone is not practical for chronic therapy since it has a short duration of action (only up to several hours) and would thus require multiple doses throughout the day to maintain pharmacologic action. In addition, naloxone is not easily administered orally due to low absorption from the gastrointestinal tract (Syed & Keating, 2013). Naltrexone is a longer-acting opioid antagonist available in oral tablets (Revia®) and an extended-release injectable suspension (Vivitrol®) (Syed & Keating, 2013). Research has shown that opioid antagonists can block the effect of opioids, and influence the dopamine system that is involved in addiction reward behaviors. Naltrexone is FDA-approved for the treatment of alcohol dependence (Jonas et al., 2014). Multiple studies have demonstrated the efficacy of naltrexone in treating the symptoms associated with pathological gambling (Grant, Kim, & Hartman, 2008; Kim, Grant, Adson, & Shin, 2001; Toneatto, Brands, & Selby, 2009). In particular, naltrexone has been found to be effective in reducing the intensity of gambling urges and has helped to lower gambling rates (Kim, Grant,

Adson, & Shin, 2001). However, side effects of nausea, and when not taken with anti-inflammatory medications, make naltrexone difficult to use in therapy (Kim, Grant, Adson, & Remmel, 2001). A newer opioid antagonist, nalmefene, has also shown promise in the treatment of pathological gambling (Grant, Odlaug, Potenza, Hollander, & Kim, 2010; Grant et al., 2006). Nalmefene is an opioid antagonist that helps fight addictive urges that relate to gambling and other addictions (Grant et al., 2006). Use of nalmefene showed significantly positive results in reducing gambling symptoms, although the side effects were similar to those treated with naltrexone (Grant et al., 2006).

TABLE 3

Medications Used to Treat Pathological Gambling*

Class	Generic Name	Trade Name	Comments
Medications showing promise in at least one controlled clinical trial			
Opioid antagonist	Naltrexone	Revia®, Vivitrol®	Multiple clinical trials have shown benefit (Grant, Kim, & Hartman, 2008; Kim, Grant, Adson, & Shin, 2001; Toneatto et al., 2009)
Opioid antagonist	Nalmefene	Revex®	Multiple clinical trials have shown benefit (Grant et al., 2010; Grant et al., 2006)
SSRI antidepressant	Paroxetine	Paxil®	Mixed results in clinical trials (Grant et al., 2003; Kim, Grant, Adson, Shin, & Zaninelli, 2002)
SSRI antidepressant	Fluvoxamine	Luvox®	Mixed results in clinical trials (Blanco, Petkova, Ibanez, & Saiz-Ruiz, 2002; Chung et al., 2009)
Mood stabilizer	Lithium	Eskalith®, Lithobid®	Single clinical trial included subjects with bipolar disorder; results may not generalize (Hollander, Pallanti, Allen, Sood, & Baldini Rossi, 2005)
Psychostimulant	Modafanil	Provigil®	Only one known clinical trial performed so far (Zack & Poulos, 2004)
Medications studied in clinical trials but with negative results			
Antidepressant	Bupropion	Wellbutrin®	Negative results compared to placebo in a single clinical trial (Black et al., 2007)
SSRI antidepressant	Sertraline	Zoloft®	Negative results compared to placebo in a single clinical trial (Saiz-Ruiz et al., 2005)
Atypical antipsychotic	Olanzapine	Zyprexa®	Negative results compared to placebo in two clinical trials (Fong, Kalechstein, Bernhard, Rosenthal, & Rugle, 2008; McElroy, Nelson, Welge, Kaehler, & Keck, 2008)
Mood stabilizer, anti-epileptic drug	Topiramate	Topamax®	Negative results compared to placebo in single clinical trial (Dannon, Lowengrub, Gonopolski, Musin, & Kotler, 2005)

* No medications are yet FDA-approved in the United States for treatment of pathological gambling. Data in table compiled from multiple sources (Bartley & Bloch, 2013; Grant et al., 2014; Labuzek et al., 2014; Stea & Hodgins, 2011; Yip & Potenza, 2014), including the citations within the table.

Antidepressants are another widely used drug that targets the serotonin system, which is associated with impulse control (Grant & Kim, 2006). SSRI medication can treat obsessive-compulsive disorder symptoms and thus, can be used with gambling disorders (Petry, 2005). While SSRIs have not shown a consistent improvement in problem gambling symptoms, they can be effective in treating gambling if they decrease impulsivity (Blanco et al., 2009). The efficacy rate of antidepressants has fluctuated widely among studies (Grant & Kim, 2006). Antidepressants have not shown significant results in treating problem gambling unless they indirectly improved symptoms by treating co-morbid disorders (e.g., depression, anxiety) (Achab & Khazaal, 2011). Studies using fluvoxamine and paroxetine have shown inconclusive data and have failed to replicate initial positive response rates to antidepressants (Blanco, Petkova, Ibáñez, & Sáiz-Ruiz, 2002; Grant et al., 2003; Hollander et al., 2000).

Mood stabilizers similarly may show a positive effect due to improvement of co-morbid bipolar disorder symptoms (Achab & Khazaal, 2011). Carbamazepine, which is a commonly used medication for bipolar disorder, may be effective in treating problem gambling (Black et al., 2008). Similar mood stabilizing drugs may help with controlling impulses. Lithium aids in self-control and mood stability (Hollander, Pallanti, Allen, Sood, & Rossi, 2005). Antipsychotic medication may have an indirect effect of treating addictive and impulsive behaviors (Achab & Khazaal, 2011).

Overall, there is much to learn about the pharmacotherapy of pathological gambling. Based on the available evidence, opioid antagonists such as naltrexone represent first-line therapy for pathological gambling. Longer-term controlled studies that include representative populations are clearly needed. The current literature does not address the optimal duration of treatment.

TREATMENT IN CORRECTIONAL SETTINGS

Treatment approaches are utilized in a different manner inside prisons compared to normal treatment programs. Inside prisons, treatment programs are used not to treat mental disorders, but to change behavioral outcomes (Weatherly et al., 2012). Correctional settings previously used punishment in their treatment plans, but rehabilitation efforts now focus on changing behaviors and helping inmates transition back into daily life (Weatherly et al., 2012). These treatment approaches include a wide range of services, including impulse-control interventions, individual therapy, drug abuse therapy, group therapy, and self-help groups (Weatherly et al., 2012). These programs do not show uniform rates of success. There have been some positive results of change, since lower recidivism rates for those involved in prison-based treatment efforts were noted, compared to those who do not use therapy (O'Neill, MacKenzie, & Bierie, 2007). Weatherly and colleagues (2012) did not find any behavioral therapy programs aimed at treating pathological gambling or even any proposals for the creation of such programs in prison settings. Considering the high risk of gambling in prisons, the prison population may be one of the largest unaddressed problematic gambling populations.

CONCLUSION

Problem and pathological gambling are significant problems in the U.S. There are many risk factors, including proximity to a casino, ineffective coping strategies, genetic factors, impulsivity, and more. Individuals with other mental health diagnoses are at increased risk to develop a pathological gambling problem (Grant & Potenza, 2004; Petry, 2005; Raylu & Oei, 2002). Individuals who engage in problem gambling are also more likely to engage in other risky behavior, which may lead to the onset of various mental health diagnoses and involvement in the criminal justice system. The lack of treatment options for inmates experiencing gambling problems may have serious implications for inmate reintegration programs. An estimated 95% of all inmates are eventually released back into the community (Harrison & Beck, 2006). The continuation of pathological gambling habits and criminal activity to compensate for losses may increase the risk of an individual's re-arrest. With the efficacy of pathological gambling treatment programs within the community, prison treatment programs have the possibility to show similar effectiveness for inmates. Currently, there is a need for the implementation of gambling-specific treatment programs within prisons and an evaluation of the efficacy rates in the individuals treated. The difficulty with utilizing prison programs is the lack of accessibility for the inmates. The implementation of gambling courts nationwide, which would be structured similar to drug courts, would make treatment for problem gambling mandatory (Williams et al., 2005). Regardless, further research is necessary to understand the network of prison gambling and develop a suitable program.

Future research should also analyze the influence of prison settings on gambling practices. No study has managed to compare individuals entering prison with fully manifested gambling problems to individuals developing gambling problems while in prison. Current studies examine the growing trend of prison gambling by grouping both together. Screening upon incarceration may help to categorize gamblers based on whether gambling is prevalent at sentencing. This approach targets changing external factors of prisons. Weatherly and colleagues (2012) also argued that populations of inmates without prior histories of gambling could be compared, based on location. Examining the gambling development rates between these populations may give rise to specific factors that increase the risk of gambling problems, such as increased leisure time. These findings may allow prison administration to change policies to reduce prison gambling, creating less of a need for gambling treatment programs.

REFERENCES

Abbott, D. A., Cramer, S. L., & Sherrets, S. D. (1995). Pathological gambling and the family: practice implications. *Families in Society: The Journal of Contemporary Human Services, 76*(4), 213-219.

Abbott, M. W., & McKenna, B. G. (2005). Gambling and problem gambling among recently sentenced women in New Zealand prisons. *Journal of Gambling Studies, 21*(4), 559-581.

Abbott, M. W., McKenna, B. G., & Giles, L. C. (2000). *Gambling and problem gambling among recently sentenced males in four New Zealand prisons.* Wellington, New Zealand: Department of Internal Affairs.

Abbott, M. W., & Volberg, R. A. (1999). A reply to Gambino's "an epidemiologic note on verification bias: Implications for estimation of rates". *Journal of Gambling Studies, 15*(3), 233-242.

Abbott, M. W., Volberg, R. A., & Rönnberg, S. (2004). Comparing the New Zealand and Swedish national surveys of gambling and problem gambling. *Journal of Gambling Studies, 20*(3), 237-258.

Aborn, R. M., & Bennett, J. (2005). *Gambling: Who's really at risk? The connection between gambling and crime.* New York, NY: Constantine & Aborn Advisory Services.

Achab, S., & Khazaal, Y. (2011). Psychopharmacological treatment in pathological gambling: a critical review. *Current pharmaceutical design, 17*(14), 1389-1395.

Achenbach, T. M., & Rescorla, L. A. (2001). *Manual for the ASEBA school-age forms & profiles.* Burlington, VT: University of Vermont, Research Center for Children, Youth, & Families.

Adamec, C. (2011). *Pathological gambling.* New York, NY: Chelsea House.

Afifi, T.O., Brownridge, D. A., MacMillan, H., & Sareen, J. (2010). The relationship of gambling to intimate partner violence and child maltreatment in a nationally representative sample. *Journal of Psychiatric Research, 44*(5), 331-337.

American Gaming Association. (2014). Gaming revenue: 10-year trend. Retrieved from http://www.american-gaming.org/industry-resources/research/fact-sheets/gaming-revenue-10-year-trends

American Psychiatric Association. (1980). *Diagnostic and statistical manual of mental disorders (3rd ed.).* Washington, DC: American Psychiatric Association.

American Psychiatric Association. (1987). *Diagnostic and statistical manual of mental disorders (3rd ed., Revised).* Washington, DC: American Psychiatric Association.

American Psychiatric Association. (1994). *Diagnostic and statistical manual of mental disorders (4th ed.).* Washington, DC: American Psychiatric Association.

American Psychiatric Association. (2013). *Diagnostic and statistical manual of mental disorders (5th ed.).* Arlington, VA: American Psychiatric Association.

American Psychiatric Association. (2013). *Diagnostic and statistical manual of mental disorders (5th ed.).* Washington, DC: Author.

Ashley, L. L., & Boehlke, K. K. (2012). Pathological gambling: A general overview. *Journal of Psychoactive Drugs, 44*(1), 27-37.

Barnes, G. M., Welte, J. W., Hoffman, J. H., & Dintcheff, B. A. (2005). Shared predictors of youthful gambling, substance use, and delinquency. *Psychology of Addictive Behaviors, 19*(2), 165-174.

Barnes, G. M., Welte, J. W., Hoffman, J. H., & Tidwell, M. O. (2011). The co-occurrence of gambling with substance use and conduct disorders among youth in the United States. *American Journal on Addictions, 20*(2), 166-173.

Bartley, C. A., & Bloch, M. H. (2013). Meta-analysis: pharmacological treatment of pathological gambling. *Expert Review of Neurotherapeutics, 13*(8), 887-894.

Battersby, M., Tolchard, B., Scurrah, M., & Thomas, L. (2006). Suicide ideation and behavior in people with pathological gambling attending a treatment service. *International Journal of Mental Health and Addiction, 4*(3), 233-246.

Beauregard, V., & Brochu, S. (2013). Gambling in detention: A source of violence? *Deviant Behavior, 34*(5), 339-360.

Bellringer, M., Abbott, M., Coombes, R., Brown, R., McKenna, B., Dyall, L., & Rossen, F. (2009). Problem gambling—formative investigation of the links between gambling (including problem gambling) and crime in New Zealand. *Report prepared for Ministry of Health, New Zealand.*

Bergh, C., & Kühlhorn, E. (1994). Social, psychological, and physical consequences of pathological gambling in Sweden. *Journal of Gambling Studies, 10*(3), 275-285.

Berman, L. & Siegel, M-E. (1992). *Behind the 8-Ball: A Recovery Guide for the Families of Gamblers.* New York, NY: Fireside/Parkside Recovery Book.

Betancourt, L. M., Brodsky, N. L., Brown, C. A., McKenna, K. A., Gianetta, J. M., Yang, W., Romer, D., & Hurt, H. (2012). Is executive functioning associated with youth gambling? *Journal of Gambling Studies, 28*(2), 225-238.

Biddle, D., Hawthorne, G., Forbes, D., & Coman, G. (2005). Problem gambling in Australian PTSD treatment-seeking veterans. *Journal of Traumatic Stress, 18*(6), 759-767.

Black, D. W., Arndt, S., Coryell, W. H., Argo, T., Forbush, K. T., Shaw, M. C., Perry, P., & Allen, J. (2007). Bupropion in the treatment of pathological gambling: A randomized, double-blind, placebo-controlled, flexible-dose study. *Journal of Clinical Psychopharmacology, 27*(2), 143-150.

Black, D. W., Shaw, M. C., & Allen, J. (2008). Extended release carbamazepine in the treatment of pathological gambling: An open-label study. *Progress in Neuro-Psychopharmacology and Biological Psychiatry, 32*(5), 1191-1194.

Blanco, C., Hasin, D. S., Petry, N., Stinson, F. S., & Grant, B. F. (2006). Sex differences in subclinical and DSM–IV pathological gambling: Results from the National Epidemiologic Survey on Alcohol and Related Conditions. *Psychological Medicine, 36*(7), 943-953.

Blanco, C., Petkova, E., Ibáñez, A., & Sáiz-Ruiz, J. (2002). A pilot placebo-controlled study of fluvoxamine for pathological gambling. *Annals of Clinical Psychiatry, 14*(1), 9-15.

Blanco, C., Potenza, M. N., Kim, S. W., Ibáñez, A., Zaninelli, R., Saiz-Ruiz, J., & Grant, J. E. (2009). A pilot study of impulsivity and compulsivity in pathological gambling. *Psychiatry Research, 167*(1), 161-168.

Blaszczynski, A., & Farrell, E. (1998). A case series of 44 completed gambling-related suicides. *Journal of Gambling Studies, 14*(2), 93-109.

Blaszczynski, A., & Nower, L. (2002). A pathways model of problem and pathological gambling. *Addiction, 97*(5), 487-499.

Borch, A. (2012). The Real of problem gambling households. *Journal of Gambling Issues, 27*, 1-27.

Breyer, J. L., Botzet, A. M., Winters, K. C., Stinchfield, R. D., August, G., & Realmuto, G. (2009). Young adult gambling behaviors and their relationship with the persistence of ADHD. *Journal of Gambling Studies, 25*(2), 227-238.

Brown, R., Killian, E., & Evans, W. P. (2003). Familial functioning as a support system for adolescents' post-detention success. *International Journal of Offender Therapy and Comparative Criminology, 47*, 529-541.

Cheung, N. W. (2014). Low self-control and co-occurrence of gambling with substance use and delinquency among Chinese adolescents. *Journal of Gambling Studies, 30*(1), 105-124.

Cheung, N. W. (2015). Social strain, couple dynamics and gender differences in gambling problems: evidence from Chinese married couples. *Addictive Behaviors, 41*, 175-184

Chung, S. K., You, I. H., Cho, G. H., Chung, G. H., Shin, Y. C., Kim, D. J., & Choi, S. W. (2009). Changes of functional MRI findings in a patient whose pathological gambling improved with fluvoxamine. *Yonsei Medical Journal, 50*(3), 441-444.

Clark, C., & Walker, D. M. (2009). Are gamblers more likely to commit crimes? An empirical analysis of a nationally representative survey of US young adults. *International Gambling Studies, 9*(2), 119-134.

Conversano, C., Marazziti, D., Carmassi, C., Baldini, S., Barnabei, G., & Dell'Osso, L. (2012). Pathological gambling: A systematic review of biochemical, neuroimaging, and neuropsychological findings. *Harvard review of psychiatry, 20*(3), 130-148.

Cowlishaw, S., Merkouris, S., Chapman, A., & Radermacher, H. (2014). Pathological and problem gambling in substance use treatment: A systematic review and meta-analysis. *Journal of Substance Abuse Treatment, 46*(2), 98-105.

Cuadrado, M., & Lieberman, L. (2012). Use of a Short Gambling Screen with an Arrestee Population: A Feasibility Study. *Journal of Gambling Studies, 28*(2), 193-205.

Dannon, P. N., Lowengrub, K., Gonopolski, Y., Musin, E., & Kotler, M. (2005). Topiramate versus fluvoxamine in the treatment of pathological gambling: A randomized, blind-rater comparison study. *Clinical Neuropharmacology, 28*(1), 6-10.

Delfabbro, P. (2013). Problem and pathological gambling: A conceptual review. *The Journal of Gambling Business and Economics, 7*(3), 35-53.

Derevensky, J., & Gupta, R. (2004). *Gambling Problems in Youth: Theoretical and Applied Perspectives*. New York, NY: Kluwer Academic/Plenum Publishers.

Derevensky, J. L., & Gupta, R. (2006). Measuring gambling problems among adolescents: Current status and future directions. *International Gambling Studies, 6*(2), 201-215.

Desai, R. A., Desai, M. M., & Potenza, M. N. (2007). Gambling, health and age: Data from the National Epidemiologic Survey on Alcohol and Related Conditions. *Psychology of Addictive Behaviors, 21*(4), 431-440.

Desai, R. A., Maciejewski, P. K., Dausey, D. J., Caldarone, B. J., & Potenza, M. N. (2004). Health correlates of recreational gambling in older adults. *American Journal of Psychiatry, 161*(9), 1672-1679.

Dowling, N. A., Jackson, A. C., Suomi, A., Lavis, T., Thomas, S. A., Patford, J., Harvey, P., Battersby, M., Koziol-McLain, J., Abbott, M., & Bellringer, M. E. (2014). Problem gambling and family violence: Prevalence and patterns in treatment-seekers. *Addictive Behaviors, 39*(12), 1713-1717.

Dowling, N., Smith, D., & Thomas, T. (2006). Treatment of female pathological gambling: The efficacy of a cognitive-behavioral approach. *Journal of Gambling Studies, 22*(4), 355-372.

Eisen, S. A., Lin, N., Lyons, M. J., Scherrer, J. F., Griffith, K., True, W. R., Goldberg, J., & Tsuang, M. T. (1998). Familial influences on gambling behavior: An analysis of 3359 twin pairs. *Addiction, 93*(9), 1375-1384.

Erickson, L., Molina, C. A., Ladd, G. T., Pietrzak, R. H., & Petry, N. M. (2005). Problem and pathological gambling are associated with poorer mental and physical health in older adults. *International Journal of Geriatric Psychiatry, 20*(8), 754-759.

Fernández-Aranda, F., Agüera, Z., Castro, R., Jiménez-Murcia, S., Ramos-Quiroga, J. A., Bosch, R., Fagundo, A.B., Granero, R., Penelo, E., Claes, L., Sánchez, I., Riesco, N., Casas, M., & Manchon, J. M. (2013). ADHD symptomatology in eating disorders: A secondary psychopathological measure of severity? *BMC Psychiatry, 13*(1), 166.

Ferris, J. & Wynne, H. (2001). *The Canadian Problem Gambling Index: Final report.* Canadian Centre on Substance Abuse (CCSA).

Folino, J. O., & Abait, P. E. (2009). Pathological gambling and criminality. *Current Opinion in Psychiatry, 22*(5), 477-481.

Fong, T., Kalechstein, A., Bernhard, B., Rosenthal, R., & Rugle, L. (2008). A double-blind, placebo-controlled trial of olanzapine for the treatment of video poker pathological gamblers. *Pharmacology Biochemistry Behavior, 89*(3), 298-303.

Forrest, D., & McHale, I. G. (2012). Gambling and problem gambling among young adolescents in Great Britain. *Journal of Gambling Studies, 28*(4), 607-622.

Gainsbury, S. M., Russell, A., Blaszczynski, A., & Hing, N. (2015). The interaction between gambling activities and modes of access: A comparison of Internet-only, land-based only, and mixed-mode gamblers. *Addictive behaviors, 41*, 34-40.

Gebauer, L., LaBrie, R., & Shaffer, H. J. (2010). Optimizing DSM-IV-TR classification accuracy: A brief biosocial screen for detecting current gambling disorders among gamblers in the general household population. *Canadian Journal of Psychiatry, 55(2)*, 82-90.

George, S. & Murali, V. (2005). Pathological gambling: An overview of assessment and treatment. *Advancements in Psychiatric Treatment, 11*, 450-456.

Gerstein, D., Murphy, S., Toce, M., Hoffman, J., Palmer, A., Chuchro, L., & Hill, M. (1999). *Gambling Impact and Behavior Study: Report to the National Gambling Impact Study Commission.* Chicago: National Opinion Research Center.

Goodie, A., MacKillop, J., Miller, J., Fortune, E., Maples, J., Lance, C., & Campbell, W. (2013). Evaluating the South Oaks Gambling Screen with DSM-IV and DSM-5 criteria: Results from a diverse community sample of gamblers. *Assessment, 20*(5), 523-531.

Goodie, A. S., & Fortune, E. E. (2013). Measuring cognitive distortions in pathological gambling: Review and meta-analyses. *Psychology of Addictive Behaviors, 27*(3), 730-743.

Gotlib, I. H., & Hammen, C. L. (Eds.). (2002). *Handbook of depression.* New York, NY: Guilford Press.

Goudriaan, A. E., Oosterlaan, J., de Beurs, E., & van den Brink, W. (2006). Neurocognitive functions in pathological gambling: A comparison with alcohol dependence, Tourette syndrome and normal controls. *Addiction, 101*(4), 534-547.

Grant, J. E., Desai, R. A., & Potenza, M. N. (2009a). Relationship of nicotine dependence, subsyndromal and pathological gambling, and other psychiatric disorders: Data from the National Epidemiologic Survey on Alcohol and Related Conditions. *The Journal of clinical psychiatry, 70*(3), 334.

Grant, J. E., Donahue, C. B., Odlaug, B. L., Kim, S. W., Miller, M. J., & Petry, N. M. (2009b). Imaginal desensitisation plus motivational interviewing for pathological gambling: Randomised controlled trial. *The British Journal of Psychiatry, 195*(3), 266-267.

Grant, J. E., & Kim, S. W. (2006). Medication management of pathological gambling. *Minnesota Medicine, 89*(9), 44-48.

Grant, J. E., Kim, S. W., & Hartman, B. K. (2008). A double-blind, placebo-controlled study of the opiate antagonist naltrexone in the treatment of pathological gambling urges. *Journal of Clinical Psychiatry, 69*(5), 783-789.

Grant, J. E., Kim, S. W., & Odlaug, B. L. (2007). N-acetyl cysteine, a glutamate-modulating agent, in the treatment of pathological gambling: a pilot study. *Biological Psychiatry, 62*(6), 652-657.

Grant, J. E., Kim, S. W., Odlaug, B. L., Buchanan, S. N., & Potenza, M. N. (2009). Late-onset pathological gambling: clinical correlates and gender differences. *Journal of Psychiatric Research, 43*(4), 380-387.

Grant, J. E., Kim, S. W., Odlaug, B. L., & Potenza, M. N. (2008). Daily tobacco smoking in treatment-seeking pathological gamblers: Clinical correlates and co-occurring psychiatric disorders. *Journal of Addiction Medicine, 2*(4), 178-184.

Grant, J. E., Kim, S. W., Potenza, M. N., Blanco, C., Ibanez, A., Stevens, L., & Zaninelli, R. (2003). Paroxetine treatment of pathological gambling: A multi-centre randomized controlled trial. *International Clinical Psychopharmacology, 18*(4), 243-249.

Grant, J. E., Odlaug, B. L., Potenza, M. N., Hollander, E., & Kim, S. W. (2010). Nalmefene in the treatment of pathological gambling: Multicentre, double-blind, placebo-controlled study. *British Journal of Psychiatry, 197*, 330-331.

Grant, J. E., Odlaug, B. L., & Schreiber, L. R. (2014). Pharmacological treatments in pathological gambling. *British Journal of Psychiatry, 77*(2), 375-381.

Grant, J. E., & Potenza, M. N. (2004). *Pathological Gambling: A Clinical Guide to Treatment.* Arlington, VA: American Psychiatric Publishing.

Grant, J. E., Potenza, M. N., Hollander, E., Cunningham-Williams, R., Nurminen, T., Smits, G., & Kallio, A. (2006). Multicenter investigation of the opioid antagonist nalmefene in the treatment of pathological gambling. *American Journal of Psychiatry, 163*(2), 303-312.

Grant, J. E., Potenza, M. N., Weinstein, A., & Gorelick, D. A. (2010). Introduction to behavioral addictions. *The American Journal of Drug and Alcohol Abuse, 36*(5), 233-241.

Grant, J. E., & Steinberg, M. A. (2005). Compulsive sexual behavior and pathological gambling. *Sexual Addiction & Compulsivity, 12*(2-3), 235-244.

Griffiths, M. (2004). Betting your life on it: Problem gambling has clear health related consequences. *British Medical Journal, 329*, 1055-1056.

Griffiths, M. (1993). Fruit machine gambling: The importance of structural characteristics. *Journal of Gambling Studies, 9*(2), 101-120.

Griffiths, M., Parke, A., & Parke, J. (2005). Gambling related violence: An issue for the police? *The Police Journal, 78*, 223-227.

Griffiths, M., Parke, A., Wood, R., & Parke, J. (2006). Internet gambling: An overview of psychosocial impacts. *Gaming Research and Review Journal, 27*(1), 27-39.

Gupta, R., & Derevensky, J. L. (1998). Adolescent gambling behavior: A prevalence study and examination of the correlates associated with problem gambling. *Journal of Gambling Studies, 14*(4), 319-345.

Gupta, R., & Derevensky, J. L. (1997). Familial and social influences on juvenile gambling behavior. *Journal of Gambling Studies, 13*(3), 179-192.

Hardoon, K., Gupta, R., & Derevensky, J. L. (2004). Psychosocial variables associated with adolescent gambling. *Psychology of Addictive Behaviors, 18*(2), 170-179.

Hardoon, K. K., & Derevensky, J. L. (2002). Child and adolescent gambling behavior: Current knowledge. *Clinical Child Psychology and Psychiatry, 7*(2), 263-281.

Harrison, P. M., & Beck, A. J. (2006). Prison and jail inmates at midyear 2005. *NCJ, 213133.*

Hodgins, D. C., Mansley, C., & Thygesen, K. (2006). Risk factors for suicide ideation and attempts among pathological gamblers. *The American Journal on Addictions, 15*(4), 303-310.

Hollander, E., DeCaria, C. M., Finkell, J. N., Begaz, T., Wong, C. M., & Cartwright, C. (2000). A randomized double-blind fluvoxamine/placebo crossover trial in pathological gambling. *Biological Psychiatry, 47*(9), 813-817.

Hollander, E., Pallanti, S., Allen, A., Sood, E., & Rossi, N. B. (2005). Does sustained-release lithium reduce impulsive gambling and affective instability versus placebo in pathological gamblers with bipolar spectrum disorders? *American Journal of Psychiatry, 162*(1), 137-145.

Hong, S. I., Sacco, P., & Cunningham-Williams, R. M. (2009). An empirical typology of lifetime and current gambling behaviors: Association with health status of older adults. *Aging and Mental Health, 13*(2), 265-273.

Huang, J. H., Jacobs, D. F., Derevensky, J. L., Gupta, R., & Paskus, T. S. (2007). Gambling and health risk behaviors among U.S. college student-athletes: Findings from a national study. *Journal of Adolescent Health, 40*(5), 390-397.

Humphrey-Jones, H. (2009). *This must be hell: A look at pathological gambling (3rd ed.).* Bloomington, IN: iUniverse.

Ibáñez, A., Blanco, C., Moreryra, P., & Sáiz-Ruiz, J. (2003). Gender differences in pathological gambling. *Journal of Clinical Psychiatry, 64*(3), 295-301.

Jacobs, D. F. (2000). Juvenile gambling in North America: An analysis of long term trends and future prospects. *Journal of Gambling Studies, 16*(2-3), 119-152.

Jacobs, D. F. (2004). Juvenile Gambling in North America: Long term trends and future prospects. In J. L. Derevensky & R. Gupta (Eds.), *Gambling problems in youth: Theoretical and applied perspectives* (pp. 1-26). New York, NY: Kluwer Academic/Plenum Publishers.

Jacobs, D. F., Marston, A. R., Singer, R. D., Widaman, K., Little, T., & Veizades, J. (1989). Children of problem gamblers. *Journal of Gambling Behavior, 5,* 261-268.

Jimenez-Murcia, S., Stinchfield, R., Alvarez-Moya, E., Jaurrieta, N., Bueno, B., Granero, R., Aymami, M.N., Gomez-Pena, M., Gimenez-Martinez, R., Fernandez-Aranda, F., & Vallejo, J. (2009). Reliability, validity and classification accuracy of a Spanish translation of a measure of DSM-IV diagnostic criteria for pathological gambling. *Journal of Gambling Studies, 25*(1), 93-104.

Jonas, D. E., Amick, H. R., Feltner, C., Bobashev, G., Thomas, K., Wines, R., & Garbutt, J. C. (2014). Pharmacotherapy for adults with alcohol use disorders in outpatient settings: A systematic review and meta-analysis. *JAMA, 311*(18), 1889-1900.

Kausch, O. (2003). Suicide attempts among veterans seeking treatment for pathological gambling. *Journal of Clinical Psychiatry, 64*(9), 1031-1038.

Kausch, O., Rugle, L., & Rowland, D. Y. (2006). Lifetime histories of trauma among pathological gamblers. *American Journal on Addictions, 15*(1), 35-43.

Kennedy, J., Muglia, P., Jain, U., & Turner, N. (2003). Identification of genetic risk factors for pathological gambling. *Ontario Problem Gambling Research Centre.*

Kennedy, J., Turner, N., & Lobo, D. (2007). Candidate gene studies in problem gambling. *Ontario Problem gambling research Centre.*

Kessler, R. C., Hwang, I., LaBrie, R. A., Petukhova, M., Sampson, N. A., Winters, K. C., & Shaffer, H. J. (2008). DSM-IV Pathological Gambling in the National Co-morbidity Survey Replication. *Psychological Medicine, 38*(9), 1351-1360.

Kim, S. (1998). Opioid antagonists in the treatment of impulse-control disorders. *Journal of Clinical Psychiatry, 59*(4), 159-164.

Kim, S., Grant, J., Adson, D., & Remmel, R. (2001). A preliminary report on possible naltrexone and nonsteroidal analgesic interactions. *Journal of Clinical Psychopharmacology, 21*(6), 632-634.

Kim, S., Grant, J., Adson, D., & Shin, Y. (2001). Double-blind naltrexone and placebo comparison study in the treatment of pathological gambling. *Biological Psychiatry, 49*(11), 914-921.

Kim, S. W., Grant, J. E., Adson, D. E., Shin, Y. C., & Zaninelli, R. (2002). A double-blind placebo-controlled study of the efficacy and safety of paroxetine in the treatment of pathological gambling. *Journal of Clinical Psychiatry, 63*(6), 501-507.

Kim, S., Grant, J., Eckert, E., Faris, P., & Hartman, B. (2006). Pathological gambling and mood disorders: Clinical associations and treatment implications. *Journal of Affective Disorders, 92*(1), 109-116.

Knezevic, B., & Ledgerwood, D. M. (2012). Gambling severity, impulsivity, and psychopathology: Comparison of treatment- and community-recruited pathological gamblers. *The American Journal on Addictions, 21*(6), 508-515.

Korman, L. M., Collins, J., Dutton, D., Dhayananthan, B., Littman-Sharp, N., & Skinner, W. (2008). Problem gambling and intimate partner violence. *Journal of Gambling Studies, 24*(1), 13-23.

Labuzek, K., Beil, S., Beil-Gawełczyk, J., Gabryel, B., Franik, G., & Okopień, B. (2014). The latest achievements in the pharmacotherapy of gambling disorder. *Pharmacological Reports, 66*(5), 811-820.

Ladd, G. T., & Petry, N. M. (2002). Disordered gambling among university-based medical and dental patients: a focus on Internet gambling. *Psychology of Addictive Behaviors, 16*(1), 76.

Ladouceur, R. & Lachance, S. (2007). *Overcoming Pathological Gambling: Therapist Guide.* New York, NY: Oxford University Press.

Ladouceur, R., Lachance, S., & Fournier, P-M. (2009). Is control a viable goal in the treatment of pathological gambling? *Behavior Research and Therapy, 47*(3), 189-197.

Lahn, J. (2005). Gambling among offenders: Results from an Australian survey. *International Journal of Offender Therapy and Comparative Criminology, 49*(3), 343-355.

Larsen, C. V. L., Curtis, T., & Bjerregaard, P. (2013). Gambling behavior and problem gambling reflecting social transition and traumatic childhood events among Greenland Inuit: A cross-sectional study in a large indigenous population undergoing rapid change. *Journal of Gambling Studies, 29*(4), 733-748.

Ledgerwood, D. M., & Petry, N. M. (2006). Post-traumatic stress disorder symptoms in treatment-seeking pathological gamblers. *Journal of Traumatic Stress, 19*(3), 411-416.

Lesieur, H. R. (1988). Altering the DSM-III criteria for pathological gambling. *Journal of Gambling Behavior, 4,* 38-47.

Lesieur, H. R. (1992). Compulsive Gambling. *Society, 29*(4), 43-50.

Lesieur, H. R. (1994). Epidemiological surveys of pathological gambling: Critique and suggestions for modification. *Journal of Gambling Studies, 10*(4), 385-398.

Lesieur, H. R., & Blume, S. B. (1987). The South Oaks gambling screen (SOGS): A new instrument for the identification of pathological gamblers. *American Journal of Psychiatry, 144*(9), 1184-1188.

Lesieur, H. R., & Blume, S. B. (1991). Evaluation of patients treated for pathological gambling in a combined alcohol, substance abuse and pathological gambling treatment unit using the Addiction Severity Index. *British Journal of Addiction, 86*(8), 1017-1028.

Lesieur, H. R., & Rosenthal, R. J. (1991). Pathological gambling: A review of the literature (prepared for the American Psychiatric Association Task Force on DSM-IV Committee on Disorders of Impulse Control Not Elsewhere Classified). *Journal of Gambling Studies, 7*(1), 5-39.

Lesieur, H. R., & Rothschild, J. (1989). Children of Gamblers Anonymous members. *Journal of Gambling Behavior, 5*(4), 269-281.

Liao, M. S. (2008). Intimate partner violence within the Chinese community in San Francisco: Problem gambling as a risk factor. *Journal of Family Violence, 23*(8), 671-678.

Lichtenberg, P. A., Martin, F., & Anderson, C. (2009). Gambling in older adults: An emerging problem for nurses. *Journal of Addictions Nursing, 20*(3), 119-123.

Lloyd, C. D., Chadwick, N., & Serin, R. C. (2014). Associations between gambling, substance misuse and recidivism among Canadian offenders: A multifaceted exploration of poor impulse control traits and behaviors. *International Gambling Studies, 14*(2), 279-300.

Lorains, F. K., Cowlishaw, S., & Thomas, S. A. (2011). Prevalence of Co-morbid disorders in problem and pathological gambling: Systematic review and meta-analysis of population surveys. *Addiction, 106*(3), 490-498.

Lorenz, V. C., & Yaffee, R. A. (1986). Pathological gambling: Psychosomatic, emotional, and marital difficulties as reported by the Gambler. *Journal of Gambling Behavior, 2*(1), 40-49.

Lussier, I. D., Derevensky, J., Gupta, R., & Vitaro, F. (2014). Risk, compensatory, protective, and vulnerability factors related to youth gambling problems. *Psychology of Addictive Behaviors, 28*(2), 404-413.

Magoon, M. E., Gupta, R., & Derevensky, J. (2005). Juvenile delinquency and adolescent gambling: Implications for the juvenile justice system. *Criminal Justice and Behavior, 32*(6), 690-713.

Marotta, J. J. (2013). Abstinence from or management of gambling in jails and prisons? Perspectives of a field worker. *Journal of Gambling Issues, 28*, 1-3.

Martins, S. S., Lee, G. P., Kim, J. H., Letourneau, E. J., & Storr, C. L. (2014). Gambling and sexual behaviors in African-American adolescents. *Addictive Behaviors, 39*(5), 854-860.

Martins, S. S., Tavares, H., da Silva Lobo, D. S., Galetti, A. M., & Gentil, V. (2004). Pathological gambling, gender, and risk-taking behaviors. *Addictive Behaviors, 29*(6), 1231-1235.

Mathews, M., & Volberg, R. A. (2013). Impact of problem gambling on financial, emotional and social well-being of Singaporean families. *International Gambling Studies, 13*(1), 127-140.

May-Chahal, C., Wilson, A., Humphreys, L., & Anderson, J. (2012). Promoting an evidence-informed approach to addressing problem gambling in UK prison populations. *The Howard Journal of Criminal Justice, 51*(4), 372-386.

McElroy, S. L., Nelson, E. B., Welge, J. A., Kaehler, L., & Keck, P. E., Jr. (2008). Olanzapine in the treatment of pathological gambling: a negative randomized placebo-controlled trial. *Journal of Clinical Psychiatry, 69*(3), 433-440.

McEvoy, A., & Spirgen, N. (2012). Gambling among prison inmates: Patterns and implications. *Journal of Gambling Studies, 28*(1), 69-76.

McGrath, D. S., & Barrett, S. P. (2009). The co-morbidity of tobacco smoking and gambling: A review of the literature. *Drug and Alcohol Review, 28*(6), 676-681.

McMullan, J. L., & Rege, A. (2010). Online crime and internet gambling. *Journal of Gambling Issues, 24*, 54-85.

McNeilly, D. P., & Burke, W. J. (2002). Disposable time and disposable income: Problem casino gambling behaviors in older adults. *Journal of Clinical Geropsychology, 8*(2), 75-85.

Mishra, S., Lalumière, M. L., Morgan, M., & Williams, R. J. (2011). An examination of the relationship between gambling and antisocial behavior. *Journal of Gambling Studies, 27*(3), 409-426.

Momper, S. L., Delva, J., Grogan-Kaylor, A., Sanchez, N., & Volberg, R. A. (2010). The association of at-risk, problem and pathological gambling with substance use, depression, and arrest history. *Journal of Gambling Issues, 24*, 7-32.

Morasco, B. J., Pietrzak, R. H., Blanco, C., Grant, B. F., Hasin, D., & Petry, N. M. (2006). Health problems and medical utilization associated with gambling disorders: Results from the National Epidemiologic Survey on Alcohol and Related Conditions. *Psychosomatic Medicine, 68*(6), 976-984.

Muelleman, R. L., DenOtter, T., Wadman, M. C., Tran, T. P., & Anderson, J. (2002). Problem gambling in the partner of the emergency department patient as a risk factor for intimate partner violence. *The Journal of Emergency Medicine, 23*(3), 307-312.

National Research Council (1999). Pathological gambling: A critical review. Washington, DC: National Academy Press.

Neal, P., Delfabbro, P. H., & O'Neil, M. (2005). Problem gambling and harm: Towards a national definition. Melbourne, Australia: Office of Gaming and Racing, Department of Justice.

Nguyen, T. A., Hahn, J. H., & Strakowski, S. M. (2013). Pharmacotherapies for treating opioid use disorder. *CNS Spectrums, 18*(6), 289-295.

Nixon, G., Leigh, G., & Nowatzki, N. (2006). Impacting attitudes towards gambling: A prison gambling awareness and prevention program. *Journal of Gambling Issues, 17*.

Nower, L. (2003). Pathological gamblers in the workplace: A primer for employers. *Employee Assistance Quarterly, 18*(4), 55-72.

Nower, L., & Blaszczynski, A. (2004). The pathways model as harm minimization for youth gamblers in educational settings. *Child and Adolescent Social Work Journal, 21*(1), 25-45.

O'Brien, C. (2011). Addiction and dependence in DSM-V. *Addiction, 106*(5), 866-867.

Ochoa, C., Álvarez-Moya, E. M., Penelo, E., Aymami, M. N., Gómez-Peña, M., Fernández-Aranda, F., Granero, R., Vallejo-Ruiloba, J., Menchón, J. M., Lawrence, N. S., & Jiménez-Murcia, S. (2013). Decision-making deficits in pathological gambling: The role of executive functions, explicit knowledge and impulsivity in relation to decisions made under ambiguity and risk. *The American Journal on Addiction, 22*(5), 492-499.

Odlaug, B. L., Stinchfield, R., Golberstein, E., & Grant, J. E. (2013). The relationship of tobacco use with gambling problem severity and gambling treatment outcome. *Psychology of Addictive Behaviors, 27*(3), 696-704.

Oleski, J., Cox, B. J., Clara, I., & Hills, A. (2011). Pathological gambling and the structure of common mental disorders. *Journal of Nervous and Mental Disease, 199*(12), 956-960.

Oliveira, M. P., & Silva, M. T. (2001). A comparison of horse-race, bingo, and video poker gamblers in Brazilian gambling settings. *Journal of Gambling Studies, 17*(2), 137-149.

O'Neill, L, MacKenzie, D. L., & Bierie, D. M. (2007). Educational opportunities within correctional institutions: Does facility type matter? *The Prison Journal, 87*(3), 311-327.

Pallesen, S., Mitsem, M., Kvale, G., Johnsen, B. H., & Molde, H. (2005). Outcome of psychological treatments of pathological gambling: A review and meta-analysis. *Addiction, 100*(10), 1412-1422.

Parehk, R., & Morano, C. (2009). Senior gambling: risk or reward? *Journal of Gerontological Social Work, 52*(7), 686-694.

347

Perlis, R. H., Huang, J., Purcell, S., Fava, M., Rush, A. J., Sullivan, P. F., Hamilton, S.P., McMahon, F.J., Schulze, T., Potash, J.B., & Zandi, P. P. (2010). Genome-wide association study of suicide attempts in mood disorder patients. *American Journal of Psychiatry, 167*(12), 1499-1507.

Petry, N. (2005). *Pathological gambling: Etiology, co-morbidity, and treatment.* Washington, D.C.: American Psychological Association.

Petry, N. M. (2000). Gambling problems in substance abusers are associated with increased sexual risk behaviors. *Addiction, 95*(7), 1089-1100.

Petry, N. M., Ammerman, Y., Bohl, J., Doersch, A., Gay, H., Kadden, R., & Steinberg, K. (2006). Cognitive behavioral therapy for pathological gamblers. *Journal of Consulting and Clinical Psychology, 74*(3), 555-567.

Petry, N. M., & Armentano, C. (1999). Prevalence, assessment, and treatment of pathological gambling: A review. *Psychiatric Services, 50*(8), 1021-1070.

Petry, N. M., Blanco, C., Jin, C., & Grant, B. F. (2014). Concordance between gambling disorder diagnoses in the DSM–IV and DSM-5: Results From the National Epidemiological Survey of Alcohol and Related Disorders. *Psychology of Addictive Behaviors, 28*(2), 586-591.

Petry, N. M., Blanco, C., Stinchfield, R., & Volberg, R. A. (2013). An empirical evaluation of proposed changes for gambling diagnosis in the DSM-5. *Addiction, 108*(3), 575-581.

Petry, N. M., & Steinberg, K. L. (2005). Childhood maltreatment in male and female treatment-seeking pathological gamblers. *Psychology of Addictive Behaviors, 19*(2), 226-229.

Petry, N. M., Stinson, F. S., & Grant, B. F. (2005). Co-morbidity of DSM-IV pathological gambling and other psychiatric disorders: Results from the National Epidemiologic Survey on Alcohol and Related Conditions. *Journal of Clinical Psychiatry, 66*(5), 564-574.

Pietrzak, R. H., Ladd, G. T., & Petry, N. M. (2003). Disordered gambling in adolescents: Epidemiology, diagnosis, and treatment. *Pediatric Drugs, 5*(9), 583-595.

Pietrzak, R. H., & Petry, N.M. (2005). Antisocial personality disorder is associated with increased severity of gambling, medical, drug and psychiatric problems among treatment-seeking pathological gamblers. *Addiction, 100*(8), 1183-1193.

Potenza, M. N. (2008). The neurobiology of pathological gambling and drug addiction: an overview and new findings. *Philosophical Transactions of the Royal Society B: Biological Sciences, 363*(1507), 3181-3189.

Potenza, M. N., Steinberg, M. A., McLaughlin, S. D., Wu, R., Rounsaville, B. J., & O'Malley, S. S. (2001). Gender-related differences in the characteristics of problem gamblers using a gambling helpline. *American Journal of Psychiatry, 158*(9), 1500-1505.

Preston, D. L., McAvoy, S., Saunders, C., Gillam, L., Saied, A., & Turner, N. E. (2012). Problem gambling and mental health co-morbidity in Canadian federal offenders. *Criminal Justice and Behavior, 39*(10), 1373-1388.

Raylu, N. & Oei, T. P. S. (2002). Pathological gambling: A comprehensive review. *Clinical Psychology Review, 22*(7), 1009-1061.

Reid, R. C., McKittrick, H. L., Davtian, M., & Fong, T. W. (2012). Self-reported differences on measures of executive function in a patient sample of pathological gamblers. *International Journal of Neuroscience, 122*(9), 500-505.

Rockloff, M. J. (2012). Validation of the Consumption Screen for Problem Gambling (CSPG). *Journal of Gambling Studies, 28*(2), 207-216.

Saiz-Ruiz, J., Blanco, C., Ibanez, A., Masramon, X., Gomez, M. M., Madrigal, M., & Díez, T. (2005). Sertraline treatment of pathological gambling: a pilot study. *Journal of Clinical Psychiatry, 66*(1), 28-33.

Scherrer, J. F. Slutske, W. S., Xian, H., Waterman, B., Shah, K. R., Volberg, R., & Eisen, S. A. (2007). Factors associated with pathological gambling at 10-year follow-up in a national sample of middle-aged men. *Addiction, 102*(6), 970-978.

Scholes-Balog, K. E., & Hemphill, S. A. (2012). Relationships between online gambling, mental health, and substance use: A review. *Cyberpsychology, Behavior, and Social Networking, 15*(12), 688-692.

Schwer, R. K., Thompson, W. N., & Nakamuro, D. (2003, February). Beyond the limits of recreation: Social costs of gambling in southern Nevada. Paper presented at the Annual Meeting of the Far West and American Popular Culture Association, Las Vegas, Nevada.

Shaffer, H. J., & Korn, D. A. (2002). Gambling and related mental disorders: A public health analysis. *Annual Review of Public Health, 23*(1), 171-212.

Shaw, M. C., Forbush, K. T., Schlinder, J., Rosenman, E., & Black, D. W. (2007). The effect of pathological gambling on families, marriages, and children. *CNS Spectrums, 12*(8), 615-622.

Slutske, W. S., Deutsch, A. R., Richmond-Rakerd, L. S., Chernyavskiy, P., Statham, D. J., & Martin, N. G. (2014). Test of a potential causal influence of earlier age of gambling initiation on gambling involvement and disorder: A multilevel discordant twin design. *Psychology of Addictive Behaviors, 28*(4), 1177-1189.

Smith, G. J., Wynne, H. J., & Hartnagel, T. F. (2003). *Examining police records to assess gambling impacts: A study of gambling-related crime in the City of Edmonton.* Edmonton: Alberta Gaming Research Institute.

Stea, J. N., & Hodgins, D. C. (2011). A critical review of treatment approaches for gambling disorders. *Current Drug Abuse Reviews, 4*(2), 67-80.

Steel, Z., & Blaszczynski, A. (1996). The factorial structure of pathological gambling. *Journal of Gambling Studies, 12*(1), 3-20.

Steel, Z., & Blaszczynski, A. (1998). Impulsivity, personality disorders and pathological gambling severity. *Addiction, 93*(6), 895-905.

Stinchfield, R. (2000). Gambling and correlates of gambling among Minnesota public school students. *Journal of Gambling Studies, 16*(2-3), 153-173.

Stinchfield, R. (2002). Reliability, Validity, and Classification Accuracy of the South Oaks Gambling Screen (SOGS). *Addictive Behaviors, 27*, 1-19.

Stinchfield, R. (2003). Reliability, validity, and classification accuracy of a measure of DSM-IV diagnostic criteria for Pathological Gambling. *American Journal of Psychiatry, 160*, 180-182.

Stinchfield, R., Govoni, R., & Frisch, R. G. (2005). DSM-IV diagnostic criteria for pathological gambling: Reliability, validity, and classification accuracy. *American Journal on Addictions, 14*, 73-82.

Strachan, M. L., & Custer, R. L. (1993). Female compulsive gamblers in Las Vegas, In W. R. Eadington, & J. A. Cornelius (Eds.), *Gambling behavior and problem gambling* (pp. 235-238). Reno, NV: Institute for the Study of Gambling and Commercial Gaming, College of Business Administration, University of Nevada Press.

Strong, D., R., & Kahler, C. W. (2007). Evaluation of the continuum of gambling problems using the DSM-IV. *Addiction, 102*, 713-721.

Subramaniam, M., Wang, P., Soh, P., Vaingankar, J. A., Chong, S. A., Browning, C. J., & Thomas, S. A. (2015). Prevalence and determinants of gambling disorder among older adults: A systematic review. *Addictive behaviors, 41*, 199-209.

Sullivan, S. (1994). Pathological gambling: Psychiatry series. *Patient Management*, 79-85.

Sullivan, S., Brown, R., & Skinner, B. (2008). Pathological and sub-clinical problem gambling in a New Zealand prison: A comparison of the eight and SOGS gambling screens. *International Journal of Mental Health Addiction, 6*(3), 369-377.

Suomi, A., Dowling, N. A., & Jackson, A. C. (2014). Problem gambling subtypes based on psychological distress, alcohol abuse and impulsivity. *Addictive Behaviors, 39*(12), 1741-1745.

Syed, Y. Y., & Keating, G. M. (2013). Extended-release intramuscular naltrexone (VIVITROL(R)): A review of its use in the prevention of relapse to opioid dependence in detoxified patients. *CNS Drugs, 27*(10), 851-861.

Sylvain, C., Ladouceur, R., & Boisvert, J. M. (1997). Cognitive and behavioral treatment of pathological gambling: A controlled study. *Journal of Consulting and Clinical Psychology, 65*(5), 727-732.

Tavares, H., Martins, S. S., Lobo, D. S., Silveira, C. M., Gentil, V., & Hodgins, D. C. (2003). Factors at play in faster progression for female pathological gamblers: An exploratory analysis. *Journal of Clinical Psychiatry, 64*(4), 433-438.

Thomas, S. A., & Jackson, A. C. (2008). *Risk and Protective Factors, Depression and Co-morbidities in Problem Gambling: A Report to Beyond Blue.* Problem Gambling Research and Treatment Centre: Monash University and University of Melbourne.

Toneatto, T., Brands, B., & Selby, P. (2009). A randomized, double-blind, placebo-controlled trial of naltrexone in the treatment of concurrent alcohol use disorder and pathological gambling. *The American Journal on Addictions, 18*(3), 219-225.

Turner, N. E., & McAvoy, S. (2011). Problem gambling in the correctional system: A brief summary report. *Gaming Law Review and Economics, 15*(10), 593-598.

Turner, N. E., Preston, D. L., Saunders, C., McAvoy, S., & Jain, U. (2009). The relationship of problem gambling to criminal behavior in a sample of Canadian male federal offenders. *Journal of Gambling Studies, 25*(2), 153-169.

Unwin, B. K., Davis, M. K., & Leeuw, J. B. (2000). Pathological gambling. *American Family Physician, 61*(3), 741-749.

van den Brink, W. (2012). Evidence-based pharmacological treatment of substance use disorders and pathological gambling. *Current Drug Abuse Reviews, 5*(1), 3-31.

Victoria State Government. (2009). *A guide to using a health promotion approach to problem gambling.* Retrieved from gamblinghelponline.org.au

Visher, C., Debus, S., & Yahner, J. (2008). *Employment after prison: A longitudinal study of releases in three states.* Urban Institute Justice Policy Center. Retrieved from http://www.urban.org/publications/411778.html

Volberg, R. A., Gupta, R., Griffiths, M. D., Ólasson, D. T., & Delfabbro, P. (2010). An international perspective on youth gambling prevalence studies. *International Journal of Adolescent Medicine and Health, 22*(1), 3-38.

Volberg, R. A., Nysse-Carris, K. L., & Gerstein, D. R. (2006). *2006 California Problem Gambling Prevalence Survey.* Sacramento, CA: California Department of Alcohol and Drug Programs, Office of Problem Gambling.

Volberg, R.A., & Wray, M. (2007). Legal gambling and problem gambling as mechanisms of social domination? Some considerations for future research. *American Behavioral Scientist, 51*(1), 56-85.

Walsh, K., & Alexander, G. (2000). Alcoholic liver disease. *Postgraduate Medical Journal, 76*(895), 280-286.

Wardle, H., Moody, A., Griffiths, M., Orford, J., & Volberg, R. (2011). Defining the online gambler and patterns of behavior integration: Evidence from the British Gambling Prevalence Survey 2010. *International Gambling Studies, 11*(3), 339-356.

Weatherly, J. N., Montes, K. S., Peters, D., & Wilson, A. (2012). Gambling behind the walls: A behavior-analytic perspective. *The Behavior Analyst Today, 13*(3-4), 2-8.

Welte, J. W., Barnes, G. M., Tidwell, M. C., & Hoffman, J. H. (2008). The prevalence of problem gambling among U.S. adolescents and young adults: Results from a national survey. *Journal of Gambling Studies, 24*(2), 119-133.

Welte, J. W., Barnes, G. M., Tidwell, M. C., & Hoffman, J. H. (2009a). The association of form of gambling with problem gambling among American youth. *Psychology of Addictive Behaviors, 23*(1), 105-112.

Welte, J. W., Barnes, G. M., Tidwell, M. C., & Hoffman, J. H. (2009b). Association between problem gambling and conduct disorder in a national survey of adolescents and young adults in the United States. *Journal of Adolescent Health, 45*(4), 396-401.

Welte, J., Barnes, G., Wieczorek, W., Tidwell, M. C., & Parker, J. (2001). Alcohol and gambling pathology among U.S. adults: prevalence, demographic patterns and co-morbidity. *Journal of Studies on Alcohol, 62*(5), 706-712.

Welte, J. W., Wieczorek, W. F., Barnes, G. M., Tidwell, M. C., & Hoffman, J. H. (2004). The relationship of ecological and geographic factors to gambling behavior and pathology. *Journal of Gambling Studies, 20*(4), 405-423.

Westphal, J. R., Rush, J. A., Stevens, L., & Johnson, L. J. (2000). Gambling behavior of Louisiana students in grades 6 through 12. *Psychiatric Services, 51*(1), 96-99.

Williams, D. J. (2008). Offender gambling in prisons and jails: Is it hidden leisure experience? *The Correctional Psychologist, 40*(3), 7-10.

Williams, D. J. (2013). Gambling in jails and prisons: Abstinence or management? *Journal of Gambling Issues, 28*, 1-4.

Williams, D. J., & Walker, G. J. (2009). Does offender gambling on the inside continue on the outside? Insights from correctional professionals on gambling and re-entry. *Journal of Offender Rehabilitation, 48*, 402-415.

Williams, R. J., Royston, J., & Hagen, B. F. (2005). Gambling and problem gambling within forensic populations: A review of the literature. *Criminal Justice and Behavior, 32*(6), 665-689.

Williams, R. J., & Wood, R. T. (2004). Final report: *The demographic sources of Ontario gaming revenue.* Ontario, Canada: Ontario Problem Gambling Research Centre.

Winters, K. C., Stinchfield, R. D., Botzet, A., & Anderson, N. (2002). A Prospective Study of Youth Gambling Behaviors. *Psychology of Addictive Behaviors, 16*(1), 3-9.

Wong, P. W., Kwok, N. C., Tang, J. Y., Blaszczynski, A., & Tse, S. (2014). Suicidal ideation and familicidal-suicidal ideation among individuals presenting to problem gambling services: A retrospective data analysis. *Crisis: The Journal of Crisis Intervention and Suicide Prevention, 35*(4), 219-232.

Xian, H., Shah, K. R., Phillips, S. M., Scherrer, J. F., Volberg, R., & Eisen, S. A. (2008). Association of cognitive distortions with problem and pathological gambling in adult male twins. *Psychiatry Research, 160*(3), 300-307.

Yi, S. (2012). Shame-prone gamblers and their coping with gambling loss. *Journal of Gambling Issues, 27*, 2-21.

Yip, S. W., Desai, R. A., Steinberg, M. A., Rugle, L., Cavallo, D. A., Krishnan-Sarin, S., & Potenza, M. N. (2011). Health/functioning characteristics, gambling behaviors, and gambling-related motivations in adolescents stratified by gambling problem severity: Findings from a high school survey. *The American Journal on Addictions, 20*(6), 495-508.

Yip, S. W., & Potenza, M. N. (2014). Treatment of Gambling Disorders. *Current Treatment Options in Psychiatry, 1*(2), 189-203.

Zack, M., & Poulos, C. X. (2004). Amphetamine primes motivation to gamble and gambling-related semantic networks in problem gamblers. *Neuropsychopharmacology, 29*(1), 195-207.

Zimmerman, M., Chelminski, I., & Young, D. (2006). Prevalence and diagnostic correlates of DSM-IV pathological gambling in psychiatric outpatients. *Journal of Gambling Studies, 22*(2), 255-262.

Zuckerman, M., & Kuhlman, D. M. (2000). Personality and risk-taking: Common biosocial factors. *Journal of Personality, 68*(6), 999-1029.

Zurhold, H., Verthein, U., & Kalke, J. (2014). Prevalence of problem gambling among the prison population in Hamburg, Germany. *Journal of Gambling Studies, 30*(2), 309-319.

CHAPTER 16

PROBLEM-SOLVING COURTS: AN OVERVIEW

ALLISON KREHBIEL & JOSEPH H. METZEN

CHAPTER OVERVIEW

The criminal justice system's approach to crime has traditionally been to arrest, prosecute, and incarcerate. However, the past two decades have seen the rise of a different criminal justice model: one that seeks to address the problems underlying the criminal behavior. The core of this alternative model is the problem-solving court, in particular the drug court. This chapter will review (1) the origin and history of problem-solving courts; (2) philosophy and principles behind problem-solving courts; (3) chemical dependency and treatment; (4) models of drug courts; (5) operations of a typical drug court; (6) the effectiveness of drug courts; and (7) other kinds of problem-solving courts. The primary goal of this chapter is to educate and inform the reader about the principles and operations of problem-solving courts as alternatives to incarceration.

INTRODUCTION

It is a routine Tuesday morning in a courtroom in Nicollet County, Minnesota. The judge sits on the bench, a stack of court files piled next to her, and peers down over defendants, all dressed in faded orange jumpers, their legs shackled and their heads down. This could be a courtroom in any community in America; in the United States, many people are under the supervision of the criminal justice system in some form or another. According to recent estimates, over 2 million Americans are incarcerated, 4.1 million are on probation, and 700,000 are on parole (Glaze & Palla, 2005). As the judge begins to call the calendar, she, like every other trial court judge in the nation, knows that most of these people have something in common: they likely have a substance use disorder. Of the nearly 7 million Americans in prison, on parole, or on probation, 80% are using drugs or alcohol regularly, have been convicted of an alcohol or other drug violation, were under the influence of alcohol or other drugs at the time of their crime, or committed a crime to support their drug use (Hora & Stalcup, 2008). In fact, as many as 53% of incarcerated populations meet the criteria for drug abuse or dependence, compared with an estimated 13% of men and 5.5% of women in community populations aged 18 or older (Belenko, Hiller, & Hamilton, 2013). Even among those individuals on probation and thus subject to strict community supervision, the rate of illicit drug use was over 26% percent (Hora & Stalcup, 2008).

Moreover, even for defendants who serve their time or successfully complete probation, recidivism is likely. Nearly 70% of all drug offenders are rearrested within three years of release from incarceration, and roughly 41% are rearrested for a specific drug offense (Hora & Stalcup, 2008). When individuals are treated for their substance abuse issues, the evidence indicates that they are less likely to engage in criminal behavior.

WHY PROBLEM-SOLVING COURTS WERE DEVELOPED

On this Tuesday morning, the judge recognizes several of the defendants appearing before her. George was here three weeks ago, and she had released him on condition that he abstain from the use of mood-altering substances. His probation agent subsequently filed a violation report, alleging that George had tested positive for methamphetamine. With three prior drug-related convictions on his record, there was little deliberation involved in the judge's decision to remand George back into custody. However, the judge, like other criminal justice professionals in Nicollet County and their counterparts in hundreds of other jurisdictions in the country, recognized the prominent role that substance abuse plays in the etiology of crime and looked for a different solution.

Criminal justice professionals have known, through decades of experience, that following the traditional criminal justice system process only leads to a "revolving door" of arrest, incarceration, and re-arrest for chemically dependent defendants. Clearly, offenders who are addicted to any substance have serious difficulty avoiding the legal consequences of their addiction without external intervention. An alternative approach to intervention, emphasizing treatment, is needed in these cases. Longitudinal studies have consistently documented the effectiveness of treatment in reducing criminal recidivism and substance abuse (National Institute for Justice, 1995). The birth of drug courts was the result of an understanding that treatment, along with continued court supervision, could increase the success for criminal defendants.

THE DEVELOPMENT AND GROWTH OF DRUG COURTS IN THE U.S.A.

The first adult drug treatment court was established in Miami, Florida, in 1989 (Hora & Stalcup, 2008). Another one was founded shortly thereafter in Portland, Oregon. Since then, the number of drug courts has continued to grow throughout the entire nation. As of 2012, there were over 2,350 drug courts in the United States (Contrino, Nochajski, Farrell, & Logsdon, 2016; Kaiser & Holtfreter, 2016). That represented a 40% increase over the previous five years. Of these drug courts, approximately 54% are adult drug courts, 19% are juvenile drug courts, 13% are family dependency treatment courts, and 7% are DWI courts. It is estimated that by December 31, 2008, approximately 116,300 people had participated in drug courts throughout the U.S. (Huddleston & Marlowe, 2011).

Essential to the drug court model is the acknowledgment that chemical dependency/addiction is a disease, rather than simply a set of irresponsible behaviors or poor decisions made by an individual. Rather than an individual choosing to repeatedly and intentionally ignore societal norms regarding acceptable substance use, the modern approach views addiction as a disease of the pleasure-producing chemistry of the brain (Charland, 2002; Leshner, 1999). Addictive drugs have a specific effect on the brain structure involved in the control of motivation and learned behaviors (McLellan, Lewis, O'Brien, & Kleber, 2000). When the areas of the brain responsible for decision-making and weighing consequences in terms of pleasure and punishment are impaired or damaged, the brain becomes more stimulus-driven; addicts no longer consider the consequences of their actions—instead, they respond almost instinctively to the drive to remain stimulated and artificially rewarded. Drugs also have marked effects on the brain's dopamine system. Addictive substances such as cocaine, opiates, and methamphetamine stimulate the reward circuitry of the brain far more than what naturally pleasurable activity would produce, leading to an urgent and intense desire to continue drug use. Permanent pathophysiological changes in the brain's reward circuitry (baseline levels of many neurotransmitters) and stress response system may persist, depending on dosage, frequency, and chronicity of the chemical use. In one study, such brain alterations persisted for 10 years after sobriety (Goldstein & Volkow, 2002). Studies of twins demonstrate a genetic component to addiction that makes some individuals more vulnerable to becoming addicts than others (Kendler & Prescott, 1998; Lal, Deb, & Kedia, 2015). The disease model is thus well-founded and well-settled. However, society and people working in the criminal justice system often fail to recognize this fact. Historically, defendants like George, who was back in court facing charges of continued drug use while on probation, were seen as weak individuals who chose to use drugs, despite the fact that their drug use left them sick and living on the periphery of mainstream society.

Co-Occurring Disorders

As drug courts across the country were developed, the needs of individual defendants became more apparent. It became obvious that many criminal defendants were arriving in court only after a lengthy history of dysfunction. A substantial number were living with undiagnosed mental illness or severe emotional issues. In those cases, substance abuse was used as a method of self-medication to deal with other underlying mental health conditions. It is estimated that 10%-15% of the population involved in the criminal justice system have mental health disorders (Peters & Hills, 1997). An estimated one-third of drug court participants have co-occurring disorders, the presence of which increases the risk of arrest. Furthermore, once arrested, individuals with co-occurring disorders are more likely to be incarcerated and to remain in jail significantly longer than neurotypical offenders. Moreover, offenders with co-occurring disorders are much more likely to cycle rapidly between the criminal justice system and other social service systems. Historically, offenders suffering from co-occurring disorders have not fared well in traditional substance abuse or mental health services. For these individuals to be successful, specialized treatment and supervision approaches are necessary (Peters, 2008). Drug courts recognize that psychiatric and/or psychological treatment must be incorporated into the individuals' overall drug court plans to increase the likelihood of success.

Treatment

Drug courts recognize the necessity of long-term treatment to address addiction. Length of time in treatment is important to the length of sobriety, and drug courts work to ensure that participants spend a significant amount of time in treatment. For an addict, long-term use results in a constant urge to use a mood-altering substance. Therefore, participation in a comprehensive treatment program is an important part of recovery. National Institute of Health studies have found that drug abuse is reduced by up to 60% with treatment (Hora & Stalcup, 2008). In treatment, individuals are encouraged to accept responsibility for behavior that not only has a detrimental impact on their life, but also adversely affects the lives of family and friends. The emotional struggles, coupled with an effort to maintain a chemical-free lifestyle, can make completing a comprehensive treatment program extremely difficult. However, because participants have intensive and frequent contact with the drug court team, drug courts substantially increase the retention rate of the participants. The Drug Abuse Outcome Study showed that half of those who checked into an outpatient treatment program on a voluntary basis stayed less than three months (Belenko, 1999). Addicts referred to treatment by the criminal justice system are more likely to complete treatment and are less likely to leave against medical advice than those patients who are not mandated into treatment (Hora & Stalcup, 2008). Knowing that completion of treatment is a requirement of the drug court program, as well as knowing that an unsuccessful treatment experience will likely result in immediate incarceration, gives drug court participants an incentive to engage in their treatment experience. The benefits of successful completion of treatment are not limited to the addict. Society also reaps rewards because individuals who are in recovery no longer need to engage in criminal activity to support their drug habits, and the community is a safer place. Individuals who misuse chemicals at times resort to violence to obtain money for future drug use. (Miller, Levy, & Cohen, 2006). Treating addicts is thus an investment in public safety.

Drug court participants are involved in recovery support groups and treatment programs for an extended period. Research indicates that the longer people stay in treatment, the lower the likelihood of recidivism (Belenko, 1999; Middleton, 2015). A national study showed that in the first year following graduation from drug court, approximately 85% of offenders did not have new arrests. Nearly 73% of graduates will not have a new arrest two years after graduation (Roman, Townsend, & Singh Bhati, 2003). Drug court participants who successfully complete long-term treatment programs and adhere to the other requirements of the drug court program begin to realize the benefits of their sobriety. Steady employment or education, repaired relationships, and a network of sober-support systems increase individual self-esteem and empower individuals to look forward to a life outside the criminal justice system.

EVIDENCE-BASED COURTS

Drug courts and other problem-solving courts are often referred to as evidence-based courts. The U.S. Department of Justice Office of Justice Programs (OJP), which plays a significant role in funding and assisting problem-solving court programs in the nation, places strong emphasis on the use of data and evidence in policy-making and program development in criminal justice. The OJP considers programs and practices to be evidence-based when their effectiveness has been demonstrated by causal evidence, generally obtained through one or more outcome evaluations. Causal evidence documents a relationship between an activity or intervention (including technology) and its intended outcome, including measuring the direction and size of a change and the extent to which a change may be attributed to the activity or intervention (National Institute for Justice, n.d.). Causal evidence depends on the use of scientific methods to rule out, to the extent possible, alternative explanations for the documented change (Flies-Away, Garrow, & Sekaquaptewa, 2014). To graduate successful participants, drug courts and other problem-solving courts carefully evaluate the effectiveness of their programs. Monitoring the recidivism rates, relapses, and general well-being of their participants over set periods guarantees the success of a drug court program.

DRUG COURT ESSENCE

Drug courts are rooted in the theory of therapeutic jurisprudence (Berman & Feinblatt, 2001; Boldt, 2014). The central premise of therapeutic jurisprudence is that interactions with the justice system have an impact on individuals' psychological well-being and that the system should be designed to minimize psychological harm and maximize benefit to the extent possible (Lucas & Hanrahn, 2016; Wexler & Winick, 1996). In the past, the court experience for defendants like George ultimately resulted in repeated incarceration and lengthy probation periods. Relying on evidence-based results, drug courts seek to offer participants one intensive, extended, and transformative interaction with the criminal justice system instead of a lifetime of repeated, brief, and ineffectual encounters (Holland, 2010).

Therapeutic jurisprudence has been described as the study of the law as a healing agent: a lens that focuses on the law's impact on emotional and psychological well-being, through which it is possible to view not only the law but also the role and behavior of legal actors (Berman & Feinblatt, 2001; Boldt, 2014; Lucas & Hanrahn, 2016). It proposes to apply the tools of the behavioral sciences to the law, to create tangible, positive change; to promote the well-being of all court actors; and to make the justice system more relevant and effective for those involved. A therapeutic or problem-solving approach to justice addresses issues (like addiction, poverty, impaired emotional or anger-management skills, low literacy, mental illness, or abuse) that underlie human causes of crime and criminal behavior (Goldberg, 2005). By focusing on the causes of criminal behavior, a therapeutic justice approach addresses the "revolving door" system that simply recycles repeat offenders through the criminal justice system.

Unlike the majority of criminal courts in the United States, drug courts recognize the need for a specialized docket, one that is specifically designated and staffed to handle cases involving non-violent, substance-abusing offenders through an intensive, judicially monitored program of drug treatment and rehabilitative services (Berman & Feinblatt, 2001; Contrino, Nochajski, Farrell, & Logsdon, 2016; Fulkerson, Keena, & O'Brien, 2012; Kaiser & Holtfreter, 2016; Lucas & Hanrahan, 2016; Mackinem & Higgins, 2009). Rather than focusing solely on punishment, as the traditional criminal court docket does, drug court judges focus on issues usually not considered by traditional trial court judges. Addressing the conditions underpinning criminal behavior, such as addiction, relationship problems, lack of job skills or stable housing, cognitive impairments and mental health needs, becomes the focus of every court hearing (Minnesota Judicial Branch, 2007). The central principles around which drug courts are constructed are often referred to as "The 10 Key Components." Adherence to these components is essential if a drug court is to be successful (Bureau of Justice Assistance, *Defining Drug Courts: The Key Components,* 2004):

1. Drug courts integrate alcohol and other drug treatment services with justice system case processing.
2. A non-adversarial approach is used; prosecution and defense counsel promote public safety while protecting participants' due process rights.
3. Eligible participants are identified early and are promptly placed in the drug court program.
4. Drug courts provide access to a continuum of alcohol, drug, and other related treatment and rehabilitation services.
5. Abstinence is monitored by frequent alcohol and another drug testing.
6. A coordinated strategy governs drug court responses to participants' compliance.
7. Ongoing judicial interaction with each drug court participant is essential.
8. Monitoring and evaluation measure the achievement of program goals and gauge effectiveness.
9. Continuing interdisciplinary education promotes effective drug court planning, implementation, and operations.
10. Forging partnerships among drug courts, public agencies, and community-based organizations generates local support and enhances drug court program effectiveness.

In a traditional criminal hearing, an adversarial approach is taken by both the prosecution and the defense. If a criminal defendant opts to participate in drug court, the adversarial approach is suspended, and the drug court focuses on the participant's recovery and law-abiding behavior (Hora & Stalcup, 2008). Both the prosecution and the defense share a common goal of successfully addressing the cause of the offender's behaviors—addiction—rather than focusing on the criminal act. In today's criminal justice system, resolution of cases moving through the traditional criminal justice system takes months, sometimes years. Drug courts strive to identify eligible participants as early as possible, to ensure their prompt placement into the drug court and the commencement of treatment (Bureau of Justice, 1997). To ensure that participants remain abstinent, frequent alcohol and other drug testing are performed, and violations are met with swift and individualized sanctions. Likewise, abstinence and other sober behaviors are recognized, and incentives are awarded to those participants who demonstrate a commitment to the program. The prosecution and the defense join efforts to ensure the move of criminal defendants out of the criminal justice system. This approach allows prosecutors to successfully promote public safety, while the criminal defense attorneys successfully maneuver a client away from the criminal justice system.

DISPOSITIONAL MODELS

The concept that a criminal court might encompass a therapeutic approach was a controversial topic among criminal justice professionals. Prosecutors, law enforcement agencies, and criminal defense attorneys are required to find common ground on which all players have equal footing. Thus, three general dispositional models of drug courts were developed to satisfy the concerns of all those players. Some courts utilize a pre-plea program, some utilize post-plea programs, and some operate a hybrid program.

In a pre-plea program, participants enter the program as part of a diversion agreement, with the understanding that the charge(s) against the participant will be dismissed upon successful completion of the program. Because the participant never formally enters a guilty plea, successful completion of the drug court program means that a formal conviction is never entered. If, on the other hand, the participant is unsuccessful, the case resumes in the traditional criminal justice system. This model was most common from the inception of drug courts until approximately the mid-1990s. For the prosecution, a pre-plea model offers the advantage of faster case processing, because the hearings and discovery may be reduced. On the other hand, the pre-plea model carried the risks of witnesses' memories fading and other evidence being no longer accessible if a participant is unsuccessfully terminated from the program (Huddleston & Marlowe, 2011). For the criminal defendant, the pre-plea model offers a chance to avoid a felony conviction and its consequences. However, when cases involve serious felony offenses, not all agencies involved in the criminal justice system are comfortable with the pre-plea model.

When an individual is charged with a serious felony offense, prosecutors and law enforcement alike can be hesitant to agree to a possible dismissal of charges. Because public safety is served when an individual's criminal history is available to the public, a conviction, or at least a record of arrest and subsequent charges, is appropriate in some cases. This concern resulted in the post-plea drug court model. As its name implies, a post-plea program requires the participant to enter a plea of guilty to the charge(s) or to stipulate to the allegations in the criminal complaint as a condition of entry. There are two sub-types of the post-plea programs. In post-plea/pre-adjudication programs, the guilty plea or stipulated agreement is held in abeyance and is vacated or withdrawn upon successful completion of the program. In a post-plea/post-adjudication program (also called term of probation program), a conviction is entered and recorded; however, participants can avoid incarceration or reduce probation obligations. The post-plea paradigm has been the most common, with approximately 58% of drug courts using this model as of December 31, 2009. A perceived advantage of post-plea models is that they provide coercive advantage over the participants, to keep them engaged in treatment and to continue to work the program. The post-plea model also eliminates the risk of the case going "cold" and the state having to try the matter with deficient evidence if a participant is terminated after a significant period (Huddleston & Marlowe, 2011).

The hybrid program is a combination of the pre-plea and post-plea models. As drug courts matured, the professionals involved in the process moved toward an individualized version, where participants are selected on a case-by-case basis. In other words, as a drug court team matures, its understanding of the ramifications of addiction increases the likelihood that plea agreements, including both dismissals and downward departure from required prison sentences, will be contemplated by the team.

THE DRUG COURT TEAM

George is charged with First Degree Burglary. He stands before the court, his head lowered. When the judge asks if he understands his rights and the charges that the State has brought against him, he slowly nods. George has four prior felony charges and an array of misdemeanor convictions for alcohol-related offenses.

The judge considers her options. George's continued use of drugs is concerning, as is his inability, or unwillingness, to comply with direct court orders. In a traditional court setting, to aid in her decision, the judge must rely on a report from the probation officer. The report is based on a short interview with George and a few collateral contacts. The defense attorney will argue that his client deserves another chance, and the prosecutor will counter that George has already been given too many chances. If George is referred to drug court, by contrast, far more information about George will be available to the judge.

In drug court, a judge serves as the leader and ultimate decision-maker of an inter-disciplinary team of professionals, all of whom have some pertinent and first-hand knowledge of each drug court participant. In addition to the judge, the team typically includes a prosecutor, a defense attorney, a law enforcement officer, a probation agent, a social services case manager, a treatment provider, and a court administrator. Staffings (i.e., meetings of the entire team) and court hearings occur on a frequent basis—typically weekly. The drug court team meets prior to each session of drug court and acts as a multi-disciplinary case manager with respect to the individual drug court participants (Minnesota Judicial Branch, 2007). Typically, the drug court team discusses each client and his or her situation and reaches a consensus about an appropriate consequence, whether positive or negative, for the various participants at the staffing (Huddleston & Marlowe, 2011). The various team members contribute the information they have about the participants and offer recommendations from the perspective of their respective disciplines. For example, law enforcement officers typically ensure that participants are abiding by a set curfew by visiting their homes. Officers are therefore able to relay information to the team. This information might include who was present at a participant's home on the day of their visit. Likewise, a therapist working with the individual participant may inform the judge that the client is experiencing a high level of anxiety or is battling serious depression. The treatment provider will report on an individual's progress in his or her treatment program. The drug court judge, armed with this additional knowledge, is better equipped to interact positively and productively with each participant in open court. In this manner, sanctions for non-compliance, as well as incentives recognizing the hard work of the participant, are meted out in a timely and fair manner (Huddleston & Marlowe, 2011). All team members work cooperatively with a single goal in mind: to reduce the participant's susceptibility to becoming involved in further criminal activities by treating his/her substance use disorder, typically known by the multidisciplinary team to be a disease (Hora & Stalcup, 2008). The focus of the whole team is to return participants to society as productive, sober members. The primary goal is to find solutions mutually beneficial to the participant, his or her family, the wider community, and any victims (Simon, 2003).

Because of the comprehensive efforts of the members of a drug court team, hearings scheduled during drug court offer the Nicollet County judge a reprieve from her normal, busy schedule. During a traditional court calendar, the judge can spend approximately five minutes on each case, hardly enough to dispense fairness and justice. However, in the drug court setting, the judge becomes more than the neutral, impersonal administrator of justice. The weekly, personalized contact with each participant results in the judge learning about the individuals standing before her. If George is admitted into drug court, the judge will learn more about his personal circumstances so she can form an opinion based on a complete person. The type of information she might need to know could include the name of his partner, the names and ages of his children, and whether he completed high school. She will know how long he has used chemicals, whether he has housing, whether he is in a relationship, and whether he is complying with the requirements of drug court. The drug court becomes an extension of treatment, while simultaneously maintaining the ultimate power it historically enjoyed in the traditional system.

Drug Court Eligibility

Adult drug courts were created to serve drug-dependent offenders who did not respond to existing correctional programs—those not adhering to standard probation, who were being rearrested for new offenses shortly after release from incarceration, and those who were repeatedly returning to court on new charges or technical violations. Drug courts most effectively focus their efforts on "high-risk/high-need" offenders: individuals who are (1) substance dependent and (2) at risk of failing in less-intensive rehabilitation programs. Drug courts that focus their efforts on these individuals reduce crime approximately twice as much as those serving less-serious offenders. Further, they return approximately 50% greater cost-benefits to the participants' communities (Marlowe, 2012).

Drug court is fundamentally designed to serve addicts who commit crimes due to their addiction; it is not meant for criminals who also happen to be addicts or users. The target population of one drug court in south-central Minnesota is adult, non-violent, felony-level offenders who have been diagnosed as chemically dependent or chemically abusive, and who appear at medium to high risk of re-offending. Typically, participants are required to be a resident of a county served by the drug court. Violent offenders are commonly disqualified, due to provisions in federal law regarding grants to drug court programs (Minnesota Judicial Branch, 2007).

Participants volunteer to be part of these programs. No one can be forced to participate in drug court. In addition to the prospect of treatment, the participants are generally presented with an incentive such as a lesser sentence, preventing incarceration, avoiding a conviction or adjudication, or being reunited with children pursuant to supervision (Minnesota Judicial Branch, 2007). For George, acceptance into the drug court means he will avoid lengthy incarceration in a state correctional facility and may be able to re-establish relationships with his family. Once individuals like George agree to participate in a drug court program, the modality of "coerced treatment" and accountability begins (Minnesota Judicial Branch, 2007).

MULTI-PHASE PROCESS

Drug courts employ a multi-phased treatment and recovery process. For example, one program in south-central Minnesota makes use of a 4-phase program that includes graduation and aftercare (Minnesota Judicial Branch, 2007). Each phase has a prescribed amount of time, and participants move through the phases based on successful completion of the requirements and his or her individual needs. The first phase of any drug court program will utilize a multitude of methods aimed at keeping participants free from alcohol and drugs. House arrest (i.e., requiring that an individual remain at home unless at work or in treatment), GPS monitoring, and even frequent law enforcement visits may be required. As the participant progresses through the program, the amount of court supervision slowly decreases. Similarly, treatment plans may be revised/updated as the participant's needs evolve. If a participant is non-compliant during later phases of the program, their supervision requirements may be increased and/or the participant may be moved back a phase. Each phase consists of specific treatment objectives, therapeutic and rehabilitative activities, and specific requirements for advancement into the next phase. Program components include supervision contacts, court appearances, treatment, support group attendance, sobriety, and chemical testing. They can also include education and/or work requirements, such as completing a GED, participating in vocational training or searching for employment. Supervision contacts refer to how often a participant must report to a probation officer or other personnel (including a law enforcement officer). Contact is usually three times per week in early phases and decreases with phase advancement. Often, contact occurs when a participant least expects it (e.g., at home or a workplace). Participants in early phases typically appear in court every week. As participants progress through the program, their required court appearances decrease, and they will report twice each month and once a month in the later stages of the program. Treatment is critical to successful completion of drug court, and active engagement in treatment is necessary for phase advancement. Sobriety is the central goal of the program, and a set number of days of negative tests for drugs/alcohol is required to attain phase advancement and, ultimately, graduation. The participant may be required to perform all or a select portion of program requirements in each phase.

Once a participant has successfully completed the criteria for each phase, the participant is a candidate for graduation (Minnesota Judicial Branch, 2007).

A full drug court program will typically take 12-18 months to complete, depending upon the participant's motivation and rate of progress (Huddleston & Marlowe, 2011). If they require residential treatment, additional time is required. The treatment phase lasts a minimum of one year, followed by six months of aftercare. Participants may also be required to comply with other court orders (e.g., child support) (Minnesota Judicial Branch, 2007). The goals of each phase are steps toward a future free from chemical use and criminal behavior. Successes, such as gaining and maintaining steady employment or pursuing additional education, positively reflect the benefits of sobriety. By the time an individual is eligible for graduation from the drug court program, he or she will have a lengthy period of sobriety and be financially stable and demonstrably dedicated to a sober support program (e.g., Alcoholics Anonymous or Narcotics Anonymous). Every requirement of the participant in each phase of drug court is based upon the drug court team's constant review of the data provided by evaluations of its program. Learning from experience is a key concept of any successful drug court.

OTHER PROBLEM-SOLVING COURTS

The success of the drug court model resulted in awareness that the traditional criminal justice model may not be the most-effective approach to curb crime and promote public safety; it also paved the way for other, non-typical avenues in the criminal justice system. Recent years have seen the development of problem-solving courts that focus on mental health, child protection, issues specific to veterans, and miscellaneous problems. In fact, as many as 3,000 problem-solving courts are in operation throughout the United States (Boldt, 2014). Regardless of which population or problem is targeted, the foundations of these specialty courts are firmly rooted in the concepts that were embraced by the very first drug courts. As their name reflects, problem-solving courts consider all aspects of the lives of criminal defendants in the criminal justice system. The commonality between all problem-solving courts is recognition of the underlying issues manifesting in illegal behavior (Berman & Feinblatt, 2001; Lucas & Hanrahan, 2016; Bullard & Thrasher, 2016).

JUVENILE DRUG COURTS

A juvenile drug court is a specialized docket within the juvenile or family court system to which selected delinquency cases and status offender cases are referred. The youths referred to the court are identified as having problems with alcohol and/or other drugs (Huddleston & Marlowe, 2011). An array of support services is provided to address the problems that contribute to juvenile involvement in the justice system. Service areas include substance abuse treatment, mental health, primary care, family, and education. Juvenile drug courts operate similarly to adult drug courts, except that the participants are underage. Thus, the court must also decide how to engage parents and other family members in supporting the participant's progress in the program. Some courts require parents or other adults in the youth's life to participate in special parent groups to provide both support and the opportunity to enhance parenting skills. There is variance among the states in the authority granted to juvenile court judges to require parents to participate in proceedings involving their children. However, most juvenile drug court judges realize that achieving parental cooperation through persuasion rather than coercion is important to the long-term effectiveness of the participant's programming.

An additional issue that can arise is how to define the participant's "family." Youths may live with various adults other than a biological parent. Juvenile drug courts thus often find it necessary to identify some adult other than a biological parent with whom the participant can work. Juvenile drug court programs may also use peer groups of other juveniles to influence participants.

Juvenile drug courts also work with schools, recognizing that completion of school is important to a participant's future and that justice system-involved youth often have problems in school, including truancy.

The court may benefit schools by reinforcing school policies (via its supervisory elements and enforcement mechanisms) and allow school-related problems to be addressed as soon as they occur. Schools may, in turn, work with the court to keep youths in school who would otherwise have been expelled for behavioral problems or possession of controlled substances on campus. Information from juvenile drug courts has indicated that more than 80% of participants returned to or remained in school full-time because of program participation, which was a significantly higher rate than would have been expected, absent the court (Cooper, 2001).

MENTAL HEALTH COURTS

Recognizing that an individual may not only suffer from chemical dependency, but also from a specific mental disorder, requires the problem-solving court to provide treatment options that treat both issues. In so doing, not only is the defendant given the opportunity to become a participating member of the community-at-large, but members of the community will experience greater public safety. Mental health courts, like drug courts, follow the legal theory of therapeutic jurisprudence (Winick, 2003). Mental health courts focus on treatment and future improvements in mental health and quality of life, rather than on the criminal charge and level of culpability (Wolff & Pogorzelski, 2005). A guiding principle of mental health courts is the assumed connection between mental illness and criminal behavior (Wolff, 2002). The structure and operation of mental health courts generally follow that of adult drug courts. The defining characteristics of mental health courts include:

1. A special docket of cases in which participants have a mental illness.
2. A collaborative and non-adversarial team comprised of a judge, prosecuting and defense attorneys, and a mental health representative.
3. A link with a local mental health provider.
4. Some form of compliance monitoring, with sanctions for non-compliance (Steadman, Davison, & Brown, 2001).

Eligibility criteria typically require that participants have a mental illness and criminal charges that are non-violent in nature (Watson, Hanrahan, Luchins, & Lurigio, 2001).

VETERANS COURTS

Many veterans caught in the criminal justice system struggle with addiction and/or mental health issues (Huddleston & Marlowe, 2011). Studies show that 81% of all justice-involved veterans had substance abuse problems prior to incarceration, and 25% were identified as mentally ill (Tanielian & Jaycox, 2008). Traumatic brain injury (TBI) and post-traumatic stress disorder (PTSD) are disorders common among veterans (Tanielian & Jaycox, 2008). Left untreated, veterans' substance abuse or mental health problems can lead to joblessness and/or homelessness. It has been estimated that 23% of the homeless population in the United States are veterans (Russell, 2009).

In 2008, Judge Robert Russell created the first Veterans Treatment Court in Buffalo, New York. This specialized, veterans-only docket was designed to address the growing number of veterans appearing before the criminal courts in Buffalo who were addicted to drugs or alcohol, or were suffering from a mental health disorder (Huddleston & Marlowe, 2008). As of June 30, 2012, there were 104 Veterans Treatment Courts in the United States (http://www.justiceforvets.org).

Veterans Treatment Courts are modeled on the Drug Court pattern. In addition, these courts make use of military and veteran culture to render services specifically to veterans. Other veterans can take part in the court's process to assist the participating veterans, making use of the feeling of camaraderie stemming from military service. Veterans Treatment Courts also function as a common point for linking veterans with necessary programs, services, and benefits (Justice for Vets, n.d.).

FAMILY DEPENDENCY COURTS

Each year in the U.S., nearly 1 million cases of child abuse and neglect are filed and substantiated. Substance abuse plays a significant part in this serious problem. In 80% of confirmed child abuse and neglect cases, experts identify parental substance abuse as a precipitating factor. Parents who abuse substances are much less likely to provide effectively for the basic needs of children, often resulting in neglect and increasing the likelihood of long-term emotional, intellectual, and physical problems (Wheeler & Fox, 2006).

Family Dependency Courts originated in Reno, Nevada, in 1995. There were over 300 programs as of July 2011 (Huddleston & Marlow, 2011). Family Dependency Courts, in general, use the drug court model. However, Family Dependency Court focuses not on criminal issues, but on protecting children and reuniting families by providing parents with support, treatment, and access to services. The Family Dependency Court team works to address the complex array of issues affecting families (Wheeler & Fox, 2006).

TRIBAL WELLNESS

Native American leaders expressed interests in the drug court model and how it could, in a non-adversarial way, help address the severe alcoholism and associated crime prevalent in Native American communities. In 1997, the Office of Justice Programs of the U.S. Department of Justice developed a program to assist Native American tribes in planning and implementing drug courts in their communities. That process led to the development of the Tribal Healing to Wellness Courts. Tribal Healing to Wellness Courts are tribal adaptations of drug courts, seeking to apply the drug court concept and its key components to meet tribal criminal, juvenile, and child welfare needs (Flies-Away, Garrow, & Sekaquaptewa, 2014).

As Native American tribes began to use the drug court model in their communities, it became apparent that using one standard version of the model might not be appropriate in the tribal context. In 2003, the Tribal Law and Policy Institute (TLPI), with funding and support from the U.S. Department of Justice's Bureau of Justice Assistance, published *Tribal Healing to Wellness Courts: The Key Components*. This document described how the 10 key components of drug court, discussed above, might apply to the tribal context. By 2014, Tribal Healing to Wellness Courts had been implemented to serve more than 120 tribal communities. These courts have been recognized by the Departments of Justice as a model alternative to incarceration and an effective tool that permits tribal nations to employ culturally based strategies (Flies-Away, Garrow, & Sekaquaptewa, 2014).

CHILD SUPPORT

Problem-solving court practices are being adapted to serve a variety of issues, including that of delinquent child support. In 2003, noncustodial parents in the United States paid less than 60% of their child support obligations, and approximately one-fourth of all custodial parents who were owed child support did not receive any money from the non-custodial parent (Legler, 2003). The payment of child support by divorced parents with full-time jobs has improved due to federal and state legislative measures taken to address the "deadbeat dad" issue (Martin & Brustin, 2015; Zingraff, 2007). However, many other noncustodial parents have problems that limit their ability to comply with child support obligations. Child support personnel in Las Vegas determined that 60% of their chronic nonpaying obligors had a substance use disorder (Rausch & Rawlings, 2008). Of child support obligors who participated in a nationwide work-skills assistance pilot program, 70% had an arrest record and 60% did not have a high school diploma or GED (Looney & Schexnayder, 2004; Reichert, 1999). Another study showed that only 43% of low-income, noncompliant obligors were participating in the labor market, and 33% had been unemployed for more than three years (Legler, 2003). These obligors clearly require more than a court order to pay a certain amount of money each month. To increase the consistency and amount of payment, underlying problems must be addressed. Several courts in the nation have attempted to do just that. A court in San Antonio, Texas, initiated the "Children First" program in 2004. That program works closely with younger obligors who express willingness to address issues such as unemployment and lack of education. Features of the program include:

1. Obligors meet with a probation officer to discuss their needs, obstacles, and progress.
2. Obligors attend frequent in-court reviews to ensure the obligor is paying current support obligations.
3. There is a zero-tolerance policy for those who do not make at least current, regular payments.

This approach has resulted in a statewide compliance rate of 65% (Rausch & Rawlings, 2008). In Wake County, North Carolina, Judge Kristin Ruth took over the child support docket in 1999 and began collaborating with other child support advocates to create a continuum of services and sanctions designed to help noncustodial parents meet their obligations. A study of Judge Ruth's court conducted by Meredith College determined that, while the compliance rates of obligors sentenced to jail for non-payment of support experienced a dramatic two-month jump after their incarceration, their subsequent payment history was erratic and inconsistent. By contrast, obligors ordered to receive services demonstrated a significantly more consistent pattern of payments following the intervention by the child support court. Further, it was estimated that Wake County saved over $3 million in incarceration costs through the court's efforts to solve obligors' problems instead of merely using punishment as a motivator (Rausch & Rawlings, 2008).

DWI COURTS

A DWI (Driving While Impaired) Court is an accountability court dedicated to changing the behavior of chronic offenders arrested for DWI (Bouffard & Bouffard, 2011; Bouffard, Richardson, & Franklin, 2010; Eckberg & Jones, 2015; Hanson, 2009; Saum, Hiller, & Nolan, 2013). Chronic offenders are defined as individuals who drive with a blood alcohol concentration of .15 or more, or who are arrested for or convicted of a repeat DWI offense (Marlowe, 2010b; National Center for DWI Courts, n.d.). As of December 2011, there were 192 designated DWI Courts (Eckberg, & Jones, 2015). In addition, there were another 406 Hybrid DWI/Drug Courts in operation. A Hybrid DWI/Drug Court is one that started as a "regular" Drug Court, but which now also accepts DWI offenders (National Center for DWI Courts, n.d.). There is evidence that DWI Court is working. An evaluation of three such courts in Georgia, funded by the National Highway Traffic Safety Administration, found that repeat DWI offenders graduating from DWI Court were up to 65% less likely to be re-arrested for a new DWI offense. Participants, regardless of whether they graduated, had a recidivism rate of 15%, compared to 35% for those not in DWI Court (National Center for DWI Courts n.d.). A three-county evaluation of DWI Courts in Michigan found that in one county, participants were 19 times less likely to reoffend (National Center for DWI Courts n.d.).

MISCELLANEOUS COURTS

Re-entry Drug Courts utilize the drug court model to facilitate the reintegration of drug-involved offenders into the community upon their release from local or state correctional facilities. These are different from "Re-entry Courts," which work on similar populations but do not use the drug court model (National Drug Court Resource Center, 2012).

Gun courts are designed for youth and young adults who have committed gun offenses that have not resulted in serious physical injury. Gun court focuses on educating participants about gun safety and allows for direct and immediate responses to violations of court orders. The goal of consolidating all the gun cases onto one docket is to reduce the number of illegal guns in circulation (National Drug Court Resource Center, 2012).

Homeless courts help homeless people charged with nuisance offenses to secure housing and obtain social services needed for stabilization. Participation in services substitutes for fines and custody. These services include substance abuse and mental health treatment, health care, life skills, literacy classes, and vocational training (National Drug Court Resource Center, 2012).

Gambling courts are for people suffering from a pathological or compulsive gambling disorder and who face criminal charges as a result. Participants enroll in a judicially supervised gambling recovery program with services that can include Gamblers Anonymous (GA), psychotherapeutic intervention, debt counseling, group and individual counseling, and drug/alcohol treatment. Participation by family members is encouraged (National Drug Court Resource Center, 2012).

Truancy courts address the underlying causes of truancy in school-aged children by reinforcing and combining efforts from the school, mental health providers, families and the community. Guidance counselors from the school submit weekly reports to the court. Truancy court is often held on school grounds, and successful completion of the program results in dismissal of any truancy petition (National Drug Court Resource Center, 2012).

Domestic violence court seeks to address the problems that traditionally accompany domestic violence cases. These include withdrawn charges by victims, threats to victims, lack of defendant accountability, and high recidivism. The court applies intense judicial scrutiny of the defendant and a close cooperation between the judiciary and social services (National Drug Court Resource Center, 2012).

Community court primarily addresses "quality of life" crimes, such as petty theft, turnstile jumping, vandalism, loitering, and prostitution. Community courts partner with neighborhood groups and local police. Their goals are to assist the offenders with their problems, while simultaneously using court leverage to encourage the offenders to give back to their community (National Drug Court Resource Center, 2012).

INTERNATIONAL PROBLEM-SOLVING COURTS

Substance abuse and the problems associated with it are not limited to the United States. An estimated 205 million people in the world use illicit drugs, including 25 million who suffer from illicit-drug dependence, which constitutes a public health, socio-economic development and security problem for both industrialized and developing countries alike (World Health Organization, 2008). To address these problems, other nations besides the United States are experimenting with the problem-solving court model.

Drug courts do not exist only in the United States. In 1998, a drug court began to operate in Toronto, Canada (Huddleston & Marlowe, 2011). By 2011, there were over 30 Drug Courts operating in countries in various parts of the world: Argentina, Belgium, Bermuda, Brazil, Canada, Chile, Cayman Islands, Ireland, Jamaica, Mexico, New Zealand, Norway, Suriname, Australia, and the United Kingdom (Huddleston & Marlowe, 2011). A study of the drug courts in 11 nations indicated that they had collectively enrolled more than 3,800 participants and successfully graduated over 500 individuals by the time of the survey (Cooper, Franklin, & Mease, 2010). It has been reported that in nearly all the countries, drug courts have been reducing recidivism better than the traditional criminal justice systems (Cooper et al., 2010).

EFFECTIVENESS OF DRUG COURTS

Convincing society that drug court is a better alternative for some criminal defendants than incarceration can be a challenge. The adage, "If you do the crime, you do the time," is reflective of the view of a large segment of society. However, meta-analyses conducted on drug courts have demonstrated that they are effective. Numerous analyses reveal that drug courts significantly reduced re-arrest or reconviction rates by an average of 8%-26%, with the "average of the averages" reflecting a reduction of 10%-15% in recidivism (Morse, Silverstein, Thomas, Bedel, & Cerulli, 2015; Shaffer, 2006). In addition, drug court participants report significantly reduced use of illegal drugs and alcohol. Longer engagement with substance abuse treatment predicts better outcomes, and drug courts are proven to retain offenders in treatment considerably longer than most other correctional programs. A meta-analysis investigating costs concluded that the courts produce an average of $2.21 in direct benefits to the criminal justice system for every $1.00 invested in the courts, a figure that rises to $3.36 per $1.00 invested when the courts targeted their services to the more serious, higher-risk offenders (Marlowe, 2010a).

In a three-year study, the New York State Court System estimated that $254 million were saved in incarceration costs by diverting 18,000 non-violent drug offenders into drug courts (Huddleston & Marlowe, 2011). Due to incarceration alternatives, New York State could close two prisons, and several others were left with a significant number of empty beds (Huddleston & Marlowe, 2011). Aside from the savings to state correctional facilities, taxpayer money can be allocated to other areas, such as child welfare organizations, emergency rooms, and other crisis-driven programs.

A study conducted on the effectiveness of the Multnomah County Drug Court in Portland, Oregon, examined approximately 11,000 offenders who had been identified as eligible for the program from 1991 to 2001. Approximately 6,500 of these offenders had participated in drug court, and approximately 4,600 had their cases processed in the traditional court system. The survey concluded that there was a significant reduction in recidivism for drug court participants for up to 14 years after drug court entry, compared to eligible offenders who were not in drug court. Including all offenders who were eligible during the 10-year period, over five years from the drug court petition hearing, the incidence of re-arrest for those who participated in drug court was reduced by nearly 30% compared to those who did not participate. The effect was statistically significant after controlling for age, gender, race, and criminal history. It was found that investment costs in the drug court program were $5,168 versus $6,560 for the traditional court system. Outcome cost savings (i.e., avoided costs) were much larger. Those savings over a 5-year period from the petition hearing were found to be $6,744 per participant, or $12,218 when victimization costs were included. Savings due to the reduced recidivism of drug court participants was estimated at $79 million over the 10-year period (Finigan, Carey, & Cox, 2007).

The Minnesota state court system conducted an evaluation of its drug courts in 2012, observing a statewide cohort of participants who entered drug court between July 1, 2007, and December 31, 2008. A follow-up analysis was subsequently conducted, and the results of that were released in February 2015. The study concluded that the drug court cohort had a lower rate of recidivism than the comparison group. For participants who reached four years of at-risk time (i.e., time after leaving the program during which an individual was not incarcerated), 28% had received a new conviction, compared to 41% of the comparison group. The percentages of individuals in the drug court cohort (86%) and in the comparison group (87%) who were incarcerated at some point during the four years was nearly identical. However, a drug court participant spent an average of 74 fewer days in jail than a comparison individual did. The result was that incarceration costs for a drug court participant were $4,288 lower than for a comparison individual (Minnesota State Court Administrator's Office, 2015).

A multi-site evaluation was performed on several adult drug courts located in different regions of the country (Florida, Georgia, Illinois, New York, Pennsylvania, South Carolina, and Washington). The study included 1,781 offenders (1,156 drug court participants and 625 comparison group members) who were interviewed at three intervals: baseline, 6 months after baseline, and 18 months after baseline. The study also administered drug tests to participants. The study found that drug courts produce significant reductions in drug relapse. Drug court participants were significantly less likely than the comparison group to report using any drugs (56% versus 76%) in the year prior to the 18-month interview, and significantly fewer drug court participants (29% versus 46%) tested positive for illegal drugs. Drug court participants were less likely to report committing crimes (40% vs. 53%) in the year prior to the 18-month interview, and those reporting criminal activities reported committing about half (43 vs. 88) as many crimes, on average, during the prior year. Drug court participants were also less likely to report a need for employment, educational, and financial services, and reported less family conflict (Rossman, Roman, Zweig, Rempel, & Lindquist, 2011).

A meta-analysis of 181 studies of drug court programs concluded that drug court participants have lower rates of recidivism, but that the size of the effect varies by type of drug court. The average effect of participation in drug court was analogous to a drop in recidivism from 50% to 38%, with those effects lasting up to three years. The study concluded that the magnitude of recidivism reduction for DWI courts was comparable to that for adult drug courts, although more rigorous studies need to be conducted. As to juvenile drug courts, the study found relatively small effects on the rate of recidivism. The study estimated the average reduction in the rate of recidivism for juvenile drug court participants to be from 50% for non-participants to 43.5% for participants—significantly less than the rate for adult drug courts. The authors theorized that the difference might be that juvenile drug courts generally provide services to relatively high-risk offenders, with typically fewer demanding interventions than adult drug courts (Mitchell, Wilson, Eggers, & MacKenzie, 2012).

Conclusion

Problem-solving courts represent a significant change from the traditional court proceedings of the adversarial system. This change is necessary and is justified on both normative and utilitarian grounds. Many of the people appearing in America's courtrooms (and courtrooms around the world) are not true criminals. They are people who suffer from chemical dependency, mental illness, or other problems. It is therefore a matter of justice to have a court process that addresses those issues instead of simply meting out punishment. Problem-solving courts are also in society's best interests; if the participants' issues can be addressed and corrected, those individuals will become productive members of society and be less likely to engage in behaviors that endanger the public and drain public resources.

References

Belenko, S., (1999). Research on drug courts: A critical review. *National Institute Review, 1,* 1-27.

Belenko, S., Hiller, M., Hamilton, L. (2013). Treating substance use disorders in the criminal justice system. *Current Psychiatry Reports, 15*(11), 414.

Berman, G. & Feinblatt, J. (2001). Problem-solving courts: A brief primer. *Law & Policy, 23*(2), 125-140.

Boldt, R. C. (2014). Problem-solving courts and pragmatism. *Maryland Law Review, 73,* 1120-1172.

Bouffard, J. A. & Bouffard, L. A. (2011). What works (or doesn't) in a DUI court? An example of expedited case processing. *Journal of Criminal Justice, 39,* 320-328.

Bouffard, J. A., Richardson, K. A. & Franklin, T. (2010). Drug courts for DWI offenders? The effectiveness of two hybrid drug courts on DWI offenders. *Journal of Criminal Justice, 38,* 25-33.

Bullard, C. E. & Thrasher, R. (2016). Evaluating mental health court by impact on jurisdictional crime rates. *Criminal Justice Policy Review, 27*(3), 227-246.

Bureau of Justice Assistance (1997). Defining drug courts: The key components. Retrieved from http://www.courts.ca.gov/documents/DefiningDC.pdf

Bureau of Justice Assistance (2004). Defining drug courts: The key components. Retrieved from http://www.courts.ca.gov/documents/DefiningDC.pdf

Charland, L. C. (2002). Cynthia's dilemma: Consenting to heroin prescription. *The American Journal of Bioethics, 2*(2), 37-47.

Contrino, K. M., Nochajski, T., Farrell, M. G., & Logsdon, E. (2016). Factors of success: Drug court graduate exit interviews. *American Journal of Criminal Justice, 41*(1), 136-150.

Cooper, C. (2001). *Juvenile drug court programs*. U.S. Department of Justice, Office of Juvenile Justice and Delinquency Programs.

Cooper, C. S., Franklin, B., & Mease, T. (2010). *Establishing drug treatment courts: Strategies, experiences, and preliminary outcomes*. American University School of Public Affairs.

Eckberg, D. A. & Jones, D. S. (2015). "I'll just do my time:" The role of motivation in the rejection of the DWI court model. *The Qualitative Report, 20*(1), 130-147.

Finigan, M., Carey, S., & Cox, A. (2007). *Impact of a mature drug court over 10 years of operation: Recidivism and costs*. NPC Research.

Flies-Away, J.T., Garrow, C., & Sekaquaptewa, P. (2014). *Tribal healing to wellness courts: The key components*. Tribal Law and Policy Institute.

Fulkerson, A., Keena, L. D., & O'Brien, E. (2013). Understanding success and nonsuccess in the Drug Court. *International journal of offender therapy and comparative criminology, 57*(10), 1297-1316.

Glaze, L. E., & Palla, S. (2005). Probation and parole in the United States in 2004 (Publication No. NCJ-210676). *Washington, DC7 US Department of Justice, Bureau of Justice Statistics*.

Goldberg, S. (2005). *Judging for the 21st century: A problem-solving approach*. National Judicial Institute, Ottawa, Ontario, Canada.

Goldstein, R., & Volkow, N. (2002). Drug addiction and its underlying neurobiological basis: Neuroimaging evidence for the involvement of the frontal cortex, *American Journal of Psychiatry, 159*, 1642-1652.

Hanson, D. J. (2009). DWI courts: *Effectively addressing drunk driving*. In Higgins, P. & Mackinem, M. B. (Eds.), Problem-solving courts: Justice for the twenty-first century? (91-113). Santa Barbara, California: ABC-CLIO, LLC.

Holland, P. (2010). Lawyering and learning in problem-solving courts. *Washington University Journal of Law and Policy, 34*, 185-238.

Hora, P., & Stalcup, T. (2008). Drug treatment courts in the twenty-first century: The evolution of the revolution in problem-solving courts. *Georgia Law Review, 42*, 717-811.

Huddleston, W., & Marlow, D. (2011). *Painting the current picture: A national report on drug courts and other problem-solving court programs in the United States*. National Drug Court Institute.

Justice for Vets (n.d.). Justice for Vets. Retrieved from http://www.justiceforvets.org

Kaiser, K. A. & Holtfreter, K. (2016). An integrated theory of specialized court programs: Using procedural justice and therapeutic jurisprudence to promote offender compliance and rehabilitation. *Criminal Justice and Behavior, 43*(1), 45-62.

Kendler, K., & Prescott, C. (1998). Cocaine use, abuse, and dependence in a population-based sample of female twins. *British Journal of Psychiatry, 173(4)*, 345-350.

Lal, R., Deb, K. S., & Kedia, S. (2015). Substance use in women: current status and future directions. *Indian journal of psychiatry, 57*(Suppl 2), S275.

Langan, P., & Levin, D. (2002). *Recidivism of prisoners Released in 1994*. Bureau of Justice Statistics, U.S. Department of Justice.

Legler, P. (2003). *Low-income fathers and child support: Starting off on the right track*. Annie E. Casey Foundation.

Leshner, A. (1999). Science-Based views of drug addiction and its treatment. *Journal of the American Medical Association, 282*, 1314-1315.

Lindquist, C., Krebs, C., Warner, T., & Lattimore, P. (2009). An exploration of treatment and supervision intensity among drug court and non-drug court participants. *Journal of Offender Rehabilitation, 48,* 167-193.

Looney, S., & Schexnayder, D. (2004). *Factors Affecting Participation in Programs for Young Low-Income Fathers: Findings from the Texas Bootstrap Project.* Texas Fragile Families Bootstrap Evaluation.

Lucas, P. A. & Hanrahan, K. H. (2016). No soldier left behind: The veterans court solution. *International Journal of Law and Psychiatry, 45,* 52-59.

Marlowe, D. (2010a). *Research update on adult drug courts.* National Association of Drug Court Professionals.

Marlowe, D. (2012). *Targeting the right participants for adult drug courts.* National Drug Court Institute.

Marlowe, D. B. (2010b). *Introductory handbook for DWI Court program evaluations.* National Center for DWI Courts.

Marlowe, D., & Carey, S. (2012). *Research Update on Family Drug Courts.*

Marlowe, D., DeMatteo, D., & Festinger, D. (2003). *A sober assessment of drug courts. Federal Sentencing Reporter, 16,* 153-157.

Martin, L. V., & Brustin, S. L. (2015). Paved with Good Intentions: Unintended Consequences of Federal Proposals to Integrate Child Support and Parenting Time. *Available at SSRN.*

McLellan, T., Lewis, D., O'Brien, C., & Kleber, H. (2000). Drug dependence, a chronic medical illness: Implications for treatment, insurance, and outcomes evaluation, *Journal of the American Medical Association, 284,* 1689-1693.

Middleton, M. (2015). *Can participation in Drug Treatment Courts reduce emergency department use? An evaluation* (Doctoral dissertation, University of Ontario Institute of Technology).

Miller, T. R., Levy, D. T., Cohen, M. A., & Cox, K. L. (2006). Costs of alcohol and drug-involved crime. *Prevention Science, 7(*4), 333-342. Minnesota Judicial Branch. (2007). Brown-Nicollet-Watonwan Multi-County Drug Court Pilot Project: Policies and Procedures. Retrieved from http://www.mncourts.gov/mncourtsgov/media/scao_library/Drug%20Courts/5th%20District/Brown-Nicollet-Watonwan%20Adult%20Drug/BNW_Guidelines_Procedures_4-07-(1).pdf

Minnesota State Court Administrator's Office. (2015). *Minnesota Statewide Adult Drug Court Evaluation – Follow-Up.*

Mitchell, O., Wilson, D., Eggers, A, & MacKenzie, D. (2012). Assessing the effectiveness of drug court on recidivism: A meta-analytic review of traditional and non-traditional drug courts. *Journal of Criminal Justice, 40,* 60-71.

Morse, D. S., Silverstein, J., Thomas, K., Bedel, P., & Cerulli, C. (2015). Finding the loopholes: a cross-sectional qualitative study of systemic barriers to treatment access for women drug court participants. *Health & Justice, 3*(1), 1-9.

Mumola, C. J. (2000). Veterans in prison or jail. *Alcohol, 23,* 30-36.

National Center for DWI Courts. (n.d.). Retrieved from http://www.dwicourts.org/learn/about-dwi-court.

National Drug Court Institute (2007). The ten guiding principles for DWI courts. Alexandra, VA.

National Drug Court Resource Center (2012). Retrieved from http://www.ndcrc.org/node/356

National Institute for Justice (n.d.). Retrieved from http://www.crimesolutions.gov

National Institute for Justice, Research Report (1995). *The Effectiveness of Treatment for Drug Abusers Under Criminal Justice Supervision.* Retrieved from https://www.ncjrs.gov/pdffiles/drugsupr.pdf

National Institute on Drug Abuse, U.S. Department of Health & Human Services. (1999). *Principles of Drug Addiction Treatment: A Research-Based Guide,* 15th ed. National Institute on Drug Abuse.

Peters, R. H. (2008). Co-occurring disorders. In C. Hardin & J.N. Kushner (Eds.), *Quality improvement for drug courts: Evidence-based practices* (pp. 51-61). Alexandria, Virginia: National Drug Court Institute, National Association of Drug Court Professionals.

Peters, R. H., & Hills, H. A. (1997). *Intervention strategies for offenders with co-occurring disorders: What works?* Delmar, NY: The National GAINS Center.

Rausch, J., & Rawlings, T. (2008). *Integrating problem-solving court practices into the child support docket.* National Council of Juvenile and Family Court Judges.

Reichert, D. (1999). *Broke but not deadbeat: Reconnecting low-income fathers and children.* National Conference of State Legislatures.

Roman, J., Townsend, W., & Singh Bhati, A. (2003). Recidivism rates for drug court graduates: Nationally based estimates, final report. *Caliber Associates & Urban Institute.*

Rossman, S., Roman, J., Zweig, J., Rempel, M., & Lindquist, C. (2011). The multi-site adult drug court evaluation: Executive summary. *Urban Institute Justice Policy Center.*

Russell, R. (2009). Veterans Treatment Court: A Proactive Approach, *New England Journal on Criminal and Civil Commitment, 35,* 2.

Saum, C. A., Hiller, M. L. & Nolan, B. A. (2013). Predictors of completion of a driving under the influence (DUI) court for repeat offenders. *Criminal Justice Review, 38*(2), 207-225.

Shaffer, D. K. (2006). *Reconsidering drug court effectiveness: A meta-analytic review.* University of Nevada.

Simon, W. (2003). Criminal defenders and community justice: The drug court example. *American Criminal Law Review, 40,* 1595.

Steadman, H. J., Davison, S., & Brown, C. (2001). Mental Health Courts: Their Promise and Unanswered Questions. *Psychiatric Services, 52,* 457-458.

Tanielian, T. L., & Jaycox, L. H. (Eds.). (2008). *Invisible wounds of war: Psychological and cognitive injuries, their consequences, and services to assist recovery.* Santa Monica, CA: RAND Corporation.

Watson, A., Hanrahan, P., Luchins, D., & Lurigio, A. (2001). Mental health courts and the complex issue of mentally ill offenders. *Psychiatric Services, 52,* 477-481.

Wexler, D. B., & Winick, B. (Ed.). (1996). *Law in a therapeutic key: Developments in therapeutic jurisprudence.* Durham, North Carolina: Carolina Academic Press.

Wheeler, M., & Fox, C. (2006). Family dependency treatment court: Applying the drug court model in child maltreatment cases. *National Drug Court Institute, 1,* 1-7.

Winick, B. (2003). Outpatient commitment: A therapeutic jurisprudence analysis. *Psychology, Public Policy, and Law, 9,* 107-144.

Wolff, N. (2002). Courts as Therapeutic Agents: Thinking Past the Novelty of Mental Health Courts. *Journal of American Academy of Psychiatry and Law, 30,* 431-437.

Wolff, N., & Pogorzelski, W. (2005). Measuring the Effectiveness of Mental Health Courts: Challenges and Recommendations. *Psychology, Public Policy, and Law, 11,* 539-569.

World Health Organization (2008). Principles of drug dependence treatment. *Geneva, Switzerland: World Health Organization.*

Zingraff, R. (2007). Extended Executive Summary: *The Effects of Differential Court Sanctions on Child Support Payment Compliance.* Retrieved from http://www.childsupportandthecourt.org/reports/diferential_court_sanctions

CHAPTER 17

SCHIZOPHRENIA: A BEGINNER'S GUIDE FOR CRIMINAL JUSTICE AND FORENSIC MENTAL HEALTH PROFESSIONALS

JERROD BROWN, BETH JORDAN, ERIN J. WATTS, CHERYL ARNDT,
MATTHEW D. KRASOWSKI, AMANDA BELTRANI, ANDREA PATRICK, ERIK ASP,
AARON TRNKA, PHYLLIS BURGER, DEBRA HUNTLEY, TRISHA M. KIVISALU,
DEBORAH A. ECKBERG, ERWIN CONCEPCION, & SAMANTHA L. CARTER

CHAPTER OVERVIEW

Schizophrenia is a chronic, severe and disabling brain disorder that typically manifests between the ages of 16 to 30 (Gold, Kool, Botvinick, Hubzin, August, & Waltz, 2015; Hall, Trent, Thomas, O'Donovan, & Owen, 2015; National Institute of Mental Health [NIMH], 2010) and plagues millions of individuals worldwide (Rajji, Miranda, & Mulsant, 2014). Symptoms of schizophrenia can include hallucinations, delusions, disordered thinking, catatonia, flat affect, and problems with working memory/executive function (NIMH, 2010).

According to the American Psychiatric Association (APA, 2013), a diagnosis of schizophrenia requires that an individual exhibit the presence of at least two symptoms for six or more months, and have at least one month of active symptoms at the time of assessment. Much research shows a direct link to brain functioning and neurochemical imbalances as significant contributors to the genesis and subsequent changes in the brain functionality (Rajji, Miranda, & Mulsant, 2014; Schiffer et al., 2012).

Those diagnosed with acute, chronic, or moderate to severe schizophrenia may experience frequent hospitalizations, suicidal ideation, social alienation, unemployment, poverty and homelessness, which can decrease the quality and length of an individual's life (Thaker, 2011). Schizophrenia has the potential to manifest itself in violent behavior, which creates unique challenges for the criminal justice system to provide effective services to individuals with this disorder. Indeed, schizophrenia is overrepresented in justice-related populations (Arboleda-Florez, 2009). In the context of criminal behavior, schizophrenia has been linked to illicit substance abuse, general violence; and domestic violence (Fazel, Grann, Carlstrom, Lichtenstein, & Långström, 2009a; Miller, 2010; Trevillion, Oram, Feder, & Howard, 2012; Wallace, Mullen, & Burgess, 2004; Walsh, Buchanan, & Fahy, 2002; Wehring & Carpenter, 2011). This chapter reviews the juxtaposition of clinical and forensic aspects of schizophrenia with a specific emphasis on applicability across various areas of the criminal justice system.

CLINICAL OVERVIEW OF SCHIZOPHRENIA

The symptoms of schizophrenia are diverse, making it difficult to ascertain its neurologic etiology and make a prognosis (Beck, Rector, Stolar, & Grant, 2009). Despite the public's fascination and ongoing research about schizophrenia, many of the symptoms are not immediately evident to criminal justice professionals (American Psychiatric Association [APA], 2013; Tandon, Gaebel, Barch, Bustillo, Gur, Heckers, & Carpenter, 2013). According to the National Institute of Mental Health (NIMH, 2010), there are three constellations of schizophrenia symptoms, which are typically characteristic of the diagnosis: positive, negative, and cognitive. Positive symptoms are referred to as any behavior or feeling that is not usually present in healthy individuals, such as hallucinations and delusions. Negative symptoms are behaviors or feelings that are absent, such as flat emotional levels or inappropriate social responses that lead to a disruption in functioning. These symptoms are among those in the low-range spectrum encompassing the less-severe subtypes of schizophrenic spectrum disorder, thus making them difficult to recognize (Pagsburg, 2013). Cognitive symptoms include disruptions in an individual's thinking and memory, such as problems with executive function, including attention, planning, and working memory (Eisenberg & Berman, 2010; Smith & Jonides, 1999).

AGE OF ONSET

The age of onset, usually first present in males between 16 and 30 years of age, is the beginning of overt symptom development or initial symptom presentation (Linke, Jankowski, & Wichniak, 2015). Early onset refers to the development of symptoms and illness presentation before the age of 20 and, in some cases, correlates with early conduct disorder behaviors, violence prior to the age of 15, and an increased risk of suicide attempts (Hor & Taylor, 2010). For females, the typical age of onset is slightly older; it may occur in the late teen years or, more commonly, into the twenties (APA, 2013). According to World Health Organization (2012), 23% of individuals diagnosed with the disorder experience the onset of schizophrenia at the age of 40 or later, or late-onset (Rajji, Ismail, & Mulsant, 2009). Individuals who experience the onset of schizophrenia at the age of 60 or later are significantly fewer in number (0.1% to 0.5%) and are characterized as exhibiting very late onset (Howard, Rabins, Seeman, & Jeste, 2000).

SYMPTOM CATEGORIES

Symptom categories are helpful in the recognition and presentation of various mental health illnesses such as schizophrenia. As previously discussed, there are positive, negative, and cognitive symptoms that are characteristic of and specific to schizophrenia. Along with these three symptom classifications, clinicians also consider prodromal symptoms in their diagnosis and treatment planning, which are symptoms that present before a formal diagnosis of schizophrenia.

POSITIVE SYMPTOMS

Positive symptoms of schizophrenia include hallucinations, delusions, and disorganized speech and behavior. Positive symptoms of schizophrenia tend to diminish over the life-span (APA, 2013) and are the most responsive to typical antipsychotic medications (King, 1998). These symptoms are usually the most easily recognized by clinicians and are necessary to receive a diagnosis of schizophrenia (Pagsberg, 2013).

HALLUCINATIONS

Hallucinations are characterized by sensory experiences that occur in the absence of a stimulus. They generate from the affected individual's brain in the form of neurochemical and electrical imbalance and can affect the perception of all five senses (touch, taste, sight, sound, smell). The individual may attempt to make sense of these imbalances and reason through a non-existing external source. Approximately 75% of people with schizophrenia report an auditory hallucination—the perception of sound with no stimulus—making it the most common symptom of schizophrenia (Nayani & David, 1996). Such hallucinations are often distressing, loud vocalizations, and may or may not make sense to the person hearing them. Voices heard may seem to come from within one's own mind or from an external source. They may command a person to do things, such as to harm either themselves or others. They may elicit feelings of paranoia and result in the individual feeling compelled to warn about the perceived ill intentions of others. Finally, the experience of hearing voices may cause an individual to talk to himself. In many of these instances, medication may help control the hallucinations but may not eliminate these experiences (Laroi & Aleman, 2011).

Visual hallucinations, though far less common than auditory hallucinations, may also be present among individuals suffering from schizophrenia (Bracha, Wolkowitz, Lohr, Karson, & Bigelow, 1989; Subramanian, Burhan, Pallaveshi, & Rudnick, 2013). Roberts (1984) suggests that visual hallucinations are usually associated with auditory hallucinations (as cited in Bracha et al., 1989). Visual hallucinations can range from simple to complex, with simple hallucinations containing lights, shapes, or colors, which create a false sense of reality. Individuals with schizophrenia have also reported complex hallucinations, which are clear and lifelike images of people, objects, or animals. The visual hallucinations may generate scenes that can either be static or appear to be dynamic and in motion (Manford & Anderman, 1998).

Olfactory hallucinations are the least common symptoms of schizophrenia (Longden, Sampson, & Read, 2015). These hallucinations involve smelling odors that do not exist. The olfactory hallucinations are typically malodorous: unpleasant odors such as urine, rotting flesh, or feces (Greenberg, 1992). Research conducted on individuals suffering from schizophrenia has identified a relationship between the experience of olfactory sensations that are not present and deficits in the amygdala and the orbitofrontal cortex of the brain (Arguedas, Langdon, & Stevenson, 2012). These abnormalities in the function of the brain can engage the senses during hallucinations, leading to their perception as realistic.

Two additional hallucination types are tactile (touch) and gustatory (taste). Commonly experienced tactile hallucinations include the sensation of bugs crawling on one's skin, formally known as formification. While this is a commonly reported symptom of those who are in the midst of a methamphetamine or cocaine-induced drug state (i.e., a "high"), those with sensory hallucinations in schizophrenia may also report similar experiences (Litt, 2009). As such, it is imperative for those in correctional and forensic settings to have an awareness of how some drug-related symptoms might also be characteristic of serious mental health disorders such as schizophrenia (Compton et al., 2009; Litt, 2009; Zhornitsky et al., 2011).

DELUSIONS

Delusions occur in approximately 60%-70% of all those diagnosed with schizophrenia (Picchioni & Murray, 2007). Torrey (2006) described four primary forms of delusions:

1. **Delusions of Grandeur** – belief that one is important or has unusual, unique powers (for example, a belief that one is the incarnation of Christ).
2. **Delusions of Persecution** – belief that others are out to harm the individual (for example, a belief that the government is spying on the individual).
3. **Delusions of Reference** – belief that an event is a sign meant only for the individual to understand

(for example, John Nash believed that red neckties were being worn to signal their allegiance to a communist conspiracy against him).

4. **Delusions of Control** – belief that the individual's body or thought process are being controlled by another party (for example, mind control by an alien).

Delusions are categorized as either bizarre or non-bizarre. Bizarre delusions are one or more false and implausible beliefs about how the world is functioning and how the individual is living or working within that world. This type of delusion was commonly experienced in what was previously classified as paranoid schizophrenia—a subtype of schizophrenia that was excluded from the most recent 5th edition of the *Diagnostic and Statistical Manual of Mental Disorders* (DSM-5) (American Psychiatric Association [APA], 2013). The skewed belief systems, which are typical in schizophrenia, are usually far more complex and influential across several domains affecting social interactions, work functioning, family systems, educational progress, and financial stability. Non-bizarre delusions are plausible but are either completely false or exaggerated truths (Butler & Braff, 1991). These beliefs (such as a sense of being followed by unseen law enforcement) cannot be readily dismissed (APA, 2013).

DISORGANIZED SPEECH AND BEHAVIOR

Characteristics such as disorganized speech and behavior are commonly associated with schizophrenia (APA, 2013). According to the DSM-5 (APA, 2013), examples of this may include the inability to track conversations or to respond appropriately to questions, and the demonstration of extremely strange behaviors that are incongruent with the current situation. These behaviors can occur individually, or several may occur simultaneously. Abnormal speech patterns exhibited by individuals with schizophrenia include neologisms (newly created words), loose associations (jumping from topic to topic randomly throughout a conversation), and word salads (the unintelligible mixture of seemingly random words and phrases). Individuals experiencing disorganized symptoms are often unaware of the incoherence their speech displays or maintains.

Individuals living with schizophrenia may exhibit disorganized behavior (described as difficulty following goal-oriented patterns of behavior) or catatonic behavior (manifested as a marked decrease in motor activity) (APA, 2013). The disorganized behavior might appear inappropriate for the situation or out of context, such as staring into a mirror for long periods of time or laughing and crying during casual conversation (Barlow & Durand, 2010). Levels of these and other behaviors, such as agitation and repetitive motor activity, could change over time (Barlow & Durand, 2010).

NEGATIVE SYMPTOMS

Negative symptoms are an absence or decrease in characteristics of typical functioning, which can include inexpressive faces, monotone speech, few gestures, a lack of interest in others, inability to feel pleasure, or inability to act spontaneously. These negative symptoms have a high impact on an individual's capacity to live independently and lead to difficulties with managing social situations (Miles, 2012). The most common forms of negative symptoms exhibited by individuals with schizophrenia are reduced emotional activity (blunt affect) and a complete absence of emotional expression (flat affect) (APA, 2013). Diminished or absent affect is often misperceived as poor attitude, callousness, an unwillingness to comply, or being "anti-social"; however, negative symptoms are caused by neurological dysfunction that inhibits emotional processing and social acuity (Bijanki, Hodis, Magnotta, Zeien, & Andreasen, 2015).

Aside from a diminished capacity to express emotions through facial expressions, many individuals with schizophrenia also show an inability to comprehend others' emotional expressions (Csukly, Stefanics, Komlósi, Czigler, & Czobor, 2014; Goghari, 2014; Kee, Green, Mintz, & Brekke, 2003; Van Donkersgoed et al., 2014). Problems recognizing others' facial features and emotions can contribute to poor social interactions. Individuals with schizophrenia may also experience a deficit specific to facial processing, which is not typically accounted for by deficits in cognitive capacity (Goghari & Sponheim, 2013). Goghari (2014) found evidence of differing facial processing skills in individuals with schizophrenia, as those individuals were more likely to attend to eye regions and less likely to attend to nose and mouth regions when assessing anger and neutral emotional expression. This deficit, in response to a differential processing method, is significant because these individuals may be unable to recognize dangerous situations. Another study found that patients treated in a high-security, forensic psychiatric hospital were better able to process expressions of disgust (Wolfkühler et al., 2012). Additionally, they outperformed non-forensic patients treated in a regular psychiatric hospital on emotional recognition in other areas. The processing of facial expressions is different among individuals with schizophrenia and needs to be considered on an individual basis.

COGNITIVE SYMPTOMS

Cognitive symptoms can be difficult to discern from the categorical "negative" symptoms. The difference between a person who has a cognitive symptom of a deficit in motivation (or avolition) and a gap in social competence (a negative symptom) is hard to discern. Additionally, the negative symptoms of alogia, or poverty of speech, are difficult to differentiate from someone who has difficulty retrieving the words, which is a cognitive symptom. Beyond this, the numerous areas affected in the brain by schizophrenia can increase the difficulty faced in recognizing cognitive symptoms (Barch & Ceaser, 2012). Negatively affected areas may include executive functioning, working memory, episodic memory, language function, sensory processing, processing speed, and attention span (Barch & Ceaser, 2012). Executive functioning essentially allows people to access information, think about options, and implement solutions. This includes the ability to anticipate outcomes and consequences, determine which action will have the most positive outcomes, and perform the tasks necessary to carry out that action. Combine insufficient executive functioning with difficulties in remembering previous experiences and applying outcomes (consequences) to the present day, a low processing speed, and impaired attention span, and the cognitive component of schizophrenia can have a significant impact on people. Barach and Ceaser (2012) opine that cognitive symptoms of schizophrenia may have more of an impact on an individual's quality of life and overall functioning than either positive or negative symptoms.

Even though cognitive impairment is a common element in schizophrenia, researchers are still examining the etiology of the disorder. Bora (2015) suggested that the cognitive impairments relate to the age of onset of cognitive symptoms and developmental impairments. Barach and Ceaser (2012) suggest the cognitive deficiencies may stem from dysfunction in the dorsolateral prefrontal cortex (DLPFC) and its interactions with other parts of the brain. However, the origin of cognitive symptoms of individuals with schizophrenia remains elusive.

PRODROMAL STAGE

It is common that many symptoms related to schizophrenia begin to develop one to two years before diagnosis, or during the prodromal stage (Barlow & Durand, 2010). Symptoms during this stage are less severe and may include ideas of reference; magical thinking; increased irritability; or mild cognitive, social, or motor coordination problems. The prodromal period is the timeframe between the appearance of these aforementioned symptoms and the onset of one's psychotic symptoms (Yung & McGorry, 1996). Since symptoms in the prodromal phase are mild and similar to a wide variety of other diagnoses, they are often overlooked until they become pervasive enough to affect functioning (Barlow & Durand, 2010).

CAUSES AND RISK FACTORS

ROLE OF GENETICS

Genetics plays a role in the etiology of schizophrenia. An individual with an immediate family member diagnosed with schizophrenia maintains the highest risk for development of the disorder (Cardno & Gottesman, 2000). If an individual has a parent or sibling with schizophrenia, the 1% chance of acquiring the disorder increases to 10%. If the sibling is an identical twin, the chance of being afflicted is 50%. The odds remain the same when identical twins grow up in different households (Plomin et al., 1997). Twin studies estimate that the hereditary risk of developing schizophrenia is approximately 64%-85% (Cardno & Gottesman, 2000) (Lichtenstein et al., 2009), supporting the influence of genetics. An alteration or modification of a specific gene may be significant, yet there has been no particular gene implicated in the development of schizophrenia at this time (Walsh & Yun, 2013). Researchers have recently demonstrated an increased probability for schizophrenia when combining a genetic risk (such as having a parent diagnosed with schizophrenia) with an environmental stressor such as significant life or occupational stressors or the experience of maternal depression during pregnancy) (Gilmore 2010). For these individuals, the likelihood of developing schizophrenia is greater than it would be for either risk factor on its own. Gilmore (2010) notes that:

> Currently, it is thought that genetic risk for schizophrenia emerges in two basic ways—the first being the polygenic interaction of multiple common variants of probably thousands of genes, each with very small individual effects. The second are rare but highly penetrant genetic events such as deletions or duplications—copy number variations. Of the environmental causes of schizophrenia, most studies have focused on pre- and perinatal environmental risk factors....especially infection, maternal depression/stress, and urban birth (p. 8).

Paternal age at the time of birth is also a significant factor in the development of schizophrenia (Sipos et al., 2004; King et al., 2010). Older paternal age was associated with higher diagnosed rates of schizophrenia, although this finding was only evident among individuals without a family history of the disease (Sipos et al., 2004). There are many studies currently examining the possible influences on the development of schizophrenia. Genes, environment, and family and social upbringing all contribute to the efforts to enrich the understanding of its complex set of symptoms and characteristics (Cantor-Graae, 2007; Howes & Kapur, 2009; King et al., 2010).

THE DOPAMINE HYPOTHESIS

The Dopamine Hypothesis attributes the symptoms of schizophrenia to an overabundance of dopamine, a naturally produced neurotransmitter, in the brain (Howes & Kapur, 2009). This is one of the oldest and most widely accepted hypotheses for the development of schizophrenia. The theory states that variations in the dopamine levels may affect a person's ability to process information and communicate clearly. Additionally, these variations may increase positive symptoms of schizophrenia (i.e., delusions and hallucinations) (Walsh & Yun, 2013). The dopamine hypothesis was first crafted in response to affirmative clinical outcomes among patients with schizophrenia who were treated with antipsychotic drugs that affect dopamine release in the brain (Delay, Deniker, & Harl, 1952). Specifically, drugs found to block dopamine receptors were found to lessen positive symptoms in psychotic patients while drugs that increase dopamine intake were shown to increase these symptoms (Seeman, 2007; Swerdlow & Koob, 1987). Researchers also found that in autopsies of such patients, there was an excess of dopamine receptors (Seeman et al., 1993; Wong et al., 1986). This seminal finding led researchers to believe that abnormal activity among dopamine pathways caused individuals to develop symptoms of schizophrenia.

Aided by the advancement of neurochemical imaging, researchers are now able to indirectly assess dopamine release and synaptic dopamine levels using radio-labelled *L*-dopa, a substance that can be converted into dopamine to determine its creation and storage (Moore, Whone, McGowan, & Brooks, 2003). The majority of studies that have used this assessment method have reported significantly higher levels of presynaptic dopamine synthesis capacity in individuals with schizophrenia, demonstrating increased levels of available dopamine (Hietala et al., 1995; Hietala et al., 1999; Howes & Kapur, 2009; Lindstrom et al., 1999). Furthermore, individuals with schizophrenia have shown increased levels of dopamine release compared to control groups (Kestler, Walker, & Vega, 2001). Such persons may also be predisposed to increased dopamine activity in response to external factors.

ENVIRONMENTAL FACTORS

As with any disorder or phenomenon in psychology, the biological aspects of schizophrenia cannot be studied exclusively; the environment of individuals must always be considered. There are a variety of environmental factors, categorized into early and late factors (McDonald & Murray, 2000), which have been shown to affect the genetic risk of schizophrenia and trigger the onset of symptoms (Howes & Kapur, 2009). These perils may begin as early as the presence of prenatal complications (Carter, 2011; McDonald & Murray, 2000), such as maternal diabetes, or factors that lead to low birth weight and oxygen deprivation during delivery (King et al., 2010). Significant associations have been reported between the later onset of schizophrenia and prenatal contact with German measles, influenza, chicken pox, herpes, and the common cold with fevers (Carter, 2011). In a study of prenatal influenza exposure, researchers suggested that the timing (occurrence during the second trimester specifically), rather than the type of viral disturbance, was the critical risk factor for developing schizophrenia (Mednick, Machon, Huttunen, & Bonett, 1988). Brown et al. (2004) studied serum samples from pregnancies which showed antibodies from exposure to influenza, and indicated that exposure during the first trimester or over multiple trimesters may increase the risk of later development of schizophrenia in the child by as much as three to seven times over the controls. This measurement of the antibodies addressed problems with earlier studies, which linked timelines of exposure based on influenza outbreaks rather than on individual measures.

Other prenatal sources linked to the development of schizophrenia include maternal alcohol use and maternal stressors, which create significant stress on the fetus. Prenatal alcohol exposure may contribute to executive functioning deficits and predict symptom development (Kodituwakku, Kalberg, & May, 2011). Exposure to these toxins can lead to increased dopamine activity; moreover, significant stress for the fetus during prenatal periods and increased stress following the birth of the child are also associated with the increased dopamine release common in schizophrenia (Kehoe, Shoemaker, Triano, Hoffman, & Arons, 1996). Another prenatal risk factor, as noted earlier, is maternal depression during pregnancy, which can cause increased stress on the fetus (Gilmore, 2010).

Beyond the prenatal period, there are certain social risk factors (such as social withdrawal, childhood abuse, and migration), which could interact with genetic risk to increase the probability of developing schizophrenia (Howes & Kapur, 2009). Past research has demonstrated an increased risk for onset of schizophrenia in certain migratory groups, especially the African-Caribbean population in England; however, the reasons for such increased risk have not yet been identified (McDonald & Murray, 2000). In addition the association between schizophrenia rates and income inequality is supported throughout the literature; the larger the rich-poor gap, the higher the rates of schizophrenia among lower income earners (Burns, Tomita, & Kapadia, 2014). Lastly, behavioral reactions to environmental stimuli are indicative of later onset schizophrenia (Morgan et al., 2002). Overall, the development of schizophrenia is impacted by the intersection of biology and environment.

FAMILY UNIT

It is important to highlight the distinction between various theories that implicate the family unit. Several theories exist regarding the family's influence on the development of schizophrenia, particularly around parenting and negative experiences in childhood. Many of these theories relied on stereotypes and presented some aspects related to contributing factors in erroneous and demeaning ways. This resulted in a tremendous amount of stigma and misunderstanding among the public, regarding the development and presentation of schizophrenia (Penn et al., 1994).

Ineffective parenting practices, especially identified with mothers, was widely believed to be a cause of schizophrenia throughout the twentieth century. Freudian theory largely influenced and perpetuated this belief (Torrey, 2006). The poorly defined mechanisms that might connect family dysfunction to psychotic disorder implicated qualities such as parents being overbearing, authoritarian, and neurotic. Furthermore, statistical support and sound methodology were completely lacking among the studies carried out by Freudian experimenters who supported such claims; as such, the association between "bad" parenting and familial units and schizophrenia has long been debunked (Andreasen, 1984). Unfortunately, due to the influence of Freudian theory on popular psychology, the general societal consensus may still be misinformed. This could potentially lead to baseless blaming of mothers and fathers, as well as the notion that individuals with schizophrenia were somehow unable to cope with normal childhood challenges and are, therefore, partly to blame for their disorder (Ferriter & Huband, 2003; Gumley et al., 2006).

Nevertheless, the role of abuse as a potential activating stressor for the risk of schizophrenia development is well established (Cantor-Graae, 2007). Symptoms common to schizophrenia and related psychoses, especially hallucinations, have been significantly associated with childhood abuse and neglect (Janssen et al., 2003; Read, van Os, Morrison, & Ross, 2005). Janssen et al. (2003) examined a large sample of individuals with schizophrenia, focusing primarily on the first onset of psychiatric symptoms, and found early childhood abuse to significantly predict the onset of positive symptoms (i.e., hallucinations, delusions, disorganized speech).

Whether or not these findings point to a causal relationship between childhood abuse and later onset of schizophrenia remains debatable. While some reviews support this relationship, other experts contend that, due to methodological problems in the current data, this connection cannot be validated (Larsson et al., 2013). In other words, given that psychotic disorders are highly heritable, instances of childhood trauma may interact with genetic factors, giving rise to the onset of schizophrenia (Larsson et al., 2013).

CHILDHOOD MALTREATMENT AND NEGLECT RISK FACTORS

Childhood adversity is a significant risk factor for individuals with schizophrenia. Childhood abuse falls under the umbrella of early stressful experiences, which developmental researchers identify as a possible risk factor for the onset of schizophrenia (Torrey, 2006). Researchers who examined the childhood backgrounds of 28 individuals with schizophrenia and a history of criminal violence found that 46.4 % of those prisoners had a history of childhood abuse and at least one form of neglect (Bennouna-Greene, Bennouna-Greene, Berna, & Defranoux, 2011). Additionally, they found that 21.4% had experienced two or more forms of abuse. Another study by Matheson, Shepherd, Pinchbeck, Laurens, and Carr (2013) reported a medium to large effect of childhood adversity as a risk factor for later development of schizophrenia. Additional research found that a common form of childhood neglect in individuals with schizophrenia is emotional neglect (Larsson et al., 2013). There is mounting evidence to suggest that childhood maltreatment and neglect are positively correlated with the development of schizophrenia (DeRosse, Nitzburg, Kompancaril, & Malhotra, 2014; Larsson et al., 2013; Morgan & Fisher, 2006).

TREATMENT

Multiple treatment programs are available for individuals living with schizophrenia, including medication management as a primary method (Bo, Abu-Akel, Kongerslev, Haahr, & Simonsen, 2011; Opler, Grennan, & Ford, 2009; Tiihonen et al., 2006). Additional therapeutic modalities are also effective, including psycho-social treatment (Bustillo et al., 2001), substance abuse treatment (if applicable) (Hellerstein, Rosenthal, & Miner, 2001), and a variety of cognitive-based therapy modalities (Richardson & Weiler, 1999).

PSYCHOPHARMACOLOGICAL INTERVENTIONS

Antipsychotics, also known as neuroleptics, are the most common medications used in the treatment of schizophrenia (Meyer, 2011). This class of drugs is diverse and continually expanding, evidenced by the number of new antipsychotics that have entered the United States market within the last decade. Antipsychotics are broadly classified into the 'typical' (first-generation) and 'atypical' (second-generation) agents, (Meyer, 2011; Leucht et al., 2013), as shown in Table 1.

TYPICAL ANTIPSYCHOTICS

Typical antipsychotics, used in clinical practice for decades, are inexpensive and deemed quite useful in the treatment of schizophrenia (Caccia, 2013; Meyer, 2011; Zhang et al., 2013). Those used for the treatment of symptoms include chlorpromazine (Thorazine®), trifluoperazine (Stelazine®), and haloperidol (Haldol®). These antipsychotic medications target biological causes, producing most of their therapeutic effect by blocking dopamine-2 receptors in the brain. Research has demonstrated support for the efficacy of typical antipsychotics, as they work toward decreasing the frequency and severity of positive symptoms (Walsh & Yun, 2013) and reducing aggressive behaviors (Walsh & Yun, 2013; Volavka, 2013). However, these drugs also affect other targets, and their long-term use may produce a host of unwanted or harmful side effects (Davis, Chen, & Glick, 2003; U.S. National Library of Medicine, 2011). This may lead to discontinuation, treatment resistance, and the inability to respond to antipsychotic medication therapy (Moncrieff, 2003). Physical side effects of such drugs can range from mild symptoms (i.e., dry mouth, blurred vision, drowsiness, dizziness) to more severe symptoms (i.e., problems with muscle control, spasms, neck and head cramps, tremors similar to symptoms of Parkinson's disease, facial tics). Additionally, long-term use of these medications has been associated with weight gain, hyperlipidemia, and hyperglycemia (Sliwa, Fu, Bossie, Turkoz, & Alphs, 2014). Moreover, several of the typical antipsychotics have been associated with fatal cardiovascular events caused by cardiac arrhythmias induced by the medications. Many antipsychotic medications and other approved drugs found to have such adverse drug reactions have been issued a "Black Box" warning (the sternest of which a medication can carry and remain on the market in the Unites States) by the the U.S. Food and Drug Administration (FDA) (Lasser et al., 2002).

ATYPICAL ANTIPSYCHOTICS

In the more recent years, atypical antipsychotics have emerged. These include risperidone (Risperdal®), olanzapine (Zyprexa®), clozapine (Clozaril®), quetiapine (Seroquel®), and aripiprazole (Abilify®). Atypical antipsychotics provide increased control over both the positive and negative symptoms of schizophrenia (Leucht et al., 2013). Recent research has indicated that these newer, atypical antipsychotics have fewer side effects than the older, typical antipsychotics, while rates of medication resistance remain high (Lieberman et al., 2005). Lieberman and colleagues (2005) compared discontinuation rates of perphenazine, a typical antipsychotic, with those of olanzapine, quetiapine, and risperidone, which are atypical antipsychotics. Their findings highlighted that both the typical and atypical medications demonstrated high rates of termination: perphenazine, 75%; olanzapine, 64%; quetiapine, 82%; and risperidone, 74% (Lieberman et al., 2005).

Atypical antipsychotics have steadily been replacing typical antipsychotics, primarily due to the increased safety and a less aversive effect profile. Atypical agents also tend to be better at treating the adverse symptoms of schizophrenia (e.g., apathy, flat affect, withdrawal) than the typical agents. Atypical antipsychotics effectively block dopamine receptors (a surplus of which is understood to trigger many of the symptoms of schizophrenia), assisting with minimizing the magnitude of schizophrenia symptoms. Unfortunately, the newer atypical medications can be substantially more expensive than the typical agents or the older atypical agents (e.g., clozapine and risperidone), as the older medications have more generic products. Some of the atypical agents (e.g., olanzapine) are also frequently associated with weight gain in patients on long-term therapy (Meyer, 2011; Rosenheck et al., 2006). However, side effects occur with all medications and may not apply to all patients or may only last for a short period of time, while many patients benefit from some type of medicine through reduction of symptoms.

PSYCHOTHERAPEUTIC INTERVENTIONS

COGNITIVE BEHAVIORAL THERAPY
Cognitive behavioral therapy (CBT) is one of the oldest evidence-based options for the treatment of schizophrenia. CBT aims to support individuals in understanding how their thoughts and feelings influence their behaviors, with its main component focused on the "here and now." Therapists work closely with their clients to develop a plan that they will follow throughout treatment to help resolve any cognitive dissonance the client may experience. There are several newer options as well, that focus on psychological assistance, promotion of coping strategies, and client self-esteem and satisfaction. Still other options, such as acceptance and commitment therapy and narrative therapy, focus only on symptom control (Dickerson & Lehman, 2011).

COGNITIVE ENHANCEMENT THERAPY
Cognitive Enhancement Therapy (CET) focuses on developmental cognitive rehabilitation of the social and non-social cognitive deficits that are associated with schizophrenia. In a randomized trial, there were robust effects of this therapy on social cognition and social adjustment, lasting up to a year after treatment ended (Eack et al., 2009). CET requires that the client is medication compliant and stable before beginning treatment. The course of treatment is approximately 18 months (National Registry of Evidence-Based Programs and Practices [NREPP], 2012). Mental health professionals who are providing CET must meet minimum standards and be specifically trained in this method of counseling (NREPP, 2012).

FAMILY THERAPY
Family therapy focuses on educating the family about the illness and improving family dynamics between the client and his or her family members (Lewis, Tarrier, & Drake, 2005). Skills training can help facilitate a less stressful atmosphere and improve problem-solving strategies within a family. Among other forms of treatment, family therapy is shown to be one of the most cost-effective (Andrew, Knapp, McCrone, Parsonage, & Trachtenberg, 2012; Walsh & Yun, 2013). Research has indicated that family therapy has proven useful among those with schizophrenia, reducing symptom relapse rates by an estimated 40% compared to controls (Pharoah, Mari, & Streiner, 2003). Family therapy has also been significantly associated with an increase in medication management adherence (Pharoah et al., 2003).

METACOGNITIVE REFLECTION AND INSIGHT THERAPY (MERIT)
Van Donkersgoed et al. (2014) studied a manual-based, individual therapy for persons with schizophrenia. Characterized by the inability to recognize personal cognitive distortions, metacognitive dysfunctions are common among individuals with schizophrenia. Deficits in metacognition also affect the person's ability

to understand others' feelings and intentions. Used to enhance metacognition in people with schizophrenia, MERIT has helped increase functioning in daily life through the stimulation of various elements, such as awareness of personal thoughts and reflection of thoughts regarding others (Van Donkersgoed et al., 2014).

TELEPSYCHIATRY
Monitoring individuals with schizophrenia who display suicidal thoughts and behaviors is critical during treatment. Telepsychiatry, or teletherapy, involves the delivery of mental health services through technology (Center for Substance Abuse Treatment, 2009). In the case of treating individuals with schizophrenia, the goal of communicating through means of technology is to closely monitor the warning signs of suicide in this population (Kasckow et al., 2014). While telepsychiatry is not currently a commonly used psychiatric service in correctional settings, it has been a recommended option for connecting inmates with more in-depth and personalized mental health care in the community, as well as for reducing overall health care costs in the criminal justice systems (Kinsella, 2004).

CO-MORBIDITY

Co-morbidity is the interaction between two or more disorders that occur at the same time (National Institute on Mental Health, 2010). An individual with schizophrenia will likely have a Co-morbid disorder; however, the risk factors for why Co-morbidity increases in magnitude among those with schizophrenia remain unclear (Buckley et al., 2009).

PHYSICAL HEALTH
Individuals with schizophrenia are likely to experience increased physical health problems compared to the general population, due in part to their low levels of physical activity, linked to increased neurocognitive deficits (Leutwyler, Hubbard, Jeste, Miller, & Vinogradov, 2013). According to Chwastiak et al. (2006), approximately 50% of individuals with schizophrenia experience at least one Co-morbid physical health concern that must be addressed concurrently with the symptoms of schizophrenia. Specifically, type-2 diabetes is the most influential factor in mortality among individuals with schizophrenia (Schoepf, Uppal, Potluri, & Huen, 2013).

CHEMICAL HEALTH
Substance abuse is a serious co-occurring condition, estimated to be present in approximately 50% of individuals with schizophrenia (Blanchard, Brown, Horan, & Sherwood, 2000). People with schizophrenia maintain higher rates of substance use disorders compared to other groups of people with mental illnesses and the general population (Mueser & Gingerich, 2006; Van Dorn, Desmarais, Young, Sellers, & Swartz, 2012). Alcohol and Psychostimulants are the most common substances that individuals with schizophrenia abuse (Batel, 2000). There are strong associations linking the use of cannabis with early onset of symptoms of schizophrenia and an elevated risk of developing psychosis (Green et al., 2004; Hambrecht & Häfner, 1996). Specifically, those who used cannabis more than 50 times before the age 18 demonstrated a greater risk of developing schizophrenia (Hill, 2014). Researchers have also found a link between methamphetamine use and the development of schizophrenia (Li et al., 2014).

People with schizophrenia are more likely to smoke and be heavier smokers than people with other diagnoses, making nicotine another substance commonly abused by patients with schizophrenia. In a literature review, Dalack, Healy, and Meador-Woodruff (1998) reported that studies found 68%-88% of patients with schizophrenia were smokers. For those individuals, smoking may stimulate an increase in dopamine levels in the brain and also stimulate processes involved with learning and cognition. This increase in dopamine levels is also linked with improvement in attention, coping, and emotional engagement and response (Kumari

& Postma, 2005). A suspected association between nicotine acetylcholine receptors and negative symptoms could explain the elevated smoking rates in individuals with schizophrenia (D'Souza et al., 2012). Despite an individual's perceived symptom alleviation by smoking, nicotine "alters the metabolism of psychiatric medications and reduces blood levels of neuroleptics and some antidepressants and benzodiazepines" (Ziedonis, Kosten, Glazer, & Frances, 1994, p. 204). Nicotine usage not only influences the efficacy of antipsychotic drugs and increases unwanted side effects, it can also affect the symptomatology of schizophrenia. Individuals who exhibit Co-morbid substance abuse are at risk for an increase in symptom severity and complications in treatment, since there is an association between Co-morbid substance abuse and less positive treatment outcomes in comparison to individuals who do not show Co-morbid abuse patterns (Lewis et al., 2005).

INTELLECTUAL DISABILITY

The general population of adults age 18 and older has an intelligence estimate traditionally expressed in the form of an Intelligence Quotient (IQ), with an average of 100. In individuals with schizophrenia, the IQ scores may be average to below average in range (Urfer Parnas et al., 2007). Intellectual deficits predating the onset of schizophrenia may account for some disability within the population (Miles et al., 2014). Extensive epidemiological studies have demonstrated that low premorbid IQs are a weak but consistent risk factor for schizophrenia. Additionally, studies have found correlations between a lower premorbid IQ and high occurrence of negative symptoms (Urfer Parnas et al., 2007).

SCHIZOPHRENIA AND CRIMINAL BEHAVIOR

Wallace et al. (2004) found that individuals with schizophrenia were significantly more likely than the general population to be convicted of a violent criminal offense, with rates of 8.1% and 1.8%, respectively. Convictions for non-violent criminal offenses were also higher among individuals with schizophrenia. Of those in the schizophrenia groups, 21.6% held prior convictions compared to a conviction rate of 7.8% among the general population (Wallace et al., 2004). Furthermore, McCabe et al. (2012) assessed a sample of criminals with schizophrenia over a ten-year period and found an arrest rate of 65% for public disorder crimes, 50% for violent crimes, and 45% for property crimes.

CONDUCT DISORDER

In some cases, symptoms of juvenile delinquency and conduct disorder (CD) displayed before age 15 have also been shown to be possible harbingers of schizophrenia (Schiffer et al., 2012; Siegel & Welsh, 2008). CD is more prevalent among people with schizophrenia than among the general population. CD prior to 15 years of age, coupled with a later diagnosis of schizophrenia, causes individuals to commit a higher frequency of violent crimes during childhood, compared to people diagnosed solely with schizophrenia (Schiffer et al., 2012; Vinokur, Levine, Roe, Krivoy, & Fischel, 2014). Those with schizophrenia who retain a childhood diagnosis of CD typically display anti-social and aggressive behaviors, substance abuse, and criminal behaviors throughout their lives (Hanlon, Coda, Cobia, & Rubin, 2012; Schiffer et al., 2012; Volavka, 2013).

CRIMINAL ACTIVITY

Criminogenic risk and mental illness are separate but related issues that need to be addressed concurrently (Wilson et al., 2014). Schizophrenia co-occurring with antisocial personality disorder and/or substance use disorder results in a high number of arrests (Hanlon et al., 2012; Harris, Oakley, & Picchioni, 2014). McCabe et al. (2012) conducted a study assessing Swiss male prisoners with schizophrenia. Of the sample, 85% met diagnostic criteria for alcohol use disorder, 60% met criteria for drug use disorder, and 68% met criteria for antisocial personality. Due to the higher predisposition for thinking styles that support criminal activity among inmates with mental illnesses, it is imperative that treatment planning incorporate interventions that address the specific risk factors of criminogenic needs and anti-social attitudes (Blank Wilson, Draine, Barrenger, Hadley, & Evans, 2014).

VIOLENT CRIME

Wallace et al. (2004) found that individuals with schizophrenia are more likely to be convicted of a violent crime. Fazel and colleagues (2009b) also found that persons with schizophrenia were significantly more likely to be convicted of a violent offense, in comparison to the general population. While it is still important to remember that the majority of individuals diagnosed with schizophrenia are not violent, another study describes the risk of violent criminal activity among these individuals as approximately 3.9 to 5.0 times higher than the general population, when coupled with Co-morbidity of substance abuse (Fazel et al., 2009b). People with schizophrenia and rape or robbery convictions are more likely to be incarcerated than people convicted of those charges who do not have diagnoses of schizophrenia (Morgan et al., 1993; Siegel, 2011). Interestingly, one study found that individuals with schizophrenia commit dangerous crimes (such as assault and arson) more commonly than less serious crimes (Siegel, 2011). Additionally, Hodgins (2008) found the most prevalent form of violent behavior among individuals with schizophrenia to be assault. Hodgins (2008) examined a sample of 205 individuals exhibiting severe symptoms of schizophrenia and found that 49.2% of the men and 38.8% of the women reported one act of physical aggression in the past six months.

Although schizophrenia is present in only 1% of the general population, research found that approximately 10% of individuals in prison who were awaiting trial for homicide met the diagnostic criteria for schizophrenia, and it is likely that this rate is underestimated due to inaccurate diagnoses (Soyka, Morhart-Klute, & Schoech, 2004; Swanson et al., 2006; Wallace et al., 2004). With mental illness considered a risk factor for criminal behavior, Ostermann and Matejkowski (2014) studied former inmates reintegrating into the community and used propensity scoring and matching to examine recidivism rates. Their findings indicated that while those former inmates with a mental illness had similar rates of recurrence compared to those without a mental illness, those with a mental illness faced higher consequences upon reoffending (Ostermann & Matejkowski, 2014).

Walsh and Yun (2013) found that individuals with schizophrenia are at a high risk for violence; however, they also indicated that these individuals are more likely to be the victim of violent crime than the aggressor. People with severe mental health disorders such as schizophrenia may have command hallucinations and visual oddities, and unknowingly get themselves into reckless and dangerous situations that put them at risk of being harmed. Increased risk of victimization is linked to the stigma associated with mental illness (Meadows & Kuehnel, 2005) and the perceived association between schizophrenia and aggression (Hanlon et al., 2012), regardless of the veracity of the claim that those with schizophrenia are violent or the outcome of violent behavior. Tiihonent et al. (1997) found that among people who had committed one or more crimes, only 4% suffered from schizophrenia. Alternatively, Wallace et al. (1998) found that while men with schizophrenia were five times more likely than the general population to commit a serious violent crime, almost none of those individuals were convicted in the course of a year. Though it is not the intention of those who suffer with schizophrenia, the symptoms of the illness cause reckless and self-endangering behaviors (APA, 2013), a concept which criminal justice professionals must consider as they interact with them and make decisions on their behalf.

The risk of aggressive behavior encompasses many interacting factors, including youth, male gender, a low socioeconomic status, substance abuse (Slijepcevic et al., 2014), and a history of violent behavior (Bo et al., 2011; Bobes, Fillat, & Arango, 2009; Chen, Hwu, & Hu, 2014). Additionally, psychological deficits that result in delusional beliefs and hallucinations (especially persecutory delusions or hallucinations) may lead to anger (Mueser & Gingerich, 2006). An impaired sense of empathy (Bragado-Jimenez & Taylor, 2012) and difficulty recognizing facial emotions correlate with violence in individuals with schizophrenia (Demirbuga et al., 2013). This is due in part to the social cognitive impairments that individuals with schizophrenia face when attempting to recognize negative facial emotions, resulting in misunderstanding others' behaviors and intentions (Demirbuga et al., 2013; Harris et al., 2014).

Other resources suggest that, because their rates similarly increased over recent years, violent offending correlates with an increase in substance abuse activity (Fazel et al., 2009b; Hanlon et al., 2012; McCabe et al., 2012; Wallace et al., 2004). Alcohol abuse has been reported as a strong predictor of violence (Fleischman, Werbeloff, Yoffe, Davidson, & Weiser, 2014; Short, Thomas, Mullen, & Ogloff, 2013; Slijepcevic et al., 2014). Miller (2010) found that a dual diagnosis of schizophrenia and substance abuse was the only combination of mental health diagnoses that posed a significantly increased risk of violent crime over the general population.

Other factors such as socioeconomic status and a history of family trauma may increase the risk of violent crime among individuals with schizophrenia (Miller, 2014; Monahan et al., 2001). Research has highlighted that family members and close friends of individuals with schizophrenia are at a greater risk of becoming victims of violence (Short et al., 2013). However, Nordström and Kullgren (2003) found that most victims were unknown to the offenders. The intensity of the violence was less in cases with unknown victims, compared to situations involving family members. In cases involving family members, female family members, especially mothers, were more likely to suffer from more extreme forms of violence (Nordström & Kullgren, 2003).

HOMICIDE

One study estimated that 6% of individuals who have committed murder suffered from schizophrenia (Richard-Devantoy, Orsat, Dumais, Turecki, & Jollant, 2014). Given the low rate of schizophrenia among the general population (approximately 1%), this estimation is worth investigating. Some factors that have been found to mediate the relationship between homicide and schizophrenia, similar to those that increase the risk of aggressive behaviors, include being of the male gender, lack of a professional career, low education levels, alcohol abuse, childhood physical abuse, and a previous history of committing a violent offense.

Neurocognitive factors linking schizophrenia with homicide have been suggested as mediating factors as well. A large-scale meta-analysis reviewed 1760 studies on schizophrenia and homicide, incorporating seven neuropsychological and twelve brain-imaging studies. Richard-Devantoy and colleagues (2014) found common brain abnormalities among individuals with schizophrenia and a history of homicidal acts. These abnormalities range from reduced inferior frontal and temporal cortices (two of four major lobes of the cerebral cortex in the human brain) to increased amygdala volumes (two almond-shaped clusters of nuclei located in the termperol lobes that perform a primary role in emotional processing, decision-making, and emotional memory. Inferior frontal (or more specifically the prefrontal) cortex remains critical for decision-making. In the limited studies highlighting a connection between homicide and schizophrenia, only volumetric analyses showed consistent results. Researchers noted that a conclusive finding could not be made regarding a specific causal link between these variations and homicidal behavior, as the abnormalities were extremely varied (Richard-Devantoy et al., 2014). Still, prior research suggested that neuropsychological deficits might lead to an increase in homicidal behavior due to uninhibited aggressive impulses, and suggested that it is a factor worthy of consideration throughout adjudication proceedings (Hanlon et al., 2012). The majority of schizophrenia-related homicides are not well-conceived plots; they are more likely to be spontaneous acts caused by inadequate management of an individual's emotional dysregulation (fear, anger, etc.). Further research is needed to examine any neurological deficits that might play a role in the intersection between schizophrenia and the risk for homicide (Hanlon et al., 2012; Richard-Devantoy et al., 2014).

Ability to Form Criminal Intent

In many court cases, Mens Rea, or the intent to commit an illegal act or cause harm, in addition to the mental state of the defendant at the time of the alleged offense, is not the central focus. The defense may attempt to decrease the sentence by stating that the defendant is suffering from a severe and persistent mental illness and, at the time of the offense, lacked the ability to form criminal intent (Morse & Hoffman, 2007). The intent to offend may be absent or nearly impossible to prove among individuals with severe mental illness such as schizophrenia.

Confabulation and Criminal Justice

False memories, known clinically as confabulations, are most often associated with memory-specific disorders such as Alzheimer's disease, dementia, and other neurological disorders (Mertz & Brown, 2016). False memories are present in healthy individuals as well, however. In schizophrenia, there is a link between delusions (false beliefs) and confabulations (false memories), though it is not present in all those diagnosed. Schnider (2008) outlined two types of false memories: delusional memory misinterpretation (which occurs when individuals with schizophrenia inappropriately attribute certain memories to their delusion) and falsification of memory (which is a recollection of an event or situation that never occurred). The steady presence of false beliefs can lead to the formation of false memories (Langdon & Turner, 2010).

Lorente-Rovira, Santos-Gómez, Moro, Villagrán, and McKenna (2010) found a statistically significant link between schizophrenia and confabulation. Although patients with schizophrenia were no more or less likely than the control group to remember the facts contained within a fable provided to them, the patients with schizophrenia were far more likely to not only endorse the original fable, but to also expand upon it—elaborations frequently called intrusion errors.

The difference between intrusion errors and fabricating information in the criminal justice system resides in the lack of intentional deceit. This has been shown to occur in healthy individuals in situations such as police interrogations and interviews as well, leading to unreliable testimony (Loftus & Guido, 1975). A recent study advanced current theory indicating that there are unique markers of confabulation in schizophrenia that differ from confabulation in other contexts (Shakeel & Docherty, 2014). Individuals with schizophrenia presented confabulations that differed from those of patients with amnesia and Alzheimer's (McKenna, Lorente-Rovira, & Berrios, 2009; Nathaniel-James & Frith, 1996; Nathaniel-James, Foong, & Frith, 1996). The presentation of evidence contrary to the individual's belief will not necessarily result in understanding or acceptance of the facts, due to the neurological nature of confabulations. Additionally, if an individual is experiencing symptoms of schizophrenia and confabulations are a product of these symptoms, confrontation may result in aggression, confusion, and other undesirable outcomes as a way of acting out when defending what they believe to be true (Mertz & Brown, 2016; Schnider, 2008; Feinberg, 2009), as the ability to filter reality is often lacking in those with psychosis (Waters, Badcock, Mayberry, & Michie, 2003). In short, when faced with a different version of reality, the individual with schizophrenia may become confused and act defensively and/or violently, due to their inability to comprehend the cognitive disconnect. When confabulation or deceit is present, the assessment of an individual's current functioning by a mental health professional is imperative before engaging in a discussion.

The risk for confabulation among individuals with schizophrenia poses serious problems for the justice system. False memories may compromise several aspects of the adjudication process and could ultimately render an offender incompetent to stand trial. In most cases, false testimony is punishable by law, and an earnestly believed confabulation may be difficult to both identify and to assign moral or legal judgment. Psychological evaluations conducted for the court should presumably involve memory tests to assist in solidifying an individual's current mental health status. Furthermore, additional efforts should be conducted to locate and obtain copies of all previous intellectual and psychological assessments, to compare the current cognitive functioning and mental health presentations or diagnostic presentations with the current outcomes (Coid et al., 2007; Stafford, 2003).

Unreliable Testimony

Individuals with schizophrenia are at an increased risk of falling victim to suggestive techniques commonly used by trained police interrogators, as one or more of the common symptoms of schizophrenia can trigger susceptibility to suggestions (Redlich, 2004). Individuals experiencing paranoia may be subject to internalizing fear, causing them to develop unlikely story plots and/or agreeing to information presented to them by a person in a position of authority, out of concern for their personal safety. Individuals with schizophrenia who are subject to confabulation may provide additional facts based on false memories, generated by intrusions (McKenna et al., 2009). Hallucinations and delusions may also significantly alter the course of an individual's verbal and behavioral responses to questioning (Stafford & Sellbom, 2013). This is particularity the case when police conduct interrogations using the Reid technique. The Reid method assumes guilt and emotional manipulating tactics are used, which can cause individuals with psychotic disorders to confabulate and give false confessions or testimony (Redlich, 2004).

In addition to the ethical considerations regarding professional behavior and individual rights, criminal justice professionals must consider the consequence that symptoms of schizophrenia place on the legal system. In defenses such as insanity or diminished capacity, criminal procedure places the burden of proof on the defendant, who must prove that their symptoms contributed to their behavior (Stafford, 2003).

Individuals suffering from a severe and persistent mental illness such as schizophrenia often have difficulties comprehending their Miranda rights (Viljoen, Roesch, & Zapf, 2002). They are also more likely to waive rights such as the privilege of representation by counsel, due to incomprehension. These individuals are also more vulnerable to divulging false information or confessions (Redlich, 2004). Follette, Davis, and Leo (2007) highlighted that deficits in cognitive processing and delusions, two characteristic symptoms of schizophrenia, are common factors of mental illness that are often associated with false confessions. Delusional episodes, especially severe episodes where voices coerce the individual, may lead to a confession regardless of the interrogation tactics (Redlich, 2004).

Competency

It is imperative that an individual is competent to stand trial throughout the entire adjudication process. Competency implies a rational amount of understanding and the ability to communicate with a lawyer to formulate a reasonable defense (Drope v. Missouri, 1975). An individual who is suffering from active hallucinations and delusions is severely limited in the extent to which he or she can understand, communicate, and assist their attorney in their defense. Researchers have demonstrated that hallucinations and delusions are related to impairments in defendants who have schizophrenia (Stafford & Sellbom, 2013), and a study by Viljoen et al. (2002) found active psychotic episodes might impair an individual's ability to comprehend legal ramifications. Psychotic impairments in relation to the criminal justice system may potentially alter the culpability at the time of the offense, the arrest, interrogation, and further participation in criminal procedure (Viljoen et al., 2002).

It is important to be aware that the presence of a serious mental illness does not equate with trial incompetency, and the majority of individuals who undergo competency evaluations are deemed competent (Stafford, 2003). A defendant considered incompetent may be sent to a psychiatric treatment center to receive services in hopes of restoring insight and legal competency. In some circumstances, the court can order the use of medication, with the hopes of restoring the individual's competency (Sell v. United States, 2003). The Supreme Court ruling in Sell v. United States (2003) imposed stringent limitations on the use of such forced medication. It is important that all professionals working within the fields of criminal justice, psychology, and law keep abreast of not only the legal codes, but also the professional ethics and current science in mental and behavioral health.

SCHIZOPHRENIA AND CRIMINAL JUSTICE

The deinstitutionalization movement progressed in both legislature and public opinion during the second half of the 20th century, following mounting evidence that supported the stance that forced institutionalization of the mentally ill was inhumane (Octophetus, 2012). This trend would ostensibly shift a portion of the responsibility for treatment of mental disorders toward the community, to promote care in local, community-based settings closer to the individual's family, community, and natural support system. President John F. Kennedy championed this cause, enacting the Community Mental Health Centers Act in October of 1963. Unfortunately, due to President Kennedy's assassination less than a month later, funding for the act was never fully allocated, and those who left the institutions lacked the support to survive in the community (Slate, Buffington-Vollum, & Johnson, 2013).

Challenges that may confront community-level settings are security and the decision each person has, based on his or her fundamental human rights, to refuse treatment. Thus, many who were released to community-based settings were released from or left the hospital care centers and, without income, shelter, or medication for mental health maintenance, were homeless and failed to receive treatment (Hoffer, 2004). Documentation from as early as 1972 showed that the number of mentally ill individuals in the correctional system was increasing proportionally to the deinstitutionalization movement—a phenomenon referred to as the criminalization of mentally disordered behavior (Torrey, 2006; Slate et al., 2013). Contact between individuals with schizophrenia and law enforcement is not surprising, due to the frequently disorganized behavior displayed by individuals with schizophrenia.

Untreated symptoms of schizophrenia within correctional institutions present serious implications for the future behavior of inmates. According to Keers, Ullrich, Destavola, and Coid (2014), numerous studies suggest that ongoing symptoms of schizophrenia, especially delusions, play a significant role in violence during imprisonment and affect an individual's release back into the community. Those with schizophrenia can be more likely to break prison rules, most notably by use of violent methods, and consequently are often on cell restriction for longer periods of time (Morgan et al., 1993). However, no behavioral benefit to cell restriction has been found (Morgan et al., 1993). Restricting individuals with schizophrenia limits access to psychiatric treatment and can have unintended consequences of increased symptomology.

Psychiatric rehabilitation within the criminal justice system is often limited, frequently due to reported budget constraints. The Policy Research Institute (2004) reported that state and federal prison costs increased in the early 1990s by 82%, and again in 2004 by 160%, due to an increase in the number of inmates with schizophrenia. Conversely, this report noted that only one-fifth of polled inmates said they had received any treatment since their incarceration (National Alliance on Mental Illness, 2004). The majority of individuals living with schizophrenia within the criminal justice system are not receiving the proper treatment, if any at all, due to economic restrictions. It is, therefore, imperative for those working in correctional facilities to make themselves aware of the mental health services, support groups, therapy, and referral resources within the correctional system that can accurately treat inmates with schizophrenia.

MEDICATION USE IN CORRECTIONS

Adherence to psychotropic medications can be a challenge when treating people with schizophrenia. Patients may purposefully cease taking their medications for a variety of reasons, from avoiding side effects to abusing substances (Dixon, 1999; Lieberman et al., 2005). Antipsychotics present a unique challenge within correctional facility systems: while seldom seen as substances of abuse in the general population, they are commonly implicated in the correctional setting (Pilkinton & Pilkinton, 2014; Tamburello, Lieberman, Baum, & Reeves, 2012). Several factors influence this phenomenon: first, for some prisoners, antipsychotic medication may be the only item of value for obtaining other desired goods; second, limited staffing in correctional facilities may lead to overuse of antipsychotics for managing disruptive behavior or vague psychiatric symptoms; and lastly, there may be a lack of knowledge among correctional staff regarding the addiction potential of antipsychotics. Workers may not realize that antipsychotics may be just as coveted as traditionally higher-abuse-liability medications, such as stimulants and opiates.

The most commonly abused antipsychotics are quetiapine (Seroquel®), chlorpromazine (Geodon®), and ziprasidone (Zeldox®) (Pilkinton & Pilkinton, 2014; Tamburello et al., 2012). Diphenhydramine and other medications used to manage adverse effects of antipsychotics are highly sought-after among patients in correctional facilities. Quetiapine and chlorpromazine are often abused for their sedative-hypnotic effects and used to offset withdrawal or other unpleasant symptoms resulting from misuse of other drugs. Pulverized quetiapine and ziprasidone tablets can be snorted for euphoric effect (Pilkinton & Pilkinton, 2014; Tamburello et al., 2012). Inmates may also attempt dangerous practices such as intravenous injection of pulverized tablets. Additionally, quetiapine may be paired with cocaine, going by the street name "Q-ball" (Malekshahi, Tioleco, Ahmed, Campbell, & Haller, 2015).

While some patients may avoid their prescribed antipsychotic regimen, it is not always straightforward to detect drug diversion (transfer of legally prescribed medication to someone else) (Pilkinton & Pilkinton, 2014). The variety of different antipsychotic formulations (Table 1 under Appendix) provides options to limit diversion. A liquid solution or rapidly disintegrating, oral tablet antipsychotic reduces chances of concealing medications or avoiding ingestion, especially when used with direct, observed therapy practices. Rapid-disintegrating tablets, if feasible, are a better option than crushing up regular oral tablets and dispersing them into applesauce or other foods, as manipulation of medications outside their intended use may interfere with effectiveness (Keith, 2006). Long-acting depot injections avoid risk of diversion altogether. A challenge for correctional facilities is that specialized formulations of medications often are more costly. Furthermore, some correctional facilities have taken stricter measures such as restricting or even removing specific antipsychotic medications from their formulary. Some of the published literature specifically addresses quetiapine, as this medication has been consistently identified as one of the most frequently abused prescription drugs within correctional facilities (Morin, 2007; Hanley & Kenna, 2008). The State of New Jersey Department of Corrections has published data regarding removal of quetiapine from their formulary (Tamburello et al., 2012), a decision likely influenced by the risk for potential abuse.

THE RIGHT TO REFUSE MEDICATION

The U.S. Supreme Court has delivered opinions on numerous cases involving patients involuntarily committed, as well as individuals within the corrections system being forced medication (Natanson v Kline, 1960; Schloendorff v Society of N.Y, Hosp., 1914). It is important to note that patients have the right to refuse treatment in most circumstances. For instance, in Riggins v. Nevada (1992), the court ruled that it was unconstitutional to force a mentally ill person to take antipsychotic medications for facilitating trial by ensuring competency. However, in Washington v. Harper (1990), the court ruled that a mentally ill individual may be forced to take antipsychotic medication if the person is dangerous to themselves or others and the prescribed medication is in the best medical interest (that is, there exists no less-intrusive manner that would quell the risk posed). Overall, the decision to force an individual living with schizophrenia to take medication is dependent on the risk to the individual and others.

Transitions Out of Corrections

When an individual with schizophrenia is scheduled to transition out of corrections, their ability to attend to basic needs must be given consideration. This is particularly true if the individual has spent significant amounts of time in an institutional setting. Persons with schizophrenia often have anxiety living independently and require services such as assisted living (Rajji et al., 2014). These individuals are often required to live in a structured community setting, due to their inability to complete basic self-care activities such as cooking, cleaning, and various forms of hygiene (Rajji et al., 2014).

Coid et al. (2007) found a 41% recidivism rate for individuals with schizophrenia released into the community being reconvicted of a violent crime—the average time frame being approximately two years after release. The most common reasons for reconvictions among this population were a breach of probationary guidelines and theft (Coid et al., 2007). This finding underlies the necessity for improving prison treatment services to be responsive to the needs of individuals living with schizophrenia. Successful treatment outcomes among individuals within prison settings may reduce recidivism rates and ultimately reduce rates of reconvictions. Creating structure and support when living in the community can lower an individual's chance of reoffending. Stable employment, housing, and positive relationships have been found to translate into lower recidivism rates compared to those who do not have supportive relationships or remain unemployed (Mullen, 2006). Considerations need to be made regarding financial concerns, living environment, and the availability of appropriate services to enable a successful transition (Morenoff & Harding, 2014), as placement upon release can affect recidivism.

Conclusion

Schizophrenia is a complex and heterogeneous mental health syndrome that affects perception, communication, cognition, behavior, affect, memory, and social interactions. The level of functioning for an individual with schizophrenia can vary greatly and is dependent on environment, medication, and other factors. A professional in the criminal justice system working with an individual diagnosed with schizophrenia must be both attuned to and aware of the individual's level of functioning at all times. This is a matter of safety for both the individual and the criminal justice professional—safety in the traditional sense of physical well-being and the behavioral health sense of stress reduction and avoidance of undesirable thoughts and behaviors. The necessity of attunement to these factors extends to interactions with individuals with schizophrenia during public contact as well as during questioning or court proceedings and during incarceration and release planning.

During the development and ongoing maintenance of policies regarding mental health in criminal justice departments, administrators should remain equally attuned to the impact of positive, negative, and cognitive symptoms that accompany schizophrenia. Educational training for professionals can enable early identification for the need to screen for mental illness. For professionals working in the judicial system, this training may allow for the development of procedures that improve the reliability and validity of confessions and testimonies provided by individuals with a diagnosis of schizophrenia. In many cases, precautions are necessary to ensure that individuals with schizophrenia receive proper representation in court and are not impulsively waiving their personal rights.

Educating professionals who work as the primary criminal justice points of contact, as well as families and friends of individuals with schizophrenia about the signs and risks of schizophrenia may be the most effective future-course of action. Those in direct observation or contact are often the most likely to notice the deteriorating symptoms characteristic of schizophrenia. Involving family, friends, and team members in the legal and treatment processes can elevate the social support of patients and lead to more positive personal and social outcomes.

References

American Psychiatric Association. (2013). *Diagnostic and statistical manual of mental disorders* (5th Ed.). Arlington, Virginia: American Psychiatric Publishing.

Andreasen, N. C. (1984). *The broken brain: The biological revolution in psychiatry* (1st ed.). New York: Harper & Row.

Andrew, A., Knapp, M., McCrone, P., Parsonage, M., & Trachtenberg, M. (2012). *Effective interventions in schizophrenia the economic case: A report prepared for the schizophrenia commission.* London, UK: Rethink Mental Illness.

Arboleda-Florez, J. (2009). Mental patients in prisons. *World psychiatry, 8*(3), 187-189.

Arguedas, D., Langdon, R., & Stevenson, R. (2012). Neuropsychological characteristics associated with olfactory hallucinations in schizophrenia. *Journal of the International Neuropsychological Society, 18*(05), 799-808.

Barch, D. M., & Ceaser, A. (2012). Cognition in schizophrenia: Core psychological and neural mechanisms. *Trends in Cognitive Sciences, 16*(1), 27-34.

Barlow, D. H., & Durand, V. M. (2010). *Abnormal psychology.* Mason, OH: Cengage Learning.

Batel, P. (2000). Addiction and schizophrenia. *European Psychiatry, 15*(2), 115-122.

Beck, A. T., Rector, N. A., Stolar, N., & Grant, P. (2009). *Schizophrenia: Cognitive theory, research, and therapy.* New York, NY: The Guilford Press.

Ben Amor, L. (2012). Antipsychotics in pediatric and adolescent patients: A review of comparative safety data. *Journal of Affective Disorders, 138*, 22-30.

Bennouna-Greene, M., Bennouna-Greene, V., Berna, F., & Defranoux, L. (2011). History of abuse and neglect in patients with schizophrenia who have a history of violence. *Child Abuse & Neglect, 35*(5), 329-332. doi:10.1016/j.chiabu.2011.01.008

Bijanki, K. R., Hodis, B., Magnotta, V. A., Zeien, E., & Andreasen, N. C. (2015). Effects of age on white matter integrity and negative symptoms in schizophrenia. *Schizophrenia Research, 161*(1), 29–35. http://doi.org/10.1016/j.schres.2014.05.031

Blanchard, J. J., Brown, S. A., Horan, W. P., & Sherwood, A. R. (2000). Substance use disorders in schizophrenia: Review, integration, and a proposed model. *Clinical Psychology Review, 20*(2), 207-234. doi:10.1016/S0272-7358(99)00033-1

Blank Wilson, A., Draine, J., Barrenger, S., Hadley, T., & Evans, A. (2014). Examining the impact of mental illness and substance use on time till reincarceration in a county jail. *Administration and Policy in Mental Health and Mental Health Services Research, 41*(3), 293-301. doi:10.1007/s10488-013-0467-7

Bo, S., Abu-Akel, A., Kongerslev, M., Haahr, U. H., & Simonsen, E. (2011). Risk factors for violence among patients with schizophrenia. *Clinical Psychology Review, 31*(5), 711-726. doi:10.1016/j.cpr.2011.03.002

Bobes, J., Fillat, O., & Arango, C. (2009). Violence among schizophrenia out-patients compliant with medication: Prevalence and associated factors. *Acta Psychiatrica Scandinavica, 119*, 218-225. doi:10.1111/j.1600-0447.2008.01302.x

Bora, E. (2015). Neurodevelopmental origin of cognitive impairment in schizophrenia. *Psychological Medicine, 45*, 1-9. doi:10.1017/S0033291714001263

Bracha, S. H., Wolkowitz, O. M., Lohr, J. B., Karson, C. N., & Bigelow, L. B. (1989). High prevalence of visual hallucinations in research subjects with chronic schizophrenia. *American Journal Psychiatry, 146*(4), 526-528.

Bragado-Jimenez, M. D., & Taylor, P. J. (2012). Empathy, schizophrenia and violence: A systematic review. *Schizophrenia Research, 141*(1), 83-90. doi:10.1016/j.chres.2012.07.019

Brown, A. S., Begg, M. D., Gravenstein, S., Schaefer, C. A., Wyatt, R. J., Bresnahan, M., Babulas, V.P., & Susser, E. S. (2004). Serologic evidence of prenatal influenza in the etiology of schizophrenia. *Archives of General Psychiatry, 61*(8), 774-780. doi:10.1001/archpsyc.61.8.774

Buckley, P., Miller, B., Lehrer, D., & Castle, D. (2009). Psychiatric Co-morbidities and schizophrenia. *Schizophrenia Bulletin, 35*(2), 383-402. doi:10.1093/schbul/sbn135

Burns, J. K., Tomita, A., & Kapadia, A. S. (2014). Income inequality and schizophrenia: Increased schizophrenia incidence in countries with high levels of income inequality. *International Journal of Social Psychiatry, 60*(2), 185-196. doi: 10.1177/0020764013481426

Bustillo, J. R., Lauriello, J., Horan, W. P., & Keith, S. J. (2001). The psychosocial treatment of schizophrenia: an update. *American Journal of Psychiatry, 158*(2), 163-175.

Butler, R. W., & Braff, D. L. (1991). Delusions: A review and integration. *Schizophrenia Bulletin, 17*(4), 633-647.

Caccia, S. (2013). Safety and pharmacokinetics of atypical antipsychotics in children and adolescents. *Paediatric Drugs, 15*(3), 217-233. doi:10.1007/s40272-013-0024-6

Callahan, L. (2004). Correctional officer attitudes toward inmates with mental disorders. *International Journal of Forensic Mental Health, 3*(1), 37-54. doi:10.1080/14999013.2004.10471195

Cantor-Graae, E. (2007). The contribution of social factors to the development of schizophrenia: A review of recent findings. *Canadian Journal of Psychiatry, 52*(2), 277-286.

Cardno, A., & Gottesman, I. (2000). Twin studies of schizophrenia: From bow-and-arrow concordances to star wars Mx and functional genomics. *American Journal of Medical Genetics, 97*(1), 12-17. doi:10.1002/(SICI)1096-8628(200021)97:13.0.CO;2-U

Carter, C. J. (2011). Schizophrenia: A pathogenetic autoimmune disease caused by viruses and pathogens and dependent on genes. *Journal of Pathogens, 2011.*

Center for Substance Abuse Treatment. (2009). *Considerations for the provision of E-therapy.* HHS Publication. No. (SMA) 09-4450. Rockville, MD: Center for Substance Abuse Treatment, Substance Abuse and Mental Health Services Administration.

Chen, S. C., Hwu, H. G., & Hu, F. C. (2014). Clinical prediction of violence among inpatients with schizophrenia using the Chinese modified version of violence scale: A prospective cohort study. *International Journal of Nursing Studies, 51*(2), 198-207. doi:10.1016/j.ijnurstu.2013.06.002

Chwastiak, L., Rosenheck, R., McEvoy, J., Keefe, R., Swartz, M., & Lieberman, M. (2006). Interrelationships of psychiatric symptom severity, medical Co-morbidity, and functioning in schizophrenia. *Psychiatric Services, 57*(8), 1102-1109.

Coid, J., Yang, M., Ullrich, S., Zhang, T., Roberts, A., Roberts, C., Rogers, R., & Farrington, C. (2007). Predicting and understanding risk of re-offending: The prisoner cohort study. *Research Summary No. 6.* Ministry of Justice.

Compton, M. T., Neubert, B. N. D., Broussard, B., McGriff, J. A., Morgan, R., & Oliva, J. R. (2009). Use of force preferences and perceived effectiveness of actions among Crisis Intervention Team (CIT) police officers and non-CIT officers in an escalating psychiatric crisis involving a subject with schizophrenia. *Schizophrenia Bulletin*, sbp146.

Csukly, G., Stefanics, G., Komlósi, S., Czigler, I., & Czobor, P. (2014). Event-related theta synchronization predicts deficit in facial affect recognition in schizophrenia. *Journal of Abnormal Psychology, 123*(1), 178-189. http://dx.doi.org/10.1037/a0035793

D'Souza, D.C., Esterlis, I., Carbuto, M., Krasenics, M., Seibyl, J., Bois, F., Pattman, B., Ranganthan, M, Cosgrove, K., & Staley, J. (2012). Lower β2*-nicotinic acetylcholine receptor availability in smoking with schizophrenia. *American Journal of Psychiatry, 169*(3), 326-334.

Dalack, G. W., Healy, D. J., & Meador-Woodruff, J. H. (1998). Nicotine dependence in schizophrenia: Clinical phenomena and laboratory findings. *American Journal of Psychiatry, 155*, 1490-1501.

Davis, J., Chen, N., & Glick, I. (2003). A meta-analysis of the efficacy of second-generation antipsychotics. *Archives of General Psychiatry, 60*(6), 553-564. doi:10.1001/archpsyc.60.6.553

Delay, J., Deniker, P., & Harl, J. (1952). Therapeutic use in psychiatry of phenothiazine of central elective action (4560 RP). *Annales Medico-Psychologiques (Paris), 110*(2), 112-117.

Demirbuga, S., Sahin, E., Ozver, I., Alustaoglu, S., Kandemir, E., Varkal, M. D., Emul, M., & Ince, H. (2013). Facial emotion recognition in patients with violent schizophrenia. *Schizophrenia Research, 144*(1-3), 142-145. doi:10.1016/j.schres.2012.12.015

DeRosse, P., Nitzburg, G. C., Kompancaril, B., & Malhotra, A. K. (2014). The relation between childhood maltreatment and psychosis in patients with schizophrenia and non-psychiatric controls. *Schizophrenia Research, 155*(1-3), 66-71. doi:10.1016/j.schres.2014.03.009

Dickerson, F. B., & Lehman, A. F. (2011). Evidence-based psychotherapy for schizophrenia, 2011 update. *The Journal of Nervous and Mental Disease, 199*(1), 520-526. doi: 10.1097/NMD.0b013e318225ee78

Dixon, L. (1999). Dual diagnosis of substance abuse in schizophrenia: Prevalence and impact on outcomes. *Schizophrenia Research, 35*(1), 93-100. doi:10.1016/S0920-9964(98)00161-3

Doctor, R. M., & Shiromoto, F. N. (2010). *The A to Z of trauma: A concise guide to the causes, symptoms, and treatment of traumatic stress disorders.* New York, NY: Checkmark Books.

Drope v. Missouri, 420 U.S. 162, 172 (1975).

Eack, S. M., Greenwald, D. P., Hogarty, S. S., Cooley, S. J., DiBarry, A. L., Montrose, D. M., & Keshavan, M. S. (2009). Cognitive enhancement therapy for early course schizophrenia: Effects of a two-year randomized controlled trial. *Psychiatric Services, 60*(11), 1468-1476. doi:10.1176/appi.ps.60.11.1468

Eisenberg, D. P., & Berman, K. F. (2010). Executive function, neural circuitry, and genetic mechanisms in schizophrenia. *Neuropsychopharmacology, 35*(1), 258-277.

Fazel, S., Grann, M., Carlström, E., Lichtenstein, P., & Långström, N. (2009a). Risk factors for violent crime in schizophrenia: A national cohort study of 13,806 patients. *Journal of Clinical Psychiatry, 70*(3), 362-369. doi: info:pmid/19284931

Fazel, S., Långström, N., Hjern, A., Grann, M., & Lichtenstein, P. (2009b). Schizophrenia, substance abuse, and violent crime. *The Journal of the American Medical Association, 301*(19), 2016-2023. doi:10.1001/jama.2009.675

Feinberg, T. (2009). Confabulation, The self, and ego functions: The ego disequilibrium theory. W. Hirstein (Ed.), *Confabulation: Views From Neuroscience, Psychiatry, Psychology, and Philosophy.* (pp. 91-108). New York, NY; Oxford University Press.

Ferriter, M., & Huband, N. (2003). Experiences of parents with a son or daughter suffering from schizophrenia. *Journal of psychiatric and mental health nursing, 10*(5), 552-560.

Fleischman, A., Werbeloff, N., Yoffe, R., Davidson, M., & Weiser, M. (2014). Schizophrenia and violent crime: A population-based study. *Psychological Medicine, 44*(14), 3051-3057. doi:10.1017/S0033291714000695

Follette, W., Davis, D., & Leo, R. (2007). Mental health status and vulnerability to police interrogation tactics. *Criminal Justice, 22*(3), 46-49.

Fusar-Poli, P., Kempton, M. J., & Rosenheck, R. A. (2013). Efficacy and safety of second-generation long-acting injections in schizophrenia: A meta-analysis of randomized-controlled trials. *International Clinical Psychopharmacology, 28*(2), 57-66. doi:10.1097/YIC.0b013e32835b091f

Gentile, S. (2013). Adverse effects associated with second-generation antipsychotic long-acting injection treatment: A comprehensive systematic review. *Pharmacotherapy, 33*(10), 1087-1106. doi:10.1002/phar.1313

Gilmore, J. H. (2010). Understanding what causes schizophrenia: A developmental perspective. *American Journal of Psychiatry, 167(1)*, 8-10. doi: 10.1176/appi.ajp.2009.09111588

Goghari, V. M. (2014). Facial emotion recognition deficits in schizophrenia: Brain mechanisms to targeted treatments. *Canadian Journal of Psychiatry, 55*(1), 41-43. doi:10.1037/a0035354

Goghari, V. M., & Sponheim, S. R. (2013). More pronounced deficits in facial emotion recognition for schizophrenia than bipolar disorder. *Comprehensive Psychiatry, 54*(4), 388-397. doi:10.1016/j.comppsych.2012.10.012

Gold, J. M., Kool, W., Botvinick, M. M., Hubzin, L., August, S., & Waltz, J. A. (2015). Cognitive effort avoidance and detection in people with schizophrenia. *Cognitive, Affective, & Behavioral Neuroscience, 15*(1), 145-154.

Green, A., Tohen, M., Hamer, R., Strakowski, S., Lieberman, J., Glick, I., Clark, W. S., & HDGH Research Group. (2004). First-episode schizophrenia-related psychosis and substance use disorders: Acute response to olanzapine and haloperidol. *Schizophrenia Research, 66*(2-3), 125-135. doi:10.1016/j.schres.2003.08.001

Greenberg, M. S. (1992). Olfactory hallucinations. In *Science of Olfaction* (pp. 467-499). Springer New York.

Gumley, A., Karatzias, A., Power, K., Reilly, J., McNay, L., & O'Grady, M. (2006). Early intervention for relapse in schizophrenia: Impact of cognitive behavioural therapy on negative beliefs about psychosis and self-esteem. *British Journal of Clinical Psychology, 45*(2), 247-260.

Hall, J., Trent, S., Thomas, K. L., O'Donovan, M. C., & Owen, M. J. (2015). Genetic risk for schizophrenia: convergence on synaptic pathways involved in plasticity. *Biological Psychiatry, 77*(1), 52-58.

Hambrecht, M., & Häfner, H. (1996). Substance abuse and the onset of schizophrenia. *Biological Psychiatry, 40*(11), 1155-1163. doi:10.1016/S0006-3223(95)00609-5

Hanley, M. J., & Kenna, G. A. (2008). Quetiapine: treatment for substance abuse and drug of abuse. *American Journal of Health-System Pharmacy, 65*(7), 611-618.

Hanlon, R. E., Coda, J. J., Cobia, D., & Rubin, L. H. (2012). Psychotic domestic murder: Neuropsychological differences between homicidal and nonhomicidal schizophrenic men. *Journal of Family Violence, 27*(2), 105-113. doi:10.1007/s10896-011-9410-4

Harris, S. T., Oakley, C., & Picchioni, M. M. (2014). A systematic review of the association between attributional bias/interpersonal style, and violence in schizophrenia/psychosis. *Aggression and Violent Behavior, 19*(3), 235-241. doi:10.1016/j.avb.2014.04.009

Hartling, L., Abou-Setta, A. M., Dursun, S., Mousavi, S. S., Pasichnyk, D., & Newton, A. S. (2012). Antipsychotics in adults with schizophrenia: Comparative effectiveness of first-generation versus second-generation medications: A systematic review and meta-analysis. *Annals of Internal Medicine, 157*(7), 498-511. doi:10.7326/0003-4819-157-7-201210020-00525

Hellerstein, D. L., Rosenthal, R. N., Miner, C. R. (2001). Integrating service for schizophrenia and substance abuse. *Psychiatric Quarterly, 72*(4), 291-306. doi:10.1023/A:1010385114289

Hietala, J., Syvälahti, E., Vilkman, H., Vuorio, K., Räkköläinen, V., Bergman, J., Haaparanta, M., Solin, O., Kuoppamäki, M., Eronen, E., & Ruotsalainen, U. (1999). Depressive symptoms and presynaptic dopamine function in neuroleptic-naive schizophrenia. *Schizophrenia Research, 35*(1), 41-50. doi:10.1016/S0920-9964(98)00113-3

Hietala, J., Syvälahti, E., Vuorio, K., Räkköläinen, V., Bergman, J., Haaparanta, M.,Ruotsalainen, U., Vuorio, K., Räkköläinen, V., Bergman, J., Solin, O., Kirvelä, O., & Salokangas, R. K. (1995). Presynaptic dopamine function in striatum of neuroleptic-naïve schizophrenic patients. *Lancet, 346*(8983), 1130-1131.

Hill, M. N. (2014). Clearing the smoke: What do we know about adolescent cannabis use and schizophrenia? *Journal of Psychiatry & Neuroscience, 39*(2), 75-77. doi:10.1503/jpn.140028

Hodgins, S. (2008). Violent behavior among people with schizophrenia: A framework for investigations of causes, and effective treatment, and prevention. *Philosophical Transactions of the Royal Society B, 363*(1503), 2505-2518. doi:10.1098/rstb.2008.0034

Hoffer, A. (2004). Healing Schizophrenia: Complementary vitamin & drug treatments. Toronto, CAN: CCNM Press.

Hor, K., & Taylor, M. (2010). Suicide and schizophrenia: A systematic review of rates and risk factors. *Journal of Psychopharmacology, 24*(4), 81-90. doi:10.1177/1359786810385490

Howard, R., Rabins, P. V., Seeman, M. V., & Jeste, D. V. (2000). Late-onset schizophrenia and very-late-onset schizophrenia-like psychosis: an international consensus. *American Journal of Psychiatry, 157,* 172-178. doi: 10.1176/appi.ajp.157.2.172

Howes, O., & Kapur, S. (2009). The dopamine hypothesis of schizophrenia: Version III- the final common pathway. *Schizophrenia Bulletin, 35*(3), 549-562. doi:10.1093/schbul/sbp006

Janssen, I., Krabbendam, L., Bak, M., Hanssen, M., Vollebergh, W., de Graaf, R., & van Os, J. (2003). Childhood abuse as a risk factor for psychotic experiences. *Acta Psychiatrica Scandinavica, 109*(1), 38-45. doi:10.1046/j.0001-690X.2003.00217.x

Kasckow, J., Zickmund, S., Rotondi, A., Mrkva, A., Gurklis, J., Chinman, M., Fox, L., Loganathan, M., Hanusa, B., & Haas, G. (2014). Development of telehealth dialogues for monitoring suicidal patients with schizophrenia: Consumer feedback. *Community Mental Health Journal, 50*(3), 339-342. doi: 10.1007/s10597-012-9589-8

Kee, K. S., Green, M. F., Mintz, J., & Brekke, J. S. (2003). Is emotion processing a predictor of functional outcome in schizophrenia? *Schizophrenia Bulletin, 29*(3), 487-497.

Keers, R., Ullrich, S., Destavola, B., & Coid, J. (2014). Association of violence with emergence of persecutory delusions in untreated schizophrenia. *The American Journal of Psychiatry, 171*(3), 332-339. doi:10.1176/appi.ajp.2013.13010134

Kehoe, P., Shoemaker, W., Triano, L., Hoffman, J., & Arons, C. (1996). Repeated isolation in the neonatal rat produces alterations in behavior and ventral striatal dopamine release in the juvenile after amphetamine challenge. *Behavioral Neuroscience, 110*(6), 1435-1444.

Keith, S. (2006). Advances in psychotropic formulations. *Progress in Neuro-psychopharmacology & Biological Psychiatry, 30*(6), 996-1008. doi:10.1016/j.pnpbp.2006.03.031

Kestler, L., Walker, E., & Vega, E. (2001). Dopamine receptors in the brains of schizophrenia patients: A meta-analysis of the findings. *Behavioral Pharmacology, 12*(5), 355-371. doi: 10.1097/00008877-200109000-00007

King, D. J. (1998). Drug treatment of the negative symptoms of schizophrenia. *European Neuropsychopharmacology, 8*(1), 33-42.

King, S., St-Hilaire, A., & Heidkamp, D. (2010). Prenatal factors in schizophrenia. *Current Directions in Psychological Science, 19*(4), 209-213.

Kinsella, C. (2004). *Corrections health care costs*. Lexington, KY: The Council of State Governments. Retrieved from http://www.prisonpolicy.org/scans/csg/Corrections+Health+Care+Costs+1-21-04.pdf

Kodituwakku, P., Kalberg, W., & May, P. (2011). Effects of prenatal alcohol exposure on executive functioning. National Institute on Alcohol Abuse and Alcoholism. Retrieved from http://pubs.niaaa.nih.gov/publications/arh25-3/192-198.htm

Kumari, V., & Postma, P. (2005). Nicotine dependence and illness severity in schizophrenia. *British Journal of Psychiatry, 29*(6), 1021-1034.

Langdon, R., & Turner, M. (2010). Delusions and confabulation: Overlapping or distinct distortions of reality? *Cognitive Neuropsychiatry, 15*(1-3), 1-13. doi:10.1080/13546800903519095

Laroi, F., & Aleman, A. (2011). Insights into hallucinations in schizophrenia: Novel treatment approaches. *Expert Review of Neurotherapeutics, 11*(7), 1007-1015. doi:10.1586/ern.11.90

Larsson, S., Adreassen, O. A., Aas, M., Rossberg, J. I., Mork, E., Steen, N. E., Barrett, E. A., Lagerberg, T. V., Peleikis, D., Agartz, I., & Melle, I. (2013). High prevalence of childhood trauma in patients with schizophrenia spectrum and affective disorder. *Comprehensive Psychiatry, 54*(2), 123-127. doi:10.1016/j.comppsych.2012.06.009

Lasser, K. E., Allen, P. D., Woolhandler, S. J., Himmelstein, D. U., Wolfe, S. M., & Bor, D. H. (2002). Timing of new black box warnings and withdrawals for prescription medications. *Journal of the American Medical Association, 287*(17), 2215-2220. doi:10.1001/jama.287.17.2215

Lenior, M., Dingemans, P., Linszen, D., de Haan, L., & Schene, A. (2001). Social functioning and the course of early-onset schizophrenia: Five-year follow-up of a psychosocial intervention. *British Journal of Psychiatry, 179*(1), 53-58. doi:10.1192/bjp.179.1.53

Leucht, S., Cipriani, A., Spineli, L., Mavridis, D., Orey, D., Richter, F., Samara, M., Barbui, C., Engel, R. R., Geddes, J. R., & Kissling, W. (2013). Comparative efficacy and tolerability of 15 antipsychotic drugs in schizophrenia: A multiple-treatments meta-analysis. *The Lancet, 382*(9896), 951-962. doi:10.1016/S0140-6736(13)60733-3

Leutwyler, H., Hubbard, E. M., Jeste, D. V., Miller, B., & Vinogradov, S. (2013). Associations of schizophrenia symptoms and neurocognition with physical activity in older adults with schizophrenia. *Biological Research for Nursing*, 1-8. doi: 10.1177/1099800413500845

Lewis, S., Tarrier, N., & Drake, R. (2005). Integrating non-drug treatments in early schizophrenia. *The British Journal of Psychiatry, 187*(48), 65-71. doi:10.1192/bjp.187.48.s65

Li, H., Lu, Q., Xiao, E., Li, Q., He, Z., & Mei, X. (2014). Methamphetamine enhances the development of schizophrenia in first-degree relatives of patients with schizophrenia. *Canadian Journal of Psychiatry. Revue Canadienne de Psychiatrie, 59*(2), 107-113.

Lichtenstein, P., Tip, B., Bjork, C., Pawitan, Y., Cannon, T., Sullivan, T., & Hultman, C. (2009). Common genetic determinants of schizophrenia and bipolar disorder in Swedish families: A population-based study. *The Lancet, 373*(9659), 234-239. doi:10.1016/S0140-6736(09)60072-6

Lieberman, J., Stroup, T., McEvoy, J., Swartz, M., Rosenheck, R., Perkins, D., Keefe, R. S., Davis, S. M., Davis, C. E., Lebowitz, B. D., & Severe, J. (2005). Effectiveness of antipsychotic drugs in patients with chronic schizophrenia. *The New England Journal of Medicine, 353*(12), 1209-1223. doi:10.1056/NEJMoa051688

Lindstrom, L., Gefvert, O., Hagberg, G., Lundberg, T. Bergstrom, M., Hartvig, P., & Långström, B. (1999). Increased dopamine synthesis rate in medial prefrontal cortex and striatum in schizophrenia indicated by L-(beta-11C) DOPA and PET. *Biological Psychiatry, 46*(5), 681-688. doi:10.1016/S0006-3223(99)00109-2

Linke, M., Jankowski, K. S., & Wichniak, A. (2015). Age or age at onset? Which of them really matters for neuro and social cognition in schizophrenia? *Psychiatry Research 225*(1-2), 197-201. doi:10.1016/j.psychres.2014.11.024

Litt, J. (2009). Formification: So what's bugging you? *Psychology Today*. Retrieved from https://www.psychologytoday.com/blog/odd-curious-and-rare/200911/formification

Loftus, E. F., & Zanni, G. (1975). Eyewitness testimony: The influence of the wording of a question. *Bulletin of the Psychonomic Society, 5*(1), 86-88.

Longden, E., Sampson, M., & Read J. (2015). Childhood adversity and psychosis: generalized or specific effects? *Epidemiology and Psychiatric Sciences, 25*, 1-11. doi:10.1017/S204579601500044X

Lorente-Rovira, E., Santos-Gómez, J. L., Moro, M., Villagrán, J. M., & McKenna, P. J. (2010). Confabulation in schizophrenia: A neuropsychological study. *Journal of the International Neuropsychological Society, 16*(6), 1018-1026. doi:10.1017/s1355617710000718

Malekshahi, T., Tioleco, N., Ahmed, N., Campbell, A. N., & Haller, D. (2015). Misuse of atypical antipsychotics in conjunction with alcohol and other drugs of abuse. *Journal of Substance Abuse Treatment, 48*(1), 8-12. doi:10.1016/j.jsat.2014.07.006

Manford, M., & Anderman, F. (1998). Complex visual hallucinations clinical and neurobiological insights. *Brain A Journal of Neurology, 121*(10), 1819-1840. doi:10.1093/brain/121.10.1819

Matheson, S. L., Shepherd, A. M., Pinchbeck, R. M., Laurens, K. R., & Carr, V. J. (2013). Childhood adversity in schizophrenia: A systematic meta-analysis. *Psychological Medicine, 43*(2), 225-238. doi:10.1017/S0033291712000785

McCabe, P. J., Christopher, P. P., Druhn, N., Roy-Bujnowski, K. M., Grudzinskas Jr., A. J., & Fisher, W. H. (2012). Arrest types and co-occurring disorders in persons with schizophrenia or related psychoses. *Journal of Behavioral Health Services and Research, 39*(3), 271-284. doi: 10.1007/s11414-011-9269-4

McDonald, C., & Murray, R. (2000). Early and late environmental factors for schizophrenia. *Brain Research Reviews, 31*(2-3), 130-137. doi:10.1016/S0165-0173(99)00030-2

McKenna, P. J., Lorente-Rovira, E., & Berrios, G. E. (2009). Confabulation as a psychiatric symptom. In W. Hirstein (Ed.), *Confabulation: Views from neuroscience, psychiatry, psychology, and philosophy* (pp. 159-172). New York, NY: Oxford University Press.

Meadows, R. J., & Kuehnel, J. (2005). *Evil minds: Understanding and responding to violent predators.* Upper Saddle River, NJ: Pearson Education.

Mednick, S. A., Machon, R. A., Huttunen, M. O., & Bonett, D. (1988). Adult schizophrenia following prenatal exposure to an influenza epidemic. *Archives of General Psychiatry, 45*(2), 189-192. doi:10.1001/archpsyc.1988.01800260109013

Mertz, C., & Brown, J. (2016). Confabulation: An Introduction for Clinical and Forensic Mental Health Professionals. *MAMFT News, 34*(2), 15-16.

Meyer, J. M. (2011). Pharmacotherapy of psychosis and mania. In L. L. Brunton, B. A. Chabner & B. C. Knollman (Eds.), *Goodman & Gilman's the pharmacological basic of therapeutics* (12th Ed., pp. 417-456). New York City, NY: McGraw-Hill Co.

Miles, A. A. A. (2012). *Stability and change in symptoms, cognition, and community outcome in schizophrenia.* Toronto, Ontario: York University Graduate Programs in Psychology.

Miles, A. A., Heinrichs, R. W., Ammari, N., Hartman, L., McDermid Vaz, S., & Muharib, E. (2014). Stability and change in symptoms, cognition, and community outcome in schizophrenia. *Schizophrenia Research, 152*(2), 435-439.

Miller, N. S. (2010). *Principles of addictions and the law: Applications in forensic, mental health, and medical practice.* Burlington, MA: Elsevier Science.

Monahan, J., Steadman, H. J., Silver, E., Appelbaum, P. S., Robbins, P. C., Mulvey, E. P., Roth, L. H., Grisso, T., & Banks, S. (2001). *Rethinking risk assessment: The Macarthur study of mental disorder and violence.* New York, NY: Oxford University Press.

Moncrieff, J. (2003). Clozapine v. conventional antipsychotic drugs for treatment-resistant schizophrenia: A re-examination. *The British Journal of Psychiatry, 183*(2), 161-166. doi:10.1192/bjp.183.2.161

Moore, R. Y., Whone, A. L., McGowan, S., & Brooks, D. J. (2003). Monoamine neuron innervation of the normal human brain: An 18F-DOPA PET study. *Brain Research, 982*(2), 137-145. doi:10.1016/S0006-8993(03)02721-5

Morenoff, J. D., & Harding, D. J. (2014). Incarceration, prisoner reentry, and communities. *Annual Review of Sociology, 40*(1), 411-429. doi:10.1146/annurev-soc-071811-145511

Morgan, C., & Fisher, H. (2006). Environmental factors in schizophrenia: Childhood trauma- a critical review. *Schizophrenia Bulletin, 33*(1), 3-10. doi:10.1093/schbul/sbl053

Morgan, D., Edwards, A., & Faulkner, L. (1993). The adaptation to prison by individuals with schizophrenia. *The Bulletin of the Academy of Psychiatry and the Law, 21*(4), 427-433.

Morgan, D., Grant, K., Gage, H., Mach, R., Kaplan, J., Prioleau, O., Nader, S. H., Buchheimer, N., Ehrenkaufer, R. L., & Nader, M. (2002). Social dominance in monkeys: Dopamine D2 receptors and cocaine self-administration. *Nature Neuroscience, 5*(2), 169-174. doi:10.1038/nn798

Morin, A. K. (2207). Possible intranasal quetiapine misuse. *American Journal of Health-System Pharmacy, 64*(7), 723-725. doi:10.2146/ajhp060226

Morse, S. J., & Hoffman, M. B. (2007). The uneasy entente between legal insanity and mens rea: Beyond Clark v. Arizona. *The Journal of Criminal Law and Criminology*, 1071-1149.

Mueser, K. T., & Gingerich, S. (2006). *The complete family guide to schizophrenia.* New York, NY: The Guilford Press.

Mullen, P. (2006). Schizophrenia and violence: From correlations to preventive strategies. *Advances in Psychiatric Treatment, 12*(4), 239-248. doi:10.1192/apt.12.4.239

Musselman, M. E., & Saely, S. (2013). Diagnosis and treatment of drug-induced hyperthermia. *American Journal of Health-System Pharmacy, 70*(1), 34-42. doi:10.2146/ajhp110543

Natanson v Kline, 186 Kan.393, 350 P. 2d 1093 (1960). National Alliance on Mental Illness. (2004). *Spending money in all the wrong places: Jails and prisons.* St. Paul, MN: Author. Retrieved from http://www2. nami.org/Template.cfm?Section=Fact_Sheets&Template=/ContentManagement/ContentDisplay. cfm&ContentID=14593

Nathaniel-James, D. A., Foong, J., & Frith, C. D. (1996). The mechanisms of confabulation in schizophrenia. *Neurocase, 2*(6), 475-483.

Nathaniel-James, D. A., & Frith, C. D. (1996). Confabulation in schizophrenia: Evidence of a new form?. *Psychological Medicine, 26*(02), 391-399.

National Alliance on Mental Illness (NAMI), (2004). Retrieved from https://www.nami.org

National Institute on Mental Health. (2010). *Schizophrenia.* Bethesda, MD: Author. Retrieved from http://www.nimh.nih.gov/health/topics/schizophrenia/index.shtml

National Registry of Evidence Based Programs and Practices. (2012). Cognitive enhancement therapy. Retrieved from http://nrepp.samhsa.gov/ViewIntervention.aspx?id=273

Nayani T. H., & David A. S. (1996). The auditory hallucination: a phenomenological survey. *Psychololgical Medicine*, 26 (1), 177-189. doi: 10.1017/S003329170003381X

Nordström, A., & Kullgren, G. (2003). Victim relations and victim gender in violent crimes committed by offenders with schizophrenia. *Social Psychiatry and Psychiatric Epidemiology, 38*(6), 326-330. doi:10.1007/s00127-003-0640-5

Octophetus. (2012). *Sick: A documentary* [Video File]. Retrieved from https://www.youtube.com/watch?v=FJjMBCN3abE

Opler, L. A., Grennan, M. S., & Ford, J. D. (2009). Pharmacotherapy. In C. Courtois & J. Ford (Eds.), *Treating complex traumatic stress disorder: An evidence-based guide* (pp. 329-349). New York, NY: The Guilford Press.

Ostermann, M., & Matejkowski, J. (2014). Estimating the impact of mental illness on costs of crimes: A matched samples comparison. *Criminal Justice and Behavior, 41*(1), 20-40. doi:10.1177/0093854813496239

Pagsberg, A. K. (2013). Schizophrenia spectrum and other psychotic disorders. *European Child & Adolescent Psychiatry, 22*(S1), 3-9. doi:10.1007/s00787-012-0354-x

Penn, D. L., Guynan, K., Daily, T., Spaulding, W. D., Garbin, C. P., & Sullivan, M. (1994). Dispelling the stigma of schizophrenia: What sort of information is best?. *Schizophrenia bulletin, 20*(3), 567-578.

Pharoah, F., Mari, J., & Streiner, D. (2003). Family intervention for schizophrenia. *Cochrane Database of Systematic Reviews, 12*, doi: 10.1002/14651858.CD000088.pub3

Picchioni, M. M., & Murray, R. M. (2007). Clinical review: Schizophrenia. *British Medical Journal, 335*, 91-95. doi:10.1136/bmj.39227.616447.BE

Pilkinton, P. D., & Pilkinton, J. C. (2014). Prescribing in prison: Minimizing psychotropic drug diversion in correctional practice. *Journal of Correctional Health Care, 20*(2), 95-104. doi:10.1177/1078345813518629

Plomin, R., Fulker, D. W., Corley, R., & DeFries, J. C. (1997). Nature, nurture, and cognitive development from 1 to 16 years: A parent-offspring adoption study. *Psychological Science*, 442-447.

Rajji, T. K., Ismail, Z., & Mulsant, B. H. (2009). Age at onset and cognition in schizophrenia: Meta-analysis. *The British Journal of Psychiatry. 195*(4), 286-293. doi:10.1192/bjp.bp.108.060723

Rajji, T. K., Miranda, D., & Mulsant, B. H. (2014). Cognition, function, and disability in patients with schizophrenia: A review of longitudinal studies. *Canadian Journal of Psychiatry, 59*(1), 13-17.

Read, J., van Os, J., Morrison, A., & Ross, C. (2005). Childhood trauma, psychosis and schizophrenia: A literature review with theoretical and clinical implications. *Acta Psychiatrica Scandinavica, 112*(5), 330-350. doi:10.1111/j.1600-0447.2005.00634.x

Redlich, A. (2004). Mental illness, police interrogations, and the potential for false confessions. *Law and Psychiatry, 55*(1), 19-21. doi:10.1176/appi.ps.55.1.19

Richard-Devantoy, S., Orsat, M., Dumais, A., Turecki, G., & Jollant, F. (2014). Neurocognitive vulnerability: Suicidal and homicidal behaviors in patients with schizophrenia. *Canadian Journal of Psychiatry, 59*(1), 18-25.

Richardson, C., & Weiler, M. (1999). Effects of Cognitive Treatment in Psychiatric Rehabilitation. *Schizophrenia Bulletin, 25*(4), 657-676.

Riggins v. Nevada, 504 U.S. 127 (1992).

Roberts, J. K. (1984). Differential diagnosis in neuropsychiatry. John Wiley & Sons Incorporated.

Rosenheck, R. A., Leslie, D. L., Sindelar, J., Miller, E. A., Lin, H., Stroup, T. S., McEvoy, J., Davis, S.M., Keefe, R.S., Swartz, M., & Perkins, D.O. (2006). Cost-effectiveness of second-generation antipsychotics and perphenazine in a randomized trial of treatment for chronic schizophrenia. *American Journal of Psychiatry, 163*(12), 2080-2089. doi:10.1176/appi.ajp.163.12.2080

Schiffer, B., Leygraf, N., Muller, B. W., Scherbaum, N., Forsting, M., Wiltfang, J., Gizewski, E. R., & Hodgins, S. (2012). Structural brain alterations associated with schizophrenia preceded by conduct disorder: A common and distinct subtype of schizophrenia? *Schizophrenia Bulletin, 39*(5), 1115-1128. doi:10.1093/schbul/sbs115

Schloendorff v. Society of N.Y. Hosp., 211 N.Y. 125, 129. 105 N.E. 92, 93 (1914).

Schnider, A. (2008). *The confabulating mind: How the brain creates reality.* Oxford, UK: University Press.

Schoepf, D., Uppal, H., Potluri, R., & Huen, R. (2013). Physical Co-morbidity and its relevance on mortality in schizophrenia: A naturalistic 12-year follow-up in general hospital admissions. *European Archives of Psychiatry and Clinical Neuroscience, 264*(1), 3-28. doi:10.1007/s00406-013-0436-x

Seeman, P. (2007). Antiparkinson therapeutic potencies correlate with their affinities at dopamine D2High receptors. *Synapse, 61*(12), 1013-1018.

Seeman, P., Guan, H. C., & Van Tol, H. H. (1993). Dopamine D4 receptors elevated in schizophrenia. *Nature, 365*(6445), 441-445.

Sell v. United States, 539 U.S. 166 (2003).

Sendt, K. V., Tracy, D. K., & Bhattacharyya, S. (2015). A systematic review of factors influencing adherence to antipsychotic medication in schizophrenia-spectrum disorders. *Psychiatry Research, 225*(1-2), 14-30. doi:10.1016/j.psychres.2014.11.002

Shakeel, M. K., & Docherty, N. M. (2014). Confabulations in schizophrenia. *Cognitive Neuropsychiatry, 20*(1), 1-13. doi:10.1080/13546805.2014.940886

Short, T., Thomas, S., Mullen, P., & Ogloff, J. R. P. (2013). Comparing violence in schizophrenia patients with and without Co-morbid substance-use disorders to community controls. *Acta Psychiatrica Scandinavica, 128*(4), 306-313. doi:10.1111/acps.12066

Siegel, L. J. (2011). Criminology (5th ed.). Stamford, CT: Cengage Learning.

Siegel, L. J., & Welsh, B. C. (2008). Juvenile delinquency. Belmont, CA: Wadsworth.

Sipos, A., Rasmussen, F., Harrison, G., Tynelius, P., Lewis, G., Leon, D., & Gunnell, D. (2004). Paternal age and schizophrenia: A population based cohort study. *British Medical Journal, 329*(7474), 1-5. doi:10.1136/bmj.38243.672396.55

Slate, R. N., Buffington-Vollum, J. K., & Johnson, W. W. (2013). *The criminalization of mental illness: Crisis and opportunity for the justice system.* Carolina Academic Press.

Slijepcevic, M. K., Jukic, V., Novalic, D., Zarkovic-Palijan, T., Milosevic, M., & Rosenzweig, I. (2014). Alcohol abuse as the strongest risk factor of violent offending in patients with paranoid schizophrenia. *Clinical Science, 55*(2), 156-162. doi:10.3325/cmj.2014.55.156

Sliwa, J. K., Fu, D. J., Bossie, C. A., Turkoz, I., & Alphs, L. (2014). Body mass index and metabolic parameters in patients with schizophrenia during long-term treatment with paliperidone palmitate. *BioMed Central Psychiatry, 14*(1), 1-11. doi:10.1186/1471-244X-14-52

Smith, E. E., & Jonides, J. (1999). Storage and executive processes in the frontal lobes. *Science, 283,* 1657-1661.

Soyka, M., Morhart-Klute, V., & Schoech, H. (2004). Delinquency and criminal offences in former schizophrenic inpatients 7-12 years following discharge. *European Archives of Psychiatry and Clinical Neuroscience, 254*(5), 289-294. doi:10.1007/s00406-004-0495-0

Stafford, K. P. (2003). Assessment of competence to stand trial. In A. Goldstein & I. Weiner (Eds.). *Handbook of Psychology Volume 11 Forensic Psychology.* (pp. 359-380). John Wiley & Sons, Inc., Hoboken, New Jersey.

Stafford, K. P., & Sellbom, M. O. (2013). Assessment of Competence to Stand Trial. In R. Otto & I. Weiner (Eds.), *Handbook of Psychology Volume 11 Forensic Psychology* (2nd Ed.; pp. 412-439). Hoboken, NJ: John Wiley & Sons.

Subramanian, P., Burhan, A., Pallaveshi, L., & Rudnick, A. (2013). The experience of patients with schizophrenia treated with repetitive transcranial magnetic stimulation for auditory hallucinations. *Case Reports in Psychiatry, 2013,* 1-5. doi:10.1155/2013/183582

Swanson, J., Swartz, M., Van Dorn, R., Elbogen, E., Wagner, H., Rosenheck, R., Stroup, T. S., McEvoy, J. P., & Lieberman, J. (2006). A national study of violent behavior in persons with schizophrenia. Archives of *General Psychiatry, 63*(5), 490-499. doi:10.1001/archpsyc.63.5.490

Swerdlow, N. R., & Koob, G. F. (1987). Dopamine, schizophrenia, mania, and depression: toward a unified hypothesis of cortico-striatopallido-thalamic function. *Behavioral and brain sciences, 10*(02), 197-208.

Tamburello, A. C., Lieberman, J. A., Baum, R. M., & Reeves, R. (2012). Successful removal of quetiapine from a correctional formulary. *The Journal of the American Academy of Psychiatry and the Law, 40*(4), 502-508.

Tandon, R., Gaebel, W., Barch, D. M., Bustillo, J., Gur, R. E., Heckers, S., & Carpenter, W. (2013). Definition and description of schizophrenia in the DSM-5. *Schizophrenia Research, 150*(1), 3-10. doi:10.1016/j.schres.2013.05.028

Thaker, G. K. (2011). Introduction: Schizophrenia spectrum disorders. *Psychiatric Times, 28*(3), 23. Retrieved from http://ezproxy.csp.edu/login?url=http://search.proquest.com/docview/856830137?accountid=26720

Tiihonen, J., Isohanni, M., Rasanen, P., Koiranen, M., & Moring, J. (1997). Specific major mental disorders and criminality: A 26-year perspective study of the 1966 northern Finland birth cohort. *American Journal of Psychiatry, 154,* 840-845.

Tiihonen, J., Walhbeck, K., Lonnqvist, J., Klaukka, T., Ioannidis, J., Volavka, J., & Haukka, J. (2006). Effectiveness of antipsychotic treatments in a nationwide cohort of patients in community care after first hospitalization due to schizophrenia and schizoaffective disorder: Observational follow-up study. *British Medical Journal, 333*(7561), 1-6. doi:10.1136/bmj.38881.382755.2F

Torrey, E. F. (2006). *Surviving schizophrenia.* New York, NY: Harper Collins.

Trevillion, K., Oram, S., Feder, G., & Howard, L. M. (2012). Experiences of domestic violence and mental disorders: A systematic review and meta-analysis. *PLoS One, 7*(12), e51740. doi:10.1371/journal.pone.0051740

Urfer Parnas, A., Jansson, L., Handest, P., Nielson, J., Saebye, D., & Parnas, J. (2007). Premorbid IQ varies across different definitions of schizophrenia. *World Psychiatry, 6*(1). 38-41.

U.S. National Library of Medicine. (2011). *Chlorpromazine.* Retrieved from https://www.nlm.nih.gov/medlineplus/druginfo/meds/a682040.html

Van Donkersgoed, R. J., De Jong, S., Van der Gaag, M., Aleman, A., Lysaker, P. H., Wunderink, L., & Pijnenborg, G. H. M. (2014). A manual-based individual therapy to improve metacognition in schizophrenia: Protocol of a multi-center RCT. *BioMed Central Psychiatry, 14*(1), 1-8. doi:10.1186/1471-244X-14-27

Van Dorn, R. A., Desmarais, S. L., Young, M. S., Sellers, B. G., & Swartz, M. S. (2012). Assessing illicit drug use among adults with schizophrenia. *Psychiatry Research, 200*(2-3), 228-236. doi:10.1016/j.psychres.2012.05.028

Viljoen, J., Roesch, R., & Zapf, P. (2002). An examination of the relationship between competency to stand trial, competency to waive interrogation rights, and psychopathology. *Law and Human Behavior, 26*(5), 481-506. doi:10.1023/A:1020299804821

Vinokur, D., Levine, S. Z., Roe, D., Krivoy, A., & Fischel, T. (2014). Age of onset group characteristics in forensic patients with Schizophrenia. *European Psychiatry, 29*(3), 149-152. doi:10.1016/j.eurpsy.2012.11.006

Volavka, J. (2013). Violence in schizophrenia and bipolar disorder. *Psychiatria Danubina, 25*(1), 24-33.

Wallace, C., Mullen, P. E., & Burgess, P. (2004). Criminal offending in schizophrenia over a 25-year period marked by deinstitutionalization and increasing prevalence of Co-morbid substance use disorders. *American Journal of Psychiatry, 161*(4), 716-727. http://dx.doi.org/10.1176/appi.ajp.161.4.716

Wallace, C., Mullen, P., Burgess, P., Palmer, S., Ruschena, D., & Browne, C. (1998). Serious criminal offending and mental disorder: Case linkage study. *British Journal of Psychology, 172,* 477-484.

Walsh, A., & Yun, I. (2013). Schizophrenia: Causes, crime, and implications for criminology and criminal justice. *International Journal of Law, Crime and Justice, 41*(2), 188-202. doi:10.1016/j.ijlcj.2013.04.003

Walsh, E., Buchanan, A., & Fahy, T. (2002). Violence and schizophrenia: Examining the evidence. *British Journal of Psychiatry, 180*(6), 490-495. doi:10.1192/bjp.180.6.490

Washington v. Harper, 494 U.S. 210 (1990).

Waters, F.A., Badcock, J.C., Maybery, M.T., & Michie, P.T. (2003). Inhibition in schizophrenia: Association with auditory hallucinations. *Schizophrenia Research, 62*(3), 275-280.

Wehring, H. J., & Carpenter, W. T. (2011). Violence and schizophrenia. *Schizophrenia Bulletin, 37*(5), 877-878. doi:10.1093/schbul/sbr094

Wilson, A. B., Farkas, K., Ishler, K. J., Gearhart, M., Morgan, R., & Ashe, M. (2014). Criminal thinking styles among people with serious mental illness in jail. *Law and Human Behavior, 38*(6), 592-601. doi:10.1037/lhb0000084

Witt, K., Hawton, K., & Fazel, S. (2014). The relationship between suicide and violence in schizophrenia: Analysis of the clinical antipsychotic trials of intervention effectiveness (CATIE) dataset. Schizophrenia Research, 154(1-3), 61-67. doi:10.1016/j.schres.2014.02.001

Wolfkühler, W., Majorek, K., Tas, C., Küper, C., Saimed, N., Juckel, G., & Brüne, M. (2012). Emotion recognition in pictures of facial affect: Is there a difference between forensic and non-forensic patients with schizophrenia? *The European Journal of Psychiatry, 26*(2), 73-85. doi:10.4321/s0213-61632012000200001

Wong, D. F., Wagner, H. N., Tune, L. E., Dannals, R. F., Pearlson, G. D., Links, J.M., Tamminga, C. A., Broussolle, E. P., Ravert, H.T., & Wilson, A. A. (1986). Positron emission tomography reveals elevated D2 dopamine receptors in drug-naïve schizophrenics. *Science, 234*(4783), 1558-1563.

World Health Organization (2012). *Mental health atlas 2011*. Geneva, Switzerland: Author.

Yung, A. R., & McGorry, P. D. (1996). The prodromal phase of first-incidence psychosis: Past and current conceptualizations. *Schizophrenia Bulletin, 22*(2), 353-370. Retrieved from http://schizophreniabulletin. oxfordjournals.org

Zhang, J. P., Gallego, J. A., Robinson, D. G., Malhotra, A. K., Kane, J. M., & Correll, C. U. (2013). Efficacy and safety of individual second-generation vs. first-generation antipsychotics in first-episode psychosis: A systematic review and meta-analysis. *International Journal of Neuropsychopharmacology, 16*(6), 1205-1218. doi:10.1017/S1461145712001277

Zhornitsky, S., Stip, E., Desfossés, J., Pampoulova, T., Rizkallah, E., Rompré, P.. . Potvin, S. (2011). Evolution of substance use, neurological and psychiatric symptoms in schizophrenia and substance use disorder patients: A 12-week, pilot, case-control trial with quetiapine. *Frontiers in Psychiatry, 2,* 22. doi:10.3389/fpsyt.2011.00022

Ziedonis, D. M., Kosten, T. R., Glazer, W. M., & Frances, R. J. (1994). Nicotine dependence and schizophrenia. *Psychiatric Services, 45*(3), 204-206.

APPENDIX

TABLE 1

Medications Used to Treat Schizophrenia and Psychosis and Available Formulations (Krakowski, 2014)

Drug Generic Name	Trade Name(s)	Tablet	Liquid Formulation	Oral-disintegrating Tablet	Intramuscular	Depot Injection
Typical (First-Generation) Agents						
Chlorpromazine	Thorazine®	Y	Y		Y	
Perphenazine	Trilafon®	Y	Y		Y	
Trifluoperazine	Stelazine®	Y	Y		Y	
Fluphenazine	Prolixin®	Y	Y		Y	Y
Molindone	Moban®	Y	Y			
Loxapine	Loxitane®	Y	Y		Y	
Haloperidol	Haldol®	Y	Y		Y	Y
Atypical (Second-Generation) Agents						
Aripiprazole	Abilify®	Y	Y	Y	Y	
Asenapine	Saphris®, Sycrest®			Y		
Clozapine	Clozaril®, Fazclo®	Y		Y		
Iloperidone	Fanapt®	Y				
Olanzapine	Zyprexa®	Y		Y	Y	
Paliperidone	Invega®, Sustenna®	Y				Y
Quetiapine	Seroquel®	Y				
Risperidone	Risperdal®, Risperdal Consta®	Y	Y	Y		Y
Sertindole	Serdolect®, Serlect®	Y				
Ziprasidone	Geodon®, Zeldox®	Y			Y	

Data compiled from multiple sources (Keith, 2006; Leucht et al., 2013; Meyer, 2011).

TABLE 2

Adverse Effects of Anti-Psychotic Agents (Krakowski, 2014)

Drug Generic Name	Risk of Weight Gain	Risk of Elevated Lipids/ Glucose	Risk of Acute Dystonic Reaction	Risk of Akathisia	Risk of Tardive Dyskinesia	Other Adverse Effects
Typical (First-Generation) Agents						
Chlorpromazine	High	High	Medium	Medium	High	Hyperprolactinemia, cardiac arrhythmias
Perphenazine	Low	Low	High	High	High	Cardiac arrhythmias
Trifluoperazine	Low	Low	High	High	High	Lower seizure threshold
Fluphenazine	Low	Low	High	High	High	Cardiac arrhythmias
Molindone	Low	Low	Medium	Medium	High	Weight loss
Loxapine	Medium	Low	Medium	Medium	High	Intense sleeping
Haloperidol	Low	Low	High	High	High	Cardiac arrhythmias
Atypical (Second-Generation) Agents						
Aripiprazole	Low	Low	Low	Medium	Low	Restlessness
Asenapine	Low	Low	Low	Low	Low	Oral numbness
Clozapine	Very high	High	Low	Low	Low	Blood disorders
Iloperidone	Medium	Low	Low	Low	Low	Hypotension
Olanzapine	Very high	High	Low	Low	Low	Weight gain may be very profound
Paliperidone	Medium	Low	Low	Low	Low	Hyperprolactinemia
Quetiapine	Medium	Low	Low	Medium	Low	Cardiac arrhythmias
Risperidone	Medium	Low	Low	Low	Low	Hyperprolactinemia
Sertindole	Low	Low	Low	Low	Low	Cardiac arrhythmias
Ziprasidone	Low	Low	Low	Low	Low	Increased mortality in elderly in dementia-related psychosis

Data compiled from multiple sources (Ben Amor, 2012; Caccia, 2013; Fusar-Poli, Kempton, & Rosenheck, 2013; Hartling et al., 2012; Meyer, 2011; Zhang et al., 2013).

CHAPTER 18

SUGGESTIBILITY: A BEGINNER'S GUIDE FOR CRIMINAL JUSTICE AND FORENSIC MENTAL HEALTH PROFESSIONALS

JERROD BROWN, ELIZABETH QUINBY, ERV WEINKAUF, CHARLOTTE GERTH HAANEN, HAL PICKETT, DANIELLE PRICE, & ERIC SKOG

CHAPTER OVERVIEW

Suggestibility can be defined as an individual's vulnerability to adopt someone else's views. Suggestibility is likely influenced by confabulation (Baumbach, 2002; Gudjonsson & Young, 2010), which is the generation of memories inspired by fictional or non-fictional events (Gudjonsson & Clare, 1995). Confabulation and suggestibility can range from slight distortions in the recall of actual events to the elaborate invention of nuanced and complex events (Guerri, Bazinet, & Riley, 2009; Moscovitch, 1989). The potential of suggestibility in children is particularly acute in comparison to adults (Ceci & Bruck, 1993; Cleveland, Quas, & Lyon, 2016), but this gap in proneness closes as children mature. Suggestibility, particularly interrogative suggestibility, is of particular concern in criminal justice and forensic settings, because many criminal justice processes (e.g., police interviews and testimony during trials) hinge on the recall of memories. Many of these processes subject individuals to repetitive lines of questioning, along with negative feedback that may increase the likelihood of suggestibility. If inaccurate, false memories could result in false confessions and wrongful convictions of innocent individuals. This chapter will review theoretical models and measurement of suggestibility and explore the impact of this phenomenon on interrogation, false confessions, and eyewitness testimony.

INTRODUCTION

Since the emergence of psychological research in the 19th century (Coffin, 1941; Polczyk et al., 2004), suggestibility has been the focus of empirical inquiry. Suggestibility can be defined as an individual's vulnerability to adopt someone else's views. For example, in response to another individual's suggestion (i.e., hint, clue, question, or statement) (Gudjonsson, 2003; Sharman & Powell, 2012), an individual can be convinced of events unfolding differently or the occurrence of events that never happened (Cole and Loftus, 1987). This is different from compliance, where an individual outwardly agrees with information from another source.

Instead, suggestibility involves the acceptance of information as truth (Gudjonsson, 2003). Driven by a combination of memory (i.e., encoding, storage, and retrieval) and personality traits (Brainerd & Poole, 1997; Ceci & Bruck, 1993; Gudjonsson, 2003), suggestibility ultimately occurs as a function of the individual's predisposition and their interactions with the demands of the social situation (Robinson & Briggs, 1997).

Suggestibility can take on many forms, as evidenced by different conceptualizations of the construct in the literature. For example, Eysenck (1943) disaggregated suggestibility into three identifiable subtypes. First, primary suggestibility is the result of verbal suggestions on the motor system. This was tested by the Body Sway test, where a blindfolded participant's physical movement was measured in response to verbal suggestions that they would fall forward or backward. Second, secondary suggestibility, which is a sensation and/or perception that results from verbal suggestions with no physical stimulation. Third, Eysenck and Furneaux (1945) later developed the concept of tertiary suggestibility, which occurs when an individual's attitude changes as a direct result of communicating with a figure of authority.

In contrast, Gudjonsson (1987a) discussed less abstract and more traditional subtypes of suggestibility. First, hypnotic suggestibility occurs when a suggestion changes a thought or attitude (Milling, Reardon, & Carosella, 2006). Second, idio-motor suggestibility is viewed as false sensory stimulation (e.g., the detection of a non-existent change in temperature) (Eysneck & Furneaux, 1945). Third, interrogative suggestibility occurs when misinformation suggested during questioning alters memories of a given event (Janosson & Vitelli, 2007). This could take the form of change in a small detail to the creation of a complicated string of events. Suggestions driving such a false memory could include misleading and repetitive questions as well as negative feedback (Gudjonsson, 1997).

Interrogative suggestibility is of particular concern in criminal justice and forensic settings (Janosson & Vitelli, 2007). Specifically, many criminal justice processes (e.g., police interviews and testimony during trials) subject individuals to repetitive lines of questioning that may increase the likelihood of suggestibility (Gudjonsson & Clare, 1995). This is due to the emphasis put on memory recall. If inaccurate, false memories could result in false confessions and false convictions of innocent individuals (Fisher, Ross, & Cahill, 2010). This chapter will review theoretical models and measurement of suggestibility and explore the impact this phenomenon has on interrogation, false confessions, and eyewitness testimony.

Suggestibility in Children

Over the last 50 years, researchers have found that the potential of suggestibility in children is particularly acute (Ceci & Bruck, 1993; Cleveland, Quas, & Lyon, 2016). Relative to adults, children are more vulnerable to the influence of individuals in a position of authority, and more likely to render inaccurate statements following questioning in an interrogative manner (Ceci, 1994; Ceci & Bruck, 1993; Dunn, 1995; Loftus, 1979). This gap in proneness to suggestibility closes as children mature into adolescents and then adults (Bruck, Ceci, & Hembrooke, 2002; Ceci & Bruck, 1993). Because the process of interviewing a witness, victim, or suspect of a crime can be acutely stressful, considerations of age and developmental maturity should be made for children to help ensure accurate performance (Cleveland, Quas, & Lyon, 2016; Carter, Bottoms, & Levine, 1996; Quas & Lench, 2007). This section reviews techniques, questions, and contexts that increase the likelihood of suggestibility in children.

As established above, interviewers and the techniques that they employ can strongly influence the likelihood of suggestibility in children (Bruck & Ceci, 1999; Cassel, Roebers, & Bjorklund, 1996; Lamb, La Rooy, Malloy, & Katz, 2011; Poole & Lindsay, 1995). Strategies that rely on coerciveness are particularly problematic for children. This could include the use of questioning in a repetitious and leading manner (Ceci, 1994; Ceci & Bruck, 1993; Dunn, 1995; Leo, 1994; Quas, Schaaf, Alexander, & Goodman, 2000; Tobey & Goodman, 1992), employing false or misleading evidence, and falsely assuring the interviewee that the crime or its consequences are not serious (Kassin, 1997; Redlich & Goodman, 2003; Russano, Meissner, Narchet, & Kassin, 2005). These strategies contribute to suggestibility because children tend to be eager to please (Gudjonsson, 2003; Ofshe, 1989) and trust (Ofshe, 1989) people in a position of authority. Further, children may be driven to protect their peers or escape the interrogation setting as soon as possible, which can lead them to say anything (Ceci & Bruck, 1993; Drizin & Leo, 2004; Grisso, 1981; Gudjonsson, 2003; Hall, 1980; Sigurdsson & Gudjonsson, 1996). Nonetheless, susceptibility to these techniques and strategies, along with proneness to suggestibility, varies by youth.

Research has established that individual differences can play an important role in increasing the likelihood of suggestibility in children (Bruck & Melnyk, 2004). Cognitive factors such as intelligence, theory of mind, and executive function are identified as key (Karpinski & Scullin, 2009). Further, social characteristics like shyness and an avoidance coping style, along with deficits in psychosocial maturity (such as responsibility and temperance), also contribute to suggestibility (Gudjonsson, 2003; Karpinski & Scullin, 2009; Steinberg & Cauffman, 1996). Despite progress in research, less is known about how these cognitive and social factors influence suggestibility across time. Nonetheless, this work indicates great concern for the performance of children in interrogations, and the situation is likely worse for children with cognitive and social capabilities diminished by developmental and intellectual disabilities (Fried & Reppucci, 2001; Scott, Reppucci, & Woolard, 1995).

In addition to the established impact of interviewing techniques on suggestibility, recent concerns have focused on the roles of suggestive questions versus contexts (Bruck & Ceci, 2004; Cleveland et al., 2016; Goodman & Quas, 2008). The likelihood of suggestibility increases when suggestive questions imply the occurrence of events that did not take place (Cleveland et al., 2016). This proneness to suggestibility is more pronounced in younger children (Cassel et al., 1996; Lamb & Fauchier, 2001; Lyon, Malloy, Quas, & Talwar, 2008). That said, the context of an interview likely plays an important role in increasing the likelihood of suggestibility. Further research is needed (Cleveland et al., 2016), but contexts could include the interviewer's statements, actions, and tone prior to and during the interview (Goodman & Quas, 2008; Leichtman & Ceci, 1995). Together, suggestive questions and contexts can create an interviewer bias that threatens the validity of information procured during the interview (Cleveland et al., 2016).

Relative to adults, children are more prone to suggestibility when interviewed with coercive techniques in stressful settings (Cleveland et al., 2016; Ceci & Bruck, 1993). Despite replicated research that identifies techniques (e.g., repeated and leading questions) (Ceci, 1994; Quas, Schaaf, Alexander, & Goodman, 2000; Tobey & Goodman, 1992) that increase the likelihood of suggestibility, a reliance on such techniques and strategies persists in criminal justice settings. In fact, even those who receive specialized training in interviewing children in criminal justice settings have a tendency to revert to suggestive techniques and reference questionable information obtained from peers (Karpinski & Scullin, 2009). As such, the field needs improved education and training programs that help increase awareness of suggestibility in children.

CONFABULATION AND SUGGESTIBILITY

Suggestibility is likely influenced by confabulation (Baumbach, 2002), which is the generation of memories inspired by fictional or non-fictional events (Gudjonsson & Clark, 1995). Confabulation can range from slight distortions in the recall of actual events, to the elaborate invention of nuanced and complex events (Guerri et al., 2009; Moscovitch, 1989). Important to note, confabulation is the genuine creation of a new memory that is believed to be true rather than a deliberate deception or lie (Gudjonsson & Clark, 1995). Occurrences of confabulation can be either spontaneous or provoked in certain situations (Dalla Barbra & Boisse, 2010). For example, individuals with memory difficulties might confabulate or create new memories during interrogations by police or intense questioning by a lawyer. In particular, the same leading and repetitive questions that result in suggestibility could lead to confabulation. In fact, Smith and Gudjonsson (1995) observed a significant relationship between suggestibility and confabulation. Because confabulation and suggestibility can have a profound impact in legal contexts through false confessions and convictions (Gudjonsson, 2003), the identification of individuals who may be at risk for these phenomena is imperative.

Both confabulation and suggestibility are linked to individuals with cognitive deficits and certain personality traits. First, deficits in cognitive capabilities such as short- and long-term memory and intellectual functioning are associated with both confabulation and suggestibility (Gathercole, 1998; Gudjonsson & Young, 2010). For example, Clare and Gudjonsson (1995) found that a group of individuals with learning disabilities (mean IQ = 65) exhibited higher levels of suggestibility and more instances of confabulation relative to a group of individuals with normal intellectual functioning (mean IQ = 99). Further, other work has reported that the occurrence of confabulation negatively relates to intelligence scores and performance on memory tasks (Gudjonsson & Young, 2010). Second, a limited body of research has found that the likelihood of confabulation and suggestibility links to personality (Gudjonsson & Young, 2010). In a study of forensic patients, Smith and Gudjonsson (1995) observed that those with personality disorders exhibited confabulation more frequently and had worse memory recall in general than those with a schizophrenia-related disorder. In light of these observations, forensic and criminal justice professionals should be wary of the possibility of confabulation and suggestibility when working with individuals who have cognitive deficits and personality disorder symptoms.

INTERROGATIVE SUGGESTIBILITY

Interrogative suggestibility is defined as a vulnerability to the incorporation of suggestions or views of a police interrogator (Gudjonsson, 1984; 1987b). Interest in this topic dates back at least to Binet (1900), who explored the impact of manipulation on suggestibility in schoolchildren (Gudjonsson, 1992). Elaborating on this initial line of inquiry, other early researchers including Stern went on to explore the impact of leading questions on suggestibility and distorted memories. As mentioned earlier, interest in this topic has been driven by the fact that interrogative suggestibility can have a profoundly deleterious influence on prone individuals (Drake, 2011; Gudjonsson, 2003) and can sometimes result in false confessions and wrongful convictions (Gudjonsson & MacKeith, 1990; Kassin & Gudjonsson, 2004). In this section, we explore how interrogative suggestibility fits within historical theoretical frameworks of suggestibility, research approaches to interrogative suggestibility, and the fundamental components of interrogative suggestibility.

Interrogative suggestibility has important distinctions from the types outlined earlier in the chapter (Gudjonsson, 1997). In particular, interrogative suggestibility has little in common with Eysenck's (1943) primary suggestibility, which is concerned with the result of verbal suggestions on the motor system. Specifically, interrogations focus on past events and memories, rather than evoking future body movements (Gudjonsson, 1997). Instead, interrogative suggestibility has more in common with Eysenck's (1943) secondary suggestibility; sensations or perceptions that result from verbal suggestions. The implanting of new memories with leading and repetitive questions is very compatible with this concept. For many of these same reasons, interrogative suggestibility likely has much in common with tertiary suggestibility (Eysenck & Furneaux, 1945), which is concerned with changes in attitude as a direct result of communicating with a figure of authority. As such, interrogative suggestibility may be some sort of combination of Eysenck's secondary and tertiary forms of suggestibility.

Research has traditionally investigated interrogative suggestibility from one of two different approaches: individual differences versus experimental approaches (Mastroberardino & Marucci, 2013). The individual differences approach largely focuses on aspects of the interviewee that defer proneness to interrogative suggestibility. This could include everything from an interviewee's cognitive and personality predispositions to coping skills and strategies used in stressful situations (Gudjonsson & Clark, 1986; Pires, Silva, & Ferreira,

2014). In contrast, the experimental approach focuses on the effectiveness of different interview techniques and strategies of manipulation in eliciting the placement of false memories (Loftus, Miller, and Burns, 1978). Together, these approaches have informed our current understanding of the many influences of suggestibility. Gudjonsson and Clark (1986) integrated these divergent research approaches to develop a theoretical model of interrogative suggestibility. This model conceptualizes interrogative suggestibility as "the extent to which, within a closed social interaction, people come to accept messages communicated during formal questioning, as the result of which their subsequent behavioral response is affected" (Gudjonsson and Clark, 1986, p.84). Gudjonsson and Clark (1986) went on to identify five interactive elements of interrogative suggestibility: (a) the essence of the social exchange, (b) the systematic questioning of an individual by one or more individuals, (c) a suggestive impetus, (d) consumption of the suggestive impetus by the interviewee, and (e) the interviewee's behavioral outcome. The dynamic interactions in this model are driven by the interviewee, interviewers, and environment (Gudjonsson & Clark, 1986).

The individual characteristics of the interviewee can play an important role in determining if suggestibility is more likely to occur because of such stimuli. Described as the "yield" component, an interviewee could possess a proneness to acquiesce to misinformation suggested by the interviewer, whether or not the interviewee possesses firm memories of the event (Gudjonsson, 1984; 1987b; 1997). Specifically, interviewees may possess certain predispositions such as cognitive capabilities (e.g., intelligence and short- and long-term memory) and personality traits (e.g., extroversion and anxiousness) that increase or decrease the likelihood of suggestibility. Further, the presence of strong strategies for coping with stressful situations may decrease the likelihood of suggestibility, as interviewees with such strategies may be more prepared to analyze and address problems and consequences that may arise in interrogative settings (Gudjonsson & Clark, 1986). This is critical because interrogative interviews are fraught with uncertainty, distrust, and fear. Although a firm consensus has not been reached (Bianco & Curci, 2015), the likelihood of suggestibility may be predicted by certain individual differences (e.g., poor memory, low levels of intelligence, and proneness to anxiety) (Gudjonsson, 1991; Boon, Gozna, & Hall, 2008; Pires et al., 2014).

The interviewer also plays an integral role in the manifestation of interrogative suggestibility. Perhaps one of the most integral aspects of interrogative suggestibility is interviewer bias, which includes prior beliefs about the event in question (Bruck & Ceci, 1997). If close-minded, the interviewer may consciously or unconsciously influence the direction of the interview to elicit statements that are consistent with his or her preconceived notions of the event (Bruck & Ceci, 1997). One of the most potentially damaging ways to influence the interviewee is with leading and repetitive questions that have a long-demonstrated impact on distorted responses (Stern, 1910; 1939). Subsequent research has confirmed that leading and repetitive questions along with negative feedback decrease the accuracy of confessions and later testimony (Cohen & Harnick, 1980; Loftus, 1979; Gudjonsson, 1984; Hünefeldt, Rossi-Arnaud, & Furia, 2009). For example, an interviewee may feel compelled to comply with an interviewer's suggestions and unknowingly integrate those suggestions into their memories of an event (Shapiro, Blackford, & Chen, 2005). This phenomenon is described as a "shift" away from accurate answers toward the answers sought by the interviewer (Gudjonsson, 1984). Taken together, this work highlights the possibility that interrogative suggestibility outcomes can vary widely by individual and interviewer (Gudjonsson, 1991).

GUDJONSSON SUGGESTIBILITY SCALE

The Gudjonsson Suggestibility Scale (GSS) (Gudjonsson, 1984) is one of the first-and-only widely available measures of suggestibility for use in forensic and criminal justice settings (Gignac & Powell, 2009). This measure was developed to assess Gudjonsson and Clark's (1986) theoretical model of interrogative suggestibility: the degree that an individual would change his/her story based on leading and repetitive questioning by someone in a position of authority. This instrument measures a person's predisposition to interrogative suggestibility with two parallel forms: GSS 1 (Gudjonsson, 1984) and GSS 2 (Gudjonsson, 1987). Not only have these scales been used in research settings (Pires et al., 2014), but the GSS 1 and GSS 2 have been extensively utilized in legal and forensic settings to explore the proneness of suspects, victims, and witnesses to interrogative suggestibility (Bianco & Curci, 2015; Gudjonsson, 2003; 2013). In this section, we will review the administration, scoring, and psychometric evidence of the GSS forms.

The administration of the GSS scales requires considerable time commitments and interpersonal interactions on the part of both the interviewer and interviewee (Gudjonsson, 1997). First, the task begins with the interviewer reading a story about a child prevented from tumbling off his/her bike. Second, the interviewee is asked to immediately recall as much of the story as possible. Third, after waiting approximately 50 minutes, the interviewee is again asked to recall as much of the story as possible. Fourth, the interviewee is asked 20 closed-ended questions, fifteen of which can be considered subtly misleading. Fifth, upon completion of these 20 questions, the interviewee is provided negative feedback (e.g., "You made many errors in responding to these questions") and required to respond to the 20 questions one more time while being urged to improve (Gudjonsson, 2003). Responses are typically audio-recorded and transcribed prior to scoring to ensure accuracy.

Responses on the GSS scales are comprised of two distinguishable factors (Gudjonsson, 1984, 1987a, 1997). First, the "yield" factor refers to interviewers eliciting agreement with inaccurate statements via misleading questions. This "yield" factor can be disaggregated into suggestibility based on misinformation ("yield 1") versus negative feedback ("yield 2") (Gudjonsson, 1992). The yield score ranges from zero to fifteen. Second, the "shift" factor demarcates alterations in interviewee responses after receiving negative feedback. The shift score ranges from zero to twenty. Scores on these scales are totaled, with higher scores indicative of increased suggestibility.

TABLE 1

Constructs with Established Links to Interrogative Suggestibility

Constructs	Relevant Research
Confabulation and Distortion of Memory	• Gudjonsson (1991) • Gudjonsson and Young (2010) • Willner (2008)
Cognitive Impairment	• Danielsdottir, Sigurgeirsdottir, Einarsdottir, and Haraldsson (1993) • Warren, Hulse-Trotter, and Tubbs (1991)
Intellectual Disability	• Henry and Gudjonsson (1999, 2003) • Young, Powell, and Dudgeon (2003)
Personality Characteristics (e.g., anxiety and acquiescence)	• Forrest, Wadkins, and Larson (2006) • Gudjonsson and Clark (1995) • Muris, Meesters, and Merckelbach (2004)

The GSS has demonstrated strong psychometric properties across diverse experimental and real-world settings. Evidence of reliability includes high levels of inter-rater reliability, temporal consistency, and internal consistency (Clare, Gudjonsson, Rutter, & Cross, 1994). The validity of the GSS and other measures is supported by research findings of significant negative associations between intelligence and suggestibility regardless of age groups (Muris et al., 2004; Polczyk, 2005; Pollard et al., 2004; Richardson & Kelly, 1995; Singh & Gudjonsson, 1992). Corroborating these findings, several other related concepts have been linked to the GSS (see Table 1 above). Such findings of reliability and validity have been observed across developmental groups (i.e., children 7 years of age and older, adolescents, and adults) and in individuals with behavioral and psychological disorders (Danielsdottir, Sigurgeirsdottir, Einarsdottir, & Haraldsson, 1993; Gudjonsson, 1987(a); 1997; 2003; 2013). Despite requiring substantial resources to administer, including at least an hour for testing, the GSS is a valuable assessment of the likelihood of interrogative suggestibility in criminal justice and forensic contexts (Frumkin, Lally, & Sexton, 2012).

WITNESS TESTIMONY AND SUGGESTIBILITY

Eyewitness testimony plays an integral role in the legal systems of most Western nations (Levy-Gigi & Vakil, 2014; Pires et al., 2014). Unfortunately, eyewitness testimony is fallible and can result in wrongful convictions (Cutler & Penrod, 1995; Wells & Olson, 2003). Inaccurate eyewitness testimony is driven, at least in part, by suggestibility (Loftus, 1979; Zaragoza, Belli, & Payment, 2007; Levy-Gigi & Vakil, 2014). Eyewitness suggestibility occurs when an eyewitness, exposed to misinformation about an event that they witnessed, incorporates this misinformation into their memory of the event (Chan, Thomas, & Bulevich, 2009). Younger children and older adults are particularly prone to eyewitness suggestibility (Chan et al., 2009). The phenomenon of eyewitness suggestibility can be particularly deleterious because eyewitness testimony is only eclipsed by confessions in terms of incriminating evidence in the U.S. legal system (Yarmey, 2006). In this section, we review how the legal process, interview techniques, and individual differences contribute to eyewitness suggestibility.

The long and complicated nature of the American legal process may contribute to the likelihood of eyewitness suggestibility. In fact, it is common for an eyewitness to testify in court months or years after an event occurred (Chan & LaPaglia, 2011). Over this extended period, eyewitnesses may be exposed to suggestions during interactions with police, lawyers, family, and peers (Gray, 1993; Whitcomb, Shapiro, & Stellwagen, 1985) or other sources of information such as media coverage (Allen & Lindsay, 1998; Lindsay, Allen, Chan, & Dahl, 2004). The process of law enforcement officers interviewing witnesses is not only necessary (Gudjonsson & Young, 2011), but is also one of the most common points where eyewitness suggestibility occurs. Examples of suggestibility can range from small details to the creation of a largely new memory (Ackil & Zaragoza, 1998; Chrobak & Zaragoza, 2008; Hanba & Zaragoza, 2007). Both dynamic and complex police interviews, characterized by repeated and misleading questions, can interact with the cognitive and personality characteristics of the interviewee to result in inaccurate testimony (Gudjonsson, 2003; 2010a). Suggestibility is particularly likely when an eyewitness is asked detailed questions about an event and is then exposed to incorrect and misleading details (Chan et al., 2009). To decrease the likelihood of eyewitness suggestibility, it is necessary to have a greater understanding of the techniques and individual differences that increase proneness to this issue.

Concerns about memory issues in eyewitness testimony have long been studied by psychologists and researchers (Davis & Loftus, 2007; Neuschatz, Lampinen, Toglia, Payne, & Cisneros, 2007; Roediger & McDermott, 2000), emerging as late as the early 1900s (Binet, 1900; Otgaar, Sauerland, & Petrila, 2013; Stern, 1910). Perhaps the most prominent research investigating the role of suggestibility in eyewitness testimony dates back to Elizabeth Loftus' seminal work beginning in the 1970s. Her research laid the groundwork for experimental studies on how misinformation, particularly suggestive questioning, leads to the generation of false memories (Otgaar et al., 2013). Across several studies, post-event information had a demonstrated impact on memory (Ainsworth, 1998; Loftus, 1979; Memon & Wright, 2000), including the impact of leading and repetitive questions on eyewitness memory in forensic settings (George & Clifford, 1992; Pearse & Gudjonsson, 1999). The likelihood of eyewitness suggestibility might increase with the degree of similarity between the actual event and suggested event (Abeles & Morton, 1999; Levy–Gigi, & Vakil, 2014; Roebers & McConkey, 2003), but other research has failed to replicate such findings (Bonto & Payne, 1991; Shaw, García, & Robles, 1997). Although there is clear evidence that memory can be influenced by the manner in which an eyewitness is questioned, this is not the only way that the likelihood of suggestibility is influenced.

Cognitive and personality characteristics of the eyewitness can have an important impact on the likelihood of suggestibility (Gudjonsson, 2003; Pires et al., 2013). On one hand, cognitive characteristics such as low levels of intelligence, short- and long-term memory issues, and attention problems, among other issues, may all increase the risk of suggestibility (Gudjonsson & Clark, 1986; Gudjonsson, 1991). On the other hand, personality characteristics including anxiety, shyness, compliance, and other traits may render an eyewitness more prone to suggestibility (Gudjonsson, 2006). When coupled with interview techniques including leading and repetitive questions, these cognitive and personality characteristics may have a detrimental real-world impact on another individual's freedom and future.

Despite empirical evidence that interview techniques and individual differences interact to result in eyewitness suggestibility, fallible memories have influenced the verdicts of an alarming number of legal cases in recent years (Pires et al., 2013). Such injustices have resulted in wrongful convictions of innocent individuals and, in some cases, long prison sentences. This dire situation calls for programs to enhance the awareness and knowledge of eyewitness suggestibility in legal professionals across America. This includes judges, who play a critical role in evaluating the accuracy and admissibility of eyewitness testimony (Otgaar et al., 2013). Wide-scale efforts involving judges, researchers, forensic professionals, law enforcement officers, and other legal professionals are needed to address this critical issue going forward.

FALSE CONFESSIONS AND SUGGESTIBILITY

A confession can be defined as a verbal or written admission of guilt for a specific crime. Before the 19th century, the courts accepted confessions at face value, even when extracted through physical torture (Wigmore, 1970). In the last century, skepticism of confessions and their reliability grew. Unreliable confessions, also labeled as false confessions, occur when a suspect provides verbal or written admission of guilt for a crime that they did not commit (Redlich & Goodman, 2003). Despite wide-scale skepticism of false confessions, a few like Hugo Münsterberg began exploring potential causal factors of false confessions (such as physical threats, promises of leniency, and suggestibility) in the early 20th century (Drake, 2011). In recent decades, the tide of skepticism has changed, with concerns about the possibility of false confessions becoming firmly entrenched in criminal justice professionals and researchers alike. Because confessions are one of the strongest factors in the determination of a defendant's guilt (Kassin, 1997; Kassin & Sukel, 1997; Redlich & Goodman, 2003), even more so than eyewitness identification and testimony (Kassin & Neumann, 1997), there is an urgent need to better understand the role that false confessions play in our legal system.

The lack of a standardized tracking system complicates the estimation of the number of false confessions (Meyer & Reppucci, 2007). Nonetheless, the most reliable estimates may come from the work of the Innocence Project. In an in-depth analysis of 273 DNA-based exonerations from 1989 to 2010, the Innocence Project reported evidence of false confessions or self-incriminating information in almost 25% of the cases (Frumkin, Lally, & Sexton, 2012; Innocence Project, 2012; Scheck, Neufeld, & Dwyer, 2000). In consideration of these false confession rates and wrongful conviction rates (Huff, Ratner, & Sagarin, 1996), Meyer and Reppucci (2007) estimate that more than 2,500 prisoners were incarcerated based on a false confession. In another study of 125 confirmed false confessions, almost one-third of those cases were juveniles at the time of the confession (Drizin & Leo, 2004). Taken together, these studies highlight the vast impact of false confessions in the criminal justice system, particularly for youthful offenders.

Before delving into the causes of false confessions, one must have a firm understanding of the criminal justice system's definition of a confession. In the United States, the Supreme Court plays an essential role in setting precedence in the area of confessions, which are "probably the most probative and damaging evidence that can be admitted" (Bruton v. U.S., 1968). In Columbe v. Connecticut (1961), the Supreme Court determined that a confession was admissible if, and only if, rendered voluntarily upon a systematic review of all relevant circumstances. The voluntary nature of a confession is typically questioned if the suspect is not notified of their Miranda rights, or in the presence of physical intimidation and harm and/or false promises of sentencing leniency (Kassin, 1997). Nonetheless, confessions elicited via psychologically coercive techniques typically remain admissible and commonplace in U.S. courts (Kassin & McNall, 1991).

The growing recognition of false confessions and their dire consequences has led researchers, legal professionals, and law enforcement officers to wonder why a suspect would inaccurately admit to a crime. In addition to type of crime, Gudjonsson (2003) identified both the interrogation (e.g., interrogation techniques and strategies) and the suspect (i.e., suggestibility) as important characteristics that influence the likelihood of a false confession. In recent decades, research has played an important role in better understanding the impact of these characteristics on the manifestation of a false confession.

Although it is unlikely that police officers would purposefully try to extract confessions from innocent people, police interrogation procedures do directly impact the likelihood of false confessions (Meyer & Reppucci, 2007). In fact, many police are still trained to utilize the psychologically manipulative interrogation techniques and strategies known to result in unreliable and inaccurate confessions (Gudjonsson, 2003; Kassin, 1997; Leo, 1992). Unfortunately, most police receive little to no training on the potentially negative consequences of these tactics in relation to the reliability of confessions (Drizin & Leo, 2004). Other than notifying suspects of their Miranda rights and not utilizing physical intimidation and false promises of sentencing leniency (Kassin, 1997), few restrictions exist on the techniques and strategies that police officers can use to obtain a confession (Mesiarik, 2008). Because questionable interrogative procedures can result in the false confession and wrongful conviction of an innocent person (Redlich & Goodman, 2003), and a growing body of evidence suggests this phenomenon is quite common (Meyer & Reppucci, 2007), police officers must consider the impact of these techniques on the reliability of confessions.

Beyond the interrogative techniques and strategies of the police, individual differences in the vulnerability of suspects may play an important role in false confessions (Kassin, 1997). One characteristic often observed among individuals who have falsely confessed is a limited understanding of legal rights (Muris et al., 2004; Redlich & Goodman, 2003; Richardson et al., 1995). As is often the case, a suspect may not comprehend the legal rights that they are foregoing when waiving the right to remain silent or to have an attorney present. Such a limited understanding of legal rights is particularly concerning in the presence of a predisposition to suggestibility (Gudjonsson, 2003; 1990; 1991).

This concept of suggestibility is associated with the elicitation of false confessions in response to tense and stressful interrogative situations (Smeets, Leppink, Jelicic, & Merckelbach, 2009; Sigurdsson & Gudjonsson, 1994). Further, suspects who have falsely confessed to a crime exhibit higher levels of suggestibility scores relative to both suspects who refuse to falsely confess and the general population (Gudjonsson, 1991). This proneness to suggestibility may be intrinsically linked to the memory capacity of a suspect (Gudjonsson, 2003; Gudjonsson & Henry, 2003). In light of these findings, a limited understanding of legal rights may interact with a vulnerability to suggestibility and result in false confessions.

As highlighted in popular media cases in the recent years, children and adolescents may be at a greater risk of false confessions in interrogation-based situations than adults (Meyer & Reppucci, 2007). Factors contributing to this propensity may include intellectual and emotional immaturity, along with a limited understanding of legal rights (Oberlander & Goldstein, 2001; McLachlan, Roesch, & Douglas, 2011). These observations generalize to experimental research settings. For example, several research studies have found that youths render false confessions in response to suggestive questioning at a higher rate than adults (Loftus, 1979; Redlich & Goodman, 2003; Richardson, Gudjonsson, & Kelly, 1995). As such, children and adolescents may be more susceptible to the techniques used by police during interrogations (Redlich & Goodman, 2003).

In light of these external and internal contributing factors, Gudjonsson (1991) identified four different categories of false confessions. First, the voluntary false confession is provided without any pressure from other individuals. This may be driven by symptoms of mental illness and personality disorders. For example, Gudjonsson (2003) described the case of a man who falsely confessed to playing a role in a murder in order to resolve free-floating guilt related to an episode of major depression. Second, coerced-compliant confessions typically occur when a suspect believes that providing the confession will result in some sort of gain in the short-term (Gudjonsson & MacKeith, 1990). For example, the suspect may simply believe that providing the confession will end the stressful interrogation. Third, coerced-internalized confessions occur when a suspect becomes convinced that they did, in fact, commit the crime (Gudjonsson & MacKeith, 1990). Fourth, coerced-reactive confessions occur when a suspect is coerced into confession of a crime by someone who is not in law enforcement (McCann, 1998). These four groups serve as a useful framework to discuss different types of false confessions, but classifying a given false confession may be tricky since such complicated events often vary in degree, rather than likeness (Frumkin, 2008; Frumkin, Lally, & Sexton, 2012).

There are a number of things law enforcement can do to prevent false confessions (DeClue, 2005; Frumkin & Garcia, 2003; Oberlander & Goldstein, 2003). First, it is necessary for police to gather collateral reports and evidence for any suspicious confession (Frumkin, Lally, & Sexton, 2012). Second, complete recordings of interrogations should be retained so that mental health experts can review them for evidence of coercion (Frumkin, 2008). Third, improved and more widely disseminated guidelines on useful and harmful interrogation strategies are needed. Going forward, research that not only identifies techniques that contribute to false confessions but also isolates techniques that protect against false confessions is imperative (Redlich & Goodman, 2003).

Conclusion

As outlined in this chapter, suggestibility can have a wide-ranging impact on memory in the criminal justice system. As described earlier, suggestibility is the degree to which an individual can be convinced of events unfolding differently, or the occurrence of events that never happened, in response to another individual's suggestion (i.e., hint, clue, question, or statement) (Gudjonsson, 2003; Cole and Loftus, 1987; Sharman & Powell, 2012). This is concerning because many criminal justice processes (e.g., police interviews, interrogations, and testimony during trials) hinge on the recall of memories. Children are far more susceptible to suggestibility than adults (Cleveland, Quas, & Lyon, 2016; Ceci & Bruck, 1993). Memory deficits driven by suggestibility can lead to doubt in everything from interrogation-based confessions to eyewitness testimony. In fact, confessions and eyewitness testimony are two of the strongest factors used in the legal system to determine guilt (Kassin, 1997; Kassin & Neumann, 1997; Kassin & Sukel, 1997; Redlich & Goodman, 2003). Steps must be taken to protect against the possibility of false memories resulting in wrongful convictions, including education of professionals in the criminal justice system. This also requires the implementation of large-scale awareness campaigns among criminal justice professionals, the utilization of interrogative suggestibility experts to evaluate recordings of confessions, and the identification and development of trainings for appropriate interrogation techniques that minimize the likelihood of false confessions.

References

Abeles, P., & Morton, J. (1999). Avoiding misinformation: Reinstating target modality. *The Quarterly Journal of Experimental Psychology Section A, 52*(3), 581-592. doi:10.1080/713755830

Ackil, J.K. & Zaragoza, M.S. (1998). Memorial consequences of forced confabulation: Age differences in susceptibility to false memories. *Developmental Psychology, 34*, 1358-1372.

Ainsworth, P. B. (1998). *Psychology, law and eyewitness testimony.* Sussex: Wiley and Sons Ltd.

Allen, B.P., & Lindsay, D.S. (1998). Amalgamations of memories: Intrusion of information from one event into reports of another. *Applied Cognitive Psychology, 12*, 277-285. doi:10.1002/(SCI)1099-0720(199806)12:3

Baumbach, J. (2002). Some implications of prenatal alcohol exposure for the treatment of adolescents with sexual offending behaviors. *Sexual Abuse: A Journal of Research and Treatment, 14*(4), 313-327. doi:10.1177/107906320201400403

Bianco, A., & Curci, A. (2015). Measuring interrogative suggestibility with the Italian version of the Gudjonsson Suggestibility Scales (GSS): Factor structure and discriminant validity. *Personality and Individual Differences, 82*, 258-265. doi:10.1016/j.paid.2015.03.035

Binet, A. (1900). La suggestibilité. Paris: Schleicher.

Bonto, M.A., & Payne, D.G. (1991). Role of environmental context in eyewitness memory. *The American Journal of Psychology, 104*(1), 117-134. doi:10.2307/1422854

Boon, J., Gozna, L. & Hall, S. (2008). Detecting 'faking bad' on the Gudjonsson Suggestibility Scales. *Personality and Individual Differences, 44*, 263-272.

Brainerd, C. J., & Poole, D. A. (1997). Long-term survival of children's false memories: A review. *Learning and Individual Differences, 9*, 125-152.

Bruck M. & Ceci S. J. (1999). The suggestibility of children's memory. *Annual Review of Psychology, 50*, 419-439.

Bruck, M., & Ceci, S. J. (2004). Forensic developmental psychology: Unveiling four scientific misconceptions. *Current Directions in Psychology, 13*, 229-232.

Bruck, M., Ceci, S.J., & Hembrooke, H. (2002). The nature of children's true and false narratives. *Developmental Review, 22*, 520-554.

Bruck, M. & Melnyk, L. (2004). Individual differences in children's suggestibility: A review and synthesis. *Applied Cognitive Psychology, 18*(8), 947-996. doi:10.002/acp.1070

Bruton v. United States, 391 U.S. 123 (1968).

Carter, C. A., Bottoms, B. L., & Levine, M. (1996). Linguistic and socioemotional influences on the accuracy of children's reports. *Law & Human Behavior, 20*, 335-358. doi:10.1007/BF01499027

Cassel, W. S., Roebers, C. E., & Bjorklund, D. F. (1996). Developmental patterns of eyewitness responses to repeated and increasingly suggestive questions. *Journal of Experimental Child Psychology, 61*, 116-133. doi: 10.1006/jecp.1996.0008

Ceci, S.J. (1994) Cognitive and social factors in children's testimony. In. B.D. Sales (Ed.), *Psychology in Litigation and Legislation. Master Lectures in Psychology.* (pp 11-54) Washington DC: American Psychological Association.

Ceci, S. J., & Bruck, M. (1993). The suggestibility of the child witness: A historical review and synthesis. *Psychological Bulletin, 113*, 403-439.

Chan, J.C.K., & LaPaglia, J.A. (2011). The dark side of testing memory: Repeated retrieval can enhance eyewitness suggestibility. *Journal of Experimental Psychology: Applied,* 1-15. doi:10.1037/a0025147

Chan, J. C. K., Thomas, A. K., & Bulevich, J. B. (2009). Recalling a witnessed event increases eyewitness suggestibility: The reversed testing effect. *Psychological Science, 20*, 66-73. doi:10.1111/j.1467-9280.2008.02245.x

Chrobak, Q.M., & Zaragoza, M.S. (2008). Inventing stories: Forcing witnesses to fabricate entire fictitious events leads to freely reported false memories. *Psychonomic Bulletin & Review, 15*(6), 1190-1195. doi:10.3758/PBR.15.6.1190

Clare, I.C.H., & Gudjonsson, G. (1993). Interrogative suggestibility, confabulation, and acquiescence in people with mild learning disabilities (mental handicap): Implications for reliability during police interrogations. *Journal of Clinical Psychology, 32*(3) 295-301.

Clare, I. C. H., & Gudjonsson, G. H. (1995). The vulnerability of suspects with intellectual disabilities during police interviews: Aa review and experimental study of decision-making. *Mental Handicap Research, 8,* 110-128.

Clare, I. C. H., Gudjonsson, G., Rutter, S. C., & Cross, P. (1994). Inter-rater reliability of the Gudjonsson Suggestibility Scale (Form 2). *British Journal of Clinical Psychology, 33,* 357-365. doi:10.1111 /j.2044-8260.1994.tb01132.x

Cleveland, K. C., Quas, J. A., & Lyon, T. D. (2016). Valence, implicated actor, and children's acquiescence to false suggestions. *Journal of Applied Developmental Psychology, 43,* 1-7. doi:10.1016/j.appdev.2015.12.003

Coffin, T. E. (1941). Some conditions of suggestion and suggestibility: A study of certain attitudinal and situational factors influencing the process of suggestion. *Psychological Monographs, 53,* 1-121.

Cohen, R.L., & Harnick, M.A. (1980). The susceptibility of child witnesses to suggestion. *Law and Human Behavior, 4,* 201-210.

Cole, C.B. & Loftus, E.F. (1987). The memory of children. In S. Ceci, M. Toglia, & D. Ross (Eds.), *Children's Eyewitness Memory* (pp. 178-208). NY: Springer-Verlag.

Columbe v. Connecticut, 367 U.S. 568 (1961).

Cutler, B. L., & Penrod, S. D. (1995). Assessing the accuracy of eyewitness identifications. In R. Bull and D. Carson (Ed.), Handbook of psychology in legal contexts (pp. 193-213) Chicester: John Wiley & Sons.

Dalla Barbra, G., & Boisse, M. (2010). Temporal consciousness and confabulation: is the medial temporal lobe "temporal"? *Cognitive Neuropsychiatry, 15*(1), 95-117. doi:10.1080/1354680090758017

Danielsdottir, G., Sigurgeirsdottir, S., Einarsdottir, H. R., & Haraldsson, E. (1993). Interrogative suggestibility in children and its relationship with memory and vocabulary. *Personalityand Individual Differences, 14,* 499-502.

Davis, D., & Loftus, E. F. (2007). Internal and external sources of misinformation in adult witness memory. In M. P. Toglia, J. D. Read, D. F. Ross, & R. C. L. Lindsay (Eds.), The handbook of eyewitness psychology: Memory for events (Vol. 1, pp. 195-237). Mahwah, NJ: Erlbaum.

DeClue, G. (2005). Interrogations and disputed confessions: A manual for forensic psychological practice. Sarasota, FL: Professional Resource Press.

Drake, K. (2011). Why might innocents make false confessions? *The British Psychological Society, 24*(10), 752-755.

Drizin, S., Leo, R. (2004). The problem of false confessions in the post-DNA world. *North Carolina Law Review, 82,* 891-1007.

Dunn, A. R. (1995). Questioning the reliability of children's testimony: An examination of the problematic events. *Law and Psychology Review,* 19, 203-215.

Eysenck, H.J. (1943). Suggestibility and hypnosis. *Journal of Neurology and Psychiatry, 6,* 22-31.

Eysenck, H.J., & Furneaux, W.D. (1945). States of heightened suggestibility: Narcosis. *Journal of Mental Science, 91,* 301-310.

Fisher, R.P., Ross, S.J., & Cahill, B.S. (2010). Interviewing witnesses and victims. In P.A. Granhang (ed.), *Forensic psychology in context: Nordic and international approaches* (pp. 56-74). Cullompton, UK: Willan Publishing.

Forrest, K. D., Wadkins, T. A., & Larson, B. A. (2006). Suspect personality, police interrogations, and false confessions: Maybe it is not just the situation. *Personality and Individual Differences, 40*, 621-628.

Fried, C.S., & Reppucci, N.D. (2001). Criminal decision making: The development of adolescent judgment, criminal responsibility, and culpability. *Law and Human Behavior, 25*(1), 45-61. doi:10.1023/A: 1005639909226

Frumkin, I. B. (2008). Psychological evaluation in Miranda waiver and confession cases. In R. Denny & J. Sullivan (Eds.), *Clinical neuropsychology in the criminal forensic setting* (pp. 135-175). New York: Guilford Press.

Frumkin, I.B., & Garcia, A. (2003). Psychological evaluations and the competency to waive Miranda rights. *Chamption Magazine, 27*. Retrieved form http://www.nacdl.org/public.nsf/$$searchChampion

Frumkin, I. B., Lally, S. J., & Sexton, J. E. (2012). A United States forensic sample for the Gudjonsson Suggestibility Scales. *Behavioral Sciences & The Law, 30*(6), 749-763. doi:10.1002/bsl.2032

Gathercole, S.E. (1998). The development of memory. *Journal of Child Psychology and Psychiatry, 39*(1), 3-27.

George, R. C. & Clifford, B. R. (1992). *Making the most of witnesses: Policing, 8,* 185-198.

Ginac, G., & Powel, M.B. (2009). A psychometric evaluation of the Gudjonsson Suggestibility Scales: Problems associated with measuring suggestibility as a difference score composite. *Personality and Individual Differences, 46*(2), 88-93. doi:10.1016/j.paid.2008.09.007

Goodman, G.S., & Quas, J.A. (2008) Repeated interviews and children's memory: It's more than just how many. *Current Directions in Psychological Science, 17*(6), 286-290. doi:10.1111/j.1467-8721.2008.00611.x

Gray, E. (1993). *Unequal justice: The prosecution of child sexual abuse.* New York, NY: Free Press.

Grisso, T. (1981). *Juveniles' waiver of rights: Legal and psychological competence.* New York: Plenum Press.

Gudjonsson, G. H. (1984). A new scale of interrogative suggestibility. *Personality and Individual Differences, 5,* 303-314. doi:10.1016/0191-8869(84)90069-2

Gudjonsson, G. H. (1987a). A parallel form of the Gudjonsson Suggestibility Scale. *British Journal of Clinical Psychology, 26,* 215-221. doi:10.1111/j.2044-8260.1987.tb01348.x

Gudjonsson, G. H. (1987b). The relationship between memory and suggestibility. *Social Behaviour, 2*(1), 29-33.

Gudjonsson, G.H. (1990). One hundred alleged false confession cases: Some normative data. *British Journal of Clinical Psychology, 29*(2). doi:10.1111/j.2044-8260.1990.tb00881.x

Gudjonsson, G. H. (1991). The effects of intelligence and memory on group differences in suggestibility and compliance. *Personality and Individual Differences, 5,* 503-505.

Gudjonsson, G. H. (1992). Interrogative suggestibility: Factor analysis of the Gudjonsson Suggestibility Scale. *Personality and Individual Differences, 13,* 479-481. doi:10.1016/0191-8869(92)90077-3

Gudjonsson, G. H. (1997). *The Gudjonsson Suggestibility Scales manual.* London: Psychology Press.

Gudjonsson, G. H. (2003). *The Psychology of Interrogations and Confessions: A Handbook.* London: UK. John Wiley & Sons.

Gudjonsson, G. H. (2006). Disputed confessions and miscarriages of justice in Britain: Expert psychological and psychiatric evidence in court of appeal. *The Manitoba Law Journal, 31,* 489-521.

Gudjonsson, G. H. (2010a). The psychology of false confessions: A review of the current evidence. In G. Daniel Lassiter & Christian. A. Meissner (Ed.), *Police Interrogations and False Confessions* (pp. 31-47). New York: American Psychological Association.

Gudjonsson, G. H. (2010b). Psychological vulnerabilities during police interviews. Why are they important? *Legal and Criminological Psychology, 15,* 161-175. doi:10.1348/13552510X5000064

Gudjonsson, G. H. (2013). *Interrogative suggestibility and compliance*. In A. M Ridley, F. Gabbert, & D. J. L. (Eds.), Suggestibility in legal contexts. *Psychological Research and Forensic Implications* (pp. 45-61). Chichester: Wiley-Blackwell.

Gudjonsson, G. H., & Clare, I. C. H. (1995). The relationship between confabulation and intellectual ability, memory, interrogative suggestibility and acquiescence. *Personality & Individual Differences, 19*, 333-338.

Gudjonsson, G. H., & Clark, N. K. (1986). A theoretical model of interrogative suggestibility. *Social Behavior, 1*(2), 83-104.

Gudjonsson, G.H., & Henry, L. (2003). Child and adult witnesses with intellectual disability: The importance of suggestibility. *Legal and Criminal Psychology, 8*(2), 241-252. doi:10.1348/135532503322363013

Gudjonsson, G.H., & MacKeith, J.A.C. (1990). A proven case of false confession: Psychological aspects of the coerced-compliant type. *Medicine, Science, and the Law, 30*, 329-335.

Gudjonsson, G. H., & Young, S. (2010). Does confabulation in memory predict suggestibility beyond IQ and memory? *Personality and Individual Differences, 49*(1), 65-67. doi:10.1016/j.paid.2010.03.014

Guerri, C., Bazinet, A., & Riley, E.P. (2009). Fetal alcohol spectrum disorders and alterations in brain and behavior. *Alcohol, 44*(2), 108-114. doi:10.1093/alcalc/agn105

Hall, G. S. (1980). Children's lies. *American Journal of Psychology, 3*, 59-70.

Hanba, J. M., & Zaragoza, M. S. (2007). Interviewer feedback in repeated interviews involving forced confabulation. *Applied Cognitive Psychology, 21*, 433-455. doi:10.1002/acp.1296

Henry L. A. & Gudjonsson G. H. (1999). Eyewitness memory and suggestibility in children with mental retardation. *American Journal on Mental Retardation, 104*, 491-508. doi:10.1023/A:1025434022699

Henry L. A. & Gudjonsson G. H. (2003). Eyewitness memory, suggestibility and repeated recall sessions in children with mild and moderate intellectual disabilities. *Law and Human Behavior, 27*(5), 481-505. doi:10.1023/A:1025434022699

Huff, C. R., Ratner, A., & Sagarin, E. (1996). *Convicted but innocent: Wrongful conviction and public policy.* Thousand Oaks, CA: Sage.

Hünefeldt, T., Rossi-Arnaud, C., & Furia, A. (2009). Effects of information type on children's interrogative suggestibility: Is Theory-of-Mind involved?. *Cognitive Processing, 10*(3), 199-207.

Innocence Project. (2012). *Facts on post-conviction dna exonerations*. Retrieved from http://www.innocenceproject.org/Content/Facts_on_PostConviction_DNA_Exonerations

Janosson, M., & Vitelli, R. (2007). Review of *Gudjonsson Suggestibility Scales*. In K.F. Geisinger,R.A. Spies, J.F. Carlson & B.S. Plake (eds.), *The seventeenth edition of the mental measurements yearbook*. UK: Buros Center.

Karpinski A. C., Scullin M. H. (2009). Suggestibility under pressure: Theory of mind, executive function, and suggestibility in preschoolers. *Journal of Applied Developmental Psychology, 30*, 749-763. 10.1016/j.appdev.2009.05.004

Kassin, S. M. (1997). The psychology of confession evidence. *American Psychologist, 5*(2), 233-251.

Kassin, S. M., & Gudjonsson, G. H. (2004). The psychology of confession evidence: A review of the literature and issues. *Psychological Science in the Public Interest, 5*, 35-69. doi: 10.1111/j.1529-1006.2004.00016.x

Kassin, S.M., & McNall, K. (1991). Police interrogations and confessions: Communicating promises and threats by pragmatic implication. *Law and Human Behavior, 15*(3), 233-251.

Kassin, S.M., & Neumann, K. (1997). On the power of confession evidence: An experimental test of the "fundamental difference" hypothesis. *Law and Human Behavior, 21*(5), 469- 484.

Kassin, S. M., & Sukel, H. (1997). Coerced confessions and the jury: An experimental test of the "harmless error" rule. *Law and Human Behavior, 21*, 27-46. doi:10.1023/A:1024814009769

Lamb M. E. & Fauchier A. (2001). The effects of question type on self-contradiction by children in the course of forensic interviews. *Applied Cognitive Development, 15*, 483-491. doi:10.1002/acp.726l

Lamb, M. E., La Rooy, D. J., Malloy, L. C., & Katz, C. (2011). *Children's testimony: A handbook of psychological research and forensic practice* (vol. 52) UK: John Wiley & Sons.

Last, U., & Aharoni-Etzioni, A. (1995). Secrets and reasons for secrecy among school-aged children: Developmental trends and gender differences. *The Journal of Genetic Psychology, 156*, 191-203. Retrieved from http://dx.doi.org/10.1080/00221325.1995.9914816

Leichtman M. D. & Ceci S. J. (1995). The effects of stereotypes and suggestions on preschoolers' reports. *Developmental Psychology, 31,* 568-578.

Leo, R. A. (1994). Police interrogation and social control. *Social & Legal Studies, 3*(1), 93-120. doi:10.1177/0964663994003300106

Levy-Gigi, E., & Vakil, E. (2014). The counterintuitive relationship between conceptual and perceptual similarities and eyewitness suggestibility. *Applied Cognitive Psychology, 28*(5), 799-804. doi:10.1002/acp.3066

Lindsay, D. S., Allen, B. P., Chan, J. C. K., & Dahl, L. C. (2004). Eyewitness suggestibility and source similarity: Intrusions of details from one event into memory reports of another event. *Journal of Memory and Language, 50*, 96-111.

Loftus, E. F. (1979). Reactions to blatantly contradictory information. *Memory & Cognition, 7*, 368-374. doi:10.3758/BF03196941

Loftus, E.F. (2005). Planting misinformation in the human mind: A 30-year investigation of the malleability of memory. *Learning and Memory, 12*, 361-366. doi:10.1101/lm.94705

Loftus, E. F., Miller, D. G., & Burns, H. J. (1978). Semantic integration of verbal information into a visual memory. *Journal of Experimental Psychology: Human Learning and Memory, 4*, 19-31.

Lyon, T. D., Malloy, L. C., Quas, J. A., & Talwar, V. A. (2008). Coaching, truth induction, and young maltreated children's false allegations and false denials. *Child Development, 79*, 914-929. Retrieved from http://dx.doi.org/10.1111/j.1467-8624.2008.01167.x

Mastroberardino, S., Marucci, F.S. (2013). Interrogative suggestibility: Was it just compliance or a genuine false memory. *Legal and Criminal Psychology, 18*(2), 274-286. doi:10.1111/j.2044-8333.2012.02048.x

McCann, J. (1998). A conceptual framework for identifying various types of false confessions. *Behavioral Sciences & the Law, 16*, 441-453. doi:10.1002/(SICI)1099-0798(199823)16:4<441::AID-BSL320>3.0. CO;2-W

McLachlan, K., Roesch, R., & Douglas, K. S. (2011). Examining the role of interrogative suggestibility in Miranda rights comprehension in adolescents. *Law and Human Behavior, 35*(3), 165. doi:10.1007s10979-009-9198-4

Memon, A. & Wright, D. (2000). Eyewitness testimony: Theoretical and practical issues, in J. McGuire, T. Mason and A. O'Kane (eds) *Behaviour, Crime and Legal Process*. Chichester: John Wiley and Sons.

Mesiarik, C.M. (2008). Gender, suggestibility, and self-reported likelihood of false confessions. (Unpublished doctoral dissertation. Drexel, Pennsylvania.

Meyer, J.R., & Reppucci, N.D. (2007). Police practices and perceptions regarding juvenile interrogation and interrogative suggestibility. *Behavioral Sciences and the Law, 25*, 757-780. doi:10.1002/bsl.774

Milling, L.S., Reardon, J.M., & Carosella, G.M. (2006). Mediation and moderation of psychological pain treatments: Response expectancies and hypnotic suggestibility. *Journal of Consulting Clinical Psychology, 74*(2), 253-262.

Moscovitch, M. (1989). Confabulation and the frontal systems: Strategic versus associative retrieval in neu-ropsychological theories of memory. In H.L. Roediger & F.I. Craik (Eds.), *Varieties of memory and consciousness: Essays in honor of Endel Tulving* (pp. 133-160). Hillsdale, NJ: Lawrence Erlbaum Associates.

Murris, P., Meesters, C., & Merckelbach, H.L.G.J. (2004). Correlates of the Gudjonsson Suggestibility Scale in delinquent adolescents. *Psycholgoical Reports, 94*(1), 264-266.

Neuschatz, J. S., Lampinen, J. M., Toglia, M. P., Payne, D.G., & Cisneros, E. P. (2007). False memory re-search: History, theory, and applied implications. In R. C. L. Lindsay, D. F. Ross, J.D. Read, & M. P. Toglia (Eds.), *The handbook of eyewitness psychology volume 1: Memory for events.* (pp. 239-260). Mahwah, NJ: Lawrence Erlbaum Associates.

Oberlander, L.B., & Goldstien, N.E. (2003). A review and update on the practice of evaluating Miranda com-prehension. *Behavioral Science and the Law, 19*(4), 453-471.

Ofshe, R. J. (1989). Coerced confessions: The logic of seemingly irrational action. *Cultic Studies Journal, 6*, 1-15.

Otgaar, H., Sauerland, M., & Petrila, J. P. (2013). Novel shifts in memory research and their impact on the legal process: Introduction to the special issue on memory formation and suggestibility in the legal process. *Behavioral Sciences & The Law, 31*(5), 531-540. doi:10.1002/bsl.2095

Pearse, J., & Gudjonsson, G.H. (1999). Measuring influential police interviewing tactics: A factor analytic approach. *Legal and Criminal Psychology, 4*(2), 221-238. doi:10.1348/13552599167860

Pires, R., Silva, D. R., & Ferreira, A. S. (2014). The Portuguese adaptation of the Gudjonsson Suggestibility Scale (GSS1) in a sample of inmates. *International Journal of Law and Psychiatry, 37*(3), 289-294.

Polczyk, R., Wesołowska, B., Gabarczyk, A., Minakowska, I., Spuska, M., & Bomba, E. (2004). Age differ-ences in interrogative suggestibility: A comparison between young and older adults. *Applied Cogni-tive Psychology, 18*, 1097-1107.

Pollard, R., Trowbridge, B., Slade, P. D., Streissguth, A. P., Laktonen, A., & Townes, B. D. (2004). Inter-rogative suggestibility in a US context: Some preliminary data on normal subjects. *Personality and Individual Differences, 37*, 1101-1108.

Poole, D. A., & Lindsay, D. S. (1995). Interviewing preschoolers: Effects of nonsuggestive techniques, pa-rental coaching, and leading questions on reports of nonexperienced events. *Journal of Experimental Child Psychology, 60*, 129-154.

Quas, J. A., & Lench, H. C. (2007). Arousal at encoding, arousal at retrieval, interviewer support, and chil-dren's memory for a mild stressor. *Applied Cognitive Psychology, 21*, 289-305.

Quas, J.A., Schaaf, J.M., Alexander, K.W., & Goodman, G.S. (2000). Do you really remember it happening or do you only remember being asked about it happening? Children's source monitoring in forensic contexts. In K.P. Roberts & M. Blades (Eds.), *Children's Source Monitoring* (pp. 197-226). Mahwah, NJ: Erlbaum.

Redlich, A.D. & Goodman, G.S. (2003). Taking responsibility for an act not committed: The influence of age and suggestibility. *Law and Human Behavior, 27*, 141-156.

Richardson, G., Gudjonsson, G. H., & Kelly, T. P. (1995). Interrogative suggestibility in an adolescent forensic population. *Journal of Adolescence, 18*, 211-216.

Richardson, G., & Kelly, T.P. (1995). The relationship between intelligence, memory and interrogative suggest-ibility in young offenders. *Psychology, Crime & Law, 1*, 283-290. doi:10.1080/10683169508411965

Robinson, J., & Briggs, P. (1997). Age trends and eye witness suggestibility and compliance. *Psychology, Crime and Law, 3*, 187-202.

Roebers, C.M., & McConkey, K.M. (2003). Mental reinstatement of the misinformation context and the misinformation effect in children and adults. *Applied Cognitive Psychology, 17*(4), 477-493. doi:10.1002/acp.886

Roediger, H.L., & McDermott, K.B. (2000). Tricks of memory. *Current Directions in Psychological Science, 9*(4), 123-127. doi:10.1111/467-8721.00075

Rossi-Arnaud, H.T., & Furia, A. (2009). Effects of information type on children's interrogative suggestibility: Is theory-of-mind involved? *Cognitions Process, 10*(3), 199-207. doi:10.1007/s10339-009-0269-8

Russano, M. B., Meissner, C. A., Narchet, F. M., & Kassin, S. M. (2005). Investigating true and false confessions within a novel experimental paradigm. *Psychological Science, 16*(6), 481-486.

Scheck, B., Neufeld, P., & Dwyer, J. (2000). *Actual innocence: Five days to execution, and other dispatches from the wrongly convicted.* New York: Doubleday.

Scott, E. S., Reppucci, N. D., & Woolard, J. L. (1995). Evaluating adolescents' decision making in legal contexts. *Law and Human Behavior, 19*, 221-244.

Shapiro, L.R., Blackford, C., & Chen, C. (2005). Eyewitness memory for a simulated misdemeanor crime: The role of temperament in suggestibility. *Applied Cognitive Psychology, 19*(3), 267-289. doi:10.1002/acp.1089

Sharman, S.J. & Powel, M.B. (2012). A comparison of adult witnesses' suggestibility across various types of leading questions. *Applied Cognitive Psychology, 26*(1), 48-53. doi:10.1002/acp.1793

Shaw, J. S., García, L. A., & Robles, B. E. (1997). Cross-language post event misinformation effects in Spanish-English bilingual witnesses. *Journal of Applied Psychology, 82*, 889- 899.

Sigurdsson, J.F. & Godjonsson, G.H. (1994). Alcohol and drug intoxication during police interrogation and the reasons why suspects confess to the police. *Addiction, 89*(8), 985-997. doi:10.111/j.1360-0443.1994.tb03358.x

Sigurdsson J. F., & Gudjonsson, G. H. (1996). The psychological characteristics of false confessor'. A study among Icelandic prison inmates and juvenile offenders. *Personality and Individual Differences, 20*, 321-329.

Singh, K. K., & Gudjonsson, G. H. (1992). Interrogative suggestibility among adolescent boys and its relationship with intelligence, memory, and cognitive set. *Journal of Adolescence, 15*, 155-161.

Smeets, T., Leppink, J., Jelicic, M., & Merckelbach, H. L. G. J. (2009). Shortened versions of the Gudjonsson Suggestibility Scale meet the standards. *Legal and criminological Psychology, 14*(1), 149-155. doi:10.1348/135532507X190207

Smith, P., & Gudjonsson, G. H. (1995). Confabulation among forensic inpatients and its relationship with memory, suggestibility, compliance, anxiety, and self-esteem. *Personality and Individual Differences, 19*, 517-523.

Smith, P., & Gudjonsson, G. H. (1995). The relationship of mental disorder to suggestibility and confabulation among forensic inpatients. *The Journal of Forensic Psychiatry, 6*, 499-515.

Steinberg L, Cauffman E. (1996). Maturity of judgment in adolescence: Psychosocial factors in adolescent decision making. *Law and Human Behavior, 20*, 249-272.

Stern, W. (1910). Abstracts of lectures on the psychology of testimony and on the study of individuality. *American Journal of Psychology, 21*, 273-282.

Stern, W. (1939). The psychology of testimony. *Journal of Abnormal and Social Psychology, 34*, 3-30.

Tobey, A.E. & Goodman, G.S. (1992). Children's eyewitness memory: Effects of participation and forensic context. *Child Abuse Neglect, 16*(6), 799-796.

Warren, A. R., Hulse-Trotter, K., & Tubbs, E. C. (1991). Inducing resistance to suggestibility in children. *Law and Human Behavior, 15*, 273-285.

Wells, G.L. & Olson, E.A. (2003). Eyewitness testimony. *Annual Review of Psychology, 54*, 277-295. doi:10.1146/annurev.psych.54.101601.145028

Whitcomb, D., Shapiro, E. R., & Stellwagen, L. D. (1985). *When the victim is` a child: Issues for judges and prosecutors*. Washington, DC: National Institute of Justice.

Wigmore, J.H. (1970). *Evidence: Volume Three*. Boston: Little, Brown.

Willner, P. (2008). Clarification of the memory artifact in the assessment of suggestibility. *Journal of Intellectual Disability Research, 52*(4), 318-326. doi:10.1111/j.1365-2788.2007.01022.x

Yarmey, D. A. (2006). Depoimentos de testemunhas oculares e auriculares [Eye and auricular witness testimony]. In M. R. Simões, M. C. T. Simões, & M. S. Pinho (Eds.), *Psicologia Forense* (pp. 227-258). Coimbra: Almedina.

Young, K., Powell, M. B., & Dudgeon, P. (2003). Individual differences in children's suggestibility: A comparison between intellectually disabled and mainstream samples. *Personality and Individual Differences, 35*(1), 31-49.

Zaragoza, M., Belli, R. F., & Payment, K. E. (2007). Misinformation effects and the suggestibility of eyewitness memory. In M. Garry & H. Hayne (Eds.), *Do justice and let the sky fall: Elizabeth F. Loftus and her contributions to science, law and academic freedom* (pp. 35-63). Mahwah, NJ: Lawrence Erlbaum Associates.

CHAPTER 19

TRAUMA-INFORMED CARE (TIC): AN OVERVIEW WITH APPLICATIONS FOR THE CRIMINAL JUSTICE SYSTEM

KATE BAILEY & JERROD BROWN

CHAPTER OVERVIEW

Trauma-Informed Care (TIC) refers to a trauma-sensitive approach to services employed within human services, mental health, education, and criminal justice systems, as well as other organizations and agencies serving populations with high rates of trauma. Research shows a high prevalence of trauma among people utilizing public mental health and substance abuse services, as well as among those who are involved in child welfare and criminal justice systems. By acknowledging the presence of trauma and recognizing the risk of retraumatizing clients in service environments, trauma-informed approaches aim to create policies, practices, and environments that improve experiences and outcomes for clients as well as service providers.

This chapter will define the problems that trauma-informed care seeks to address: the pervasiveness of trauma; the life-shaping impact of trauma on physical, social, and emotional health and well-being; and the inherent risk of retraumatization in service environments. The chapter will then explore the principles of trauma-informed care and its applications across the criminal justice system. Resources for further research on topics of trauma-informed care training and trauma-informed treatments will also be provided.

DEFINING TRAUMA

The term *trauma*, used broadly, can refer to a single or prolonged overwhelming experience or multiple personal experiences, including actual or threatened serious injury or harm to one's physical integrity, witnessing violence toward another person, loss, war, natural disasters, and other circumstances resulting in feelings of intense fear, helplessness or horror (Mailloux, 2014; Black, Woodworth, Tremblay, & Carpenter, 2012; American Psychiatric Association, 2013). The term *complex trauma* is used to describe exposure to multiple traumatic events, often of an interpersonal nature and occurring in childhood (Bath, 2008; Buffington, Dierkhising, & Marsh, 2010; van der Kolk, 2005; National Child Traumatic Stress Network, 2015).

Historical trauma refers to multigenerational trauma most often experienced by specific cultural groups that have faced severe levels of oppression, poverty, or loss and are still suffering as a result (Sotero,

2006). These populations include American Indians, people of color, immigrants, and families experiencing intergenerational poverty (Substance Abuse and Mental Health Services Administration, n.d.). According to Brown (2008), some cultural minorities have "...post-trauma distress and dysfunction arising from doing battle every day against an army of small toxic agents" (p. 106).

The term *vicarious trauma* (also known as *secondary trauma*) refers to occurrences in which professionals' perspectives and beliefs about the world become altered due to repeated and prolonged involvement and exposure to the trauma of others (Hesse, 2002; Mailloux, 2014; McCann & Pearlman, 1990). Vicarious trauma may also result in therapist retraumatization, in the event that the therapist has endured his/her own trauma previously (Mailloux, 2014). Vicarious trauma is distinct from *burnout* in that it specifically refers to exposure to emotionally trying images and descriptions of suffering, as well as the experience of symptoms resembling those of post-trauma individuals (Hesse, 2002; McCann & Pearlman, 1990).

PREVALENCE AND IMPLICATIONS OF TRAUMA

Research on trauma-informed care emerged in response to growing awareness of the prevalence of trauma and the accompanying impact that trauma can have on a life course. The most prominent research about the pervasiveness of trauma and its implications comes from the Adverse Childhood Experiences (ACE) Study.

The ACE Study was a collaborative research project between the Centers for Disease Control and Prevention (CDC) and Kaiser Permanente's Department of Preventative Medicine in San Diego. In the late 1990s, in the largest study of its kind, Dr. Robert Anda and Dr. Vincent Felitti studied more than 17,000 participants to assess exposure to Adverse Childhood Experiences (ACEs) and to examine health-related outcomes. The study looked specifically at ten types of childhood adversity, including emotional, physical, and sexual abuse; emotional and physical neglect; and growing up in a household where someone was an alcoholic, a drug user, mentally ill, suicidal, where the mother was treated violently, or where a household member had been imprisoned during the participant's childhood (Felitti et al., 1998).

From the study, Anda and Felitti discovered that ACEs were common and interrelated. Two-thirds of participants reported exposure to at least one ACE, and one in six reported exposures to four or more ACEs. For participants reporting any single category of exposure, the probability of exposure to an additional ACE category ranged from 65%–93%, with a median of 80% (Felitti et al., 1998). The study also found that the effects of ACEs were cumulative: compared to persons with an ACE score of zero, those reporting four or more ACEs were twice as likely to be smokers, twelve times more likely to have attempted suicide, seven times more likely to be an alcoholic, and ten times more likely to have injected street drugs (Redding, 2003).

It should be noted that the vast majority of participants in the ACE Study were white, middle-class, and highly educated, and all participants had health insurance (Felitti et al., 1998). More recent studies have demonstrated that the incidence of childhood adversity is higher among Native Americans (Koss et al., 2003) and African Americans and low-income populations in urban settings (The Research and Evaluation Group, 2013). Historical trauma may also be a factor in explaining disproportionately high exposure to ACEs among American Indian and African American populations. Intergenerational trauma theories and the minority stress model have explained how racial minority groups often experience worse health outcomes due to a variety of stressors (Coleman, 2016). According to Duran, Duran, & Braveheart (1998), unresolved trauma is intergenerationally cumulative, thus compounding the health and social problems of succeeding generations.

The framework for understanding the link between childhood adversity and negative health outcomes is shown in Figure 1. The biological stress-response systems of children exposed to trauma can change as they shift their focus from a developmentally appropriate investment in interests and activities that can promote growth to a need to ensure safety (Anda & Felitti, 2010; Bath, 2008; Levenson, 2014). For example, normal biological stress responses include temporarily increased heart rate, blood pressure, and stress hormones such as cortisol; when experiencing chronic stress, the body is consistently utilizing stress-response systems, which can cause damage to the brain and organ systems. These physical adaptations in the brain and body that result from exposure to toxic stress can be directly connected to a multitude of long-term health consequences, such as coronary disease later in life (Anda & Felitti, 2010; Harvard University Center for the Developing Child, n.d.).

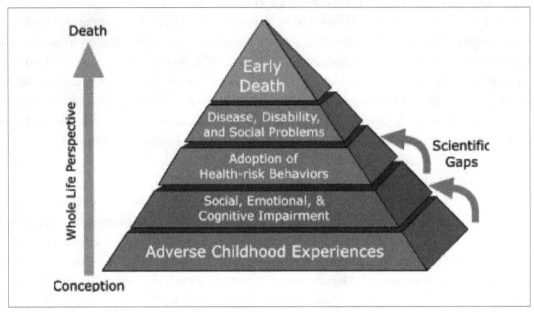

FIGURE 1

The ACE Pyramid. Centers for Disease Control and Prevention.

Research has also found support for a relationship between toxic stress in childhood and subsequent engagement in behaviors resembling those of Post-Traumatic Stress Disorder (PTSD), such as hypervigilance and reactivity, which often led to anxiety, depression, and health-risk behaviors such as smoking and substance abuse (Eames et al., 2014). The adoption of coping, health-risk behaviors is another way that ACEs can be linked to chronic disease and early death. According to the ACE Study, the relationship between ACEs and negative health outcomes is strong and proportionate, with negative outcomes steadily increasing with the number of ACEs experienced in childhood (Felitti et al., 1998).

Research has also shown that children who have suffered complex trauma may meet the diagnostic criteria for many disorders, including PTSD (Black et al., 2012). Symptoms of PTSD include nightmares, flashbacks, and other involuntary re-experiencing of the terror and helplessness; a focus on avoiding cues and reminders of trauma; hyperarousal; hypervigilance; and difficulty concentrating (American Psychiatric Association, 2013). Many of these symptoms also describe those experienced by individuals suffering from vicarious trauma (Molden & Firestone, 2007).

EVOLUTION OF TRAUMA-INFORMED CARE

In light of the pervasiveness of trauma and the implications of trauma on all areas of life, the concept of trauma-informed care *(also referred to as trauma-informed practice)*, evolved in the late 1990s and early 2000s as an approach for organizations and systems to address the potential impacts of trauma on their clients and, by doing so, to provide services in a manner that improves outcomes. Among the leading researchers in the field of trauma-informed care are Maxine Harris, Roger Fallot, and Sandra Bloom. Harris and Fallot coined the term "trauma informed" in 2001, defining a trauma-informed approach as threefold: knowing the trauma histories of clients, understanding the impact of victimization on the lives of clients, and using that understanding to deliver services in a manner that accommodates the vulnerabilities of trauma survivors (Harris & Fallot, 2001).

Because trauma survivors are less likely to seek help for trauma-related symptoms, trauma-informed care is particularly crucial in public systems such as education, human services, and criminal justice, which come into contact with individuals within this population and are presented with a unique opportunity to provide interventions (Schreiber, Renneberg, & Maercker, 2010). In this way, teachers, counselors, direct-care workers, case managers, corrections officers, and others are in a position to utilize trauma-informed practices to help trauma survivors heal (Greenwald, 2005).

Harris and Fallot were foundational in applying trauma-informed philosophy and practice, particularly in mental health and substance abuse service settings. As part of their "Self-Assessment and Planning Protocol" tool for creating cultures of trauma-informed care, Fallot and Harris defined five key values of trauma-informed care that are often referred to today: safety, trustworthiness, choice, collaboration, and empowerment (Fallot & Harris, 2002). In 2005, Elliott, Bjelajac, Fallot, Markoff and Reed framed the values of trauma-informed care as a set of ten core principles. Sandra Bloom, who began theorizing about nonviolent service environments in the late 1990s and in the early 2000s, developed the Sanctuary Model (a trauma-informed organizational model) and focused her trauma-informed care philosophy on seven cultural commitments: nonviolence, emotional intelligence, social learning, open communication, democracy, social responsibility, and growth and change (Bloom & Sreedhar, 2008).

Below is a synthesized list of the most commonly discussed principles of trauma-informed care. Today these core values and principles are used in fields including mental health, juvenile justice, corrections, substance abuse treatment, child welfare, and education. In addition to a trauma-informed care approach, many mental health settings also utilize trauma-informed treatment (or trauma-specific treatment), which refers to therapeutic intervention models designed to help clients understand and address past trauma. Trauma-informed treatment is distinct from trauma-informed care and will be highlighted in a later section.

PRINCIPLES OF TRAUMA-INFORMED CARE

- *Understanding Trauma* – Service providers must be informed regarding the prevalence of trauma and its potential cognitive, physical, social, and emotional implications. This includes training service providers about the nature of trauma as well as providing opportunities to gain competence in the screening of clients for histories and symptoms of trauma.
- *Ensuring Safety* – Clients with a history of trauma may be wary of trusting service providers. Creating a consistent, reliable, and transparent service environment can improve the effectiveness of care by establishing safety and trust between service providers and clients.
- *Minimizing Trauma* – Service environment, policies, and practices are designed to prevent client retraumatization, as well as secondary or vicarious trauma among service providers. Foundational to the concept of trauma-informed care is that service providers do no harm.
- *Building Self-Regulation Skills* – Trauma frequently results in impulsive emotional responses. In a service environment where trauma is prevalent, service providers and clients need to be supported in learning ways to prevent triggering previous trauma and, instead, fostering positive interactions.
- *Fostering Connections* – Positive relationships are essential for growth and healing after the experience of trauma. Service providers have a unique opportunity to model respectful and supportive connections, helping clients to develop positive emotions about building healthy relationships with others.
- *Utilizing Strengths-Based and Culturally Competent Approaches* – Services must be provided through a holistic lens with the client at the center. Service providers are expected to focus on the strengths of each individual by recognizing and tailoring services to their unique histories, while valuing their role within the therapeutic process as an influential agent of change.

- ***Ensuring Choice and Involvement*** – It is important that clients are empowered within the service environment, in order to overcome feelings of helplessness caused by trauma. Client collaboration and choice increases participation, buy-in, and the likelihood of success.
- ***Integrating Reflection and Evaluation*** – In order to evaluate the effectiveness and efficiency of trauma-informed approaches, service providers and clients must reflect often on processes and practices. A culture that supports honest reflection can continually adapt and improve services to meet the needs of clients, service providers, and administrators.

In addition to these commonly discussed principles, trauma-informed approaches also discuss the importance of reframing the question "What's wrong with you?" to "What happened to you?" when working with clients. This shift moves the implication from blame and shame to openness and understanding. Changing this question allows clients an opportunity to better understand how what happened to them in the past is affecting their present lives (Bloom & Sreedhar, 2008).

BENEFITS OF TRAUMA-INFORMED CARE

Research has shown that utilizing trauma-informed principles, policies, and practices in service environments can be beneficial for clients, service providers, and administrators.

- Service providers better understand their clients and more effectively meet their needs (Brown, Harris, & Fallot, 2013; Levenson, 2014; Miller & Najavits, 2012).
- Organization/agency staff are supported by policies and practices designed to cultivate self-regulation and prevent secondary trauma, making them more effective in serving clients (Berger & Quiros, 2014; Ford & Blaustein, 2013; Mailloux, 2014).
- Clients are involved in the design and implementation of services and, as a result, are more engaged throughout the process and invested in achieving shared goals for service outcomes (Elliott, Bjelajac, Fallot, Markoff, & Reed, 2005; Ford & Blaustein, 2013).
- Clients' symptoms of trauma are reduced; they are empowered to recognize negative patterns, build new skills, develop healthy interpersonal relationships, and improve their overall well-being (Berger & Quiros, 2014; Levenson, 2014; Substance Abuse and Mental Health Administration, n.d.).
- Providing integrated trauma-informed services, such as trauma-informed treatment and substance abuse treatment, results in more sustainable positive outcomes for clients and may also be more cost-effective for service providers (Berger & Guiros, 2014; Farro, 2011; Substance Abuse and Mental Health Services Administration, n.d.).
- Rehabilitation through trauma-informed care can be a more successful means of reducing relapse and recidivism than punitive measures such as surveillance and enforcement (Levenson, 2014; Miller & Najavits, 2012; Substance Abuse and Mental Health Services Administration, n.d.).

APPLYING TRAUMA-INFORMED CARE TO THE CRIMINAL JUSTICE SYSTEM

As was stated earlier, trauma is a common experience among individuals involved in the criminal justice system. Research indicates that at least three in four youths in the juvenile justice system have been exposed to traumatic victimization, particularly in the form of child maltreatment (Dierkhising et al., 2013; Ford & Blaustein, 2013; Ko et al., 2008). Among adult correctional populations, just under half of women and one-tenth of men report histories of physical and/or sexual abuse. A history of sexual abuse is actually considered a risk factor for criminal behavior and, in general, people who have been sexually abused are more likely to be arrested (Hubbard, 2002; Levenson, Willis, & Prescott, 2016; Miller & Najavits, 2012).

Due to the high prevalence of trauma within the criminal justice system, there is increasing support for the integration of trauma-informed approaches into service provisions across the system, from law enforcement to re-entry and community corrections. The Substance Abuse and Mental Health Services Administration (SAMHSA) Sequential Intercept Model, shown in Figure 2, provides a helpful framework for examining the various settings in which trauma-informed care can be implemented in the criminal justice system to better address trauma, prevent retraumatization, and improve outcomes for offenders. This model has demonstrated success in improving the lives of women involved in the criminal justice system by helping them recognize and heal from past trauma, restore relationships, and reduce incidences of conflict and recidivism (Substance Abuse and Mental Health Services Administration, n.d.).

Using the Sequential Intercept Model as a guide, this section will discuss applications of trauma-informed care in four central settings of the criminal justice system: law enforcement, courts, corrections, and rehabilitative treatment programs.

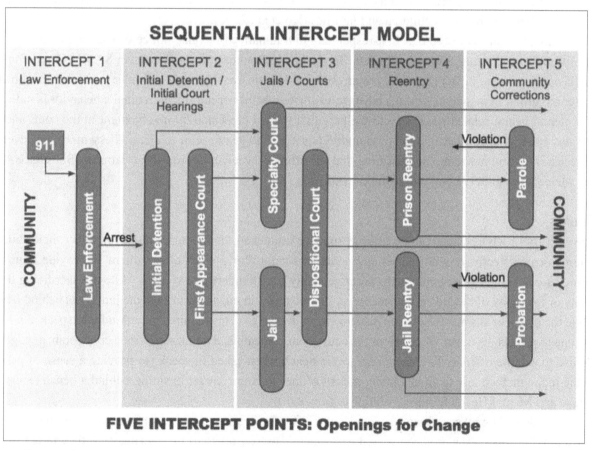

FIGURE 2

SAMSHA's Criminal Justice Sequential Intercept Model. With permission from SAMHSA's GAINS Center, operated by Policy Research Associates, Inc. 2015.

LAW ENFORCEMENT

First responders, such as law enforcement and emergency medical services, encounter traumatized children and families every day. Due to the role of first responders in making the initial contact with victims of trauma, they are in a unique position to reduce the immediate stress of victims and witnesses; they are also at increased risk of re-traumatizing victims if they are unprepared to respond to the physical and psychological effects of trauma. For example, while police officers have protocols in place for investigating and responding to traumatic incidents involving children, few officers have formal training for assisting children in dealing with psychological trauma (Ko et al., 2008). It should also be noted that police officers are at increased risk for PTSD as a result of multiple exposures to traumatic events in the line of duty; trauma-informed support for police officers, including a focus on social resiliency and coping strategies for managing intense emotions, are important for the well-being of police officers (Marchand, Nadeau, Beaulieu-Prevost, Boyer, & Martin, 2015; Violanti, 2006).

When police officers are trained and supported by trauma specialists, they can be influential in helping decrease victim and witness exposure to further traumatic stress, providing safety and structure, and making necessary referrals (Ko et al., 2008). In 1991, the Yale Child Study Center, in collaboration with the New Haven Connecticut Department of Police Service, developed a trauma-informed model for integrating children's mental health services with law enforcement procedures. The Child Development Community Policing Program (CD-CP) partnered mental health professionals with police officers to offer early intervention services when working with children following exposure to trauma (Marans, Murphy, & Berkowitz, 2002). This model has since been nationally recognized as an effective way for mental health providers to support law enforcement in addressing trauma in children and families (Ko et al., 2008).

In addition to their role as first-responders to traumatized victims, police officers are responsible for identifying and arresting criminal offenders. To do this in a trauma-informed manner, SAMHSA recommends that law enforcement officers consider pre-arrest diversion, such as taking the offender to a mental health crisis center or calling in mental health specialists to evaluate whether or not the individual's behavior is indicative of a mental health-related issue. Due to the potential trauma presented by involvement in the court and corrections systems, careful evaluation of an individual's mental health prior to arrest is essential for preventing unnecessary retraumatization and ensuring that the offender receives appropriate treatment (Substance Abuse and Mental Health Services Administration, n.d.).

COURTS

The courtroom environment can be intimidating for trauma survivors, and stress may affect their ability to communicate effectively with judges and court personnel. For a court environment to provide trauma-informed services, the goal should be to promote safety for offenders and victims while not sacrificing the security or formality of the judicial proceedings. For example, in most courtrooms the judge sits behind a bench while the offender sits at a table some distance from the bench. This requires the offender to speak at a higher volume to project his or her voice across the courtroom. Instead, in a trauma-informed courtroom, a judge may choose to ask the offender to come closer to the bench when asked to speak (to provide a sense of privacy) or the judge may choose to sit at a table in front of the court in contrast to sitting behind a bench (Substance Abuse and Mental Health Services Administration, n.d.).

Judges, like other service providers, have difficulty distinguishing trauma survivors from non-trauma impacted. For this reason, it is considered best practice to treat all court participants as if they might be trauma survivors and seek to prevent retraumatization (Elliott et al., 2005). It is also important to assess potential PTSD symptoms in court, given the prevalence of PTSD in some populations (Bottalico & Bruni, 2012). Judges who are trauma-informed expect the presence of trauma, take care not to cause trauma, and understand that trauma may affect an offender's behavior as well as success in rehabilitation. Trauma-informed judges also work closely with other court personnel as well as attorneys and case managers to maximize opportunities for positive outcomes (Substance Abuse and Mental Health Services Administration, n.d.).

Interactions between judges or other court personnel and offenders can offer an opportunity for modeling support and encouraging healing. Many judges have found that expressing concern and using less negative, punitive, or judgmental language has had a positive impact on court participants (Substance Abuse and Mental Health Services Administration, n.d.). In a recent study, staff members and administrators from several agencies involved in a California county-level drug court reported that an assessment of their agency's services using a trauma-informed lens heightened their awareness of what parents have to go through and increased their sensitivity and respect for parents, which helped them find improved ways to affirm parents in their parenting roles (Drabble, Jones, & Brown, 2013).

JUVENILE JUSTICE

Childhood trauma is an almost universal experience among youth in the juvenile justice system. As a result of being exposed to abuse or neglect, youth may cope with indifference, defiance, or aggression as a means of self-protection. As stated by Ko and colleagues (2008), "These defensive attempts to overcome or resist the helplessness and isolation caused by victimization often are motivated by the desire to regain the ability to feel safe and in control rather than by the callous indifference often assumed to be driving delinquency" (p. 400). This assumption, that delinquency is driven by malice or indifference, can prevent juvenile justice program staff and administrators from viewing youth offenders as needing (or deserving) assistance in building self-regulation skills (Caldwell, 2007).

Juvenile justice residential programs offer unique opportunities to educate youth and begin to equip them with self-regulation skills, since the youth in these programs are literally a "captive audience" (Ford & Blaustein, 2013). In Connecticut, a trauma-informed education and self-regulation skill-building program was recently implemented in juvenile justice residential facilities over a period of several years. Incrementally, through ongoing modeling and support for administrators, staff, and youth, trauma-informed principles and self-regulation skills were integrated into each facility environment. Evidence indicated that this shift resulted in positive outcomes, including greater freedom for youth as they demonstrated that they could act with appropriate self-regulation, fewer violent incidents, a greater sense of mutual understanding between staff and youth, reduced staff absenteeism and turnover, and an improved safety record (Ford & Blaustein, 2013; Ford & Hawke, 2012).

CORRECTIONS

The phrase "hurt people hurt people" speaks to the recurring nature of trauma and how it is transmitted to others (Bloom & Farragher, 2011). This concept is evident in the corrections system, where higher rates of trauma, particularly in early childhood, are associated with increased violence and victimization in prison (Komarovskaya, 2009). Prisoners abused prior to incarceration are more likely than non-abused inmates to be incarcerated for a murder, violent offense, or sexual crime. Among state-prison inmates, one in twenty men and one in four women report childhood sexual abuse, and one in ten men and one in four women report physical abuse in childhood (Harlow, 1999; Levenson, 2014).

Research conducted in correctional institutions has demonstrated that in the absence of trauma-informed care, the environment and programming of correctional institutions are frequently ineffective. The culture of the corrections system is often punitive and pathologizing (Ford & Blaustein, 2013), with imbalanced power dynamics that can result in perceived disparities in humanity – as demonstrated by the famous Stanford Prison Experiment of 1971 led by Philip Zimbardo (Gwinn, Judd, & Park, 2013). As a result, trauma survivors in the system are at risk of experiencing shame, dehumanization, and retraumatization, which can, in turn, lead to a sense of injustice and a violent response (Gilligan, 1996). In addition to risking physical and emotional harm, there is also empirical evidence that sanctions and punitive measures used in prisons, without treatment, are the least-effective means of reducing recidivism (Andrews et al., 1990; Miller & Najavits, 2012).

Treatment and rehabilitation are more likely to be a successful means of reducing recidivism than surveillance and enforcement (Gendreau, Goggin, Cullen, & Andrews, 2000). Evidence has shown that the use of cognitive-behavioral and coping-skills treatments with strong educational components have helped stabilize inmates with PTSD (Zlotnick, Najavits, Rohsenow, & Johnson, 2003). Some trauma-informed treatments (e.g., Seeking Safety) can be conducted by a broad range of staff, are cost effective, and are known to be safe. Even when these types of trauma-informed therapies are not used in correctional settings, integrating trauma-informed principles into facility environments can still help improve inmate outcomes (Miller & Najavits, 2012).

Using trauma-informed approaches in corrections institutions benefits not only inmates, but also corrections staff. In the absence of effective trauma-informed practices, prison systems may develop institutional trauma, becoming highly reactive to crises (Miller & Najavits, 2012). According to Ford and Blaustein (2013), administrators and staff in correctional systems "have become dysregulated as a result of a combination of vicarious trauma, direct exposure in the line of duty to traumatic stressors, and political and economic pressures, constraints, and threats" (p. 668). For this reason, trauma-informed training for corrections staff must emphasize the importance of self-care and also reinforce the values of compassion and intuition in recognizing and building successful strategies for interacting with inmates. Values such as compassionate care and empathy may be perceived as weak or ineffective due to the traditional corrections milieu, so involving seasoned staff and administrators in training is a critical component in gaining buy-in from all facility personnel (Miller & Najavits, 2012).

REHABILITATIVE TREATMENT

Rehabilitative programs and services, because they are generally aimed at reducing relapse by improving self-awareness and self-regulation skills, have tended to be early adopters of trauma-informed care concepts. Due to the link between trauma and subsequent development of mental health issues, as well as substance abuse and other addictive behaviors, it follows that trauma-informed care is of critical importance in these settings. Evidence has even shown that trauma-exposed clients may be more receptive to treatments than those who have not experienced trauma: a recent study of participants in a substance abuse treatment program for individuals under criminal justice supervision showed that people with trauma histories reported a greater desire for help managing their stress and developing healthy relationships than those without traumatic backgrounds (Clark, Reiland, Thorne, & Cropsey, 2014). While there are many types of rehabilitative treatment that a client may encounter in the criminal justice system, this section will briefly touch on three types of treatment, with consideration of efforts to integrate trauma-informed care into services provided.

SEX OFFENDER TREATMENT

Sex offenders have been shown to have significantly higher ACE scores than the general population (Levenson, Willis, & Prescott, 2016; Reavis, Looman, Franco, & Rojas, 2013) and are more than three times more likely to have been sexually abused than non-sex offenders (Jespersen, Lalumier, & Seto, 2009). Research has also shown a link between ACE scores and risk factors for recidivism. Due to these associations, the role of early adversity in the development of sexual aggression is a relevant consideration in treatment (Levenson, Willis, & Prescott, 2016).

Sex offender treatment programs have traditionally emphasized relapse prevention, focusing on management of triggers and high-risk situations (Laws, 1989; Levenson, 2014). These programs often use confrontational strategies that risk re-traumatizing clients. Modern approaches to the treatment of sex offenders is shifting toward a more individualized approach that looks at the unique history behind each offender's actions. Two such models that are gaining traction include the Risks, Needs and Responsivity (RNR) model, which seeks to assess and respond flexibly to each client's unique personal characteristics that may motivate or serve as a potential barrier to effective treatment (Levenson & Prescott, 2007), and the Good Lives Model (GLM), which helps clients self-actualize goals while improving behavioral self-regulation (Ward & Brown, 2004). According to Andrews and Bonta (2010), therapeutic models incorporating RNR have been shown to significantly diminish recidivism for sex offenders.

Reentry into society can be particularly challenging for sex offenders due to the stigma caused by sex offender registration, which can be a barrier to reintegration and social support (Levenson, 2014). This is problematic because a lack of intimacy and social support has been correlated with sex offense recidivism (Hanson & Harris, 2001). Due to trauma-informed programming's emphasis on the modeling of safe and healthy intimacy while mitigating the isolation and loneliness often felt by sex offenders research suggests that it may prove effective in reducing recidivism if incorporated into sex offender reintegration programming (Levinson, 2014).

SUBSTANCE ABUSE TREATMENT

As was stated previously, the ACE Study demonstrated that ACEs can be correlated to coping-risk behaviors such as alcohol and substance abuse. It is not surprising then, that most men and women in substance abuse treatment programs have histories of trauma and abuse (Ouimette, Kimerling, Shaw, & Moos, 2000). Although approximately 35% to 50% of individuals in addiction treatment have a lifetime diagnosis of PTSD, historically, addiction treatment programs did not address trauma for fear of exacerbating trauma symptoms and endangering client recovery. Studies have shown, however, that not addressing client trauma may lead to inadequate recovery and negative outcomes such as early termination of treatment (Brown, Harris, & Fallot, 2013).

Consequently, in order to be effective, therapists must create a safe and trusting space for clients to talk openly about traumatic experiences, serving to diminish the shame often associated with trauma in society (Becker-Blease & Freyd, 2006). The SAMHSA-funded National Women with Co-Occurring Disorders and Violence Study (WCDVS) of 1998 found that attending to trauma in addiction and mental health treatment improves treatment outcomes for women. In addition, the study showed that women with serious mental illness and addiction found trauma-informed integrative treatment to better meet their needs and those of their children (Brown, Harris & Fallot, 2013; Substance Abuse and Mental Health Services Administration, n.d.).

MENTAL HEALTH TREATMENT

Many evidence-based mental health service models exist specifically to treat trauma. These trauma-informed treatments and services are designed to help individuals understand how their past experiences shape their present behavior (Substance Abuse and Mental Health Services Administration, n.d.). Trauma-informed mental health treatments recognize that because trauma often occurs in relationships, healing from trauma also needs to take place in the context of relationships (Herman, 1992). In mental health settings, therapists can model respectful interaction, build trust, and facilitate new positive experiences that help to heal the soul and also allow the brain to discover neural pathways to new behaviors (Creeden, 2009).

According to Courouis and Gold (2009), graduate programs for mental health professionals do not offer enough trauma-informed training. The authors state, "The vast majority of those professionals interested in developing expertise on psychological trauma must find a way to accomplish it on their own, often after their graduate studies are completed" (p.4). Without formal, comprehensive training on psychological trauma, professionals have to rely on piecemeal resources such as readings and specialized conferences to develop their knowledge and skills.

While formal training on trauma in educational institutions may still be needed, the number of trauma-informed treatment and intervention models has grown over the past decade. The most studied and endorsed treatment model is Trauma-Informed Cognitive Behavioral Therapy (TI-CBT), developed in 2006, which has been shown to reduce trauma symptoms among children and adults across different cultures and races (Black et al., 2012). The topic of trauma-informed treatment models is beyond the scope of the current chapter; however, a list of prominent models can be found in Figure 3 for further research.

FIGURE 3

Trauma-Informed and Trauma-Specific Treatment Models

Addictions and Trauma Recovery Integration Model (ATRIUM)	ATRIUM is a model intended to bring together peer support, psychosocial education, interpersonal-skills training, meditation, creative expression, spirituality, and community action to support survivors in addressing and healing from trauma.
Attachment, Self-Regulation and Competency (ARC) Clinical Services	ARC is a flexible framework, within which three core domains (attachment, self-regulation, and competency) and ten building blocks of trauma-informed treatment and service are identified.
Life Space Crisis Intervention (LSCI)	LSCI teaches staff the therapeutic talking strategies they will need to help children during stressful moments, as well as the awareness and skills to understand and manage their own feelings and counter-aggressive tendencies when intervening with aggressive or out-of-control behaviors.
Seeking Safety	Seeking Safety is an evidence-based present-focused counseling model to help people attain safety from trauma and/or substance abuse. It directly addresses both trauma and addiction, but without requiring clients to delve into the trauma narrative (the detailed account of disturbing trauma memories).
Structured Psychotherapy for Adolescents Responding to Chronic Stress (SPARCS)	SPARCS is a group intervention that was specifically designed to address the needs of chronically traumatized adolescents who may still be living with ongoing stress and are experiencing problems in several areas of functioning.
Trauma, Addiction, Mental Health and Recovery (TAMAR)	The TAMAR Treatment Group Model is a structured, manualized, 15-week intervention combining psycho-educational approaches with expressive therapies. It is designed for women and men with histories of trauma in correctional systems.
Trauma Affect Regulation: Guide for Education and Therapy (TARGET)	TARGET is an educational and therapeutic approach for the prevention and treatment of complex Post-Traumatic Stress Disorder.
Trauma-Informed Cognitive Behavioral Therapy (TI-CBT) or Trauma-Focused Cognitive Behavioral Therapy (TF-CBT)	Trauma-Focused Cognitive Behavioral Therapy (TF-CBT) is a psychosocial treatment model designed to treat post-traumatic stress and related emotional and behavioral problems in children and adolescents. This therapy can also be applied to adults.
Trauma Recovery and Empowerment Model (TREM and M-TREM)	The Trauma Recovery and Empowerment Model is intended for trauma survivors, particularly those with exposure to physical or sexual violence. This model is gender-specific: TREM for women and M-TREM for men.
Trauma Systems Therapy (TST)	TST is a community-based program designed to facilitate enhanced ability of the child to regulate emotional and behavioral response to social environmental stressors. The program is designed to address barriers toward families' engagement in treatment.

TRAINING RESOURCES FOR BECOMING TRAUMA-INFORMED

Training resources for individuals and organizations seeking to become trauma-informed vary in length and depth. Individuals can enhance their knowledge and practice by utilizing both public and proprietary evidence-based toolkits and resources online. In addition, many national and local organizations offer intensive trainings as well as ongoing technical assistance to help organizations and systems learn about trauma, apply trauma-informed care best practices to their service environment, and design a plan for implementation. A list of prominent organizations and agencies offering trauma-informed care training and resources for whole organizations and agencies is shown below in Figure 4.

FIGURE 4

Prominent Organizations and Agencies Offering Trauma-Informed Care Training and Resources

Center for Gender and Justice	http://www.centerforgenderandjustice.org
Community Connections Trauma Informed Care	http://www.ccdc1.org/
National Assoc. of State Mental Health Program Directors	http://www.nasmhpd.org/TA/nctic.aspx
National Child Traumatic Stress Network	http://www.nctsn.org/
National Council for Behavioral Health	http://www.thenationalcouncil.org
Sanctuary Model	http://www.sanctuaryweb.com
Sidran Institute	http://www.sidran.org
Substance Abuse & Mental Health Services Administration	http://www.samhsa.gov/nctic

RECOMMENDATIONS FOR FURTHER RESEARCH

Recent research has highlighted that although literature on the topic of trauma-informed care is burgeoning, the definition of trauma-informed care remains somewhat vague and inconsistent; while the principles of trauma-informed care are generally understood, how the principles are operationalized in organizational culture is often unclear (Hanson & Lang, 2016). A study of child-service providers in a large Midwestern state demonstrated that service providers are very aware of the importance of trauma-informed practices and need a plan for implementing trauma-informed practices (Donisch, Bray, & Gewirtz, 2016). Additional research is needed to identify more specific, evidence-based, trauma-informed practices that can be applied in service settings.

Further, while trauma-informed care and trauma-informed treatments have been documented in a variety of settings, further research can be done in unique service environments and communities. Beyond sector-specific, trauma-informed approaches, effective regionally specific and culturally specific, trauma-informed practices are also opportunities for further research. Within the criminal justice context, further research is needed on trauma-informed practices with individuals affected by trauma who have autism spectrum disorder (ASD), fetal alcohol spectrum disorder (FASD), traumatic brain injury (TBI), developmental disabilities, and other serious and persistent mental illnesses.

In addition, much of the research on the implications of trauma on health and well-being focuses on the negative outcomes associated with trauma. Future directions for research include protective factors that mediate the impact of trauma on the life course. By identifying factors that buffer children from the consequences of toxic stress, the prevention of negative health and social effects of trauma is possible, which could, in turn, reduce the need for costly interventions in adulthood and prevent the intergenerational transmission of trauma from parents to their children.

CONCLUSION

Trauma is prevalent and has lasting consequences for trauma survivors, their families, service providers, and the broader society. In light of the prevalence and widespread implications of trauma, the responsibility to address trauma is not limited to the behavioral health system, but is integral to other collaborating systems, including criminal justice, education, and health and human services, among others.

By understanding the impacts of trauma and integrating the principles of trauma-informed care into service environments, providers can more effectively engage and better serve clients who have experienced trauma. Evidence shows that trauma-informed care offers an intuitive, low-cost, and potentially transformative framework for preventing retraumatization of survivors while improving service experiences and outcomes for trauma survivors as well as staff and administrators. In addition to trauma-informed care, many trauma-informed treatments have proven to be effective tools for addressing trauma, improving self-regulation, reducing rates of recidivism, and facilitating healing and recovery from trauma.

Due to the potential for traumatization within the criminal justice system (e.g., interactions with police, courts, imprisonment, and mandatory treatment programs), it is important for direct-service staff as well as administrators across the system to recognize how interactions with offenders could be reframed in order to support the key principles of trauma-informed care. Rather than asking "What's wrong with you?" a trauma-informed lens asks, "What happened to you?" This chapter provided examples of how practitioners within the criminal justice system have integrated trauma-informed care into their service environments and, as a result, improved outcomes for offenders and staff.

Awareness of and demand for trauma-informed care is growing, and examples of successful trauma-informed care efforts across systems and cultures are being published and discussed across disciplines. Best practices in trauma-informed care and trauma-informed treatment will continue to emerge as more organizations and agencies implement and evaluate trauma-informed services in unique service environments.

REFERENCES

American Psychiatric Association. (2013). *Diagnostic and statistical manual of mental disorders* (5th ed.). Washington, D.C.

Anda, R. & Felitti, V. (2010). The relationship of Adverse Childhood Experiences to adult medical disease, psychiatric disorders, and sexual behavior: Implications for healthcare. In R. Lanius, E. Vermetten & C. Pain (Eds.), *The hidden epidemic: The impact of early life trauma on health and disease*, (77-87). Cambridge: Cambridge University Press.

Andrews, D. & Bonta, J. (2010). Rehabilitating criminal justice policy and practice. *Psychology, Public Policy, and Law, 16*(1), 39-55.

Andrews, D., Zinger, I., Hoge, R.D., Bonta, J., Gendreau, P., & Cullen, F. (1990). Does correctional treatment work? A psychologically informed meta-analysis. *Criminology, 28*(3), 369-404.

Bath, H. (2008). The three pillars of trauma-informed care. *Reclaiming Children and Youth, 17*(3), 17-21.

Becker-Blease, K. & Freyd, J. (2006). Research participants telling the truth about their lives: The ethics of asking and not asking about abuse. *American Psychologist, 61*, 218-226.

Berger, R., & Quiros, L. (2014). Supervision for trauma-informed practice. *Traumatology, 20*(4), 296-301.

Black, P., Woodworth, M., Tremblay, M. & Carpenter, T. (2012). A review of trauma informed treatment for adolescents. *Canadian Psychology, 53*(3), 192-203.

Bloom, S. & Farragher, B. (2011). *Destroying sanctuary: The crisis in human service delivery systems.* New York: Oxford University.

Bloom, S. & Sreedhar, S. (2008). The sanctuary model of trauma-informed organizational change. *Reclaiming Children and Youth, 17*(3), 48-53.

Bottalico, B., & Bruni, T. (2012). Post traumatic stress disorder, neuroscience, and the law. *International Journal of Law and Psychiatry, 35,* 112-120.

Brown, L. (2008). *Cultural competence in trauma therapy: Beyond the flashback.* Washington, DC. American Psychological Association.

Brown, V.B., Harris, M., & Fallot, R. (2013). Moving toward trauma-informed practice in addiction treatment: A collaborative model of agency assessment. *Journal of Psychoactive Drugs, 45*(5), 358-393.

Brown, V.B. & Worth, D. (2000). *Recruiting, training and maintaining consumer staff; Strategies used and lessons learned.* Culver City, CA: PROTOTYPES.

Buffington, K., Dierkhising, C., & Marsh, S. (2010). *Ten things every juvenile court judge should know about trauma and delinquency.* National Council of Juvenile and Family Court Judges. Retrieved from http://www.ncjfcj.org/sites/default/files/trauma%20bulletin_1.pdf

Caldwell, A. (2007). Attitudes of juvenile justice staff towards intellectual, psychiatric, and physical disabilities. *Intellectual and Developmental Disabilities, 45*(2), 77-89.

Clark, C., Reiland, S., Thorne, C., & Cropsey, K. (2014). Relationship of trauma exposure and substance abuse to self-reported violence among men and women in substance abuse treatment. *Journal of Interpersonal Violence, 29*(5), 1514-1530.

Coleman, J. (2016). Racial differences in Post Traumatic Stress Disorder in military personnel: Intergenerational transmission of trauma as a theoretical lens. *Journal of Aggression, Maltreatment & Trauma, 25*(6), 561-579.

Courouis, C. & Gold, S. (2009). The need for inclusion of psychological trauma in the professional curriculum: A call to action. *Psychological Trauma: Theory, Research, Practice and Policy, 1,* 3-23.

Creeden, K. (2009). How trauma and attachment can impact neurodevelopment: Informing our understanding and treatment of sexual behavior problems. *Journal of Sexual Aggression, 15,* 261-273.

Dierkhising, C., Ko, S., Woods-Jaeger, B., Briggs, E., Lee, R., & Pynoos, R. (2013). Trauma histories among justice-involved youth: Findings from the National Child Traumatic Stress Network. *European Journal of Psychotraumatology, 4.* doi:10.3402/ejpt.v4i0. 20274

Donisch, K., Bray, C., & Gewirtz, A. (2016). Child welfare, juvenile justice, mental health, and education providers' conceptualizations of trauma-informed practice. *Child Maltreatment, 2*(2), 125-134.

Drabble, L.A., Jones, S. & Brown, V. (2013). Advancing trauma-informed systems change in a family drug treatment court context. *Journal of Social Work Practice in the Addictions, 13*(1), 91-113.

Duran, B., Duran, E. & Brave Heart, M.Y.H., (1998). Native Americans and the trauma of history. In R. Thorton (Ed.), *Studying native America: Problems and prospects.* Madison, WI: University of Wisconsin Press.

Eames, S., Businelle, M., Suris, A., Walker, R., Rao, U., North, C., Xiao, H., & Adinoff, B. (2014). Stress moderates the effect of childhood trauma and adversity on recent drinking in treatment-seeking alcohol-dependent men. *Journal of Consulting and Clinical Psychology, 82*(3), 441-447.

Elliott, D., Bjelajac, P., Fallot, R., Markoff, L., & Reed, B. (2005). Trauma-informed or trauma denied: Principles and implementation of trauma-informed services for women. *Journal of Community Psychology, 33*(4), 461-477.

Fallot. R. & Harris, M. (2002). Trauma-informed services: A self-assessment and planning protocol. Washington, DC: Community Connections.

Farro, S.A., Clark, C., & Eyles, C.H. (2011). Assessing trauma-informed care readiness in behavioral health: An organizational case study. *Journal of Dual Diagnosis, 7*(4), 228-241.

Felitti, V., Anda, R., Nordenberg, D., Williamson, D., Spitz, A., Edwards, V., Koss, M., & Marks, J. (1998). Relationship of childhood abuse and household dysfunction to many of the leading causes of death in adults: The Adverse Childhood Experiences (ACE) study. *American Journal of Preventive Medicine, 14(4),* 245-258.

Ford, J. & Blaustein, M. (2013). Systemic self-regulation: A framework for trauma informed services in residential juvenile justice. *Journal of Family Violence, 28,* 665-677.

Ford, J. & Hawke, J. (2012). Trauma affect regulation psychoeducational group attendance is associated with reduced disciplinary incidents and sanctions in juvenile justice facilities. *Journal of Aggression, Maltreatment, and Trauma, 21,* 365-384.

Gendreau, P., Goggin, C., Cullen, F., & Andrews, D. (2000). The effects of community sanctions and incarceration on recidivism. *Forum on Corrections Research, 12*(2), 10-13.

Gilligan, J. (1996). *Violence: Reflections on a national epidemic.* New York: Vintage Books.

Greenwald, R. (2005). *Child trauma handbook: A guide for helping trauma-exposed children and adolescents.* New York: The Haworth Maltreatment and Trauma Press.

Gwinn, J., Judd, C., & Park, B. (2013). Less power = less human? Effects of power differentials on dehumanization. *Journal of Experimental Social Psychology, 49*(3), 464-470.

Hanson, R. & Harris, A. (2001). A structured approach to evaluating change among sexual offenders. *Sexual Abuse: A Journal of Research and Treatment, 13*(2), 105-122.

Hanson, R. & Lang, J. (2016). A critical look at trauma-informed care among agencies and systems serving maltreated youth and their families. *Child Maltreatment, 2*(2), 95-100.

Harlow, C.W. (1999). Prior abuse reported by inmates and probationers. Rockville, MD: U.S. Department of Justice.

Harris, M. & , R. (Eds.) (2001). *Using trauma theory to design service systems. New directions for mental health services.* San Francisco: Jossey-Bass.

Harvard University Center for the Developing Child. (n.d.) *Key concepts: Toxic stress.* Retrieved from http://developingchild.harvard.edu/key_concepts/toxic_stress_response/

Herman, J. (1992). *Trauma and recovery.* New York: Basic Books.

Hesse, A. (2002). Secondary trauma: How working with trauma survivors affects therapists. *Clinical Social Work Journal, 30*(3), 293-309.

Hubbard, D. J. (2002). Cognitive-behavioral treatment: An analysis of gender and other responsivity characteristics and their effects on success in offender rehabilitation. A dissertation submitted to the Division of Research and Advanced Studies of the University of Cincinnati in partial fulfillment of the requirements for the degree of Doctorate of Philosophy in the division of Criminal Justice of the College of Education.

Jesperson, A., Lalumiere, M., & Seto, M. (2009). Sexual abuse history among adult sex offenders and non-sex offenders: A meta-analysis. *Child Abuse & Neglect, 33,* 179, 192.

Ko, S., Kassam-Adams, N., Wilson, C., Ford, J. Berkowitz, S., Wong, M., Brymer, M., & Layne, C. (2008). Creating trauma-informed systems: Child welfare, education, first responders, health care, juvenile justice. *Professional Psychology: Research and Practice, 39*(4), 369-404.

Komarovskaya, I. (2009). Trauma, PTSD, and the cycle of violence among incarcerated men and women. A dissertation presented to the faculty of the Curry School of Education University of Virginia in partial fulfillment of the requirements for the degree Doctor of Philosophy by M.Ed. August, 2009.

Koss, M., Yuan, N., Dightman, D., Prince, R., Polacca, M., Sanderson, B. & Goldman, D. (2003). Adverse childhood exposures and alcohol dependence among seven Native American tribes. *American Journal of Preventive Medicine, 25*(3), 238-244.

Laws, D. (1989). *Relapse prevention with sex offenders.* New York, NY: Guilford Press.

Levenson, J. (2014). Incorporating trauma-informed care into evidence-based sex offender treatment. *Journal of Sexual Aggression, 20*(1), 9-22.

Levenson, J. & Prescott, D (2007). Considerations in evaluating the effectiveness of sex offender treatment. In D. Prescott (Ed.), *Applying knowledge to practice: Challenges in the treatment and supervision of sexual abusers.* Oklahoma City, OK: Wood and Barnes.

Levenson, J., Wilis, G., & Prescott, D. (2016). Adverse Childhood Experiences in the lives of male sex offenders: Implications for trauma-informed care. *Sexual Abuse: A Journal of Research and Treatment, 28*(4), 340-359.

Mailloux, S. (2014). The ethical imperative: Special considerations in the trauma counseling process. *Traumatology, 20*(1), 50-60.

Marans, S. & Cohen, D. (1993). Children and inner-city violence: Strategies for intervention. In L. Leavitt & N Fox (Eds.), *Psychological effects of war and violence on children.* Hillsdale, NJ: Erlbaum.

Marans, S., Murphy, R. A., & Berkowitz, S. J. (2002). Police-mental health responses to children exposed to violence: The child development-community policing program. In M. Lewis (Ed.), *Child and adolescent psychiatry: A comprehensive textbook.* Baltimore, MD: Williams & Wilkins.

Marchand, A., Nadeau, C., Beaulieu-Prevost, D., Boyer, R., & Martin, M. (2015). Predictors of post-traumatic stress disorder among police officers; A prospective study. *Psychological Trauma: Theory, Research, Practice, and Policy, 7*(3), 212-221.

McCann, L. & Pearlman, L. (1990). Vicarious trauma: A framework for understanding the psychological effects of working with victims. *Journal of Traumatic Stress, 3*, 131-152.

Miller, N. & Najavits, L. (2012). Creating trauma-informed correctional care: A balance of goals and environment. *European Journal of Psychotraumatology. 3*, 17246. doi: 10.3402/ejpt.v3i0.17246

Molden, H., & Firestone, P. (2007). Vicarious traumatization: The impact on therapists who work with sexual offenders. *Trauma, Violence & Abuse, 8*, 67-83.

National Child Traumatic Stress Network. (2015). *Complex Trauma.* Retrieved from http://www.nctsn.org/trauma-types/complex-trauma

Ouimette, P., Kimerling, R., Shaw, J. & Moos, R. (2000). Physical and sexual abuse among women and men with substance abuse disorders. *Alcoholism Quarterly, 18*(3), 7-17.

Reavis, J., Looman, J., Franco, K. & Rojas, B. (2013). Adverse childhood experiences and adult criminality: How long must we live before we possess our own lives? *The Permanente Journal, 17*(2), 44-48.

Redding, C. (Ed.) (2003). Origins and essence of the study. *ACE Reporter, 1*(1), 1-4.

Schreiber, V., Renneberg, B. & Maercker, A. (2010). Social influences on mental health help seeking after interpersonal traumatization: A quantitative analysis. *Biomedical Central Public Health, 10*, 643. doi:10.1186/1471-2458-10-634

Sotero, M. (2006). A conceptual model of historical trauma: Implications for public health practice and research. *Journal of Health Disparities Research and Practice, 1*(1), 92-108.

Substance Abuse and Mental Health Services Administration. (n.d.). *Creating a trauma informed criminal justice system for women: Why and how.* Retrieved from http://gainscenter.samhsa.gov/cms-assets/documents/73437-12763.ticjforwmn-2.pdf

Substance Abuse and Mental Health Services Administration. (n.d.). *Essential components of trauma-informed judicial practice.* Retrieved from http://www.nasmhpd.org/docs/NCTIC/JudgesEssential_5%201%20 2013finaldraft.pdf

Substance Abuse and Mental Health Services Administration: GAINS Center for Behavioral Health and Justice Transformation. (n.d.). *Fact sheet: Historical trauma.* Retrieved from http://gainscenter.samhsa. gov/cms-assets/documents/93078-842830.historicaltrauma.pdf

The Research and Evaluation Group. (2013). *Findings from the Philadelphia Urban ACE Study.* Retrieved from http://www.instituteforsafefamilies.org/

van der Kolk, B. (2005). Developmental trauma disorder: Towards a rational diagnosis for children with complex trauma histories. *Psychiatric Annals, 33*(5), 401-408.

Violanti, J. (2006). The police: Perspectives on trauma and resiliency. *Traumatology, 12*(3), 167-169.

Ward, T. & Brown, M. (2004). The Good Lives Model and conceptual issues in offender rehabilitation. *Psychology, Crime & Law, 10,* 243-257.

Zlotnick, C., Najavits, L., Rohsenow, D., & Johnson, D. (2003). A Cognitive-Behavioral Treatment for incarcerated women with substance abuse disorder and post-traumatic stress disorder: Findings from a pilot study. *Journal of Substance Abuse Treatment, 25,* 99-105.

CHAPTER 20

TRAUMATIC BRAIN INJURY IN THE CRIMINAL JUSTICE SYSTEM: A PRACTITIONER'S GUIDE

ERWIN CONCEPCION, JERROD BROWN, DEBORAH ECKBERG, MARGARET WIMBERLEY, CAMERON WILEY, & JEFFREY RILEY

CHAPTER OVERVIEW

"Traumatic Brain Injury" (TBI) is the terminology commonly used by the medical community to describe a condition that may not only result in physical adversity, but is also seen as a source of behavioral change. Individuals with TBI may be found to experience altered emotions, reduced cognitive functions, changes in personality, and a greater propensity for aggression and abuse of drugs and alcohol. It is no surprise that individuals who have sustained a TBI, as well as groups prone to TBI, are significantly represented in criminal justice-involved populations. Ironically, the effects of TBI put these individuals at a disadvantage when moving through the various stages of the criminal justice system. To make matters worse, justice professionals often lack the appropriate education and training necessary to effectively identify and treat criminal justice-involved individuals with a history of TBI. Recognition of TBI and other brain-related disorders is now seen as part of a paradigm shift in the study of criminology, as the causal role of biosocial factors on criminal behavior has come to be viewed with increasing acceptance. The identification, management, and treatment of TBI in this population is crucial to better understanding these injuries and their effects on the criminal justice system, as well as to improve the chances for this population to have independent, sustainable lives (Behnken, DeLisi, Toulson, & Vaughn, 2015).

INTRODUCTION

Traumatic brain injury (TBI) is defined as an alteration in the function and pathology of the brain that is caused by an external, physical force in the form of a strike, blow, or percussive blast (Brain Injury Association of America, 2015; Centers for Disease Control, 2015b; Troncoso & Pletnikova, 2010). TBI is recognized as an important topic in relation to the criminal justice system, due to the high percentage of defendants and incarcerated individuals who have sustained one or more brain injury events. Studies in the United States indicate that 25%-87% of inmates in jails and prisons have been subjected to TBI (Shiroma, Ferguson, & Pickelsimer, 2012), compared to only 8.5% in the general population (Silver, Kramer, Greenwalk, & Weissman, 2001). An estimated 25%-35% of individuals with TBI may experience changes in behavior and character, as well as an onset of aggression within months or years after their injury (Aaronson & Lloyd, 2015). Findings also suggest that even a mild traumatic brain injury (mTBI), such as a concussion, may provoke negative and aggressive behavior (Collins, Pastorek, Tharp, & Kent, 2012; Jeter, Hergenroeder, Hylin, Redell, Moore, & Dash, 2013; Silver, McAllister, & Arciniegas, 2009).

Since the earliest medical writing, physicians have pointed to brain injury as a leading cause of death and other severe side-effects (Finger, 1994). The correlation between the specific locations of head wounds and consistent changes in types of behaviors prompted the understanding that differing regions of the brain have specialized behavioral dominance (Fleischman, 2002; Wood & Liossi, 2006). This includes the observation that wounds to the prefrontal region of the brain may alter impulse control, pro-social affect, and empathy, all of which are prominent factors in the study of forensic mental health (Shamay-Tsoory, Tomer, Berger, & Aharon-Peretz, 2003). Many credit this realization to the 1848 case of Phineas Gage, who sustained severe brain trauma when an iron rod completely penetrated his prefrontal lobe (Capruso & Levin, 2006; Fleischman, 2002). Miraculously, Gage lived for over a decade after his injury, but his personality shifted from that of a polite, respectable hard-worker to that of a volatile, vulgar, antisocial pariah. Following the accident, his doctor noted "Gage was no longer Gage" (Fleischman, 2002, pg. 2).

In recent years, TBI has emerged as a serious and pervasive phenomenon. In the United States, combined rates for TBI incidents involving death, hospitalization, and emergency room visits rose from 521 to 823.7 per 100,000 between 2001 and 2010, with an estimated 1.4 million people sustaining a TBI every year (CDC, 2015b; Troncoso & Pletnikova, 2010). Propensities for certain injuries vary by age group, with falls being the most prominent in cases of children ages 4 and under, and in adults ages 65 and older. Young adults aged 15-24 have the highest rates of TBI associated with motor vehicle incidents (CDC, 2015c; Troncoso & Pletnikova, 2010). Case studies following up on accident survivors with TBI have shown a high incidence of behavioral change resulting from their head injuries, specifically marked by disinhibition, increased anger, and aggression (Langlois, Rutland-Brown, & Thomas, 2004). Ten percent of TBI cases are attributed to assault, although it is likely this figure is underestimated due to the high number of assault victims, especially in domestic violence cases, who do not report their victimization (Langlois, Rutland-Brown, & Thomas, 2004). Also underreported are assaults in prisons and jails, where more than 2 million incarcerated individuals in the United States live in conditions where brain injury and violence co-occur (Langlois, Rutland-Brown, & Thomas, 2004).

In this chapter, we first focus on understanding populations prone to TBI and the likely effects of their brain injuries. In doing so, we establish the relevancy of TBI to forensic study. Afterward, we provide a review of what can occur when the brain experiences trauma from an outside force, and identify risk factors and sociological correlations between TBI and poverty, childhood maltreatment, substance abuse, and incarceration. These risk factors and sociological variables may exacerbate TBI deficits. We also present common terminology used in the discussion of TBI. Finally, we discuss the implications of brain injury for individuals in the criminal justice system and recommend approaches to mediate negative outcomes.

EPIDEMIOLOGY OF TBI-PRONE POPULATIONS

Even though TBI can happen to any individual, numerous factors (including involvement in athletics, military service, or criminal activity) statistically increase the risk of sustaining a brain injury. Understanding the factors that contribute to an increased risk of TBI in certain populations may serve to enhance awareness of the epidemiology of TBI, as well as aid in its prevention.

SPORTS

The wealth of TBI research in recent decades has primarily stemmed from concerns regarding brain injuries that take place during sports activities and the military service (Neal, Wilson, Hsu, & Powers, 2012). A sports injury study of a large population in the United States estimated that 63,000 concussions occur among high school athletes per year in 10 major sports, with 63% of these injuries sustained by football players (Vastag, 2002). Even a relatively minor brain injury, such as a concussion, has the potential to compromise the brain's blood flow and regulatory systems (Meany & Smith, 2011). Such events may lead to balance deficits and a dysregulation of cognitive processing, predisposing the injured person to another injury, thereby increasing the likelihood of significant neurocognitive impairment (Betzen et al., 2009; Dambinova, Sowell, & Maroon, 2013). These conditions often increase susceptibility to secondary concussions or another TBI before the brain has had time to fully heal – a problem especially likely to occur in sports where players are committed to participating throughout an entire season (Guskiewicz, Weaver, Padua, & Garrett, 2000; Zemper, 2003). Subsequent brain injuries have been found to contribute to significant deficits in memory functioning, as well as behavioral and personality changes (Grindel, 2003; McKee et al., 2009). The effects of these secondary traumas are referred to as Second Impact Syndrome (SIS) (Blyth & Bazarian, 2010; Dessy, Rasouli, & Choudhri, 2015; Saunders & Harbaugh, 1984). Some sports doctors prefer the term "diffuse cerebral swelling" (Vastag, 2002, pg. 438). One of the possible consequences that may result from this condition is a disturbance in gait, contributing to an increased likelihood of falls and further brain injury (Martini, Sabin, DePesa, Leal, Negrete, Sosnoff, & Broglio, 2011). Studies of football players with concussion indicate that a player who has sustained a concussion is five times more likely to experience repeat concussions than a player who has never had such an injury (Levy, Ozgur, Berry, Aryan, & Apuzzo, 2004).

MILITARY

Since 2001, the United States armed forces have been engaged in the longest span of military conflict in the history of the country. During this time, it is estimated that 20% of active military personnel have experienced some form of traumatic brain injury (Tanielian & Jaycox, 2008; Arriola & Rozelle, 2016). Along with the cognitive and neurological deficits common to TBI, members of the military often experience co-occurring Post-Traumatic Stress Disorder (PTSD), presenting a greater challenge for diagnosis and subsequent treatment (Barnett, Miller-Perrin, & Perrin, 2010; Bryant, Marosszeky, Crooks, & Gurka, 2000; Mooney & Speed, 2001; Arriola & Rozelle, 2016; Tanielian & Jaycox, 2008). The shared clinical symptomology of the two disorders includes impulsive behavior, anxiety, depression, headaches, ataxia, memory deficits, depressed reaction time, high levels of sensitivity to stimuli, and sleep disturbances (Savitsky, Illingworth, & Dulaney, 2009), along with an increase in Intimate Partner Violence (IPV) among active personnel and veterans (Stamm, 2009). Due to the elevated frequency of co-occurrence, it is essential that current and former active personnel who are symptomatic be tested for biomarkers associated with TBI and mTBI (mild TBI) to determine proper diagnosis and treatment, and to ensure medications and therapy are correct for the patient (Raji, Willeumier, Taylor, Tarzwell, Newberg, Henderson, & Amen 2015). Co-occurrence of TBI with substance abuse has also been found to be prominent in veteran populations (Jenkins, 2014). While veterans with mTBI and Alcohol Use Disorder (AUD) have a 60% incidence rate of mood disorders such as depression, only 37% of veterans with mTBI and no substance abuse exhibit mood disorders (Jorge et al., 2005).

Co-morbidity of TBI and PTSD occurs in an estimated 33%-42% of all veterans (Hoge et al., 2004; Lew, 2005; Tanielan & Jaycox, 2008). Computed tomography (CT) and magnetic resonance imaging (MRI) are unlikely to highlight the subtle structural damages common to TBI, often leaving those with TBI and mTBI undiagnosed (Van Boven et al., 2009). Single Photon Emission Computed Tomography (SPECT), however, is widely noted as being effective in differentiating the biomarkers of TBI and PTSD, and functional MRI (fMRI) has been used to identify patients with TBI (Kim et al., 2012). Concomitant symptomology in men and women who return from military service with TBI includes depression, impatience, a lack of interest in demonstrating authority, and difficulties relating to and communicating with their children (Sogomonyan & Cooper, 2010). Sadly, this has played out in statistics as well. Since 2002, maltreatment of the children of active service personnel has shifted from being statistically lower in veteran families (compared to the general population) to significantly higher.

GENDER

Gender disparities associated with concussion and mild TBI in college and high school athletes show that males are more likely to experience post-concussive vomiting, sadness, amnesia, confusion, and disorientation; while females are more inclined to have impairments in visual memory tasks, cognitive function, drowsiness, and noise sensitivity (Covassin, Schatz, & Swanik, 2007). Overall, females sustaining a mild TBI have been found to have significantly poorer outcomes than males (Bazarian, Blyth, Mookerjee, He, & McDermott, 2010; Tanielian et al., 2008).

HOMELESSNESS

Studies show a positive correlation between homelessness and TBI, ranging from 8% to 53%, with only one study reporting a correlation under 20% (Mackelprang et al., 2014). Among the homeless, TBI is reported to have most likely occurred during late adolescence and prior to homelessness (Hwang et al., 2008; Oddy, Moir, Fortescue, & Chadwick, 2012). People who experienced their first TBI after becoming homeless were more likely to be younger, have a past suicide attempt, and have poor coping strategies (Cleverley & Kidd, 2011; Mackelprang et al., 2014). Among homeless people, substance abuse is more likely to occur among those with TBI, as is exposure to assault (Mackelprang et al., 2014).

Statistically, the intersection of the long-term effects of TBI, mTBI, and at-risk populations is associated with a wide spectrum of head-trauma-related health and neurological issues. These can include cognitive deficits leading to employment difficulties and eventual homelessness, increased rates of substance abuse, aggressive or violent behavior, and a greater likelihood of exhibiting antisocial behaviors. Research conducted in the United States and Canada to determine the prevalence of TBI among people who are homeless has produced a wide range of results: 48% in Milwaukee, Wisconsin; 67% in Boston, Massachusetts; 24% in Fort Lauderdale, Florida; 98% in Hamilton, Ontario, and 53% in Toronto, Ontario (Topoloviec-Vraniz et al., 2012).

Medical costs associated with TBI also contribute to homelessness. It is estimated that 62% of personal bankruptcies, a factor commonly leading to homelessness, are caused by medical debt (Himmelstein, Thorne, Warren, & Woolhandler, 2009). Such circumstances are typically exacerbated by the lack of available medical care for homeless people. Some forms of mental illness, such as schizophrenia, may be a contributing factor in a person's homelessness and may be aggravated by the presence of a head injury. Schizophrenia has been found to occur twice as often after a brain injury in cases where there is a genetic predisposition to the disorder (Malaspina et al., 2001).

INTIMATE PARTNER VIOLENCE (IPV)

Intimate Partner Violence (IPV) is positively associated with TBI for both the victim and the abuser, although the incidence rate of TBI-related intimate partner violence is not known (Kwako et al., 2011). An "intimate partner" is defined as a spouse, current or past boyfriend, or current or past girlfriend (Barnett, Miller-Perrin, & Perrin, 2005). This definition extends to same-sex partners. Not only has TBI been found to cause the aggressive behavior and disinhibition associated with IPV, it can also contribute to a victim's lack of insight and judgment (Langlois, 2008). From a sample of 53 women who were victims of battery, 92% said they have received blows to the head, and 40% of these women also said they had lost consciousness (Jackson, Philip, Nuttall, & Diller, 2002).

Statistically, the most vulnerable time for a victim of IPV is during the process of leaving the relationship. TBI may negatively affect this, causing mental deficits in victims and leading to an inability to work or to be financially independent of their abusive partners. Additionally, communication difficulties associated with TBI thwart the victim's capacity to explain the abusive relationship. Furthermore, by inhibiting financial and social independence, symptoms associated with TBI may produce an instance where the victim fears she or he will be considered unacceptable as the custodian of their children. Typically, victims will continue to experience abuse rather than leave their children in the hands of their abuser (Reichard, Langlois, Sample, Wald, & Pickelsimer, 2007; St. Ivany & Schminkey, 2016).

MENTALLY ILL POPULATIONS

Anxiety and depression are particularly prevalent among people with TBI (Reeves & Laizer, 2012), with depression widely viewed as the most common psychiatric sequelae, manifesting within six months of the traumatic incident (Malaspina et al., 2001). Depression is estimated to occur in 39% of mild injury cases and 77% of severe cases (Malaspina et al., 2001). In one study, individuals with TBI were reported to have increased hopelessness, with 23% possessing suicidal ideation and 18% having attempted suicide (Silver, Kramer, Greenwalk, & Weissman, 2001). Major depression is believed to be related to the severity of the TBI and the duration of its symptoms, which may persist for many years for more severe injuries (Reeves & Laizer, 2012). In another study, patients with TBI who had mental illness and co-occurring substance abuse issues were 21 times more likely to attempt suicide (Simpson & Tate, 2002). An Australian study of prisoners' health found that 57% of inmates with mental illness had a brain injury that led to loss of consciousness at some point in their lives. Out of 46 other physical illnesses that ranged from asthma to hemorrhoids, TBI was the most frequent coexisting ailment to the inmates' mental illness (Butler, Allnut, & Yang, 2007). Among prisoners in the study who were not mentally ill, 40% had a TBI, although these injuries were the third-ranking physical ailment among this group, behind established diagnoses of Hepatitis A (46.8%) and Hepatitis C (42.4%) (Butler, Allnut, & Yang, 2007).

ANTISOCIAL PERSONALITY DISORDER (ASPD)

Antisocial Personality Disorder (ASPD) is a psychological disorder described in The Diagnostic and Statistical Manual of Mental Disorders (5th ed.; DSM-5) (American Psychiatric Association, 2013) as primarily consisting of behavior that leads individuals to be deceitful, violate the rights of others, demonstrate aggression to people, engage in theft, and violate rules (APA, 2013). Cerebral dysfunction in the orbitofrontal or ventromedial prefrontal cortex because of brain injury (or TBI) is often positively associated with antisocial behavior (Glenn & Raine, 2011). Patients can understand what is morally acceptable but do not appear to be guided by mental controls that are common to others (Koenigs et al., 2007).

SCHIZOPHRENIA

The incidence of psychosis and schizophrenia may increase after TBI, making proper diagnosis more difficult (Silver, Kramer, Greenwald, & Weisman, 2001). Numerous studies, including one associated with a 10,000-member cohort in Finland, found that people who are genetically predisposed to schizophrenia are two to three times more likely to develop the disorder should a TBI occur (Achte, Jarho, Kyykka, & Vesterinen, 1991; Fazel, Långstrom, Hjern, Grann, & Lichtenstein, 2009; Malaspina et al., 2001). In one study the severity of TBI did not factor into this rate of manifestation (Arciniegas, Harris, & Brousseau, 2003). What remains to be understood is if premorbid conditions in individuals who eventually develop schizophrenia contribute to an increased incidence of TBI, or if TBI itself is capable of triggering psychosis (Rapp et al., 2013). The greatest predictability factor for schizophrenia is found in individuals with TBI who have blood relatives positively diagnosed with schizophrenia (Molloy, Conroy, Cotter, & Cannon, 2011).

Epilepsy and Other Medical Considerations

The development of epilepsy after a traumatic brain injury in adults is a relatively common risk that typically manifests within 5 years. Epilepsy most often manifests after an injury where the brain is penetrated (Chen, Ruff, Eavy, & Wasterlain, 2009). Partial seizures have been mistaken for PTSD, presenting a possible risk of misdiagnosis and incorrect treatment (Chen et al., 2009). Seizure remission typically occurs in 25% to 40% of cases; in tests performed on Vietnam veterans, remission was more likely to occur among those whose injury did not include penetration of the brain (Salazar et al., 1985). The risk of epilepsy following TBI in both children and young adults has been studied as well. Development of epilepsy was found to be highest in children with a family history of epilepsy, as well as in young adults over the age of 15, although less markedly so. Females were more likely than males to develop epilepsy after brain injury (Christensen et al., 2009). A longitudinal study conducted in Sweden between 1973 and 2009 compared the connection between patients with epilepsy and violent crime and patients with TBI and violent crime. The study included roughly 22,000 participants in each category and did not involve patients with epilepsy who also had a TBI. The correlation between epilepsy and violent crime was low (1.7% greater than controls), and this was further mitigated when adjusted for substance use (Fazel, Philipson, Gardiner, Merritt, & Grann, 2009). However, in cases involving TBI, patients were 3 times more likely to have committed a violent crime. Individuals with TBI who had siblings who are criminal offenders were found to be twice as likely to commit a violent crime after having a TBI (Fazel, Långstrom, Hjern, & Lichtenstein, 2009).

TBI is known to affect many other internal processes, and researchers continue to study these relationships. These other physical ailments include increased intestinal permeability, compromised intestinal mucosa, an increase of inflammatory pathways, glycemic dysregulation in diabetes, imbalance of immunological responses, alteration of brain energy metabolism, breakdown of the blood-brain barrier, dysautonomia, a compromised immune system, hypoadrenalism, fatigue (Brock et al., 2013), Postural Orthostatic Tachycardia Syndrome (POTS) (Heyer et al., 2016), and a predisposition to pituitary gland injury that can lead to disruption of sex hormones, hypogonadism, and consequential sleep disturbances (Schneider, Schneider, & Stalla, 2005).

Identifying TBI

Individuals who have sustained a TBI may lack awareness regarding the extent of their injuries and limitations, and misrepresent themselves when questioned (Curtiss, 2007). Collateral medical information for inmates may also vary in reliability (Diamond & Magaletta, 2006); in corrections populations, research typically relies on self-report to identify medical conditions. Self-report of medical conditions applied to populations stereotyped as dishonest, such as prisoners, may be viewed as unreliable (Schofield, Butler, Hollis, & D'Este, 2011). Other factors, such as substance abuse, low socio-economic status, and mental illness, may also affect the accuracy of self-report (Bergmann, Byers, Freedman, & Mokad, 1998; De Boer, Den Tonkelaar, Burger, & Van Leeuwen, 2005; Fishbain, Cutler, Rosomoff, & Rosomoff, 1999; Okura, Urban, Mahoney, Jacobsen, & Rodeheffer, 2004). TBI resulting from abuse, violence, and substance misuse may also be undisclosed (Perron & Howard, 2008), further complicating the accuracy of self-reports. Not all self-reporting by offenders has been found to be inaccurate, however. In a study of 200 inmates conducted by Schofield and colleagues (2011), 112 participants reported having had a TBI with hospitalization. Corresponding hospital medical records were found for 78 (70 percent). These findings suggested that prisoners' self-reports of TBI were generally accurate when compared with the widely accepted standard of the hospital medical record.

Interview technique may play a significant role in gaining accurate data from offender populations regarding past TBI experiences. A 2007 study conducted by Dr. Pamela Diamond and colleagues showed that, during their intake screening, only 10 (1%) of inmates reported having had a head injury, compared to the 826 (82.8%) who acknowledged this on a more-detailed TBI screening questionnaire (Diamond, Harzke, Magaletta, Cummins, & Frankowski, 2007). Corrigan and Bogner (2007a) have described the process of self-report through interview by a professional as the "gold standard" (p. 316) for determining the existence of one or more incidents of TBI in a person's history; but, as indicated by the Diamond 2007 study, accuracy appears to be largely dependent on the interviewer's skill. By providing examples of possible causes of TBI and using simple language rather than medical terminology, interviewers can typically uncover many potential incidents of undocumented injury. Exceptions to this occur (particularly in cases where brain injury occurred at an early age and continues to present ongoing medical effects), dependent upon whether the individual being questioned can recall the TBI experience (Diamond & Magaletta, 2006).

To better estimate the prevalence of brain injury, regular screening for TBI among forensic mental health populations is recommended (Colantonio, Kim, Allen, Asbridge, Petgrave, & Brochu, 2014; Colantonio, Stamenova, Abramowitz, Clarke, & Christensen, 2007). Routine TBI screening of youth involved in the criminal justice system is also suggested (Vaughn, Salas-Wright, DeLisi, & Perron, 2014). Timely identification of adolescents who have experienced a TBI may serve to prevent future criminal justice involvement and promote prosocial behavior (Williams, Cordan, Mewse, Tonks, & Burgess, 2010a). Given their age groups' elevated risk of falling, it is also important to seek information from children and adolescents regarding their known history of falls. Answers to similar questions directed to adult populations may be unavailable, partially available, or inaccurately reported due to the lapse of time and increased difficulty in obtaining accurate, remote autobiographical data.

Given the apparently high base rate of TBI in the corrections population, an approach similar to how other co-morbid conditions such as substance use disorders, PTSD, and epilepsy are addressed is warranted. Taking this approach requires staff to consider the likelihood of a TBI as an expectation rather than an exception. One of the keys to effective screening is to avoid formal medical terminology and identify examples of events associated with possible physical, psychosocial, and psychological conditions and their symptoms. Asking whether the individual has ever had a brain injury may lead to a response in the negative. In contrast, when interviewers include the question in context, such as by asking if the person has ever been in a car accident in which they hit their head, or if the individual has ever been knocked out, they may gather better information and more open responses (Hux, Schneider, & Bennett, 2009).

The more-challenging aspect of screening procedures involves determining whether any long-term effects exist because of one or more instances of brain injury. To obtain this information, screeners must question respondents about changes in cognitive, physical, social, or emotional status coinciding with or following an identified incident. Potential screeners are cautioned that, for some individuals, sustaining an injury in childhood may not lead to immediate evidence of behavioral challenges. Some children do not display learning or social difficulties until reaching late elementary or middle school years, since these deficits are more obviously apparent when challenged by more difficult learning and greater academic demands (Anderson, Damasio, Tranel, & Damasio, 2000; Ylvisaker et al., 2001).

Identifying individuals with histories of TBI has several advantages. Most important is the ability for practitioners to implement timely and effective education and intervention methods to assist the individual with their brain injury, as well as to assist their families with the associated challenges that may arise over time (Dams-O'Connor et al., 2014). Among several areas of service, the prison system is one in which screening is essential to providing the benefits of intervention as early as possible. Yet, despite the ease with which screening can be conducted and the known benefits of identifying individuals with brain injury, routine use of such procedures is rare (Diamond, Magaletta, Harzke, & Baxter, 2008).

There are various tools used for screening purposes, with different levels of questioning involved in each process. Table 1 includes a few of these screening tools (Hux, Schneider, & Bennett, 2009; Picard, Scarisbrick, & Paluck, 1991).

Table 1

TBI Tools

- HELPS Screening Tool
- Total Symptom Severity Scale (TSSS)
- Total Symptom Frequency Scale (TSFS)
- Traumatic Brain Injury Questionnaire (TBIQ)
- Glasgow Coma Scores (GCS)
- Ranchos Los Amigos Scale

One instrument used to help detect the possibility of TBI and determine if further assessment is needed is HELPS (Hux, Schneider, & Bennet, 2009; Picard et al., 1991), an acronym for the prompting questions of the screen:

H – Have you ever *Hit your Head* or been *Hit on the Head*?

E – Were you ever seen in the *Emergency room*, hospital, or by a doctor because of an injury to your head?

L – Did you ever *Lose consciousness* or experience a period of being dazed and confused because of an injury to your head?

P – Do you experience any of these *Problems in your daily life* since you hit your head: headaches; dizziness; anxiety; depression; difficulty concentrating; difficulty remembering; difficulty reading, writing or calculating; poor problem-solving; difficulty performing your job/school work; change in relationships with others; or poor judgment (e.g. being fired from jobs, being arrested, being in fights)?

S – Have you had any *Significant Sicknesses*?

Note that the questions are comprised of a sample of items that identify circumstances in which a brain injury may have been sustained, including immediate consequences of injury, residual or lingering problems because of the injury, and illnesses that may account for other neurological causes. A positive TBI screen is generated when a respondent meets three criteria: 1) responds in the affirmative to the existence of an event that could have caused a brain injury (i.e., questions H, E, or S), and 2) has had a medical assessment for a head injury or loss of consciousness associated with the event, indicating that the injury was of sufficient severity to result in brain damage (i.e., questions E or L), and 3) has two or more chronic problems resulting from the sustained injury (i.e., question P). As with other screening procedures, a positive result is not sufficient for a formal diagnosis of TBI. However, it strongly suggests the need for further assessment and investigation of the possibility that the person has sustained a TBI of sufficient severity to cause reported symptoms, challenging behaviors, educational and learning difficulties, vocational problems, or social-emotional challenges (Hux et al., 2009). In some instances, TBI may be misdiagnosed as either a learning disability or as any number of other conditions (León-Carrión & Ramos, 2003).

Key to the purpose behind conducting a thorough screening of all individuals entering the correctional system is that programs for inmates who are known to have sustained a TBI can be tailored to include substance abuse treatment, strategies to decrease risk for victims of violence (TBI is a known predictor of increased risk for more victimization), management of aggressive behavior, and to create appropriate work assignments (Wald, Helgeson, & Langlois, 2008). For some individuals, screening is only the first step in a process that requires a more thorough assessment of cognitive functioning to identify the person's strengths and needs. Ultimately, such an assessment can enable practitioners to provide tailored recommendations for accommodation and remediation. The high percentage of individuals within correctional settings who have a history of TBI presents a compelling argument that brain injury should be one of the factors considered in determining why higher rates of mental illness are often found in this population (Schofield et al., 2006a). Further research is needed to examine other variables that may also contribute to mental illness.

CONSEQUENCES OF TBI

IMPACT OF INJURY

Traumatic brain injuries are generally classified as either focal injuries (which involves impact directly to the head or brain itself, leading to either a contusion or an extra or subdural hemorrhage) or diffuse injuries (caused by forces that present as rapid acceleration or deceleration) (Walker & Tesco, 2013). Diffuse damage to the brain is more often associated with closed head-injury (CHI), which causes widespread effects via shearing, tearing, and bruising of neuronal cells (Ashley, Masel, & Nagele, 2016; Teasdale & Jennett, 1974). Regardless of the site of the CHI impact, the areas of maximum injury are the frontal and lower surfaces of the temporal and frontal lobes, where contusions are caused by the bony ridges of the skull in those areas (Adams, Mitchell, Graham, & Doyle, 1977; Walker & Tesco, 2013).

Brain damage typically is the result of the combined effects of three forces. The first is the rapid jolting of the brain within the skull as the head is struck by or against an object. This action causes the long nerve bodies that make up the deep-structure white matter to stretch. When these neurons stretch beyond their limits, damage to the nerve axons results in axonal shearing (Walker & Tesco, 2013). The second action is the rapid rotation of the head (Ashley et al., 2016). Very few blows to the head occur straight on. Rotational injuries can result in the damage and swelling of deep subcortical brain tissue near the base of the brain. Finally, damage from CHI can occur at both the site of impact and the site directly opposite the initial impact, in what is called a coup-contrecoup injury. This type of injury involves the force of the brain's own mass, when struck, to collide against the interior of the skull on the opposite side of impact. The "coup" site is that area of the brain directly struck by or against the object. The "contrecoup" site is the area opposite the side that was struck and sometimes receives even greater damage than the area that sustained the direct blow (Ashley et al., 2016).

LEVEL OF SEVERITY

A bump, blow, or jolt to the head, or a penetrating head injury that disrupts the normal function of the brain does not always automatically indicate that the person has had a TBI. Consequences from TBI can be variable and range from mild, which involves a brief change in mental status or consciousness, to severe, involving an extended period of unconsciousness or loss of memory following the injury. Most TBIs can be categorized as mild and are typically referred to as concussions (CDC, 2003). Factors determining the nature and severity of neuropsychological impairments include the site and type of injury, the resulting effects on systemic and intracranial processes, the consumption of alcohol, and a history of previously sustained TBIs (Eames, 1990; Gronwall, Wrightson, & Waddell, 1990; Kolb & Whishaw, 2009; Morse & Montgomery, 1992). Even a mild concussion can cause severe and long-lasting damage if it is followed by another concussion, which creates a condition referred to as "Second Impact Syndrome," (Dessy, Rasouli, & Choudhri, 2015).

There are standard measures for categorizing the severity of a brain injury which depend on whether the injury is a closed head injury or involves a penetrating wound (Stein, 1996). One commonly used measure is the Glasgow Coma Scale (GCS), developed by Teasdale and Jennet (Teasdale & Jennett, 1974; 1976). This system has been particularly useful when attempting to categorize the severity of brain injury sustained by individuals with closed head injury, especially when there is no obvious visual damage or entry wound (Rapp, Rosenberg, Keyser, Nathan, Toruno, Cellucci, & Bashore, 2013).

The GCS is a 15-item scale that measures an individual's responsiveness along three dimensions (eye opening, verbal response, and motor response) which correspond with the patient's ability to react and respond to visual, auditory, and tactile stimuli. The visual dimension is rated from 1 (unable to respond) to 4 (spontaneous eye opening). Response to sound is rated from 1 (no response) to 5 (oriented conversation). Finally, motor response is rated from 1 (unable to respond) to 6 (obeys commands). From these measures, a total GCS score ranging from 3 to 15 is generated. Scores of 13 to 15 indicate mild injury, scores of 9 to 12 indicate moderate injury, and scores of 3 to 8 place the brain injury in the severe category. This battery has been accepted as a standard and aids the measuring process as a prognosticator of future patient outcomes for individuals who have sustained moderate to severe injuries (Jennett, Snoek, Bond, & Brooks, 1981; Teasdale, Maas, Lecky, Manley, Stocchetti, & Murray, 2014).

One of the challenges of the GCS is its low level of sensitivity to mild TBI/concussions when there is no loss of consciousness. A better measure for these types of injuries is the length of post-traumatic amnesia (PTA). PTA is defined as the length of time between injury and the point when consistent memories are again being formed by the individual, as noted by consistent orientation and the resolution of confusion regarding their situation and environment. Brain injury does not require a measure of PTA, but it is almost certain that an individual with a period of PTA has sustained a brain injury (Gass, Rogers, & Kinne, 2016). The resolution of PTA is often demonstrated via a process known as "islands of memory." The ability to recall information and establish ongoing memories does not snap into place at one time, but instead, slowly returns with increasing periods of lucidity and awareness of the present. This does not equate to the ability to remember the events that occurred during the period of PTA itself, since these memories are usually lost permanently. They are not stored due to the disruption in brain functioning.

To categorize severity of injury using PTA, individuals with less than 1 day of PTA fall in the mild TBI or concussion range; those with PTA greater than 1 day but less than 7 days are in the moderate TBI range; and patients sustaining injuries resulting in PTA of greater than 7 days are identified as having a severe TBI. Another measure used is loss of consciousness (LOC). Individuals who have lost consciousness for less than 30 minutes are categorized as having a mild brain injury; those with LOC between 30 minutes and 24 hours are categorized as having a moderate brain injury; and those with LOC lasting greater than 24 hours are categorized as having sustained a severe brain injury (Langlois Orman, Kraus, Zaloshnja, & Miller, 2011).

BEHAVIORAL, COGNITIVE, AND PHYSICAL CONSEQUENCES OF TBI

Secondary consequences associated with TBI may place a significant burden on correctional mental health care settings (Piccolino & Solberg, 2014). Such consequences may include a host of behavioral, emotional, and physical health complaints (Bennett & Raymond, 2008; Miller & Donders, 2001).

Mild TBI may include symptoms such as headache, confusion, light-headedness, dizziness, blurred vision, ringing in the ears, bad taste in the mouth, fatigue, change in sleep pattern, behavioral or mood changes, and difficulty with cognitive functions such as attention, concentration, and memory (McAllister, 2011). Moderate to severe TBI is usually associated with neuropsychological deficits, behavioral problems, and poor social outcomes (Stambrook, Moore, Peers, Deviaene, & Hawryluk, 1990). Symptoms of severe TBI may include headaches that worsen or do not go away, repeated vomiting or nausea, convulsions or seizures, an inability to awaken from sleep, dilation of one or both pupils of the eyes, slurred speech, weakness or numbness in the extremities, loss of coordination, increased confusion, and restlessness or agitation. Mild TBI resulting in less than 10 minutes of LOC is not usually associated with such persisting problems. However, when injuries are complex or cumulative, there can be adverse reactions which affect the brain's attention and executive systems (Williams, Potter, & Ryland, 2010). Neuropsychological effects may limit those individuals' capacity to fully engage in forensic rehabilitation, thereby hindering the possibility of behavioral improvement. Unfortunately, such important issues may not be fully appreciated within the justice system, where behavior change is mandated (Williams, Mewse, Tonks, Burgess, & Cordan, 2010b). It is interesting to note, however, that repeat offenders are frequently described as impulsive and lacking affective empathy–a characteristic noted in individuals with TBI (Colantonio et al., 2007; Jolliffe et al., 2003). Table 2 highlights a more comprehensive list of consequences that may result from a TBI.

The range of severity for TBI in inmates reflects that of the general population, with symptoms and their consequences varying from mild to severe. Difficulties associated with TBI can affect numerous areas in a person's life. The greater the severity, the more likely TBI is to encompass three major areas of mental functioning: thinking, feeling, and behavior (CDC, 2015a). Depending on the amount of neuronal, vascular, and cellular damage, an individual may present a wide variety of cognitive symptoms immediately following injury, or symptoms may develop later. One key to understanding these consequences is to remember that TBI-related behavior may not have been explained to the individual as being part of a medical problem.

TABLE 2

Possible Consequences Associated with TBI

• Aggression	• Low Frustration Tolerance	• Nausea
• Agitation	• Headaches	• Organization and Planning Deficits
• Chronic Body Pain	• Impulsivity	
• Communication Difficulties	• Information-Processing Deficits	• Perseveration
• Confusion		• Poor Insight
• Decreased Ability to Empathize	• Language and Speech Deficits	• Seizure Disorders
		• Sensory Integration Problems
• Dizziness	• Loss of Sense of Smell	• Sleep Disorders
• Emotional and Behavioral Problems	• Memory Impairments	• Social Skills Deficits
	• Misperception of Social Cues	• Uncontrolled Laughing and/or Crying
• Fatigue	• Mobility Limitations	
• Flat Affect	• Mood Swings	• Visual-Spatial Impairments

The consequences for those affected by TBI may include:

ATTENTION AND CONCENTRATION

Some of the greatest challenges faced by individuals with TBI involve the difficulties they have maintaining attention and concentration. Attention problems make it difficult for inmates with TBI to focus on a required task or respond to directions given by a corrections officer. When this issue arises, it is sometimes misinterpreted as intentional defiance toward the officer (Schofield et al., 2006b). Strategies for individuals with attention problems usually involve minimizing distraction in the environment, asking the person with TBI to repeat what has been said (to verify understanding), having them write down the steps necessary for successful completion of a task (or providing them with written material if unable to write), and providing additional time to complete tasks (Williams et al., 2010b).

LEARNING AND MEMORY

New learning and memory deficits are common long-term effects of TBI (Schofield et al., 2006a; Levin et al., 1979). While these functions are different from each other, it often helps to consider both as factors in a continuum that involves grasping new information and being able to later recall the same information. Problems in this area present challenges to inmates who display difficulty remembering rules and directions, which may lead to disciplinary action by corrections staff (Merbitz, Jain, Good, & Jain, 1995). Accommodations for problems with learning and memory should include explaining rules and directions at a slow pace, using step-by-step instructions, asking the individual to repeat the steps, and instructing the inmate to ask questions when uncertain or confused about what to do.

IRRITABILITY AND ANGER

Irritability and anger may also be evident. Individuals with a history of TBI may have a diminished ability to manage their emotions, which can lead to incidents with other prisoners or correctional officers and cause harm to themselves and others (Cohen, Rosenbaum, Kane, Warnken, & Benjamin, 1999; Maruschak & Beck, 2001). Anger, irritability and aggression are behaviors commonly viewed as consequential to TBI (Arciniegas & Beresford, 2001; Max, Robertson, & Lansing, 2001; Silver, McAllister, & Yudovsky, 2011). Negative and difficult personalities, often concomitant with easily irritated individuals, may significantly complicate their recovery process (Wood & Thomas, 2013).

VERBAL PROCESSING

Slowed verbal processing and physical reactions may be characterized by delayed responses, difficulty with verbal comprehension and communication, and a slow pace in completing tasks. These behaviors may be misinterpreted by corrections officers as modes of resistance or uncooperativeness (Kaufman, 2001). As with many areas of dysfunction, the best approach is to allow the individual with TBI to have adequate time to think and process information, to ensure that he or she is tracking and attending to the information given. Repetition of information and the chance to practice required tasks in a variety of settings may also facilitate this process.

DISINHIBITED AND IMPULSIVE BEHAVIOR

Closed head injury may adversely affect individuals' behavioral functioning, as well as their ability to comply with correctional authorities' demands and perform activities of daily living. Effects include poor anger control, increased aggression, impaired judgment, and memory dysfunction (Iverson, Franzen, Demarest, & Hammond, 1993; Krakowski, Convit, Jaeger, Lin, & Volavka, 1989; National Institute of Health, 1999). The nature of this type of injury is of great concern, as the frontal regions of the brain are associated with the highest levels of cognition, including problem solving, reasoning, perspective taking, self-awareness, directing attention, and behavioral control. Disinhibited and impulsive behavior, including a low threshold for anger management and displays of unacceptable and unsafe sexual behavior, may provoke other prisoners or lead to disciplinary action by staff (Jaffe, O'Neill, Vandergoot, Gordon, & Small, 2000; Kramer, Nelson, & Li, 1993; Young, Justice, Erdberg, 2004).

In non-correctional settings, various cognitive, medical, behavioral, educational, and other rehabilitative approaches have been shown to be effective in improving various aspects of functioning following TBI (Braverman et al., 1999; Eames and Wood, 1985; Fann, Uomoto, & Katon, 2000; Fann, Uomoto, & Katon, 2001; Mateer & Mapou, 1996; National Institute of Health, 1999; Paniak, Toller-Lobe, Durand, & Nagy, 1998; Silver & Yudofsky, 1985). These individuals respond best to calm but direct prompts that underline the inappropriate nature of their behavior. Depending on the frequency and severity of the behavior displayed, staff may need to obtain help from mental health professionals with additional expertise in brain injury and behavioral management.

CHRONIC PAIN

TBI can also contribute to chronic pain concerns (Nampiaparampil, 2008). As previously stated, it is possible for a TBI (regardless of severity) to produce cascading disturbances that can become recurring issues long after the initial injury. What may be considered a mild impact to the head could potentially cause chronic headaches in the future. Severe injuries that result in major cognitive or behavioral deficits can lead to the development of seemingly unrelated issues later in life, such as emotional instability and disinhibited aggression. Compounded with the preexisting effects of the TBI, these issues can continue to persist throughout the lifespan and further complicate the victim's chances for recovery.

SUICIDAL IDEATION

Suicidal thinking is yet another major concern for some individuals affected by TBI (Bahraini, Simpson, Brenner, Hoffberg, & Schneider, 2013; Seel & Kreutzer, 2003; Tsaousides, Cantor, & Gordon, 2011; Wood, Williams, & Lewis, 2010). Suicide rates are higher among individuals with TBI, compared to the general population (Brenner, Ignacio, & Blow, 2011; Harrison-Felix et al., 2009; Tate, Simpson, Flanagan, & Coffey, 1997; Teasdale & Engberg, 2001; Ventura et al., 2010). Adolescents with a history of TBI have been found to be more likely to be bullied, cyber-bullied, or threatened with a weapon at school—all known causes of adolescent suicidal ideation (Ilie et al., 2014). Other factors contributing to suicidal ideation include increased depression, anxiety, physical pain, (Zaninotto et al., 2016), and sleep disturbances, including insomnia and hypersomnia (Hou et al., 2013). Additional training and awareness regarding suicide risk assessment and intervention are crucial for clinicians serving individuals with a history of TBI (Mackelprang et al., 2014).

VICTIMIZATION

Few studies have examined the possible connection between TBI and increased victimization (Marge, 2003). TBI can lead to impaired decision-making abilities, substance misuse, memory dysfunction, and a reduced capacity to detect unsafe situations. These and other factors may increase risk of victimization among individuals affected by TBI (Kim, 2002; Kwasnica & Heinemann, 1994; Levin, 1999; Li et al., 2000). TBI has been found to play a role in trauma in some cases of assault, Intimate Partner Violence (IPV), human trafficking, and prostitution. The perspective of the trauma-bonded victim involves adapting to victimization to survive, rendering these individuals susceptible to future cases of assault or victimization. Trauma bonding will typically subject the victim to repeated assault interspersed with occasional moments of kindness, leading to the belief that succumbing will allow the victim to survive. Some research indicates that this is not a conscious reaction and may be evolutionary, as it is a behavior found not only in humans, but also in other mammals. It is believed that trauma bonding in IPV cases may play a role in the underreporting of TBI and other forms of assault (Reid, Haskell, Dillahunt-Aspillaga, & Thor, 2013).

BEHAVIORAL HEALTH CONSEQUENCES

There is strong evidence in the general population that TBI is associated with psychiatric problems, especially mood and anxiety disorders (Jorge & Arcinegas, 2015), as well as changes in personality (Silver et al., 2011). Following injury, it is common for individuals to experience emotional and behavioral problems resulting in a diagnosis of a mental health condition, which may impact the individual for many years. One study conducted by Koponen and colleagues (2002) found the presence of mental health problems following a TBI persisting for up to 30 years.

Risk factors for the development of neuropsychiatric complications following TBI include low educational attainment, psychosocial stress, a history of psychiatric illness, substance abuse, and recurrent TBI (Schiehser, Delano-Wood, Jak, Hanson, Sorg, Orff, & Clark, 2016; Walker, Hiller, Staton, & Leukefeld, 2003). Research consistently demonstrates a relationship between TBI, aggression, and violence (Brooks, Campsie, Symington, Beattie, & McKinlay, 1986). Impulsivity and aggression may be both risk factors for and results of TBI, with both having clear relevance to offending behavior (Eysenk & McGurk, 1980; Horvath & Zuckerman, 1993; Krueger et al., 1994; Allnut, Wedgwood, Wilhelm, & Butler, 2008). A sample of 50 inmates from a county jail, consisting of 25 individuals with TBI in the prior year and 25 without, revealed that the former group had anger and aggression scores that were significantly worse (Slaughter, Fann, & Ehde, 2003).

SEIZURE DISORDERS

TBI may increase the risk of seizure disorders (Morrell, Merbitz, Jain, & Jain, 1998; Salinsky, Parko, Rutecki, Boudreau, & Storzbach, 2016). Brain injuries are most frequently the result of falling, being struck by a blunt object, and automotive collision (CDC, 2015b). Many of these injuries involve impact sustained by the brain's frontal regions, which is also the common area of origin for seizures and epilepsy. Additionally, the occurrence of loss of consciousness (LOC) or subdural bleeding following injury may also leave the individual more susceptible to epileptic episodes. Annegers and Coan (2000) found that the incidence of seizures among males aged 15-24 increased with the severity of the sustained TBI, using measures of relative risk – a ratio that compares the probability of a seizure occurring in an adolescent male TBI population to the probability of a seizure occurring in a general adolescent male population. This study found a relative risk of 1.5 for mild injuries, 2.9 for moderate injuries, and 17.2 for severe injuries. Persons in positions of authority overseeing incarcerated individuals who have a history of TBI need to be aware that seizures may occur.

IMPLICATIONS FOR THE CRIMINAL JUSTICE SYSTEM

TBI is believed to be significantly overrepresented within forensic settings (Freckelton, 2012; Lewis et al., 1988; Lewis, Pincus, Feldman, Jackson, & Bard, 1986; Shiroma, Ferguson, & Pickelsimer, 2010a). It is a significant medical concern that should demand the attention of correctional staff and administration (Williams et al., 2010). Within the criminal justice system, TBI is an invisible disability (Rushworth, 2008). Defendants with a history of TBI who proceed through the various stages of the judicial process should warrant the attention and consideration of justice professionals (Schofield et al., 2006b). An increased awareness and understanding of TBI among this population is also highly warranted (Williams et al., 2010b).

JUVENILE JUSTICE SETTINGS

Juveniles in the criminal justice system with a history of being runaways or homeless have significantly high levels of TBI histories (Mackelprang, Harpin, Grubenhoff, & Rivara (2014). Juvenile detention officers should be aware of the possibility of TBI when interacting with offending adolescent populations (Williams et al., 2010). Identifying incarcerated juveniles who have experienced a previous head injury may create opportunities for additional rehabilitation and treatment. Identification and subsequent treatment of justice-involved individuals impacted by TBI may diminish the possibility of future maladaptive behaviors (Williams et al., 2010b). Therefore, criminal justice professionals should identify juvenile offenders who have a history of TBI and provide appropriate care and services to aid in their recovery process (Colantonio et al., 2014; Schofield et al., 2006b).

ADOLESCENT CONSIDERATIONS

Adolescence is a risk period for both offending and TBI—itself a risk factor for offending and a known contributor to poor mental health. A Finnish study of more than 12,000 people revealed that those who sustained a TBI during childhood or adolescence were four times more at risk for the development of a mental disorder later in life (Timonen et al., 2002). TBI is largely neglected when managing the mental health needs of young offending individuals. Williams and colleagues (2010b) sought to establish the rate and frequency of self-reported TBI, of all severities and causes, in a representative population of adolescent male offenders. These researchers also sought to explore whether self-reported TBI was associated with an increased number of convictions, violent offending, mental health problems, and drug misuse. In a sample of 186 young males (justice-involved participants aged 11 to 19 years); they found that the frequency of self-reported TBI was, in fact, associated with more convictions. Furthermore, three or more self-reported TBIs were linked to greater violence in offenses. Those with self-reported TBI were also at a greater risk for mental health problems as well as cannabis misuse. Additionally, TBI may be associated with offending behavior and poorer mental health outcomes due to neuropsychological dysfunction. Deficits in executive function and attention may be linked to irritability and disinhibited behavior. Findings related to repeat offenders suggest that neurocognitive factors might be contributing to an individual's limited ability for behavioral change once they become enmeshed with custodial systems. Improved management of justice-involved individuals with TBI within the justice system may reduce the risk of future offending (Williams et al., 2010b).

ARREST

Considering the high rates of TBI among prison populations, professionals who work in the criminal justice system should regularly seize the opportunity to screen for the presence of brain injury among adults and juveniles who are arrested, incarcerated, homeless, victims, or who have found themselves caught up in the system (Kaba, Diamond, Haque, MacDonald, & Venters, 2014). The presentation of TBI in an individual can range from no noticeable signs or symptoms of dysfunction to overt demonstrations of impairment, including inarticulate speech, problems with balance, slowed processing speed, and inattention. Unfortunately, individuals under the influence of alcohol or illicit substances also display similar signs, including slurred speech, stumbling or unsteady gait, latency of response, and trouble focusing. Law enforcement personnel are encouraged to mimic the approaches of trained mental health professionals when encountering these individuals, given that these approaches are effective in avoiding unnecessary confrontation. Helping to assess the person and situation and establish rapport in a clear and nonthreatening manner can help resolve situations safely and efficiently.

JUDICIAL HEARING

Individuals with moderate to severe brain injury may present a combination of cognitive or behavioral deficits that greatly hinder their ability to effectively participate in their own defense. In cases involving patients with moderate to severe brain injury who have developed psychiatric symptoms (i.e., paranoid thinking), it is extremely difficult for the affected individual to participate on their own behalf. Delusional thinking can arise either as a direct neuropsychiatric consequence of brain injury or as a secondary consequence of amnesia, with variable response to medication and psychosocial interventions. In some cases, they may even suspect people in the court of plotting against them. The process may become particularly challenging due to the individual's lack of awareness regarding what they are doing, how it affects others, and the repercussions on their case (O'Brien & Ferguson, 2015). Impaired memory and time-line confusion may also prompt confabulation and lead to an accusation of lying, even though the accused believes his or her false memory to be true (Szczepanski & Knight, 2014). These issues are further described in the chapter on confabulation.

INCARCERATION

Inmates with a TBI demonstrate a greater risk of maladaptive behavior than inmates with no TBI (Merbitz,

Jain, Good, & Jain, 1995; Shiroma et al., 2010), especially when appropriate supports and services are not in place. Individuals with a history of TBI in a correctional setting often experience adjustment issues and find themselves more challenged in following rules when compared to other incarcerated individuals (Merbitz et al., 1995; Shiroma et al., 2010). Therefore, TBI is a concern that jail administrators and staff must consider (Slaughter, Fann, & Ehde, 2003). Because TBI can significantly impair one's ability to comprehend and learn new information, such impairments may increase an inmate's risk of behavioral infractions (Aaronson & Lloyd, 2015; Bannon, Salis, & O'Leary, 2015; Merbitz et al., 1995), especially when the TBI is undetected by confinement staff.

There are select aspects of incarceration that may be identified by corrections staff as serving individuals with TBI effectively: the use of predictable routines, clear rules to follow, daily structure, and the development of an understanding of social hierarchy (Colantonio, 2014; Schofield et al., 2006b). However, as previously mentioned, deficits in memory and low frustration tolerance can present a challenge for TBI-affected inmates. Even when staff and former inmates say that the high level of structure and daily routine provided are advantageous to their functioning, this should not be mistaken or equated with thinking that people with brain injury automatically thrive in such a highly regulated and regimented environment. This environment and the structure within it may present a double-edged sword. On one hand, the predictability and limited choices minimize the need for planning ahead in areas such as housekeeping, meal planning and food preparation, selecting clean clothes, or performing household chores. On the other hand, the rules of conduct and high degree of regimentation can pose problems for individuals who may struggle to understand the rules, remember them, or know the right time and context to apply them (Merbitz et al., 1995). What is key for working with individuals with TBI is to understand the extent to which such difficulties may be expected. This understanding may be best seen as part of a treatment process, based on information gained through a combination of observation, clinical interview, and evaluation (Colantonio, 2014).

One study examined the association between medically attended TBI and in-prison behavioral infractions in a statewide adult population of 16,299 males and 1,270 females over an 11-year period, with the goal of understanding rates of infractions in inmates with and without TBI. The in-prison behavioral infraction rate (violent and nonviolent occurrences) was significantly increased in males with TBI, compared to those with no TBI. Similarly, the violent behavioral infraction rate was significantly increased in females with TBI, compared to those without (Shiroma et al., 2010).

TREATMENT

Treatment is the logical next step for individuals identified as having TBI in the criminal justice system. Scientific study continues to make progress in identifying particular brain areas and their relation to anti-social behavior (Johnson, Emmons, Anderson, Glanz, Romig-Martin, Narayanan, & Radley, 2016; Lebow & Chen, 2016). The "frontal" system, which includes the amygdala, hippocampus, the bed nucleus of the stria terminalis (BNST), and insular areas, are involved in responses to situations that require critical socio-affective capabilities such as impulse control, empathy response, and consideration of consequences. (Birbaumer et al., 2005; Lebow & Chen, 2016). Unfortunately, these systems are also often affected adversely by TBI, leading to frontal lobe dysfunction. Treatment for TBI has evolved to not only focus on behavioral programs, but may (in cases where available) focus on therapeutic treatment that targets specific regions of the brain where damage has occurred. (Franke, Walker, Hoke, & Wares, 2016; Thornton & Cormody, 2009).

Untreated TBI within prison populations may increase the risk for unmanageable anger (Schofield et al., 2006b). A comprehensive treatment plan includes proper attention in all steps of the judicial process, including sentencing, incarceration (if appropriate), and community integration. Incarcerated individuals with TBI have an increased susceptibility to various forms of abuse and maltreatment while in prison, and insufficient care at one or more levels of the criminal justice system may not only exacerbate their deficits, but also increase their risk of reoffending (Slaughter et al., 2003). The development of specialized programs within prisons, jails, and detention centers is essential to the proper treatment of individuals affected by TBI. Additionally, therapies and rehabilitation methods should cater to the specific needs of the individual, such as anger management (for emotional disturbances) and cognitive-behavioral therapy.

Increasing numbers of facilities have started programs that address the need for increased TBI awareness and identification. These facilities now conduct staff training in TBI-related issues, introduce screening processes, and identify inmates' unique needs upon release.

COMMUNITY RELEASE

The absence of identification and intervention of TBI among forensic populations may result in poor outcomes upon re-entry into the community (O'Brien & Ferguson, 2015). A familiarity with these individuals, their needs, and the impact of their brain injuries should be given additional consideration to ensure that part of the release plan addresses rehabilitation, effective resources for health care, and a follow-up schedule that caters toward individuals with brain injury. Community care providers and correctional professionals who serve individuals reintegrating into the community should participate in training to increase awareness of the impact TBI has on the criminal population (Fowles, 1988; León-Carrión & Ramos, 2003; Sarapata, Herrmann, Johnson, & Aycock, 1998).

TABLE 3
Possible Care Team Specialties

• Adult Rehabilitative Mental Health Services (ARMHS)	• Occupational Therapy
• Case Management	• Physical Therapy
• Educational Specialist	• Psychiatry
• Independent Living Skills Specialist	• Recreational Therapy
• Neurology	• Social Work
• Neuropsychology	• Speech Therapy
	• Vocational Specialist

Numerous issues can hinder the success of community integration. For persons with TBI, these may include rule infractions, long delays in thinking, problems with understanding and communicating, trouble learning and remembering, challenges with attention, poor self-regulation of temper and behavior, being unable to generate new solutions to daily problems, and initiating planned and adaptive actions. If the TBI occurred during incarceration, the released individual may have to cope not only with being newly released, but also finding himself or herself having to manage any disembodied feelings (Buzan, Kupfer, Eastridge, & Lema-Hincapie, 2014). Understanding and having realistic expectations for the common occurrence of these problems will help staff provide effective rehabilitation through education, accommodation, behavioral intervention, and positive behavioral and environmental supports.

CONCLUSION

TBI is overrepresented and under-identified in corrections populations. This paradox will persist so long as the criminal justice system fails to appreciate the profound association between brain injury and its resultant behavioral and cognitive deficits that can lead to offending, especially among individuals in at-risk populations. Furthermore, community services used by members of the public who have TBI are less likely to be utilized by at-risk individuals with TBI, mostly because the debilitating deficits they live with every day create conditions that isolate them from support (Slaughter et al., 2003). This isolation is typically worse in cases where the individual has been or is incarcerated (Reichard, Langlois, Sample, Wald, & Pickelsimer, 2007). As a society, it is as important to support community efforts for rehabilitation of TBI as it is for any mental or physical disorder, so that when these individuals re-join society, they may be able to cope with increased aggression, cognitive deficits, and other psycho-social problems that not only lead to recidivism, but also diminish the quality of our population, our neighborhoods, and who we are as a culture. Based on the statistically significant occurrence of Co-morbidity between TBI and various psychiatric disorders (Fann et al., 1996; Van Reekum, Bolago, Finlayson, Garner, & Links, 1996; Van Reekum, Cohen, & Wong, 2000) concurrent treatment of mental conditions along with treatment for TBI may be beneficial (Slaughter et al., 2003). These findings need to be considered in the management and rehabilitation of individuals involved in the criminal justice system. Traumatic brain injury, although acute in its initial presentation, has emerged in recent medical literature as a condition increasingly seen as chronic for individuals sustaining more severe injury. TBI treatment needs to be included in rehabilitation considerations for individuals within the criminal justice system. Managing these injuries could be essential to enabling positive behavioral changes, as well as decreasing the risk of re-offending by criminals with TBI (Williams et al., 2010b).

REFERENCES

Aaronson, A., & Lloyd, R. B. (2015). Aggression after traumatic brain injury: A review of the current literature. *Psychiatric Annals, 45*(8), 422-426.

Achté, K., Jarho, L., Kyykkä, T., & Vesterinen, E. (1991). Paranoid disorders following war brain damage. *Psychopathology, 24*(5), 309-315.

Adams, J.H., Mitchell, D. E., Graham, D. I., & Doyle, D. (1977). Diffuse brain damage of immediate impact type. Its relationship to 'primary brain-stem damage' in head injury. *Brain: A Journal of Neurology, 100*(3), 489-502.

Allnutt, S., Wedgwood, L., Wilhelm, K., & Butler, T. (2008). Temperament, substance use and psychopathology in a prisoner population: implications for treatment. *Australian and New Zealand Journal of Psychiatry, 42*(11), 969-975.

Alway, Y., Gould, K. R., Johnston, L., *McKenzie*, D., & Ponsford, J. (2016). A prospective examination of Axis I psychiatric disorders in the first 5 years following moderate to severe traumatic brain injury. *Psychological medicine, 46*(06), 1331-1341.

American Psychiatric Association. (2013). *Diagnostic and statistical manual of mental disorders (5th Ed.)*. Washington, D.C.

Anderson, S. W., Damasio, H., Tranel, D., & Damasio, A. R. (2000). Long-term sequelae of prefrontal cortex damage acquired in early childhood. *Developmental Neuropsychology, 18*(3), 281-296.

Andrews, T.K., Rose, F.D., & Johnson, D.A., (1998). Social and behavioural effects of traumatic brain injury in children. *Brain Injury, 12*(2), 133-138.

Annegers, J.F. & Coan, S.P. (2000). The risks of epilepsy after traumatic brain injury. *Seizure, 9*(7), 453-457.

Arciniegas, D.B. & Beresford, T.P. (2001). *Neuropsychiatry: An introductory approach*. Cambridge: Cambridge University Press.

Arciniegas, D.B., Harris, S.N., & Brousseau, K. M. (2003). Psychosis following traumatic brain injury. *International Revue of Psychiatry, 15*(4), 328-340.

Arriola, V. D., & Rozelle, J. W. (2016). Traumatic Brain Injury in United States Operation Enduring Freedom/ Operation Iraqi Freedom (OEF/OIF) Hispanic Veterans—A Review Using the PRISMA Method. *Behavioral Sciences, 6*(1), 3.

Ashley, M.J., Masel, B.E., & Nagele, D.A. (2016). Brain injury overview. In H. Reyst (Ed.), The Essential Brain Injury Guide (Fifth ed., pp. 286-317). Brain Injury Association of America.

Baguley, I. J., Cooper, J., & Felmingham, K. (2006). Aggressive behavior following traumatic brain injury: how common is common? *The Journal of head trauma rehabilitation, 21*(1), 45-56.

Bahraini, N. H., Simpson, G. K., Brenner, L. A., Hoffberg, A. S., & Schneider, A. L. (2013). Suicidal ideation and behaviours after traumatic brain injury: A systematic review. *Brain Impairment, 14*(1), 92-112.

Bannon, S. M., Salis, K. L., & O'Leary, K. D. (2015). Structural brain abnormalities in aggression and violent behavior. *Aggression and Violent Behavior, 25,* 323-331.

Barnett, O., Miller-Perrin, C. L., & Perrin, R. D. (2010). *Family violence across the lifespan: An introduction, 3rd ed.* Thousand Oaks, CA: Sage Publications, Inc.

Barnett, O.W., Miller-Perrin, C.L., & Perrin, R.D. (2011). Family violence across the lifespan: An introduction (Third ed.). Thousand Oaks, CA, SAGE Publications.

Barnfield, T.V., & Leathem, J.M. (1998). Neuropsychological outcomes of traumatic brain injury and substance abuse in a New Zealand prison population. *Brain Injury, 12*(11), 951-962.

Barrash, J., Tranel, D., & Anderson, S. W. (2000). Acquired personality disturbances associated with bilateral damage to the ventromedial prefrontal region. *Developmental Neuropsychology, 18*(3), 355-381.

Barth, J.T., Macciocchi, S.N., Giordani, B., Rimel, R., Jane, J.A., & Boll, T.J. (1983). Neuropsychological sequelae of minor head injury. *Neurosurgery, 13*(5), 529-533.

Bazarian, J. J., Blyth, B., Mookerjee, S., He, H., & McDermott, M. P. (2010). Sex differences in outcome after mild traumatic brain injury. *Journal of Neurotrauma, 27*(3), 527-539.

Behnken, M.P., DeLisi, M., Trulson, C.R., & Vaugn, M.G. (2015). Blackout: Traumatic brain injury associated with career criminality withstands powerful confounds. In M. DeLisi & M. Vaughn (Eds.), *The Routledge international handbook of biosocial criminology* (pp. 418-429). New York, NY: Routledge.

Bennett, T. L., & Raymond, M. J. (2008). The neuropsychology of traumatic brain injury. In Horton, AM & Wedding, D. (3ª Ed.). *The handbook of neuropsychology* (pp. 533-570). New York, NY: Springer.

Bergmann, M. M., Byers, T., Freedman, D. S., & Mokdad, A. (1998). Validity of self-reported diagnoses leading to hospitalization: A comparison of self-reports with hospital records in a prospective study of American adults. *American Journal of Epidemiology, 147*(10), 969-977.

Betzen, C., White, R., Zehendner, C.M., Pietrowski, E., Bender, B. et al. (2009). Oxidative stress upregulates the NMDA receptor on cerebrovascular endothelium. *Free Radical Biology & Medicine. 47*(8), 1212-1220.

Birbaumer, N., Veit, R., Lotze, M., Erb, M., Hermann, C., Grodd, W., & Flor, H. (2005). Deficient fear onditioning in psychopathy: a functional magnetic resonance imaging study. *Archives of General Psychiatry, 62*(7), 799-805.

Blaauw, E., Arensman, E., Kraaij, V., Winkel, F.W., & Bout, R. (2002). Traumatic life events and suicide risk among jail inmates: the influence of types of events, time period and significant others. *Journal of Traumatic Stress, 15*(1), 9-16.

Blyth, B.J. & Bazarian, J.J. (2010). Traumatic alterations of consciousness: Traumatic brain injury. *Emergency Medical Clinics of North America, 28*(3), 571-594.

Butler, T., Allnutt, S., & Yang, B. (2007). Mentally ill prisoners in Australia have poor physical health. *International Journal of Prisoner Health, 3*(2), 99-110.

Bond, M.R. (1986). Neurobehavioral sequelae of closed head injury. In I. Grant & K. Adams (Eds.), *Neuro-psychological assessment of neuropsychiatric disorders*. Oxford: Oxford University Press.

Brain Injury Association of America, National Brain Injury Information Center. (2015). Brain injury statistics: Traumatic brain injury. Retrieved from www.biausa.org

Braverman, S.E., Spector, J., Warden, D.L., Wilson, B.C., Ellis, T.E., Bamdad, M.J., & Salazar, A.M. (1999). A multidisciplinary TBI inpatient rehabilitation programme for active duty service members as part of a randomized clinical trial. *Brain Injury, 13*(6), 405-415.

Brenner, L.A., Ignacio, R.V., & Blow, F.C. (2011). Suicide and traumatic brain injury among individuals seeking Veterans Health Administration services. *Journal of Head Trauma Rehabilitation, 26*(4), 257-264.

Brewer Smyth, K., Burgess, A.W., & Shults, J. (2004). Physical and sexual abuse, salivary cortical, and neurologic correlates of violent criminal behavior in female prison inmates. *Biological Psychiatry, 55*(1), 21-31.

Brismar, B., Engström, A., & Rydberg, U. (1982). Head injury and intoxication: a diagnostic and therapeutic dilemma. *Acta Chirurgica Scandinavica, 149*(1), 11-14.

Brock, J.B., Yanuck, S., Pierce, M., Powell, M., Geanolulos, S., Noseworthy, S., Kharrazian, D., Turnpaugh, C., Comey, A, & Zielinski, G. (2013). The potential impact of various physiological mechanisms on outcomes in TBI, mTBI, concussion and PPCS. *Functional Neurology, Rehabilitation, and Ergonomics, 3*(2/3), 215-256.

Brooks, N., Campsi, L., Symington, C., Beattie, A., & McKinlay, W. (1986). The five-year outcome of severe blunt head injury: A relative's view. *Journal of Neurology, Neurosurgery, and Psychiatry, 49*(7), 764-770.

Brower, M. C., & Price, B. H. (2001). Neuropsychiatry of frontal lobe dysfunction in violent and criminal behaviour: A critical review. *Journal of Neurology, Neurosurgery & Psychiatry, 71*(6), 720-726.

Bryant, E., Scott, M., Golden, C. & Tori, C. (1984) Neuropsychological deficits, learning disability, and violent behavior. *Journal of Consulting and Clinical Psychology, 52*, 323-324.

Bryant, R. A., Marosszeky, J. E., Crooks, J., & Gurka, J. A. (2000). Post-traumatic stress disorder after severe traumatic brain injury. *American Journal of Psychiatry, 157*(4), 629-631.

Burgess, P.W. & Wood, R.L.I. (1990). Neuropsychology of behavioral disorders following brain injury. In R.L.I. Wood (Ed.), *Neuro-behavioral sequelae of traumatic brain injury* (110-133). London: Burgess Science Press.

Butler, T., Allnutt, S., & Yang, B. (2007). Mentally ill prisoners in Australia have poor physical health. *International Journal of Prisoner Health, 3*(2), 99-110.

Butterworth, P., Anstey, K., Jorm, A. F., & Rodgers, B. (2004). A community survey demonstrated cohort differences in the lifetime prevalence of self-reported head injury. *Journal of Clinical Epidemiology, 57*(7), 742-748.

Buzan, R. D., Kupfer, J., Eastridge, D., & Lema-Hincapie, A. (2014). Philosophy of mind: Coming to terms with traumatic brain injury. *NeuroRehabilitation, 34*(4), 601-611.

Capruso, D.X., & Levin, H.S. (2006). Neurobehavioral outcome of head trauma. In R.W. Evans (Ed.), *Neurology & trauma* (pp. 192-229). New York, NY: Oxford University Press.

Cassidy, J. W. (1990). Neurochemical substrates of aggression: Toward a model for improved intervention. *The Journal of Head Trauma Rehabilitation, 5*(2), 83-86.

Centers for Disease Control and Prevention (CDC). (2003). *National Center for Injury Prevention and Control. Report to Congress on mild traumatic brain injury in the United States: Steps to prevent a serious public health problem*. Atlanta (GA), Centers for Disease Control and prevention.

Centers for Disease Control and Prevention. (2011). Nonfatal traumatic brain injuries related to sports and recreation activities among persons aged <19 years – United States, 2001-2009. *MMWR, 60*(39), 1337-1342.

Centers for Disease Control and Prevention (2015a). *Traumatic brain injury in prisons and jails: An unrecognized problem.* Online. Available from URL: www.cdc.gov/traumaticbraininjury/pdf/ Prisoner_TBI_Prof-a.pdf

Centers for Disease Control and Prevention (2015b). *Traumatic brain injury in the United States: Fact sheet.* Online. Available from URL: www.cdc.gov/traumaticbraininjury/get_the_facts.html

Centers for Disease Control and Prevention. (2015c). *National TBI estimates: Injury prevention & control.* Online. Available from URL: www.cdc.gov/traumaticbraininjury/statistics.html

Chandler, R.K., Fletcher, B., & Volkow, N. (2009). Treating drug abuse and addiction in the criminal justice system. *Journal of the American Medical Association, 301*(2), 183-190.

Chen, J.W.Y., Ruff, R.L., Eavy, R., & Wasterlain, C.G. (2009). Post-traumatic epilepsy and treatment. *Journal of Rehabilitation Research and Development, 46*(6), 685-696.

Christensen, J., Pedersen, M. G., Pedersen, C. B., Sidenius, P., Olsen, J., & Vestergaard, M. (2009). Long-term risk of epilepsy after traumatic brain injury in children and young adults: A population-based cohort study. *The Lancet, 373*(9669), 1105-1110.

Christian, C.W. & Block, R. (2009). Abusive head trauma in infants and children. *Pediatrics, 123*, 1409.

Cleverley, K. & Kidd, S.A. (2011). Resilience and suicidality among homeless youth. *Journal of Adolescence,* 34(5), 1049-1054.

Cochrane, B.N., Stewart, A.J., Ginzler, J.A., & Cauce, A.M. (2002). Challenges faced by homeless youth and young adults. *American Journal of Public Health, 95*(5), 773-777.

Cohen, R.A., Rosenbaum, A., Kane, R.L., Warnken, W.J., & Benjamin, S. (1999). Neuropsychological correlates of domestic violence. *Violence and Victims, 14*(4), 397-411.

Colantonio, A., Kim, H., Allen, S., Asbridge, M., Petgrave, J., & Brochu, S. (2014). Traumatic brain injury and early life experiences among men and women in a prison population. *Journal of Correctional Health Care, 20*(4), 271-279.

Colantonio, A., Stamenova, V., Abramowitz, C., Clarke, D., & Christensen, B. (2007). Brain injury in forensic psychiatry population. *Brain Injury, 21*(13-14), 1353-1360.

Cole, W.R., Gerring, J.P., Gray, R.M., Vasa, R.A., Salorio, C.F., Grados, M., Christensen, J.R., & Slomine, B.S. (2008). Prevalence of aggressive behavior after severe pediatric traumatic brain injury. *Brain Injury, 22*(12), 932-939.

Collins, R. L., Pastorek, N. J., Tharp, A. T., & Kent, T. A. (2012). Behavioral and psychiatric Co-morbidities of TBI. In *Traumatic brain injury* (pp. 223-244). Springer New York.

Corrigan, J. D., & Bogner, J. (2007a). Initial reliability and validity of the Ohio State University TBI identification method. *The Journal of Head Trauma Rehabilitation, 22*(6), 318-329.

Corrigan, J.D., & Bogner, J. (2007b). Screening and identification of TBI. *The Journal of Head Trauma Rehabilitation, 22*(6), 315-317.

Corrigan, J.D., Bogner, J., & Holloman, C. (2012). Lifetime history of traumatic brain injury among persons with substance use disorders. *Brain Injury, 26*(2), 139-150.

Corrigan, J.D., & Deutschle Jr, J.J. (2008). The presence and impact of traumatic brain injury among clients in treatment for co-occurring mental illness and substance abuse. *Brain Injury, 22*(3), 223-231.

Covassin, T., Schatz, P., & Swanik, C.B. (2007). Sex differences in neuropsychological function and post-concussion symptoms of concussed collegiate athletes. *Neurosurgery, 61*(2), 345-351.

Covassin, T., Schatz, P., & Swanik, C.B. (2007). Sex differences in neuropsychological function and post-concussion symptoms of concussed collegiate athletes. *Neurosurgery, 61*, 345-351. PubMed doi:10.1227/01.NEU.0000279972.95060.CB

Crosson, B. (1987). Treatment of interpersonal deficits for head-trauma patients in inpatient rehabilitation settings. *The Clinical Neuropsychologist, 1*(4), 335-352.

Curtiss, G. (2007). Awareness problems following moderate to severe traumatic brain injury: Prevalence, assessment methods, and injury correlates. *Journal of Rehabilitation Research and Development, 44*(7), 937.

Dahm, J. & Ponsford, J. (2015). Comparison of long-term outcomes following traumatic injury: What is the unique experience for those with brain injury compared with orthopaedic injury? *Injury, 46*(1), 142-149.

Dambinova, S. A., Sowell, R. L., & Maroon, J. C. (2013). Gradual return to play: Potential role of neurotoxicity biomarkers in assessment of concussions severity. *Journal of Molecular Biomarkers & Diagnosis, 3*, 003.

Dams-O'Connor, K., Cantor, J. B., Brown, M., Dijkers, M. P., Spielman, L. A., & Gordon, W. A. (2014). Screening for traumatic brain injury: Findings and public health implications. *The Journal of Head Trauma Rehabilitation, 29*(6), 479-489. http://doi.org/10.1097/HTR.0000000000000099

Davies, R. C., Williams, W. H., Hinder, D., Burgess, C. N., & Mounce, L. T. (2012). Self-reported traumatic brain injury and post-concussion symptoms in incarcerated youth. *The Journal of Head Trauma Rehabilitation, 27*(3), E21-E27.

De Boer, E. J., Den Tonkelaar, I., Burger, C. W., & Van Leeuwen, F. E. (2005). Validity of self-reported causes of subfertility. *American Journal of Epidemiology, 161*(10), 978-986.

DelBello, M. P., Soutullo, C. A., Zimmerman, M. E., Sax, K. W., Williams, J. R., McElroy, S. L., & Strakowski, S. M. (1999). Traumatic brain injury in individuals convicted of sexual offenses with and without bipolar disorder. *Psychiatry Research, 89*(3), 281-286.

Department of Justice (US), Office of Justice Programs, Bureau of Justice Statistics. (2006a). *Medical problems of jail inmates.* Retrieved from www.bjs.gov/content/pub/pdf/mpji.pdf

Department of Justice (US). Office of Justice Programs. Bureau of Justice Statistics. (2006b). Prison and jail inmates at midyear 2005. In P.M. Harrison & A.J. Beck (Eds.), *Bureau of Justice Statistics Special Report. No. (NCJ) 213133.* Washington D. C.; U.S. Department of Justice.

Dessy, A. M., Rasouli, J., & Choudhri, T. F. (2015). Second impact syndrome: A rare, devastating consequence of repetitive head injuries. *Neurosurgery Quarterly, 25*(3), 423-426.

Diamond, P. M., Harzke, A. J., Magaletta, P. R., Cummins, A. G., & Frankowski, R. (2007). Screening for traumatic brain injury in an offender sample: A first look at the reliability and validity of the Traumatic Brain Injury Questionnaire. *The Journal of Head Trauma Rehabilitation, 22*(6), 330-338.

Diamond, P. & Magaletta, P. (2006). *TBI in the Federal prison: Assessing history of traumatic brain injury in a prison population.* A lecture given at the national Center for Injury Prevention and Control. Centers for Disease Control and Prevention. Atlanta, GA.

Diamond, P. M., Magaletta, P. R., Harzke, A. J., & Baxter, J. (2008). Who requests psychological services upon admission to prison? *Psychological Services, 5*(2), 97.

Dikmen, S., McLean, A., & Temkin, N. (1986). Neuropsychological and psychosocial consequences of minor head injury. *Journal of Neurology, Neurosurgery & Psychiatry, 49*(11), 1227-1232.

Dikmen, S.S., Temkin, N., Armsden, G., Levin, H.S., Eisenberg, H.M., & Benton, A.L. (1989). Neuropsychological recovery: Relationship to psychosocial functioning and post concussional complaints. Mild head injury. New York: Oxford University Press.

Dooley, J.J., Anderson, V., Hemphill, S.A., & Ohan, J. (2008). Aggression after pediatric traumatic brain injury: A theoretical approach. *Brain Injury, 22*(11), 836-846.

Dunlop, T.W., Udvarhelyi, G.B., Stedem, A.F., O'Connor, J.M., Isaacs, M.L., Puig, J.G., & Mather, J.H. (1991). Comparison of patients with and without emotional/behavioral deterioration during the first year after traumatic brain injury. *The Journal of Neuropsychiatry and Clinical Neurosciences, 3*, 150-156.

Eames, P. (1990). Organic bases of behavioral disorders following traumatic brain injury. In R.L.I Wood (Ed.), *Neuro-behavioral sequelae of traumatic brain injury*. London, Burgess Science Press, pp. 134-150.

Eames, P., & Wood, R. (1985). Rehabilitation after severe brain injury: A follow-up study of a behaviour modification approach. *Journal of Neurology, Neurosurgery & Psychiatry, 48*(7), 613-619.

Edna, T. H. (1981). Alcohol influence and head injury. *Acta Chirurgica Scandinavica, 148*(3), 209-212.

Elmer, O., & Lim Jr, R. C. (1985). Influence of acute alcohol intoxication on the outcome of severe non-neurologic trauma. *Acta Chirurgica Scandinavica, 151*(4), 305-308.

Evans, D.C.L. (2006). Reading neuroscience: ventriloquism as a metaphor for multiple readings of self. University of Plymouth.

Eysenk, S.B., & McGurk, B.J. (1980). Impulsiveness and venturesomeness in a detention center population. *Psychological Reports, 3*(47), 1299-1306.

Fann, J., Katon, W., Uomoto, J., & Esselman, P. (1996). Psychiatric disorders and functional disability in outpatients with traumatic brain injuries. *The Journal of Head Trauma Rehabilitation, 11*(4), 96-97.

Fann, J. R., Uomoto, J. M., & Katon, W. J. (2000). Sertraline in the treatment of major depression following mild traumatic brain injury. *The Journal of Neuropsychiatry and Clinical neurosciences, 12*(2), 226-232.

Fann, J.R., Uomoto, J.M., & Katon, W.J. (2001). Cognitive improvement with treatment of depression following mild traumatic brain injury. *Psychosomatics, 42*(1), 48-54.

Farrel, M., Boys, P., Brugha, T., Coid, J., Jenkins, R., Lewis, G., Meltzer, H., Marsden, J., Singleton, N., & Taylor, C. (2002). Psychosis and drug dependence: Results from a national survey of prisoners. *The British Journal of Psychiatry, 181*(5), 393-398.

Farrer, T.J., Frost, R.B., & Hedges, D.W. (2013). Prevalence of traumatic brain injury in juvenile offenders: A meta-analysis. *Child Neuropsychology, 19*(3), 225-234.

Farrer, T.J., & Hedges, D.W. (2011). Prevalence of traumatic brain injury in incarcerated groups compared to the general population: A meta-analysis. *Progress in Neuro-Psychopharmacology & Biological Psychiatry, 3*(2), 390-394.

Faul, M., Xu, L., Wald, M.M., & Coronado, V.G. (2010). *Traumatic brain injury in the United States: Emergency department visits, hospitalizations and deaths 2002-2006*. Atlanta (GA), Centers for Disease Control and Prevention, National Center for Injury Prevention and Control.

Fazel, S., Långström, N., Hjern, A., Grann, M., & Lichtenstein, P. (2009). Schizophrenia, substance abuse, and violent crime. *Journal of the American Medical Association, 301*(19), 2016-2023.

Fazel, S., Lichtenstein, P., Grann, M., & Långström, N. (2011). Risk of violent crime in individuals with epilepsy and traumatic brain injury: A 35-year Swedish population study. *PLoS Med, 8*(12), e1001150.

Fazel, S., Philipson, J., Gardiner, L., Merritt, R., & Grann, M. (2009). Neurological disorders and violence: A systematic review and meta-analysis with a focus on epilepsy and traumatic brain injury. *Journal of Neurology, 256*(10), 1591-1602.

Felde, A.B., Westermeyer, J., & Thuras, P. (2006). Co-morbid traumatic brain injury and substance use disorder: Childhood predictors and adult correlates. *Brain Injury, 20*(1), 41-49.

Fenton, G., McClelland, R., Montgomery, A., MacFlynn, G., & Rutherford, W. (1993). The postconcussional syndrome: Social antecedents and psychological sequelae. *The British Journal of Psychiatry, 162*(4), 493-497.

Ferguson, P. L., Pickelsimer, E. E., Corrigan, J. D., Bogner, J. A., & Wald, M. (2012). Prevalence of traumatic brain injury among prisoners in South Carolina. *The Journal of Head Trauma Rehabilitation, 27*(3), E11-E20.

Finger, S. (1994). *Origins of neuroscience: A history of explorations into brain function.* New York: Oxford University Press, 3-9.

Fishbain, D. A., Cutler, R. B., Rosomoff, H. L., & Rosomoff, R. S. (1999). Validity of self-reported drug use in chronic pain patients. *The Clinical Journal of Pain, 15*(3), 184-191.

Fleischman, J. (2002). *Phineas Gage: A gruesome but true story about brain science.* Boston, Massachusetts: Houghton Mifflin Company. p. 2.

Fleminger, S., & Ponsford, J. (2005). Long term outcome after traumatic brain injury: More attention needs to be paid to neuropsychiatric functioning. *British Medical Journal, 331*(7530), 1419.

Forrest, C. B., Tambor, E., Riley, A. W., Ensminger, M. E., & Starfield, B. (2000). The health profile of incarcerated male youths. *Pediatrics, 105*(2), 286-291.

Fowles, G. P. (1988). Neuropsychologically impaired offenders: Considerations for assessment and treatment. *Psychiatric Annals, 18*(12), 692-697.

Franke, L. M., Walker, W. C., Hoke, K. W., & Wares, J. R. (2016). Distinction in EEG slow oscillations between chronic mild traumatic brain injury and PTSD. *International Journal of Psychophysiology, 106*, 21-29.

Freckelton, I. (2012). Expert evidence by mental health professionals: The communication challenge posed by evidence about Autism Spectrum Disorder, brain injuries, and Huntington's Disease. *International Journal of Law and Psychiatry, 35*(5), 372-379.

Freedman, D., & Hemenway, D. (2000). Precursors of lethal violence: A death row sample. *Social Science and Medicine, 50*(12), 1757-1770.

Ganesalingam, K., Yeates, K.O., Sanson, A., & Anderson, V. (2007). Social problem-solving skills following childhood traumatic brain injury and its association with self-regulation and social and behavioural functioning. *Journal of Neuropsychology, 1*(2), 149-170.

Gass, C. S., Rogers, D., & Kinne, E. (2016). Psychological characteristics in acute mild traumatic brain injury: an MMPI-2 study. *Applied Neuropsychology: Adult*, 1-8.

Geraldina, P., Mariarosaria, L., Annarita, A., Susanna, G., Michela, S., Alessandro, D., Sandra, S., & Enrico, C. (2003). Neuropsychiatric sequelae in TBI: A comparison across different age groups. *Brain Injury, 17*(10), 835-846.

Girard, P., Meyer, K., Schneider, J.C., & Trudel, T. (2016). Military populations. In H. Reyst (Ed.), The Essential Brain Injury Guide (Fifth ed., pp. 376-394). Brain Injury Association of America.

Glaze, L.E. (2011). *Correctional populations in the United States, 2010 (NCJ 236319).* Bureau of Justice Statistics. Retrieved from http://bjs.ojp.usdoj.gov/content/pub/pdf/cpus10.pdf

Gleason, W.J. (1993). Mental disorders in battered women: An empirical study. *Violence and Victims, 8*(1), 53-68.

Glenn, A.L. & Raine, A. (2011). Antisocial personality disorders. In J. Decety & J. Cacioppo (Eds.), *The Oxford Handbook of Social Neuroscience* (pp. 885-894). New York: Oxford University Press.

Godfrey, H. P., Marsh, N. V., & Partridge, F. M. (1987). Severe traumatic head injury and social behaviour: A review. *New Zealand Journal of Psychology, 16*(2), 49-57.

Greer, B. G. (1986). Substance abuse among people with disabilities: A problem of too much accessibility. *Journal of Rehabilitation, 52*(1), 34.

Grindel, S.H. (2003). Epidemiology and pathophysiology of minor traumatic brain injury. *Current Sports Medicine Reports, 2*(1), 18-23.

Gronwall, D. (1991). Minor head injury. *Neuropsychology, 5*(4), 253-265.

Gronwall, D., Wrightson, P., & Waddell, P. (1990). *Head injury: The facts. A guide for families and caregivers.* New York: Oxford University Press.

Gualtieri, T., & Cox, D. R. (1991). The delayed neurobehavioural sequelae of traumatic brain injury. *Brain Injury, 5*(3), 219-232.

Guskiewicz, K.M., Weaver, N L., Padua, D.A., & Garrett, W.E. (2000). Epidemiology of concussion in collegiate and high school football players. *The American Journal of Sports Medicine, 28*(5), 643-650.

Hall, K.M., Karzmark, P., Stevens, M., Englander, J., O'Hare, P., & Wright, J. (1994). Family stressors in traumatic brain injury: A two-year follow-up. *Archives of Physical Medicine and Rehabilitation, 74*(8), 876-884.

Hanlon, R. E., Rubin, L. H., Jensen, M., & Daoust, S. (2010). Neuropsychological features of indigent murder defendants and death row inmates in relation to homicidal aspects of their crimes. *Archives of Clinical Neuropsychology, 25*(1), 1-13.

Hannay, H.J., Howieson, D.B., Loring, D.B., Fischer, J.S., & Lezak, M.D. (2004). Neuropathology for neuropsychologists. In M.D. Lezak, D.B. Howieson, & D.W. Loring (Eds.), *Neuropsychological Assessment*, 4th edition (pp. 157-285). New York: Oxford University Press.

Harris Interactive Inc. (2000). *The full Harris poll results on the public perceptions of brain and head injuries.* Unpublished raw data. From Brain Injury Association, Inc.

Harrison-Felix, C.L., Whiteneck, G.G., Jha, A., DeVivo, M.J., Hammond, F.M., & Hart, D.M. (2009). Mortality over four decades after traumatic brain injury rehabilitation: A retrospective cohort study. *Archive of Physical Medicine and Rehabilitation, 90*(9), 1506-1513.

Hawley, C.A. (2003). Reported problems and their resolution following mild, moderate and severe traumatic brain injury amongst children and adolescents in the UK. *Brain Injury, 17*(2), 105-129.

Hayman-Abello, S., Rourke, B., & Fuerst, D. (2003). Psychosocial status after pediatric traumatic brain injury: A subtype analysis using the Child Behavior Checklist. *Journal of the International Neuropsychological Society, 9*, 887-898.

Heyer, G. L., Fischer, A., Wilson, J., MacDonald, J., Cribbs, S., Ravindran, R., ... & Cuff, S. (2016). Orthostatic intolerance and autonomic dysfunction in youth with persistent postconcussion symptoms: A head-upright tilt table study. *Clinical Journal of Sport Medicine, 26*(1), 40-45.

Hibbard, M., Bogdany, J., Uysal, S., Kepler, K., Silver, J., Gordon, W., & Haddad, L. (2000). Axis II psychopathology in individuals with traumatic brain injury. *Brain Injury, 14*(1), 45-61.

Hibbard, M., Uysal, S., Kepler, K., Bogdany, J., & Silver, J. (1998). Axis I psychopathology in individuals with traumatic brain injury. *Journal of Head Trauma Rehabilitation, 13*(4), 24-39.

Himmelstein, D.U., Thornes, D., Warren, E., & Woolhandler, S. (2009). Medical bankruptcy in the United States, 2007: Results of a national study. *The American Journal of Medicine, 122*(8), 741-746.

Hoge, C.W., Castro, C.A., Messer, S.C., McGurk, D., Cotting, D.I., & Koffman, R.L. (2004). Combat duty in Iraq and Afghanistan, mental health problems, and barriers to care. *New England Journal of Medicine. 351*(1), 70161-70163.

Horvath, P. & Zuckerman, M. (1993). Sensation seeking, risk appraisal, and risky behavior. *Personality and Individual Differences, 14*(1), 41-52.

Hou, L., Han, X., Sheng, P., Tong, W., Li, Z., Xu, D., ... Dong, Y. (2013). Risk factors associated with sleep disturbance following traumatic brain injury: Clinical findings and questionnaire based study. *PLoS ONE, 8*(10), e76087. http://doi.org/10.1371/journal.pone.0076087

Hux, K., Bong, V., Skinner, S., Belau, D., & Sanger, D. (1998). Parental report of occurrences and consequences of traumatic brain injury among delinquent and non-delinquent. *Brain Injury, 12*, 667-681.

Hux, K., Schneider, T., & Bennett, K. (2009). Screening for traumatic brain injury. *Brain Injury, 23*(1), 8-14.

Hwang, S.W., Colantonio, A., Chiu, S., Tolomiczenko, G., Kiss, A., Cowan, L., Redelmeier, D.A. & Levinson, W. (2008). The effect of traumatic brain injury on the health of homeless people. *Canadian Medical Association Journal, 179*(8), 779-784.

Ilie, G., Mann, R. E., Boak, A., Adlaf, E. M., Hamilton, H., Asbridge, M., ... Cusimano, M. D. (2014). Suicidality, bullying and other conduct and mental health correlates of traumatic brain injury in adolescents. *PLoS ONE, 9*(4), e94936. http://doi.org/10.1371/journal.pone.0094936

Iverson, G.L., Franzen, M.D., Demarest, D.S., & Hammond, J.A. (1993). Neuropsychological screening in correctional settings. *Criminal Justice and Behavior, 20*(4), 347-358.

Jackson, H., Philip, E., Nuttall, R.L., & Diller, L. (2002). Traumatic brain injury: A hidden consequence for battered women. *Professional Psychology: Research & Practices, 3*(1), 39-45.

Jaffe, M.P., O'Neill, J., Vandergoot, D., Gordon, W.A., & Small, B. (2000). The unveiling of traumatic brain injury in an HIV/AIDS population. *Brain Injury, 14*(1), 35-44.

Janusz, J.A., Kirkwood, M.W., Yeates, K.O., & Taylor, H.G. (2002). Social problem-solving skills in children with traumatic brain injury: Long-term outcomes and prediction of social competence. *Child Neuropsychology: A Journal on Normal and Abnormal Development in Childhood and Adolescence, 8*(3), 179-194.

Jenkins, S. (2014). Alcohol use and craving among Veterans with mental health disorders and mild traumatic brain injury. *Journal of Rehabilitation Research and Development, 51*(9), 1397.

Jennet, B. & Teasdale, G. (1981). *Management of head injuries.* Philadelphia, F.A. Davis.

Jennett, B., Snoek, J., Bond, M. R., & Brooks, N. (1981). Disability after severe head injury: observations on the use of the Glasgow Outcome Scale. *Journal of Neurology, Neurosurgery & Psychiatry, 44*(4), 285-293.

Jeter, C. B., Hergenroeder, G. W., Hylin, M. J., Redell, J. B., Moore, A. N., & Dash, P. K. (2013). Biomarkers for the diagnosis and prognosis of mild traumatic brain injury/concussion. *Journal of Neurotrauma, 30*(8), 657-670.

Jiang, J.Y., Gao, G.Y., Li, W.P., Yu, M.K., & Zhu, C. (2002). Early indicators of prognosis in 846 cases of severe traumatic brain injury. *Journal of Neurotrauma, 19*(7), 869-874.

Johnson, S. B., Emmons, E. B., Anderson, R. M., Glanz, R. M., Romig-Martin, S. A., Narayanan, N. S., ... & Radley, J. J. (2016). A Basal Forebrain Site Coordinates the Modulation of Endocrine and Behavioral Stress Responses via Divergent Neural Pathways. *The Journal of Neuroscience, 36*(33), 8687-8699.

Johnson, D., Roethig-Johnston, K., & Richards, D. (1993). Biochemical and physiological parameters of recovery in acute severe head injury: Responses to multisensory stimulation. *Brain Injury, 7*(6), 491-499.

Jolliffe, D., Farrington, D.P., Hawkins, J.D., Catalano, R.F., Hill, K.G., & Kosterman, R. (2003). Predictive, concurrent, prospective and retrospective validity reported delinquency. *Criminal Behavior and Mental Health, 13*(3), 179-197.

Jones, G. A. (1989). Alcohol abuse and traumatic brain injury. *Alcohol Health & Research World, 13*(2), 104-110.

Jorge, R. E., & Arciniegas, D. B. (2014). Mood disorders after TBI. *The Psychiatric Clinics of North America, 37*(1), 13-29. http://doi.org/10.1016/j.psc.2013.11.005

Jorge, R.E., Robinsonm R.G., & Arndt, S. (1993). Are there symptoms that are specific for depressed mood in patients with traumatic brain injury? *The Journal of Nervous and Mental Disease, 181*(2), 91-99.

Jorge, R.E., Starkstein, S.E., Arndt, S., Moser, D., Crespo-Facorro, B., & Robinson, R.G. (2005) Alcohol misuse and mood disorders following traumatic brain injury. *Archives of General Psychiatry, 62*(7), 742-749.

Jorgensen, C., Anderson, N. E., & Barnes, J. C. (2016). Bad brains: Crime and drug abuse from a neurocriminological perspective. *American Journal of Criminal Justice, 41*(1), 47-69.

Kaba, F., Diamond, P., Haque, A., MacDonald, R., & Venters, H. (2014). Traumatic brain injury among newly admitted adolescents in the New York City jail system. *Journal of Adolescent Health, 54*(5), 615-617.

Kaplan, C.A., & Corrigan, J.D. (1992). Effects of blood alcohol level on recovery from severe closed head injury. *Brain Injury, 6*(4), 337-349.

Kaufman, C.W. (2001). *Handbook for correction officers and other institutional staff to identify and manage inmates with traumatic brain injuries* (Doctoral Dissertation). Miami (FL), Carlos Albizu University 2001. Available from: University Microfilms, Ann Arbor, MI. (UMI No. AAT3040762)

Kelly, M.P., Johnson, C.T., Knoller, N., Drubach, D.A., & Winslow, M.M. (1997). Substance abuse, traumatic brain injury and neuropsychological outcome. *Brain Injury, 11*(6), 391-402.

Kennedy, J.E., Jaffee, M.S., Leskin, G.A., Stokes, J.W., Leal, F.O., & Fitzpatrick, P.J. (2007). Post-traumatic stress disorder and post-traumatic stress disorder-like symptoms and mild traumatic brain injury. *Journal of Rehabilitation Research & Development, 44*(7), 895-920.

Kim, E. (2002). Agitation, aggression, and disinhibition syndromes after traumatic brain injury. *Neurorehabilitation, 17*(4), 297-310.

Kim, J., Whyte, J., Patel, S., Europa, E., Slattery, J., Coslett, H.B., & Detre, J.A. (2012). A perfusion fMRI study of the neural correlates of sustained-attention and working-memory deficits in chronic traumatic brain injury. *Neurorehabilitation and Neural Repair, 26*(7), 870-880.

Klabunde, C. N., Reeve, B. B., Harlan, L. C., Davis, W. W., & Potosky, A. L. (2005). Do patients consistently report Co-morbid conditions over time? Results from the prostate cancer outcomes study. *Medical Care, 43*(4), 391-400.

Koch, L., Merz, M. A., & Lynch, R. T. (1995). Screening for mild traumatic brain injury: A guide for rehabilitation counselors. *Journal of Rehabilitation, 61*(4), 50.

Koenigs, M., Young, L., Adolphs, R., Tranel, D., Cushman, F., Hauser, M., & Damasio, A. (2007). Damage to the prefrontal cortex increases utilitarian moral judgements. *Nature, 446*(7138), 908-911.

Kolb, B., & Whishaw, I. Q. (2009). *Fundamentals of human neuropsychology*. New York, NY: Worth Publishing.

Koponen, S., Taiminen, T., Portin, R., Himanen, L., Isoniemi, H., Heinonen, H., Hinkka, S. & Tenovuo, O. (2002). Axis I and II psychiatric disorders after traumatic brain injury: A 30-year follow-up study. *American Journal of Psychiatry, 159*(8), 1315-1321.

Krakowski, M.I., Convit, A., Jaeger, J., Lin, S., & Volavka, J. (1989). Inpatient violence: Trait and state. *Journal of Psychiatric Research, 23*(1), 57-64.

Kramer, T.H., Nelson, D.F., & Li, P.W. (1993). AIDS knowledge and risk behaviors among traumatic brain injury survivors with coexisting substance abuse. *Brain Injury, 7*(3), 209-217.

Krueger, R.F., Schmutte, P.S., Caspi, A., Moffitt, T.E., Campbell, K., & Silva, P.A. (1994). Personality traits are linked to crime among men and women: evidence from a birth cohort. *Journal of abnormal psychology, 103*(2), 328.

Krueger, R.F, Schutte, P.S., Caspi, A., Moffitt, T.E., Campbell, K., Silva, P.A., & Levin, H.S. (1999). Neurocognitive/behavioral outcomes in children and adults. In K.T. Ragnarsson (Ed.). *Report of the NIH consensus development conference on the rehabilitation of persons with traumatic brain injury* (p. 49-54).

Kwako, L. E., Glass, N., Campbell, J., Melvin, K. C., Barr, T., & Gill, J. M. (2011). Traumatic brain injury in intimate partner violence: A critical review of outcomes and mechanisms. *Trauma, Violence, & Abuse, 12*(3), 115-126.

Kwasnica, C.M., & Heinemann, A. (1994). Coping with traumatic brain injury: Representative case studies. *Archives of Physical Medicine & Rehabilitation, 75*(4), 384-389.

Langevin, R. (2006). Sexual offenses and traumatic brain injury. *Brain and Cognition, 60*(2), 206-207.

Langley, M.J., Lindsay, W.P., Lam, C.S., & Priddy, D.A. (1990). Programme development. *Brain Injury, 4*(1), 77-86.

Langlois, J. (2008). *Heads up: Brain injury in your practice. A tool kit for physicians.* Atlanta, GA: Centers for Disease Control and Prevention.

Langlois, J.A., Rutland-Brown, W., & Thomas, K.E. (2004). *Traumatic brain injury in the United States: Emergency department visits, hospitalizations, and deaths.* Atlanta, GA: US Department of Health and Human Services, Centers for Disease Control and Prevention, National Center for Injury Prevention and Control.

Langlois Orman, J.A., Kraus, J.F., Zaloshnja, E., & Miller, T. (2011). In J.M. Silver, T.W. McAllister, & S.C. Yudofsky (Eds.), *Textbook of Traumatic Brain Injury, Second Edition*, London, England: American Psychiatric Publishing Inc.

Lebow, M. A., & Chen, A. (2016). Overshadowed by the amygdala: The bed nucleus of the stria terminalis emerges as key to psychiatric disorders. *Molecular Psychiatry, 21*(4), 450-463. http://doi.org/10.1038/mp.2016.1

Leininger, B.E., Gramling, S.E., Farrell, A.D., Kreutzer, J.S., & Peck, E.A. (1990). Neuropsychological deficits in symptomatic minor head injury patients after concussion and mild concussion. *Journal of Neurology, Neurosurgery & Psychiatry, 53*(4), 293-296.

Leon-Carrion, J. & Ramos, F.J. (2003). Blows to the head during development can predispose to violent criminal behavior: Rehabilitation of consequences of head injury is a measure of crime prevention. *Brain Injury, 17*(3), 207-216.

Levin, H.S. (1999). Neurocognitive/behavioral outcomes in children and adults. In: Ragnarsson KT, editor. *Report of the NIH consensus development conference on the rehabilitation of persons with traumatic brain injury* (p. 49-54). Washington (DC): Department of Health and Human Services (US), Public Health Service, National Institutes of Health.

Levin, H.S. (1990). Predicting the neurobehavioral sequelae of closed head injury. In R.L.I. Wood (Ed.), *Neuro-behavioral Sequelae of Traumatic Brain Injury*, London, Burgess Science Press. 89-109.

Levin, H., Brown, S., Song, J., McCauley, S., Boake, C., Contant, C., Goodman, H., & Kotria, K. (2001). Depression and post-traumatic stress disorder at three months after mild to moderate traumatic brain injury. *Journal of Clinical and Experimental Neuropsychology, 23*(6), 754-769.

Levin, H.S., & Grossman, R.G. (1978). Behavioral sequelae of closed head injury: a quantitative study. *Archives of Neurology, 35*(11), 720.

Levin, H.S., Grossman, R.G., & Rose, J.E. (1979). Long-term neuropsychological outcome of closed head injury. *Journal of Neurosurgery, 50*(4), 412-422.

Levy, M.L., Ozgur, B.M., Berry, C., Aryan, H.E., & Apuzzo, M.L. (2004). Analysis and evolution of head injury in football. *Neurosurgery, 55*(3), 649-655.

Lew, H.L. (2005). Rehabilitation needs of an increasing population of patients: Traumatic brain injury, poly-trauma, and blast-related injuries. *Journal of Rehabilitation Research & Development. 42*(4), xiii-xvi.

Lewis, D.O., Pincus, J.H., Bard, B., Richardson. E., Prichep, L.S., Feldman, M., & Yeager, C. (1988). Neuropsychiatric, psychoeducational and family characteristics of 14 juveniles condemned to death in the USA. *The American Journal of Psychiatry, 145*(5), 584-589.

Lewis, D.O., Pincus, J.H., Feldman, M., Jackson, L., & Bard, B. (1986). Psychiatric, neurological, and psycho-educational characteristics of 15 death row inmates in the United States. *American Journal of Psychiatry, 143*(7), 838-845.

Li, L., Ford, J.A., & Moore, D. (2000). An exploratory study of violence, substance abuse, disability, and gender. *Social Behavior & Personality, 28*(1), 61-71.

Mackelprang, J.L., Bombardier, C.H., Fann, J.R., Temkin, N.R., Barber, J.K., & Dikmen, S.S. (2014). Rates and predictors of suicidal ideation during the first year after traumatic brain injury. *American Journal of Public Health, 104*(7), e100-e107.

Mackelprang, J.L., Harpin, S.B., Grubenhoff, J.A., & Rivara, F.P. (2014). Adverse outcomes among homeless adolescents and young adults who report a history of traumatic brain injury. *American Journal of Public Health, 104*(10), 1986-1992.

Malaspina, D., Harlap, S., Fennig, S., Heiman, D., Nahon, D., Feldman, D., & Susser, E. S. (2001). Advancing paternal age and the risk of schizophrenia. *Archives of General Psychiatry, 58*(4), 361-367.

Malaspina, D., Goetz, R.R., Friedman, J.H., Kaufmann, C.A., Faraone, S.V., Tsuang, M., Cloninger, C.R., Nurnberger Jr, J.I., & Blehar, M.C. (2001). Traumatic brain injury and schizophrenia in members of schizophrenia and bipolar disorder pedigrees. *American Journal of Psychiatry, 158*(3), 440-446.

Malia, K., Powell, G., & Torode, S. (1995). Personality and psychosocial function after brain injury. *Brain Injury, 9*(7), 697-712.

Marge, K. (2003). Introduction to violence and disability. In: Marge K, editor. A call to action: Ending crimes of violence against children and adults with disabilities, a report to the nation (p. 1-16). Syracuse: State University of New York, Upstate Medical University.

Marsh, N.V., & Knight, R.G. (1991). Relationship between cognitive deficits and social skill after head injury. *Neuropsychology, 5*(2), 107-117.

Marsh, N.V., & Martinovich, W.M. (2006). Executive dysfunction and domestic violence. *Brain Injury, 20*(1), 61-66.

Martini, D. N., Sabin, M. J., DePesa, S. A., Leal, E. W., Negrete, T. N., Sosnoff, J. J., & Broglio, S. P. (2011). The chronic effects of concussion on gait. *Archives of Physical Medicine and Rehabilitation, 92*(4), 585-589.

Maruschak, L.M. & Beck, A.J. (2001). *Medical problems of inmates, 1997*. Department of Justice (US), Office of Justice Programs, Bureau of Justice Statistics. (online). Available from URL: http://bjs.gov/content/pub/pdf/mpi97.pdf

Mateer, C.A. & Mapou, R.I. (1996). Understanding, evaluating and managing attention disorders following traumatic brain injury. *Journal of Head Trauma Rehabilitation, 11,* 1-16.

Max, J.E., Robertson, B.A.M., & Lansing, A.E. (2001). The phenomenology of personality change due to traumatic brain injury in children and adolescents. *The Journal of Neuropsychiatry and Clinical Neurosciences, 13*(2), 161-170.

McAllister, T.W. (2011). Mild brain injury. In J.M. Silver, T.W. McAllister, & S.C. Yudofsky (Eds.), *Textbook of Traumatic Brain Injury*, Second Edition. (pp. 239-264). London, England: American Psychiatric Publishing Inc.

McCrea, M.A. (2008). *Mild traumatic brain injury and postconcussion syndrome*. New York, NY: Oxford University Press.

McCrea, M., Prichep, L., Powell, M.R., Chabot, R., & Barr, W.B. (2010). Acute Effects and Recovery After Sport-Related Concussion: A Neurocognitive and Quantitative Brain Electrical Activity Study. *The Journal of head trauma rehabilitation, 25*(4), 283-292.

McGuire, L.M., Burright, R.G., Williams, R., & Donovick, P.J. (1998). Prevalence of traumatic brain injury in psychiatric and non-psychiatric subjects. *Brain Injury, 12*(3), 207-214.

McKee, A. C., Cantu, R. C., Nowinski, C. J., Hedley-Whyte, E. T., Gavett, B. E., Budson, A. E., ... & Stern, R. A. (2009). Chronic traumatic encephalopathy in athletes: progressive tauopathy after repetitive head injury. *Journal of Neuropathology & Experimental Neurology, 68*(7), 709-735.

McKinlay, A., Grace, R.C., Horwood, L.J., Fergusson, D.M., Ridder, E.M., & MacFarlane, M.R (2008). Prevalence of traumatic brain injury among children, adolescents and young adults: prospective evidence from a birth cohort. *Brain Injury, 22*(2), 175-181.

Meaney, D. F., & Smith, D. H. (2011). Biomechanics of concussion. *Clinics in Sports Medicine, 30*(1), 19-31.

Meek, P.S., Clark, H.W., & Solana, V.L. (1989). Neurocognitive impairment: The unrecognized component of dual diagnosis in substance abuse treatment. *Journal of Psychoactive Drugs, 21*(2), 153-160.

Merbitz, C., Jain, S., Good, G.L., & Jain, A. (1995). Reported head injury and disciplinary rule infractions in prison. *Journal of Offender Rehabilitation, 22*(3-4), 11-19.

Miller, E. (2002). Brain injury as a contributory factor in offending. In J. Glickson (Ed.), *The neurobiology of criminal behavior* (pp. 137-153). Norwell, MA: Kluwer Academic Publishers.

Miller, E. (1999). Head injury and offending. *The Journal of Forensic Psychiatry, 10*(1), 157-166.

Miller, L. (1992). Neuropsychology, personality, and substance abuse in the head injury case: Clinical and forensic issues. *International Journal of Law and Psychiatry, 15*(3), 303-316.

Miller, L. J., & Donders, J. (2001). Subjective symptomatology after traumatic head injury. *Brain Injury, 15*(4), 297-304.

Misic-Pavkov, G., Novovic, Z., Bozic, K., Kolundzija, K., Kovacevic, S.I., Drakip, D., Lukic, T., & Jelkić, M. (2012). Forensic aspect of late subjective complaints after traumatic brain injury. *European Review for Medical and Pharmacological Sciences, 16*(13), 1806-1813.

Mobbs, D., Lau, H. C., Jones, O. D., & Frith, C. D. (2007). Law, responsibility, and the brain. *PLoS Biology, 5*(4), e103.

Molloy, C., Conroy, R. M., Cotter, D. R., & Cannon, M. (2011). Is traumatic brain injury a risk factor for schizophrenia? A meta-analysis of case-controlled population-based studies. *Schizophrenia Bulletin, 37*(6), 1104-1110. http://doi.org/10.1093/schbul/sbr091

Mooney, G., & Speed, J. (2001). The association between mild traumatic brain injury and psychiatric conditions. *Brain Injury, 15*(10), 865-877.

Morrell, R.F., Merbitz, C.T., Jain, S., & Jain, S. (1998). Traumatic brain injury in prisoners. *Journal of Offender Rehabilitation, 27*(3-4), 1-8.

Morse, P.A. & Montgomery, C.E. (1992). Neuropsychological evaluation of traumatic brain injury. In R.F. White (Ed.), *Clinical syndromes in adult neuropsychology. The practitioner's handbook.* Elsevier Science Publishers. 85-176.

Murray, G.D., Teasdale, G.M., Braakman, R., Cohadon, F., Dearden, M., Iannotti, F., Karimi, A., Lapierre, F., Maas, A., Ohman, J., & Persson, L. (1999). The European brain injury consortium survey of head injuries. *Acta Neurochirurgica, 141*(3), 223-236.

Nampiaparampil, D.E. (2008). Prevalence of chronic pain after traumatic brain injury: A systematic review. *Journal of the American Medical Association, 300*(6), 711-719.

National Center for Injury Prevention and Control (US). (2003). Report to Congress on mild traumatic brain injury in the United States: Steps to prevent a serious public health problem. Centers for Disease Control and Prevention.

National Institute for Neurological Disorders and Stroke. (2012). Retrieved from http://www.ninds.nih.gov/disorders/tbi/detail_tbi.htm#193613218

National Institutes of Health Consensus Development Panel on Rehabilitation of Persons with Traumatic Brain injury: Rehabilitation of persons with traumatic brain injury. (1999). *Journal of the American Medical Association, 282*, 974-983.

Neal, M., Wilson, J., Hsu, W., & Powers, A. (2012). Concussions: What a neurosurgeon should know about current scientific evidence and management strategies. *Surgical Neurology International, 3*, 16.

Novack, T. A., Roth, D. L., & Boll, T. J. (1988). Treatment alternatives following mild head injury. *Rehabilitation Counseling Bulletin, 31*(4), 313-324.

O'Brien, S.D. & Ferguson, K. (2015). Traumatic brain injury and the law: Introduction. *UMKC Law Review, 84*, 287-575.

Oddy, M., Moir, J.F., Fortescue, D., & Chadwick, S. (2012). The prevalence of traumatic brain injury in the homeless community in a UK city. *Brain Injury, 26*(9), 1058-1064.

Okura, Y., Urban, L.H., Mahoney, D.W., Jacobsen, S.J., & Rodeheffer, R.J. (2004). Agreement between self-reported questionnaires and medical record data was substantial for diabetes, hypertension, myocardial infarction and stroke but not for heart failure. *Journal of Clinical Epidemiology, 57*(10), 1096-1103.

Paniak, C., Toller-Lobe, G., Durand, A., & Nagy, J. (1998). A randomized trial of two treatments for mild traumatic brain injury. *Brain Injury, 12*(12), 1011-1023.

O'Keeffe, F.M., Dockree, P.M., Moloney, P., Carton, S., & Robertson, I.H. (2007). Characterising error-awareness of attentional lapses and inhibitory control failures in patients with traumatic brain injury. *Experimental Brain Research, 180*(1), 59-67.

Perkes, I., Shofield, P.W., Butler, T., & Hollis, S.J. (2011). Traumatic brain injury rates and sequelae: A comparison of prisoners with a matched community sample in Australia. *Brain Injury, 25*(2), 131-141.

Perron, B.E. & Howard, M.O. (2008). Prevalence and correlates of traumatic brain injury among delinquent youths. *Criminal Behavior and Mental Health, 18*(4), 43-255.

Picard, M., Scarisbrick, D., & Paluck, R. (1991). HELPS TBI screening tool. International Center for the Disabled, TBI-NET, *US Department of Education, Rehabilitation Services Administration.*

Piccolino, A.L., & Solberg, K.B. (2014). The impact of traumatic brain injury on prison health services and offender management. *Journal of Correctional Health Care, 20*(3), 203-212.

Prigatano, G.P. (1991). Disturbances of self-awareness of deficit after traumatic brain injury. In G.P. Prigatano & D.L. Schacter (Eds.), *Awareness of deficit after brain injury: Clinical and theoretical issues.* New York: Oxford University Press, pp. 116-126.

Prigatano, G.P. (1992). Personality disturbances associated with traumatic brain injury. *Journal of Consulting and Clinical Psychology, 60*(3), 360-368.

Prigatano, G. P., & Fordyce, D. J. (1986). Cognitive dysfunction and psychosocial adjustment after brain injury. *Neuropsychological Rehabilitation After Brain Injury, 47*, 1-17.

Prins, H. A. (2016). *Offenders, deviants or patients?: An introduction to clinical criminology* (Fifth ed.). London/New York, Routledge: Taylor & Francis Group.

Raine, A., Buchsbaum, M.S., Stanley, J., Lottenberg, S., Abel, L., & Stoddard, J. (1994). Selective reductions in prefrontal glucose metabolism in murderers. *Biological Psychiatry, 36*(6), 365-373.

Raji, C. A., Willeumier, K., Taylor, D., Tarzwell, R., Newberg, A., Henderson, T. A., & Amen, D. G. (2015). Functional neuroimaging with default mode network regions distinguishes PTSD from TBI in a military veteran population. *Brain Imaging and Behavior, 9*(3), 527-534.

Rao, V., Rosenberg, P., Bertrand, M., Salehinia, S., Spiro, J., Vaishnavi, S., Rastogi, P., Noll, K., Schretlen, D.J., Brandt, J., & Cornwell, E. (2009). Aggression after traumatic brain injury: prevalence and correlates. *The Journal of neuropsychiatry and clinical neurosciences, 21*(4),420-429.

Rapoport, M., McCullagh, S., Streiner, D., & Feinstein, A. (2003). The clinical significance of major depression following mild traumatic brain injury. *Psychosomatics, 44*(1), 31-37.

Rapp, P. E., Rosenberg, B. M., Keyser, D. O., Nathan, D., Toruno, K. M., Cellucci, C. J., ... & Bashore, T. R. (2013). Patient characterization protocols for psychophysiological studies of traumatic brain injury and post-TBI psychiatric disorders. *Frontiers in Neurology, 4,* 91.

Reeves, R.R., & Laizer, J.T. (2012). Traumatic brain injury and suicide. *Journal of Psychosocial Nursing, 50*(3), 32-38.

Reichard, A.A., Langlois, J.A., Sample, P.L., Wald, M.M., & Pickelsimer, E.E. (2007). Violence, abuse, and neglect among people with traumatic brain injuries. *Journal of Head Trauma Rehabilitation, 12*(6), 390-402.

Reid, J. A., Haskell, R. A., Dillahunt-Aspillaga, C., & Thor, J. A. (2013). Contemporary review of empirical and clinical studies of trauma bonding in violent or exploitative relationships. *International Journal of Psychology Research, 8*(1), 37-73. Retrieved from http://search.proquest.com/docview/1625577532?accountid=35803

Rimel, R.W., Giordani, B., Barth, J.T., & Jane, J.A. (1982). Moderate head injury: Completing the clinical spectrum of brain trauma. *Neurosurgery, 11*(3), 344-351.

Rockhill, C.M., Fann, J.R., Fan, M.Y., Hollingworth, W., & Katon, J. (2010). Healthcare costs associated with mild traumatic brain injury and psychological distress in children and adolescents. *Brain Injury, 42*(9), 1051-1060.

Roebuck-Spencer, T. & Sherer, M. (2008). Moderate and severe traumatic brain injury. In J.E. Morgan & J.H. Ricker (Eds.), *Textbook of clinical neuropsychology* (pp. 411-439). New York: Taylor & Francis.

Rosenbaum, A., Hoge, S.K., Adelman, S.A., Warnken, W.J., Fletcher, K.E., & Kane, R.L. (1994). Head injury in partner-abusive men. *Journal of consulting and clinical psychology, 62*(6), 1187.

Rosenbaum, I., & Hoge, H.K. (1989). Head injury and marital aggression. *American Journal of Psychiatry, 146*(8), 1048-1051.

Rosenthal, M., Christensen, B. K., & Ross, T. P. (1998). Depression following traumatic brain injury. *Archives of Physical Medicine and Rehabilitation, 79*(1), 90-103.

Rushworth, N. (2008). Brain Injury Australia: Submission to the Australian Government's National Mental Health and Disability Employment Strategy.

Rushworth, N. (2011). Out of sight, out of mind: People with an acquired brain injury and the criminal justice system. Brain Injury Australia.

Russell, W.R. (1932). Cerebral involvement in head injury: A study based on the examination of two hundred cases. *Brain, 55,* 549-603.

Salazar, A.M., Jabbari, B., Vance, S.C., Grafman, J., Amin, D., & Dillon, J.D. (1985). Epilepsy after penetrating head injury: A report of the Vietnam Head Injury Study. *Neurology, 35*(10), 1406-1414.

Salcido, R., & Costich, J.F. (1992). Recurrent traumatic brain injury. *Brain Injury, 6*(3), 293-298.

Salinsky, M., Parko, K., Rutecki, P., Boudreau, E., & Storzbach, D. (2016). Attributing seizures to TBI: Validation of a brief patient questionnaire. *Epilepsy & Behavior, 57,* 141-144.

Sarapata, M., Herrman, D., Johnson, T., & Aycock, R. (1998). The role of head injury in cognitive functioning, emotional adjustment and criminal behavior. *Brain Injury, 12*(10), 821-842.

Saunders, R.L. & Harbaugh, R.E. (1984). The second impact in catastrophic contact-sports head trauma. *Journal of the American Medical Association, 252*(4), 538-539.

Savitsky, L., Illingworth, M., & DuLaney, M. (2009). Civilian social work: Serving the military and veteran populations. *Social Work, 54*(4), 327-339.

Schiehser, D. M., Delano-Wood, L., Jak, A. J., Hanson, K. L., Sorg, S. F., Orff, H., & Clark, A. L. (2016). Predictors of cognitive and physical fatigue in post-acute mild–moderate traumatic brain injury. *Neuropsychological Rehabilitation*, 1-16.

Schneider, M., Schneider, H. J., & Stalla, G. K. (2005). Anterior pituitary hormone abnormalities following traumatic brain injury. *Journal of Neurotrauma, 22*(9), 937-946.

Schofield, P., Butler, T., Hollis, S., & D'Este, C. (2011). Are prisoners reliable survey respondents? A validation of self-reported traumatic brain injury (TBI) against hospital medical records. *Brain Injury, 25*(1), 74-82.

Schofield, P. W., Butler, T. G., Hollis, S. J., Smith, N. E., Lee, S. J., & Kelso, W. M. (2006a). Neuropsychiatric correlates of traumatic brain injury (TBI) among Australian prisoner entrants. *Brain Injury, 20*(13-14), 1409-1418.

Schofield, P. W., Butler, T. G., Hollis, S. J., Smith, N. E., Lee, S. J., & Kelso, W. M. (2006b). Traumatic brain injury among Australian prisoners: Rates, recurrence and sequelae. *Brain Injury, 20*(5), 499-506.

Schofield, P.W., Malacova, E., Preen, D.B., D'Este, C. Tate, R., Reekie, J., Wand, H., & Butler, T. (2015). Does traumatic brain injury lead to criminality? A whole-population retrospective cohort study using linked data. *PLoS One, 10*(7), e0132558.

Seel, R.T., & Kreutzer, J.S. (2003). Depression assessment after traumatic brain injury: an empirically based classification method. *Archives of Physical Medicine and Rehabilitation, 84*(11), 1621-1628.

Sentencing Commission (US). (2014). *Guidelines Manual*. Online. Available from URL: http://www.ussc.gov/guidelines-manual/2014/2014-ussc-guidelines-manual

Shamay-Tsoory, S.G., Tomer, R., Berger, B.D., & Aharon-Peretz, J. (2003). Characterization of empathy deficits following prefrontal brain damage: The role of the right ventromedial prefrontal cortex. *Journal of Cognitive Neuroscience, 15*(3), 324-337.

Shiroma, E.J., Ferguson, P.L., & Pickelsimer, E.E. (2010a). Prevalence of traumatic brain injury in an offender population: A meta-analysis. *Journal of Correctional Health Care, 16*(2), 147-159.

Shiroma, E. J., Ferguson, P. L., & Pickelsimer, E. E. (2012). Prevalence of traumatic brain injury in an offender population: A meta-analysis. *The Journal of Head Trauma Rehabilitation, 27*(3), E1-E10.

Shiroma, E.J., Pickelsimer, E.E., Ferguson, P.L., Gebregziabher, M., Lattimore, P.K., Nicholas, J.S., Dukes, T., & Hunt, K.J. (2010b). Association of medically attended traumatic brain injury and in-prison behavioral infractions: A statewide longitudinal study. *Journal of Correctional Health Care, 16*(4), 273-286.

Silver, J.M., Caton, C.L.M., Shrout, P.E., & Dominguez, B. (1993, May). Traumatic brain injury and schizophrenia. In 1993 Annual Meeting New Research Program and Abstracts. Washington, DC, American Psychiatric Association.

Silver, J.M., Kramer, R., Greenwald, S., & Weissman, M. (2001). The association between head injuries and psychiatric disorders: Findings from the New Haven NIMH Epidemiological Catchment Area Study. *Brain Injury, 15*(11), 935-945.

Silver, J. M., McAllister, T. W., & Arciniegas, D. B. (2009). Depression and cognitive complaints following mild traumatic brain injury. *American Journal of Psychiatry, 166*(6), 653-661.

Silver, J.M., McAllister, T.W., & Yudofsky, S.C. (2011). *Textbook of traumatic brain injury.* London, England, American Psychiatric Publishing Inc.

Silver, J. M., & Yudofsky, S. (1985). Propranolol for aggression: Literature review and clinical guidelines. *International Drug Therapy Newsletter, 20,* 9-12.

Simpson, G., & Tate, R. (2002). Suicidality after traumatic brain injury: Demographic, injury and c l i n i c a l correlates. *Psychological Medicine, 32*(4), 687-697.

Simpson, J.M., & Tate, R. (2002). Suicidality after traumatic brain injury: Demographic, injury, and clinical correlates. *Psychological Medicine, 32,* 687-697.

Slaughter, B., Fann, J.R., & Ehde, D. (2003). Traumatic brain injury in a county jail population: Relevance, neuropsychological functioning and psychiatric disorders. *Brain Injury, 17*(9), 731-741.

Sliwinski, M., Gordon, W.A., & Bogdany, J. (1998). The Beck Depression Inventory: Is it a suitable measure of depression for individuals with traumatic brain injury? *Journal of Head Trauma Rehabilitation, 13*(4), 40-46.

Sogomonyan, F., & Cooper, J.L. (2010). Trauma faced by children of military families: What every policymaker should know. *National Center for Children in Poverty.* Retrieved from http://hdl.handle.net/10022//AC:P:8857

Spikman, J.M., Deelman, B.G., & van Zomeren, A.H. (2000). Executive functioning, attention, and frontal lesions in patients with chronic CHI. *Journal of Clinical and Experimental Neuropsychology, 22*(3), 325-338.

Stambrook, M., Moore, A.D., Peers, L.C., Deviaene, C., & Hawryluk, G.A. (1990). Effects of mild, moderate and severe closed head injury on long-term vocational status. *Brain Injury, 4*(2), 183-190.

Stein, S.C. (1996). Classification of head injury. In R.K. Narayn, J.E. Wilberger, & J.T. Povlishock (Eds.), *Neurotrauma.* Philadelphia: W.B. Saunders. p. 43.

St Ivany, A., & Schminkey, D. (2016). Intimate partner violence and traumatic brain injury. *Family and Community Health*, 39(2), 129. Retrieved from http://search.proquest.com/docview/1778078970?accountid=35803

Streeter, C., Van Reekum, R., Shorr, R., & Bachman, D. (1995) Prior head injury in male veterans with borderline personality disorder. *Journal of Nervous and Mental Disorders, 183*(9), 577-581.

Stuss, D. T., & Gow, C. A. (1992). "Frontal dysfunction" after traumatic brain injury. *Cognitive and Behavioral Neurology, 5*(4), 272-282.

Stuss, D. T., Gow, C. A., & Hetherington, C. R. (1992). "No longer Gage": Frontal lobe dysfunction and emotional changes. *Journal of Consulting and Clinical Psychology, 60*(3), 349-359.

Subrahmanyam, B.V., & Agrawal, A. (2012). Medico-legal issues in patients of traumatic brain: Indian perspective. *The Indian Journal of Neurotrauma, 9*(2), 117-122.

Sweet, J.J., Goldman, D.J., Breting, G., & Leslie, M. (2013). Traumatic brain injury: Guidance in a forensic context from outcome, dose–response, and response bias research. *Behavioral Sciences & the Law, 31*(6), 756-778.

Szczepanski, S. M., & Knight, R. T. (2014). Insights into human behavior from lesions to the prefrontal cortex. *Neuron, 83*(5), 1002-1018. http://doi.org/10.1016/j.neuron.2014.08.011

Tanielan, T. & Jaycox, L.H. (2008). Invisible wounds of war: Psychological and cognitive injuries, their consequences, and services to assist recovery. RAND Corporation, Santa Monica, CA.

Tanielian, T., Jaycox, L.H., Schell, T.L. Marshall, G. M., Burnam, M.A., Eibner, C., Karney, B. R.,Meredith, L.S., Ringel, J.S., & Vaiana, M.E. (2008). Invisible wounds: Mental health and cognitive care needs of America's returning Veterans. RAND Corporation. Retrieved from http://www.rand.org/pubs/research_briefs/RB9336.html

Taousides, T., Cantor, J.B., & Gordon, W.A. (2011). Suicidal ideation following traumatic brain injury: Prevalence rates and correlates in adults living in the community. *Journal of Head Trauma Rehabilitation, 26*(4), 265-275.

Tate, R., Simpson, G., Flanagan, S., & Coffey, M. (1997). Completed suicide after traumatic brain injury. *Journal of Head Trauma Rehabilitation, 12*(6), 16-28.

Teasdale, G., & Jennett, B. (1974). Assessment of coma and impaired consciousness, *The Lancet, 304*(7872), 81-84.

Teasdale, G., & Jennett, B. (1976). Assessment and prognosis of coma after head injury. *Acta Neurocher, 34*(1-4), 45-55.

Teasdale, G. & Jennett, B. (1978). Assessment of coma and severity of brain damage. *The Journal of the American Society of Anesthesiologists, 49*(3), 225-225.

Teasdale, G., Maas, A., Lecky, F., Manley, G., Stocchetti, N., & Murray, G. (2014). The Glasgow Coma Scale at 40 years: Standing the test of time. *The Lancet Neurology, 13*(8), 844-854.

Teasdale, T.W., & Engberg, A.W. (2001). Suicide after traumatic brain injury: A population study. *Journal of Neurology, Neurosurgery & Psychiatry, 71*(4), 436-440.

Templer, D.I., Kasiraj, J., Trent, N., Trent, A., Hughey, B., Keller, W., Orling, R., & Thomas-Dobson, S. (1992). Exploration of head injury without medical attention. *Perceptual and Motor Skills, 75*, 195-202.

Thornton, K. E., & Carmody, D. P. (2009). Traumatic brain injury rehabilitation: QEEG biofeedback treatment protocols. *Applied psychophysiology and biofeedback, 34*(1), 59-68.

Thurman, D.J., Alverson, C., Dunn, K.A., Guerrero, J., & Sniezek, J.E. (1999). Traumatic brain injury in the United States: a public health perspective. *The Journal of Head Trauma Rehabilitation, 14*(6), 602-615.

Thurman, D.J., Coronado, V., & Selassie, A. (2007). The epidemiology of TBI: Implications for public health. In N.D. Zasler, D.I. Katz, & R.D. Zafonte (Eds.), *Brain injury medicine: Principles and practice* (p. 45-56). New York, NY: Demos Medical.

Timonen, M., Miettunen, J., Hakko, H., Zitting, P., Veijola, J., vonWendt, L., & Räsänen, P. (2002). The association of preceding traumatic brain injury with mental disorders, alcoholism and criminality: The Northern Finland 1966 birth cohort study. *Psychiatry Research, 113*(3), 217-226.

Topolovec-Vranic, J., Ennis, N., Colantonio, A., Cusimano, M.D., Hwang, S.W., Kontos, P. Ouchterlony, D., & Stergiopoulos, V. (2012). Traumatic brain injury among people who are homeless: A systematic review. *BMC Public Health, 12*(1), 1059.

Troncoso, J.C. & Pletnikova, O. (2010). Traumatic brain injuries and dural hemorrhages. In J. C. Troncoso, A. Rubio, & D. R. Fowler (Authors), *Essential forensic neuropathology* (pp. 71-81). Baltimore, MD: Wolters Kluwer Health/Lippincott Williams & Wilkins.

Tsaousides, T., Cantor, J.B., & Gordon, W.A. (2011). Suicidal ideation following traumatic brain injury: prevalence rates and correlates in adults living in the community. *The Journal of Head Trauma Rehabilitation, 26*(4), 265-275.

Turkstr, L., Jones, D., & Toler, H.L. (2003). Brain injury and violent crime. *Brain Injury, 17*(1), 39-47.

Van Boven, R.W., Harrington, G.S., Hackney, D.B., Ebel, A., Gauger, G., Bremner, J.D., D'Esposito, M., Detre, J.A., Haacke, E.M., Jack Jr, C.R., & Jagust, W.J. (2009). Advances in neuroimaging of traumatic brain injury and post-traumatic stress disorder. *Journal of Rehabilitation Research & Development, 46*(6), 717-757.

Van Reekum, R., Bolago, I., Finlayson, M.A.J., Garner, S., & Links, P.S. (1996). Psychiatric disorders after traumatic brain injury. *Brain Injury, 10*(5), 319-328.

Van Reekum, R., Cohen, B.A., & Wong, J. (2000). Can traumatic brain injury cause psychiatric disorder? *Journal of Neuropsychiatry and Clinical Neuroscience, 12*(3), 316-327.

Van Reekum, R., Conway, C., Gansler, D., White, R., & Bachman, D. (1993). Neurobehavioral study of borderline personality disorder. *Journal of Psychiatry and Neuroscience, 18*(3), 121-129.

Vastag, B. (2002). Football brain injuries draw increased scrutiny. *Journal of American Medical Association, 287*(4), 437-439.

Vaughn, M.G., Salas-Wright, C.P., DeLisi, M., & Perron, B. (2014). Correlates of traumatic brain injury among juvenile offenders: A multi-site study. *Criminal Behaviour and Mental Health, 24*(3), 188-203.

Ventura, T., Harrison-Felix, C., Carlson, N., DiGuiseppi, C., Gabella, B., Brown, A., DeVivo, M., & Whiteneck, G. (2010). Mortality after discharge from acute care hospitalization with traumatic brain injury: a population-based study. *Archives of Physical Medicine and Rehabilitation, 91*(1), 20-29.

Wald, M.M., Helgeson, S.R., & Langlois, J.A. (2008). Traumatic brain injury among prisoners. *Brain Injury Professional Magazine.* Online. Available from URL: http://www.brainline.org/content/2008/11/traumatic-brain-injury-among-prisoners_pageall.html

Walker, K. R, & Tesco, G. (2013). Molecular mechanisms of cognitive dysfunction following traumatic brain injury. *Frontiers in Aging Neuroscience, 5,* 29.

Walker, R., Hiller, M., Staton, M., & Leukefield, C.G. (2003). Head injury among drug abusers: An indicator of co-occurring problems. *Journal of Psychoactive Drugs, 35*(3), 343-353.

Washington (DC): Department of Health and Human Services (US), Public Health Service, National Institutes of Health. (1994). Personality traits are linked to crime among men and women: Evidence from a birth cohort. *Journal of Abnormal Psychology, 103,* 328-338.

Williams, W.H., Cordan, G., Mewse, A.J., Tonks, J., & Burgess, C.N.W. (2010a). Self-reported traumatic brain injury in male young offenders: A risk factor for re-offending, poor mental health and violence? *Neuropsychological Rehabilitation, 20(*6), 801-812.

Williams, W.H., Mewse, A.J., Tonks, J., Mills, S., Burgess, C.N.W., & Cordan, G. (2010b). Traumatic brain injury in a prison population: Prevalence and risk for re-offending. *Brain Injury, 24*(10), 1184-1188.

Williams, W.H., Potter, S., & Ryland, H. (2010). Mild traumatic brain injury and postconcussion syndrome: A neuropsychological perspective. *Journal of Neurology, Neurosurgery and psychiatry, 81*(10), 1116-1122.

Wood, R.L., & Liossi, C. (2006). Neuropsychological and neurobehavioral correlates of aggression following traumatic brain injury. *The Journal of Neuropsychiatry and Clinical Neurosciences. 18*(3), 333-341.

Wood, R.L., & Thomas, R.H. (2013). Impulsive and episodic disorders of aggressive behaviour following traumatic brain injury. *Brain Injury, 27*(3), 253-261.

Wood, R.L., Williams, C., & Lewis, R. (2010). Role of alexithymia in suicide ideation after traumatic brain injury. *Journal of the International Neuropsychological Society, 16*(6), 1108-1114.

Yates, P.J., Williams, W.H., Harris, A., & Round, A. (2006). An epidemiological study of head injuries in a UK population attending an emergency department. *Journal of Neurology, Neurosurgery, and Psychiatry, 77*(5), 699-701.

Yeager, C.A., & Lewis, D.O. (2000). Mental illness, neuropsychologic deficits, child abuse, and violence. *Child & Adolescent Psychiatric Clinics of North America, 9*(4), 793-813.

Ylvisaker, M., Todis, B., Glang, A., Urbanczyk, B., Franklin, C., DePompei, R., Feeney, T., Maxwell, N.M., Pearson, S., & Tyler, J.S. (2001). Educating students with TBI: Themes and recommendations. *Journal of Head Trauma Rehabilitation, 16*(1), 76-93.

Young, M.H., Justice, J.V., & Erdberg, P. (2004). Assault in prison and assault in prison psychiatric treatment. *Journal of Forensic Science, 49*(1), 1-9.

Zaninotto, A. L., Vicentini, J. E., Fregni, F., Rodrigues, P. A., Botelho, C., de Lucia, M. C. S., & Paiva, W. S. (2016). Updates and current perspectives of psychiatric assessments after traumatic brain injury: A systematic review. *Frontiers in Psychiatry, 7,* 95. Retrieved from http://doi.org/10.3389/fpsyt.2016.00095

Zemper, E. D. (2003). Two-year prospective study of relative risk of a second cerebral concussion. *American Journal of Physical Medicine & Rehabilitation, 82*(9), 653-659.

Zielinski, R., Theroux-Fichera, S., Rayls, K., Tremont, G., & Mittenberg, W. (1995). The effects of alcohol on neuropsychological functioning following head injury. *Archives of Clinical Neuropsychology, 10*(4), 409.

SUBJECT INDEX

A

Abandonment 50, 63, 67, 130

Abstinence 346, 351, 357

Abusive Head Trauma (AHT) 299, 300-309, 310

Accidental Trauma 303, 304, 308

Actuarial Assessment 187, 191

Actus Reus (Criminal Act) 31

Addiction 45, 106-107, 155, 176, 178, 216, 234-236, 280, 288, 340-343, 346-350, 369, 390, 420, 432
  Addictions 10, 13, 324, 335, 337, 343, 396
  Addictive Disorders 275, 318, 321

Adjudicative Competence(s) 84, 86, 89

Adjudicative Incompetence 92

Adjudicative System 84

Adult Drug Court 369

Adult Protective Services (APS) 128

Adverse Childhood Effects (ACE) 151, 423-424, 430-431, 436-438

Aggression 23, 26-27, 36-38, 40-41, 58, 67, 78, 79, 80, 117, 131, 133, 147-148, 155, 158, 169, 186, 201, 212, 275, 280-281, 319, 326, 333, 383, 385, 393, 429, 430, 435-437, 439, 440, 443, 449-452, 456-458, 461, 465, 470, 472, 474
  Aggression Replacement Training (ART) 148

Agrammatic 120, 122

Alcohol Dependence 38,
156, 270, 328, 336, 342, 436
  Alcoholic 423

Alcohol-Related Birth Defects (ARBD) 161, 163-164

Alcohol Use Disorder (AUD) 74, 181, 344, 441

Alzheimer's Disease 100, 112, 116, 121, 125, 134, 136

American Academy of Neurology 123, 135

American Bar Association Commission on Law and Aging 131, 135

American Psychiatric Association (APA) 21-22, 25, 27, 47, 68, 90, 115, 117-122, 124, 128-128, 135, 139, 143, 247-248, 264, 269, 272, 278, 371-372, 374, 383, 443

Amnesia 95-96, 100, 102-103, 109-111, 180, 242-244, 250, 254, 260, 262-264, 266, 385, 442, 448, 453

Amphetamine 216-218, 225-227, 231-233, 235-236, 394

Amyotrophic Lateral Sclerosis (ALS) 15, 120, 203

Angel Dust (PCP) 223, 227, 240

Anosognosia 197

Antidepressant 337

Antipsychotic 198, 324, 338

Antisocial 50, 55, 58, 67, 72, 76, 146, 249, 262-63, 275, 290, 326, 348, 374, 382-383, 443, 545, 462
  Antisocial Behavior 23, 184-185, 290, 326, 347, 443
  Antisocial Cognition 290

Antisocial Personality

Disorder (APD) 50, 55,
58, 72, 249, 326, 443

Anxiety 22, 24-25, 29, 33, 37, 43, 47, 51-52, 59, 117, 119, 193, 196, 200, 208, 220, 228-230, 243- 244, 249, 262-263, 268-272, 275-278, 280, 282, 288, 319-320, 323, 325-326, 334, 336, 338, 359, 389, 408, 409, 411, 420, 424, 441, 446, 451

Apnea 303, 309

Asperger 21-22, 36-47, 181, 186, 269
  Asperger Syndrome 40-41

Asphyxiation 300

Assault 11, 27, 67, 147, 170, 190, 208, 228-229, 235-236, 288, 332, 383, 440, 442, 451, 474

Assessment of Capacity to Consent to Treatment (ACCT) 126, 139

Atkins v. Virginia (2002) 246

At-Risk Population 161, 319, 442, 455

Attachment 30, 40, 45, 52-53, 55, 61, 63, 72, 74-75, 77-80, 102, 105-108, 185, 258, 270, 277, 334, 432, 435
  Attachment Theory 77, 102, 105

Attention and Concentration Loss 300

Attention-Deficit Hyperactivity Disorder (ADHD) 22, 38, 55, 79, 85, 94, 108, 162, 165, 225-226, 261, 264, 272, 319, 324-326, 341, 342

Autism Spectrum Disorder (ASD) 6, 10-12, 14, 18, 21-48, , 85, 165, 180, 182, 212, 282, 433, 462

B

Balance Deficits 441

Bankruptcy 333, 463

Bath Salts Drugs 300

Behavioral Variant FTD 121

Benzodiazepine 228-229, 235, 236

Betting 317-318, 320, 322, 331-332

Biopsychosocial Model 54

Bipolar 52, 59, 208, 288, 328
  Bipolar Disorder (BD) 228

Birth Defects 161, 163, 176

Bizarre Delusion 300

Bona Fide Doubt Standard 83

Borderline Personality (BPD) 18, 49, 52, 60, 66-67, 71- 80, 150-151, 156, 326

Brain Damage 13, 106, 118, 160-161, 164, 169, 171, 176, 300, 305, 310-311, 446, 456, 471, 473
  Irreversible Brain Damage 300

Brain Injury 6, 10, 12, 16, 66, 101, 105-106, 109, 113, 116, 166, 249, 251, 257-258, 261, 263, 309-315, 362, 422, 439-448, 451, 453-475

Bullying 28,-29, 33, 41, 48, 57, 464

Burnout 151, 423

C

Cannabis 216-217, 219, 230-231, 234, 241, 381, 394, 453

Capacity to Consent to Treatment Instrument (CCTI) 126

Cardiovascular Disease 196, 288

Casino 317, 320, 322, 325, 330, 338, 347

Catatonia 244, 371

Centers for Disease Control and Prevention (CDC) 22, 114, 162, 163, 183, 300, 314, 423, 440, 447, 449, 452, 458

Cerebral Atrophy 52, 173, 269, 287, 288, 364, 371

Cerebral Edema/Damage 303

Chemical Dependency 65, 200, 204, 208, 353, 354, 362, 367

Chemical-Free Lifestyle 355

Chemical Testing 360

Child Abuse and Neglect 47, 302, 305-306, 309, 310, 312, 315, 329
    Childhood Abuse 38, 56, 67, 78, 103, 324, 377-378, 436
    Child Maltreatment 45, 47, 78, 205, 310, 316, 333, 435, 436

Child Development Community Policing Program (CD-CP) 428

Childhood Adversity 378, 423

Childhood Trauma 15, 102, 113, 156, 174, 378, 395, 435

Child Pornography 276

Child Support Court 52, 173, 269, 287-288, 364, 371

Child Support Worker 52, 173, 269, 287-288, 364, 371

Child Welfare Services 189

Chi-Squared Automatic Interaction Detection (CHAID) 187

Chorea 93, 194, 198, 206-212

Chronic Lying 318

Chronic Pain 451

Chronic Stress 167, 328, 423

Clinical Method 52, 173, 269, 287-288, 364, 371

Clinical Negligence 189, 371

Clinical Relevance 99

Cocaine 216-218, 224-225, 227-229, 233-235, 354, 373, 388, 397

Codeine 220, 239

Cognition 73, 92, 96, 108-109, 114, 118-121, 124, 127, 136, 183, 252, 290, 325, 380-381, 389, 396, 398, 450

Cognitive
    Cognitive and Personality Characteristics 410, 411
    Cognitive Behavioral Therapy (CBT) 60-61, 68, 147-148, 280, 291, 335, 380, 431-432
    Cognitive Deficits 300
    Cognitive Enhancement Therapy (CET) 380
    Cognitive Filters 300
    Cognitive Functioning 85
    Cognitive Impairment 409
    Cognitive Processing 417
    Cognitive Symptoms 119, 120, 122, 193, 302, 372, 375, 389, 449

Columbia Suicide Severity Rating Scale (C-SSRS) 201

Community-Based Intervention 300

Community Supervision 7, 8, 143, 188, 284, 285, 292, 353

Co-Morbid 22, 23, 27, 34, 43, 49, 51, 52, 58, 63-64, 71, 74, 76, 160, 165-168, 200, 242, 259, 268, 270, 272, 279, 281, 318, 320, 325-326, 328, 333, 335, 338, 346, 381-382, 399, 401, 461, 465
    Co-Morbidities 73, 146
    Co-Morbidity 441

Competency to Stand Trial (CST) 18, 82-88

Complex Hallucinations 300

Complex Trauma 150, 422, 424, 437-438

Compulsive Behavior 275-277
    Compulsive Ritual 277

Computerized Tomography (CT) 77, 123, 303, 305, 306, 399, 441

Conditions of Release 286, 287, 292

Conduct Disorder 165, 319

Confabulation 6, 15, 18, 93-113, 117, 167, 171, 174, 176-178, 180, 199, 211, 213-214, 259, 261, 263, 265, 385-386, 392, 395, 397, 404, 406, 407, 409, 413, 415, 417, 419-420, 453
    Forced confabulation 113

Conners' Continuous Performance Test–II (CPT–II) 255

Consumer Financial Protection Bureau 131

Controlled Substance(s) 220, 225, 228-229, 300

Conviction 220, 225, 228-229

Co-Occurring Disorder 71

Court-Ordered 30, 33-34, 171
    Court-Ordered Evaluation 30, 33-34, 171

Criminal Intent 208, 385

Criminal Justice System 18, 19, 20-21, 23, 49, 66, 73, 114, 131, 159, 168, 268, 330, 422, 426, 439, 452

Criminal Responsibility 300

Criminological Malingering 300

Crisis De-Escalation 300

Cybercrime 24

D

Date Rape Drug (GHB) 216-217, 228-229, 240

D.E.A.R. 173

Debt-Relief Counseling 335

Deception 11, 91, 93-94, 101, 253, 258-259, 264-265, 406

Decision-Making Impairment 300

Dehumanization 429, 436

Deliberate Interference 171, 247

Delinquent 30, 363, 419, 463, 300, 469

Delusional Memories 101

Delusions 70, 85, 101, 117, 119-120, 231, 244, 250, 371- 374, 376, 378, 383, 385-387, 394

Dementia 18, 110, 114-141, 181, 193-194, 197-198, 208, 242-243, 251, 254, 269, 272, 385, 403
    Dementia with Lewy Bodies (DLB) 118-120
    Mixed Dementia 123

Depression 29, 33, 43, 47, 52, 60, 64-65, 68, 118-121, 149, 151, 156, 167-168, 193, 199, 200-202, 205, 208, 211, 215, 220-222, 228, 243, 244, 254-265, 269, 272, 281, 288, 302, 319, 323, 325-326, 334, 338, 342, 347, 359, 376-377, 400, 413, 424, 441-443, 446, 451, 461, 470, 472

Designer Drugs 216, 233-234

Developmental Disability (DD) 161

Developmental Maturity 86, 169, 405

Developmental Stage 53

Diabetes 53-55, 78-80

Diagnostic and Statistical Manual of Mental Disorders (DSM) 15, 21-22, 35, 49, 50, 74, 75, 101, 105, 112, 115, 119, 121-122, 124, 135, 161, 181, 249, 262, 266, 268-269, 271-272, 275, 278, 280-281, 317-318, 321-323, 340, 342, 344-349, 352, 374, 400, 443
    DSM-5 15, 21, 22, 49, 50, 101, 115, 119, 121-122, 124, 135, 161, 181, 249, 269, 271-272, 275, 278, 318, 321-322, 342, 348, 374, 400, 443
    DSM-IV 15, 21, 35, 75, 115, 266, 268, 278, 317, 321-322, 342, 344-346, 348-349, 352

Diagnostic Criteria 21, 28,

49, 165, 251, 408, 412, 443

Dialectical Behavioral Therapy (DBT) 14, 16, 54, 60-61, 64, 66-67, 71, 77-78, 80, 147, 150-151, 155

Differential Processing 300

Digit Recognition Test (DRT) 254, 300

Disabilities 6, 11, 37, 39, 40, 43-47, 106, 110, 125, 140, 156, 164, 166, 176, 178-180, 435

Disorganized Speech 193, 231, 372, 374, 378

Dissimulation 259

Dissociation 51, 64, 102

Distortion of Memory 409

DLB 118- 120

Doctor Shopping 230

Domestic Violence 15, 167-168, 193, 204-206, 277, 329, 333, 334, 365, 371, 400, 440, 459, 467

Dopamine Hypothesis 376

Driving While Impaired Court 300

Drug Abuse 67, 142, 216, 224, 227, 232-233, 235, 237, 293, 295-296, 327-338, 349, 353, 355, 459, 465-368

Drug Court 356, 358. 360, 366-368

Drug Enforcement Administration (DEA) 217-218, 221, 227, 230-231

Drug-of-Abuse Testing 216, 218, 219

Drug of Abuse Warning Network (DAWN) 221, 223

Drug Use 154, 329

Dunn v. Johnson (1998) 171, 177, 300

Durham Rule 300

Dusky Standard 31, 300

Dusky v. United States (1960) 83, 88

Dynamic Deconstructive Psychotherapy (DDP) 60, 63, 64

Dynamic Factors 30, 33-34, 171

Dynamic Interaction 300

Dysarthia 300

Dysphagia 196

Dysregulation 53-54, 57, 60, 64, 67, 70, 73, 80, 150-151, 384, 441, 444

Dystonia 198

E

Early Onset 327, 381

Ecstasy (MDMA) 217, 223, 226-227, 233, 236, 240

Elder Abuse 129-131, 136-137, 139, 281

Elder Juustice Act (2002) 171

Electronic Monitoring 287

Emotional Dysregulation 53, 57, 60, 64, 67, 73, 150, 384

Emotional Intensity Disorder (EID) 62

Emotional Regulation 53, 57, 60, 64, 67, 73, 150, 384

Empathy 23, 43, 49, 51-52, 58, 63-64, 71, 74, 76, 160, 165-168, 200, 242, 259, 268, 270, 272, 279, 281, 318, 320, 325-326, 328, 333, 335, 338, 346, 381-382, 399, 401, 461, 465

Empirical Method 300

Environmental Factors 377

Environmental Stimuli 377

Epilepsy 23, 28, 37, 39, 41, 44, 47, 311, 444, 470

Episodic Memory 113, 137, 375

Evidence-Based Courts 356

Evidence-Based Practices (EBP) 142-144, 146, 153, 289

Excited Delirium 23, 43, 49, 51-52, 58, 63-64, 71, 74, 76, 160, 165-168, 200, 242, 259, 268, 270, 272, 279, 281, 318, 320, 325-326, 328, 333, 335, 338, 346, 381-382, 399, 401, 461, 465

Executive Functioning 96,

99-100, 105, 109, 118, 122, 129, 160, 165, 167, 171, 183, 193, 203, 270, 272, 307, 324, 325, 340, 375, 377, 395

Executive Functioning Deficits 325

Experiential Avoidance 300

Expert Testimony 8, 35

Extraversion 23, 43, 49, 51-52, 58, 63-64, 71, 74, 76, 160, 165-168, 200, 242, 259, 268, 270, 272, 279, 281, 318, 320, 325-326, 328, 333, 335, 338, 346, 381-382, 399, 401, 461, 465

Eyewitness Testimony 93, 96, 104, 404-405, 410-411, 413-414

F

Facial Dysmorphology 164, 180

Factitious Presentation 245

False Confession 94, 96, 101, 103, 105, 108-110, 169, 171, 386, 398, 404-405, 407, 411-413, 415-418, 420

False Memory 93, 95, 98, 100-101, 103-105, 109-111, 113, 171, 254, 259, 385- 386, 404-405, 408, 410, 413-414, 418, 453

False Negatives 300

False Positive 323

False Testimony 94, 103, 385

Familial Heritability 300

Family-Based Therapy 291

Family Dependency Treatment Court 300

Family-Focused Instrument (FCI-9) 300

Family Therapy 209, 380

Family Trauma 384

Feigned Dysfunction 291

Fentanyl 216-218, 220, 222-224, 236, 239

Fetal Alcohol Spectrum Disorder (FASD) 6, 9-10, 13-14, 16, 18, 85,

99-100, 110-111, 160-183, 433

Financial Capacity Instrument (FCI-9) 127

Financial Exploitation 130, 131

Financial Insecurity 300

First responders 427

Fitness Interview Test-Revised (FIT-R) 87

Flashbacks 249, 424

Flashbulb Memory 98

Flat Affect 371, 374, 380, 449

Food and Drug Administration (FDA) 118, 208, 217, 336-337, 379

Forced Choice Test and the Portland Digit Recognition Test (PDRT) 255

Forensic Risk Assessment 19, 184, 186, 189

Fragments of Memories 102

Frontotemporal Dementias (FTD) 120,-123, 132-135, 141

Functional Analytic Psychotherapy 276

Functionally Illiterate 287

G

Gamblers Anonymous (GA) 136, 175, 322, 335, 365, 458, 460-461, 466

Gambling Courts 300

Gambling Disorder 318, 321

Gas Chromatography/Mass Spectrometry (GC/MS) 219

Gender Identity Disorder (GID) 60

Gene Mutation 199

Genetic Information Non-discrimination Act (GINA) 195

Global Brain Dysfunction 199

Godinez v. Moran (1993) 83

Good Lives Model (GLM) 430

Gudjonsson Suggestibility Scale (GSS) 172, 408-410, 414

H

Hallucinations 120, 198, 227, 250, 373, 386

Harm Reduction 277, 282

Head Trauma 23, 43, 49, 51-52, 58, 63-64, 71, 74, 76, 160, 165-168, 200, 242, 259, 268, 270, 272, 279, 281, 318, 320, 325-326, 328, 333, 335, 338, 346, 381-382, 399, 401, 461, 465

Health Risk Behaviors 23, 43, 49-52, 58, 63-64, 71, 74, 76, 160, 165-168, 200, 242, 259, 268, 270, 272, 279, 281, 300, 318, 320, 325- 326, 328, 333, 335, 338, 346, 381-382, 399, 401, 461, 465

HELPS Screening Instrument 300

Heritable Vulnerability 300

Heroin 220, 239

High-Risk Factor 54

Historical Trauma 422-423, 438

Histrionic Personality Disorder 50

Hoarding 122, 268-283
Hoarding Disorder (HD) 13, 15, 193-210, 212, 214, 270-271

Home Confinement 23, 43, 49, 51-52, 58, 63-64, 71, 74, 76, 160, 165-168, 200, 242, 259, 268, 270, 272, 279, 281, 318, 320, 325-326, 328, 333, 335, 338, 346, 381-382, 399, 401, 461, 465

Homelessness 173, 329, 442

Honest Lying 300

Hopemont Capacity Assessment Interview (HCAI) 126

Hopkins Competency Assessment Test (HCAT) 126

Human Immunodeficiency

Syndrome (HIV) 124, 231, 288, 296, 464

Huntington Disease (HD) 13, 15, 193-210, 212, 214-215, 270-271
Huntington Disease Society of America 164, 413

Hydrocodone 217, 221, 239

Hyperactivity 55, 85, 94, 162, 164-165, 319, 326

Hyperarousal 424

Hypervigilance 424

Hypnotic Suggestibility 23, 43, 49-52, 58, 63-64, 71, 74, 76, 160, 165-168, 200, 242, 259, 268, 270, 272, 279, 281, 318, 320, 325-326, 328, 333, 335, 338, 346, 381-382, 399, 401, 461, 465

Hypothalamic-Pituitary-Adrenal Axis (HPA) 54

I

Idio-Motor Sugggestibility 300

Illicit Substance Abuse 300

Illness Management Recovery (IMR) 149

Improves Outcomes 424

Impulse Control Disorders 321

Informed Consent 300

Injury Impact 300

Innocence Project 11, 94, 111, 411, 417

Insanity Defense 32, 39, 42, 44
Insanity Defense Reform Act of 1984 32, 44

Insecure Attachment Pathology 300

Integrated Dual Disorders Training (IDDT) 147, 149

Intellectual Disability (ID) 36, 73, 161, 246

Intergenerational 423, 435

Intergenerational trauma 423

Internet Gambling 300

Interpersonal Interactions 300

Interrogation Techniques 300
Interrogative Suggestibility 407, 409
Interview Dynamics 300

Intimate Partner Violence 206, 441-442, 451

Intracranial Abnormalities 300

Invalidating Environment 300

invalidation 53-55, 78-80

Inventory of Legal Knowledge 87

Invisibility Disability 300

J

Jackson v. Indiana (1972) 87, 133

Jesness Inventory 86

Judicial Process 300

Juvenile Drug Court 300

Juvenile Huntington's Disease (JHD) 194, 202

Juvenile Offenders 30, 156, 245, 260, 293, 420, 452, 461, 474

L

Law Enforcement 7-8, 12, 24-25, 29, 35, 38, 94, 104, 112, 124, 131-134, 166, 172, 174, 183, 193-194, 200, 203, 206-207, 209, 219, 223, 225, 227, 229, 233, 286, 294, 315, 358-360, 374, 387, 410-413, 427-428

Leading Questions 300

Learning Disabilities 11, 40, 44, 166

Legal Rights 300

Lessard v. Schmidt (1972) 300

Levels of Service/Case Management Inventory (LS/CMI) 164, 413

Liquid Chromatography/ Tandem Mass Spectrometry (LC/MS/ MS) 219

Litigation Response Syndrome (LRS) 244

Long Response Latency 164, 413

Low Social-Economic Status 164, 413

M

MacArthur Competence Assessment Tool—Criminal Adjudication (MacCAT-CA) 87

Magical Thinking 375

Magnetic Resonance Imaging (MRI) 123, 276, 303, 305-306, 341, 441

Maladaptive Behavior 33, 249, 453

Maladaptive Social Skills 164

Malicious Coaching 23, 43, 49, 51-52, 58, 63-64, 71, 74, 76, 160, 165-168, 200, 242, 259, 268, 270, 272, 279, 281, 318, 320, 325-326, 328, 333, 335, 338, 346, 381-382, 399, 401, 461, 465

Malingered Neurocognitive Dysfunction (MND) 256

Malingering 19, 87, 92, 242, 244-246, 249, 251-252, 254, 257-267

Mandatory Minimum Sentence 23, 43, 49, 51-52, 58, 63-64, 71, 74, 76, 160, 165-168, 200, 242, 259, 268, 270, 272, 279-281, 318, 320, 325-326, 328, 333, 335, 338, 346, 381-382, 399, 401, 461, 465

Manifestation 21, 28, 49, 165, 251, 408, 412, 443

Manipulated 98

Marijuana and Synthetic Cannabinoids
Cannabinoids 233-234
Marijuana 230, 233-234, 241
Synthetic Cannabinoids 234

MBT 60, 63, 64

McArthur Competence Assessment Tool

for Treatment (MacCAT-T) 126, 137

Medical Model 164, 413

Medical Symptom Validity Test (MSVT) 255, 257, 260

Medication Management 164, 413

Memory 92, 106-112, 119, 123, 133, 164, 166, 171, 181, 251, 254-261, 263-266, 409, 413, 415, 418-419, 449-450

Mens Rea 5-16, 21-39, 41-106, 108, 110, 112-136, 138, 141- 238, 242-470, 472-475

Mental Health Court 54, 80

Mental Illness 32, 44, 56, 65, 77, 84, 147, 158, 292, 387, 390, 397

Mentalization-Based Therapy (MBT) 60, 63, 64

Metacognitive Reflection and Insight Therapy (MERIT) 380, 381

Methadone 221, 239

Methamphetamine 216-217, 219, 223, 225-226, 233, 238, 240, 354, 373, 381, 395

Meth Lab 23, 43, 49, 51-52, 58, 63-64, 71, 74, 76, 160, 165-168, 200, 242, 259, 268, 270, 272, 279, 281, 318, 320, 325-326, 328, 333, 335, 338, 346, 381-382, 399, 401, 461, 465

Mild Cognitive Impairment (MCI) 115

Miller Forensic Assessment Test (M-FAST) 254, 263

Millon Adolescent Clinical Inventory (MACI) 86, 90

Mini-Mental Status Exam (MMSE) 124

Minnesota Multiphasic Personality Inventory (MMPI) 88, 89, 253, 258, 259, 262, 264, 462

Minnesota Multiphasic Personality Inventory –

Adolescent 86 MMPI 88-89, 253, 258, 259, 262, 264, 462

Miranda Warning 54, 80

Misinformation 42, 97, 98, 105, 107, 131, 405, 408-410, 413, 415, 418, 420

Misinterpretation 24, 33

M'Naghten Rule 39, 164, 413

Model Penal Code 5-16, 21-39, 41--106, 108, 110, 112- 282, 284-461, 463, 465-470, 472-475

Montreal Cognitive Assessment (MoCA) 124, 129

Mood Altering Chemicals 54, 80

Mood Dysregulation 54

Moral Recognition Therapy (MRT) 148

Morphine 220, 239

Motivational Interviewing (MI) 147, 150, 182, 465

Motivational Interviewing Treatment Integrity (MITI) 150

Motor Skill Development 54, 80

mTBI (mild TBI, mTBI) 54, 80, 440-442, 448, 458

Multigenerational Trauma 422

Munchausen Syndrome 248

Muscle Tone 23, 43, 49-52, 58, 63-64, 71, 74, 76, 160, 165-168, 200, 242, 259, 268, 270, 272, 279, 281, 318, 320, 325-326, 328, 333, 335, 338, 346, 381-382, 399, 401, 461, 465

N

Narcissistic Personality Disorder 50

Narcotic Addict Treatment Act 222

National Alliance for Mental Illness (NAMI) 56, 65, 397

National Autistic Society 25, 28, 34-35, 40, 44

National Center for Elder Abuse 131

National Women with Co-Occurring Disorders and Violence Study (WCDVS) 431

Negative Symptoms 374

Neglect 13, 23, 54, 56, 129-131, 136, 141, 167, 193, 205-206, 212, 219, 273-274, 281, 306, 316, 333-334, 363, 378, 390, 423, 429, 470

Neurochemical Imbalance 54, 80

Neurocognitive Impairment 54, 80

Neurodegenerative 115-116, 118-120, 124, 127, 132-134, 193-195, 203, 210

Neurodegenerative Dementia 54, 80

Neurodegenerative Disorders 120, 124, 132-134

Neuroleptic 208, 394

Neurological Growth 54, 80

Neuron 215, 472

Neuropsychological Testing 124

Neuroticism 54, 80

Neurotransmitter 223, 376

Nicotine 328, 343, 381-382

Non-Bizarre Delusion 54, 80

Not Guilty by Reason of Insanity (NGRI) 173, 246

Nuisance Crimes 204, 273, 278, 365

O

Obsession 23, 43, 49, 51-52, 58, 63-64, 71, 74, 76, 160, 165-168, 200, 242, 259, 268, 270, 272, 279, 281, 318, 320, 325-326, 328, 333, 335, 338, 346, 381-382, 399, 401, 461, 465

Obsessive 19, 24, 268, 269, 271, 275, 278, 279, 280, 281

Obsessive-compulsive Disorder (OCD) 19, 268-273, 275-277, 279-282

Offender 6, 9, 13-15, 26, 33-34, 36, 70, 134, 143-145, 148, 152, 154, 157-158, 169, 175-176, 186, 188, 205, 250, 284- 287, 289- 291, 295-298, 332, 351, 357, 361, 468, 385, 428, 430-431, 436-438, 444, 460, 469, 471

Offender Reentry 19, 173, 284

Office of Justice Programs 44, 158- 159, 356, 363, 460, 467

Olfactory Hallucinations 300

Opiates 220

Opiods 300

Oppositional Defiant Disorder (ODD) 22, 319

Overdose 228

Oxycodone 221, 236, 239

P

Paranoia 198

Parkinson 15, 118-120, 123, 127, 195, 203, 213, 379

Parkinson Disease Dementia (PDD) 22, 118-120

Parole 192, 285, 286, 297

Party Drug 23, 43, 49, 51-52, 58, 63-64, 71, 74, 76, 160, 165-168, 200, 242, 259, 268, 270, 272, 279, 281, 318, 320, 325-326, 328, 333, 335, 338, 346, 381-382, 399, 401, 461, 465

Pathological Gambling 212, 275, 280, 318, 320, 322-326, 328, 330-331, 333-352

Pathological Gambling (PG) 317, 321

Pattern of Performance Method (PPM) 255

Pediatric Abusive Head Trauma 19, 299

Pedophilia 23, 43, 49, 51-52, 58, 63-64, 71, 74, 76, 160, 165, 166-168, 200, 242, 259, 268, 270, 272, 276-277, 279-281, 318, 320, 325-326, 328, 333, 335, 338, 346, 381-382, 399, 401, 461, 465

Performance Enhancing Drugs 358

Perinatal Shaken Baby Syndrome Prevention Program (PSBSPP) 308

Perpetrator 28, 129, 169, 170, 451

Perske's List 94, 111

Personality Behavior Clusters 54, 80

Personality Disorder 18, 49, 50, 52, 55, 58, 60, 66, 72-74, 76-80, 150-151, 156, 249, 326, 443

Pervasive Developmental Disability 21

Pet Abuse 274

Pharmacological Interventions 336, 358

Pharmacological Therapy 54, 80

Pharmacological Treatment 149, 340, 350

Pharmacotherapy 236, 237, 344, 393, 396, 398

Phobia 427

Pick's Disease 54, 80

Placebo 72, 97, 336, 337, 340, 342-346, 350

Poor Effort 23, 43, 49, 51, 52, 58, 63, 64, 71, 74, 76, 160, 165-168, 200, 242, 259, 268, 270, 272, 279, 281, 318, 320, 325- 326, 328, 333, 335, 338, 346, 381-382, 399, 401, 461, 465

Pornography 276

Positive Stimulation 54, 80

Post-Plea Drug Court Model 358

Post-Traumatic Amnesia (PTA) 448

Post-Traumatic Stress Disorder (PTSD) 10, 12, 51, 59, 165, 246, 249-250, 260-264, 267, 272, 288, 326-327, 340, 362, 424, 428-429, 431, 436, 441, 444-445, 462, 470

Poverty 12, 57, 269, 356, 371, 375, 422-423, 440

Predictive Accuracy 191

Prenatal 16, 100, 107, 111, 160, 164-167, 175-183, 377, 391, 395-396, 414

Prenatal Alcohol Exposure (PAE) 99, 160-163, 167, 169, 171, 174, 177

Prenatal Risk Factors 54, 80

Pre-Plea Drug Court Model 358

Prescription Medications 19

Prevalence Rates 54, 80

Primary Caregiver 54, 80

Primary Progressive Aphasia (PPA) 122-123, 358

Primary Suggestibility 54, 80

Probation 10, 33-34, 39, 42, 296, 329, 368

Problem Gambling 6, 13, 19, 317-319, 322, 329, 342, 344, 348, 350-351

Problem Gambling Severity Index (PGSI) Test 322-323

Problem Solving 60-61, 72, 75, 147, 151, 154, 156

Problem Solving Courts 23, 43, 49, 51-52, 58, 63-64, 71, 74, 76, 160, 165-168, 200, 242, 259, 268, 270, 272, 279, 281, 318, 320, 325-326, 328, 333, 335, 338, 346, 381-382, 399, 401, 461, 465

Prodromal Symptoms 358

Protective Factors 185, 190, 350

Provoked Confabulation 97

PSBSPP 308

Psychological Disorder 358

Psychological Trauma 80, 435, 437

Psychosocial Maturity 358

Psychosocial Treatment 358

Psychotherapy 18, 39, 60, 62-63, 73-77, 80-81, 109, 142, 154-157, 192, 276, 280, 432

Psychotic Disorder 85, 378

Public Health Problems 273

Public Mental Health Services 358

Rapid Eye Movement (REM) Sleep Behavior Disorder 118, 119, 120

Reactive Attachment Disorder (RAD) 165

Recidivism 8, 30, 34-36, 58, 65, 66, 70-73, 79, 142-158, 169, 173-174, 185-189, 192, 274, 278, 280, 284-286, 288, 289- 298, 338, 346, 353-356, 364-367, 369, 383, 389, 426-427, 429-431, 434, 436, 456

Recidivism 70, 74, 158, 173, 286, 295-296, 358, 368, 370

Reclusiveness 196

Recovery Support Group 23, 43, 49, 51-52, 58, 63-64, 71, 74, 76, 160, 165-168, 200, 242, 259, 268, 270, 272, 279, 281, 318, 320, 325-326, 328, 333, 335, 338, 346, 381-382, 399, 401, 461, 465

Rehabilitation 13, 14, 16, 33-34, 36-37, 40, 66, 71, 77, 143-144, 154-155, 157-158, 178-179, 260-261, 285-286, 297, 312-313, 338, 351, 357, 360, 368-369, 380, 387, 398, 426, 428-429, 436, 438, 449, 452, 455-475

Rehabilitative Treatment 430

Reid Technique 358

Reintegration 296

Relapse 358

Relationship Obsessive-compulsive Disorder (ROCDO) 276

Residential Treatment 23, 43, 49-52, 58, 63-64, 71, 74, 76, 160, 165-168, 200, 242, 259, 268, 270, 272, 279, 281, 318, 320, 325-326, 328, 333, 335, 338, 346, 381, 382, 399, 401, 461, 465

Retaliation 277

Retinal Hemorrhages (RH)

304, 307, 309, 310

Retraumatization 422-423, 425, 427-429, 434

Re-Traumatization Risks 5-16, 21-37, 39, 41-47, 49-73, 76-79, 82, 83, 84-106, 108, 110, 112-136, 138, 141,-238, 242-260, 262-266, 268-315, 317-392, 394-396, 397-398, 400-401, 405-416, 418-463, 465-470, 472-475

Revolving-Door Phenomenon 273

Rey Complex Figure and Recognition Test (ROCFT) 255

Riggins v. Nevada (1992) 388

Risk Assessment 19, 70, 144, 184, 186, 189-190

Risk Assessment Tool Evaluation Directory 190

Risk Factors 23, 28-29, 34, 41, 47, 52, 70, 71, 76-78, 80, 118, 131, 133, 137, 145, 157, 168, 180, 185, 187-188, 190, 201, 211, 290, 292, 299, 301-302, 324, 335, 338, 344, 376-378, 381, 383, 394, 430, 440, 452

Risk Needs Responsivity (RNR) 5-16, 21-39, 41- 47, 49-106, 108, 110, 112-138, 141-158, 160-351, 353-470, 472-475

Risk Needs Assessment (RNR) 358

Risk Reduction Strategy 273

Rule 82 Assessment 323

SAMHSA 50, 51, 59, 65, 78, 157-158, 183, 291-292, 427-428, 431

Sanctuary Model 425, 433

Saving Inventory-Revised (SI-R) 270

Schedule of Controlled Substances 217-218, 221, 223, 227-231, 237

Schema-Focused Therapy (SFT) 60-61, 64

R

S

Schizophrenia   12, 14, 19, 43, 59, 85, 101, 104, 107, 110, 149, 157, 189, 191, 244, 250-251, 269, 272, 282, 288, 293, 371-402, 407, 442-443, 467-468, 471

Secondary Disabilities   54, 80

Secondary Suggestibility   54, 80

Secondary Trauma   300, 423, 426

Second Chance Act   273

Second Impact Syndrome (SIS)   441

Sedative Hypnotics   164, 413

Seizure   23, 28, 41-42, 236, 288, 307, 314, 403, 452

Self-Injurious Behavior (SIB)   27

Self-Medication   355

Self-Mutilation   51, 78

Self-Reflection   164, 413

Self-Regulation   42, 164-165, 179, 301, 413, 426, 429, 430, 432, 434, 436, 455, 462

Sell v. U.S. (2003)   54, 80

Semantic PPA   122

Sensory Processing   166, 375

Sentencing Guideline   204, 273, 278, 365

Sequential Intercept Model   427

Serotonin Syndrome   204, 273, 278, 365

Sexual Abuse   25, 47, 54, 102, 107, 109, 113, 130, 155. 157, 170, 175, 191, 205, 299, 324, 414, 416, 423, 426, 429, 436-437, 458

Sexual Exploitation   358

Sexual Violence Risk-20 (SVR-20)   188-189, 192

Shaken Baby Prevention   358

Shaken Baby Syndrome (SBS)   299, 300-301, 303, 309-310, 315

Short-Term Assessment of Risk and Treatability (START)   188-189, 192

Shoulson-Fahn Scale   358

Simple Hallucinations   358

Single Photon Emission Computed Tomography (SPECT)   281, 441

Sleep   62, 118, 119, 120, 220, 358, 441, 444, 448-449, 451, 463

Sleep Disturbance   358
Sleeping Pills   164, 413

Sobriety   65, 70, 355-356, 360-361

Social   11-12, 14-16, 24, 33, 37, 38, 41-42, 44-45, 47, 68, 72, 76-77, 80, 103, 107, 111-113, 137, 158-159, 173, 191, 213, 278-279, 281, 288, 291, 295, 297, 302, 340-341, 347, 349, 391, 395, 397, 416-418, 420, 435-437, 449, 455-456, 461-462, 464, 467, 471

Social Alienation   371
Social Functioning   22, 38, 123
Social Isolation   54, 80
Social Phobias   54, 80
Social Resiliency   54, 80
Social Stigma   54, 80

Somatoform Disorders   358

South Oaks Gambling Screen—Revised (SOGS-R)   322-323

Specialty Guidelines for Forensic Psychology   87

Spontaneous Confabulation   96

Sports Betting   273

Stalking   9, 24, 273, 276-277

Static Factors   290

Static Risk Factors   54, 80

Stigma   67, 70, 72, 149, 194, 203, 206-207, 210, 248, 320, 336, 378, 383, 398, 431
Stigmatization   288

Stimulants   216, 224-225, 228, 232, 236, 388

Strategies   6, 8-9, 11-12, 14, 16, 34, 38, 41, 47, 63, 70-71, 73-75, 77, 79, 81, 91, 126, 136-137, 144, 146-147, 149-151, 154-159, 161, 173, 175, 181, 191-192, 222, 258, 273, 277, 281-282, 334-335, 338, 341-343, 350-351, 355, 360, 362, 368-370, 379, 381, 391, 396-398, 405, 414, 429-432, 435-438, 449, 454, 460, 469

Stress-Management   308, 358

Structural Neuroimaging   358

Structured Interview of Reported Symptoms - 2 (SIRS-2)   87, 91, 254, 265

Structured Inventory of Malingered Symptomatology (SIMS)   254, 261

Structured Professional Judgment (SPJ)   188

Subdural hematoma (SDH)   303, 310

Substance Abuse   15, 38, 55, 59, 70-71, 73, 80, 109, 147, 149, 155-157, 166, 200, 291, 341-342, 381, 391, 396, 423, 426-428, 431, 433, 437-438

Substance Abuse and Mental Health Service Administration (SAMHSA)   50-51, 59, 65, 78, 157-158, 183, 291-292, 427-428, 431

Substance Abuse Services   156

Substance-Related and Addictive Disorders   275, 318, 321

Substance Use Disorder (SUD)   23, 27, 166, 167

Suggestibility   19, 172, 176, 251, 358, 404-411, 414-420

Suicide   15, 27, 43, 44, 51, 68-69, 73, 78, 80, 168, 178-179, 201, 210, 327-329, 340, 344, 351, 394, 451, 458, 473
Suicidal Ideation (SI)   358
Suicide and Self-Injurous Behavior (SIB)   358

Support System   22, 34, 56, 69, 168, 174, 341, 387

Synthetic Cannabinoids   234

Systems Training for Emotional Predictability and Problem Solving (STEPPS)   60-61, 72, 151, 154

T

Tactile   226, 258, 373, 448

Tactile Hallucinations   373

Tarasoff Liability   189

Tarasoff v. Regents of the University of California (1976)   189

Teletherapy   54, 80

Tertiary Suggestibility   358

Testimony   8, 25, 31, 35, 42, 93-96, 99, 103, 104, 106, 108, 110-112, 171-172, 176, 212, 385-386, 396, 404-405, 408, 410-411, 413-415, 418, 420-421

Testimony   31, 103, 108, 386, 410

Test of Memory Malingering (TOMM)   254, 264-266

The Centers for Disease Control and Prevention (CDC)   162, 300

The Competence Assessment for Standing Trial for Defendants with Mental Retardation (CAST-MR)   86

The Diagnostic and Statistical Manual of Mental Disorders (DSM)   21

The Hudson Valley Shaken Baby Prevention Initiative   309

The Juvenile Adjudicative Competence Interview (JACI)   86

Theoetical Method   358

Theory of Mind (TOM)   27

The Period of PURPLE Crying Program   358

Therapeutic   178, 296, 356, 370, 392

Therapeutic Intervention Models   358

Therapeutic Jurisprudence 358

Therapeutic Models 430

Thinking for a Change (T4C) 6, 147-148

Three Strike Law 204, 273, 278, 365

Tonic-Clonic Seizures 54, 80

Tough-On-Crime Policies 358

Transference Focused Psychotherapy (TFP) 60

Transitional Housing Placements 358

Transition from Prison to Community (TPC) 358

Trauma 9-13, 15, 52, 54-57, 66, 70, 80, 101-102, 109, 113, 150-152, 154, 156-157, 168, 174, 211, 218, 224-225, 246, 249-250, 258, 266, 272, 280, 288, 299-301, 303-308, 310-315, 326, 344, 378, 384, 392, 395, 397-398, 422-438, 440, 442, 451, 457-461, 466, 468, 470-471
  Trauma Affect Regulation: Guide for Education and Therapy (TARGET) 152
  Trauma-Informed 9, 12, 151, 157, 422-437
    Trauma-Informed Care (TIC) 151
    Trauma-Informed Cognitive Behavioral Therapy (TI-CBT) 358, 431-432
  Trauma Recovery and Empowerment Model (TREM) 147, 152, 432, 358
  M-TREM 152, 432

Traumatic Brain Injury (TBI) 101

Traumatic Childhood Events 358

Traumatic Victimization 358

Trauma Vulnerability 54, 80

Treatment 6, 8, 9, 11-12, 14, 16, 34, 38, 41, 47, 63, 70-71, 73-75, 77, 79, 81, 91, 126, 136-137, 144, 146-147, 149-151, 154-159, 161, 175, 181, 191-192, 222, 258, 273, 277, 281-282, 334-335, 338, 341-343, 350-351, 355, 360, 362, 369-370, 379, 381, 391, 396-398, 414, 429-432, 436-438, 454, 460, 469
  Treatment Strategies 358

Tribal Healing to Wellness Courts 363

Truancy Courts 54, 80

Truth-In Sentencing Laws 54, 80

Type I and Type II Errors 358

U

Unconsciousness 23, 43, 49, 51-52, 58, 63, 64, 71, 74, 76, 160, 165-168, 200, 242, 259, 268, 270, 272, 279, 281, 318, 320, 325-326, 328, 333, 335, 338, 346, 381, 382, 399, 401, 461, 465

Undiagnosed 23, 43, 49, 51-52, 58, 63-64, 71, 74, 76, 160, 165-168, 200, 242, 259, 268, 270, 272, 279, 281, 318, 320, 325-326, 328, 333, 335, 338, 346, 381-382, 399, 401, 461, 465

Undiagnosed Mental Illness 355

Unemployment 52, 173, 269, 287-288, 364, 371

Uniform Guardianship and Protective Proceedings Act (UGPPA) 23, 43, 49, 51- 52, 58, 63, 64, 71, 74, 76, 128, 160, 165-168, 200, 242, 259, 268, 270, 272, 279, 281, 318, 320, 325-326, 328, 333, 335, 338, 346, 381-382, 399, 401, 461, 465

Unstructured Clinical Judgment (UCI) 358

V

Vascular Dementia 54, 80, 117, 135

Veteran 23, 43, 49, 51-52, 58, 63-64, 71, 74, 76, 160, 165-168, 200, 242, 259, 268, 270, 272, 279, 281, 318, 320, 325-326, 328, 333, 335, 338, 346, 381, 382, 399, 401, 461, 465
  Veterans Court 54, 80

Vicarious Trauma 423-425, 430

Victimization 7, 23, 25, 28-29, 33, 47, 71, 112, 129, 131, 165, 169, 170, 173, 183, 206, 262, 289, 366, 383, 424, 426, 429, 440, 447, 451

Violence Risk Appraisal Guide (VRAG-R) 187, 192, 358
  Violence Risk Appraisal Guide (VRAG) 187

Visuospacial Awareness 54, 80

Vulnerable 23, 43, 49, 51-52, 58, 63-64, 71, 74, 76, 160, 165-168, 200, 242, 259, 268, 270, 272, 279, 281, 318, 320, 325-326, 328, 333, 335, 338, 346, 381-382, 399, 401, 461, 465

W

Washington v. Harper (1990) 388

Wechsler Adult Intelligence Scale 256, 263

Wechsler Intelligence Scales for Children –V 86

Weeks v. State (1998) 172

Wisconsin State Mental Health Act 184

Witness 23, 43, 49, 51-52, 58, 63-64, 71, 74, 76, 160, 165-168, 200, 242, 259, 268, 270, 272, 279, 281, 318, 320, 325-326, 328, 333, 335, 338, 346, 381-382, 399, 401, 410, 461, 465

Word Memory Test (WMT) 255

Working Memory 111, 164, 166, 174, 181-182, 324- 325, 371-372, 375

Y

Yale-Brown Obsessive Compulsive Scale 271, 279

CPSIA information can be obtained
at www.ICGtesting.com
Printed in the USA
LVHW061400230819
628737LV00010B/115/P